Planning Algorithms

Planning algorithms are impacting technical disciplines and industries around the world, including robotics, computer-aided design, manufacturing, computer graphics, aerospace applications, drug design, and protein folding. This coherent and comprehensive book unifies material from several sources, including robotics, control theory, artificial intelligence, and algorithms. The treatment is centered on robot motion planning but integrates material on planning in discrete spaces. A major part of the book is devoted to planning under uncertainty, including decision theory, Markov decision processes, and information spaces, which are the "configuration spaces" of all sensor-based planning problems. The last part of the book delves into planning under differential constraints that arise when automating the motions of virtually any mechanical system.

Developed from courses taught by the author, the book is intended for students, engineers, and researchers in robotics, artificial intelligence, and control theory as well as computer graphics, algorithms, and computational biology.

Steven M. LaValle is Associate Professor of Computer Science at the University of Illinois at Urbana-Champaign. He has worked in motion planning and robotics for more than a decade and has published dozens of articles in the field. He is the main developer of the rapidly exploring random tree (RRT) algorithm, which has been used in numerous research labs and industrial products around the world. He has taught material on which the book is based at Stanford University, Iowa State University, the Tec de Monterrey, and the University of Illinois.

Planning Algorithms

Steven M. LaValle

University of Illinois

CAMBRIDGE
UNIVERSITY PRESS

CAMBRIDGE UNIVERSITY PRESS
Cambridge, New York, Melbourne, Madrid, Cape Town, Singapore, São Paulo

Cambridge University Press
40 West 20th Street, New York, NY 10011-4211, USA

www.cambridge.org
Information on this title: www.cambridge.org/9780521862059

First published 2006

Printed in the United States of America

A catalog record for this publication is available from the British Library.

Library of Congress Cataloging in Publication Data

LaValle, Steven M. (Steven Michael), 1968–
Planning algorithms / Steven M. LaValle.
p. cm.
Includes bibliographical references and index.
ISBN 0-521-86205-1 (hardback)
1. Robots – Motion – Planning.   2. Algorithms.   I. Title.
TJ211.4.L385   2006
629.8′932 – dc22   2006010125

ISBN-13   978-0-521-86205-9 hardback
ISBN-10   0-521-86205-1 hardback

For my wife, Tammy, and my sons, Alexander and Ethan

Contents

Preface

What is meant by "planning algorithms"?

Due to many exciting developments in the fields of robotics, artificial intelligence, and control theory, three topics that were once quite distinct are presently on a collision course. In robotics, motion planning was originally concerned with problems such as how to move a piano from one room to another in a house without hitting anything. The field has grown, however, to include complications such as uncertainties, multiple bodies, and dynamics. In artificial intelligence, planning originally meant a search for a sequence of logical operators or actions that transform an initial world state into a desired goal state. Presently, planning extends beyond this to include many decision-theoretic ideas such as Markov decision processes, imperfect state information, and game-theoretic equilibria. Although control theory has traditionally been concerned with issues such as stability, feedback, and optimality, there has been growing interest in designing algorithms that find feasible open-loop trajectories for nonlinear systems. In some of this work, the term "motion planning" has been applied, with a different interpretation from its use in robotics. Thus, even though each originally considered different problems, the fields of robotics, artificial intelligence, and control theory have expanded their scope to share an interesting common ground.

In this text, I use the term *planning* in a broad sense that encompasses this common ground. This does not, however, imply that the term is meant to cover everything important in the fields of robotics, artificial intelligence, and control theory. The presentation focuses on *algorithm* issues relating to planning. Within robotics, the focus is on designing algorithms that generate useful motions by processing complicated geometric models. Within artificial intelligence, the focus is on designing systems that use decision-theoretic models to compute appropriate actions. Within control theory, the focus is on algorithms that compute feasible trajectories for systems, with some additional coverage of feedback and optimality. Analytical techniques, which account for the majority of control theory literature, are not the main focus here.

The phrase "planning and control" is often used to identify complementary issues in developing a system. Planning is often considered as a higher level process than control. In this text, I make no such distinctions. Ignoring historical connotations that come with the terms, "planning" and "control" can be used interchangeably. Either refers to some kind of decision making in this text, with no associated notion of "high" or "low" level. A hierarchical approach can be developed, and either level could be called "planning" or "control" without any difference in meaning.

Who is the intended audience?

The text is written primarily for computer science and engineering students at the advanced-undergraduate or beginning-graduate level. It is also intended as an introduction to recent techniques for researchers and developers in robotics, artificial intelligence, and control theory. It is expected that the presentation here would be of interest to those working in other areas such as computational biology (drug design, protein folding), virtual prototyping, manufacturing, video game development, and computer graphics. Furthermore, this book is intended for those working in industry who want to design and implement planning approaches to solve their problems.

I have attempted to make the book as self-contained and readable as possible. Advanced mathematical concepts (beyond concepts typically learned by undergraduates in computer science and engineering) are introduced and explained. For readers with deeper mathematical interests, directions for further study are given.

Where does this book fit?

Here is where this book fits with respect to other well-known subjects:

Robotics

This book addresses the planning part of robotics, which includes motion planning, trajectory planning, and planning under uncertainty. This is only one part of the big picture in robotics, which includes issues not directly covered here, such as mechanism design, dynamical system modeling, feedback control, sensor design, computer vision, inverse kinematics, and humanoid robotics.

Artificial intelligence

Machine learning is currently one of the largest and most successful divisions of artificial intelligence. This book (perhaps along with [384]) represents the important complement to machine learning, which can be thought of as "machine planning." Subjects such as reinforcement learning and decision theory lie in the boundary between the two and are covered in this book. Once learning is being successfully performed, what decisions should be made? This enters into planning.

Control theory

Historically, control theory has addressed what may be considered here as planning in continuous spaces under differential constraints. Dynamics, optimality, and feedback have been paramount in control theory. This book is complementary in that most of the focus is on open-loop control laws, feasibility as opposed to optimality, and dynamics may or may not be important. Nevertheless, feedback, optimality, and dynamics concepts appear in many places throughout the book. However, the techniques in this book are mostly algorithmic, as opposed to the analytical techniques that are typically developed in control theory.

Computer graphics

Animation has been a hot area in computer graphics in recent years. Many techniques in this book have either been applied or can be applied to animate video game characters, virtual humans, or mechanical systems. Planning algorithms allow users to specify tasks at a high level, which avoids having to perform tedious specifications of low-level motions (e.g., key framing).

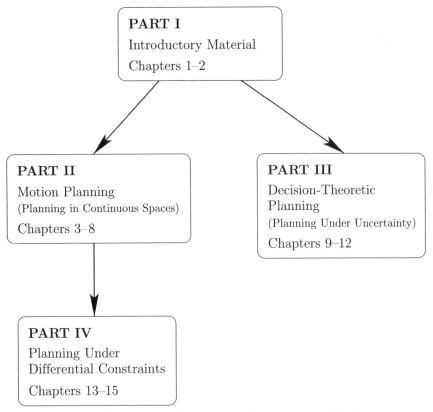

Figure 1: The dependencies between the four main parts of the book.

Algorithms

As the title suggests, this book may fit under algorithms, which is a discipline within computer science. Throughout the book, typical issues from combinatorics and complexity arise. In some places, techniques from computational geometry and computational real algebraic geometry, which are also divisions of algorithms, become important. On the other hand, this is not a pure algorithms book in that much of the material is concerned with characterizing various decision processes that arise in applications. This book does not focus purely on complexity and combinatorics.

Other fields

At the periphery, many other fields are touched by planning algorithms. For example, motion planning algorithms, which form a major part of this book, have had a substantial impact on such diverse fields as computational biology, virtual prototyping in manufacturing, architectural design, aerospace engineering, and computational geography.

Suggested use

The ideas should flow naturally from chapter to chapter, but at the same time, the text has been designed to make it easy to skip chapters. The dependencies between the four main parts are illustrated in Figure 1.

If you are only interested in robot motion planning, it is only necessary to read Chapters 3–8, possibly with the inclusion of some discrete planning algorithms from Chapter 2

Motion planning
Core: 2.1–2.2, 3.1–3.3, 4.1–4.3, 5.1–5.6, 6.1–6.3
Optional: 3.4–3.5, 4.4, 6.4–6.5, 7.1–7.7, 8.1–8.5
Planning under uncertainty
Core: 2.1–2.3, 9.1–9.2, 10.1–10.4, 11.1–11.6, 12.1–12.3
Optional: 9.3–9.5, 10.5–10.6, 11.7, 12.4–12.5
Planning under differential constraints
Core: 8.3, 13.1–13.3, 14.1–14.4, 15.1, 15.3–15.4
Optional: 13.4–13.5, 14.5–14.7, 15.2, 15.5

Figure 2: Based on Parts II, III, and IV, there are three themes of core material and optional topics.

because they arise in motion planning. Chapters 3 and 4 provide the foundations needed to understand basic robot motion planning. Chapters 5 and 6 present algorithmic techniques to solve this problem. Chapters 7 and 8 consider extensions of the basic problem. If you are additionally interested in nonholonomic planning and other problems that involve differential constraints, then it is safe to jump ahead to Chapters 13–15, after completing Part II.

Chapters 11 and 12 cover problems in which there is sensing uncertainty. These problems live in an *information space*, which is detailed in Chapter 11. Chapter 12 covers algorithms that plan in the information space.

If you are interested mainly in decision-theoretic planning, then you can read Chapter 2 and then jump straight to Chapters 9–12. The material in these later chapters does not depend much on Chapters 3–8, which cover motion planning. Thus, if you are not interested in motion planning, the chapters may be easily skipped.

There are many ways to design a semester or quarter course from the book material. Figure 2 may help in deciding between core material and some optional topics. For an advanced undergraduate-level course, I recommend covering one core and some optional topics. For a graduate-level course, it may be possible to cover a couple of cores and some optional topics, depending on the initial background of the students. A two-semester sequence can also be developed by drawing material from all three cores and including some optional topics. Also, two independent courses can be made in a number of different ways. If you want to avoid continuous spaces, a course on discrete planning can be offered from Sections 2.1–2.5, 9.1–9.5, 10.1–10.5, 11.1–11.3, 11.7, and 12.1–12.3. If you are interested in teaching some game theory, there is roughly a chapter's worth of material in Sections 9.3–9.4, 10.5, 11.7, and 13.5. Material that contains the most prospects for future research appears in Chapters 7, 8, 11, 12, and 14. In particular, research on information spaces is still in its infancy.

To facilitate teaching, there are more than 500 examples and exercises throughout the book. The exercises in each chapter are divided into written problems and implementation projects. For motion planning projects, students often become bogged down with low-level implementation details. One possibility is to use the Motion Strategy Library (MSL):

http://msl.cs.uiuc.edu/msl/

as an object-oriented software base on which to develop projects. I have had great success with this for both graduate and undergraduate students.

For additional material, updates, and errata, see the Web page associated with this book:

http://planning.cs.uiuc.edu/

You may also download a free electronic copy of this book for your own personal use.

For further reading, consult the numerous references given at the end of chapters and throughout the text. Most can be found with a quick search of the Internet, but I did not give too many locations because these tend to be unstable over time. Unfortunately, the literature surveys are shorter than I had originally planned; thus, in some places, only a list of papers is given, which is often incomplete. I have tried to make the survey of material in this book as impartial as possible, but there is undoubtedly a bias in some places toward my own work. This was difficult to avoid because my research efforts have been closely intertwined with the development of this book.

Acknowledgments

I am very grateful to many students and colleagues who have given me extensive feedback and advice in developing this text. It evolved over many years through the development and teaching of courses at Stanford, Iowa State, and the University of Illinois. These universities have been very supportive of my efforts.

Many ideas and explanations throughout the book were inspired through numerous collaborations. For this reason, I am particularly grateful to the helpful insights and discussions that arose through collaborations with Michael Branicky, Francesco Bullo, Jeff Erickson, Emilio Frazzoli, Rob Ghrist, Leo Guibas, Seth Hutchinson, Lydia Kavraki, James Kuffner, Jean-Claude Latombe, Rajeev Motwani, Rafael Murrieta, Rajeev Sharma, Thierry Siméon, and Giora Slutzki. Over years of interaction, their ideas helped me to shape the perspective and presentation throughout the book.

Many valuable insights and observations were gained through collaborations with students, especially Peng Cheng, Hamid Chitsaz, Prasanth Konkimalla, Steve Lindemann, Jason O'Kane, Stjepan Rajko, Shai Sachs, Boris Simov, Benjamin Tovar, Jeff Yakey, Libo Yang, and Anna Yershova. I am grateful for the opportunities to work with them and appreciate their interaction as it helped to develop my own understanding and perspective.

While writing the text, at many times I recalled being strongly influenced by one or more technical discussions with colleagues. Undoubtedly, the following list is incomplete, but, nevertheless, I would like to thank the following colleagues for their helpful insights and stimulating discussions: Pankaj Agarwal, Srinivas Akella, Nancy Amato, Devin Balkcom, Tamer Başar, Antonio Bicchi, Robert Bohlin, Joel Burdick, Stefano Carpin, Howie Choset, Juan Cortés, Jerry Dejong, Bruce Donald, Ignacy Duleba, Mike Erdmann, Roland Geraerts, Malik Ghallab, Ken Goldberg, Pekka Isto, Vijay Kumar, Andrew Ladd, Jean-Paul Laumond, Kevin Lynch, Matt Mason, Pascal Morin, David Mount, Dana Nau, Mark Overmars, Jean Ponce, Elon Rimon, and Al Rizzi.

Many thanks go to Karl Bohringer, Marco Bressan, Stefano Carpin, John Cassel, Peng Cheng, Hamid Chitsaz, Ignacy Duleba, Claudia Esteves, Eleonora Fantini, Brian Gerkey, Ken Goldberg, Björn Hein, Sanjit Jhala, Marcelo Kallmann, James Kuffner, Olivier Lefebvre, Mong Leng, Steve Lindemann, Dennis Nieuwenhuisen, Jason O'Kane, Neil Petroff, Mihail Pivtoraiko, Stephane Redon, Gildardo Sanchez, Wiktor Schmidt, Fabian

Schöfeld, Robin Schubert, Sanketh Shetty, Mohan Sirchabesan, James Solberg, Domenico Spensieri, Kristian Spoerer, Tony Stentz, Morten Strandberg, Ichiro Suzuki, Benjamin Tovar, Zbynek Winkler, Anna Yershova, Jingjin Yu, George Zaimes, and Liangjun Zhang for pointing out numerous mistakes in the online manuscript. I also appreciate the efforts of graduate students in my courses who scribed class notes that served as an early draft for some parts. These include students at Iowa State and the University of Illinois: Peng Cheng, Brian George, Shamsi Tamara Iqbal, Xiaolei Li, Steve Lindemann, Shai Sachs, Warren Shen, Rishi Talreja, Sherwin Tam, and Benjamin Tovar.

I sincerely thank Krzysztof Kozlowski and his staff, Joanna Gawecka, Wirginia Król, and Marek Lawniczak, at the Politechnika Poznańska (Technical University of Poznan) for all of their help and hospitality during my sabbatical in Poland. I also thank Heather Hall for managing my U.S.-based professional life while I lived in Europe. I am grateful to the National Science Foundation, the Office of Naval Research, and DARPA for research grants that helped to support some of my sabbatical and summer time during the writing of this book. The Department of Computer Science at the University of Illinois was also very generous in its support of this huge effort.

I am very fortunate to have artistically talented friends. I am deeply indebted to James Kuffner for creating the image on the front cover and to Audrey de Malmazet de Saint Andeol for creating the art on the first page of each of the four main parts.

Finally, I thank my editor, Lauren Cowles, my copy editor, Elise Oranges, and the rest of the people involved with Cambridge University Press for their efforts and advice in preparing the manuscript for publication.

Steve LaValle
Urbana, Illinois, U.S.A.

PART I

Introductory Material

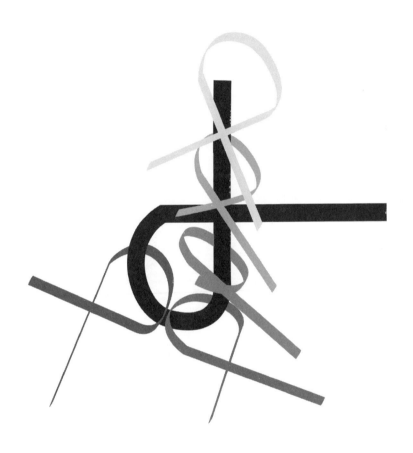

1

Introduction

1.1 Planning to plan

Planning is a term that means different things to different groups of people. *Robotics* addresses the automation of mechanical systems that have sensing, actuation, and computation capabilities (similar terms, such as *autonomous systems* are also used). A fundamental need in robotics is to have algorithms that convert high-level specifications of tasks from humans into low-level descriptions of how to move. The terms *motion planning* and *trajectory planning* are often used for these kinds of problems. A classical version of motion planning is sometimes referred to as the *Piano Mover's Problem*. Imagine giving a precise computer-aided design (CAD) model of a house and a piano as input to an algorithm. The algorithm must determine how to move the piano from one room to another in the house without hitting anything. Most of us have encountered similar problems when moving a sofa or mattress up a set of stairs. Robot motion planning usually ignores dynamics and other differential constraints and focuses primarily on the translations and rotations required to move the piano. Recent work, however, does consider other aspects, such as uncertainties, differential constraints, modeling uncertainties, and optimality. Trajectory planning usually refers to the problem of taking the solution from a robot motion planning algorithm and determining how to move along the solution in a way that respects the mechanical limitations of the robot.

Control theory has historically been concerned with designing inputs to physical systems described by differential equations. These could include mechanical systems such as cars or aircraft, electrical systems such as noise filters, or even systems arising in areas as diverse as chemistry, economics, and sociology. Classically, control theory has developed *feedback policies*, which enable an adaptive response during execution, and has focused on *stability*, which ensures that the dynamics do not cause the system to become wildly out of control. A large emphasis is also placed on optimizing criteria to minimize resource consumption, such as energy or time. In recent control theory literature, *motion planning* sometimes refers to the construction of inputs to a nonlinear dynamical system that drives it from an initial state to a specified goal state. For example, imagine trying to operate a remote-controlled hovercraft that glides over the surface of a frozen pond. Suppose we would like the hovercraft to leave its current resting location and come to rest at another specified location. Can an algorithm be designed that computes the desired inputs, even in an ideal simulator that neglects uncertainties that arise from model inaccuracies? It is possible to add other considerations, such as uncertainties, feedback, and optimality; however, the problem is already challenging enough without these.

In *artificial intelligence*, the terms *planning* and *AI planning* take on a more discrete flavor. Instead of moving a piano through a continuous space, as in the robot motion planning problem, the task might be to solve a puzzle, such as the Rubik's cube or a sliding-tile puzzle, or to achieve a task that is modeled discretely, such as building a stack of blocks. Although such problems could be modeled with continuous spaces, it seems natural to define a finite set of actions that can be applied to a discrete set of states and to construct a solution by giving the appropriate sequence of actions. Historically, planning has been considered different from *problem solving*; however, the distinction seems to have faded away in recent years. In this book, we do not attempt to make a distinction between the two. Also, substantial effort has been devoted to representation language issues in planning. Although some of this will be covered, it is mainly outside of our focus. Many decision-theoretic ideas have recently been incorporated into the AI planning problem, to model uncertainties, adversarial scenarios, and optimization. These issues are important and are considered in detail in Part III.

Given the broad range of problems to which the term planning has been applied in the artificial intelligence, control theory, and robotics communities, you might wonder whether it has a specific meaning. Otherwise, just about anything could be considered as an instance of planning. Some common elements for planning problems will be discussed shortly, but first we consider planning as a branch of algorithms. Hence, this book is entitled *Planning Algorithms*. The primary focus is on algorithmic and computational issues of planning problems that have arisen in several disciplines. On the other hand, this does not mean that planning algorithms refers to an existing community of researchers within the general algorithms community. This book it not limited to combinatorics and asymptotic complexity analysis, which is the main focus in pure algorithms. The focus here includes numerous concepts that are not necessarily algorithmic but aid in modeling, solving, and analyzing planning problems.

Natural questions at this point are, What is a plan? How is a plan represented? How is it computed? What is it supposed to achieve? How is its quality evaluated? Who or what is going to use it? This chapter provides general answers to these questions. Regarding the user of the plan, it clearly depends on the application. In most applications, an algorithm executes the plan; however, the user could even be a human. Imagine, for example, that the planning algorithm provides you with an investment strategy.

In this book, the user of the plan will frequently be referred to as a *robot* or a *decision maker*. In artificial intelligence and related areas, it has become popular in recent years to use the term *agent*, possibly with adjectives to yield an *intelligent agent* or *software agent*. Control theory usually refers to the decision maker as a *controller*. The plan in this context is sometimes referred to as a *policy* or *control law*. In a game-theoretic context, it might make sense to refer to decision makers as *players*. Regardless of the terminology used in a particular discipline, this book is concerned with planning algorithms that find a strategy for one or more decision makers. Therefore, remember that terms such as *robot*, *agent*, and *controller* are interchangeable.

1.2 Motivational examples and applications

Planning problems abound. This section surveys several examples and applications to inspire you to read further.

Why study planning algorithms? There are at least two good reasons. First, it is fun to try to get machines to solve problems for which even humans have great difficulty. This involves exciting challenges in modeling planning problems, designing efficient algorithms, and developing robust implementations. Second, planning algorithms have achieved widespread successes in several industries and academic disciplines, including robotics, manufacturing, drug design, and aerospace applications. The rapid growth in

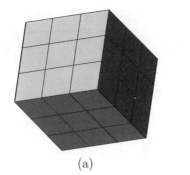

(a)   (b)

Figure 1.1: The Rubik's cube (a), sliding-tile puzzle (b), and other related puzzles are examples of discrete planning problems.

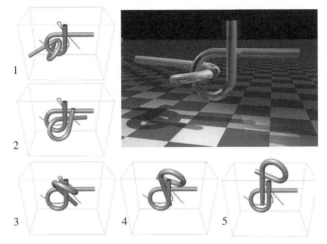

Figure 1.2: Remember puzzles like this? Imagine trying to solve one with an algorithm. The goal is to pull the two bars apart. This example is called the Alpha 1.0 Puzzle. It was created by Boris Yamrom and posted as a research benchmark by Nancy Amato at Texas A&M University. This solution and animation were made by James Kuffner (see [561] for the full movie).

recent years indicates that many more fascinating applications may be on the horizon. These are exciting times to study planning algorithms and contribute to their development and use.

Discrete puzzles, operations, and scheduling

Chapter 2 covers discrete planning, which can be applied to solve familiar puzzles, such as those shown in Figure 1.1. They are also good at games such as chess or bridge [899]. Discrete planning techniques have been used in space applications, including a rover that traveled on Mars and the Earth Observing One satellite [209, 384, 897]. When combined with methods for planning in continuous spaces, they can solve complicated tasks such as determining how to bend sheet metal into complicated objects [422]; see Section 7.5 for the related problem of folding cartons.

A motion planning puzzle

The puzzles in Figure 1.1 can be easily discretized because of the regularity and symmetries involved in moving the parts. Figure 1.2 shows a problem that lacks these properties

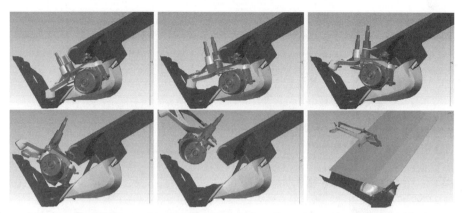

Figure 1.3: An automotive assembly task that involves inserting or removing a windshield wiper motor from a car body cavity. This problem was solved for clients using the motion planning software of Kineo CAM (courtesy of Kineo CAM).

and requires planning in a continuous space. Such problems are solved by using the motion planning techniques of Part II. This puzzle was designed to frustrate both humans and motion planning algorithms. It can be solved in a few minutes on a standard personal computer (PC) using the techniques in Section 5.5. Many other puzzles have been developed as benchmarks for evaluating planning algorithms.

An automotive assembly puzzle

Although the problem in Figure 1.2 may appear to be pure fun and games, similar problems arise in important applications. For example, Figure 1.3 shows an automotive assembly problem for which software is needed to determine whether a wiper motor can be inserted (and removed) from the car body cavity. Traditionally, such a problem is solved by constructing physical models. This costly and time-consuming part of the design process can be virtually eliminated in software by directly manipulating the CAD models.

The wiper example is just one of many. The most widespread impact on industry comes from motion planning software developed at Kineo CAM. It has been integrated into Robcad (eM-Workplace) from Tecnomatix, which is a leading tool for designing robotic workcells in numerous factories around the world. Their software has also been applied to assembly problems by Renault, Ford, Airbus, Optivus, and many other major corporations. Other companies and institutions are also heavily involved in developing and delivering motion planning tools for industry (many are secret projects, which unfortunately cannot be described here). One of the first instances of motion planning applied to real assembly problems is documented in [188].

Sealing cracks in automotive assembly

Figure 1.4 shows a simulation of robots performing sealing at the Volvo Cars assembly plant in Torslanda, Sweden. Sealing is the process of using robots to spray a sticky substance along the seams of a car body to prevent dirt and water from entering and causing corrosion. The entire robot workcell is designed using CAD tools, which automatically provide the necessary geometric models for motion planning software. The solution shown in Figure 1.4 is one of many problems solved for Volvo Cars and others using motion planning software developed by the Fraunhofer Chalmers Centre (FCC). Using motion planning software, engineers need only specify the high-level task of performing the

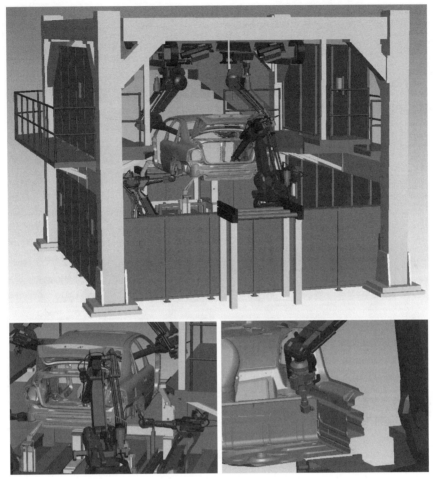

Figure 1.4: An application of motion planning to the sealing process in automotive manufacturing. Planning software developed by the Fraunhofer Chalmers Centre (FCC) is used at the Volvo Cars plant in Sweden (courtesy of Volvo Cars and FCC).

sealing, and the robot motions are computed automatically. This saves enormous time and expense in the manufacturing process.

Moving furniture

Returning to pure entertainment, the problem shown in Figure 1.5 involves moving a grand piano across a room using three mobile robots with manipulation arms mounted on them. The problem is humorously inspired by the phrase *Piano Mover's Problem*. Collisions between robots and with other pieces of furniture must be avoided. The problem is further complicated because the robots, piano, and floor form closed kinematic chains, which are covered in Sections 4.4 and 7.4.

Navigating mobile robots

A more common task for mobile robots is to request them to navigate in an indoor environment, as shown in Figure 1.6a. A robot might be asked to perform tasks such as building a map of the environment, determining its precise location within a map, or arriving at a particular place. Acquiring and manipulating information from sensors is quite challenging and is covered in Chapters 11 and 12. Most robots operate in spite of

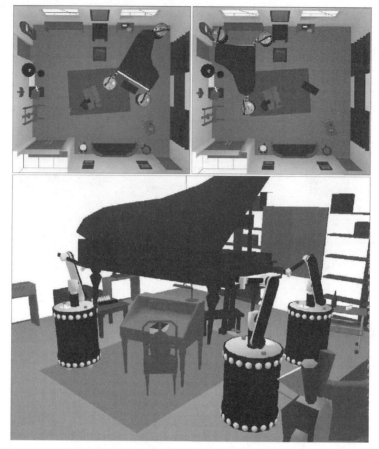

Figure 1.5: Using mobile robots to move a piano [246].

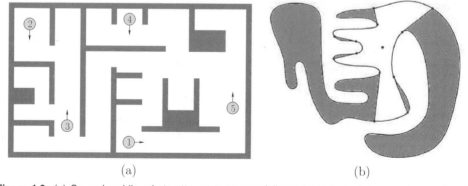

(a)   (b)

Figure 1.6: (a) Several mobile robots attempt to successfully navigate in an indoor environment while avoiding collisions with the walls and each other. (b) Imagine using a lantern to search a cave for missing people.

large uncertainties. At one extreme, it may appear that having many sensors is beneficial because it could allow precise estimation of the environment and the robot position and orientation. This is the premise of many existing systems, as shown for the robot system in Figure 1.7, which constructs a map of its environment. It may alternatively be preferable to develop low-cost and reliable robots that achieve specific tasks with little

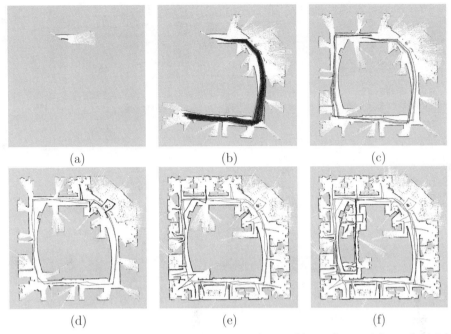

(a) (b) (c)

(d) (e) (f)

Figure 1.7: A mobile robot can reliably construct a good map of its environment (here, the Intel Research Lab) while simultaneously localizing itself. This is accomplished using laser scanning sensors and performing efficient Bayesian computations on the information space [353].

or no sensing. These trade-offs are carefully considered in Chapters 11 and 12. Planning under uncertainty is the focus of Part III.

If there are multiple robots, then many additional issues arise. How can the robots communicate? How can their information be integrated? Should their coordination be centralized or distributed? How can collisions between them be avoided? Do they each achieve independent tasks, or are they required to collaborate in some way? If they are competing in some way, then concepts from game theory may apply. Therefore, some game theory appears in Sections 9.3, 9.4, 10.5, 11.7, and 13.5.

Playing hide and seek

One important task for a mobile robot is playing the game of hide and seek. Imagine entering a cave in complete darkness. You are given a lantern and asked to search for any people who might be moving about, as shown in Figure 1.6b. Several questions might come to mind. Does a strategy even exist that guarantees I will find everyone? If not, then how many other searchers are needed before this task can be completed? Where should I move next? Can I keep from exploring the same places multiple times? This scenario arises in many robotics applications. The robots can be embedded in surveillance systems that use mobile robots with various types of sensors (motion, thermal, cameras, etc.). In scenarios that involve multiple robots with little or no communication, the strategy could help one robot locate others. One robot could even try to locate another that is malfunctioning. Outside of robotics, software tools can be developed that assist people in systematically searching or covering complicated environments, for applications such as law enforcement, search and rescue, toxic cleanup, and in the architectural design of secure buildings. The problem is extremely difficult because the status of the pursuit must be carefully computed to avoid unnecessarily allowing the evader to sneak

Figure 1.8: Across the top, a motion computed by a planning algorithm, for a digital actor to reach into a refrigerator [502]. In the lower left, a digital actor plays chess with a virtual robot [547]. In the lower right, a planning algorithm computes the motions of 100 digital actors moving across terrain with obstacles [594].

back to places already searched. The information-space concepts of Chapter 11 become critical in solving the problem. For an algorithmic solution to the hide-and-seek game, see Section 12.4.

Making smart video game characters

The problem in Figure 1.6b might remind you of a video game. In the arcade classic *Pacman*, the ghosts are programmed to seek the player. Modern video games involve human-like characters that exhibit much more sophisticated behavior. Planning algorithms can enable game developers to program character behaviors at a higher level, with the expectation that the character can determine on its own how to move in an intelligent way.

At present there is a large separation between the planning-algorithm and video-game communities. Some developers of planning algorithms are recently considering more of the particular concerns that are important in video games. Video-game developers have to invest too much energy at present to adapt existing techniques to their problems. For recent books that are geared for game developers, see [154, 373].

Virtual humans and humanoid robots

Beyond video games, there is broader interest in developing virtual humans. See Figure 1.8. In the field of computer graphics, computer-generated animations are a primary focus. Animators would like to develop digital actors that maintain many elusive style characteristics of human actors while at the same time being able to design motions for them from high-level descriptions. It is extremely tedious and time consuming to specify all motions frame-by-frame. The development of planning algorithms in this context is rapidly expanding.

Figure 1.9: (a) This is a picture of the H7 humanoid robot and one of its developers, S. Kagami. It was developed in the JSK Laboratory at the University of Tokyo. (b) Bringing virtual reality and physical reality together. A planning algorithm computes stable motions for a humanoid to grab an obstructed object on the floor [564].

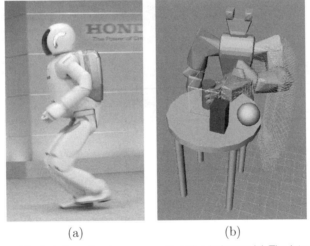

Figure 1.10: Humanoid robots from the Japanese automotive industry: (a) The latest Asimo robot from Honda can run at 3 km/hr (courtesy of Honda); (b) planning is incorporated with vision in the Toyota humanoid so that it plans to grasp objects [451].

Why stop at *virtual* humans? The Japanese robotics community has inspired the world with its development of advanced humanoid robots. In 1997, Honda shocked the world by unveiling an impressive humanoid that could walk up stairs and recover from lost balance. Since that time, numerous corporations and institutions have improved humanoid designs. Although most of the mechanical issues have been worked out, two principle difficulties that remain are sensing and planning. What good is a humanoid robot if it cannot be programmed to accept high-level commands and execute them autonomously? Figure 1.9 shows work from the University of Tokyo for which a plan computed in simulation for a humanoid robot is actually applied on a real humanoid. Figure 1.10 shows humanoid projects from the Japanese automotive industry.

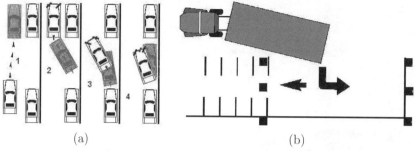

(a)   (b)

Figure 1.11: Some parking illustrations from government manuals for driver testing: (a) parking a car (from the 2005 *Missouri Driver Guide*); (b) parking a tractor trailer (published by the Pennsylvania Division of Motor Vehicles). Both humans and planning algorithms can solve these problems.

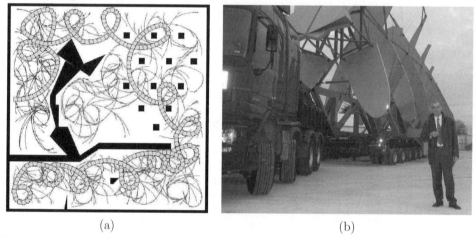

(a)   (b)

Figure 1.12: (a) Having a little fun with differential constraints. An obstacle-avoiding path is shown for a car that must move forward and can only turn left. Could you have found such a solution on your own? This is an easy problem for several planning algorithms. (b) This gigantic truck was designed to transport portions of the Airbus A380 across France. Kineo CAM developed nonholonomic planning software that plans routes through villages that avoid obstacles and satisfy differential constraints imposed by 20 steering axles. Jean-Paul Laumond, a pioneer of nonholonomic planning, is also pictured.

Parking cars and trailers

The planning problems discussed so far have not involved differential constraints, which are the main focus in Part IV. Consider the problem of parking slow-moving vehicles, as shown in Figure 1.11. Most people have a little difficulty with parallel parking a car and much greater difficulty parking a truck with a trailer. Imagine the difficulty of parallel parking an airport baggage train! See Chapter 13 for many related examples. What makes these problems so challenging? A car is constrained to move in the direction that the rear wheels are pointing. Maneuvering the car around obstacles therefore becomes challenging. If all four wheels could turn to any orientation, this problem would vanish. The term *nonholonomic planning* encompasses parking problems and many others. Figure 1.12a shows a humorous driving problem. Figure 1.12b shows an extremely complicated vehicle for which nonholonomic planning algorithms were developed and applied in industry.

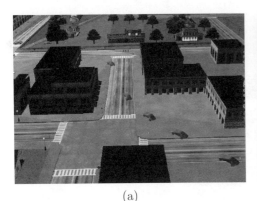
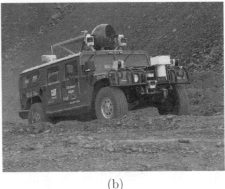

(a)   (b)

Figure 1.13: Reckless driving: (a) Using a planning algorithm to drive a car quickly through an obstacle course [201]. (b) A contender developed by the Red Team from Carnegie Mellon University in the DARPA Grand Challenge for autonomous vehicles driving at high speeds over rugged terrain (courtesy of the Red Team).

"Wreckless" driving

Now consider driving the car at high speeds. As the speed increases, the car must be treated as a dynamical system due to momentum. The car is no longer able to instantaneously start and stop, which was reasonable for parking problems. Although there exist planning algorithms that address such issues, there are still many unsolved research problems. The impact on industry has not yet reached the level achieved by ordinary motion planning, as shown in Figures 1.3 and 1.4. By considering dynamics in the design process, performance and safety evaluations can be performed before constructing the vehicle. Figure 1.13 shows a solution computed by a planning algorithm that determines how to steer a car at high speeds through a town while avoiding collisions with buildings. A planning algorithm could even be used to assess whether a sports utility vehicle tumbles sideways when stopping too quickly. Tremendous time and costs can be spared by determining design flaws early in the development process via simulations and planning. One related problem is *verification*, in which a mechanical system design must be thoroughly tested to make sure that it performs as expected in spite of all possible problems that could go wrong during its use. Planning algorithms can also help in this process. For example, the algorithm can try to violently crash a vehicle, thereby establishing that a better design is needed.

Aside from aiding in the design process, planning algorithms that consider dynamics can be directly embedded into robotic systems. Figure 1.13b shows an application that involves a difficult combination of most of the issues mentioned so far. Driving across rugged, unknown terrain at high speeds involves dynamics, uncertainties, and obstacle avoidance. Numerous unsolved research problems remain in this context.

Flying through the air or in space

Driving naturally leads to flying. Planning algorithms can help to navigate autonomous helicopters through obstacles. They can also compute thrusts for a spacecraft so that collisions are avoided around a complicated structure, such as a space station. In Section 14.1.3, the problem of designing entry trajectories for a reusable spacecraft is described. Mission planning for interplanetary spacecraft, including solar sails, can even be performed using planning algorithms [439].

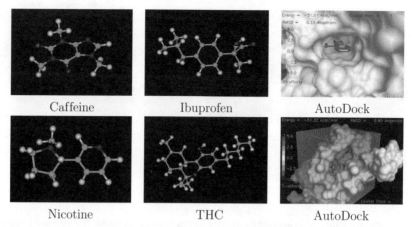

| Caffeine | Ibuprofen | AutoDock |
| Nicotine | THC | AutoDock |

Figure 1.14: On the left, several familiar drugs are pictured as ball-and-stick models (courtesy of the New York University MathMol Library [737]). On the right, 3D models of protein-ligand docking are shown from the AutoDock software package (courtesy of the Scripps Research Institute).

Designing better drugs

Planning algorithms are even impacting fields as far away from robotics as computational biology. Two major problems are protein folding and drug design. In both cases, scientists attempt to explain behaviors in organisms by the way large organic molecules interact. Such molecules are generally flexible. Drug molecules are small (see Figure 1.14), and proteins usually have thousands of atoms. The *docking problem* involves determining whether a flexible molecule can insert itself into a protein cavity, as shown in Figure 1.14, while satisfying other constraints, such as maintaining low energy. Once geometric models are applied to molecules, the problem looks very similar to the assembly problem in Figure 1.3 and can be solved by motion planning algorithms. See Section 7.5 and the literature at the end of Chapter 7.

Perspective

Planning algorithms have been applied to many more problems than those shown here. In some cases, the work has progressed from modeling, to theoretical algorithms, to practical software that is used in industry. In other cases, substantial research remains to bring planning methods to their full potential. The future holds tremendous excitement for those who participate in the development and application of planning algorithms.

1.3 Basic ingredients of planning

Although the subject of this book spans a broad class of models and problems, there are several basic ingredients that arise throughout virtually all of the topics covered as part of planning.

State

Planning problems involve a *state space* that captures all possible situations that could arise. The *state* could, for example, represent the position and orientation of a robot, the locations of tiles in a puzzle, or the position and velocity of a helicopter. Both discrete (finite, or countably infinite) and continuous (uncountably infinite) state spaces will be allowed. One recurring theme is that the state space is usually represented *implicitly* by a planning algorithm. In most applications, the size of the state space (in terms of number of states or combinatorial complexity) is much too large to be explicitly represented. Nevertheless, the definition of the state space is an important component in the formulation of a planning problem and in the design and analysis of algorithms that solve it.

Time

All planning problems involve a sequence of decisions that must be applied over time. Time might be explicitly modeled, as in a problem such as driving a car as quickly as possible through an obstacle course. Alternatively, time may be implicit, by simply reflecting the fact that actions must follow in succession, as in the case of solving the Rubik's cube. The particular time is unimportant, but the proper sequence must be maintained. Another example of implicit time is a solution to the Piano Mover's Problem; the solution to moving the piano may be converted into an animation over time, but the particular speed is not specified in the plan. As in the case of state spaces, time may be either discrete or continuous. In the latter case, imagine that a continuum of decisions is being made by a plan.

Actions

A plan generates *actions* that manipulate the state. The terms *actions* and *operators* are common in artificial intelligence; in control theory and robotics, the related terms are *inputs* and *controls*. Somewhere in the planning formulation, it must be specified how the state changes when actions are applied. This may be expressed as a state-valued function for the case of discrete time or as an ordinary differential equation for continuous time. For most motion planning problems, explicit reference to time is avoided by directly specifying a path through a continuous state space. Such paths could be obtained as the integral of differential equations, but this is not necessary. For some problems, actions could be chosen by *nature*, which interfere with the outcome and are not under the control of the decision maker. This enables uncertainty in predictability to be introduced into the planning problem; see Chapter 10.

Initial and goal states

A planning problem usually involves starting in some initial state and trying to arrive at a specified goal state or any state in a set of goal states. The actions are selected in a way that tries to make this happen.

A criterion

This encodes the desired outcome of a plan in terms of the state and actions that are executed. There are generally two different kinds of planning concerns based on the type of criterion:

1. **Feasibility:** Find a plan that causes arrival at a goal state, regardless of its efficiency.
2. **Optimality:** Find a feasible plan that optimizes performance in some carefully specified manner, in addition to arriving in a goal state.

For most of the problems considered in this book, feasibility is already challenging enough; achieving optimality is considerably harder for most problems. Therefore, much of the focus is on finding feasible solutions to problems, as opposed to optimal solutions. The majority of literature in robotics, control theory, and related fields focuses on optimality,

Figure 1.15: According to the Church-Turing thesis, the notion of an algorithm is equivalent to the notion of a Turing machine.

but this is not necessarily important for many problems of interest. In many applications, it is difficult to even formulate the right criterion to optimize. Even if a desirable criterion can be formulated, it may be impossible to obtain a practical algorithm that computes optimal plans. In such cases, feasible solutions are certainly preferable to having no solutions at all. Fortunately, for many algorithms the solutions produced are not too far from optimal in practice. This reduces some of the motivation for finding optimal solutions. For problems that involve probabilistic uncertainty, however, optimization arises more frequently. The probabilities are often utilized to obtain the best performance in terms of expected costs. Feasibility is often associated with performing a worst-case analysis of uncertainties.

A plan

In general, a plan imposes a specific strategy or behavior on a decision maker. A plan may simply specify a sequence of actions to be taken; however, it could be more complicated. If it is impossible to predict future states, then the plan can specify actions as a function of state. In this case, regardless of the future states, the appropriate action is determined. Using terminology from other fields, this enables *feedback* or *reactive plans*. It might even be the case that the state cannot be measured. In this case, the appropriate action must be determined from whatever information is available up to the current time. This will generally be referred to as an *information state*, on which the actions of a plan are conditioned.

1.4 Algorithms, planners, and plans

1.4.1 Algorithms

What is a planning algorithm? This is a difficult question, and a precise mathematical definition will not be given in this book. Instead, the general idea will be explained, along with many examples of planning algorithms. A more basic question is, What is an algorithm? One answer is the classical Turing machine model, which is used to define an algorithm in theoretical computer science. A *Turing machine* is a finite state machine with a special head that can read and write along an infinite piece of tape, as depicted in Figure 1.15. The Church-Turing thesis states that an algorithm *is* a Turing machine (see [465, 892] for more details). The *input* to the algorithm is encoded as a string of symbols (usually a binary string) and then is written to the tape. The Turing machine reads the string, performs computations, and then decides whether to *accept* or *reject* the string. This version of the Turing machine only solves *decision problems*; however, there are straightforward extensions that can yield other desired outputs, such as a
.n.

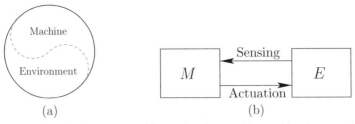

Figure 1.16: (a) The boundary between machine and environment is considered as an arbitrary line that may be drawn in many ways depending on the context. (b) Once the boundary has been drawn, it is assumed that the machine, *M*, interacts with the environment, *E*, through sensing and actuation.

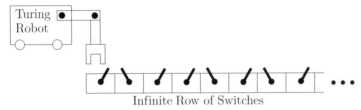

Figure 1.17: A robot and an infinite sequence of switches could be used to simulate a Turing machine. Through manipulation, however, many other kinds of behavior could be obtained that fall outside of the Turing model.

The Turing model is reasonable for many of the algorithms in this book; however, others may not exactly fit. The trouble with using the Turing machine in some situations is that plans often interact with the physical world. As indicated in Figure 1.16, the boundary between the machine and the environment is an arbitrary line that varies from problem to problem. Once drawn, sensors provide information about the environment; this provides input to the machine during execution. The machine then executes actions, which provides actuation to the environment. The actuation may alter the environment in some way that is later measured by sensors. Therefore, the machine and its environment are closely coupled during execution. This is fundamental to robotics and many other fields in which planning is used.

Using the Turing machine as a foundation for algorithms usually implies that the physical world must be first carefully modeled and written on the tape before the algorithm can make decisions. If changes occur in the world during execution of the algorithm, then it is not clear what should happen. For example, a mobile robot could be moving in a cluttered environment in which people are walking around. As another example, a robot might throw an object onto a table without being able to precisely predict how the object will come to rest. It can take measurements of the results with sensors, but it again becomes a difficult task to determine how much information should be explicitly modeled and written on the tape. The *on-line algorithm* model is more appropriate for these kinds of problems [513, 771, 893]; however, it still does not capture a notion of algorithms that is broad enough for all of the topics of this book.

Processes that occur in a physical world are more complicated than the interaction between a state machine and a piece of tape filled with symbols. It is even possible to simulate the tape by imagining a robot that interacts with a long row of switches as depicted in Figure 1.17. The switches serve the same purpose as the tape, and the robot

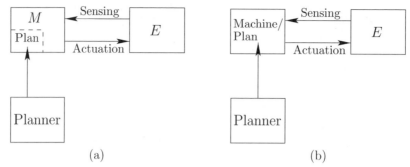

Figure 1.18: (a) A planner produces a plan that may be executed by the machine. The planner may either be a machine itself or even a human. (b) Alternatively, the planner may design the entire machine.

carries a computer that can simulate the finite state machine.[1] The complicated interaction allowed between a robot and its environment could give rise to many other models of computation.[2] Thus, the term *algorithm* will be used somewhat less formally than in the theory of computation. Both *planners* and *plans* are considered as algorithms in this book.

1.4.2 Planners

A planner simply constructs a plan and may be a machine or a human. If the planner is a machine, it will generally be considered as a planning algorithm. In many circumstances it is an algorithm in the strict Turing sense; however, this is not necessary. In some cases, humans become planners by developing a plan that works in all situations. For example, it is perfectly acceptable for a human to design a state machine that is connected to the environment (see Section 12.3.1). There are no additional inputs in this case because the human fulfills the role of the algorithm. The planning model is given as input to the human, and the human "computes" a plan.

1.4.3 Plans

Once a plan is determined, there are three ways to use it:

1. **Execution:** Execute it either in simulation or in a mechanical device (robot) connected to the physical world.

2. **Refinement:** Refine it into a better plan.

3. **Hierarchical Inclusion:** Package it as an action in a higher level plan.

Each of these will be explained in succession.

Execution

A plan is usually executed by a machine. A human could alternatively execute it; however, the case of machine execution is the primary focus of this book. There are two general types of machine execution. The first is depicted in Figure 1.18a, in which the planner

---

[1] Of course, having infinitely long tape seems impossible in the physical world. Other versions of Turing machines exist in which the tape is finite but as long as necessary to process the given input. This may be more appropriate for the discussion.

[2] Performing computations with mechanical systems is discussed in [818]. Computation models over the reals are covered in [120].

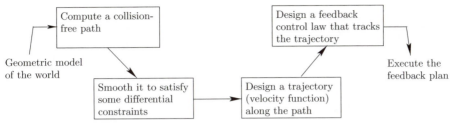

Figure 1.19: A refinement approach that has been used for decades in robotics.

produces a *plan*, which is encoded in some way and given as input to the machine. In this case, the machine is considered *programmable* and can accept possible plans from a planner before execution. It will generally be assumed that once the plan is given, the machine becomes autonomous and can no longer interact with the planner. Of course, this model could be extended to allow machines to be improved over time by receiving better plans; however, we want a strict notion of autonomy for the discussion of planning in this book. This approach does not prohibit the updating of plans in practice; however, this is not preferred because plans should already be designed to take into account new information during execution.

The second type of machine execution of a plan is depicted in Figure 1.18b. In this case, the plan produced by the planner encodes an entire machine. The plan *is* a special-purpose machine that is designed to solve the specific tasks given originally to the planner. Under this interpretation, one may be a *minimalist* and design the simplest machine possible that sufficiently solves the desired tasks. If the plan is encoded as a finite state machine, then it can sometimes be considered as an algorithm in the Turing sense (depending on whether connecting the machine to a tape preserves its operation).

Refinement

If a plan is used for refinement, then a planner accepts it as input and determines a new plan that is hopefully an improvement. The new plan may take more problem aspects into account, or it may simply be more efficient. Refinement may be applied repeatedly, to produce a sequence of improved plans, until the final one is executed. Figure 1.19 shows a refinement approach used in robotics. Consider, for example, moving an indoor mobile robot. The first plan yields a collision-free path through the building. The second plan transforms the route into one that satisfies differential constraints based on wheel motions (recall Figure 1.11). The third plan considers how to move the robot along the path at various speeds while satisfying momentum considerations. The fourth plan incorporates feedback to ensure that the robot stays as close as possible to the planned path in spite of unpredictable behavior. Further elaboration on this approach and its trade-offs appears in Section 14.6.1.

Hierarchical inclusion

Under hierarchical inclusion, a plan is incorporated as an action in a larger plan. The original plan can be imagined as a subroutine in the larger plan. For this to succeed, it is important for the original plan to guarantee *termination*, so that the larger plan can execute more actions as needed. Hierarchical inclusion can be performed any number of times, resulting in a rooted *tree* of plans. This leads to a general model of *hierarchical planning*. Each vertex in the tree is a plan. The root vertex represents the *master plan*. The children of any vertex are plans that are incorporated as actions in the plan of the

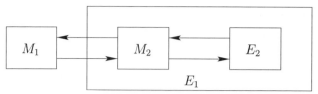

Figure 1.20: In a hierarchical model, the environment of one machine may itself contain a machine.

vertex. There is no limit to the tree depth or number of children per vertex. In hierarchical planning, the line between machine and environment is drawn in multiple places. For example, the environment, E_1, with respect to a machine, M_1, might actually include another machine, M_2, that interacts with its environment, E_2, as depicted in Figure 1.20. Examples of hierarchical planning appear in Sections 7.3.2 and 12.5.1.

1.5 Organization of the book

Here is a brief overview of the book. See also the overviews at the beginning of Parts II–IV.

PART I: Introductory Material
This provides very basic background for the rest of the book.

- **Chapter 1: Introductory Material**
  This chapter offers some general perspective and includes some motivational examples and applications of planning algorithms.

- **Chapter 2: Discrete Planning**
  This chapter covers the simplest form of planning and can be considered as a springboard for entering into the rest of the book. From here, you can continue to Part II, or even head straight to Part III. Sections 2.1 and 2.2 are most important for heading into Part II. For Part III, Section 2.3 is additionally useful.

PART II: Motion Planning
The main source of inspiration for the problems and algorithms covered in this part is robotics. The methods, however, are general enough for use in other applications in other areas, such as computational biology, computer-aided design, and computer graphics. An alternative title that more accurately reflects the kind of planning that occurs is "Planning in Continuous State Spaces."

- **Chapter 3: Geometric Representations and Transformations**
  The chapter gives important background for expressing a motion planning problem. Section 3.1 describes how to construct geometric models, and the remaining sections indicate how to transform them. Sections 3.1 and 3.2 are important for later chapters.

- **Chapter 4: The Configuration Space**
  This chapter introduces concepts from topology and uses them to formulate the *configuration space*, which is the state space that arises in motion planning. Sections 4.1, 4.2, and 4.3.1 are important for understanding most of the material in later chapters. In addition to the previously mentioned sections, all of Section 4.3 provides useful background for the combinatorial methods of Chapter 6.

- **Chapter 5: Sampling-Based Motion Planning**
  This chapter introduces motion planning algorithms that have dominated the literature in recent years and have been applied in fields both in and out of robotics. If you understand

the basic idea that the configuration space represents a continuous state space, most of the concepts should be understandable. They even apply to other problems in which continuous state spaces emerge, in addition to motion planning and robotics. Chapter 14 revisits sampling-based planning, but under differential constraints.

- **Chapter 6: Combinatorial Motion Planning**
  The algorithms covered in this section are sometimes called *exact algorithms* because they build discrete representations without losing any information. They are *complete*, which means that they must find a solution if one exists; otherwise, they report failure. The sampling-based algorithms have been more useful in practice, but they only achieve weaker notions of completeness.

- **Chapter 7: Extensions of Basic Motion Planning**
  This chapter introduces many problems and algorithms that are extensions of the methods from Chapters 5 and 6. Most can be followed with basic understanding of the material from these chapters. Section 7.4 covers planning for closed kinematic chains; this requires an understanding of the additional material, from Section 4.4

- **Chapter 8: Feedback Motion Planning**
  This is a transitional chapter that introduces feedback into the motion planning problem but still does not introduce differential constraints, which are deferred until Part IV. The previous chapters of Part II focused on computing *open-loop* plans, which means that any errors that might occur during execution of the plan are ignored, yet the plan will be executed as planned. Using feedback yields a *closed-loop* plan that responds to unpredictable events during execution.

PART III: Decision-Theoretic Planning

An alternative title to Part III is "Planning Under Uncertainty." Most of Part III addresses discrete state spaces, which can be studied immediately following Part I. However, some sections cover extensions to continuous spaces; to understand these parts, it will be helpful to have read some of Part II.

- **Chapter 9: Basic Decision Theory**
  The main idea in this chapter is to design the best decision for a decision maker that is confronted with interference from other decision makers. The others may be true opponents in a game or may be fictitious in order to model uncertainties. The chapter focuses on making a decision in a single step and provides a building block for Part III because planning under uncertainty can be considered as multi-step decision making.

- **Chapter 10: Sequential Decision Theory**
  This chapter takes the concepts from Chapter 9 and extends them by chaining together a sequence of basic decision-making problems. Dynamic programming concepts from Section 2.3 become important here. For all of the problems in this chapter, it is assumed that the current state is always known. All uncertainties that exist are with respect to prediction of future states, as opposed to measuring the current state.

- **Chapter 11: Sensors and Information Spaces**
  The chapter extends the formulations of Chapter 10 into a framework for planning when the current state is unknown during execution. Information regarding the state is obtained from sensor observations and the memory of actions that were previously applied. The information space serves a similar purpose for problems with sensing uncertainty as the configuration space has for motion planning.

- **Chapter 12: Planning Under Sensing Uncertainty**
  This chapter covers several planning problems and algorithms that involve sensing uncertainty. This includes problems such as localization, map building, pursuit-evasion, and

manipulation. All of these problems are unified under the idea of planning in information spaces, which follows from Chapter 11.

PART IV: Planning Under Differential Constraints

This can be considered as a continuation of Part II. Here there can be both global (obstacles) and local (differential) constraints on the continuous state spaces that arise in motion planning. Dynamical systems are also considered, which yields state spaces that include both position and velocity information (this coincides with the notion of a *state space* in control theory or a *phase space* in physics and differential equations).

- **Chapter 13: Differential Models**
  This chapter serves as an introduction to Part IV by introducing numerous models that involve differential constraints. This includes constraints that arise from wheels rolling as well as some that arise from the dynamics of mechanical systems.

- **Chapter 14: Sampling-Based Planning Under Differential Constraints**
  Algorithms for solving planning problems under the models of Chapter 13 are presented. Many algorithms are extensions of methods from Chapter 5. All methods are sampling-based because very little can be accomplished with combinatorial techniques in the context of differential constraints.

- **Chapter 15: System Theory and Analytical Techniques**
  This chapter provides an overview of the concepts and tools developed mainly in control theory literature. They are complementary to the algorithms of Chapter 14 and often provide important insights or components in the development of planning algorithms under differential constraints.

2

Discrete Planning

This chapter provides introductory concepts that serve as an entry point into other parts of the book. The planning problems considered here are the simplest to describe because the state space will be finite in most cases. When it is not finite, it will at least be countably infinite (i.e., a unique integer may be assigned to every state). Therefore, no geometric models or differential equations will be needed to characterize the discrete planning problems. Furthermore, no forms of uncertainty will be considered, which avoids complications such as probability theory. All models are completely known and predictable.

There are three main parts to this chapter. Sections 2.1 and 2.2 define and present search methods for feasible planning, in which the only concern is to reach a goal state. The search methods will be used throughout the book in numerous other contexts, including motion planning in continuous state spaces. Following feasible planning, Section 2.3 addresses the problem of optimal planning. The *principle of optimality*, or the *dynamic programming principle*, [86] provides a key insight that greatly reduces the computation effort in many planning algorithms. The *value-iteration* method of dynamic programming is the main focus of Section 2.3. The relationship between Dijkstra's algorithm and value iteration is also discussed. Finally, Sections 2.4 and 2.5 describe logic-based representations of planning and methods that exploit these representations to make the problem easier to solve; material from these sections is not needed in later chapters.

Although this chapter addresses a form of planning, it encompasses what is sometimes referred to as *problem solving*. Throughout the history of artificial intelligence research, the distinction between *problem solving* [738] and *planning* has been rather elusive. The widely used textbook by Russell and Norvig [842] provides a representative, modern survey of the field of artificial intelligence. Two of its six main parts are termed "problem-solving" and "planning"; however, their definitions are quite similar. The problem-solving part begins by stating, "Problem solving agents decide what to do by finding sequences of actions that lead to desirable states" ([842], p. 59). The planning part begins with, "The task of coming up with a sequence of actions that will achieve a goal is called planning" ([842], p. 375). Also, the STRIPS system [339] is widely considered as a seminal planning algorithm, and the "PS" part of its name stands for "Problem Solver." Thus, problem solving and planning appear to be synonymous. Perhaps the term "planning" carries connotations of future time, whereas "problem solving" sounds somewhat more general. A problem-solving task might be to take evidence from a crime scene and piece together the actions taken by suspects. It might seem odd to call this a "plan" because it occurred in the past.

Since it is difficult to make clear distinctions between problem solving and planning, we will simply refer to both as planning. This also helps to keep with the theme of this book. Note, however, that some of the concepts apply to a broader set of problems than what is often meant by planning.

2.1 Introduction to discrete feasible planning

2.1.1 Problem formulation

The discrete feasible planning model will be defined using state-space models, which will appear repeatedly throughout this book. Most of these will be natural extensions of the model presented in this section. The basic idea is that each distinct situation for the world is called a *state*, denoted by x, and the set of all possible states is called a *state space*, X. For discrete planning, it will be important that this set is countable; in most cases it will be finite. In a given application, the state space should be defined carefully so that irrelevant information is not encoded into a state (e.g., a planning problem that involves moving a robot in France should not encode information about whether certain light bulbs are on in China). The inclusion of irrelevant information can easily convert a problem that is amenable to efficient algorithmic solutions into one that is intractable. On the other hand, it is important that X is large enough to include all information that is relevant to solve the task.

The world may be transformed through the application of *actions* that are chosen by the planner. Each action, u, when applied from the current state, x, produces a new state, x', as specified by a *state transition function*, f. It is convenient to use f to express a *state transition equation*,

$$x' = f(x, u). \tag{2.1}$$

Let $U(x)$ denote the *action space* for each state x, which represents the set of all actions that could be applied from x. For distinct $x, x' \in X$, $U(x)$ and $U(x')$ are not necessarily disjoint; the same action may be applicable in multiple states. Therefore, it is convenient to define the set U of all possible actions over all states:

$$U = \bigcup_{x \in X} U(x). \tag{2.2}$$

As part of the planning problem, a set $X_G \subset X$ of *goal states* is defined. The task of a planning algorithm is to find a finite sequence of actions that when applied, transforms the initial state x_I to some state in X_G. The model is summarized as:

Formulation 2.1 (Discrete feasible planning)

1. A nonempty *state space* X, which is a finite or countably infinite set of *states*.
2. For each state $x \in X$, a finite *action space* $U(x)$.
3. A *state transition function* f that produces a state $f(x, u) \in X$ for every $x \in X$ and $u \in U(x)$. The *state transition equation* is derived from f as $x' = f(x, u)$.
4. An *initial state* $x_I \in X$.
5. A *goal set* $X_G \subset X$.

It is often convenient to express Formulation 2.1 as a directed *state transition graph*. The set of vertices is the state space X. A directed edge from $x \in X$ to $x' \in X$ exists in the graph if and only if there exists an action $u \in U(x)$ such that $x' = f(x, u)$. The initial state and goal set are designated as special vertices in the graph, which completes the representation of Formulation 2.1 in graph form.

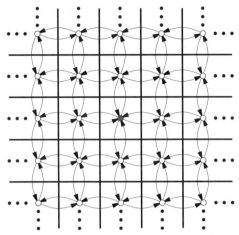

Figure 2.1: The state transition graph for an example problem that involves walking around on an infinite tile floor.

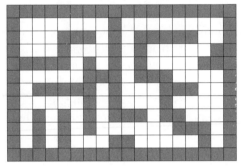

Figure 2.2: Interesting planning problems that involve exploring a labyrinth can be made by shading in tiles.

2.1.2 Examples of discrete planning

Example 2.1 (Moving on a 2D Grid) Suppose that a robot moves on a grid in which each grid point has integer coordinates of the form (i, j). The robot takes discrete steps in one of four directions (up, down, left, right), each of which increments or decrements one coordinate. The motions and corresponding state transition graph are shown in Figure 2.1, which can be imagined as stepping from tile to tile on an infinite tile floor.

This will be expressed using Formulation 2.1. Let X be the set of all integer pairs of the form (i, j), in which $i, j \in \mathbb{Z}$ ($\mathbb{Z}$ denotes the set of all integers). Let $U = \{(0, 1), (0, -1), (1, 0), (-1, 0)\}$. Let $U(x) = U$ for all $x \in X$. The state transition equation is $f(x, u) = x + u$, in which $x \in X$ and $u \in U$ are treated as two-dimensional vectors for the purpose of addition. For example, if $x = (3, 4)$ and $u = (0, 1)$, then $f(x, u) = (3, 5)$. Suppose for convenience that the initial state is $x_I = (0, 0)$. Many interesting goal sets are possible. Suppose, for example, that $X_G = \{(100, 100)\}$. It is easy to find a sequence of inputs that transforms the state from $(0, 0)$ to $(100, 100)$.

The problem can be made more interesting by shading in some of the square tiles to represent obstacles that the robot must avoid, as shown in Figure 2.2. In this case, any tile that is shaded has its corresponding vertex and associated edges deleted from the state transition graph. An outer boundary can be made to fence in a bounded region so that X becomes finite. Very complicated labyrinths can be constructed.   ■

Example 2.2 (Rubik's Cube Puzzle)   Many puzzles can be expressed as discrete planning problems. For example, the Rubik's cube is a puzzle that looks like an array of $3 \times 3 \times 3$ little cubes, which together form a larger cube as shown in Figure 1.1a (Section 1.2). Each face of the larger cube is painted one of six colors. An action may be applied to the cube by rotating a 3×3 sheet of cubes by 90 degrees. After applying many actions to the Rubik's cube, each face will generally be a jumble of colors. The state space is the set of configurations for the cube (the orientation of the entire cube is irrelevant). For each state there are 12 possible actions. For some arbitrarily chosen configuration of the Rubik's cube, the planning task is to find a sequence of actions that returns it to the configuration in which each one of its six faces is a single color.   ■

It is important to note that a planning problem is usually specified without explicitly representing the entire state transition graph. Instead, it is revealed incrementally in the planning process. In Example 2.1, very little information actually needs to be given to specify a graph that is infinite in size. If a planning problem is given as input to an algorithm, close attention must be paid to the encoding when performing a complexity analysis. For a problem in which X is infinite, the input length must still be finite. For some interesting classes of problems it may be possible to compactly specify a model that is equivalent to Formulation 2.1. Such representation issues have been the basis of much research in artificial intelligence over the past decades as different representation logics have been proposed; see Section 2.4 and [384]. In a sense, these representations can be viewed as input compression schemes.

Readers experienced in computer engineering might recognize that when X is finite, Formulation 2.1 appears almost identical to the definition of a *finite state machine* or *Mealy/Moore machines*. Relating the two models, the actions can be interpreted as *inputs* to the state machine, and the output of the machine simply reports its state. Therefore, the feasible planning problem (if X is finite) may be interpreted as determining whether there exists a sequence of inputs that makes a finite state machine eventually report a desired output. From a planning perspective, it is assumed that the planning algorithm has a complete specification of the machine transitions and is able to read its current state at any time.

Readers experienced with theoretical computer science may observe similar connections to a *deterministic finite automaton* (DFA), which is a special kind of finite state machine that reads an *input string* and makes a decision about whether to *accept* or *reject* the string. The input string is just a finite sequence of inputs, in the same sense as for a finite state machine. A DFA definition includes a set of *accept states*, which in the planning context can be renamed to the *goal set*. This makes the feasible planning problem (if X is finite) equivalent to determining whether there exists an input string that is accepted by a given DFA. Usually, a *language* is associated with a DFA, which is the set of all strings it accepts. DFAs are important in the theory of computation because their languages correspond precisely to regular expressions. The planning problem amounts to determining whether the empty language is associated with the DFA.

Thus, there are several ways to represent and interpret the discrete feasible planning problem that sometimes lead to a very compact, implicit encoding of the problem. This

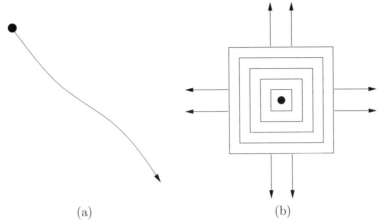

(a)   (b)

Figure 2.3: (a) Many search algorithms focus too much on one direction, which may prevent them from being systematic on infinite graphs. (b) If, for example, the search carefully expands in wavefronts, then it becomes systematic. The requirement to be systematic is that, in the limit, as the number of iterations tends to infinity, all reachable vertices are reached.

issue will be revisited in Section 2.4. Until then, basic planning algorithms are introduced in Section 2.2, and discrete optimal planning is covered in Section 2.3.

2.2 Searching for feasible plans

The methods presented in this section are just graph search algorithms, but with the understanding that the state transition graph is revealed incrementally through the application of actions, instead of being fully specified in advance. The presentation in this section can therefore be considered as visiting graph search algorithms from a planning perspective. An important requirement for these or any search algorithms is to be *systematic*. If the graph is finite, this means that the algorithm will visit every reachable state, which enables it to correctly declare in finite time whether or not a solution exists. To be systematic, the algorithm should keep track of states already visited; otherwise, the search may run forever by cycling through the same states. Ensuring that no redundant exploration occurs is sufficient to make the search systematic.

   If the graph is infinite, then we are willing to tolerate a weaker definition for being systematic. If a solution exists, then the search algorithm still must report it in finite time; however, if a solution does not exist, it is acceptable for the algorithm to search forever. This systematic requirement is achieved by ensuring that, in the limit, as the number of search iterations tends to infinity, every reachable vertex in the graph is explored. Since the number of vertices is assumed to be countable, this must always be possible.

   As an example of this requirement, consider Example 2.1 on an infinite tile floor with no obstacles. If the search algorithm explores in only one direction, as depicted in Figure 2.3a, then in the limit most of the space will be left uncovered, even though no states are revisited. If instead the search proceeds outward from the origin in wavefronts, as depicted in Figure 2.3b, then it may be systematic. In practice, each search algorithm has to be carefully analyzed. A search algorithm could expand in multiple directions, or even in wavefronts, but still not be systematic. If the graph is finite, then it is much simpler: Virtually any search algorithm is systematic, provided that it marks visited states to avoid revisiting the same states indefinitely.

FORWARD_SEARCH
1      $Q.Insert(x_I)$ and mark x_I as visited
2   **while** Q not empty **do**
3            $x \leftarrow Q.GetFirst()$
4   **if** $x \in X_G$
5   **return** SUCCESS
6   **forall** $u \in U(x)$
7                  $x' \leftarrow f(x, u)$
8   **if** x' not visited
9   Mark x' as visited
10                       $Q.Insert(x')$
11   **else**
12   Resolve duplicate x'
13   **return** FAILURE

Figure 2.4: A general template for forward search.

2.2.1 General forward search

Figure 2.4 gives a general template of search algorithms, expressed using the state-space representation. At any point during the search, there will be three kinds of states:

1. **Unvisited:** States that have not been visited yet. Initially, this is every state except x_I.

2. **Dead:** States that have been visited, and for which every possible next state has also been visited. A *next state* of x is a state x' for which there exists a $u \in U(x)$ such that $x' = f(x, u)$. In a sense, these states are *dead* because there is nothing more that they can contribute to the search; there are no new leads that could help in finding a feasible plan. Section 2.3.3 discusses a variant in which dead states can become alive again in an effort to obtain optimal plans.

3. **Alive:** States that have been encountered and possibly some adjacent states that have not been visited. These are considered *alive*. Initially, the only alive state is x_I.

The set of alive states is stored in a priority queue, Q, for which a priority function must be specified. The only significant difference between various search algorithms is the particular function used to sort Q. Many variations will be described later, but for the time being, it might be helpful to pick one. Therefore, assume for now that Q is a common FIFO (First-In First-Out) queue; whichever state has been waiting the longest will be chosen when $Q.GetFirst()$ is called. The rest of the general search algorithm is quite simple. Initially, Q contains the initial state x_I. A **while** loop is then executed, which terminates only when Q is empty. This will only occur when the entire graph has been explored without finding any goal states, which results in a FAILURE (unless the reachable portion of X is infinite, in which case the algorithm should never terminate). In each **while** iteration, the highest ranked element, x, of Q is removed. If x lies in X_G, then it reports SUCCESS and terminates; otherwise, the algorithm tries applying every possible action, $u \in U(x)$. For each next state, $x' = f(x, u)$, it must determine whether x' is being encountered for the first time. If it is unvisited, then it is inserted into Q; otherwise, there is no need to consider it because it must be either dead or already in Q.

The algorithm description in Figure 2.4 omits several details that often become important in practice. For example, how efficient is the test to determine whether $x \in X_G$ in line 4? This depends, of course, on the size of the state space and on the particular representations chosen for x and X_G. At this level, we do not specify a particular method because the representations are not given.

One important detail is that the existing algorithm only indicates whether a solution exists, but does not seem to produce a plan, which is a sequence of actions that achieves the goal. This can be fixed by inserting a line after line 7 that associates with x' its parent, x. If this is performed each time, one can simply trace the pointers from the final state to the initial state to recover the plan. For convenience, one might also store which action was taken, in addition to the pointer from x' to x.

Lines 8 and 9 are conceptually simple, but how can one tell whether x' has been visited? For some problems the state transition graph might actually be a tree, which means that there are no repeated states. Although this does not occur frequently, it is wonderful when it does because there is no need to check whether states have been visited. If the states in X all lie on a grid, one can simply make a lookup table that can be accessed in constant time to determine whether a state has been visited. In general, however, it might be quite difficult because the state x' must be compared with every other state in Q and with all of the dead states. If the representation of each state is long, as is sometimes the case, this will be very costly. A good hashing scheme or another clever data structure can greatly alleviate this cost, but in many applications the computation time will remain high. One alternative is to simply allow repeated states, but this could lead to an increase in computational cost that far outweighs the benefits. Even if the graph is very small, search algorithms could run in time exponential in the size of the state transition graph, or the search may not terminate at all, even if the graph is finite.

One final detail is that some search algorithms will require a cost to be computed and associated with every state. If the same state is reached multiple times, the cost may have to be updated, which is performed in line 12, if the particular search algorithm requires it. Such costs may be used in some way to sort the priority queue, or they may enable the recovery of the plan on completion of the algorithm. Instead of storing pointers, as mentioned previously, the optimal cost to return to the initial state could be stored with each state. This cost alone is sufficient to determine the action sequence that leads to any visited state. Starting at a visited state, the path back to x_I can be obtained by traversing the state transition graph backward in a way that decreases the cost as quickly as possible in each step. For this to succeed, the costs must have a certain monotonicity property, which is obtained by Dijkstra's algorithm and A^* search, and will be introduced in Section 2.2.2. More generally, the costs must form a *navigation function*, which is considered in Section 8.2.2 as feedback is incorporated into discrete planning.

2.2.2 Particular forward search methods

This section presents several search algorithms, each of which constructs a search tree. Each search algorithm is a special case of the algorithm in Figure 2.4, obtained by defining a different sorting function for Q. Most of these are just classical graph search algorithms [245].

Breadth first

The method given in Section 2.2.1 specifies Q as a First-In First-Out (FIFO) queue, which selects states using the first-come, first-serve principle. This causes the search frontier to grow uniformly and is therefore referred to as *breadth-first search*. All plans that have k steps are exhausted before plans with $k + 1$ steps are investigated. Therefore, breadth first guarantees that the first solution found will use the smallest number of steps. On detection that a state has been revisited, there is no work to do in line 12. Since the search progresses in a series of wavefronts, breadth-first search is systematic. In fact, it even remains systematic if it does not keep track of repeated states (however, it will waste time considering irrelevant cycles).

The asymptotic running time of breadth-first search is $O(|V| + |E|)$, in which $|V|$ and $|E|$ are the numbers of vertices and edges, respectively, in the state transition graph (recall, however, that the graph is usually not the input; for example, the input may be the rules of the Rubik's cube). This assumes that all basic operations, such as determining whether a state has been visited, are performed in constant time. In practice, these operations will typically require more time and must be counted as part of the algorithm's complexity. The running time can be expressed in terms of the other representations. Recall that $|V| = |X|$ is the number of states. If the same actions U are available from every state, then $|E| = |U||X|$. If the action sets $U(x_1)$ and $U(x_2)$ are pairwise disjoint for any $x_1, x_2 \in X$, then $|E| = |U|$.

Depth first

By making Q a stack (Last-In, First-Out; or LIFO), aggressive exploration of the state transition graph occurs, as opposed to the uniform expansion of breadth-first search. The resulting variant is called *depth-first search* because the search dives quickly into the graph. The preference is toward investigating longer plans very early. Although this aggressive behavior might seem desirable, note that the particular choice of longer plans is arbitrary. Actions are applied in the **forall** loop in whatever order they happen to be defined. Once again, if a state is revisited, there is no work to do in line 12. Depth-first search is systematic for any finite X but not for an infinite X because it could behave like Figure 2.3a. The search could easily focus on one "direction" and completely miss large portions of the search space as the number of iterations tends to infinity. The running time of depth first search is also $O(|V| + |E|)$.

Dijkstra's algorithm

Up to this point, there has been no reason to prefer one action over any other in the search. Section 2.3 will formalize optimal discrete planning and will present several algorithms that find optimal plans. Before going into that, we present a systematic search algorithm that finds optimal plans because it is also useful for finding feasible plans. The result is the well-known Dijkstra's algorithm for finding single-source shortest paths in a graph [275], which is a special form of dynamic programming. More general dynamic programming computations appear in Section 2.3 and throughout the book.

Suppose that every edge, $e \in E$, in the graph representation of a discrete planning problem has an associated nonnegative cost $l(e)$, which is the cost to apply the action. The cost $l(e)$ could be written using the state-space representation as $l(x, u)$, indicating that it costs $l(x, u)$ to apply action u from state x. The total cost of a plan is just the sum of the edge costs over the path from the initial state to a goal state.

The priority queue, Q, will be sorted according to a function $C : X \to [0, \infty]$, called the *cost-to-come*. For each state x, the value $C^*(x)$ is called the *optimal*[1] *cost-to-come* from the initial state x_I. This optimal cost is obtained by summing edge costs, $l(e)$, over

---

[1] As in optimization literature, we will use * to mean *optimal*.

all possible paths from x_I to x and using the path that produces the least cumulative cost. If the cost is not known to be optimal, then it is written as $C(x)$.

The cost-to-come is computed incrementally during the execution of the search algorithm in Figure 2.4. Initially, $C^*(x_I) = 0$. Each time the state x' is generated, a cost is computed as $C(x') = C^*(x) + l(e)$, in which e is the edge from x to x' (equivalently, we may write $C(x') = C^*(x) + l(x, u)$). Here, $C(x')$ represents the best cost-to-come that is known so far, but we do not write C^* because it is not yet known whether x' was reached optimally. Due to this, some work is required in line 12. If x' already exists in Q, then it is possible that the newly discovered path to x' is more efficient. If so, then the cost-to-come value $C(x')$ must be lowered for x', and Q must be reordered accordingly.

When does $C(x)$ finally become $C^*(x)$ for some state x? Once x is removed from Q using $Q.GetFirst()$, the state becomes dead, and it is known that x cannot be reached with a lower cost. This can be argued by induction. For the initial state, $C^*(x_I)$ is known, and this serves as the base case. Now assume that every dead state has its optimal cost-to-come correctly determined. This means that their cost-to-come values can no longer change. For the first element, x, of Q, the value must be optimal because any path that has a lower total cost would have to travel through another state in Q, but these states already have higher costs. All paths that pass only through dead states were already considered in producing $C(x)$. Once all edges leaving x are explored, then x can be declared as dead, and the induction continues. This is not enough detail to constitute a proof of optimality; more arguments appear in Section 2.3.3 and in [245]. The running time is $O(|V| \lg |V| + |E|)$, in which $|V|$ and $|E|$ are the numbers of edges and vertices, respectively, in the graph representation of the discrete planning problem. This assumes that the priority queue is implemented with a Fibonacci heap, and that all other operations, such as determining whether a state has been visited, are performed in constant time. If other data structures are used to implement the priority queue, then higher running times may be obtained.

A-star

The A^* (pronounced "ay star") search algorithm is an extension of Dijkstra's algorithm that tries to reduce the total number of states explored by incorporating a heuristic estimate of the cost to get to the goal from a given state. Let $C(x)$ denote the cost-to-come from x_I to x, and let $G(x)$ denote the cost-to-go from x to some state in X_G. It is convenient that $C^*(x)$ can be computed incrementally by dynamic programming; however, there is no way to know the true optimal cost-to-go, G^*, in advance. Fortunately, in many applications it is possible to construct a reasonable underestimate of this cost. As an example of a typical underestimate, consider planning in the labyrinth depicted in Figure 2.2. Suppose that the cost is the total number of steps in the plan. If one state has coordinates (i, j) and another has (i', j'), then $|i' - i| + |j' - j|$ is an underestimate because this is the length of a straightforward plan that ignores obstacles. Once obstacles are included, the cost can only increase as the robot tries to get around them (which may not even be possible). Of course, zero could also serve as an underestimate, but that would not provide any helpful information to the algorithm. The aim is to compute an estimate that is as close as possible to the optimal cost-to-go and is also guaranteed to be no greater. Let $\hat{G}^*(x)$ denote such an estimate.

The A^* search algorithm works in exactly the same way as Dijkstra's algorithm. The only difference is the function used to sort Q. In the A^* algorithm, the sum $C^*(x') + \hat{G}^*(x')$ is used, implying that the priority queue is sorted by estimates of the optimal cost from x_I to X_G. If $\hat{G}^*(x)$ is an underestimate of the true optimal cost-to-go for all $x \in X$, the

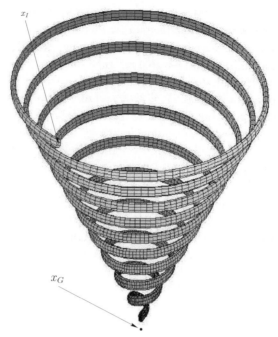

x_I

x_G

Figure 2.5: Here is a troublesome example for best-first search. Imagine trying to reach a state that is directly below the spiral tube. If the initial state starts inside of the opening at the top of the tube, the search will progress around the spiral instead of leaving the tube and heading straight for the goal.

A^* algorithm is guaranteed to find optimal plans [339, 780]. As $\hat{G}^*$ becomes closer to G^*, fewer vertices tend to be explored in comparison with Dijkstra's algorithm. This would always seem advantageous, but in some problems it is difficult or impossible to find a heuristic that is both efficient to evaluate and provides good search guidance. Note that when $\hat{G}^*(x) = 0$ for all $x \in X$, then A^* degenerates to Dijkstra's algorithm. In any case, the search will always be systematic.

Best first

For *best-first search*, the priority queue is sorted according to an estimate of the optimal cost-to-go. The solutions obtained in this way are not necessarily optimal; therefore, it does not matter whether the estimate exceeds the true optimal cost-to-go, which was important to maintain optimality for A^* search. Although optimal solutions are not found, in many cases, far fewer vertices are explored, which results in much faster running times. There is no guarantee, however, that this will happen. The worst-case performance of best-first search is worse than that of A^* search and dynamic programming. The algorithm is often too greedy because it prefers states that "look good" very early in the search. Sometimes the price must be paid for being greedy! Figure 2.5 shows a contrived example in which the planning problem involves taking small steps in a 3D world. For any specified number, k, of steps, it is easy to construct a spiral example that wastes at least k steps in comparison to Dijkstra's algorithm. Note that best-first search is not systematic.

Iterative deepening

The *iterative deepening* approach is usually preferable if the search tree has a large branching factor (i.e., there are many more vertices in the next level than in the current level). This could occur if there are many actions per state and only a few states are revisited. The idea is to use depth-first search and find all states that are distance i or less from x_I. If the goal is not found, then the previous work is discarded, and depth first is applied to find all states of distance $i + 1$ or less from x_I. This generally iterates from $i = 1$ and proceeds indefinitely until the goal is found. Iterative deepening can be viewed as a way of converting depth-first search into a systematic search method. The motivation for discarding the work of previous iterations is that the number of states reached for $i + 1$ is expected to far exceed (e.g., by a factor of 10) the number reached for i. Therefore, once the commitment has been made to reach level $i + 1$, the cost of all previous iterations is negligible.

The iterative deepening method has better worst-case performance than breadth-first search for many problems. Furthermore, the space requirements are reduced because the queue in breadth-first search is usually much larger than for depth-first search. If the nearest goal state is i steps from x_I, breadth-first search in the worst case might reach nearly all states of distance $i + 1$ before terminating successfully. This occurs each time a state $x \notin X_G$ of distance i from x_I is reached because all new states that can be reached in one step are placed onto Q. The A^* idea can be combined with iterative depending to yield IDA^*, in which i is replaced by $C^*(x') + \hat{G}^*(x')$. In each iteration of IDA^*, the allowed total cost gradually increases [780].

2.2.3 Other general search schemes

This section covers two other general templates for search algorithms. The first one is simply a "backward" version of the tree search algorithm in Figure 2.4. The second one is a bidirectional approach that grows two search trees, one from the initial state and one from a goal state.

Backward search

Backward versions of any of the forward search algorithms of Section 2.2.2 can be made. For example, a backward version of Dijkstra's algorithm can be made by starting from x_G. To create backward search algorithms, suppose that there is a single goal state, x_G. For many planning problems, it might be the case that the branching factor is large when starting from x_I. In this case, it might be more efficient to start the search at a goal state and work backward until the initial state is encountered. A general template for this approach is given in Figure 2.6. For forward search, recall that an action $u \in U(x)$ is applied from $x \in X$ to obtain a new state, $x' = f(x, u)$. For backward search, a frequent computation will be to determine for some x', the preceding state $x \in X$, and action $u \in U(x)$ such that $x' = f(x, u)$. The template in Figure 2.6 can be extended to handle a goal region, X_G, by inserting all $x_G \in X_G$ into Q in line 1 and marking them as visited.

For most problems, it may be preferable to precompute a representation of the state transition function, f, that is "backward" to be consistent with the search algorithm. Some convenient notation will now be constructed for the backward version of f. Let $U^{-1} = \{(x, u) \in X \times U \mid x \in X, u \in U(x)\}$, which represents the set of all state-action pairs and can also be considered as the domain of f. Imagine from a given state $x' \in X$, the set of all $(x, u) \in U^{-1}$ that map to x' using f. This can be considered as a *backward action space*, defined formally for any $x' \in X$ as

$$U^{-1}(x') = \{(x, u) \in U^{-1} \mid x' = f(x, u)\}. \tag{2.3}$$

BACKWARD_SEARCH
1      $Q.Insert(x_G)$ and mark x_G as visited
2   **while** Q not empty **do**
3          $x' \leftarrow Q.GetFirst()$
4   **if** $x = x_I$
5   **return** SUCCESS
6   **forall** $u^{-1} \in U^{-1}(x)$
7              $x \leftarrow f^{-1}(x', u^{-1})$
8   **if** x not visited
9   Mark x as visited
10                 $Q.Insert(x)$
11   **else**
12   Resolve duplicate x
13   **return** FAILURE

Figure 2.6: A general template for backward search.

For convenience, let u^{-1} denote a state-action pair (x, u) that belongs to some $U^{-1}(x')$. From any $u^{-1} \in U^{-1}(x')$, there is a unique $x \in X$. Thus, let f^{-1} denote a *backward state transition function* that yields x from x' and $u^{-1} \in U^{-1}(x)$. This defines a *backward state transition equation*, $x = f^{-1}(x', u^{-1})$, which looks very similar to the forward version, $x' = f(x, u)$.

The interpretation of f^{-1} is easy to capture in terms of the state transition graph: reverse the direction of every edge. This makes finding a plan in the reversed graph using backward search equivalent to finding one in the original graph using forward search. The backward state transition function is the variant of f that is obtained after reversing all of the edges. Each u^{-1} is a reversed edge. Since there is a perfect symmetry with respect to the forward search of Section 2.2.1, any of the search algorithm variants from Section 2.2.2 can be adapted to the template in Figure 2.6, provided that f^{-1} has been defined.

Bidirectional search

Now that forward and backward search have been covered, the next reasonable idea is to conduct a bidirectional search. The general search template given in Figure 2.7 can be considered as a combination of the two in Figures 2.4 and 2.6. One tree is grown from the initial state, and the other is grown from the goal state (assume again that X_G is a singleton, $\{x_G\}$). The search terminates with success when the two trees meet. Failure occurs if either priority queue has been exhausted. For many problems, bidirectional search can dramatically reduce the amount of required exploration. There are Dijkstra and A^* variants of bidirectional search, which lead to optimal solutions. For best-first and other variants, it may be challenging to ensure that the two trees meet quickly. They might come very close to each other and then fail to connect. Additional heuristics may help in some settings to guide the trees into each other. One can even extend this framework to allow any number of search trees. This may be desirable in some applications, but connecting the trees becomes even more complicated and expensive.

BIDIRECTIONAL_SEARCH
1    $Q_I.Insert(x_I)$ and mark x_I as visited
2    $Q_G.Insert(x_G)$ and mark x_G as visited
3   **while** Q_I not empty **and** Q_G not empty **do**
4   **if** Q_I not empty
5            $x \leftarrow Q_I.GetFirst()$
6   **if** $x = x_G$ **or** $x \in Q_G$
7   **return** SUCCESS
8   **forall** $u \in U(x)$
9                $x' \leftarrow f(x, u)$
10   **if** x' not visited
11   Mark x' as visited
12                    $Q_I.Insert(x')$
13   **else**
14   Resolve duplicate x'
15   **if** Q_G not empty
16            $x' \leftarrow Q_G.GetFirst()$
17   **if** $x' = x_I$ **or** $x' \in Q_I$
18   **return** SUCCESS
19   **forall** $u^{-1} \in U^{-1}(x')$
20                $x \leftarrow f^{-1}(x', u^{-1})$
21   **if** x not visited
22   Mark x as visited
23                    $Q_G.Insert(x)$
24   **else**
25   Resolve duplicate x
26   **return** FAILURE

Figure 2.7: A general template for bidirectional search.

2.2.4 A unified view of the search methods

It is convenient to summarize the behavior of all search methods in terms of several basic steps. Variations of these steps will appear later for more complicated planning problems. For example, in Section 5.4, a large family of sampling-based motion planning algorithms can be viewed as an extension of the steps presented here. The extension in this case is made from a discrete state space to a continuous state space (called the configuration space). Each method incrementally constructs a *search graph*, $\mathcal{G}(V, E)$, which is the subgraph of the state transition graph that has been explored so far.

All of the planning methods from this section followed the same basic template:

1. **Initialization:** Let the search graph, $\mathcal{G}(V, E)$, be initialized with E empty and V containing some starting states. For forward search, $V = \{x_I\}$; for backward search, $V = \{x_G\}$. If bidirectional search is used, then $V = \{x_I, x_G\}$. It is possible to grow more than two trees and merge them during the search process. In this case, more states can be initialized in V. The search graph will incrementally grow to reveal more and more of the state transition graph.

2. **Select Vertex:** Choose a vertex $n_{cur} \in V$ for expansion; this is usually accomplished by maintaining a priority queue. Let x_{cur} denote the state associated with n_{cur}.

3. **Apply an Action:** In either a forward or backward direction, a new state, x_{new}, is obtained. This may arise from $x_{new} = f(x, u)$ for some $u \in U(x)$ (forward) or $x = f(x_{new}, u)$ for some $u \in U(x_{new})$ (backward).

4. **Insert a Directed Edge into the Graph:** If certain algorithm-specific tests are passed, then generate an edge from x to x_{new} for the forward case, or an edge from x_{new} to x for the backward case. If x_{new} is not yet in V, it will be inserted into V.[2]

5. **Check for Solution:** Determine whether $\mathcal{G}$ encodes a path from x_I to x_G. If there is a single search tree, then this is trivial. If there are two or more search trees, then this step could be expensive.

6. **Return to Step 2:** Iterate unless a solution has been found or an early termination condition is satisfied, in which case the algorithm reports failure.

Note that in this summary, several iterations may have to be made to generate one iteration in the previous formulations. The forward search algorithm in Figure 2.4 tries all actions for the first element of Q. If there are k actions, this corresponds to k iterations in the template above.

2.3 Discrete optimal planning

This section extends Formulation 2.1 to allow optimal planning problems to be defined. Rather than being satisfied with any sequence of actions that leads to the goal set, suppose we would like a solution that optimizes some criterion, such as time, distance, or energy consumed. Three important extensions will be made: 1) A stage index will be used to conveniently indicate the current plan step; 2) a cost functional will be introduced, which behaves like a taxi meter by indicating how much cost accumulates during the plan execution; and 3) a termination action will be introduced, which intuitively indicates when it is time to stop the plan and fix the total cost.

The presentation involves three phases. First, the problem of finding optimal paths of a fixed length is covered in Section 2.3.1. The approach, called *value iteration*, involves iteratively computing optimal cost-to-go functions over the state space. Although this case is not very useful by itself, it is much easier to understand than the general case of variable-length plans. Once the concepts from this section are understood, their extension to variable-length plans will be much clearer and is covered in Section 2.3.2. Finally, Section 2.3.3 explains the close relationship between value iteration and Dijkstra's algorithm, which was covered in Section 2.2.1.

With nearly all optimization problems, there is the arbitrary, symmetric choice of whether to define a criterion to *minimize* or *maximize*. If the cost is a kind of energy or expense, then minimization seems sensible, as is typical in robotics and control theory. If the cost is a kind of reward, as in investment planning or in most AI books, then maximization is preferred. Although this issue remains throughout the book, we will choose to minimize everything. If maximization is instead preferred, then multiplying the costs by -1 and swapping minimizations with maximizations should suffice.

---

[2] In some variations, the vertex could be added without a corresponding edge. This would start another tree in a multiple-tree approach

The fixed-length optimal planning formulation will be given shortly, but first we introduce some new notation. Let π_K denote a K-*step plan*, which is a sequence $(u_1, u_2, \ldots, u_K)$ of K actions. If π_K and x_I are given, then a sequence of states, $(x_1, x_2, \ldots, x_{K+1})$, can be derived using the state transition function, f. Initially, $x_1 = x_I$, and each subsequent state is obtained by $x_{k+1} = f(x_k, u_k)$.

The model is now given; the most important addition with respect to Formulation 2.1 is L, the cost functional.

Formulation 2.2 (Discrete Fixed-Length Optimal Planning)

1. All of the components from Formulation 2.1 are inherited directly: X, $U(x)$, f, x_I, and X_G, except here it is assumed that X is finite (some algorithms may easily extend to the case in which X is countably infinite, but this will not be considered here).

2. A number, K, of *stages*, which is the exact length of a plan (measured as the number of actions, $u_1, u_2, \ldots, u_K$). States may also obtain a stage index. For example, x_{k+1} denotes the state obtained after u_k is applied.

3. Let L denote a stage-additive cost (or loss) functional, which is applied to a K-step plan, π_K. This means that the sequence $(u_1, \ldots, u_K)$ of actions and the sequence $(x_1, \ldots, x_{K+1})$ of states may appear in an expression of L. For convenience, let F denote the *final stage*, $F = K + 1$ (the application of u_K advances the stage to $K + 1$). The *cost functional* is

$$L(\pi_K) = \sum_{k=1}^{K} l(x_k, u_k) + l_F(x_F). \tag{2.4}$$

The *cost term* $l(x_k, u_k)$ yields a real value for every $x_k \in X$ and $u_k \in U(x_k)$. The *final term* $l_F(x_F)$ is outside of the sum and is defined as $l_F(x_F) = 0$ if $x_F \in X_G$, and $l_F(x_F) = \infty$ otherwise.

An important comment must be made regarding l_F. Including l_F in (2.4) is actually unnecessary if it is agreed in advance that L will only be applied to evaluate plans that reach X_G. It would then be undefined for all other plans. The algorithms to be presented shortly will also function nicely under this assumption; however, the notation and explanation can become more cumbersome because the action space must always be restricted to ensure that successful plans are produced. Instead of this, the domain of L is extended to include all plans, and those that do not reach X_G are penalized with infinite cost so that they are eliminated automatically in any optimization steps. At some point, the role of l_F may become confusing, and it is helpful to remember that it is just a trick to convert feasibility constraints into a straightforward optimization ($L(\pi_K) = \infty$ means *not feasible* and $L(\pi_K) < \infty$ means *feasible with cost* $L(\pi_K)$).

Now the task is to find a plan that minimizes L. To obtain a feasible planning problem like Formulation 2.1 but restricted to K-step plans, let $l(x, u) \equiv 0$. To obtain a planning problem that requires minimizing the number of stages, let $l(x, u) \equiv 1$. The possibility also exists of having goals that are less "crisp" by letting $l_F(x)$ vary for different $x \in X_G$, as opposed to $l_F(x) = 0$. This is much more general than what was allowed with feasible planning because now states may take on any value, as opposed to being classified as inside or outside of X_G.

2.3.1 Optimal fixed-length plans

Consider computing an optimal plan under Formulation 2.2. One could naively generate all length-K sequences of actions and select the sequence that produces the best cost, but this would require $O(|U|^K)$ running time (imagine K nested loops, one for each stage), which is clearly prohibitive. Luckily, the dynamic programming principle helps. We first say in words what will appear later in equations. The main observation is that portions of optimal plans are themselves optimal. It would be absurd to be able to replace a portion of an optimal plan with a portion that produces lower total cost; this contradicts the optimality of the original plan.

The principle of optimality leads directly to an iterative algorithm, called *value iteration*,[3] that can solve a vast collection of optimal planning problems, including those that involve variable-length plans, stochastic uncertainties, imperfect state measurements, and many other complications. The idea is to iteratively compute optimal cost-to-go (or cost-to-come) functions over the state space. In some cases, the approach can be reduced to Dijkstra's algorithm; however, this only occurs under some special conditions. The *value-iteration* algorithm will be presented next, and Section 2.3.3 discusses its connection to Dijkstra's algorithm.

2.3.1.1 Backward value iteration

As for the search methods, there are both forward and backward versions of the approach. The backward case will be covered first. Even though it may appear superficially to be easier to progress from x_I, it turns out that progressing backward from X_G is notationally simpler. The forward case will then be covered once some additional notation is introduced.

The key to deriving long optimal plans from shorter ones lies in the construction of optimal cost-to-go functions over X. For k from 1 to F, let G_k^* denote the cost that accumulates from stage k to F under the execution of the optimal plan:

$$G_k^*(x_k) = \min_{u_k,\dots,u_K} \left\{ \sum_{i=k}^{K} l(x_i, u_i) + l_F(x_F) \right\}. \tag{2.5}$$

Inside of the min of (2.5) are the last $F - k$ terms of the cost functional, (2.4). The optimal cost-to-go for the boundary condition of $k = F$ reduces to

$$G_F^*(x_F) = l_F(x_F). \tag{2.6}$$

This makes intuitive sense: Since there are no stages in which an action can be applied, the final stage cost is immediately received.

Now consider an algorithm that makes K passes over X, each time computing G_k^* from G_{k+1}^*, as k ranges from F down to 1. In the first iteration, G_F^* is copied from l_F without significant effort. In the second iteration, G_K^* is computed for each $x_K \in X$ as

$$G_K^*(x_K) = \min_{u_K} \left\{ l(x_K, u_K) + l_F(x_F) \right\}. \tag{2.7}$$

Since $l_F = G_F^*$ and $x_F = f(x_K, u_K)$, substitutions can be made into (2.7) to obtain

$$G_K^*(x_K) = \min_{u_K} \left\{ l(x_K, u_K) + G_F^*(f(x_K, u_K)) \right\}, \tag{2.8}$$

---

[3] The "value" here refers to the optimal cost-to-go or cost-to-come. Therefore, an alternative name could be *cost-to-go iteration*.

which is straightforward to compute for each $x_K \in X$. This computes the costs of all optimal one-step plans from stage K to stage $F = K + 1$.

It will be shown next that G_k^* can be computed similarly once G_{k+1}^* is given. Carefully study (2.5) and note that it can be written as

$$G_k^*(x_k) = \min_{u_k} \left\{ \min_{u_{k+1},\dots,u_K} \left\{ l(x_k, u_k) + \sum_{i=k+1}^{K} l(x_i, u_i) + l_F(x_F) \right\} \right\} \qquad (2.9)$$

by pulling the first term out of the sum and by separating the minimization over u_k from the rest, which range from u_{k+1} to u_K. The second min does not affect the $l(x_k, u_k)$ term; thus, $l(x_k, u_k)$ can be pulled outside to obtain

$$G_k^*(x_k) = \min_{u_k} \left\{ l(x_k, u_k) + \min_{u_{k+1},\dots,u_K} \left\{ \sum_{i=k+1}^{K} l(x_i, u_i) + l(x_F) \right\} \right\}. \qquad (2.10)$$

The inner min is exactly the definition of the optimal cost-to-go function G_{k+1}^*. Upon substitution, this yields the recurrence

$$G_k^*(x_k) = \min_{u_k} \left\{ l(x_k, u_k) + G_{k+1}^*(x_{k+1}) \right\}, \qquad (2.11)$$

in which $x_{k+1} = f(x_k, u_k)$. Now that the right side of (2.11) depends only on x_k, u_k, and G_{k+1}^*, the computation of G_k^* easily proceeds in $O(|X||U|)$ time. This computation is called a *value iteration*. Note that in each value iteration, some states receive an infinite value only because they are not reachable; a $(K - k)$-step plan from x_k to X_G does not exist. This means that there are no actions, $u_k \in U(x_k)$, that bring x_k to a state $x_{k+1} \in X$ from which a $(K - k - 1)$-step plan exists that terminates in X_G.

Summarizing, the value iterations proceed as follows:

$$G_F^* \;\rightarrow\; G_K^* \;\rightarrow\; G_{K-1}^* \;\cdots\; G_k^* \;\rightarrow\; G_{k-1}^* \;\cdots\; G_2^* \;\rightarrow\; G_1^* \qquad (2.12)$$

until finally G_1^* is determined after $O(K|X||U|)$ time. The resulting G_1^* may be applied to yield $G_1^*(x_I)$, the optimal cost to go to the goal from x_I. It also conveniently gives the optimal cost-to-go from any other initial state. This cost is infinity for states from which X_G cannot be reached in K stages.

It seems convenient that the cost of the optimal plan can be computed so easily, but how is the actual plan extracted? One possibility is to store the action that satisfied the min in (2.11) from every state, and at every stage. Unfortunately, this requires $O(K|X|)$ storage, but it can be reduced to $O(|X|)$ using the tricks to come in Section 2.3.2 for the more general case of variable-length plans.

Example 2.3 (A Five-State Optimal Planning Problem) Figure 2.8 shows a graph representation of a planning problem in which $X = \{a, c, b, d, e\}$. Suppose that $K = 4$, $x_I = a$, and $X_G = \{d\}$. There will hence be four value iterations, which construct G_4^*, G_3^*, G_2^*, and G_1^*, once the final-stage cost-to-go, G_5^*, is given.

The cost-to-go functions are shown in Figure 2.9. Figures 2.10 and 2.11 illustrate the computations. For computing G_4^*, only b and c receive finite values because only they can reach d in one stage. For computing G_3^*, only the values $G_4^*(b) = 4$ and $G_4^*(c) = 1$ are important. Only paths that reach b or c can possibly lead to d in stage $k = 5$. Note that the minimization in (2.11) always chooses the action that produces the lowest total cost when arriving at a vertex in the next stage.   ∎

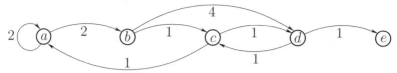

Figure 2.8: A five-state example. Each vertex represents a state, and each edge represents an input that can be applied to the state transition equation to change the state. The weights on the edges represent $l(x_k, u_k)$ (x_k is the originating vertex of the edge).

	a	b	c	d	e
G_5^*	∞	∞	∞	0	∞
G_4^*	∞	4	1	∞	∞
G_3^*	6	2	∞	2	∞
G_2^*	4	6	3	∞	∞
G_1^*	6	4	5	4	∞

Figure 2.9: The optimal cost-to-go functions computed by backward value iteration.

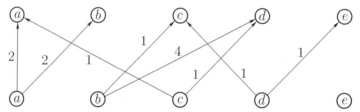

Figure 2.10: The possibilities for advancing forward one stage. This is obtained by making two copies of the states from Figure 2.8, one copy for the current state and one for the potential next state.

2.3.1.2 Forward value iteration

The ideas from Section 2.3.1.1 may be recycled to yield a symmetrically equivalent method that computes optimal *cost-to-come* functions from the initial stage. Whereas backward value iterations were able to find optimal plans from all initial states simultaneously, forward value iterations can be used to find optimal plans to all states in X. In the backward case, X_G must be fixed, and in the forward case, x_I must be fixed.

The issue of maintaining feasible solutions appears again. In the forward direction, the role of l_F is not important. It may be applied in the last iteration, or it can be dropped altogether for problems that do not have a predetermined X_G. However, one must force all plans considered by forward value iteration to originate from x_I. We again have the choice of either making notation that imposes constraints on the action spaces or simply adding a term that forces infeasible plans to have infinite cost. Once again, the latter will be chosen here.

Let C_k^* denote the *optimal cost-to-come* from stage 1 to stage k, optimized over all $(k-1)$-step plans. To preclude plans that do not start at x_I, the definition of C_1^* is given by

$$C_1^*(x_1) = l_I(x_1), \tag{2.13}$$

in which l_I is a new function that yields $l_I(x_I) = 0$, and $l_I(x) = \infty$ for all $x \neq x_I$. Thus, any plans that try to start from a state other than x_I will immediately receive infinite cost.

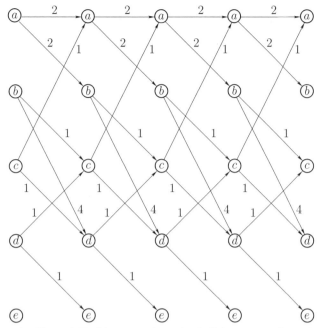

Figure 2.11: By turning Figure 2.10 sideways and copying it K times, a graph can be drawn that easily shows all of the ways to arrive at a final state from an initial state by flowing from left to right. The computations automatically select the optimal route.

For an intermediate stage, $k \in \{2, \dots, K\}$, the following represents the optimal cost-to-come:

$$C_k^*(x_k) = \min_{u_1, \dots, u_{k-1}} \left\{ l_I(x_1) + \sum_{i=1}^{k-1} l(x_i, u_i) \right\}. \qquad (2.14)$$

Note that the sum refers to a sequence of states, $x_1, \dots, x_{k-1}$, which is the result of applying the action sequence $(u_1, \dots, u_{k-2})$. The last state, x_k, is not included because its cost term, $l(x_k, u_k)$, requires the application of an action, u_k, which has not been chosen. If it is possible to write the cost additively, as $l(x_k, u_k) = l_1(x_k) + l_2(u_k)$, then the $l_1(x_k)$ part could be included in the cost-to-come definition, if desired. This detail will not be considered further.

As in (2.5), it is assumed in (2.14) that $u_i \in U(x_i)$ for every $i \in \{1, \dots, k-1\}$. The resulting x_k, obtained after applying u_{k-1}, must be the same x_k that is named in the argument on the left side of (2.14). It might appear odd that x_1 appears inside of the min above; however, this is not a problem. The state x_1 can be completely determined once $u_1, \dots, u_{k-1}$ and x_k are given.

The final forward value iteration is the arrival at the final stage, F. The cost-to-come in this case is

$$C_K^*(x_F) = \min_{u_1, \dots, u_K} \left\{ l_I(x_1) + \sum_{i=1}^{K} l(x_i, u_i) \right\}. \qquad (2.15)$$

This equation looks the same as (2.8), but l_I is used instead of l_F. This has the effect of filtering the plans that are considered to include only those that start at x_I. The forward value iterations find optimal plans to any reachable final state from x_I. This behavior is complementary to that of backward value iteration. In that case, X_G was fixed, and

	a	b	c	d	e
C_1^*	0	∞	∞	∞	∞
C_2^*	2	2	∞	∞	∞
C_3^*	4	4	3	6	∞
C_4^*	4	6	5	4	7
C_5^*	6	6	5	6	5

Figure 2.12: The optimal cost-to-come functions computed by forward value iteration.

optimal plans from any initial state were found. For forward value iteration, this is reversed.

To express the dynamic-programming recurrence, one further issue remains. Suppose that C_{k-1}^* is known by induction, and we want to compute $C_k^*(x_k)$ for a particular x_k. This means that we must start at some state x_{k-1} and arrive in state x_k by applying some action. Once again, the backward state transition equation from Section 2.2.3 is useful. Using the stage indices, it is written here as $x_{k-1} = f^{-1}(x_k, u_k^{-1})$.

The recurrence is

$$C_k^*(x_k) = \min_{u^{-1} \in U^{-1}(x_k)} \left\{ C_{k-1}^*(x_{k-1}) + l(x_{k-1}, u_{k-1}) \right\}, \tag{2.16}$$

in which $x_{k-1} = f^{-1}(x_k, u_k^{-1})$ and $u_{k-1} \in U(x_{k-1})$ is the input to which $u_k^{-1} \in U^{-1}(x_k)$ corresponds. Using (2.16), the final cost-to-come is iteratively computed in $O(K|X||U|)$ time, as in the case of computing the first-stage cost-to-go in the backward value-iteration method.

Example 2.4 (Forward Value Iteration)   Example 2.3 is revisited for the case of forward value iterations with a fixed plan length of $K = 4$. The cost-to-come functions shown in Figure 2.12 are obtained by direct application of (2.16). It will be helpful to refer to Figures 2.10 and 2.11 once again. The first row corresponds to the immediate application of l_I. In the second row, finite values are obtained for a and b, which are reachable in one stage from $x_I = a$. The iterations continue until $k = 5$, at which point that optimal cost-to-come is determined for every state.   ■

2.3.2 Optimal plans of unspecified lengths

The value-iteration method for fixed-length plans can be generalized nicely to the case in which plans of different lengths are allowed. There will be no bound on the maximal length of a plan; therefore, the current case is truly a generalization of Formulation 2.1 because arbitrarily long plans may be attempted in efforts to reach X_G. The model for the general case does not require the specification of K but instead introduces a special action, u_T.

Formulation 2.3 (Discrete Optimal Planning)

1.   All of the components from Formulation 2.1 are inherited directly: X, $U(x)$, f, x_I, and X_G. Also, the notion of stages from Formulation 2.2 is used.

2. Let L denote a stage-additive cost functional, which may be applied to any K-step plan, π_K, to yield

$$L(\pi_K) = \sum_{k=1}^{K} l(x_k, u_k) + l_F(x_F). \tag{2.17}$$

In comparison with L from Formulation 2.2, the present expression does not consider K as a predetermined constant. It will now vary, depending on the length of the plan. Thus, the domain of L is much larger.

3. Each $U(x)$ contains the special *termination action*, u_T. If u_T is applied at x_k, then the action is repeatedly applied forever, the state remains unchanged, and no more cost accumulates. Thus, for all $i \geq k$, $u_i = u_T$, $x_i = x_k$, and $l(x_i, u_T) = 0$.

The termination action is the key to allowing plans of different lengths. It will appear throughout this book. Suppose that value iterations are performed up to $K = 5$, and for the problem there exists a two-step solution plan, (u_1, u_2), that arrives in X_G from x_I. This plan is equivalent to the five-step plan $(u_1, u_2, u_T, u_T, u_T)$ because the termination action does not change the state, nor does it accumulate cost. The resulting five-step plan reaches X_G and costs the same as (u_1, u_2). With this simple extension, the forward and backward value iteration methods of Section 2.3.1 may be applied for any fixed K to optimize over all plans of length K or less (instead of fixing K).

The next step is to remove the dependency on K. Consider running backward value iterations indefinitely. At some point, G_1^* will be computed, but there is no reason why the process cannot be continued onward to G_0^*, G_{-1}^*, and so on. Recall that x_I is not utilized in the backward value-iteration method; therefore, there is no concern regarding the starting initial state of the plans. Suppose that backward value iteration was applied for $K = 16$ and was executed down to G_{-8}^*. This considers all plans of length 25 or less. Note that it is harmless to add 9 to all stage indices to shift all of the cost-to-go functions. Instead of running from G_{-8}^* to G_{16}^*, they can run from G_1^* to G_{25}^* without affecting their values. The index shifting is allowed because none of the costs depend on the particular index that is given to the stage. The only important aspect of the value iterations is that they proceed backward and consecutively from stage to stage.

Eventually, enough iterations will have been executed so that an optimal plan is known from every state that can reach X_G. From that stage, say k, onward, the cost-to-go values from one value iteration to the next will be *stationary*, meaning that for all $i \leq k$, $G_{i-1}^*(x) = G_i^*(x)$ for all $x \in X$. Once the stationary condition is reached, the cost-to-go function no longer depends on a particular stage k. In this case, the stage index may be dropped, and the recurrence becomes

$$G^*(x) = \min_u \left\{ l(x, u) + G^*(f(x, u)) \right\}. \tag{2.18}$$

Are there any conditions under which backward value iterations could be executed forever, with each iteration producing a cost-to-go function for which some values are different from the previous iteration? If $l(x, u)$ is nonnegative for all $x \in X$ and $u \in U(x)$, then this could never happen. It could certainly be true that, for any fixed K, longer plans will exist, but this cannot be said of *optimal* plans. From every $x \in X$, there either exists a plan that reaches X_G with finite cost or there is no solution. For each state from which there exists a plan that reaches X_G, consider the number of stages in the optimal plan. Consider the maximum number of stages taken from all states that can reach X_G. This serves as an upper bound on the number of value iterations before the cost-to-go becomes stationary. Any further iterations will just consider solutions that are worse than the ones already considered (some may be equivalent due to the termination action and shifting of stages). Some trouble might occur if $l(x, u)$ contains negative values. If the state transition graph contains a cycle for which total cost is negative, then it is preferable to execute a plan that travels around the cycle forever, thereby reducing the total cost to $-\infty$. Therefore, we will assume that the cost functional is defined in a sensible way so that negative cycles do not exist. Otherwise, the optimization model itself appears flawed. Some negative values for $l(x, u)$, however, are allowed as long as there are no negative cycles. (It is straightforward to detect and report negative cycles before running the value iterations.)

Since the particular stage index is unimportant, let $k = 0$ be the index of the final stage, which is the stage at which the backward value iterations begin. Hence, G_0^* is the final stage cost, which is obtained directly from l_F. Let $-K$ denote the stage index at which the cost-to-go values all become stationary. At this stage, the optimal cost-to-go function, $G^* : X \to \mathbb{R} \cup \{\infty\}$, is expressed by assigning $G^* = G_{-K}^*$. In other words, the particular stage index no longer matters. The value $G^*(x)$ gives the optimal cost to go from state $x \in X$ to the specific goal state x_G.

If the optimal actions are not stored during the value iterations, the optimal cost-to-go, G^*, can be used to efficiently recover them. Consider starting from some $x \in X$. What is the optimal next action? This is given by

$$u^* = \operatorname*{argmin}_{u \in U(x)} \left\{ l(x, u) + G^*(f(x, u)) \right\}, \tag{2.19}$$

in which argmin denotes the argument that achieves the minimum value of the expression. The action minimizes an expression that is very similar to (2.11). The only differences between (2.19) and (2.11) are that the stage indices are dropped in (2.19) because the cost-to-go values no longer depend on them, and argmin is used so that u^* is selected. After applying u^*, the state transition equation is used to obtain $x' = f(x, u^*)$, and (2.19) may be applied again on x'. This process continues until a state in X_G is reached. This procedure is based directly on the dynamic programming recurrence; therefore, it recovers the optimal plan. The function G^* serves as a kind of guide that leads the system from any initial state into the goal set optimally. This can be considered as a special case of a *navigation function*, which will be covered in Section 8.2.2.

As in the case of fixed-length plans, the direction of the value iterations can be reversed to obtain a forward value-iteration method for the variable-length planning problem. In this case, the backward state transition equation, f^{-1}, is used once again. Also, the initial cost term l_I is used instead of l_F, as in (2.14). The forward value-iteration method starts at $k = 1$, and then iterates until the cost-to-come becomes stationary. Once again, the termination action, u_T, preserves the cost of plans that arrived at a state in earlier iterations. Note that it is not required to specify X_G. A counterpart to G^* may be obtained, from which optimal actions can be recovered. When the cost-to-come values become stationary, an optimal cost-to-come function, $C^* : X \to \mathbb{R} \cup \{\infty\}$, may be expressed by assigning $C^* = C_F^*$, in which F is the final stage reached when the algorithm terminates. The value $C^*(x)$ gives the cost of an optimal plan that starts from x_I and reaches x. The optimal action sequence for any specified goal $x_G \in X$ can be obtained using

$$\operatorname*{argmin}_{u^{-1} \in U^{-1}} \left\{ C^*(f^{-1}(x, u^{-1})) + l(f^{-1}(x, u^{-1}), u') \right\}, \tag{2.20}$$

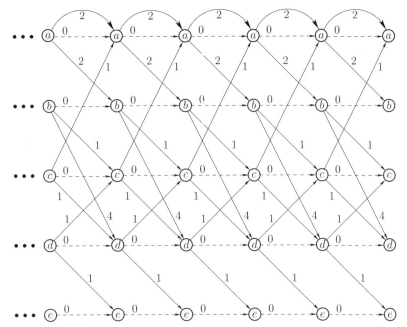

Figure 2.13: Compare this figure to Figure 2.11, for which K was fixed at 4. The effect of the termination action is depicted as dashed-line edges that yield 0 cost when traversed. This enables plans of all finite lengths to be considered. Also, the stages extend indefinitely to the left (for the case of backward value iteration).

	a	b	c	d	e
G_0^*	∞	∞	∞	0	∞
G_{-1}^*	∞	4	1	0	∞
G_{-2}^*	6	2	1	0	∞
G_{-3}^*	4	2	1	0	∞
G_{-4}^*	4	2	1	0	∞
G^*	4	2	1	0	∞

Figure 2.14: The optimal cost-to-go functions computed by backward value iteration applied in the case of variable-length plans.

which is the forward counterpart of (2.19). The u' is the action in $U(f^{-1}(x, u^{-1}))$ that yields x when the state transition function, f, is applied. The iterations proceed backward from x_G and terminate when x_I is reached.

Example 2.5 (Value Iteration for Variable-Length Plans) Once again, Example 2.3 is revisited; however, this time the plan length is not fixed due to the termination action. Its effect is depicted in Figure 2.13 by the superposition of new edges that have zero cost. It might appear at first that there is no incentive to choose nontermination actions, but remember that any plan that does not terminate in state $x_G = d$ will receive infinite cost.

See Figure 2.14. After a few backward value iterations, the cost-to-go values become stationary. After this point, the termination action is being applied from all reachable states and no further cost accumulates. The final cost-to-go function is defined to be G^*. Since d is not reachable from e, $G^*(e) = \infty$.

	a	b	c	d	e
C_1^*	∞	0	∞	∞	∞
C_2^*	∞	0	1	4	∞
C_3^*	2	0	1	2	5
C_4^*	2	0	1	2	3
C^*	2	0	1	2	3

Figure 2.15: The optimal cost-to-come functions computed by forward value iteration applied in the case of variable-length plans.

As an example of using (2.19) to recover optimal actions, consider starting from state a. The action that leads to b is chosen next because the total cost $2 + G^*(b) = 4$ is better than $2 + G^*(a) = 6$ (the 2 comes from the action cost). From state b, the optimal action leads to c, which produces total cost $1 + G^*(c) = 1$. Similarly, the next action leads to $d \in X_G$, which terminates the plan.

Using forward value iteration, suppose that $x_I = b$. The following cost-to-come functions shown in Figure 2.15 are obtained. For any finite value that remains constant from one iteration to the next, the termination action was applied. Note that the last value iteration is useless in this example. Once C_3^* is computed, the optimal cost-to-come to every possible state from x_I is determined, and future cost-to-come functions are identical. Therefore, the final cost-to-come is renamed C^*. ∎

2.3.3 Dijkstra revisited

So far two different kinds of dynamic programming have been covered. The value-iteration method of Section 2.3.2 involves repeated computations over the entire state space. Dijkstra's algorithm from Section 2.2.2 flows only once through the state space, but with the additional overhead of maintaining which states are *alive*.

Dijkstra's algorithm can be derived by focusing on the forward value iterations, as in Example 2.5, and identifying exactly where the "interesting" changes occur. Recall that for Dijkstra's algorithm, it was assumed that all costs are nonnegative. For any states that are not reachable, their values remain at infinity. They are precisely the *unvisited* states. States for which the optimal cost-to-come has already become stationary are *dead*. For the remaining states, an initial cost is obtained, but this cost may be lowered one or more times until the optimal cost is obtained. All states for which the cost is finite, but possibly not optimal, are in the queue, Q.

After understanding value iteration, it is easier to understand why Dijkstra's form of dynamic programming correctly computes optimal solutions. It is clear that the unvisited states will remain at infinity in both algorithms because no plan has reached them. It is helpful to consider the forward value iterations in Example 2.5 for comparison. In a sense, Dijkstra's algorithm is very much like the value iteration, except that it efficiently maintains the set of states within which cost-to-go values can change. It correctly inserts any states that are reached for the first time, changing their cost-to-come from infinity to a finite value. The values are changed in the same manner as in the value iterations. At the end of both algorithms, the resulting values correspond to the stationary, optimal cost-to-come, C^*.

FORWARD_LABEL_CORRECTING(x_G)
1   Set $C(x) = \infty$ for all $x \neq x_I$, and set $C(x_I) = 0$
2     $Q.Insert(x_I)$
3   **while** Q not empty **do**
4          $x \leftarrow Q.GetFirst()$
5   **forall** $u \in U(x)$
6               $x' \leftarrow f(x, u)$
7   **if** $C(x) + l(x, u) < \min\{C(x'), C(x_G)\}$ **then**
8                    $C(x') \leftarrow C(x) + l(x, u)$
9   **if** $x' \neq x_G$ **then**
10                        $Q.Insert(x')$

Figure 2.16: A generalization of Dijkstra's algorithm, which upon termination produces an optimal plan (if one exists) for any prioritization of Q, as long as X is finite. Compare this to Figure 2.4.

If Dijkstra's algorithm seems so clever, then why have we spent time covering the value-iteration method? For some problems it may become too expensive to maintain the sorted queue, and value iteration could provide a more efficient alternative. A more important reason is that value iteration extends easily to a much broader class of problems. Examples include optimal planning over continuous state spaces (Sections 8.5.2 and 14.5), stochastic optimal planning (Section 10.2), and computing dynamic game equilibria (Section 10.5). In some cases, it is still possible to obtain a Dijkstra-like algorithm by focusing the computation on the "interesting" region; however, as the model becomes more complicated, it may be inefficient or impossible in practice to maintain this region. Therefore, it is important to have a good understanding of both algorithms to determine which is most appropriate for a given problem.

Dijkstra's algorithm belongs to a broader family of *label-correcting algorithms*, which all produce optimal plans by making small modifications to the general forward-search algorithm in Figure 2.4. Figure 2.16 shows the resulting algorithm. The main difference is to allow states to become alive again if a better cost-to-come is found. This enables other cost-to-come values to be improved accordingly. This is not important for Dijkstra's algorithm and A^* search because they only need to visit each state once. Thus, the algorithms in Figures 2.4 and 2.16 are essentially the same in this case. However, the label-correcting algorithm produces optimal solutions for any sorting of Q, including FIFO (breadth first) and LIFO (depth first), as long as X is finite. If X is not finite, then the issue of systematic search dominates because one must guarantee that states are revisited sufficiently many times to guarantee that optimal solutions will eventually be found.

Another important difference between label-correcting algorithms and the standard forward-search model is that the label-correcting approach uses the cost at the goal state to prune away many candidate paths; this is shown in line 7. Thus, it is only formulated to work for a single goal state; it can be adapted to work for multiple goal states, but performance degrades. The motivation for including $C(x_G)$ in line 7 is that there is no need to worry about improving costs at some state, x', if its new cost-to-come would be higher than $C(x_G)$; there is no way it could be along a path that improves the cost to go to x_G. Similarly, x_G is not inserted in line 10 because there is no need to consider plans that have x_G as an intermediate state. To recover the plan, either pointers can be stored from

x to x' each time an update is made in line 7, or the final, optimal cost-to-come, C^*, can be used to recover the actions using (2.20).

2.4 Using logic to formulate discrete planning

For many discrete planning problems that we would like a computer to solve, the state space is enormous (e.g., 10^{100} states). Therefore, substantial effort has been invested in constructing *implicit* encodings of problems in hopes that the entire state space does not have to be explored by the algorithm to solve the problem. This will be a recurring theme throughout this book; therefore, it is important to pay close attention to representations. Many planning problems can appear trivial once everything has been explicitly given.

Logic-based representations have been popular for constructing such implicit representations of discrete planning. One historical reason is that such representations were the basis of the majority of artificial intelligence research during the 1950s–1980s. Another reason is that they have been useful for representing certain kinds of planning problems very compactly. It may be helpful to think of these representations as compression schemes. A string such as 010101010101... may compress very nicely, but it is impossible to substantially compress a random string of bits. Similar principles are true for discrete planning. Some problems contain a kind of regularity that enables them to be expressed compactly, whereas for others it may be impossible to find such representations. This is why there has been a variety of representation logics proposed through decades of planning research.

Another reason for using logic-based representations is that many discrete planning algorithms are implemented in large software systems. At some point, when these systems solve a problem, they must provide the complete plan to a user, who may not care about the internals of planning. Logic-based representations have seemed convenient for producing output that logically explains the steps involved to arrive at some goal. Other possibilities may exist, but logic has been a first choice due to its historical popularity.

In spite of these advantages, one shortcoming with logic-based representations is that they are difficult to generalize. It is important in many applications to enable concepts such as continuous spaces, unpredictability, sensing uncertainty, and multiple decision makers to be incorporated into planning. This is the main reason why the state-space representation has been used so far: It will be easy to extend and adapt to the problems covered throughout this book. Nevertheless, it is important to study logic-based representations to understand the relationship between the vast majority of discrete planning research and other problems considered in this book, such as motion planning and planning under differential constraints. There are many recurring themes throughout these different kinds of problems, even though historically they have been investigated by separate research communities. Understanding these connections well provides powerful insights into planning issues across all of these areas.

2.4.1 A STRIPS-like representation

STRIPS-like representations have been the most common logic-based representations for discrete planning problems. This refers to the STRIPS system, which is considered one of the first planning algorithms and representations [339]; its name is derived from the STanford Research Institute Problem Solver. The original representation used first-order logic, which had great expressive power but many technical difficulties. Therefore, the representation was later restricted to only propositional logic use [746], which is similar to the form introduced in this section. There are many variations of STRIPS-like representations. Here is one formulation:

Formulation 2.4 (STRIPS-Like Planning)

1. A finite, nonempty set I of *instances*.

2. A finite, nonempty set P of *predicates*, which are binary-valued (partial) functions of one of more instances. Each application of a predicate to a specific set of instances is called a *positive literal*. A logically negated positive literal is called a *negative literal*.

3. A finite, nonempty set O of *operators*, each of which has: 1) *preconditions*, which are positive or negative literals that must hold for the operator to apply, and 2) *effects*, which are positive or negative literals that are the result of applying the operator.

4. An *initial set S* which is expressed as a set of *positive literals*. Negative literals are implied. For any positive literal that does not appear in S, its corresponding negative literal is assumed to hold initially.

5. A *goal set G* which is expressed as a set of both *positive* and *negative literals*.

Formulation 2.4.1 provides a definition of discrete feasible planning expressed in a STRIPS-like representation. The three most important components are the sets of *instances* I, *predicates* P, and *operators* O. Informally, the instances characterize the complete set of distinct things that exist in the world. They could, for example, be books, cars, trees, and so on. The predicates correspond to basic properties or statements that can be formed regarding the instances. For example, a predicate called $Under$ might be used to indicate things like $Under(Book, Table)$ (the book is under the table) or $Under(Dirt, Rug)$. A predicate can be interpreted as a kind of function that yields TRUE or FALSE values; however, it is important to note that it is only a partial function because it might not be desirable to allow any instance to be inserted as an argument to the predicate.

If a predicate is evaluated on an instance, for example, $Under(Dirt, Rug)$, the expression is called a *positive literal*. The set of all possible positive literals can be formed by applying all possible instances to the domains over which the predicates are defined. Every positive literal has a corresponding *negative literal*, which is formed by negating the positive literal. For example, $\neg Under(Dirt, Rug)$ is the negative literal that corresponds to the positive literal $Under(Dirt, Rug)$, and $\neg$ denotes negation. Let a *complementary pair* refer to a positive literal together with its counterpart negative literal. The various components of the planning problem are expressed in terms of positive and negative literals.

The role of an operator is to change the world. To be applicable, a set of *preconditions* must all be satisfied. Each element of this set is a positive or negative literal that must hold TRUE for the operator to be applicable. Any complementary pairs that can be formed from the predicates, but are not mentioned in the preconditions, may assume any value without affecting the applicability of the operator. If the operator is applied, then the world is updated in a manner precisely specified by the set of *effects*, which indicates positive and negative literals that result from the application of the operator. It is assumed that the truth values of all unmentioned complementary pairs are not affected.

Multiple operators are often defined in a single statement by using variables. For example, $Insert(i)$ may allow any instance $i \in I$ to be inserted. In some cases, this dramatically reduces the space required to express the problem.

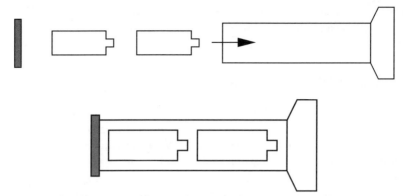

Figure 2.17: An example that involves putting batteries into a flashlight.

The planning problem is expressed in terms of an initial set S of positive literals and a goal set G of positive and negative literals. A state can be defined by selecting either the positive or negative literal for every possible complementary pair. The initial set S specifies such a state by giving the positive literals only. For all possible positive literals that do not appear in S, it is assumed that their negative counterparts hold in the initial state. The goal set G actually refers to a set of states because, for any unmentioned complementary pair, the positive or negative literal may be chosen, and the goal is still achieved. The task is to find a sequence of operators that when applied in succession will transform the world from the initial state into one in which all literals of G are TRUE. For each operator, the preconditions must also be satisfied before it can be applied. The following example illustrates Formulation 2.4.

Example 2.6 (Putting Batteries into a Flashlight) Imagine a planning problem that involves putting two batteries into a flashlight, as shown in Figure 2.17. The set of instances are

$$I = \{Battery1, Battery2, Cap, Flashlight\}. \qquad (2.21)$$

Two different predicates will be defined, On and In, each of which is a partial function on I. The predicate On may only be applied to evaluate whether the Cap is On the $Flashlight$ and is written as $On(Cap, Flashlight)$. The predicate In may be applied in the following two ways: $In(Battery1, Flashlight)$, $In(Battery2, Flashlight)$, to indicate whether either battery is in the flashlight. Recall that predicates are only partial functions in general. For the predicate In, it is not desirable to apply any instance to any argument. For example, it is meaningless to define $In(Battery1, Battery1)$ and $In(Flashlight, Battery2)$ (they could be included in the model, always retaining a negative value, but it is inefficient).

The initial set is

$$S = \{On(Cap, Flashlight)\}. \qquad (2.22)$$

Based on S, both $\neg In(Battery1, Flashlight)$ and $\neg In(Battery2, Flashlight)$ are assumed to hold. Thus, S indicates that the cap is on the flashlight, but the batteries are outside.

Name	Preconditions	Effects
PlaceCap	$\{\neg On(Cap, Flashlight)\}$	$\{On(Cap, Flashlight)\}$
RemoveCap	$\{On(Cap, Flashlight)\}$	$\{\neg On(Cap, Flashlight)\}$
Insert(i)	$\{\neg On(Cap, Flashlight), \neg In(i, Flashlight)\}$	$\{In(i, Flashlight)\}$

Figure 2.18: Three operators for the flashlight problem. Note that an operator can be expressed with variable argument(s) for which different instances could be substituted.

The goal state is

$$G = \{On(Cap, Flashlight), In(Battery1, Flashlight),$$
$$In(Battery2, Flashlight)\}, \tag{2.23}$$

which means that both batteries must be in the flashlight, and the cap must be on.

The set O consists of the four operators, which are shown in Figure 2.18. Here is a plan that reaches the goal state in the smallest number of steps:

$$(RemoveCap, Insert(Battery1), Insert(Battery2), PlaceCap). \tag{2.24}$$

In words, the plan simply says to take the cap off, put the batteries in, and place the cap back on.

This example appears quite simple, and one would expect a planning algorithm to easily find such a solution. It can be made more challenging by adding many more instances to I, such as more batteries, more flashlights, and a bunch of objects that are irrelevant to achieving the goal. Also, many other predicates and operators can be added so that the different combinations of operators become overwhelming. ∎

A large number of complexity results exist for planning expressed using logic. The graph search problem is solved efficiently in polynomial time; however, a state transition graph is not given as the input. An input that is expressed using Formulation 2.4 may describe an enormous state transition graph using very few instances, predicates, and operators. In a sense, the model is highly compressed when using some logic-based formulations. This brings it closer to the *Kolmogorov complexity* [250, 633] of the state transition graph, which is the shortest bit size to which it can possibly be compressed and then fully recovered by a Turing machine. This has the effect of making the planning problem appear more difficult. Concise inputs may encode very challenging planning problems. Most of the known hardness results are surveyed in Chapter 3 of [384]. Under most formulations, logic-based planning is NP-hard. The particular level of hardness (NP, PSPACE, EXPTIME, etc.) depends on the precise problem conditions. For example, the complexity depends on whether the operators are fixed in advance or included in the input. The latter case is much harder. Separate complexities are also obtained based on whether negative literals are allowed in the operator effects and also whether they are allowed in preconditions. The problem is generally harder if both positive and negative literals are allowed in these cases.

2.4.2 Converting to the state-space representation

It is useful to characterize the relationship between Formulation 2.4 and the original formulation of discrete feasible planning, Formulation 2.1. One benefit is that it immediately shows how to adapt the search methods of Section 2.2 to work for logic-based representations. It is also helpful to understand the relationships between the algorithmic complexities of the two representations.

Up to now, the notion of "state" has been only vaguely mentioned in the context of the STRIPS-like representation. Now consider making this more concrete. Suppose that every predicate has k arguments, and any instance could appear in each argument. This means that there are $|P||I|^k$ complementary pairs, which corresponds to all of the ways to substitute instances into all arguments of all predicates. To express the state, a positive or negative literal must be selected from every complementary pair. For convenience, this selection can be encoded as a binary string by imposing a linear ordering on the instances and predicates. Using Example 2.6, the state might be specified in order as

$$(On(Cap, Flashlight), \neg In(Battery1, Flashlight1), In(Battery2, Flashlight)). \tag{2.25}$$

Using a binary string, each element can be "0" to denote a negative literal or "1" to denote positive literal. The encoded state is $x = 101$ for (2.25). If any instance can appear in the argument of any predicate, then the length of the string is $|P||I|^k$. The total number of possible states of the world that could possibly be distinguished corresponds to the set of all possible bit strings. This set has size

$$2^{|P||I|^k}. \tag{2.26}$$

The implication is that with a very small number of instances and predicates, an enormous state space can be generated. Even though the search algorithms of Section 2.2 may appear efficient with respect to the size of the search graph (or the number of states), the algorithms appear horribly inefficient with respect to the sizes of P and I. This has motivated substantial efforts on the development of techniques to help guide the search by exploiting the structure of specific representations. This is the subject of Section 2.5.

The next step in converting to a state-space representation is to encode the initial state x_I as a string. The goal set, X_G, is the set of all strings that are consistent with the positive and negative goal literals. This can be compressed by extending the string alphabet to include a "don't care" symbol, δ. A single string that has a "0" for each negative literal, a "1" for each positive literal, and a "δ" for all others would suffice in representing any X_G that is expressed with positive and negative literals.

Now convert the operators. For each state, $x \in X$, the set $U(x)$ represents the set of operators with preconditions that are satisfied by x. To apply the search techniques of Section 2.2, note that it is not necessary to determine $U(x)$ explicitly in advance for all $x \in X$. Instead, $U(x)$ can be computed whenever each x is encountered for the first time in the search. The effects of the operator are encoded by the state transition equation. From a given $x \in X$, the next state, $f(x, u)$, is obtained by flipping the bits as prescribed by the effects part of the operator.

All of the components of Formulation 2.1 have been derived from the components of Formulation 2.4. Adapting the search techniques of Section 2.2 is straightforward. It is also straightforward to extend Formulation 2.4 to represent optimal planning. A cost can be associated with each operator and set of literals that capture the current state. This would express $l(x, u)$ of the cost functional, L, from Section 2.3. Thus, it is even possible to adapt the value-iteration method to work under the logic-based representation, yielding optimal plans.

2.5 Logic-based planning methods

A huge body of research has been developed over the last few decades for planning using logic-based representations [384, 842]. These methods usually exploit some structure that is particular to the representation. Furthermore, numerous heuristics for accelerating performance have been developed from implementation studies. The main ideas behind some of the most influential approaches are described in this section, but without presenting particular heuristics.

Rather than survey all logic-based planning methods, this section focuses on some of the main approaches that exploit logic-based representations. Keep in mind that the searching methods of Section 2.2 also apply. Once a problem is given using Formulation 2.4, the state transition graph is incrementally revealed during the search. In practice, the search graph may be huge relative to the size of the problem description. One early attempt to reduce the size of this graph was the STRIPS planning algorithm [339, 746]; it dramatically reduced the branching factor but unfortunately was not complete. The methods presented in this section represent other attempts to reduce search complexity in practice while maintaining completeness. For each method, there are some applications in which the method may be more efficient, and others for which performance may be worse. Thus, there is no clear choice of method that is independent of its particular use.

2.5.1 Searching in a space of partial plans

One alternative to searching directly in X is to construct partial plans without reference to particular states. By using the operator representation, partial plans can be incrementally constructed. The idea is to iteratively achieve required subgoals in a partial plan while ensuring that no conflicts arise that could destroy the solution developed so far.

A *partial plan* σ is defined as

1. A set O_σ of operators that need to be applied. If the operators contain variables, these may be filled in by specific values or left as variables. The same operator may appear multiple times in O_σ, possibly with different values for the variables.

2. A partial ordering relation $\prec_\sigma$ on O_σ, which indicates for some pairs $o_1, o_2 \in O_\sigma$ that one must appear before other: $o_1 \prec_\sigma o_2$.

3. A set B_σ of *binding constraints*, in which each indicates that some variables across operators must take on the same value.

4. A set C_σ of *causal links*, in which each is of the form (o_1, l, o_2) and indicates that o_1 achieves the literal l for the purpose of satisfying a precondition of o_2.

Example 2.7 (A Partial Plan) Each partial plan encodes a *set* of possible plans. Recall the model from Example 2.6. Suppose

$$O_\sigma = \{RemoveCap, Insert(Battery1)\}. \tag{2.27}$$

A sensible ordering constraint is that

$$RemoveCap \prec_\sigma Insert(Battery1). \tag{2.28}$$

A causal link,

$$(RemoveCap, \neg On(Cap, Flashlight), Insert(Battery1)), \tag{2.29}$$

PLAN-SPACE PLANNING

1. Start with any initial partial plan, σ.

2. Find a flaw in σ, which may be 1) an operator precondition that has not achieved, or 2) an operator in O_σ that threatens a causal constraint in C_σ.

3. If there is no flaw, then report that σ is a complete solution and compute a linear ordering of O_σ that satisfies all constraints.

4. If the flaw is an unachieved precondition, l, for some operator o_2, then find an operator, o_1, that achieves it and record a new causal constraint, (o_1, l, o_2).

5. If the flaw is a threat on a causal link, then the threat must be removed by updating $\prec_\sigma$ to induce an appropriate operator ordering, or by updating B_σ to bind the operators in a way that resolves the threat.

6. Return to Step 2.

Figure 2.19: Planning in the plan space is achieved by iteratively finding a flaw in the plan and fixing it.

indicates that the *RemoveCap* operator achieves the literal $\neg On(Cap, Flashlight)$, which is a precondition of *Insert*(*Battery*1). There are no binding constraints for this example. The partial plan implicitly represents the set of all plans for which *RemoveCap* appears before *Insert*(*Battery*1), under the constraint that the causal link is not violated. ∎

Several algorithms have been developed to search in the space of partial plans. To obtain some intuition about the partial-plan approach, a planning algorithm is described in Figure 2.19. A vertex in the partial-plan search graph is a partial plan, and an edge is constructed by extending one partial plan to obtain another partial plan that is closer to completion. Although the general template is simple, the algorithm performance depends critically on the choice of initial plan and the particular flaw that is resolved in each iteration. One straightforward generalization is to develop multiple partial plans and decide which one to refine in each iteration.

In early works, methods based on partial plans seemed to offer substantial benefits; however, they are currently considered to be not "competitive enough" in comparison to methods that search the state space [384]. One problem is that it becomes more difficult to develop application-specific heuristics without explicit references to states. Also, the vertices in the partial-plan search graph are costly to maintain and manipulate in comparison to ordinary states.

2.5.2 Building a planning graph

Blum and Furst introduced the notion of a *planning graph*, which is a powerful data structure that encodes information about which states may be reachable [119]. For the logic-based problem expressed in Formulation 2.4, consider performing reachability analysis. Breadth-first search can be used from the initial state to expand the state transition graph. In terms of the input representation, the resulting graph may be of exponential size in the number of stages. This gives precise reachability information and is guaranteed to find the goal state.

The idea of Blum and Furst is to construct a graph that is much smaller than the state transition graph and instead contains only partial information about reachability. The resulting *planning graph* is polynomial in size and can be efficiently constructed for some challenging problems. The trade-off is that the planning graph indicates states that can *possibly* be reached. The true reachable set is overapproximated, by eliminating many impossible states from consideration. This enables quick elimination of impossible alternatives in the search process. Planning algorithms have been developed that extract a plan from the planning graph. In the worst case, this may take exponential time, which is not surprising because the problem in Formulation 2.4 is NP-hard in general. Nevertheless, dramatic performance improvements were obtained on some well-known planning benchmarks. Another way to use the planning graph is as a source of information for developing search heuristics for a particular problem.

Planning graph definition

A *layered graph* is a graph that has its vertices partitioned into a sequence of *layers*, and its edges are only permitted to connect vertices between successive layers. The *planning graph* is a layered graph in which the layers of vertices form an alternating sequence of literals and operators:

$$(L_1, O_1, L_2, O_2, L_3, O_3, \ldots, L_k, O_k, L_{k+1}). \tag{2.30}$$

The edges are defined as follows. To each operator $o_i \in O_i$, a directed edge is made from each $l_i \in L_i$ that is a precondition of o_i. To each literal $l_i \in L_i$, an edge is made from each operator $o_{i-1} \in O_{i-1}$ that has l_i as an effect.

One important requirement is that no variables are allowed in the operators. Any operator from Formulation 2.4 that contains variables must be converted into a set that contains a distinct copy of the operator for every possible substitution of values for the variables.

Layer-by-layer construction

The planning graph is constructed layer by layer, starting from L_1. In the first stage, L_1 represents the initial state. Every positive literal in S is placed into L_1, along with the negation of every positive literal not in S. Now consider stage i. The set O_i is the set of all operators for which their preconditions are a subset of L_i. The set L_{i+1} is the union of the effects of all operators in O_i. The iterations continue until the planning graph stabilizes, which means that $O_{i+1} = O_i$ and $L_{i+1} = L_i$. This situation is very similar to the stabilization of value iterations in Section 2.3.2. A trick similar to the termination action, u_T, is needed even here so that plans of various lengths are properly handled. In Section 2.3.2, one job of the termination action was to prevent state transitions from occurring. The same idea is needed here. For each possible literal, l, a *trivial operator* is constructed for which l is the only precondition and effect. The introduction of trivial operators ensures that once a literal is reached, it is maintained in the planning graph for every subsequent layer of literals. Thus, each O_i may contain some trivial operators, in addition to operators from the initially given set O. These are required to ensure that the planning graph expansion reaches a steady state, in which the planning graph is identical for all future expansions.

Mutex conditions

During the construction of the planning graph, information about the conflict between operators and literals within a layer is maintained. A conflict is called a *mutex condition*, which means that a pair of literals[4] or pair of operators is mutually exclusive. Both cannot

---

[4] The pair of literals need not be a complementary pair, as defined in Section 2.4.1.

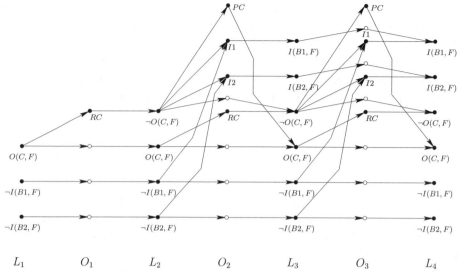

Figure 2.20: The planning graph for the flashlight example. The unlabeled operator vertices correspond to trivial operators. For clarity, the operator and literal names are abbreviated.

be chosen simultaneously without leading to some kind of conflict. A pair in conflict is called *mutex*. For each layer, a *mutex relation* is defined that indicates which pairs satisfy the mutex condition. A pair, $o, o' \in O_i$, of operators is defined to be *mutex* if any of these conditions is met:

1. **Inconsistent effects:** An effect of o is the negated literal of an effect of o'.
2. **Interference:** An effect of o is the negated literal of a precondition of o'.
3. **Competing needs:** A pair of preconditions, one from each of o and o', are mutex in L_i.

The last condition relies on the definition of mutex for literals, which is presented next. Any pair, $l, l' \in L_i$, of literals is defined to be *mutex* if at least one of the two conditions is met:

1. **Negated literals:** l and l' form a complementary pair.
2. **Inconsistent support:** Every pair of operators, $o, o' \in O_{i-1}$, that achieve l and l' is mutex. In this case, one operator must achieve l, and the other must achieve l'. If there exists an operator that achieves both, then this condition is false, regardless of the other pairs of operators.

The mutex definition depends on the layers; therefore, it is computed layer by layer during the planning graph construction.

Example 2.8 (The Planning Graph for the Flashlight) Figure 2.20 shows the planning graph for Example 2.6. In the first layer, L_1 expresses the initial state. The only applicable operator is *RemoveCap*. The operator layer O_1 contains *RemoveCap* and three trivial operators, which are needed to maintain the literals from L_1. The appearance of $\neg On(Cap, Flashlight)$ enables the battery-insertion operator to apply. Since variables are not allowed in operator definitions in a planning graph, two different operators (labeled as $I1$ and $I2$) appear, one for each battery. Notice the edges drawn to $I1$ and $I2$ from their preconditions. The cap may also be replaced; hence, *PlaceCap* is included in O_2. At the L_3 layer, all possible literals have been obtained. At O_3, all possible operators, including the trivial ones, are included. Finally, $L_4 = L_3$, and O_4 will be the same as O_3. This implies that the planning graph has stabilized. ∎

Plan extraction

Suppose that the planning graph has been constructed up to L_i. At this point, the planning graph can be searched for a solution. If no solution is found and the planning graph has stabilized, then no solution exists to the problem in general (this was shown in [119]; see also [384]). If the planning graph has not stabilized, then it can be extended further by adding O_i and L_{i+1}. The extended graph can then be searched for a solution plan. A planning algorithm derived from the planning graph interleaves the graph extensions and the searches for solutions. Either a solution is reported at some point or the algorithm correctly reports that no solution exists after the planning graph stabilizes. The resulting algorithm is complete. One of the key observations in establishing completeness is that the literal and operator layers each increase monotonically as i increases. Furthermore, the sets of pairs that are mutex decrease monotonically, until all possible conflicts are resolved.

Rather than obtaining a fully specified plan, the planning graph yields a *layered plan*, which is a special form of partial plan. All of the necessary operators are included, and the layered plan is specified as

$$(A_1, A_2, \ldots, A_k), \tag{2.31}$$

in which each A_i is a set of operators. Within any A_i, the operators are nonmutex and may be applied in any order without altering the state obtained by the layered plan. The only constraint is that for each i from 1 to k, every operator in A_i must be applied before any operators in A_{i+1} can be applied. For the flashlight example, a layered plan that would be constructed from the planning graph in Figure 2.20 is

$$(\{RemoveCap\}, \{Insert(Battery1), Insert(Battery2)\}, \{PlaceCap\}). \tag{2.32}$$

To obtain a fully specified plan, the layered plan needs to be linearized by specifying a linear ordering for the operators that is consistent with the layer constraints. For (2.32), this results in (2.24). The actual plan execution usually involves more stages than the number in the planning graph. For complicated planning problems, this difference is expected to be huge. With a small number of stages, the planning graph can consider very long plans because it can apply several nonmutex operators in a single layer.

At each level, the search for a plan could be quite costly. The idea is to start from L_i and perform a backward *and/or search*. To even begin the search, the goal literals G must be a subset of L_i, and no pairs are allowed to be mutex; otherwise, immediate failure is declared. From each literal $l \in G$, an "or" part of the search tries possible operators that produce l as an effect. The "and" part of the search must achieve all literals in the precondition of an operator chosen at the previous "or" level. Each of these preconditions must be achieved, which leads to another "or" level in the search. The idea is applied recursively until the initial set L_1 of literals is obtained. During the and/or search, the computed mutex relations provide information that immediately eliminates some branches. Frequently, triples and higher order tuples are checked for being mutex together, even though they are not pairwise mutex. A hash table is constructed to efficiently retrieve this information as it is considered multiple times in the search. Although the plan extraction is quite costly, superior performance was shown in [119] on several important benchmarks. In the worst case, the search could require exponential time (otherwise, a polynomial-time algorithm would have been found to an NP-hard problem).

2.5.3 Planning as satisfiability

Another interesting approach is to convert the planning problem into an enormous Boolean satisfiability problem. This means that the planning problem of Formulation 2.4 can be solved by determining whether some assignment of variables is possible for a Boolean expression that leads to a TRUE value. Generic methods for determining satisfiability can be directly applied to the Boolean expression that encodes the planning problem. The *Davis-Putnam procedure* is one of the most widely known algorithms for satisfiability. It performs a depth-first search by iteratively trying assignments for variables and backtracking when assignments fail. During the search, large parts of the expression can be eliminated due to the current assignments. The algorithm is complete and reasonably efficient. Its use in solving planning problems is surveyed in [384]. In practice, stochastic local search methods provide a reasonable alternative to the Davis-Putnam procedure [462].

Suppose a planning problem has been given in terms of Formulation 2.4. All literals and operators will be tagged with a stage index. For example, a literal that appears in two different stages will be considered distinct. This kind of tagging is similar to *situation calculus* [380]; however, in that case, variables are allowed for the tags. To obtain a finite, Boolean expression the total number of stages must be declared. Let K denote the number of stages at which operators can be applied. As usual, the fist stage is $k = 1$ and the final stage is $k = F = K + 1$. Setting a stage limit is a significant drawback of the approach because this is usually not known before the problem is solved. A planning algorithm can assume a small value for F and then gradually increase it each time the resulting Boolean expression is not satisfied. If the problem is not solvable, however, this approach iterates forever.

Let $\vee$ denote logical OR, and let $\wedge$ denote logical AND. The Boolean expression is written as a conjunction[5] of many terms, which arise from five different sources:

1. **Initial state:** A conjunction of all literals in S is formed, along with the negation of all positive literals not in S. These are all tagged with 1, the initial stage index.

2. **Goal state:** A conjunction of all literals in G, tagged with the final stage index, $F = K + 1$.

3. **Operator encodings:** Each operator must be copied over the stages. For each $o \in O$, let o_k denote the operator applied at stage k. A conjunction is formed over all operators at all stages. For each o_k, the expression is

$$\neg o_k \vee (p_1 \wedge p_2 \wedge \cdots \wedge p_m \wedge e_1 \wedge e_2 \wedge \cdots \wedge e_n), \tag{2.33}$$

in which $p_1, \ldots, p_m$ are the preconditions of o_k, and $e_1, \ldots, e_n$ are the effects of o_k.

4. **Frame axioms:** The next part is to encode the implicit assumption that every literal that is not an effect of the applied operator remains unchanged in the next stage. This can alternatively be stated as follows: If a literal l becomes negated to $\neg l$, then an operator that includes $\neg l$ as an effect must have been executed. (If l was already a negative literal, then $\neg l$ is a positive literal.) For each stage and literal, an expression is needed. Suppose

---

[5] Conjunction means logical AND.

that l_k and l_{k+1} are the same literal but are tagged for different stages. The expression is

$$(l_k \vee \neg l_{k+1}) \vee (o_{k,1} \vee o_{k,2} \vee \cdots \vee o_{k,j}), \tag{2.34}$$

in which $o_{k,1}, \ldots, o_{k,j}$ are the operators, tagged for stage k, that contain l_{k+1} as an effect. This ensures that if $\neg l_k$ appears, followed by l_{k+1}, then some operator must have caused the change.

5. **Complete exclusion axiom:** This indicates that only one operator applies at every stage. For every stage k, and any pair of stage-tagged operators o_k and o'_k, the expression is

$$\neg o_k \vee \neg o'_k, \tag{2.35}$$

which is logically equivalent to $\neg(o_k \wedge o'_k)$ (meaning, "not both at the same stage").

It is shown in [515] that a solution plan exists if and only if the resulting Boolean expression is satisfiable.

The following example illustrates the construction.

Example 2.9 (The Flashlight Problem as a Boolean Expression) A Boolean expression will be constructed for Example 2.6. Each of the expressions given below is joined into one large expression by connecting them with $\wedge$'s.

The expression for the initial state is

$$O(C, F, 1) \wedge \neg I(B1, F, 1) \wedge \neg I(B2, F, 1), \tag{2.36}$$

which uses the abbreviated names, and the stage tag has been added as an argument to the predicates. The expression for the goal state is

$$O(C, F, 5) \wedge I(B1, F, 5) \wedge I(B2, F, 5), \tag{2.37}$$

which indicates that the goal must be achieved at stage $k = 5$. This value was determined because we already know the solution plan from (2.24). The method will also work correctly for a larger value of k. The expressions for the operators are

$$
\begin{aligned}
&\neg PC_k \vee (\neg O(C, F, k) \wedge O(C, F, k + 1)) \\
&\neg RC_k \vee (O(C, F, k) \wedge \neg O(C, F, k + 1)) \\
&\neg I1_k \vee (\neg O(C, F, k) \wedge \neg I(B1, F, k) \wedge I(B1, F, k + 1)) \\
&\neg I2_k \vee (\neg O(C, F, k) \wedge \neg I(B2, F, k) \wedge I(B2, F, k + 1))
\end{aligned}
\tag{2.38}
$$

for each k from 1 to 4.

The frame axioms yield the expressions

$$
\begin{aligned}
&(O(C, F, k) \vee \neg O(C, F, k + 1)) \vee (PC_k) \\
&(\neg O(C, F, k) \vee O(C, F, k + 1)) \vee (RC_k) \\
&(I(B1, F, k) \vee \neg I(B1, F, k + 1)) \vee (I1_k) \\
&(\neg I(B1, F, k) \vee I(B1, F, k + 1)) \\
&(I(B2, F, k) \vee \neg I(B2, F, k + 1)) \vee (I2_k) \\
&(\neg I(B2, F, k) \vee I(B2, F, k + 1)),
\end{aligned}
\tag{2.39}
$$

for each k from 1 to 4. No operators remove batteries from the flashlight. Hence, two of the expressions list no operators.

Finally, the complete exclusion axiom yields the expressions

$$\neg RC_k \vee \neg PC_k \qquad \neg RC_k \vee \neg O1_k \qquad \neg RC_k \vee \neg O2_k \qquad (2.40)$$
$$\neg PC_k \vee \neg O1_k \qquad \neg PC_k \vee \neg O2_k \qquad \neg O1_k \vee \neg O2_k,$$

for each k from 1 to 4. The full problem is encoded by combining all of the given expressions into an enormous conjunction. The expression is satisfied by assigning TRUE values to RC_1, $IB1_2$, $IB2_3$, and PC_4. An alternative solution is RC_1, $IB2_2$, $IB1_3$, and PC_4. The stage index tags indicate the order that the actions are applied in the recovered plan. ∎

Further reading

Most of the ideas and methods in this chapter have been known for decades. Most of the search algorithms of Section 2.2 are covered in algorithms literature as graph search [245, 406, 695, 859] and in AI literature as planning or search methods [554, 746, 747, 780, 842, 975]. Many historical references to search in AI appear in [842]. Bidirectional search was introduced in [800, 801] and is closely related to *means-end analysis* [738]; more discussion of bidirectional search appears in [187, 186, 500, 572, 842]. The development of good search heuristics is critical to many applications of discrete planning. For substantial material on this topic, see [384, 553, 780]. For the relationship between planning and scheduling, see [268, 384, 897].

The dynamic programming principle forms the basis of optimal control theory and many algorithms in computer science. The main ideas follow from Bellman's principle of optimality [86, 87]. These classic works led directly to the value-iteration methods of Section 2.3. For more recent material on this topic, see [97], which includes Dijkstra's algorithm and its generalization to label-correcting algorithms. An important special version of Dijkstra's algorithm is Dial's algorithm [274] (see [946] and Section 8.2.3). Throughout this book, there are close connections between planning methods and control theory. One step in this direction was taken earlier in [269].

The foundations of logic-based planning emerged from early work of Nilsson [339, 746], which contains most of the concepts introduced in Section 2.4. Over the last few decades, an enormous body of literature has been developed. Section 2.5 briefly surveyed some of the highlights; however, several more chapters would be needed to do this subject justice. For a comprehensive, recent treatment of logic-based planning, see [384]; topics beyond those covered here include constraint-satisfaction planning, scheduling, and temporal logic. Other sources for logic-based planning include [380, 842, 963, 984]. A critique of benchmarks used for comparisons of logic-based planning algorithms appears in [467].

Too add uncertainty or multiple decision makers to the problems covered in this chapter, jump ahead to Chapter 10 (this may require some background from Chapter 9). To move from searching in discrete to continuous spaces, try Chapters 5 and 6 (some background from Chapters 3 and 4 is required).

Exercises

1. Consider the planning problem shown in Figure 2.21. Let a be the initial state, and let e be the goal state.

   (a) Use backward value iteration to determine the stationary cost-to-go.

   (b) Do the same but instead use forward value iteration.

2. Try to construct a worst-case example for best-first search that has properties similar to that shown in Figure 2.5, but instead involves moving in a 2D world with obstacles, as introduced in Example 2.1.

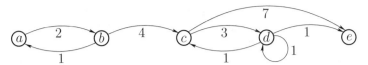

Figure 2.21: Another five-state discrete planning problem.

3. It turns out that value iteration can be generalized to a cost functional of the form

$$L(\pi_K) = \sum_{k=1}^{K} l(x_k, u_k, x_{k+1}) + l_F(x_F), \qquad (2.41)$$

in which $l(x_k, u_k)$ in (2.4) has been replaced by $l(x_k, u_k, x_{k+1})$.

(a) Show that the dynamic programming principle can be applied in this more general setting to obtain forward and backward value iteration methods that solve the fixed-length optimal planning problem.

(b) Do the same but for the more general problem of variable-length plans, which uses termination conditions.

4. The cost functional can be generalized to being *stage-dependent*, which means that the cost might depend on the particular stage k in addition to the state, x_k and the action u_k. Extend the forward and backward value iteration methods of Section 2.3.1 to work for this case, and show that they give optimal solutions. Each term of the more general cost functional should be denoted as $l(x_k, u_k, k)$.

5. Recall from Section 2.3.2 the method of defining a termination action u_T to make the value iterations work correctly for variable-length planning. Instead of requiring that one remains at the same state, it is also possible to formulate the problem by creating a special state, called the *terminal state*, x_T. Whenever u_T is applied, the state becomes x_T. Describe in detail how to modify the cost functional, state transition equation, and any other necessary components so that the value iterations correctly compute shortest plans.

6. Dijkstra's algorithm was presented as a kind of forward search in Section 2.2.1.

(a) Develop a backward version of Dijkstra's algorithm that starts from the goal. Show that it always yields optimal plans.

(b) Describe the relationship between the algorithm from part (a) and the backward value iterations from Section 2.3.2.

(c) Derive a backward version of the A^* algorithm and show that it yields optimal plans.

7. Reformulate the general forward search algorithm of Section 2.2.1 so that it is expressed in terms of the STRIPS-like representation. Carefully consider what needs to be explicitly constructed by a planning algorithm and what is considered only implicitly.

8. Rather than using bit strings, develop a set-based formulation of the logic-based planning problem. A state in this case can be expressed as a set of positive literals.

9. Extend Formulation 2.4 to allow disjunctive goal sets (there are alternative sets of literals that must be satisfied). How does this affect the binary string representation?

10. Make a *Remove* operator for Example 2.17 that takes a battery away from the flashlight. For this operator to apply, the battery must be in the flashlight and must not be blocked by another battery. Extend the model to allow enough information for the *Remove* operator to function properly.

11. Model the operation of the sliding-tile puzzle in Figure 1.1b using the STRIPS-like representation. You may use variables in the operator definitions.

12. Find the complete set of plans that are implicitly encoded by Example 2.7.

13. Explain why, in Formulation 2.4, G needs to include both positive and negative literals, whereas S only needs positive literals. As an alternative definition, could S have contained only negative literals? Explain.

14. Using Formulation 2.4, model a problem in which a robot checks to determine whether a room is dark, moves to a light switch, and flips on the light. Predicates should indicate whether the robot is at the light switch and whether the light is on. Operators that move the robot and flip the switch are needed.

15. Construct a planning graph for the model developed in Exercise 14.

16. Express the model in Exercise 14 as a Boolean satisfiability problem.

17. In the worst case, how many terms are needed for the Boolean expression for planning as satisfiability? Express your answer in terms of $|I|$, $|P|$, $|O|$, $|S|$, and $|G|$.

Implementations

18. Using A^* search, the performance degrades substantially when there are many alternative solutions that are all optimal, or at least close to optimal. Implement A^* search and evaluate it on various grid-based problems, based on Example 2.1. Compare the performance for two different cases:

    (a) Using $|i' - i| + |j' - j|$ as the heuristic, as suggested in Section 2.2.2.

    (b) Using $\sqrt{(i' - i)^2 + (j' - j)^2}$ as the heuristic.

    Which heuristic seems superior? Explain your answer.

19. Implement A^*, breadth-first, and best-first search for grid-based problems. For each search algorithm, design and demonstrate examples for which one is clearly better than the other two.

20. Experiment with bidirectional search for grid-based planning. Try to understand and explain the trade-off between exploring the state space and the cost of connecting the trees.

21. Try to improve the method used to solve Exercise 18 by detecting when the search might be caught in a local minimum and performing random walks to try to escape. Try using best-first search instead of A^*. There is great flexibility in possible approaches. Can you obtain better performance on average for any particular examples?

22. Implement backward value iteration and verify its correctness by reconstructing the costs obtained in Example 2.5. Test the implementation on some complicated examples.

23. For a planning problem under Formulation 2.3, implement both Dijkstra's algorithm and forward value iteration. Verify that these find the same plans. Comment on their differences in performance.

24. Consider grid-based problems for which there are mostly large, open rooms. Attempt to develop a multi-resolution search algorithm that first attempts to take larger steps, and only takes smaller steps as larger steps fail. Implement your ideas, conduct experiments on examples, and refine your approach accordingly.

PART II
Motion Planning

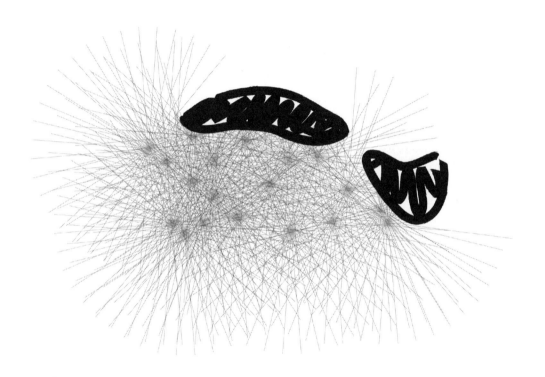

Overview of Part II: Motion planning

Planning in continuous spaces

Part II makes the transition from discrete to continuous state spaces. Two alternative titles are appropriate for this part: 1) *motion planning*, or 2) *planning in continuous state spaces*. Chapters 3–8 are based on research from the field of motion planning, which has been building since the 1970s; therefore, the name *motion planning* is widely known to refer to the collection of models and algorithms that will be covered. On the other hand, it is convenient to also think of Part II as *planning in continuous spaces* because this is the primary distinction with respect to most other forms of planning.

In addition, motion planning will frequently refer to motions of a *robot* in a 2D or 3D *world* that contains *obstacles*. The robot could model an actual robot, or any other collection of moving bodies, such as humans or flexible molecules. A *motion plan* involves determining what motions are appropriate for the robot so that it reaches a goal state without colliding into obstacles. Recall the examples from Section 1.2.

Many issues that arose in Chapter 2 appear once again in motion planning. Two themes that may help to see the connection are as follows.

1. Implicit representations

A familiar theme from Chapter 2 is that planning algorithms must deal with *implicit* representations of the state space. In motion planning, this will become even more important because the state space is uncountably infinite. Furthermore, a complicated transformation exists between the world in which the models are defined and the space in which the planning occurs. Chapter 3 covers ways to model motion planning problems, which includes defining 2D and 3D geometric models and transforming them. Chapter 4 introduces the state space that arises for these problems. Following motion planning literature [660, 591], we will refer to this state space as the *configuration space*. The dimension of the configuration space corresponds to the number of degrees of freedom of the robot. Using the configuration space, motion planning will be viewed as a kind of search in a high-dimensional configuration space that contains implicitly represented obstacles. One additional complication is that configuration spaces have unusual topological structure that must be correctly characterized to ensure correct operation of planning algorithms. A motion plan will then be defined as a continuous path in the configuration space.

2. Continuous → discrete

A central theme throughout motion planning is to transform the continuous model into a discrete one. Due to this transformation, many algorithms from Chapter 2 are embedded in motion planning algorithms. There are two alternatives to achieving this transformation, which are covered in Chapters 5 and 6, respectively. Chapter 6 covers *combinatorial motion planning*, which means that from the input model the algorithms build a discrete representation that *exactly* represents the original problem. This leads to *complete* planning approaches, which are guaranteed to find a solution when it exists, or correctly report failure if one does not exist. Chapter 5 covers *sampling-based motion planning*, which refers to algorithms that use collision detection methods to sample the configuration space and conduct discrete searches that utilize these samples. In this case, completeness is sacrificed, but it is often replaced with a weaker notion, such as *resolution completeness* or *probabilistic completeness*. It is important to study both Chapters 5 and 6 because each methodology has its strengths and weaknesses. Combinatorial methods can solve virtually any motion planning problem, and in some restricted cases, very elegant solutions may be efficiently constructed in practice. However, for the majority of "industrial-grade" motion planning problems, the running times and implementation difficulties of these algorithms make them unappealing. Sampling-based algorithms have fulfilled much of this need in recent years by solving challenging problems in several settings, such as automobile assembly, humanoid robot planning, and conformational analysis in drug design. Although the completeness guarantees are weaker, the efficiency and ease of implementation of these methods have bolstered interest in applying motion planning algorithms to a wide variety of applications.

Two additional chapters appear in Part II. Chapter 7 covers several extensions of the basic motion planning problem from the earlier chapters. These extensions include avoiding moving obstacles, multiple robot coordination, manipulation planning, and planning with closed kinematic chains. Algorithms that solve these problems build on the principles of earlier chapters, but each extension involves new challenges.

Chapter 8 is a transitional chapter that involves many elements of motion planning but is additionally concerned with gracefully recovering from unexpected deviations during execution. Although uncertainty in predicting the future is not explicitly modeled until Part III, Chapter 8 redefines the notion of a plan to be a function over state space, as opposed to being a path through it. The function gives the appropriate actions to take during execion, regardless of what configuration is entered. This allows the true configuration to drift away from the commanded configuration. In Part III such uncertainties will be explicitly modeled, but this comes at greater modeling and computational costs. It is worthwhile to develop effective ways to avoid this.

3

Geometric Representations
and Transformations

This chapter provides important background material that will be needed for Part II. Formulating and solving motion planning problems require defining and manipulating complicated geometric models of a system of bodies in space. Section 3.1 introduces geometric modeling, which focuses mainly on semi-algebraic modeling because it is an important part of Chapter 6. If your interest is mainly in Chapter 5, then understanding semi-algebraic models is not critical. Sections 3.2 and 3.3 describe how to transform a single body and a chain of bodies, respectively. This will enable the robot to "move." These sections are essential for understanding all of Part II and many sections beyond. It is expected that many readers will already have some or all of this background (especially Section 3.2, but it is included for completeness). Section 3.4 extends the framework for transforming chains of bodies to transforming trees of bodies, which allows modeling of complicated systems, such as humanoid robots and flexible organic molecules. Finally, Section 3.5 briefly covers transformations that do not assume each body is rigid.

3.1 Geometric modeling

A wide variety of approaches and techniques for geometric modeling exist, and the particular choice usually depends on the application and the difficulty of the problem. In most cases, there are generally two alternatives: 1) a *boundary representation*, and 2) a *solid representation*. Suppose we would like to define a model of a planet. Using a boundary representation, we might write the equation of a sphere that roughly coincides with the planet's surface. Using a solid representation, we would describe the set of all points that are contained in the sphere. Both alternatives will be considered in this section.

The first step is to define the *world* $\mathcal{W}$ for which there are two possible choices: 1) a 2D world, in which $\mathcal{W} = \mathbb{R}^2$, and 2) a 3D world, in which $\mathcal{W} = \mathbb{R}^3$. These choices should be sufficient for most problems; however, one might also want to allow more complicated worlds, such as the surface of a sphere or even a higher dimensional space. Such generalities are avoided in this book because their current applications are limited. Unless otherwise stated, the world generally contains two kinds of entities:

1. **Obstacles:** Portions of the world that are "permanently" occupied, for example, as in the walls of a building.

2. **Robots:** Bodies that are modeled geometrically and are controllable via a motion plan.

Based on the terminology, one obvious application is to model a robot that moves around in a building; however, many other possibilities exist. For example, the robot could be a flexible molecule, and the obstacles could be a folded protein. As another example, the robot could be a virtual human in a graphical simulation that involves obstacles (imagine the family of Doom-like video games).

This section presents a method for systematically constructing representations of obstacles and robots using a collection of primitives. Both obstacles and robots will be considered as (closed) subsets of $\mathcal{W}$. Let the *obstacle region* $\mathcal{O}$ denote the set of all points in $\mathcal{W}$ that lie in one or more obstacles; hence, $\mathcal{O} \subseteq \mathcal{W}$. The next step is to define a systematic way of representing $\mathcal{O}$ that has great expressive power while being computationally efficient. Robots will be defined in a similar way; however, this will be deferred until Section 3.2, where transformations of geometric bodies are defined.

3.1.1 Polygonal and polyhedral models

In this and the next subsection, a solid representation of $\mathcal{O}$ will be developed in terms of a combination of *primitives*. Each primitive H_i represents a subset of $\mathcal{W}$ that is easy to represent and manipulate in a computer. A complicated obstacle region will be represented by taking finite, Boolean combinations of primitives. Using set theory, this implies that $\mathcal{O}$ can also be defined in terms of a finite number of unions, intersections, and set differences of primitives.

Convex polygons

First consider $\mathcal{O}$ for the case in which the obstacle region is a convex, polygonal subset of a 2D world, $\mathcal{W} = \mathbb{R}^2$. A subset $X \subset \mathbb{R}^n$ is called *convex* if and only if, for any pair of points in X, all points along the line segment that connects them are contained in X. More precisely, this means that for any $x_1, x_2 \in X$ and $\lambda \in [0, 1]$,

$$\lambda x_1 + (1 - \lambda)x_2 \in X. \tag{3.1}$$

Thus, interpolation between x_1 and x_2 always yields points in X. Intuitively, X contains no pockets or indentations. A set that is not convex is called *nonconvex* (as opposed to *concave*, which seems better suited for lenses).

A boundary representation of $\mathcal{O}$ is an m-sided polygon, which can be described using two kinds of *features*: vertices and edges. Every *vertex* corresponds to a "corner" of the polygon, and every *edge* corresponds to a line segment between a pair of vertices. The polygon can be specified by a sequence, $(x_1, y_1), (x_2, y_2), \ldots, (x_m, y_m)$, of m points in $\mathbb{R}^2$, given in counterclockwise order.

A solid representation of $\mathcal{O}$ can be expressed as the intersection of m half-planes. Each half-plane corresponds to the set of all points that lie to one side of a line that is common to a polygon edge. Figure 3.1 shows an example of an octagon that is represented as the intersection of eight half-planes.

An edge of the polygon is specified by two points, such as (x_1, y_1) and (x_2, y_2). Consider the equation of a line that passes through (x_1, y_1) and (x_2, y_2). An equation can be determined of the form $ax + by + c = 0$, in which $a, b, c \in \mathbb{R}$ are constants that are determined from x_1, y_1, x_2, and y_2. Let $f : \mathbb{R}^2 \to \mathbb{R}$ be the function given by $f(x, y) = ax + by + c$. Note that $f(x, y) < 0$ on one side of the line, and $f(x, y) > 0$ on the other. (In fact, f may be interpreted as a signed Euclidean distance from (x, y) to the line.) The sign of $f(x, y)$ indicates a half-plane that is bounded by the line, as depicted in Figure 3.2. Without loss of generality, assume that $f(x, y)$ is defined so that $f(x, y) < 0$ for all points to the left of the edge from (x_1, y_1) to (x_2, y_2) (if it is not, then multiply $f(x, y)$ by -1).

Let $f_i(x, y)$ denote the f function derived from the line that corresponds to the edge from (x_i, y_i) to (x_{i+1}, y_{i+1}) for $1 \leq i < m$. Let $f_m(x, y)$ denote the line equation that

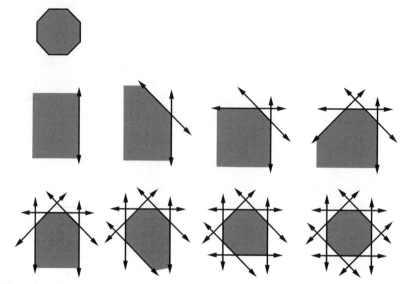

Figure 3.1: A convex polygonal region can be identified by the intersection of half-planes.

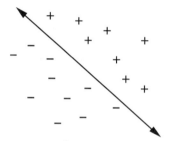

Figure 3.2: The sign of the $f(x, y)$ partitions $\mathbb{R}^2$ into three regions: two half-planes given by $f(x, y) < 0$ and $f(x, y) > 0$, and the line $f(x, y) = 0$.

corresponds to the edge from (x_m, y_m) to (x_1, y_1). Let a *half-plane* H_i for $1 \leq i \leq m$ be defined as a subset of $\mathcal{W}$:

$$H_i = \{(x, y) \in \mathcal{W} \mid f_i(x, y) \leq 0\}. \tag{3.2}$$

Above, H_i is a primitive that describes the set of all points on one side of the line $f_i(x, y) = 0$ (including the points on the line). A convex, m-sided, polygonal obstacle region $\mathcal{O}$ is expressed as

$$\mathcal{O} = H_1 \cap H_2 \cap \cdots \cap H_m. \tag{3.3}$$

Nonconvex polygons

The assumption that $\mathcal{O}$ is convex is too limited for most applications. Now suppose that $\mathcal{O}$ is a nonconvex, polygonal subset of $\mathcal{W}$. In this case $\mathcal{O}$ can be expressed as

$$\mathcal{O} = \mathcal{O}_1 \cup \mathcal{O}_2 \cup \cdots \cup \mathcal{O}_n, \tag{3.4}$$

in which each $\mathcal{O}_i$ is a convex, polygonal set that is expressed in terms of half-planes using (3.3). Note that $\mathcal{O}_i$ and $\mathcal{O}_j$ for $i \neq j$ need not be disjoint. Using this representation, very complicated obstacle regions in $\mathcal{W}$ can be defined. Although these regions may contain multiple components and holes, if $\mathcal{O}$ is bounded (i.e., $\mathcal{O}$ will fit inside of a big enough rectangular box), its boundary will consist of linear segments.

In general, more complicated representations of $\mathcal{O}$ can be defined in terms of any finite combination of unions, intersections, and set differences of primitives; however, it is always possible to simplify the representation into the form given by (3.3) and (3.4). A set difference can be avoided by redefining the primitive. Suppose the model requires removing a set defined by a primitive H_i that contains[1] $f_i(x, y) < 0$. This is equivalent to keeping all points such that $f_i(x, y) \geq 0$, which is equivalent to $-f_i(x, y) \leq 0$. This can be used to define a new primitive H_i', which when taken in union with other sets, is equivalent to the removal of H_i. Given a complicated combination of primitives, once set differences are removed, the expression can be simplified into a finite union of finite intersections by applying Boolean algebra laws.

Note that the representation of a nonconvex polygon is not unique. There are many ways to decompose $\mathcal{O}$ into convex components. The decomposition should be carefully selected to optimize computational performance in whatever algorithms that model will be used. In most cases, the components may even be allowed to overlap. Ideally, it seems that it would be nice to represent $\mathcal{O}$ with the minimum number of primitives, but automating such a decomposition may lead to an NP-hard problem (see Section 6.5.1 for a brief overview of NP-hardness). One efficient, practical way to decompose $\mathcal{O}$ is to apply the vertical cell decomposition algorithm, which will be presented in Section 6.2.2

Defining a logical predicate

What is the value of the previous representation? As a simple example, we can define a logical predicate that serves as a collision detector. Recall from Section 2.4.1 that a predicate is a Boolean-valued function. Let ϕ be a predicate defined as $\phi : \mathcal{W} \to$ {TRUE, FALSE}, which returns TRUE for a point in $\mathcal{W}$ that lies in $\mathcal{O}$, and FALSE otherwise. For a line given by $f(x, y) = 0$, let $e(x, y)$ denote a logical predicate that returns TRUE if $f(x, y) \leq 0$, and FALSE otherwise.

A predicate that corresponds to a convex polygonal region is represented by a logical conjunction,

$$\alpha(x, y) = e_1(x, y) \wedge e_2(x, y) \wedge \cdots \wedge e_m(x, y). \tag{3.5}$$

The predicate $\alpha(x, y)$ returns TRUE if the point (x, y) lies in the convex polygonal region, and FALSE otherwise. An obstacle region that consists of n convex polygons is represented by a logical disjunction of conjuncts,

$$\phi(x, y) = \alpha_1(x, y) \vee \alpha_2(x, y) \vee \cdots \vee \alpha_n(x, y). \tag{3.6}$$

Although more efficient methods exist, ϕ can check whether a point (x, y) lies in $\mathcal{O}$ in time $O(n)$, in which n is the number of primitives that appear in the representation of $\mathcal{O}$ (each primitive is evaluated in constant time).

Note the convenient connection between a logical predicate representation and a set-theoretic representation. Using the logical predicate, the unions and intersections of the set-theoretic representation are replaced by logical ORs and ANDs. It is well known from

---

[1] In this section, we want the resulting set to include all of the points along the boundary. Therefore, $<$ is used to model a set for removal, as opposed to $\leq$.

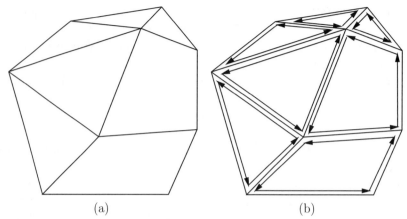

Figure 3.3: (a) A polyhedron can be described in terms of faces, edges, and vertices. (b) The edges of each face can be stored in a circular list that is traversed in counterclockwise order with respect to the outward normal vector of the face.

Boolean algebra that any complicated logical sentence can be reduced to a logical disjunction of conjunctions (this is often called "sum of products" in computer engineering). This is equivalent to our previous statement that $\mathcal{O}$ can always be represented as a union of intersections of primitives.

Polyhedral models

For a 3D world, $\mathcal{W} = \mathbb{R}^3$, and the previous concepts can be nicely generalized from the 2D case by replacing polygons with polyhedra and replacing half-plane primitives with half-space primitives. A boundary representation can be defined in terms of three features: vertices, edges, and faces. Every face is a "flat" polygon embedded in $\mathbb{R}^3$. Every edge forms a boundary between two faces. Every vertex forms a boundary between three or more edges.

Several data structures have been proposed that allow one to conveniently "walk" around the polyhedral features. For example, the *doubly connected edge list* [266] data structure contains three types of records: faces, half-edges, and vertices. Intuitively, a half-edge is a directed edge. Each vertex record holds the point coordinates and a pointer to an arbitrary half-edge that touches the vertex. Each face record contains a pointer to an arbitrary half-edge on its boundary. Each face is bounded by a circular list of half-edges. There is a pair of directed half-edge records for each edge of the polyhedon. Each half-edge is shown as an arrow in Figure 3.3b. Each half-edge record contains pointers to five other records: 1) the vertex from which the half-edge originates; 2) the "twin" half-edge, which bounds the neighboring face, and has the opposite direction; 3) the face that is bounded by the half-edge; 4) the next element in the circular list of edges that bound the face; and 5) the previous element in the circular list of edges that bound the face. Once all of these records have been defined, one can conveniently traverse the structure of the polyhedron.

Now consider a solid representation of a polyhedron. Suppose that $\mathcal{O}$ is a convex polyhedron, as shown in Figure 3.3. A solid representation can be constructed from the vertices. Each face of $\mathcal{O}$ has at least three vertices along its boundary. Assuming these vertices are not collinear, an equation of the plane that passes through them can be determined of the form

$$ax + by + cz + d = 0, \tag{3.7}$$

in which $a, b, c, d \in \mathbb{R}$ are constants.

Once again, f can be constructed, except now $f : \mathbb{R}^3 \to \mathbb{R}$ and

$$f(x, y, z) = ax + by + cz + d. \tag{3.8}$$

Let m be the number of faces. For each face of $\mathcal{O}$, a *half-space* H_i is defined as a subset of $\mathcal{W}$:

$$H_i = \{(x, y, z) \in \mathcal{W} \mid f_i(x, y, z) \le 0\}. \tag{3.9}$$

It is important to choose f_i so that it takes on negative values inside of the polyhedron. In the case of a polygonal model, it was possible to consistently define f_i by proceeding in counterclockwise order around the boundary. In the case of a polyhedron, the half-edge data structure can be used to obtain for each face the list of edges that form its boundary in counterclockwise order. Figure 3.3b shows the edge ordering for each face. For every edge, the arrows point in opposite directions, as required by the half-edge data structure. The equation for each face can be consistently determined as follows. Choose three consecutive vertices, p_1, p_2, p_3 (they must not be collinear) in counterclockwise order on the boundary of the face. Let v_{12} denote the vector from p_1 to p_2, and let v_{23} denote the vector from p_2 to p_3. The cross product $v = v_{12} \times v_{23}$ always yields a vector that points out of the polyhedron and is normal to the face. Recall that the vector $[a \ b \ c]$ is parallel to the normal to the plane. If its components are chosen as $a = v[1]$, $b = v[2]$, and $c = v[3]$, then $f(x, y, z) \le 0$ for all points in the half-space that contains the polyhedron.

As in the case of a polygonal model, a convex polyhedron can be defined as the intersection of a finite number of half-spaces, one for each face. A nonconvex polyhedron can be defined as the union of a finite number of convex polyhedra. The predicate $\phi(x, y, z)$ can be defined in a similar manner, in this case yielding TRUE if $(x, y, z) \in \mathcal{O}$, and FALSE otherwise.

3.1.2 Semi-algebraic models

In both the polygonal and polyhedral models, f was a linear function. In the case of a semi-algebraic model for a 2D world, f can be any polynomial with real-valued coefficients and variables x and y. For a 3D world, f is a polynomial with variables x, y, and z. The class of semi-algebraic models includes both polygonal and polyhedral models, which use first-degree polynomials. A point set determined by a single polynomial primitive is called an *algebraic set*; a point set that can be obtained by a finite number of unions and intersections of algebraic sets is called a *semi-algebraic set*.

Consider the case of a 2D world. A solid representation can be defined using *algebraic primitives* of the form

$$H = \{(x, y) \in \mathcal{W} \mid f(x, y) \le 0\}. \tag{3.10}$$

As an example, let $f = x^2 + y^2 - 4$. In this case, H represents a disc of radius 2 that is centered at the origin. This corresponds to the set of points (x, y) for which $f(x, y) \le 0$, as depicted in Figure 3.4a.

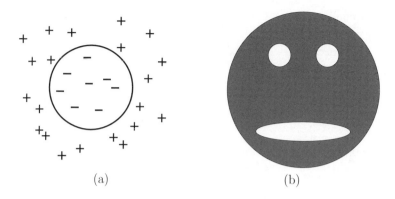

(a)   (b)

Figure 3.4: (a) Once again, f is used to partition $\mathbb{R}^2$ into two regions. In this case, the algebraic primitive represents a disc-shaped region. (b) The shaded "face" can be exactly modeled using only four algebraic primitives.

Example 3.1 (Gingerbread Face)   Consider constructing a model of the shaded region shown in Figure 3.4b. Let the center of the outer circle have radius r_1 and be centered at the origin. Suppose that the "eyes" have radius r_2 and r_3 and are centered at (x_2, y_2) and (x_3, y_3), respectively. Let the "mouth" be an ellipse with major axis a and minor axis b and is centered at $(0, y_4)$. The functions are defined as

$$\begin{aligned}
f_1 &= x^2 + y^2 - r_1^2, \\
f_2 &= -\big((x - x_2)^2 + (y - y_2)^2 - r_2^2\big), \\
f_3 &= -\big((x - x_3)^2 + (y - y_3)^2 - r_3^2\big), \\
f_4 &= -\big(x^2/a^2 + (y - y_4)^2/b^2 - 1\big).
\end{aligned} \tag{3.11}$$

For f_2, f_3, and f_4, the familiar circle and ellipse equations were multiplied by -1 to yield algebraic primitives for all points outside of the circle or ellipse. The shaded region $\mathcal{O}$ is represented as

$$\mathcal{O} = H_1 \cap H_2 \cap H_3 \cap H_4. \tag{3.12}$$

∎

   In the case of semi-algebraic models, the intersection of primitives does not necessarily result in a convex subset of $\mathcal{W}$. In general, however, it might be necessary to form $\mathcal{O}$ by taking unions and intersections of algebraic primitives.

   A logical predicate, $\phi(x, y)$, can once again be formed, and collision checking is still performed in time that is linear in the number of primitives. Note that it is still very efficient to evaluate every primitive; f is just a polynomial that is evaluated on the point (x, y, z).

   The semi-algebraic formulation generalizes easily to the case of a 3D world. This results in algebraic primitives of the form

$$H = \{(x, y, z) \in \mathcal{W} \mid f(x, y, z) \le 0\}, \tag{3.13}$$

which can be used to define a solid representation of a 3D obstacle $\mathcal{O}$ and a logical predicate ϕ.

   Equations (3.10) and (3.13) are sufficient to express any model of interest. One may define many other primitives based on different relations, such as $f(x, y, z) \ge 0$,

$f(x, y, z) = 0$, $f(x, y, z) < 0$, $f(x, y, z) = 0$, and $f(x, y, z) \neq 0$; however, most of them do not enhance the set of models that can be expressed. They might, however, be more convenient in certain contexts. To see that some primitives do not allow new models to be expressed, consider the primitive

$$H = \{(x, y, z) \in \mathcal{W} \mid f(x, y, z) \geq 0\}. \tag{3.14}$$

The right part may be alternatively represented as $-f(x, y, z) \leq 0$, and $-f$ may be considered as a new polynomial function of x, y, and z. For an example that involves the $=$ relation, consider the primitive

$$H = \{(x, y, z) \in \mathcal{W} \mid f(x, y, z) = 0\}. \tag{3.15}$$

It can instead be constructed as $H = H_1 \cap H_2$, in which

$$H_1 = \{(x, y, z) \in \mathcal{W} \mid f(x, y, z) \leq 0\} \tag{3.16}$$

and

$$H_2 = \{(x, y, z) \in \mathcal{W} \mid -f(x, y, z) \leq 0\}. \tag{3.17}$$

The relation $<$ does add some expressive power if it is used to construct primitives.[2] It is needed to construct models that do not include the outer boundary (for example, the set of all points *inside* of a sphere, which does not include points *on* the sphere). These are generally called *open sets* and are defined Chapter 4.

3.1.3 Other models

The choice of a model often depends on the types of operations that will be performed by the planning algorithm. For combinatorial motion planning methods, to be covered in Chapter 6, the particular representation is critical. On the other hand, for sampling-based planning methods, to be covered in Chapter 5, the particular representation is important only to the collision detection algorithm, which is treated as a "black box" as far as planning is concerned. Therefore, the models given in the remainder of this section are more likely to appear in sampling-based approaches and may be invisible to the designer of a planning algorithm (although it is never wise to forget completely about the representation).

Nonconvex polygons and polyhedra

The method in Section 3.1.1 required nonconvex polygons to be represented as a union of convex polygons. Instead, a boundary representation of a nonconvex polygon may be directly encoded by listing vertices in a specific order; assume that counterclockwise order is used. Each polygon of m vertices may be encoded by a list of the form (x_1, y_1), (x_2, y_2), $\ldots$, (x_m, y_m). It is assumed that there is an edge between each (x_i, y_i) and (x_{i+1}, y_{i+1}) for each i from 1 to $m - 1$, and also an edge between (x_m, y_m) and (x_1, y_1). Ordinarily, the vertices should be chosen in a way that makes the polygon *simple*, meaning that no edges intersect. In this case, there is a well-defined interior of the polygon, which is to the left of every edge, if the vertices are listed in counterclockwise order.

What if a polygon has a hole in it? In this case, the boundary of the hole can be expressed as a polygon, but with its vertices appearing in the clockwise direction. To the

---

[2] An alternative that yields the same expressive power is to still use $\leq$, but allow set complements, in addition to unions and intersections.

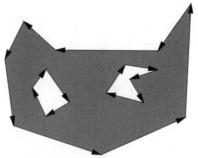

Figure 3.5: A polygon with holes can be expressed by using different orientations: counterclockwise for the outer boundary and clockwise for the hole boundaries. Note that the shaded part is always to the left when following the arrows.

Figure 3.6: Triangle strips and triangle fans can reduce the number of redundant points.

left of each edge is the interior of the outer polygon, and to the right is the hole, as shown in Figure 3.5.

Although the data structures are a little more complicated for three dimensions, boundary representations of nonconvex polyhedra may be expressed in a similar manner. In this case, instead of an edge list, one must specify faces, edges, and vertices, with pointers that indicate their incidence relations. Consistent orientations must also be chosen, and holes may be modeled once again by selecting opposite orientations.

3D triangles

Suppose $\mathcal{W} = \mathbb{R}^3$. One of the most convenient geometric models to express is a set of triangles, each of which is specified by three points, (x_1, y_1, z_1), (x_2, y_2, z_2), (x_3, y_3, z_3). This model has been popular in computer graphics because graphics acceleration hardware primarily uses triangle primitives. It is assumed that the interior of the triangle is part of the model. Thus, two triangles are considered as "colliding" if one pokes into the interior of another. This model offers great flexibility because there are no constraints on the way in which triangles must be expressed; however, this is also one of the drawbacks. There is no coherency that can be exploited to easily declare whether a point is "inside" or "outside" of a 3D obstacle. If there is at least some coherency, then it is sometimes preferable to reduce redundancy in the specification of triangle coordinates (many triangles will share the same corners). Representations that remove this redundancy are called a *triangle strip*, which is a sequence of triangles such that each adjacent pair shares a common edge, and a *triangle fan*, which is a triangle strip in which all triangles share a common vertex. See Figure 3.6.

Nonuniform rational B-splines (NURBS)

These are used in many engineering design systems to allow convenient design and adjustment of curved surfaces, in applications such as aircraft or automobile body design. In contrast to semi-algebraic models, which are implicit equations, NURBS and other splines are parametric equations. This makes computations such as rendering easier;

however, others, such as collision detection, become more difficult. These models may be defined in any dimension. A brief 2D formulation is given here.

A curve can be expressed as

$$C(u) = \frac{\displaystyle\sum_{i=0}^{n} w_i P_i N_{i,k}(u)}{\displaystyle\sum_{i=0}^{n} w_i N_{i,k}(u)}, \tag{3.18}$$

in which $w_i \in \mathbb{R}$ are *weights* and P_i are control points. The $N_{i,k}$ are normalized basis functions of degree k, which can be expressed recursively as

$$N_{i,k}(u) = \left(\frac{u - t_i}{t_{i+k} - t_i}\right) N_{i,k-1}(u) + \left(\frac{t_{i+k+1} - u}{t_{i+k+1} - t_{i+1}}\right) N_{i+1,k-1}(u). \tag{3.19}$$

The basis of the recursion is $N_{i,0}(u) = 1$ if $t_i \le u < t_{i+1}$, and $N_{i,0}(u) = 0$ otherwise. A *knot vector* is a nondecreasing sequence of real values, $\{t_0, t_1, \ldots, t_m\}$, that controls the intervals over which certain basic functions take effect.

Bitmaps

For either $\mathcal{W} = \mathbb{R}^2$ or $\mathcal{W} = \mathbb{R}^3$, it is possible to discretize a bounded portion of the world into rectangular cells that may or may not be occupied. The resulting model looks very similar to Example 2.1. The resolution of this discretization determines the number of cells per axis and the quality of the approximation. The representation may be considered as a binary image in which each "1" in the image corresponds to a rectangular region that contains at least one point of $\mathcal{O}$, and "0" represents those that do not contain any of $\mathcal{O}$. Although bitmaps do not have the elegance of the other models, they often arise in applications. One example is a digital map constructed by a mobile robot that explores an environment with its sensors. One generalization of bitmaps is a *gray-scale map* or *occupancy grid*. In this case, a numerical value may be assigned to each cell, indicating quantities such as "the probability that an obstacle exists" or the "expected difficulty of traversing the cell." The latter interpretation is often used in terrain maps for navigating planetary rovers.

Superquadrics

Instead of using polynomials to define f_i, many generalizations can be constructed. One popular primitive is a *superquadric*, which generalizes quadric surfaces. One example is a superellipsoid, which is given for $\mathcal{W} = \mathbb{R}^3$ by

$$\left(|x/a|^{n_1} + |y/b|^{n_2}\right)^{n_1/n_2} + |z/c|^{n_1} - 1 \le 0, \tag{3.20}$$

in which $n_1 \ge 2$ and $n_2 \ge 2$. If $n_1 = n_2 = 2$, an ellipse is generated. As n_1 and n_2 increase, the superellipsoid becomes shaped like a box with rounded corners.

Generalized cylinders

A *generalized cylinder* is a generalization of an ordinary cylinder. Instead of being limited to a line, the center axis is a continuous *spine curve*, $(x(s), y(s), z(s))$, for some parameter $s \in [0, 1]$. Instead of a constant radius, a radius function $r(s)$ is defined along the spine. The value $r(s)$ is the radius of the circle obtained as the cross section of the generalized cylinder at the point $(x(s), y(s), z(s))$. The normal to the cross-section plane is the tangent to the spine curve at s.

3.2 Rigid-body transformations

Any of the techniques from Section 3.1 can be used to define both the obstacle region and the robot. Let $\mathcal{O}$ refer to the *obstacle region*, which is a subset of $\mathcal{W}$. Let $\mathcal{A}$ refer to the robot, which is a subset of $\mathbb{R}^2$ or $\mathbb{R}^3$, matching the dimension of $\mathcal{W}$. Although $\mathcal{O}$ remains fixed in the world, $\mathcal{W}$, motion planning problems will require "moving" the robot, $\mathcal{A}$.

3.2.1 General concepts

Before giving specific transformations, it will be helpful to define them in general to avoid confusion in later parts when intuitive notions might fall apart. Suppose that a rigid robot, $\mathcal{A}$, is defined as a subset of $\mathbb{R}^2$ or $\mathbb{R}^3$. A *rigid-body transformation* is a function, $h : \mathcal{A} \rightarrow \mathcal{W}$, that maps every point of $\mathcal{A}$ into $\mathcal{W}$ with two requirements: 1) The distance between any pair of points of $\mathcal{A}$ must be preserved, and 2) the orientation of $\mathcal{A}$ must be preserved (no "mirror images").

Using standard function notation, $h(a)$ for some $a \in \mathcal{A}$ refers to the point in $\mathcal{W}$ that is "occupied" by a. Let

$$h(\mathcal{A}) = \{h(a) \in \mathcal{W} \mid a \in \mathcal{A}\}, \tag{3.21}$$

which is the image of h and indicates all points in $\mathcal{W}$ occupied by the transformed robot.

Transforming the robot model

Consider transforming a robot model. If $\mathcal{A}$ is expressed by naming specific points in $\mathbb{R}^2$, as in a boundary representation of a polygon, then each point is simply transformed from a to $h(a) \in \mathcal{W}$. In this case, it is straightforward to transform the entire model using h. However, there is a slight complication if the robot model is expressed using primitives, such as

$$H_i = \{a \in \mathbb{R}^2 \mid f_i(a) \le 0\}. \tag{3.22}$$

This differs slightly from (3.2) because the robot is defined in $\mathbb{R}^2$ (which is not necessarily $\mathcal{W}$), and also a is used to denote a point $(x, y) \in \mathcal{A}$. Under a transformation h, the primitive is transformed as

$$h(H_i) = \{h(a) \in \mathcal{W} \mid f_i(a) \le 0\}. \tag{3.23}$$

To transform the primitive completely, however, it is better to directly name points in $w \in \mathcal{W}$, as opposed to $h(a) \in \mathcal{W}$. Using the fact that $a = h^{-1}(w)$, this becomes

$$h(H_i) = \{w \in \mathcal{W} \mid f_i(h^{-1}(w)) \le 0\}, \tag{3.24}$$

in which the inverse of h appears in the right side because the original point $a \in A$ needs to be recovered to evaluate f_i. Therefore, it is important to be careful because either h or h^{-1} may be required to transform the model. This will be observed in more specific contexts in some coming examples.

A parameterized family of transformations

It will become important to study families of transformations, in which some parameters are used to select the particular transformation. Therefore, it makes sense to generalize h to accept two variables: a parameter vector, $q \in \mathbb{R}^n$, along with $a \in \mathcal{A}$. The resulting transformed point a is denoted by $h(q, a)$, and the entire robot is transformed to $h(q, \mathcal{A}) \subset \mathcal{W}$.

The coming material will use the following shorthand notation, which requires the specific h to be inferred from the context. Let $h(q, a)$ be shortened to $a(q)$, and let $h(q, \mathcal{A})$ be shortened to $\mathcal{A}(q)$. This notation makes it appear that by adjusting the parameter q, the robot $\mathcal{A}$ travels around in $\mathcal{W}$ as different transformations are selected from the predetermined family. This is slightly abusive notation, but it is convenient. The expression $\mathcal{A}(q)$ can be considered as a set-valued function that yields the set of points in $\mathcal{W}$ that are occupied by $\mathcal{A}$ when it is transformed by q. Most of the time the notation does not cause trouble, but when it does, it is helpful to remember the definitions from this section, especially when trying to determine whether h or h^{-1} is needed.

Defining frames

It was assumed so far that $\mathcal{A}$ is defined in $\mathbb{R}^2$ or $\mathbb{R}^3$, but before it is transformed, it is not considered to be a subset of $\mathcal{W}$. The transformation h *places* the robot in $\mathcal{W}$. In the coming material, it will be convenient to indicate this distinction using coordinate frames. The origin and coordinate basis vectors of $\mathcal{W}$ will be referred to as the *world frame*.[3] Thus, any point $w \in \mathcal{W}$ is expressed in terms of the world frame.

The coordinates used to define $\mathcal{A}$ are initially expressed in the *body frame*, which represents the origin and coordinate basis vectors of $\mathbb{R}^2$ or $\mathbb{R}^3$. In the case of $\mathcal{A} \subset \mathbb{R}^2$, it can be imagined that the body frame is painted on the robot. Transforming the robot is equivalent to converting its model from the body frame to the world frame. This has the effect of *placing*[4] $\mathcal{A}$ into $\mathcal{W}$ at some position and orientation. When multiple bodies are covered in Section 3.3, each body will have its own body frame, and transformations require expressing all bodies with respect to the world frame.

3.2.2 2D transformations

Translation

A rigid robot $\mathcal{A} \subset \mathbb{R}^2$ is *translated* by using two parameters, $x_t, y_t \in \mathbb{R}$. Using definitions from Section 3.2.1, $q = (x_t, y_t)$, and h is defined as

$$h(x, y) = (x + x_t, y + y_t). \qquad (3.25)$$

A boundary representation of $\mathcal{A}$ can be translated by transforming each vertex in the sequence of polygon vertices using (3.25). Each point, (x_i, y_i), in the sequence is replaced by $(x_i + x_t, y_i + y_t)$.

Now consider a solid representation of $\mathcal{A}$, defined in terms of primitives. Each primitive of the form

$$H_i = \{(x, y) \in \mathbb{R}^2 \mid f(x, y) \le 0\} \qquad (3.26)$$

---

[3] The world frame serves the same purpose as an inertial frame in Newtonian mechanics. Intuitively, it is a frame that remains fixed and from which all measurements are taken. See Section 13.3.1.

[4] Technically, this placement is a function called an *orientation-preserving isometric embedding*.

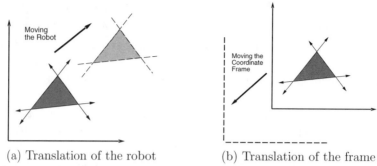

(a) Translation of the robot   (b) Translation of the frame

Figure 3.7: Every transformation has two interpretations.

is transformed to

$$h(H_i) = \{(x, y) \in \mathcal{W} \mid f(x - x_t, y - y_t) \le 0\}. \tag{3.27}$$

Example 3.2 (Translating a Disc) For example, suppose the robot is a disc of unit radius, centered at the origin. It is modeled by a single primitive,

$$H_i = \{(x, y) \in \mathbb{R}^2 \mid x^2 + y^2 - 1 \le 0\}. \tag{3.28}$$

Suppose $\mathcal{A} = H_i$ is translated x_t units in the x direction and y_t units in the y direction. The transformed primitive is

$$h(H_i) = \{(x, y) \in \mathcal{W} \mid (x - x_t)^2 + (y - y_t)^2 - 1 \le 0\}, \tag{3.29}$$

which is the familiar equation for a disc centered at (x_t, y_t). In this example, the inverse, h^{-1} is used, as described in Section 3.2.1. ■

The translated robot is denoted as $\mathcal{A}(x_t, y_t)$. Translation by $(0, 0)$ is the *identity transformation*, which results in $\mathcal{A}(0, 0) = \mathcal{A}$, if it is assumed that $\mathcal{A} \subset \mathcal{W}$ (recall that $\mathcal{A}$ does not necessarily have to be initially embedded in $\mathcal{W}$). It will be convenient to use the term *degrees of freedom* to refer to the maximum number of independent parameters that are needed to completely characterize the transformation applied to the robot. If the set of allowable values for x_t and y_t forms a two-dimensional subset of $\mathbb{R}^2$, then the degrees of freedom is two.

Suppose that $\mathcal{A}$ is defined directly in $\mathcal{W}$ with translation. As shown in Figure 3.7, there are two interpretations of a rigid-body transformation applied to $\mathcal{A}$: 1) The world frame remains fixed and the robot is transformed; 2) the robot remains fixed and the world frame is translated. The first one characterizes the effect of the transformation from a fixed world frame, and the second one indicates how the transformation appears from the robot's perspective. Unless stated otherwise, the first interpretation will be used when we refer to motion planning problems because it often models a robot moving in a physical world. Numerous books cover coordinate transformations under the second interpretation. This has been known to cause confusion because the transformations may sometimes appear "backward" from what is desired in motion planning.

Rotation

The robot, $\mathcal{A}$, can be *rotated* counterclockwise by some angle $\theta \in [0, 2\pi)$ by mapping every $(x, y) \in \mathcal{A}$ as

$$(x, y) \mapsto (x \cos \theta - y \sin \theta, \ x \sin \theta + y \cos \theta). \tag{3.30}$$

Using a 2×2 rotation matrix,

$$R(\theta) = \begin{pmatrix} \cos\theta & -\sin\theta \\ \sin\theta & \cos\theta \end{pmatrix}, \tag{3.31}$$

the transformation can be written as

$$\begin{pmatrix} x\cos\theta - y\sin\theta \\ x\sin\theta + y\cos\theta \end{pmatrix} = R(\theta)\begin{pmatrix} x \\ y \end{pmatrix}. \tag{3.32}$$

Using the notation of Section 3.2.1, $R(\theta)$ becomes $h(q)$, for which $q = \theta$. For linear transformations, such as the one defined by (3.32), recall that the column vectors represent the basis vectors of the new coordinate frame. The column vectors of $R(\theta)$ are unit vectors, and their inner product (or dot product) is zero, indicating that they are orthogonal. Suppose that the x and y coordinate axes, which represent the body frame, are "painted" on $\mathcal{A}$. The columns of $R(\theta)$ can be derived by considering the resulting directions of the x- and y-axes, respectively, after performing a counterclockwise rotation by the angle θ. This interpretation generalizes nicely for higher dimensional rotation matrices.

Note that the rotation is performed about the origin. Thus, when defining the model of $\mathcal{A}$, the origin should be placed at the intended axis of rotation. Using the semi-algebraic model, the entire robot model can be rotated by transforming each primitive, yielding $\mathcal{A}(\theta)$. The inverse rotation, $R(-\theta)$, must be applied to each primitive.

Combining translation and rotation

Suppose a rotation by θ is performed, followed by a translation by x_t, y_t. This can be used to place the robot in any desired position and orientation. Note that translations and rotations do not commute! If the operations are applied successively, each $(x, y) \in \mathcal{A}$ is transformed to

$$\begin{pmatrix} x\cos\theta - y\sin\theta + x_t \\ x\sin\theta + y\cos\theta + y_t \end{pmatrix}. \tag{3.33}$$

The following matrix multiplication yields the same result for the first two vector components:

$$\begin{pmatrix} \cos\theta & -\sin\theta & x_t \\ \sin\theta & \cos\theta & y_t \\ 0 & 0 & 1 \end{pmatrix}\begin{pmatrix} x \\ y \\ 1 \end{pmatrix} = \begin{pmatrix} x\cos\theta - y\sin\theta + x_t \\ x\sin\theta + y\cos\theta + y_t \\ 1 \end{pmatrix}. \tag{3.34}$$

This implies that the 3×3 matrix,

$$T = \begin{pmatrix} \cos\theta & -\sin\theta & x_t \\ \sin\theta & \cos\theta & y_t \\ 0 & 0 & 1 \end{pmatrix}, \tag{3.35}$$

represents a rotation followed by a translation. The matrix T will be referred to as a *homogeneous transformation matrix*. It is important to remember that T represents a rotation *followed by* a translation (not the other way around). Each primitive can be transformed using the inverse of T, resulting in a transformed solid model of the robot. The transformed robot is denoted by $\mathcal{A}(x_t, y_t, \theta)$, and in this case there are three degrees of freedom. The homogeneous transformation matrix is a convenient representation of the combined transformations; therefore, it is frequently used in robotics, mechanics, computer graphics, and elsewhere. It is called homogeneous because over $\mathbb{R}^3$ it is just a

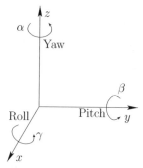

Figure 3.8: Any three-dimensional rotation can be described as a sequence of yaw, pitch, and roll rotations.

linear transformation without any translation. The trick of increasing the dimension by one to absorb the translational part is common in projective geometry [807].

3.2.3 3D transformations

Rigid-body transformations for the 3D case are conceptually similar to the 2D case; however, the 3D case appears more difficult because rotations are significantly more complicated.

3D translation

The robot, $\mathcal{A}$, is *translated* by some $x_t, y_t, z_t \in \mathbb{R}$ using

$$(x, y, z) \mapsto (x + x_t, y + y_t, z + z_t). \tag{3.36}$$

A primitive of the form

$$H_i = \{(x, y, z) \in \mathcal{W} \mid f_i(x, y, z) \le 0\} \tag{3.37}$$

is transformed to

$$\{(x, y, z) \in \mathcal{W} \mid f_i(x - x_t, y - y_t, z - z_t) \le 0\}. \tag{3.38}$$

The translated robot is denoted as $\mathcal{A}(x_t, y_t, z_t)$.

Yaw, pitch, and roll rotations

A 3D body can be rotated about three orthogonal axes, as shown in Figure 3.8. Borrowing aviation terminology, these rotations will be referred to as yaw, pitch, and roll:

1. A *yaw* is a counterclockwise rotation of α about the z-axis. The rotation matrix is given by

$$R_z(\alpha) = \begin{pmatrix} \cos\alpha & -\sin\alpha & 0 \\ \sin\alpha & \cos\alpha & 0 \\ 0 & 0 & 1 \end{pmatrix}. \tag{3.39}$$

Note that the upper left entries of $R_z(\alpha)$ form a 2D rotation applied to the x and y coordinates, whereas the z coordinate remains constant.

2. A *pitch* is a counterclockwise rotation of β about the y-axis. The rotation matrix is given by

$$R_y(\beta) = \begin{pmatrix} \cos\beta & 0 & \sin\beta \\ 0 & 1 & 0 \\ -\sin\beta & 0 & \cos\beta \end{pmatrix}. \tag{3.40}$$

3. A *roll* is a counterclockwise rotation of γ about the x-axis. The rotation matrix is given by

$$R_x(\gamma) = \begin{pmatrix} 1 & 0 & 0 \\ 0 & \cos\gamma & -\sin\gamma \\ 0 & \sin\gamma & \cos\gamma \end{pmatrix}. \tag{3.41}$$

Each rotation matrix is a simple extension of the 2D rotation matrix, (3.31). For example, the yaw matrix, $R_z(\alpha)$, essentially performs a 2D rotation with respect to the x and y coordinates while leaving the z coordinate unchanged. Thus, the third row and third column of $R_z(\alpha)$ look like part of the identity matrix, while the upper right portion of $R_z(\alpha)$ looks like the 2D rotation matrix.

The yaw, pitch, and roll rotations can be used to place a 3D body in any orientation. A single rotation matrix can be formed by multiplying the yaw, pitch, and roll rotation matrices to obtain

$$R(\alpha, \beta, \gamma) = R_z(\alpha)\, R_y(\beta)\, R_x(\gamma) =$$

$$\begin{pmatrix} \cos\alpha\cos\beta & \cos\alpha\sin\beta\sin\gamma - \sin\alpha\cos\gamma & \cos\alpha\sin\beta\cos\gamma + \sin\alpha\sin\gamma \\ \sin\alpha\cos\beta & \sin\alpha\sin\beta\sin\gamma + \cos\alpha\cos\gamma & \sin\alpha\sin\beta\cos\gamma - \cos\alpha\sin\gamma \\ -\sin\beta & \cos\beta\sin\gamma & \cos\beta\cos\gamma \end{pmatrix}. \tag{3.42}$$

It is important to note that $R(\alpha, \beta, \gamma)$ performs the roll first, then the pitch, and finally the yaw. If the order of these operations is changed, a different rotation matrix would result. Be careful when interpreting the rotations. Consider the final rotation, a yaw by α. Imagine sitting inside of a robot $\mathcal{A}$ that looks like an aircraft. If $\beta = \gamma = 0$, then the yaw turns the plane in a way that feels like turning a car to the left. However, for arbitrary values of β and γ, the final rotation axis will not be vertically aligned with the aircraft because the aircraft is left in an unusual orientation before α is applied. The yaw rotation occurs about the z-axis of the world frame, not the body frame of $\mathcal{A}$. Each time a new rotation matrix is introduced from the left, it has no concern for original body frame of $\mathcal{A}$. It simply rotates every point in $\mathbb{R}^3$ in terms of the world frame. Note that 3D rotations depend on three parameters, α, β, and γ, whereas 2D rotations depend only on a single parameter, θ. The primitives of the model can be transformed using $R(\alpha, \beta, \gamma)$, resulting in $\mathcal{A}(\alpha, \beta, \gamma)$.

Determining yaw, pitch, and roll from a rotation matrix

It is often convenient to determine the α, β, and γ parameters directly from a given rotation matrix. Suppose an arbitrary rotation matrix

$$\begin{pmatrix} r_{11} & r_{12} & r_{13} \\ r_{21} & r_{22} & r_{23} \\ r_{31} & r_{32} & r_{33} \end{pmatrix} \tag{3.43}$$

is given. By setting each entry equal to its corresponding entry in (3.42), equations are obtained that must be solved for α, β, and γ. Note that $r_{21}/r_{11} = \tan\alpha$ and $r_{32}/r_{33} = \tan\gamma$. Also, $r_{31} = -\sin\beta$ and $\sqrt{r_{32}^2 + r_{33}^2} = \cos\beta$. Solving for each angle yields

$$\alpha = \tan^{-1}(r_{11}/r_{21}), \tag{3.44}$$

$$\beta = \tan^{-1}\left(\sqrt{r_{32}^2 + r_{33}^2}/-r_{31}\right), \tag{3.45}$$

and

$$\gamma = \tan^{-1}(r_{32}/r_{33}). \tag{3.46}$$

There is a choice of four quadrants for the inverse tangent functions. How can the correct quadrant be determined? Each quadrant should be chosen by using the signs of the numerator and denominator of the argument. The numerator sign selects whether the direction will be to the left or right of the y-axis, and the denominator selects whether the direction will be above or below the x-axis. This is the same as the atan2 function in the C programming language, which nicely expands the range of the arctangent to $[0, 2\pi)$. This can be applied to express (3.44), (3.45), and (3.46) as

$$\alpha = \operatorname{atan2}(r_{11}, r_{21}), \tag{3.47}$$

$$\beta = \operatorname{atan2}\left(\sqrt{r_{32}^2 + r_{33}^2}, -r_{31}\right), \tag{3.48}$$

and

$$\gamma = \operatorname{atan2}(r_{32}, r_{33}). \tag{3.49}$$

Note that this method assumes $r_{21} \neq 0$ and $r_{33} \neq 0$.

The homogeneous transformation matrix for 3D bodies

As in the 2D case, a homogeneous transformation matrix can be defined. For the 3D case, a 4×4 matrix is obtained that performs the rotation given by $R(\alpha, \beta, \gamma)$, followed by a translation given by x_t, y_t, z_t. The result is

$$T = \begin{pmatrix} \cos\alpha\cos\beta & \cos\alpha\sin\beta\sin\gamma - \sin\alpha\cos\gamma & \cos\alpha\sin\beta\cos\gamma + \sin\alpha\sin\gamma & x_t \\ \sin\alpha\cos\beta & \sin\alpha\sin\beta\sin\gamma + \cos\alpha\cos\gamma & \sin\alpha\sin\beta\cos\gamma - \cos\alpha\sin\gamma & y_t \\ -\sin\beta & \cos\beta\sin\gamma & \cos\beta\cos\gamma & z_t \\ 0 & 0 & 0 & 1 \end{pmatrix}. \tag{3.50}$$

Once again, the order of operations is critical. The matrix T in (3.50) represents the following sequence of transformations:

1. Roll by γ 3. Yaw by α
2. Pitch by β 4. Translate by (x_t, y_t, z_t).

The robot primitives can be transformed to yield $\mathcal{A}(x_t, y_t, z_t, \alpha, \beta, \gamma)$. A 3D rigid body that is capable of translation and rotation therefore has six degrees of freedom.

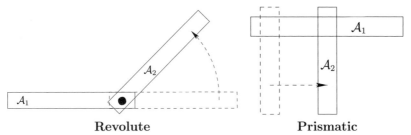

Revolute   Prismatic

Figure 3.9: Two types of 2D joints: a revolute joint allows one link to rotate with respect to the other, and a prismatic joint allows one link to translate with respect to the other.

3.3 Transforming kinematic chains of bodies

The transformations become more complicated for a chain of attached rigid bodies. For convenience, each rigid body is referred to as a *link*. Let $\mathcal{A}_1, \mathcal{A}_2, \ldots, \mathcal{A}_m$ denote a set of m links. For each i such that $1 \leq i < m$, link $\mathcal{A}_i$ is "attached" to link $\mathcal{A}_{i+1}$ in a way that allows $\mathcal{A}_{i+1}$ some constrained motion with respect to $\mathcal{A}_i$. The motion constraint must be explicitly given, and will be discussed shortly. As an example, imagine a trailer that is attached to the back of a car by a hitch that allows the trailer to rotate with respect to the car. In general, a set of attached bodies will be referred to as a *linkage*. This section considers bodies that are attached in a single chain. This leads to a particular linkage called a *kinematic chain*.

3.3.1 A 2D kinematic chain

Before considering a kinematic chain, suppose $\mathcal{A}_1$ and $\mathcal{A}_2$ are unattached rigid bodies, each of which is capable of translating and rotating in $\mathcal{W} = \mathbb{R}^2$. Since each body has three degrees of freedom, there is a combined total of six degrees of freedom; the independent parameters are x_1, y_1, θ_1, x_2, y_2, and θ_2.

Attaching bodies

When bodies are attached in a kinematic chain, degrees of freedom are removed. Figure 3.9 shows two different ways in which a pair of 2D links can be attached. The place at which the links are attached is called a *joint*. For a *revolute joint*, one link is capable only of rotation with respect to the other. For a *prismatic joint* is shown, one link slides along the other. Each type of joint removes two degrees of freedom from the pair of bodies. For example, consider a revolute joint that connects $\mathcal{A}_1$ to $\mathcal{A}_2$. Assume that the point $(0, 0)$ in the body frame of $\mathcal{A}_2$ is permanently fixed to a point (x_a, y_a) in the body frame of $\mathcal{A}_1$. This implies that the translation of $\mathcal{A}_2$ is completely determined once x_a and y_a are given. Note that x_a and y_a depend on x_1, y_1, and θ_1. This implies that $\mathcal{A}_1$ and $\mathcal{A}_2$ have a total of four degrees of freedom when attached. The independent parameters are x_1, y_1, θ_1, and θ_2. The task in the remainder of this section is to determine exactly how the models of $\mathcal{A}_1, \mathcal{A}_2, \ldots, \mathcal{A}_m$ are transformed when they are attached in a chain, and to give the expressions in terms of the independent parameters.

Consider the case of a kinematic chain in which each pair of links is attached by a revolute joint. The first task is to specify the geometric model for each link, $\mathcal{A}_i$. Recall that for a single rigid body, the origin of the body frame determines the axis of rotation. When defining the model for a link in a kinematic chain, excessive complications can be avoided by carefully placing the body frame. Since rotation occurs about a revolute

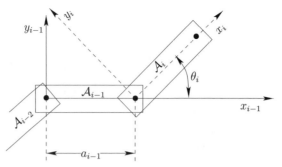

Figure 3.10: The body frame of each $\mathcal{A}_i$, for $1 < i < m$, is based on the joints that connect $\mathcal{A}_i$ to $\mathcal{A}_{i-1}$ and $\mathcal{A}_{i+1}$.

joint, a natural choice for the origin is the joint between $\mathcal{A}_i$ and $\mathcal{A}_{i-1}$ for each $i > 1$. For convenience that will soon become evident, the x_i-axis for the body frame of $\mathcal{A}_i$ is defined as the line through the two joints that lie in $\mathcal{A}_i$, as shown in Figure 3.10. For the last link, $\mathcal{A}_m$, the x_m-axis can be placed arbitrarily, assuming that the origin is placed at the joint that connects $\mathcal{A}_m$ to $\mathcal{A}_{m-1}$. The body frame for the first link, $\mathcal{A}_1$, can be placed using the same considerations as for a single rigid body.

Homogeneous transformation matrices for 2D chains

We are now prepared to determine the location of each link. The location in $\mathcal{W}$ of a point in $(x, y) \in \mathcal{A}_1$ is determined by applying the 2D homogeneous transformation matrix (3.35),

$$
T_1 = \begin{pmatrix} \cos\theta_1 & -\sin\theta_1 & x_t \\ \sin\theta_1 & \cos\theta_1 & y_t \\ 0 & 0 & 1 \end{pmatrix}. \tag{3.51}
$$

As shown in Figure 3.10, let a_{i-1} be the distance between the joints in $\mathcal{A}_{i-1}$. The orientation difference between $\mathcal{A}_i$ and $\mathcal{A}_{i-1}$ is denoted by the angle θ_i. Let T_i represent a 3×3 homogeneous transformation matrix (3.35), specialized for link $\mathcal{A}_i$ for $1 < i \leq m$,

$$
T_i = \begin{pmatrix} \cos\theta_i & -\sin\theta_i & a_{i-1} \\ \sin\theta_i & \cos\theta_i & 0 \\ 0 & 0 & 1 \end{pmatrix}. \tag{3.52}
$$

This generates the following sequence of transformations:

1. Rotate counterclockwise by θ_i.

2. Translate by a_{i-1} along the x-axis.

The transformation T_i expresses the difference between the body frame of $\mathcal{A}_i$ and the body frame of $\mathcal{A}_{i-1}$. The application of T_i moves $\mathcal{A}_i$ from its body frame to the body frame of $\mathcal{A}_{i-1}$. The application of $T_{i-1}T_i$ moves both $\mathcal{A}_i$ and $\mathcal{A}_{i-1}$ to the body frame of $\mathcal{A}_{i-2}$. By following this procedure, the location in $\mathcal{W}$ of any point $(x, y) \in \mathcal{A}_m$ is determined by multiplying the transformation matrices to obtain

$$
T_1 T_2 \cdots T_m \begin{pmatrix} x \\ y \\ 1 \end{pmatrix}. \tag{3.53}
$$

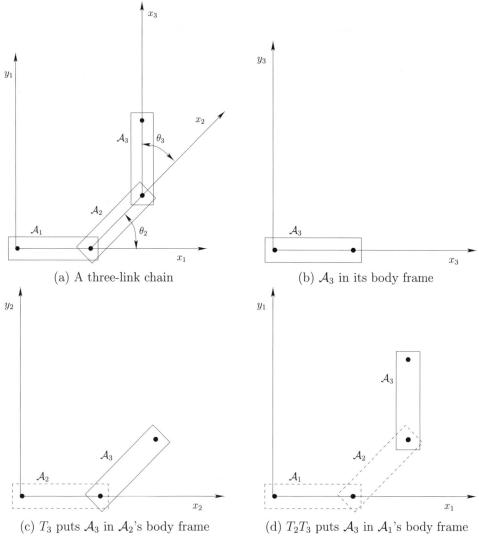

Figure 3.11: Applying the transformation $T_2 T_3$ to the model of $\mathcal{A}_3$. If T_1 is the identity matrix, then this yields the location in $\mathcal{W}$ of points in $\mathcal{A}_3$.

Example 3.3 (A 2D Chain of Three Links) To gain an intuitive understanding of these transformations, consider determining the configuration for link $\mathcal{A}_3$, as shown in Figure 3.11. Figure 3.11a shows a three-link chain in which $\mathcal{A}_1$ is at its initial configuration and the other links are each offset by $\pi/4$ from the previous link. Figure 3.11b shows the frame in which the model for $\mathcal{A}_3$ is initially defined. The application of T_3 causes a rotation of θ_3 and a translation by a_2. As shown in Figure 3.11c, this places $\mathcal{A}_3$ in its appropriate configuration. Note that $\mathcal{A}_2$ can be placed in its initial configuration, and it will be attached correctly to $\mathcal{A}_3$. The application of T_2 to the previous result places both $\mathcal{A}_3$ and $\mathcal{A}_2$ in their proper configurations, and $\mathcal{A}_1$ can be placed in its initial configuration. ■

For revolute joints, the a_i parameters are constants, and the θ_i parameters are variables. The transformed mth link is represented as $\mathcal{A}_m(x_t, y_t, \theta_1, \ldots, \theta_m)$. In some cases, the first link might have a fixed location in the world. In this case, the revolute joints account for

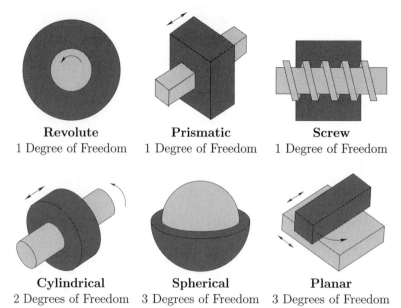

Revolute   **Prismatic**   **Screw**
1 Degree of Freedom   1 Degree of Freedom   1 Degree of Freedom

Cylindrical   **Spherical**   **Planar**
2 Degrees of Freedom 3 Degrees of Freedom   3 Degrees of Freedom

Figure 3.12: Types of 3D joints arising from the 2D surface contact between two bodies.

all degrees of freedom, yielding $\mathcal{A}_m(\theta_1, \ldots, \theta_m)$. For prismatic joints, the a_i parameters are variables, instead of the θ_i parameters. It is straightforward to include both types of joints in the same kinematic chain.

3.3.2 A 3D kinematic chain

As for a single rigid body, the 3D case is significantly more complicated than the 2D case due to 3D rotations. Also, several more types of joints are possible, as shown in Figure 3.12. Nevertheless, the main ideas from the transformations of 2D kinematic chains extend to the 3D case. The following steps from Section 3.3.1 will be recycled here:

1.   The body frame must be carefully placed for each $\mathcal{A}_i$.
2.   Based on joint relationships, several parameters are measured.
3.   The parameters define a homogeneous transformation matrix, T_i.
4.   The location in $\mathcal{W}$ of any point in $\mathcal{A}_m$ is given by applying the matrix $T_1 T_2 \cdots T_m$.

Consider a kinematic chain of m links in $\mathcal{W} = \mathbb{R}^3$, in which each $\mathcal{A}_i$ for $1 \leq i < m$ is attached to $\mathcal{A}_{i+1}$ by a revolute joint. Each link can be a complicated, rigid body as shown in Figure 3.13. For the 2D problem, the coordinate frames were based on the points of attachment. For the 3D problem, it is convenient to use the axis of rotation of each revolute joint (this is equivalent to the point of attachment for the 2D case). The axes of rotation will generally be skew lines in $\mathbb{R}^3$, as shown in Figure 3.14. Let the z_i-axis be the axis of rotation for the revolute joint that holds $\mathcal{A}_i$ to $\mathcal{A}_{i-1}$. Between each pair of axes in succession, let the x_i-axis join the closest pair of points between the z_i- and z_{i+1}-axes, with the origin on the z_i-axis and the direction pointing towards the nearest point of the z_{i+1}-axis. This axis is uniquely defined if the z_i- and z_{i+1}-axes are not parallel. The recommended body frame for each $\mathcal{A}_i$ will be given with respect to the z_i- and x_i-axes, which are shown in Figure 3.14. Assuming a right-handed coordinate system, the y_i-axis points away from us in Figure 3.14. In the transformations that will appear shortly, the

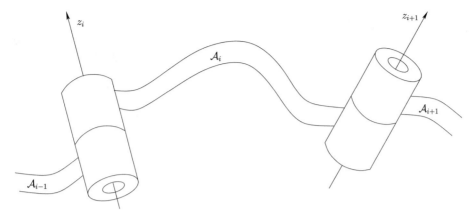

Figure 3.13: The rotation axes for a generic link attached by revolute joints.

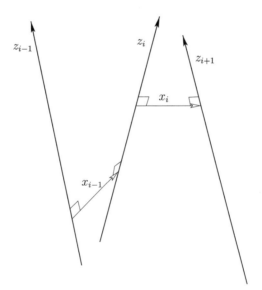

Figure 3.14: The rotation axes of the generic links are skew lines in $\mathbb{R}^3$.

coordinate frame given by x_i, y_i, and z_i will be most convenient for defining the model for $\mathcal{A}_i$. It might not always appear convenient because the origin of the frame may even lie outside of $\mathcal{A}_i$, but the resulting transformation matrices will be easy to understand.

In Section 3.3.1, each T_i was defined in terms of two parameters, a_{i-1} and θ_i. For the 3D case, four parameters will be defined: d_i, θ_i, a_{i-1}, and α_{i-1}. These are referred to as *Denavit-Hartenberg (DH) parameters* [437]. The definition of each parameter is indicated in Figure 3.15. Figure 3.15a shows the definition of d_i. Note that the x_{i-1}- and x_i-axes contact the z_i-axis at two different places. Let d_i denote signed distance between these points of contact. If the x_i-axis is above the x_{i-1}-axis along the z_i-axis, then d_i is positive; otherwise, d_i is negative. The parameter θ_i is the angle between the x_i- and x_{i-1}-axes, which corresponds to the rotation about the z_i-axis that moves the x_{i-1}-axis to coincide with the x_i-axis. The parameter a_i is the distance between the z_i- and z_{i-1}-axes; recall these are generally skew lines in $\mathbb{R}^3$. The parameter α_{i-1} is the angle between the z_i- and z_{i-1}-axes.

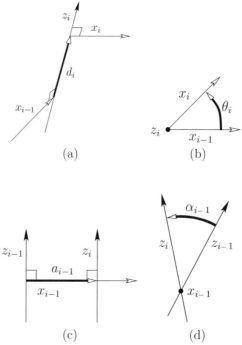

Figure 3.15: Definitions of the four DH parameters: d_i, θ_i, a_{i-1}, α_{i-1}. The z_i- and x_{i-1}-axes in (b) and (d), respectively, are pointing outward. Any parameter may be positive, zero, or negative.

Two screws

The homogeneous transformation matrix T_i will be constructed by combining two simpler transformations. The transformation

$$
R_i = \begin{pmatrix}
\cos\theta_i & -\sin\theta_i & 0 & 0 \\
\sin\theta_i & \cos\theta_i & 0 & 0 \\
0 & 0 & 1 & d_i \\
0 & 0 & 0 & 1
\end{pmatrix}
\tag{3.54}
$$

causes a rotation of θ_i about the z_i-axis, and a translation of d_i along the z_i-axis. Notice that the rotation by θ_i and translation by d_i commute because both operations occur with respect to the same axis, z_i. The combined operation of a translation and rotation with respect to the same axis is referred to as a *screw* (as in the motion of a screw through a nut). The effect of R_i can thus be considered as a screw about the z_i-axis. The second transformation is

$$
Q_{i-1} = \begin{pmatrix}
1 & 0 & 0 & a_{i-1} \\
0 & \cos\alpha_{i-1} & -\sin\alpha_{i-1} & 0 \\
0 & \sin\alpha_{i-1} & \cos\alpha_{i-1} & 0 \\
0 & 0 & 0 & 1
\end{pmatrix},
\tag{3.55}
$$

which can be considered as a screw about the x_{i-1}-axis. A rotation of α_{i-1} about the x_{i-1}-axis and a translation of a_{i-1} are performed.

The homogeneous transformation matrix

The transformation T_i, for each i such that $1 < i \leq m$, is

$$
T_i = Q_{i-1} R_i = \begin{pmatrix} \cos\theta_i & -\sin\theta_i & 0 & a_{i-1} \\ \sin\theta_i \cos\alpha_{i-1} & \cos\theta_i \cos\alpha_{i-1} & -\sin\alpha_{i-1} & -\sin\alpha_{i-1} d_i \\ \sin\theta_i \sin\alpha_{i-1} & \cos\theta_i \sin\alpha_{i-1} & \cos\alpha_{i-1} & \cos\alpha_{i-1} d_i \\ 0 & 0 & 0 & 1 \end{pmatrix}. \quad (3.56)
$$

This can be considered as the 3D counterpart to the 2D transformation matrix, (3.52). The following four operations are performed in succession:

1. Translate by d_i along the z_i-axis.
2. Rotate counterclockwise by θ_i about the z_i-axis.
3. Translate by a_{i-1} along the x_{i-1}-axis.
4. Rotate counterclockwise by α_{i-1} about the x_{i-1}-axis.

As in the 2D case, the first matrix, T_1, is special. To represent any position and orientation of $\mathcal{A}_1$, it could be defined as a general rigid-body homogeneous transformation matrix, (3.50). If the first body is only capable of rotation via a revolute joint, then a simple convention is usually followed. Let the a_0, α_0 parameters of T_1 be assigned as $a_0 = \alpha_0 = 0$ (there is no z_0-axis). This implies that Q_0 from (3.55) is the identity matrix, which makes $T_1 = R_1$.

The transformation T_i for $i > 1$ gives the relationship between the body frame of $\mathcal{A}_i$ and the body frame of $\mathcal{A}_{i-1}$. The position of a point (x, y, z) on $\mathcal{A}_m$ is given by

$$
T_1 T_2 \cdots T_m \begin{pmatrix} x \\ y \\ z \\ 1 \end{pmatrix}. \quad (3.57)
$$

For each revolute joint, θ_i is treated as the only variable in T_i. Prismatic joints can be modeled by allowing a_i to vary. More complicated joints can be modeled as a sequence of degenerate joints. For example, a spherical joint can be considered as a sequence of three zero-length revolute joints; the joints perform a roll, a pitch, and a yaw. Another option for more complicated joints is to abandon the DH representation and directly develop the homogeneous transformation matrix. This might be needed to preserve topological properties that become important in Chapter 4.

Example 3.4 (Puma 560) This example demonstrates the 3D chain kinematics on a classic robot manipulator, the PUMA 560, shown in Figure 3.16. The current parameterization here is based on [37, 558]. The procedure is to determine appropriate body frames to represent each of the links. The first three links allow the hand (called an end-effector) to make large movements in $\mathcal{W}$, and the last three enable the hand to achieve a desired orientation. There are six degrees of freedom, each of which arises from a revolute joint. The body frames are shown in Figure 3.16, and the corresponding DH parameters are given in Figure 3.17. Each transformation matrix T_i is a function of θ_i; hence, it is written $T_i(\theta_i)$. The other parameters are fixed for this example. Only $\theta_1, \theta_2, \ldots, \theta_6$ are allowed to vary.

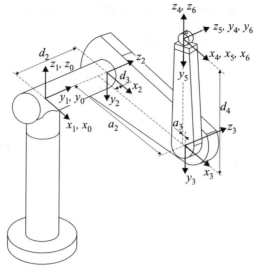

Figure 3.16: The Puma 560 is shown along with the DH parameters and body frames for each link in the chain. This figure is borrowed from [558] by courtesy of the authors.

Matrix	α_{i-1}	a_{i-1}	θ_i	d_i
$T_1(\theta_1)$	0	0	θ_1	0
$T_2(\theta_2)$	$-\pi/2$	0	θ_2	d_2
$T_3(\theta_3)$	0	a_2	θ_3	d_3
$T_4(\theta_4)$	$\pi/2$	a_3	θ_4	d_4
$T_5(\theta_5)$	$-\pi/2$	0	θ_5	0
$T_6(\theta_6)$	$\pi/2$	0	θ_6	0

Figure 3.17: The DH parameters are shown for substitution into each homogeneous transformation matrix (3.56). Note that a_3 and d_3 are negative in this example (they are signed displacements, not distances).

The parameters from Figure 3.17 may be substituted into the homogeneous transformation matrices to obtain

$$T_1(\theta_1) = \begin{pmatrix} \cos\theta_1 & -\sin\theta_1 & 0 & 0 \\ \sin\theta_1 & \cos\theta_1 & 0 & 0 \\ 0 & 0 & 1 & 0 \\ 0 & 0 & 0 & 1 \end{pmatrix}, \tag{3.58}$$

$$T_2(\theta_2) = \begin{pmatrix} \cos\theta_2 & -\sin\theta_2 & 0 & 0 \\ 0 & 0 & 1 & d_2 \\ -\sin\theta_2 & -\cos\theta_2 & 0 & 0 \\ 0 & 0 & 0 & 1 \end{pmatrix}, \tag{3.59}$$

$$T_3(\theta_3) = \begin{pmatrix} \cos\theta_3 & -\sin\theta_3 & 0 & a_2 \\ \sin\theta_3 & \cos\theta_3 & 0 & 0 \\ 0 & 0 & 1 & d_3 \\ 0 & 0 & 0 & 1 \end{pmatrix}, \tag{3.60}$$

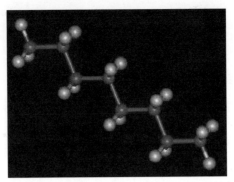

Figure 3.18: A hydrocarbon (octane) molecule with 8 carbon atoms and 18 hydrogen atoms (courtesy of the New York University MathMol Library).

$$T_4(\theta_4) = \begin{pmatrix} \cos\theta_4 & -\sin\theta_4 & 0 & a_3 \\ 0 & 0 & -1 & -d_4 \\ \sin\theta_4 & \cos\theta_4 & 0 & 0 \\ 0 & 0 & 0 & 1 \end{pmatrix}, \qquad (3.61)$$

$$T_5(\theta_5) = \begin{pmatrix} \cos\theta_5 & -\sin\theta_5 & 0 & 0 \\ 0 & 0 & 1 & 0 \\ -\sin\theta_5 & -\cos\theta_5 & 0 & 0 \\ 0 & 0 & 0 & 1 \end{pmatrix}, \qquad (3.62)$$

and

$$T_6(\theta_6) = \begin{pmatrix} \cos\theta_6 & -\sin\theta_6 & 0 & 0 \\ 0 & 0 & -1 & 0 \\ \sin\theta_6 & \cos\theta_6 & 0 & 0 \\ 0 & 0 & 0 & 1 \end{pmatrix}. \qquad (3.63)$$

A point (x, y, z) in the body frame of the last link $\mathcal{A}_6$ appears in $\mathcal{W}$ as

$$T_1(\theta_1)T_2(\theta_2)T_3(\theta_3)T_4(\theta_4)T_5(\theta_5)T_6(\theta_6)\begin{pmatrix} x \\ y \\ z \\ 1 \end{pmatrix}. \qquad (3.64)$$

Example 3.5 (Transforming Octane) Figure 3.18 shows a ball-and-stick model of an octane molecule. Each "ball" is an atom, and each "stick" represents a bond between a pair of atoms. There is a linear chain of eight carbon atoms, and a bond exists between each consecutive pair of carbons in the chain. There are also numerous hydrogen atoms, but we will ignore them. Each bond between a pair of carbons is capable of twisting, as shown in Figure 3.19. Studying the configurations (called *conformations*) of molecules is an important part of computational biology. It is assumed that there are seven degrees of freedom, each of which arises from twisting a bond. The techniques from this section can be applied to represent these transformations.

Note that the bonds correspond exactly to the axes of rotation. This suggests that the z_i axes should be chosen to coincide with the bonds. Since consecutive bonds meet at

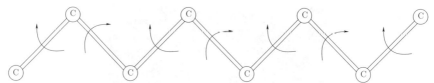

Figure 3.19: Consider transforming the spine of octane by ignoring the hydrogen atoms and allowing the bonds between carbons to rotate. This can be easily constructed with balls and sticks (e.g., Tinkertoys). If the first link is held fixed, then there are six degrees of freedom. The rotation of the last link is ignored.

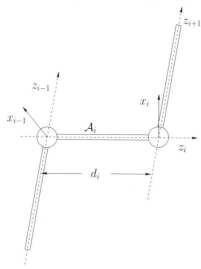

Figure 3.20: Each bond may be interpreted as a "link" of length d_i that is aligned with the z_i-axis. Note that most of $\mathcal{A}_i$ appears in the $-z_i$ direction.

atoms, there is no distance between them. From Figure 3.15c, observe that this makes $a_i = 0$ for all i. From Figure 3.15a, it can be seen that each d_i corresponds to a *bond length*, the distance between consecutive carbon atoms. See Figure 3.20. This leaves two angular parameters, θ_i and α_i. Since the only possible motion of the links is via rotation of the z_i-axes, the angle between two consecutive axes, as shown in Figure 3.15d, must remain constant. In chemistry, this is referred to as the *bond angle* and is represented in the DH parameterization as α_i. The remaining θ_i parameters are the variables that represent the degrees of freedom. However, looking at Figure 3.15b, observe that the example is degenerate because each x_i-axis has no frame of reference because each $a_i = 0$. This does not, however, cause any problems. For visualization purposes, it may be helpful to replace x_{i-1} and x_i by z_{i-1} and z_{i+1}, respectively. This way it is easy to see that as the bond for the z_i-axis is twisted, the observed angle changes accordingly. Each bond is interpreted as a link, $\mathcal{A}_i$. The origin of each $\mathcal{A}_i$ must be chosen to coincide with the intersection point of the z_i- and z_{i+1}-axes. Thus, most of the points in $\mathcal{A}_i$ will lie in the $-z_i$ direction; see Figure 3.20.

The next task is to write down the matrices. Attach a world frame to the first bond, with the second atom at the origin and the bond aligned with the z-axis, in the negative direction; see Figure 3.20. To define T_1, recall that $T_1 = R_1$ from (3.54) because Q_0 is dropped. The parameter d_1 represents the distance between the intersection points of the

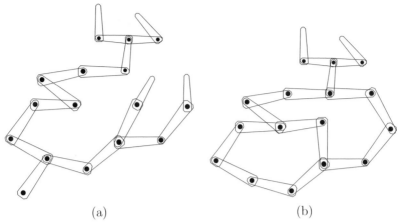

(a)   (b)

Figure 3.21: General linkages: (a) Instead of a chain of rigid bodies, a "tree" of rigid bodies can be considered. (b) If there are loops, then parameters must be carefully assigned to ensure that the loops are closed.

x_0- and x_1-axes along the z_1 axis. Since there is no x_0-axis, there is freedom to choose d_1; hence, let $d_1 = 0$ to obtain

$$T_1(\theta_1) = R_1(\theta_1) = \begin{pmatrix} \cos\theta_1 & -\sin\theta_1 & 0 & 0 \\ \sin\theta_1 & \cos\theta_1 & 0 & 0 \\ 0 & 0 & 1 & 0 \\ 0 & 0 & 0 & 1 \end{pmatrix}. \tag{3.65}$$

The application of T_1 to points in $\mathcal{A}_1$ causes them to rotate around the z_1-axis, which appears correct.

The matrices for the remaining six bonds are

$$T_i(\theta_i) = \begin{pmatrix} \cos\theta_i & -\sin\theta_i & 0 & 0 \\ \sin\theta_i\cos\alpha_{i-1} & \cos\theta_i\cos\alpha_{i-1} & -\sin\alpha_{i-1} & -\sin\alpha_{i-1}d_i \\ \sin\theta_i\sin\alpha_{i-1} & \cos\theta_i\sin\alpha_{i-1} & \cos\alpha_{i-1} & \cos\alpha_{i-1}d_i \\ 0 & 0 & 0 & 1 \end{pmatrix}, \tag{3.66}$$

for $i \in \{2, \dots, 7\}$. The position of any point, $(x, y, z) \in \mathcal{A}_7$, is given by

$$T_1(\theta_1)T_2(\theta_2)T_3(\theta_3)T_4(\theta_4)T_5(\theta_5)T_6(\theta_6)T_7(\theta_7) \begin{pmatrix} x \\ y \\ z \\ 1 \end{pmatrix}. \tag{3.67}$$

∎

3.4 Transforming kinematic trees

Motivation

For many interesting problems, the linkage is arranged in a "tree" as shown in Figure 3.21a. Assume here that the links are not attached in ways that form loops (i.e., Figure 3.21b); that case is deferred until Section 4.4, although some comments are also made at the end of this section. The human body, with its joints and limbs attached to the torso, is an example that can be modeled as a tree of rigid links. Joints such as knees and elbows are

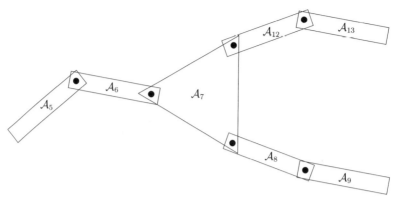

Figure 3.22: Now it is possible for a link to have more than two joints, as in $\mathcal{A}_7$.

considered as revolute joints. A shoulder joint is an example of a spherical joint, although it cannot achieve any orientation (without a visit to the emergency room!). As mentioned in Section 1.4, there is widespread interest in animating humans in virtual environments and also in developing humanoid robots. Both of these cases rely on formulations of kinematics that mimic the human body.

Another problem that involves kinematic trees is the conformational analysis of molecules. Example 3.5 involved a single chain; however, most organic molecules are more complicated, as in the familiar drugs shown in Figure 1.14a (Section 1.2). The bonds may twist to give degrees of freedom to the molecule. Moving through the space of conformations requires the formulation of a kinematic tree. Studying these conformations is important because scientists need to determine for some candidate drug whether the molecule can twist the right way so that it docks nicely (i.e., requires low energy) with a protein cavity; this induces a pharmacological effect, which hopefully is the desired one. Another important problem is determining how complicated protein molecules fold into certain configurations. These molecules are orders of magnitude larger (in terms of numbers of atoms and degrees of freedom) than typical drug molecules. For more information, see Section 7.5.

Common joints for $\mathcal{W} = \mathbb{R}^2$

First consider the simplest case in which there is a 2D tree of links for which every link has only two points at which revolute joints may be attached. This corresponds to Figure 3.21a. A single link is designated as the *root*, $\mathcal{A}_1$, of the tree. To determine the transformation of a body, $\mathcal{A}_i$, in the tree, the tools from Section 3.3.1 are directly applied to the chain of bodies that connects $\mathcal{A}_i$ to $\mathcal{A}_1$ while ignoring all other bodies. Each link contributes a θ_i to the total degrees of freedom of the tree. This case seems quite straightforward; unfortunately, it is not this easy in general.

Junctions with more than two rotation axes

Now consider modeling a more complicated collection of attached links. The main novelty is that one link may have joints attached to it in more than two locations, as in $\mathcal{A}_7$ in Figure 3.22. A link with more than two joints will be referred to as a *junction*.

If there is only one junction, then most of the complications arising from junctions can be avoided by choosing the junction as the root. For example, for a simple humanoid model, the torso would be a junction. It would be sensible to make this the root of the tree, as opposed to the right foot. The legs, arms, and head could all be modeled as independent

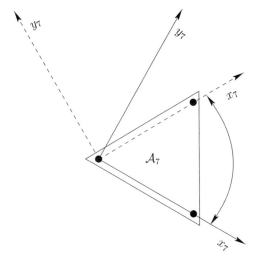

Figure 3.23: The junction is assigned two different frames, depending on which chain was followed. The solid axes were obtained from transforming $\mathcal{A}_9$, and the dashed axes were obtained from transforming $\mathcal{A}_{13}$.

chains. In each chain, the only concern is that the first link of each chain does not attach to the same point on the torso. This can be solved by inserting a fixed, fictitious link that connects from the origin of the torso to the attachment point of the limb.

The situation is more interesting if there are multiple junctions. Suppose that Figure 3.22 represents part of a 2D system of links for which the root, $\mathcal{A}_1$, is attached via a chain of links to $\mathcal{A}_5$. To transform link $\mathcal{A}_9$, the tools from Section 3.3.1 may be directly applied to yield a sequence of transformations,

$$T_1 \cdots T_5 T_6 T_7 T_8 T_9 \begin{pmatrix} x \\ y \\ 1 \end{pmatrix}, \tag{3.68}$$

for a point $(x, y) \in \mathcal{A}_9$. Likewise, to transform T_{13}, the sequence

$$T_1 \cdots T_5 T_6 T_7 T_{12} T_{13} \begin{pmatrix} x \\ y \\ 1 \end{pmatrix} \tag{3.69}$$

can be used by ignoring the chain formed by $\mathcal{A}_8$ and $\mathcal{A}_9$. So far everything seems to work well, but take a close look at $\mathcal{A}_7$. As shown in Figure 3.23, its body frame was defined in two different ways, one for each chain. If both are forced to use the same frame, then at least one must abandon the nice conventions of Section 3.3.1 for choosing frames. This situation becomes worse for 3D trees because this would suggest abandoning the DH parameterization. The Khalil-Kleinfinger parameterization is an elegant extension of the DH parameterization and solves these frame assignment issues [527].

Constraining parameters

Fortunately, it is fine to use different frames when following different chains; however, one extra piece of information is needed. Imagine transforming the whole tree. The variable θ_7 will appear twice, once from each of the upper and lower chains. Let θ_{7u} and θ_{7l} denote these θ's. Can θ really be chosen two different ways? This would imply that the tree is instead as pictured in Figure 3.24, in which there are two independently moving links,

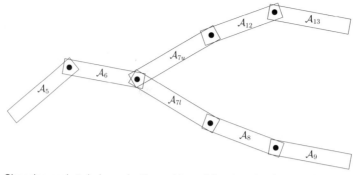

Figure 3.24: Choosing each θ_7 independently would result in a tree that ignores that fact that $\mathcal{A}_7$ is rigid.

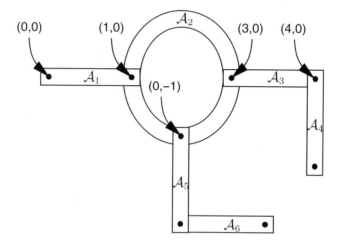

Figure 3.25: A tree of bodies in which the joints are attached in different places.

$\mathcal{A}_{7u}$ and $\mathcal{A}_{7l}$. To fix this problem, a constraint must be imposed. Suppose that θ_{7l} is treated as an independent variable. The parameter θ_{7u} must then be chosen as $\theta_{7l} + \phi$, in which ϕ is as shown in Figure 3.23.

Example 3.6 (A 2D Tree of Bodies) Figure 3.25 shows a 2D example that involves six links. To transform $(x, y) \in \mathcal{A}_6$, the only relevant links are $\mathcal{A}_5$, $\mathcal{A}_2$, and $\mathcal{A}_1$. The chain of transformations is

$$T_1 T_{2l} T_5 T_6 \begin{pmatrix} x \\ y \\ 1 \end{pmatrix}, \tag{3.70}$$

in which

$$T_1 = \begin{pmatrix} \cos\theta_1 & -\sin\theta_1 & x_t \\ \sin\theta_1 & \cos\theta_1 & y_t \\ 0 & 0 & 1 \end{pmatrix} = \begin{pmatrix} \cos\theta_1 & -\sin\theta_1 & 0 \\ \sin\theta_1 & \cos\theta_1 & 0 \\ 0 & 0 & 1 \end{pmatrix}, \tag{3.71}$$

$$T_{2l} = \begin{pmatrix} \cos\theta_{2l} & -\sin\theta_{2l} & a_1 \\ \sin\theta_{2l} & \cos\theta_{2l} & 0 \\ 0 & 0 & 1 \end{pmatrix} = \begin{pmatrix} \cos\theta_2 & -\sin\theta_2 & 1 \\ \sin\theta_2 & \cos\theta_2 & 0 \\ 0 & 0 & 1 \end{pmatrix}, \tag{3.72}$$

$$T_5 = \begin{pmatrix} \cos\theta_5 & -\sin\theta_5 & a_2 \\ \sin\theta_5 & \cos\theta_5 & 0 \\ 0 & 0 & 1 \end{pmatrix} = \begin{pmatrix} \cos\theta_5 & -\sin\theta_5 & \sqrt{2} \\ \sin\theta_5 & \cos\theta_5 & 0 \\ 0 & 0 & 1 \end{pmatrix}, \qquad (3.73)$$

and

$$T_6 = \begin{pmatrix} \cos\theta_6 & -\sin\theta_6 & a_5 \\ \sin\theta_6 & \cos\theta_6 & 0 \\ 0 & 0 & 1 \end{pmatrix} = \begin{pmatrix} \cos\theta_6 & -\sin\theta_6 & 1 \\ \sin\theta_6 & \cos\theta_6 & 0 \\ 0 & 0 & 1 \end{pmatrix}. \qquad (3.74)$$

The matrix T_{2l} in (3.72) denotes the fact that the lower chain was followed. The transformation for points in $\mathcal{A}_4$ is

$$T_1 T_{2u} T_4 T_5 \begin{pmatrix} x \\ y \\ 1 \end{pmatrix}, \qquad (3.75)$$

in which T_1 is the same as in (3.71), and

$$T_3 = \begin{pmatrix} \cos\theta_3 & -\sin\theta_3 & a_2 \\ \sin\theta_3 & \cos\theta_3 & 0 \\ 0 & 0 & 1 \end{pmatrix} = \begin{pmatrix} \cos\theta_3 & -\sin\theta_3 & \sqrt{2} \\ \sin\theta_3 & \cos\theta_3 & 0 \\ 0 & 0 & 1 \end{pmatrix}, \qquad (3.76)$$

and

$$T_4 = \begin{pmatrix} \cos\theta_4 & -\sin\theta_4 & a_4 \\ \sin\theta_4 & \cos\theta_4 & 0 \\ 0 & 0 & 1 \end{pmatrix} = \begin{pmatrix} \cos\theta_4 & -\sin\theta_4 & 0 \\ \sin\theta_4 & \cos\theta_4 & 0 \\ 0 & 0 & 1 \end{pmatrix}. \qquad (3.77)$$

The interesting case is

$$T_{2u} = \begin{pmatrix} \cos\theta_{2u} & -\sin\theta_{2u} & a_1 \\ \sin\theta_{2u} & \cos\theta_{2u} & 0 \\ 0 & 0 & 1 \end{pmatrix} = \begin{pmatrix} \cos(\theta_{2l}+\pi/4) & -\sin(\theta_{2l}+\pi/4) & a_1 \\ \sin(\theta_{2l}+\pi/4) & \cos(\theta_{2l}+\pi/4) & 0 \\ 0 & 0 & 1 \end{pmatrix}, \quad (3.78)$$

in which the constraint $\theta_{2u} = \theta_{2l} + \pi/4$ is imposed to enforce the fact that $\mathcal{A}_2$ is a junction. ∎

For a 3D tree of bodies the same general principles may be followed. In some cases, there will not be any complications that involve special considerations of junctions and constraints. One example of this is the transformation of flexible molecules because all consecutive rotation axes intersect, and junctions occur directly at these points of intersection. In general, however, the DH parameter technique may be applied for each chain, and then the appropriate constraints have to be determined and applied to represent the true degrees of freedom of the tree. The Khalil-Kleinfinger parameterization conveniently captures the resulting solution [527].

What if there are loops?

The most general case includes links that are connected in loops, as shown in Figure 3.26. These are generally referred to as *closed kinematic chains*. This arises in many applications. For example, with humanoid robotics or digital actors, a loop is formed when both feet touch the ground. As another example, suppose that two robot manipulators, such as the Puma 560 from Example 3.4, cooperate together to carry an object. If each robot grasps the same object with its hand, then a loop will be formed. A complicated

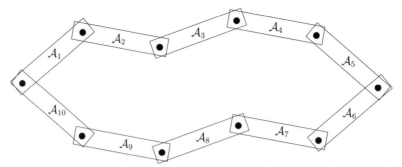

Figure 3.26: There are ten links and ten revolute joints arranged in a loop. This is an example of a closed kinematic chain.

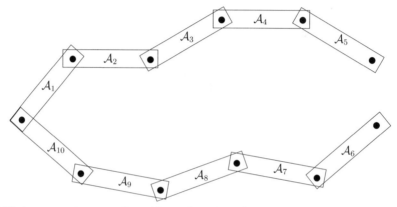

Figure 3.27: Loops may be opened to enable tree-based transformations to be applied; however, a closure constraint must still be satisfied.

example of this was shown in Figure 1.5, in which mobile robots moved a piano. Outside of robotics, a large fraction of organic molecules have flexible loops. Exploring the space of their conformations requires careful consideration of the difficulties imposed by these loops.

The main difficulty of working with closed kinematic chains is that it is hard to determine which parameter values are within an acceptable range to ensure closure. If these values are given, then the transformations are handled in the same way as the case of trees. For example, the links in Figure 3.26 may be transformed by breaking the loop into two different chains. Suppose we forget that the joint between $\mathcal{A}_5$ and $\mathcal{A}_6$ exists, as shown in Figure 3.27. Consider two different kinematic chains that start at the joint on the extreme left. There is an upper chain from $\mathcal{A}_1$ to $\mathcal{A}_5$ and a lower chain from $\mathcal{A}_{10}$ to $\mathcal{A}_6$. The transformations for any of these bodies can be obtained directly from the techniques of Section 3.3.1. Thus, it is easy to transform the bodies, but how do we choose parameter values that ensure $\mathcal{A}_5$ and $\mathcal{A}_6$ are connected at their common joint? Using the upper chain, the position of this joint may be expressed as

$$T_1(\theta_1)T_2(\theta_2)T_3(\theta_3)T_4(\theta_4)T_5(\theta_5)\begin{pmatrix} a_5 \\ 0 \\ 1 \end{pmatrix}, \tag{3.79}$$

in which $(a_5, 0) \in \mathcal{A}_5$ is the location of the joint of $\mathcal{A}_5$ that is supposed to connect to $\mathcal{A}_6$. The position of this joint may also be expressed using the lower chain as

$$T_{10}(\theta_{10})T_9(\theta_9)T_8(\theta_8)T_7(\theta_7)T_6(\theta_6) \begin{pmatrix} a_6 \\ 0 \\ 1 \end{pmatrix}, \tag{3.80}$$

with $(a_6, 0)$ representing the position of the joint in the body frame of $\mathcal{A}_6$. If the loop does not have to be maintained, then any values for $\theta_1, \ldots, \theta_{10}$ may be selected, resulting in ten degrees of freedom. However, if a loop must maintained, then (3.79) and (3.80) must be equal,

$$T_1(\theta_1)T_2(\theta_2)T_3(\theta_3)T_4(\theta_4)T_5(\theta_5) \begin{pmatrix} a_5 \\ 0 \\ 1 \end{pmatrix} = T_{10}(\theta_{10})T_9(\theta_9)T_8(\theta_8)T_7(\theta_7)T_6(\theta_6) \begin{pmatrix} a_6 \\ 0 \\ 1 \end{pmatrix}, \tag{3.81}$$

which is quite a mess of nonlinear, trigonometric equations that must be solved. The set of solutions to (3.81) could be very complicated. For the example, the true degrees of freedom is eight because two were removed by making the joint common. Since the common joint allows the links to rotate, exactly two degrees of freedom are lost. If $\mathcal{A}_5$ and $\mathcal{A}_6$ had to be rigidly attached, then the total degrees of freedom would be only seven. For most problems that involve loops, it will not be possible to obtain a nice parameterization of the set of solutions. This a form of the well-known *inverse kinematics problem* [254, 696, 778, 994].

In general, a complicated arrangement of links can be imagined in which there are many loops. Each time a joint along a loop is "ignored," as in the procedure just described, then one less loop exists. This process can be repeated iteratively until there are no more loops in the graph. The resulting arrangement of links will be a tree for which the previous techniques of this section may be applied. However, for each joint that was "ignored" an equation similar to (3.81) must be introduced. All of these equations must be satisfied simultaneously to respect the original loop constraints. Suppose that a set of value parameters is already given. This could happen, for example, using motion capture technology to measure the position and orientation of every part of a human body in contact with the ground. From this the solution parameters could be computed, and all of the transformations are easy to represent. However, as soon as the model moves, it is difficult to ensure that the new transformations respect the closure constraints. The foot of the digital actor may push through the floor, for example. Further information on this problem appears in Section 4.4.

3.5 Nonrigid transformations

One can easily imagine motion planning for nonrigid bodies. This falls outside of the families of transformations studied so far in this chapter. Several kinds of nonrigid transformations are briefly surveyed here.

Linear transformations

A rotation is a special case of a linear transformation, which is generally expressed by an $n \times n$ matrix, M, assuming the transformations are performed over $\mathbb{R}^n$. Consider

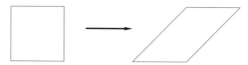

Figure 3.28: Shearing transformations may be performed.

transforming a point (x, y) in a 2D robot, $\mathcal{A}$, as

$$
\begin{pmatrix} m_{11} & m_{12} \\ m_{21} & m_{22} \end{pmatrix} \begin{pmatrix} x \\ y \end{pmatrix}. \tag{3.82}
$$

If M is a rotation matrix, then the size and shape of $\mathcal{A}$ will remain the same. In some applications, however, it may be desirable to distort these. The robot can be *scaled* by m_{11} along the x-axis and m_{22} along the y-axis by applying

$$
\begin{pmatrix} m_{11} & 0 \\ 0 & m_{22} \end{pmatrix} \begin{pmatrix} x \\ y \end{pmatrix}, \tag{3.83}
$$

for positive real values m_{11} and m_{22}. If one of them is negated, then a mirror image of $\mathcal{A}$ is obtained. In addition to scaling, $\mathcal{A}$ can be *sheared* by applying

$$
\begin{pmatrix} 1 & m_{12} \\ 0 & 1 \end{pmatrix} \begin{pmatrix} x \\ y \end{pmatrix} \tag{3.84}
$$

for $m_{12} \neq 0$. The case of $m_{12} = 1$ is shown in Figure 3.28.

The scaling, shearing, and rotation matrices may be multiplied together to yield a general transformation matrix that explicitly parameterizes each effect. It is also possible to extend the M from $n \times n$ to $(n + 1) \times (n + 1)$ to obtain a homogeneous transformation matrix that includes translation. Also, the concepts extend in a straightforward way to $\mathbb{R}^3$ and beyond. This enables the additional effects of scaling and shearing to be incorporated directly into the concepts from Sections 3.2-3.4.

Flexible materials

In some applications there is motivation to move beyond linear transformations. Imagine trying to warp a flexible material, such as a mattress, through a doorway. The mattress could be approximated by a 2D array of links; however, the complexity and degrees of freedom would be too cumbersome. For another example, suppose that a snake-like robot is designed by connecting 100 revolute joints together in a chain. The tools from Section 3.3 may be used to transform it with 100 rotation parameters, $\theta_1, \ldots, \theta_{100}$, but this may become unwieldy for use in a planning algorithm. An alternative is to approximate the snake with a deformable curve or shape.

For problems such as these, it is desirable to use a parameterized family of curves or surfaces. Spline models are often most appropriate because they are designed to provide easy control over the shape of a curve through the adjustment of a small number of parameters. Other possibilities include the generalized-cylinder and superquadric models that were mentioned in Section 3.1.3.

One complication is that complicated constraints may be imposed on the space of allowable parameters. For example, each joint of a snake-like robot could have a small range of rotation. This would be easy to model using a kinematic chain; however, determining which splines from a spline family satisfy this extra constraint may be difficult. Likewise, for manipulating flexible materials, there are usually complicated constraints based on the elasticity of the material. Even determining its correct shape under the application of some forces requires integration of an elastic energy function over the material [580].

Further reading

Section 3.1 barely scratches the surface of geometric modeling. Most literature focuses on parametric curves and surfaces [378, 721, 791]. These models are not as popular for motion planning because obtaining efficient collision detection is most important in practice, and processing implicit algebraic surfaces is most important in theoretical methods. A thorough coverage of solid and boundary representations, including semi-algebraic models, can be found in [457]. Theoretical algorithm issues regarding semi-algebraic models are covered in [707, 708]. For a comparison of the doubly connected edge list to its variants, see [525].

The material of Section 3.2 appears in virtually any book on robotics, computer vision, or computer graphics. Consulting linear algebra texts may be helpful to gain more insight into rotations. There are many ways to parameterize the set of all 3D rotation matrices. The yaw-pitch-roll formulation was selected because it is the easiest to understand. There are generally 12 different variants of the yaw-pitch-roll formulation (also called *Euler angles*) based on different rotation orderings and axis selections. This formulation, however, it not well suited for the development of motion planning algorithms. It is easy (and safe) to use for making quick 3D animations of motion planning output, but it incorrectly captures the structure of the state space for planning algorithms. Section 4.2 introduces the quaternion parameterization, which correctly captures this state space; however, it is harder to interpret when constructing examples. Therefore, it is helpful to understand both. In addition to Euler angles and quaternions, there is still motivation for using many other parameterizations of rotations, such as spherical coordinates, Cayley-Rodrigues parameters, and stereographic projection. Chapter 5 of [212] provides extensive coverage of 3D rotations and different parameterizations.

The coverage in Section 3.3 of transformations of chains of bodies was heavily influenced by two classic robotics texts [254, 778]. The DH parameters were introduced in [437] and later extended to trees and loops in [527]. An alternative to DH parameters is exponential coordinates [728], which simplify some computations; however, determining the parameters in the modeling stage may be less intuitive. A fascinating history of mechanisms appears in [438]. Other texts on kinematics include [29, 312, 534, 692]. The standard approach in many robotics books [368, 858, 908, 994] is to introduce the kinematic chain formulations and DH parameters in the first couple of chapters, and then move on to topics that are crucial for controlling robot manipulators, including dynamics modeling, singularities, manipulability, and control. Since this book is concerned instead with planning algorithms, we depart at the point where dynamics would usually be covered and move into a careful study of the configuration space in Chapter 4.

Exercises

1. Define a semi-algebraic model that removes a triangular "nose" from the region shown in Figure 3.4.

2. For distinct values of yaw, pitch, and roll, it is possible to generate the same rotation. In other words, $R(\alpha, \beta, \gamma) = R(\alpha', \beta', \gamma')$ for some cases in which at least $\alpha \neq \alpha$, $\beta \neq \beta'$, or $\gamma \neq \gamma'$. Characterize the sets of angles for which this occurs.

3. Using rotation matrices, prove that 2D rotation is commutative but 3D rotation is not.

4. An alternative to the yaw-pitch-roll formulation from Section 3.2.3 is considered here. Consider the following Euler angle representation of rotation (there are many other variants). The first rotation is $R_z(\gamma)$, which is just (3.39) with α replaced by γ. The next two rotations are identical to the yaw-pitch-roll formulation: $R_y(\beta)$ is applied, followed by $R_z(\alpha)$. This yields $R_{euler}(\alpha, \beta, \gamma) = R_z(\alpha)R_y(\beta)R_z(\gamma)$.

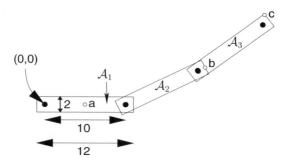

Figure 3.29: A chain of three bodies.

(a) Determine the matrix R_{euler}.

(b) Show that $R_{euler}(\alpha, \beta, \gamma) = R_{euler}(\alpha - \pi, -\beta, \gamma - \pi)$.

(c) Suppose that a rotation matrix is given as shown in (3.43). Show that the Euler angles are

$$\alpha = \text{atan2}(r_{23}, r_{13}), \tag{3.85}$$

$$\beta = \text{atan2}(\sqrt{1 - r_{33}^2}, r_{33}), \tag{3.86}$$

and

$$\gamma = \text{atan2}(r_{32}, -r_{31}). \tag{3.87}$$

5. There are 12 different variants of yaw-pitch-roll (or Euler angles), depending on which axes are used and the order of these axes. Determine all of the possibilities, using only notation such as $R_z(\alpha)R_y(\beta)R_z(\gamma)$ for each one. Give brief arguments that support why or why not specific combinations of rotations are included in your list of 12.

6. Let $\mathcal{A}$ be a unit disc, centered at the origin, and $\mathcal{W} = \mathbb{R}^2$. Assume that $\mathcal{A}$ is represented by a single, algebraic primitive, $H = \{(x, y) \mid x^2 + y^2 \leq 1\}$. Show that the transformed primitive is unchanged after any rotation is applied.

7. Consider the articulated chain of bodies shown in Figure 3.29. There are three identical rectangular bars in the plane, called $\mathcal{A}_1, \mathcal{A}_2, \mathcal{A}_3$. Each bar has width 2 and length 12. The distance between the two points of attachment is 10. The first bar, $\mathcal{A}_1$, is attached to the origin. The second bar, $\mathcal{A}_2$, is attached to $\mathcal{A}_1$, and $\mathcal{A}_3$ is attached to $\mathcal{A}_2$. Each bar is allowed to rotate about its point of attachment. The configuration of the chain can be expressed with three angles, $(\theta_1, \theta_2, \theta_3)$. The first angle, θ_1, represents the angle between the segment drawn between the two points of attachment of $\mathcal{A}_1$ and the x-axis. The second angle, θ_2, represents the angle between $\mathcal{A}_2$ and $\mathcal{A}_1$ ($\theta_2 = 0$ when they are parallel). The third angle, θ_3, represents the angle between $\mathcal{A}_3$ and $\mathcal{A}_2$. Suppose the configuration is $(\pi/4, \pi/2, -\pi/4)$.

   (a) Use the homogeneous transformation matrices to determine the locations of points a, b, and c.

   (b) Characterize the set of all configurations for which the final point of attachment (near the end of $\mathcal{A}_3$) is at $(0, 0)$ (you should be able to figure this out without using the matrices).

8. A three-link chain of bodies that moves in a 2D world is shown Figure 3.30. The first link, $\mathcal{A}_1$, is attached at $(0, 0)$ but can rotate. Each remaining link is attached to another link with a revolute joint. The second link, $\mathcal{A}_2$, is a rigid ring, and the other two links are rectangular bars.

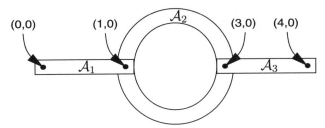

Figure 3.30: Another exercise involving a chain of bodies.

Assume that the structure is shown in the zero configuration. Suppose that the linkage is moved to the configuration $(\theta_1, \theta_2, \theta_3) = (\frac{\pi}{4}, \frac{\pi}{2}, \frac{\pi}{4})$, in which θ_1 is the angle of $\mathcal{A}_1$, θ_2 is the angle of $\mathcal{A}_2$ with respect to $\mathcal{A}_1$, and θ_3 is the angle of $\mathcal{A}_3$ with respect to $\mathcal{A}_2$. Using homogeneous transformation matrices, compute the position of the point at $(4, 0)$ in Figure 3.30, when the linkage is at configuration $(\frac{\pi}{4}, \frac{\pi}{2}, \frac{\pi}{4})$ (the point is attached to $\mathcal{A}_3$).

9. Approximate a spherical joint as a chain of three short, perpendicular links that are attached by revolute joints and give the sequence of transformation matrices. Show that as the link lengths approach zero, the resulting sequence of transformation matrices converges to exactly representing the freedom of a spherical joint. Compare this approach to directly using a full rotation matrix, (3.42), to represent the joint in the homogeneous transformation matrix.

10. Figure 3.12 showed six different ways in which 2D surfaces can slide with respect to each other to produce a joint.

    (a) Suppose that two bodies contact each other along a one-dimensional curve. Characterize as many different kinds of "joints" as possible, and indicate the degrees of freedom of each.

    (b) Suppose that the two bodies contact each other at a point. Indicate the types of rolling and sliding that are possible, and their corresponding degrees of freedom.

11. Suppose that two bodies form a screw joint in which the axis of the central axis of the screw aligns with the x-axis of the first body. Determine an appropriate homogeneous transformation matrix to use in place of the DH matrix. Define the matrix with the screw radius, r, and displacement-per-revolution, d, as parameters.

12. Recall Example 3.6. How should the transformations be modified so that the links are in the positions shown in Figure 3.25 at the zero configuration ($\theta_i = 0$ for every revolute joint whose angle can be independently chosen)?

13. Generalize the shearing transformation of (3.84) to enable shearing of 3D models.

Implementations

14. Develop and implement a kinematic model for 2D linkages. Enable the user to display the arrangement of links in the plane.

15. Implement the kinematics of molecules that do not have loops and show them graphically as a "ball and stick" model. The user should be able to input the atomic radii, bond connections, bond lengths, and rotation ranges for each bond.

16. Design and implement a software system in which the user can interactively attach various links to make linkages that resemble those possible from using Tinkertoys (or another popular construction set that allows pieces to move). There are several rods of various lengths, which fit into holes in the center and around the edge of several coin-shaped pieces. Assume that all joints are revolute. The user should be allowed to change parameters and see the resulting positions of all of the links.

17. Construct a model of the human body as a tree of links in a 3D world. For simplicity, the geometric model may be limited to spheres and cylinders. Design and implement a system that displays the virtual human and allows the user to click on joints of the body to enable them to rotate.

18. Develop a simulator with 3D graphics for the Puma 560 model shown in Figure 3.4.

4

The Configuration Space

Chapter 3 only covered how to model and transform a collection of bodies; however, for the purposes of planning it is important to define the state space. The state space for motion planning is a set of possible transformations that could be applied to the robot. This will be referred to as the *configuration space*, based on Lagrangian mechanics and the seminal work of Lozano-Pérez [659, 663, 660], who extensively utilized this notion in the context of planning (the idea was also used in early collision avoidance work by Udupa [947]). The motion planning literature was further unified around this concept by Latombe's book [591]. Once the configuration space is clearly understood, many motion planning problems that appear different in terms of geometry and kinematics can be solved by the same planning algorithms. This level of abstraction is therefore very important.

This chapter provides important foundational material that will be very useful in Chapters 5 to 8 and other places where planning over continuous state spaces occurs. Many of the concepts introduced in this chapter come directly from mathematics, particularly from topology. Therefore, Section 4.1 gives a basic overview of topological concepts. Section 4.2 uses the concepts from Chapter 3 to define the configuration space. After reading this, you should be able to precisely characterize the configuration space of a robot and understand its structure. In Section 4.3, obstacles in the world are transformed into obstacles in the configuration space, but it is important to understand that this transformation may not be explicitly constructed. The implicit representation of the state space is a recurring theme throughout planning. Section 4.4 covers the important case of kinematic chains that have loops, which was mentioned in Section 3.4. This case is so difficult that even the space of transformations usually cannot be explicitly characterized (i.e., parameterized).

4.1 Basic topological concepts

This section introduces basic topological concepts that are helpful in understanding configuration spaces. Topology is a challenging subject to understand in depth. The brief treatment given here provides only a brief overview and is designed to stimulate further study (see the literature overview at the end of the chapter). To advance further in this chapter, it is not necessary to understand all of the material of this section; however, the more you understand, the deeper will be your understanding of motion planning in general.

4.1.1 Topological spaces

Recall the concepts of open and closed intervals in the set of real numbers $\mathbb{R}$. The open interval $(0, 1)$ includes all real numbers between 0 and 1, *except* 0 and 1. However, for either endpoint, an infinite sequence may be defined that converges to it. For example, the sequence $1/2, 1/4, \ldots, 1/2^i$ converges to 0 as i tends to infinity. This means that we can choose a point in $(0, 1)$ within any small, positive distance from 0 or 1, but we cannot pick one exactly on the boundary of the interval. For a closed interval, such as $[0, 1]$, the boundary points are included.

The notion of an open set lies at the heart of topology. The open set definition that will appear here is a substantial generalization of the concept of an open interval. The concept applies to a very general collection of subsets of some larger space. It is general enough to easily include any kind of configuration space that may be encountered in planning.

A set X is called a *topological space* if there is a collection of subsets of X called *open sets* for which the following axioms hold:

1. The union of a countable number of open sets is an open set.
2. The intersection of a finite number of open sets is an open set.
3. Both X and $\emptyset$ are open sets.

Note that in the first axiom, the union of an infinite number of open sets may be taken, and the result must remain an open set. Intersecting an infinite number of open sets, however, does not necessarily lead to an open set.

For the special case of $X = \mathbb{R}$, the open sets include open intervals, as expected. Many sets that are not intervals are open sets because taking unions and intersections of open intervals yields other open sets. For example, the set

$$\bigcup_{i=1}^{\infty} \left(\frac{1}{3^i}, \frac{2}{3^i} \right), \tag{4.1}$$

which is an infinite union of pairwise-disjoint intervals, is an open set.

Closed sets

Open sets appear directly in the definition of a topological space. It next seems that closed sets are needed. Suppose X is a topological space. A subset $C \subset X$ is defined to be a *closed set* if and only if $X \setminus C$ is an open set. Thus, the complement of any open set is closed, and the complement of any closed set is open. Any closed interval, such as $[0, 1]$, is a closed set because its complement, $(-\infty, 0) \cup (1, \infty)$, is an open set. For another example, $(0, 1)$ is an open set; therefore, $\mathbb{R} \setminus (0, 1) = (-\infty, 0] \cup [1, \infty)$ is a closed set. The use of "(" may seem wrong in the last expression, but "[" cannot be used because $-\infty$ and ∞ do not belong to $\mathbb{R}$. Thus, the use of "(" is just a notational quirk.

Are all subsets of X either closed or open? Although it appears that open sets and closed sets are opposites in some sense, the answer is *no.* For $X = \mathbb{R}$, the interval $[0, 2\pi)$ is neither open nor closed (consider its complement: $[2\pi, \infty)$ is closed, and $(-\infty, 0)$ is open). Note that for any topological space, X and $\emptyset$ are both open and closed!

Special points

From the definitions and examples so far, it should seem that points on the "edge" or "border" of a set are important. There are several terms that capture where points are relative to the border. Let X be a topological space, and let U be any subset of X. Furthermore, let x be any point in X. The following terms capture the position of point x relative to U (see Figure 4.1):

- If there exists an open set O_1 such that $x \in O_1$ and $O_1 \subseteq U$, then x is called an *interior point* of U. The set of all interior points in U is called the *interior of U* and is denoted by int(U).

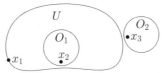

Figure 4.1: An illustration of the boundary definition. Suppose $X = \mathbb{R}^2$, and U is a subset as shown. Three kinds of points appear: 1) x_1 is a boundary point, 2) x_2 is an interior point, and 3) x_3 is an exterior point. Both x_1 and x_2 are limit points of U.

- If there exists an open set O_2 such that $x \in O_2$ and $O_2 \subseteq X \setminus U$, then x is called an *exterior point* with respect to U.

- If x is neither an interior point nor an exterior point, then it is called a *boundary point* of U. The set of all boundary points in X is called the *boundary of U* and is denoted by ∂U.

- All points in $x \in X$ must be one of the three above; however, another term is often used, even though it is redundant given the other three. If x is either an interior point or a boundary point, then it is called a *limit point* (or *accumulation point*) of U. The set of all limit points of U is a closed set called the *closure* of U, and it is denoted by $\mathrm{cl}(U)$. Note that $\mathrm{cl}(U) = \mathrm{int}(U) \cup \partial U$.

For the case of $X = \mathbb{R}$, the boundary points are the endpoints of intervals. For example, 0 and 1 are boundary points of intervals, $(0, 1)$, $[0, 1]$, $[0, 0)$, and $(0, 1]$. Thus, U may or may not include its boundary points. All of the points in $(0, 1)$ are interior points, and all of the points in $[0, 1]$ are limit points. The motivation of the name "limit point" comes from the fact that such a point might be the limit of an infinite sequence of points in U. For example, 0 is the limit point of the sequence generated by $1/2^i$ for each $i \in \mathbb{N}$, the natural numbers.

There are several convenient consequences of the definitions. A closed set C contains the limit point of any sequence that is a subset of C. This implies that it contains all of its boundary points. The closure, cl, always results in a closed set because it adds all of the boundary points to the set. On the other hand, an open set contains none of its boundary points. These interpretations will come in handy when considering obstacles in the configuration space for motion planning.

Some examples

The definition of a topological space is so general that an incredible variety of topological spaces can be constructed.

Example 4.1 (The Topology of $\mathbb{R}^n$) We should expect that $X = \mathbb{R}^n$ for any integer n is a topological space. This requires characterizing the open sets. An *open ball* $B(x, \rho)$ is the set of points in the interior of a sphere of radius ρ, centered at x. Thus,

$$B(x, \rho) = \{x' \in \mathbb{R}^n \mid \|x' - x\| < \rho\}, \tag{4.2}$$

in which $\| \cdot \|$ denotes the Euclidean norm (or magnitude) of its argument. The open balls are open sets in $\mathbb{R}^n$. Furthermore, all other open sets can be expressed as a countable union of open balls.[1] For the case of $\mathbb{R}$, this reduces to representing any open set as a union of intervals, which was done so far.

---

[1] Such a collection of balls is often referred to as a *basis*.

Even though it is possible to express open sets of $\mathbb{R}^n$ as unions of balls, we prefer to use other representations, with the understanding that one could revert to open balls if necessary. The primitives of Section 3.1 can be used to generate many interesting open and closed sets. For example, any algebraic primitive expressed in the form $H = \{x \in \mathbb{R}^n \mid f(x) \leq 0\}$ produces a closed set. Taking finite unions and intersections of these primitives will produce more closed sets. Therefore, all of the models from Sections 3.1.1 and 3.1.2 produce an obstacle region $\mathcal{O}$ that is a closed set. As mentioned in Section 3.1.2, sets constructed only from primitives that use the $<$ relation are open. ∎

Example 4.2 (Subspace Topology) A new topological space can easily be constructed from a subset of a topological space. Let X be a topological space, and let $Y \subset X$ be a subset. The *subspace topology* on Y is obtained by defining the open sets to be every subset of Y that can be represented as $U \cap Y$ for some open set $U \subseteq X$. Thus, the open sets for Y are almost the same as for X, except that the points that do not lie in Y are trimmed away. New subspaces can be constructed by intersecting open sets of $\mathbb{R}^n$ with a complicated region defined by semi-algebraic models. This leads to many interesting topological spaces, some of which will appear later in this chapter. ∎

Example 4.3 (The Trivial Topology) For any set X, there is always one trivial example of a topological space that can be constructed from it. Declare that X and $\emptyset$ are the only open sets. Note that all of the axioms are satisfied. ∎

Example 4.4 (A Strange Topology) It is important to keep in mind the almost absurd level of generality that is allowed by the definition of a topological space. A topological space can be defined for any set, as long as the declared open sets obey the axioms. Suppose a four-element set is defined as

$$X = \{\text{CAT, DOG, TREE, HOUSE}\}. \tag{4.3}$$

In addition to $\emptyset$ and X, suppose that $\{\text{CAT}\}$ and $\{\text{DOG}\}$ are open sets. Using the axioms, $\{\text{CAT, DOG}\}$ must also be an open set. Closed sets and boundary points can be derived for this topology once the open sets are defined. ∎

After the last example, it seems that topological spaces are so general that not much can be said about them. Most spaces that are considered in topology and analysis satisfy more axioms. For $\mathbb{R}^n$ and any configuration spaces that arise in this book, the following is satisfied:

Hausdorff axiom: For any distinct $x_1, x_2 \in X$, there exist open sets O_1 and O_2 such that $x_1 \in O_1$, $x_2 \in O_2$, and $O_1 \cap O_2 = \emptyset$.

In other words, it is possible to separate x_1 and x_2 into nonoverlapping open sets. Think about how to do this for $\mathbb{R}^n$ by selecting small enough open balls. Any topological space X that satisfies the Hausdorff axiom is referred to as a *Hausdorff space*. Section 4.1.2 will introduce manifolds, which happen to be Hausdorff spaces and are general enough to capture the vast majority of configuration spaces that arise. We will have no need in this book to consider topological spaces that are not Hausdorff spaces.

Continuous functions

A very simple definition of continuity exists for topological spaces. It nicely generalizes the definition from standard calculus. Let $f : X \to Y$ denote a function between topological spaces X and Y. For any set $B \subseteq Y$, let the *preimage* of B be denoted and defined by

$$f^{-1}(B) = \{x \in X \mid f(x) \in B\}. \tag{4.4}$$

Note that this definition does not require f to have an inverse.

The function f is called *continuous* if $f^{-1}(O)$ is an open set for every open set $O \subseteq Y$. Analysis is greatly simplified by this definition of continuity. For example, to show that any composition of continuous functions is continuous requires only a one-line argument that the preimage of the preimage of any open set always yields an open set. Compare this to the cumbersome classical proof that requires a mess of δ's and ϵ's. The notion is also so general that continuous functions can even be defined on the absurd topological space from Example 4.4.

Homeomorphism: Making a donut into a coffee cup

You might have heard the expression that to a topologist, a donut and a coffee cup appear the same. In many branches of mathematics, it is important to define when two basic objects are equivalent. In graph theory (and group theory), this equivalence relation is called an *isomorphism*. In topology, the most basic equivalence is a homeomorphism, which allows spaces that appear quite different in most other subjects to be declared equivalent in topology. The surfaces of a donut and a coffee cup (with one handle) are considered equivalent because both have a single hole. This notion needs to be made more precise!

Suppose $f : X \to Y$ is a bijective (one-to-one and onto) function between topological spaces X and Y. Since f is bijective, the inverse f^{-1} exists. If both f and f^{-1} are continuous, then f is called a *homeomorphism*. Two topological spaces X and Y are said to be *homeomorphic*, denoted by $X \cong Y$, if there exists a homeomorphism between them. This implies an equivalence relation on the set of topological spaces (verify that the reflexive, symmetric, and transitive properties are implied by the homeomorphism).

Example 4.5 (Interval Homeomorphisms) Any open interval of $\mathbb{R}$ is homeomorphic to any other open interval. For example, $(0, 1)$ can be mapped to $(0, 5)$ by the continuous mapping $x \mapsto 5x$. Note that $(0, 1)$ and $(0, 5)$ are each being interpreted here as topological subspaces of $\mathbb{R}$. This kind of homeomorphism can be generalized substantially using linear algebra. If a subset, $X \subset \mathbb{R}^n$, can be mapped to another, $Y \subset \mathbb{R}^n$, via a nonsingular linear transformation, then X and Y are homeomorphic. For example, the rigid-body transformations of the previous chapter were examples of homeomorphisms applied to the robot. Thus, the topology of the robot does not change when it is translated or rotated. (In this example, note that the robot itself is the topological space. This will not be the case for the rest of the chapter.)

Be careful when mixing closed and open sets. The space $[0, 1]$ is not homeomorphic to $(0, 1)$, and neither is homeomorphic to $[0, 1)$. The endpoints cause trouble when trying to make a bijective, continuous function. Surprisingly, a bounded and unbounded set may be homeomorphic. A subset X of $\mathbb{R}^n$ is called *bounded* if there exists a ball $B \subset \mathbb{R}^n$ such that $X \subset B$. The mapping $x \mapsto 1/x$ establishes that $(0, 1)$ and $(1, \infty)$ are homeomorphic. The mapping $x \mapsto \tan^{-1}(\pi x/2)$ establishes that $(-1, 1)$ and all of $\mathbb{R}$ are homeomorphic! ∎

Example 4.6 (Topological Graphs) Let X be a topological space. The previous example can be extended nicely to make homeomorphisms look like graph isomorphisms. Let a

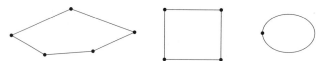

Figure 4.2: Even though the graphs are not isomorphic, the corresponding topological spaces may be homeomorphic due to useless vertices. The example graphs map into $\mathbb{R}^2$, and are all homeomorphic to a circle.

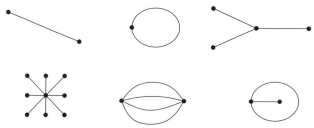

Figure 4.3: These topological graphs map into subsets of $\mathbb{R}^2$ that are not homeomorphic to each other.

topological graph[2] be a graph for which every vertex corresponds to a point in X and every edge corresponds to a continuous, injective (one-to-one) function, $\tau : [0, 1] \to X$. The image of τ connects the points in X that correspond to the endpoints (vertices) of the edge. The images of different edge functions are not allowed to intersect, except at vertices. Recall from graph theory that two graphs, $G_1(V_1, E_1)$ and $G_2(V_2, E_2)$, are called *isomorphic* if there exists a bijective mapping, $f : V_1 \to V_2$ such that there is an edge between v_1 and v_1' in G_1, if and only if there exists an edge between $f(v_1)$ and $f(v_1')$ in G_2.

The bijective mapping used in the graph isomorphism can be extended to produce a homeomorphism. Each edge in E_1 is mapped continuously to its corresponding edge in E_2. The mappings nicely coincide at the vertices. Now you should see that two topological graphs are homeomorphic if they are isomorphic under the standard definition from graph theory.[3] What if the graphs are not isomorphic? There is still a chance that the topological graphs may be homeomorphic, as shown in Figure 4.2. The problem is that there appear to be "useless" vertices in the graph. By removing vertices of degree two that can be deleted without affecting the connectivity of the graph, the problem is fixed. In this case, graphs that are not isomorphic produce topological graphs that are not homeomorphic. This allows many distinct, interesting topological spaces to be constructed. A few are shown in Figure 4.3. ∎

4.1.2 Manifolds

In motion planning, efforts are made to ensure that the resulting configuration space has nice properties that reflect the true structure of the space of transformations. One important kind of topological space, which is general enough to include most of the configuration spaces considered in Part II, is called a manifold. Intuitively, a manifold can be considered as a "nice" topological space that behaves at every point like our intuitive notion of a surface.

---

[2] In topology this is called a 1-complex [442].

[3] Technically, the images of the topological graphs, as subspaces of X, are homeomorphic, not the graphs themselves.

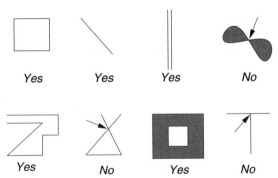

Figure 4.4: Some open subsets of $\mathbb{R}^2$ that may or may not be manifolds. For the three that are not, the point that prevents them from being manifolds is indicated.

Manifold definition

A topological space $M \subseteq \mathbb{R}^m$ is a *manifold*[4] if for every $x \in M$, an open set $O \subset M$ exists such that: 1) $x \in O$, 2) O is homeomorphic to $\mathbb{R}^n$, and 3) n is fixed for all $x \in M$. The fixed n is referred to as the *dimension* of the manifold, M. The second condition is the most important. It states that in the vicinity of any point, $x \in M$, the space behaves just like it would in the vicinity of any point $y \in \mathbb{R}^n$; intuitively, the set of directions that one can move appears the same in either case. Several simple examples that may or may not be manifolds are shown in Figure 4.4.

One natural consequence of the definitions is that $m \geq n$. According to Whitney's embedding theorem [452], $m \leq 2n + 1$. In other words, $\mathbb{R}^{2n+1}$ is "big enough" to hold any n-dimensional manifold.[5] Technically, it is said that the n-dimensional manifold M is *embedded* in $\mathbb{R}^m$, which means that an injective mapping exists from M to $\mathbb{R}^m$ (if it is not injective, then the topology of M could change).

As it stands, it is impossible for a manifold to include its boundary points because they are not contained in open sets. A *manifold with boundary* can be defined requiring that the neighborhood of each boundary point of M is homeomorphic to a half-space of dimension n (which was defined for $n = 2$ and $n = 3$ in Section 3.1) and that the interior points must be homeomorphic to $\mathbb{R}^n$.

The presentation now turns to ways of constructing some manifolds that frequently appear in motion planning. It is important to keep in mind that two manifolds will be considered equivalent if they are homeomorphic (recall the donut and coffee cup).

Cartesian products

There is a convenient way to construct new topological spaces from existing ones. Suppose that X and Y are topological spaces. The *Cartesian product*, $X \times Y$, defines a new topological space as follows. Every $x \in X$ and $y \in Y$ generates a point (x, y) in $X \times Y$.

---

[4] Manifolds that are not subsets of $\mathbb{R}^m$ may also be defined. This requires that M is a Hausdorff space and is second countable, which means that there is a countable number of open sets from which any other open set can be constructed by taking a union of some of them. These conditions are automatically satisfied when assuming $M \subseteq \mathbb{R}^m$; thus, it avoids these extra complications and is still general enough for our purposes. Some authors use the term *manifold* to refer to a *smooth manifold*. This requires the definition of a smooth structure, and the homeomorphism is replaced by diffeomorphism. This extra structure is not needed here but will be introduced when it is needed in Section 8.3.

[5] One variant of the theorem is that for smooth manifolds, $\mathbb{R}^{2n}$ is sufficient. This bound is tight because $\mathbb{RP}^n$ (n-dimensional projective space, which will be introduced later in this section), cannot be embedded in $\mathbb{R}^{2n-1}$.

Each open set in $X \times Y$ is formed by taking the Cartesian product of one open set from X and one from Y. Exactly one open set exists in $X \times Y$ for every pair of open sets that can be formed by taking one from X and one from Y. No other open sets appear in $X \times Y$; therefore, its open sets are automatically determined.

A familiar example of a Cartesian product is $\mathbb{R} \times \mathbb{R}$, which is equivalent to $\mathbb{R}^2$. In general, $\mathbb{R}^n$ is equivalent to $\mathbb{R} \times \mathbb{R}^{n-1}$. The Cartesian product can be taken over many spaces at once. For example, $\mathbb{R} \times \mathbb{R} \times \cdots \times \mathbb{R} = \mathbb{R}^n$. In the coming text, many important manifolds will be constructed via Cartesian products.

1D manifolds

The set $\mathbb{R}$ of reals is the most obvious example of a 1D manifold because $\mathbb{R}$ certainly looks like (via homeomorphism) $\mathbb{R}$ in the vicinity of every point. The range can be restricted to the unit interval to yield the manifold $(0, 1)$ because they are homeomorphic (recall Example 4.5).

Another 1D manifold, which is not homeomorphic to $(0, 1)$, is a circle, $\mathbb{S}^1$. In this case $\mathbb{R}^m = \mathbb{R}^2$, and let

$$\mathbb{S}^1 = \{(x, y) \in \mathbb{R}^2 \mid x^2 + y^2 = 1\}. \tag{4.5}$$

If you are thinking like a topologist, it should appear that this particular circle is not important because there are numerous ways to define manifolds that are homeomorphic to $\mathbb{S}^1$. For any manifold that is homeomorphic to $\mathbb{S}^1$, we will sometimes say that the manifold *is* $\mathbb{S}^1$, just represented in a different way. Also, $\mathbb{S}^1$ will be called a *circle*, but this is meant only in the topological sense; it only needs to be homeomorphic to the circle that we learned about in high school geometry. Also, when referring to $\mathbb{R}$, we might instead substitute $(0, 1)$ without any trouble. The alternative representations of a manifold can be considered as changing *parameterizations*, which are formally introduced in Section 8.3.2.

Identifications

A convenient way to represent $\mathbb{S}^1$ is obtained by *identification*, which is a general method of declaring that some points of a space are identical, even though they originally were distinct.[6] For a topological space X, let $X/\sim$ denote that X has been redefined through some form of identification. The open sets of X become redefined. Using identification, $\mathbb{S}^1$ can be defined as $[0, 1]/\sim$, in which the identification declares that 0 and 1 are equivalent, denoted as $0 \sim 1$. This has the effect of "gluing" the ends of the interval together, forming a closed loop. To see the homeomorphism that makes this possible, use polar coordinates to obtain $\theta \mapsto (\cos 2\pi\theta, \sin 2\pi\theta)$. You should already be familiar with 0 and 2π leading to the same point in polar coordinates; here they are just normalized to 0 and 1. Letting θ run from 0 up to 1, and then "wrapping around" to 0 is a convenient way to represent $\mathbb{S}^1$ because it does not need to be curved as in (4.5).

It might appear that identifications are cheating because the definition of a manifold requires it to be a subset of $\mathbb{R}^m$. This is not a problem because Whitney's theorem, as mentioned previously, states that any n-dimensional manifold can be embedded in $\mathbb{R}^{2n+1}$. The identifications just reduce the number of dimensions needed for visualization. They are also convenient in the implementation of motion planning algorithms.

---

[6] This is usually defined more formally and called a *quotient topology*.

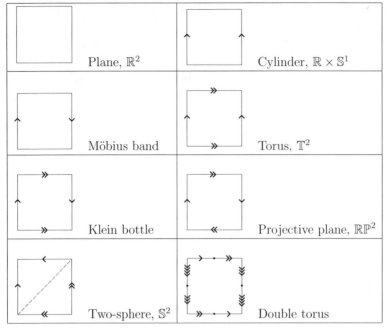

Figure 4.5: Some 2D manifolds that can be obtained by identifying pairs of points along the boundary of a square region.

2D manifolds

Many important, 2D manifolds can be defined by applying the Cartesian product to 1D manifolds. The 2D manifold $\mathbb{R}^2$ is formed by $\mathbb{R} \times \mathbb{R}$. The product $\mathbb{R} \times \mathbb{S}^1$ defines a manifold that is equivalent to an infinite cylinder. The product $\mathbb{S}^1 \times \mathbb{S}^1$ is a manifold that is equivalent to a torus (the surface of a donut).

Can any other 2D manifolds be defined? See Figure 4.5. The identification idea can be applied to generate several new manifolds. Start with an open square $M = (0, 1) \times (0, 1)$, which is homeomorphic to $\mathbb{R}^2$. Let (x, y) denote a point in the plane. A *flat cylinder* is obtained by making the identification $(0, y) \sim (1, y)$ for all $y \in (0, 1)$ and adding all of these points to M. The result is depicted in Figure 4.5 by drawing arrows where the identification occurs.

A *Möbius band* can be constructed by taking a strip of paper and connecting the ends after making a 180-degree twist. This result is not homeomorphic to the cylinder. The Möbius band can also be constructed by putting the twist into the identification, as $(0, y) \sim (1, 1 - y)$ for all $y \in (0, 1)$. In this case, the arrows are drawn in opposite directions. The Möbius band has the famous properties that it has only one side (trace along the paper strip with a pencil, and you will visit both sides of the paper) and is nonorientable (if you try to draw it in the plane, without using identification tricks, it will always have a twist).

For all of the cases so far, there has been a boundary to the set. The next few manifolds will not even have a boundary, even though they may be bounded. If you were to live in one of them, it means that you could walk forever along any trajectory and never encounter the edge of your universe. It might seem like our physical universe is unbounded, but it would only be an illusion. Furthermore, there are several distinct possibilities for the universe that are not homeomorphic to each other. In higher dimensions, such possibilities are the subject of cosmology, which is a branch of astrophysics that uses topology to characterize the structure of our universe.

A *torus* can be constructed by performing identifications of the form $(0, y) \sim (1, y)$, which was done for the cylinder, and also $(x, 0) \sim (x, 1)$, which identifies the top and bottom. Note that the point $(0, 0)$ must be included and is identified with three other points. Double arrows are used in Figure 4.5 to indicate the top and bottom identification. All of the identification points must be added to M. Note that there are no twists. A funny interpretation of the resulting *flat torus* is as the universe appears for a spacecraft in some 1980s-style *Asteroids*-like video games. The spaceship flies off of the screen in one direction and appears somewhere else, as prescribed by the identification.

Two interesting manifolds can be made by adding twists. Consider performing all of the identifications that were made for the torus, except put a twist in the side identification, as was done for the Möbius band. This yields a fascinating manifold called the *Klein bottle*, which can be embedded in $\mathbb{R}^4$ as a closed 2D surface in which the inside and the outside are the same! (This is in a sense similar to that of the Möbius band.) Now suppose there are twists in both the sides and the top and bottom. This results in the most bizarre manifold yet: the real projective plane, $\mathbb{RP}^2$. This space is equivalent to the set of all lines in $\mathbb{R}^3$ that pass through the origin. The 3D version, $\mathbb{RP}^3$, happens to be one of the most important manifolds for motion planning!

Let $\mathbb{S}^2$ denote the unit sphere, which is defined as

$$\mathbb{S}^2 = \{(x, y, z) \in \mathbb{R}^3 \mid x^2 + y^2 + z^2 = 1\}. \tag{4.6}$$

Another way to represent $\mathbb{S}^2$ is by making the identifications shown in the last row of Figure 4.5. A dashed line is indicated where the equator might appear, if we wanted to make a distorted wall map of the earth. The poles would be at the upper left and lower right corners. The final example shown in Figure 4.5 is a *double torus*, which is the surface of a two-holed donut.

Higher dimensional manifolds

The construction techniques used for the 2D manifolds generalize nicely to higher dimensions. Of course, $\mathbb{R}^n$, is an n-dimensional manifold. An n-dimensional torus, $\mathbb{T}^n$, can be made by taking a Cartesian product of n copies of $\mathbb{S}^1$. Note that $\mathbb{S}^1 \times \mathbb{S}^1 \neq \mathbb{S}^2$. Therefore, the notation $\mathbb{T}^n$ is used for $(\mathbb{S}^1)^n$. Different kinds of n-dimensional cylinders can be made by forming a Cartesian product $\mathbb{R}^i \times \mathbb{T}^j$ for positive integers i and j such that $i + j = n$. Higher dimensional spheres are defined as

$$\mathbb{S}^n = \{x \in \mathbb{R}^{n+1} \mid \|x\| = 1\}, \tag{4.7}$$

in which $\|x\|$ denotes the Euclidean norm of x, and n is a positive integer. Many interesting spaces can be made by identifying faces of the cube $(0, 1)^n$ (or even faces of a polyhedron or polytope), especially if different kinds of twists are allowed. An n-dimensional projective space can be defined in this way, for example. *Lens spaces* are a family of manifolds that can be constructed by identification of polyhedral faces [837].

Due to its coming importance in motion planning, more details are given on projective spaces. The standard definition of an *n-dimensional real projective space* $\mathbb{RP}^n$ is the set of all lines in $\mathbb{R}^{n+1}$ that pass through the origin. Each line is considered as a point in $\mathbb{RP}^n$. Using the definition of $\mathbb{S}^n$ in (4.7), note that each of these lines in $\mathbb{R}^{n+1}$ intersects $\mathbb{S}^n \subset \mathbb{R}^{n+1}$ in exactly two places. These intersection points are called *antipodal*, which means that they are as far from each other as possible on $\mathbb{S}^n$. The pair is also unique for each line. If we identify all pairs of antipodal points of $\mathbb{S}^n$, a homeomorphism can be defined between each line through the origin of $\mathbb{R}^{n+1}$ and each antipodal pair on the sphere. This means that the resulting manifold, $\mathbb{S}^n / \sim$, is homeomorphic to $\mathbb{RP}^n$.

Another way to interpret the identification is that $\mathbb{RP}^n$ is just the upper half of $\mathbb{S}^n$, but with every equatorial point identified with its antipodal point. Thus, if you try to walk into the southern hemisphere, you will find yourself on the other side of the world walking north. It is helpful to visualize the special case of $\mathbb{RP}^2$ and the upper half of $\mathbb{S}^2$. Imagine warping the picture of $\mathbb{RP}^2$ from Figure 4.5 from a square into a circular disc, with opposite points identified. The result still represents $\mathbb{RP}^2$. The center of the disc can now be lifted out of the plane to form the upper half of $\mathbb{S}^2$.

4.1.3 Paths and connectivity

Central to motion planning is determining whether one part of a space is reachable from another. In Chapter 2, one state was reached from another by applying a sequence of actions. For motion planning, the analog to this is connecting one point in the configuration space to another by a continuous path. Graph connectivity is important in the discrete planning case. An analog to this for topological spaces is presented in this section.

Paths

Let X be a topological space, which for our purposes will also be a manifold. A *path* is a continuous function, $\tau : [0, 1] \to X$. Alternatively, $\mathbb{R}$ may be used for the domain of τ. Keep in mind that a path is a function, not a set of points. Each point along the path is given by $\tau(s)$ for some $s \in [0, 1]$. This makes it appear as a nice generalization to the sequence of states visited when a plan from Chapter 2 is applied. Recall that there, a countable set of stages was defined, and the states visited could be represented as $x_1, x_2, \ldots$. In the current setting $\tau(s)$ is used, in which s replaces the stage index. To make the connection clearer, we could use x instead of τ to obtain $x(s)$ for each $s \in [0, 1]$.

Connected vs. path connected

A topological space X is said to be *connected* if it cannot be represented as the union of two disjoint, nonempty, open sets. While this definition is rather elegant and general, if X is connected, it does not imply that a path exists between any pair of points in X thanks to crazy examples like the *topologist's sine curve*:

$$X = \{(x, y) \in \mathbb{R}^2 \mid x = 0 \text{ or } y = \sin(1/x)\}. \tag{4.8}$$

Consider plotting X. The $\sin(1/x)$ part creates oscillations near the y-axis in which the frequency tends to infinity. After union is taken with the y-axis, this space is connected, but there is no path that reaches the y-axis from the sine curve.

How can we avoid such problems? The standard way to fix this is to use the path definition directly in the definition of connectedness. A topological space X is said to be *path connected* if for all $x_1, x_2 \in X$, there exists a path τ such that $\tau(0) = x_1$ and $\tau(1) = x_2$. It can be shown that if X is path connected, then it is also connected in the sense defined previously.

Another way to fix it is to make restrictions on the kinds of topological spaces that will be considered. This approach will be taken here by assuming that all topological spaces

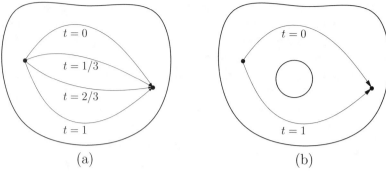

Figure 4.6: (a) Homotopy continuously warps one path into another. (b) The image of the path cannot be continuously warped over a hole in $\mathbb{R}^2$ because it causes a discontinuity. In this case, the two paths are not homotopic.

are manifolds. In this case, no strange things like (4.8) can happen,[7] and the definitions of connected and path connected coincide [454]. Therefore, we will just say a space is *connected*. However, it is important to remember that this definition of connected is sometimes inadequate, and one should really say that X is *path connected*.

Simply connected

Now that the notion of connectedness has been established, the next step is to express different kinds of connectivity. This may be done by using the notion of homotopy, which can intuitively be considered as a way to continuously "warp" or "morph" one path into another, as depicted in Figure 4.6a.

Two paths τ_1 and τ_2 are called *homotopic* (with endpoints fixed) if there exists a continuous function $h : [0, 1] \times [0, 1] \to X$ for which the following four conditions are met:

1. **(Start with first path)** $h(s, 0) = \tau_1(s)$ for all $s \in [0, 1]$.
2. **(End with second path)** $h(s, 1) = \tau_2(s)$ for all $s \in [0, 1]$.
3. **(Hold starting point fixed)** $h(0, t) = h(0, 0)$ for all $t \in [0, 1]$.
4. **(Hold ending point fixed)** $h(1, t) = h(1, 0)$ for all $t \in [0, 1]$.

The parameter t can be interpreted as a knob that is turned to gradually deform the path from τ_1 into τ_2. The first two conditions indicate that $t = 0$ yields τ_1 and $t = 1$ yields τ_2, respectively. The remaining two conditions indicate that the path endpoints are held fixed.

During the warping process, the path image cannot make a discontinuous jump. In $\mathbb{R}^2$, this prevents it from moving over holes, such as the one shown in Figure 4.6b. The key to preventing homotopy from jumping over some holes is that h must be continuous. In higher dimensions, however, there are many different kinds of holes. For the case of $\mathbb{R}^3$, for example, suppose the space is like a block of Swiss cheese that contains air bubbles. Homotopy can go around the air bubbles, but it cannot pass through a hole that is drilled through the entire block of cheese. Air bubbles and other kinds of holes that appear in higher dimensions can be characterized by generalizing homotopy to the warping of higher dimensional surfaces, as opposed to paths [442].

---

[7] The topologist's sine curve is not a manifold because all open sets that contain the point $(0, 0)$ contain some of the points from the sine curve. These open sets are not homeomorphic to $\mathbb{R}$.

It is straightforward to show that homotopy defines an equivalence relation on the set of all paths from some $x_1 \in X$ to some $x_2 \in X$. The resulting notion of "equivalent paths" appears frequently in motion planning, control theory, and many other contexts. Suppose that X is path connected. If all paths fall into the same equivalence class, then X is called *simply connected*; otherwise, X is called *multiply connected*.

Groups

The equivalence relation induced by homotopy starts to enter the realm of algebraic topology, which is a branch of mathematics that characterizes the structure of topological spaces in terms of algebraic objects, such as groups. These resulting groups have important implications for motion planning. Therefore, we give a brief overview. First, the notion of a group must be precisely defined. A *group* is a set, G, together with a binary operation, $\circ$, such that the following *group axioms* are satisfied:

1. (**Closure**) For any $a, b \in G$, the product $a \circ b \in G$.

2. (**Associativity**) For all $a, b, c \in G$, $(a \circ b) \circ c = a \circ (b \circ c)$. Hence, parentheses are not needed, and the product may be written as $a \circ b \circ c$.

3. (**Identity**) There is an element $e \in G$, called the *identity*, such that for all $a \in G$, $e \circ a = a$ and $a \circ e = a$.

4. (**Inverse**) For every element $a \in G$, there is an element a^{-1}, called the *inverse* of a, for which $a \circ a^{-1} = e$ and $a^{-1} \circ a = e$.

Here are some examples.

Example 4.7 (Simple Examples of Groups) The set of integers $\mathbb{Z}$ is a group with respect to addition. The identity is 0, and the inverse of each i is $-i$. The set $\mathbb{Q} \setminus 0$ of rational numbers with 0 removed is a group with respect to multiplication. The identity is 1, and the inverse of every element, q, is $1/q$ (0 was removed to avoid division by zero). ∎

An important property, which only some groups possess, is *commutativity*: $a \circ b = b \circ a$ for any $a, b \in G$. The group in this case is called *commutative* or *Abelian*. We will encounter examples of both kinds of groups, both commutative and noncommutative. An example of a commutative group is vector addition over $\mathbb{R}^n$. The set of all 3D rotations is an example of a noncommutative group.

The fundamental group

Now an interesting group will be constructed from the space of paths and the equivalence relation obtained by homotopy. The *fundamental group*, $\pi_1(X)$ (or *first homotopy group*), is associated with any topological space, X. Let a (continuous) path for which $f(0) = f(1)$ be called a *loop*. Let some $x_b \in X$ be designated as a *base point*. For some arbitrary but fixed base point, x_b, consider the set of all loops such that $f(0) = f(1) = x_b$. This can be made into a group by defining the following binary operation. Let $\tau_1 : [0, 1] \to X$ and $\tau_2 : [0, 1] \to X$ be two loop paths with the same base point. Their product $\tau = \tau_1 \circ \tau_2$ is defined as

$$\tau(t) = \begin{cases} \tau_1(2t) & \text{if } t \in [0, 1/2) \\ \tau_2(2t - 1) & \text{if } t \in [1/2, 1]. \end{cases} \tag{4.9}$$

This results in a continuous loop path because τ_1 terminates at x_b, and τ_2 begins at x_b. In a sense, the two paths are concatenated end-to-end.

Suppose now that the equivalence relation induced by homotopy is applied to the set of all loop paths through a fixed point, x_b. It will no longer be important which particular path was chosen from a class; any representative may be used. The equivalence relation also applies when the set of loops is interpreted as a group. The group operation actually occurs over the set of equivalences of paths.

Consider what happens when two paths from different equivalence classes are concatenated using $\circ$. Is the resulting path homotopic to either of the first two? Is the resulting path homotopic if the original two are from the same homotopy class? The answers in general are *no* and *no*, respectively. The fundamental group describes how the equivalence classes of paths are related and characterizes the connectivity of X. Since fundamental groups are based on paths, there is a nice connection to motion planning.

Example 4.8 (A Simply Connected Space)   Suppose that a topological space X is simply connected. In this case, all loop paths from a base point x_b are homotopic, resulting in one equivalence class. The result is $\pi_1(X) = \mathbf{1_G}$, which is the group that consists of only the identity element.   ■

Example 4.9 (The Fundamental Group of $\mathbb{S}^1$)   Suppose $X = \mathbb{S}^1$. In this case, there is an equivalence class of paths for each $i \in \mathbb{Z}$, the set of integers. If $i > 0$, then it means that the path winds i times around $\mathbb{S}^1$ in the counterclockwise direction and then returns to x_b. If $i < 0$, then the path winds around i times in the clockwise direction. If $i = 0$, then the path is equivalent to one that remains at x_b. The fundamental group is $\mathbb{Z}$, with respect to the operation of addition. If τ_1 travels i_1 times counterclockwise, and τ_2 travels i_2 times counterclockwise, then $\tau = \tau_1 \circ \tau_2$ belongs to the class of loops that travel around $i_1 + i_2$ times counterclockwise. Consider additive inverses. If a path travels seven times around $\mathbb{S}^1$, and it is combined with a path that travels seven times in the opposite direction, the result is homotopic to a path that remains at x_b. Thus, $\pi_1(\mathbb{S}^1) = \mathbb{Z}$.   ■

Example 4.10 (The Fundamental Group of $\mathbb{T}^n$)   For the torus, $\pi_1(\mathbb{T}^n) = \mathbb{Z}^n$, in which the ith component of $\mathbb{Z}^n$ corresponds to the number of times a loop path wraps around the ith component of $\mathbb{T}^n$. This makes intuitive sense because $\mathbb{T}^n$ is just the Cartesian product of n circles. The fundamental group $\mathbb{Z}^n$ is obtained by starting with a simply connected subset of the plane and drilling out n disjoint, bounded holes. This situation arises frequently when a mobile robot must avoid collision with n disjoint obstacles in the plane.   ■

By now it seems that the fundamental group simply keeps track of how many times a path travels around holes. This next example yields some very bizarre behavior that helps to illustrate some of the interesting structure that arises in algebraic topology.

Example 4.11 (The Fundamental Group of $\mathbb{RP}^2$)   Suppose $X = \mathbb{RP}^2$, the projective plane. In this case, there are only two equivalence classes on the space of loop paths. All paths that "wrap around" an even number of times are homotopic. Likewise, all paths that wrap around an odd number of times are homotopic. This strange behavior is illustrated in Figure 4.7. The resulting fundamental group therefore has only two elements: $\pi_1(\mathbb{RP}^2) = \mathbb{Z}_2$, the cyclic group of order 2, which corresponds to addition mod 2. This makes intuitive sense because the group keeps track of whether a sum of integers is odd

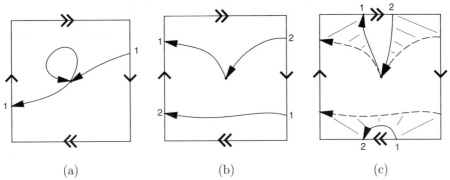

(a)   (b)   (c)

Figure 4.7: An illustration of why $\pi_1(\mathbb{RP}^2) = \mathbb{Z}_2$. The integers 1 and 2 indicate precisely where a path continues when it reaches the boundary. (a) Two paths are shown that are not equivalent. (b) A path that winds around twice is shown. (c) This is homotopic to a loop path that does not wind around at all. Eventually, the part of the path that appears at the bottom is pulled through the top. It finally shrinks into an arbitrarily small loop.

or even, which in this application corresponds to the total number of traversals over the square representation of $\mathbb{RP}^2$. The fundamental group is the same for $\mathbb{RP}^3$, which arises in Section 4.2.2 because it is homeomorphic to the set of 3D rotations. Thus, there are surprisingly only two path classes for the set of 3D rotations. ■

Unfortunately, two topological spaces may have the same fundamental group even if the spaces are not homeomorphic. For example, $\mathbb{Z}$ is the fundamental group of $\mathbb{S}^1$, the cylinder, $\mathbb{R} \times \mathbb{S}^1$, and the Möbius band. In the last case, the fundamental group does not indicate that there is a "twist" in the space. Another problem is that spaces with interesting connectivity may be declared as simply connected. The fundamental group of the sphere $\mathbb{S}^2$ is just $\mathbf{1}_G$, the same as for $\mathbb{R}^2$. Try envisioning loop paths on the sphere; it can be seen that they all fall into one equivalence class. Hence, $\mathbb{S}^2$ is simply connected. The fundamental group also neglects bubbles in $\mathbb{R}^3$ because the homotopy can warp paths around them. Some of these troubles can be fixed by defining second-order homotopy groups. For example, a continuous function, $[0, 1] \times [0, 1] \to X$, of two variables can be used instead of a path. The resulting homotopy generates a kind of sheet or surface that can be warped through the space, to yield a homotopy group $\pi_2(X)$ that wraps around bubbles in $\mathbb{R}^3$. This idea can be extended beyond two dimensions to detect many different kinds of holes in higher dimensional spaces. This leads to the *higher order homotopy groups*. A stronger concept than simply connected for a space is that its homotopy groups of all orders are equal to the identity group. This prevents all kinds of holes from occurring and implies that a space, X, is *contractible*, which means a kind of homotopy can be constructed that shrinks X to a point [442]. In the plane, the notions of *contractible* and *simply connected* are equivalent; however, in higher dimensional spaces, such as those arising in motion planning, the term *contractible* should be used to indicate that the space has no interior obstacles (holes).

An alternative to basing groups on homotopy is to derive them using *homology*, which is based on the structure of cell complexes instead of homotopy mappings. This subject is much more complicated to present, but it is more powerful for proving theorems in topology. See the literature overview at the end of the chapter for suggested further reading on algebraic topology.

4.2 Defining the configuration space

This section defines the manifolds that arise from the transformations of Chapter 3. If the robot has n degrees of freedom, the set of transformations is usually a manifold of dimension n. This manifold is called the *configuration space* of the robot, and its name is often shortened to *C-space*. In this book, the C-space may be considered as a special state space. To solve a motion planning problem, algorithms must conduct a search in the C-space. The C-space provides a powerful abstraction that converts the complicated models and transformations of Chapter 3 into the general problem of computing a path that traverses a manifold. By developing algorithms directly for this purpose, they apply to a wide variety of different kinds of robots and transformations. In Section 4.3 the problem will be complicated by bringing obstacles into the configuration space, but in Section 4.2 there will be no obstacles.

4.2.1 2D rigid bodies: $SE(2)$

Section 3.2.2 expressed how to transform a rigid body in $\mathbb{R}^2$ by a homogeneous transformation matrix, T, given by (3.35). The task in this chapter is to characterize the set of all possible rigid-body transformations. Which manifold will this be? Here is the answer and brief explanation. Since any $x_t, y_t \in \mathbb{R}$ can be selected for translation, this alone yields a manifold $M_1 = \mathbb{R}^2$. Independently, any rotation, $\theta \in [0, 2\pi)$, can be applied. Since 2π yields the same rotation as 0, they can be identified, which makes the set of 2D rotations into a manifold, $M_2 = \mathbb{S}^1$. To obtain the manifold that corresponds to all rigid-body motions, simply take $\mathcal{C} = M_1 \times M_2 = \mathbb{R}^2 \times \mathbb{S}^1$. The answer to the question is that the C-space is a kind of cylinder.

Now we give a more detailed technical argument. The main purpose is that such a simple, intuitive argument will not work for the 3D case. Our approach is to introduce some of the technical machinery here for the 2D case, which is easier to understand, and then extend it to the 3D case in Section 4.2.2.

Matrix groups

The first step is to consider the set of transformations as a group, in addition to a topological space.[8] We now derive several important groups from sets of matrices, ultimately leading to $SO(n)$, the group of $n \times n$ rotation matrices, which is very important for motion planning. The set of all nonsingular $n \times n$ real-valued matrices is called the *general linear group*, denoted by $GL(n)$, with respect to matrix multiplication. Each matrix $A \in GL(n)$ has an inverse $A^{-1} \in GL(n)$, which when multiplied yields the identity matrix, $AA^{-1} = I$. The matrices must be nonsingular for the same reason that 0 was removed from $\mathbb{Q}$. The analog of division by zero for matrix algebra is the inability to invert a singular matrix.

Many interesting groups can be formed from one group, G_1, by removing some elements to obtain a *subgroup*, G_2. To be a subgroup, G_2 must be a subset of G_1 and satisfy the group axioms. We will arrive at the set of rotation matrices by constructing subgroups. One important subgroup of $GL(n)$ is the *orthogonal group*, $O(n)$, which is the set of all

---

[8] The groups considered in this section are actually Lie groups because they are smooth manifolds [64]. We will not use that name here, however, because the notion of a smooth structure has not yet been defined. Readers familiar with Lie groups, however, will recognize most of the coming concepts. Some details on Lie groups appear later in Sections 15.4.3 and 15.5.1.

matrices $A \in GL(n)$ for which $AA^T = I$, in which A^T denotes the matrix *transpose* of A. These matrices have orthogonal columns (the inner product of any pair is zero) and the determinant is always 1 or -1. Thus, note that AA^T takes the inner product of every pair of columns. If the columns are different, the result must be 0; if they are the same, the result is 1 because $AA^T = I$. The *special orthogonal group*, $SO(n)$, is the subgroup of $O(n)$ in which every matrix has determinant 1. Another name for $SO(n)$ is the *group of n-dimensional rotation matrices.*

A chain of groups, $SO(n) \leq O(n) \leq GL(n)$, has been described in which $\leq$ denotes "a subgroup of." Each group can also be considered as a topological space. The set of all $n \times n$ matrices (which is not a group with respect to multiplication) with real-valued entries is homeomorphic to $\mathbb{R}^{n^2}$ because n^2 entries in the matrix can be independently chosen. For $GL(n)$, singular matrices are removed, but an n^2-dimensional manifold is nevertheless obtained. For $O(n)$, the expression $AA^T = I$ corresponds to n^2 algebraic equations that have to be satisfied. This should substantially drop the dimension. Note, however, that many of the equations are redundant (pick your favorite value for n, multiply the matrices, and see what happens). There are only $\binom{n}{2}$ ways (pairwise combinations) to take the inner product of pairs of columns, and there are n equations that require the magnitude of each column to be 1. This yields a total of $n(n+1)/2$ independent equations. Each independent equation drops the manifold dimension by one, and the resulting dimension of $O(n)$ is $n^2 - n(n+1)/2 = n(n-1)/2$, which is easily remembered as $\binom{n}{2}$. To obtain $SO(n)$, the constraint $\det A = 1$ is added, which eliminates exactly half of the elements of $O(n)$ but keeps the dimension the same.

Example 4.12 (Matrix Subgroups) It is helpful to illustrate the concepts for $n = 2$. The set of all 2×2 matrices is

$$\left\{ \begin{pmatrix} a & b \\ c & d \end{pmatrix} \; \middle| \; a, b, c, d \in \mathbb{R} \right\}, \tag{4.10}$$

which is homeomorphic to $\mathbb{R}^4$. The group $GL(2)$ is formed from the set of all nonsingular 2×2 matrices, which introduces the constraint that $ad - bc \neq 0$. The set of singular matrices forms a 3D manifold with boundary in $\mathbb{R}^4$, but all other elements of $\mathbb{R}^4$ are in $GL(2)$; therefore, $GL(2)$ is a 4D manifold.

Next, the constraint $AA^T = I$ is enforced to obtain $O(2)$. This becomes

$$\begin{pmatrix} a & b \\ c & d \end{pmatrix} \begin{pmatrix} a & c \\ b & d \end{pmatrix} = \begin{pmatrix} 1 & 0 \\ 0 & 1 \end{pmatrix}, \tag{4.11}$$

which directly yields four algebraic equations:

$$a^2 + b^2 = 1 \tag{4.12}$$

$$ac + bd = 0 \tag{4.13}$$

$$ca + db = 0 \tag{4.14}$$

$$c^2 + d^2 = 1. \tag{4.15}$$

Note that (4.14) is redundant. There are two kinds of equations. One equation, given by (4.13), forces the inner product of the columns to be 0. There is only one because $\binom{n}{2} = 1$ for $n = 2$. Two other constraints, (4.12) and (4.15), force the rows to be unit vectors. There are two because $n = 2$. The resulting dimension of the manifold is $\binom{n}{2} = 1$ because we started with $\mathbb{R}^4$ and lost three dimensions from (4.12), (4.13), and (4.15). What does this manifold look like? Imagine that there are two different two-dimensional unit vectors,

(a, b) and (c, d). Any value can be chosen for (a, b) as long as $a^2 + b^2 = 1$. This looks like $\mathbb{S}^1$, but the inner product of (a, b) and (c, d) must also be 0. Therefore, for each value of (a, b), there are two choices for c and d: 1) $c = b$ and $d = -a$, or 2) $c = -b$ and $d = a$. It appears that there are two circles! The manifold is $\mathbb{S}^1 \sqcup \mathbb{S}^1$, in which $\sqcup$ denotes the union of disjoint sets. Note that this manifold is not connected because no path exists from one circle to the other.

The final step is to require that $\det A = ad - bc = 1$, to obtain $SO(2)$, the set of all 2D rotation matrices. Without this condition, there would be matrices that produce a rotated mirror image of the rigid body. The constraint simply forces the choice for c and d to be $c = -b$ and $a = d$. This throws away one of the circles from $O(2)$, to obtain a single circle for $SO(2)$. We have finally obtained what you already knew: $SO(2)$ is homeomorphic to $\mathbb{S}^1$. The circle can be parameterized using polar coordinates to obtain the standard 2D rotation matrix, (3.31), given in Section 3.2.2. ∎

Special Euclidean group

Now that the group of rotations, $SO(n)$, is characterized, the next step is to allow both rotations and translations. This corresponds to the set of all $(n + 1) \times (n + 1)$ transformation matrices of the form

$$\left\{ \begin{pmatrix} R & v \\ 0 & 1 \end{pmatrix} \,\middle|\, R \in SO(n) \text{ and } v \in \mathbb{R}^n \right\}. \tag{4.16}$$

This should look like a generalization of (3.52) and (3.56), which were for $n = 2$ and $n = 3$, respectively. The R part of the matrix achieves rotation of an n-dimensional body in $\mathbb{R}^n$, and the v part achieves translation of the same body. The result is a group, $SE(n)$, which is called the *special Euclidean group*. As a topological space, $SE(n)$ is homeomorphic to $\mathbb{R}^n \times SO(n)$, because the rotation matrix and translation vectors may be chosen independently. In the case of $n = 2$, this means $SE(2)$ is homeomorphic to $\mathbb{R}^2 \times \mathbb{S}^1$, which verifies what was stated at the beginning of this section. Thus, the C-space of a 2D rigid body that can translate and rotate in the plane is

$$\mathcal{C} = \mathbb{R}^2 \times \mathbb{S}^1. \tag{4.17}$$

To be more precise, $\cong$ should be used in the place of $=$ to indicate that $\mathcal{C}$ could be any space homeomorphic to $\mathbb{R}^2 \times \mathbb{S}^1$; however, this notation will mostly be avoided.

Interpreting the C-space

It is important to consider the topological implications of $\mathcal{C}$. Since $\mathbb{S}^1$ is multiply connected, $\mathbb{R} \times \mathbb{S}^1$ and $\mathbb{R}^2 \times \mathbb{S}^1$ are multiply connected. It is difficult to visualize $\mathcal{C}$ because it is a 3D manifold; however, there is a nice interpretation using identification. Start with the open unit cube, $(0, 1)^3 \subset \mathbb{R}^3$. Include the boundary points of the form $(x, y, 0)$ and $(x, y, 1)$, and make the identification $(x, y, 0) \sim (x, y, 1)$ for all $x, y \in (0, 1)$. This means that when traveling in the x and y directions, there is a "frontier" to the C-space; however, traveling in the z direction causes a wraparound.

It is very important for a motion planning algorithm to understand that this wraparound exists. For example, consider $\mathbb{R} \times \mathbb{S}^1$ because it is easier to visualize. Imagine a path planning problem for which $\mathcal{C} = \mathbb{R} \times \mathbb{S}^1$, as depicted in Figure 4.8. Suppose the top and bottom are identified to make a cylinder, and there is an obstacle across the middle. Suppose the task is to find a path from q_I to q_G. If the top and bottom were not identified,

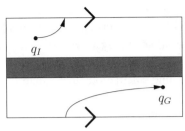

Figure 4.8: A planning algorithm may have to cross the identification boundary to find a solution path.

then it would not be possible to connect q_I to q_G; however, if the algorithm realizes it was given a cylinder, the task is straightforward. In general, it is very important to understand the topology of $\mathcal{C}$; otherwise, potential solutions will be lost.

The next section addresses $SE(n)$ for $n = 3$. The main difficulty is determining the topology of $SO(3)$. At least we do not have to consider $n > 3$ in this book.

4.2.2 3D rigid bodies: $SE(3)$

One might expect that defining $\mathcal{C}$ for a 3D rigid body is an obvious extension of the 2D case; however, 3D rotations are significantly more complicated. The resulting C-space will be a six-dimensional manifold, $\mathcal{C} = \mathbb{R}^3 \times \mathbb{RP}^3$. Three dimensions come from translation and three more come from rotation.

The main quest in this section is to determine the topology of $SO(3)$. In Section 3.2.3, yaw, pitch, and roll were used to generate rotation matrices. These angles are convenient for visualization, performing transformations in software, and also for deriving the DH parameters. However, these were concerned with applying a single rotation, whereas the current problem is to characterize the set of all rotations. It is possible to use α, β, and γ to parameterize the set of rotations, but it causes serious troubles. There are some cases in which nonzero angles yield the identity rotation matrix, which is equivalent to $\alpha = \beta = \gamma = 0$. There are also cases in which a continuum of values for yaw, pitch, and roll angles yield the same rotation matrix. These problems destroy the topology, which causes both theoretical and practical difficulties in motion planning.

Consider applying the matrix group concepts from Section 4.2.1. The general linear group $GL(3)$ is homeomorphic to $\mathbb{R}^9$. The orthogonal group, $O(3)$, is determined by imposing the constraint $AA^T = I$. There are $\binom{3}{2} = 3$ independent equations that require distinct columns to be orthogonal, and three independent equations that force the magnitude of each column to be 1. This means that $O(3)$ has three dimensions, which matches our intuition since there were three rotation parameters in Section 3.2.3. To obtain $SO(3)$, the last constraint, $\det A = 1$, is added. Recall from Example 4.12 that $SO(2)$ consists of two circles, and the constraint $\det A = 1$ selects one of them. In the case of $O(3)$, there are two three-spheres, $\mathbb{S}^3 \sqcup \mathbb{S}^3$, and $\det A = 1$ selects one of them. However, there is one additional complication: Antipodal points on these spheres generate the same rotation matrix. This will be seen shortly when quaternions are used to parameterize $SO(3)$.

Using complex numbers to represent SO(2)

Before introducing quaternions to parameterize 3D rotations, consider using complex numbers to parameterize 2D rotations. Let the term *unit complex number* refer to any complex number, $a + bi$, for which $a^2 + b^2 = 1$.

The set of all unit complex numbers forms a group under multiplication. It will be seen that it is "the same" group as $SO(2)$. This idea needs to be made more precise. Two groups, G and H, are considered "the same" if they are *isomorphic*, which means that there exists a bijective function $f : G \to H$ such that for all $a, b \in G$, $f(a) \circ f(b) = f(a \circ b)$. This means that we can perform some calculations in G, map the result to H, perform more calculations, and map back to G without any trouble. The sets G and H are just two alternative ways to express the same group.

The unit complex numbers and $SO(2)$ are isomorphic. To see this clearly, recall that complex numbers can be represented in polar form as $re^{i\theta}$; a unit complex number is simply $e^{i\theta}$. A bijective mapping can be made between 2D rotation matrices and unit complex numbers by letting $e^{i\theta}$ correspond to the rotation matrix (3.31).

If complex numbers are used to represent rotations, it is important that they behave algebraically in the same way. If two rotations are combined, the matrices are multiplied. The equivalent operation is multiplication of complex numbers. Suppose that a 2D robot is rotated by θ_1, followed by θ_2. In polar form, the complex numbers are multiplied to yield $e^{i\theta_1} e^{i\theta_2} = e^{i(\theta_1+\theta_2)}$, which clearly represents a rotation of $\theta_1 + \theta_2$. If the unit complex number is represented in Cartesian form, then the rotations corresponding to $a_1 + b_1 i$ and $a_2 + b_2 i$ are combined to obtain $(a_1 a_2 - b_1 b_2) + (a_1 b_2 + a_2 b_1)i$. Note that here we have not used complex numbers to express the solution to a polynomial equation, which is their more popular use; we simply borrowed their nice algebraic properties. At any time, a complex number $a + bi$ can be converted into the equivalent rotation matrix

$$R(a, b) = \begin{pmatrix} a & -b \\ b & a \end{pmatrix}. \tag{4.18}$$

Recall that only one independent parameter needs to be specified because $a^2 + b^2 = 1$. Hence, it appears that the set of unit complex numbers is the same manifold as $SO(2)$, which is the circle $\mathbb{S}^1$ (recall, that "same" means in the sense of homeomorphism).

Quaternions

The manner in which complex numbers were used to represent 2D rotations will now be adapted to using quaternions to represent 3D rotations. Let $\mathbb{H}$ represent the set of *quaternions*, in which each quaternion, $h \in \mathbb{H}$, is represented as $h = a + bi + cj + dk$, and $a, b, c, d \in \mathbb{R}$. A quaternion can be considered as a four-dimensional vector. The symbols i, j, and k are used to denote three "imaginary" components of the quaternion. The following relationships are defined: $i^2 = j^2 = k^2 = ijk = -1$, from which it follows that $ij = k$, $jk = i$, and $ki = j$. Using these, multiplication of two quaternions, $h_1 = a_1 + b_1 i + c_1 j + d_1 k$ and $h_2 = a_2 + b_2 i + c_2 j + d_2 k$, can be derived to obtain $h_1 \cdot h_2 = a_3 + b_3 i + c_3 j + d_3 k$, in which

$$\begin{aligned} a_3 &= a_1 a_2 - b_1 b_2 - c_1 c_2 - d_1 d_2 \\ b_3 &= a_1 b_2 + a_2 b_1 + c_1 d_2 - c_2 d_1 \\ c_3 &= a_1 c_2 + a_2 c_1 + b_2 d_1 - b_1 d_2 \\ d_3 &= a_1 d_2 + a_2 d_1 + b_1 c_2 - b_2 c_1. \end{aligned} \tag{4.19}$$

Using this operation, it can be shown that $\mathbb{H}$ is a group with respect to quaternion multiplication. Note, however, that the multiplication is not commutative! This is also true of 3D rotations; there must be a good reason.

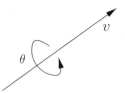

Figure 4.9: Any 3D rotation can be considered as a rotation by an angle θ about the axis given by the unit direction vector $v = [v_1 \ v_2 \ v_3]$.

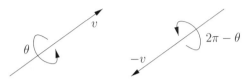

Figure 4.10: There are two ways to encode the same rotation.

For convenience, quaternion multiplication can be expressed in terms of vector multiplications, a dot product, and a cross product. Let $v = [b \ c \ d]$ be a three-dimensional vector that represents the final three quaternion components. The first component of $h_1 \cdot h_2$ is $a_1 a_2 - v_1 \cdot v_2$. The final three components are given by the three-dimensional vector $a_1 v_2 + a_2 v_1 - v_1 \times v_2$.

In the same way that *unit* complex numbers were needed for $SO(2)$, *unit quaternions* are needed for $SO(3)$, which means that $\mathbb{H}$ is restricted to quaternions for which $a^2 + b^2 + c^2 + d^2 = 1$. Note that this forms a subgroup because the multiplication of unit quaternions yields a unit quaternion, and the other group axioms hold.

The next step is to describe a mapping from unit quaternions to $SO(3)$. Let the unit quaternion $h = a + bi + cj + dk$ map to the matrix

$$R(h) = \begin{pmatrix} 2(a^2 + b^2) - 1 & 2(bc - ad) & 2(bd + ac) \\ 2(bc + ad) & 2(a^2 + c^2) - 1 & 2(cd - ab) \\ 2(bd - ac) & 2(cd + ab) & 2(a^2 + d^2) - 1 \end{pmatrix}, \quad (4.20)$$

which can be verified as orthogonal and $\det R(h) = 1$. Therefore, it belongs to $SO(3)$. It is not shown here, but it conveniently turns out that h represents the rotation shown in Figure 4.9, by making the assignment

$$h = \cos\frac{\theta}{2} + \left(v_1 \sin\frac{\theta}{2}\right) i + \left(v_2 \sin\frac{\theta}{2}\right) j + \left(v_3 \sin\frac{\theta}{2}\right) k. \quad (4.21)$$

Unfortunately, this representation is not unique. It can be verified in (4.20) that $R(h) = R(-h)$. A nice geometric interpretation is given in Figure 4.10. The quaternions h and $-h$ represent the same rotation because a rotation of θ about the direction v is equivalent to a rotation of $2\pi - \theta$ about the direction $-v$. Consider the quaternion representation of the second expression of rotation with respect to the first. The real part is

$$\cos\left(\frac{2\pi - \theta}{2}\right) = \cos\left(\pi - \frac{\theta}{2}\right) = -\cos\left(\frac{\theta}{2}\right) = -a. \quad (4.22)$$

The i, j, and k components are

$$-v \sin\left(\frac{2\pi - \theta}{2}\right) = -v \sin\left(\pi - \frac{\theta}{2}\right) = -v \sin\left(\frac{\theta}{2}\right) = [-b \ -c \ -d]. \quad (4.23)$$

The quaternion $-h$ has been constructed. Thus, h and $-h$ represent the same rotation. Luckily, this is the only problem, and the mapping given by (4.20) is two-to-one from the set of unit quaternions to $SO(3)$.

This can be fixed by the identification trick. Note that the set of unit quaternions is homeomorphic to $\mathbb{S}^3$ because of the constraint $a^2 + b^2 + c^2 + d^2 = 1$. The algebraic properties of quaternions are not relevant at this point. Just imagine each h as an element of $\mathbb{R}^4$, and the constraint $a^2 + b^2 + c^2 + d^2 = 1$ forces the points to lie on $\mathbb{S}^3$. Using identification, declare $h \sim -h$ for all unit quaternions. This means that the antipodal points of $\mathbb{S}^3$ are identified. Recall from the end of Section 4.1.2 that when antipodal points are identified, $\mathbb{RP}^n \cong \mathbb{S}^n / \sim$. Hence, $SO(3) \cong \mathbb{RP}^3$, which can be considered as the set of all lines through the origin of $\mathbb{R}^4$, but this is hard to visualize. The representation of $\mathbb{RP}^2$ in Figure 4.5 can be extended to $\mathbb{RP}^3$. Start with $(0, 1)^3 \subset \mathbb{R}^3$, and make three different kinds of identifications, one for each pair of opposite cube faces, and add all of the points to the manifold. For each kind of identification a twist needs to be made (without the twist, $\mathbb{T}^3$ would be obtained). For example, in the z direction, let $(x, y, 0) \sim (1 - x, 1 - y, 1)$ for all $x, y \in [0, 1]$.

One way to force uniqueness of rotations is to require staying in the "upper half" of $\mathbb{S}^3$. For example, require that $a \geq 0$, as long as the boundary case of $a = 0$ is handled properly because of antipodal points at the equator of $\mathbb{S}^3$. If $a = 0$, then require that $b \geq 0$. However, if $a = b = 0$, then require that $c \geq 0$ because points such as $(0, 0, -1, 0)$ and $(0, 0, 1, 0)$ are the same rotation. Finally, if $a = b = c = 0$, then only $d = 1$ is allowed. If such restrictions are made, it is important, however, to remember the connectivity of $\mathbb{RP}^3$. If a path travels across the equator of $\mathbb{S}^3$, it must be mapped to the appropriate place in the "northern hemisphere." At the instant it hits the equator, it must move to the antipodal point. These concepts are much easier to visualize if you remove a dimension and imagine them for $\mathbb{S}^2 \subset \mathbb{R}^3$, as described at the end of Section 4.1.2.

Using quaternion multiplication

The representation of rotations boiled down to picking points on $\mathbb{S}^3$ and respecting the fact that antipodal points give the same element of $SO(3)$. In a sense, this has nothing to do with the algebraic properties of quaternions. It merely means that $SO(3)$ can be parameterized by picking points in $\mathbb{S}^3$, just like $SO(2)$ was parameterized by picking points in $\mathbb{S}^1$ (ignoring the antipodal identification problem for $SO(3)$).

However, one important reason why the quaternion arithmetic was introduced is that the group of unit quaternions is also isomorphic to $SO(3)$. This means that a sequence of rotations can be multiplied together using quaternion multiplication instead of matrix multiplication. This is important because fewer operations are required for quaternion multiplication in comparison to matrix multiplication. At any point, (4.20) can be used to convert the result back into a matrix; however, this is not even necessary. It turns out that a point in the world, $(x, y, z) \in \mathbb{R}^3$, can be transformed by directly using quaternion arithmetic. An analog to the complex conjugate from complex numbers is needed. For any $h = a + bi + cj + dk \in \mathbb{H}$, let $h^* = a - bi - cj - dk$ be its *conjugate*. For any point $(x, y, z) \in \mathbb{R}^3$, let $p \in \mathbb{H}$ be the quaternion $0 + xi + yj + zk$. It can be shown (with a lot of algebra) that the rotated point (x, y, z) is given by $h \cdot p \cdot h^*$. The i, j, k components of the resulting quaternion are new coordinates for the transformed point. It is equivalent to having transformed (x, y, z) with the matrix $R(h)$.

Finding quaternion parameters from a rotation matrix

Recall from Section 3.2.3 that given a rotation matrix (3.43), the yaw, pitch, and roll parameters could be directly determined using the atan2 function. It turns out that the quaternion representation can also be determined directly from the matrix. This is the inverse of the function in (4.20).[9]

For a given rotation matrix (3.43), the quaternion parameters $h = a + bi + cj + dk$ can be computed as follows [212]. The first component is

$$a = \tfrac{1}{2}\sqrt{r_{11} + r_{22} + r_{33} + 1}, \tag{4.24}$$

and if $a \neq 0$, then

$$b = \frac{r_{32} - r_{23}}{4a}, \tag{4.25}$$

$$c = \frac{r_{13} - r_{31}}{4a}, \tag{4.26}$$

and

$$d = \frac{r_{21} - r_{12}}{4a}. \tag{4.27}$$

If $a = 0$, then the previously mentioned equator problem occurs. In this case,

$$b = \frac{r_{13}r_{12}}{\sqrt{r_{12}^2 r_{13}^2 + r_{12}^2 r_{23}^2 + r_{13}^2 r_{23}^2}}, \tag{4.28}$$

$$c = \frac{r_{12}r_{23}}{\sqrt{r_{12}^2 r_{13}^2 + r_{12}^2 r_{23}^2 + r_{13}^2 r_{23}^2}}, \tag{4.29}$$

and

$$d = \frac{r_{13}r_{23}}{\sqrt{r_{12}^2 r_{13}^2 + r_{12}^2 r_{23}^2 + r_{13}^2 r_{23}^2}}. \tag{4.30}$$

This method fails if $r_{12} = r_{23} = 0$ or $r_{13} = r_{23} = 0$ or $r_{12} = r_{23} = 0$. These correspond precisely to the cases in which the rotation matrix is a yaw, (3.39), pitch, (3.40), or roll, (3.41), which can be detected in advance.

Special Euclidean group

Now that the complicated part of representing $SO(3)$ has been handled, the representation of $SE(3)$ is straightforward. The general form of a matrix in $SE(3)$ is given by (4.16), in which $R \in SO(3)$ and $v \in \mathbb{R}^3$. Since $SO(3) \cong \mathbb{RP}^3$, and translations can be chosen independently, the resulting C-space for a rigid body that rotates and translates in $\mathbb{R}^3$ is

$$\mathcal{C} = \mathbb{R}^3 \times \mathbb{RP}^3, \tag{4.31}$$

which is a six-dimensional manifold. As expected, the dimension of $\mathcal{C}$ is exactly the number of degrees of freedom of a free-floating body in space.

---

[9] Since that function was two-to-one, it is technically not an inverse until the quaternions are restricted to the upper hemisphere, as described previously.

4.2.3 Chains and trees of bodies

If there are multiple bodies that are allowed to move independently, then their C-spaces can be combined using Cartesian products. Let C_i denote the C-space of $\mathcal{A}_i$. If there are n free-floating bodies in $\mathcal{W} = \mathbb{R}^2$ or $\mathcal{W} = \mathbb{R}^3$, then

$$C = C_1 \times C_2 \times \cdots \times C_n. \tag{4.32}$$

If the bodies are attached to form a kinematic chain or kinematic tree, then each C-space must be considered on a case-by-case basis. There is no general rule that simplifies the process. One thing to generally be careful about is that the full range of motion might not be possible for typical joints. For example, a revolute joint might not be able to swing all of the way around to enable any $\theta \in [0, 2\pi)$. If θ cannot wind around $\mathbb{S}^1$, then the C-space for this joint is homeomorphic to $\mathbb{R}$ instead of $\mathbb{S}^1$. A similar situation occurs for a spherical joint. A typical ball joint cannot achieve any orientation in $SO(3)$ due to mechanical obstructions. In this case, the C-space is not $\mathbb{RP}^3$ because part of $SO(3)$ is missing.

Another complication is that the DH parameterization of Section 3.3.2 is designed to facilitate the assignment of coordinate frames and computation of transformations, but it neglects considerations of topology. For example, a common approach to representing a spherical robot wrist is to make three zero-length links that each behave as a revolute joint. If the range of motion is limited, this might not cause problems, but in general the problems would be similar to using yaw, pitch, and roll to represent $SO(3)$. There may be multiple ways to express the same arm configuration.

Several examples are given below to help in determining C-spaces for chains and trees of bodies. Suppose $\mathcal{W} = \mathbb{R}^2$, and there is a chain of n bodies that are attached by revolute joints. Suppose that the first joint is capable of rotation only about a fixed point (e.g., it spins around a nail). If each joint has the full range of motion $\theta_i \in [0, 2\pi)$, the C-space is

$$C = \mathbb{S}^1 \times \mathbb{S}^1 \times \cdots \times \mathbb{S}^1 = \mathbb{T}^n. \tag{4.33}$$

However, if each joint is restricted to $\theta_i \in (-\pi/2, \pi/2)$, then $C = \mathbb{R}^n$. If any transformation in $SE(2)$ can be applied to $\mathcal{A}_1$, then an additional $\mathbb{R}^2$ is needed. In the case of restricted joint motions, this yields $\mathbb{R}^{n+2}$. If the joints can achieve any orientation, then $C = \mathbb{R}^2 \times \mathbb{T}^n$. If there are prismatic joints, then each joint contributes $\mathbb{R}$ to the C-space.

Recall from Figure 3.12 that for $\mathcal{W} = \mathbb{R}^3$ there are six different kinds of joints. The cases of revolute and prismatic joints behave the same as for $\mathcal{W} = \mathbb{R}^2$. Each screw joint contributes $\mathbb{R}$. A cylindrical joint contributes $\mathbb{R} \times \mathbb{S}^1$, unless its rotational motion is restricted. A planar joint contributes $\mathbb{R}^2 \times \mathbb{S}^1$ because any transformation in $SE(2)$ is possible. If its rotational motions are restricted, then it contributes $\mathbb{R}^3$. Finally, a spherical joint can theoretically contribute $\mathbb{RP}^3$. In practice, however, this rarely occurs. It is more likely to contribute $\mathbb{R}^2 \times \mathbb{S}^1$ or $\mathbb{R}^3$ after restrictions are imposed. Note that if the first joint is a free-floating body, then it contributes $\mathbb{R}^3 \times \mathbb{RP}^3$.

Kinematic trees can be handled in the same way as kinematic chains. One issue that has not been mentioned is that there might be collisions between the links. This has been ignored up to this point, but obviously this imposes very complicated restrictions. The concepts from Section 4.3 can be applied to handle this case and the placement of additional obstacles in $\mathcal{W}$. Reasoning about these kinds of restrictions and the path connectivity of the resulting space is indeed the main point of motion planning.

4.3 Configuration space obstacles

Section 4.2 defined $\mathcal{C}$, the manifold of robot transformations in the absence of any collision constraints. The current section removes from $\mathcal{C}$ the configurations that either cause the robot to collide with obstacles or cause some specified links of the robot to collide with each other. The removed part of $\mathcal{C}$ is referred to as the obstacle region. The leftover space is precisely what a solution path must traverse. A motion planning algorithm must find a path in the leftover space from an initial configuration to a goal configuration. Finally, after the models of Chapter 3 and the previous sections of this chapter, the motion planning problem can be precisely described.

4.3.1 Definition of the basic motion planning problem

Obstacle region for a rigid body

Suppose that the world, $\mathcal{W} = \mathbb{R}^2$ or $\mathcal{W} = \mathbb{R}^3$, contains an obstacle region, $\mathcal{O} \subset \mathcal{W}$. Assume here that a rigid robot, $\mathcal{A} \subset \mathcal{W}$, is defined; the case of multiple links will be handled shortly. Assume that both $\mathcal{A}$ and $\mathcal{O}$ are expressed as semi-algebraic models (which includes polygonal and polyhedral models) from Section 3.1. Let $q \in \mathcal{C}$ denote the *configuration* of $\mathcal{A}$, in which $q = (x_t, y_t, \theta)$ for $\mathcal{W} = \mathbb{R}^2$ and $q = (x_t, y_t, z_t, h)$ for $\mathcal{W} = \mathbb{R}^3$ (h represents the unit quaternion).

The *obstacle region*, $\mathcal{C}_{obs} \subseteq \mathcal{C}$, is defined as

$$\mathcal{C}_{obs} = \{q \in \mathcal{C} \mid \mathcal{A}(q) \cap \mathcal{O} \neq \emptyset\}, \tag{4.34}$$

which is the set of all configurations, q, at which $\mathcal{A}(q)$, the transformed robot, intersects the obstacle region, $\mathcal{O}$. Since $\mathcal{O}$ and $\mathcal{A}(q)$ are closed sets in $\mathcal{W}$, the obstacle region is a closed set in $\mathcal{C}$.

The leftover configurations are called the *free space*, which is defined and denoted as $\mathcal{C}_{free} = \mathcal{C} \setminus \mathcal{C}_{obs}$. Since $\mathcal{C}$ is a topological space and $\mathcal{C}_{obs}$ is closed, $\mathcal{C}_{free}$ must be an open set. This implies that the robot can come arbitrarily close to the obstacles while remaining in $\mathcal{C}_{free}$. If $\mathcal{A}$ "touches" $\mathcal{O}$,

$$\text{int}(\mathcal{O}) \cap \text{int}(\mathcal{A}(q)) = \emptyset \text{ and } \mathcal{O} \cap \mathcal{A}(q) \neq \emptyset, \tag{4.35}$$

then $q \in \mathcal{C}_{obs}$ (recall that int means the interior). The condition above indicates that only their boundaries intersect.

The idea of getting arbitrarily close may be nonsense in practical robotics, but it makes a clean formulation of the motion planning problem. Since $\mathcal{C}_{free}$ is open, it becomes impossible to formulate some optimization problems, such as finding the shortest path. In this case, the closure, $\text{cl}(\mathcal{C}_{free})$, should instead be used, as described in Section 7.7.

Obstacle region for multiple bodies

If the robot consists of multiple bodies, the situation is more complicated. The definition in (4.34) only implies that the robot does not collide with the obstacles; however, if the robot consists of multiple bodies, then it might also be appropriate to avoid collisions between different links of the robot. Let the robot be modeled as a collection, $\{\mathcal{A}_1, \mathcal{A}_2, \ldots, \mathcal{A}_m\}$, of m links, which may or may not be attached together by joints. A single configuration vector q is given for the entire collection of links. We will write $\mathcal{A}_i(q)$ for each link, i,

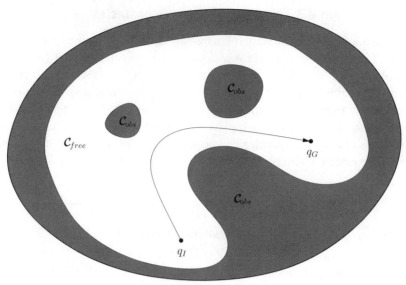

Figure 4.11: The basic motion planning problem is conceptually very simple using C-space ideas. The task is to find a path from q_I to q_G in $\mathcal{C}_{free}$. The entire blob represents $\mathcal{C} = \mathcal{C}_{free} \cup \mathcal{C}_{obs}$.

even though some of the parameters of q may be irrelevant for moving link $\mathcal{A}_i$. For example, in a kinematic chain, the configuration of the second body does not depend on the angle between the ninth and tenth bodies.

Let P denote the set of *collision pairs*, in which each collision pair, $(i, j) \in P$, represents a pair of link indices $i, j \in \{1, 2, \ldots, m\}$, such that $i \neq j$. If (i, j) appears in P, it means that A_i and A_j are not allowed to be in a configuration, q, for which $\mathcal{A}_i(q) \cap \mathcal{A}_j(q) \neq \emptyset$. Usually, P does not represent all pairs because consecutive links are in contact all of the time due to the joint that connects them. One common definition for P is that each link must avoid collisions with any links to which it is not attached by a joint. For m bodies, P is generally of size $O(m^2)$; however, in practice it is often possible to eliminate many pairs by some geometric analysis of the linkage. Collisions between some pairs of links may be impossible over all of $\mathcal{C}$, in which case they do not need to appear in P.

Using P, the consideration of robot self-collisions is added to the definition of $\mathcal{C}_{obs}$ to obtain

$$\mathcal{C}_{obs} = \left(\bigcup_{i=1}^{m} \{q \in \mathcal{C} \mid \mathcal{A}_i(q) \cap \mathcal{O} \neq \emptyset\} \right) \bigcup \left(\bigcup_{[i,j] \in P} \{q \in \mathcal{C} \mid \mathcal{A}_i(q) \cap \mathcal{A}_j(q) \neq \emptyset\} \right). \quad (4.36)$$

Thus, a configuration $q \in \mathcal{C}$ is in $\mathcal{C}_{obs}$ if at least one link collides with $\mathcal{O}$ or a pair of links indicated by P collide with each other.

Definition of basic motion planning

Finally, enough tools have been introduced to precisely define the motion planning problem. The problem is conceptually illustrated in Figure 4.11. The main difficulty is that it is neither straightforward nor efficient to construct an explicit boundary or solid representation of either C_{free} or C_{obs}. The components are as follows:

Formulation 4.1 (The Piano Mover's Problem)

1. A *world* W in which either $W = \mathbb{R}^2$ or $W = \mathbb{R}^3$.

2. A semi-algebraic *obstacle region* $\mathcal{O} \subset W$ in the world.

3. A semi-algebraic *robot* is defined in W. It may be a rigid robot $\mathcal{A}$ or a collection of m links, $\mathcal{A}_1, \mathcal{A}_2, \ldots, \mathcal{A}_m$.

4. The *configuration space* C determined by specifying the set of all possible transformations that may be applied to the robot. From this, C_{obs} and C_{free} are derived.

5. A configuration $q_I \in C_{free}$ designated as the *initial configuration*.

6. A configuration $q_G \in C_{free}$ designated as the *goal configuration*. The initial and goal configurations together are often called a *query pair* (or *query*) and designated as (q_I, q_G).

7. A complete algorithm must compute a (continuous) *path*, $\tau : [0, 1] \to C_{free}$, such that $\tau(0) = q_I$ and $\tau(1) = q_G$, or correctly report that such a path does not exist.

It was shown by Reif [820] that this problem is PSPACE-hard, which implies NP-hard. The main problem is that the dimension of C is unbounded.

4.3.2 Explicitly modeling C_{obs}: The translational case

It is important to understand how to construct a representation of C_{obs}. In some algorithms, especially the combinatorial methods of Chapter 6, this represents an important first step to solving the problem. In other algorithms, especially the sampling-based planning algorithms of Chapter 5, it helps to understand why such constructions are avoided due to their complexity.

The simplest case for characterizing C_{obs} is when $C = \mathbb{R}^n$ for $n = 1, 2$, and 3, and the robot is a rigid body that is restricted to translation only. Under these conditions, C_{obs} can be expressed as a type of convolution. For any two sets $X, Y \subset \mathbb{R}^n$, let their *Minkowski difference*[10] be defined as

$$X \ominus Y = \{x - y \in \mathbb{R}^n \mid x \in X \text{ and } y \in Y\}, \qquad (4.37)$$

in which $x - y$ is just vector subtraction on $\mathbb{R}^n$. The Minkowski difference between X and Y can also be considered as the Minkowski sum of X and $-Y$. The *Minkowski sum* $\oplus$ is obtained by simply adding elements of X and Y in (4.37), as opposed to subtracting them. The set $-Y$ is obtained by replacing each $y \in Y$ by $-y$.

In terms of the Minkowski difference, $C_{obs} = \mathcal{O} \ominus \mathcal{A}(0)$. To see this, it is helpful to consider a one-dimensional example.

Example 4.13 (One-Dimensional C-Space Obstacle) In Figure 4.12, both the robot $\mathcal{A} = [-1, 2]$ and obstacle region $\mathcal{O} = [0, 4]$ are intervals in a one-dimensional world, $W = \mathbb{R}$. The negation, $-\mathcal{A}$, of the robot is shown as the interval $[-2, 1]$. Finally, by applying the Minkowski sum to $\mathcal{O}$ and $-\mathcal{A}$, the C-space obstacle, $C_{obs} = [-2, 5]$, is obtained. ∎

---

[10] In some contexts, which include mathematics and image processing, the Minkowski difference or *Minkowski subtraction* is defined differently (instead, it is a kind of "erosion"). For this reason, some authors prefer to define all operations in terms of the Minkowski sum, $\oplus$, which is consistently defined in all contexts. Following this convention, we would define $X \oplus (-Y)$, which is equivalent to $X \ominus Y$.

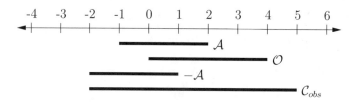

Figure 4.12: A one-dimensional C-space obstacle.

Figure 4.13: A triangular robot and a rectangular obstacle.

The Minkowski difference is often considered as a *convolution*. It can even be defined to appear the same as studied in differential equations and system theory. For a one-dimensional example, let $f : \mathbb{R} \to \{0, 1\}$ be a function such that $f(x) = 1$ if and only if $x \in \mathcal{O}$. Similarly, let $g : \mathbb{R} \to \{0, 1\}$ be a function such that $g(x) = 1$ if and only if $x \in \mathcal{A}$. The convolution

$$h(x) = \int_{-\infty}^{\infty} f(\tau)g(x - \tau)d\tau, \qquad (4.38)$$

yields a function h, for which $h(x) = 1$ if $x \in \mathcal{C}_{obs}$, and $h(x) = 0$ otherwise.

A polygonal C-space obstacle

A simple algorithm for computing $\mathcal{C}_{obs}$ exists in the case of a 2D world that contains a convex polygonal obstacle $\mathcal{O}$ and a convex polygonal robot $\mathcal{A}$ [660]. This is often called the *star algorithm*. For this problem, $\mathcal{C}_{obs}$ is also a convex polygon. Recall that nonconvex obstacles and robots can be modeled as the union of convex parts. The concepts discussed below can also be applied in the nonconvex case by considering $\mathcal{C}_{obs}$ as the union of convex components, each of which corresponds to a convex component of $\mathcal{A}$ colliding with a convex component of $\mathcal{O}$.

The method is based on sorting normals to the edges of the polygons on the basis of angles. The key observation is that every edge of $\mathcal{C}_{obs}$ is a translated edge from either $\mathcal{A}$ or $\mathcal{O}$. In fact, every edge from $\mathcal{O}$ and $\mathcal{A}$ is used exactly once in the construction of $\mathcal{C}_{obs}$. The only problem is to determine the ordering of these edges of $\mathcal{C}_{obs}$. Let $\alpha_1, \alpha_2, \ldots, \alpha_n$ denote the angles of the inward edge normals in counterclockwise order around $\mathcal{A}$. Let $\beta_1, \beta_2, \ldots, \beta_n$ denote the outward edge normals to $\mathcal{O}$. After sorting both sets of angles in circular order around $\mathbb{S}^1$, $\mathcal{C}_{obs}$ can be constructed incrementally by using the edges that correspond to the sorted normals, in the order in which they are encountered.

Example 4.14 (A Triangular Robot and Rectangular Obstacle) To gain an understanding of the method, consider the case of a triangular robot and a rectangular obstacle, as shown in Figure 4.13. The black dot on $\mathcal{A}$ denotes the origin of its body frame. Consider sliding the robot around the obstacle in such a way that they are always in contact, as shown in Figure 4.14a. This corresponds to the traversal of all of the configurations in $\partial \mathcal{C}_{obs}$ (the boundary of $\mathcal{C}_{obs}$). The origin of $\mathcal{A}$ traces out the edges of $\mathcal{C}_{obs}$, as shown in Figure 4.14b. There are seven edges, and each edge corresponds to either an edge of $\mathcal{A}$ or

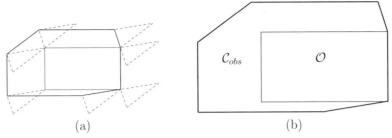

Figure 4.14: (a) Slide the robot around the obstacle while keeping them both in contact. (b) The edges traced out by the origin of $\mathcal{A}$ form $\mathcal{C}_{obs}$.

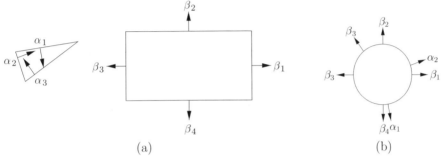

Figure 4.15: (a) Take the inward edge normals of $\mathcal{A}$ and the outward edge normals of $\mathcal{O}$. (b) Sort the edge normals around $\mathbb{S}^1$. This gives the order of edges in $\mathcal{C}_{obs}$.

an edge of $\mathcal{O}$. The directions of the normals are defined as shown in Figure 4.15a. When sorted as shown in Figure 4.15b, the edges of $\mathcal{C}_{obs}$ can be incrementally constructed. ∎

The running time of the algorithm is $O(n + m)$, in which n is the number of edges defining $\mathcal{A}$, and m is the number of edges defining $\mathcal{O}$. Note that the angles can be sorted in linear time because they already appear in counterclockwise order around $\mathcal{A}$ and $\mathcal{O}$; they only need to be merged. If two edges are collinear, then they can be placed end-to-end as a single edge of $\mathcal{C}_{obs}$.

Computing the boundary of $\mathcal{C}_{obs}$

So far, the method quickly identifies each edge that contributes to $\mathcal{C}_{obs}$. It can also construct a solid representation of $\mathcal{C}_{obs}$ in terms of half-planes. This requires defining $n + m$ linear equations (assuming there are no collinear edges).

There are two different ways in which an edge of $\mathcal{C}_{obs}$ is generated, as shown in Figure 4.16 [284, 660]. *Type EV* contact refers to the case in which an edge of $\mathcal{A}$ is in contact with a vertex of $\mathcal{O}$. Type EV contacts contribute to n edges of $\mathcal{C}_{obs}$, once for each edge of $\mathcal{A}$. *Type VE* contact refers to the case in which a vertex of $\mathcal{A}$ is in contact with an edge of $\mathcal{O}$. This contributes to m edges of $\mathcal{C}_{obs}$. The relationships between the edge normals are also shown in Figure 4.16. For Type EV, the inward edge normal points between the outward edge normals of the obstacle edges that share the contact vertex. Likewise for Type VE, the outward edge normal of $\mathcal{O}$ points between the inward edge normals of $\mathcal{A}$.

Using the ordering shown in Figure 4.15b, Type EV contacts occur precisely when an edge normal of $\mathcal{A}$ is encountered, and Type VE contacts occur when an edge normal of $\mathcal{O}$ is encountered. The task is to determine the line equation for each occurrence. Consider

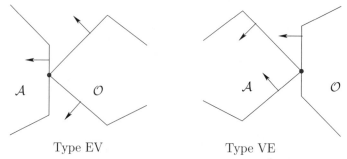

Type EV   Type VE

Figure 4.16: Two different types of contact, each of which generates a different kind of $\mathcal{C}_{obs}$ edge [282, 660].

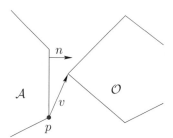

Figure 4.17: Contact occurs when n and v are perpendicular.

the case of a Type EV contact; the Type VE contact can be handled in a similar manner. In addition to the constraint on the directions of the edge normals, the contact vertex of $\mathcal{O}$ must lie on the contact edge of $\mathcal{A}$. Recall that convex obstacles were constructed by the intersection of half-planes. Each edge of $\mathcal{C}_{obs}$ can be defined in terms of a supporting half-plane; hence, it is only necessary to determine whether the vertex of $\mathcal{O}$ lies on the line through the contact edge of $\mathcal{A}$. This condition occurs precisely as n and v are perpendicular, as shown in Figure 4.17, and yields the constraint $n \cdot v = 0$.

Note that the normal vector n does not depend on the configuration of $\mathcal{A}$ because the robot cannot rotate. The vector v, however, depends on the translation $q = (x_t, y_t)$ of the point p. Therefore, it is more appropriate to write the condition as $n \cdot v(x_t, y_t) = 0$. The transformation equations are linear for translation; hence, $n \cdot v(x_t, y_t) = 0$ is the equation of a line in $\mathcal{C}$. For example, if the coordinates of p are $(1, 2)$ for $\mathcal{A}(0, 0)$, then the expression for p at configuration (x_t, y_t) is $(1 + x_t, 2 + y_t)$. Let $f(x_t, y_t) = n \cdot v(x_t, y_t)$. Let $H = \{(x_t, y_t) \in \mathcal{C} \mid f(x_t, y_t) \leq 0\}$. Observe that any configurations not in H must lie in $\mathcal{C}_{free}$. The half-plane H is used to define one edge of $\mathcal{C}_{obs}$. The obstacle region $\mathcal{C}_{obs}$ can be completely characterized by intersecting the resulting half-planes for each of the Type EV and Type VE contacts. This yields a convex polygon in $\mathcal{C}$ that has $n + m$ sides, as expected.

Example 4.15 (The Boundary of $\mathcal{C}_{obs}$) Consider building a geometric model of $\mathcal{C}_{obs}$ for the robot and obstacle shown in Figure 4.18. Suppose that the orientation of $\mathcal{A}$ is fixed as shown, and $\mathcal{C} = \mathbb{R}^2$. In this case, $\mathcal{C}_{obs}$ will be a convex polygon with seven sides. The contact conditions that occur are shown in Figure 4.19. The ordering as the normals appear around $\mathbb{S}^1$ (using inward edge normals for $\mathcal{A}$ and outward edge normals for $\mathcal{O}$). The $\mathcal{C}_{obs}$ edges and their corresponding contact types are shown in Figure 4.19. ∎

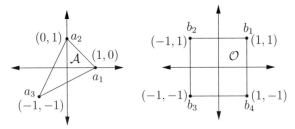

Figure 4.18: Consider constructing the obstacle region for this example.

Type	Vtx.	Edge	n	v	Half-Plane
VE	a_3	b_4-b_1	$[1,0]$	$[x_t - 2, y_t]$	$\{q \in \mathcal{C} \mid x_t - 2 \le 0\}$
VE	a_3	b_1-b_2	$[0,1]$	$[x_t - 2, y_t - 2]$	$\{q \in \mathcal{C} \mid y_t - 2 \le 0\}$
EV	b_2	a_3-a_1	$[1,-2]$	$[-x_t, 2 - y_t]$	$\{q \in \mathcal{C} \mid -x_t + 2y_t - 4 \le 0\}$
VE	a_1	b_2-b_3	$[-1,0]$	$[2 + x_t, y_t - 1]$	$\{q \in \mathcal{C} \mid -x_t - 2 \le 0\}$
EV	b_3	a_1-a_2	$[1,1]$	$[-1 - x_t, -y_t]$	$\{q \in \mathcal{C} \mid -x_t - y_t - 1 \le 0\}$
VE	a_2	b_3-b_4	$[0,-1]$	$[x_t + 1, y_t + 2]$	$\{q \in \mathcal{C} \mid -y_t - 2 \le 0\}$
EV	b_4	a_2-a_3	$[-2,1]$	$[2 - x_t, -y_t]$	$\{q \in \mathcal{C} \mid 2x_t - y_t - 4 \le 0\}$

Figure 4.19: The various contact conditions are shown in the order as the edge normals appear around $\mathbb{S}^1$ (using inward normals for $\mathcal{A}$ and outward normals for $\mathcal{O}$).

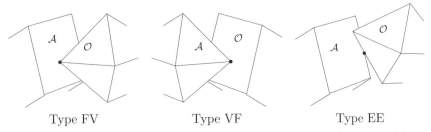

Type FV   Type VF   Type EE

Figure 4.20: Three different types of contact, each of which generates a different kind of $\mathcal{C}_{obs}$ face.

A polyhedral C-space obstacle

Most of the previous ideas generalize nicely for the case of a polyhedral robot that is capable of translation only in a 3D world that contains polyhedral obstacles. If $\mathcal{A}$ and $\mathcal{O}$ are convex polyhedra, the resulting $\mathcal{C}_{obs}$ is a convex polyhedron.

There are three different kinds of contacts that each lead to half-spaces in $\mathcal{C}$:

1. **Type FV:** A face of $\mathcal{A}$ and a vertex of $\mathcal{O}$

2. **Type VF:** A vertex of $\mathcal{A}$ and a face of $\mathcal{O}$

3. **Type EE:** An edge of $\mathcal{A}$ and an edge of $\mathcal{O}$.

These are shown in Figure 4.20. Each half-space defines a face of the polyhedron, $\mathcal{C}_{obs}$. The representation of $\mathcal{C}_{obs}$ can be constructed in $O(n + m + k)$ time, in which n is the number of faces of $\mathcal{A}$, m is the number of faces of $\mathcal{O}$, and k is the number of faces of $\mathcal{C}_{obs}$, which is at most nm [414].

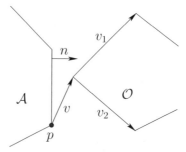

Figure 4.21: An illustration to help in constructing $\mathcal{C}_{obs}$ when rotation is allowed.

4.3.3 Explicitly modeling $\mathcal{C}_{obs}$: The general case

Unfortunately, the cases in which $\mathcal{C}_{obs}$ is polygonal or polyhedral are quite limited. Most problems yield extremely complicated C-space obstacles. One good point is that $\mathcal{C}_{obs}$ can be expressed using semi-algebraic models, for any robots and obstacles defined using semi-algebraic models, even after applying any of the transformations from Sections 3.2 to 3.4. It might not be true, however, for other kinds of transformations, such as warping a flexible material [32, 580].

Consider the case of a convex polygonal robot and a convex polygonal obstacle in a 2D world. Assume that any transformation in $SE(2)$ may be applied to $\mathcal{A}$; thus, $\mathcal{C} = \mathbb{R}^2 \times \mathbb{S}^1$ and $q = (x_t, y_t, \theta)$. The task is to define a set of algebraic primitives that can be combined to define $\mathcal{C}_{obs}$. Once again, it is important to distinguish between Type EV and Type VE contacts. Consider how to construct the algebraic primitives for the Type EV contacts; Type VE can be handled in a similar manner.

For the translation-only case, we were able to determine all of the Type EV contacts by sorting the edge normals. With rotation, the ordering of edge normals depends on θ. This implies that the applicability of a Type EV contact depends on θ, the robot orientation. Recall the constraint that the inward normal of $\mathcal{A}$ must point between the outward normals of the edges of $\mathcal{O}$ that contain the vertex of contact, as shown in Figure 4.21. This constraint can be expressed in terms of inner products using the vectors v_1 and v_2. The statement regarding the directions of the normals can equivalently be formulated as the statement that the angle between n and v_1, and between n and v_2, must each be less than $\pi/2$. Using inner products, this implies that $n \cdot v_1 \geq 0$ and $n \cdot v_2 \geq 0$. As in the translation case, the condition $n \cdot v = 0$ is required for contact. Observe that n now depends on θ. For any $q \in \mathcal{C}$, if $n(\theta) \cdot v_1 \geq 0$, $n(\theta) \cdot v_2 \geq 0$, and $n(\theta) \cdot v(q) > 0$, then $q \in \mathcal{C}_{free}$. Let H_f denote the set of configurations that satisfy these conditions. These conditions imply that a point is in $\mathcal{C}_{free}$. Furthermore, any other Type EV and Type VE contacts could imply that more points are in $\mathcal{C}_{free}$. Ordinarily, $H_f \subset \mathcal{C}_{free}$, which implies that the complement, $\mathcal{C} \setminus H_f$, is a superset of $\mathcal{C}_{obs}$ (thus, $\mathcal{C}_{obs} \subset \mathcal{C} \setminus H_f$). Let $H_A = \mathcal{C} \setminus H_f$. Using the primitives

$$H_1 = \{q \in \mathcal{C} \mid n(\theta) \cdot v_1 \leq 0\}, \tag{4.39}$$

$$H_2 = \{q \in \mathcal{C} \mid n(\theta) \cdot v_2 \leq 0\}, \tag{4.40}$$

and

$$H_3 = \{q \in \mathcal{C} \mid n(\theta) \cdot v(q) \leq 0\}, \tag{4.41}$$

let $H_A = H_1 \cup H_2 \cup H_3$.

It is known that $\mathcal{C}_{obs} \subseteq H_A$, but H_A may contain points in $\mathcal{C}_{free}$. The situation is similar to what was explained in Section 3.1.1 for building a model of a convex polygon from half-planes. In the current setting, it is only known that any configuration outside of H_A must be in $\mathcal{C}_{free}$. If H_A is intersected with all other corresponding sets for each possible Type EV and Type VE contact, then the result is $\mathcal{C}_{obs}$. Each contact has the opportunity to remove a portion of $\mathcal{C}_{free}$ from consideration. Eventually, enough pieces of $\mathcal{C}_{free}$ are removed so that the only configurations remaining must lie in $\mathcal{C}_{obs}$. For any Type EV contact, $(H_1 \cup H_2) \setminus H_3 \subseteq \mathcal{C}_{free}$. A similar statement can be made for Type VE contacts. A logical predicate, similar to that defined in Section 3.1.1, can be constructed to determine whether $q \in \mathcal{C}_{obs}$ in time that is linear in the number of $\mathcal{C}_{obs}$ primitives.

One important issue remains. The expression $n(\theta)$ is not a polynomial because of the $\cos \theta$ and $\sin \theta$ terms in the rotation matrix of $SO(2)$. If polynomials could be substituted for these expressions, then everything would be fixed because the expression of the normal vector (not a unit normal) and the inner product are both linear functions, thereby transforming polynomials into polynomials. Such a substitution can be made using stereographic projection (see [591]); however, a simpler approach is to use complex numbers to represent rotation. Recall that when $a + bi$ is used to represent rotation, each rotation matrix in $SO(2)$ is represented as (4.18), and the 3×3 homogeneous transformation matrix becomes

$$T(a, b, x_t, y_t) = \begin{pmatrix} a & -b & x_t \\ b & a & y_t \\ 0 & 0 & 1 \end{pmatrix}. \tag{4.42}$$

Using this matrix to transform a point $[x \ y \ 1]$ results in the point coordinates $(ax - by + x_t, bx + ay + y_t)$. Thus, any transformed point on $\mathcal{A}$ is a linear function of a, b, x_t, and y_t.

This was a simple trick to make a nice, linear function, but what was the cost? The dependency is now on a and b instead of θ. This appears to increase the dimension of $\mathcal{C}$ from 3 to 4, and $\mathcal{C} = \mathbb{R}^4$. However, an algebraic primitive must be added that constrains a and b to lie on the unit circle.

By using complex numbers, primitives in $\mathbb{R}^4$ are obtained for each Type EV and Type VE contact. By defining $\mathcal{C} = \mathbb{R}^4$, the following algebraic primitives are obtained for a Type EV contact:

$$H_1 = \{(x_t, y_t, a, b) \in \mathcal{C} \mid n(x_t, y_t, a, b) \cdot v_1 \leq 0\}, \tag{4.43}$$

$$H_2 = \{(x_t, y_t, a, b) \in \mathcal{C} \mid n(x_t, y_t, a, b) \cdot v_2 \leq 0\}, \tag{4.44}$$

and

$$H_3 = \{(x_t, y_t, a, b) \in \mathcal{C} \mid n(x_t, y_t, a, b) \cdot v(x_t, y_t, a, b) \leq 0\}. \tag{4.45}$$

This yields $H_A = H_1 \cup H_2 \cup H_3$. To preserve the correct $\mathbb{R}^2 \times \mathbb{S}^1$ topology of $\mathcal{C}$, the set

$$H_s = \{(x_t, y_t, a, b) \in \mathcal{C} \mid a^2 + b^2 - 1 = 0\} \tag{4.46}$$

is intersected with H_A. The set H_s remains fixed over all Type EV and Type VE contacts; therefore, it only needs to be considered once.

Example 4.16 (A Nonlinear Boundary for $\mathcal{C}_{obs}$) Consider adding rotation to the model described in Example 4.15. In this case, all possible contacts between pairs of edges must be considered. For this example, there are 12 Type EV contacts and 12 Type VE contacts. Each contact produces 3 algebraic primitives. With the inclusion of H_s, this simple example produces 73 primitives! Rather than construct all of these, we derive the primitives for a single contact. Consider the Type VE contact between a_3 and b_4-b_1. The outward edge normal n remains fixed at $n = [1, 0]$. The vectors v_1 and v_2 are derived from the edges adjacent to a_3, which are a_3-a_2 and a_3-a_1. Note that each of a_1, a_2, and a_3 depend on the configuration. Using the 2D homogeneous transformation (3.35), a_1 at configuration (x_t, y_t, θ) is $(\cos\theta + x_t, \sin\theta + y_t)$. Using $a + bi$ to represent rotation, the expression of a_1 becomes $(a + x_t, b + y_t)$. The expressions of a_2 and a_3 are $(-b + x_t, a + y_t)$ and $(-a + b + x_t, -b - a + y_t)$, respectively. It follows that $v_1 = a_2 - a_3 = [a - 2b, 2a + b]$ and $v_2 = a_1 - a_3 = [2a - b, a + 2b]$. Note that v_1 and v_2 depend only on the orientation of $\mathcal{A}$, as expected. Assume that v is drawn from b_4 to a_3. This yields $v = a_3 - b_4 = [-a + b + x_t - 1, -a - b + y_t + 1]$. The inner products $v_1 \cdot n$, $v_2 \cdot n$, and $v \cdot n$ can easily be computed to form H_1, H_2, and H_3 as algebraic primitives.

One interesting observation can be made here. The only nonlinear primitive is $a^2 + b^2 = 1$. Therefore, $\mathcal{C}_{obs}$ can be considered as a linear polytope (like a polyhedron, but one dimension higher) in $\mathbb{R}^4$ that is intersected with a cylinder.   ■

3D rigid bodies

For the case of a 3D rigid body to which any transformation in $SE(3)$ may be applied, the same general principles apply. The quaternion parameterization once again becomes the right way to represent $SO(3)$ because using (4.20) avoids all trigonometric functions in the same way that (4.18) avoided them for $SO(2)$. Unfortunately, (4.20) is not linear in the configuration variables, as it was for (4.18), but it is at least polynomial. This enables semi-algebraic models to be formed for $\mathcal{C}_{obs}$. Type FV, VF, and EE contacts arise for the $SE(3)$ case. From all of the contact conditions, polynomials that correspond to each patch of $\mathcal{C}_{obs}$ can be made. These patches are polynomials in seven variables: x_t, y_t, z_t, a, b, c, and d. Once again, a special primitive must be intersected with all others; here, it enforces the constraint that unit quaternions are used. This reduces the dimension from 7 back down to 6. Also, constraints should be added to throw away half of $\mathbb{S}^3$, which is redundant because of the identification of antipodal points on $\mathbb{S}^3$.

Chains and trees of bodies

For chains and trees of bodies, the ideas are conceptually the same, but the algebra becomes more cumbersome. Recall that the transformation for each link is obtained by a product of homogeneous transformation matrices, as given in (3.53) and (3.57) for the 2D and 3D cases, respectively. If the rotation part is parameterized using complex numbers for $SO(2)$ or quaternions for $SO(3)$, then each matrix consists of polynomial entries. After the matrix product is formed, polynomial expressions in terms of the configuration variables are obtained. Therefore, a semi-algebraic model can be constructed. For each link, all of the contact types need to be considered. Extrapolating from Examples 4.15 and 4.16, you can imagine that no human would ever want to do all of that by hand, but it can at least be automated. The ability to construct this representation automatically is also very important for the existence of theoretical algorithms that solve the motion planning problem combinatorially; see Section 6.4.

If the kinematic chains were formulated for $\mathcal{W} = \mathbb{R}^3$ using the DH parameterization, it may be inconvenient to convert to the quaternion representation. One way to avoid this is to use complex numbers to represent each of the θ_i and α_i variables that appear as configuration variables. This can be accomplished because only cos and sin functions appear in the transformation matrices. They can be replaced by the real and imaginary parts, respectively, of a complex number. The dimension will be increased, but this will be appropriately reduced after imposing the constraints that all complex numbers must have unit magnitude.

4.4 Closed kinematic chains

This section continues the discussion from Section 3.4. Suppose that a collection of links is arranged in a way that forms loops. In this case, the C-space becomes much more complicated because the joint angles must be chosen to ensure that the loops remain closed. This leads to constraints such as that shown in (3.80) and Figure 3.26, in which some links must maintain specified positions relative to each other. Consider the set of all configurations that satisfy such constraints. Is this a manifold? It turns out, unfortunately, that the answer is generally *no*. However, the C-space belongs to a nice family of spaces from algebraic geometry called *varieties*. Algebraic geometry deals with characterizing the solution sets of polynomials. As seen so far in this chapter, all of the kinematics can be expressed as polynomials. Therefore, it may not be surprising that the resulting constraints are a system of polynomials whose solution set represents the C-space for closed kinematic linkages. Although the algebraic varieties considered here need not be manifolds, they can be decomposed into a finite collection of manifolds that fit together nicely.[11]

Unfortunately, a parameterization of the variety that arises from closed chains is available in only a few simple cases. Even the topology of the variety is extremely difficult to characterize. To make matters worse, it was proved in [492] that for every closed, bounded real algebraic variety that can be embedded in $\mathbb{R}^n$, there exists a linkage whose C-space is homeomorphic to it. These troubles imply that most of the time, motion planning algorithms need to work directly with implicit polynomials. For the algebraic methods of Section 6.4.2, this does not pose any conceptual difficulty because the methods already work directly with polynomials. Sampling-based methods usually rely on the ability to efficiently sample configurations, which cannot be easily adapted to a variety without a parameterization. Section 7.4 covers recent methods that extend sampling-based planning algorithms to work for varieties that arise from closed chains.

4.4.1 Mathematical concepts

To understand varieties, it will be helpful to have definitions of polynomials and their solutions that are more formal than the presentation in Chapter 3.

Fields

Polynomials are usually defined over a *field*, which is another object from algebra. A field is similar to a group, but it has more operations and axioms. The definition is given below, and while reading it, keep in mind several familiar examples of fields: the rationals, $\mathbb{Q}$; the

---

[11] This is called a Whitney stratification [175, 968].

reals, $\mathbb{R}$; and the complex plane, $\mathbb{C}$. You may verify that these fields satisfy the following six axioms.

A *field* is a set $\mathbb{F}$ that has two binary operations, $\cdot : \mathbb{F} \times \mathbb{F} \to \mathbb{F}$ (called *multiplication*) and $+ : \mathbb{F} \times \mathbb{F} \to \mathbb{F}$ (called *addition*), for which the following axioms are satisfied:

1. **(Associativity)** For all $a, b, c \in \mathbb{F}$, $(a + b) + c = a + (b + c)$ and $(a \cdot b) \cdot c = a \cdot (b \cdot c)$.
2. **(Commutativity)** For all $a, b \in \mathbb{F}$, $a + b = b + a$ and $a \cdot b = b \cdot a$.
3. **(Distributivity)** For all $a, b, c \in \mathbb{F}$, $a \cdot (b + c) = a \cdot b + a \cdot c$.
4. **(Identities)** There exist $0, 1 \in \mathbb{F}$, such that $a + 0 = a \cdot 1 = a$ for all $a \in \mathbb{F}$.
5. **(Additive Inverses)** For every $a \in \mathbb{F}$, there exists some $b \in \mathbb{F}$ such that $a + b = 0$.
6. **(Multiplicative Inverses)** For every $a \in F$, except $a = 0$, there exists some $c \in \mathbb{F}$ such that $a \cdot c = 1$.

Compare these axioms to the group definition from Section 4.2.1. Note that a field can be considered as two different kinds of groups, one with respect to multiplication and the other with respect to addition. Fields additionally require commutativity; hence, we cannot, for example, build a field from quaternions. The distributivity axiom appears because there is now an interaction between two different operations, which was not possible with groups.

Polynomials

Suppose there are n variables, $x_1, x_2, \ldots, x_n$. A *monomial* over a field $\mathbb{F}$ is a product of the form

$$x_1^{d_1} \cdot x_2^{d_2} \cdot \cdots \cdot x_n^{d_n}, \tag{4.47}$$

in which all of the exponents $d_1, d_2, \ldots, d_n$ are positive integers. The *total degree* of the monomial is $d_1 + \cdots + d_n$.

A *polynomial* f in variables $x_1, \ldots, x_n$ with coefficients in $\mathbb{F}$ is a finite linear combination of monomials that have coefficients in $\mathbb{F}$. A polynomial can be expressed as

$$\sum_{i=1}^{m} c_i m_i, \tag{4.48}$$

in which m_i is a monomial as shown in (4.47), and $c_i \in \mathbb{F}$ is a *coefficient*. If $c_i \neq 0$, then each $c_i m_i$ is called a *term*. Note that the exponents d_i may be different for every term of f. The *total degree of* f is the maximum total degree among the monomials of the terms of f. The set of all polynomials in $x_1, \ldots, x_n$ with coefficients in $\mathbb{F}$ is denoted by $\mathbb{F}[x_1, \ldots, x_n]$.

Example 4.17 (Polynomials) The definitions correspond exactly to our intuitive notion of a polynomial. For example, suppose $\mathbb{F} = \mathbb{Q}$. An example of a polynomial in $\mathbb{Q}[x_1, x_2, x_3]$ is

$$x_1^4 - \tfrac{1}{2} x_1 x_2 x_3^3 + x_1^2 x_2^2 + 4. \tag{4.49}$$

Note that 1 is a valid monomial; hence, any element of $\mathbb{F}$ may appear alone as a term, such as the $4 \in \mathbb{Q}$ in the polynomial above. The total degree of (4.49) is 5 due to the second term. An equivalent polynomial may be written using nicer variables. Using x, y, and z as variables yields

$$x^4 - \tfrac{1}{2} xyz^3 + x^2 y^2 + 4, \tag{4.50}$$

which belongs to $\mathbb{Q}[x, y, z]$. ∎

The set $\mathbb{F}[x_1, \ldots, x_n]$ of polynomials is actually a group with respect to addition; however, it is not a field. Even though polynomials can be multiplied, some polynomials do not have a multiplicative inverse. Therefore, the set $\mathbb{F}[x_1, \ldots, x_n]$ is often referred to as a *commutative ring* of polynomials. A commutative ring is a set with two operations for which every axiom for fields is satisfied except the last one, which would require a multiplicative inverse.

Varieties

For a given field $\mathbb{F}$ and positive integer n, the n-dimensional *affine space* over $\mathbb{F}$ is the set

$$\mathbb{F}^n = \{(c_1, \ldots, c_n) \mid c_1, \ldots, c_n \in \mathbb{F}\}. \tag{4.51}$$

For our purposes in this section, an affine space can be considered as a vector space (for an exact definition, see [441]). Thus, $\mathbb{F}^n$ is like a vector version of the scalar field $\mathbb{F}$. Familiar examples of this are $\mathbb{Q}^n$, $\mathbb{R}^n$, and $\mathbb{C}^n$.

A polynomial in $f \in \mathbb{F}[x_1, \ldots, x_n]$ can be converted into a function,

$$f : \mathbb{F}^n \to \mathbb{F}, \tag{4.52}$$

by substituting elements of $\mathbb{F}$ for each variable and evaluating the expression using the field operations. This can be written as $f(a_1, \ldots, a_n) \in \mathbb{F}$, in which each a_i denotes an element of $\mathbb{F}$ that is substituted for the variable x_i.

We now arrive at an interesting question. For a given f, what are the elements of $\mathbb{F}^n$ such that $f(a_1, \ldots, a_n) = 0$? We could also ask the question for some nonzero element, but notice that this is not necessary because the polynomial may be redefined to formulate the question using 0. For example, what are the elements of $\mathbb{R}^2$ such that $x^2 + y^2 = 1$? This familiar equation for $\mathbb{S}^1$ can be reformulated to yield: What are the elements of $\mathbb{R}^2$ such that $x^2 + y^2 - 1 = 0$?

Let $\mathbb{F}$ be a field and let $\{f_1, \ldots, f_k\}$ be a set of polynomials in $\mathbb{F}[x_1, \ldots, x_n]$. The set

$$V(f_1, \ldots, f_k) = \{(a_1, \ldots, a_n) \in \mathbb{F} \mid f_i(a_1, \ldots, a_n) = 0 \text{ for all } 1 \le i \le k\} \tag{4.53}$$

is called the *(affine) variety* defined by $f_1, \ldots, f_k$. One interesting fact is that unions and intersections of varieties are varieties. Therefore, they behave like the semi-algebraic sets from Section 3.1.2, but for varieties only equality constraints are allowed. Consider the varieties $V(f_1, \ldots, f_k)$ and $V(g_1, \ldots, g_l)$. Their intersection is given by

$$V(f_1, \ldots, f_k) \cap V(g_1, \ldots, g_l) = V(f_1, \ldots, f_k, g_1, \ldots, g_l), \tag{4.54}$$

because each element of $\mathbb{F}^n$ must produce a 0 value for each of the polynomials in $\{f_1, \ldots, f_k, g_1, \ldots, g_l\}$.

To obtain unions, the polynomials simply need to be multiplied. For example, consider the varieties $V_1, V_2 \subset \mathbb{F}$ defined as

$$V_1 = \{(a_1, \ldots, a_n) \in \mathbb{F} \mid f_1(a_1, \ldots, a_n) = 0\} \tag{4.55}$$

and

$$V_2 = \{(a_1, \ldots, a_n) \in \mathbb{F} \mid f_2(a_1, \ldots, a_n) = 0\}. \tag{4.56}$$

The set $V_1 \cup V_2 \subset \mathbb{F}$ is obtained by forming the polynomial $f = f_1 f_2$. Note that $f(a_1, \ldots, a_n) = 0$ if either $f_1(a_1, \ldots, a_n) = 0$ or $f_2(a_1, \ldots, a_n) = 0$. Therefore, $V_1 \cup V_2$

is a variety. The varieties V_1 and V_2 were defined using a single polynomial, but the same idea applies to any variety. All pairs of the form $f_i g_j$ must appear in the argument of $V(\cdot)$ if there are multiple polynomials.

4.4.2 Kinematic chains in $\mathbb{R}^2$

To illustrate the concepts it will be helpful to study a simple case in detail. Let $\mathcal{W} = \mathbb{R}^2$, and suppose there is a chain of links, $\mathcal{A}_1, \ldots, \mathcal{A}_n$, as considered in Example 3.3 for $n = 3$. Suppose that the first link is attached at the origin of $\mathcal{W}$ by a revolute joint, and every other link, $\mathcal{A}_i$ is attached to $\mathcal{A}_{i-1}$ by a revolute joint. This yields the C-space

$$\mathcal{C} = \mathbb{S}^1 \times \mathbb{S}^1 \times \cdots \times \mathbb{S}^1 = \mathbb{T}^n, \tag{4.57}$$

which is the n-dimensional torus.

Two links

If there are three links, $\mathcal{A}_1$ and $\mathcal{A}_2$, then the C-space can be nicely visualized as a 3D cube with opposite faces identified. Each coordinate, θ_1 and θ_2, ranges from 0 to 2π, for which $0 \sim 2\pi$. Suppose that each link has length 1. This yields $a_1 = 1$. A point $(x, y) \in \mathcal{A}_2$ is transformed as

$$\begin{pmatrix} \cos\theta_1 & -\sin\theta_1 & 0 \\ \sin\theta_1 & \cos\theta_1 & 0 \\ 0 & 0 & 1 \end{pmatrix} \begin{pmatrix} \cos\theta_2 & -\sin\theta_2 & 1 \\ \sin\theta_2 & \cos\theta_2 & 0 \\ 0 & 0 & 1 \end{pmatrix} \begin{pmatrix} x \\ y \\ 1 \end{pmatrix}. \tag{4.58}$$

To obtain polynomials, the technique from Section 4.2.2 is applied to replace the trigonometric functions using $a_i = \cos\theta_i$ and $b_i = \sin\theta_i$, subject to the constraint $a_i^2 + b_i^2 = 1$. This results in

$$\begin{pmatrix} a_1 & -b_1 & 0 \\ b_1 & a_1 & 0 \\ 0 & 0 & 1 \end{pmatrix} \begin{pmatrix} a_2 & -b_2 & 1 \\ b_2 & a_2 & 0 \\ 0 & 0 & 1 \end{pmatrix} \begin{pmatrix} x \\ y \\ 1 \end{pmatrix}, \tag{4.59}$$

for which the constraints $a_i^2 + b_i^2 = 1$ for $i = 1, 2$ must be satisfied. This preserves the torus topology of $\mathcal{C}$, but now the C-space is embedded in $\mathbb{R}^4$. The coordinates of each point are $(a_1, b_1, a_2, b_2) \in \mathbb{R}^4$; however, there are only two degrees of freedom because each a_i, b_i pair must lie on a unit circle.

Multiplying the matrices in (4.59) yields the polynomials, $f_1, f_2 \in \mathbb{R}[a_1, b_1, a_2, b_2]$,

$$f_1 = x a_1 a_2 - y a_1 b_2 - x b_1 b_2 + y a_2 b_1 + a_1 \tag{4.60}$$

and

$$f_2 = -y a_1 a_2 + x a_1 b_2 + x a_2 b_1 - y b_1 b_2 + b_1, \tag{4.61}$$

for the x and y coordinates, respectively. Note that the polynomial variables are configuration parameters; x and y are not polynomial variables. For a given point $(x, y) \in \mathcal{A}_2$, all coefficients are determined.

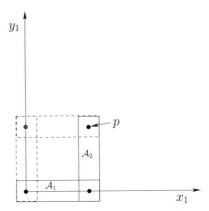

Figure 4.22: Two configurations hold the point p at $(1, 1)$.

A zero-dimensional variety

Now a kinematic closure constraint will be imposed. Fix the point $(1, 0)$ in the body frame of $\mathcal{A}_2$ at $(1, 1)$ in $\mathcal{W}$. This yields the constraints

$$f_1 = a_1 a_2 - b_1 b_2 + a_1 = 1 \qquad (4.62)$$

and

$$f_2 = a_1 b_2 + a_2 b_1 + b_1 = 1, \qquad (4.63)$$

by substituting $x = 1$ and $y = 0$ into (4.60) and (4.61). This yields the variety

$$V(a_1 a_2 - b_1 b_2 + a_1 - 1, a_1 b_2 + a_2 b_1 + b_1 - 1, a_1^2 + b_1^2 - 1, a_2^2 + b_2^2 - 1), \qquad (4.64)$$

which is a subset of $\mathbb{R}^4$. The polynomials are slightly modified because each constraint must be written in the form $f = 0$.

Although (4.64) represents the constrained configuration space for the chain of two links, it is not very explicit. Without an explicit characterization (i.e., a parameterization), it complicates motion planning. From Figure 4.22 it can be seen that there are only two solutions. These occur for $\theta_1 = 0$, $\theta_2 = \pi/2$ and $\theta_1 = \pi/2$, $\theta_2 = -\pi/2$. In terms of the polynomial variables, (a_1, b_1, a_2, b_2), the two solutions are $(1, 0, 0, 1)$ and $(0, 1, 0, -1)$. These may be substituted into each polynomial in (4.64) to verify that 0 is obtained. Thus, the variety represents two points in $\mathbb{R}^4$. This can also be interpreted as two points on the torus, $\mathbb{S}^1 \times \mathbb{S}^1$.

It might not be surprising that the set of solutions has dimension zero because there are four independent constraints, shown in (4.64), and four variables. Depending on the choices, the variety may be empty. For example, it is physically impossible to bring the point $(1, 0) \in \mathcal{A}_2$ to $(1000, 0) \in \mathcal{W}$.

A one-dimensional variety

The most interesting and complicated situations occur when there is a continuum of solutions. For example, if one of the constraints is removed, then a one-dimensional set of solutions can be obtained. Suppose only one variable is constrained for the example in Figure 4.22. Intuitively, this should yield a one-dimensional variety. Set the x coordinate to 0, which yields

$$a_1 a_2 - b_1 b_2 + a_1 = 0, \qquad (4.65)$$

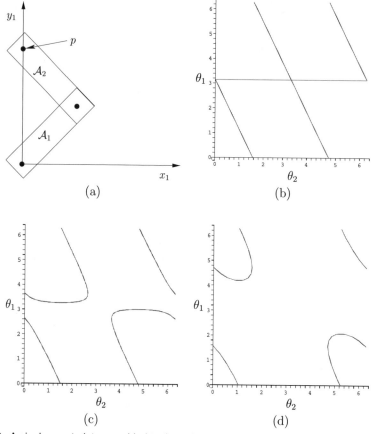

Figure 4.23: A single constraint was added to the point p on $\mathcal{A}_2$, as shown in (a). The curves in (b), (c), and (d) depict the variety for the cases of $f_1 = 0$, $f_1 = 1/8$, and $f_1 = 1$, respectively.

and allow any possible value for y. As shown in Figure 4.23a, the point p must follow the y-axis. (This is equivalent to a three-bar linkage that can be constructed by making a third joint that is prismatic and forced to stay along the y-axis.) Figure 4.23b shows the resulting variety $V(a_1 a_2 - b_1 b_2 + a_1)$ but plotted in $\theta_1 - \theta_2$ coordinates to reduce the dimension from 4 to 2 for visualization purposes. To correctly interpret the figures in Figure 4.23, recall that the topology is $\mathbb{S}^1 \times \mathbb{S}^1$, which means that the top and bottom are identified, and also the sides are identified. The center of Figure 4.23b, which corresponds to $(\theta_1, \theta_2) = (\pi, \pi)$, prevents the variety from being a manifold. The resulting space is actually homeomorphic to two circles that touch at a point. Thus, even with such a simple example, the nice manifold structure may disappear. Observe that at (π, π) the links are completely overlapped, and the point p of $\mathcal{A}_2$ is placed at $(0, 0)$ in $\mathcal{W}$. The horizontal line in Figure 4.23b corresponds to keeping the two links overlapping and swinging them around together by varying θ_1. The diagonal lines correspond to moving along configurations such as the one shown in Figure 4.23a. Note that the links and the y-axis always form an isosceles triangle, which can be used to show that the solution set is any pair of angles, θ_1, θ_2 for which $\theta_2 = \pi - \theta_1$. This is the reason why the diagonal curves in Figure 4.23b are linear. Figures 4.23c and 4.23d show the varieties for the constraints

$$a_1 a_2 - b_1 b_2 + a_1 = \tfrac{1}{8}, \qquad\qquad (4.66)$$

and

$$a_1 a_2 - b_1 b_2 + a_1 = 1, \tag{4.67}$$

respectively. In these cases, the point $(0, 1)$ in $\mathcal{A}_2$ must follow the $x = 1/8$ and $x = 1$ axes, respectively. The varieties are manifolds, which are homeomorphic to $\mathbb{S}^1$. The sequence from Figure 4.23b to 4.23d can be imagined as part of an animation in which the variety shrinks into a small circle. Eventually, it shrinks to a point for the case $a_1 a_2 - b_1 b_2 + a_1 = 2$, because the only solution is when $\theta_1 = \theta_2 = 0$. Beyond this, the variety is the empty set because there are no solutions. Thus, by allowing one constraint to vary, four different topologies are obtained: 1) two circles joined at a point, 2) a circle, 3) a point, and 4) the empty set.

Three links

Since visualization is still possible with one more dimension, suppose there are three links, $\mathcal{A}_1$, $\mathcal{A}_2$, and $\mathcal{A}_3$. The C-space can be visualized as a 3D cube with opposite faces identified. Each coordinate θ_i ranges from 0 to 2π, for which $0 \sim 2\pi$. Suppose that each link has length 1 to obtain $a_1 = a_2 = 1$. A point $(x, y) \in \mathcal{A}_3$ is transformed as

$$\begin{pmatrix} \cos\theta_1 & -\sin\theta_1 & 0 \\ \sin\theta_1 & \cos\theta_1 & 0 \\ 0 & 0 & 1 \end{pmatrix} \begin{pmatrix} \cos\theta_2 & -\sin\theta_2 & 10 \\ \sin\theta_2 & \cos\theta_2 & 0 \\ 0 & 0 & 1 \end{pmatrix} \begin{pmatrix} \cos\theta_3 & -\sin\theta_3 & 10 \\ \sin\theta_3 & \cos\theta_3 & 0 \\ 0 & 0 & 1 \end{pmatrix} \begin{pmatrix} x \\ y \\ 1 \end{pmatrix}. \tag{4.68}$$

To obtain polynomials, let $a_i = \cos\theta_i$ and $b_i = \sin\theta_i$, which results in

$$\begin{pmatrix} a_1 & -b_1 & 0 \\ b_1 & a_1 & 0 \\ 0 & 0 & 1 \end{pmatrix} \begin{pmatrix} a_2 & -b_2 & 1 \\ b_2 & a_2 & 0 \\ 0 & 0 & 1 \end{pmatrix} \begin{pmatrix} a_3 & -b_3 & 1 \\ b_3 & a_3 & 0 \\ 0 & 0 & 1 \end{pmatrix} \begin{pmatrix} x \\ y \\ 1 \end{pmatrix}, \tag{4.69}$$

for which the constraints $a_i^2 + b_i^2 = 1$ for $i = 1, 2, 3$ must also be satisfied. This preserves the torus topology of $\mathcal{C}$, but now it is embedded in $\mathbb{R}^6$. Multiplying the matrices yields the polynomials $f_1, f_2 \in \mathbb{R}[a_1, b_1, a_2, b_2, a_3, b_3]$, defined as

$$f_1 = 2a_1 a_2 a_3 - a_1 b_2 b_3 + a_1 a_2 - 2b_1 b_2 a_3 - b_1 a_2 b_3 + a_1, \tag{4.70}$$

and

$$f_2 = 2b_1 a_2 a_3 - b_1 b_2 b_3 + b_1 a_2 + 2a_1 b_2 a_3 + a_1 a_2 b_3, \tag{4.71}$$

for the x and y coordinates, respectively.

Again, consider imposing a single constraint,

$$2a_1 a_2 a_3 - a_1 b_2 b_3 + a_1 a_2 - 2b_1 b_2 a_3 - b_1 a_2 b_3 + a_1 = 0, \tag{4.72}$$

which constrains the point $(1, 0) \in \mathcal{A}_3$ to traverse the y-axis. The resulting variety is an interesting manifold, depicted in Figure 4.24 (remember that the sides of the cube are identified).

Increasing the required f_1 value for the constraint on the final point causes the variety to shrink. Snapshots for $f_1 = 7/8$ and $f_1 = 2$ are shown in Figure 4.25. At $f_1 = 1$, the variety is not a manifold, but it then changes to $\mathbb{S}^2$. Eventually, this sphere is reduced to a point at $f_1 = 3$, and then for $f_1 > 3$ the variety is empty.

Instead of the constraint $f_1 = 0$, we could instead constrain the y coordinate of p to obtain $f_2 = 0$. This yields another 2D variety. If both constraints are enforced simultaneously, then the result is the intersection of the two original varieties. For example, suppose $f_1 = 1$

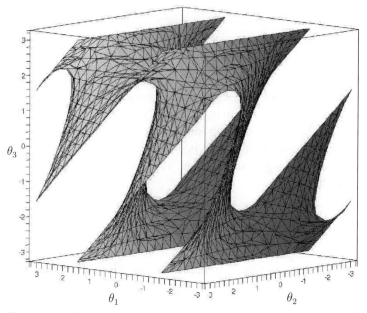

Figure 4.24: The variety for the three-link chain with $f_1 = 0$ is a 2D manifold.

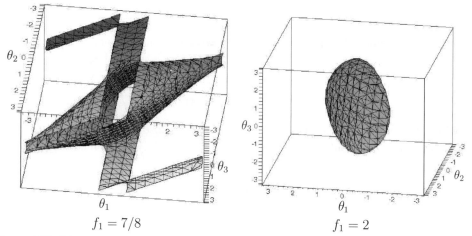

$$f_1 = 7/8 \qquad\qquad f_1 = 2$$

Figure 4.25: If $f_1 > 0$, then the variety shrinks. If $1 < p < 3$, the variety is a sphere. At $f_1 = 0$ it is a point, and for $f_1 > 3$ it completely vanishes.

and $f_2 = 0$. This is equivalent to a kind of *four-bar mechanism* [312], in which the fourth link, $\mathcal{A}_4$, is fixed along the x-axis from 0 to 1. The resulting variety,

$$V(2a_1a_2a_3 - a_1b_2b_3 + a_1a_2 - 2b_1b_2a_3 - b_1a_2b_3 + a_1 - 1,$$
$$2b_1a_2a_3 - b_1b_2b_3 + b_1a_2 + 2a_1b_2a_3 + a_1a_2b_3), \tag{4.73}$$

is depicted in Figure 4.26. Using the $\theta_1, \theta_2, \theta_3$ coordinates, the solution may be easily parameterized as a collection of line segments. For all $t \in [0, \pi]$, there exist solution points at $(0, 2t, \pi)$, $(t, 2\pi - t, \pi + t)$, $(2\pi - t, t, \pi - t)$, $(2\pi - t, \pi, \pi + t)$, and $(t, \pi, \pi - t)$. Note that once again the variety is not a manifold. A family of interesting varieties can be generated for the four-bar mechanism by selecting different lengths for the links. The topologies of these mechanisms have been determined for 2D and a 3D extension that uses spherical joints (see [701]).

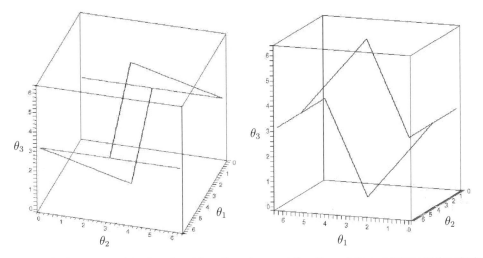

Figure 4.26: If two constraints, $f_1 = 1$ and $f_2 = 0$, are imposed, then the varieties are intersected to obtain a 1D set of solutions. The example is equivalent to a well-studied four-bar mechanism.

4.4.3 Defining the variety for general linkages

We now describe a general methodology for defining the variety. Keeping the previous examples in mind will help in understanding the formulation. In the general case, each constraint can be thought of as a statement of the form:

The ith coordinate of a point $p \in \mathcal{A}_j$ needs to be held at the value x in the body frame of $\mathcal{A}_k$.

For the variety in Figure 4.23b, the first coordinate of a point $p \in \mathcal{A}_2$ was held at the value 0 in $\mathcal{W}$ in the body frame of $\mathcal{A}_1$. The general form must also allow a point to be fixed with respect to the body frames of links other than $\mathcal{A}_1$; this did not occur for the example in Section 4.4.2

Suppose that n links, $\mathcal{A}_1, \ldots, \mathcal{A}_n$, move in $\mathcal{W} = \mathbb{R}^2$ or $\mathcal{W} = \mathbb{R}^3$. One link, $\mathcal{A}_1$ for convenience, is designated as the root as defined in Section 3.4. Some links are attached in pairs to form joints. A *linkage graph*, $\mathcal{G}(V, E)$, is constructed from the links and joints. Each vertex of $\mathcal{G}$ represents a link in L. Each edge in $\mathcal{G}$ represents a joint. This definition may seem somewhat backward, especially in the plane because links often look like edges and joints look like vertices. This alternative assignment is also possible, but it is not easy to generalize to the case of a single link that has more than two joints. If more than two links are attached at the same point, each generates an edge of $\mathcal{G}$.

The steps to determine the polynomial constraints that express the variety are as follows:

1. Define the linkage graph $\mathcal{G}$ with one vertex per link and one edge per joint. If a joint connects more than two bodies, then one body must be designated as a junction. See Figures 4.27 and 4.28a. In Figure 4.28, links 4, 13, and 23 are designated as junctions in this way.

2. Designate one link as the root, $\mathcal{A}_1$. This link may either be fixed in $\mathcal{W}$, or transformations may be applied. In the latter case, the set of transformations could be $SE(2)$ or $SE(3)$, depending on the dimension of $\mathcal{W}$. This enables the entire linkage to move independently of its internal motions.

3. Eliminate the loops by constructing a spanning tree T of the linkage graph, $\mathcal{G}$. This implies that every vertex (or link) is reachable by a path from the root). Any spanning tree may be used. Figure 4.28b shows a resulting spanning tree after deleting the edges shown with dashed lines.

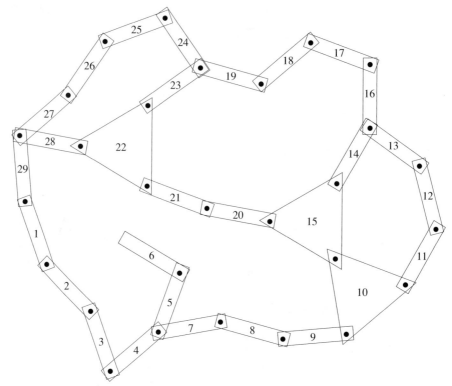

Figure 4.27: A complicated linkage that has 29 links, several loops, links with more than two bodies, and bodies with more than two links. Each integer i indicates link $\mathcal{A}_i$.

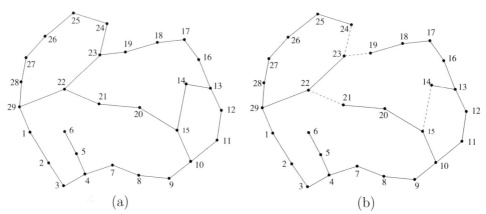

(a) (b)

Figure 4.28: (a) One way to make the linkage graph that corresponds to the linkage in Figure 4.27. (b) A spanning tree is indicated by showing the removed edges with dashed lines.

4. Apply the techniques of Section 3.4 to assign body frames and transformations to the resulting tree of links.

5. For each edge of $\mathcal{G}$ that does not appear in T, write a set of constraints between the two corresponding links. In Figure 4.28b, it can be seen that constraints are needed between four pairs of links: 14–15, 21–22, 23–24, and 19–23.

   This is perhaps the trickiest part. For examples like the one shown in Figure 3.27, the constraint may be formulated as in (3.81). This is equivalent to what was done to obtain the example in Figure 4.26, which means that there are actually two constraints, one for each of the x and y coordinates. This will also work for the example shown in Figure 4.27 if all joints are revolute. Suppose instead that two bodies, $\mathcal{A}_j$ and $\mathcal{A}_k$, must be rigidly attached. This requires adding one more constraint that prevents mutual rotation. This could be achieved by selecting another point on $\mathcal{A}_j$ and ensuring that one of its coordinates is in the correct position in the body frame of $\mathcal{A}_k$. If four equations are added, two from each point, then one of them would be redundant because there are only three degrees of freedom possible for $\mathcal{A}_j$ relative to $\mathcal{A}_k$ (which comes from the dimension of $SE(2)$).

A similar but more complicated situation occurs for $\mathcal{W} = \mathbb{R}^3$. Holding a single point fixed produces three constraints. If a single point is held fixed, then $\mathcal{A}_j$ may achieve any rotation in $SO(3)$ with respect to $\mathcal{A}_k$. This implies that $\mathcal{A}_j$ and $\mathcal{A}_k$ are attached by a spherical joint. If they are attached by a revolute joint, then two more constraints are needed, which can be chosen from the coordinates of a second point. If $\mathcal{A}_j$ and $\mathcal{A}_k$ are rigidly attached, then one constraint from a third point is needed. In total, however, there can be no more than six independent constraints because this is the dimension of $SE(3)$.

6. Convert the trigonometric functions to polynomials. For any 2D transformation, the familiar substitution of complex numbers may be made. If the DH parameterization is used for the 3D case, then each of the $\cos\theta_i$, $\sin\theta_i$ expressions can be parameterized with one complex number, and each of the $\cos\alpha_i$, $\sin\alpha_i$ expressions can be parameterized with another. If the rotation matrix for $SO(3)$ is directly used in the parameterization, then the quaternion parameterization should be used. In all of these cases, polynomial expressions are obtained.

7. List the constraints as polynomial equations of the form $f = 0$. To write the description of the variety, all of the polynomials must be set equal to zero, as was done for the examples in Section 4.4.2.

Is it possible to determine the dimension of the variety from the number of independent constraints? The answer is generally *no*, which can be easily seen from the chains of links in Section 4.4.2; they produced varieties of various dimensions, depending on the particular equations. Techniques for computing the dimension exist but require much more machinery than is presented here (see the literature overview at the end of the chapter). However, there is a way to provide a simple upper bound on the number of degrees of freedom. Suppose the total degrees of freedom of the linkage in spanning tree form is m. Each independent constraint can remove at most one degree of freedom. Thus, if there are l independent constraints, then the variety can have no more than $m - l$ dimensions. One expression of this for a general class of mechanisms is the Kutzbach criterion; the planar version of this is called Grübler's formula [312].

One final concern is the obstacle region, $\mathcal{C}_{obs}$. Once the variety has been identified, the obstacle region and motion planning definitions in (4.34) and Formulation 4.1 do not need to be changed. The configuration space $\mathcal{C}$ must be redefined, however, to be the set of configurations that satisfy the closure constraints.

Further reading

Section 4.1 introduced the basic definitions and concepts of topology. Further study of this fascinating subject can provide a much deeper understanding of configuration spaces. There are many books on topology, some of which may be intimidating, depending on your level of math training. For a heavily illustrated, gentle introduction to topology, see [538]. Another gentle introduction appears in [499]. An excellent text at the graduate level is available on-line: [442]. Other sources include [38, 454]. To understand the motivation for many technical definitions in topology, [912] is helpful. The manifold coverage in Section 4.1.2 was simpler than that found in most sources because most sources introduce *smooth manifolds*, which are complicated by differentiability requirements (these were not needed in this chapter); see Section 8.3.2 for smooth manifolds. For the configuration spaces of points moving on a topological graph, see [5].

Section 4.2 provided basic C-space definitions. For further reading on matrix groups and their topological properties, see [64], which provides a transition into more advanced material on Lie group theory. For more about quaternions in engineering, see [212, 566]. The remainder of Section 4.2 and most of Section 4.3 were inspired by the coverage in [591]. C-spaces are also covered in [222]. For further reading on computing representations of $\mathcal{C}_{obs}$, see [516, 739] for bitmaps, and Chapter 6 and [867] for combinatorial approaches.

Much of the presentation in Section 4.4 was inspired by the nice introduction to algebraic varieties in [252], which even includes robotics examples; methods for determining the dimension of a variety are also covered. More algorithmic coverage appears in [707]. See [696] for detailed coverage of robots that are designed with closed kinematic chains.

Exercises

1. Consider the set $X = \{1, 2, 3, 4, 5\}$. Let X, $\emptyset$, $\{1, 3\}$, $\{1, 2\}$, $\{2, 3\}$, $\{1\}$, $\{2\}$, and $\{3\}$ be the collection of all subsets of X that are designated as *open sets*.

   (a) Is X a topological space?

   (b) Is it a topological space if $\{1, 2, 3\}$ is added to the collection of open sets? Explain.

   (c) What are the closed sets (assuming $\{1, 2, 3\}$ is included as an open set)?

   (d) Are any subsets of X neither open nor closed?

2. Continuous functions for the strange topology:

   (a) Give an example of a continuous function, $f : X \to X$, for the strange topology in Example 4.4.

   (b) Characterize the set of all possible continuous functions.

3. For the letters of the Russian alphabet, А, Б, В, Г, Д, Е, Ё, Ж, З, И, Й, К, Л, М, Н, О, П, Р, С, Т, У, Ф, Х, Ц, Ч, Ш, Щ, Ъ, Ы, Ь, Э, Ю, Я, determine which pairs are homeomorphic. Imagine each as a 1D subset of $\mathbb{R}^2$ and draw them accordingly before solving the problem.

4. Prove that homeomorphisms yield an equivalence relation on the collection of all topological spaces.

5. What is the dimension of the C-space for a cylindrical rod that can translate and rotate in $\mathbb{R}^3$? If the rod is rotated about its central axis, it is assumed that the rod's position and orientation are not changed in any detectable way. Express the C-space of the rod in terms of a Cartesian product of simpler spaces (such as $\mathbb{S}^1$, $\mathbb{S}^2$, $\mathbb{R}^n$, P^2, etc.). What is your reasoning?

6. Let $\tau_1 : [0, 1] \to \mathbb{R}^2$ be a loop path that traverses the unit circle in the plane, defined as $\tau_1(s) = (\cos(2\pi s), \sin(2\pi s))$. Let $\tau_2 : [0, 1] \to \mathbb{R}^2$ be another loop path: $\tau_1(s) = (-2 + 3\cos(2\pi s), \frac{1}{2}\sin(2\pi s))$. This path traverses an ellipse that is centered at $(-2, 0)$. Show that τ_1 and τ_2 are homotopic (by constructing a continuous function with an additional parameter that "morphs" τ_1 into τ_2).

7. Prove that homotopy yields an equivalence relation on the set of all paths from some $x_1 \in X$ to some $x_2 \in X$, in which x_1 and x_2 may be chosen arbitrarily.

8. Determine the C-space for a spacecraft that can translate and rotate in a 2D *Asteroids*-style video game. The sides of the screen are identified. The top and bottom are also identified. There are no "twists" in the identifications.

9. Repeat the derivation of H_A from Section 4.3.3, but instead consider Type VE contacts.

10. Determine the C-space for a car that drives around on a huge sphere (such as the earth with no mountains or oceans). Assume the sphere is big enough so that its curvature may be neglected (e.g., the car rests flatly on the earth without wobbling). [Hint: It is not $\mathbb{S}^2 \times \mathbb{S}^1$.]

11. Suppose that A and O are each defined as equilateral triangles, with coordinates $(0, 0)$, $(2, 0)$, and $(1, \sqrt{3})$. Determine the C-space obstacle. Specify the coordinates of all of its vertices and indicate the corresponding contact type for each edge.

12. Show that (4.20) is a valid rotation matrix for all unit quaternions.

13. Show that $\mathbb{F}[x_1, \ldots, x_n]$, the set of polynomials over a field $\mathbb{F}$ with variables $x_1, \ldots, x_n$, is a group with respect to addition.

14. Quaternions:

    (a) Define a unit quaternion h_1 that expresses a rotation of $-\frac{\pi}{2}$ around the axis given by the vector $[\frac{1}{\sqrt{3}} \ \frac{1}{\sqrt{3}} \ \frac{1}{\sqrt{3}}]$.

    (b) Define a unit quaternion h_2 that expresses a rotation of π around the axis given by the vector $[0 \ 1 \ 0]$.

    (c) Suppose the rotation represented by h_1 is performed, followed by the rotation represented by h_2. This combination of rotations can be represented as a single rotation around an axis given by a vector. Find this axis and the angle of rotation about this axis.

15. What topological space is contributed to the C-space by a spherical joint that achieves any orientation except the identity?

16. Suppose five polyhedral bodies float freely in a 3D world. They are each capable of rotating and translating. If these are treated as "one" composite robot, what is the topology of the resulting C-space (assume that the bodies are *not* attached to each other)? What is its dimension?

17. Suppose a goal region $G \subseteq W$ is defined in the C-space by requiring that the *entire* robot is contained in G. For example, a car may have to be parked entirely within a space in a parking lot.

    (a) Give a definition of C_{goal} that is similar to (4.34) but pertains to containment of A inside of G.

    (b) For the case in which A and G are convex and polygonal, develop an algorithm for efficiently computing C_{goal}.

18. Figure 4.29a shows the Möbius band defined by identification of sides of the unit square. Imagine that scissors are used to cut the band along the two dashed lines. Describe the resulting topological space. Is it a manifold? Explain.

19. Consider Figure 4.29b, which shows the set of points in $\mathbb{R}^2$ that are remaining after a closed disc of radius $1/4$ with center (x, y) is removed for every value of (x, y) such that x and y are both integers.

    (a) Is the remaining set of points a manifold? Explain.

    (b) Now remove discs of radius 1 instead of $1/4$. Is a manifold obtained?

    (c) Finally, remove disks of radius $3/2$. Is a manifold obtained?

20. Show that the solution curves shown in Figure 4.26 correctly illustrate the variety given in (4.73).

21. Find the number of faces of C_{obs} for a cube and regular tetrahedron, assuming C is $SE(3)$. How many faces of each contact type are obtained?

22. Following the analysis matrix subgroups from Section 4.2, determine the dimension of $SO(4)$, the group of 4×4 rotation matrices. Can you characterize this topological space?

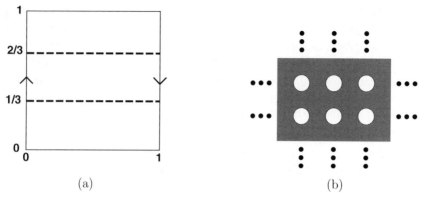

(a)   (b)

Figure 4.29: (a) What topological space is obtained after slicing the Möbius band? (b) Is a manifold obtained after tearing holes out of the plane?

23. Suppose that a kinematic chain of spherical joints is given. Show how to use (4.20) as the rotation part in each homogeneous transformation matrix, as opposed to using the DH parameterization. Explain why using (4.20) would be preferable for motion planning applications.

24. Suppose that the constraint that c is held to position $(10, 10)$ is imposed on the mechanism shown in Figure 3.29. Using complex numbers to represent rotation, express this constraint using polynomial equations.

25. The Tangle toy is made of 18 pieces of macaroni-shaped joints that are attached together to form a loop. Each attachment between joints forms a revolute joint. Each link is a curved tube that extends around $1/4$ of a circle. What is the dimension of the variety that results from maintaining the loop? What is its configuration space (accounting for internal degrees of freedom), assuming the toy can be placed anywhere in $\mathbb{R}^3$?

Implementations

26. Computing C-space obstacles:

    (a) Implement the algorithm from Section 4.3.2 to construct a convex, polygonal C-space obstacle.

    (b) Now allow the robot to rotate in the plane. For any convex robot and obstacle, compute the orientations at which the C-space obstacle fundamentally changes due to different Type EV and Type VE contacts becoming active.

    (c) Animate the changing C-space obstacle by using the robot orientation as the time axis in the animation.

27. Consider "straight-line" paths that start at the origin (lower left corner) of the manifolds shown in Figure 4.5 and leave at a particular angle, which is input to the program. The lines must respect identifications; thus, as the line hits the edge of the square, it may continue onward. Study the conditions under which the lines fill the entire space versus forming a finite pattern (i.e., a segment, stripes, or a tiling).

5

Sampling-Based Motion Planning

There are two main philosophies for addressing the motion planning problem, in Formulation 4.1 from Section 4.3.1. This chapter presents one of the philosophies, *sampling-based motion planning*, which is outlined in Figure 5.1. The main idea is to avoid the explicit construction of C_{obs}, as described in Section 4.3, and instead conduct a search that probes the C-space with a sampling scheme. This probing is enabled by a collision detection module, which the motion planning algorithm considers as a "black box." This enables the development of planning algorithms that are independent of the particular geometric models. The collision detection module handles concerns such as whether the models are semi-algebraic sets, 3D triangles, nonconvex polyhedra, and so on. This general philosophy has been very successful in recent years for solving problems from robotics, manufacturing, and biological applications that involve thousands and even millions of geometric primitives. Such problems would be practically impossible to solve using techniques that explicitly represent C_{obs}.

Notions of completeness

It is useful to define several notions of completeness for sampling-based algorithms. These algorithms have the drawback that they result in weaker guarantees that the problem will be solved. An algorithm is considered *complete* if for any input it correctly reports whether there is a solution in a finite amount of time. If a solution exists, it must return one in finite time. The combinatorial motion planning methods of Chapter 6 will achieve this. Unfortunately, such completeness is not achieved with sampling-based planning. Instead, weaker notions of completeness are tolerated. The notion of denseness becomes important, which means that the samples come arbitrarily close to any configuration as the number of iterations tends to infinity. A deterministic approach that samples densely will be called *resolution complete*. This means that if a solution exists, the algorithm will find it in finite time; however, if a solution does not exist, the algorithm may run forever. Many sampling-based approaches are based on random sampling, which is dense with probability one. This leads to algorithms that are *probabilistically complete*, which means that with enough points, the probability that it finds an existing solution converges to one. The most relevant information, however, is the rate of convergence, which is usually very difficult to establish.

Section 5.1 presents metric and measure space concepts, which are fundamental to nearly all sampling-based planning algorithms. Section 5.2 presents general sampling concepts and quality criteria that are effective for analyzing the performance of sampling-based algorithms. Section 5.3 gives a brief overview of collision detection algorithms, to gain an understanding of the information available to a planning algorithm and the computation price that must be paid to obtain it. Section 5.4 presents a framework that defines algorithms which solve motion planning problems by integrating sampling and discrete planning (i.e., searching) techniques. These approaches can be considered *single*

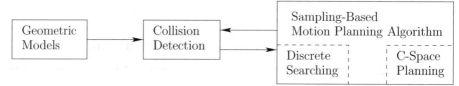

Figure 5.1: The sampling-based planning philosophy uses collision detection as a "black box" that separates the motion planning from the particular geometric and kinematic models. C-space sampling and discrete planning (i.e., searching) are performed.

query in the sense that a single pair, (q_I, q_G), is given, and the algorithm must search until it finds a solution (or it may report early failure). Section 5.5 focuses on *rapidly exploring random trees* (RRTs) and *rapidly exploring dense trees* (RDTs), which are used to develop efficient single-query planning algorithms. Section 5.6 covers *multiple-query* algorithms, which invest substantial preprocessing effort to build a data structure that is later used to obtain efficient solutions for many initial-goal pairs. In this case, it is assumed that the obstacle region $\mathcal{O}$ remains the same for every query.

5.1 Distance and volume in C-space

Virtually all sampling-based planning algorithms require a function that measures the distance between two points in $\mathcal{C}$. In most cases, this results in a *metric space*, which is introduced in Section 5.1.1. Useful examples for motion planning are given in Section 5.1.2. It will also be important in many of these algorithms to define the volume of a subset of $\mathcal{C}$. This requires a *measure space*, which is introduced in Section 5.1.3. Section 5.1.4 introduces invariant measures, which should be used whenever possible.

5.1.1 Metric spaces

It is straightforward to define Euclidean distance in $\mathbb{R}^n$. To define a distance function over any $\mathcal{C}$, however, certain axioms will have to be satisfied so that it coincides with our expectations based on Euclidean distance.

The following definition and axioms are used to create a function that converts a topological space into a metric space.[1] A *metric space* (X, ρ) is a topological space X equipped with a function $\rho : X \times X \to \mathbb{R}$ such that for any $a, b, c \in X$:

1. **Nonnegativity:** $\rho(a, b) \geq 0$.
2. **Reflexivity:** $\rho(a, b) = 0$ if and only if $a = b$.
3. **Symmetry:** $\rho(a, b) = \rho(b, a)$.
4. **Triangle inequality:** $\rho(a, b) + \rho(b, c) \geq \rho(a, c)$.

The function ρ defines distances between points in the metric space, and each of the four conditions on ρ agrees with our intuitions about distance. The final condition implies that ρ is optimal in the sense that the distance from a to c will always be less than or equal to

---

[1] Some topological spaces are not *metrizable*, which means that no function exists that satisfies the axioms. Many metrization theorems give sufficient conditions for a topological space to be metrizable [454], and virtually any space that has arisen in motion planning will be metrizable.

the total distance obtained by traveling through an intermediate point b on the way from a to c.

L_p metrics

The most important family of metrics over $\mathbb{R}^n$ is given for any $p \geq 1$ as

$$\rho(x, x') = \left(\sum_{i=1}^{n} |x_i - x_i'|^p \right)^{1/p}. \tag{5.1}$$

For each value of p, (5.1) is called an L_p *metric* (pronounced "el pee"). The three most common cases are

1. L_2: The *Euclidean metric*, which is the familiar Euclidean distance in $\mathbb{R}^n$.
2. L_1: The *Manhattan metric*, which is often nicknamed this way because in $\mathbb{R}^2$ it corresponds to the length of a path that is obtained by moving along an axis-aligned grid. For example, the distance from $(0, 0)$ to $(2, 5)$ is 7 by traveling "east two blocks" and then "north five blocks".
3. L_∞: The L_∞ *metric* must actually be defined by taking the limit of (5.1) as p tends to infinity. The result is

$$L_\infty(x, x') = \max_{1 \leq i \leq n} \{|x_i - x_i'|\}, \tag{5.2}$$

which seems correct because the larger the value of p, the more the largest term of the sum in (5.1) dominates.

An L_p metric can be derived from a norm on a vector space. An L_p *norm* over $\mathbb{R}^n$ is defined as

$$\|x\|_p = \left(\sum_{i=1}^{n} |x_i|^p \right)^{1/p}. \tag{5.3}$$

The case of $p = 2$ is the familiar definition of the magnitude of a vector, which is called the *Euclidean norm*. For example, assume the vector space is $\mathbb{R}^n$, and let $\| \cdot \|$ be the standard Euclidean norm. The L_2 metric is $\rho(x, y) = \|x - y\|$. Any L_p metric can be written in terms of a vector subtraction, which is notationally convenient.

Metric subspaces

By verifying the axioms, it can be shown that any subspace Y of a metric space (X, ρ) itself becomes a metric space by restricting the domain of ρ to Y. This conveniently provides metrics on any of the manifolds and varieties from Chapter 4 by simply using any L_p metric on $\mathbb{R}^m$, the space in which the manifold or variety is embedded.

Cartesian products of metric spaces

Metrics extend nicely across Cartesian products, which is very convenient because C-spaces are often constructed from Cartesian products, especially in the case of multiple bodies. Let (X, ρ_x) and (Y, ρ_y) be two metric spaces. A metric space (Z, ρ_z) can be constructed for the Cartesian product $Z = X \times Y$ by defining the metric ρ_z as

$$\rho_z(z, z') = \rho_z(x, y, x', y') = c_1 \rho_x(x, x') + c_2 \rho_y(y, y'), \tag{5.4}$$

in which $c_1 > 0$ and $c_2 > 0$ are any positive real constants, and $x, x' \in X$ and $y, y' \in Y$. Each $z \in Z$ is represented as $z = (x, y)$.

Other combinations lead to a metric for Z; for example,

$$\rho_z(z, z') = \Big(c_1\big[\rho_x(x, x')\big]^p + c_2\big[\rho_y(y, y')\big]^p\Big)^{1/p}, \qquad (5.5)$$

is a metric for any positive integer p. Once again, two positive constants must be chosen. It is important to understand that many choices are possible, and there may not necessarily be a "correct" one.

5.1.2 Important metric spaces for motion planning

This section presents some metric spaces that arise frequently in motion planning.

Example 5.1 ($SO(2)$ Metric Using Complex Numbers) If $SO(2)$ is represented by unit complex numbers, recall that the C-space is the subset of $\mathbb{R}^2$ given by $\{(a, b) \in \mathbb{R}^2 \mid a^2 + b^2 = 1\}$. Any L_p metric from $\mathbb{R}^2$ may be applied. Using the Euclidean metric,

$$\rho(a_1, b_1, a_2, b_2) = \sqrt{(a_1 - a_2)^2 + (b_1 - b_2)^2}, \qquad (5.6)$$

for any pair of points (a_1, b_1) and (a_2, b_2). ∎

Example 5.2 ($SO(2)$ Metric by Comparing Angles) You might have noticed that the previous metric for $SO(2)$ does not give the distance traveling along the circle. It instead takes a shortcut by computing the length of the line segment in $\mathbb{R}^2$ that connects the two points. This distortion may be undesirable. An alternative metric is obtained by directly comparing angles, θ_1 and θ_2. However, in this case special care has to be given to the identification, because there are two ways to reach θ_2 from θ_1 by traveling along the circle. This causes a min to appear in the metric definition:

$$\rho(\theta_1, \theta_2) = \min\big\{|\theta_1 - \theta_2|, 2\pi - |\theta_1 - \theta_2|\big\}, \qquad (5.7)$$

for which $\theta_1, \theta_2 \in [0, 2\pi]/\sim$. This may alternatively be expressed using the complex number representation $a + bi$ as an angle between two vectors:

$$\rho(a_1, b_1, a_2, b_2) = \cos^{-1}(a_1 a_2 + b_1 b_2), \qquad (5.8)$$

for two points (a_1, b_1) and (a_2, b_2). ∎

Example 5.3 (An $SE(2)$ Metric) Again by using the subspace principle, a metric can easily be obtained for $SE(2)$. Using the complex number representation of $SO(2)$, each element of $SE(2)$ is a point $(x_t, y_t, a, b) \in \mathbb{R}^4$. The Euclidean metric, or any other L_p metric on $\mathbb{R}^4$, can be immediately applied to obtain a metric. ∎

Example 5.4 ($SO(3)$ Metrics Using Quaternions) As usual, the situation becomes more complicated for $SO(3)$. The unit quaternions form a subset $\mathbb{S}^3$ of $\mathbb{R}^4$. Therefore, any L_p metric may be used to define a metric on $\mathbb{S}^3$, but this will not be a metric for $SO(3)$ because antipodal points need to be identified. Let $h_1, h_2 \in \mathbb{R}^4$ represent two unit quaternions (which are being interpreted here as elements of $\mathbb{R}^4$ by ignoring the quaternion algebra).

Taking the identifications into account, the metric is

$$\rho(h_1, h_2) = \min \{ \|h_1 - h_2\|, \|h_1 + h_2\| \}, \tag{5.9}$$

in which the two arguments of the min correspond to the distances from h_1 to h_2 and $-h_2$, respectively. The $h_1 + h_2$ appears because h_2 was negated to yield its antipodal point, $-h_2$.

As in the case of $SO(2)$, the metric in (5.9) may seem distorted because it measures the length of line segments that cut through the interior of $\mathbb{S}^3$, as opposed to traveling along the surface. This problem can be fixed to give a very natural metric for $SO(3)$, which is based on *spherical linear interpolation*. This takes the line segment that connects the points and pushes it outward onto $\mathbb{S}^3$. It is easier to visualize this by dropping a dimension. Imagine computing the distance between two points on $\mathbb{S}^2$. If these points lie on the equator, then spherical linear interpolation yields a distance proportional to that obtained by traveling along the equator, as opposed to cutting through the interior of $\mathbb{S}^2$ (for points not on the equator, use the *great circle* through the points).

It turns out that this metric can easily be defined in terms of the inner product between the two quaternions. Recall that for unit vectors v_1 and v_2 in $\mathbb{R}^n$, $v_1 \cdot v_2 = \cos \theta$, in which θ is the angle between the vectors. This angle is precisely what is needed to give the proper distance along $\mathbb{S}^3$. The resulting metric is a surprisingly simple extension of (5.8). The distance along $\mathbb{S}^3$ between two quaternions is

$$\rho_s(h_1, h_2) = \cos^{-1}(a_1 a_2 + b_1 b_2 + c_1 c_2 + d_1 d_2), \tag{5.10}$$

in which each $h_i = (a_i, b_i, c_i, d_i)$. Taking identification into account yields the metric

$$\rho(h_1, h_2) = \min \{ \rho_s(h_1, h_2), \rho_s(h_1, -h_2) \}. \tag{5.11}$$

■

Example 5.5 (Another $SE(2)$ Metric) For many C-spaces, the problem of relating different kinds of quantities arises. For example, any metric defined on $SE(2)$ must compare both distance in the plane and an angular quantity. For example, even if $c_1 = c_2 = 1$, the range for $\mathbb{S}^1$ is $[0, 2\pi)$ using radians but $[0, 360)$ using degrees. If the same constant c_2 is used in either case, two very different metrics are obtained. The units applied to $\mathbb{R}^2$ and $\mathbb{S}^1$ are completely incompatible. ■

Example 5.6 (Robot Displacement Metric) Sometimes this incompatibility problem can be fixed by considering the robot displacement. For any two configurations $q_1, q_2 \in \mathcal{C}$, a robot displacement metric can be defined as

$$\rho(q_1, q_2) = \max_{a \in \mathcal{A}} \{ \|a(q_1) - a(q_2)\| \}, \tag{5.12}$$

in which $a(q_i)$ is the position of the point a in the world when the robot $\mathcal{A}$ is at configuration q_i. Intuitively, the robot displacement metric yields the maximum amount in $\mathcal{W}$ that any part of the robot is displaced when moving from configuration q_1 to q_2. The difficulty and efficiency with which this metric can be computed depend strongly on the particular robot geometric model and kinematics. For a convex polyhedral robot that can translate and rotate, it is sufficient to check only vertices. The metric may appear to be ideal, but efficient algorithms are not known for most situations. ■

Example 5.7 ($\mathbb{T}^n$ Metrics) Next consider making a metric over a torus $\mathbb{T}^n$. The Cartesian product rules such as (5.4) and (5.5) can be extended over every copy of $\mathbb{S}^1$ (one for each parameter θ_i). This leads to n arbitrary coefficients $c_1, c_2, \ldots, c_n$. Robot displacement could be used to determine the coefficients. For example, if the robot is a chain of links, it might make sense to weight changes in the first link more heavily because the entire chain moves in this case. When the last parameter is changed, only the last link moves; in this case, it might make sense to give it less weight. ∎

Example 5.8 ($SE(3)$ Metrics) Metrics for $SE(3)$ can be formed by applying the Cartesian product rules to a metric for $\mathbb{R}^3$ and a metric for $SO(3)$, such as that given in (5.11). Again, this unfortunately leaves coefficients to be specified. These issues will arise again in Section 5.3.4, where more details appear on robot displacement. ∎

Pseudometrics

Many planning algorithms use functions that behave somewhat like a distance function but may fail to satisfy all of the metric axioms. If such distance functions are used, they will be referred to as *pseudometrics*. One general principle that can be used to derive pseudometrics is to define the distance to be the optimal cost-to-go for some criterion (recall discrete cost-to-go functions from Section 2.3). This will become more important when differential constraints are considered in Chapter 14.

In the continuous setting, the cost could correspond to the distance traveled by a robot or even the amount of energy consumed. Sometimes, the resulting pseudometric is not symmetric. For example, it requires less energy for a car to travel downhill as opposed to uphill. Alternatively, suppose that a car is only capable of driving forward. It might travel a short distance to go forward from q_1 to some q_2, but it might have to travel a longer distance to reach q_1 from q_2 because it cannot drive in reverse. These issues arise for the Dubins car, which is covered in Sections 13.1.2 and 15.3.1.

An important example of a pseudometric from robotics is a *potential function*, which is an important part of the randomized potential field method, which is discussed in Section 5.4.3. The idea is to make a scalar function that estimates the distance to the goal; however, there may be additional terms that attempt to repel the robot away from obstacles. This generally causes local minima to appear in the distance function, which may cause potential functions to violate the triangle inequality.

5.1.3 Basic measure theory definitions

This section briefly indicates how to define volume in a metric space. This provides a basis for defining concepts such as integrals or probability densities. Measure theory is an advanced mathematical topic that is well beyond the scope of this book; however, it is worthwhile to briefly introduce some of the basic definitions because they sometimes arise in sampling-based planning.

Measure can be considered as a function that produces real values for subsets of a metric space, (X, ρ). Ideally, we would like to produce a nonnegative value, $\mu(A) \in [0, \infty]$, for any subset $A \subseteq X$. Unfortunately, due to the Banach-Tarski paradox, if $X = \mathbb{R}^n$, there are some subsets for which trying to assign volume leads to a contradiction. If X is finite, this cannot happen. Therefore, it is hard to visualize the problem; see [839] for a construction of the bizarre nonmeasurable sets. Due to this problem, a workaround was developed by defining a collection of subsets that avoids the paradoxical sets. A collection $\mathcal{B}$ of subsets of X is called a *sigma algebra* if the following axioms are satisfied:

1. The empty set is in $\mathcal{B}$.
2. If $B \in \mathcal{B}$, then $X \setminus B \in \mathcal{B}$.
3. For any collection of a countable number of sets in $\mathcal{B}$, their union must also be in $\mathcal{B}$.

Note that the last two conditions together imply that the intersection of a countable number of sets in $\mathcal{B}$ is also in $\mathcal{B}$. The sets in $\mathcal{B}$ are called the *measurable sets*.

A nice sigma algebra, called the *Borel sets*, can be formed from any metric space (X, ρ) as follows. Start with the set of all open balls in X. These are the sets of the form

$$B(x, r) = \{x' \in X \mid \rho(x, x') < r\} \tag{5.13}$$

for any $x \in X$ and any $r \in (0, \infty)$. From the open balls, the *Borel sets* $\mathcal{B}$ are the sets that can be constructed from these open balls by using the sigma algebra axioms. For example, an open square in $\mathbb{R}^2$ is in $\mathcal{B}$ because it can be constructed as the union of a countable number of balls (infinitely many are needed because the curved balls must converge to covering the straight square edges). By using Borel sets, the nastiness of nonmeasurable sets is safely avoided.

Example 5.9 (Borel Sets) A simple example of $\mathcal{B}$ can be constructed for $\mathbb{R}$. The open balls are just the set of all open intervals, $(x_1, x_2) \subset \mathbb{R}$, for any $x_1, x_2 \in \mathbb{R}$ such that $x_1 < x_2$. ∎

Using $\mathcal{B}$, a *measure* μ is now defined as a function $\mu : \mathcal{B} \to [0, \infty]$ such that the *measure axioms* are satisfied:

1. For the empty set, $\mu(\emptyset) = 0$.
2. For any collection, $E_1, E_2, E_3, \ldots$, of a countable (possibly finite) number of pairwise disjoint, measurable sets, let E denote their union. The measure μ must satisfy

$$\mu(E) = \sum_i \mu(E_i), \tag{5.14}$$

in which i counts over the whole collection.

Example 5.10 (Lebesgue Measure) The most common and important measure is the *Lebesgue measure*, which becomes the standard notions of length in $\mathbb{R}$, area in $\mathbb{R}^2$, and volume in $\mathbb{R}^n$ for $n \geq 3$. One important concept with Lebesgue measure is the existence of sets of *measure zero*. For any countable set A, the Lebesgue measure yields $\mu(A) = 0$. For example, what is the total length of the point $\{1\} \subset \mathbb{R}$? The length of any single point must be zero. To satisfy the measure axioms, sets such as $\{1, 3, 4, 5\}$ must also have measure zero. Even infinite subsets such as $\mathbb{Z}$ and $\mathbb{Q}$ have measure zero in $\mathbb{R}$. If the dimension of a set $A \subseteq \mathbb{R}^n$ is m for some integer $m < n$, then $\mu(A) = 0$, according to the Lebesgue measure on $\mathbb{R}^n$. For example, the set $\mathbb{S}^2 \subset \mathbb{R}^3$ has measure zero because the sphere has no volume. However, if the measure space is restricted to $\mathbb{S}^2$ and then the surface area is defined, then nonzero measure is obtained. ∎

Example 5.11 (The Counting Measure) If (X, ρ) is finite, then the *counting measure* can be defined. In this case, the measure can be defined over the entire power set of X.

For any $A \subset X$, the counting measure yields $\mu(A) = |A|$, the number of elements in A. Verify that this satisfies the measure axioms.   ∎

Example 5.12 (Probability Measure)   Measure theory even unifies discrete and continuous probability theory. The measure μ can be defined to yield probability mass. The probability axioms (see Section 9.1.2) are consistent with the measure axioms, which therefore yield a measure space. The integrals and sums needed to define expectations of random variables for continuous and discrete cases, respectively, unify into a single measure-theoretic integral.   ∎

Measure theory can be used to define very general notions of integration that are much more powerful than the Riemann integral that is learned in classical calculus. One of the most important concepts is the *Lebesgue integral*. Instead of being limited to partitioning the domain of integration into intervals, virtually any partition into measurable sets can be used. Its definition requires the notion of a *measurable function* to ensure that the function domain is partitioned into measurable sets. For further study, see [348, 549, 839].

5.1.4 Using the correct measure

Since many metrics and measures are possible, it may sometimes seem that there is no "correct" choice. This can be frustrating because the performance of sampling-based planning algorithms can depend strongly on these. Conveniently, there is a natural measure, called the Haar measure, for some transformation groups, including $SO(N)$. Good metrics also follow from the Haar measure, but unfortunately, there are still arbitrary alternatives.

The basic requirement is that the measure does not vary when the sets are transformed using the group elements. More formally, let G represent a matrix group with real-valued entries, and let μ denote a measure on G. If for any measurable subset $A \subseteq G$, and any element $g \in G$, $\mu(A) = \mu(gA) = \mu(Ag)$, then μ is called the *Haar measure*[2] for G. The notation gA represents the set of all matrices obtained by the product ga, for any $a \in A$. Similarly, Ag represents all products of the form ag.

Example 5.13 (Haar Measure for $SO(2)$)   The Haar measure for $SO(2)$ can be obtained by parameterizing the rotations as $[0, 1]/ \sim$ with 0 and 1 identified, and letting μ be the Lebesgue measure on the unit interval. To see the invariance property, consider the interval $[1/4, 1/2]$, which produces a set $A \subset SO(2)$ of rotation matrices. This corresponds to the set of all rotations from $\theta = \pi/2$ to $\theta = \pi$. The measure yields $\mu(A) = 1/4$. Now consider multiplying every matrix $a \in A$ by a rotation matrix, $g \in SO(2)$, to yield Ag. Suppose g is the rotation matrix for $\theta = \pi$. The set Ag is the set of all rotation matrices from $\theta = 3\pi/2$ up to $\theta = 2\pi = 0$. The measure $\mu(Ag) = 1/4$ remains unchanged. Invariance for gA may be checked similarly. The transformation g translates the intervals in $[0, 1]/ \sim$. Since the measure is based on interval lengths, it is invariant with respect to translation. Note that μ can be multiplied by a fixed constant (such as 2π) without affecting the invariance property.

An invariant metric can be defined from the Haar measure on $SO(2)$. For any points $x_1, x_2 \in [0, 1]$, let $\rho = \mu([x_1, x_2])$, in which $[x_1, x_2]$ is the shortest length (smallest

---

[2] Such a measure is unique up to scale and exists for any locally compact topological group [348, 839].

measure) interval that contains x_1 and x_2 as endpoints. This metric was already given in Example 5.2.

To obtain examples that are not the Haar measure, let μ represent probability mass over $[0, 1]$ and define any nonuniform probability density function (the uniform density yields the Haar measure). Any shifting of intervals will change the probability mass, resulting in a different measure.

Failing to use the Haar measure weights some parts of $SO(2)$ more heavily than others. Sometimes imposing a bias may be desirable, but it is at least as important to know how to eliminate bias. These ideas may appear obvious, but in the case of $SO(3)$ and many other groups it is more challenging to eliminate this bias and obtain the Haar measure. ∎

Example 5.14 (Haar Measure for $SO(3)$) For $SO(3)$ it turns out once again that quaternions come to the rescue. If unit quaternions are used, recall that $SO(3)$ becomes parameterized in terms of $\mathbb{S}^3$, but opposite points are identified. It can be shown that the surface area on $\mathbb{S}^3$ is the Haar measure. (Since $\mathbb{S}^3$ is a 3D manifold, it may more appropriately be considered as a surface "volume.") It will be seen in Section 5.2.2 that uniform random sampling over $SO(3)$ must be done with a uniform probability density over $\mathbb{S}^3$. This corresponds exactly to the Haar measure. If instead $SO(3)$ is parameterized with Euler angles, the Haar measure will not be obtained. An unintentional bias will be introduced; some rotations in $SO(3)$ will have more weight than others for no particularly good reason. ∎

5.2 Sampling theory

5.2.1 Motivation and basic concepts

The state space for motion planning, $\mathcal{C}$, is uncountably infinite, yet a sampling-based planning algorithm can consider at most a countable number of samples. If the algorithm runs forever, this may be countably infinite, but in practice we expect it to terminate early after only considering a finite number of samples. This mismatch between the cardinality of $\mathcal{C}$ and the set that can be probed by an algorithm motivates careful consideration of sampling techniques. Once the sampling component has been defined, discrete planning methods from Chapter 2 may be adapted to the current setting. Their performance, however, hinges on the way the C-space is sampled.

Since sampling-based planning algorithms are often terminated early, the particular order in which samples are chosen becomes critical. Therefore, a distinction is made between a sample *set* and a sample *sequence*. A unique sample set can always be constructed from a sample sequence, but many alternative sequences can be constructed from one sample set.

Denseness

Consider constructing an infinite sample sequence over $\mathcal{C}$. What would be some desirable properties for this sequence? It would be nice if the sequence eventually reached every point in $\mathcal{C}$, but this is impossible because $\mathcal{C}$ is uncountably infinite. Strangely, it is still possible for a sequence to get arbitrarily close to every element of $\mathcal{C}$ (assuming $\mathcal{C} \subseteq \mathbb{R}^m$). In topology, this is the notion of denseness. Let U and V be any subsets of a topological space. The set U is said to be *dense* in V if $\text{cl}(U) = V$ (recall the closure of a set from Section 4.1.1). This means adding the boundary points to U produces V. A simple example is that $(0, 1) \subset \mathbb{R}$ is dense in $[0, 1] \subset \mathbb{R}$. A more interesting example is that the set $\mathbb{Q}$ of rational numbers is both countable and dense in $\mathbb{R}$. Think about why. For any real number, such as $\pi \in \mathbb{R}$, there exists a sequence of fractions that converges to it. This sequence of fractions must be a subset of $\mathbb{Q}$. A sequence (as opposed to a set) is called *dense* if its underlying set is dense. The bare minimum for sampling methods is that they produce a dense sequence. Stronger requirements, such as uniformity and regularity, will be explained shortly.

A random sequence is probably dense

Suppose that $C = [0, 1]$. One of the simplest ways conceptually to obtain a dense sequence is to pick points at random. Suppose $I \subset [0, 1]$ is an interval of length e. If k samples are chosen independently at random,[3] the probability that none of them falls into I is $(1 - e)^k$. As k approaches infinity, this probability converges to zero. This means that the probability that any nonzero-length interval in $[0, 1]$ contains no points converges to zero. One small technicality exists. The infinite sequence of independently, randomly chosen points is only dense *with probability one*, which is not the same as being guaranteed. This is one of the strange outcomes of dealing with uncountably infinite sets in probability theory. For example, if a number between $[0, 1]$ is chosen at random, the probably that $\pi/4$ is chosen is zero; however, it is still possible. (The probability is just the Lebesgue measure, which is zero for a set of measure zero.) For motion planning purposes, this technicality has no practical implications; however, if k is not very large, then it might be frustrating to obtain only probabilistic assurances, as opposed to absolute guarantees of coverage. The next sequence is guaranteed to be dense because it is deterministic.

The van der Corput sequence

A beautiful yet underutilized sequence was published in 1935 by van der Corput, a Dutch mathematician [952]. It exhibits many ideal qualities for applications. At the same time, it is based on a simple idea. Unfortunately, it is only defined for the unit interval. The quest to extend many of its qualities to higher dimensional spaces motivates the formal quality measures and sampling techniques in the remainder of this section.

To explain the van der Corput sequence, let $C = [0, 1]/ \sim$, in which $0 \sim 1$, which can be interpreted as $SO(2)$. Suppose that we want to place 16 samples in C. An ideal choice is the set $S = \{i/16 \mid 0 \le i < 16\}$, which evenly spaces the points at intervals of length $1/16$. This means that no point in C is further than $1/32$ from the nearest sample. What if we want to make S into a sequence? What is the best ordering? What if we are not even sure that 16 points are sufficient? Maybe 16 is too few or even too many.

The first two columns of Figure 5.2 show a naive attempt at making S into a sequence by sorting the points by increasing value. The problem is that after $i = 8$, half of C has been neglected. It would be preferable to have a nice covering of C for any i. Van der Corput's clever idea was to reverse the order of the bits, when the sequence is represented with binary decimals. In the original sequence, the most significant bit toggles only once,

---

[3] See Section 9.1.2 for a review of probability theory.

i	Naive Sequence	Binary	Reverse Binary	Van der Corput	Points in $[0,1]/\sim$
1	0	.0000	.0000	0	
2	1/16	.0001	.1000	1/2	
3	1/8	.0010	.0100	1/4	
4	3/16	.0011	.1100	3/4	
5	1/4	.0100	.0010	1/8	
6	5/16	.0101	.1010	5/8	
7	3/8	.0110	.0110	3/8	
8	7/16	.0111	.1110	7/8	
9	1/2	.1000	.0001	1/16	
10	9/16	.1001	.1001	9/16	
11	5/8	.1010	.0101	5/16	
12	11/16	.1011	.1101	13/16	
13	3/4	.1100	.0011	3/16	
14	13/16	.1101	.1011	11/16	
15	7/8	.1110	.0111	7/16	
16	15/16	.1111	.1111	15/16	

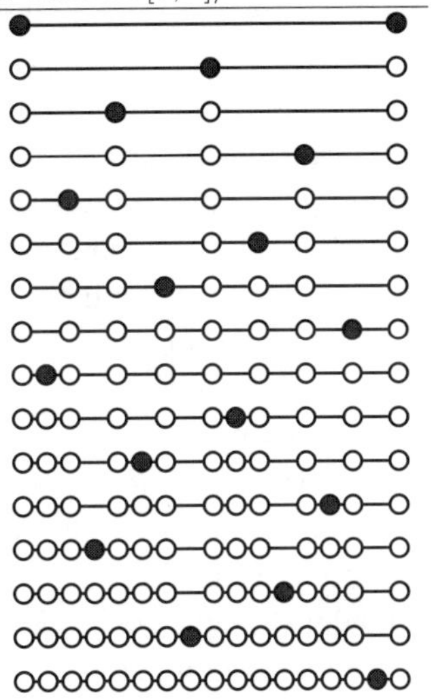

Figure 5.2: The van der Corput sequence is obtained by reversing the bits in the binary decimal representation of the naive sequence.

whereas the least significant bit toggles in every step. By reversing the bits, the most significant bit toggles in every step, which means that the sequence alternates between the lower and upper halves of $\mathcal{C}$. The third and fourth columns of Figure 5.2 show the original and reversed-order binary representations. The resulting sequence dances around $[0, 1]/\sim$ in a nice way, as shown in the last two columns of Figure 5.2. Let $\nu(i)$ denote the ith point of the van der Corput sequence.

In contrast to the naive sequence, each $\nu(i)$ lies far away from $\nu(i + 1)$. Furthermore, the first i points of the sequence, for any i, provide reasonably uniform coverage of $\mathcal{C}$. When i is a power of 2, the points are perfectly spaced. For other i, the coverage is still good in the sense that the number of points that appear in any interval of length l is roughly il. For example, when $i = 10$, every interval of length $1/2$ contains roughly 5 points.

The length, 16, of the naive sequence is actually not important. If instead 8 is used, the same $\nu(1), \ldots, \nu(8)$ are obtained. Observe in the reverse binary column of Figure 5.2 that this amounts to removing the last zero from each binary decimal representation, which does not alter their values. If 32 is used for the naive sequence, then the same $\nu(1), \ldots, \nu(16)$ are obtained, and the sequence continues nicely from $\nu(17)$ to $\nu(32)$. To obtain the van der Corput sequence from $\nu(33)$ to $\nu(64)$, six-bit sequences are reversed (corresponding to the case in which the naive sequence has 64 points). The process repeats to produce an infinite sequence that does not require a fixed number of points to be specified a priori. In addition to the nice uniformity properties for every i, the infinite van der Corput sequence is also dense in $[0, 1]/\sim$. This implies that every open subset must contain at least one sample.

You have now seen ways to generate nice samples in a unit interval both randomly and deterministically. Sections 5.2.2–5.2.4 explain how to generate dense samples with nice properties in the complicated spaces that arise in motion planning.

5.2.2 Random sampling

Now imagine moving beyond $[0, 1]$ and generating a dense sample sequence for any bounded C-space, $\mathcal{C} \subseteq \mathbb{R}^m$. In this section the goal is to generate *uniform random* samples. This means that the probability density function $p(q)$ over $\mathcal{C}$ is uniform. Wherever relevant, it also will mean that the probability density is also consistent with the Haar measure. We will not allow any artificial bias to be introduced by selecting a poor parameterization. For example, picking uniform random Euler angles does *not* lead to uniform random samples over $SO(3)$. However, picking uniform random unit quaternions works perfectly because quaternions use the same parameterization as the Haar measure; both choose points on $\mathbb{S}^3$.

Random sampling is the easiest of all sampling methods to apply to C-spaces. One of the main reasons is that C-spaces are formed from Cartesian products, and independent random samples extend easily across these products. If $X = X_1 \times X_2$, and uniform random samples x_1 and x_2 are taken from X_1 and X_2, respectively, then (x_1, x_2) is a uniform random sample for X. This is very convenient in implementations. For example, suppose the motion planning problem involves 15 robots that each translate for any $(x_t, y_t) \in [0, 1]^2$; this yields $\mathcal{C} = [0, 1]^{30}$. In this case, 30 points can be chosen uniformly at random from $[0, 1]$ and combined into a 30-dimensional vector. Samples generated this way are uniformly randomly distributed over $\mathcal{C}$. Combining samples over Cartesian products is much more difficult for nonrandom (deterministic) methods, which are presented in Sections 5.2.3 and 5.2.4.

Generating a random element of $SO(3)$

One has to be very careful about sampling uniformly over the space of rotations. The probability density must correspond to the Haar measure, which means that a random rotation should be obtained by picking a point at random on $\mathbb{S}^3$ and forming the unit quaternion. An extremely clever way to sample $SO(3)$ uniformly at random is given in [46] and is reproduced here. Choose three points $u_1, u_2, u_3 \in [0, 1]$ uniformly at random. A uniform, random quaternion is given by the simple expression

$$h = (\sqrt{1 - u_1} \sin 2\pi u_2, \ \sqrt{1 - u_1} \cos 2\pi u_2, \ \sqrt{u_1} \sin 2\pi u_3, \ \sqrt{u_1} \cos 2\pi u_3). \qquad (5.15)$$

A full explanation of the method is given in [46], and a brief intuition is given here. First drop down a dimension and pick $u_1, u_2 \in [0, 1]$ to generate points on $\mathbb{S}^2$. Let u_1 represent the value for the third coordinate, $(0, 0, u_1) \in \mathbb{R}^3$. The slice of points on $\mathbb{S}^2$ for which u_1 is fixed for $0 < u_1 < 1$ yields a circle on $\mathbb{S}^2$ that corresponds to some line of latitude on $\mathbb{S}^2$. The second parameter selects the longitude, $2\pi u_2$. Unfortunately, the points are not uniformly distributed over $\mathbb{S}^2$. Why? Imagine $\mathbb{S}^2$ as the crust on a spherical loaf of bread that is run through a bread slicer. The slices are cut in a direction parallel to the equator and are of equal thickness. The crusts of each slice do not have equal area; therefore, the points are not uniformly distributed. However, for $\mathbb{S}^3$, the 3D crusts happen to have the same area (or measure); this can be shown by evaluating surface integrals. This implies that a (infinitesimal) slice can be selected uniformly at random with u_1, and a point on the crust is selected uniformly at random by u_2 and u_3. For $\mathbb{S}^4$ and beyond, the measure of the crusts vary, which means this elegant scheme only works for $\mathbb{S}^3$. To respect the antipodal identification for rotations, any quaternion h found in the lower hemisphere (i.e., $a < 0$) can be negated to yield $-h$. This does not distort the uniform random distribution of the samples.

Generating random directions

Some sampling-based algorithms require choosing motion directions at random.[4] From a configuration q, the possible directions of motion can be imagined as being distributed around a sphere. In an $(n + 1)$-dimensional C-space, this corresponds to sampling on $\mathbb{S}^n$. For example, choosing a direction in $\mathbb{R}^2$ amounts to picking an element of $\mathbb{S}^1$; this can be parameterized as $\theta \in [0, 2\pi]/\sim$. If $n = 4$, then the previously mentioned trick for $SO(3)$ should be used. If $n = 3$ or $n > 4$, then samples can be generated using a slightly more expensive method that exploits spherical symmetries of the multidimensional Gaussian density function [343]. The method is explained for $\mathbb{R}^{n+1}$; boundaries and identifications must be taken into account for other spaces. For each of the $n + 1$ coordinates, generate a sample u_i from a zero-mean Gaussian distribution with the same variance for each coordinate. Following from the Central Limit Theorem, u_i can be approximately obtained by generating k samples at random over $[-1, 1]$ and adding them ($k \geq 12$ is usually sufficient in practice). The vector $(u_1, u_2, \dots, u_{n+1})$ gives a random direction in $\mathbb{R}^{n-1}$ because each u_i was obtained independently, and the level sets of the resulting probability density function are spheres. We did not use uniform random samples for each u_i because this would bias the directions toward the corners of a cube; instead, the Gaussian yields spherical symmetry. The final step is to normalize the vector by taking $u_i/\|u\|$ for each coordinate.

Pseudorandom number generation

Although there are advantages to uniform random sampling, there are also several disadvantages. This motivates the consideration of deterministic alternatives. Since there are trade-offs, it is important to understand how to use both kinds of sampling in motion planning. One of the first issues is that computer-generated numbers are not random.[5] A *pseudorandom number generator* is usually employed, which is a deterministic method that simulates the behavior of randomness. Since the samples are not truly random, the advantage of extending the samples over Cartesian products does not necessarily hold. Sometimes problems are caused by unforeseen deterministic dependencies. One of the best pseudorandom number generators for avoiding such troubles is the Mersenne twister [687], for which implementations can be found on the Internet.

To help see the general difficulties, the classical *linear congruential* pseudorandom number generator is briefly explained [622, 741]. The method uses three integer parameters, M, a, and c, which are chosen by the user. The first two, M and a, must be relatively prime, meaning that $\gcd(M, a) = 1$. The third parameter, c, must be chosen to satisfy $0 \leq c < M$. Using modular arithmetic, a sequence can be generated as

$$y_{i+1} = ay_i + c \mod M, \tag{5.16}$$

by starting with some arbitrary seed $1 \leq y_0 \leq M$. Pseudorandom numbers in $[0, 1]$ are generated by the sequence

$$x_i = y_i/M. \tag{5.17}$$

---

[4] The directions will be formalized in Section 8.3.2 when smooth manifolds are introduced. In that case, the directions correspond to the set of possible velocities that have unit magnitude. Presently, the notion of a direction is only given informally.

[5] There are exceptions, which use physical phenomena as a random source [811].

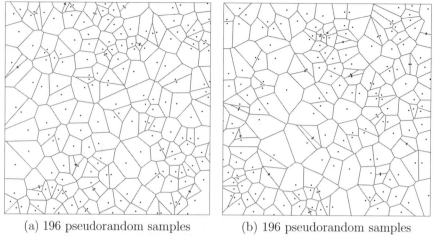

(a) 196 pseudorandom samples   (b) 196 pseudorandom samples

Figure 5.3: Irregularity in a collection of (pseudo)random samples can be nicely observed with Voronoi diagrams.

The sequence is periodic; therefore, M is typically very large (e.g., $M = 2^{31} - 1$). Due to periodicity, there are potential problems of regularity appearing in the samples, especially when applied across a Cartesian product to generate points in $\mathbb{R}^n$. Particular values must be chosen for the parameters, and statistical tests are used to evaluate the samples either experimentally or theoretically [741].

Testing for randomness

Thus, it is important to realize that even the "random" samples are deterministic. They are designed to optimize performance on statistical tests. Many sophisticated statistical tests of uniform randomness are used. One of the simplest, the *chi-square test*, is described here. This test measures how far computed statistics are from their expected value. As a simple example, suppose $\mathcal{C} = [0, 1]^2$ and is partitioned into a 10 by 10 array of 100 square boxes. If a set P of k samples is chosen at random, then intuitively each box should receive roughly $k/100$ of the samples. An error function can be defined to measure how far from true this intuition is:

$$e(P) = \sum_{i=1}^{100} (b_i - k/100)^2, \tag{5.18}$$

in which b_i is the number of samples that fall into box i. It is shown [524] that $e(P)$ follows a *chi-squared* distribution. A surprising fact is that the goal is not to minimize $e(P)$. If the error is too small, we would declare that the samples are too uniform to be random! Imagine $k = 1,000,000$ and exactly $10,000$ samples appear in each of the 100 boxes. This yields $e(P) = 0$, but how likely is this to ever occur? The error must generally be larger (it appears in many statistical tables) to account for the irregularity due to randomness.

This irregularity can be observed in terms of *Voronoi diagrams*, as shown in Figure 5.3. The Voronoi diagram partitions $\mathbb{R}^2$ into regions based on the samples. Each sample x has an associated *Voronoi region* $\text{Vor}(x)$. For any point $y \in \text{Vor}(x)$, x is the closest sample to y using Euclidean distance. The different sizes and shapes of these regions give some indication of the required irregularity of random sampling. This irregularity may be undesirable for sampling-based motion planning and is somewhat repaired by the

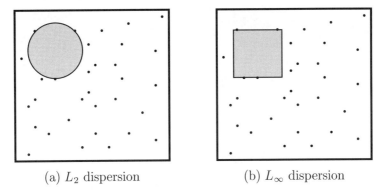

(a) L_2 dispersion   (b) L_∞ dispersion

Figure 5.4: Reducing the dispersion means reducing the radius of the largest empty ball.

deterministic sampling methods of Sections 5.2.3 and 5.2.4 (however, these methods also have drawbacks).

5.2.3 Low-dispersion sampling

This section describes an alternative to random sampling. Here, the goal is to optimize a criterion called *dispersion* [741]. Intuitively, the idea is to place samples in a way that makes the largest uncovered area be as small as possible. This generalizes of the idea of *grid resolution*. For a grid, the *resolution* may be selected by defining the step size for each axis. As the step size is decreased, the resolution increases. If a grid-based motion planning algorithm can increase the resolution arbitrarily, it becomes resolution complete. Using the concepts in this section, it may instead reduce its dispersion arbitrarily to obtain a resolution complete algorithm. Thus, dispersion can be considered as a powerful generalization of the notion of "resolution."

Dispersion definition

The *dispersion*[6] of a set P of samples in a metric space (X, ρ) is[7]

$$\delta(P) = \sup_{x \in X} \left\{ \min_{p \in P} \left\{ \rho(x, p) \right\} \right\}. \tag{5.19}$$

Figure 5.4 gives an interpretation of the definition for two different metrics. An alternative way to consider dispersion is as the radius of the largest empty ball (for the L_∞ metric, the balls are actually cubes). Note that at the boundary of X (if it exists), the empty ball becomes truncated because it cannot exceed the boundary. There is also a nice interpretation in terms of Voronoi diagrams. Figure 5.3 can be used to help explain L_2 dispersion in $\mathbb{R}^2$. The *Voronoi vertices* are the points at which three or more Voronoi regions meet. These are points in $\mathcal{C}$ for which the nearest sample is far. An open, empty disc can be placed at any Voronoi vertex, with a radius equal to the distance to the three (or more) closest samples. The radius of the largest disc among those placed at all Voronoi vertices is the dispersion. This interpretation also extends nicely to higher dimensions.

---

[6] The definition is unfortunately backward from intuition. Lower dispersion means that the points are nicely dispersed. Thus, more dispersion is bad, which is counterintuitive.

[7] The sup represents the *supremum*, which is the least upper bound. If X is closed, then the sup becomes a max. See Section 9.1.1 for more details.

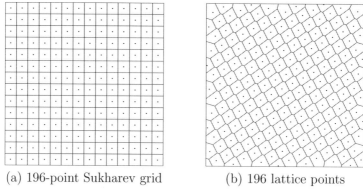

(a) 196-point Sukharev grid   (b) 196 lattice points

Figure 5.5: The Sukharev grid and a nongrid lattice.

Making good grids

Optimizing dispersion forces the points to be distributed more uniformly over $\mathcal{C}$. This causes them to fail statistical tests, but the point distribution is often better for motion planning purposes. Consider the best way to reduce dispersion if ρ is the L_∞ metric and $X = [0, 1]^n$. Suppose that the number of samples, k, is given. Optimal dispersion is obtained by partitioning $[0, 1]$ into a grid of cubes and placing a point at the center of each cube, as shown for $n = 2$ and $k = 96$ in Figure 5.5a. The number of cubes per axis must be $\lfloor k^{\frac{1}{n}} \rfloor$, in which $\lfloor \cdot \rfloor$ denotes the *floor*. If $k^{\frac{1}{n}}$ is not an integer, then there are leftover points that may be placed anywhere without affecting the dispersion. Notice that $k^{\frac{1}{n}}$ just gives the number of points per axis for a grid of k points in n dimensions. The resulting grid will be referred to as a *Sukharev grid* [923].

The dispersion obtained by the Sukharev grid is the best possible. Therefore, a useful lower bound can be given for *any* set P of k samples [923]:

$$\delta(P) \geq \frac{1}{2 \lfloor N^{\frac{1}{d}} \rfloor}. \tag{5.20}$$

This implies that keeping the dispersion fixed *requires* exponentially many points in the dimension, d.

At this point you might wonder why L_∞ was used instead of L_2, which seems more natural. This is because the L_2 case is extremely difficult to optimize (except in $\mathbb{R}^2$, where a tiling of equilateral triangles can be made, with a point in the center of each one). Even the simple problem of determining the best way to distribute a fixed number of points in $[0, 1]^3$ is unsolved for most values of k. See [243] for extensive treatment of this problem.

Suppose now that other topologies are considered instead of $[0, 1]^n$. Let $X = [0, 1]/\sim$, in which the identification produces a torus. The situation is quite different because X no longer has a boundary. The Sukharev grid still produces optimal dispersion, but it can also be shifted without increasing the dispersion. In this case, a *standard grid* may also be used, which has the same number of points as the Sukharev grid but is translated to the origin. Thus, the first grid point is $(0, 0)$, which is actually the same as $2^n - 1$ other points by identification. If X represents a cylinder and the number of points, k, is given, then it is best to just use the Sukharev grid. It is possible, however, to shift each coordinate that behaves like $\mathbb{S}^1$. If X is rectangular but not a square, a good grid can still be made by tiling the space with cubes. In some cases this will produce optimal dispersion. For complicated spaces such as $SO(3)$, no grid exists in the sense defined so far. It is possible, however, to generate grids on the faces of an inscribed Platonic solid [253] and lift the samples to

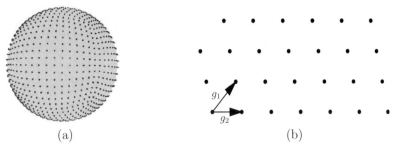

(a) (b)

Figure 5.6: (a) A distorted grid can even be placed over spheres and $SO(3)$ by putting grids on the faces of an inscribed cube and lifting them to the surface [987]. (b) A lattice can be considered as a grid in which the generators are not necessarily orthogonal.

$\mathbb{S}^n$ with relatively little distortion [987]. For example, to sample $\mathbb{S}^2$, Sukharev grids can be placed on each face of a cube. These are lifted to obtain the warped grid shown in Figure 5.6a.

Example 5.15 (Sukharev Grid)   Suppose that $n = 2$ and $k = 9$. If $X = [0, 1]^2$, then the Sukharev grid yields points for the nine cases in which either coordinate may be $1/6$, $1/2$, or $5/6$. The L_∞ dispersion is $1/6$. The spacing between the points along each axis is $1/3$, which is twice the dispersion. If instead $X = [0, 1]^2/\sim$, which represents a torus, then the nine points may be shifted to yield the standard grid. In this case each coordinate may be 0, $1/3$, or $2/3$. The dispersion and spacing between the points remain unchanged. ■

One nice property of grids is that they have a lattice structure. This means that neighboring points can be obtained very easily be adding or subtracting vectors. Let g_j be an n-dimensional vector called a *generator*. A point on a lattice can be expressed as

$$x = \sum_{j=1}^{n} k_j g_j \qquad (5.21)$$

for n independent generators, as depicted in Figure 5.6b. In a 2D grid, the generators represent "up" and "right." If $X = [0, 100]^2$ and a standard grid with integer spacing is used, then the neighbors of the point $(50, 50)$ are obtained by adding $(0, 1)$, $(0, -1)$, $(-1, 0)$, or $(1, 0)$. In a general lattice, the generators need not be orthogonal. An example is shown in Figure 5.5b. In Section 5.4.2, lattice structure will become important and convenient for defining the search graph.

Infinite grid sequences

Now suppose that the number, k, of samples is not given. The task is to define an infinite sequence that has the nice properties of the van der Corput sequence but works for any dimension. This will become the notion of a *multi-resolution grid*. The resolution can be iteratively doubled. For a multi-resolution standard grid in $\mathbb{R}^n$, the sequence will first place one point at the origin. After 2^n points have been placed, there will be a grid with two points per axis. After 4^n points, there will be four points per axis. Thus, after 2^{ni} points for any positive integer i, a grid with 2^i points per axis will be represented. If only complete grids are allowed, then it becomes clear why they appear inappropriate for high-dimensional problems. For example, if $n = 10$, then full grids appear after 1, 2^{10}, 2^{20}, 2^{30}, and so on, samples. Each doubling in resolution multiplies the number of points by 2^n. Thus, to use grids in high dimensions, one must be willing to accept *partial grids* and define an infinite sequence that places points in a nice way.

The van der Corput sequence can be extended in a straightforward way as follows. Suppose $X = \mathbb{T}^2 = [0, 1]^2 / \sim$. The original van der Corput sequence started by counting in binary. The least significant bit was used to select which half of $[0, 1]$ was sampled. In the current setting, the two least significant bits can be used to select the quadrant of $[0, 1]^2$. The next two bits can be used to select the quadrant within the quadrant. This procedure continues recursively to obtain a complete grid after $k = 2^{2i}$ points, for any positive integer i. For any k, however, there is only a partial grid. The points are distributed with optimal L_∞ dispersion. This same idea can be applied in dimension n by using n bits at a time from the binary sequence to select the orthant (n-dimensional quadrant). Many other orderings produce L_∞-optimal dispersion. Selecting orderings that additionally optimize other criteria, such as discrepancy or L_2 dispersion, are covered in [642, 647]. Unfortunately, it is more difficult to make a multi-resolution Sukharev grid. The base becomes 3 instead of 2; after every 3^{ni} points a complete grid is obtained. For example, in one dimension, the first point appears at $1/2$. The next two points appear at $1/6$ and $5/6$. The next complete one-dimensional grid appears after there are 9 points.

Dispersion bounds

Since the sample sequence is infinite, it is interesting to consider asymptotic bounds on dispersion. It is known that for $X = [0, 1]^n$ and any L_p metric, the best possible asymptotic dispersion is $O(k^{-1/n})$ for k points and n dimensions [741]. In this expression, k is the variable in the limit and n is treated as a constant. Therefore, any function of n may appear as a constant (i.e., $O(f(n)k^{-1/n}) = O(k^{-1/n})$ for any positive $f(n)$). An important practical consideration is the size of $f(n)$ in the asymptotic analysis. For example, for the van der Corput sequence from Section 5.2.1, the dispersion is bounded by $1/k$, which means that $f(n) = 1$. This does not seem good because for values of k that are powers of two, the dispersion is $1/2k$. Using a multi-resolution Sukharev grid, the constant becomes $3/2$ because it takes a longer time before a full grid is obtained. Nongrid, low-dispersion infinite sequences exist that have $f(n) = 1/\ln 4$ [741]; these are not even uniformly distributed, which is rather surprising.

5.2.4 Low-discrepancy sampling

In some applications, selecting points that align with the coordinate axis may be undesirable. Therefore, extensive sampling theory has been developed to determine methods that avoid alignments while distributing the points uniformly. In sampling-based motion planning, grids sometimes yield unexpected behavior because a row of points may align nicely with a corridor in $\mathcal{C}_{free}$. In some cases, a solution is obtained with surprisingly few samples, and in others, too many samples are necessary. These alignment problems, when they exist, generally drive the variance higher in computation times because it is difficult to predict when they will help or hurt. This provides motivation for developing sampling techniques that try to reduce this sensitivity.

Discrepancy theory and its corresponding sampling methods were developed to avoid these problems for numerical integration [741]. Let X be a measure space, such as $[0, 1]^n$. Let $\mathcal{R}$ be a collection of subsets of X that is called a *range space*. In most cases, $\mathcal{R}$ is chosen as the set of all axis-aligned rectangular subsets; hence, this will be assumed from this point onward. With respect to a particular point set, P, and range space, $\mathcal{R}$, the

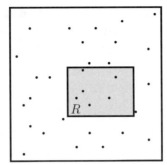

Figure 5.7: Discrepancy measures whether the right number of points fall into boxes. It is related to the chi-square test but optimizes over all possible boxes.

discrepancy [965] for k samples is defined as (see Figure 5.7)

$$D(P, \mathcal{R}) = \sup_{R \in \mathcal{R}} \left\{ \left| \frac{|P \cap R|}{k} - \frac{\mu(R)}{\mu(X)} \right| \right\}, \tag{5.22}$$

in which $|P \cap R|$ denotes the number of points in $P \cap R$. Each term in the supremum considers how well P can be used to estimate the volume of R. For example, if $\mu(R)$ is $1/5$, then we would hope that about $1/5$ of the points in P fall into R. The discrepancy measures the largest volume estimation error that can be obtained over all sets in $\mathcal{R}$.

Asymptotic bounds

There are many different asymptotic bounds for discrepancy, depending on the particular range space and measure space [685]. The most widely referenced bounds are based on the standard range space of axis-aligned rectangular boxes in $[0, 1]^n$. There are two different bounds, depending on whether the number of points, k, is given. The best possible asymptotic discrepancy for a single sequence is $O(k^{-1} \log^n k)$. This implies that k is not specified. If, however, for every k a new set of points can be chosen, then the best possible discrepancy is $O(k^{-1} \log^{n-1} k)$. This bound is lower because it considers the best that can be achieved by a sequence of points sets, in which every point set may be completely different. In a single sequence, the next set must be extended from the current set by adding a single sample.

Relating dispersion and discrepancy

Since balls have positive volume, there is a close relationship between discrepancy, which is measure-based, and dispersion, which is metric-based. For example, for any $P \subset [0, 1]^n$,

$$\delta(P, L_\infty) \leq D(P, \mathcal{R})^{1/d}, \tag{5.23}$$

which means low-discrepancy implies low-dispersion. Note that the converse is not true. An axis-aligned grid yields high discrepancy because of alignments with the boundaries of sets in $\mathcal{R}$, but the dispersion is very low. Even though low-discrepancy implies low-dispersion, lower dispersion can usually be obtained by ignoring discrepancy (this is one less constraint to worry about). Thus, a trade-off must be carefully considered in applications.

Low-discrepancy sampling methods

Due to the fundamental importance of numerical integration and the intricate link between discrepancy and integration error, most sampling literature has led to low-discrepancy sequences and point sets [741, 894, 937]. Although motion planning is quite different from integration, it is worth evaluating these carefully constructed and well-analyzed samples. Their potential use in motion planning is no less reasonable than using pseudo-random sequences, which were also designed with a different intention in mind (satisfying statistical tests of randomness).

Low-discrepancy sampling methods can be divided into three categories: 1) Halton/Hammersley sampling; 2) (t,s)-sequences and (t,m,s)-nets; and 3) lattices. The first category represents one of the earliest methods, and is based on extending the van der Corput sequence. The *Halton sequence* is an n-dimensional generalization of the van der Corput sequence, but instead of using binary representations, a different basis is used for each coordinate [433]. The result is a reasonable deterministic replacement for random samples in many applications. The resulting discrepancy (and dispersion) is lower than that for random samples (with high probability). Figure 5.8a shows the first 196 Halton points in $\mathbb{R}^2$.

Choose n relatively prime integers $p_1, p_2, \ldots, p_n$ (usually the first n primes, $p_1 = 2$, $p_2 = 3, \ldots$, are chosen). To construct the ith sample, consider the base-p representation for i, which takes the form $i = a_0 + pa_1 + p^2 a_2 + p^3 a_3 + \ldots$. The following point in [0, 1] is obtained by reversing the order of the bits and moving the decimal point (as was done in Figure 5.2):

$$r(i, p) = \frac{a_0}{p} + \frac{a_1}{p^2} + \frac{a_2}{p^3} + \frac{a_3}{p^4} + \cdots . \tag{5.24}$$

For $p = 2$, this yields the ith point in the van der Corput sequence. Starting from $i = 0$, the ith sample in the Halton sequence is

$$\bigl(r(i, p_1), r(i, p_2), \ldots, r(i, p_n)\bigr). \tag{5.25}$$

Suppose instead that k, the required number of points, is known. In this case, a better distribution of samples can be obtained. The *Hammersley point set* [434] is an adaptation of the Halton sequence. Using only $d - 1$ distinct primes and starting at $i = 0$, the ith sample in a Hammersley point set with k elements is

$$\bigl(i/k, r(i, p_1), \ldots, r(i, p_{n-1})\bigr). \tag{5.26}$$

Figure 5.8b shows the Hammersley set for $n = 2$ and $k = 196$.

The construction of Halton/Hammersley samples is simple and efficient, which has led to widespread application. They both achieve asymptotically optimal discrepancy; however, the constant in their asymptotic analysis increases more than exponentially with dimension [741]. The constant for the dispersion also increases exponentially, which is much worse than for the methods of Section 5.2.3.

Improved constants are obtained for sequences and finite points by using (t,s)-sequences, and (t,m,s)-nets, respectively [741]. The key idea is to enforce zero discrepancy over particular subsets of $\mathcal{R}$ known as *canonical rectangles*, and all remaining ranges in $\mathcal{R}$ will contribute small amounts to discrepancy. The most famous and widely used (t,s)-sequences are Sobol' and Faure (see [741]). The Niederreiter-Xing (t,s)-sequence has the best-known asymptotic constant, $(a/n)^n$, in which a is a small positive constant [742].

The third category is *lattices*, which can be considered as a generalization of grids that allows nonorthogonal axes [685, 894, 959]. As an example, consider Figure 5.5b, which shows 196 lattice points generated by the following technique. Let α be a positive irrational number. For a fixed k, generate the ith point according to $(i/k, \{i\alpha\})$, in which

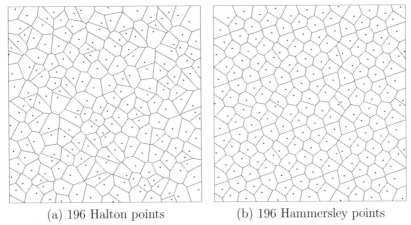

(a) 196 Halton points   (b) 196 Hammersley points

Figure 5.8: The Halton and Hammersley points are easy to construct and provide a nice alternative to random sampling that achieves more regularity. Compare the Voronoi regions to those in Figure 5.3. Beware that although these sequences produce asymptotically optimal discrepancy, their performance degrades substantially in higher dimensions (e.g., beyond 10).

$\{\cdot\}$ denotes the fractional part of the real value (modulo-one arithmetic). In Figure 5.5b, $\alpha = (\sqrt{5} + 1)/2$, the *golden ratio*. This procedure can be generalized to n dimensions by picking $n - 1$ distinct irrational numbers. A technique for choosing the α parameters by using the roots of irreducible polynomials is discussed in [685]. The ith sample in the lattice is

$$\left(\frac{i}{k}, \{i\alpha_1\}, \dots, \{i\alpha_{n-1}\} \right). \tag{5.27}$$

Recent analysis shows that some lattice sets achieve asymptotic discrepancy that is very close to that of the best-known nonlattice sample sets [448, 938]. Thus, restricting the points to lie on a lattice seems to entail little or no loss in performance, but has the added benefit of a regular neighborhood structure that is useful for path planning. Historically, lattices have required the specification of k in advance; however, there has been increasing interest in extensible lattices, which are infinite sequences [449, 938].

5.3 Collision detection

Once it has been decided where the samples will be placed, the next problem is to determine whether the configuration is in collision. Thus, collision detection is a critical component of sampling-based planning. Even though it is often treated as a black box, it is important to study its inner workings to understand the information it provides and its associated computational cost. In most motion planning applications, the majority of computation time is spent on collision checking.

A variety of collision detection algorithms exist, ranging from theoretical algorithms that have excellent computational complexity to heuristic, practical algorithms whose performance is tailored to a particular application. The techniques from Section 4.3 can be used to develop a collision detection algorithm by defining a logical predicate using the geometric model of $\mathcal{C}_{obs}$. For the case of a 2D world with a convex robot and obstacle, this leads to an linear-time collision detection algorithm. In general, however, it can be determined whether a configuration is in collision more efficiently by avoiding the full construction of $\mathcal{C}_{obs}$.

5.3.1 Basic concepts

As in Section 3.1.1, collision detection may be viewed as a logical predicate. In the current setting it appears as $\phi : \mathcal{C} \to \{\text{TRUE, FALSE}\}$, in which the domain is $\mathcal{C}$ instead of $\mathcal{W}$. If $q \in \mathcal{C}_{obs}$, then $\phi(q) = \text{TRUE}$; otherwise, $\phi(q) = \text{FALSE}$.

Distance between two sets

For the Boolean-valued function ϕ, there is no information about how far the robot is from hitting the obstacles. Such information is very important in planning algorithms. A *distance function* provides this information and is defined as $d : \mathcal{C} \to [0, \infty)$, in which the real value in the range of f indicates the distance in the world, $\mathcal{W}$, between the closest pair of points over all pairs from $\mathcal{A}(q)$ and $\mathcal{O}$. In general, for two closed, bounded subsets, E and F, of $\mathbb{R}^n$, the *distance* is defined as

$$\rho(E, F) = \min_{e \in E} \left\{ \min_{f \in F} \left\{ \|e - f\| \right\} \right\}, \tag{5.28}$$

in which $\| \cdot \|$ is the Euclidean norm. Clearly, if $E \cap F \neq \emptyset$, then $\rho(E, F) = 0$. The methods described in this section may be used to either compute distance or only determine whether $q \in \mathcal{C}_{obs}$. In the latter case, the computation is often much faster because less information is required.

Two-phase collision detection

Suppose that the robot is a collection of m attached links, $\mathcal{A}_1, \mathcal{A}_2, \ldots, \mathcal{A}_m$, and that $\mathcal{O}$ has k connected components. For this complicated situation, collision detection can be viewed as a two-phase process.

1. **Broad Phase:** In the *broad phase*, the task is to avoid performing expensive computations for bodies that are far away from each other. Simple bounding boxes can be placed around each of the bodies, and simple tests can be performed to avoid costly collision checking unless the boxes overlap. Hashing schemes can be employed in some cases to greatly reduce the number of pairs of boxes that have to be tested for overlap [706]. For a robot that consists of multiple bodies, the pairs of bodies that should be considered for collision must be specified in advance, as described in Section 4.3.1.

2. **Narrow Phase:** In the *narrow phase*, individual pairs of bodies are each checked carefully for collision. Approaches to this phase are described in Sections 5.3.2 and 5.3.3.

5.3.2 Hierarchical methods

In this section, suppose that two complicated, nonconvex bodies, E and F, are to be checked for collision. Each body could be part of either the robot or the obstacle region. They are subsets of $\mathbb{R}^2$ or $\mathbb{R}^3$, defined using any kind of geometric primitives, such as triangles in $\mathbb{R}^3$. *Hierarchical methods* generally decompose each body into a tree. Each vertex in the tree represents a *bounding region* that contains some subset of the body. The bounding region of the root vertex contains the whole body.

There are generally two opposing criteria that guide the selection of the type of bounding region:

1. The region should fit the intended body points as tightly as possible.
2. The intersection test for two regions should be as efficient as possible.

Several popular choices are shown in Figure 5.9 for an L-shaped body.

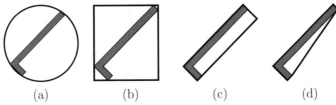

(a)   (b)   (c)   (d)

Figure 5.9: Four different kinds of bounding regions: (a) sphere, (b) axis-aligned bounding box (AABB), (c) oriented bounding box (OBB), and (d) convex hull. Each usually provides a tighter approximation than the previous one but is more expensive to test for overlapping pairs.

Figure 5.10: The large circle shows the bounding region for a vertex that covers an L-shaped body. After performing a split along the dashed line, two smaller circles are used to cover the two halves of the body. Each circle corresponds to a child vertex.

The tree is constructed for a body, E (or alternatively, F) recursively as follows. For each vertex, consider the set X of all points in E that are contained in the bounding region. Two child vertices are constructed by defining two smaller bounding regions whose union covers X. The split is made so that the portion covered by each child is of similar size. If the geometric model consists of primitives such as triangles, then a split could be made to separate the triangles into two sets of roughly the same number of triangles. A bounding region is then computed for each of the children. Figure 5.10 shows an example of a split for the case of an L-shaped body. Children are generated recursively by making splits until very simple sets are obtained. For example, in the case of triangles in space, a split is made unless the vertex represents a single triangle. In this case, it is easy to test for the intersection of two triangles.

Consider the problem of determining whether bodies E and F are in collision. Suppose that the trees T_e and T_f have been constructed for E and F, respectively. If the bounding regions of the root vertices of T_e and T_f do not intersect, then it is known that T_e and T_f are not in collision without performing any additional computation. If the bounding regions do intersect, then the bounding regions of the children of T_e are compared to the bounding region of T_f. If either of these intersect, then the bounding region of T_f is replaced with the bounding regions of its children, and the process continues recursively. As long as the bounding regions overlap, lower levels of the trees are traversed, until eventually the leaves are reached. If triangle primitives are used for the geometric models, then at the leaves the algorithm tests the individual triangles for collision, instead of bounding regions. Note that as the trees are traversed, if a bounding region from the vertex v_1 of T_e does not intersect the bounding region from a vertex, v_2, of T_f, then no children of v_1 have to be compared to children of v_1. Usually, this dramatically reduces the number of comparisons, relative in a naive approach that tests all pairs of triangles for intersection.

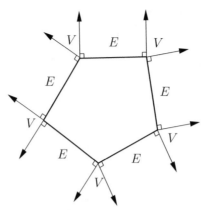

Figure 5.11: The Voronoi regions alternate between being edge-based and vertex-based. The Voronoi regions of vertices are labeled with a "V" and the Voronoi regions of edges are labeled with an "E."

It is possible to extend the hierarchical collision detection scheme to also compute distance. The closest pair of points found so far serves as an upper bound that prunes aways some future pairs from consideration. If a pair of bounding regions has a distance greater than the smallest distance computed so far, then their children do not have to be considered [641]. In this case, an additional requirement usually must be imposed. Every bounding region must be a proper subset of its parent bounding region [810]. If distance information is not needed, then this requirement can be dropped.

5.3.3 Incremental methods

This section focuses on a particular approach called *incremental distance computation*, which assumes that between successive calls to the collision detection algorithm, the bodies move only a small amount. Under this assumption the algorithm achieves "almost constant time" performance for the case of convex polyhedral bodies [639, 705]. Nonconvex bodies can be decomposed into convex components.

These collision detection algorithms seem to offer wonderful performance, but this comes at a price. The models must be *coherent*, which means that all of the primitives must fit together nicely. For example, if a 2D model uses line segments, all of the line segments must fit together perfectly to form polygons. There can be no isolated segments or chains of segments. In three dimensions, polyhedral models are required to have all faces come together perfectly to form the boundaries of 3D shapes. The model cannot be an arbitrary collection of 3D triangles.

The method will be explained for the case of 2D convex polygons, which are interpreted as convex subsets of $\mathbb{R}^2$. Voronoi regions for a convex polygon will be defined in terms of features. The *feature set* is the set of all vertices and edges of a convex polygon. Thus, a polygon with n edges has $2n$ features. Any point outside of the polygon has a closest feature in terms of Euclidean distance. For a given feature, F, the set of all points in $\mathbb{R}^2$ from which F is the closest feature is called the Voronoi region of F and is denoted $\text{Vor}(F)$. Figure 5.11 shows all ten Voronoi regions for a pentagon. Each feature is considered as a point set in the discussion below.

For any two convex polygons that do not intersect, the closest point is determined by a pair of points, one on each polygon (the points are unique, except in the case of parallel edges). Consider the feature for each point in the closest pair. There are only three possible combinations:

- **Vertex-Vertex** Each point of the closest pair is a vertex of a polygon.
- **Edge-Vertex** One point of the closest pair lies on an edge, and the other lies on a vertex.
- **Edge-Edge** Each point of the closest pair lies on an edge. In this case, the edges must be parallel.

Let P_1 and P_2 be two convex polygons, and let F_1 and F_2 represent any feature pair, one from each polygon. Let $(x_1, y_1) \in F_1$ and $(x_2, y_2) \in F_2$ denote the closest pair of points, among all pairs of points in F_1 and F_2, respectively. The following condition implies that the distance between (x_1, y_1) and (x_2, y_2) is the distance between P_1 and P_2:

$$(x_1, y_1) \in \text{Vor}(F_2) \text{ and } (x_2, y_2) \in \text{Vor}(F_1). \qquad (5.29)$$

If (5.29) is satisfied for a given feature pair, then the distance between P_1 and P_2 equals the distance between F_1 and F_2. This implies that the distance between P_1 and P_2 can be determined in constant time. The assumption that P_1 moves only a small amount relative to P_2 is made to increase the likelihood that the closest feature pair remains the same. This is why the phrase "almost constant time" is used to describe the performance of the algorithm. Of course, it is possible that the closest feature pair will change. In this case, neighboring features are tested using the condition above until the new closest pair of features is found. In this worst case, this search could be costly, but this violates the assumption that the bodies do not move far between successive collision detection calls.

The 2D ideas extend to 3D convex polyhedra [249, 639, 705]. The primary difference is that three kinds of features are considered: faces, edges, and vertices. The cases become more complicated, but the idea is the same. Once again, the condition regarding mutual Voronoi regions holds, and the resulting incremental collision detection algorithm has "almost constant time" performance.

5.3.4 Checking a path segment

Collision detection algorithms determine whether a configuration lies in $\mathcal{C}_{free}$, but motion planning algorithms require that an entire path maps into $\mathcal{C}_{free}$. The interface between the planner and collision detection usually involves validation of a path segment (i.e., a path, but often a short one). This cannot be checked point-by-point because it would require an uncountably infinite number of calls to the collision detection algorithm.

Suppose that a path, $\tau : [0, 1] \to \mathcal{C}$, needs to be checked to determine whether $\tau([0, 1]) \subset \mathcal{C}_{free}$. A common approach is to sample the interval $[0, 1]$ and call the collision checker only on the samples. What resolution of sampling is required? How can one ever guarantee that the places where the path is not sampled are collision-free? There are both practical and theoretical answers to these questions. In practice, a fixed $\Delta q > 0$ is often chosen as the C-space step size. Points $t_1, t_2 \in [0, 1]$ are then chosen close enough together to ensure that $\rho(\tau(t_1), \tau(t_2)) \leq \Delta q$, in which ρ is the metric on $\mathcal{C}$. The value of Δq is often determined experimentally. If Δq is too small, then considerable time is wasted on collision checking. If Δq is too large, then there is a chance that the robot could jump through a thin obstacle.

Setting Δq empirically might not seem satisfying. Fortunately, there are sound algorithmic ways to verify that a path is collision-free. In some applications the methods are still

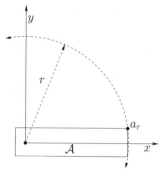

Figure 5.12: The furthest point on $\mathcal{A}$ from the origin travels the fastest when $\mathcal{A}$ is rotated. At most it can be displaced by $2\pi r$, if x_t and y_t are fixed.

not used because they are trickier to implement and they often yield worse performance. Therefore, both methods are presented here, and you can decide which is appropriate, depending on the context and your personal tastes.

Ensuring that $\tau([0,1]) \subset \mathcal{C}_{free}$ requires the use of both distance information and bounds on the distance that points on $\mathcal{A}$ can travel in $\mathbb{R}$. Such bounds can be obtained by using the robot displacement metric from Example 5.6. Before expressing the general case, first we will explain the concept in terms of a rigid robot that translates and rotates in $\mathcal{W} = \mathbb{R}^2$. Let $x_t, y_t \in \mathbb{R}^2$ and $\theta \in [0, 2\pi]/ \sim$. Suppose that a collision detection algorithm indicates that $\mathcal{A}(q)$ is at least d units away from collision with obstacles in $\mathcal{W}$. This information can be used to determine a region in $\mathcal{C}_{free}$ that contains q. Suppose that the next candidate configuration to be checked along τ is q'. If no point on $\mathcal{A}$ travels more than distance d when moving from q to q' along τ, then q' and all configurations between q and q' must be collision-free. This assumes that on the path from q to q', every visited configuration must lie between q_i and q'_i for the ith coordinate and any i from 1 to n. If the robot can instead take any path between q and q', then no such guarantee can be made).

When $\mathcal{A}$ undergoes a translation, all points move the same distance. For rotation, however, the distance traveled depends on how far the point on $\mathcal{A}$ is from the rotation center, $(0,0)$. Let $a_r = (x_r, y_r)$ denote the point on $\mathcal{A}$ that has the largest magnitude, $r = \sqrt{x_r^2 + y_r^2}$. Figure 5.12 shows an example. A transformed point $a \in \mathcal{A}$ may be denoted by $a(x_t, y_t, \theta)$. The following bound is obtained for any $a \in \mathcal{A}$, if the robot is rotated from orientation θ to θ':

$$\|a(x_t, y_t, \theta) - a(x_t, y_t, \theta')\| \leq \|a_r(x_t, y_t, \theta) - a_r(x_t, y_t, \theta')\| < r|\theta - \theta'|, \qquad (5.30)$$

assuming that a path in $\mathcal{C}$ is followed that interpolates between θ and θ' (using the shortest path in $\mathbb{S}^1$ between θ and θ'). Thus, if $\mathcal{A}(q)$ is at least d away from the obstacles, then the orientation may be changed without causing collision as long as $r|\theta - \theta'| < d$. Note that this is a loose upper bound because a_r travels along a circular arc and can be displaced by no more than $2\pi r$.

Similarly, x_t and y_t may individually vary up to d, yielding $|x_t - x'_t| < d$ and $|y_t - y'_t| < d$. If all three parameters vary simultaneously, then a region in $\mathcal{C}_{free}$ can be defined as

$$\{(x'_t, y'_t, \theta') \in \mathcal{C} \mid |x_t - x'_t| + |y_t - y'_t| + r|\theta - \theta'| < d\}. \qquad (5.31)$$

Such bounds can generally be used to set a step size, Δq, for collision checking that guarantees the intermediate points lie in $\mathcal{C}_{free}$. The particular value used may vary depending on d and the direction[8] of the path.

For the case of $SO(3)$, once again the displacement of the point on $\mathcal{A}$ that has the largest magnitude can be bounded. It is best in this case to express the bounds in terms of quaternion differences, $\|h - h'\|$. Euler angles may also be used to obtain a straightforward generalization of (5.31) that has six terms, three for translation and three for rotation. For each of the three rotation parts, a point with the largest magnitude in the plane perpendicular to the rotation axis must be chosen.

If there are multiple links, it becomes much more complicated to determine the step size. Each point $a \in \mathcal{A}_i$ is transformed by some nonlinear function based on the kinematic expressions from Sections 3.3 and 3.4. Let $a : \mathcal{C} \to \mathcal{W}$ denote this transformation. In some cases, it might be possible to derive a *Lipschitz condition* of the form

$$\|a(q) - a(q')\| < c\|q - q'\|, \tag{5.32}$$

in which $c \in (0, \infty)$ is a fixed constant, a is any point on $\mathcal{A}_i$, and the expression holds for any $q, q' \in \mathcal{C}$. The goal is to make the *Lipschitz constant*, c, as small as possible; this enables larger variations in q.

A better method is to individually bound the link displacement with respect to each parameter,

$$\|a(q_1, \ldots, q_{i-1}, q_i, q_{i+1}, \ldots, q_n) - a(q_1, \ldots, q_{i-1}, q_i', q_{i+1}, \ldots, q_n)\| < c_i |q_i - q_i'|, \tag{5.33}$$

to obtain the Lipschitz constants $c_1, \ldots, c_n$. The bound on robot displacement becomes

$$\|a(q) - a(q')\| < \sum_{i=1}^{n} c_i |q_i - q_i'|. \tag{5.34}$$

The benefit of using individual parameter bounds can be seen by considering a long chain. Consider a 50-link chain of line segments in $\mathbb{R}^2$, and each link has length 10. The C-space is $\mathbb{T}^{50}$, which can be parameterized as $[0, 2\pi]^{50}/\sim$. Suppose that the chain is in a straight-line configuration ($\theta_i = 0$ for all $1 \leq i \leq 50$), which means that the last point is at $(500, 0) \in \mathcal{W}$. Changes in θ_1, the orientation of the first link, dramatically move $\mathcal{A}_{50}$. However, changes in θ_{50} move $\mathcal{A}_{50}$ a smaller amount. Therefore, it is advantageous to pick a different Δq_i for each $1 \leq i \leq 50$. In this example, a smaller value should be used for $\Delta \theta_1$ in comparison to $\Delta \theta_{50}$.

Unfortunately, there are more complications. Suppose the 50-link chain is in a configuration that folds all of the links on top of each other ($\theta_i = \pi$ for each $1 \leq i \leq n$). In this case, $\mathcal{A}_{50}$ does not move as fast when θ_1 is perturbed, in comparison to the straight-line configuration. A larger step size for θ_1 could be used for this configuration, relative to other parts of $\mathcal{C}$. The implication is that, although Lipschitz constants can be made to hold over all of $\mathcal{C}$, it might be preferable to determine a better bound in a local region around $q \in \mathcal{C}$. A linear method could be obtained by analyzing the Jacobian of the transformations, such as (3.53) and (3.57).

Another important concern when checking a path is the order in which the samples are checked. For simplicity, suppose that Δq is constant and that the path is a constant-speed

---

[8] To formally talk about directions, it would be better to define a differentiable structure on $\mathcal{C}$. This will be deferred to Section 15.4, where it seems unavoidable.

parameterization. Should the collision checker step along from 0 up to 1? Experimental evidence indicates that it is best to use a recursive binary strategy [381]. This makes no difference if the path is collision-free, but it often saves time if the path is in collision. This is a kind of sampling problem over [0, 1], which is addressed nicely by the van der Corput sequence, ν. The last column in Figure 5.2 indicates precisely where to check along the path in each step. Initially, $\tau(1)$ is checked. Following this, points from the van der Corput sequence are checked in order: $\tau(0)$, $\tau(1/2)$, $\tau(1/4)$, $\tau(3/4)$, $\tau(1/8)$, ... The process terminates if a collision is found or when the dispersion falls below Δq. If Δq is not constant, then it is possible to skip over some points of ν in regions where the allowable variation in q is larger.

5.4 Incremental sampling and searching

5.4.1 The general framework

The algorithms of Sections 5.4 and 5.5 follow the *single-query model*, which means (q_I, q_G) is given only once per robot and obstacle set. This means that there are no advantages to precomputation, and the sampling-based motion planning problem can be considered as a kind of search. The *multiple-query model*, which favors precomputation, is covered in Section 5.6.

The sampling-based planning algorithms presented in the present section are strikingly similar to the family of search algorithms summarized in Section 2.2.4. The main difference lies in step 3 below, in which applying an action, u, is replaced by generating a path segment, τ_s. Another difference is that the search graph, $\mathcal{G}$, is undirected, with edges that represent paths, as opposed to a directed graph in which edges represent actions. It is possible to make these look similar by defining an action space for motion planning that consists of a collection of paths, but this is avoided here. In the case of motion planning with differential constraints, this will actually be required; see Chapter 14.

Most single-query, sampling-based planning algorithms follow this template:

1. **Initialization:** Let $\mathcal{G}(V, E)$ represent an undirected *search graph*, for which V contains at least one vertex and E contains no edges. Typically, V contains q_I, q_G, or both. In general, other points in $\mathcal{C}_{free}$ may be included.

2. **Vertex Selection Method (VSM):** Choose a vertex $q_{cur} \in V$ for expansion.

3. **Local Planning Method (LPM):** For some $q_{new} \in \mathcal{C}_{free}$ that may or may not be represented by a vertex in V, attempt to construct a path $\tau_s : [0, 1] \to \mathcal{C}_{free}$ such that $\tau(0) = q_{cur}$ and $\tau(1) = q_{new}$. Using the methods of Section 5.3.4, τ_s must be checked to ensure that it does not cause a collision. If this step fails to produce a collision-free path segment, then go to step 2.

4. **Insert an Edge in the Graph:** Insert τ_s into E, as an edge from q_{cur} to q_{new}. If q_{new} is not already in V, then it is inserted.

5. **Check for a Solution:** Determine whether $\mathcal{G}$ encodes a solution path. As in the discrete case, if there is a single search tree, then this is trivial; otherwise, it can become complicated and expensive.

6. **Return to Step 2:** Iterate unless a solution has been found or some termination condition is satisfied, in which case the algorithm reports failure.

In the present context, $\mathcal{G}$ is a topological graph, as defined in Example 4.6. Each vertex is a configuration and each edge is a path that connects two configurations. In this chapter,

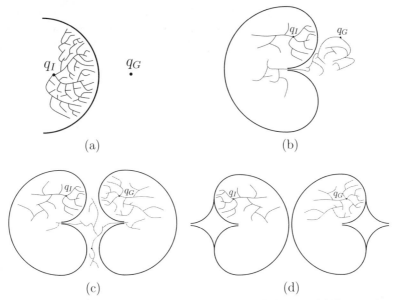

Figure 5.13: All of these depict high-dimensional obstacle regions in C-space. (a) The search must involve some sort of multi-resolution aspect, otherwise, that algorithm may explore too many points within a cavity. (b) Sometimes the problem is like a bug trap, in which case bidirectional search can help. (c) For a double bug trap, multi-directional search may be needed. (d) This example is hard to solve even for multi-directional search.

it will be simply referred to as a graph when there is no chance of confusion. Some authors refer to such a graph as a *roadmap*; however, we reserve the term roadmap for a graph that contains enough paths to make any motion planning query easily solvable. This case is covered in Section 5.6 and throughout Chapter 6.

A large family of sampling-based algorithms can be described by varying the implementations of steps 2 and 3. Implementations of the other steps may also vary, but this is less important and will be described where appropriate. For convenience, step 2 will be called the vertex selection method (VSM) and step 3 will be called the *local planning method* (LPM). The role of the VSM is similar to that of the priority queue, Q, in Section 2.2.1. The role of the LPM is to compute a collision-free path segment that can be added to the graph. It is called *local* because the path segment is usually simple (e.g., the shortest path) and travels a short distance. It is not *global* in the sense that the LPM does not try to solve the entire planning problem; it is expected that the LPM may often fail to construct path segments.

It will be formalized shortly, but imagine for the time being that any of the search algorithms from Section 2.2 may be applied to motion planning by approximating C with a high-resolution grid. The resulting problem looks like a multi-dimensional extension of Example 2.1 (the "labyrinth" walls are formed by C_{obs}). For a high-resolution grid in a high-dimensional space, most classical discrete searching algorithms have trouble getting trapped in a local minimum. There could be an astronomical number of configurations that fall within a concavity in C_{obs} that must be escaped to solve the problem, as shown in Figure 5.13a. Imagine a problem in which the C-space obstacle is a giant "bowl" that can trap the configuration. This figure is drawn in two dimensions, but imagine that the C has many dimensions, such as six for $SE(3)$ or perhaps dozens for a linkage. If the discrete planning algorithms from Section 2.2 are applied to a high-resolution grid approximation of $\mathcal{C}$, then they will all waste their time filling up the bowl before being able to escape to q_G. The number of grid points in this bowl would typically be on the order of 100^n for an n-dimensional C-space. Therefore, sampling-based motion planning algorithms combine sampling and searching in a way that attempts to overcome this difficulty.

As in the case of discrete search algorithms, there are several classes of algorithms based on the number of search trees.

Unidirectional (single-tree) methods: In this case, the planning appears very similar to discrete forward search, which was given in Figure 2.4. The main difference between algorithms in this category is how they implement the VSM and LPM. Figure 5.13b shows a *bug trap*[9] example for which forward-search algorithms would have great trouble; however, the problem might not be difficult for backward search, if the planner incorporates some kind of greedy, best-first behavior. This example, again in high dimensions, can be considered as a kind of "bug trap." To leave the trap, a path must be found from q_I into the narrow opening. Imagine a fly buzzing around through the high-dimensional trap. The escape opening might not look too difficult in two dimensions, but if it has a small range with respect to each configuration parameter, it is nearly impossible to find the opening. The tip of the "volcano" would be astronomically small compared to the rest of the bug trap. Examples such as this provide some motivation for bidirectional algorithms. It might be easier for a search tree that starts in q_G to arrive in the bug trap.

Bidirectional (two-tree) methods: Since it is not known whether q_I or q_G might lie in a bug trap (or another challenging region), a bidirectional approach is often preferable. This follows from an intuition that two propagating wavefronts, one centered on q_I and the other on q_G, will meet after covering less area in comparison to a single wavefront centered at q_I that must arrive at q_G. A bidirectional search is achieved by defining the VSM to alternate between trees when selecting vertices. The LPM sometimes generates paths that explore new parts of $\mathcal{C}_{free}$, and at other times it tries to generate a path that connects the two trees.

Multi-directional (more than two trees) methods: If the problem is so bad that a double bug trap exists, as shown in Figure 5.13c, then it might make sense to grow trees from other places in the hopes that there are better chances to enter the traps in the other direction. This complicates the problem of connecting trees, however. Which pairs of trees should be selected in each iteration for possible connection? How often should the same pair be selected? Which vertex pairs should be selected? Many heuristic parameters may arise in practice to answer these questions.

Of course, one can play the devil's advocate and construct the example in Figure 5.13d, for which virtually all sampling-based planning algorithms are doomed. Even harder versions can be made in which a sequence of several narrow corridors must be located and traversed. We must accept the fact that some problems are hopeless to solve using sampling-based planning methods, unless there is some problem-specific structure that can be additionally exploited.

5.4.2 Adapting discrete search algorithms

One of the most convenient and straightforward ways to make sampling-based planning algorithms is to define a grid over $\mathcal{C}$ and conduct a discrete search using the algorithms of

---

[9] This principle is actually used in real life to trap flying bugs. This analogy was suggested by James O'Brien in a discussion with James Kuffner.

Section 2.2. The resulting planning problem actually looks very similar to Example 2.1. Each edge now corresponds to a path in $\mathcal{C}_{free}$. Some edges may not exist because of collisions, but this will have to be revealed incrementally during the search because an explicit representation of $\mathcal{C}_{obs}$ is too expensive to construct (recall Section 4.3).

Assume that an n-dimensional C-space is represented as a unit cube, $\mathcal{C} = [0, 1]^n / \sim$, in which $\sim$ indicates that identifications of the sides of the cube are made to reflect the C-space topology. Representing $\mathcal{C}$ as a unit cube usually requires a reparameterization. For example, an angle $\theta \in [0, 2\pi)$ would be replaced with $\theta / 2\pi$ to make the range lie within $[0, 1]$. If quaternions are used for $SO(3)$, then the upper half of $\mathbb{S}^3$ must be deformed into $[0, 1]^3 / \sim$.

Discretization

Assume that $\mathcal{C}$ is *discretized* by using the *resolutions* $k_1, k_2, \ldots$, and k_n, in which each k_i is a positive integer. This allows the resolution to be different for each C-space coordinate. Either a standard grid or a Sukharev grid can be used. Let

$$\Delta q_i = [0 \ \cdots \ 0 \ 1/k_i \ 0 \ \cdots \ 0], \qquad (5.35)$$

in which the first $i - 1$ components and the last $n - i$ components are 0. A *grid point* is a configuration $q \in \mathcal{C}$ that can be expressed in the form[10]

$$\sum_{i=1}^{n} j_i \Delta q_i, \qquad (5.36)$$

in which each $j_i \in \{0, 1, \ldots, k_i\}$. The integers $j_1, \ldots, j_n$ can be imagined as array indices for the grid. Let the term *boundary grid point* refer to a grid point for which $j_i = 0$ or $j_i = k_i$ for some i. Due to identifications, boundary grid points might have more than one representation using (5.36).

Neighborhoods

For each grid point q we need to define the set of nearby grid points for which an edge may be constructed. Special care must be given to defining the neighborhood of a boundary grid point to ensure that identifications and the C-space boundary (if it exists) are respected. If q is not a boundary grid point, then the *1-neighborhood* is defined as

$$N_1(q) = \{q + \Delta q_1, \ldots, q + \Delta q_n, q - \Delta q_1, \ldots, q - \Delta q_n\}. \qquad (5.37)$$

For an n-dimensional C-space there at most $2n$ 1-neighbors. In two dimensions, this yields at most four 1-neighbors, which can be thought of as "up," "down," "left," and "right." There are *at most* four because some directions may be blocked by the obstacle region.

A *2-neighborhood* is defined as

$$N_2(q) = \{q \pm \Delta q_i \pm \Delta q_j \mid 1 \leq i, j \leq n, \ i \neq j\} \cup N_1(q). \qquad (5.38)$$

Similarly, a *k-neighborhood* can be defined for any positive integer $k \leq n$. For an n-neighborhood, there are at most $3^n - 1$ neighbors; there may be fewer due to boundaries or collisions. The definitions can be easily extended to handle the boundary points.

---

[10] Alternatively, the general lattice definition in (5.21) could be used.

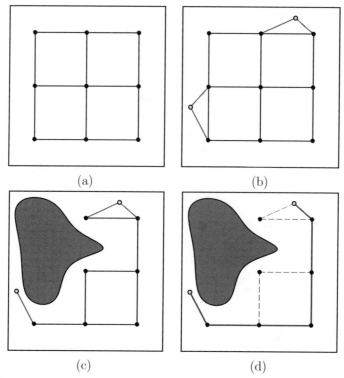

Figure 5.14: A topological graph can be constructed during the search and can successfully solve a motion planning problem using very few samples.

Obtaining a discrete planning problem

Once the grid and neighborhoods have been defined, a discrete planning problem is obtained. Figure 5.14 depicts the process for a problem in which there are nine Sukharev grid points in $[0, 1]^2$. Using 1-neighborhoods, the potential edges in the search graph, $\mathcal{G}(V, E)$, appear in Figure 5.14a. Note that $\mathcal{G}$ is a topological graph, as defined in Example 4.6, because each vertex is a configuration and each edge is a path. If q_I and q_G do not coincide with grid points, they need to be connected to some nearby grid points, as shown in Figure 5.14b. What grid points should q_I and q_G be connected to? As a general rule, if k-neighbors are used, then one should try connecting q_I and q_G to any grid points that are at least as close as the furthest k-neighbor from a typical grid point.

Usually, all of the vertices and edges shown in Figure 5.14b do not appear in $\mathcal{G}$ because some intersect with $\mathcal{C}_{obs}$. Figure 5.14c shows a more typical situation, in which some of the potential vertices and edges are removed because of collisions. This representation could be computed in advance by checking all potential vertices and edges for collision. This would lead to a roadmap, which is suited for multiple queries and is covered in Section 5.6. In this section, it is assumed that $\mathcal{G}$ is revealed "on the fly" during the search. This is the same situation that occurs for the discrete planning methods from Section 2.2. In the current setting, the potential edges of $\mathcal{G}$ are validated during the search. The candidate edges to evaluate are given by the definition of the k-neighborhoods. During the search, any edge or vertex that has been checked for collision explicitly appears in a data structure so that it does not need to be checked again. At the end of the search, a path is found, as depicted in Figure 5.14d.

Grid resolution issues

The method explained so far will nicely find the solution to many problems when provided with the correct resolution. If the number of points per axis is too high, then the search may be too slow. This motivates selecting fewer points per axis, but then solutions might be missed. This trade-off is fundamental to sampling-based motion planning. In a more general setting, if other forms of sampling and neighborhoods are used, then enough samples have to be generated to yield a sufficiently small dispersion.

There are two general ways to avoid having to select this resolution (or more generally, dispersion):

1. Iteratively refine the resolution until a solution is found. In this case, sampling and searching become interleaved. One important variable is how frequently to alternate between the two processes. This will be presented shortly.

2. An alternative is to abandon the adaptation of discrete search algorithms and develop algorithms directly for the continuous problem. This forms the basis of the methods in Sections 5.4.3, 5.4.4, and 5.5.

The most straightforward approach is to iteratively improve the grid resolution. Suppose that initially a standard grid with 2^n points total and 2 points per axis is searched using one of the discrete search algorithms, such as best-first or A^*. If the search fails, what should be done? One possibility is to double the resolution, which yields a grid with 4^n points. Many of the edges can be reused from the first grid; however, the savings diminish rapidly in higher dimensions. Once the resolution is doubled, the search can be applied again. If it fails again, then the resolution can be doubled again to yield 8^n points. In general, there would be a full grid for 2^{ni} points, for each i. The problem is that if n is large, then the rate of growth is too large. For example, if $n = 10$, then there would initially be 1024 points; however, when this fails, the search is not performed again until there are over one million points! If this also fails, then it might take a very long time to reach the next level of resolution, which has 2^{30} points.

A method similar to iterative deepening from Section 2.2.2 would be preferable. Simply discard the efforts of the previous resolution and make grids that have i^n points per axis for each iteration i. This yields grids of sizes 2^n, 3^n, 4^n, and so on, which is much better. The amount of effort involved in searching a larger grid is insignificant compared to the time wasted on lower resolution grids. Therefore, it seems harmless to discard previous work.

A better solution is not to require that a complete grid exists before it can be searched. For example, the resolution can be increased for one axis at a time before attempting to search again. Even better yet may be to tightly interleave searching and sampling. For example, imagine that the samples appear as an infinite, dense sequence α. The graph can be searched after every 100 points are added, assuming that neighborhoods can be defined or constructed even though the grid is only partially completed. If the search is performed too frequently, then searching would dominate the running time. An easy way make this efficient is to apply the *union-find algorithm* [245, 826] to iteratively keep track of connected components in $\mathcal{G}$ instead of performing explicit searching. If q_I and q_G become part of the same connected component, then a solution path has been found. Every time a new point in the sequence α is added, the "search" is performed in nearly[11] constant time by the union-find algorithm. This is the tightest interleaving of the sampling

---

[11] It is not constant because the running time is proportional to the inverse Ackerman function, which grows very, very slowly. For all practical purposes, the algorithm operates in constant time. See Section 6.5.2.

and searching, and results in a nice sampling-based algorithm that requires no resolution parameter. It is perhaps best to select a sequence α that contains some lattice structure to facilitate the determination of neighborhoods in each iteration.

What if we simply declare the resolution to be outrageously high at the outset? Imagine there are 100^n points in the grid. This places all of the burden on the search algorithm. If the search algorithm itself is good at avoiding local minima and has built-in multi-resolution qualities, then it may perform well without the iterative refinement of the sampling. The method of Section 5.4.3 is based on this idea by performing best-first search on a high-resolution grid, combined with random walks to avoid local minima. The algorithms of Section 5.5 go one step further and search in a multi-resolution way without requiring resolutions and neighborhoods to be explicitly determined. This can be considered as the limiting case as the number of points per axis approaches infinity.

Although this section has focused on grids, it is also possible to use other forms of sampling from Section 5.2. This requires defining the neighborhoods in a suitable way that generalizes the k-neighborhoods of this section. In every case, an infinite, dense sample sequence must be defined to obtain resolution completeness by reducing the dispersion to zero in the limit. Methods for obtaining neighborhoods for irregular sample sets have been developed in the context of sampling-based roadmaps; see Section 5.6. The notion of improving resolution becomes generalized to adding samples that improve dispersion (or even discrepancy).

5.4.3 Randomized potential fields

Adapting the discrete algorithms from Section 2.2 works well if the problem can be solved with a small number of points. The number of points per axis must be small or the dimension must be low, to ensure that the number of points, k^n, for k points per axis and n dimensions is small enough so that every vertex in g can be reached in a reasonable amount of time. If, for example, the problem requires 50 points per axis and the dimension is 10, then it is impossible to search all of the 50^{10} samples. Planners that exploit best-first heuristics might find the answer without searching most of them; however, for a simple problem such as that shown in Figure 5.13a, the planner will take too long exploring the vertices in the bowl.[12]

The *randomized potential field* [71, 73, 591] approach uses random walks to attempt to escape local minima when best-first search becomes stuck. It was one of the first sampling-based planners that developed specialized techniques beyond classical discrete search, in an attempt to better solve challenging motion planning problems. In many cases, remarkable results were obtained. In its time, the approach was able to solve problems up to 31 degrees of freedom, which was well beyond what had been previously possible. The main drawback, however, was that the method involved many heuristic parameters that had to be adjusted for each problem. This frustration eventually led to the development of better approaches, which are covered in Sections 5.4.4, 5.5, and 5.6. Nevertheless, it is worthwhile to study the clever heuristics involved in this earlier method because they illustrate many interesting issues, and the method was very influential in the development of other sampling-based planning algorithms.[13]

---

[12] Of course, that problem does not appear to need so many points per axis; fewer may be used instead, if the algorithm can adapt the sampling resolution or dispersion.

[13] The exciting results obtained by the method even helped inspire me many years ago to work on motion planning.

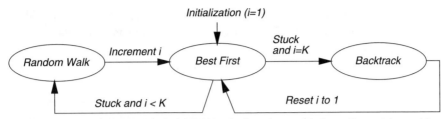

Figure 5.15: The randomized potential field method can be modeled as a three-state machine.

The most complicated part of the algorithm is the definition of a *potential function*, which can be considered as a pseudometric that tries to estimate the distance from any configuration to the goal. In most formulations, there is an *attractive* term, which is a metric on $\mathcal{C}$ that yields the distance to the goal, and a *repulsive* term, which penalizes configurations that come too close to obstacles. The construction of potential functions involves many heuristics and is covered in great detail in [591]. One of the most effective methods involves constructing cost-to-go functions over $\mathcal{W}$ and lifting them to $\mathcal{C}$ [72]. In this section, it will be sufficient to assume that some potential function, $g(q)$, is defined, which is the same notation (and notion) as a cost-to-go function in Section 2.2.2. In this case, however, there is no requirement that $g(q)$ is optimal or even an underestimate of the true cost to go.

When the search becomes stuck and a random walk is needed, it is executed for some number of iterations. Using the discretization procedures of Section 5.4.2, a high-resolution grid (e.g., 50 points per axis) is initially defined. In each iteration, the current configuration is modified as follows. Each coordinate, q_i, is increased or decreased by Δq_i (the grid step size) based on the outcome of a fair coin toss. Topological identifications must be respected, of course. After each iteration, the new configuration is checked for collision, or whether it exceeds the boundary of $\mathcal{C}$ (if it has a boundary). If so, then it is discarded, and another attempt is made from the previous configuration. The failures can repeat indefinitely until a new configuration in $\mathcal{C}_{free}$ is obtained.

The resulting planner can be described in terms of a three-state machine, which is shown in Figure 5.15. Each state is called a *mode* to avoid confusion with earlier state-space concepts. The VSM and LPM are defined in terms of the mode. Initially, the planner is in the BEST FIRST mode and uses q_I to start a gradient descent. While in the BEST FIRST mode, the VSM selects the newest vertex, $v \in V$. In the first iteration, this is q_I. The LPM creates a new vertex, v_n, in a neighborhood of v, in a direction that minimizes g. The direction sampling may be performed using randomly selected or deterministic samples. Using random samples, the sphere sampling method from Section 5.2.2 can be applied. After some number of tries (another parameter), if the LPM is unsuccessful at reducing g, then the mode is changed to RANDOM WALK because the best-first search is stuck in a local minimum of g.

In the RANDOM WALK mode, a random walk is executed from the newest vertex. The random walk terminates if either g is lowered or a specified limit of iterations is reached. The limit is actually sampled from a predetermined random variable (which contains parameters that also must be selected). When the RANDOM WALK mode terminates, the mode is changed back to BEST FIRST. A counter is incremented to keep track of the number of times that the random walk was attempted. A parameter K determines the maximum number of attempted random walks (a reasonable value is $K = 20$ [72]). If BEST FIRST fails after K random walks have been attempted, then the BACKTRACK mode is entered.

The BACKTRACK mode selects a vertex at random from among the vertices in V that were obtained during a random walk. Following this, the counter is reset, and the mode is changed back to BEST FIRST.

Due to the random walks, the resulting paths are often too complicated to be useful in applications. Fortunately, it is straightforward to transform a computed path into a simpler one that is still collision-free. A common approach is to iteratively pick pairs of points at random along the domain of the path and attempt to replace the path segment with a straight-line path (in general, the shortest path in C). For example, suppose $t_1, t_2 \in [0, 1]$ are chosen at random, and $\tau : [0, 1] \to C_{free}$ is the computed solution path. This path is transformed into a new path,

$$
\tau'(t) = \begin{cases} \tau(t) & \text{if } 0 \leq t \leq t_1 \\ a\tau(t_1) + (1-a)\tau(t_2) & \text{if } t_1 \leq t \leq t_2 \\ \tau(t) & \text{if } t_2 \leq t \leq 1, \end{cases} \tag{5.39}
$$

in which $a \in [0, 1]$ represents the fraction of the way from t_1 to t_2. Explicitly, $a = (t_2 - t)/(t_2 - t_1)$. The new path must be checked for collision. If it passes, then it replaces the old path; otherwise, it is discarded and a new pair t_1, t_2, is chosen.

The randomized potential field approach can escape high-dimensional local minima, which allow interesting solutions to be found for many challenging high-dimensional problems. Unfortunately, the heavy amount of parameter tuning caused most people to abandon the method in recent times, in favor of newer methods.

5.4.4 Other methods

Several influential sampling-based methods are given here. Each of them appears to offer advantages over the randomized potential field method. All of them use randomization, which was perhaps inspired by the potential field method.

Ariadne's clew algorithm

This approach grows a search tree that is biased to explore as much new territory as possible in each iteration [691, 690]. There are two modes, SEARCH and EXPLORE, which alternate over successive iterations. In the EXPLORE mode, the VSM selects a vertex, v_e, at random, and the LPM finds a new configuration that can be easily connected to v_e and is as far as possible from the other vertices in G. A global optimization function that aggregates the distances to other vertices is optimized using a genetic algorithm. In the SEARCH mode, an attempt is made to extend the vertex added in the EXPLORE mode to the goal configuration. The key idea from this approach, which influenced both the next approach and the methods in Section 5.5, is that some of the time must be spent exploring the space, as opposed to focusing on finding the solution. The greedy behavior of the randomized potential field led to some efficiency but was also its downfall for some problems because it was all based on escaping local minima with respect to the goal instead of investing time on global exploration. One disadvantage of Ariadne's Clew algorithm is that it is very difficult to solve the optimization problem for placing a new vertex in the EXPLORE mode. Genetic algorithms were used in [690], which are generally avoided for motion planning because of the required problem-specific parameter tuning.

Expansive-space planner

This method [470, 847] generates samples in a way that attempts to explore new parts of the space. In this sense, it is similar to the explore mode of the Ariadne's Clew algorithm. Furthermore, the planner is made more efficient by borrowing the bidirectional search idea from discrete search algorithms, as covered in Section 2.2.3. The VSM selects a vertex, v_e, from $\mathcal{G}$ with a probability that is inversely proportional to the number of other vertices of $\mathcal{G}$ that lie within a predetermined neighborhood of v_e. Thus, "isolated" vertices are more likely to be chosen. The LPM generates a new vertex v_n at random within a predetermined neighborhood of v_e. It will decide to insert v_n into $\mathcal{G}$ with a probability that is inversely proportional to the number of other vertices of $\mathcal{G}$ that lie within a predetermined neighborhood of v_n. For a fixed number of iterations, the VSM repeatedly chooses the same vertex, until moving on to another vertex. The resulting planner is able to solve many interesting problems by using a surprisingly simple criterion for the placement of points. The main drawbacks are that the planner requires substantial parameter tuning, which is problem-specific (or at least specific to a similar family of problems), and the performance tends to degrade if the query requires systematically searching a long labyrinth. Choosing the radius of the predetermined neighborhoods essentially amounts to determining the appropriate resolution.

Random-walk planner

A surprisingly simple and efficient algorithm can be made entirely from random walks [181]. To avoid parameter tuning, the algorithm adjusts its distribution of directions and magnitude in each iteration, based on the success of the past k iterations (perhaps k is the only parameter). In each iteration, the VSM just selects the vertex that was most recently added to $\mathcal{G}$. The LPM generates a direction and magnitude by generating samples from a multivariate Gaussian distribution whose covariance parameters are adaptively tuned. The main drawback of the method is similar to that of the previous method. Both have difficulty traveling through long, winding corridors. It is possible to combine adaptive random walks with other search algorithms, such as the potential field planner [180].

5.5 Rapidly exploring dense trees

This section introduces an incremental sampling and searching approach that yields good performance in practice without any parameter tuning.[14] The idea is to incrementally construct a search tree that gradually improves the resolution but does not need to explicitly set any resolution parameters. In the limit, the tree densely covers the space. Thus, it has properties similar to space filling curves [845], but instead of one long path, there are shorter paths that are organized into a tree. A dense sequence of samples is used as a guide in the incremental construction of the tree. If this sequence is random, the resulting tree is called a *rapidly exploring random tree (RRT)*. In general, this family of trees, whether the sequence is random or deterministic, will be referred to as *rapidly exploring dense trees (RDTs)* to indicate that a dense covering of the space is obtained. This method was originally developed for motion planning under differential constraints [611, 614]; that case is covered in Section 14.4.3.

---

[14] The original RRT [601] was introduced with a step size parameter, but this is eliminated in the current presentation. For implementation purposes, one might still want to revert to this older way of formulating the algorithm because the implementation is a little easier. This will be discussed shortly.

SIMPLE_RDT(q_0)
1    $\mathcal{G}$.init(q_0);
2   **for** $i = 1$ **to** k **do**
3        $\mathcal{G}$.add_vertex($\alpha(i)$);
4        $q_n \leftarrow$ NEAREST($S(\mathcal{G})$, $\alpha(i)$);
5        $\mathcal{G}$.add_edge(q_n, $\alpha(i)$);

Figure 5.16: The basic algorithm for constructing RDTs (which includes RRTs as a special case) when there are no obstacles. It requires the availability of a dense sequence, α, and iteratively connects from $\alpha(i)$ to the nearest point among all those reached by $\mathcal{G}$.

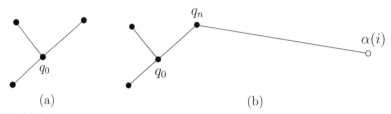

(a)   (b)

Figure 5.17: (a) Suppose inductively that this tree has been constructed so far using the algorithm in Figure 5.16. (b) A new edge is added that connects from the sample $\alpha(i)$ to the nearest point in S, which is the vertex q_n.

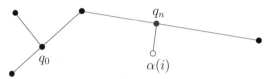

Figure 5.18: If the nearest point in S lies in an edge, then the edge is split into two, and a new vertex is inserted into $\mathcal{G}$.

5.5.1 The exploration algorithm

Before explaining how to use these trees to solve a planning query, imagine that the goal is to get as close as possible to every configuration, starting from an initial configuration. The method works for any dense sequence. Once again, let α denote an infinite, dense sequence of samples in $\mathcal{C}$. The ith sample is denoted by $\alpha(i)$. This may possibly include a uniform, random sequence, which is only dense with probability one. Random sequences that induce a nonuniform bias are also acceptable, as long as they are dense with probability one.

An RDT is a topological graph, $\mathcal{G}(V, E)$. Let $S \subset \mathcal{C}_{free}$ indicate the set of all points reached by $\mathcal{G}$. Since each $e \in E$ is a path, this can be expressed as the *swath*, S, of the graph, which is defined as

$$S = \bigcup_{e \in E} e([0, 1]). \tag{5.40}$$

In (5.40), $e([0, 1]) \subseteq \mathcal{C}_{free}$ is the image of the path e.

The exploration algorithm is first explained in Figure 5.16 without any obstacles or boundary obstructions. It is assumed that $\mathcal{C}$ is a metric space. Initially, a vertex is made at q_0. For k iterations, a tree is iteratively grown by connecting $\alpha(i)$ to its nearest point in the swath, S. The connection is usually made along the shortest possible path. In every iteration, $\alpha(i)$ becomes a vertex. Therefore, the resulting tree is dense. Figures 5.17–5.18

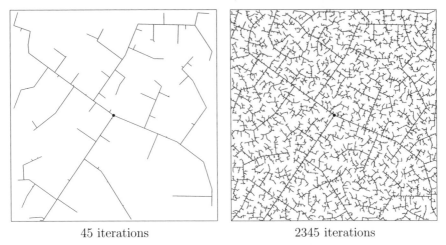

| 45 iterations | 2345 iterations |

Figure 5.19: In the early iterations, the RRT quickly reaches the unexplored parts. However, the RRT is dense in the limit (with probability one), which means that it gets arbitrarily to any point in the space.

illustrate an iteration graphically. Suppose the tree has three edges and four vertices, as shown in Figure 5.17a. If the nearest point, $q_n \in S$, to $\alpha(i)$ is a vertex, as shown in Figure 5.17b, then an edge is made from q_n to $\alpha(i)$. However, if the nearest point lies in the interior of an edge, as shown in Figure 5.18, then the existing edge is split so that q_n appears as a new vertex, and an edge is made from q_n to $\alpha(i)$. The edge splitting, if required, is assumed to be handled in line 4 by the method that adds edges. Note that the total number of edges may increase by one or two in each iteration.

The method as described here does not fit precisely under the general framework from Section 5.4.1; however, with the modifications suggested in Section 5.5.2, it can be adapted to fit. In the RDT formulation, the NEAREST function serves the purpose of the VSM, but in the RDT, a point may be selected from anywhere in the swath of the graph. The VSM can be generalized to a *swath-point selection method*, SSM. This generalization will be used in Section 14.3.4. The LPM tries to connect $\alpha(i)$ to q_n along the shortest path possible in $\mathcal{C}$.

Figure 5.19 shows an execution of the algorithm in Figure 5.16 for the case in which $\mathcal{C} = [0, 1]^2$ and $q_0 = (1/2, 1/2)$. It exhibits a kind of fractal behavior.[15] Several main branches are first constructed as it rapidly reaches the far corners of the space. Gradually, more and more area is filled in by smaller branches. From the pictures, it is clear that in the limit, the tree densely fills the space. Thus, it can be seen that the tree gradually improves the resolution (or dispersion) as the iterations continue. This behavior turns out to be ideal for sampling-based motion planning.

Recall that in sampling-based motion planning, the obstacle region $\mathcal{C}_{obs}$ is not explicitly represented. Therefore, it must be taken into account in the construction of the tree. Figure 5.20 indicates how to modify the algorithm in Figure 5.16 so that collision checking is taken into account. The modified algorithm appears in Figure 5.21. The procedure STOPPING-CONFIGURATION yields the nearest configuration possible to the boundary of $\mathcal{C}_{free}$, along the direction toward $\alpha(i)$. The nearest point $q_n \in S$ is defined to be same (obstacles are ignored); however, the new edge might not reach to $\alpha(i)$. In this case, an

---

[15] If α is uniform, random, then a *stochastic fractal* [589] is obtained. Deterministic fractals can be constructed using sequences that have appropriate symmetries.

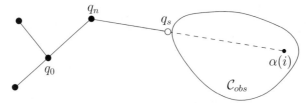

Figure 5.20: If there is an obstacle, the edge travels up to the obstacle boundary, as far as allowed by the collision detection algorithm.

RDT(q_0)
1    $\mathcal{G}$.init(q_0);
2   **for** $i = 1$ **to** k **do**
3        $q_n \leftarrow$ NEAREST($S, \alpha(i)$);
4        $q_s \leftarrow$ STOPPING-CONFIGURATION($q_n, \alpha(i)$);
5   **if** $q_s \neq q_n$ **then**
6            $\mathcal{G}$.add_vertex(q_s);
7            $\mathcal{G}$.add_edge(q_n, q_s);

Figure 5.21: The RDT with obstacles.

edge is made from q_n to q_s, the last point possible before hitting the obstacle. How close can the edge come to the obstacle boundary? This depends on the method used to check for collision, as explained in Section 5.3.4. It is sometimes possible that q_n is already as close as possible to the boundary of $\mathcal{C}_{free}$ in the direction of $\alpha(i)$. In this case, no new edge or vertex is added that for that iteration.

5.5.2 Efficiently finding nearest points

There are several interesting alternatives for implementing the NEAREST function in line 3 of the algorithm in Figure 5.16. There are generally two families of methods: *exact* or *approximate*. First consider the exact case.

Exact solutions

Suppose that all edges in $\mathcal{G}$ are line segments in $\mathbb{R}^m$ for some dimension $m \geq n$. An edge that is generated early in the construction process will be split many times in later iterations. For the purposes of finding the nearest point in S, however, it is best to handle this as a single segment. For example, see the three large branches that extend from the root in Figure 5.19. As the number of points increases, the benefit of agglomerating the segments increases. Let each of these agglomerated segments be referred to as a *supersegment*. To implement NEAREST, a primitive is needed that computes the distance between a point and a line segment. This can be performed in constant time with simple vector calculus. Using this primitive, NEAREST is implemented by iterating over all supersegments and taking the point with minimum distance among all of them. It may be possible to improve performance by building hierarchical data structures that can eliminate large sets of supersegments, but this remains to be seen experimentally.

In some cases, the edges of $\mathcal{G}$ may not be line segments. For example, the shortest paths between two points in $SO(3)$ are actually circular arcs along $\mathbb{S}^3$. One possible solution is to maintain a separate parameterization of $\mathcal{C}$ for the purposes of computing the NEAREST

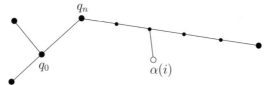

Figure 5.22: For implementation ease, intermediate vertices can be inserted to avoid checking for close points along line segments. The trade-off is that the number of vertices is increased dramatically.

function. For example, $SO(3)$ can be represented as $[0, 1]^3 / \sim$, by making the appropriate identifications to obtain $\mathbb{RP}^3$. Straight-line segments can then be used. The problem is that the resulting metric is not consistent with the Haar measure, which means that an accidental bias would result. Another option is to tightly enclose $\mathbb{S}^3$ in a 4D cube. Every point on $\mathbb{S}^3$ can be mapped outward onto a cube face. Due to antipodal identification, only four of the eight cube faces need to be used to obtain a bijection between the set of all rotation and the cube surface. Linear interpolation can be used along the cube faces, as long as both points remain on the same face. If the points are on different faces, then two line segments can be used by bending the shortest path around the corner between the two faces. This scheme will result in less distortion than mapping $SO(3)$ to $[0, 1]^3 / \sim$; however, some distortion will still exist.

Another approach is to avoid distortion altogether and implement primitives that can compute the distance between a point and a curve. In the case of $SO(3)$, a primitive is needed that can find the distance between a circular arc in $\mathbb{R}^m$ and a point in $\mathbb{R}^m$. This might not be too difficult, but if the curves are more complicated, then an exact implementation of the NEAREST function may be too expensive computationally.

Approximate solutions

Approximate solutions are much easier to construct, however, a resolution parameter is introduced. Each path segment can be approximated by inserting intermediate vertices along long segments, as shown in Figure 5.22. The intermediate vertices should be added each time a new sample, $\alpha(i)$, is inserted into $\mathcal{G}$. A parameter Δq can be defined, and intermediate samples are inserted to ensure that no two consecutive vertices in $\mathcal{G}$ are ever further than Δq from each other. Using intermediate vertices, the interiors of the edges in $\mathcal{G}$ are ignored when finding the nearest point in S. The approximate computation of NEAREST is performed by finding the closest vertex to $\alpha(i)$ in $\mathcal{G}$. This approach is by far the simplest to implement. It also fits precisely under the incremental sampling and searching framework from Section 5.4.1.

When using intermediate vertices, the trade-offs are clear. The computation time for each evaluation of NEAREST is linear in the number of vertices. Increasing the number of vertices improves the quality of the approximation, but it also dramatically increases the running time. One way to recover some of this cost is to insert the vertices into an efficient data structure for nearest-neighbor searching. One of the most practical and widely used data structures is the *Kd-tree* [266, 367, 761]. A depiction is shown in Figure 5.23 for 14 points in $\mathbb{R}^2$. The Kd-tree can be considered as a multi-dimensional generalization of a binary search tree. The Kd-tree is constructed for points, P, in $\mathbb{R}^2$ as follows. Initially, sort the points with respect to the x coordinate. Take the median point, $p \in P$, and divide P into two sets, depending on which side of a vertical line through p the other points fall. For each of the two sides, sort the points by the y coordinate and find their medians. Points are divided at this level based on whether they are above or below horizontal lines. At the

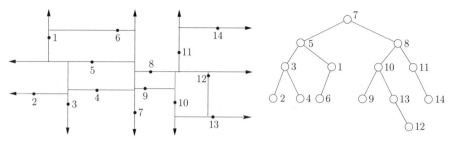

Figure 5.23: A Kd-tree can be used for efficient nearest-neighbor computations.

next level of recursion, vertical lines are used again, followed by horizontal again, and so on. The same idea can be applied in $\mathbb{R}^n$ by cycling through the n coordinates, instead of alternating between x and y, to form the divisions. In [53], the Kd-tree is extended to topological spaces that arise in motion planning and is shown to yield good performance for RRTs and sampling-based roadmaps. The Kd-tree can be constructed in $O(n \lg k)$ time. Topological identifications must be carefully considered when traversing the tree. To find the nearest point in the tree to some given point, the query algorithm descends to a leaf vertex whose associated region contains the query point, finds all distances from the data points in this leaf to the query point, and picks the closest one. Next, it recursively visits those surrounding leaf vertices that are further from the query point than the closest point found so far [48, 53]. The nearest point can be found in time logarithmic in k.

Unfortunately, these bounds hide a constant that increases exponentially with the dimension, n. In practice, the Kd-tree is useful in motion planning for problems of up to about 20 dimensions. After this, the performance usually degrades too much. As an empirical rule, if there are more than 2^n points, then the Kd-tree should be more efficient than naive nearest neighbors. In general, the trade-offs must be carefully considered in a particular application to determine whether exact solutions, approximate solutions with naive nearest-neighbor computations, or approximate solutions with Kd-trees will be more efficient. There is also the issue of implementation complexity, which probably has caused most people to prefer the approximate solution with naive nearest-neighbor computations.

5.5.3 Using the trees for planning

So far, the discussion has focused on exploring $\mathcal{C}_{free}$, but this does not solve a planning query by itself. RRTs and RDTs can be used in many ways in planning algorithms. For example, they could be used to escape local minima in the randomized potential field planner of Section 5.4.3.

Single-tree search

A reasonably efficient planner can be made by directly using the algorithm in Figure 5.21 to grow a tree from q_I and periodically check whether it is possible to connect the RDT to q_G. An easy way to achieve this is to start with a dense sequence α and periodically insert q_G at regularly spaced intervals. For example, every 100th sample could be q_G. Each time this sample is reached, an attempt is made to reach q_G from the closest vertex in the RDT. If the sample sequence is random, which generates an RRT, then the following modification works well. In each iteration, toss a biased coin that has probability $99/100$ of being HEADS and $1/100$ of being TAILS. If the result is HEADS, then set $\alpha(i)$, to be the next element of the pseudorandom sequence; otherwise, set $\alpha(i) = q_G$. This forces the

---

RDT_BALANCED_BIDIRECTIONAL(q_I, q_G)
1   T_a.init(q_I); T_b.init(q_G);
2   **for** $i = 1$ **to** K **do**
3        $q_n \leftarrow$ NEAREST(S_a, $\alpha(i)$);
4        $q_s \leftarrow$ STOPPING-CONFIGURATION(q_n, $\alpha(i)$);
5   **if** $q_s \neq q_n$ **then**
6   T_a.add_vertex(q_s);
7   T_a.add_edge(q_n, q_s);
8            $q'_n \leftarrow$ NEAREST(S_b, q_s);
9            $q'_s \leftarrow$ STOPPING-CONFIGURATION(q'_n, q_s);
10   **if** $q'_s \neq q'_n$ **then**
11   T_b.add_vertex(q'_s);
12   T_b.add_edge(q'_n, q'_s);
13   **if** $q'_s = q_s$ **then return** SOLUTION;
14   **if** $|T_b| > |T_a|$ **then** SWAP(T_a, T_b);
15   **return** FAILURE

Figure 5.24: A bidirectional RDT-based planner.

RRT to occasionally attempt to make a connection to the goal, q_G. Of course, $1/100$ is arbitrary, but it is in a range that works well experimentally. If the bias is too strong, then the RRT becomes too greedy like the randomized potential field. If the bias is not strong enough, then there is no incentive to connect the tree to q_G. An alternative is to consider other dense, but not necessarily nonuniform sequences in $\mathcal{C}$. For example, in the case of random sampling, the probability density function could contain a gentle bias towards the goal. Choosing such a bias is a difficult heuristic problem; therefore, such a technique should be used with caution (or avoided altogether).

Balanced, bidirectional search

Much better performance can usually be obtained by growing two RDTs, one from q_I and the other from q_G. This is particularly valuable for escaping one of the bug traps, as mentioned in Section 5.4.1. For a grid search, it is straightforward to implement a bidirectional search that ensures that the two trees meet. For the RDT, special considerations must be made to ensure that the two trees will connect while retaining their "rapidly exploring" property. One additional idea is to make sure that the bidirectional search is balanced [563], which ensures that both trees are the same size.

Figure 5.24 gives an outline of the algorithm. The graph $\mathcal{G}$ is decomposed into two trees, denoted by T_a and T_b. Initially, these trees start from q_I and q_G, respectively. After some iterations, T_a and T_b are swapped; therefore, keep in mind that T_a is not always the tree that contains q_I. In each iteration, T_a is grown exactly the same way as in one iteration of the algorithm in Figure 5.16. If a new vertex, q_s, is added to T_a, then an attempt is made in lines 10–12 to extend T_b. Rather than using $\alpha(i)$ to extend T_b, the new vertex q_s of T_a is used. This causes T_b to try to grow toward T_a. If the two connect, which is tested in line 13, then a solution has been found.

Line 14 represents an important step that balances the search. This is particularly important for a problem such as the bug trap shown in Figure 5.13b or the puzzle shown in Figure 1.2. If one of the trees is having trouble exploring, then it makes sense to focus more energy on it. Therefore, new exploration is always performed for the smaller tree. How is "smaller" defined? A simple criterion is to use the total number of vertices. Another reasonable criterion is to use the total length of all segments in the tree.

An unbalanced bidirectional search can instead be made by forcing the trees to be swapped in every iteration. Once the trees are swapped, then the roles are reversed. For example, after the first swap, T_b is extended in the same way as an integration in Figure 5.16, and if a new vertex q_s is added then an attempt is made to connect T_a to q_s.

One important concern exists when α is deterministic. It might be possible that even though α is dense, when the samples are divided among the trees, each may not receive a dense set. If each uses its own deterministic sequence, then this problem can be avoided. In the case of making a bidirectional RRT planner, the same (pseudo)random sequence can be used for each tree without encountering such troubles.

More than two trees

If a dual-tree approach offers advantages over a single tree, then it is natural to ask whether growing three or more RDTs might be even better. This is particularly helpful for problems like the double bug trap in Figure 5.13c. New trees can be grown from parts of $\mathcal{C}$ that are difficult to reach. Controlling the number of trees and determining when to attempt connections between them is difficult. Some interesting recent work has been done in this direction [84, 919, 920].

These additional trees could be started at arbitrary (possibly random) configurations. As more trees are considered, a complicated decision problem arises. The computation time must be divided between attempting to explore the space and attempting to connect trees to each other. It is also not clear which connections should be attempted. Many research issues remain in the development of this and other RRT-based planners. A limiting case would be to start a new tree from every sample in $\alpha(i)$ and to try to connect nearby trees whenever possible. This approach results in a graph that covers the space in a nice way that is independent of the query. This leads to the main topic of the next section.

5.6 Roadmap methods for multiple queries

Previously, it was assumed that a single initial-goal pair was given to the planning algorithm. Suppose now that numerous initial-goal queries will be given to the algorithm, while keeping the robot model and obstacles fixed. This leads to a *multiple-query* version of the motion planning problem. In this case, it makes sense to invest substantial time to preprocess the models so that future queries can be answered efficiently. The goal is to construct a topological graph called a *roadmap*, which efficiently solves multiple initial-goal queries. Intuitively, the paths on the roadmap should be easy to reach from each of q_I and q_G, and the graph can be quickly searched for a solution. The general framework presented here was mainly introduced in [519] under the name *probabilistic roadmaps (PRMs)*. The probabilistic aspect, however, is not important to the method. Therefore, we call this family of methods *sampling-based roadmaps*. This distinguishes them from *combinatorial roadmaps*, which will appear in Chapter 6.

5.6.1 The basic method

Once again, let $\mathcal{G}(V, E)$ represent a topological graph in which V is a set of vertices and E is the set of paths that map into $\mathcal{C}_{free}$. Under the multiple-query philosophy, motion planning is divided into two phases of computation:

BUILD_ROADMAP
1 $\mathcal{G}$.init(); $i \leftarrow 0$;
2 **while** $i < N$
3   **if** $\alpha(i) \in \mathcal{C}_{free}$ **then**
4          $\mathcal{G}$.add_vertex($\alpha(i)$); $i \leftarrow i + 1$;
5   **for each** $q \in$ NEIGHBORHOOD($\alpha(i),\mathcal{G}$)
6   **if** ((**not** $\mathcal{G}$.same_component($\alpha(i), q$)) **and** CONNECT($\alpha(i), q$)) **then**
7                  $\mathcal{G}$.add_edge($\alpha(i), q$);

Figure 5.25: The basic construction algorithm for sampling-based roadmaps. Note that i is not incremented if $\alpha(i)$ is in collision. This forces i to correctly count the number of vertices in the roadmap.

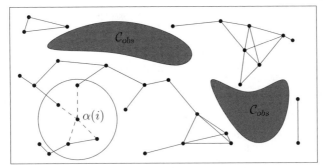

Figure 5.26: The sampling-based roadmap is constructed incrementally by attempting to connect each new sample, $\alpha(i)$, to nearby vertices in the roadmap.

Preprocessing Phase: During the preprocessing phase, substantial effort is invested to build $\mathcal{G}$ in a way that is useful for quickly answering future queries. For this reason, it is called a *roadmap*, which in some sense should be accessible from every part of $\mathcal{C}_{free}$.

Query Phase: During the query phase, a pair, q_I and q_G, is given. Each configuration must be connected easily to $\mathcal{G}$ using a local planner. Following this, a discrete search is performed using any of the algorithms in Section 2.2 to obtain a sequence of edges that forms a path from q_I to q_G.

Generic preprocessing phase

Figure 5.25 presents an outline of the basic preprocessing phase, and Figure 5.26 illustrates the algorithm. As seen throughout this chapter, the algorithm utilizes a uniform, dense sequence α. In each iteration, the algorithm must check whether $q \in \mathcal{C}_{free}$. If $q \in \mathcal{C}_{obs}$, then it must continue to iterate until a collision-free sample is obtained. Once $\alpha(i) \in \mathcal{C}_{free}$, then in line 4 it is inserted as a vertex of $\mathcal{G}$. The next step is to try to connect $\alpha(i)$ to some nearby vertices, q, of $\mathcal{G}$. Each connection is attempted by the CONNECT function, which is a typical LPM (local planning method) from Section 5.4.1. In most implementations, this simply tests the shortest path between $\alpha(i)$ and q. Experimentally, it seems most efficient to use the multi-resolution, van der Corput–based method described at the end of Section 5.3.4 [381]. Instead of the shortest path, it is possible to use more sophisticated connection methods, such as the bidirectional algorithm in Figure 5.24. If the path is collision-free, then CONNECT returns TRUE.

The same_component condition in line 6 checks to make sure $\alpha(i)$ and q are in different components of $\mathcal{G}$ before wasting time on collision checking. This ensures that every time a connection is made, the number of connected components of $\mathcal{G}$ is decreased. This can be implemented very efficiently (near constant time) using the previously mentioned *union-find algorithm* [245, 826]. In some implementations this step may be ignored, especially if it is important to generate multiple, alternative solutions. For example, it may be desirable to generate solution paths from different homotopy classes. In this case the condition (**not** $\mathcal{G}$.same_component($\alpha(i), q$)) is replaced with $\mathcal{G}$.vertex_degree(q) $< K$, for some fixed K (e.g., K = 15).

Selecting neighboring samples

Several possible implementations of line 5 can be made. In all of these, it seems best to sort the vertices that will be considered for connection in order of increasing distance from $\alpha(i)$. This makes sense because shorter paths are usually less costly to check for collision, and they also have a higher likelihood of being collision-free. If a connection is made, this avoids costly collision checking of longer paths to configurations that would eventually belong to the same connected component.

Several useful implementations of NEIGHBORHOOD are

1. **Nearest K:** The K closest points to $\alpha(i)$ are considered. This requires setting the parameter K (a typical value is 15). If you are unsure which implementation to use, try this one.

2. **Component K:** Try to obtain up to K nearest samples from each connected component of $\mathcal{G}$. A reasonable value is $K = 1$; otherwise, too many connections would be tried.

3. **Radius:** Take all points within a ball of radius r centered at $\alpha(i)$. An upper limit, K, may be set to prevent too many connections from being attempted. Typically, $K = 20$. A radius can be determined adaptively by shrinking the ball as the number of points increases. This reduction can be based on dispersion or discrepancy, if either of these is available for α. Note that if the samples are highly regular (e.g., a grid), then choosing the nearest K and taking points within a ball become essentially equivalent. If the point set is highly irregular, as in the case of random samples, then taking the nearest K seems preferable.

4. **Visibility:** In Section 5.6.2, a variant will be described for which it is worthwhile to try connecting α to all vertices in $\mathcal{G}$.

Note that all of these require $\mathcal{C}$ to be a metric space. One variation that has not yet been given much attention is to ensure that the directions of the NEIGHBORHOOD points relative to $\alpha(i)$ are distributed uniformly. For example, if the 20 closest points are all clumped together in the same direction, then it may be preferable to try connecting to a further point because it is in the opposite direction.

Query phase

In the query phase, it is assumed that $\mathcal{G}$ is sufficiently complete to answer many queries, each of which gives an initial configuration, q_I, and a goal configuration, q_G. First, the query phase pretends as if q_I and q_G were chosen from α for connection to $\mathcal{G}$. This requires running two more iterations of the algorithm in Figure 5.25. If q_I and q_G are successfully connected to other vertices in $\mathcal{G}$, then a search is performed for a path that connects the vertex q_I to the vertex q_G. The path in the graph corresponds directly to a path in $\mathcal{C}_{free}$, which is a solution to the query. Unfortunately, if this method fails, it cannot be determined conclusively whether a solution exists. If the dispersion is known for a sample sequence, α, then it is at least possible to conclude that no solution exists for the resolution of the planner. In other words, if a solution does exist, it would require the path to travel through a corridor no wider than the radius of the largest empty ball [603].

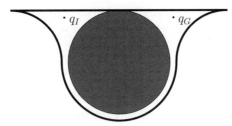

Figure 5.27: An example such as this is difficult for sampling-based roadmaps (in higher dimensional C-spaces) because some samples must fall along many points in the curved tube. Other methods, however, may be able to easily solve it.

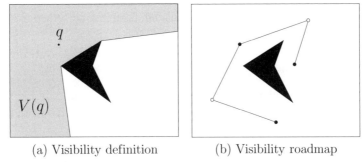

(a) Visibility definition   (b) Visibility roadmap

Figure 5.28: (a) $V(q)$ is the set of points reachable by the LPM from q. (b) A visibility roadmap has two kinds of vertices: guards, which are shown in black, and connectors, shown in white. Guards are not allowed to see other guards. Connectors must see at least two guards.

Some analysis

There have been many works that analyze the performance of sampling-based roadmaps. The basic idea from one of them [70] is briefly presented here. Consider problems such as the one in Figure 5.27, in which the CONNECT method will mostly likely fail in the thin tube, even though a connection exists. The higher dimensional versions of these problems are even more difficult. Many planning problems involve moving a robot through an area with tight clearance. This generally causes narrow channels to form in $\mathcal{C}_{free}$, which leads to a challenging planning problem for the sampling-based roadmap algorithm. Finding the escape of a bug trap is also challenging, but for the roadmap methods, even traveling through a single corridor is hard (unless more sophisticated LPMs are used [482]).

Let $V(q)$ denote the set of all configurations that can be connected to q using the CONNECT method. Intuitively, this is considered as the set of all configurations that can be "seen" using line-of-sight visibility, as shown in Figure 5.28a

The ϵ-goodness of $\mathcal{C}_{free}$ is defined as

$$\epsilon(\mathcal{C}_{free}) = \min_{q \in \mathcal{C}_{free}} \left\{ \frac{\mu(V(q))}{\mu(\mathcal{C}_{free})} \right\}, \tag{5.41}$$

in which μ represents the measure. Intuitively, $\epsilon(\mathcal{C}_{free})$ represents the small fraction of $\mathcal{C}_{free}$ that is visible from any point. In terms of ϵ and the number of vertices in $\mathcal{G}$, bounds can be established that yield the probability that a solution will be found [70]. The main difficulties are that the ϵ-goodness concept is very conservative (it uses worst-case analysis over all configurations), and ϵ-goodness is defined in terms of the structure of $\mathcal{C}_{free}$, which cannot be computed efficiently. This result and other related results help to gain a better understanding of sampling-based planning, but such bounds are difficult to apply to particular problems to determine whether an algorithm will perform well.

5.6.2 Visibility roadmap

One of the most useful variations of sampling-based roadmaps is the *visibility roadmap* [886]. The approach works very hard to ensure that the roadmap representation is small yet covers C_{free} well. The running time is often greater than the basic algorithm in Figure 5.25, but the extra expense is usually worthwhile if the multiple-query philosophy is followed to its fullest extent.

The idea is to define two different kinds of vertices in $\mathcal{G}$:

> **Guards:** To become a *guard*, a vertex, q must not be able to see other guards. Thus, the visibility region, $V(q)$, must be empty of other guards.

> **Connectors:** To become a *connector*, a vertex, q, must see at least two guards. Thus, there exist guards q_1 and q_2, such that $q \in V(q_1) \cap V(q_2)$.

The roadmap construction phase proceeds similarly to the algorithm in Figure 5.25. The *neighborhood function* returns all vertices in $\mathcal{G}$. Therefore, for each new sample $\alpha(i)$, an attempt is made to connect it to every other vertex in $\mathcal{G}$.

The main novelty of the visibility roadmap is using a strong criterion to determine whether to keep $\alpha(i)$ and its associated edges in $\mathcal{G}$. There are three possible cases for each $\alpha(i)$:

1. The new sample, $\alpha(i)$, is not able to connect to any guards. In this case, $\alpha(i)$ earns the privilege of becoming a guard itself and is inserted into $\mathcal{G}$.

2. The new sample can connect to guards from at least two different connected components of $\mathcal{G}$. In this case, it becomes a connector that is inserted into $\mathcal{G}$ along with its associated edges, which connect it to these guards from different components.

3. Neither of the previous two conditions were satisfied. This means that the sample could only connect to guards in the same connected component. In this case, $\alpha(i)$ is discarded.

The final condition causes a dramatic reduction in the number of roadmap vertices.

One problem with this method is that it does not allow guards to be deleted in favor of better guards that might appear later. The placement of guards depends strongly on the order in which samples appear in α. The method may perform poorly if guards are not positioned well early in the sequence. It would be better to have an adaptive scheme in which guards could be reassigned in later iterations as better positions become available. Accomplishing this efficiently remains an open problem. Note the algorithm is still probabilistically complete using random sampling or resolution complete if α is dense, even though many samples are rejected.

5.6.3 Heuristics for improving roadmaps

The quest to design a good roadmap through sampling has spawned many heuristic approaches to sampling and making connections in roadmaps. Most of these exploit properties that are specific to the shape of the C-space and/or the particular geometry and kinematics of the robot and obstacles. The emphasis is usually on finding ways to dramatically reduce the number or required samples. Several of these methods are briefly described here.

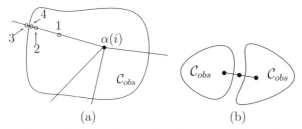

Figure 5.29: (a) To obtain samples along the boundary, binary search is used along random directions from a sample in $\mathcal{C}_{obs}$. (b) The bridge test finds narrow corridors by examining a triple of nearby samples along a line.

Vertex enhancement [519]

This heuristic strategy focuses effort on vertices that were difficult to connect to other vertices in the roadmap construction algorithm in Figure 5.25. A probability distribution, $P(v)$, is defined over the vertices $v \in V$. A number of iterations are then performed in which a vertex is sampled from V according to $P(v)$, and then some random motions are performed from v to try to reach new configurations. These new configurations are added as vertices, and attempts are made to connect them to other vertices, as selected by the NEIGHBORHOOD function in an ordinary iteration of the algorithm in Figure 5.25. A recommended heuristic [519] for defining $P(v)$ is to define a statistic for each v as $n_f/(n_t + 1)$, in which n_t is the total number of connections attempted for v, and n_f is the number of times these attempts failed. The probability $P(v)$ is assigned as $n_f/(n_t + 1)m$, in which m is the sum of the statistics over all $v \in V$ (this normalizes the statistics to obtain a valid probability distribution).

Sampling on the $\mathcal{C}_{free}$ boundary [22, 26]

This scheme is based on the intuition that it is sometimes better to sample along the boundary, $\partial \mathcal{C}_{free}$, rather than waste samples on large areas of $\mathcal{C}_{free}$ that might be free of obstacles. Figure 5.29a shows one way in which this can be implemented. For each sample of $\alpha(i)$ that falls into $\mathcal{C}_{obs}$, a number of random directions are chosen in $\mathcal{C}$; these directions can be sampled using the $\mathbb{S}^n$ sampling method from Section 5.2.2. For each direction, a binary search is performed to get a sample in $\mathcal{C}_{free}$ that is as close as possible to $\mathcal{C}_{obs}$. The order of point evaluation in the binary search is shown in Figure 5.29a. Let $\tau : [0, 1]$ denote the path for which $\tau(0) \in \mathcal{C}_{obs}$ and $\tau(1) \in \mathcal{C}_{free}$. In the first step, test the midpoint, $\tau(1/2)$. If $\tau(1/2) \in \mathcal{C}_{free}$, this means that $\partial \mathcal{C}_{free}$ lies between $\tau(0)$ and $\tau(1/2)$; otherwise, it lies between $\tau(1/2)$ and $\tau(1)$. The next iteration selects the midpoint of the path segment that contains $\partial \mathcal{C}_{free}$. This will be either $\tau(1/4)$ or $\tau(3/4)$. The process continues recursively until the desired resolution is obtained.

Gaussian sampling [134]

The Gaussian sampling strategy follows some of the same motivation for sampling on the boundary. In this case, the goal is to obtain points near $\partial \mathcal{C}_{free}$ by using a Gaussian distribution that biases the samples to be closer to $\partial \mathcal{C}_{free}$, but the bias is gentler, as prescribed by the variance parameter of the Gaussian. The samples are generated as follows. Generate one sample, $q_1 \in \mathcal{C}$, uniformly at random. Following this, generate another sample, $q_2 \in \mathcal{C}$, according to a Gaussian with mean q_1; the distribution must be adapted for any topological identifications and/or boundaries of $\mathcal{C}$. If one of q_1 or q_2 lies

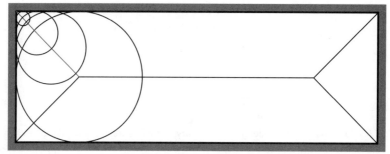

Figure 5.30: The medial axis is traced out by the centers of the largest inscribed balls. The five line segments inside of the rectangle correspond to the medial axis.

in $\mathcal{C}_{free}$ and the other lies in $\mathcal{C}_{obs}$, then the one that lies in $\mathcal{C}_{free}$ is kept as a vertex in the roadmap. For some examples, this dramatically prunes the number of required vertices.

Bridge-test sampling [468]

The Gaussian sampling strategy decides to keep a point based in part on testing a pair of samples. This idea can be carried one step further to obtain a *bridge test*, which uses three samples along a line segment. If the samples are arranged as shown in Figure 5.29b, then the middle sample becomes a roadmap vertex. This is based on the intuition that narrow corridors are thin in at least one direction. The bridge test indicates that a point lies in a thin corridor, which is often an important place to locate a vertex.

Medial-axis sampling [458, 638, 971]

Rather than trying to sample close to the boundary, another strategy is to force the samples to be as far from the boundary as possible. Let (X, ρ) be a metric space. Let a *maximal ball* be a ball $B(x, r) \subseteq X$ such that no other ball can be a proper subset. The centers of all maximal balls trace out a one-dimensional set of points referred to as the *medial axis*. A simple example of a medial axis is shown for a rectangular subset of $\mathbb{R}^2$ in Figure 5.30. The medial axis in $\mathcal{C}_{free}$ is based on the largest balls that can be inscribed in $cl(\mathcal{C}_{free})$. Sampling on the medial axis is generally difficult, especially because the representation of $\mathcal{C}_{free}$ is implicit. Distance information from collision checking can be used to start with a sample, $\alpha(i)$, and iteratively perturb it to increase its distance from $\partial \mathcal{C}_{free}$ [638, 971]. Sampling on the medial axis of $\mathcal{W} \setminus \mathcal{O}$ has also been proposed [458]. In this case, the medial axis in $\mathcal{W} \setminus \mathcal{O}$ is easier to compute, and it can be used to heuristically guide the placement of good roadmap vertices in $\mathcal{C}_{free}$.

Further reading

Unlike the last two chapters, the material of Chapter 5 is a synthesis of very recent research results. Some aspects of sampling-based motion planning are still evolving. Early approaches include [71, 146, 195, 282, 284, 331, 332, 661, 763]. The Gilbert-Johnson-Keerthi algorithm [390] is an early collision detection approach that helped inspire sampling-based motion planning; see [475] and [591] for many early references. In much of the early work, randomization appeared to be the main selling point; however, more recently it has been understood that deterministic sampling can work at least as well while obtaining resolution completeness. For a more recent survey of sampling-based motion planning, see [643].

Section 5.1 is based on material from basic mathematics books. For a summary of basic theorems and numerous examples of metric spaces, see [699]. More material appears in basic point-set topology books (e.g., [454, 499]) and analysis books (e.g., [348]). Metric issues in the context of sampling-based motion planning are discussed in [21, 612]. Measure theory is most often introduced in the context of real analysis [348, 428, 549, 839, 840]. More material on Haar measure appears in [428].

Section 5.2 is mainly inspired by literature on Monte Carlo and quasi–Monte Carlo methods for numerical integration and optimization. An excellent source of material is [741]. Other important references for further reading include [193, 543, 685, 937, 938]. Sampling issues in the context of motion planning are considered in [382, 562, 603, 642, 987]. Comprehensive introductions to pure Monte Carlo algorithms appear in [343, 505]. The original source for the Monte Carlo method is [698]. For a survey on algorithms that compute Voronoi diagrams, see [55].

For further reading on collision detection (beyond Section 5.3), see the surveys in [491, 640, 641, 706]. Hierarchical collision detection is covered in [408, 641, 705]. The incremental collision detection ideas in Section 5.3.3 were inspired by the algorithm [639] and V-Clip [249, 705]. Distance computation is covered in [169, 308, 389, 408, 416, 705, 810]. A method suited for detecting self-collisions of linkages appears in [656]. A combinatorial approach to collision detection for motion planning appears in [857]. Numerous collision detection packages are available for use in motion planning research. One of the most widely used is PQP because it works well for any mess of 3D triangles [948].

The incremental sampling and searching framework was synthesized by unifying ideas from many planning methods. Some of these include grid-based search [72, 551, 623] and probabilistic roadmaps (PRMs) [519]. Although the PRM was developed for multiple queries, the single-query version developed in [127] helped shed light on the connection to earlier planning methods. This even led to grid-based variants of PRMs [125, 603]. Another single-query variant is presented in [413].

RDTs were developed in the literature mainly as RRTs, and were introduced in [601, 613]. RRTs have been used in several applications, and many variants have been developed [84, 140, 152, 202, 226, 246, 267, 364, 395, 498, 501, 502, 531, 634, 644, 645, 919, 920, 949, 979, 986]. Originally, they were developed for planning under differential constraints, but most of their applications to date have been for ordinary motion planning. For more information on efficient nearest-neighbor searching, see the recent survey [478], and [47, 48, 49, 53, 101, 232, 367, 479, 541, 761, 909, 989].

Section 5.6 is based mainly on the PRM framework [519]. The "probabilistic" part is not critical to the method; thus, it was referred to here as a *sampling-based roadmap*. A related precursor to the PRM was proposed in [392, 393]. The PRM has been widely used in practice, and many variants have been proposed [1, 23, 62, 63, 127, 163, 183, 246, 482, 547, 603, 630, 631, 743, 787, 795, 886, 901, 950, 971, 979, 995]. An experimental comparison of many of these variants appears in [382]. Some analysis of PRMs appears in [70, 470, 576]. In some works, the term PRM has been applied to virtually any sampling-based planning algorithm (e.g., [470]); however, in recent years the term has been used more consistently with its original meaning in [519].

Many other methods and issues fall outside of the scope of this chapter. Several interesting methods based on *approximate cell decomposition* [146, 330, 649, 661] can be considered as a form of sampling-based motion planning. A sampling-based method of developing global potential functions appears in [126]. Other sampling-based planning algorithms appear in [196, 350, 420, 421, 466]. The algorithms of this chapter are generally unable to guarantee that a solution does not exist for a motion planning problem. It is possible, however, to use sampling-based techniques to establish in finite time that no solution exists [77]. Such a result is called a *disconnection proof*. Parallelization issues have also been investigated in the context of sampling-based motion planning [84, 179, 185, 259, 798].

Exercises

1. Prove that the Cartesian product of a metric space is a metric space by taking a linear combination as in (5.4).

2. Prove or disprove: If ρ is a metric, then ρ^2 is a metric.

3. Determine whether the following function is a metric on any topological space: X: $\rho(x, x') = 1$ is $x \neq x'$; otherwise, $\rho(x, x') = 0$.

4. State and prove whether or not (5.28) yields a metric space on $\mathcal{C} = SE(3)$, assuming that the two sets are rigid bodies.

5. The dispersion definition given in (5.19) is based on the worst case. Consider defining the *average dispersion*:

$$\bar{\delta}(P) = \int_X \min_{p \in P}\{\rho(x, p)\}dx. \tag{5.42}$$

Describe a Monte Carlo (randomized) method to approximately evaluate (5.42).

6. Determine the average dispersion for the van der Corput sequence (base 2) on $[0, 1]/\sim$.

7. Show that using the Lebesgue measure on $\mathbb{S}^3$ (spreading mass around uniformly on $\mathbb{S}^3$) yields the Haar measure for $SO(3)$.

8. Is the Haar measure useful in selecting an appropriate C-space metric? Explain.

9. Determine an expression for the (worst-case) dispersion of the ith sample in the base-p (Figure 5.2 shows base-2) van der Corput sequence in $[0, 1]/\sim$, in which 0 and 1 are identified.

10. Determine the dispersion of the following sequence on $[0, 1]$. The first point is $\alpha(1) = 1$. For each $i > 1$, let $c_i = \ln(2i - 3)/\ln 4$ and $\alpha(i) = c_i - \lfloor c_i \rfloor$. It turns out that this sequence achieves the best asymptotic dispersion possible, even in terms of the preceding constant. Also, the points are not uniformly distributed. Can you explain why this happens? [It may be helpful to plot the points in the sequence.]

11. Prove that (5.20) holds.

12. Prove that (5.23) holds.

13. Show that for any given set of points in $[0, 1]^n$, a range space $\mathcal{R}$ can be designed so that the discrepancy is as close as desired to 1.

14. Suppose $\mathcal{A}$ is a rigid body in $\mathbb{R}^3$ with a fixed orientation specified by a quaternion, h. Suppose that h is perturbed a small amount to obtain another quaternion, h' (no translation occurs). Construct a good upper bound on distance traveled by points on $\mathcal{A}$, expressed in terms of the change in the quaternion.

15. Design combinations of robots and obstacles in $\mathcal{W}$ that lead to C-space obstacles resembling bug traps.

16. How many k-neighbors can there be at most in an n-dimensional grid with $1 \leq k \leq n$?

17. In a high-dimensional grid, it becomes too costly to consider all $3^n - 1$ n-neighbors. It might not be enough to consider only $2n$ 1-neighbors. Determine a scheme for selecting neighbors that are spatially distributed in a good way, but without requiring too many. For example, what is a good way to select 50 neighbors for a grid in $\mathbb{R}^{10}$?

18. Explain the difference between searching an implicit, high-resolution grid and growing search trees directly on the C-space without a grid.

19. Improve the bound in (5.31) by considering the fact that rotating points trace out a circle, instead of a straight line.

20. (Open problem) Prove there are $n + 1$ main branches for an RRT starting from the center of an "infinite" n-dimensional ball in $\mathbb{R}^n$. The directions of the branches align with the vertices of a regular simplex centered at the initial configuration.

21. Implement 2D incremental collision checking for convex polygons to obtain "near constant time" performance.

22. Implement the sampling-based roadmap approach. Select an appropriate family of motion planning problems: 2D rigid bodies, 2D chains of bodies, 3D rigid bodies, etc.

(a) Compare the roadmaps obtained using visibility-based sampling to those obtained for the ordinary sampling method.

(b) Study the sensitivity of the method with respect to the particular NEIGHBORHOOD method.

(c) Compare random and deterministic sampling methods.

(d) Use the bridge test to attempt to produce better samples.

23. Implement the balanced, bidirectional RRT planning algorithm.

    (a) Study the effect of varying the amount of intermediate vertices created along edges.

    (b) Try connecting to the random sample using more powerful descent functions.

    (c) Explore the performance gains from using Kd-trees to select nearest neighbors.

24. Make an RRT-based planning algorithm that uses more than two trees. Carefully resolve issues such as the maximum number of allowable trees, when to start a tree, and when to attempt connections between trees.

25. Implement both the expansive-space planner and the RRT, and conduct comparative experiments on planning problems. For the full set of problems, keep the algorithm parameters fixed.

26. Implement a sampling-based algorithm that computes collision-free paths for a rigid robot that can translate or rotate on any of the flat 2D manifolds shown in Figure 4.5.

6

Combinatorial Motion Planning

Combinatorial approaches to motion planning find paths through the continuous configuration space without resorting to approximations. Due to this property, they are alternatively referred to as *exact* algorithms. This is in contrast to the sampling-based motion planning algorithms from Chapter 5.

6.1 Introduction

All of the algorithms presented in this chapter are *complete*, which means that for any problem instance (over the space of problems for which the algorithm is designed), the algorithm will either find a solution or will correctly report that no solution exists. By contrast, in the case of sampling-based planning algorithms, weaker notions of completeness were tolerated: resolution completeness and probabilistic completeness.

Representation is important

When studying combinatorial motion planning algorithms, it is important to carefully consider the definition of the input. What is the representation used for the robot and obstacles? What set of transformations may be applied to the robot? What is the dimension of the world? Are the robot and obstacles convex? Are they piecewise linear? The specification of possible inputs defines a set of problem instances on which the algorithm will operate. If the instances have certain convenient properties (e.g., low dimensionality, convex models), then a combinatorial algorithm may provide an elegant, practical solution. If the set of instances is too broad, then a requirement of both completeness and practical solutions may be unreasonable. Many general formulations of general motion planning problems are PSPACE-hard[1]; therefore, such a hope appears unattainable. Nevertheless, there exist general, complete motion planning algorithms. Note that focusing on the representation is the opposite philosophy from sampling-based planning, which hides these issues in the collision detection module.

Reasons to study combinatorial methods

There are generally two good reasons to study combinatorial approaches to motion planning:

1. In many applications, one may only be interested in a special class of planning problems. For example, the world might be 2D, and the robot might only be capable of translation. For many special classes, elegant and efficient algorithms can be developed. These algorithms are complete, do not depend on approximation, and can offer much better performance than sampling-based planning methods, such as those in Chapter 5.

---

[1] This implies NP-hard. An overview of such complexity statements appears in Section 6.5.1.

2. It is both interesting and satisfying to know that there are complete algorithms for an extremely broad class of motion planning problems. Thus, even if the class of interest does not have some special limiting assumptions, there still exist general-purpose tools and algorithms that can solve it. These algorithms also provide theoretical upper bounds on the time needed to solve motion planning problems.

Warning: Some methods are impractical

Be careful not to make the wrong assumptions when studying the algorithms of this chapter. A few of them are efficient and easy to implement, but many might be neither. Even if an algorithm has an amazing asymptotic running time, it might be close to impossible to implement. For example, one of the most famous algorithms from computational geometry can split a simple[2] polygon into triangles in $O(n)$ time for a polygon with n edges [192]. This is so amazing that it was covered in the *New York Times*, but the algorithm is so complicated that it is doubtful that anyone will ever implement it. Sometimes it is preferable to use an algorithm that has worse theoretical running time but is much easier to understand and implement. In general, though, it is valuable to understand both kinds of methods and decide on the trade-offs for yourself. It is also an interesting intellectual pursuit to try to determine how efficiently a problem can be solved, even if the result is mainly of theoretical interest. This might motivate others to look for simpler algorithms that have the same or similar asymptotic running times.

Roadmaps

Virtually all combinatorial motion planning approaches construct a *roadmap* along the way to solving queries. This notion was introduced in Section 5.6, but in this chapter stricter requirements are imposed in the roadmap definition because any algorithm that constructs one needs to be complete. Some of the algorithms in this chapter first construct a cell decomposition of $\mathcal{C}_{free}$ from which the roadmap is consequently derived. Other methods directly construct a roadmap without the consideration of cells.

Let $\mathcal{G}$ be a topological graph (defined in Example 4.6) that maps into $\mathcal{C}_{free}$. Furthermore, let $S \subset \mathcal{C}_{free}$ be the swath, which is set of all points reached by $\mathcal{G}$, as defined in (5.40). The graph $\mathcal{G}$ is called a *roadmap* if it satisfies two important conditions:

1. **Accessibility:** From any $q \in \mathcal{C}_{free}$, it is simple and efficient to compute a path $\tau : [0, 1] \to \mathcal{C}_{free}$ such that $\tau(0) = q$ and $\tau(1) = s$, in which s may be any point in S. Usually, s is the closest point to q, assuming $\mathcal{C}$ is a metric space.

2. **Connectivity-preserving:** Using the first condition, it is always possible to connect some q_I and q_G to some s_1 and s_2, respectively, in S. The second condition requires that if there exists a path $\tau : [0, 1] \to \mathcal{C}_{free}$ such that $\tau(0) = q_I$ and $\tau(1) = q_G$, then there also exists a path $\tau' : [0, 1] \to S$, such that $\tau'(0) = s_1$ and $\tau'(1) = s_2$. Thus, solutions are not missed because $\mathcal{G}$ fails to capture the connectivity of $\mathcal{C}_{free}$. This ensures that complete algorithms are developed.

By satisfying these properties, a roadmap provides a discrete representation of the continuous motion planning problem without losing any of the original connectivity information needed to solve it. A query, (q_I, q_G), is solved by connecting each query point to the roadmap and then performing a discrete graph search on $\mathcal{G}$. To maintain completeness,

---

[2] A polygonal region that has no holes.

the first condition ensures that any query can be connected to $\mathcal{G}$, and the second condition ensures that the search always succeeds if a solution exists.

6.2 Polygonal obstacle regions

Rather than diving into the most general forms of combinatorial motion planning, it is helpful to first see several methods explained for a case that is easy to visualize. Several elegant, straightforward algorithms exist for the case in which $\mathcal{C} = \mathbb{R}^2$ and $\mathcal{C}_{obs}$ is polygonal. Most of these cannot be directly extended to higher dimensions; however, some of the general principles remain the same. Therefore, it is very instructive to see how combinatorial motion planning approaches work in two dimensions. There are also applications where these algorithms may directly apply. One example is planning for a small mobile robot that may be modeled as a point moving in a building that can be modeled with a 2D polygonal floor plan.

After covering representations in Section 6.2.1, Sections 6.2.2–6.2.4 present three different algorithms to solve the same problem. The one in Section 6.2.2 first performs *cell decomposition* on the way to building the roadmap, and the ones in Sections 6.2.3 and 6.2.4 directly produce a roadmap. The algorithm in Section 6.2.3 computes maximum clearance paths, and the one in Section 6.2.4 that computes shortest paths (which consequently have no clearance).

6.2.1 Representation

Assume that $\mathcal{W} = \mathbb{R}^2$; the obstacles, $\mathcal{O}$, are polygonal; and the robot, $\mathcal{A}$, is a polygonal body that is only capable of translation. Under these assumptions, $\mathcal{C}_{obs}$ will be polygonal. For the special case in which $\mathcal{A}$ is a point in $\mathcal{W}$, $\mathcal{O}$ maps directly to $\mathcal{C}_{obs}$ without any distortion. Thus, the problems considered in this section may also be considered as planning for a *point robot*. If $\mathcal{A}$ is not a point robot, then the Minkowski difference, (4.37), of $\mathcal{O}$ and $\mathcal{A}$ must be computed. For the case in which both $\mathcal{A}$ and each component of $\mathcal{O}$ are convex, the algorithm in Section 4.3.2 can be applied to compute each component of $\mathcal{C}_{obs}$. In general, both $\mathcal{A}$ and $\mathcal{O}$ may be nonconvex. They may even contain holes, which results in a $\mathcal{C}_{obs}$ model such as that shown in Figure 6.1. In this case, $\mathcal{A}$ and $\mathcal{O}$ may be decomposed into convex components, and the Minkowski difference can be computed for each pair of components. The decompositions into convex components can actually be performed by adapting the cell decomposition algorithm that will be presented in Section 6.2.2. Once the Minkowski differences have been computed, they need to be merged to obtain a representation that can be specified in terms of simple polygons, such as those in Figure 6.1. An efficient algorithm to perform this merging is given in Section 2.4 of [266]. It can also be based on many of the same principles as the planning algorithm in Section 6.2.2.

To implement the algorithms described in this section, it will be helpful to have a data structure that allows convenient access to the information contained in a model such as Figure 6.1. How is the outer boundary represented? How are holes inside of obstacles represented? How do we know which holes are inside of which obstacles? These questions can be efficiently answered by using the doubly connected edge list data structure, which was described in Section 3.1.3 for consistent labeling of polyhedral faces. We will need to represent models, such as the one in Figure 6.1, and any other information that planning algorithms need to maintain during execution. There are three different records:

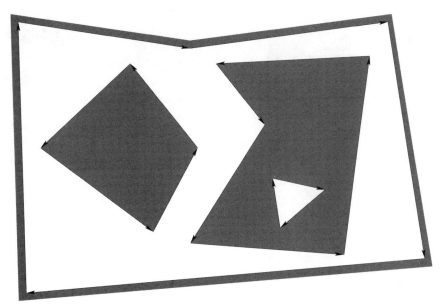

Figure 6.1: A polygonal model specified by four oriented simple polygons.

Vertices: Every vertex v contains a pointer to a point $(x, y) \in \mathcal{C} = \mathbb{R}^2$ and a pointer to some half-edge that has v as its origin.

Faces: Every face has one pointer to a half-edge on the boundary that surrounds the face; the pointer value is NIL if the face is the outermost boundary. The face also contains a list of pointers for each connected component (i.e., hole) that is contained inside of that face. Each pointer in the list points to a half-edge of the component's boundary.

Half-edges: Each half-edge is directed so that the obstacle portion is always to its left. It contains five different pointers. There is a pointer to its *origin vertex*. There is a *twin* half-edge pointer, which may point to a half-edge that runs in the opposite direction (see Section 3.1.3). If the half-edge borders an obstacle, then this pointer is NIL. Half-edges are always arranged in circular chains to form the boundary of a face. Such chains are oriented so that the obstacle portion (or a twin half-edge) is always to its left. Each half-edge stores a pointer to its internal face. It also contains pointers to the next and previous half-edges in the circular chain of half-edges.

For the example in Figure 6.1, there are four circular chains of half-edges that each bound a different face. The face record of the small triangular hole points to the obstacle face that contains the hole. Each obstacle contains a pointer to the face represented by the outermost boundary. By consistently assigning orientations to the half-edges, circular chains that bound an obstacle always run counterclockwise, and chains that bound holes run clockwise. There are no twin half-edges because all half-edges bound part of $\mathcal{C}_{obs}$. The doubly connected edge list data structure is general enough to allow extra edges to be inserted that slice through $\mathcal{C}_{free}$. These edges will not be on the border of $\mathcal{C}_{obs}$, but they can be managed using twin half-edge pointers. This will be useful for the algorithm in Section 6.2.2.

6.2.2 Vertical cell decomposition

Cell decompositions will be defined formally in Section 6.3, but here we use the notion informally. Combinatorial methods must construct a finite data structure that exactly

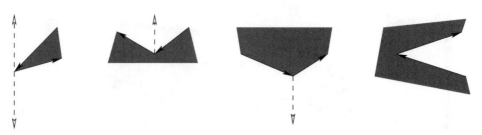

Figure 6.2: There are four general cases: 1) extending upward and downward, 2) upward only, 3) downward only, and 4) no possible extension.

encodes the planning problem. Cell decomposition algorithms achieve this partitioning of $\mathcal{C}_{free}$ into a finite set of regions called *cells*. The term *k-cell* refers refer to a k-dimensional cell. The cell decomposition should satisfy three properties:

1. Computing a path from one point to another inside of a cell must be trivially easy. For example, if every cell is convex, then any pair of points in a cell can be connected by a line segment.

2. Adjacency information for the cells can be easily extracted to build the roadmap.

3. For a given q_I and q_G, it should be efficient to determine which cells contain them.

If a cell decomposition satisfies these properties, then the motion planning problem is reduced to a graph search problem. Once again the algorithms of Section 2.2 may be applied; however, in the current setting, the entire graph, $\mathcal{G}$, is usually known in advance.[3] This was not assumed for discrete planning problems.

Defining the vertical decomposition

We next present an algorithm that constructs a *vertical cell decomposition* [191], which partitions $\mathcal{C}_{free}$ into a finite collection of 2-cells and 1-cells. Each 2-cell is either a trapezoid that has vertical sides or a triangle (which is a degenerate trapezoid). For this reason, the method is sometimes called *trapezoidal decomposition*. The decomposition is defined as follows. Let P denote the set of vertices used to define $\mathcal{C}_{obs}$. At every $p \in P$, try to extend rays upward and downward through $\mathcal{C}_{free}$, until $\mathcal{C}_{obs}$ is hit. There are four possible cases, as shown in Figure 6.2, depending on whether or not it is possible to extend in each of the two directions. If $\mathcal{C}_{free}$ is partitioned according to these rays, then a vertical decomposition results. Extending these rays for the example in Figure 6.3a leads to the decomposition of $\mathcal{C}_{free}$ shown in Figure 6.3b. Note that only trapezoids and triangles are obtained for the 2-cells in $\mathcal{C}_{free}$.

Every 1-cell is a vertical segment that serves as the border between two 2-cells. We must ensure that the topology of $\mathcal{C}_{free}$ is correctly represented. Recall that $\mathcal{C}_{free}$ was defined to be an open set. Every 2-cell is actually defined to be an open set in $\mathbb{R}^2$; thus, it is the interior of a trapezoid or triangle. The 1-cells are the interiors of segments. It is tempting to make 0-cells, which correspond to the endpoints of segments, but these are not allowed because they lie in $\mathcal{C}_{obs}$.

---

[3] Exceptions to this are some algorithms mentioned in Section 6.5.3, which obtain greater efficiency by only maintaining one connected component of $\mathcal{C}_{obs}$.

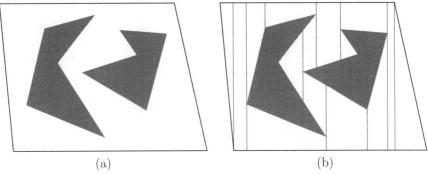

(a)   (b)

Figure 6.3: The vertical cell decomposition method uses the cells to construct a roadmap, which is searched to yield a solution to a query.

General position issues

What if two points along $\mathcal{C}_{obs}$ lie on a vertical line that slices through $\mathcal{C}_{free}$? What happens when one of the edges of $\mathcal{C}_{obs}$ is vertical? These are special cases that have been ignored so far. Throughout much of combinatorial motion planning it is common to ignore such special cases and assume $\mathcal{C}_{obs}$ is in *general position*. This usually means that if all of the data points are perturbed by a small amount in some random direction, the probability that the special case remains is zero. Since a vertical edge is no longer vertical after being slightly perturbed, it is not in general position. The general position assumption is usually made because it greatly simplifies the presentation of an algorithm (and, in some cases, its asymptotic running time is even lower). In practice, however, this assumption can be very frustrating. Most of the implementation time is often devoted to correctly handling such special cases. Performing random perturbations may avoid this problem, but it tends to unnecessarily complicate the solutions. For the vertical decomposition, the problems are not too difficult to handle without resorting to perturbations; however, in general, it is important to be aware of this difficulty, which is not as easy to fix in most other settings.

Defining the roadmap

To handle motion planning queries, a roadmap is constructed from the vertical cell decomposition. For each cell C_i, let q_i denote a designated *sample point* such that $q_i \in C_i$. The sample points can be selected as the cell centroids, but the particular choice is not too important. Let $\mathcal{G}(V, E)$ be a topological graph defined as follows. For every cell, C_i, define a vertex $q_i \in V$. There is a vertex for every 1-cell and every 2-cell. For each 2-cell, define an edge from its sample point to the sample point of every 1-cell that lies along its boundary. Each edge is a line-segment path between the sample points of the cells. The resulting graph is a roadmap, as depicted in Figure 6.4. The accessibility condition is satisfied because every sample point can be reached by a straight-line path thanks to the convexity of every cell. The connectivity condition is also satisfied because $\mathcal{G}$ is derived directly from the cell decomposition, which also preserves the connectivity of $\mathcal{C}_{free}$. Once the roadmap is constructed, the cell information is no longer needed for answering planning queries.

Solving a query

Once the roadmap is obtained, it is straightforward to solve a motion planning query, (q_I, q_G). Let C_0 and C_k denote the cells that contain q_I and q_G, respectively. In the graph

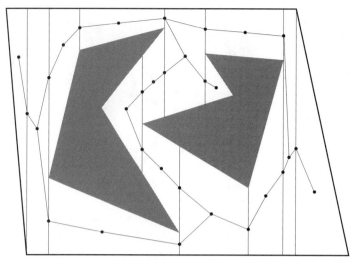

Figure 6.4: The roadmap derived from the vertical cell decomposition.

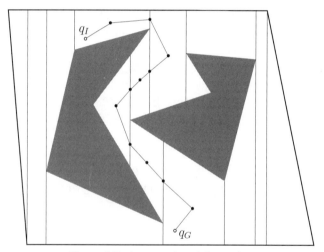

Figure 6.5: An example solution path.

$\mathcal{G}$, search for a path that connects the sample point of C_0 to the sample point of C_k. If no such path exists, then the planning algorithm correctly declares that no solution exists. If one does exist, then let $C_1, C_2, \ldots, C_{k-1}$ denote the sequence of 1-cells and 2-cells visited along the computed path in $\mathcal{G}$ from C_0 to C_k.

A solution path can be formed by simply "connecting the dots." Let $q_0, q_1, q_2, \ldots, q_{k-1}, q_k$, denote the sample points along the path in $\mathcal{G}$. There is one sample point for every cell that is crossed. The solution path, $\tau : [0, 1] \to \mathcal{C}_{free}$, is formed by setting $\tau(0) = q_I$, $\tau(1) = q_G$, and visiting each of the points in the sequence from q_0 to q_k by traveling along the shortest path. For the example, this leads to the solution shown in Figure 6.5. In selecting the sample points, it was important to ensure that each path segment from the sample point of one cell to the sample point of its neighboring cell is collision-free.[4]

---

[4] This is the reason why the approach is defined differently from Chapter 1 of [591]. In that case, sample points were not placed in the interiors of the 2-cells, and collision could result for some queries.

Computing the decomposition

The problem of efficiently computing the decomposition has not yet been considered. Without concern for efficiency, the problem appears simple enough that all of the required steps can be computed by brute-force computations. If C_{obs} has n vertices, then this approach would take at least $O(n^2)$ time because intersection tests have to be made between each vertical ray and each segment. This even ignores the data structure issues involved in finding the cells that contain the query points and in building the roadmap that holds the connectivity information. By careful organization of the computation, it turns out that all of this can be nicely handled, and the resulting running time is only $O(n \lg n)$.

Plane-sweep principle

The algorithm is based on the *plane-sweep* (or *line-sweep*) principle from computational geometry [129, 266, 304], which forms the basis of many combinatorial motion planning algorithms and many other algorithms in general. Much of computational geometry can be considered as the development of data structures and algorithms that generalize the sorting problem to multiple dimensions. In other words, the algorithms carefully "sort" geometric information.

The word "sweep" is used to refer to these algorithms because it can be imagined that a line (or plane, etc.) sweeps across the space, only to stop where some critical change occurs in the information. This gives the intuition, but the sweeping line is not explicitly represented by the algorithm. To construct the vertical decomposition, imagine that a vertical line sweeps from $x = -\infty$ to $x = \infty$, using (x, y) to denote a point in $C = \mathbb{R}^2$.

From Section 6.2.1, note that the set P of C_{obs} vertices are the only data in $\mathbb{R}^2$ that appear in the problem input. It therefore seems reasonable that interesting things can only occur at these points. Sort the points in P in increasing order by their X coordinate. Assuming general position, no two points have the same X coordinate. The points in P will now be visited in order of increasing x value. Each visit to a point will be referred to as an *event*. Before, after, and in between every event, a list, L, of some C_{obs} edges will be maintained. This list must be maintained at all times in the order that the edges appear when stabbed by the vertical sweep line. The ordering is maintained from lower to higher.

Algorithm execution

Figures 6.6 and 6.7 show how the algorithm proceeds. Initially, L is empty, and a doubly connected edge list is used to represent C_{free}. Each connected component of C_{free} yields a single face in the data structure. Suppose inductively that after several events occur, L is correctly maintained. For each event, one of the four cases in Figure 6.2 occurs. By maintaining L in a balanced binary search tree [245], the edges above and below p can be determined in $O(\lg n)$ time. This is much better than $O(n)$ time, which would arise from checking every segment. Depending on which of the four cases from Figure 6.2 occurs, different updates to L are made. If the first case occurs, then two different edges are inserted, and the face of which p is on the border is split two times by vertical line segments. For each of the two vertical line segments, two half-edges are added, and all faces and half-edges must be updated correctly (this operation is local in that only

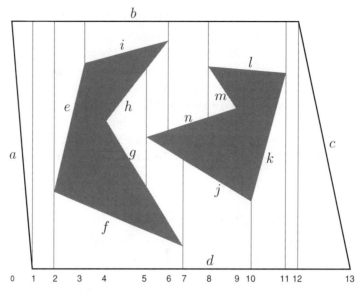

Figure 6.6: There are 14 events in this example.

Event	Sorted Edges in L	Event	Sorted Edges in L
0	$\{a, b\}$	7	$\{d, j, n, b\}$
1	$\{d, b\}$	8	$\{d, j, n, m, l, b\}$
2	$\{d, f, e, b\}$	9	$\{d, j, l, b\}$
3	$\{d, f, i, b\}$	10	$\{d, k, l, b\}$
4	$\{d, f, g, h, i, b\}$	11	$\{d, b\}$
5	$\{d, f, g, j, n, h, i, b\}$	12	$\{d, c\}$
6	$\{d, f, g, j, n, b\}$	13	$\{\}$

Figure 6.7: The status of L is shown after each of 14 events occurs. Before the first event, L is empty.

records adjacent to where the change occurs need to be updated). The next two cases in Figure 6.2 are simpler; only a single face split is made. For the final case, no splitting occurs.

Once the face splitting operations have been performed, L needs to be updated. When the sweep line crosses p, two edges are always affected. For example, in the first and last cases of Figure 6.2, two edges must be inserted into L (the mirror images of these cases cause two edges to be deleted from L). If the middle two cases occur, then one edge is replaced by another in L. These insertion and deletion operations can be performed in $O(\lg n)$ time. Since there are n events, the running time for the construction algorithm is $O(n \lg n)$.

The roadmap $\mathcal{G}$ can be computed from the face pointers of the doubly connected edge list. A more elegant approach is to incrementally build $\mathcal{G}$ at each event. In fact, all of the pointer maintenance required to obtain a consistent doubly connected edge list can be ignored if desired, as long as $\mathcal{G}$ is correctly built and the sample point is obtained for each cell along the way. We can even go one step further, by forgetting about the cell decomposition and directly building a topological graph of line-segment paths between all sample points of adjacent cells.

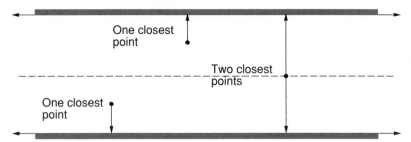

Figure 6.8: The maximum clearance roadmap keeps as far away from the C_{obs} as possible. This involves traveling along points that are equidistant from two or more points on the boundary of C_{obs}.

6.2.3 Maximum-clearance roadmaps

A *maximum-clearance roadmap* tries to keep as far as possible from C_{obs}, as shown for the corridor in Figure 6.8. The resulting solution paths are sometimes preferred in mobile robotics applications because it is difficult to measure and control the precise position of a mobile robot. Traveling along the maximum-clearance roadmap reduces the chances of collisions due to these uncertainties. Other names for this roadmap are *generalized Voronoi diagram* and *retraction method* [752]. It is considered as a generalization of the Voronoi diagram (recall from Section 5.2.2) from the case of points to the case of polygons. Each point along a roadmap edge is equidistant from two points on the boundary of C_{obs}. Each roadmap vertex corresponds to the intersection of two or more roadmap edges and is therefore equidistant from three or more points along the boundary of C_{obs}.

The retraction term comes from topology and provides a nice intuition about the method. A subspace S is a *deformation retract* of a topological space X if the following continuous homotopy, $h : X \times [0, 1] \rightarrow X$, can be defined as follows [454]:

1. $h(x, 0) = x$ for all $x \in X$.
2. $h(x, 1)$ is a continuous function that maps every element of X to some element of S.
3. For all $t \in [0, 1]$, $h(s, t) = s$ for any $s \in S$.

The intuition is that C_{free} is gradually thinned through the homotopy process, until a skeleton, S, is obtained. An approximation to this shrinking process can be imagined by shaving off a thin layer around the whole boundary of C_{free}. If this is repeated iteratively, the maximum-clearance roadmap is the only part that remains (assuming that the shaving always stops when thin "slivers" are obtained).

To construct the maximum-clearance roadmap, the concept of *features* from Section 5.3.3 is used again. Let the *feature set* refer to the set of all edges and vertices of C_{obs}. Candidate paths for the roadmap are produced by every pair of features. This leads to a naive $O(n^4)$ time algorithm as follows. For every edge-edge feature pair, generate a line as shown in Figure 6.9a. For every vertex-vertex pair, generate a line as shown in Figure 6.9b. The maximum-clearance path between a point and a line is a parabola. Thus, for every edge-point pair, generate a parabolic curve as shown in Figure 6.9c. The portions of the paths that actually lie on the maximum-clearance roadmap are determined by intersecting the curves. Several algorithms exist that provide better asymptotic running times [619, 629], but they are considerably more difficult to implement. The best-known algorithm runs in $O(n \lg n)$ time in which n is the number of roadmap curves [867].

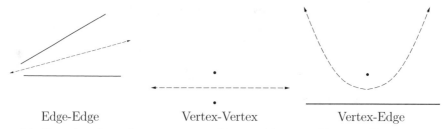

| Edge-Edge | Vertex-Vertex | Vertex-Edge |

Figure 6.9: Voronoi roadmap pieces are generated in one of three possible cases. The third case leads to a quadratic curve.

Figure 6.10: A bitangent edge must touch two reflex vertices that are mutually visible from each other, and the line must extend outward past each of them without poking into $\mathcal{C}_{obs}$.

6.2.4 Shortest-path roadmaps

Instead of generating paths that maximize clearance, suppose that the goal is to find shortest paths. This leads to the *shortest-path roadmap*, which is also called the *reduced visibility graph* in [591]. The idea was first introduced in [745] and may perhaps be the first example of a motion planning algorithm. The shortest-path roadmap is in direct conflict with maximum clearance because shortest paths tend to graze the corners of $\mathcal{C}_{obs}$. In fact, the problem is ill posed because $\mathcal{C}_{free}$ is an open set. For any path $\tau : [0, 1] \to \mathcal{C}_{free}$, it is always possible to find a shorter one. For this reason, we must consider the problem of determining shortest paths in $\mathrm{cl}(\mathcal{C}_{free})$, the closure of $\mathcal{C}_{free}$. This means that the robot is allowed to "touch" or "graze" the obstacles, but it is not allowed to penetrate them. To actually use the computed paths as solutions to a motion planning problem, they need to be slightly adjusted so that they come very close to $\mathcal{C}_{obs}$ but do not make contact. This slightly increases the path length, but the additional cost can be made arbitrarily small as the path gets arbitrarily close to $\mathcal{C}_{obs}$.

The *shortest-path roadmap*, $\mathcal{G}$, is constructed as follows. Let a *reflex vertex* be a polygon vertex for which the interior angle (in $\mathcal{C}_{free}$) is greater than π. All vertices of a convex polygon (assuming that no three consecutive vertices are collinear) are reflex vertices. The vertices of $\mathcal{G}$ are the reflex vertices. Edges of $\mathcal{G}$ are formed from two different sources:

> **Consecutive reflex vertices:** If two reflex vertices are the endpoints of an edge of $\mathcal{C}_{obs}$, then an edge between them is made in $\mathcal{G}$.
>
> **Bitangent edges:** If a *bitangent line* can be drawn through a pair of reflex vertices, then a corresponding edge is made in $\mathcal{G}$. A bitangent line, depicted in Figure 6.10, is a line that is incident to two reflex vertices and does not poke into the interior of $\mathcal{C}_{obs}$ at any of these vertices. Furthermore, these vertices must be mutually visible from each other.

An example of the resulting roadmap is shown in Figure 6.11. Note that the roadmap may have isolated vertices, such as the one at the top of the figure. To solve a query, q_I and q_G are connected to all roadmap vertices that are visible; this is shown in Figure 6.12. This makes an extended roadmap that is searched for a solution. If Dijkstra's algorithm is

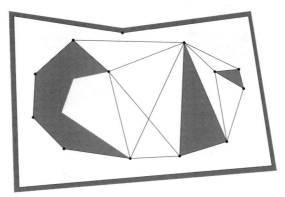

Figure 6.11: The shortest-path roadmap includes edges between consecutive reflex vertices on $\mathcal{C}_{obs}$ and also bitangent edges.

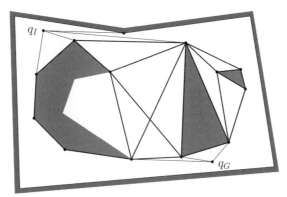

Figure 6.12: To solve a query, q_I and q_G are connected to all visible roadmap vertices, and graph search is performed.

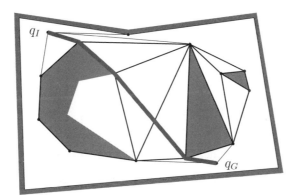

Figure 6.13: The shortest path in the extended roadmap is the shortest path between q_I and q_G.

used, and if each edge is given a cost that corresponds to its path length, then the resulting solution path is the shortest path between q_I and q_G. The shortest path for the example in Figure 6.12 is shown in Figure 6.13.

If the bitangent tests are performed naively, then the resulting algorithm requires $O(n^3)$ time, in which n is the number of vertices of $\mathcal{C}_{obs}$. There are $O(n^2)$ pairs of reflex vertices that need to be checked, and each check requires $O(n)$ time to make certain that no other edges prevent their mutual visibility. The plane-sweep principle from Section 6.2.2 can

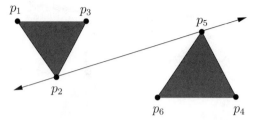

Figure 6.14: Potential bitangents can be identified by checking for left turns, which avoids the use of trigonometric functions and their associated numerical problems.

be adapted to obtain a better algorithm, which takes only $O(n^2 \lg n)$ time. The idea is to perform a *radial sweep* from each reflex vertex, v. A ray is started at $\theta = 0$, and events occur when the ray touches vertices. A set of bitangents through v can be computed in this way in $O(n \lg n)$ time. Since there are $O(n)$ reflex vertices, the total running time is $O(n^2 \lg n)$. See Chapter 15 of [266] for more details. There exists an algorithm that can compute the shortest-path roadmap in time $O(n \lg n + m)$, in which m is the total number of edges in the roadmap [386]. If the obstacle region is described by a simple polygon, the time complexity can be reduced to $O(n)$; see [712] for many shortest-path variations and references.

To improve numerical robustness, the shortest-path roadmap can be implemented without the use of trigonometric functions. For a sequence of three points, p_1, p_2, p_3, define the *left-turn predicate*, $f_l : \mathbb{R}^2 \times \mathbb{R}^2 \times \mathbb{R}^2 \to \{\text{TRUE, FALSE}\}$, as $f_l(p_1, p_2, p_3) = \text{TRUE}$ if and only if p_3 is to the left of the ray that starts at p_1 and pierces p_2. A point p_2 is a reflex vertex if and only if $f_l(p_1, p_2, p_3) = \text{TRUE}$, in which p_1 and p_3 are the points before and after, respectively, along the boundary of $\mathcal{C}_{obs}$. The bitangent test can be performed by assigning points as shown in Figure 6.14. Assume that no three points are collinear and the segment that connects p_2 and p_5 is not in collision. The pair, p_2, p_5, of vertices should receive a bitangent edge if the following sentence is FALSE:

$$\big(f_l(p_1, p_2, p_5) \oplus f_l(p_3, p_2, p_5)\big) \vee \big(f_l(p_4, p_5, p_2) \oplus f_l(p_6, p_5, p_2)\big), \qquad (6.1)$$

in which $\oplus$ denotes logical "exclusive or." The f_l predicate can be implemented without trigonometric functions by defining

$$M(p_1, p_2, p_3) = \begin{pmatrix} 1 & x_1 & y_1 \\ 1 & x_2 & y_2 \\ 1 & x_3 & y_3 \end{pmatrix}, \qquad (6.2)$$

in which $p_i = (x_i, y_i)$. If $\det(M) > 0$, then $l_f(p_1, p_2, p_3) = \text{TRUE}$; otherwise, $l_f(p_1, p_2, p_3) = \text{FALSE}$.

6.3 Cell decompositions

Section 6.2.2 introduced the vertical cell decomposition to solve the motion planning problem when $\mathcal{C}_{obs}$ is polygonal. It is important to understand, however, that this is just one choice among many for the decomposition. Some of these choices may not be preferable in 2D; however, they might generalize better to higher dimensions. Therefore, other cell decompositions are covered in this section, to provide a smoother transition from vertical cell decomposition to cylindrical algebraic decomposition in Section 6.4, which solves the motion planning problem in any dimension for any semi-algebraic model. Along the way, a cylindrical decomposition will appear in Section 6.3.4 for the special case of a line-segment robot in $\mathcal{W} = \mathbb{R}^2$.

6.3.1 General definitions

In this section, the term *complex* refers to a collection of cells together with their boundaries. A partition into cells can be derived from a complex, but the complex contains additional information that describes how the cells must fit together. The term *cell decomposition* still refers to the partition of the space into cells, which is derived from a *complex*.

It is tempting to define complexes and cell decompositions in a very general manner. Imagine that any partition of $\mathcal{C}_{free}$ could be called a cell decomposition. A cell could be so complicated that the notion would be useless. Even $\mathcal{C}_{free}$ itself could be declared as one big cell. It is more useful to build decompositions out of simpler cells, such as ones that contain no holes. Formally, this requires that every k-dimensional cell is homeomorphic to $B^k \subset \mathbb{R}^k$, an open k-dimensional unit ball. From a motion planning perspective, this still yields cells that are quite complicated, and it will be up to the particular cell decomposition method to enforce further constraints to yield a complete planning algorithm.

Two different complexes will be introduced. The *simplicial complex* is explained because it is one of the easiest to understand. Although it is useful in many applications, it is not powerful enough to represent all of the complexes that arise in motion planning. Therefore, the *singular complex* is also introduced. Although it is more complicated to define, it encompasses all of the cell complexes that are of interest in this book. It also provides an elegant way to represent topological spaces. Another important cell complex, which is not covered here, is the *CW-complex* [442].

Simplicial complex

For this definition, it is assumed that $X = \mathbb{R}^n$. Let $p_1, p_2, \ldots, p_{k+1}$, be $k + 1$ linearly independent[5] points in $\mathbb{R}^n$. A k-simplex, $[p_1, \ldots, p_{k+1}]$, is formed from these points as

$$[p_1, \ldots, p_{k+1}] = \left\{ \sum_{i=1}^{k+1} \alpha_i p_i \in \mathbb{R}^n \;\middle|\; 0 \leq \alpha_i \leq 1 \text{ for any } 1 \leq i \leq k + 1 \right\}, \qquad (6.3)$$

in which $\alpha_i p_i$ is the scalar multiplication of α_i by each of the point coordinates. Another way to view (6.3) is as the convex hull of the $k + 1$ points (i.e., all ways to linearly interpolate between them). If $k = 2$, a triangular region is obtained. For $k = 3$, a tetrahedron is produced.

For any k-simplex and any i such that $1 \leq i \leq k + 1$, let $\alpha_i = 0$. This yields a $(k - 1)$-dimensional simplex that is called a *face* of the original simplex. A 2-simplex has three faces, each of which is a 1-simplex that may be called an edge. Each 1-simplex (or edge) has two faces, which are 0-simplexes called *vertices*.

To form a complex, the simplexes must fit together in a nice way. This yields a high-dimensional notion of a *triangulation*, which in $\mathbb{R}^2$ is a tiling composed of triangular

---

[5] Form k vectors by subtracting p_1 from the other k points for some positive integer k such that $k \leq n$. Arrange the vectors into a $k \times n$ matrix. For linear independence, there must be at least one $k \times k$ cofactor with a nonzero determinant. For example, if $k = 2$, then the three points cannot be collinear.

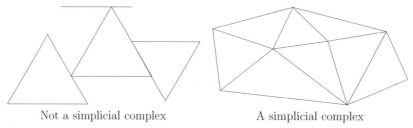

Not a simplicial complex   A simplicial complex

Figure 6.15: To become a simplicial complex, the simplex faces must fit together nicely.

regions. A *simplicial complex*, $\mathcal{K}$, is a finite set of simplexes that satisfies the following:

1. Any face of a simplex in $\mathcal{K}$ is also in $\mathcal{K}$.
2. The intersection of any two simplexes in $\mathcal{K}$ is either a common face of both of them or the intersection is empty.

Figure 6.15 illustrates these requirements. For $k > 0$, a k-cell of $\mathcal{K}$ is defined to be interior, $\text{int}([p_1, \ldots, p_{k+1}])$, of any k-simplex. For $k = 0$, every 0-simplex is a 0-cell. The union of all of the cells forms a partition of the point set covered by $\mathcal{K}$. This therefore provides a *cell decomposition* in a sense that is consistent with Section 6.2.2.

Singular complex

Simplicial complexes are useful in applications such as geometric modeling and computer graphics for computing the topology of models. Due to the complicated topological spaces, implicit, nonlinear models, and decomposition algorithms that arise in motion planning, they are insufficient for the most general problems. A *singular complex* is a generalization of the *simplicial complex*. Instead of being limited to $\mathbb{R}^n$, a singular complex can be defined on any manifold, X (it can even be defined on any Hausdorff topological space). The main difference is that, for a simplicial complex, each simplex is a subset of $\mathbb{R}^n$; however, for a singular complex, each *singular simplex* is actually a homeomorphism from a (simplicial) simplex in $\mathbb{R}^n$ to a subset of X.

To help understand the idea, first consider a 1D singular complex, which happens to be a topological graph (as introduced in Example 4.6). The interval $[0, 1]$ is a 1-simplex, and a continuous path $\tau : [0, 1] \to X$ is a *singular 1-simplex* because it is a homeomorphism of $[0, 1]$ to the image of τ in X. Suppose $\mathcal{G}(V, E)$ is a topological graph. The cells are subsets of X that are defined as follows. Each point $v \in V$ is a 0-cell in X. To follow the formalism, each is considered as the image of a function $f : \{0\} \to X$, which makes it a *singular 0-simplex*, because $\{0\}$ is a 0-simplex. For each path $\tau \in E$, the corresponding 1-cell is

$$\{x \in X \mid \tau(s) = x \text{ for some } s \in (0, 1)\}. \tag{6.4}$$

Expressed differently, it is $\tau((0, 1))$, the image of the path τ, except that the endpoints are removed because they are already covered by the 0-cells (the cells must form a partition).

These principles will now be generalized to higher dimensions. Since all balls and simplexes of the same dimension are homeomorphic, balls can be used instead of a simplex in the definition of a singular simplex. Let $B^k \subset \mathbb{R}^k$ denote a closed, k-dimensional unit ball,

$$D^k = \{x \in \mathbb{R}^n \mid \|x\| \le 1\}, \tag{6.5}$$

in which $\| \cdot \|$ is the Euclidean norm. A *singular k-simplex* is a continuous mapping $\sigma : D^k \to X$. Let $\text{int}(D^k)$ refer to the interior of D^k. For $k \geq 1$, the *k-cell*, C, corresponding to a singular k-simplex, σ, is the image $C = \sigma(\text{int}(D^k)) \subseteq X$. The 0-cells are obtained directly as the images of the 0 singular simplexes. Each singular 0-simplex maps to the 0-cell in X. If σ is restricted to $\text{int}(D^k)$, then it actually defines a homeomorphism between D^k and C. Note that both of these are open sets if $k > 0$.

A simplicial complex requires that the simplexes fit together nicely. The same concept is applied here, but topological concepts are used instead because they are more general. Let $\mathcal{K}$ be a set of singular simplexes of varying dimensions. Let S_k denote the union of the images of all singular i-simplexes for all $i \leq k$.

A collection of singular simplexes that map into a topological space X is called a *singular complex* if:

1. For each dimension k, the set $S_k \subseteq X$ must be closed. This means that the cells must all fit together nicely.

2. Each k-cell is an open set in the topological subspace S_k. Note that 0-cells are open in S_0, even though they are usually closed in X.

Example 6.1 (Vertical Decomposition) The vertical decomposition of Section 6.2.2 is a nice example of a singular complex that is not a simplicial complex because it contains trapezoids. The interior of each trapezoid and triangle forms a 2-cell, which is an open set. For every pair of adjacent 2-cells, there is a 1-cell on their common boundary. There are no 0-cells because the vertices lie in $\mathcal{C}_{obs}$, not in $\mathcal{C}_{free}$. The subspace S_2 is formed by taking the union of all 2-cells and 1-cells to yield $S_2 = \mathcal{C}_{free}$. This satisfies the closure requirement because the complex is built in $\mathcal{C}_{free}$ only; hence, the topological space is $\mathcal{C}_{free}$. The set $S_2 = \mathcal{C}_{free}$ is both open and closed. The set S_1 is the union of all 1-cells. This is also closed because the 1-cell endpoints all lie in $\mathcal{C}_{obs}$. Each 1-cell is also an open set.

One way to avoid some of these strange conclusions from the topology restricted to $\mathcal{C}_{free}$ is to build the vertical decomposition in $\text{cl}(\mathcal{C}_{free})$, the closure of $\mathcal{C}_{free}$. This can be obtained by starting with the previously defined vertical decomposition and adding a new 1-cell for every edge of $\mathcal{C}_{obs}$ and a 0-cell for every vertex of $\mathcal{C}_{obs}$. Now $S_3 = \text{cl}(\mathcal{C}_{free})$, which is closed in $\mathbb{R}^2$. Likewise, S_2, S_1, and S_0, are closed in the usual way. Each of the individual k-dimensional cells, however, is open in the topological space S_k. The only strange case is that the 0-cells are considered open, but this is true in the discrete topological space S_0. ∎

6.3.2 2D decompositions

The vertical decomposition method of Section 6.2.2 is just one choice of many cell decomposition methods for solving the problem when $\mathcal{C}_{obs}$ is polygonal. It provides a nice balance between the number of cells, computational efficiency, and implementation ease. It is usually possible to decompose $\mathcal{C}_{obs}$ into far fewer convex cells. This would be preferable for multiple-query applications because the roadmap would be smaller. It is unfortunately quite difficult to optimize the number of cells. Determining the decomposition of a polygonal $\mathcal{C}_{obs}$ with holes that uses the smallest number of convex cells is NP-hard [522, 648]. Therefore, we are willing to tolerate nonoptimal decompositions.

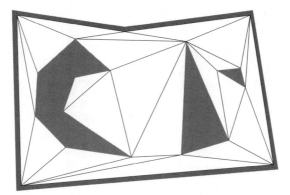

Figure 6.16: A triangulation of $\mathcal{C}_{obs}$.

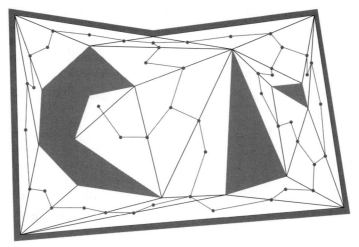

Figure 6.17: A roadmap obtained from the triangulation.

Triangulation

One alternative to the vertical decomposition is to perform a *triangulation*, which yields a simplicial complex over $\mathcal{C}_{free}$. Figure 6.16 shows an example. Since $\mathcal{C}_{free}$ is an open set, there are no 0-cells. Each 2-simplex (triangle) has either one, two, or three faces, depending on how much of its boundary is shared with $\mathcal{C}_{obs}$. A roadmap can be made by connecting the samples for 1-cells and 2-cells as shown in Figure 6.17. Note that there are many ways to triangulate $\mathcal{C}_{free}$ for a given problem. Finding good triangulations, which for example means trying to avoid thin triangles, is given considerable attention in computational geometry [129, 266, 304].

How can the triangulation be computed? It might seem tempting to run the vertical decomposition algorithm of Section 6.2.2 and split each trapezoid into two triangles. Even though this leads to triangular cells, it does not produce a simplicial complex (two triangles could abut the same side of a triangle edge). A naive approach is to incrementally split faces by attempting to connect two vertices of a face by a line segment. If this segment does not intersect other segments, then the split can be made. This process can be iteratively performed over all vertices of faces that have more than three vertices, until a triangulation is eventually obtained. Unfortunately, this results in an $O(n^3)$ time algorithm because $O(n^2)$ pairs must be checked in the worst case, and each check requires

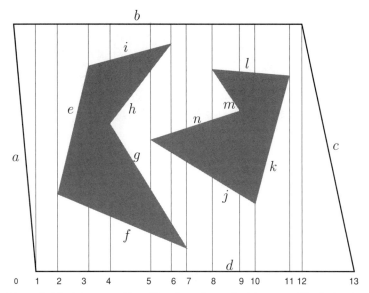

Figure 6.18: The cylindrical decomposition differs from the vertical decomposition in that the rays continue forever instead of stopping at the nearest edge. Compare this figure to Figure 6.6.

$O(n)$ time to determine whether an intersection occurs with other segments. This can be easily reduced to $O(n^2 \lg n)$ by performing radial sweeping. Chapter 3 of [266] presents an algorithm that runs in $O(n \lg n)$ time by first partitioning $\mathcal{C}_{free}$ into *monotone polygons*, and then efficiently triangulating each monotone polygon. If $\mathcal{C}_{free}$ is simply connected, then, surprisingly, a triangulation can be computed in linear time [192]. Unfortunately, this algorithm is too complicated to use in practice (there are, however, simpler algorithms for which the complexity is close to $O(n)$; see [92] and the end of Chapter 3 of [266] for surveys).

Cylindrical decomposition

The *cylindrical decomposition* is very similar to the vertical decomposition, except that when any of the cases in Figure 6.2 occurs, then a vertical line slices through all faces, all the way from $y = -\infty$ to $y = \infty$. The result is shown in Figure 6.18, which may be considered as a singular complex. This may appear very inefficient in comparison to the vertical decomposition; however, it is presented here because it generalizes nicely to any dimension, any C-space topology, and any semi-algebraic model. Therefore, it is presented here to ease the transition to more general decompositions. The most important property of the cylindrical decomposition is shown in Figure 6.19. Consider each vertical strip between two events. When traversing a strip from $y = -\infty$ to $y = \infty$, the points alternate between being $\mathcal{C}_{obs}$ and $\mathcal{C}_{free}$. For example, between events 4 and 5, the points below edge f are in $\mathcal{C}_{free}$. Points between f and g lie in $\mathcal{C}_{obs}$. Points between g and h lie in $\mathcal{C}_{free}$, and so forth. The cell decomposition can be defined so that 2D cells are also created in $\mathcal{C}_{obs}$. Let $S(x, y)$ denote the logical predicate (3.6) from Section 3.1.1. When traversing a strip, the value of $S(x, y)$ also alternates. This behavior is the main reason to construct a cylindrical decomposition, which will become clearer in Section 6.4.2. Each vertical strip is actually considered to be a *cylinder*, hence, the name cylindrical decomposition (i.e., there are not necessarily any cylinders in the 3D geometric sense).

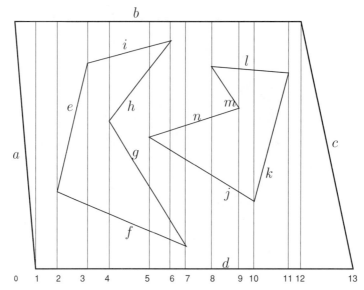

Figure 6.19: The cylindrical decomposition produces vertical strips. Inside of a strip, there is a stack of collision-free cells, separated by $\mathcal{C}_{obs}$.

6.3.3 3D vertical decomposition

It turns out that the vertical decomposition method of Section 6.2.2 can be extended to any dimension by recursively applying the sweeping idea. The method requires, however, that $\mathcal{C}_{obs}$ is piecewise linear. In other words, $\mathcal{C}_{obs}$ is represented as a semi-algebraic model for which all primitives are linear. Unfortunately, most of the general motion planning problems involve nonlinear algebraic primitives because of the nonlinear transformations that arise from rotations. Recall the complicated algebraic $\mathcal{C}_{obs}$ model constructed in Section 4.3.3. To handle generic algebraic models, powerful techniques from computational algebraic geometry are needed. This will be covered in Section 6.4.

One problem for which $\mathcal{C}_{obs}$ is piecewise linear is a polyhedral robot that can translate in $\mathbb{R}^3$, and the obstacles in $\mathcal{W}$ are polyhedra. Since the transformation equations are linear in this case, $\mathcal{C}_{obs} \subset \mathbb{R}^3$ is polyhedral. The polygonal faces of $\mathcal{C}_{obs}$ are obtained by forming geometric primitives for each of the Type FV, Type VF, and Type EE cases of contact between $\mathcal{A}$ and $\mathcal{O}$, as mentioned in Section 4.3.2.

Figure 6.20 illustrates the algorithm that constructs the 3D vertical decomposition. Compare this to the algorithm in Section 6.2.2. Let (x, y, z) denote a point in $\mathcal{C} = \mathbb{R}^3$. The vertical decomposition yields convex 3-cells, 2-cells, and 1-cells. Neglecting degeneracies, a generic 3-cell is bounded by six planes. The cross section of a 3-cell for some fixed x value yields a trapezoid or triangle, exactly as in the 2D case, but in a plane parallel to the yz plane. Two sides of a generic 3-cell are parallel to the yz plane, and two other sides are parallel to the xz plane. The 3-cell is bounded above and below by two polygonal faces of $\mathcal{C}_{obs}$.

Initially, sort the $\mathcal{C}_{obs}$ vertices by their x coordinate to obtain the events. Now consider sweeping a plane perpendicular to the x-axis. The plane for a fixed value of x produces a 2D polygonal slice of $\mathcal{C}_{obs}$. Three such slices are shown at the bottom of Figure 6.20. Each slice is parallel to the yz plane and appears to look exactly like a problem that can be solved by the 2D vertical decomposition method. The 2-cells in a slice are actually slices of 3-cells in the 3D decomposition. The only places in which these 3-cells can critically

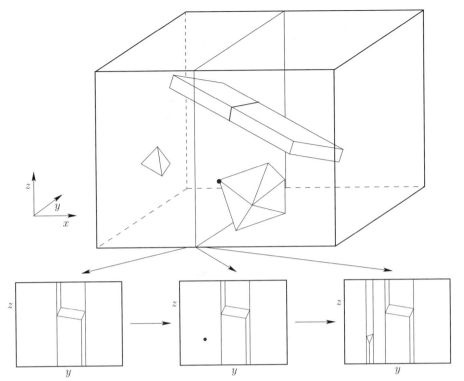

Figure 6.20: In higher dimensions, the sweeping idea can be applied recursively.

change is when the sweeping plane stops at some x value. The center slice in Figure 6.20 corresponds to the case in which a vertex of a convex polyhedron is encountered, and all of the polyhedron lies to right of the sweep plane (i.e., the rest of the polyhedron has not been encountered yet). This corresponds to a place where a critical change must occur in the slices. These are 3D versions of the cases in Figure 6.2, which indicate how the vertical decomposition needs to be updated. The algorithm proceeds by first building the 2D vertical decomposition at the first x event. At each event, the 2D vertical decomposition must be updated to take into account the critical changes. During this process, the 3D cell decomposition and roadmap can be incrementally constructed, as in the 2D case.

The roadmap is constructed by placing a sample point in the center of each 3-cell and 2-cell. The vertices are the sample points, and edges are added to the roadmap by connecting the sample points for each case in which a 3-cell is adjacent to a 2-cell.

This same principle can be extended to any dimension, but the applications to motion planning are limited because the method requires linear models (or at least it is very challenging to adapt to nonlinear models; in some special cases, this can be done). See [429] for a summary of the complexity of vertical decompositions for various geometric primitives and dimensions.

6.3.4 A decomposition for a line-segment robot

This section presents one of the simplest cell decompositions that involves nonlinear models, yet it is already fairly complicated. This will help to give an appreciation of the difficulty of combinatorial planning in general. Consider the planning problem shown in Figure 6.21. The robot, $\mathcal{A}$, is a single line segment that can translate or rotate in

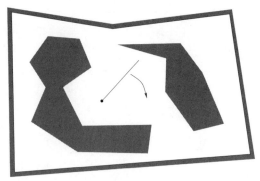

Figure 6.21: Motion planning for a line segment that can translate and rotate in a 2D world.

$\mathcal{W} = \mathbb{R}^2$. The dot on one end of $\mathcal{A}$ is used to illustrate its origin and is not part of the model. The C-space, $\mathcal{C}$, is homeomorphic to $\mathbb{R}^2 \times \mathbb{S}^1$. Assume that the parameterization $\mathbb{R}^2 \times [0, 2\pi] / \sim$ is used in which the identification equates $\theta = 0$ and $\theta = 2\pi$. A point in $\mathcal{C}$ is represented as (x, y, θ).

An approximate solution

First consider making a cell decomposition for the case in which the segment can only translate. The method from Section 4.3.2 can be used to compute $\mathcal{C}_{obs}$ by treating the robot-obstacle interaction with Type EV and Type VE contacts. When the interior of $\mathcal{A}$ touches an obstacle vertex, then Type EV is obtained. An endpoint of $\mathcal{A}$ touching an object interior yields Type VE. Each case produces an edge of $\mathcal{C}_{obs}$, which is polygonal. Once this is represented, the vertical decomposition can be used to solve the problem. This inspires a reasonable numerical approach to the rotational case, which is to discretize θ into K values, $i \Delta\theta$, for $0 \le i \le K$, and $\Delta\theta = 2\pi/K$ [20]. The obstacle region, $\mathcal{C}_{obs}$, is polygonal for each case, and we can imagine having a stack of K polygonal regions. A roadmap can be formed by connecting sampling points inside of a slice in the usual way, and also by connecting samples between corresponding cells in neighboring slices. If K is large enough, this strategy works well, but the method is not complete because a sufficient value for K cannot be determined in advance. The method is actually an interesting hybrid between combinatorial and sampling-based motion planning. A resolution-complete version can be imagined.

In the limiting case, as K tends to infinity, the surfaces of $\mathcal{C}_{obs}$ become curved along the θ direction. The conditions in Section 4.3.3 must be applied to generate the actual obstacle regions. This is possible, but it yields a semi-algebraic representation of $\mathcal{C}_{obs}$ in terms of implicit polynomial primitives. It is no easy task to determine an explicit representation in terms of simple cells that can be used for motion planning. The method of Section 6.3.3 cannot be used because $\mathcal{C}_{obs}$ is not polyhedral. Therefore, special analysis is warranted to produce a cell decomposition.

The general idea is to construct a cell decomposition in $\mathbb{R}^2$ by considering only the translation part, (x, y). Each cell in $\mathbb{R}^2$ is then lifted into $\mathcal{C}$ by considering θ as a third axis that is "above" the xy plane. A cylindrical decomposition results in which each cell in the xy plane produces a cylindrical stack of cells for different θ values. Recall the cylinders in Figures 6.18 and 6.19. The vertical axis corresponds to θ in the current setting, and the horizontal axis is replaced by two axes, x and y.

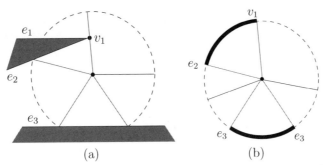

Figure 6.22: Fix (x, y) and swing the segment around for all values of $\theta \in [0, 2\pi]/\sim$. (a) Note the vertex and edge features that are hit by the segment. (b) Record orientation intervals over which the robot is not in collision.

To construct the decomposition in $\mathbb{R}^2$, consider the various robot-obstacle contacts shown in Figure 6.22. In Figure 6.22a, the segment swings around from a fixed (x, y). Two different kinds of contacts arise. For some orientation (value of θ), the segment contacts v_1, forming a Type EV contact. For three other orientations, the segment contacts an edge, forming Type VE contacts. Once again using the *feature* concept, there are four orientations at which the segment contacts a feature. Each feature may be either a vertex or an edge. Between the two contacts with e_2 and e_3, the robot is not in collision. These configurations lie in $\mathcal{C}_{free}$. Also, configurations for which the robot is between contacts e_3 (the rightmost contact) and v_1 are also in $\mathcal{C}_{free}$. All other orientations produce configurations in $\mathcal{C}_{obs}$. Note that the line segment cannot get from being between e_2 and e_3 to being between e_3 and v_1, unless the (x, y) position is changed. It therefore seems sensible that these must correspond to different cells in whatever decomposition is made.

Radar maps

Figure 6.22b illustrates which values of θ produce collision. We will refer to this representation as a *radar map*. The four contact orientations are indicated by the contact feature. The notation $[e_3, v_1]$ and $[e_2, e_3]$ identifies the two intervals for which $(x, y, \theta) \in \mathcal{C}_{free}$. Now imagine changing (x, y) by a small amount, to obtain (x', y'). How would the radar map change? The precise angles at which the contacts occur would change, but the notation $[e_3, v_1]$ and $[e_2, e_3]$, for configurations that lie in $\mathcal{C}_{free}$, remains unchanged. Even though the angles change, there is no interesting change in terms of the contacts; therefore, it makes sense to declare (x, y, θ) and (x, y, θ') to lie in the same cell in $\mathcal{C}_{free}$ because θ and θ' both place the segment between the same contacts. Imagine a column of two 3-cells above a small area around (x, y). One 3-cell is for orientations in $[e_3, v_1]$, and the other is for orientations in $[e_2, e_3]$. These appear to be 3D regions in $\mathcal{C}_{free}$ because each of x, y, and θ can be perturbed a small amount without leaving the cell.

Of course, if (x, y) is changed enough, then eventually we expect a dramatic change to occur in the radar map. For example, imagine e_3 is infinitely long, and the x value is gradually increased in Figure 6.22a. The black band between v_1 and e_2 in Figure 6.22b shrinks in length. Eventually, when the distance from (x', y') to v_1 is greater than the length of $\mathcal{A}$, the black band disappears. This situation is shown in Figure 6.23. The change is very important to notice because after that region vanishes, any orientation θ' between e_3 and e_3, traveling the long way around the circle, produces a configuration $(x', y', \theta') \in \mathcal{C}_{free}$. This seems very important because it tells us that we can travel between the original two cells by moving the robot further way from v_1, rotating the robot, and then moving

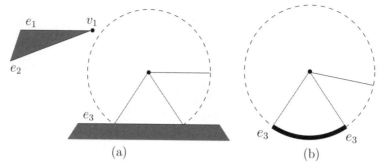

Figure 6.23: If x is increased enough, a critical change occurs in the radar map because v_1 can no longer be reached by the robot.

back. Now move from the position shown in Figure 6.23 into the positive y direction. The remaining black band begins to shrink and finally disappears when the distance to e_3 is further than the robot length. This represents another critical change.

The radar map can be characterized by specifying a circular ordering

$$([f_1, f_2], [f_3, f_4], [f_5, f_6], \ldots, [f_{2k-1}, f_{2k}]), \tag{6.6}$$

when there are k orientation intervals over which the configurations lie in $\mathcal{C}_{free}$. For the radar map in Figure 6.22b, this representation yields $([e_3, v_1], [e_2, e_3])$. Each f_i is a feature, which may be an edge or a vertex. Some of the f_i may be identical; the representation for Figure 6.23b is $([e_3, e_3])$. The intervals are specified in counterclockwise order around the radar map. Since the ordering is circular, it does not matter which interval is specified first. There are two degenerate cases. If $(x, y, \theta) \in \mathcal{C}_{free}$ for all $\theta \in [0, 2\pi)$, then we write () for the ordering. On the other hand, if $(x, y, \theta) \in \mathcal{C}_{obs}$ for all $\theta \in [0, 2\pi)$, then we write $\emptyset$.

Critical changes in cells

Now we are prepared to explain the cell decomposition in more detail. Imagine traveling along a path in $\mathbb{R}^2$ and producing an animated version of the radar map in Figure 6.22b. We say that a *critical change* occurs each time the circular ordering representation of (6.6) changes. Changes occur when intervals: 1) appear, 2) disappear, 3) split apart, 4) merge into one, or 5) when the feature of an interval changes. The first task is to partition $\mathbb{R}^2$ into maximal 2-cells over which no critical changes occur. Each one of these 2-cells, R, represents the projection of a strip of 3-cells in $\mathcal{C}_{free}$. Each 3-cell is defined as follows. Let $\{R, [f_i, f_{i+1}]\}$ denote the 3D region in $\mathcal{C}_{free}$ for which $(x, y) \in R$ and θ places the segment between contacts f_i and f_{i+1}. The *cylinder* of cells above R is given by $\{R, [f_i, f_{i+1}]\}$ for each interval in the circular ordering representation, (6.6). If any orientation is possible because $\mathcal{A}$ never contacts an obstacle while in R, then we write $\{R\}$.

What are the positions in $\mathbb{R}^2$ that cause critical changes to occur? It turns out that there are five different cases to consider, each of which produces a set of *critical curves* in $\mathbb{R}^2$. When one of these curves is crossed, a critical change occurs. If none of these curves is crossed, then no critical change can occur. Therefore, these curves precisely define the boundaries of the desired 2-cells in $\mathbb{R}^2$. Let L denote the length of the robot (which is the line segment).

Consider how the five cases mentioned above may occur. Two of the five cases have already been observed in Figures 6.22 and 6.23. These appear in Figures 6.24a and Figures 6.24b, and occur if (x, y) is within L of an edge or a vertex. The third and fourth

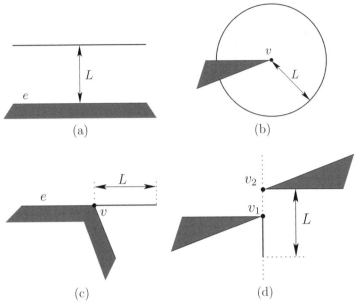

Figure 6.24: Four of the five cases that produce critical curves in $\mathbb{R}^2$.

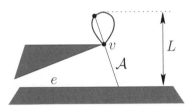

Figure 6.25: The fifth case is the most complicated. It results in a fourth-degree algebraic curve called the Conchoid of Nicomedes.

cases are shown in Figures 6.24c and 6.24d, respectively. The third case occurs because crossing the curve causes $\mathcal{A}$ to change between being able to touch e and being able to touch v. This must be extended from any edge at an endpoint that is a reflex vertex (interior angle is greater than π). The fourth case is actually a return of the bitangent case from Figure 6.10, which arose for the shortest path graph. If the vertices are within L of each other, then a linear critical curve is generated because $\mathcal{A}$ is no longer able to touch v_2 when crossing it from right to left. Bitangents always produce curves in pairs; the curve above v_2 is not shown. The final case, shown in Figure 6.25, is the most complicated. It is a fourth-degree algebraic curve called the Conchoid of Nicomedes, which arises from $\mathcal{A}$ being in simultaneous contact between v and e. Inside of the teardrop-shaped curve, $\mathcal{A}$ can contact e but not v. Just outside of the curve, it can touch v. If the xy coordinate frame is placed so that v is at $(0, 0)$, then the equation of the curve is

$$(x^2 - y^2)(y + d)^2 - y^2 L^2 = 0, \tag{6.7}$$

in which d is the distance from v to e.

Putting all of the curves together generates a cell decomposition of $\mathbb{R}^2$. There are *noncritical regions*, over which there is no change in (6.6); these form the 2-cells. The boundaries between adjacent 2-cells are sections of the critical curves and form 1-cells. There are also 0-cells at places where critical curves intersect. Figure 6.26 shows an

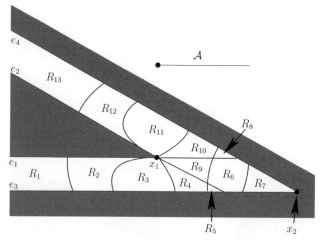

Figure 6.26: The critical curves form the boundaries of the noncritical regions in $\mathbb{R}^2$.

example adapted from [591]. Note that critical curves are not drawn if their corresponding configurations are all in C_{obs}. The method still works correctly if they are included, but unnecessary cell boundaries are made. Just for fun, they could be used to form a nice cell decomposition of C_{obs}, in addition to C_{free}. Since C_{obs} is avoided, is seems best to avoid wasting time on decomposing it. These unnecessary cases can be detected by imagining that $\mathcal{A}$ is a laser with range L. As the laser sweeps around, only features that are contacted by the laser are relevant. Any features that are hidden from view of the laser correspond to unnecessary boundaries.

After the cell decomposition has been constructed in $\mathbb{R}^2$, it needs to be lifted into $\mathbb{R}^2 \times [0, 2\pi]/ \sim$. This generates a cylinder of 3-cells above each 2D noncritical region, R. The roadmap could easily be defined to have a vertex for every 3-cell and 2-cell, which would be consistent with previous cell decompositions; however, vertices at 2-cells are not generated here to make the coming example easier to understand. Each 3-cell,$\{R, [f_i, f_{i+1}]\}$, corresponds to the vertex in a roadmap. The roadmap edges connect neighboring 3-cells that have a 2-cell as part of their common boundary. This means that in $\mathbb{R}^2$ they share a one-dimensional portion of a critical curve.

Constructing the roadmap

The problem is to determine which 3-cells are actually adjacent. Figure 6.27 depicts the cases in which connections need to be made. The xy plane is represented as one axis (imagine looking in a direction parallel to it). Consider two neighboring 2-cells (noncritical regions), R and R', in the plane. It is assumed that a 1-cell (critical curve) in $\mathbb{R}^2$ separates them. The task is to connect together 3-cells in the cylinders above R and R'. If neighboring cells share the same feature pair, then they are connected. This means that $\{R, [f_i, f_{i+1}]\}$ and $\{R', [f_i, f_{i+1}]\}$ must be connected. In some cases, one feature may change, while the interval of orientations remains unchanged. This may happen, for example, when the robot changes from contacting an edge to contacting a vertex of the edge. In these cases, a connection must also be made. One case illustrated in Figure 6.27 is when a splitting or merging of orientation intervals occurs. Traveling from R to R', the figure shows two regions merging into one. In this case, connections must be made from each of the original two 3-cells to the merged 3-cell. When constructing the roadmap edges, sample points of both the 3-cells and 2-cells should be used to ensure

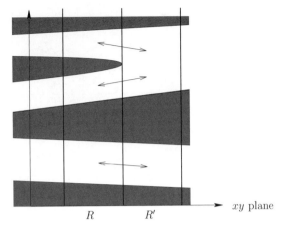

Figure 6.27: Connections are made between neighboring 3-cells that lie above neighboring noncritical regions.

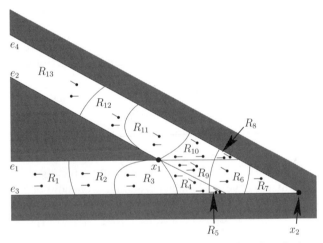

Figure 6.28: A depiction of the 3-cells above the noncritical regions. Sample rod orientations are shown for each cell (however, the rod length is shortened for clarity). Edges between cells are shown in Figure 6.29.

collision-free paths are obtained, as in the case of the vertical decomposition in Section 6.2.2. Figure 6.28 depicts the cells for the example in Figure 6.26. Each noncritical region has between one and three cells above it. Each of the various cells is indicated by a shortened robot that points in the general direction of the cell. The connections between the cells are also shown. Using the noncritical region and feature names from Figure 6.26, the resulting roadmap is depicted abstractly in Figure 6.29. Each vertex represents a 3-cell in $\mathcal{C}_{free}$, and each edge represents the crossing of a 2-cell between adjacent 3-cells. To make the roadmap consistent with previous roadmaps, we could insert a vertex into every edge and force the path to travel through the sample point of the corresponding 2-cell.

Once the roadmap has been constructed, it can be used in the same way as other roadmaps in this chapter to solve a query. Many implementation details have been neglected here. Due to the fifth case, some of the region boundaries in $\mathbb{R}^2$ are fourth-degree algebraic curves. Ways to prevent the explicit characterization of every noncritical region

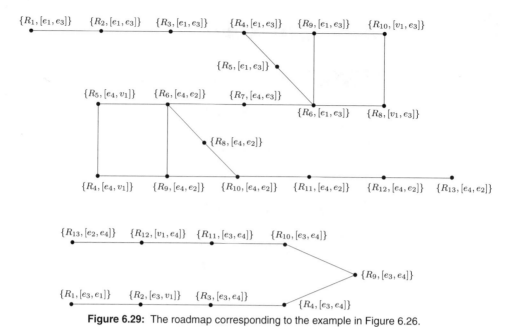

Figure 6.29: The roadmap corresponding to the example in Figure 6.26.

boundary, and other implementation details, are covered in [57]. Some of these details are also summarized in [591].

Complexity

How many cells can there possibly be in the worst case? First count the number of noncritical regions in $\mathbb{R}^2$. There are $O(n)$ different ways to generate critical curves of the first three types because each corresponds to a single feature. Unfortunately, there are $O(n^2)$ different ways to generate bitangents and the Conchoid of Nicomedes because these are based on pairs of features. Assuming no self-intersections, a collection of $O(n^2)$ curves in $\mathbb{R}^2$, may intersect to generate at most $O(n^4)$ regions. Above each noncritical region in $\mathbb{R}^2$, there could be a cylinder of $O(n)$ 3-cells. Therefore, the size of the cell decomposition is $O(n^5)$ in the worst case. In practice, however, it is highly unlikely that all of these intersections will occur, and the number of cells is expected to be reasonable. In [853], an $O(n^5)$-time algorithm is given to construct the cell decomposition. Algorithms that have much better running time are mentioned in Section 6.5.3, but they are more complicated to understand and implement.

6.4 Computational algebraic geometry

This section presents algorithms that are so general that they solve any problem of Formulation 4.1 and even the closed-chain problems of Section 4.4. It is amazing that such algorithms exist; however, it is also unfortunate that they are both extremely challenging to implement and not efficient enough for most applications. The concepts and tools of this section were mostly developed in the context of computational real algebraic geometry [79, 252]. They are powerful enough to conquer numerous problems in robotics, computer vision, geometric modeling, computer-aided design, and geometric theorem proving. One of these problems happens to be motion planning, for which the connection to computational algebraic geometry was first recognized in [854].

6.4.1 Basic definitions and concepts

This section builds on the semi-algebraic model definitions from Section 3.1 and the polynomial definitions from Section 4.4.1. It will be assumed that $\mathcal{C} \subseteq \mathbb{R}^n$, which could for example arise by representing each copy of $SO(2)$ or $SO(3)$ in its 2×2 or 3×3 matrix form. For example, in the case of a 3D rigid body, we know that $\mathcal{C} = \mathbb{R}^3 \times \mathbb{RP}^3$, which is a six-dimensional manifold, but it can be embedded in $\mathbb{R}^{12}$, which is obtained from the Cartesian product of $\mathbb{R}^3$ and the set of all 3×3 matrices. The constraints that force the matrices to lie in $SO(2)$ or $SO(3)$ are polynomials, and they can therefore be added to the semi-algebraic models of $\mathcal{C}_{obs}$ and $\mathcal{C}_{free}$. If the dimension of $\mathcal{C}$ is less than n, then the algorithm presented below is sufficient, but there are some representation and complexity issues that motivate using a special parameterization of $\mathcal{C}$ to make both dimensions the same while altering the topology of $\mathcal{C}$ to become homeomorphic to $\mathbb{R}^n$. This is discussed briefly in Section 6.4.2.

Suppose that the models in $\mathbb{R}^n$ are all expressed using polynomials from $\mathbb{Q}[x_1, \ldots, x_n]$, the set of polynomials[6] over the field of rational numbers $\mathbb{Q}$. Let $f \in \mathbb{Q}[x_1, \ldots, x_n]$ denote a polynomial.

Tarski sentences

Recall the logical predicates that were formed in Section 3.1. They will be used again here, but now they are defined with a little more flexibility. For any $f \in \mathbb{Q}[x_1, \ldots, x_n]$, an *atom* is an expression of the form $f \bowtie 0$, in which $\bowtie$ may be any relation in the set $\{=, \neq, <, >, \leq, \geq\}$. In Section 3.1, such expressions were used to define logical predicates. Here, we assume that relations other than $\leq$ can be used and that the vector of polynomial variables lies in $\mathbb{R}^n$.

A *quantifier-free formula*, $\phi(x_1, \ldots, x_n)$, is a logical predicate composed of atoms and logical connectives, "and," "or," and "not," which are denoted by $\wedge$, $\vee$, and $\neg$, respectively. Each atom itself is considered as a logical predicate that yields TRUE if and only if the relation is satisfied when the polynomial is evaluated at the point $(x_1, \ldots, x_n) \in \mathbb{R}^n$.

Example 6.2 (An Example Predicate) Let ϕ be a predicate over $\mathbb{R}^3$, defined as

$$\phi(x_1, x_2, x_3) = (x_1^2 x_3 - x_2^4 < 0) \vee \left(\neg(3x^2 x^3 \neq 0) \wedge (2x_3^2 - x_1 x_2 x_3 + 2 \geq 0) \right). \tag{6.8}$$

The precedence order of the connectives follows the laws of Boolean algebra. ∎

Let a *quantifier* Q be either of the symbols, $\forall$, which means "for all," or $\exists$, which means "there exists." A *Tarski sentence* Φ is a logical predicate that may additionally involve quantifiers on some or all of the variables. In general, a Tarski sentence takes the form

$$\Phi(x_1, \ldots, x_{n-k}) = (Qz_1)(Qz_2)\ldots(Qz_k)\, \phi(z_1, \ldots, z_k, x_1, \ldots, x_{n-k}), \tag{6.9}$$

in which the z_i are the *quantified variables*, the x_i are the *free variables*, and ϕ is a quantifier-free formula. The quantifiers do not necessarily have to appear at the left to be a valid Tarski sentence; however, any expression can be manipulated into an equivalent expression that has all quantifiers in front, as shown in (6.9). The procedure for moving quantifiers to the front is as follows [708]: 1) Eliminate any redundant quantifiers; 2) rename some of the variables to ensure that the same variable does not appear both free

---

[6] It will be explained shortly why $\mathbb{Q}[x_1, \ldots, x_n]$ is preferred over $\mathbb{R}[x_1, \ldots, x_n]$.

and bound; 3) move negation symbols as far inward as possible; and 4) push the quantifiers to the left.

Example 6.3 (Several Tarski Sentences)   Tarski sentences that have no free variables are either TRUE or FALSE in general because there are no arguments on which the results depend. The sentence

$$\Phi = \forall x \exists y \ (x^2 - y < 0), \tag{6.10}$$

is TRUE because for any $x \in \mathbb{R}$, some $y \in \mathbb{R}$ can always be chosen so that $y > x^2$. In the general notation of (6.9), this example becomes $\mathcal{Q}z_1 = \forall x$, $\mathcal{Q}z_2 = \exists y$, and $\phi(z_1, z_2) = (x^2 - y < 0)$.

Swapping the order of the quantifiers yields the Tarski sentence

$$\Phi = \exists y \forall x \ (x^2 - y < 0), \tag{6.11}$$

which is FALSE because for any y, there is always an x such that $x^2 > y$.

Now consider a Tarski sentence that has a free variable:

$$\Phi(z) = \exists y \forall x \ (x^2 - zx^2 - y < 0). \tag{6.12}$$

This yields a function $\Phi : \mathbb{R} \to \{\text{TRUE, FALSE}\}$, in which

$$\Phi(z) = \begin{cases} \text{TRUE} & \text{if } z > 1 \\ \text{FALSE} & \text{if } z \leq 1. \end{cases} \tag{6.13}$$

An equivalent quantifier-free formula ϕ can be defined as $\phi(z) = (z > 1)$, which takes on the same truth values as the Tarski sentence in (6.12). This might make you wonder whether it is always possible to make a simplification that eliminates the quantifiers. This is called the *quantifier-elimination problem*, which will be explained shortly. ∎

The decision problem

The sentences in (6.10) and (6.11) lead to an interesting problem. Consider the set of all Tarski sentences that have no free variables. The subset of these that are TRUE comprise the *first-order theory of the reals*. Can an algorithm be developed to determine whether such a sentence is true? This is called the *decision problem* for the first-order theory of the reals. At first it may appear hopeless because $\mathbb{R}^n$ is uncountably infinite, and an algorithm must work with a finite set. This is a familiar issue faced throughout motion planning. The sampling-based approaches in Chapter 5 provided one kind of solution. This idea could be applied to the decision problem, but the resulting lack of completeness would be similar. It is not possible to check all possible points in $\mathbb{R}^n$ by sampling. Instead, the decision problem can be solved by constructing a combinatorial representation that exactly represents the decision problem by partitioning $\mathbb{R}^n$ into a finite collection of regions. Inside of each region, only one point needs to be checked. This should already seem related to cell decompositions in motion planning; it turns out that methods developed to solve the decision problem can also conquer motion planning.

The quantifier-elimination problem

Another important problem was exemplified in (6.12). Consider the set of all Tarski sentences of the form (6.9), which may or may not have free variables. Can an algorithm be developed that takes a Tarski sentence Φ and produces an equivalent quantifier-free formula ϕ? Let $x_1, \ldots, x_n$ denote the free variables. To be equivalent, both must take on the same true values over $\mathbb{R}^n$, which is the set of all assignments $(x_1, \ldots, x_n)$ for the free variables.

Given a Tarski sentence, (6.9), the *quantifier-elimination problem* is to find a quantifier-free formula ϕ such that

$$\Phi(x_1, \ldots, x_n) = \phi(x_1, \ldots, x_n) \qquad (6.14)$$

for all $(x_1, \ldots, x_n) \in \mathbb{R}^n$. This is equivalent to constructing a semi-algebraic model because ϕ can always be expressed in the form

$$\phi(x_1, \ldots, x_n) = \bigvee_{i=1}^{k} \bigwedge_{j=1}^{m_i} \left(f_{i,j}(x_1, \ldots, x_n) \bowtie 0 \right), \qquad (6.15)$$

in which $\bowtie$ may be either $<$, $=$, or $>$. This appears to be the same (3.6), except that (6.15) uses the relations $<$, $=$, and $>$ to allow open and closed semi-algebraic sets, whereas (3.6) only used $\leq$ to construct closed semi-algebraic sets for $\mathcal{O}$ and $\mathcal{A}$.

Once again, the problem is defined on $\mathbb{R}^n$, which is uncountably infinite, but an algorithm must work with a finite representation. This will be achieved by the cell decomposition technique presented in Section 6.4.2.

Semi-algebraic decomposition

As stated in Section 6.3.1, motion planning inside of each cell in a complex should be trivial. To solve the decision and quantifier-elimination problems, a cell decomposition was developed for which these problems become trivial in each cell. The decomposition is designed so that only a single point in each cell needs to be checked to solve the decision problem.

The semi-algebraic set $Y \subseteq \mathbb{R}^n$ that is expressed with (6.15) is

$$Y = \bigcup_{i=1}^{k} \bigcap_{j=1}^{m_i} \left\{ (x_1, \ldots, x_n) \in \mathbb{R}^n \mid \text{sgn}(f_{i,j}(x_1, \ldots, x_n)) = s_{i,j} \right\}, \qquad (6.16)$$

in which sgn is the sign function, and each $s_{i,j} \in \{-1, 0, 1\}$, which is the range of sgn. Once again the nice relationship between set-theory and logic, which was described in Section 3.1, appears here. We convert from a set-theoretic description to a logical predicate by changing $\cup$ and $\cap$ to $\vee$ and $\wedge$, respectively.

Let $\mathcal{F}$ denote the set of $m = \sum_{i=1}^{k} m_i$ polynomials that appear in (6.16). A *sign assignment* with respect to $\mathcal{F}$ is a vector-valued function, $\text{sgn}_{\mathcal{F}} : \mathbb{R}^n \to \{-1, 0, 1\}^m$. Each $f \in \mathcal{F}$ has a corresponding position in the sign assignment vector. At this position, the sign, $\text{sgn}(f(x_1, \ldots, x_n)) \in \{-1, 0, 1\}$, appears. A *semi-algebraic decomposition* is a partition of $\mathbb{R}^n$ into a finite set of connected regions that are each *sign invariant*. This means that inside of each region, $\text{sgn}_{\mathcal{F}}$ must remain constant. The regions will not be called *cells* because a semi-algebraic decomposition is not necessarily a singular complex as defined in Section 6.3.1; the regions here may contain holes.

Example 6.4 (Sign assignment) Recall Example 3.1 and Figure 3.4 from Section 3.1.2. Figure 3.4a shows a sign assignment for a case in which there is only one polynomial, $\mathcal{F} = \{x^2 + y^2 - 4\}$. The sign assignment is defined as

$$\text{sgn}_{\mathcal{F}}(x, y) = \begin{cases} -1 & \text{if } x^2 + y^2 - 4 < 0 \\ 0 & \text{if } x^2 + y^2 - 4 = 0 \\ 1 & \text{if } x^2 + y^2 - 4 > 0. \end{cases} \qquad (6.17)$$

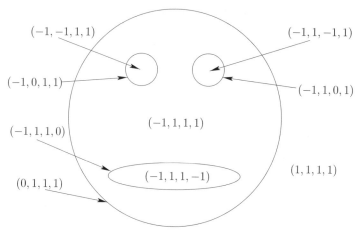

Figure 6.30: A semi-algebraic decomposition of the gingerbread face yields 9 sign-invariant regions.

Now consider the sign assignment $\text{sgn}_\mathcal{F}$, shown in Figure 6.30 for the gingerbread face of Figure 3.4b. The polynomials of the semi-algebraic model are $\mathcal{F} = \{f_1, f_2, f_3, f_4\}$, as defined in Example 3.1. In order, these are the "head," "left eye," "right eye," and "mouth." The sign assignment produces a four-dimensional vector of signs. Note that if (x, y) lies on one of the zeros of a polynomial in $\mathcal{F}$, then a 0 appears in the sign assignment. If the curves of two or more of the polynomials had intersected, then the sign assignment would produce more than one 0 at the intersection points.

For the semi-algebraic decomposition for the gingerbread face in Figure 6.30, there are nine regions. Five 2D regions correspond to: 1) being outside of the face, 2)inside of the left eye, 3) inside of the right eye, 4) inside of the mouth, and 5) inside of the face but outside of the mouth and eyes. There are four 1D regions, each of which corresponds to points that lie on one of the zero sets of a polynomial. The resulting decomposition is not a singular complex because the $(-1, 1, 1, 1)$ region contains three holes.   ■

A decomposition such as the one in Figure 6.30 would not be very useful for motion planning because of the holes in the regions. Further refinement is needed for motion planning, which is fortunately produced by cylindrical algebraic decomposition. On the other hand, any semi-algebraic decomposition is quite useful for solving the decision problem. Only one point needs to be checked inside of each region to determine whether some Tarski sentence that has no free variables is true. Why? If the polynomial signs cannot change over some region, then the TRUE/FALSE value of the corresponding logical predicate, Φ, cannot change. Therefore, it sufficient only to check one point per sign-invariant region.

6.4.2 Cylindrical algebraic decomposition

Cylindrical algebraic decomposition is a general method that produces a cylindrical decomposition in the same sense considered in Section 6.3.2 for polygons in $\mathbb{R}^2$ and also the decomposition in Section 6.3.4 for the line-segment robot. It is also referred to as *Collins decomposition* after its original developer [40, 234, 235]. The decomposition in Figure 6.19 can even be considered as a cylindrical algebraic decomposition for a semi-algebraic set in which every geometric primitive is a linear polynomial. In this section, such a decomposition is generalized to any semi-algebraic set in $\mathbb{R}^n$.

The idea is to develop a sequence of projections that drops the dimension of the semi-algebraic set by one each time. Initially, the set is defined over $\mathbb{R}^n$, and after one projection, a semi-algebraic set is obtained in $\mathbb{R}^{n-1}$. Eventually, the projection reaches $\mathbb{R}$, and a univariate polynomial is obtained for which the zeros are at the critical places where cell boundaries need to be formed. A cell decomposition of 1-cells (intervals) and 0-cells is formed by partitioning $\mathbb{R}$. The sequence is then reversed, and decompositions are formed from $\mathbb{R}^2$ up to $\mathbb{R}^n$. Each iteration starts with a cell decomposition in $\mathbb{R}^i$ and lifts it to obtain a cylinder of cells in $\mathbb{R}^{i+1}$. Figure 6.35 shows how the decomposition looks for the gingerbread example; since $n = 2$, it only involves one projection and one lifting.

Semi-algebraic projections are semi-algebraic

The following is implied by the *Tarski-Seidenberg Theorem* [79]:

A projection of a semi-algebraic set from dimension n to dimension $n - 1$ is a semi-algebraic set.

This gives a kind of closure of semi-algebraic sets under projection, which is required to ensure that every projection of a semi-algebraic set in $\mathbb{R}^i$ leads to a semi-algebraic set in $\mathbb{R}^{i-1}$. This property is actually not true for (real) algebraic varieties, which were introduced in Section 4.4.1. Varieties are defined using only the $=$ relation and are not closed under the projection operation. Therefore, it is a good thing (not just a coincidence!) that we are using semi-algebraic sets.

Real algebraic numbers

As stated previously, the sequence of projections ends with a univariate polynomial over $\mathbb{R}$. The sides of the cells will be defined based on the precise location of the roots of this polynomial. Furthermore, representing a sample point for a cell of dimension k in a complex in $\mathbb{R}^n$ for $k < n$ requires perfect precision. If the coordinates are slightly off, the point will lie in a different cell. This raises the complicated issue of how these roots are represented and manipulated in a computer.

For univariate polynomials of degree 4 or less, formulas exist to compute all of the roots in terms of functions of square roots and higher order roots. From Galois theory [472, 772], it is known that such formulas and nice expressions for roots do not exist for most higher degree polynomials, which can certainly arise in the complicated semi-algebraic models that are derived in motion planning. The roots in $\mathbb{R}$ could be any real number, and many real numbers require infinite representations.

One way of avoiding this mess is to assume that only polynomials in $\mathbb{Q}[x_1, \ldots, x_n]$ are used, instead of the more general $\mathbb{R}[x_1, \ldots, x_n]$. The field $\mathbb{Q}$ is not *algebraically closed* because zeros of the polynomials lie outside of $\mathbb{Q}^n$. For example, if $f(x_1) = x_1^2 - 2$, then $f = 0$ for $x_1 = \pm\sqrt{2}$, and $\sqrt{2} \notin \mathbb{Q}$. However, some elements of $\mathbb{R}$ can never be roots of a polynomial in $\mathbb{Q}[x_1, \ldots, x_n]$.

The set $\mathbb{A}$ of all real roots to all polynomials in $\mathbb{Q}[x]$ is called the set of *real algebraic numbers*. The set $\mathbb{A} \subset \mathbb{R}$ actually represents a field (recall from Section 4.4.1). Several nice algorithmic properties of the numbers in $\mathbb{A}$ are 1) they all have finite representations, 2) addition and multiplication operations on elements of $\mathbb{A}$ can be computed in polynomial time, and 3) conversions between different representations of real algebraic numbers can be performed in polynomial time. This means that all operations can be computed efficiently without resorting to some kind of numerical approximation. In some applications, such approximations are fine; however, for algebraic decompositions, they destroy critical information by potentially confusing roots (e.g., how can we know for sure whether a polynomial has multiple roots or just two roots that are very close together?).

The details are not presented here, but there are several methods for representing real algebraic numbers and the corresponding algorithms for manipulating them efficiently. The running time of cylindrical algebraic decomposition ultimately depends on this representation. In practice, a numerical root-finding method that has a precision parameter, ϵ, can be used by choosing ϵ small enough to ensure that roots will not be confused. A sufficiently small value can be determined by applying *gap theorems*, which give lower bounds on the amount of real root separation, expressed in terms of the polynomial coefficients [175]. Some methods avoid requiring a precision parameter. One well-known example is the derivation of a Sturm sequence of polynomials based on the given polynomial. The polynomials in the Sturm sequence are then used to find isolating intervals for each of the roots [79]. The polynomial, together with its isolating interval, can be considered as an exact root representation. Algebraic operations can even be performed using this representation in time $O(d \lg^2 d)$, in which d is the degree of the polynomial [854]. See [79, 175, 854] for detailed presentations on the exact representation and calculation with real algebraic numbers.

One-dimensional decomposition

To explain the cylindrical algebraic decomposition method, we first perform a semi-algebraic decomposition of $\mathbb{R}$, which is the final step in the projection sequence. Once this is explained, then the multi-dimensional case follows more easily.

Let $\mathcal{F}$ be a set of m univariate polynomials,

$$\mathcal{F} = \{ f_i \in \mathbb{Q}[x] \mid i = 1, \ldots, m \}, \tag{6.18}$$

which are used to define some semi-algebraic set in $\mathbb{R}$. The polynomials in $\mathcal{F}$ could come directly from a quantifier-free formula ϕ (which could even appear inside of a Tarski sentence, as in (6.9)).

Define a single polynomial as $f = \prod_{i=1}^{m} f_i$. Suppose that f has k distinct, real roots, which are sorted in increasing order:

$$-\infty < \beta_1 < \beta_2 < \cdots < \beta_{i-1} < \beta_i < \beta_{i+1} < \cdots < \beta_k < \infty. \tag{6.19}$$

The one-dimensional semi-algebraic decomposition is given by the following sequence of alternating 1-cells and 0-cells:

$$(-\infty, \beta_1), \ [\beta_1, \beta_1], \ (\beta_1, \beta_2), \ \ldots, \ (\beta_{i-1}, \beta_i), \ [\beta_i, \beta_i],$$
$$(\beta_i, \beta_{i+1}), \ \ldots, \ [\beta_k, \beta_k], \ (\beta_k, \infty). \tag{6.20}$$

Any semi-algebraic set that can be expressed using the polynomials in $\mathcal{F}$ can also be expressed as the union of some of the 0-cells and 1-cells given in (6.20). This can also be considered as a singular complex (it can even be considered as a simplicial complex, but this does not extend to higher dimensions).

Sample points can be generated for each of the cells as follows. For the unbounded cells $[-\infty, \beta_1)$ and $(\beta_k, \infty]$, valid samples are $\beta_1 - 1$ and $\beta_k + 1$, respectively. For each finite 1-cell, (β_i, β_{i+1}), the midpoint $(\beta_i + \beta_{i+1})/2$ produces a sample point. For each 0-cell, $[\beta_i, \beta_i]$, the only choice is to use β_i as the sample point.

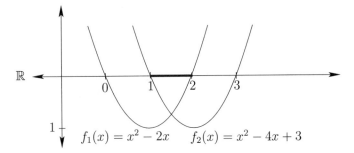

Figure 6.31: Two parabolas are used to define the semi-algebraic set [1, 2].

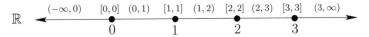

Figure 6.32: A semi-algebraic decomposition for the polynomials in Figure 6.31.

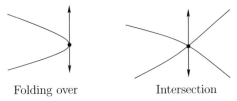

Figure 6.33: Critical points occur either when the surface folds over in the vertical direction or when surfaces intersect.

Example 6.5 (One-Dimensional Decomposition) Figure 6.31 shows a semi-algebraic subset of $\mathbb{R}$ that is defined by two polynomials, $f_1(x) = x^2 - 2x$ and $f_2(x) = x^2 - 4x + 3$. Here, $\mathcal{F} = \{f_1, f_2\}$. Consider the quantifier-free formula

$$\phi(x) = (x^2 - 2x \geq 0) \wedge (x^2 - 4x + 3 \geq 0). \tag{6.21}$$

The semi-algebraic decomposition into five 1-cells and four 0-cells is shown in Figure 6.32. Each cell is sign invariant. The sample points for the 1-cells are $-1, 1/2, 3/2, 5/2$, and 4, respectively. The sample points for the 0-cells are 0, 1, 2, and 3, respectively.

A decision problem can be nicely solved using the decomposition. Suppose a Tarski sentence that uses the polynomials in $\mathcal{F}$ has been given. Here is one possibility:

$$\Phi = \exists x [(x^2 - 2x \geq 0) \wedge (x^2 - 4x + 3 = 0)] \tag{6.22}$$

The sample points alone are sufficient to determine whether Φ is TRUE or FALSE. Once $x = 1$ is attempted, it is discovered that Φ is TRUE. The quantifier-elimination problem cannot yet be considered because more dimensions are needed. ∎

The inductive step to higher dimensions

Now consider constructing a cylindrical algebraic decomposition for $\mathbb{R}^n$ (note the decomposition is actually semi-algebraic). Figure 6.35 shows an example for $\mathbb{R}^2$. First consider how to iteratively project the polynomials down to $\mathbb{R}$ to ensure that when the decomposition of $\mathbb{R}^n$ is constructed, the sign-invariant property is maintained. The resulting decomposition corresponds to a singular complex.

There are two cases that cause cell boundaries to be performed, as shown in Figure 6.33. Let $\mathcal{F}_n$ denote the original set of polynomials in $\mathbb{Q}[x_1, \ldots, x_n]$ that are used to define the semi-algebraic set (or Tarski sentence) in $\mathbb{R}^n$. Form a single polynomial $f = \prod_{i=1}^{m} f_i$. Let $f' = \partial f / \partial x_n$, which is also a polynomial. Let $g = GCD(f, f')$, which is the greatest common divisor of f and f'. The set of zeros of g is the set of all points that are zeros of both f and f'. Being a zero of f' means that the surface given by $f = 0$ does not vary locally when perturbing x_n. These are places where a cell boundary needs to be formed because the surface may fold over itself in the x_n direction, which is not permitted for a cylindrical decomposition. Another place where a cell boundary needs to be formed is at the intersection of two or more polynomials in $\mathcal{F}_n$. The projection technique from $\mathbb{R}^n$ to $\mathbb{R}^{n-1}$ generates a set, $\mathcal{F}_{n-1}$, of polynomials in $\mathbb{Q}[x_1, \ldots, x_{n-1}]$ that satisfies these requirements. The polynomials $\mathcal{F}_{n-1}$ have the property that at least one contains a zero point below every point in $x \in \mathbb{R}^n$ for which $f(x) = 0$ and $f'(x) = 0$, or polynomials in $\mathcal{F}_n$ intersect. The projection method that constructs $\mathcal{F}_{n-1}$ involves computing *principle subresultant coefficients*, which are covered in [79, 855]. Resultants, of which the subresultants are an extension, are covered in [252].

The polynomials in $\mathcal{F}_{n-1}$ are then projected to $\mathbb{R}^{n-2}$ to obtain $\mathcal{F}_{n-2}$. This process continues until $\mathcal{F}_1$ is obtained, which is a set of polynomials in $\mathbb{Q}[x_1]$. A one-dimensional decomposition is formed, as defined earlier. From $\mathcal{F}_1$, a single polynomial is formed by taking the product, and $\mathbb{R}$ is partitioned into 0-cells and 1-cells. We next describe the process of lifting a decomposition over $\mathbb{R}^{i-1}$ up to $\mathbb{R}^i$. This technique is applied iteratively until $\mathbb{R}^n$ is reached.

Assume inductively that a cylindrical algebraic decomposition has been computed for a set of polynomials $\mathcal{F}_{i-1}$ in $\mathbb{Q}[x_1, \ldots, x_{i-1}]$. The decomposition consists of k-cells for which $0 \leq k \leq i$. Let $p = (x_1, \ldots, x_{i-1}) \in \mathbb{R}^{i-1}$. For each one of the k-cells C_{i-1}, a *cylinder* over C_{i-1} is defined as the $(k + 1)$-dimensional set

$$\{(p, x_i) \in \mathbb{R}^i \mid p \in C_{i-1}\}. \tag{6.23}$$

The cylinder is sliced into a strip of k-dimensional and $k + 1$-dimensional cells by using polynomials in $\mathcal{F}_i$. Let f_j denote one of the ℓ slicing polynomials in the cylinder, sorted in increasing x_i order as $f_1, f_2, \ldots, f_j, f_{j+1}, \ldots, f_\ell$. The following kinds of cells are produced (see Figure 6.34):

1. **Lower unbounded sector:**

$$\{(p, x_i) \in \mathbb{R}^i \mid p \in C_{i-1} \text{ and } x_i < f_1(p)\}. \tag{6.24}$$

2. **Section:**

$$\{(p, x_i) \in \mathbb{R}^i \mid p \in C_{i-1} \text{ and } x_i = f_j(p)\}. \tag{6.25}$$

3. **Bounded sector:**

$$\{(p, x_i) \in \mathbb{R}^i \mid p \in C_{i-1} \text{ and } f_j(p) < x_i < f_{j+1}(p)\}. \tag{6.26}$$

4. **Upper unbounded sector:**

$$\{(p, x_i) \in \mathbb{R}^i \mid p \in C_{i-1} \text{ and } f_\ell(p) < x_i\}. \tag{6.27}$$

There is one degenerate possibility in which there are no slicing polynomials and the cylinder over C_{i-1} can be extended into one unbounded cell. In general, the sample points are computed by picking a point in $p \in C_{i-1}$ and making a vertical column of samples of the form (p, x_i). A polynomial in $\mathbb{Q}[x_i]$ can be generated, and the samples are placed using the same assignment technique that was used for the one-dimensional decomposition.

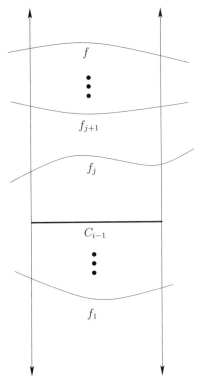

Figure 6.34: A cylinder over every k-cell C_{i-1} is formed. A sequence of polynomials, $f_1, \ldots, f_\ell$, slices the cylinder into k-dimensional sections and $(k+1)$-dimensional sectors.

Example 6.6 (Mutilating the Gingerbread Face) Figure 6.35 shows a cylindrical algebraic decomposition of the gingerbread face. Observe that the resulting complex is very similar to that obtained in Figure 6.19. ∎

Note that the cells do not necessarily project onto a rectangular set, as in the case of a higher dimensional vertical decomposition. For example, a generic n-cell C_n for a decomposition of $\mathbb{R}^n$ is described as the open set of $(x_1, \ldots, x_n) \in \mathbb{R}^n$ such that

- $C_0 < x_n < C_0'$ for some 0-cells $C_0, C_0' \in \mathbb{R}$, which are roots of some $f, f' \in \mathcal{F}_1$.
- (x_{n-1}, x_n) lies between C_1 and C_1' for some 1-cells C_1, C_1', which are zeros of some $f, f' \in \mathcal{F}_2$.
  $\vdots$
- $(x_{n-i+1}, \ldots, x_n)$ lies between C_{i-1} and C_{i-1}' for some i-cells C_{i-1}, C_{i-1}', which are zeros of some $f, f' \in \mathcal{F}_i$.
  $\vdots$
- $(x_1, \ldots, x_n)$ lies between C_{n-1} and C_{n-1}' for some $(n-1)$-cells C_{n-1}, C_{n-1}', which are zeros of some $f, f' \in \mathcal{F}_n$.

The resulting decomposition is sign invariant, which allows the decision and quantifier-elimination problems to be solved in finite time. To solve a decision problem, the polynomials in $\mathcal{F}_n$ are evaluated at every sample point to determine whether one of them satisfies the Tarski sentence. To solve the quantifier-elimination problem, note that any semi-algebraic sets that can be constructed from $\mathcal{F}_n$ can be defined as a union of some

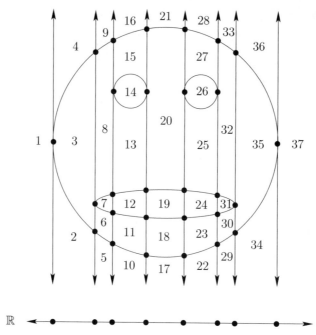

Figure 6.35: A cylindrical algebraic decomposition of the gingerbread face. There are 37 2-cells, 64 1-cells, and 28 0-cells. The straight 1-cells are intervals of the vertical lines, and the curved ones are portions of the zero set of a polynomial in $\mathcal{F}$. The decomposition of $\mathbb{R}$ is also shown.

cells in the decomposition. For the given Tarski sentence, $\mathcal{F}_n$ is formed from all polynomials that are mentioned in the sentence, and the cell decomposition is performed. Once obtained, the sign information is used to determine which cells need to be included in the union. The resulting union of cells is designed to include only the points in $\mathbb{R}^n$ at which the Tarski sentence is TRUE.

Solving a motion planning problem

Cylindrical algebraic decomposition is also capable of solving any of the motion planning problems formulated in Chapter 4. First assume that $\mathcal{C} = \mathbb{R}^n$. As for other decompositions, a roadmap is formed in which every vertex is an n-cell and edges connect every pair of adjacent n-cells by traveling through an $(n-1)$-cell. It is straightforward to determine adjacencies inside of a cylinder, but there are several technical details associated with determining adjacencies of cells from different cylinders (pages 152–154 of [79] present an example that illustrates the problem). The cells of dimension less than $n-1$ are not needed for motion planning purposes (just as vertices were not needed for the vertical decomposition in Section 6.2.2). The query points q_I and q_G are connected to the roadmap depending on the cell in which they lie, and a discrete search is performed.

If $\mathcal{C} \subset \mathbb{R}^n$ and its dimension is k for $k < n$, then all of the interesting cells are of lower dimension. This occurs, for example, due to the constraints on the matrices to force them to lie in $SO(2)$ or $SO(3)$. This may also occur for problems from Section 4.4, in which closed chains reduce the degrees of freedom. The cylindrical algebraic decomposition method can still solve such problems; however, the exact root representation problem becomes more complicated when determining the cell adjacencies. A discussion of these issues appears in [854]. For the case of $SO(2)$ and $SO(3)$, this complication can be avoided by using *stereographic projection* to map $\mathbb{S}^1$ or $\mathbb{S}^3$ to $\mathbb{R}$ or $\mathbb{R}^3$, respectively. This mapping removes a single point from each, but the connectivity of $\mathcal{C}_{free}$ remains unharmed. The antipodal identification problem for unit quaternions represented by $\mathbb{S}^3$ also does not present a problem; there is a redundant copy of $\mathcal{C}$, which does not affect the connectivity.

The running time for cylindrical algebraic decomposition depends on many factors, but in general it is polynomial in the number of polynomials in $\mathcal{F}_n$, polynomial in the maximum algebraic degree of the polynomials, and doubly exponential in the dimension. Complexity issues are covered in more detail in Section 6.5.3.

6.4.3 Canny's roadmap algorithm

The doubly exponential running time of cylindrical algebraic decomposition inspired researchers to do better. It has been shown that quantifier elimination requires doubly exponential time [264]; however, motion planning is a different problem. Canny introduced a method that produces a roadmap directly from the semi-algebraic set, rather than constructing a cell decomposition along the way. Since there are doubly exponentially many cells in the cylindrical algebraic decomposition, avoiding this construction pays off. The resulting roadmap method of Canny solves the motion planning problem in time that is again polynomial in the number of polynomials and polynomial in the algebraic degree, but it is only singly exponential in dimension [172, 175]; see also [79].

Much like the other combinatorial motion planning approaches, it is based on finding critical curves and critical points. The main idea is to construct linear mappings from $\mathbb{R}^n$ to $\mathbb{R}^2$ that produce *silhouette curves* of the semi-algebraic sets. Performing one such mapping on the original semi-algebraic set yields a roadmap, but it might not preserve the original connectivity. Therefore, linear mappings from $\mathbb{R}^{n-1}$ to $\mathbb{R}^2$ are performed on some $(n-1)$-dimensional slices of the original semi-algebraic set to yield more roadmap curves. This process is applied recursively until the slices are already one-dimensional. The resulting roadmap is formed from the union of all of the pieces obtained in the recursive calls. The resulting roadmap has the same connectivity as the original semi-algebraic set [175].

Suppose that $\mathcal{C} = \mathbb{R}^n$. Let $\mathcal{F} = \{f_1, \ldots, f_m\}$ denote the set of polynomials that define the semi-algebraic set, which is assumed to be a disjoint union of manifolds. Assume that each $f_i \in \mathbb{Q}[x_1, \ldots, x_n]$. First, a small perturbation to the input polynomials $\mathcal{F}$ is performed to ensure that every sign-invariant set of $\mathbb{R}^n$ is a manifold. This forces the polynomials into a kind of general position, which can be achieved with probability one using random perturbations; there are also deterministic methods to solve this problem. The general position requirements on the input polynomials and the 2D projection directions are fairly strong, which has stimulated more recent work that eliminates many of the problems [79]. From this point onward, it will be assumed that the polynomials are in general position.

Recall the sign-assignment function from Section 6.4.1. Each sign-invariant set is a manifold because of the general position assumption. Canny's method computes a roadmap for any k-dimensional manifold for $k < n$. Such a manifold has precisely $n - k$ signs that are 0 (which means that points lie precisely on the zero sets of $n - k$ polynomials in $\mathcal{F}$). At least one of the signs must be 0, which means that Canny's roadmap actually lies in $\partial \mathcal{C}_{free}$ (this technically is not permitted, but the algorithm nevertheless correctly decides whether a solution path exists through $\mathcal{C}_{free}$).

Recall that each f_i is a function, $f_i : \mathbb{R}^n \to \mathbb{R}$. Let x denote $(x_1, \ldots, x_n) \in \mathbb{R}^n$. The k polynomials that have zero signs can be put together sequentially to produce a mapping $\psi : \mathbb{R}^n \to \mathbb{R}^k$. The ith component of the vector $\psi(x)$ is $\psi_i(x) = f_i(x)$. This is closely

related to the sign assignment function of Section 6.4.1, except that now the real value
from each polynomial is directly used, rather than taking its sign.

Now introduce a function $g : \mathbb{R}^n \to \mathbb{R}^j$, in which either $j = 1$ or $j = 2$ (the general
concepts presented below work for other values of j, but 1 and 2 are the only values
needed for Canny's method). The function g serves the same purpose as a projection in
cylindrical algebraic decomposition, but note that g immediately drops from dimension n
to dimension 2 or 1, instead of dropping to $n - 1$ as in the case of cylindrical projections.

Let $h : \mathbb{R}^n \to \mathbb{R}^{k+j}$ denote a mapping constructed directly from ψ and g as follows.
For the ith component, if $i \leq k$, then $h_i(x) = \psi_i(x) = f_i(x)$. Assume that $k + j \leq n$. If
$i > k$, then $h_i(x) = g_{i-k}(x)$. Let $J_x(h)$ denote the *Jacobian* of h and be defined at x as

$$J_x(h) = \begin{pmatrix} \dfrac{\partial h_1(x)}{\partial x_1} & \cdots & \dfrac{\partial h_1(x)}{\partial x_n} \\ \vdots & & \vdots \\ \dfrac{\partial h_{m+k}(x)}{\partial x_1} & \cdots & \dfrac{\partial h_{m+k}(x)}{\partial x_n} \end{pmatrix} = \begin{pmatrix} \dfrac{\partial f_1(x)}{\partial x_1} & \cdots & \dfrac{\partial f_1(x)}{\partial x_n} \\ \vdots & & \vdots \\ \dfrac{\partial f_k(x)}{\partial x_1} & \cdots & \dfrac{\partial f_k(x)}{\partial x_n} \\ \dfrac{\partial g_1(x)}{\partial x_1} & \cdots & \dfrac{\partial g_1(x)}{\partial x_n} \\ \vdots & & \vdots \\ \dfrac{\partial g_j(x)}{\partial x_1} & \cdots & \dfrac{\partial g_j(x)}{\partial x_n} \end{pmatrix}. \tag{6.28}$$

A point $x \in \mathbb{R}^n$ at which $J_x(h)$ is singular is called a *critical point*. The matrix is defined
to be *singular* if every $(m + k) \times (m + k)$ subdeterminant is zero. Each of the first k
rows of $J_x(h)$ calculates the surface normal to $f_i(x) = 0$. If these normals are not linearly
independent of the directions given by the last j rows, then the matrix becomes singular.
The following example from [171] nicely illustrates this principle.

Example 6.7 (Canny's Roadmap Algorithm)   Let $n = 3$, $k = 1$, and $j = 1$. The zeros
of a single polynomial f_1 define a 2D subset of $\mathbb{R}^3$. Let f_1 be the unit sphere, $\mathbb{S}^2$, defined
as the zeros of the polynomial

$$f_1(x_1, x_2, x_3) = x_1^2 + x_2^2 + x_3^2 - 1. \tag{6.29}$$

Suppose that $g : \mathbb{R}^3 \to \mathbb{R}$ is defined as $g(x_1, x_2, x_3) = x_1$. The Jacobian, (6.28), becomes

$$\begin{pmatrix} 2x_1 & 2x_2 & 2x_3 \\ 1 & 0 & 0 \end{pmatrix} \tag{6.30}$$

and is singular when all three of the possible 2×2 subdeterminants are zero. This occurs
if and only if $x_2 = x_3 = 0$. This yields the critical points $(-1, 0, 0)$ and $(1, 0, 0)$ on $\mathbb{S}^2$.
Note that this is precisely when the surface normals of $\mathbb{S}^2$ are parallel to the vector [1 0 0].

Now suppose that $j = 2$ to obtain $g : \mathbb{R}^3 \to \mathbb{R}^2$, and suppose $g(x_1, x_2, x_3) = (x_1, x_2)$.
In this case, (6.28) becomes

$$\begin{pmatrix} 2x_1 & 2x_2 & 2x_3 \\ 1 & 0 & 0 \\ 0 & 1 & 0 \end{pmatrix}, \tag{6.31}$$

which is singular if and only if $x_3 = 0$. The critical points are therefore the x_1x_2 plane
intersected with $\mathbb{S}^3$, which yields the equator points (all $(x_1, x_2) \in \mathbb{R}^2$ such that $x_1^2 +
x_2^2 = 1$). In this case, more points are generated because the matrix becomes degenerate

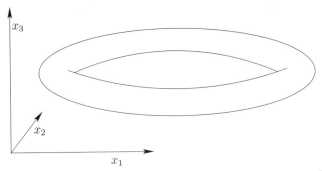

Figure 6.36: Suppose that the semi-algebraic set is a solid torus in $\mathbb{R}^3$.

for any surface normal of $\mathbb{S}^2$ that is parallel to [1 0 0], [0 1 0] or any linear combination of these. ∎

The first mapping in Example 6.7 yielded two isolated critical points, and the second mapping yielded a one-dimensional set of critical points, which is referred to as a *silhouette*. The union of the silhouette and the isolated critical points yields a roadmap for $\mathbb{S}^2$. Now consider generalizing this example to obtain the full algorithm for general n and k. A linear mapping $g : \mathbb{R}^n \to \mathbb{R}^2$ is constructed that might not be axis-aligned as in Example 6.7 because it must be chosen in general position (otherwise degeneracies might arise in the roadmap). Define ψ to be the set of polynomials that become zero on the desired manifold on which to construct a roadmap. Form the matrix (6.28) and determine the silhouette. This is accomplished in general using subresultant techniques that were also needed for cylindrical algebraic decomposition; see [79, 175] for details. Let g_1 denote the first component of g, which yields a mapping $g_1 : \mathbb{R}^n \to \mathbb{R}$. Forming (6.28) using g_1 yields a finite set of critical points. Taking the union of the critical points and the silhouette produces part of the roadmap.

So far, however, there are no guarantees that the connectivity is preserved. To handle this problem, Canny's algorithm proceeds recursively. For each of the critical points $x \in \mathbb{R}^n$, an $n - 1$-dimensional hyperplane through x is chosen for which the g_1 row of (6.28) is the normal (hence it is perpendicular in some sense to the flow of g_1). Inside of this hyperplane, a new g mapping is formed. This time a new direction is chosen, and the mapping takes the form $g : \mathbb{R}^{n-1} \to \mathbb{R}^2$. Once again, the silhouettes and critical points are founded and added to the roadmap. This process is repeated recursively until the base case in which the silhouettes and critical points are directly obtained without forming g.

It is helpful to consider an example. Since the method involves a *sequence* of 2D projections, it is difficult to visualize. Problems in $\mathbb{R}^4$ and higher involve two or more 2D projections and would therefore be more interesting. An example over $\mathbb{R}^3$ is presented here, even though it unfortunately has only one projection; see [175] for another example over $\mathbb{R}^3$.

Example 6.8 (Canny's Algorithm on a Torus) Consider the 3D algebraic set shown in Figure 6.36. After defining the mapping $g(x_1, x_2, x_3) = (x_1, x_2)$, the roadmap shown in Figure 6.37 is obtained. The silhouettes are obtained from g, and the critical points are obtained from g_1 (this is the first component of g). Note that the original connectivity of the solid torus is not preserved because the inner ring does not connect to the outer ring. This illustrates the need to also compute the roadmap for lower dimensional slices. For each of the four critical points, the critical curves are computed for a plane that is parallel

Figure 6.37: The projection into the $x_1 x_2$ plane yields silhouettes for the inner and outer rings and also four critical points.

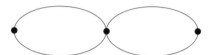

Figure 6.38: A slice taken for the inner critical points is parallel to the $x_2 x_3$ plane. The roadmap for the slice connects to the silhouettes from Figure 6.37, thereby preserving the connectivity of the original set in Figure 6.36.

Figure 6.39: All of the silhouettes and critical points are merged to obtain the roadmap.

to the $x_2 x_3$ plane and for which the x_1 position is determined by the critical point. The slice for one of the inner critical points is shown in Figure 6.38. In this case, the slice already has two dimensions. New silhouette curves are added to the roadmap to obtain the final result shown in Figure 6.39. ∎

To solve a planning problem, the query points q_I and q_G are artificially declared to be critical points in the top level of recursion. This forces the algorithm to generate curves that connect them to the rest of the roadmap.

The completeness of the method requires very careful analysis, which is thoroughly covered in [79, 175]. The main elements of the analysis are showing that: 1) the polynomials can be perturbed and g can be chosen to ensure general position, 2) the singularity conditions on (6.28) lead to algebraic sets (varieties), and 3) the resulting roadmap has the required properties mentioned in Section 6.1 of being accessible and connectivity-preserving for $\mathcal{C}_{free}$ (actually it is shown for $\partial \mathcal{C}_{free}$). The method explained above computes the roadmap for each sign-invariant set, but to obtain a roadmap for the planning problem, the roadmaps from each sign-invariant set must be connected together correctly; fortunately, this has been solved via the Linking Lemma of [171]. A major problem, however, is that even after knowing the connectivity of the roadmap, it is a considerable challenge to obtain a parameterization of each curve on the roadmap. For this and many other technical reasons, no general implementation of Canny's algorithm appears to exist at present. Another problem is the requirement of a Whitney stratification (which can be fixed by perturbation of the input). The *Basu-Pollack-Roy roadmap algorithm* overcomes this problem [79].

6.5 Complexity of motion planning

This section summarizes theoretical work that characterizes the complexity of motion planning problems. Note that this is not equivalent to characterizing the running time of particular algorithms. The existence of an algorithm serves as an *upper bound* on the problem's difficulty because it is a proof by example that solving the problem requires no more time than what is needed by the algorithm. On the other hand, *lower bounds* are also very useful because they give an indication of the difficulty of the problem itself. Suppose, for example, you are given an algorithm that solves a problem in time $O(n^2)$. Does it make sense to try to find a more efficient algorithm? Does it make sense to try to find a general-purpose motion algorithm that runs in time that is polynomial in the dimension? Lower bounds provide answers to questions such as this. Usually lower bounds are obtained by concocting bizarre, complicated examples that are allowed by the problem definition but were usually not considered by the person who first formulated the problem. In this line of research, progress is made by either raising the lower bound (unless it is already tight) or by showing that a narrower version of the problem still allows such bizarre examples. The latter case occurs often in motion planning.

6.5.1 Lower bounds

Lower bounds have been established for a variety of motion planning problems and also a wide variety of planning problems in general. To interpret these bounds a basic understanding of the *theory of computation* is required [465, 892]. This fascinating subject will be unjustly summarized in a few paragraphs. A *problem* is a set of *instances* that are each carefully encoded as a binary string. An *algorithm* is formally considered as a *Turing machine*, which is a finite-state machine that can read and write bits to an unbounded piece of tape. Other models of computation also exist, such as integer RAM and real RAM (see [120]); there are debates as to which model is most appropriate, especially when performing geometric computations with real numbers. The standard Turing machine model will be assumed from here onward. Algorithms are usually formulated to make a binary output, which involves *accepting* or *rejecting* a problem instance that is initially written to the tape and given to the algorithm. In motion planning, this amounts to deciding whether a solution path exists for a given problem instance.

Languages

A *language* is a set of binary strings associated with a problem. It represents the complete set of instances of a problem. An algorithm is said to *decide* a language if in finite time it correctly accepts all strings that belong to it and rejects all others. The interesting question is: How much time or space is required to decide a language? This question is asked of the problem, under the assumption that the best possible algorithm would be used to decide it. (We can easily think of inefficient algorithms that waste resources.)

A *complexity class* is a set of languages that can all be decided within some specified resource bound. The class P is the set of all languages (and hence problems) for which a polynomial-time algorithm exists (i.e., the algorithm runs in time $O(n^k)$ for some integer

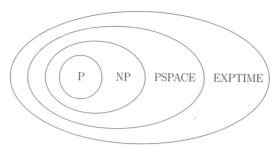

Figure 6.40: It is known that P $\subset$ EXPTIME is a strict subset; however, it is not known precisely how large NP and PSPACE are.

k). By definition, an algorithm is called *efficient* if it decides its associated language in polynomial time.[7] If no efficient algorithm exists, then the problem is called *intractable*. The relationship between several other classes that often emerge in theoretical motion planning is shown in Figure 6.40. The class NP is the set of languages that can be solved in polynomial time by a *nondeterministic Turing machine*. Some discussion of nondeterministic machines appears in Section 11.3.2. Intuitively, it means that solutions can be verified in polynomial time because the machine magically knows which choices to make while trying to make the decision. The class PSPACE is the set of languages that can be decided with no more than a polynomial amount of storage space during the execution of the algorithm (NPSPACE=PSPACE, so there is no nondeterministic version). The class EXPTIME is the set of languages that can be decided in time $O(2^{n^k})$ for some integer k. It is known that EXPTIME is larger than P, but it is not known precisely where the boundaries of NP and PSPACE lie. It might be the case that P = NP = PSPACE (although hardly anyone believes this), or it could be that NP = PSPACE = EXPTIME.

Hardness and completeness

Since an easier class is included as a subset of a harder one, it is helpful to have a notion of a language (i.e., problem) being among the hardest possible within a class. Let X refer to either P, NP, PSPACE, or EXPTIME. A language A is called *X-hard* if every language B in class X is *polynomial-time reducible* to A. In short, this means that in polynomial time, any language in B can be translated into instances for language A, and then the decisions for A can be correctly translated back in polynomial time to correctly decide B. Thus, if A can be decided, then within a polynomial-time factor, every language in X can be decided. The hardness concept can even be applied to a language (problem) that does not belong to the class. For example, we can declare that a language A is NP-hard even if $A \notin NP$ (it could be harder and lie in EXPTIME, for example). If it is known that the language is both hard for some class X and is also a member of X, then it is called *X-complete* (i.e., NP-complete, PSPACE-complete, etc.).[8] Note that because of this uncertainty regarding P, NP, and PSPACE, one cannot say that a problem is intractable if it is NP-hard or PSPACE-hard, but one can, however, if the problem is EXPTIME-hard. One additional remark: it is useful to remember that PSPACE-hard implies NP-hard.

---

[7] Note that this definition may be absurd in practice; an algorithm that runs in time $O(n^{90125})$ would probably not be too efficient for most purposes.

[8] If you remember hearing that a planning problem is NP-something, but cannot remember whether it was NP-hard or NP-complete, then it is safe to say NP-hard because NP-complete implies NP-hard. This can similarly be said for other classes, such as PSPACE-complete vs. PSPACE-hard.

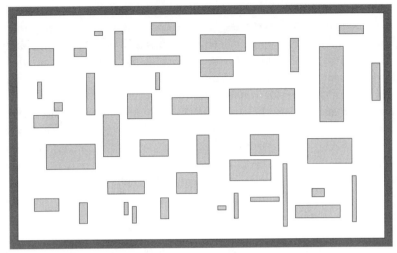

Figure 6.41: Even motion planning for a bunch of translating rectangles inside of a rectangular box in $\mathbb{R}^2$ is PSPACE-hard (and hence, NP-hard).

Lower bounds for motion planning

The general motion planning problem, Formulation 4.1, was shown in 1979 to be PSPACE-hard by Reif [820]. In fact, the problem was restricted to polyhedral obstacles and a finite number of polyhedral robot bodies attached by spherical joints. The coordinates of all polyhedra are assumed to be in $\mathbb{Q}$ (this enables a finite-length string encoding of the problem instance). The proof introduces a fascinating motion planning instance that involves many attached, dangling robot parts that must work their way through a complicated system of tunnels, which together simulates the operation of a *symmetric Turing machine*. Canny later established that the problem in Formulation 4.1 (expressed using polynomials that have rational coefficients) lies in PSPACE [175]. Therefore, the general motion planning problem is PSPACE-complete.

Many other lower bounds have been shown for a variety of planning problems. One famous example is the Warehouseman's problem shown in Figure 6.41. This problem involves a finite number of translating, axis-aligned rectangles in a rectangular world. It was shown in [464] to be PSPACE-hard. This example is a beautiful illustration of how such a deceptively simple problem formulation can lead to such a high lower bound. More recently, it was even shown that planning for Sokoban, which is a warehouseman's problem on a discrete 2D grid, is also PSPACE-hard [257]. Other general motion planning problems that were shown to be PSPACE-hard include motion planning for a chain of bodies in the plane [463, 493] and motion planning for a chain of bodies among polyhedral obstacles in $\mathbb{R}^3$. Many lower bounds have been established for a variety of extensions and variations of the general motion planning problem. For example, in [174] it was established that a certain form of planning under uncertainty for a robot in a 3D polyhedral environment is NEXPTIME-hard, which is harder than any of the classes shown in Figure 6.40; the hardest problems in this NEXPTIME are believed to require doubly exponential time to solve.

The lower bound or hardness results depend significantly on the precise representation of the problem. For example, it is possible to make problems look easier by making instance encodings that are exponentially longer than they should be. The running time or space required is expressed in terms of n, the input size. If the motion planning problem instances are encoded with exponentially more bits than necessary, then a language that belongs to P is obtained. As long as the instance encoding is within a polynomial factor of the optimal encoding (this can be made precise using Kolmogorov complexity [633]), then this bizarre behavior is avoided. Another important part of the representation is to pay attention to how parameters in the problem formulation can vary. We can redefine motion planning to be all instances for which the dimension of C is never greater than 2^{1000}. The number of dimensions is sufficiently large for virtually any application. The resulting language for this problem belongs to P because cylindrical algebraic decomposition and Canny's algorithm can solve any motion planning problem in polynomial time. Why? This is because now the dimension parameter in the time-complexity expressions can be replaced by 2^{1000}, which is a constant. This formally implies that an *efficient* algorithm is already known for any motion planning problem that we would ever care about. This implication has no practical value, however. Thus, be very careful when interpreting theoretical bounds.

The lower bounds may appear discouraging. There are two general directions to go from here. One is to weaken the requirements and tolerate algorithms that yield some kind of resolution completeness or probabilistic completeness. This approach was taken in Chapter 5 and leads to many efficient algorithms. Another direction is to define narrower problems that do not include the bizarre constructions that lead to bad lower bounds. For the narrower problems, it may be possible to design interesting, efficient algorithms. This approach was taken for the methods in Sections 6.2 and 6.3. In Section 6.5.3, upper bounds for some algorithms that address these narrower problems will be presented, along with bounds for the general motion planning algorithms. Several of the upper bounds involve Davenport-Schinzel sequences, which are therefore covered next.

6.5.2 Davenport-Schinzel sequences

Davenport-Schinzel sequences provide a powerful characterization of the structure that arises from the lower or upper envelope of a collection of functions. The lower envelope of five functions is depicted in Figure 6.42. Such envelopes arise in many problems throughout computational geometry, including many motion planning problems. They are an important part of the design and analysis of many modern algorithms, and the resulting algorithm's time complexity usually involves terms that follow directly from the sequences. Therefore, it is worthwhile to understand some of the basics before interpreting some of the results of Section 6.5.3. Much more information on Davenport-Schinzel sequences and their applications appears in [868]. The brief introduction presented here is based on [867].

For positive integers n and s, an (n, s) *Davenport-Schinzel sequence* is a sequence $(u_1, \ldots, u_m)$ composed from a set of n *symbols* such that:

1. The same symbol may not appear consecutively in the sequence. In other words, $u_i \neq u_{i+1}$ for any i such that $1 \leq i < m$.

2. The sequence does not contain any alternating subsequence that uses two symbols and has length $s + 2$. A subsequence can be formed by deleting any elements in the original sequence. The condition can be expressed as: There do not exist $s + 2$ indices $i_1 < i_2 < \cdots < i_{s+2}$ for which $u_{i_1} = u_{i_3} = u_{i_5} = a$ and $u_{i_2} = u_{i_4} = u_{i_6} = b$, for some symbols a and b.

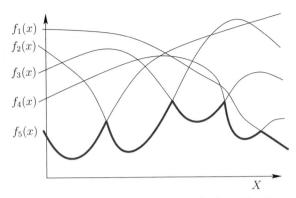

Figure 6.42: The lower envelope of a collection of functions.

As an example, an $(n, 3)$ sequence cannot appear as $(a \cdots b \cdots a \cdots b \cdots a)$, in which each $\cdots$ is filled in with any sequence of symbols. Let $\lambda_s(n)$ denote the maximum possible length of an (n, s) Davenport-Schinzel sequence.

The connection between Figure 6.42 and these sequences can now be explained. Consider the sequence of function indices that visit the lower envelope. In the example, this sequence is $(5, 2, 3, 4, 1)$. Suppose it is known that each pair of functions intersects in at most s places. If there are n real-valued continuous functions, then the sequence of function indices must be an (n, s) Davenport-Schinzel sequence. It is amazing that such sequences cannot be very long. For a fixed s, they are close to being linear.

The standard bounds for Davenport-Schinzel sequences are [867][9]

$$\lambda_1(n) = n \tag{6.32}$$

$$\lambda_2(n) = 2n - 1 \tag{6.33}$$

$$\lambda_3(n) = \Theta(n\alpha(n)) \tag{6.34}$$

$$\lambda_4(n) = \Theta(n \cdot 2^{\alpha(n)}) \tag{6.35}$$

$$\lambda_{2s}(n) \leq n \cdot 2^{\alpha(n)^{s-1} + C_{2s}(n)} \tag{6.36}$$

$$\lambda_{2s+1}(n) \leq n \cdot 2^{\alpha(n)^{s-1} \lg \alpha(n) + C'_{2s+1}(n)} \tag{6.37}$$

$$\lambda_{2s}(n) = \Omega(n \cdot 2^{\frac{1}{(s-1)!}\alpha(n)^{s-1} + C'_{2s}(n)}). \tag{6.38}$$

In the expressions above $C_r(n)$ and $C'_r(n)$ are terms that are smaller than their leading exponents. The $\alpha(n)$ term is the inverse Ackerman function, which is an extremely slow-growing function that appears frequently in algorithms. The *Ackerman function* is defined as follows. Let $A_1(m) = 2m$ and $A_{n+1}(m)$ represent m applications of A_n. Thus, $A_1(m)$ performs doubling, $A_2(m)$ performs exponentiation, and $A_3(m)$ performs *tower exponentiation*, which makes a stack of 2's,

$$2^{2^{2^{\cdot^{\cdot^{\cdot^{2^2}}}}}}, \tag{6.39}$$

that has height m. The *Ackerman function* is defined as $A(n) = A_n(n)$. This function grows so fast that $A(4)$ is already an exponential tower of 2's that has height 65536. Thus,

---

[9] The following asymptotic notion is used: $O(f(n))$ denotes an upper bound, $\Omega(f(n))$ denotes a lower bound, and $\Theta(f(n))$ means that the bound is tight (both upper and lower). This notation is used in most books on algorithms [245].

the *inverse Ackerman function*, α, grows very slowly. If n is less than or equal to an exponential tower of 65536 2's, then $\alpha(n) \leq 4$. Even when it appears in exponents of the Davenport-Schinzel bounds, it does not represent a significant growth rate.

Example 6.9 (Lower Envelope of Line Segments) One interesting application of Davenport-Schinzel applications is to the lower envelope of a set of line segments in $\mathbb{R}^2$. Since segments in general position can intersect in at most one place, the number of edges in the lower envelope is $\Theta(\lambda_3(n)) = \Theta(n\alpha(n))$. There are actually arrangements of segments in $\mathbb{R}^2$ that reach this bound; see [868]. ∎

6.5.3 Upper bounds

The upper bounds for motion planning problems arise from the existence of complete algorithms that solve them. This section proceeds by starting with the most general bounds, which are based on the methods of Section 6.4, and concludes with bounds for simpler motion planning problems.

General algorithms

The first upper bound for the general motion planning problem of Formulation 4.1 came from the application of cylindrical algebraic decomposition [854]. Let n be the dimension of $\mathcal{C}$. Let m be the number of polynomials in $\mathcal{F}$, which are used to define $\mathcal{C}_{obs}$. Recall from Section 4.3.3 how quickly this grows for simple examples. Let d be the maximum degree among the polynomials in $\mathcal{F}$. The maximum degree of the resulting polynomials is bounded by $O(d^{2^{n-1}})$, and the total number of polynomials is bounded by $O((md)^{3^{n-1}})$. The total running time required to use cylindrical algebraic decomposition for motion planning is bounded by $(md)^{O(1)^n}$.[10] Note that the algorithm is doubly exponential in dimension n but polynomial in m and d. It can theoretically be declared to be *efficient* on a space of motion planning problems of bounded dimension (although, it certainly is not efficient for motion planning in any practical sense).

Since the general problem is PSPACE-complete, it appears unavoidable that a complete, general motion planning algorithm will require a running time that is exponential in dimension. Since cylindrical algebraic decomposition is doubly exponential, it led many in the 1980s to wonder whether this upper bound could be lowered. This was achieved by Canny's roadmap algorithm, for which the running time is bounded by $m^n(\lg m)d^{O(n^4)}$. Hence, it is singly exponential, which appears very close to optimal because it is up against the lower bound that seems to be implied by PSPACE-hardness (and the fact that problems exist that require a roadmap with $(md)^n$ connected components [79]). Much of the algorithm's complexity is due to finding a suitable deterministic perturbation to put the input polynomials into general position. A randomized algorithm can alternatively be used, for which the randomized expected running time is bounded by $m^n(\lg m)d^{O(n^2)}$. For a *randomized algorithm* [722], the *randomized expected* running time is still a worst-case upper bound, but averaged over random "coin tosses" that are introduced internally in the algorithm; it does *not* reflect any kind of average over the expected input distribution. Thus, these two bounds represent the best-known upper bounds for the general motion

---

[10] It may seem odd for $O(\cdot)$ to appear in the middle of an expression. In this context, it means that there exists some $c \in [0, \infty)$ such that the running time is bounded by $(md)^{c^n}$. Note that another O is not necessary in front of the whole formula.

planning problem. Canny's algorithm may also be applied to solve the kinematic closure problems of Section 4.4, but the complexity does not reflect the fact that the dimension, k, of the algebraic variety is less than n, the dimension of $\mathcal{C}$. A roadmap algorithm that is particularly suited for this problem is introduced in [78], and its running time is bounded by $m^{k+1}d^{O(n^2)}$. This serves as the best-known upper bound for the problems of Section 4.4.

Specialized algorithms

Now upper bounds are summarized for some narrower problems, which can be solved more efficiently than the general problem. All of the problems involve either two or three degrees of freedom. Therefore, we expect that the bounds are much lower than those for the general problem. In many cases, the Davenport-Schinzel sequences of Section 6.5.2 arise. Most of the bounds presented here are based on algorithms that are not practical to implement; they mainly serve to indicate the best asymptotic performance that can be obtained for a problem. Most of the bounds mentioned here are included in [867].

Consider the problem from Section 6.2, in which the robot translates in $\mathcal{W} = \mathbb{R}^2$ and $\mathcal{C}_{obs}$ is polygonal. Suppose that $\mathcal{A}$ is a convex polygon that has k edges and $\mathcal{O}$ is the union of m disjoint, convex polygons with disjoint interiors, and their total number of edges is n. In this case, the boundary of $\mathcal{C}_{free}$ (computed by Minkowski difference; see Section 4.3.2) has at most $6m - 12$ nonreflex vertices (interior angles less than π) and $n + km$ reflex vertices (interior angles greater than π). The free space, $\mathcal{C}_{free}$, can be decomposed and searched in time $O((n + km)\lg^2 n)$ [521, 867]. Using randomized algorithms, the bound reduces to $O((n + km) \cdot 2^{\alpha(n)} \lg n)$ randomized expected time. Now suppose that $\mathcal{A}$ is a single nonconvex polygonal region described by k edges and that $\mathcal{O}$ is a similar polygonal region described by n edges. The Minkowski difference could yield as many as $\Omega(k^2 n^2)$ edges for $\mathcal{C}_{obs}$. This can be avoided if the search is performed within a single connected component of $\mathcal{C}_{free}$. Based on analysis that uses Davenport-Schinzel sequences, it can be shown that the worst connected component may have complexity $\Theta(kn\alpha(k))$, and the planning problem can be solved in time $O(kn\lg^2 n)$ deterministically or for a randomized algorithm, $O(kn \cdot 2^{\alpha(n)} \lg n)$ randomized expected time is needed. More generally, if $\mathcal{C}_{obs}$ consists of n algebraic curves in $\mathbb{R}^2$, each with degree no more than d, then the motion planning problem for translation only can be solved deterministically in time $O(\lambda_{s+2}(n)\lg^2 n)$, or with a randomized algorithm in $O(\lambda_{s+2}(n)\lg n)$ randomized expected time. In these expressions, $\lambda_{s+2}(n)$ is the bound (6.37) obtained from the $(n, s + 2)$ Davenport-Schinzel sequence, and $s \leq d^2$.

For the case of the line-segment robot of Section 6.3.4 in an obstacle region described with n edges, an $O(n^5)$-time algorithm was given. This is not the best possible running time for solving the line-segment problem, but the method is easier to understand than others that are more efficient. In [751], a roadmap algorithm based on retraction is given that solves the problem in $O(n^2 \lg n \lg^* n)$ time, in which $\lg^* n$ is the number of times that $\lg$ has to be iterated on n to yield a result less than or equal to 1 (i.e., it is a very small, insignificant term; for practical purposes, you can imagine that the running time is $O(n^2 \lg n)$). The tightest known upper bound is $O(n^2 \lg n)$ [628]. It is established in [520] that there exist examples for which the solution path requires $\Omega(n^2)$ length to encode. For the case of a line segment moving in $\mathbb{R}^3$ among polyhedral obstacles with a total of n vertices, a complete algorithm that runs in time $O(n^4 + \epsilon)$ for any $\epsilon > 0$ was given in [550]. In [520] it was established that solution paths of complexity $\Omega(n^4)$ exist.

Now consider the case for which $\mathcal{C} = SE(2)$, $\mathcal{A}$ is a convex polygon with k edges, and $\mathcal{O}$ is a polygonal region described by n edges. The boundary of $\mathcal{C}_{free}$ has no more

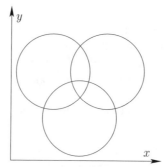

Figure 6.43: Determine the cylindrical algebraic decomposition obtained by projecting onto the *x*-axis.

than $O(kn\lambda_6(kn))$ edges and can be computed to solve the motion planning problem in time $O(kn\lambda_6(kn)\lg kn)$ [10, 11]. An algorithm that runs in time $O(k^4n\lambda_3(n)\lg n)$ and provides better clearance between the robot and obstacles is given in [207]. In [56] (some details also appear in [591]), an algorithm is presented, and even implemented, that solves the more general case in which $\mathcal{A}$ is nonconvex in time $O(k^3n^3\lg(kn))$. The number of faces of $\mathcal{C}_{obs}$ could be as high as $\Omega(k^3n^3)$ for this problem. By explicitly representing and searching only one connected component, the best-known upper bound for the problem is $O((kn)^{2+\epsilon})$, in which $\epsilon > 0$ may be chosen arbitrarily small [431].

In the final case, suppose that $\mathcal{A}$ translates in $\mathcal{W} = \mathbb{R}^3$ to yield $\mathcal{C} = \mathbb{R}^3$. For a polyhedron or polyhedral region, let its *complexity* be the total number of faces, edges, and vertices. If $\mathcal{A}$ is a polyhedron with complexity k, and $\mathcal{O}$ is a polyhedral region with complexity n, then the boundary of $\mathcal{C}_{free}$ is a polyhedral surface of complexity $\Theta(k^3n^3)$. As for other problems, if the search is restricted to a single component, then the complexity is reduced. The motion planning problem in this case can be solved in time $O((kn)^{2+\epsilon})$ [42]. If $\mathcal{A}$ is convex and there are m convex obstacles, then the best-known bound is $O(kmn\lg^2 m)$ time. More generally, if $\mathcal{C}_{obs}$ is bounded by n algebraic patches of constant maximum degree, then a vertical decomposition method solves the motion planning problem within a single connected component of $\mathcal{C}_{free}$ in time $O(n^{2+\epsilon})$.

Further reading

Most of the literature on combinatorial planning is considerably older than the sampling-based planning literature. A nice collection of early papers appears in [856]; this includes [463, 751, 752, 820, 853, 854, 855]. The classic motion planning textbook of Latombe [591] covers most of the methods presented in this chapter. The coverage here does not follow [591], which makes separate categories for cell decomposition methods and roadmap methods. A cell decomposition is constructed to produce a roadmap; hence, they are unified in this chapter. An excellent reference for material in combinatorial algorithms, computational geometry, and complete algorithms for motion planning is the collection of survey papers in [405].

Section 6.2 follows the spirit of basic algorithms from computational geometry. For a gentle introduction to computational geometry, including a nice explanation of vertical composition, see [266]. Other sources for computational geometry include [129, 304, 809]. To understand the difficulties in computing optimal decompositions of polygons, see [760]. See [653, 712, 835] for further reading on computing shortest paths.

Cell decompositions and cell complexes are very important in computational geometry and algebraic topology. Section 6.3 provided a brief perspective that was tailored to motion planning. For simplicial complexes in algebraic topology, see [499, 538, 837]; for singular complexes, see [837]. In computational geometry, various kinds of cell decompositions arise. Some of the most widely studied decompositions are *triangulations* [92] and *arrangements* [429], which are regions generated by a collection of primitives, such as lines or circles in the plane. For early cell decomposition methods in motion planning, see [856]. A survey of computational topology appears in [954].

The most modern and complete reference for the material in Section 6.4 is [79]. A gentle introduction to computational algebraic geometry is given in [252]. For details regarding algebraic computations with polynomials, see [707]. A survey of computational algebraic geometry appears in [708]. In addition to [79], other general references to cylindrical algebraic decomposition are [40, 234]. For its use in motion planning, see [591, 854]. The main reference for Canny's roadmap algorithm is [175]. Alternative high-level overviews to the one presented in Section 6.4.3 appear in [222, 591]. Variations and improvements to the algorithm are covered in [79]. A potential function-based extension of Canny's roadmap algorithm is developed in [178].

For further reading on the complexity of motion planning, consult the numerous references given in Section 6.5.

Exercises

1. Extend the vertical decomposition algorithm to correctly handle the case in which C_{obs} has two or more points that lie on the same vertical line. This includes the case of vertical segments. Random perturbations are not allowed.

2. Fully describe and prove the correctness of the bitangent computation method shown in Figure 6.14, which avoids trigonometric functions. Make certain that all types of bitangents (in general position) are considered.

3. Develop an algorithm that uses the plane-sweep principle to efficiently compute a representation of the union of two nonconvex polygons.

4. Extend the vertical cell decomposition algorithm of Section 6.2.2 to work for obstacle boundaries that are described as chains of circular arcs and line segments.

5. Extend the short-path roadmap algorithm of Section 6.2.4 to work for obstacle boundaries that are described as chains of circular arcs and line segments.

6. Derive the equation for the Conchoid of Nicomedes, shown in Figure 6.24, for the case of a line-segment robot contacting an obstacle vertex and edge simultaneously.

7. Propose a resolution-complete algorithm for motion planning of the line-segment robot in a polygonal obstacle region. The algorithm should compute exact C-space obstacle slices for any fixed orientation, θ; however, the algorithm should use van der Corput sampling over the set $[0, 2\pi)$ of orientations.

8. Determine the result of cylindrical algebraic decomposition for unit spheres $\mathbb{S}^1$, $\mathbb{S}^2$, $\mathbb{S}^3$, $\mathbb{S}^4$, ... Each $\mathbb{S}^n$ is expressed as a unit sphere in $\mathbb{R}^{n+1}$. Graphically depict the cases of $\mathbb{S}^1$ and $\mathbb{S}^2$. Also, attempt to develop an expression for the number of cells as a function of n.

9. Determine the cylindrical algebraic decomposition for the three intersecting circles shown in Figure 6.43. How many cells are obtained?

10. Using the matrix in (6.28), show that the result of Canny's roadmap for the torus, shown in Figure 6.39, is correct. Use the torus equation

$$(x_1^2 + x_2^2 + x_3^2 - (r_1^2 + r_2^2))^2 - 4r_1^2(r_2^2 - x_3^2) = 0, \qquad (6.40)$$

in which r_1 is the major circle, r_2 is the minor circle, and $r_1 > r_2$.

11. Propose a vertical decomposition algorithm for a polygonal robot that can translate in the plane and even continuously vary its scale. How would the algorithm be modified to instead work for a robot that can translate or be sheared?

12. Develop a shortest-path roadmap algorithm for a flat torus, defined by identifying opposite edges of a square. Use Euclidean distance but respect the identifications when determining the shortest path. Assume the robot is a point and the obstacles are polygonal.

Implementations

13. Implement the vertical cell decomposition planning algorithm of Section 6.2.2.

14. Implement the maximum-clearance roadmap planning algorithm of Section 6.2.3.

15. Implement a planning algorithm for a point robot that moves in $\mathcal{W} = \mathbb{R}^3$ among polyhedral obstacles. Use vertical decomposition.

16. Implement an algorithm that performs a cylindrical decomposition of a polygonal obstacle region.

17. Implement an algorithm that computes the cell decomposition of Section 6.3.4 for the line-segment robot.

18. Experiment with cylindrical algebraic decomposition. The project can be greatly facilitated by utilizing existing packages for performing basic operations in computational algebraic geometry.

19. Implement the algorithm proposed in Exercise 7.

7

Extensions of Basic Motion Planning

This chapter presents many extensions and variations of the motion planning problem considered in Chapters 3 to 6. Each one of these can be considered as a "spin-off" that is fairly straightforward to describe using the mathematical concepts and algorithms introduced so far. Unlike the previous chapters, there is not much continuity in Chapter 7. Each problem is treated independently; therefore, it is safe to jump to whatever sections in the chapter you find interesting without fear of missing important details.

In many places throughout the chapter, a state space X will arise. This is consistent with the general planning notation used throughout the book. In Chapter 4, the C-space, $\mathcal{C}$, was introduced, which can be considered as a special state space: It encodes the set of transformations that can be applied to a collection of bodies. Hence, Chapters 5 and 6 addressed planning in $X = \mathcal{C}$. The C-space alone is insufficient for many of the problems in this chapter; therefore, X will be used because it appears to be more general. For most cases in this chapter, however, X is derived from one or more C-spaces. Thus, C-space and state space terminology will be used in combination.

7.1 Time-varying problems

This section brings time into the motion planning formulation. Although the robot has been allowed to move, it has been assumed so far that the obstacle region $\mathcal{O}$ and the goal configuration, $q_G \in \mathcal{C}_{free}$, are stationary for all time. It is now assumed that these entities may vary over time, although their motions are predictable. If the motions are not predictable, then some form of feedback is needed to respond to observations that are made during execution. Such problems are much more difficult and will be handled in Chapters 8 and throughout Part IV.

7.1.1 Problem formulation

The formulation is designed to allow the tools and concepts learned so far to be applied directly. Let $T \subset \mathbb{R}$ denote the *time interval*, which may be *bounded* or *unbounded*. If T is bounded, then $T = [0, t_f]$, in which 0 is the *initial time* and t_f is the *final time*. If T is unbounded, then $T = [0, \infty)$. An initial time other than 0 could alternatively be defined without difficulty, but this will not be done here.

Let the state space X be defined as $X = \mathcal{C} \times T$, in which $\mathcal{C}$ is the usual C-space of the robot, as defined in Chapter 4. A state x is represented as $x = (q, t)$, to indicate the configuration q and time t components of the state vector. The planning will occur directly in X, and in many ways it can be treated as any C-space seen to far, but there is one critical difference: *Time marches forward*. Imagine a path that travels through X. If it first reaches a state $(q_1, 5)$, and then later some state $(q_2, 3)$, some traveling backward through time is required! There is no mathematical problem with allowing such time travel, but it is not realistic for most applications. Therefore, paths in X are forced to follow a constraint that they must move forward in time.

Now consider making the following time-varying versions of the items used in Formulation 4.1 for motion planning.

Formulation 7.1 (The Time-Varying Motion Planning Problem)

1. A *world* W in which either $W = \mathbb{R}^2$ or $W = \mathbb{R}^3$. This is the same as in Formulation 4.1.

2. A *time interval* $T \subset \mathbb{R}$ that is either *bounded* to yield $T = [0, t_f]$ for some *final time*, $t_f > 0$, or *unbounded* to yield $T = [0, \infty)$.

3. A semi-algebraic, time-varying *obstacle region* $\mathcal{O}(t) \subset W$ for every $t \in T$. It is assumed that the obstacle region is a finite collection of rigid bodies that undergoes continuous, time-dependent rigid-body transformations.

4. The *robot* $\mathcal{A}$ (or $\mathcal{A}_1, \ldots, \mathcal{A}_m$ for a linkage) and *configuration space* $\mathcal{C}$ definitions are the same as in Formulation 4.1.

5. The *state space* X is the Cartesian product $X = \mathcal{C} \times T$ and a state $x \in X$ is denoted as $x = (q, t)$ to denote the configuration q and time t components. See Figure 7.1. The obstacle region, X_{obs}, in the state space is defined as

$$X_{obs} = \{(q, t) \in X \mid \mathcal{A}(q) \cap \mathcal{O}(t) \neq \emptyset\}, \tag{7.1}$$

and $X_{free} = X \setminus X_{obs}$. For a given $t \in T$, slices of X_{obs} and X_{free} are obtained. These are denoted as $\mathcal{C}_{obs}(t)$ and $\mathcal{C}_{free}(t)$, respectively, in which (assuming $\mathcal{A}$ is one body)

$$\mathcal{C}_{obs}(t) = \{q \in \mathcal{C} \mid \mathcal{A}(q) \cap \mathcal{O}(t) \neq \emptyset\} \tag{7.2}$$

and $\mathcal{C}_{free} = \mathcal{C} \setminus \mathcal{C}_{obs}$.

6. A state $x_I \in X_{free}$ is designated as the *initial state*, with the constraint that $x_I = (q_I, 0)$ for some $q_I \in \mathcal{C}_{free}(0)$. In other words, at the initial time the robot cannot be in collision.

7. A subset $X_G \subset X_{free}$ is designated as the *goal region*. A typical definition is to pick some $q_G \in \mathcal{C}$ and let $X_G = \{(q_G, t) \in X_{free} \mid t \in T\}$, which means that the goal is *stationary* for all time.

8. A complete algorithm must compute a continuous, time-monotonic *path*, $\tau[0, 1] \to X_{free}$, such that $\tau(0) = x_I$ and $\tau(1) \in X_G$, or correctly report that such a path does not exist. To be *time-monotonic* implies that for any $s_1, s_2 \in [0, 1]$ such that $s_1 < s_2$, we have $t_1 < t_2$, in which $(q_1, t_1) = \tau(s_1)$ and $(q_2, t_2) = \tau(s_2)$.

Example 7.1 (Piecewise-Linear Obstacle Motion)   Figure 7.1 shows an example of a convex, polygonal robot $\mathcal{A}$ that translates in $W = \mathbb{R}^2$. There is a single, convex, polygonal obstacle $\mathcal{O}$. The two of these together yield a convex, polygonal C-space obstacle, $\mathcal{C}_{obs}(t)$, which is shown for times t_1, t_2, and t_3. The obstacle moves with a *piecewise-linear motion model*, which means that transformations applied to $\mathcal{O}$ are a piecewise-linear function of time. For example, let (x, y) be a fixed point on the obstacle. To be a linear motion model, this point must transform as $(x + c_1 t, y + c_2 t)$ for some constants $c_1, c_2 \in \mathbb{R}$. To be piecewise-linear, it may change to a different linear motion at a finite number of critical times. Between these critical times, the motion must remain linear. There are two critical times in the example. If $\mathcal{C}_{obs}(t)$ is polygonal, and a piecewise-linear motion model is used, then X_{obs} is polyhedral, as depicted in Figure 7.1. A stationary goal is also shown, which appears as a line that is parallel to the T-axis.   ∎

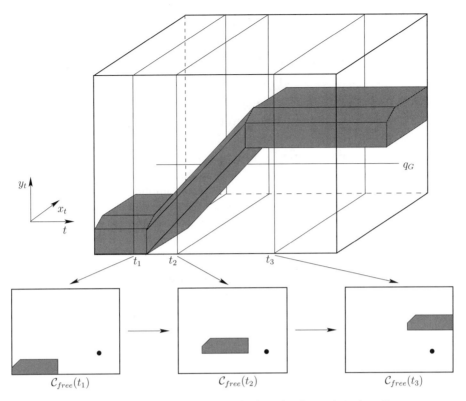

Figure 7.1: A time-varying example with piecewise-linear obstacle motion.

In the general formulation, there are no additional constraints on the path, τ, which means that the robot motion model allows infinite acceleration and unbounded speed. The robot velocity may change instantaneously, but the path through $\mathcal{C}$ must always be continuous. These issues did not arise in Chapter 4 because there was no need to mention time. Now it becomes necessary.[1]

7.1.2 Direct solutions

Sampling-based methods

Many sampling-based methods can be adapted from $\mathcal{C}$ to X without much difficulty. The time dependency of obstacle models must be taken into account when verifying that path segments are collision-free; the techniques from Section 5.3.4 can be extended to handle this. One important concern is the metric for X. For some algorithms, it may be important to permit the use of a pseudometric because symmetry is broken by time (going backward in time is not as easy as going forward).

For example, suppose that the C-space $\mathcal{C}$ is a metric space, $(\mathcal{C}, \rho)$. The metric can be extended across time to obtain a pseudometric, ρ_X, as follows. For a pair of states,

---

[1] The infinite acceleration and unbounded speed assumptions may annoy those with mechanics and control backgrounds. In this case, assume that the present models approximate the case in which every body moves slowly, and the dynamics can be consequently neglected. If this is still not satisfying, then jump ahead to Part IV, where general nonlinear systems are considered. It is still helpful to consider the implications derived from the concepts in this chapter because the issues remain for more complicated problems that involve dynamics.

$x = (q, t)$ and $x' = (q', t')$, let

$$\rho_X(x, x') = \begin{cases} 0 & \text{if } q = q' \\ \infty & \text{if } q \neq q' \text{ and } t' \leq t \\ \rho(q, q') & \text{otherwise.} \end{cases} \qquad (7.3)$$

Using ρ_X, several sampling-based methods naturally work. For example, RDTs from Section 5.5 can be adapted to X. Using ρ_X for a single-tree approach ensures that all path segments travel forward in time. Using bidirectional approaches is more difficult for time-varying problems because X_G is usually not a single point. It is not clear which (q, t) should be the starting vertex for the tree from the goal; one possibility is to initialize the goal tree to an entire time-invariant segment. The sampling-based roadmap methods of Section 5.6 are perhaps the most straightforward to adapt. The notion of a *directed roadmap* is needed, in which every edge must be directed to yield a time-monotonic path. For each pair of states, (q, t) and (q', t'), such that $t \neq t'$, exactly one valid direction exists for making a potential edge. If $t = t'$, then no edge can be attempted because it would require the robot to instantaneously "teleport" from one part of $\mathcal{W}$ to another. Since forward time progress is already taken into account by the directed edges, a symmetric metric may be preferable instead of (7.3) for the sampling-based roadmap approach.

Combinatorial methods

In some cases, combinatorial methods can be used to solve time-varying problems. If the motion model is *algebraic* (i.e., expressed with polynomials), then X_{obs} is semi-algebraic. This enables the application of general planners from Section 6.4, which are based on computational real algebraic geometry. The key issue once again is that the resulting roadmap must be directed with all edges being time-monotonic. For Canny's roadmap algorithm, this requirement seems difficult to ensure. Cylindrical algebraic decomposition is straightforward to adapt, provided that time is chosen as the last variable to be considered in the sequence of projections. This yields polynomials in $\mathbb{Q}[t]$, and $\mathbb{R}$ is nicely partitioned into time intervals and time instances. Connections can then be made for a cell of one cylinder to an adjacent cell of a cylinder that occurs later in time.

If X_{obs} is polyhedral as depicted in Figure 7.1, then vertical decomposition can be used. It is best to first sweep the plane along the time axis, stopping at the critical times when the linear motion changes. This yields nice sections, which are further decomposed recursively, as explained in Section 6.3.3, and also facilitates the connection of adjacent cells to obtain time-monotonic path segments. It is not too difficult to imagine the approach working for a four-dimensional state space, X, for which $\mathcal{C}_{obs}(t)$ is polyhedral as in Section 6.3.3, and time adds the fourth dimension. Again, performing the first sweep with respect to the time axis is preferable.

If X is not decomposed into cylindrical slices over each noncritical time interval, then cell decompositions may still be used, but be careful to correctly connect the cells. Figure 7.2 illustrates the problem, for which transitivity among adjacent cells is broken. This complicates sample point selection for the cells.

Bounded speed

There has been no consideration so far of the speed at which the robot must move to avoid obstacles. It is obviously impractical in many applications if the solution requires the robot to move arbitrarily fast. One step toward making a realistic model is to enforce a bound on the speed of the robot. (More steps towards realism are taken in Chapter 13.)

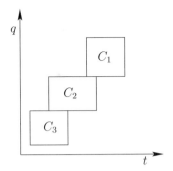

Figure 7.2: Transitivity is broken if the cells are not formed in cylinders over T. A time-monotonic path exists from C_1 to C_2, and from C_2 to C_3, but this does not imply that one exists from C_1 to C_3.

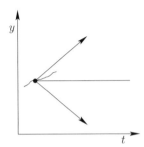

Figure 7.3: A projection of the cone constraint for the bounded-speed problem.

For simplicity, suppose $C = \mathbb{R}^2$, which corresponds to a translating rigid robot, A, that moves in $W = \mathbb{R}^2$. A configuration, $q \in C$, is represented as $q = (y, z)$ (since x already refers to the whole state vector). The *robot velocity* is expressed as $v = (\dot{y}, \dot{z}) \in \mathbb{R}^2$, in which $\dot{y} = dy/dt$ and $\dot{z} = dz/dt$. The *robot speed* is $\|v\| = \sqrt{\dot{y}^2 + \dot{z}^2}$. A *speed bound*, b, is a positive constant, $b \in (0, \infty)$, for which $\|v\| \leq b$.

In terms of Figure 7.1, this means that the slope of a solution path τ is bounded. Suppose that the domain of τ is $T = [0, t_f]$ instead of $[0, 1]$. This yields $\tau : T \to X$ and $\tau(t) = (y, z, t)$. Using this representation, $d\tau_1/dt = \dot{y}$ and $d\tau_2/dt = \dot{z}$, in which τ_i denotes the ith component of τ (because it is a vector-valued function). Thus, it can seen that b constrains the slope of $\tau(t)$ in X. To visualize this, imagine that only motion in the y direction occurs, and suppose $b = 1$. If τ holds the robot fixed, then the speed is zero, which satisfies any bound. If the robot moves at speed 1, then $d\tau_1/dt = 1$ and $d\tau_2/dt = 0$, which satisfies the speed bound. In Figure 7.1 this generates a path that has slope 1 in the yt plane and is horizontal in the zt plane. If $d\tau_1/dt = d\tau_2/dt = 1$, then the bound is exceeded because the speed is $\sqrt{2}$. In general, the velocity vector at any state (y, z, t) points into a cone that starts at (y, z) and is aligned in the positive t direction; this is depicted in Figure 7.3. At time $t + \Delta t$, the state must stay within the cone, which means that

$$\big(y(t + \Delta t) - y(t)\big)^2 + \big(z(t + \Delta t) - z(t)\big)^2 \leq b^2(\Delta t)^2. \tag{7.4}$$

This constraint makes it considerably more difficult to adapt the algorithms of Chapters 5 and 6. Even for piecewise-linear motions of the obstacles, the problem has been established to be PSPACE-hard [821, 822, 929]. A complete algorithm is presented in [822] that is similar to the shortest-path roadmap algorithm of Section 6.2.4. The sampling-based roadmap of Section 5.6 is perhaps one of the easiest of the sampling-based algorithms

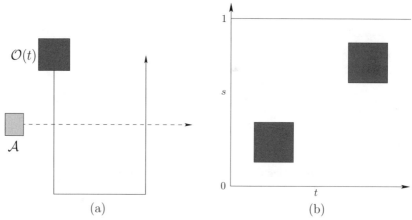

Figure 7.4: An illustration of path tuning. (a) If the robot follows its computed path, it may collide with the moving obstacle. (b) The resulting state space.

to adapt for this problem. The neighbors of point q, which are determined for attempted connections, must lie within the cone that represents the speed bound. If this constraint is enforced, a resolution complete or probabilistically complete planning algorithm results.

7.1.3 The velocity-tuning method

An alternative to defining the problem in $\mathcal{C} \times T$ is to decouple it into a *path planning* part and a *motion timing* part [509]. Algorithms based on this method are not complete, but velocity tuning is an important idea that can be applied elsewhere. Suppose there are both *stationary obstacles* and *moving obstacles*. For the stationary obstacles, suppose that some path $\tau : [0, 1] \to \mathcal{C}_{free}$ has been computed using any of the techniques described in Chapters 5 and 6.

The timing part is then handled in a second phase. Design a *timing function* (or *time scaling*), $\sigma : T \to [0, 1]$, that indicates for time, t, the location of the robot along the path, τ. This is achieved by defining the composition $\phi = \tau \circ \sigma$, which maps from T to $\mathcal{C}_{free}$ via $[0, 1]$. Thus, $\phi : T \to \mathcal{C}_{free}$. The configuration at time $t \in T$ is expressed as $\phi(t) = \tau(\sigma(t))$.

A 2D state space can be defined as shown in Figure 7.4. The purpose is to convert the design of σ (and consequently ϕ) into a familiar planning problem. The robot must move along its path from $\tau(0)$ to $\tau(1)$ while an obstacle, $\mathcal{O}(t)$, moves along its path over the time interval T. Let $S = [0, 1]$ denote the domain of τ. A state space, $X = T \times S$, is shown in Figure 7.4b, in which each point (t, s) indicates the time $t \in T$ and the position along the path, $s \in [0, 1]$. The obstacle region in X is defined as

$$X_{obs} = \{(t, s) \in X \mid \mathcal{A}(\tau(s)) \cap \mathcal{O}(t) \neq \emptyset\}. \tag{7.5}$$

Once again, X_{free} is defined as $X_{free} = X \setminus X_{obs}$. The task is to find a continuous path $g : [0, 1] \to X_{free}$. If g is time-monotonic, then a position $s \in S$ is assigned for every time, $t \in T$. These assignments can be nicely organized into the timing function, $\sigma : T \to S$, from which ϕ is obtained by $\phi = \tau \circ \sigma$ to determine where the robot will be at each time. Being time-monotonic in this context means that the path must always progress from left to right in Figure 7.4b. It can, however, be nonmonotonic in the positive s direction.

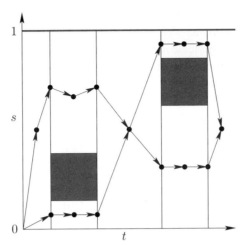

Figure 7.5: Vertical cell decomposition can solve the path tuning problem. Note that this example is not in general position because vertical edges exist. The goal is to reach the horizontal line at the top, which can be accomplished from any adjacent 2-cell. For this example, it may even be accomplished from the first 2-cell if the robot is able to move quickly enough.

This corresponds to moving back and forth along τ, causing some configurations to be revisited.

Any of the methods described in Formulation 7.1 can be applied here. The dimension of X in this case is always 2. Note that X_{obs} is polygonal if $\mathcal{A}$ and $\mathcal{O}$ are both polygonal regions and their paths are piecewise-linear. In this case, the vertical decomposition method of Section 6.2.2 can be applied by sweeping along the time axis to yield a complete algorithm (it is complete after having committed to τ, but it is not complete for Formulation 7.1). The result is shown in Figure 7.5. The cells are connected only if it is possible to reach one from the other by traveling in the forward time direction. As an example of a sampling-based approach that may be preferable when X_{obs} is not polygonal, place a grid over X and apply one of the classical search algorithms described in Section 5.4.2. Once again, only path segments in X that move forward in time are allowed.

7.2 Multiple robots

Suppose that multiple robots share the same world, $\mathcal{W}$. A path must be computed for each robot that avoids collisions with obstacles and with other robots. In Chapter 4, each robot could be a rigid body, $\mathcal{A}$, or it could be made of k attached bodies, $\mathcal{A}_1, \ldots, \mathcal{A}_k$. To avoid confusion, superscripts will be used in this section to denote different robots. The ith robot will be denoted by $\mathcal{A}^i$. Suppose there are m robots, $\mathcal{A}^1, \mathcal{A}^2, \ldots, \mathcal{A}^m$. Each robot, $\mathcal{A}^i$, has its associated C-space, $\mathcal{C}^i$, and its initial and goal configurations, q^i_{init} and q^i_{goal}, respectively.

7.2.1 Problem formulation

A state space is defined that considers the configurations of all robots simultaneously,

$$X = \mathcal{C}^1 \times \mathcal{C}^2 \times \cdots \times \mathcal{C}^m. \tag{7.6}$$

A state $x \in X$ specifies all robot configurations and may be expressed as $x = (q^1, q^2, \ldots, q^m)$. The dimension of X is N, which is $N = \sum_{i=1}^{m} \dim(\mathcal{C}^i)$.

There are two sources of obstacle regions in the state space: 1) *robot-obstacle* collisions, and 2) *robot-robot* collisions. For each i such that $1 \leq i \leq m$, the subset of X that corresponds to robot $\mathcal{A}^i$ in collision with the obstacle region, $\mathcal{O}$, is

$$X_{obs}^i = \{x \in X \mid \mathcal{A}^i(q^i) \cap \mathcal{O} \neq \emptyset\}. \tag{7.7}$$

This only models the robot-obstacle collisions.

For each pair, $\mathcal{A}^i$ and $\mathcal{A}^j$, of robots, the subset of X that corresponds to $\mathcal{A}^i$ in collision with $\mathcal{A}^j$ is

$$X_{obs}^{ij} = \{x \in X \mid \mathcal{A}^i(q^i) \cap \mathcal{A}^j(q^j) \neq \emptyset\}. \tag{7.8}$$

Both (7.7) and (7.8) will be combined in (7.10) later to yield X_{obs}.

Formulation 7.2 (Multiple-Robot Motion Planning)

1. The *world* $\mathcal{W}$ and *obstacle region* $\mathcal{O}$ are the same as in Formulation 4.1.
2. There are m *robots*, $\mathcal{A}^1, \ldots, \mathcal{A}^m$, each of which may consist of one or more bodies.
3. Each robot $\mathcal{A}^i$, for i from 1 to m, has an associated *configuration space*, $\mathcal{C}^i$.
4. The *state space* X is defined as the Cartesian product

$$X = \mathcal{C}^1 \times \mathcal{C}^2 \times \cdots \times \mathcal{C}^m. \tag{7.9}$$

   The obstacle region in X is

$$X_{obs} = \left(\bigcup_{i=1}^{m} X_{obs}^i \right) \bigcup \left(\bigcup_{ij,\ i \neq j} X_{obs}^{ij} \right), \tag{7.10}$$

   in which X_{obs}^i and X_{obs}^{ij} are the robot-obstacle and robot-robot collision states from (7.7) and (7.8), respectively.

5. A state $x_I \in X_{free}$ is designated as the *initial state*, in which $x_I = (q_I^1, \ldots, q_I^m)$. For each i such that $1 \leq i \leq m$, q_I^i specifies the initial configuration of $\mathcal{A}^i$.
6. A state $x_G \in X_{free}$ is designated as the *goal state*, in which $x_G = (q_G^1, \ldots, q_G^m)$.
7. The task is to compute a continuous path $\tau : [0, 1] \to X_{free}$ such that $\tau(0) = x_{init}$ and $\tau(1) \in x_{goal}$.

An ordinary motion planning problem?

On the surface it may appear that there is nothing unusual about the multiple-robot problem because the formulations used in Chapter 4 already cover the case in which the robot consists of multiple bodies. They do not have to be attached; therefore, X can be considered as an ordinary C-space. The planning algorithms of Chapters 5 and 6 may be applied without adaptation. The main concern, however, is that the dimension of X grows linearly with respect to the number of robots. For example, if there are 12 rigid bodies for which each has $\mathcal{C}^i = SE(3)$, then the dimension of X is $6 \cdot 12 = 72$. Complete algorithms require time that is at least exponential in dimension, which makes them unlikely candidates for such problems. Sampling-based algorithms are more likely to scale well in practice when there many robots, but the dimension of X might still be too high.

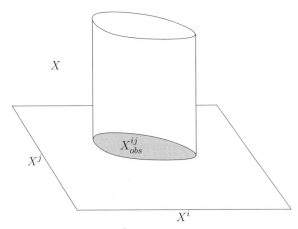

Figure 7.6: The set X_{obs}^{ij} and its cylindrical structure on X.

Reasons to study multi-robot motion planning

Even though multiple-robot motion planning can be handled like any other motion planning problem, there are several reasons to study it separately:

1. The motions of the robots can be decoupled in many interesting ways. This leads to several interesting methods that first develop some kind of partial plan for the robots independently, and then consider the plan interactions to produce a solution. This idea is referred to as *decoupled planning*.

2. The part of X_{obs} due to robot-robot collisions has a cylindrical structure, depicted in Figure 7.6, which can be exploited to make more efficient planning algorithms. Each X_{obs}^{ij} defined by (7.8) depends only on two robots. A point, $x = (q^1, \ldots, q^m)$, is in X_{obs} if there exists i, j such that $1 \leq i, j \leq m$ and $\mathcal{A}^i(q^i) \cap \mathcal{A}^j(q^j) \neq \emptyset$, regardless of the configurations of the other $m - 2$ robots. For some decoupled methods, this even implies that X_{obs} can be completely characterized by 2D projections, as depicted in Figure 7.9.

3. If optimality is important, then a unique set of issues arises for the case of multiple robots. It is not a standard optimization problem because the performance of each robot has to be optimized. There is no clear way to combine these objectives into a single optimization problem without losing some critical information. It will be explained in Section 7.7.2 that Pareto optimality naturally arises as the appropriate notion of optimality for multiple-robot motion planning.

Assembly planning

One important variant of multiple-robot motion planning is called *assembly planning*; recall from Section 1.2 its importance in applications. In automated manufacturing, many complicated objects are assembled step-by-step from individual parts. It is convenient for robots to manipulate the parts one-by-one to insert them into the proper locations (see Section 7.3.2). Imagine a collection of parts, each of which is interpreted as a robot, as shown in Figure 7.7a. The goal is to assemble the parts into one coherent object, such as that shown in Figure 7.7b. The problem is generally approached by starting with the goal configuration, which is tightly constrained, and working outward. The problem formulation may allow that the parts touch, but their interiors cannot overlap. In general, the assembly planning problem with arbitrarily many parts is NP-hard. Polynomial-time algorithms have been developed in several special cases. For the case in which parts can

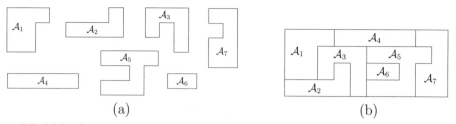

Figure 7.7: (a) A collection of pieces used to define an assembly planning problem; (b) assembly planning involves determining a sequence of motions that assembles the parts. The object shown here is assembled from the parts.

be removed by a sequence of straight-line paths, a polynomial-time algorithm is given in [973, 974].

7.2.2 Decoupled planning

Decoupled approaches first design motions for the robots while ignoring robot-robot interactions. Once these interactions are considered, the choices available to each robot are already constrained by the designed motions. If a problem arises, these approaches are typically unable to reverse their commitments. Therefore, completeness is lost. Nevertheless, decoupled approaches are quite practical, and in some cases completeness can be recovered.

Prioritized planning

A straightforward approach to decoupled planning is to sort the robots by priority and plan for higher priority robots first [322, 951]. Lower priority robots plan by viewing the higher priority robots as moving obstacles. Suppose the robots are sorted as $\mathcal{A}^1, \ldots, \mathcal{A}^m$, in which $\mathcal{A}^1$ has the highest priority.

Assume that collision-free paths, $\tau_i : [0, 1] \to \mathcal{C}^i_{free}$, have been computed for i from 1 to n. The prioritized planning approach proceeds inductively as follows:

Base case: Use any motion planning algorithm from Chapters 5 and 6 to compute a collision-free path, $\tau_1 : [0, 1] \to \mathcal{C}^1_{free}$ for $\mathcal{A}^1$. Compute a timing function, σ_1, for τ_1, to yield $\phi_1 = \tau_1 \circ \sigma_1 : T \to \mathcal{C}^1_{free}$.

Inductive step: Suppose that $\phi_1, \ldots, \phi_{i-1}$ have been designed for $\mathcal{A}^1, \ldots, \mathcal{A}^{i-1}$, and that these functions avoid robot-robot collisions between any of the first $i - 1$ robots. Formulate the first $i - 1$ robots as moving obstacles in $\mathcal{W}$. For each $t \in T$ and $j \in \{1, \ldots, i - 1\}$, the configuration q^j of each $\mathcal{A}^j$ is $\phi_j(t)$. This yields $\mathcal{A}^j(\phi_j(t)) \subset \mathcal{W}$, which can be considered as a subset of the obstacle $\mathcal{O}(t)$. Design a path, τ_i, and timing function, σ_i, using any of the time-varying motion planning methods from Section 7.1 and form $\phi_i = \tau_i \circ \sigma_i$.

Although practical in many circumstances, Figure 7.8 illustrates how completeness is lost.

A special case of prioritized planning is to design all of the paths, $\tau_1, \tau_2, \ldots, \tau_m$, in the first phase and then formulate each inductive step as a velocity tuning problem. This yields a sequence of 2D planning problems that can be solved easily. This comes at a greater expense, however, because the choices are even more constrained. The idea of preplanned paths, and even roadmaps, for all robots independently can lead to a powerful method if the coordination of the robots is approached more carefully. This is the next topic.

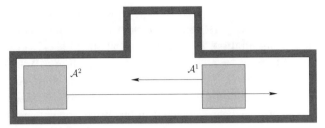

Figure 7.8: If $\mathcal{A}^1$ neglects the query for $\mathcal{A}^2$, then completeness is lost when using the prioritized planning approach. This example has a solution in general, but prioritized planning fails to find it.

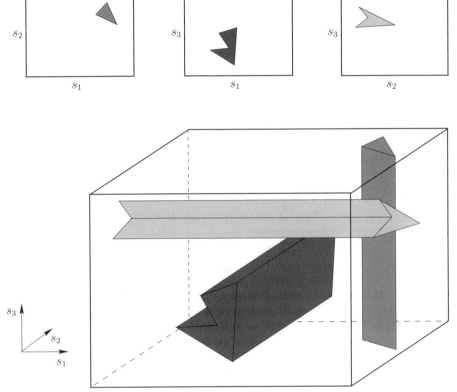

Figure 7.9: The obstacles that arise from coordinating m robots are always cylindrical. The set of all $\frac{1}{2}m(m-1)$ axis-aligned 2D projections completely characterizes X_{obs}.

Fixed-path coordination

Suppose that each robot $\mathcal{A}^i$ is constrained to follow a path $\tau_i : [0, 1] \to \mathcal{C}^i_{free}$, which can be computed using any ordinary motion planning technique. For m robots, an m-dimensional state space called a *coordination space* is defined that schedules the motions of the robots along their paths so that they will not collide [749]. One important feature is that time will only be *implicitly* represented in the coordination space. An algorithm must compute a path in the coordination space, from which explicit timings can be easily extracted.

For m robots, the *coordination space* X is defined as the m-dimensional unit cube $X = [0, 1]^m$. Figure 7.9 depicts an example for which $m = 3$. The ith coordinate of X represents the domain, $S_i = [0, 1]$, of the path τ_i. Let s_i denote a point in S_i (it is also the ith component of x). A state, $x \in X$, indicates the configuration of every robot. For each i, the configuration $q^i \in \mathcal{C}^i$ is given by $q^i = \tau_i(s_i)$. At state $(0, \ldots, 0) \in X$, every robot is in its initial configuration, $q_I^i = \tau_i(0)$, and at state $(1, \ldots, 1) \in X$, every robot is in its goal configuration, $q_G^i = \tau_i(1)$. Any continuous path, $h : [0, 1] \to X$, for which $h(0) = (0, \ldots, 0)$ and $h(1) = (1, \ldots, 1)$, moves the robots to their goal configurations. The path h does not even need to be monotonic, in contrast to prioritized planning.

One important concern has been neglected so far. What prevents us from designing h as a straight-line path between the opposite corners of $[0, 1]^m$? We have not yet taken into account the collisions between the robots. This forms an obstacle region X_{obs} that must be avoided when designing a path through X. Thus, the task is to design $h : [0, 1] \to X_{free}$, in which $X_{free} = X \setminus X_{obs}$.

The definition of X_{obs} is very similar to (7.8) and (7.10), except that here the state-space dimension is much smaller. Each q^i is replaced by a single parameter. The cylindrical structure, however, is still retained, as shown in Figure 7.9. Each cylinder of X_{obs} is

$$X_{obs}^{ij} = \{(s_1, \ldots, s_m) \in X \mid \mathcal{A}^i(\tau_i(s_i)) \cap \mathcal{A}^j(\tau_j(s_j)) \neq \emptyset\}, \qquad (7.11)$$

which are combined to yield

$$X_{obs} = \bigcup_{ij, \, i \neq j} X_{obs}^{ij}. \qquad (7.12)$$

Standard motion planning algorithms can be applied to the coordination space because there is no monotonicity requirement on h. If 1) $\mathcal{W} = \mathbb{R}^2$, 2) $m = 2$ (two robots), 3) the obstacles and robots are polygonal, and 4) the paths, τ_i, are piecewise-linear, then X_{obs} is a polygonal region in X. This enables the methods of Section 6.2, for a polygonal $\mathcal{C}_{obs}$, to directly apply after the representation of X_{obs} is explicitly constructed. For $m > 2$, the multi-dimensional version of vertical cell decomposition given for $m = 3$ in Section 6.3.3 can be applied. For general coordination problems, cylindrical algebraic decomposition or Canny's roadmap algorithm can be applied. For the problem of robots in $\mathcal{W} = \mathbb{R}^2$ that either translate or move along circular paths, a resolution complete planning method based on the exact determination of X_{obs} using special collision detection methods is given in [887].

For very challenging coordination problems, sampling-based solutions may yield practical solutions. Perhaps one of the simplest solutions is to place a grid over X and adapt the classical search algorithms, as described in Section 5.4.2 [609, 749]. Other possibilities include using the RDTs of Section 5.5 or, if the multiple-query framework is appropriate, then the sampling-based roadmap methods of 5.6 are suitable. Methods for validating the path segments, which were covered in Section 5.3.4, can be adapted without trouble to the case of coordination spaces.

Thus far, the particular speeds of the robots have been neglected. For explanation purposes, consider the case of $m = 2$. Moving vertically or horizontally in X holds one robot fixed while the other moves at some maximum speed. Moving diagonally in X moves both robots, and their relative speeds depend on the slope of the path. To carefully regulate these speeds, it may be necessary to reparameterize the paths by distance. In this case each axis of X represents the distance traveled, instead of $[0, 1]$.

Fixed-roadmap coordination

The fixed-path coordination approach still may not solve the problem in Figure 7.8 if the paths are designed independently. Fortunately, fixed-path coordination can be extended to enable each robot to move over a roadmap or topological graph. This still yields a coordination space that has only one dimension per robot, and the resulting planning methods are much closer to being complete, assuming each robot utilizes a roadmap that has many alternative paths. There is also motivation to study this problem by itself because of automated guided vehicles (AGVs), which often move in factories on a network of predetermined paths. In this case, coordinating the robots *is* the planning problem, as opposed to being a simplification of Formulation 7.2.

One way to obtain completeness for Formulation 7.2 is to design the independent roadmaps so that each robot has its own *garage* configuration. The conditions for a configuration, q^i, to be a *garage* for $\mathcal{A}^i$ are 1) while at configuration q^i, it is impossible for any other robots to collide with it (i.e., in all coordination states for which the ith coordinate is q^i, no collision occurs); and 2) q^i is always reachable by $\mathcal{A}^i$ from x_I. If each robot has a roadmap and a garage, and if the planning method for X is complete, then the overall planning algorithm is complete. If the planning method in X uses some weaker notion of completeness, then this is also maintained. For example, a resolution complete planner for X yields a resolution complete approach to the problem in Formulation 7.2.

Cube complex

How is the coordination space represented when there are multiple paths for each robot? It turns out that a *cube complex* is obtained, which is a special kind of singular complex (recall from Section 6.3.1). The coordination space for m fixed paths can be considered as a singular m-simplex. For example, the problem in Figure 7.9 can be considered as a singular 3-simplex, $[0, 1]^3 \to X$. In Section 6.3.1, the domain of a k-simplex was defined using B^k, a k-dimensional ball; however, a cube, $[0, 1]^k$, also works because B^k and $[0, 1]^k$ are homeomorphic.

For a topological space, X, let a *k-cube* (which is also a singular k-simplex), $\Box_k$, be a continuous mapping $\sigma : [0, 1]^k \to X$. A cube complex is obtained by connecting together k-cubes of different dimensions. Every k-cube for $k \geq 1$ has $2k$ *faces*, which are $(k - 1)$-cubes that are obtained as follows. Let $(s_1, \ldots, s_k)$ denote a point in $[0, 1]^k$. For each $i \in \{1, \ldots, k\}$, one face is obtained by setting $s_i = 0$ and another is obtained by setting $s_i = 1$.

The cubes must fit together nicely, much in the same way that the simplexes of a simplicial complex were required to fit together. To be a *cube complex*, $\mathcal{K}$ must be a collection of simplexes that satisfy the following requirements:

1. Any face, $\Box_{k-1}$, of a cube $\Box_k \in \mathcal{K}$ is also in $\mathcal{K}$.
2. The intersection of the images of any two k-cubes $\Box_k, \Box'_k \in \mathcal{K}$, is either empty or there exists some cube, $\Box_i \in \mathcal{K}$ for $i < k$, which is a common face of both $\Box_k$ and $\Box'_k$.

Let $\mathcal{G}_i$ denote a topological graph (which may also be a roadmap) for robot $\mathcal{A}^i$. The graph edges are paths of the form $\tau : [0, 1] \to \mathcal{C}^i_{free}$. Before covering formal definitions of the resulting complex, consider Figure 7.10a, in which $\mathcal{A}^1$ moves along three paths connected in a "T" junction and $\mathcal{A}^2$ moves along one path. In this case, three 2D fixed-path coordination spaces are attached together along one common edge, as shown in Figure 7.10b. The resulting cube complex is defined by three 2-cubes (i.e., squares), one 1-cube (i.e., line segment), and eight 0-cubes (i.e., corner points).

Now suppose more generally that there are two robots, $\mathcal{A}^1$ and $\mathcal{A}^2$, with associated topological graphs, $\mathcal{G}_1(V_1, E_1)$ and $\mathcal{G}_2(V_2, E_2)$, respectively. Suppose that $\mathcal{G}$ and $\mathcal{G}_2$ have

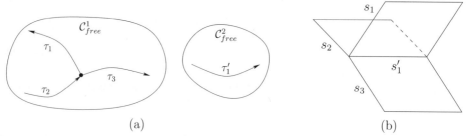

Figure 7.10: (a) An example in which $\mathcal{A}^1$ moves along three paths, and $\mathcal{A}^2$ moves along one. (b) The corresponding coordination space.

n_1 and n_2 edges, respectively. A 2D cube complex, $\mathcal{K}$, is obtained as follows. Let τ_i denote the ith path of $\mathcal{G}_1$, and let σ_j denote the jth path of $\mathcal{G}_2$. A 2-cube (square) exists in $\mathcal{K}$ for every way to select an edge from each graph. Thus, there are $n_1 n_2$ 2-cubes, one for each pair (τ_i, σ_j), such that $\tau_i \in E_1$ and $\sigma_j \in E_2$. The 1-cubes are generated for pairs of the form (v_i, σ_j) for $v_i \in V_1$ and $\sigma_j \in E_2$, or (τ_i, v_j) for $\tau_i \in E_1$ and $v_j \in V_2$. The 0-cubes (corner points) are reached for each pair (v_i, v_j) such that $v_i \in V_1$ and $v_j \in V_2$.

If there are m robots, then an m-dimensional cube complex arises. Every m-cube corresponds to a unique combination of paths, one for each robot. The $(m - 1)$-cubes are the faces of the m-cubes. This continues iteratively until the 0-cubes are reached.

Planning on the cube complex

Once again, any of the planning methods described in Chapters 5 and 6 can be adapted here, but the methods are slightly complicated by the fact that X is a complex. To use sampling-based methods, a dense sequence should be generated over X. For example, if random sampling is used, then an m-cube can be chosen at random, followed by a random point in the cube. The local planning method (LPM) must take into account the connectivity of the cube complex, which requires recognizing when branches occur in the topological graph. Combinatorial methods must also take into account this connectivity. For example, a sweeping technique can be applied to produce a vertical cell decomposition, but the sweep-line (or sweep-plane) must sweep across the various m-cells of the complex.

7.3 Mixing discrete and continuous spaces

Many important applications involve a mixture of discrete and continuous variables. This results in a state space that is a Cartesian product of the C-space and a finite set called the *mode space*. The resulting space can be visualized as having layers of C-spaces that are indexed by the modes, as depicted in Figure 7.11. The main application given in this section is manipulation planning; many others exist, especially when other complications such as dynamics and uncertainties are added to the problem. The framework of this section is inspired mainly from *hybrid systems* in the control theory community [411], which usually model mode-dependent dynamics. The main concern in this section is that the allowable robot configurations and/or the obstacles depend on the mode.

7.3.1 Hybrid systems framework

As illustrated in Figure 7.11, a hybrid system involves interaction between discrete and continuous spaces. The formal model will first be given, followed by some explanation.

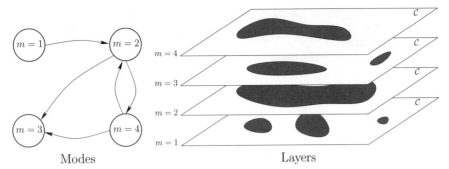

Modes   Layers

Figure 7.11: A hybrid state space can be imagined as having layers of C-spaces that are indexed by modes.

This formulation can be considered as a combination of the components from discrete feasible planning, Formulation 2.1, and basic motion planning, Formulation 4.1.

Formulation 7.3 (Hybrid-System Motion Planning)

1. The $\mathcal{W}$ and $\mathcal{C}$ components from Formulation 4.1 are included.

2. A nonempty *mode space*, M that is a finite or countably infinite set of *modes*.

3. A semi-algebraic *obstacle region* $\mathcal{O}(m)$ for each $m \in M$.

4. A semi-algebraic *robot* $\mathcal{A}(m)$, for each $m \in M$. It may be a rigid robot or a collection of links. It is assumed that the C-space is not mode-dependent; only the geometry of the robot can depend on the mode. The robot, transformed to configuration q, is denoted as $\mathcal{A}(q, m)$.

5. A *state space* X is defined as the Cartesian product $X = \mathcal{C} \times M$. A state is represented as $x = (q, m)$, in which $q \in \mathcal{C}$ and $m \in M$. Let

$$X_{obs} = \{(q, m) \in X \mid \mathcal{A}(q, m) \cap \mathcal{O}(m) \neq \emptyset\}, \qquad (7.13)$$

and $X_{free} = X \setminus X_{obs}$.

6. For each state, $x \in X$, there is a finite *action space*, $U(x)$. Let U denote the set of all possible actions (the union of $U(x)$ over all $x \in X$).

7. There is a *mode transition function* f_m that produces a mode, $f_m(x, u) \in M$, for every $x \in X$ and $u \in U(x)$. It is assumed that f_m is defined in a way that does not produce race conditions (oscillations of modes within an instant of time). This means that if q is fixed, the mode can change at most once. It then remains constant and can change only if q is changed.

8. There is a *state transition function*, f, that is derived from f_m by changing the mode and holding the configuration fixed. Thus, $f(x, u) = (q, f_m(x, u))$.

9. A configuration $x_I \in X_{free}$ is designated as the *initial state*.

10. A set $X_G \in X_{free}$ is designated as the *goal region*. A region is defined instead of a point to facilitate the specification of a goal configuration that does not depend on the final mode.

11. An algorithm must compute a (continuous) *path* $\tau : [0, 1] \to X_{free}$ and an *action trajectory* $\sigma : [0, 1] \to U$ such that $\tau(0) = x_I$ and $\tau(1) \in X_G$, or the algorithm correctly reports that such a combination of a path and an action trajectory does not exist.

The obstacle region and robot may or may not be mode-dependent, depending on the problem. Examples of each will be given shortly. Changes in the mode depend on the action taken by the robot. From most states, it is usually assumed that a "do nothing"

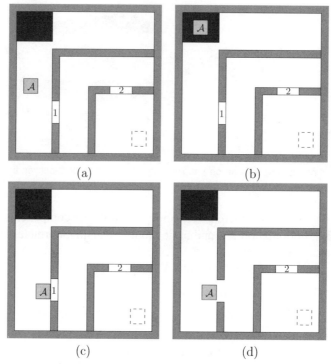

Figure 7.12: In the upper left (at the portiernia), the robot can pick up and drop off keys that open one of two doors. If the robot contacts a door while holding the correct key, then it opens.

action exists, which leaves the mode unchanged. From certain states, the robot may select an action that changes the mode as desired. An interesting degenerate case exists in which there is only a single action available. This means that the robot has no control over the mode from that state. If the robot arrives in such a state, a mode change could unavoidably occur.

The solution requirement is somewhat more complicated because both a path and an action trajectory need to be specified. It is insufficient to specify a path because it is important to know what action was applied to induce the correct mode transitions. Therefore, σ indicates when these occur. Note that τ and σ are closely coupled; one cannot simply associate any σ with a path τ; it must correspond to the actions required to generate τ.

Example 7.2 (The Power of the Portiernia)   In this example, a robot, $\mathcal{A}$, is modeled as a square that translates in $\mathcal{W} = \mathbb{R}^2$. Therefore, $\mathcal{C} = \mathbb{R}^2$. The obstacle region in $\mathcal{W}$ is mode-dependent because of two doors, which are numbered "1" and "2" in Figure 7.12a. In the upper left sits the *portiernia*,[2] which is able to give a key to the robot, if the robot is in a configuration as shown in Figure 7.12b. The portiernia only trusts the robot with one key at a time, which may be either for Door 1 or Door 2. The robot can return a key by revisiting the portiernia. As shown in Figures 7.12c and 7.12d, the robot can open a door by making contact with it, as long as it holds the correct key.

The set, M, of modes needs to encode which key, if any, the robot holds, and it must also encode the status of the doors. The robot may have: 1) the key to Door 1; 2) the key

---

[2] This is a place where people guard the keys at some public facilities in Poland.

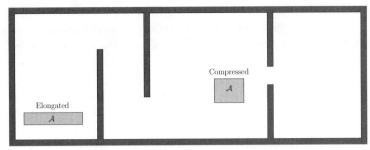

Figure 7.13: An example in which the robot must reconfigure itself to solve the problem. There are two modes: *elongated* and *compressed*.

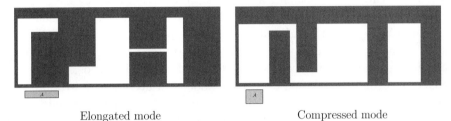

Elongated mode   Compressed mode

Figure 7.14: When the robot reconfigures itself, $\mathcal{C}_{free}(m)$ changes, enabling the problem to be solved.

to Door 2; or 3) no keys. The doors may have the status: 1) both open; 2) Door 1 open, Door 2 closed; 3) Door 1 closed, Door 2 open; or 4) both closed. Considering keys and doors in combination yields 12 possible modes.

If the robot is at a portiernia configuration as shown in Figure 7.12b, then its available actions correspond to different ways to pick up and drop off keys. For example, if the robot is holding the key to Door 1, it can drop it off and pick up the key to Door 2. This changes the mode, but the door status and robot configuration must remain unchanged when f is applied. The other locations in which the robot may change the mode are when it comes in contact with Door 1 or Door 2. The mode changes only if the robot is holding the proper key. In all other configurations, the robot only has a single action (i.e., no choice), which keeps the mode fixed.

The task is to reach the configuration shown in the lower right with dashed lines. The problem is solved by: 1) picking up the key for Door 1 at the portiernia; 2) opening Door 1; 3) swapping the key at the portiernia to obtain the key for Door 2; or 4) entering the innermost room to reach the goal configuration. As a final condition, we might want to require that the robot returns the key to the portiernia. ∎

Example 7.2 allows the robot to change the obstacles in $\mathcal{O}$. The next example involves a robot that can change its shape. This is an illustrative example of a *reconfigurable robot*. The study of such robots has become a popular topic of research [211, 387, 555, 990]; the reconfiguration possibilities in that research area are much more complicated than the simple example considered here.

Example 7.3 (Reconfigurable Robot) To solve the problem shown in Figure 7.13, the robot must change its shape. There are two possible shapes, which correspond directly to the modes: *elongated* and *compressed*. Examples of each are shown in the figure. Figure 7.14 shows how $\mathcal{C}_{free}(m)$ appears for each of the two modes. Suppose the robot starts initially from the left while in the elongated mode and must travel to the last room on the right. This problem must be solved by 1) reconfiguring the robot into the compressed mode; 2) passing through the corridor into the center; 3) reconfiguring the robot into the elongated mode; and 4) passing through the corridor to the rightmost room. The robot has actions that directly change the mode by reconfiguring itself. To make the problem more interesting, we could require the robot to reconfigure itself in specific locations (e.g., where there is enough clearance, or possibly at a location where another robot can assist it).   ∎

The examples presented so far barely scratch the surface on the possible hybrid motion planning problems that can be defined. Many such problems can arise, for example, in the context making automated video game characters or digital actors. To solve these problems, standard motion planning algorithms can be adapted if they are given information about how to change the modes. Locations in X from which the mode can be changed may be expressed as subgoals. Much of the planning effort should then be focused on attempting to change modes, in addition to trying to directly reach the goal. Applying sampling-based methods requires the definition of a metric on X that accounts for both changes in the mode and the configuration. A wide variety of hybrid problems can be formulated, ranging from those that are impossible to solve in practice to those that are straightforward extensions of standard motion planning. In general, the hybrid motion planning model is useful for formulating a hierarchical approach, as described in Section 1.4. One particularly interesting class of problems that fit this model, for which successful algorithms have been developed, will be covered next.

7.3.2 Manipulation planning

This section presents an overview of manipulation planning; the concepts explained here are mainly due to [16, 17]. Returning to Example 7.2, imagine that the robot must carry a key that is so large that it changes the connectivity of C_{free}. For the manipulation planning problem, the robot is called a *manipulator*, which interacts with a *part*. In some configurations it is able to *grasp* the part and move it to other locations in the environment. The *manipulation task* usually requires moving the part to a specified location in W, without particular regard as to how the *manipulator* can accomplish the task. The model considered here greatly simplifies the problems of grasping, stability, friction, mechanics, and uncertainties and instead focuses on the geometric aspects (some of these issues will be addressed in Section 12.5). For a thorough introduction to these other important aspects of manipulation planning, see [684]; see also Sections 13.1.3 and 12.5.

Admissible configurations

Assume that W, O, and A from Formulation 4.1 are used. For manipulation planning, A is called the *manipulator*, and let C^a refer to the *manipulator configuration space*. Let P denote a *part*, which is a rigid body modeled in terms of geometric primitives, as described in Section 3.1. It is assumed that P is allowed to undergo rigid-body transformations and will therefore have its own *part configuration space*, $C^p = SE(2)$ or $C^p = SE(3)$. Let $q^p \in C^p$ denote a *part configuration*. The transformed part model is denoted as $P(q^p)$.

The combined *configuration space*, C, is defined as the Cartesian product

$$C = C^a \times C^p,$$

(7.14)

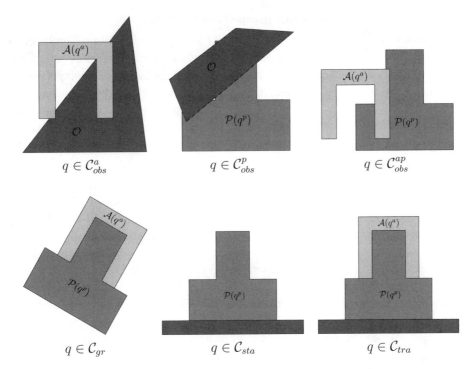

Figure 7.15: Examples of several important subsets of $\mathcal{C}$ for manipulation planning.

in which each configuration $q \in \mathcal{C}$ is of the form $q = (q^a, q^p)$. The first step is to remove all configurations that must be avoided. Parts of Figure 7.15 show examples of these sets. Configurations for which the manipulator collides with obstacles are

$$\mathcal{C}^a_{obs} = \{(q^a, q^p) \in \mathcal{C} \mid \mathcal{A}(q^a) \cap \mathcal{O} \neq \varnothing\}. \tag{7.15}$$

The next logical step is to remove configurations for which the part collides with obstacles. It will make sense to allow the part to "touch" the obstacles. For example, this could model a part sitting on a table. Therefore, let

$$\mathcal{C}^p_{obs} = \{(q^a, q^p) \in \mathcal{C} \mid \text{int}(\mathcal{P}(q^p)) \cap \mathcal{O} \neq \varnothing\} \tag{7.16}$$

denote the open set for which the interior of the part intersects $\mathcal{O}$. Certainly, if the part penetrates $\mathcal{O}$, then the configuration should be avoided.

Consider $\mathcal{C} \setminus (\mathcal{C}^a_{obs} \cup \mathcal{C}^p_{obs})$. The configurations that remain ensure that the robot and part do not inappropriately collide with $\mathcal{O}$. Next consider the interaction between $\mathcal{A}$ and $\mathcal{P}$. The manipulator must be allowed to touch the part, but penetration is once again not allowed. Therefore, let

$$\mathcal{C}^{ap}_{obs} = \{(q^a, q^p) \in \mathcal{C} \mid \mathcal{A}(q^a) \cap \text{int}(\mathcal{P}(q^p)) \neq \varnothing\}. \tag{7.17}$$

Removing all of these bad configurations yields

$$\mathcal{C}_{adm} = \mathcal{C} \setminus (\mathcal{C}^a_{obs} \cup \mathcal{C}^p_{obs} \cup \mathcal{C}^{ap}_{obs}), \tag{7.18}$$

which is called the set of *admissible configurations*.

Stable and grasped configurations

Two important subsets of C_{adm} are used in the manipulation planning problem. See Figure 7.15. Let C_{sta}^p denote the set of *stable part configurations*, which are configurations at which the part can safely rest without any forces being applied by the manipulator. This means that a part cannot, for example, float in the air. It also cannot be in a configuration from which it might fall. The particular stable configurations depend on properties such as the part geometry, friction, mass distribution, and so on. These issues are not considered here. From this, let $C_{sta} \subseteq C_{adm}$ be the corresponding *stable configurations*, defined as

$$C_{sta} = \{(q^a, q^p) \in C_{adm} \mid q^p \in C_{sta}^p\}. \tag{7.19}$$

The other important subset of C_{adm} is the set of all configurations in which the robot is grasping the part (and is capable of carrying it, if necessary). Let this denote the *grasped configurations*, denoted by $C_{gr} \subseteq C_{adm}$. For every configuration, $(q^a, q^p) \in C_{gr}$, the manipulator touches the part. This means that $\mathcal{A}(q^a) \cap \mathcal{P}(q^p) \neq \emptyset$ (penetration is still not allowed because $C_{gr} \subseteq C_{adm}$). In general, many configurations at which $\mathcal{A}(q^a)$ contacts $\mathcal{P}(q^p)$ will not necessarily be in C_{gr}. The conditions for a point to lie in C_{gr} depend on the particular characteristics of the manipulator, the part, and the contact surface between them. For example, a typical manipulator would not be able to pick up a block by making contact with only one corner of it. This level of detail is not defined here; see [684] for more information about grasping.

We must always ensure that either $x \in C_{sta}$ or $x \in C_{gr}$. Therefore, let $C_{free} = C_{sta} \cup C_{gr}$, to reflect the subset of C_{adm} that is permissible for manipulation planning.

The mode space, M, contains two modes, which are named the *transit mode* and the *transfer mode*. In the transit mode, the manipulator is not carrying the part, which requires that $q \in C_{sta}$. In the transfer mode, the manipulator carries the part, which requires that $q \in C_{gr}$. Based on these simple conditions, the only way the mode can change is if $q \in C_{sta} \cap C_{gr}$. Therefore, the manipulator has two available actions only when it is in these configurations. In all other configurations the mode remains unchanged. For convenience, let $C_{tra} = C_{sta} \cap C_{gr}$ denote the set of *transition configurations*, which are the places in which the mode may change.

Using the framework of Section 7.3.1, the mode space, M, and C-space, C, are combined to yield the *state space*, $X = C \times M$. Since there are only two modes, there are only two copies of C, one for each mode. State-based sets, X_{free}, X_{tra}, X_{sta}, and X_{gr}, are directly obtained from C_{free}, C_{tra}, C_{sta}, and C_{gr} by ignoring the mode. For example,

$$X_{tra} = \{(q, m) \in X \mid q \in C_{tra}\}. \tag{7.20}$$

The sets X_{free}, X_{sta}, and X_{gr} are similarly defined.

The task can now be defined. An *initial part configuration*, $q_{init}^p \in C_{sta}$, and a *goal part configuration*, $q_{goal}^p \in C_{sta}$, are specified. Compute a path $\tau : [0, 1] \to X_{free}$ such that $\tau(0) = q_{init}^p$ and $\tau(1) = q_{goal}^p$. Furthermore, the *action trajectory* $\sigma : [0, 1] \to U$ must be specified to indicate the appropriate mode changes whenever $\tau(s) \in X_{tra}$. A solution can be considered as an alternating sequence of *transit paths* and *transfer paths*, whose names follow from the mode. This is depicted in Figure 7.16.

Manipulation graph

The manipulation planning problem generally can be solved by forming a manipulation graph, $\mathcal{G}_m$ [16, 17]. Let a *connected component* of X_{tra} refer to any connected component

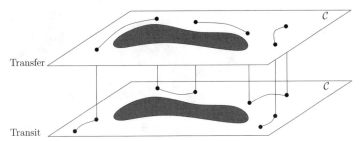

Figure 7.16: The solution to a manipulation planning problem alternates between the two layers of X. The transitions can only occur when $x \in X_{tra}$.

of C_{tra} that is lifted into the state space by ignoring the mode. There are two copies of the connected component of C_{tra}, one for each mode. For each connected component of X_{tra}, a vertex exists in $\mathcal{G}_m$. An edge is defined for each transfer path or transit path that connects two connected components of X_{tra}. The general approach to manipulation planning then is as follows:

1. Compute the connected components of X_{tra} to yield the vertices of $\mathcal{G}_m$.

2. Compute the edges of $\mathcal{G}_m$ by applying ordinary motion planning methods to each pair of vertices of $\mathcal{G}_m$.

3. Apply motion planning methods to connect the initial and goal states to every possible vertex of X_{tra} that can be reached without a mode transition.

4. Search $\mathcal{G}_m$ for a path that connects the initial and goal states. If one exists, then extract the corresponding solution as a sequence of transit and transfer paths (this yields σ, the actions that cause the required mode changes).

This can be considered as an example of hierarchical planning, as described in Section 1.4.

Multiple parts

The manipulation planning framework nicely generalizes to multiple parts, $\mathcal{P}_1, \ldots, \mathcal{P}_k$. Each part has its own C-space, and C is formed by taking the Cartesian product of all part C-spaces with the manipulator C-space. The set C_{adm} is defined in a similar way, but now part-part collisions also have to be removed, in addition to part-manipulator, manipulator-obstacle, and part-obstacle collisions. The definition of C_{sta} requires that all parts be in stable configurations; the parts may even be allowed to stack on top of each other. The definition of C_{gr} requires that one part is grasped and all other parts are stable. There are still two modes, depending on whether the manipulator is grasping a part. Once again, transitions occur only when the robot is in $C_{tra} = C_{sta} \cap C_{gr}$. The task involves moving each part from one configuration to another. This is achieved once again by defining a manipulation graph and obtaining a sequence of transit paths (in which no parts move) and transfer paths (in which one part is carried and all other parts are fixed). Challenging manipulation problems solved by motion planning algorithms are shown in Figures 7.17 and 7.18.

Other generalizations are possible. A generalization to k robots would lead to 2^k modes, in which each mode indicates whether each robot is grasping the part. Multiple robots could even grasp the same object. Another generalization could allow a single robot to grasp more than one object.

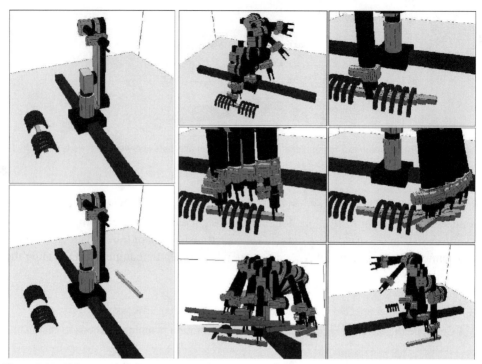

Figure 7.17: This example was solved in [246] using the manipulation planning framework and the visibility-based roadmap planner. It is very challenging because the same part must be regrasped in many places.

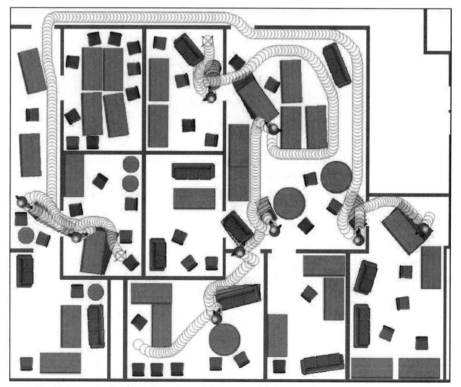

Figure 7.18: This manipulation planning example was solved in [916] and involves 90 movable pieces of furniture. Some of them must be dragged out of the way to solve the problem. Paths for two different queries are shown.

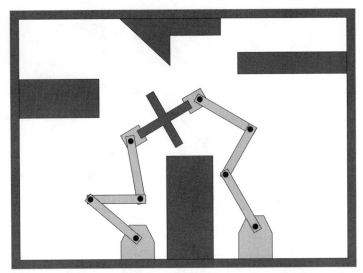

Figure 7.19: Two or more manipulators manipulating the same object causes closed kinematic chains. Each black disc corresponds to a revolute joint.

7.4 Planning for closed kinematic chains

This section continues where Section 4.4 left off. The subspace of C that results from maintaining kinematic closure was defined and illustrated through some examples. Planning in this context requires that paths remain on a lower dimensional variety for which a parameterization is not available. Many important applications require motion planning while maintaining these constraints. For example, consider a manipulation problem that involves multiple manipulators grasping the same object, which forms a closed loop as shown in Figure 7.19. A loop exists because both manipulators are attached to the ground, which may itself be considered as a link. The development of virtual actors for movies and video games also involves related manipulation problems. Loops also arise in this context when more than one human limb is touching a fixed surface (e.g., two feet on the ground). A class of robots called *parallel manipulators* are intentionally designed with internal closed loops [696]. For example, consider the Stewart-Gough platform [409, 915] illustrated in Figure 7.20. The lengths of each of the six arms, $A_1, \ldots, A_6$, can be independently varied while they remain attached via spherical joints to the ground and to the *platform*, which is A_7. Each arm can actually be imagined as two links that are connected by a prismatic joint. Due to the total of 6 degrees of freedom introduced by the variable lengths, the platform actually achieves the full 6 degrees of freedom (hence, some six-dimensional region in $SE(3)$ is obtained for A_7). Planning the motion of the Stewart-Gough platform, or robots that are based on the platform (the robot shown in Figure 7.27 uses a stack of several of these mechanisms), requires handling many closure constraints that must be maintained simultaneously. Another application is computational biology, in which the C-space of molecules is searched, many of which are derived from molecules that have closed, flexible chains of bonds [247].

7.4.1 Adaptation of motion planning algorithms

All of the components from the general motion planning problem of Formulation 4.1 are included: $W, O, A_1, \ldots, A_m, C, q_I$, and q_G. It is assumed that the robot is a collection of r links that are possibly attached in loops.

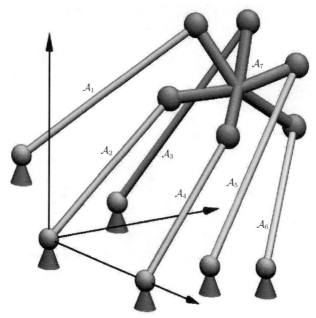

Figure 7.20: An illustration of the Stewart-Gough platform (adapted from a figure made by Frank Sottile).

It is assumed in this section that $C = \mathbb{R}^n$. If this is not satisfactory, there are two ways to overcome the assumption. The first is to represent $SO(2)$ and $SO(3)$ as $\mathbb{S}^1$ and $\mathbb{S}^3$, respectively, and include the circle or sphere equation as part of the constraints considered here. This avoids the topology problems. The other option is to abandon the restriction of using $\mathbb{R}^n$ and instead use a parameterization of C that is of the appropriate dimension. To perform calculus on such manifolds, a *smooth structure* is required, which is introduced in Section 8.3.2. In the presentation here, however, vector calculus on $\mathbb{R}^n$ is sufficient, which intentionally avoids these extra technicalities.

Closure constraints

The closure constraints introduced in Section 4.4 can be summarized as follows. There is a set, $\mathcal{P}$, of polynomials $f_1, \ldots, f_k$ that belong to $\mathbb{Q}[q_1, \ldots, q_n]$ and express the constraints for particular points on the links of the robot. The determination of these is detailed in Section 4.4.3. As mentioned previously, polynomials that force points to lie on a circle or sphere in the case of rotations may also be included in $\mathcal{P}$.

Let n denote the dimension of C. The *closure space* is defined as

$$\mathcal{C}_{clo} = \{q \in \mathcal{C} \mid \forall f_i \in \mathcal{P}, \, f_i(q_1, \ldots, q_n) = 0\}, \qquad (7.21)$$

which is an m-dimensional subspace of C that corresponds to all configurations that satisfy the closure constants. The obstacle set must also be taken into account. Once again, $\mathcal{C}_{obs}$ and $\mathcal{C}_{free}$ are defined using (4.34). The *feasible space* is defined as $\mathcal{C}_{fea} = \mathcal{C}_{clo} \cap \mathcal{C}_{free}$, which are the configurations that satisfy closure constraints and avoid collisions.

The motion planning problem is to find a path $\tau : [0, 1] \to \mathcal{C}_{fea}$ such that $\tau(0) = q_I$ and $\tau(1) = q_G$. The new challenge is that there is no explicit parameterization of $\mathcal{C}_{fea}$, which is further complicated by the fact that $m < n$ (recall that m is the dimension of $\mathcal{C}_{clo}$).

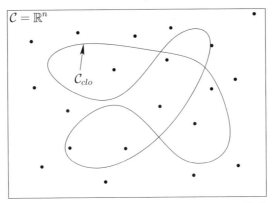

Figure 7.21: For the RDT, the samples can be drawn from a region in $\mathbb{R}^n$, the space in which $\mathcal{C}_{clo}$ is embedded.

Combinatorial methods

Since the constraints are expressed with polynomials, it may not be surprising that the computational algebraic geometry methods of Section 6.4 can solve the general motion planning problem with closed kinematic chains. Either cylindrical algebraic decomposition or Canny's roadmap algorithm may be applied. As mentioned in Section 6.5.3, an adaptation of the roadmap algorithm that is optimized for problems in which $m < n$ is given in [78].

Sampling-based methods

Most of the methods of Chapter 5 are not easy to adapt because they require sampling in $\mathcal{C}_{fea}$, for which a parameterization does not exist. If points in a bounded region of $\mathbb{R}^n$ are chosen at random, the probability is zero that a point on $\mathcal{C}_{fea}$ will be obtained. Some incremental sampling and searching methods can, however, be adapted by the construction of a local planning method (LPM) that is suited for problems with closure constraints. The sampling-based roadmap methods require many samples to be generated directly on $\mathcal{C}_{fea}$. Section 7.4.2 presents some techniques that can be used to generate such samples for certain classes of problems, enabling the development of efficient sampling-based planners and also improving the efficiency of incremental search planners. Before covering these techniques, we first present a method that leads to a more general sampling-based planner and is easier to implement. However, if designed well, planners based on the techniques of Section 7.4.2 are more efficient.

Now consider adapting the RDT of Section 5.5 to work for problems with closure constraints. Similar adaptations may be possible for other incremental sampling and searching methods covered in Section 5.4, such as the randomized potential field planner. A dense sampling sequence, α, is generated over a bounded n-dimensional subset of $\mathbb{R}^n$, such as a rectangle or sphere, as shown in Figure 7.21. The samples are not actually required to lie on $\mathcal{C}_{clo}$ because they do not necessarily become part of the topological graph, $\mathcal{G}$. They mainly serve to pull the search tree in different directions. One concern in choosing the bounding region is that it must include $\mathcal{C}_{clo}$ (at least the connected component that includes q_I) but it must not be unnecessarily large. Such bounds are obtained by analyzing the motion limits for a particular linkage.

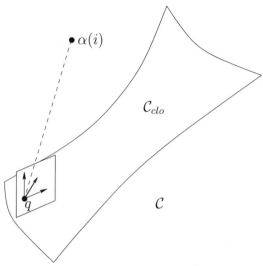

Figure 7.22: For each sample $\alpha(i)$ the nearest point, $q_n \in \mathcal{C}$, is found, and then the local planner generates a motion that lies in the local tangent plane. The motion is the project of the vector from q_n to $\alpha(i)$ onto the tangent plane.

Stepping along $\mathcal{C}_{clo}$

The RDT algorithm given Figure 5.21 can be applied directly; however, the STOPPING-CONFIGURATION function in line 4 must be changed to account for both obstacles and the constraints that define $\mathcal{C}_{clo}$. Figure 7.22 shows one general approach that is based on *numerical continuation* [18]. An alternative is to use inverse kinematics, which is part of the approach described in Section 7.4.2. The nearest RDT vertex, $q \in \mathcal{C}$, to the sample $\alpha(i)$ is first computed. Let $v = \alpha(i) - q$, which indicates the direction in which an edge would be made from q if there were no constraints. A local motion is then computed by projecting v into the tangent plane[3] of $\mathcal{C}_{clo}$ at the point q. Since $\mathcal{C}_{clo}$ is generally nonlinear, the local motion produces a point that is not precisely on $\mathcal{C}_{clo}$. Some numerical tolerance is generally accepted, and a small enough step is taken to ensure that the tolerance is maintained. The process iterates by computing v with respect to the new point and moving in the direction of v projected into the new tangent plane. If the error threshold is surpassed, then motions must be executed in the normal direction to return to $\mathcal{C}_{clo}$. This process of executing tangent and normal motions terminates when progress can no longer be made, due either to the alignment of the tangent plane (nearly perpendicular to v) or to an obstacle. This finally yields q_s, the stopping configuration. The new path followed in $\mathcal{C}_{fea}$ is no longer a "straight line" as was possible for some problems in Section 5.5; therefore, the approximate methods in Section 5.5.2 should be used to create intermediate vertices along the path.

In each iteration, the tangent plane computation is computed at some $q \in \mathcal{C}_{clo}$ as follows. The differential configuration vector dq lies in the tangent space of a constraint $f_i(q) = 0$ if

$$\frac{\partial f_i(q)}{\partial q_1}dq_1 + \frac{\partial f_i(q)}{\partial q_2}dq_2 + \cdots + \frac{\partial f_i(q)}{\partial q_n}dq_n = 0. \tag{7.22}$$

---

[3] Tangent planes are defined rigorously in Section 8.3.

This leads to the following homogeneous system for all of the k polynomials in $\mathcal{P}$ that define the closure constraints

$$
\begin{pmatrix}
\dfrac{\partial f_1(q)}{\partial q_1} & \dfrac{\partial f_1(q)}{\partial q_2} & \cdots & \dfrac{\partial f_1(q)}{\partial q_n} \\[2ex]
\dfrac{\partial f_2(q)}{\partial q_1} & \dfrac{\partial f_2(q)}{\partial q_2} & \cdots & \dfrac{\partial f_2(q)}{\partial q_n} \\[1ex]
\vdots & \vdots & & \vdots \\[1ex]
\dfrac{\partial f_k(q)}{\partial q_1} & \dfrac{\partial f_k(q)}{\partial q_2} & \cdots & \dfrac{\partial f_k(q)}{\partial q_n}
\end{pmatrix}
\begin{pmatrix}
dq_1 \\ dq_2 \\ \vdots \\ dq_n
\end{pmatrix} = \mathbf{0}.
\tag{7.23}
$$

If the rank of the matrix is $m \leq n$, then m configuration displacements can be chosen independently, and the remaining $n - m$ parameters must satisfy (7.23). This can be solved using linear algebra techniques, such as singular value decomposition (SVD) [401, 961], to compute an orthonormal basis for the tangent space at q. Let $e_1, \ldots, e_m$, denote these n-dimensional basis vectors. The components of the motion direction are obtained from $v = \alpha(i) - q_n$. First, construct the inner products, $a_1 = v \cdot e_1, a_2 = v \cdot e_2, \ldots$, $a_m = v \cdot e_m$. Using these, the projection of v in the tangent plane is the n-dimensional vector w given by

$$
w = \sum_i^m a_i e_i,
\tag{7.24}
$$

which is used as the direction of motion. The magnitude must be appropriately scaled to take sufficiently small steps. Since $\mathcal{C}_{clo}$ is generally curved, a linear motion leaves $\mathcal{C}_{clo}$. A motion in the inward normal direction is then required to move back onto $\mathcal{C}_{clo}$.

Since the dimension m of $\mathcal{C}_{clo}$ is less than n, the procedure just described can only produce numerical approximations to paths in $\mathcal{C}_{clo}$. This problem also arises in implicit curve tracing in graphics and geometric modeling [457]. Therefore, each constraint $f_i(q_1, \ldots, q_n) = 0$ is actually slightly weakened to $|f_i(q_1, \ldots, q_n)| < \epsilon$ for some fixed tolerance $\epsilon > 0$. This essentially "thickens" $\mathcal{C}_{clo}$ so that its dimension is n. As an alternative to computing the tangent plane, motion directions can be sampled directly inside of this thickened region without computing tangent planes. This results in an easier implementation, but it is less efficient [979].

7.4.2 Active-passive link decompositions

An alternative sampling-based approach is to perform an *active-passive decomposition*, which is used to generate samples in $\mathcal{C}_{clo}$ by directly sampling *active* variables, and computing the closure values for *passive* variables using inverse kinematics methods. This method was introduced in [435] and subsequently improved through the development of the *random loop generator* in [246, 248]. The method serves as a general framework that can adapt virtually any of the methods of Chapter 5 to handle closed kinematic chains, and experimental evidence suggests that the performance is better than the method of Section 7.4.1. One drawback is that the method requires some careful analysis of the linkage to determine the best decomposition and also bounds on its mobility. Such analysis exists for very general classes of linkages [246].

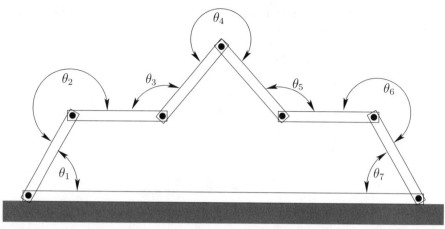

Figure 7.23: A chain of links in the plane. There are seven links and seven joints, which are constrained to form a loop. The dimension of $\mathcal{C}$ is seven, but the dimension of $\mathcal{C}_{clo}$ is four.

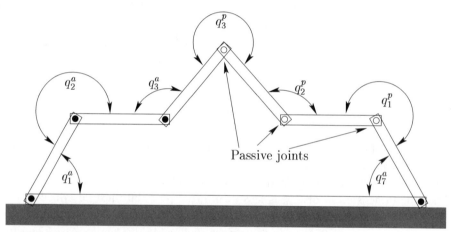

Figure 7.24: Three of the joint variables can be determined automatically by inverse kinematics. Therefore, four of the joints be designated as *active*, and the remaining three will be passive.

Active and passive variables

In this section, let $\mathcal{C}$ denote the C-space obtained from all joint variables, instead of requiring $\mathcal{C} = \mathbb{R}^n$, as in Section 7.4.1. This means that $\mathcal{P}$ includes only polynomials that encode closure constraints, as opposed to allowing constraints that represent rotations. Using the tree representation from Section 4.4.3, this means that $\mathcal{C}$ is of dimension n, arising from assigning one variable for each revolute joint of the linkage in the absence of any constraints. Let $q \in \mathcal{C}$ denote this vector of configuration variables. The *active-passive decomposition* partitions the variables of q to form two vectors, q^a, called the *active variables* and q^p, called the *passive variables*. The values of passive variables are always determined from the active variables by enforcing the closure constraints and using inverse kinematics techniques. If m is the dimension of $\mathcal{C}_{clo}$, then there are always m active variables and $n - m$ passive variables.

Temporarily, suppose that the linkage forms a single loop as shown in Figure 7.23. One possible decomposition into active q^a and passive q^p variables is given in Figure 7.24. If constrained to form a loop, the linkage has four degrees of freedom, assuming the bottom link is rigidly attached to the ground. This means that values can be chosen for four

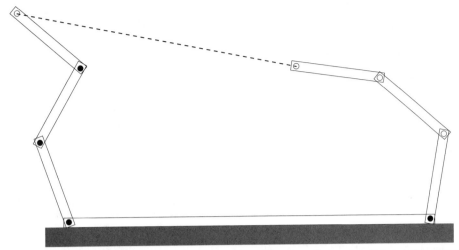

Figure 7.25: In this case, the active variables are chosen in a way that makes it impossible to assign passive variables that close the loop.

active joint angles q^a and the remaining three q^p can be derived from solving the inverse kinematics. To determine q^p, there are three equations and three unknowns. Unfortunately, these equations are nonlinear and fairly complicated. Nevertheless, efficient solutions exist for this case, and the 3D generalization [678]. For a 3D loop formed of revolute joints, there are six passive variables. The number, 3, of passive links in $\mathbb{R}^2$ and the number 6 for $\mathbb{R}^3$ arise from the dimensions of $SE(2)$ and $SE(3)$, respectively. This is the freedom that is stripped away from the system by enforcing the closure constraints. Methods for efficiently computing inverse kinematics in two and three dimensions are given in [30]. These can also be applied to the RDT stepping method in Section 7.4.1, instead of using continuation.

If the maximal number of passive variables is used, there is at most a finite number of solutions to the inverse kinematics problem; this implies that there are often several choices for the passive variable values. It could be the case that for some assignments of active variables, there are no solutions to the inverse kinematics. An example is depicted in Figure 7.25. Suppose that we want to generate samples in $\mathcal{C}_{clo}$ by selecting random values for q^a and then using inverse kinematics for q^p. What is the probability that a solution to the inverse kinematics exists? For the example shown, it appears that solutions would not exist in most trials.

Loop generator

The *random loop generator* greatly improves the chance of obtaining closure by iteratively restricting the range on each of the active variables. The method requires that the active variables appear sequentially along the chain (i.e., there is no interleaving of active and passive variables). The m coordinates of q^a are obtained sequentially as follows. First, compute an interval, I_1, of allowable values for q_1^a. The interval serves as a loose bound in the sense that, for any value $q_1^a \notin I_1$, it is known for certain that closure cannot be obtained. This is ensured by performing a careful geometric analysis of the linkage, which will be explained shortly. The next step is to generate a sample in $q_1^a \in I_1$, which is accomplished in [246] by picking a random point in I_1. Using the value q_1^a, a bounding interval I_2 is computed for allowable values of q_2^a. The value q_2^a is obtained by sampling

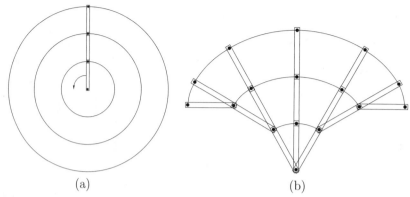

Figure 7.26: (a) If any joint angle is possible, then the links sweep out a circle in the limit. (b) If there are limits on the joint angles, then a tighter bound can be obtained for the reachability of the linkage.

in I_2. This process continues iteratively until I_m and q_m^a are obtained, unless it terminates early because some $I_i = \emptyset$ for $i < m$. If successful termination occurs, then the active variables q^a are used to find values q^p for the passive variables. This step still might fail, but the probability of success is now much higher. The method can also be applied to linkages in which there are multiple, common loops, as in the Stewart-Gough platform, by breaking the linkage into a tree and closing loops one at a time using the loop generator. The performance depends on how the linkage is decomposed [246].

Computing bounds on joint angles

The main requirement for successful application of the method is the ability to compute bounds on how far a chain of links can travel in $\mathcal{W}$ over some range of joint variables. For example, for a planar chain that has revolute joints with no limits, the chain can sweep out a circle as shown in Figure 7.26a. Suppose it is known that the angle between links must remain between $-\pi/6$ and $\pi/6$. A tighter bounding region can be obtained, as shown in Figure 7.26b. Three-dimensional versions of these bounds, along with many necessary details, are included in [246]. These bounds are then used to compute I_i in each iteration of the sampling algorithm.

Now that there is an efficient method that generates samples directly in $\mathcal{C}_{clo}$, it is straightforward to adapt any of the sampling-based planning methods of Chapter 5. In [246] many impressive results are obtained for challenging problems that have the dimension of $\mathcal{C}$ up to 97 and the dimension of $\mathcal{C}_{clo}$ up to 25; see Figure 7.27. These methods are based on applying the new sampling techniques to the RDTs of Section 5.5 and the visibility sampling-based roadmap of Section 5.6.2. For these algorithms, the local planning method is applied to the active variables, and inverse kinematics algorithms are used for the passive variables in the path validation step. This means that inverse kinematics and collision checking are performed together, instead of only collision checking, as described in Section 5.3.4.

One important issue that has been neglected in this section is the existence of *kinematic singularities*, which cause the dimension of $\mathcal{C}_{clo}$ to drop in the vicinity of certain points. The methods presented here have assumed that solving the motion planning problem does not require passing through a singularity. This assumption is reasonable for robot systems that have many extra degrees of freedom, but it is important to understand that completeness is lost in general because the sampling-based methods do not explicitly

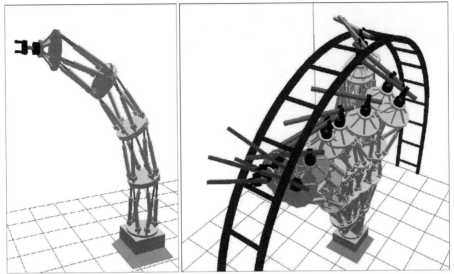

Figure 7.27: Planning for the Logabex LX4 robot [189]. This solution was computed in less than a minute by applying active-passive decomposition to an RDT-based planner [246]. In this example, the dimension of $\mathcal{C}$ is 97 and the dimension of $\mathcal{C}_{clo}$ is 25.

handle these degeneracies. In a sense, they occur below the level of sampling resolution. For more information on kinematic singularities and related issues, see [696].

7.5 Folding problems in robotics and biology

A growing number of motion planning applications involve some form of folding. Examples include automated carton folding, computer-aided drug design, protein folding, modular reconfigurable robots, and even robotic origami. These problems are generally modeled as a linkage in which all bodies are connected by revolute joints. In robotics, self-collision between pairs of bodies usually must be avoided. In biological applications, energy functions replace obstacles. Instead of crisp obstacle boundaries, energy functions can be imagined as "soft" obstacles, in which a real value is defined for every $q \in \mathcal{C}$, instead of defining a set $\mathcal{C}_{obs} \subset \mathcal{C}$. For a given threshold value, such energy functions can be converted into an obstacle region by defining $\mathcal{C}_{obs}$ to be the configurations that have energy above the threshold. However, the energy function contains more information because such thresholds are arbitrary. This section briefly shows some examples of folding problems and techniques from the recent motion planning literature.

Carton folding

An interesting application of motion planning to the automated folding of boxes is presented in [664]. Figure 7.28 shows a carton in its original flat form and in its folded form. As shown in Figure 7.29, the problem can be modeled as a tree of bodies connected by revolute joints. Once this model has been formulated, many methods from Chapters 5 and 6 can be adapted for this problem. In [664], a planning algorithm optimized particularly for box folding is presented. It is an adaptation of an approximate cell decomposition algorithm developed for kinematic chains in [661]. Its complexity is exponential in the degrees of freedom of the carton, but it gives good performance on practical examples. One such solution that was found by motion planning is shown in Figure 7.30. To use these

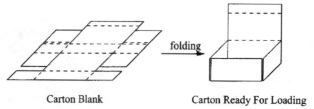

Figure 7.28: An important packaging problem is to automate the folding of a perforated sheet of cardboard into a carton.

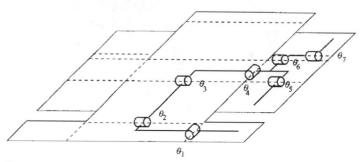

Figure 7.29: The carton can be cleverly modeled as a tree of bodies that are attached by revolute joints.

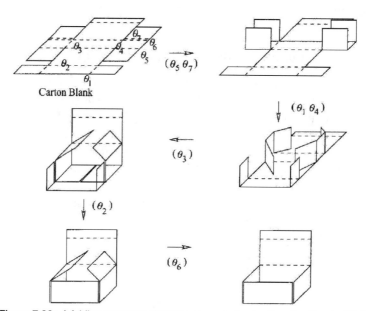

Figure 7.30: A folding sequence that was computed using the algorithm in [664].

solutions in a factory, the manipulation problem has to be additionally considered. For example, as demonstrated in [664], a manipulator arm robot can be used in combination with a well-designed set of fixtures. The fixtures help hold the carton in place while the manipulator applies pressure in the right places, which yields the required folds. Since the feasibility with fixtures depends on the particular folding path, the planning algorithm generates all possible distinct paths from the initial configuration (at which the box is completely unfolded).

Simplifying knots

A *knot* is a closed curve that does not intersect itself, is embedded in $\mathbb{R}^3$, and cannot be untangled to produce a simple loop (such as a circular path). If the knot is allowed to intersect itself, then any knot can be untangled; therefore, a careful definition of what it means to untangle a knot is needed. For a closed curve, $\tau : [0, 1] \to \mathbb{R}^3$, embedded in $\mathbb{R}^3$ (it cannot intersect itself), let the set $\mathbb{R}^3 \setminus \tau([0, 1])$ of points not reached by the curve be called the *ambient space* of τ. In knot theory, an *ambient isotopy* between two closed curves, τ_1 and τ_2, embedded in $\mathbb{R}^3$ is a homeomorphism between their ambient spaces. Intuitively, this means that τ_1 can be warped into τ_2 without allowing any self-intersections. Therefore, determining whether two loops are equivalent seems closely related to motion planning. Such equivalence gives rise to groups that characterize the space of knots and are closely related to the fundamental group described in Section 4.1.3. For more information on knot theory, see [8, 454, 514].

A motion planning approach was developed in [574] to determine whether a closed curve is equivalent to the *unknot*, which is completely untangled. This can be expressed as a curve that maps onto $\mathbb{S}^1$, embedded in $\mathbb{R}^3$. The algorithm takes as input a knot expressed as a circular chain of line segments embedded in $\mathbb{R}^3$. In this case, the unknot can be expressed as a triangle in $\mathbb{R}^3$. One of the most challenging examples solved by the planner is shown in Figure 7.31. The planner is sampling-based and shares many similarities with the RDT algorithm of Section 5.5 and the Ariadne's clew and expansive space planners described in Section 5.4.4. Since the task is not to produce a collision-free path, there are several unique aspects in comparison to motion planning. An energy function is defined over the collection of segments to try to guide the search toward simpler configurations. There are two kinds of local operations that are made by the planner: 1) Try to move a vertex toward a selected subgoal in the ambient space. This is obtained by using random sampling to grow a search tree. 2) Try to delete a vertex, and connect the neighboring vertices by a straight line. If no collision occurs along the intermediate configurations, then the knot has been simplified. The algorithm terminates when it is unable to further simplify the knot.

Drug design

A sampling-based motion planning approach to pharmaceutical drug design is taken in [604]. The development of a drug is a long, incremental process, typically requiring years of research and experimentation. The goal is to find a relatively small molecule called a *ligand*, typically comprising a few dozen atoms, that docks with a receptor cavity in a specific protein [618]; Figure 1.14 (Section 1.2) illustrated this. Examples of drug molecules were also given in Figure 1.14. Protein-ligand docking can stimulate or inhibit some biological activity, ultimately leading to the desired pharmacological effect. The problem of finding suitable ligands is complicated due to both energy considerations and the flexibility of the ligand. In addition to satisfying structural considerations, factors such as synthetic accessibility, drug pharmacology and toxicology greatly complicate and lengthen the search for the most effective drug molecules.

One popular model used by chemists in the context of drug design is a *pharmacophore*, which serves as a template for the desired ligand [231, 341, 385, 862]. The pharmacophore is expressed as a set of *features* that an effective ligand should possess and a set of *spatial constraints* among the features. Examples of features are specific atoms, centers of benzene rings, positive or negative charges, hydrophobic or hydrophilic centers, and

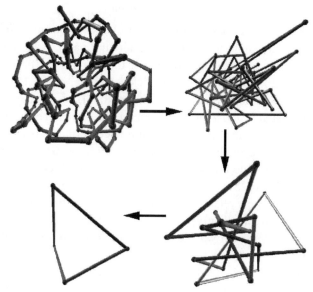

Figure 7.31: The planner in [574] untangles the famous Ochiai unknot benchmark in a few minutes on a standard PC.

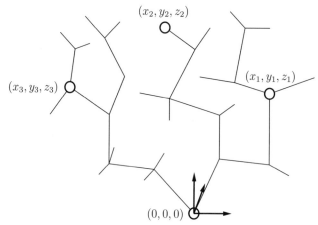

Figure 7.32: A pharmacophore is a model used by chemists to simplify the interaction process between a ligand (candidate drug molecule) and a protein. It often amounts to holding certain features of the molecule fixed in $\mathbb{R}^3$. In this example, the positions of three atoms must be fixed relative to the body frame of an arbitrarily designated root atom. It is assumed that these features interact with some complementary features in the cavity of the protein.

hydrogen bond donors or acceptors. Features generally require that parts of the molecule must remain fixed in $\mathbb{R}^3$, which induces kinematic closure constraints. These features are developed by chemists to encapsulate the assumption that ligand binding is due primarily to the interaction of some features of the ligand to "complementary" features of the receptor. The interacting features are included in the pharmacophore, which is a template for screening candidate drugs, and the rest of the ligand atoms merely provide a scaffold for holding the pharmacophore features in their spatial positions. Figure 7.32 illustrates the pharmacophore concept.

Candidate drug molecules (ligands), such as the ones shown in Figure 1.14, can be modeled as a tree of bodies as shown in Figure 7.33. Some bonds can rotate, yielding

Root Atom

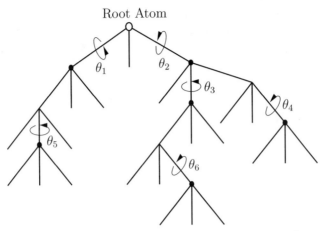

Figure 7.33: The modeling of a flexible molecule is similar to that of a robot. One atom is designated as the root, and the remaining bodies are arranged in a tree. If there are cyclic chains in the molecules, then constraints as described in Section 4.4 must be enforced. Typically, only some bonds are capable of rotation, whereas others must remain rigid.

revolute joints in the model; other bonds must remain fixed. The drug design problem amounts to searching the space of configurations (called *conformations*) to try to find a low-energy configuration that also places certain atoms in specified locations in $\mathbb{R}^3$. This additional constraint arises from the pharmacophore and causes the planning to occur on $\mathcal{C}_{clo}$ from Section 7.4 because the pharmacophores can be expressed as closure constraints.

An energy function serves a purpose similar to that of a collision detector. The evaluation of a ligand for drug design requires determining whether it can achieve low-energy conformations that satisfy the pharmacophore constraints. Thus, the task is different from standard motion planning in that there is no predetermined goal configuration. One of the greatest difficulties is that the energy functions are extremely complicated, nonlinear, and empirical. Here is typical example (used in [604]):

$$
\begin{aligned}
e(q) = \ & \sum_{bonds} \frac{1}{2} K_b (R - R')^2 + \sum_{ang} \frac{1}{2} K_a (\alpha - \alpha')^2 \\
& + \sum_{torsions} K_d [1 + \cos(p\theta - \theta')] \\
& + \sum_{i,j} \left\{ 4\epsilon_{ij} \left[\left(\frac{\sigma_{ij}}{r_{ij}} \right)^{12} - \left(\frac{\sigma_{ij}}{r_{ij}} \right)^6 \right] + \frac{c_i c_j}{\epsilon r_{ij}} \right\}.
\end{aligned}
\tag{7.25}
$$

The energy accounts for torsion-angle deformations, van der Waals potential, and Coulomb potentials. In (7.25), the first sum is taken over all bonds, the second over all bond angles, the third over all rotatable bonds, and the last is taken over all pairs of atoms. The variables are the force constants, K_b, K_a, and K_d; the dielectric constant, ϵ; a periodicity constant, p; the Lennard-Jones radii, σ_{ij}; well depth, ϵ_{ij}; partial charge, c_i; measured bond length, R; equilibrium bond length, R'; measured bond angle, α; equilibrium bond angle, α'; measured torsional angle, θ; equilibrium torsional angle, θ'; and distance between atom centers, r_{ij}. Although the energy expression is very complicated, it only depends on the configuration variables; all others are constants that are estimated in advance.

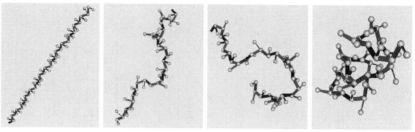

Figure 7.34: Protein folding for a polypeptide, computed by a sampling-based roadmap planning algorithm [24]

Protein folding

In computational biology, the problem of protein folding shares many similarities with drug design in that the molecules have rotatable bonds and energy functions are used to express good configurations. The problems are much more complicated, however, because the protein molecules are generally much larger than drug molecules. Instead of a dozen degrees of freedom, which is typical for a drug molecule, proteins have hundreds or thousands of degrees of freedom. When proteins appear in nature, they are usually in a folded, low-energy configuration. The *structure problem* involves determining precisely how the protein is folded so that its biological activity can be completely understood. In some studies, biologists are even interested in the pathway that a protein takes to arrive in its folded state [24, 25]. This leads directly to an extension of motion planning that involves arriving at a goal state in which the molecule is folded. In [24, 25], sampling-based planning algorithms were applied to compute folding pathways for proteins. The protein starts in an unfolded configuration and must arrive in a specified folded configuration without violating energy constraints along the way. Figure 7.34 shows an example from [25]. That work also draws interesting connections between protein folding and box folding, which was covered previously.

7.6 Coverage planning

Imagine automating the motion of a lawnmower for an estate that has many obstacles, such as a house, trees, garage, and a complicated property boundary. What are the best zig-zag motions for the lawnmower? Can the amount of redundant traversals be minimized? Can the number of times the lawnmower needs to be stopped and rotated be minimized? This is one example of *coverage planning*, which is motivated by applications such as lawn mowing, automated farming, painting, vacuum cleaning, and mine sweeping. A survey of this area appears in [219]. Even for a region in $\mathcal{W} = \mathbb{R}^2$, finding an optimal-length solution to coverage planning is NP-hard, by reduction to the closely related Traveling Salesman Problem [36, 712]. Therefore, we are willing to tolerate approximate or even heuristic solutions to the general coverage problem, even in $\mathbb{R}^2$.

Boustrophedon decomposition

One approach to the coverage problem is to decompose $\mathcal{C}_{free}$ into cells and perform boustrophedon (from the Greek "ox turning") motions in each cell as shown in Figure 7.35 [224]. It is assumed that the robot is a point in $\mathcal{W} = \mathbb{R}^2$, but it carries a *tool* of thickness ϵ that hangs evenly over the sides of the robot. This enables it to paint or mow part of $\mathcal{C}_{free}$

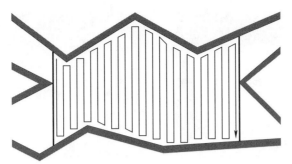

Figure 7.35: An example of the ox plowing motions.

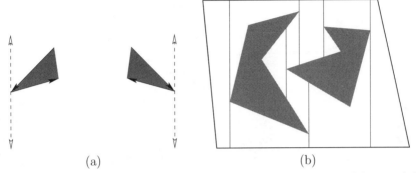

(a)   (b)

Figure 7.36: (a) Only the first case from Figure 6.2 is needed: extend upward and downward. All other cases are neglected. (b) The resulting decomposition is shown, which has fewer cells than that of the vertical decomposition in Figure 6.3.

up to distance $\epsilon/2$ from either side of the robot as it moves forward. Such motions are often used in printers to reduce the number of carriage returns.

If C_{obs} is polygonal, a reasonable decomposition can be obtained by adapting the vertical decomposition method of Section 6.2.2. In that algorithm, critical events were defined for several cases, some of which are not relevant for the boustrophedon motions. The only events that need to be handled are shown in Figure 7.36a [218]. This produces a decomposition that has fewer cells, as shown in Figure 7.36b. Even though the cells are nonconvex, they can always be sliced nicely into vertical strips, which makes them suitable for boustrophedon motions. The original vertical decomposition could also be used, but the extra cell boundaries would cause unnecessary repositioning of the robot. A similar method, which furthermore optimizes the number of robot turns, is presented in [471].

Spanning tree covering

An interesting approximate method was developed by Gabriely and Rimon; it places a tiling of squares inside of C_{free} and computes the spanning tree of the resulting connectivity graph [374, 375]. Suppose again that C_{free} is polygonal. Consider the example shown in Figure 7.37a. The first step is to tile the interior of C_{free} with squares, as shown in Figure 7.37b. Each square should be of width ϵ, for some constant $\epsilon > 0$. Next, construct a roadmap $\mathcal{G}$ by placing a vertex in the center of each square and by defining an edge that connects the centers of each pair of adjacent cubes. The next step is to compute a *spanning tree* of $\mathcal{G}$. This is a connected subgraph that has no cycles and touches every vertex of $\mathcal{G}$; it can be computed in $O(n)$ time, if $\mathcal{G}$ has n edges [686]. There are many possible spanning

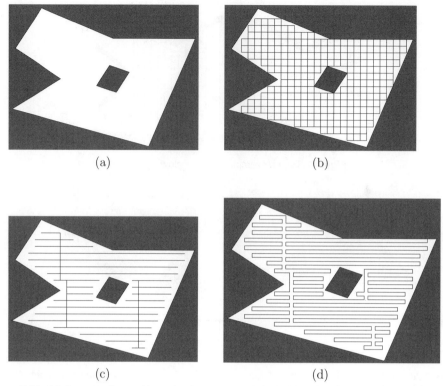

Figure 7.37: (a) An example used for spanning tree covering. (b) The first step is to tile the interior with squares. (c) The spanning tree of a roadmap formed from grid adjacencies. (d) The resulting coverage path.

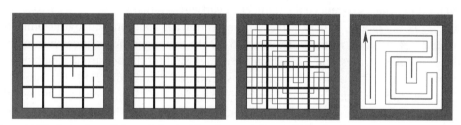

Figure 7.38: A circular path is made by doubling the resolution and following the perimeter of the spanning tree.

trees, and a criterion can be defined and optimized to induce preferences. One possible spanning tree is shown Figure 7.37c.

Once the spanning tree is made, the robot path is obtained by starting at a point near the spanning tree and following along its perimeter. This path can be precisely specified as shown in Figure 7.38. Double the resolution of the tiling, and form the corresponding roadmap. Part of the roadmap corresponds to the spanning tree, but also included is a loop path that surrounds the spanning tree. This path visits the centers of the new squares. The resulting path for the example of Figure 7.37a is shown in Figure 7.37d. In general, the method yields an optimal route, once the approximation is given. A bound on the uncovered area due to approximation is given in [374]. Versions of the method that do not require an initial map are also given in [374, 375]; this involves reasoning about information spaces, which are covered in Chapter 11.

Figure 7.39: For a polyhedral environment, the shortest paths do not have to cross vertices. Therefore, the shortest-path roadmap method from Section 6.2.4 does not extend to three dimensions.

7.7 Optimal motion planning

This section can be considered transitional in many ways. The main concern so far with motion planning has been *feasibility* as opposed to *optimality*. This placed the focus on finding *any* solution, rather than further requiring that a solution be optimal. In later parts of the book, especially as uncertainty is introduced, optimality will receive more attention. Even the most basic forms of decision theory (the topic of Chapter 9) center on making optimal choices. The requirement of optimality in very general settings usually requires an exhaustive search over the state space, which amounts to computing continuous cost-to-go functions. Once such functions are known, a feedback plan is obtained, which is much more powerful than having only a path. Thus, optimality also appears frequently in the design of feedback plans because it sometimes comes at no additional cost. This will become clearer in Chapter 8. The quest for optimal solutions also raises interesting issues about how to approximate a continuous problem as a discrete problem. The interplay between time discretization and space discretization becomes very important in relating continuous and discrete planning problems.

7.7.1 Optimality for one robot

Euclidean shortest paths

One of the most straightforward notions of optimality is the Euclidean shortest path in $\mathbb{R}^2$ or $\mathbb{R}^3$. Suppose that $\mathcal{A}$ is a rigid body that translates only in either $\mathcal{W} = \mathbb{R}^2$ or $\mathcal{W} = \mathbb{R}^3$, which contains an obstacle region $\mathcal{O} \subset \mathcal{W}$. Recall that, ordinarily, $\mathcal{C}_{free}$ is an open set, which means that any path, $\tau : [0, 1] \rightarrow \mathcal{C}_{free}$, can be shortened. Therefore, shortest paths for motion planning must be defined on the closure $\mathrm{cl}(\mathcal{C}_{free})$, which allows the robot to make contact with the obstacles; however, their interiors must not intersect.

For the case in which $\mathcal{C}_{obs}$ is a polygonal region, the shortest-path roadmap method of Section 6.2.4 has already been given. This can be considered as a kind of multiple-query approach because the roadmap completely captures the structure needed to construct the shortest path for any query. It is possible to make a single-query algorithm using the *continuous Dijkstra paradigm* [446, 711]. This method propagates a *wavefront* from q_I and keeps track of critical events in maintaining the wavefront. As events occur, the wavefront becomes composed of *wavelets*, which are arcs of circles centered on obstacle vertices. The possible events that can occur are 1) a wavelet disappears, 2) a wavelet collides with an obstacle vertex, 3) a wavelet collides with another wavelet, or 4) a wavelet collides with a point in the interior of an obstacle edge. The method can be made to run in time $O(n \lg n)$ and uses $O(n \lg n)$ space. A roadmap is constructed that uses $O(n)$ space. See Section 8.4.3 for a related method.

Such elegant methods leave the impression that finding shortest paths is not very difficult, but unfortunately they do not generalize nicely to $\mathbb{R}^3$ and a polyhedral $\mathcal{C}_{obs}$. Figure 7.39 shows a simple example in which the shortest path does not have to cross a vertex of $\mathcal{C}_{obs}$. It may cross anywhere in the interior of an edge; therefore, it is not clear where to draw the bitangent lines that would form the shortest-path roadmap. The lower bounds for this problem are also discouraging. It was shown in [174] that the 3D shortest-path problem in a polyhedral environment is NP-hard. Most of the difficulty arises because of the precision required to represent 3D shortest paths. Therefore, efficient polynomial-time approximation algorithms exist [217, 766].

General optimality criteria

It is difficult to even define optimality for more general C-spaces. What does it mean to have a shortest path in $SE(2)$ or $SE(3)$? Consider the case of a planar, rigid robot that can translate and rotate. One path could minimize the amount of rotation whereas another tries to minimize the amount of translation. Without more information, there is no clear preference. Ulam's distance is one possibility, which is to minimize the distance traveled by k fixed points [477]. In Chapter 13, differential models will be introduced, which lead to meaningful definitions of optimality. For example, the shortest paths for a slow-moving car are shown in Section 15.3; these require a precise specification of the constraints on the motion of the car (it is more costly to move a car sideways than forward).

This section formulates some optimal motion planning problems, to provide a smooth transition into the later concepts. Up until now, actions were used in Chapter 2 for discrete planning problems, but they were successfully avoided for basic motion planning by directly describing paths that map into $\mathcal{C}_{free}$. It will be convenient to use them once again. Recall that they were convenient for defining costs and optimal planning in Section 2.3.

To avoid for now the complications of differential equations, consider making an approximate model of motion planning in which every path must be composed of a sequence of shortest-path segments in $\mathcal{C}_{free}$. Most often these are line segments; however, for the case of $SO(3)$, circular arcs obtained by spherical linear interpolation may be preferable. Consider extending Formulation 2.3 from Section 2.3.2 to the problem of motion planning.

Let the C-space $\mathcal{C}$ be embedded in $\mathbb{R}^m$ (i.e., $\mathcal{C} \subset \mathbb{R}^m$). An action will be defined shortly as an m-dimensional vector. Given a scaling constant ϵ and a configuration q, an action u produces a new configuration, $q' = q + \epsilon u$. This can be considered as a *configuration transition equation*, $q' = f(q, u)$. The path segment represented by the action u is the shortest path (usually a line segment) between q and q'. Following Section 2.3, let π_K denote a *K-step plan*, which is a sequence $(u_1, u_2, \ldots, u_K)$ of K actions. Note that if π_K and q_I are given, then a sequence of states, $q_1, q_2, \ldots, q_{K+1}$, can be derived using f. Initially, $q_1 = q_I$, and each following state is obtained by $q_{k+1} = f(q_k, u_k)$. From this a path, $\tau : [0, 1] \to \mathcal{C}$, can be derived.

An approximate optimal planning problem is formalized as follows:

Formulation 7.4 (Approximate Optimal Motion Planning)

1. The following components are defined the same as in Formulation 4.1: $\mathcal{W}, \mathcal{O}, \mathcal{A}, \mathcal{C}, \mathcal{C}_{obs}$, $\mathcal{C}_{free}$, and q_I. It is assumed that $\mathcal{C}$ is an n-dimensional manifold.

2. For each $q \in \mathcal{C}$, a possibly infinite *action space*, $U(q)$. Each $u \in U$ is an n-dimensional vector.

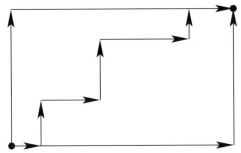

Figure 7.40: Under the Manhattan (L_1) motion model, all monotonic paths that follow the grid directions have equivalent length.

3. A positive constant $\epsilon > 0$ called the *step size*.

4. A set of *stages*, each denoted by k, which begins at $k = 1$ and continues indefinitely. Each stage is indicated by a subscript, to obtain q_k and u_k.

5. A *configuration transition function* $f(q, u) = q + \epsilon u$ in which $q + \epsilon u$ is computed by vector addition on $\mathbb{R}^m$.

6. Instead of a goal state, a goal region X_G is defined.

7. Let L denote a real-valued cost functional, which is applied to a K-step plan, π_K. This means that the sequence $(u_1, \ldots, u_K)$ of actions and the sequence $(q_1, \ldots, q_{K+1})$ of configurations may appear in an expression of L. Let $F = K + 1$. The *cost functional* is

$$L(\pi_K) = \sum_{k=1}^{K} l(q_k, u_k) + l_F(q_F). \tag{7.26}$$

The final term $l_F(q_F)$ is outside of the sum and is defined as $l_F(q_F) = 0$ if $q_F \in X_G$ and $l_F(q_F) = \infty$ otherwise. As in Formulation 2.3, K is not necessarily a constant.

8. Each $U(q)$ contains the special *termination action* u_T, which behaves the same way as in Formulation 2.3. If u_T is applied to q_k at stage k, then the action is repeatedly applied forever, the configuration remains in q_k forever, and no more cost accumulates.

The task is to compute a sequence of actions that optimizes (7.26). Formulation 7.4 can be used to define a variety of optimal planning problems. The parameter ϵ can be considered as the resolution of the approximation. In many formulations it can be interpreted as a *time step*, $\epsilon = \Delta t$; however, note that no explicit time reference is necessary because the problem only requires constructing a path through $\mathcal{C}_{free}$. As ϵ approaches zero, the formulation approaches an exact optimal planning problem. To properly express the exact problem, differential equations are needed. This is deferred until Part IV.

Example 7.4 (Manhattan Motion Model) Suppose that in addition to u_T, the action set $U(q)$ contains $2n$ vectors in which only one component is nonzero and must take the value 1 or -1. For example, if $\mathcal{C} = \mathbb{R}^2$, then

$$U(q) = \{(1, 0), (-1, 0), (0, -1), (0, 1), u_T\}. \tag{7.27}$$

When used in the configuration transition equation, this set of actions produces "up," "down," "left," and "right" motions and a "terminate" command. This produces a topological graph according to the 1-neighborhood model, (5.37), which was given in Section 5.4.2. The action set for this example and the following two examples are shown in Figure 7.41 for comparison. The cost term $l(q_k, u_k)$ is defined to be 1 for all $q_k \in \mathcal{C}_{free}$ and

Manhattan   Independent   Euclidean
Joint

Figure 7.41: Depictions of the actions sets, $U(q)$, for Examples 7.4, 7.5, and 7.6.

u_k. If $q_k \in \mathcal{C}_{obs}$, then $l(q_k, u_k) = \infty$. Note that the set of configurations reachable by these actions lies on a grid, in which the spacing between 1-neighbors is ϵ. This corresponds to a convenient special case in which time discretization (implemented by ϵ) leads to a regular space discretization. Consider Figure 7.40. It is impossible to take a shorter path along a diagonal because the actions do not allow it. Therefore, all monotonic paths along the grid produce the same costs.

Optimal paths can be obtained by simply applying the dynamic programming algorithms of Chapter 2. This example provides a nice unification of concepts from Section 2.2, which introduced grid search, and Section 5.4.2, which explained how to adapt search methods to motion planning. In the current setting, only algorithms that produce optimal solutions on the corresponding graph are acceptable.

This form of optimization might not seem relevant because it does not represent the Euclidean shortest-path problem for $\mathbb{R}^2$. The next model adds more actions, and does correspond to an important class of optimization problems in robotics. ∎

Example 7.5 (Independent-Joint Motion Model) Now suppose that $U(q)$ includes u_T and the set of all 3^n vectors for which every element is either -1, 0, or 1. Under this model, a path can be taken along any diagonal. This still does not change the fact that all reachable configurations lie on a grid. Therefore, the standard grid algorithms can be applied once again. The difference is that now there are $3^n - 1$ edges emanating from every vertex, as opposed to $2n$ in Example 7.4. This model is appropriate for robots that are constructed from a collection of links attached by revolute joints. If each joint is operated independently, then it makes sense that each joint could be moved either forward, backward, or held stationary. This corresponds exactly to the actions. However, this model cannot nicely approximate Euclidean shortest paths; this motivates the next example. ∎

Example 7.6 (Euclidean Motion Model) To approximate Euclidean shortest paths, let $U(q) = \mathbb{S}^{n-1} \cup \{u_T\}$, in which $\mathbb{S}^{n-1}$ is the m-dimensional unit sphere centered at the origin of $\mathbb{R}^n$. This means that in k stages, any piecewise-linear path in which each segment has length ϵ can be formed by a sequence of inputs. Therefore, the set of reachable states is no longer confined to a grid. Consider taking $\epsilon = 1$, and pick any point, such as $(\pi, \pi) \in \mathbb{R}^2$. How close can you come to this point? It turns out that the set of points reachable with this model is dense in $\mathbb{R}^n$ if obstacles are neglected. This means that we can come arbitrarily close to any point in $\mathbb{R}^n$. Therefore, a finite grid cannot be used to represent the problem. Approximate solutions can still be obtained by numerically computing an optimal cost-to-go function over $\mathcal{C}$. This approach is presented in Section 8.5.2.

One additional issue for this problem is the precision defined for the goal. If the goal region is very small relative to ϵ, then complicated paths may have to be selected to arrive precisely at the goal. ∎

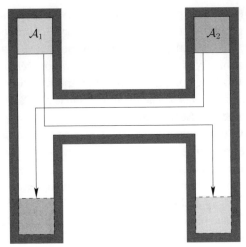

Figure 7.42: There are two Pareto-optimal coordination plans for this problem, depending on which robot has to wait.

Example 7.7 (Weighted-Region Problem) In outdoor and planetary navigation applications, it does not make sense to define obstacles in the crisp way that has been used so far. For each patch of terrain, it is more convenient to associate a cost that indicates the estimated difficulty of its traversal. This is sometimes considered as a "grayscale" model of obstacles. The model can be easily captured in the cost term $l(q_k, u_k)$. The action spaces can be borrowed from Examples 7.4 or 7.5. Stentz's algorithm [914], which is introduced in Section 12.3.2, generates optimal navigation plans for this problem, even assuming that the terrain is initially unknown. Theoretical bounds for optimal weighted-region planning problems are given in [712, 713]. An approximation algorithm appears in [823]. ∎

7.7.2 Multiple-robot optimality

Suppose that there are two robots as shown in Figure 7.42. There is just enough room to enable the robots to translate along the corridors. Each would like to arrive at the bottom, as indicated by arrows; however, only one can pass at a time through the horizontal corridor. Suppose that at any instant each robot can either be *on* or *off*. When it is *on*, it moves at its maximum speed, and when it is *off*, it is stopped.[4] Now suppose that each robot would like to reach its goal as quickly as possible. This means each would like to minimize the total amount of time that it is *off*. In this example, there appears to be only two sensible choices: 1) $\mathcal{A}_1$ stays *on* and moves straight to its goal while $\mathcal{A}_2$ is *off* just long enough to let $\mathcal{A}_1$ pass, and then moves to its goal. 2) The opposite situation occurs, in which $\mathcal{A}_2$ stays *on* and $\mathcal{A}_1$ must wait. Note that when a robot waits, there are multiple locations at which it can wait and still yield the same time to reach the goal. The only important information is how long the robot was *off*.

Thus, the two interesting plans are that either $\mathcal{A}_2$ is *off* for some amount of time, $t_{off} > 0$, or $\mathcal{A}_1$ is *off* for time t_{off}. Consider a vector of costs of the form (L_1, L_2), in which each component represents the cost for each robot. The costs of the plans could be measured in terms of time wasted by waiting. This yields $(0, t_{off})$ and $(t_{off}, 0)$ for the cost

---

[4] This model allows infinite acceleration. Imagine that the speeds are slow enough to allow this approximation. If this is still not satisfactory, then jump ahead to Chapter 13.

vectors associated with the two plans (we could equivalently define cost to be the total time traveled by each robot; the time on is the same for both robots and can be subtracted from each for this simple example). The two plans are better than or equivalent to any others. Plans with this property are called *Pareto optimal* (or *nondominated*). For example, if $\mathcal{A}_2$ waits 1 second too long for $\mathcal{A}_1$ to pass, then the resulting costs are $(0, t_{off} + 1)$, which is clearly worse than $(0, t_{off})$. The resulting plan is not Pareto optimal. More details on Pareto optimality appear in Section 9.1.1.

Another way to solve the problem is to scalarize the costs by mapping them to a single value. For example, we could find plans that optimize the average wasted time. In this case, one of the two best plans would be obtained, yielding t_{off} average wasted time. However, no information is retained about which robot had to make the sacrifice. Scalarizing the costs usually imposes some kind of artificial preference or prioritization among the robots. Ultimately, only one plan can be chosen, which might make it seem inappropriate to maintain multiple solutions. However, finding and presenting the alternative Pareto-optimal solutions could provide valuable information if, for example, these robots are involved in a complicated application that involves many other time-dependent processes. Presenting the Pareto-optimal solutions is equivalent to discarding all of the worse plans and showing the best alternatives. In some applications, priorities between robots may change, and if a scheduler of robots has access to the Pareto-optimal solutions, it is easy to change priorities by switching between Pareto-optimal plans without having to generate new plans each time.

Now the Pareto-optimality concept will be made more precise and general. Suppose there are m robots, $\mathcal{A}^1, \ldots, \mathcal{A}^m$. Let γ refer to a motion plan that gives the paths and timing functions for all robots. For each $\mathcal{A}^i$, let L_i denote its cost functional, which yields a value $L_i(\gamma) \in [0, \infty]$ for a given plan, γ. An m-dimensional vector, $L(\gamma)$, is defined as

$$L(\gamma) = (L_1(\gamma), L_2(\gamma), \ldots, L_m(\gamma)). \qquad (7.28)$$

Two plans, γ and γ', are called *equivalent* if $L(\gamma) = L(\gamma')$. A plan γ is said to *dominate* a plan γ' if they are not equivalent and $L_i(\gamma) \leq L_i(\gamma')$ for all i such that $1 \leq i \leq m$. A plan is called *Pareto optimal* if it is not dominated by any others. Since many Pareto-optimal plans may be equivalent, the task is to determine one representative from each equivalence class. This will be called finding the *unique* Pareto-optimal plans. For the example in Figure 7.42, there are two unique Pareto-optimal plans, which were already given.

Scalarization

For the motion planning problem, a Pareto-optimal solution is also optimal for a scalar cost functional that is constructed as a linear combination of the individual costs. Let $\alpha_1, \ldots, \alpha_m$ be positive real constants, and let

$$l(\gamma) = \sum_{i=1}^{m} \alpha_i L_i(\gamma). \qquad (7.29)$$

It is easy to show that any plan that is optimal with respect to (7.29) is also a Pareto-optimal solution [609]. If a Pareto optimal solution is generated in this way, however, there is no easy way to determine what alternatives exist.

Computing Pareto-optimal plans

Since optimization for one robot is already very difficult, it may not be surprising that computing Pareto-optimal plans is even harder. For some problems, it is even possible that a continuum of Pareto-optimal solutions exist (see Example 9.3), which is very discouraging. Fortunately, for the problem of coordinating robots on topological graphs, as considered in Section 7.2.2, there is only a finite number of solutions [388]. A grid-based algorithm, which is based on dynamic programming and computes all unique Pareto-optimal coordination plans, is presented in [609]. For the special case of two polygonal robots moving on a tree of piecewise-linear paths, a complete algorithm is presented in [214].

Further reading

This chapter covered some of the most direct extensions of the basic motion planning problem. Extensions that involve uncertainties are covered throughout Part III, and the introduction of differential constraints to motion planning is the main focus of Part IV. Numerous other extensions can be found by searching through robotics research publications or the Internet.

The treatment of time-varying motion planning in Section 7.1 assumes that all motions are predictable. Most of the coverage is based on early work [155, 509, 821, 822]; other related work includes [369, 370, 535, 815, 877, 906]. To introduce uncertainties into this scenario, see Chapter 10. The logic-based representations of Section 2.4 have been extended to *temporal logics* to allow time-varying aspects of discrete planning problems (see Part IV of [384]).

For more on multiple-robot motion planning, see [15, 34, 41, 321, 322, 347, 366, 410, 609, 783, 887]. Closely related is the problem of planning for modular reconfigurable robots [182, 211, 387, 555, 990]. In both contexts, nonpositive curvature (NPC) is an important condition that greatly simplifies the structure of optimal paths [141, 387, 388]. For points moving on a topological graph, the topology of $\mathcal{C}_{free}$ is described in [5]. Over the last few years there has also been a strong interest in the coordination of a team or swarm of robots [167, 230, 276, 302, 307, 338, 363, 668].

The complexity of assembly planning is studied in [400, 518, 736, 972]. The problem is generally NP-hard; however, for some special cases, polynomial-time algorithms have been developed [9, 432, 973, 974]. Other works include [188, 430, 456, 461, 545].

Hybrid systems have attracted widespread interest over the past decade. Most of this work considers how to design control laws for piecewise-smooth systems [139, 637]. Early sources of hybrid control literature appear in [411]. The manipulation planning framework of Section 7.3.2 is based on [16, 17, 168]. The manipulation planning framework presented in this chapter ignores grasping issues. For analyses and algorithms for grasping, see [258, 490, 684, 784, 802, 803, 829, 830, 921]. Manipulation on a microscopic scale is considered in [128].

To read beyond Section 7.4 on sampling-based planning for closed kinematic chains, see [246, 248, 435, 979]. A complete planner for some closed chains is presented in [700]. For related work on inverse kinematics, see [311, 696]. The power of redundant degrees of freedom in robot systems was shown in [160].

Section 7.5 is a synthesis of several applications. The application of motion planning techniques to problems in computational biology is a booming area; see [24, 25, 33, 247, 517, 592, 604, 657, 1001] for some representative papers. The knot-planning coverage is based on [575]. The box-folding presentation is based on [664]. A robotic system and planning technique for creating origami is presented in [66].

The coverage planning methods presented in Section 7.6 are based on [224] and [374, 375]. A survey of coverage planning appears in [219]. Other references include [6, 7, 166, 376, 447, 471, 976]. For discrete environments, approximation algorithms for the problem of optimally visiting all states in a goal set (the *orienteering problem*) are presented and analyzed in [117, 190].

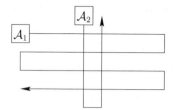

Figure 7.43: Two translating robots moving along piecewise-linear paths.

Beyond two dimensions, optimal motion planning is extremely difficult. See Section 8.5.2 for dynamic programming-based approximations. See [217, 766] for approximate shortest paths in $\mathbb{R}^3$. The weighted region problem is considered in [712, 713]. Pareto-optimal coordination is considered in [214, 388, 609].

Exercises

1. Consider the obstacle region, (7.1), in the state space for time-varying motion planning.

   (a) To ensure that X_{obs} is polyhedral, what kind of paths should be allowed? Show how the model primitives H_i that define $\mathcal{O}$ are expressed in general, using t as a parameter.

   (b) Repeat the exercise, but for ensuring that X_{obs} is semi-algebraic.

2. Propose a way to adapt the sampling-based roadmap algorithm of Section 5.6 to solve the problem of time-varying motion planning with bounded speed.

3. Develop an efficient algorithm for computing the obstacle region for two translating polygonal robots that each follow a linear path.

4. Sketch the coordination space for the two robots moving along the fixed paths shown in Figure 7.43.

5. Suppose there are two robots, and each moves on its own roadmap of three paths. The paths in each roadmap are arranged end-to-end in a triangle.

   (a) Characterize the fixed-roadmap coordination space that results, including a description of its topology.

   (b) Now suppose there are n robots, each on a triangular roadmap, and characterize the fixed-roadmap coordination space.

6. Consider the state space obtained as the Cartesian product of the C-spaces of n identical robots. Suppose that each robot is labeled with a unique integer. Show that X can be partitioned nicely into $n!$ regions in which X_{obs} appears identical and the only difference is the labels (which indicate the particular robots that are in collision).

7. Suppose there are two robots, and each moves on its own roadmap of three paths. The paths in one roadmap are arranged end-to-end in a triangle, and the paths in the other are arranged as a Y. Characterize the fixed-roadmap coordination space that results, including a description of its topology.

8. Design an efficient algorithm that takes as input a graph representation of the connectivity of a linkage and computes an active-passive decomposition. Assume that all links are revolute. The algorithm should work for either 2D or 3D linkages (the dimension is also an input). Determine the asymptotic running time of your algorithm.

9. Consider the problem of coordinating the motion of two robots that move along precomputed paths but in the presence of predictable moving obstacles. Develop a planning algorithm for this problem.

10. Consider a manipulator in $\mathcal{W} = \mathbb{R}^2$ made of four links connected in a chain by revolute joints. There is unit distance between the joints, and the first joint is attached at $(0,0)$ in

$\mathcal{W} = \mathbb{R}^2$. Suppose that the end of the last link, which is position $(1, 0)$ in its body frame, is held at $(0, 2) \in \mathcal{W}$.

(a) Use kinematics expressions to express the closure constraints for a configuration $q \in \mathcal{C}$.

(b) Convert the closure constraints into polynomial form.

(c) Use differentiation to determine the constraints on the allowable velocities that maintain closure at a configuration $q \in \mathcal{C}$.

Implementations

11. Implement the vertical decomposition algorithm to solve the path-tuning problem, as shown in Figure 7.5.

12. Use grid-based sampling and a search algorithm to compute collision-free motions of three robots moving along predetermined paths.

13. Under the conditions of Exercise 12, compute Pareto-optimal coordination strategies that optimize the time (number of stages) that each robot takes to reach its goal. Design a wavefront propagation algorithm that keeps track of the complete (ignoring equivalent strategies) set of minimal Pareto-optimal coordination strategies at each reached state. Avoid storing entire plans at each discretized state.

14. To gain an appreciation of the difficulties of planning for closed kinematic chains, try motion planning for a point on a torus among obstacles using only the implicit torus constraint given by (6.40). To simplify collision detection, the obstacles can be a collection of balls in $\mathbb{R}^3$ that intersect the torus. Adapt a sampling-based planning technique, such as the bidirectional RRT, to traverse the torus and solve planning problems.

15. Implement the spanning-tree coverage planning algorithm of Section 7.6.

16. Develop an RRT-based planning algorithm that causes the robot to chase an unpredictable moving target in a planar environment that contains obstacles. The algorithm should run quickly enough so that replanning can occur during execution. The robot should execute the first part of the most recently computed path while simultaneously computing a better plan for the next time increment.

17. Modify Exercise 16 so that the robot assumes the target follows a predictable, constant-velocity trajectory until some deviation is observed.

18. Show how to handle unexpected obstacles by using a fast enough planning algorithm. For simplicity, suppose the robot is a point moving in a polygonal obstacle region. The robot first computes a path and then starts to execute it. If the obstacle region changes, then a new path is computed from the robot's current position. Use vertical decomposition or another algorithm of your choice (provided it is fast enough). The user should be able to interactively place or move obstacles during plan execution.

19. Use the manipulation planning framework of Section 7.3.2 to develop an algorithm that solves the famous Towers of Hanoi problem by a robot that carries the rings [168]. For simplicity, suppose a polygonal robot moves polygonal parts in $\mathcal{W} = \mathbb{R}^2$ and rotation is not allowed. Make three pegs, and initially place all parts on one peg, sorted from largest to smallest. The goal is to move all of the parts to another peg while preserving the sorting.

20. Use grid-based approximation to solve optimal planning problems for a point robot in the plane. Experiment with using different neighborhoods and metrics. Characterize the combinations under which good and bad approximations are obtained.

8

Feedback Motion Planning

So far in Part II it has been assumed that a continuous path sufficiently solves a motion planning problem. In many applications, such as computer-generated animation and virtual prototyping, there is no need to challenge this assumption because models in a virtual environment usually behave as designed. In applications that involve interaction with the physical world, future configurations may not be predictable. A traditional way to account for this in robotics is to use the refinement scheme that was shown in Figure 1.19 to design a feedback control law that attempts to follow the computed path as closely as possible. Sometimes this is satisfactory, but it is important to recognize that this approach is highly decoupled. Feedback and dynamics are neglected in the construction of the original path; the computed path may therefore not even be usable.

Section 8.1 motivates the consideration of feedback in the context of motion planning. Section 8.2 presents the main concepts of this chapter, but only for the case of a discrete state space. This requires less mathematical concepts than the continuous case, making it easier to present feedback concepts. Section 8.3 then provides the mathematical background needed to extend the feedback concepts to continuous state spaces (which includes C-spaces). Feedback motion planning methods are divided into complete methods, covered in Section 8.4, and sampling-based methods, covered in Section 8.5.

8.1 Motivation

For most problems involving the physical world, some form of feedback is needed. This means the actions of a plan should depend in some way on information gathered during execution. The need for feedback arises from the unpredictability of future states. In this chapter, every state space will be either discrete, or $X = \mathcal{C}$, which is a configuration space as considered in Chapter 4.

Two general ways to model uncertainty in the predictability of future states are

1. **Explicitly:** Develop models that explicitly account for the possible ways that the actual future state can drift away from the planned future state. A planning algorithm must take this uncertainty directly into account. Such explicit models of uncertainty are introduced and incorporated into the planning model in Part III.

2. **Implicitly:** The model of state transitions indicates that no uncertainty is possible; however, a feedback plan is constructed to ensure that it knows which action to apply, just in case it happens to be in some unexpected state during execution. This approach is taken in this chapter.

The implicit way to handle this uncertainty may seem strange at first; therefore, some explanation is required. It will be seen in Part III that explicitly modeling uncertainty is extremely challenging and complicated. The requirements for expressing reliable models are much stronger; the complexity of the problem increases, making algorithm design

	Open Loop	Feedback
Free motions	Traditional motion planning	Chapter 8
Dynamics	Chapters 14 and 15	Traditional control theory

Figure 8.1: By separating the issue of dynamics from feedback, two less-investigated topics emerge.

more difficult and leading to greater opportunities to make modeling errors. The implicit way of handling uncertainty in predictability arose in control theory [110, 124, 689]. It is well known that a feedback control law is needed to obtain reliable performance, yet it is peculiar that the formulation of dynamics used in most contexts does not explicitly account for this. Classical control theory has always assumed that feedback is crucial; however, only in modern branches of the field, such as *stochastic control* and *robust control*, does this uncertainty get explicitly modeled. Thus, there is a widely accepted and successful practice of designing feedback control laws that use state feedback to implicitly account for the fact that future states may be unpredictable. Given the widespread success of this control approach across numerous applications over the past century, it seems valuable to utilize this philosophy in the context of motion planning as well (if you still do not like it, then jump to Chapter 10).

Due to historical reasons in the development of feedback control, it often seems that feedback and dynamics are inseparable. This is mainly because control theory was developed to reliably alter the behavior of dynamical systems. In traditional motion planning, neither feedback nor dynamics is considered. A solution path is considered *open loop*, which means there is no feedback of information during execution to *close* the loop. Dynamics are also not handled because the additional complications of differential constraints and higher dimensional phase spaces arise (see Part IV).

By casting history aside and separating feedback from dynamics, four separate topics can be made, as shown in Figure 8.1. The topic of open-loop planning that involves dynamics has received increasing attention in recent years. This is the focus throughout most of Part IV. Those fond of classical control theory may criticize it for failing to account for feedback; however, such open-loop trajectories (paths in a phase space) are quite useful in applications that involve simulations. Furthermore, a trajectory that accounts for dynamics is more worthwhile in a decoupled approach than using a path that ignores dynamics, which has been an acceptable practice for decades. These issues will be elaborated upon further in Part IV.

The other interesting topic that emerges in Figure 8.1 is to develop feedback plans for problems in which there are no explicit models of dynamics or other differential constraints. If it was reasonable to solve problems in classical motion planning by ignoring differential constraints, one should certainly feel no less guilty designing feedback motion plans that still neglect differential constraints.[1] This uses the implicit model of uncertainty in predictability without altering any of the other assumptions previously applied in traditional motion planning.

Even if there are no unpredictability issues, another important use of feedback plans is for problems in which the initial state is not known. A feedback plan indicates what action to take from every state. Therefore, the specification of an initial condition is not important. The analog of this in graph algorithms is the single-source shortest-paths problem, which

---

[1] Section 8.4.4 will actually consider some simple differential constraints, such as acceleration bounds; the full treatment of differential constraints is deferred until Part IV.

indicates how to arrive at a particular vertex optimally from any other vertex. Due to this connection, the next section presents feedback concepts for discrete state spaces, before extending the ideas to continuous spaces, which are needed for motion planning.

For these reasons, feedback motion planning is considered in this chapter. As a module in a decoupled approach used in robotics, feedback motion plans are at least as useful as a path computed by the previous techniques. We expect feedback solutions to be more reliable in general, when used in the place of open-loop paths computed by traditional motion planning algorithms.

8.2 Discrete state spaces

This section is provided mainly to help to explain similar concepts that are coming in later sections. The presentation is limited to discrete spaces, which are much simpler to formulate and understand. Following this, an extension to configuration spaces and other continuous state spaces can be made. The discussion here is also relevant background for the feedback planning concepts that will be introduced in Section 8.4.1. In that case, uncertainty will be explicitly modeled. The resulting formulation and concepts can be considered as an extension of this section.

8.2.1 Defining a feedback plan

Consider a discrete planning problem similar to the ones defined in Formulations 2.1 and 2.3, except that the initial state is not given. Due to this, the cost functional cannot be expressed only as a function of a plan. It is instead defined in terms of the *state history* and *action history*. At stage k, these are defined as

$$\tilde{x}_k = (x_1, x_2, \ldots, x_k) \tag{8.1}$$

and

$$\tilde{u}_k = (u_1, u_2, \ldots, u_k), \tag{8.2}$$

respectively. Sometimes, it will be convenient to alternatively refer to $\tilde{x}_k$ as the *state trajectory*.

The resulting formulation is

Formulation 8.1 (Discrete Optimal Feedback Planning)

1. A finite, nonempty *state space* X.
2. For each state, $x \in X$, a finite *action space* $U(x)$.
3. A *state transition function* f that produces a state, $f(x, u) \in X$, for every $x \in X$ and $u \in U(x)$. Let U denote the union of $U(x)$ for all $x \in X$.
4. A set of *stages*, each denoted by k, that begins at $k = 1$ and continues indefinitely.
5. A *goal set*, $X_G \subset X$.
6. Let L denote a stage-additive *cost functional*,

$$L(\tilde{x}_F, \tilde{u}_K) = \sum_{k=1}^{K} l(x_k, u_k) + l_F(x_F), \tag{8.3}$$

in which $F = K + 1$.

There is one other difference in comparison to the formulations of Chapter 2. The state space is assumed here to be finite. This facilitates the construction of a feedback plan, but it is not necessary in general.

Consider defining a plan that solves Formulation 8.1. If the initial condition is given, then a sequence of actions could be specified, as in Chapter 2. Without having the initial condition, one possible approach is to determine a sequence of actions for each possible initial state, $x_1 \in X$. Once the initial state is given, the appropriate action sequence is known. This approach, however, wastes memory. Suppose some x is given as the initial state and the first action is applied, leading to the next state x'. What action should be applied from x'? The second action in the sequence at x can be used; however, we can also imagine that x' is now the initial state and use its first action. This implies that keeping an action sequence for every state is highly redundant. It is sufficient at each state to keep only the first action in the sequence. The application of that action produces the next state, at which the next appropriate action is stored. An execution sequence can be imagined from an initial state as follows. Start at some state, apply the action stored there, arrive at another state, apply its action, arrive at the next state, and so on, until the goal is reached.

It therefore seems appropriate to represent a feedback plan as a function that maps every state to an action. Therefore, a *feedback plan* π is defined as a function $\pi : X \to U$. From every state, $x \in X$, the plan indicates which action to apply. If the goal is reached, then the termination action should be applied. This is specified as part of the plan: $\pi(x) = u_T$, if $x \in X_G$. A feedback plan is called a *solution* to the problem if it causes the goal to be reached from every state that is reachable from the goal.

If an initial state x_1 and a feedback plan π are given, then the state and action histories can be determined. This implies that the execution cost, (8.3), also can be determined. It can therefore be alternatively expressed as $L(\pi, x_1)$, instead of $L(\tilde{x}_F, \tilde{u}_K)$. This relies on future states always being predictable. In Chapter 10, it will not be possible to make this direct correspondence due to uncertainties (see Section 10.1.3).

Feasibility and optimality

The notions of feasible and optimal plans need to be reconsidered in the context of feedback planning because the initial condition is not given. A plan π is called a solution to the *feasible* planning problem if from *every* $x \in X$ from which X_G is reachable the goal set is indeed reached by executing π from x. This means that the cost functional is ignored (an alternative to Formulation 8.1 can be defined in which the cost functional is removed). For convenience, π will be called a *feasible* feedback plan.

Now consider optimality. From a given state x, it is clear that an optimal plan exists using the concepts of Section 2.3. Is it possible that a different optimal plan needs to be associated with every $x \in X$ that can reach X_G? It turns out that only one plan is needed to encode optimal paths from every initial state to X_G. Why is this true? Suppose that the optimal cost-to-go is computed over X using Dijkstra's algorithm or value iteration, as covered in Section 2.3. Every cost-to-go value at some $x \in X$ indicates the cost received under the implementation of the optimal open-loop plan from x. The first step in this optimal plan can be determined by (2.19), which yields a new state $x' = f(x, u)$. From x', (2.19) can be applied once again to determine the next optimal action. The cost at x' represents both the optimal cost-to-go if x' is the initial condition and also the optimal cost-to-go when continuing on the optimal path from x. The two must be equivalent because of the dynamic programming principle. Since all such costs must coincide, a single feedback plan can be used to obtain the optimal cost-to-go from every initial condition.

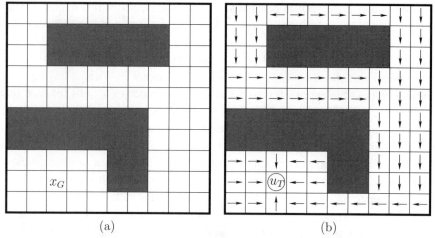

Figure 8.2: a) A 2D grid-planning problem. b) A solution feedback plan.

A feedback plan π is therefore defined as *optimal* if from *every* $x \in X$, the total cost, $L(\pi, x)$, obtained by executing π is the lowest among all possible plans. The requirement that this holds for every initial condition is important for feedback planning.

Example 8.1 (Feedback Plan on a 2D Grid)   This example uses the 2D grid model explained in Example 2.1. A robot moves on a grid, and the possible actions are up ($\uparrow$), down ($\downarrow$), left ($\leftarrow$), right ($\rightarrow$), and terminate (u_T); some directions are not available from some states. A solution feedback plan is depicted in Figure 8.2. Many other possible solutions plans exist. The one shown here happens to be optimal in terms of the number of steps to the goal. Some alternative feedback plans are also optimal (figure out which arrows can be changed). To apply the plan from any initial state, simply follow the arrows to the goal. In each stage, the application of the action represented by the arrow leads to the next state. The process terminates when u_T is applied at the goal.   ∎

8.2.2 Feedback plans as navigation functions

It conveniently turns out that tools for computing a feedback plan were already given in Chapter 2. Methods such as Dijkstra's algorithm and value iteration produce information as a side effect that can be used to represent a feedback plan. This section explains how this information is converted into a feedback plan. To achieve this, a feedback plan will be alternatively expressed as a potential function over the state space (recall potential functions from Section 5.4.3). The potential values are computed by planning algorithms and can be used to recover the appropriate actions during execution. In some cases, an *optimal* feedback plan can even be represented using potential functions.

Navigation functions

Consider a (discrete) *potential function*, defined as $\phi : X \rightarrow [0, \infty]$. The potential function can be used to define a feedback plan through the use of a *local operator*, which is a function that selects the action that reduces the potential as much as possible. First, consider the case of a feasible planning problem. The potential function, ϕ, defines a feedback plan by selecting u through the *local operator*,

$$u^* = \operatorname*{argmin}_{u \in U(x)} \left\{ \phi(f(x, u)) \right\},
\tag{8.4}$$

which means that $u^* \in U(x)$ is chosen to reduce ϕ as much as possible. The local operator yields a kind of *greedy* descent of the potential. Note that the action u^* may not be unique. In the continuous-space analog to this, the corresponding local operator performs a descent along the negative gradient (often referred to as *gradient descent*).

In the case of optimal planning, the local operator is defined as

$$u^* = \operatorname*{argmin}_{u \in U(x)} \left\{ l(x, u) + \phi(f(x, u)) \right\},
\tag{8.5}$$

which looks similar to the dynamic programming condition, (2.19). It becomes identical to (2.19) if ϕ is interpreted as the optimal cost-to-go. A simplification of (8.5) can be made if the planning problem is *isotropic*, which means that the cost is the same in every direction: $l(x, u) = l(x, u')$ for all $u, u' \in U(x)$. In this case, the cost term $l(x, u)$ does not affect the minimization in (8.5). A common example in which this assumption applies is if the cost functional counts the number of stages required to reach the goal. The costs of particular actions chosen along the way are not important. Using the isotropic property, (8.5) simplifies back to (8.4).

When is a potential function useful? Many useless potential functions can be defined that fail to reach the goal, or cause states to cycle indefinitely, and so on. The most desirable potential function is one that for any initial state causes arrival in X_G, if it is reachable. This requires only a few simple properties. A potential function that satisfies these will be called a *navigation function*.[2]

Suppose that the cost functional is isotropic. Let $x' = f(x, u^*)$, which is the state reached after applying the action $u^* \in U(x)$ that was selected by (8.4). A potential function, ϕ, is called a *(feasible) navigation function* if

1. $\phi(x) = 0$ for all $x \in X_G$.
2. $\phi(x) = \infty$ if and only if no point in X_G is reachable from x.
3. For every state, $x \in X \setminus X_G$, the local operator produces a state x' for which $\phi(x') < \phi(x)$.

The first condition requires the goal to have zero potential (this condition is actually not necessary but is included for convenience). The second condition requires that ∞ serves as a special indicator that the goal is not reachable from some state. The third condition means that the potential function has no local minima except at the goal. This means that the execution of the resulting feedback plan will progress without cycling and the goal region will eventually be reached.

An *optimal navigation function* is defined as the optimal cost-to-go, G^*. This means that in addition to the three properties above, the navigation function must also satisfy the principle of optimality:

$$\phi(x) = \min_{u \in U(x)} \left\{ l(x, u) + \phi(f(x, u)) \right\},
\tag{8.6}$$

which is just (2.18) with G^* replaced by ϕ. See Section 15.2.1 for more on this connection.

---

[2] This term was developed for continuous configuration spaces in [544, 832]; it will be used more broadly in this book but still retains the basic idea.

22	21	22	21	20	19	18	17	16	17
21	20							15	16
20	19							14	15
19	18	17	16	15	14	13	12	13	14
18	17	16	15	14	13	12	11	12	13
							10	11	12
							9	10	11
3	2	1	2	3			8	9	10
2	1	0	1	2			7	8	9
3	2	1	2	3	4	5	6	7	8

Figure 8.3: The cost-to-go values serve as a navigation function.

Example 8.2 (Navigation Function on a 2D Grid) Return to the planning problem in Example 8.1. Assume that an isotropic cost model is used: $l(x, u) = 1$ if $u \neq u_T$. Figure 8.3 shows a navigation function. The numbers shown in the tiles represent ϕ. Verify that ϕ satisfies the three requirements for a navigation function.

At any state, an action is applied that reduces the potential value. This corresponds to selecting the action using (8.4). The process may be repeated from any state until X_G is reached. This example clearly illustrates how a navigation function can be used as an alternative definition of a feedback plan.   ∎

Example 8.3 (Airport Terminal) You may have found yourself using a navigation function to find the exit after arriving in an unfamiliar airport terminal. Many terminals are tree-structured, with increasing gate numbers as the distance to the terminal exit increases. If you wish to leave the terminal, you should normally walk toward the lower numbered gates.   ∎

Computing navigation functions

There are many ways to compute navigation functions. The cost-to-go function determined by Dijkstra's algorithm working backward from X_G yields an *optimal navigation function*. The third condition of a navigation function under the anisotropic case is exactly the stationary dynamic programming equation, (2.18), if the navigation function ϕ is defined as the optimal cost-to-go G^*. It was mentioned previously that the optimal actions can be recovered using only the cost-to-go. This was actually an example of using a navigation function, and the resulting procedure could have been considered as a feedback plan. If optimality is not important, then virtually any backward search algorithm from Section 2.2 can be used, provided that it records the distance to the goal from every reached state. The distance does not have to be optimal. It merely corresponds to the cost obtained if the current vertex in the search tree is traced back to the root vertex (or back to any vertex in X_G, if there are multiple goal states).

If the planning problem does not even include a cost functional, as in Formulation 2.1, then a cost functional can be invented for the purposes of constructing a navigation function. At each $x \in X$ from which X_G is reachable, the number of edges in the search graph that would be traversed from x to X_G can be stored as the cost. If Dijkstra's algorithm is used to construct the navigation function, then the resulting feedback plan yields executions that are shortest in terms of the number of stages required to reach the goal.

The navigation function itself serves as the representation of the feedback plan, by recovering the actions from the local operator. Thus, a function, $\pi : X \to U$, can be recovered from a navigation function, $\phi : X \to [0, \infty]$. Likewise, a navigation function, ϕ, can be constructed from π. Therefore, the π and ϕ can be considered as interchangeable representations of feedback plans.

8.2.3 Grid-based navigation functions for motion planning

To consider feedback plans for continuous spaces, vector fields and other basic definitions from differential geometry will be needed. These will be covered in Section 8.3; however, before handling such complications, we first will describe how to use the ideas presented so far in Section 8.2 as a discrete approximation to feedback motion planning.

Examples 8.1 and 8.2 have already defined feedback plans and navigation functions for 2D grids that contain obstacles. Imagine that this model is used to approximate a motion planning problem for which $\mathcal{C} \subset \mathbb{R}^2$. Section 5.4.2 showed how to make a topological graph that approximates the motion planning problem with a grid of samples. The motions used in Example 8.1 correspond to the 1-neighborhood definition, (5.37). This idea was further refined in Section 7.7.1 to model approximate optimal motion planning by moving on a grid; see Formulation 7.4. By choosing the Manhattan motion model, as defined in Example 7.4, a grid with the same motions considered in Example 8.1 is produced.

To construct a navigation function that may be useful in mobile robotics, a high-resolution (e.g., 50 to 100 points per axis) grid is usually required. In Section 5.4.2, only a few points per axis were needed because feedback was not assumed. It was possible in some instances to find a collision-free path by investigating only a few points per axis. During the execution of a feedback plan, it is assumed that the future states of the robot are not necessarily predictable. Wherever the robot may end up, the navigation function in combination with the local operator must produce the appropriate action. If the current state (or configuration) is approximated by a grid, then it is important to reduce the approximation error as much as possible. This is accomplished by setting the grid resolution high. In the feedback case, the grid can be viewed as "covering" the whole configuration space, whereas in Section 5.4.2 the grid only represented a topological graph of paths that cut across the space.[3]

Wavefront propagation algorithms

Once the approximation has been made, any of the methods discussed in Section 8.2.2 can be used to compute a navigation function. An optimal navigation function can be easily computed using Dijkstra's algorithm from the goal. If each motion has unit cost, then a useful simplification can be made. Figure 8.4 describes a wavefront propagation algorithm that computes an optimal navigation function. It can be considered as a special case of Dijkstra's algorithm that avoids explicit construction of the priority queue. In Dijkstra's algorithm, the cost of the smallest element in the queue is monotonically nondecreasing during the execution of the algorithm. In the case of each motion having unit cost, there will be many states in the queue that have the same cost. Dijkstra's algorithm could remove in parallel all elements that have the same, smallest cost. Suppose the common, smallest cost value is i. These states are organized into a *wavefront*, W_i. The initial wavefront is

---

[3] Difficulty in distinguishing between these two caused researchers for many years to believe that grids yield terrible performance for the open-loop path planning problems of Chapter 5. This was mainly because it was assumed that a high-resolution grid was necessary. For many problems, however, they could terminate early after only considering a few points per axis.

WAVEFRONT PROPAGATION ALGORITHM

1. Initialize $W_0 = X_G$; $i = 0$.

2. Initialize $W_{i+1} = \emptyset$.

3. For every $x \in W_i$, assign $\phi(x) = i$ and insert all unexplored neighbors of x into W_{i+1}.

4. If $W_{i+1} = \emptyset$, then terminate; otherwise, let $i := i + 1$ and go to Step 2.

Figure 8.4: The wavefront propagation algorithm is a specialized version of Dijkstra's algorithm that optimizes the number of stages to reach the goal.

W_0, which represents the states in X_G. The algorithm can immediately assign an optimal cost-to-go value of 1 to every state that can be reached in one stage from any state in W_0. These must be optimal because no other cost value is optimal. The states that receive cost 1 can be organized into the wavefront W_1. The unexplored neighbors of W_1 are assigned cost 2, which also must be optimal. This process repeats inductively from i to $i + 1$ until all reachable states have been reached. In the end, the optimal cost-to-go is computed in $O(n)$ time, in which n is the number of reachable grid states. For any states that were not reached, the value $\phi(x) = \infty$ can be assigned. The navigation function shown in Figure 8.3 can actually be computed using the wavefront propagation algorithm.

Maximum clearance

One problem that typically arises in mobile robotics is that optimal motion plans bring robots too close to obstacles. Recall from Section 6.2.4 that the shortest Euclidean paths for motion planning in a polygonal environment must be allowed to touch obstacle vertices. This motivated the maximum clearance roadmap, which was covered in Section 6.2.3. A grid-based approximate version of the maximum clearance roadmap can be made. Furthermore, a navigation function can be defined that guides the robot onto the roadmap, then travels along the roadmap, and finally deposits the robot at a specified goal. In [591], the resulting navigation function is called *NF2*.

Assume that there is a single goal state, $x_G \in X$. The computation of a maximum clearance navigation function proceeds as follows:

1. Instead of X_G, assign W_0 to be the set of all states from which motion in at least one direction is blocked. These are the states on the boundary of the discretized collision-free space.

2. Perform wavefront iterations that propagate costs in waves outward from the obstacle boundaries.

3. As the wavefronts propagate, they will meet approximately at the location of the maximum clearance roadmap for the original, continuous problem. Mark any state at which two wavefront points arrive from opposing directions as a *skeleton state*. It may be the case that the wavefronts simply touch each other, rather than arriving at a common state; in this case, one of the two touching states is chosen as the skeleton state. Let S denote the set of all skeleton states.

4. After the wavefront propagation ends, connect x_G to the skeleton by inserting x_G and all states along the path to the skeleton into S. This path can be found using any search algorithm.

5. Compute a navigation function ϕ_1 over S by treating all other states as if they were obstacles and using the wavefront propagation algorithm. This navigation function guides any point in S to the goal.

6. Treat S as a goal region and compute a navigation function ϕ_2 using the wavefront propagation algorithm. This navigation function guides the state to the nearest point on the skeleton.

7. Combine ϕ_1 and ϕ_2 as follows to obtain ϕ. For every $x \in S$, let $\phi(x) = \phi_1(x)$. For every remaining state, the value $\phi(x) = \phi_1(x') + \phi_2(x)$ is assigned, in which x' is the nearest state to x such that $x' \in S$. The state x' can easily be recorded while ϕ_2 is computed.

If C_{free} is multiply connected, then there may be multiple ways to each x_G by traveling around different obstacles (the paths are not homotopic). The method described above does not take into account the problem that one route may have a tighter clearance than another. The given approach only optimizes the distance traveled along the skeleton; it does not, however, maximize the nearest approach to an obstacle, if there are multiple routes.

Dial's algorithm

Now consider generalizing the wavefront propagation idea. Wavefront propagation can be applied to any discrete planning problem if $l(x, u) = 1$ for any $x \in X$ and $u \in U(x)$ (except $u = u_T$). It is most useful when the transition graph is sparse (imagine representing the transition graph using an adjacency matrix). The grid problem is a perfect example where this becomes important. More generally, if the cost terms assume integer values, then *Dial's algorithm* [274] results, which is a generalization of wavefront propagation, and a specialization of Dijkstra's algorithm. The idea is that the priority queue can be avoided by assigning the alive vertices to buckets that correspond to different possible cost-to-go values. In the wavefront propagation case, there are never more than two buckets needed at a time. Dial's algorithm allows all states in the smallest cost bucket to be processed in parallel. The scheme was enhanced in [939] to yield a linear-time algorithm.

Other extensions

Several ideas from this section can be generalized to produce other navigation functions. One disadvantage of the methods discussed so far is that undesirable staircase motions (as shown in Figure 7.40) are produced. If the 2-neighborhood, as defined in (5.38), is used to define the action spaces, then the motions will generally be shorter. Dial's algorithm can be applied to efficiently compute an optimal navigation function in this case.

A grid approximation can be made to higher dimensional configuration spaces. Since a high resolution is needed, however, it is practical only for a few dimensions (e.g., 3 or 4). If the 1-neighborhood is used, then wavefront propagation can be easily applied to compute navigation functions. Dial's algorithm can be adapted for general k-neighborhoods.

Constructing navigation functions over grids may provide a practical solution in many applications. In other cases it may be unacceptable that staircase motions occur. In many cases, it may not even be possible to compute the navigation function quickly enough. Factors that influence this problem are 1) very high accuracy, and a hence high-resolution grid may be necessary; 2) the dimension of the configuration space may be high; and 3) the environment may be frequently changing, and a real-time response is required. To address these issues, it is appealing to abandon grid approximations. This will require defining potential functions and velocities directly on the configuration space. Section 8.3 presents the background mathematical concepts to make this transition.

8.3 Vector fields and integral curves

To consider feedback motion plans over continuous state spaces, including configuration spaces, we will need to define a vector field and the trajectory that is obtained by integrating the vector field from an initial point. A vector field is ideal for characterizing a feedback plan over a continuous state space. It can be viewed as providing the continuous-space analog to the feedback plans on grids, as shown in Figure 8.2b.

This section presents two alternative presentations of the background mathematical concepts. Section 8.3.1 assumes that $X = \mathbb{R}^n$, which leads to definitions that appear very similar to those you may have learned in basic calculus and differential equations courses. Section 8.3.2 covers the more general case of vector fields on manifolds. This requires significantly more technical concepts and builds on the manifold definitions of Section 4.1.2.

Some readers may have already had some background in differentiable manifolds. If, however, you are seeing it for the first time, then it may be difficult to comprehend on the first reading. In addition to rereading, here are two other suggestions. First, try studying background material on this subject, which is suggested at the end of the chapter. Second, disregard the manifold technicalities in the subsequent sections and pretend that $X = \mathcal{C} = \mathbb{R}^n$. Nearly everything will make sense without the additional technicalities. Imagine that a manifold is defined as a cube, $[0, 1]^n$, with some sides identified, as in Section 4.1.2. The concepts that were presented for $\mathbb{R}^n$ can be applied everywhere except at the boundary of the cube. For example, if $\mathbb{S}^1$ is defined as $[0, 1]/\sim$, and a function f is defined on $\mathbb{S}^1$, how can we define the derivative at $f(0)$? The technical definitions of Section 8.3.2 fix this problem. Sometimes, the technicalities can be avoided in practice by cleverly handling the identification points.

8.3.1 Vector fields on $\mathbb{R}^n$

This section revisits some basic concepts from introductory courses such as calculus, linear algebra, and differential equations. You may have learned most of these for $\mathbb{R}^2$ and $\mathbb{R}^3$. We eventually want to describe velocities in $\mathbb{R}^n$ and on manifolds, and then use the notion of a vector field to express a feedback plan in Section 8.4.1.

Vector spaces

Before defining a vector field, it is helpful to be precise about what is meant by a *vector*. A *vector space* (or *linear space*) is defined as a set, V, that is closed under two algebraic operations called *vector addition* and *scalar multiplication* and satisfies several axioms, which will be given shortly. The vector space used in this section is $\mathbb{R}^n$, in which the scalars are real numbers, and a vector is represented as a sequence of n real numbers. Scalar multiplication multiplies each component of the vector by the scalar value. Vector addition forms a new vector by adding each component of two vectors.

A *vector space* V can be defined over any field $\mathbb{F}$ (recall the definition from Section 4.4.1). The field $\mathbb{F}$ represents the *scalars*, and V represents the *vectors*. The concepts presented below generalize the familiar case of the vector space $\mathbb{R}^n$. In this case, $V = \mathbb{R}^n$ and $\mathbb{F} = \mathbb{R}$. In the definitions that follow, you may make these substitutions, if desired. We will not develop vector spaces that are more general than this; the definitions are nevertheless given in terms of V and $\mathbb{F}$ to clearly separate scalars from vectors. The *vector addition* is denoted by $+$, and the *scalar multiplication* is denoted by $\cdot$. These operations must satisfy the following axioms (a good exercise is to verify these for the case of $\mathbb{R}^n$ treated as a vector space over the field $\mathbb{R}$):

1. **(Commutative Group Under Vector Addition)** The set V is a commutative group with respect to vector addition, $+$.

2. **(Associativity of Scalar Multiplication)** For any $v \in V$ and any $\alpha, \beta \in \mathbb{F}$, $\alpha(\beta v) = (\alpha\beta)v$.

3. **(Distributivity of Scalar Sums)** For any $v \in V$ and any $\alpha, \beta \in \mathbb{F}$, $(\alpha + \beta)v = \alpha v + \beta v$.

4. **(Distributivity of Vector Sums)** For any $v, w \in V$ and any $\alpha \in \mathbb{F}$, $\alpha(v + w) = \alpha v + \alpha w$.

5. **(Scalar Multiplication Identity)** For any $v \in V$, $1v = v$ for the multiplicative identity $1 \in \mathbb{F}$.

The first axiom allows vectors to be added in any order. The rest of the axioms require that the scalar multiplication interacts with vectors in the way that we would expect from the familiar vector space $\mathbb{R}^n$ over $\mathbb{R}$.

A *basis* of a vector space V is defined as a set, $v_1, \ldots, v_n$, of vectors for which every $v \in V$ can be uniquely written as a *linear combination*:

$$v = \alpha_1 v_1 + \alpha_2 v_2 + \cdots + \alpha_n v_n, \tag{8.7}$$

for some $\alpha_1, \ldots, \alpha_n \in \mathbb{F}$. This means that every vector has a unique representation as a linear combination of basis elements. In the case of $\mathbb{R}^3$, a familiar basis is $[0 \ 0 \ 1]$, $[0 \ 1 \ 0]$, and $[1 \ 0 \ 0]$. All vectors can be expressed as a linear combination of these three. Remember that a basis is not necessarily unique. From linear algebra, recall that any three linearly independent vectors can be used as a basis for $\mathbb{R}^3$. In general, the basis must only include linearly independent vectors. Even though a basis is not necessarily unique, the number of vectors in a basis is the same for any possible basis over the same vector space. This number, n, is called the *dimension* of the vector space. Thus, we can call $\mathbb{R}^n$ an n-dimensional vector space over $\mathbb{R}$.

Example 8.4 (The Vector Space $\mathbb{R}^n$ Over $\mathbb{R}$) As indicated already, $\mathbb{R}^n$ can be considered as a vector space. A natural basis is the set of n vectors in which, for each $i \in \{1, \ldots, n\}$, a unit vector is constructed as follows. Let $x_i = 1$ and $x_j = 0$ for all $j \neq i$. Since there are n basis vectors, $\mathbb{R}^n$ is an n-dimensional vector space. The basis is not unique. Any set of n linearly independent vectors may be used, which is familiar from linear algebra, in which nonsingular $n \times n$ matrices are used to transform between them. ∎

To illustrate the power of these general vector space definitions, consider the following example.

Example 8.5 (A Vector Space of Functions) The set of all continuous, real-valued functions $f : [0, 1] \to \mathbb{R}$, for which

$$\int_0^1 f(x)dx \tag{8.8}$$

is finite, forms a vector space over $\mathbb{R}$. It is straightforward to verify that the vector space axioms are satisfied. For example, if two functions f_1 and f_2 are added, the integral remains finite. Furthermore, $f_1 + f_2 = f_2 + f_1$, and all of the group axioms are satisfied with respect to addition. Any function f that satisfies (8.8) can be multiplied by a scalar in $\mathbb{R}$, and the integral remains finite. The axioms that involve scalar multiplication can also be verified.

It turns out that this vector space is infinite-dimensional. One way to see this is to restrict the functions to the set of all those for which the Taylor series exists and converges to the function (these are called *analytic functions*). Each function can be expressed via a Taylor series as a polynomial that may have an infinite number of terms. The set of all monomials, x, x^2, x^3, and so on, represents a basis. Every continuous function can be considered as an infinite vector of coefficients; each coefficient is multiplied by one of the monomials to produce the function. This provides a simple example of a *function space*; with some additional definitions, this leads to a *Hilbert space*, which is crucial in functional analysis, a subject that characterizes spaces of functions [839, 841]. ■

The remainder of this chapter considers only finite-dimensional vector spaces over $\mathbb{R}$. It is important, however, to keep in mind the basic properties of vector spaces that have been provided.

Vector fields

A vector field looks like a "needle diagram" over $\mathbb{R}^n$, as depicted in Figure 8.5. The idea is to specify a direction at each point $p \in \mathbb{R}^n$. When used to represent a feedback plan, it indicates the direction that the robot needs to move if it finds itself at p.

For every $p \in \mathbb{R}^n$, associate an n-dimensional vector space called the *tangent space* at p, which is denoted as $T_p(\mathbb{R}^n)$. Why not just call it a vector space at p? The use of the word "tangent" here might seem odd; it is motivated by the generalization to manifolds, for which the tangent spaces will be "tangent" to points on the manifold.

A *vector field*[4] $\vec{V}$ on $\mathbb{R}^n$ is a function that assigns a vector $v \in T_p(\mathbb{R}^n)$ to every $p \in \mathbb{R}^n$. What is the range of this function? The vector $\vec{V}(p)$ at each $p \in \mathbb{R}^n$ actually belongs to a different tangent space. The range of the function is therefore the union

$$T(\mathbb{R}^n) = \bigcup_{p \in \mathbb{R}^n} T_p(\mathbb{R}^n), \qquad (8.9)$$

which is called the *tangent bundle* on $\mathbb{R}^n$. Even though the way we describe vectors from $T_p(\mathbb{R}^n)$ may appear the same for any $p \in \mathbb{R}^n$, each tangent space is assumed to produce distinct vectors. To maintain distinctness, a point in the tangent bundle can be expressed with $2n$ coordinates, by specifying p and v together. This will become important for defining phase space concepts in Part IV. In the present setting, it is sufficient to think of the range of $\vec{V}$ as $\mathbb{R}^n$ because $T_p(\mathbb{R}^n) = \mathbb{R}^n$ for every $p \in \mathbb{R}^n$.

A vector field can therefore be expressed using n real-valued functions on $\mathbb{R}^n$. Let $f_i(x_1, \ldots, x_n)$ for i from 1 to n denote such functions. Using these, a vector field is specified as

$$f(x) = [f_1(x_1, \ldots, x_n) \ \ f_2(x_1, \ldots, x_n) \ \cdots \ f_n(x_1, \ldots, x_n)]. \qquad (8.10)$$

In this case, it appears that a vector field is a function f from $\mathbb{R}^n$ into $\mathbb{R}^n$. Therefore, standard function notation will be used from this point onward to denote a vector field.

Now consider some examples of vector fields over $\mathbb{R}^2$. Let a point in $\mathbb{R}^2$ be represented as $p = (x, y)$. In standard vector calculus, a vector field is often specified as $[f_1(x, y) \ \ f_2(x, y)]$, in which f_1 and f_2 are functions on $\mathbb{R}^2$

---

[4] Unfortunately, the term *field* appears in two unrelated places: in the definition of a vector space and in the term *vector field*. Keep in mind that this is an accidental collision of terms.

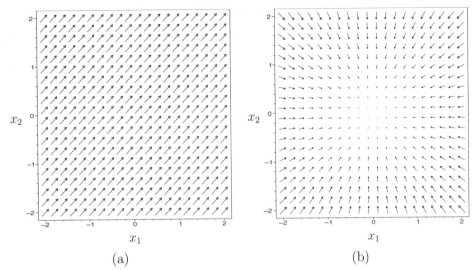

Figure 8.5: (a) A constant vector field, $f(x, y) = [1 \ \ 1]$. (b) A vector field, $f(x, y) = [-x \ \ -y]$ in which all vectors point to the origin.

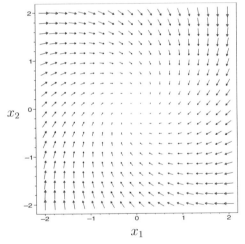

Figure 8.6: A swirling vector field, $f(x, y) = [(y - x) \ \ (-x - y)]$.

Example 8.6 (Constant Vector Field) Figure 8.5a shows a *constant vector field*, which assigns the vector $[1 \ \ 2]$ to every $(x, y) \in \mathbb{R}^2$. ∎

Example 8.7 (Inward Flow) Figure 8.5b depicts a vector field that assigns $[-x \ \ -y]$ to every $(x, y) \in \mathbb{R}^2$. This causes all vectors to point to the origin. ∎

Example 8.8 (Swirl) The vector field in Figure 8.6 assigns $[(y - x) \ \ (-x - y)]$ to every $(x, y) \in \mathbb{R}^2$. ∎

Due to obstacles that arise in planning problems, it will be convenient to sometimes restrict the domain of a vector field to an open subset of $\mathbb{R}^n$. Thus, for any open subset $O \subset \mathbb{R}^n$, a vector field $f : O \to \mathbb{R}^n$ can be defined.

Smoothness

A function f_i from a subset of $\mathbb{R}^n$ into $\mathbb{R}$ is called a *smooth function* if derivatives of any order can be taken with respect to any variables, at any point in the domain of f_i. A vector field is said to be *smooth* if every one of its n defining functions, $f_1, \ldots, f_n$, is smooth. An alternative name for a smooth function is a C^∞ *function*. The superscript represents the order of differentiation that can be taken. For a C^k *function*, its derivatives can be taken at least up to order k. A C^0 *function* is an alternative name for a continuous function. The notion of a homeomorphism can be extended to a *diffeomorphism*, which is a homeomorphism that is a smooth function. Two topological spaces are called *diffeomorphic* if there exists a diffeomorphism between them.

Vector fields as velocity fields

We now give a particular interpretation to vector fields. A vector field expressed using (8.10) can be used to define a set of first-order differential equations as

$$\frac{dx_1}{dt} = f_1(x_1, \ldots, x_n)$$

$$\frac{dx_2}{dt} = f_2(x_1, \ldots, x_n)$$

$$\vdots$$

$$\frac{dx_n}{dt} = f_n(x_1, \ldots, x_n). \tag{8.11}$$

Each equation represents the derivative of one coordinate with respect to time. For any point $x \in \mathbb{R}^n$, a *velocity vector* is defined as

$$\frac{dx}{dt} = \begin{bmatrix} \dfrac{dx_1}{dt} & \dfrac{dx_2}{dt} & \cdots & \dfrac{dx_n}{dt} \end{bmatrix}. \tag{8.12}$$

This enables f to be interpreted as a *velocity field*.

It is customary to use the short notation $\dot{x} = dx/dt$. Each velocity component can be shortened to $\dot{x}_i = dx_i/dt$. Using f to denote the vector of functions $f_1, \ldots, f_n$, (8.11) can be shorted to

$$\dot{x} = f(x). \tag{8.13}$$

The use of f here is an intentional coincidence with the use of f for the state transition equation. In Part IV, we will allow vector fields to be parameterized by actions. This leads to a continuous-time state transition equation that looks like $\dot{x} = f(x, u)$ and is very similar to the transition equations defined over discrete stages in Chapter 2.

The differential equations expressed in (8.11) are often referred to as *autonomous* or *stationary* because f does not depend on time. A time-varying vector field could alternatively be defined, which yields $\dot{x} = f(x(t), t)$. This will not be covered, however, in this chapter.

An integral curve

If a vector field f is given, then a velocity vector is defined at each point using (8.10). Imagine a point that starts at some $x_0 \in \mathbb{R}^n$ at time $t = 0$ and then moves according to the velocities expressed in f. Where should it travel? Its *trajectory* starting from x_0 can be expressed as a function $\tau : [0, \infty) \to \mathbb{R}^n$, in which the domain is a time interval, $[0, \infty)$. A trajectory represents an *integral curve* (or *solution trajectory*) of the differential equations with initial condition $\tau(0) = x_0$ if

$$\frac{d\tau}{dt}(t) = f(\tau(t)) \tag{8.14}$$

for every time $t \in [0, \infty)$. This is sometimes expressed in integral form as

$$\tau(t) = x_0 + \int_0^t f(\tau(s))ds \tag{8.15}$$

and is called a solution to the differential equations in the *sense of Caratheodory*. Intuitively, the integral curve starts at x_0 and flows along the directions indicated by the velocity vectors. This can be considered as the continuous-space analog of following the arrows in the discrete case, as depicted in Figure 8.2b.

Example 8.9 (Integral Curve for a Constant Velocity Field) The simplest case is a constant vector field. Suppose that a constant field $x_1 = 1$ and $x_2 = 2$ is defined on $\mathbb{R}^2$. The integral curve from $(0, 0)$ is $\tau(t) = (t, 2t)$. It can be easily seen that (8.14) holds for all $t \geq 0$. ■

Example 8.10 (Integral Curve for a Linear Velocity Field) Consider a velocity field on $\mathbb{R}^2$. Let $\dot{x}_1 = -2x_1$ and $\dot{x}_2 = -x_2$. The function $\tau(t) = (e^{-2t}, e^{-t})$ represents the integral curve from $(1, 1)$. At $t = 0$, $\tau(0) = (1, 1)$, which is the initial state. If can be verified that for all $t > 0$, (8.14) holds. This is a simple example of a linear velocity field. In general, if each f_i is a linear function of the coordinate variables $x_1, \ldots, x_n$, then a linear velocity field is obtained. The integral curve is generally found by determining the eigenvalues of the matrix A when the velocity field is expressed as $\dot{x} = Ax$. See [194] for numerous examples. ■

A basic result from differential equations is that a unique integral curve exists to $\dot{x} = f(x)$ if f is smooth. An alternative condition is that a unique solution exists if f satisfies a *Lipschitz condition*. This means that there exists some constant $c \in (0, \infty)$ such that

$$\|f(x) - f(x')\| \leq c\|x - x'\| \tag{8.16}$$

for all $x, x' \in X$, and $\|\cdot\|$ denotes the Euclidean norm (vector magnitude). The constant c is often called a *Lipschitz constant*. Note that if f satisfies the Lipschitz condition, then it is continuous. Also, if all partial derivatives of f over all of X can be bounded by a constant, then f is Lipschitz. The expression in (8.16) is preferred, however, because it is more general (it does not even imply that f is differentiable everywhere).

Piecewise-smooth vector fields

It will be important to allow vector fields that are smooth only over a finite number of patches. At a *switching boundary* between two patches, a discontinuous jump may occur. For example, suppose that an $(n-1)$-dimensional switching boundary, $S \subset \mathbb{R}^n$, is defined as

$$S = \{x \in \mathbb{R}^n \mid s(x) = 0\}, \tag{8.17}$$

in which s is a function $s : \mathbb{R}^n \to \mathbb{R}$. If $\mathbb{R}^n$ has dimension n and s is not singular, then S has dimension $n - 1$. Define

$$S_+ = \{x \in \mathbb{R}^n \mid s(x) > 0\} \qquad (8.18)$$

and

$$S_- = \{x \in \mathbb{R}^n \mid s(x) < 0\}. \qquad (8.19)$$

The definitions are similar to the construction of implicit models using geometric primitives in Section 3.1.2. Suppose that $f(x)$ is smooth over S_+ and S_- but experiences a discontinuous jump at S. Such differential equations model *hybrid systems* in control theory [139, 411, 637]. The task there is to design a *hybrid control system*. Can we still determine a solution trajectory in this case? Under special conditions, we can obtain what is called a solution to the differential equations in the *sense of Filipov* [340, 848].

Let $B(x, \delta)$ denote an open ball of radius δ centered at x. Let $f(B(x, \delta))$ denote the set

$$f(B(x, \delta)) = \{x' \in X \mid \exists x'' \in B(x, \delta) \text{ for which } x' = f(x'')\}. \qquad (8.20)$$

Let X_0 denote any subset of $\mathbb{R}^n$ that has measure zero (i.e., $\mu(X_0) = 0$). Let $\text{hull}(A)$ denote the convex hull of a set, A, of points in $\mathbb{R}^n$. A path $\tau : [0, t_f] \to \mathbb{R}^n$ is called a *solution in the sense of Filipov* if for almost all $t \in [0, t_f]$,

$$\frac{d\tau}{dt}(t) \in \bigcap_{\delta > 0} \left\{ \bigcap_{X_0} \text{hull}(f(B(\tau(t), \delta) \setminus X_0)) \right\}, \qquad (8.21)$$

in which the intersections are taken over all possible $\delta > 0$ and sets, X_0, of measure zero. The expression (8.21) is actually called a *differential inclusion* [54] because a set of choices is possible for $\dot{x}$. The "for almost all" requirement means that the condition can even fail to hold on a set of measure zero in $[0, t_f]$. Intuitively, it says that almost all of the velocity vectors produced by τ must point "between" the velocity vectors given by f in the vicinity of $\tau(x(t))$. The "between" part comes from using the convex hull. Filipov's sense of solution is an incredible generalization of the solution concept in the sense of Caratheodory. In that case, every velocity vector produced by τ must agree with $f(x(t))$, as given in (8.14). The condition in (8.21) allows all sorts of sloppiness to appear in the solution, even permitting f to be discontinuous.

Many bizarre vector fields can yield solutions in the sense of Filipov. The switching boundary model is relatively simple among those permitted by Filipov's condition. Figure 8.7 shows various cases that can occur at the switching boundary S. For the case of consistent flow, solutions occur as you may intuitively expect. Filipov's condition, (8.21), requires that at S the velocity vector of τ points between vectors before and after crossing S (for example, it can point down, which is the average of the two directions). The magnitude must also be between the two magnitudes. For the inward flow case, the integral curve moves along S, assuming the vectors inside of S point in the same direction (within the convex hull) as the vectors on either side of the boundary. In applications that involve physical systems, this may lead to oscillations around S. This can be alleviated by regularization, which thickens the boundary [848] (the subject of *sliding-mode control* addresses this issue [305]). The outward flow case can lead to nonuniqueness if the initial state lies in S. However, trajectories that start outside of S will not cross S, and there will be no such troubles. If the flow is tangent on both sides of a boundary, then other forms of nonuniqueness may occur. The tangent-flow case will be avoided in this chapter.

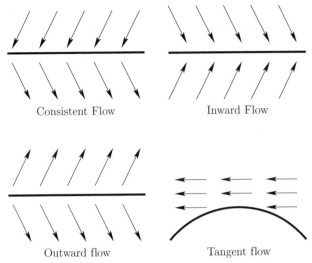

Figure 8.7: Different kinds of flows around a switching boundary.

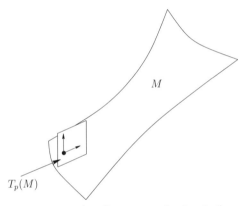

Figure 8.8: Intuitively, the tangent space is a linear approximation to the manifold in a neighborhood around p.

8.3.2 Smooth manifolds

The manifold definition given in Section 4.1.2 is often called a *topological manifold*. A manifold defined in this way does not necessarily have enough axioms to ensure that calculus operations, such as differentiation and integration, can be performed. We would like to talk about velocities on the configuration space $\mathcal{C}$ or in general for a continuous state space X. As seen in Chapter 4, the configuration space could be a manifold such as $\mathbb{RP}^3$. Therefore, we need to define some more qualities that a manifold should possess to enable calculus. This leads to the notion of a *smooth manifold*.

Assume that M is a topological manifold, as defined in Section 4.1.2. For example, M could represent $SO(3)$, the set of all rotation matrices for $\mathbb{R}^3$. A simpler example that will be helpful to keep in mind is $M = \mathbb{S}^2$, which is a sphere in $\mathbb{R}^3$. We want to extend the concepts of Section 8.3.1 from $\mathbb{R}^n$ to manifolds. One of the first definitions will be the tangent space $\mathbb{T}_p(M)$ at a point $p \in M$. As you might imagine intuitively, the tangent vectors are tangent to a surface, as shown in Figure 8.8. These will indicate possible velocities with which we can move along the manifold from p. This is more difficult to define for a manifold than for $\mathbb{R}^n$ because it is easy to express any point in $\mathbb{R}^n$ using n

coordinates, and all local coordinate frames for the tangent spaces at every $p \in \mathbb{R}^n$ are perfectly aligned with each other. For a manifold such as $\mathbb{S}^2$, we must define tangent spaces in a way that is not sensitive to coordinates and handles the fact that the tangent plane rotates as we move around on $\mathbb{S}^2$.

First think carefully about what it means to assign coordinates to a manifold. Suppose M has dimension n and is embedded in $\mathbb{R}^m$. For $M = SO(3)$, $n = 3$ and $m = 9$. For $M = \mathbb{S}^2$, $n = 2$ and $m = 3$. The number of coordinates should be n, the dimension of M; however, manifolds embedded in $\mathbb{R}^m$ are often expressed as a subset of $\mathbb{R}^m$ for which some equality constraints must be obeyed. We would like to express some part of M in terms of coordinates in $\mathbb{R}^n$.

Coordinates and parameterizations

For any open set $U \subseteq M$ and function $\phi : U \to \mathbb{R}^n$ such that ϕ is a homeomorphism onto a subset of $\mathbb{R}^n$, the pair (U, ϕ) is called a *coordinate neighborhood* (or *chart* in some literature). The values $\phi(p)$ for some $p \in U$ are called the *coordinates* of p.

Example 8.11 (Coordinate Neighborhoods on $\mathbb{S}^1$) A simple example can be obtained for the circle $M = \mathbb{S}^1$. Suppose M is expressed as the unit circle embedded in $\mathbb{R}^2$ (the set of solutions to $x^2 + y^2 = 1$). Let (x, y) denote a point in $\mathbb{R}^2$. Let U be the subset of $\mathbb{S}^1$ for which $x > 0$. A coordinate function $\phi : U \to (-\pi/2, \pi/2)$, can be defined as $\phi(x, y) = \tan^{-1}(y/x)$.

Let $W = \phi(U)$ (the range of ϕ) for some coordinate neighborhood (U, ϕ). Since U and W are homeomorphic via ϕ, the inverse function ϕ^{-1} can also be defined. It turns out that the inverse is the familiar idea of a *parameterization*. Continuing Example 8.11, ϕ^{-1} yields the mapping $\theta \mapsto (\cos\theta, \sin\theta)$, which is the familiar parameterization of the circle but restricted to $\theta \in (-\pi/2, \pi/2)$. ∎

To make differentiation work at a point $p \in M$, it will be important to have a coordinate neighborhood defined over an open subset of M that contains p. This is mainly because defining derivatives of a function at a point requires that an open set exists around the point. If the coordinates appear to have no boundary, then this will be possible. It is unfortunately not possible to cover all of M with a single coordinate neighborhood, unless $M = \mathbb{R}^n$ (or M is at least homeomorphic to $\mathbb{R}^n$). We must therefore define multiple neighborhoods for which the domains cover all of M. Since every domain is an open set, some of these domains must overlap. What happens in this case? We may have two or more alternative coordinates for the same point. Moving from one set of coordinates to another is the familiar operation used in calculus called a *change of coordinates*. This will now be formalized.

Suppose that (ϕ, U) and (ψ, V) are coordinate neighborhoods on some manifold M, and $U \cap V \neq \emptyset$. Figure 8.9 indicates how to change coordinates from ϕ to ψ. This change of coordinates is expressed using function composition as $\psi \circ \phi^{-1} : \mathbb{R}^n \to \mathbb{R}^n$ (ϕ^{-1} maps from $\mathbb{R}^n$ into M, and ψ maps from a subset of M to $\mathbb{R}^n$).

Example 8.12 (Change of Coordinates) Consider changing from Euler angles to quaternions for $M = SO(3)$. Since $SO(3)$ is a 3D manifold, $n = 3$. This means that any coordinate neighborhood must map a point in $SO(3)$ to a point in $\mathbb{R}^3$. We can construct a coordinate function $\phi : SO(3) \to \mathbb{R}^3$ by computing Euler angles from a given rotation matrix. The functions are actually defined in (3.47), (3.48), and (3.49). To make this a coordinate neighborhood, an open subset U of M must be specified.

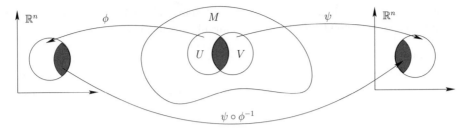

Figure 8.9: An illustration of a change of coordinates.

We can construct another coordinate function $\psi : SO(3) \to \mathbb{R}^3$ by using quaternions. This may appear to be a problem because quaternions have four components; however, the fourth component can be determined from the other three. Using (4.24) to (4.26), the a, b, and c coordinates can be determined.

Now suppose that we would like to change from Euler angles to quaternions in the overlap region $U \cap V$, in which V is an open set on which the coordinate neighborhood for quaternions is defined. The task is to construct a change of coordinates, $\psi \circ \phi^{-1}$. We first have to invert ϕ over U. This means that we instead need a parameterization of M in terms of Euler angles. This is given by (3.42), which yields a rotation matrix, $\phi^{-1}(\alpha, \beta, \gamma) \in SO(3)$ for α, β, and γ. Once this matrix is determined, then ψ can be applied to it to determine the quaternion parameters, a, b, and c. This means that we have constructed three real-valued functions, f_1, f_2, and f_3, which yield $a = f_1(\alpha, \beta, \gamma)$, $b = f_2(\alpha, \beta, \gamma)$, and $c = f_3(\alpha, \beta, \gamma)$. Together, these define $\psi \circ \phi^{-1}$. ∎

There are several reasons for performing coordinate changes in various contexts. Example 8.12 is motivated by a change that frequently occurs in motion planning. Imagine, for example, that a graphics package displays objects using quaternions, but a collision-detection algorithm uses Euler angles. It may be necessary in such cases to frequently change coordinates. From studies of calculus, you may recall changing coordinates to simplify an integral. In the definition of a smooth manifold, another motivation arises. Since coordinate neighborhoods are based on homeomorphisms of open sets, several may be required just to cover all of M. For example, even if we decide to use quaternions for $SO(3)$, several coordinate neighborhoods that map to quaternions may be needed. On the intersections of their domains, a change of coordinates is necessary.

Now we are ready to define a smooth manifold. Changes of coordinates will appear in the manifold definition, and they must satisfy a smoothness condition. A *smooth structure*[5] on a (topological) manifold M is a family[6] $\mathcal{U} = \{U_\alpha, \phi_\alpha\}$ of coordinate neighborhoods such that:

1. The union of all U_α contains M. Thus, it is possible to obtain coordinates in $\mathbb{R}^n$ for any point in M.

2. For any (U, ϕ) and (V, ϕ) in $\mathcal{U}$, if $U \cap V \neq \emptyset$, then the changes of coordinates, $\psi \circ \phi^{-1}$ and $\phi \circ \psi^{-1}$, are smooth functions on $U \cap V$. The changes of coordinates must produce diffeomorphisms on the intersections. In this case, the coordinate neighborhoods are called *compatible*.

---

[5] Alternative names are *differentiable structure* and C^∞ *structure*.

[6] In literature in which the coordinate neighborhoods are called *charts*, this family is called an *atlas*.

3. The family $\mathcal{U}$ is maximal in the sense that if some (U, ϕ) is compatible with every coordinate neighborhood in $\mathcal{U}$, then (U, ϕ) must be included in $\mathcal{U}$.

A well-known theorem (see [135], p. 54) states that if a set of compatible neighborhoods covers all of M, then a unique smooth structure exists that contains them.[7] This means that a differential structure can often be specified by a small number of neighborhoods, and the remaining ones are implied.

A manifold, as defined in Section 4.1.2, together with a smooth structure is called a *smooth manifold*.[8]

Example 8.13 ($\mathbb{R}^n$ as a Smooth Manifold)   We should expect that the concepts presented so far apply to $\mathbb{R}^n$, which is the most straightforward family of manifolds. A single coordinate neighborhood $\mathbb{R}^n \to \mathbb{R}^n$ can be used, which is the identity map. For all integers $n \in \{1, 2, 3\}$ and $n > 4$, this is the only possible smooth structure on $\mathbb{R}^n$. It is truly amazing that for $\mathbb{R}^4$, there are uncountably many incompatible smooth structures, called *exotic* $\mathbb{R}^4$ [293]. There is no need to worry, however; just use the one given by the identity map for $\mathbb{R}^4$.   ∎

Example 8.14 ($\mathbb{S}^n$ as a Smooth Manifold)   One way to define $\mathbb{S}^n$ as a smooth manifold uses $2(n + 1)$ coordinate neighborhoods and results in simple expressions. Let $\mathbb{S}^n$ be defined as

$$\mathbb{S}^n = \{(x_1, \ldots, x_{n+1}) \in \mathbb{R}^{n+1} \mid x_1^2 + \cdots + x_{n+1}^2 = 1\}. \tag{8.22}$$

The domain of each coordinate neighborhood is defined as follows. For each i from 1 to $n + 1$, there are two neighborhoods:

$$U_i^+ = \{(x_1, \ldots, x_{n+1}) \in \mathbb{R}^{n+1} \mid x_i > 0\} \tag{8.23}$$

and

$$U_i^- = \{(x_1, \ldots, x_{n+1}) \in \mathbb{R}^{n+1} \mid x_i < 0\}. \tag{8.24}$$

Each neighborhood is an open set that covers half of $\mathbb{S}^n$ but misses the great circle at $x_i = 0$. The coordinate functions can be defined by projection down to the $(n - 1)$-dimensional hyperplane that contains the great circle. For each i,

$$\phi_i^+(x_1, \ldots, x_{n+1}) = (x_1, \ldots, x_{i-1}, x_{i+1}, \ldots, x_n) \tag{8.25}$$

over U_i^+. Each ϕ_i^- is defined the same way, but over U_i^-. Each coordinate function is a homeomorphism from an open subset of $\mathbb{S}^n$ to an open subset of $\mathbb{R}^n$, as required. On the subsets in which the neighborhoods overlap, the changes of coordinate functions are smooth. For example, consider changing from ϕ_i^+ to ϕ_j^- for some $i \neq j$. The change of coordinates is a function $\phi_j^- \circ (\phi_i^+)^{-1}$. The inverse of ϕ_i^+ is expressed as

$$(\phi_i^+)^{-1}(x_1, \ldots, x_{i-1}, x_{i+1}, \ldots, x_n) =$$
$$(x_1, \ldots, x_{i-1}, 1 - \sqrt{1 - x_1^2 - \cdots - x_{i-1}^2 - x_{i+1}^2 - \cdots - x_n^2}, x_{i+1}, \ldots, x_{n+1}). \tag{8.26}$$

---

[7] This is under the assumption that M is Hausdorff and has a countable basis of open sets, which applies to the manifolds considered here.

[8] Alternative names are *differentiable manifold* and C^∞ *manifold*.

When composed with ϕ_j^-, the jth coordinate is dropped. This yields

$$\phi_k^- \circ (\phi_i^+)^{-1}(x_1, \ldots, x_{i-1}, x_{i+1}, \ldots, x_n) =$$
$$(x_1, \ldots, x_{i-1}, 1 - \sqrt{1 - x_1^2 - \cdots - x_{i-1}^2 - x_{i+1}^2 - \cdots - x_n^2},$$
$$x_{i+1}, \ldots, x_{j-1}, x_{j+1}, \ldots, x_n), \tag{8.27}$$

which is a smooth function over the domain U_i^+. Try visualizing the changes of coordinates for the circle $\mathbb{S}^1$ and sphere $\mathbb{S}^2$.

The smooth structure can alternatively be defined using only two coordinate neighborhoods by using *stereographic projection*. For $\mathbb{S}^2$, one coordinate function maps almost every point $x \in \mathbb{S}^2$ to $\mathbb{R}^2$ by drawing a ray from the north pole to x and mapping to the point in the $x_3 = 0$ plane that is crossed by the ray. The only excluded point is the north pole itself. A similar mapping can be constructed from the south pole. ∎

Example 8.15 ($\mathbb{RP}^n$ as a Smooth Manifold) This example is particularly important because $\mathbb{RP}^3$ is the same manifold as $SO(3)$, as established in Section 4.2.2. Recall from Section 4.1.2 that $\mathbb{RP}^n$ is defined as the set of all lines in $\mathbb{R}^{n+1}$ that pass through the origin. This means that for any $\alpha \in \mathbb{R}$ such that $\alpha \neq 0$, and any $x \in \mathbb{R}^{n+1}$, both x and αx are identified. In projective space, scale does not matter.

A smooth structure can be specified by only $n + 1$ coordinate neighborhoods. For each i from 1 to $n + 1$, let

$$\phi_i(x_1, \ldots, x_{n+1}) = (x_1/x_i, \ldots, x_{i-1}/x_i, x_{i+1}/x_i, \ldots, x_n/x_i), \tag{8.28}$$

over the open set of all points in $\mathbb{R}^{n+1}$ for which $x_i \neq 0$. The inverse coordinate function is given by

$$\phi_i^{-1}(z_1, \ldots, z_n) = (z_1, \ldots, z_{i-1}, 1, z_i, \ldots, z_{n+1}). \tag{8.29}$$

It is not hard to verify that these simple transformations are smooth on overlapping neighborhoods.

A smooth structure over $SO(3)$ can be derived as a special case because $SO(3)$ is topologically equivalent to $\mathbb{RP}^3$. Suppose elements of $SO(3)$ are expressed using unit quaternions. Each (a, b, c, d) is considered as a point on $\mathbb{S}^3$. There are four coordinate neighborhoods. For example, one of them is

$$\phi_b(a, b, c, d) = (a/b, \ c/b, \ d/b), \tag{8.30}$$

which is defined over the subset of $\mathbb{R}^4$ for which $b \neq 0$. The inverse of $\phi_b(a, b, c, d)$ needs to be defined so that a point on $SO(3)$ maps to a point in $\mathbb{R}^4$ that has unit magnitude. ∎

Tangent spaces on manifolds

Now consider defining tangent spaces on manifolds. Intuitively, the tangent space $T_p(M)$ at a point p on an n-dimensional manifold M is an n-dimensional hyperplane in $\mathbb{R}^m$ that best approximates M around p, when the hyperplane origin is translated to p. This is depicted in Figure 8.8. The notion of a tangent was actually used in Section 7.4.1 to describe local motions for motion planning of closed kinematic chains (see Figure 7.22).

To define a tangent space on a manifold, we first consider a more complicated definition of the tangent space at a point in $\mathbb{R}^n$, in comparison to what was given in Section 8.3.1. Suppose that $M = \mathbb{R}^2$, and consider taking directional derivatives of a smooth function

$f : \mathbb{R}^2 \to \mathbb{R}$ at a point $p \in \mathbb{R}^2$. For some (unnormalized) direction vector, $v \in \mathbb{R}^2$, the directional derivative of f at p can be defined as

$$\nabla_v(f)\Big|_p = v_1 \frac{\partial f}{\partial x_1}\Big|_p + v_2 \frac{\partial f}{\partial x_2}\Big|_p. \tag{8.31}$$

The directional derivative used here does not normalize the direction vector (contrary to basic calculus). Hence, $\nabla_v(f) = \nabla(f) \cdot v$, in which "$\cdot$" denotes the inner product or dot product, and $\nabla(f)$ denotes the gradient of f. The set of all possible direction vectors that can be used in this construction forms a two-dimensional vector space that happens to be the tangent space $T_p(\mathbb{R}^2)$, as defined previously. This can be generalized to n dimensions to obtain

$$\nabla_v(f)\Big|_p = \sum_{i=1}^{n} v_i \frac{\partial f}{\partial x_i}\Big|_p, \tag{8.32}$$

for which all possible direction vectors represent the tangent space $T_p(\mathbb{R}^n)$. The set of all directions can be interpreted for our purposes as the set of possible velocity vectors.

Now consider taking (unnormalized) directional derivatives of a smooth function, $f : M \to \mathbb{R}$, on a manifold. For an n-dimensional manifold, the tangent space $T_p(M)$ at a point $p \in M$ can be considered once again as the set of all unnormalized directions. These directions must intuitively be tangent to the manifold, as depicted in Figure 8.8. There exists a clever way to define them without even referring to specific coordinate neighborhoods. This leads to a definition of $T_p(M)$ that is intrinsic to the manifold.

At this point, you may accept that $T_p(M)$ is an n-dimensional vector space that is affixed to M at p and oriented as shown in Figure 8.8. For the sake of completeness, however, a technical definition of $T_p(M)$ from differential geometry will be given; more details appear in [135, 874]. The construction is based on characterizing the set of all possible directional derivative operators. Let $C^\infty(p)$ denote the set of all smooth functions that have domains that include p. Now make the following identification. Any two functions $f, g \in C^\infty(p)$ are defined to be *equivalent* if there exists an open set $U \subset M$ such that for any $p \in U$, $f(p) = g(p)$. There is no need to distinguish equivalent functions because their derivatives must be the same at p. Let $\tilde{C}^\infty(p)$ denote C^∞ under this identification. A directional derivative operator at p can be considered as a function that maps from $\tilde{C}^\infty(p)$ to $\mathbb{R}$ for some direction. In the case of $\mathbb{R}^n$, the operator appears as ∇_v for each direction v. Think about the set of all directional derivative operators that can be made. Each one must assign a real value to every function in $\tilde{C}^\infty(p)$, and it must obey two axioms from calculus regarding directional derivatives. Let ∇_v denote a directional derivative operator at some $p \in M$ (be careful, however, because here v is not explicitly represented since there are no coordinates). The directional derivative operator must satisfy two axioms:

1. **Linearity:** For any $\alpha, \beta \in \mathbb{R}$ and $f, g \in \tilde{C}^\infty(p)$,

$$\nabla_v(\alpha f + \beta g) = \alpha \nabla_v f + \beta \nabla_v g. \tag{8.33}$$

2. **Leibniz Rule (or Derivation):** For any $f, g \in \tilde{C}^\infty(p)$,

$$\nabla_v(fg) = \nabla_v f \, g(p) + f(p) \nabla_v g. \tag{8.34}$$

You may recall these axioms from standard vector calculus as properties of the directional derivative. It can be shown that the set of all possible operators that satisfy these axioms forms an n-dimensional vector space [135]. This vector space is called the *tangent space*,

$T_p(M)$, at p. This completes the definition of the tangent space without referring to coordinates.

It is helpful, however, to have an explicit way to express vectors in $T_p(M)$. A basis for the tangent space can be obtained by using coordinate neighborhoods. An important theorem from differential geometry states that if $F : M \rightarrow N$ is a diffeomorphism onto an open set $U \subset N$, then the tangent space, $T_p(M)$, is isomorphic to $T_{F(p)}(N)$. This means that by using a parameterization (the inverse of a coordinate neighborhood), there is a bijection between velocity vectors in $T_p(M)$ and velocity vectors in $T_{F(p)}(N)$. Small perturbations in the parameters cause motions in the tangent directions on the manifold N. Imagine, for example, making a small perturbation to three quaternion parameters that are used to represent $SO(3)$. If the perturbation is small enough, motions that are tangent to $SO(3)$ occur. In other words, the perturbed matrices will lie very close to $SO(3)$ (they will not lie in $SO(3)$ because $SO(3)$ is defined by nonlinear constraints on $\mathbb{R}^9$, as discussed in Section 4.1.2).

Example 8.16 (The Tangent Space for $\mathbb{S}^2$) The discussion can be made more concrete by developing the tangent space for $\mathbb{S}^2$, which is embedded in $\mathbb{R}^3$ as the set of all points $(x, y, z) \in \mathbb{R}^3$ for which $x^2 + y^2 + z^2 = 1$. A coordinate neighborhood can be defined that covers most of $\mathbb{S}^2$ by using standard spherical coordinates. Let f denote the coordinate function, which maps from (x, y, z) to angles (θ, ϕ). The domain of f is the open set defined by $\theta \in (0, 2\pi)$ and $\phi \in (0, \pi)$ (this excludes the poles). The standard formulas are $\theta = \text{atan2}(y, x)$ and $\phi = \cos^{-1} z$. The inverse, f^{-1}, yields a parameterization, which is $x = \cos\theta \sin\phi$, $y = \sin\theta \sin\phi$, and $z = \cos\phi$.

Now consider different ways to express the tangent space at some point $p \in \mathbb{S}^2$, other than the poles (a change of coordinates is needed to cover these). Using the coordinates (θ, ϕ), velocities can be defined as vectors in $\mathbb{R}^2$. We can imagine moving in the plane defined by θ and ϕ, provided that the limits $\theta \in (0, 2\pi)$ and $\phi \in (0, \pi)$ are respected.

We can also use the parameterization to derive basis vectors for the tangent space as vectors in $\mathbb{R}^3$. Since the tangent space has only two dimensions, we must obtain a plane that is "tangent" to the sphere at p. These can be found by taking derivatives. Let f^{-1} be denoted as $x(\theta, \phi)$, $y(\theta, \phi)$, and $z(\theta, \phi)$. Two basis vectors for the tangent plane at p are

$$\left[\frac{dx(\theta, \phi)}{d\theta} \quad \frac{dy(\theta, \phi)}{d\theta} \quad \frac{dz(\theta, \phi)}{d\theta} \right] \tag{8.35}$$

and

$$\left[\frac{dx(\theta, \phi)}{d\phi} \quad \frac{dy(\theta, \phi)}{d\phi} \quad \frac{dz(\theta, \phi)}{d\phi} \right]. \tag{8.36}$$

Computing these derivatives and normalizing yields the vectors $[-\sin\theta \quad \cos\theta \quad 0]$ and $[\cos\theta \cos\phi \quad \sin\theta \cos\phi \quad -\sin\phi]$. These can be imagined as the result of making small perturbations of θ and ϕ at p. The vector space obtained by taking all linear combinations of these vectors is the tangent space at $\mathbb{R}^2$. Note that the direction of the basis vectors depends on $p \in \mathbb{S}^2$, as expected.

The tangent vectors can now be imagined as lying in a plane that is tangent to the surface, as shown in Figure 8.8. The normal vector to a surface specified as $g(x, y, z) = 0$ is ∇g, which yields $[x \quad y \quad z]$ after normalizing. This could alternatively be obtained by taking the cross product of the two vectors above and using the parameterization f^{-1} to express it in terms of x, y, and z. For a point $p = (x_0, y_0, z_0)$, the plane equation is

$$x_0(x - x_0) + y_0(y - y_0) + z_0(z - z_0) = 0. \tag{8.37}$$

∎

Vector fields and velocity fields on manifolds

The notation for a tangent space on a manifold looks the same as for $\mathbb{R}^n$. This enables the vector field definition and notation to extend naturally from $\mathbb{R}^n$ to smooth manifolds. A *vector field* on a manifold M assigns a vector in $T_p(M)$ for every $p \in M$. It can once again be imagined as a needle diagram, but now the needle diagram is spread over the manifold, rather than lying in $\mathbb{R}^n$.

The velocity field interpretation of a vector field can also be extended to smooth manifolds. This means that $\dot{x} = f(x)$ now defines a set of n differential equations over M and is usually expressed using a coordinate neighborhood of the smooth structure. If f is a smooth vector field, then a *solution trajectory*, $\tau : [0, \infty) \to M$, can be defined from any $x_0 \in M$. Solution trajectories in the sense of Filipov can also be defined, for the case of piecewise-smooth vector fields.

8.4 Complete methods for continuous spaces

A complete feedback planning algorithm must compute a feedback solution if one exists; otherwise, it must report failure. Section 8.4.1 parallels Section 8.2 by defining feedback plans and navigation functions for the case of a continuous state space. Section 8.4.2 indicates how to define a feasible feedback plan from a cell complex that was computed using cell decomposition techniques. Section 8.4.3 presents a combinatorial approach to computing an optimal navigation function and corresponding feedback plan in $\mathbb{R}^2$. Sections 8.4.2 and 8.4.3 allow the feedback plan to be a discontinuous vector field. In many applications, especially those in which dynamics dominate, some conditions need to be enforced on the navigation functions and their resulting vector fields. Section 8.4.4 therefore considers constraints on the allowable vector fields and navigation functions. This coverage includes navigation functions in the sense of Rimon-Koditschek [832], from which the term navigation function was introduced.

8.4.1 Feedback motion planning definitions

Using the concepts from Section 8.3, we are now ready to define feedback motion planning over configuration spaces or other continuous state spaces. Recall Formulation 4.1, which defined the basic motion planning problem in terms of configuration space. The differences in the current setting are that there is no initial condition, and the requirement of a solution path is replaced by a solution vector field. The formulation here can be considered as a continuous-time adaptation to Formulation 8.1.

Formulation 8.2 (Feedback Motion Planning)

1. A *state space*, X, which is a smooth manifold. The state space will most often be $\mathcal{C}_{free}$, as defined in Section 4.3.1.[9]

---

[9] Note that X already excludes the obstacle region. For some problems in Part IV, the state space will be $X = \mathcal{C}$, which includes the obstacle region.

2. For each state, $x \in X$, an *action space*, $U(x) = T_x(X)$. The zero velocity, $0 \in T_x(X)$, is designated as the termination action, u_T. Using this model, the robot is capable of selecting its velocity at any state.[10]

3. An unbounded *time interval*, $T = [0, \infty)$.

4. A *state transition (differential) equation*,

$$\dot{x} = u, \tag{8.38}$$

which is expressed using a coordinate neighborhood and yields the velocity, $\dot{x}$, directly assigned by the action u. The velocity produced by u_T is $0 \in T_x(X)$ (which means "stop").

5. A *goal set*, $X_G \subset X$.

A *feedback plan*, π, for Formulation 8.2 is defined as a function π, which produces an action $u \in U(x)$ for each $x \in X$. A feedback plan can equivalently be considered as a vector field on X because each $u \in U(x)$ specifies a velocity vector (u_T specifies zero velocity). Since the initial state is not fixed, it becomes slightly more complicated to define what it means for a plan to be a solution to the problem. Let $X_r \subset X$ denote the set of all states from which X_G is *reachable*. More precisely, a state x_I belongs to X_r if and only if a continuous path $\tau : [0, 1] \to X$ exists for which $\tau(0) = x_I$ and $\tau(1) = x_G$ for some $x_G \in X_G$. This means that a solution path exists from x_I for the "open-loop" motion planning problem, which was considered in Chapter 4.

8.4.1.1 Solution concepts

A feedback plan, π, is called a *solution* to the problem in Formulation 8.2 if from all $x_I \in X_r$, the integral curves of π (considered as a vector field) arrive in X_G, at which point the termination action is applied. Some words of caution must be given about what it means to "arrive" in X_G. Notions of stability from control theory [526, 848] are useful for distinguishing different cases; see Section 15.1. If X_G is a small ball centered on x_G, then the ball will be reached after finite time using the inward vector field shown in Figure 8.5b. Now suppose that X_G is a single point, x_G. The inward vector field produces velocities that bring the state closer and closer to the origin, but when is it actually reached? It turns out that convergence to the origin in this case is only *asymptotic*; the origin is reached in the limit as the time approaches infinity. Such stability often arises in control theory from smooth vector fields. We may allow such asymptotic convergence to the goal (if the vector field is smooth and the goal is a point, then this is unavoidable). If any integral curves result in only asymptotic convergence to the goal, then a solution plan is called an *asymptotic solution plan*. Note that in general it may be impossible to require that π is a smooth (or even continuous) nonzero vector field. For example, due to the *hairy ball theorem* [837], it is known that no such vector field exists for $\mathbb{S}^n$ for any even integer n. Therefore, the strongest possible requirement is that π is smooth except on a set of measure zero; see Section 8.4.4. We may also allow solutions π for which *almost all* integral curves arrive in X_G.

However, it will be assumed by default in this chapter that a solution plan converges to x_G in finite time. For example, if the inward field is normalized to produce unit speed everywhere except the origin, then the origin will be reached in finite time. A constraint

---

[10] This allows discontinuous changes in velocity, which is unrealistic in many applications. Additional constraints, such as imposing acceleration bounds, will also be discussed. For a complete treatment of differential constraints, see Part IV.

can be placed on the set of allowable vector fields without affecting the existence of a solution plan. As in the basic motion planning problem, the speed along the path is not important. Let a *normalized vector field* be any vector field for which either $\| f(x) \| = 1$ or $f(x) = 0$, for all $x \in X$. This means that all velocity vectors are either unit vectors or the zero vector, and the speed is no longer a factor. A normalized vector field provides either a direction of motion or no motion. Note that any vector field f can be converted into a normalized vector field by dividing the velocity vector $f(x)$ by its magnitude (unless the magnitude is zero), for each $x \in X$.

In many cases, unit speed does not necessarily imply a constant speed in some true physical sense. For example, if the robot is a floating rigid body, there are many ways to parameterize position and orientation. The speed of the body is sensitive to this parameterization. Therefore, other constraints may be preferable instead of $\| f(x) \| = 1$; however, it is important to keep in mind that the constraint is imposed so that $f(x)$ provides a *direction* at x. The particular magnitude is assumed unimportant.

So far, consideration has been given only to a *feasible feedback motion planning problem*. An *optimal feedback motion planning problem* can be defined by introducing a cost functional. Let $\tilde{x}_t$ denote the function $\tilde{x}_t : [0, t] \to X$, which is called the *state trajectory* (or *state history*). This is a continuous-time version of the state history, which was defined previously for problems that have discrete stages. Similarly, let $\tilde{u}_t$ denote the *action trajectory* (or *action history*), $\tilde{u}_t : [0, t] \to U$. Let L denote a cost functional, which may be applied from any x_I to yield

$$L(\tilde{x}_{t_F}, \tilde{u}_{t_F}) = \int_0^{t_F} l(x(t), u(t))dt + l_F(x(t_F)), \qquad (8.39)$$

in which t_F is the time at which the termination action is applied. The term $l(x(t), u(t))$ can alternatively be expressed as $l(x(t), \dot{x}(t))$ by using the state transition equation (8.38). A normalized vector field that optimizes (8.39) from all initial states that can reach the goal is considered as an *optimal feedback motion plan*.

Note that the state trajectory can be determined from an action history and initial state. In fact, we could have used action trajectories to define a solution path to the motion planning problem of Chapter 4. Instead, a solution was defined there as a path $\tau : [0, 1] \to \mathcal{C}_{free}$ to avoid having to introduce velocity fields on smooth manifolds. That was the only place in the book in which the action space seemed to disappear, and now you can see that it was only hiding to avoid inessential notation.

8.4.1.2 Navigation functions

As in Section 8.2.2, potential functions can be used to represent feedback plans, assuming that a local operator is developed that works for continuous state spaces. In the discrete case, the local operator selects an action that reduces the potential value. In the continuous case, the local operator must convert the potential function into a vector field. In other words, a velocity vector must be defined at each state. By default, it will be assumed here that the vector fields derived from the navigation function are not necessarily normalized.

Assume that $\pi(x) = u_T$ is defined for all $x \in X_G$, regardless of the potential function. Suppose that a potential function $\phi : X \to \mathbb{R}$ has been defined for which the gradient

$$\nabla \phi = \left[\frac{\partial \phi}{\partial x_1} \quad \frac{\partial \phi}{\partial x_2} \quad \cdots \quad \frac{\partial \phi}{\partial x_n} \right] \qquad (8.40)$$

exists over all of $X \setminus X_G$. The corresponding feedback plan can then be defined as $\pi(x) = -\nabla \phi|_x$. This defines the local operator, which means that the velocity is taken in the direction of the steepest descent of ϕ. The idea of using potential functions in this way was proposed for robotics by Khatib [528, 529] and can be considered as a form of *gradient descent*, which is a general optimization technique.

It is also possible to work with potential functions for which the gradient does not exist everywhere. In these cases, a continuous-space version of (8.4) can be defined for a small, fixed Δt as

$$u^* = \operatorname*{argmin}_{u \in U(x)} \left\{ \phi(x') \right\}, \qquad (8.41)$$

in which x' is the state obtained by integrating velocity u from x for time Δt. One problem is that Δt should be chosen to use the smallest possible neighborhood around ϕ. It is best to allow only potential functions for which Δt can be made arbitrarily small at every x without affecting the decision in (8.41). To be precise, this means that an infinite sequence of u^* values can be determined from a sequence of Δt values that converges to 0. A potential function should then be chosen to ensure after some point in the sequence, u^*, exists and the same u^* can be chosen to satisfy (8.41) as Δt approaches 0. A special case of this is if the gradient of ϕ exists; the infinite sequence in this case converges to the negative gradient.

A potential function, ϕ, is called a *navigation function* if the vector field that is derived from it is a solution plan. The optimal cost-to-go serves as an *optimal navigation function*. If multiple vector fields can be derived from the same ϕ, then every possible derived vector field must yield a solution feedback plan. If designed appropriately, the potential function can be viewed as a kind of "ski slope" that guides the state to X_G. If there are extra local minima that cause the state to become trapped, then X_G will not be reached. To be a navigation function, such local minima outside of X_G are not allowed. Furthermore, there may be additional requirements to ensure that the derived vector field satisfies additional constraints, such as bounded acceleration.

Example 8.17 (Quadratic Potential Function)   As a simple example, suppose $X = \mathbb{R}^2$, there are no obstacles, and $q_{goal} = (0, 0)$. A quadratic function $\phi(x, y) = \frac{1}{2}x_1^2 + \frac{1}{2}x_2^2$ serves as a good potential function to guide the state to the goal. The feedback motion strategy is defined as $f = -\nabla \phi = [-x_1 \quad -x_2]$, which is the inward vector field shown in Figure 8.5b.

If the goal is instead at some $(x_1', x_2') \in \mathbb{R}^2$, then a potential function that guides the state to the goal is $\phi(x_1, x_2) = (x_1 - x_1')^2 + (x_2 - x_2')^2$.   ∎

Suppose the state space represents a configuration space that contains point obstacles. The previous function ϕ can be considered as an attractive potential because the configuration is attracted to the goal. One can also construct a repulsive potential that repels the configuration from the obstacles to avoid collision. Let ϕ_a denote the attractive component and ϕ_r denote a repulsive potential that is summed over all obstacle points. A potential function of the form $\phi = \phi_a + \phi_r$ can be defined to combine both effects. The robot should be guided to the goal while avoiding obstacles. The problem is that it is difficult in general to ensure that the potential function will not contain multiple local minima. The configuration could become trapped at a local minimum that is not in the goal region. This was an issue with the planner from Section 5.4.3.

8.4.2 Vector fields over cell complexes

This section describes how to construct a piecewise-smooth vector field over a cell complex. Only normalized vector fields will be considered. It is assumed that each cell in the complex has a simple shape over which it is easy to define a patch of the vector field. In many cases, the cell decomposition techniques that were introduced in Chapter 6 for motion planning can be applied to construct a feedback plan.

Suppose that an n-dimensional state space X has been decomposed into a cell complex, such as a simplicial complex or singular complex, as defined in Section 6.3.1. Assume that the goal set is a single point, x_G. Defining a feedback plan π over X requires placing a vector field on X for which all integral curves lead to x_G (if x_G is reachable). This is accomplished by defining a smooth vector field for each n-cell. Each $(n-1)$-cell is a switching boundary, as considered in Section 8.3.1. This leads directly to solution trajectories in the sense of Filipov. If π is allowed to be discontinuous, then it is actually not important to specify values on any of the cells of dimension $n-1$ or less.

A hierarchical approach is taken to the construction of π:

1. Define a discrete planning problem over the n-cells. The cell that contains x_G is designated as the goal, and a discrete navigation function is defined over the cells.

2. Define a vector field over each n-cell. The field should cause all states in the cell to flow into the next cell as prescribed by the discrete navigation function.

One additional consideration that is important in applications is to try to reduce the effect of the discontinuity across the boundary as much as possible. It may be possible to eliminate the discontinuity, or even construct a smooth transition between n-cells. This issue will not be considered here, but it is nevertheless quite important [237, 646].

The approach will now be formalized. Suppose that a cell complex has been defined over a continuous state space, X. Let $\check{X}$ denote the set of n-cells, which can be interpreted as a finite state space. A discrete planning problem will be defined over $\check{X}$. To avoid confusion with the original continuous problem, the prefix *super* will be applied to the discrete planning components. Each superstate $\check{x} \in \check{X}$ corresponds to an n-cell. From each $\check{x}$, a superaction, $\check{u} \in \check{U}(\check{x})$ exists for each neighboring n-cell (to be neighboring, the two cells must share an $(n-1)$-dimensional boundary). Let the goal superstate $\check{x}_g$ be the n-cell that contains x_G. Assume that the cost functional is defined for the discrete problem so that every action (other than u_T) produces a unit cost. Now the concepts from Section 8.2 can be applied to the discrete problem. A discrete navigation function, $\check{\phi} : \check{X} \to \mathbb{R}$, can be computed using Dijkstra's algorithm (or another algorithm, particularly if optimality is not important). Using the discrete local operator from Section 8.2.2, this results in a discrete feedback plan, $\check{\pi} : \check{X} \to \check{U}$.

Based on the discrete feedback plan, there are two kinds of n-cells. The first is the goal cell, $\check{x}_g$, for which a vector field needs to be defined so that all integral curves lead to X_g in finite time.[11] A termination action can be applied when x_G is actually reached. The remaining n-cells are of the second kind. For each cell $\check{x}$, the boundary that is shared with the cell reached by applying $\check{u} = \check{\pi}(\check{x})$ is called the *exit face*. The vector field over the n-cell $\check{x}$ must be defined so that all integral curves lead to the exit face. When the exit

---

[11] This is possible in finite time, even if X_g is a single point, because the vector field is not continuous. Otherwise, only asymptotic convergence may be possible.

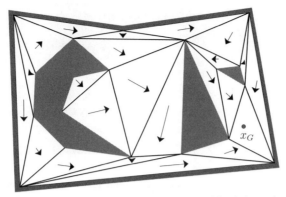

Figure 8.10: A triangulation is used to define a vector field over X. All solution trajectories lead to the goal.

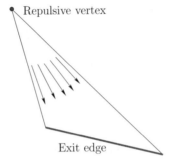

Figure 8.11: A vector field can be defined for each triangle by repelling from a vertex that opposes the exit edge.

face is reached, a transition will occur into the next n-cell. If the n-cells are convex, then defining this transition is straightforward (unless there are additional requirements on the field, such as smoothness at the boundary). For more complicated cells, one possibility is to define a vector field that retracts all points onto a single curve in the cell.

A simple example of the approach is illustrated for the case of $X = \mathcal{C}_{free} \subset \mathbb{R}^2$, in which the boundary of $\mathcal{C}_{free}$ is polygonal. This motion planning problem was considered in Section 6.2, but without feedback. Suppose that a triangulation of X has been computed, as described in Section 6.3.2. An example was shown in Figure 6.16. A discrete feedback plan is shown for a particular goal state in Figure 8.10. Each 2-cell (triangle) is labeled with an arrow that points to the next cell.

For the cell that contains x_G, a normalized version of the inward vector field shown in Figure 8.5b can be formed by dividing each nonzero vector by its magnitude. It can then be translated to move its origin to x_G. For each remaining 2-cell, a vector field must be constructed that flows into the appropriate neighboring cell. Figure 8.11 illustrates a simple way to achieve this. An outward vector field can be made by negating the field shown in Figure 8.5b to obtain $f = [x \ y]$. This field can be normalized and translated to move the origin to the triangle vertex that is not incident to the exit edge. This is called the *repulsive vertex* in Figure 8.11. This generates a vector field that pushes all points in the triangle to the ext edge. If the fields are constructed in this way for each triangle, then the global vector field represents a solution feedback plan for the problem. Integral curves (in the sense of Filipov) lead to x_G in finite time.

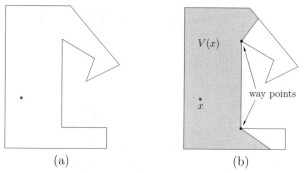

Figure 8.12: (a) A point, x, in a simple polygon. (b) The visibility polygon, V(x).

8.4.3 Optimal navigation functions

The vector fields developed in the last section yield feasible trajectories, but not necessarily optimal trajectories unless the initial and goal states are in the same convex n-cell. If $X = \mathbb{R}^2$, then it is possible to make a continuous version of Dijkstra's algorithm [711]. This results in an exact cost-to-go function over X based on the Euclidean shortest path to a goal, x_G. The cost-to-go function serves as the navigation function, from which the feedback plan is defined by using a local steepest descent.

Suppose that X is bounded by a simple polygon (no holes). Assume that only normalized vector fields are allowed. The cost functional is assumed to be the Euclidean distance traveled along a state trajectory. Recall from Section 6.2.4 that for optimal path planning, $X = \text{cl}(\mathcal{C}_{free})$ must be used. Assume that $\mathcal{C}_{free}$ and $\text{cl}(\mathcal{C}_{free})$ have the same connectivity.[12] This technically interferes with the definition of tangent spaces from Section 8.3 because each point of X must be contained in an open neighborhood. Nevertheless, we allow vectors along the boundary, provided that they "point" in a direction tangent to the boundary. This can be formally defined by considering boundary regions as separate manifolds.

Consider computing the optimal cost-to-go to a point x_G for a problem such as that shown in Figure 8.12a. For any $x \in X$, let the *visibility polygon* $V(x)$ refer to the set of all points visible from x, which is illustrated in Figure 8.12b. A point x' lies in $V(x)$ if and only if the line segment from x' to x is contained in X. This implies that the cost-to-go from x' to x is just the Euclidean distance from x' to x. The optimal navigation function can therefore be immediately defined over $V(x_G)$ as

$$\phi(x) = \|x - x_G\|. \tag{8.42}$$

Level sets at regularly spaced values of this navigation function are shown in Figure 8.13a.

How do we compute the optimal cost-to-go values for the points in $X \setminus V(x_G)$? For the segments on the boundary of $V(x)$ for any $x \in X$, some edges are contained in the boundary of X, and others cross the interior of X. For the example in Figure 8.12b, there are two edges that cross the interior. For each segment that crosses the interior, let the closer of the two vertices to x be referred to as a *way point*. Two way points are indicated in Figure 8.12b. The way points of $V(x_G)$ are places through which some optimal paths must cross. Let $W(x)$ for any $x \in X$ denote the set of way points of $V(x)$.

---

[12] This precludes a choice of $\mathcal{C}_{free}$ for which adding the boundary point enables a homotopically distinct path to be made through the boundary point. An example of this is when two square obstacles in $\mathbb{R}^2$ contact each other only at a pair of corners.

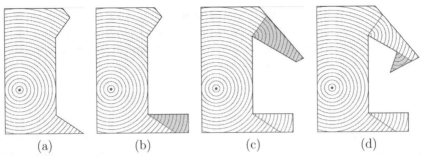

Figure 8.13: The optimal navigation function is computed in four iterations. In each iteration, the navigation function is extended from a new way point.

A straightforward algorithm proceeds as follows. Let Z_i denote the set of points over which ϕ has been defined, in the ith iteration of the algorithm. In the first iteration, $Z_1 = V(x_G)$, which is the case shown in Figure 8.13a. The way points of $V(x_G)$ are placed in a queue, Q. In each following iteration, a way point x is removed from Q. Let Z_i denote the domain over which ϕ is defined so far. The domain of ϕ is extended to include all new points visible from x. These new points are $V(x) \setminus Z_i$. This yields $Z_{i+1} = Z_i \cup V(x)$, the extended domain of ϕ. The values of $\phi(x')$ for $x' \in Z_{i+1} \setminus Z_i$ are defined by

$$\phi(x') = \phi(x) + \|x' - x\|, \tag{8.43}$$

in which x is the way point that was removed from Q (the optimal cost-to-go value of x was already computed). The way points of $V(x)$ that do not lie in Z_{i+1} are added to Q. Each of these will yield new portions of X that have not yet been seen. The algorithm terminates when Q is empty, which implies that $Z_k = X$ for some k. The execution of the algorithm is illustrated in Figure 8.13.

The visibility polygon can be computed in time $O(n \lg n)$ if X is described by n edges. This is accomplished by performing a *radial sweep*, which is an adaptation of the method applied in Section 6.2.2 for vertical cell decomposition. The difference for computing $V(x)$ is that a ray anchored at x is swept radially (like a radar sweep). The segments that intersect the ray are sorted by their distance from x. For the algorithm that constructs the navigation function, no more than $O(n)$ visibility polygons are computed because each one is computed from a unique way point. This implies $O(n^2 \lg n)$ running time for the whole algorithm. Unfortunately, there is no extension to higher dimensions; recall from Section 7.7.1 that computing shortest paths in a 3D environment is NP-hard [174].

The algorithm given here is easy to describe, but it is not the most general, nor the most efficient. If X has holes, then the level set curves can collide by arriving from different directions when traveling around an obstacle. The queue, Q, described above can be sorted as in Dijkstra's algorithm, and special data structures are needed to identify when critical events occur as the cost-to-go is propagated outward. It was shown in [446] that this can be done in time $O(n \lg n)$ and space $O(n \lg n)$.

8.4.4 A step toward considering dynamics

If dynamics is an important factor, then the discontinuous vector fields considered so far are undesirable. Due to momentum, a mechanical system cannot instantaneously change its velocity (see Section 13.3). In this context, vector fields should be required to satisfy additional constraints, such as smoothness or bounded acceleration. This represents only a step toward considering dynamics. Full consideration is given in Part IV, in which precise equations of motions of dynamical systems are expressed as part of the model. The approach in this section is to make vector fields that are "dynamics-ready" rather than carefully considering particular equations of motion.

A framework has been developed by defining a navigation function that satisfies some desired constraints over a simple region, such as a disc [832]. A set of transformations is then designed that are proved to preserve the constraints while adapting the navigation function to more complicated environments. For a given problem, a complete algorithm for constructing navigation functions is obtained by applying the appropriate series of transformations from some starting shape.

This section mostly focuses on constraints that are maintained under this transformation-based framework. Sections 8.4.2 and 8.4.3 worked with normalized vector fields. Under this constraint, virtually any vector field could be defined, provided that the resulting algorithm constructs fields for which integral curves exist in the sense of Filipov. In this section, we remove the constraint that vector fields must be normalized, and then consider other constraints. The velocity given by the vector field is now assumed to represent the true speed that must be executed when the vector field is applied as a feedback plan.

One implication of adding constraints to the vector field is that optimal solutions may not satisfy them. For example, the optimal navigation functions of Section 8.4.3 lead to discontinuous vector fields, which violate the constraints to be considered in this section. The required constraints restrict the set of allowable vector fields. Optimality must therefore be defined over the restricted set of vector fields. In some cases, an optimal solution may not even exist (see the discussion of open sets and optimality in Section 9.1.1). Therefore, this section focuses only on feasible solutions.

8.4.4.1 An acceleration-based control model

To motivate the introduction of constraints, consider a control model proposed in [237, 833]. The action space, defined as $U(x) = T_x(X)$ in Formulation 8.2, produces a velocity for each action $u \in U(x)$. Therefore, $\dot{x} = u$. Suppose instead that each action produces an acceleration. This can be expressed as $\ddot{x} = u$, in which $\ddot{x}$ is an *acceleration vector*,

$$\ddot{x} = \frac{d\dot{x}}{dt} = \left[\frac{d^2 x_1}{dt^2} \quad \frac{d^2 x_2}{dt^2} \quad \cdots \quad \frac{d^2 x_n}{dt^2} \right]. \tag{8.44}$$

The velocity $\dot{x}$ is obtained by integration over time. The state trajectory, $\tilde{x} : T \rightarrow X$, is obtained by integrating (8.44) twice.

Suppose that a vector field is given in the form $\dot{x} = f(x)$. How can a feedback plan be derived? Consider how the velocity vectors specified by $f(x)$ change as x varies. Assume that $f(x)$ is smooth (or at least C^1), and let

$$\nabla_{\dot{x}} f(x) = [\nabla_{\dot{x}} f_1(x) \quad \nabla_{\dot{x}} f_2(x) \quad \cdots \quad \nabla_{\dot{x}} f_n(x)], \tag{8.45}$$

in which $\nabla_{\dot{x}}$ denotes the unnormalized directional derivative in the direction of $\dot{x}$: $\nabla f_i \cdot \dot{x}$. Suppose that an initial state x_I is given, and that the initial velocity is $\dot{x} = f(x_I)$. The feedback plan can now be defined as

$$u = \nabla_{\dot{x}} f(x). \tag{8.46}$$

This is equivalent to the previous definition of a feedback plan from Section 8.4.1; the only difference is that now two integrations are needed (which requires both x and $\dot{x} = f(x_I)$ as initial conditions) and a differentiability condition must be satisfied for the vector field.

Now the relationship between $\dot{x}$ and $f(x)$ will be redefined. Suppose that $\dot{x}$ is the true measured velocity during execution and that $f(x)$ is the prescribed velocity, obtained from the vector field f. During execution, it is assumed that $\dot{x}$ and $f(x)$ are not necessarily the same, but the task is to keep them as close to each other as possible. A discrepancy between them may occur due to dynamics that have not been modeled. For example, if the field $f(x)$ requests that the velocity must suddenly change, a mobile robot may not be able to make a sharp turn due to its momentum.

Using the new interpretation, the difference, $f(x) - \dot{x}$, can be considered as a discrepancy or error. Suppose that a vector field f has been computed. A feedback plan becomes the *acceleration-based control* model

$$u = K(f(x) - \dot{x}) + \nabla_{\dot{x}} f(x), \qquad (8.47)$$

in which K is a scalar *gain constant*. A larger value of K will make the control system more aggressively attempt to reduce the error. If K is too large, then acceleration or energy constraints may be violated. Note that if $\dot{x} = f(x)$, then $u = \nabla_{\dot{x}} f(x)$, which becomes equivalent to the earlier formulation.

8.4.4.2 Velocity and acceleration constraints

Considering the acceleration-based control model, some constraints can be placed on the set of allowable vector fields. A *bounded-velocity model* means that $\|\dot{x}\| < v_{max}$, for some positive real value v_{max} called the *maximum speed*. This could indicate, for example, that the robot has a maximum speed for safety reasons. It is also possible to bound individual components of the velocity vector. For example, there may be separate bounds for the maximum angular and linear velocities of an aircraft. Intuitively, velocity bounds imply that the functions f_i, which define the vector field, cannot take on large values.

A *bounded-acceleration model* means that $\|\ddot{x}\| \leq a_{max}$, in which a_{max} is a positive real value called the *maximum acceleration*. Intuitively, acceleration bounds imply that the velocity cannot change too quickly while traveling along an integral curve. Using the control model $\ddot{x} = u$, this implies that $\|u\| \leq a_{max}$. It also imposes the constraint that vector fields must satisfy $\|\nabla_{\dot{x}} f(x)\| \leq a_{max}$ for all $\dot{x}$ and $x \in X$. The condition $\|u\| \leq a_{max}$ is very important in practice because higher accelerations are generally more expensive (bigger motors are required, more fuel is consumed, etc.). The action u may correspond directly to the torques that are applied to motors. In this case, each motor usually has an upper limit.

As has already been seen, setting an upper bound on velocity generally does not affect the existence of a solution. Imagine that a robot can always decide to travel more slowly. If there is also an upper bound on acceleration, then the robot can attempt to travel more slowly to satisfy the bound. Imagine slowing down in a car to make a sharp turn. If you would like to go faster, then it may be more difficult to satisfy acceleration constraints. Nevertheless, in most situations, it is preferable to go faster.

A discontinuous vector field fails to satisfy any acceleration bound because it essentially requires infinite acceleration at the discontinuity to cause a discontinuous jump in the velocity vector. If the vector field satisfies the Lipschitz condition (8.16) for some constant C, then it satisfies the acceleration bound if $C < a_{max}$.

In Chapter 13, we will precisely specify $U(x)$ at every $x \in X$, which is more general than imposing simple velocity and acceleration bounds. This enables virtually any physical system to be modeled.

8.4.4.3 Navigation function in the sense of Rimon-Koditschek

Now consider constructing a navigation function from which a vector field can be derived that satisfies constraints motivated by the acceleration-based control model, (8.47). As usual, the definition of a navigation function begins with the consideration of a potential function, $\phi : X \to \mathbb{R}$. What properties does a potential function need to have so that it may be considered as a navigation function as defined in Section 8.4.1 and also yield a vector field that satisfies an acceleration bound? Sufficient conditions will be given that imply that a potential function will be a navigation function that satisfies the bound.

To give the conditions, it will first be important to characterize extrema of multivariate functions. Recall from basic calculus that a function $f : \mathbb{R} \to \mathbb{R}$ has a critical point when the first derivative is zero. At such points, the sign of the second derivative indicates whether the critical point is a minimum or maximum. These ideas can be generalized to higher dimensions. A *critical point* of ϕ is one for which $\nabla \phi = 0$. The *Hessian* of ϕ is defined as the matrix

$$
H(\phi) = \begin{pmatrix}
\dfrac{\partial^2 \phi}{\partial^2 x_1^2} & \dfrac{\partial^2 \phi}{\partial x_1 \partial x_2} & \cdots & \dfrac{\partial^2 \phi}{\partial x_1 \partial x_n} \\[2mm]
\dfrac{\partial^2 \phi}{\partial x_2 \partial x_1} & \dfrac{\partial^2 \phi}{\partial x_2^2} & \cdots & \dfrac{\partial^2 \phi}{\partial x_2 \partial x_n} \\[2mm]
\vdots & \vdots & & \vdots \\[2mm]
\dfrac{\partial^2 \phi}{\partial x_n \partial x_1} & \dfrac{\partial^2 \phi}{\partial x_n \partial x_2} & \cdots & \dfrac{\partial^2 \phi}{\partial x_n^2}
\end{pmatrix} .
\tag{8.48}
$$

At each critical point, the Hessian gives some information about the extremum. If the rank of $H(\phi)$ at x is n, then the Hessian indicates the kind of extremum. If (8.48) is positive definite,[13] then the ϕ achieves a *local minimum* at x. If (8.48) is negative definite,[14] then the ϕ achieves a *local minimum* at x. In all other cases, x is a *saddle point*. If the rank of $H(\phi)$ at x is less than n, then the Hessian is *degenerate*. In this case the Hessian cannot classify the type of extremum. An example of this occurs when x lies in a plateau (there is no direction in which ϕ increases or decreases. Such behavior is obviously bad for a potential function because the local operator would not be able to select a direction.

Suppose that the navigation function is required to be smooth, to ensure the existence of a gradient at every point. This enables gradient descent to be performed. If X is not contractible, then it turns out there must exist some critical points other than x_G at which $\nabla \phi(x) = 0$. The critical points can even be used to infer the topology of X, which is the basic idea in the subject of *Morse theory* [704, 236]. Unfortunately, this implies that there does not exist a solution navigation function for such spaces because the definition

[13] Positive definite for an $n \times n$ matrix A means that for all $x \in \mathbb{R}^n$, $x^T A x > 0$. If A is symmetric (which applies to $H(\phi)$), then this is equivalent to A having all positive eigenvalues.

[14] Negative definite means that for all $x \in \mathbb{R}^n$, $x^T A x < 0$. If A is symmetric, then this is equivalent to A having all negative eigenvalues.

in Section 8.4.1 required that the integral curve from any state that can reach x_G must reach it using the vector field derived from the navigation function. If the initial state is a critical point, the integral curve is constant (the state remains at the critical point). Therefore, under the smoothness constraint, the definition of a navigation function should be modified to allow critical points at a small number of places (only on a set that has measure zero). It is furthermore required that the set of states from which the integral curves arrive at each critical point (i.e., the domain of attraction of each critical point) has measure zero. From all possible initial states, except from a set of measure zero, the integral curves must reach x_G, if it is reachable. This is ensured in the following definition.

A function $\phi : X \to \mathbb{R}$ is called a *navigation function in the sense of Rimon-Koditschek* if [832]:

1. It is smooth (or at least C^2).

2. Among all values on the connected component of $\mathcal{C}_{free}$ that contains x_G, there is only one local minimum, which is at x_G.[15]

3. It is maximal and constant on $\partial \mathcal{C}_{free}$, the boundary of $\mathcal{C}_{free}$.

4. It is a Morse function [704], which means that at each critical point x (i.e., $\nabla \phi|_x = 0$), the Hessian of ϕ is not degenerate.[16] Such functions are known to exist on any smooth manifold.

If ϕ is smooth in the C^∞ sense, then by Sard's Theorem [236] the set of critical points has measure zero.

Methods for constructing navigation functions are outlined in [832] for a general family of problems in which $\mathcal{C}_{free}$ has a semi-algebraic description. The basic idea is to start with simple shapes over which a navigation function can be easily defined. One example of this is a spherical subset of $\mathbb{R}^n$, which contains spherical obstacles. A set of distorting transformations is then developed to adapt the navigation functions to other shapes while ensuring that the four properties above are maintained. One such transformation extends a ball into any visibility region (in the sense defined in Section 8.4.3). This is achieved by smoothly stretching out the ball into the shape of the visibility region. (Such regions are sometimes called *star-shaped*.) The transformations given in [832] can be combined to define navigation functions for a large family of configuration spaces. The main problem is that the configuration space obstacles and the connectivity of $\mathcal{C}_{free}$ are represented only implicitly, which makes it difficult to correctly apply the method to complicated high-dimensional problems. One of the advantages of the approach is that proving convergence to the goal is simplified. In many cases, Lyapunov stability analysis can be performed (see Section 15.1.1).

8.4.4.4 Harmonic potential functions

Another important family of navigation functions is constructed from harmonic functions [238, 241, 242, 484, 532]. A function ϕ is called a *harmonic function* if it satisfies the differential equation

$$\nabla^2 \phi = \sum_{i=1}^{n} \frac{\partial^2 \phi}{\partial x_i^2} = 0. \tag{8.49}$$

---

[15] Some authors do not include the global minimum as a local minimum. In this case, one would say that there are no local minima.

[16] Technically, to be Morse, the values of the function must also be distinct at each critical point.

There are many possible solutions to the equation, depending on the conditions along the boundary of the domain over which ϕ is defined. A simple disc-based example is given in [237] for which an analytical solution exists. Complicated navigation functions are generally defined by imposing constraints on ϕ along the boundary of C_{free}. A *Dirichlet boundary condition* means that the boundary must be held to a constant value. Using this condition, a harmonic navigation function can be developed that guides the state into a goal region from anywhere in a simply connected state space. If there are interior obstacles, then a *Neumann boundary condition* forces the velocity vectors to be tangent to the obstacle boundary. By solving (8.49) under a combination of both boundary conditions, a harmonic navigation function can be constructed that avoids obstacles by moving parallel to their boundaries and eventually landing in the goal. It has been shown under general conditions that navigation functions can be produced [242, 241]; however, the main problems are that the boundary of C_{free} is usually not constructed explicitly (recall why this was avoided in Chapter 5) and that a numerical solution to (8.49) is expensive to compute. This can be achieved, for example, by using Gauss-Seidel iterations (as indicated in [242]), which are related to value iteration (see [98] for the distinction). A sampling-based approach to constructing navigation functions via harmonic functions is presented in [126]. Value iteration will be used to produce approximate, optimal navigation functions in Section 8.5.2.

8.5 Sampling-based methods for continuous spaces

The methods in Section 8.4 can be considered as the feedback-case analogs to the combinatorial methods of Chapter 6. Although such methods provide elegant solutions to the problem, the issue arises once again that they are either limited to lower dimensional problems or problems that exhibit some special structure. This motivates the introduction of sampling-based methods. This section presents the feedback-case analog to Chapter 5.

8.5.1 Computing a composition of funnels

Mason introduced the concept of a *funnel* as a metaphor for motions that converge to the same small region of the state space, regardless of the initial position [682]. As grains of sand in a funnel, they follow the slope of the funnel until they reach the opening at the bottom. A navigation function can be imagined as a funnel that guides the state into the goal. For example, the cost-to-go function depicted in Figure 8.13d can be considered as a complicated funnel that sends each piece of sand along an optimal path to the goal.

Rather than designing a single funnel, consider decomposing the state space into a collection of simple, overlapping regions. Over each region, a funnel can be designed that leads the state into another funnel; see Figure 8.14. As an example, the approach in [164] places a *Lyapunov function* (such functions are covered in Section 15.1.2) over each funnel to ensure convergence to the next funnel. A feedback plan can be constructed by composing several funnels. Starting from some initial state in X, a sequence of funnels is visited until the goal is reached. Each funnel essentially solves the subgoal of reaching the next funnel. Eventually, a funnel is reached that contains the goal, and a navigation function on this funnel causes the goal to be reached. In the context of sensing uncertainty, for which the funnel metaphor was developed, the composition of funnels becomes the preimage planning framework [662], which is covered in Section 12.5.1. In this section, however, it is assumed that the current state is always known.

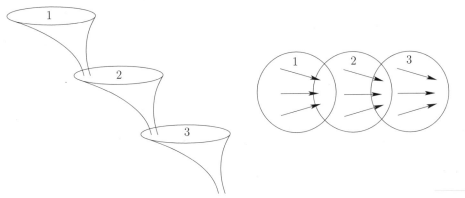

Figure 8.14: A navigation function and corresponding vector field can be designed as a composition of funnels.

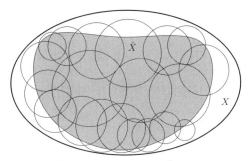

Figure 8.15: An approximate cover is shown. Every point of $\tilde{X}$ is contained in at least one neighborhood, and $\tilde{X}$ is a subset of X.

8.5.1.1 An approximate cover

Figure 8.15 illustrates the notion of an approximate cover, which will be used to represent the funnel domains. Let $\tilde{X}$ denote a subset of a state space X. A *cover* of $\tilde{X}$ is a collection $\mathcal{O}$ of sets for which

1. $O \subseteq X$ for each $O \in \mathcal{O}$.

2. $\tilde{X}$ is a subset of the union of all sets in the cover:

$$\tilde{X} \subseteq \bigcup_{O \in \mathcal{O}} O. \tag{8.50}$$

Let each $O \in \mathcal{O}$ be called a *neighborhood*. The notion of a cover was actually used in Section 8.3.2 to define a smooth manifold using a cover of coordinate neighborhoods.

In general, a cover allows the following:

1. Any number of neighborhoods may overlap (have nonempty intersection).

2. Any neighborhood may contain points that lie outside of $\tilde{X}$.

A cell decomposition, which was introduced in Section 6.3.1, is a special kind of cover for which the neighborhoods form a partition of $\tilde{X}$, and they must fit together nicely (recall Figure 6.15).

So far, no constraints have been placed on the neighborhoods. They should be chosen in practice to greatly simplify the design of a navigation function over each one. For the original motion planning problem, cell decompositions were designed to make the

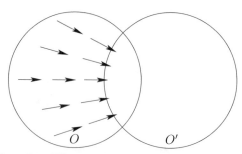

Figure 8.16: A transition from O to O' is caused by a vector field on O for which all integral curves lead into $O \cap O'$.

determination of a collision-free path trivial in each cell. The same idea applies here, except that we now want to construct a feedback plan. Therefore, it is usually assumed that the cells have a simple shape.

A cover is called *approximate* if $\tilde{X}$ is a strict subset of X. Ideally, we would like to develop an *exact cover*, which implies that $\tilde{X} = X$ and each neighborhood has some nice property, such as being convex. Developing such covers is possible in practice for state spaces that are either low-dimensional or exhibit some special structure. This was observed for the cell decomposition methods of Chapter 6.

Consider constructing an approximate cover for X. The goal should be to cover as much of X as possible. This means that $\mu(X \setminus \tilde{X})$ should be made as small as possible, in which μ denotes Lebesgue measure, as defined in Section 5.1.3. It is also desirable to ensure that $\tilde{X}$ preserves the connectivity of X. In other words, if a path between two points exists in X, then it should also exist in $\tilde{X}$.

8.5.1.2 Defining a feedback plan over a cover

The ideas from Section 8.4.2 can be adapted to define a feedback plan over $\tilde{X}$ using a cover. Let $\check{X}$ denote a discrete state space in which each superstate is a neighborhood. Most of the components of the associated discrete planning problems are the same as in Section 8.4.2. The only difference is in the definition of superactions because neighborhoods can overlap in a cover. For each neighborhood $O \in \mathcal{O}$, a superaction exists for each other neighborhood, $O' \in \mathcal{O}$ such that $O \cap O' \neq \emptyset$ (usually, their interiors overlap to yield $\operatorname{int}(O) \cap \operatorname{int}(O') \neq \emptyset$).

Note that in the case of a cell decomposition, this produces no superactions because it is a partition. To follow the metaphor of composing funnels, the domains of some funnels should overlap, as shown in Figure 8.14. A transition from one neighborhood, O, to another, O', is obtained by defining a vector field on O that sends all states from $O \setminus O'$ into $O \cap O'$; see Figure 8.16. Once O' is reached, the vector field of O is no longer followed; instead, the vector field of O' is used. Using the vector field of O', a transition may be applied to reach another neighborhood. Note that the jump from the vector field of O to that of O' may cause the feedback plan to be a discontinuous vector field on $\tilde{X}$. If the cover is designed so that $O \cap O'$ is large (if they intersect), then gradual transitions may be possible by blending the vector fields from O and O'.

Once the discrete problem has been defined, a discrete feedback plan can be computed over $\check{X}$, as defined in Section 8.2. This is converted into a feedback plan over X by defining a vector field on each neighborhood that causes the appropriate transitions. Each $\check{x} \in \check{X}$ can be interpreted both as a superstate and a neighborhood. For each $\check{x}$, the discrete

INCREMENTAL COVER CONSTRUCTION

1. Initialize $\mathcal{O} = \emptyset$ and $i = 1$.

2. Let $x = \alpha(i)$, and let d be the distance returned by the collision detection algorithm applied at x.

3. If $d > 0$ (which implies that $x \in \mathcal{C}_{free}$) and $x \notin O$ for all $O \in \mathcal{O}$, then insert a new neighborhood, O_n, into $\mathcal{O}$. The neighborhood size and shape are determined from x and d.

4. If the termination condition is not satisfied, then let $i := i + 1$, and go to Step 1.

5. Remove any neighborhoods from $\mathcal{O}$ that are contained entirely inside of another neighborhood.

Figure 8.17: The cover is incrementally extended by adding new neighborhoods that are guaranteed to be collision-free.

feedback plan produces a superaction $\check{u} = \pi(\check{x})$, which yields a new neighborhood $\check{x}'$. The vector field over $\check{x} = O$ is then designed to send all states into $\check{x}' = O'$.

If desired, a navigation function ϕ over X can even be derived from a navigation function, $\check{\phi}$, over $\check{X}$. Suppose that $\check{\phi}$ is constructed so that every $\check{\phi}(\check{x})$ is distinct for every $\check{x} \in \check{X}$. Any navigation function can be easily transformed to satisfy this constraint (because $\check{X}$ is finite). Let ϕ_O denote a navigation function over some $O \in \mathcal{O}$. Assume that X_G is a point, x_G (extensions can be made to more general cases). For every neighborhood $O \in \mathcal{O}$ such that $x_G \notin O$, ϕ_O is defined so that performing gradient descent leads into the overlapping neighborhood for which $\check{\phi}(\check{x})$ is smallest. If O contains x_G, the navigation function ϕ_O simply guides the state to x_G.

The navigation functions over each $O \in \mathcal{O}$ can be easily pieced together to yield a navigation function over all of X. In places where multiple neighborhoods overlap, ϕ is defined to be the navigation function associated with the neighborhood for which $\check{\phi}(\check{x})$ is smallest. This can be achieved by adding a large constant to each ϕ_O. Let c denote a constant for which $\phi_O(x) < c$ over all $O \in \mathcal{O}$ and $x \in O$ (it is assumed that each ϕ_O is bounded). Suppose that $\check{\phi}$ assumes only integer values. Let $\mathcal{O}(x)$ denote the set of all $O \in \mathcal{O}$ such that $x \in O$. The navigation function over X is defined as

$$\phi(x) = \min_{O \in \mathcal{O}(x)} \left\{ \phi_O(x) + c\,\check{\phi}(O) \right\}. \tag{8.51}$$

8.5.1.3 A sampling-based approach

There are numerous alternative ways to construct a cover. To illustrate the ideas, an approach called the *sampling-based neighborhood graph* is presented here [983]. Suppose that $X = \mathcal{C}_{free}$, which is a subset of some configuration space. As introduced in Section 5.4, let α be a dense, infinite sequence of samples in X. Assume that a collision detection algorithm is available that returns the distance, (5.28), between the robot and obstacles in the world. Such algorithms were described in Section 5.3.

An incremental algorithm is given in Figure 8.17. Initially, $\mathcal{O}$ is empty. In each iteration, if $\alpha(i) \in \mathcal{C}_{free}$ and it is not already contained in some neighborhood, then a new neighborhood is added to $\mathcal{O}$. The two main concerns are 1) how to define a new neighborhood, O, such that $O \subset \mathcal{C}_{free}$, and 2) when to terminate. At any given time, the cover is approximate. The union of all neighborhoods is $\tilde{X}$, which is a strict subset of X. In comparison to Figure 8.15, the cover is a special case in which the neighborhoods do not extend beyond $\tilde{X}$.

Defining new neighborhoods

For defining new neighborhoods, it is important to keep them simple because during execution, the neighborhoods that contain the state x must be determined quickly. Suppose that all neighborhoods are open balls:

$$B(x, r) = \{x' \in X \mid \rho(x, x') < r\}, \tag{8.52}$$

in which ρ is the metric on $\mathcal{C}$. There are efficient algorithms for determining whether $x \in O$ for some $O \in \mathcal{O}$, assuming all of the neighborhoods are balls [703]. In practice, methods based on Kd-trees yield good performance [48, 53] (recall Section 5.5.2). A new ball, $B(x, r)$, can be constructed in Step 3 for $x = \alpha(i)$, but what radius can be assigned? For a point robot that translates in $\mathbb{R}^2$ or $\mathbb{R}^3$, the Hausdorff distance d between the robot and obstacles in $\mathcal{W}$ is precisely the distance to $\mathcal{C}_{obs}$ from $\alpha(i)$. This implies that we can set $r = d$, and $B(x, r)$ is guaranteed to be collision-free.

In a general configuration space, it is possible to find a value of r such that $B(x, r) \subseteq \mathcal{C}_{free}$, but in general $r < d$. This issue arose in Section 5.3.4 for checking path segments. The transformations of Sections 3.2 and 3.3 become important in the determination of r. For illustrative purposes, suppose that $\mathcal{C} = \mathbb{R}^2 \times \mathbb{S}^1$, which corresponds to a rigid robot, $\mathcal{A}$, that can translate and rotate in $\mathcal{W} = \mathbb{R}^2$. Each point $a \in \mathcal{A}$ is transformed using (3.35). Now imagine starting with some configuration $q = (x, y, \theta)$ and perturbing each coordinate by some Δx, Δy, and $\Delta \theta$. What is the maximum distance that a point on $\mathcal{A}$ could travel? Translation affects all points on $\mathcal{A}$ the same way, but rotation affects points differently. Recall Figure 5.12 from Section 5.3.4. Let $a_r \in \mathcal{A}$ denote the point that is furthest from the origin $(0, 0)$. Let r denote the distance from a_r to the origin. If the rotation is perturbed by some small amount, $\Delta \theta$, then the displacement of any $a \in \mathcal{A}$ is no more than $r \Delta \theta$. If all three configuration parameters are perturbed, then

$$(\Delta x)^2 + (\Delta y)^2 + (r \Delta \theta)^2 < d^2 \tag{8.53}$$

is the constraint that must be satisfied to ensure that the resulting ball is contained in $\mathcal{C}_{free}$. This is actually the equation of a solid ellipsoid, which becomes a ball if $r = 1$. This can be made into a ball by reparameterizing $SE(2)$ so that $\Delta \theta$ has the same affect as Δx and Δy. A transformation $h : \theta \mapsto r\theta$ maps θ into a new domain $Z = [0, 2\pi r)$. In this new space, the equation of the ball is

$$(\Delta x)^2 + (\Delta y)^2 + (\Delta z)^2 < d^2, \tag{8.54}$$

in which Δz represents the change in $z \in Z$. The reparameterized version of (3.35) is

$$T = \begin{pmatrix} \cos(\theta/r) & -\sin(\theta/r) & x_t \\ \sin(\theta/r) & \cos(\theta/r) & y_t \\ 0 & 0 & 1 \end{pmatrix}. \tag{8.55}$$

For a 3D rigid body, similar reparameterizations can be made to Euler angles or quaternions to generate six-dimensional balls. Extensions can be made to chains of bodies [983]. One of the main difficulties, however, is that the balls are not the largest possible. In higher dimensions the problem becomes worse because numerous balls are needed, and the radii constructed as described above tend to be much smaller than what is possible. The number

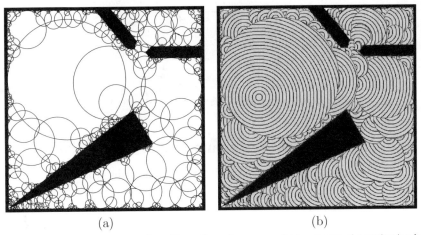

Figure 8.18: (a) A approximate cover for a 2D configuration space. (b) Level sets of a navigation function.

of balls can be reduced by also allowing axis-aligned cylinders, but it still remains difficult to construct a cover over a large fraction of $\mathcal{C}_{free}$ in more than six dimensions.

Termination

The sampling-based planning algorithms in Chapter 5 were designed to terminate upon finding a solution path. In the current setting, termination is complicated by the fact that we are interested in solutions from all initial configurations. Since α is dense, the volume of uncovered points in $\mathcal{C}_{free}$ tends to zero. After some finite number of iterations, it would be nice to measure the quality of the approximation and then terminate when the desired quality is achieved. This was also possible with the visibility sampling-based roadmap in Section 5.6.2. Using random samples, an estimate of the fraction of $\mathcal{C}_{free}$ can be obtained by recording the percentage of failures in obtaining a sample in $\mathcal{C}_{free}$ that is outside of the cover. For example, if a new neighborhood is created only once in 1000 iterations, then it can be estimated that 99.9 percent of $\mathcal{C}_{free}$ is covered. High-probability bounds can also be determined. Termination conditions are given in [983] that ensure with probability greater than P_c that at least a fraction $\alpha \in (0, 1)$ of $\mathcal{C}_{free}$ has been covered. The constants P_c and α are given as parameters to the algorithm, and it will terminate when the condition has been satisfied using rigorous statistical tests. If deterministic sampling is used, then termination can be made to occur based on the dispersion, which indicates the largest ball in $\mathcal{C}_{free}$ that does not contain the center of another neighborhood. One problem with volume-based criteria, such as those suggested here, is that there is no way to ensure that the cover preserves the connectivity of $\mathcal{C}_{free}$. If two portions of $\mathcal{C}_{free}$ are connected by a narrow passage, the cover may miss a neighborhood that has very small volume yet is needed to connect the two portions.

Example 8.18 (2D Example of Computed Funnels)   Figure 8.18 shows a 2D example that was computed using random samples and the algorithm in Figure 8.17. Note that once a cover is computed, it can be used to rapidly compute different navigation functions and vector fields for various goals. This example is mainly for illustrative purposes. For the case of a polygonal environment, constructing covers based on convex polygons would be more efficient. ∎

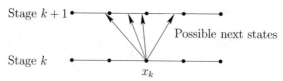

Figure 8.19: Even though x_k is a sample point, the next state, x_{k+1}, may land between sample points. For each $u_k \in U(x_k)$, interpolation may be needed for the resulting next state, $x_{k+1} = f(x_k, u_k)$.

8.5.2 Dynamic programming with interpolation

This section concludes Part II by solving the motion planning problem with value iteration, which was introduced in Section 2.3. It has already been applied to obtain discrete feedback plans in Section 8.2. It will now be adapted to continuous spaces by allowing interpolation first over a continuous state space and then by additionally allowing interpolation over a continuous action space. This yields a numerical approach to computing optimal navigation functions and feedback plans for motion planning. The focus will remain on backward value iteration; however, the interpolation concepts may also be applied in the forward direction. The approach here views optimal feedback motion planning as a discrete-time optimal control problem [28, 86, 153, 586].

8.5.2.1 Using interpolation for continuous state spaces

Consider a problem formulation that is identical to Formulation 8.1 except that X is allowed to be continuous. Assume that X is bounded, and assume for now that the action space, $U(x)$, it finite for all $x \in X$. Backward value iteration can be applied. The dynamic programming arguments and derivation are identical to those in Section 2.3. The resulting recurrence is identical to (2.11) and is repeated here for convenience:

$$G_k^*(x_k) = \min_{u_k \in U(x_k)} \left\{ l(x_k, u_k) + G_{k+1}^*(x_{k+1}) \right\}. \tag{8.56}$$

The only difficulty is that $G_k^*(x_k)$ cannot be stored for every $x_k \in X$ because X is continuous. There are two general approaches. One is to approximate G_k^* using a parametric family of surfaces, such as polynomials or nonlinear basis functions derived from neural networks [99]. The other is to store G_k^* only over a finite set of sample points and use interpolation to obtain its value at all other points [585, 586].

Suppose that a finite set $S \subset X$ of samples is used to represent cost-to-go functions over X. The evaluation of (8.56) using interpolation is depicted in Figure 8.19. In general, the samples should be chosen to reduce the dispersion (defined in Section 5.2.3) as much as possible. This prevents attempts to approximate the cost-to-go function on large areas that contain no sample points. The rate of convergence ultimately depends on the dispersion [94] (in combination with Lipschitz conditions on the state transition equation and the cost functional). To simplify notation and some other issues, assume that S is a grid of regularly spaced points in $\mathbb{R}^n$.

First, consider the case in which $X = [0, 1] \subset \mathbb{R}$. Let $S = \{s_0, s_1, \ldots, s_r\}$, in which $s_i = i/r$. For example, if $r = 3$, then $S = \{0, 1/3, 2/3, 1\}$. Note that this always yields points on the boundary of X, which ensures that for any point in $(0, 1)$ there are samples both above and below it. Let i be the largest integer such that $s_i < x$. This implies that $s_{i+1} > x$. The samples s_i and s_{i+1} are called *interpolation neighbors* of x.

The value of G^*_{k+1} in (8.56) at any $x \in [0, 1]$ can be obtained via *linear interpolation* as

$$G^*_{k+1}(x) \approx \alpha G^*_{k+1}(s_i) + (1 - \alpha)G^*_{k+1}(s_{i+1}), \tag{8.57}$$

in which the coefficient $\alpha \in [0, 1]$ is computed as

$$\alpha = 1 - \frac{x - s_i}{r}. \tag{8.58}$$

If $x = s_i$, then $\alpha = 1$, and (8.57) reduces to $G^*_{k+1}(s_i)$, as expected. If $x = s_{i+1}$, then $\alpha = 0$, and (8.57) reduces to $G^*_{k+1}(s_{i+1})$. At all points in between, (8.57) blends the cost-to-go values at s_i and s_{i+1} using α to provide the appropriate weights.

The interpolation idea can be naturally extended to multiple dimensions. Let X be a bounded subset of $\mathbb{R}^n$. Let S represent an n-dimensional grid of points in $\mathbb{R}^n$. Each sample in S is denoted by $s(i_1, i_2, \ldots, i_n)$. For some $x \in X$, there are 2^n interpolation neighbors that "surround" it. These are the corners of an n-dimensional cube that contains x. Let $x = (x_1, \ldots, x_n)$. Let i_j denote the largest integer for which the jth coordinate of $s(i_1, i_2, \ldots, i_n)$ is less than x_j. The 2^n samples are all those for which either i_j or $i_j + 1$ appears in the expression $s(\cdot, \cdot, \ldots, \cdot)$, for each $j \in \{1, \ldots, n\}$. This requires that samples exist in S for all of these cases. Note that X may be a complicated subset of $\mathbb{R}^n$, provided that for any $x \in X$, all of the required 2^n interpolation neighbors are in S. Using the 2^n interpolation neighbors, the value of G^*_{k+1} in (8.56) on any $x \in X$ can be obtained via *multi-linear interpolation*. In the case of $n = 2$, this is expressed as

$$\begin{aligned}
G^*_{k+1}(x) \approx \;& \alpha_1 \alpha_2 \; G^*_{k+1}(s(i_1, i_2)) \\
& + \alpha_1(1 - \alpha_2) \; G^*_{k+1}(s(i_1, i_2 + 1)) \\
& + (1 - \alpha_1)\alpha_2 \; G^*_{k+1}(s(i_1 + 1, i_2)) \\
& + (1 - \alpha_1)(1 - \alpha_2) \; G^*_{k+1}(s(i_1 + 1, i_2 + 1)),
\end{aligned} \tag{8.59}$$

in which α_1 and α_2 are defined similarly to α in (8.58) but are based on distances along the x_1 and x_2 directions, respectively. The expressions for multi-linear interpolation in higher dimensions are similar but are more cumbersome to express. Higher order interpolation, such a quadratic interpolation may alternatively be used [586].

Unfortunately, the number of interpolation neighbors grows exponentially with the dimension, n. Instead of using all 2^n interpolation neighbors, one improvement is to decompose the cube defined by the 2^n samples into simplexes. Each simplex has only $n + 1$ samples as its vertices. Only the vertices of the simplex that contains x are declared to be the interpolation neighbors of x; this reduces the cost of evaluating $G^*_{k+1}(x)$ to $O(n)$ time. The problem, however, is that determining the simplex that contains x may be a challenging *point-location problem* (a common problem in computational geometry [266]). If barycentric subdivision is used to decompose the cube using the midpoints of all faces, then the point-location problem can be solved in $O(n \lg n)$ time [265, 610, 724], which is an improvement over the $O(2^n)$ scheme described above. Examples of this decomposition are shown for two and three dimensions in Figure 8.20. This is sometimes called the *Coxeter-Freudenthal-Kuhn triangulation*. Even though n is not too large due to practical performance considerations (typically, $n \leq 6$), substantial savings occur in implementations, even for $n = 3$.

It will be convenient to refer directly to the set of all points in X for which all required interpolation neighbors exist. For any finite set $S \subseteq X$ of sample points, let the *interpolation region* $R(S)$ be the set of all $x \in X \setminus S$ for which $G^*(x)$ can be computed by

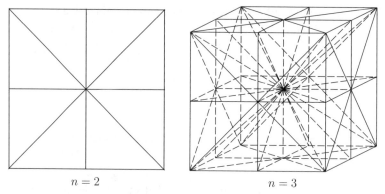

$$n = 2 \qquad\qquad n = 3$$

Figure 8.20: Barycentric subdivision can be used to partition each cube into simplexes, which allows interpolation to be performed in $O(n \lg n)$ time, instead of $O(2^n)$.

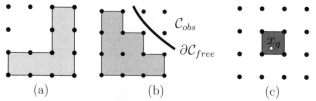

$$\text{(a)} \qquad\qquad \text{(b)} \qquad\qquad \text{(c)}$$

Figure 8.21: (a) An interpolation region, $R(S)$, is shown for a set of sample points, S. (b) The interpolation region that arises due to obstacles. (c) The interpolation region for goal points must not be empty.

interpolation. This means that $x \in R(S)$ if and only if all interpolation neighbors of x lie in S. Figure 8.21a shows an example. Note that some sample points may not contribute any points to R. If a grid of samples is used to approximate G^*, then the volume of $X \setminus R(S)$ approaches zero as the sampling resolution increases.

Continuous action spaces

Now suppose that $U(x)$ is continuous, in addition to X. Assume that $U(x)$ is both a closed and bounded subset of $\mathbb{R}^n$. Once again, the dynamic programming recurrence, (8.56), remains the same. The trouble now is that the *min* represents an optimization problem over an uncountably infinite number of choices. One possibility is to employ nonlinear optimization techniques to select the optimal $u \in U(x)$. The effectiveness of this depends heavily on $U(x)$, X, and the cost functional.

Another approach is to evaluate (8.56) over a finite set of samples drawn from $U(x)$. Again, it is best to choose samples that reduce the dispersion as much as possible. In some contexts, it may be possible to eliminate some actions from consideration by carefully utilizing the properties of the cost-to-go function and its representation via interpolation.

8.5.2.2 The connection to feedback motion planning

The tools have now been provided to solve motion planning problems using value iteration. The configuration space is a continuous state space; let $X = \mathcal{C}_{free}$. The action space is also continuous, $U(x) = T_x(X)$. For motion planning problems, $0 \in T_x(X)$ is only obtained only when u_T is applied. Therefore, it does not need to be represented separately. To compute optimal cost-to-go functions for motion planning, the main concerns are as follows:

1. The action space must be bounded.

2. A discrete-time approximation must be made to derive a state transition equation that works over stages.

3. The cost functional must be discretized.

4. The obstacle region, $\mathcal{C}_{obs}$, must be taken into account.

5. At least some interpolation region must yield $G^*(x) = 0$, which represents the goal region.

We now discuss each of these.

Bounding the action space

Recall that using normalized vector fields does not alter the existence of solutions. This is convenient because $U(x)$ needs to be bounded to approximate it with a finite set of samples. It is useful to restrict the action set to obtain

$$U(x) = \{u \in \mathbb{R}^n \mid \|u\| \le 1\}. \tag{8.60}$$

To improve performance, it is sometimes possible to use only those u for which $\|u\| = 1$ or $u = 0$; however, numerical instability problems may arise. A finite sample set for $U(x)$ should have low dispersion and always include $u = 0$.

Obtaining a state transition equation

Value iterations occur over discrete stages; however, the integral curves of feedback plans occur over continuous time. Therefore, the time interval T needs to be sampled. Let Δt denote a small positive constant that represents a fixed interval of time. Let the stage index k refer to time $(k - 1)\Delta t$. Now consider representing a velocity field $\dot{x}$ over $\mathbb{R}^n$. By definition,

$$\frac{dx}{dt} = \lim_{\Delta t \to 0} \frac{x(t + \Delta t) - x(t)}{\Delta t}. \tag{8.61}$$

In Section 8.3.1, a velocity field was defined by assigning some $u \in U(x)$ to each $x \in X$. If the velocity vector u is integrated from $x(t)$ over a small Δt, then a new state, $x(t + \Delta t)$, results. If u remains constant, then

$$x(t + \Delta t) = x(t) + \Delta t\, u, \tag{8.62}$$

which is called an *Euler approximation*. If a feedback plan is executed, then u is determined from x via $u = \pi(x(t))$. In general, this means that u could vary as the state is integrated forward. In this case, (8.62) is only approximate,

$$x(t + \Delta t) \approx x(t) + \Delta t\, \pi(x(t)). \tag{8.63}$$

The expression in (8.62) can be considered as a state transition equation that works over stages. Let $x_{k+1} = x(t + \Delta t)$ and $x_k = x(t)$. The transitions can now be expressed as

$$x_{k+1} = f(x_k, u) = x_k + \Delta t\, u. \tag{8.64}$$

The quality of the approximation improves as Δt decreases. Better approximations can be made by using more sample points along time. The most widely known approximations are the Runge-Kutta family. For optimal motion planning, it turns out that the direction vector almost always remains constant along the integral curve. For example, in Figure 8.12, observe that piecewise-linear paths are obtained by performing gradient descent of the optimal navigation function. The direction vector is constant over most of the resulting integral curve (it changes only as obstacles are contacted). Therefore, approximation problems tend not to arise in motion planning problems. When approximating dynamical systems, such as those presented in Chapter 13, then better approximations are needed; see Section 14.3.2. One important concern is that Δt is chosen in a way that is compatible with the grid resolution. If Δt is so small that the actions to not change the state enough to yield new interpolation neighbors, then the interpolated cost-to-go values will remain constant. This implies that Δt must be chosen to ensure that $x(t + \Delta t)$ has a different set of interpolation neighbors than $x(t)$.

An interesting connection can be made to the approximate motion planning problem that was developed in Section 7.7. Formulation 7.4 corresponds precisely to the approximation defined here, except that ϵ was used instead of Δt because velocities were not yet considered (also, the initial condition was specified because there was no feedback). Recall the different possible action spaces shown in Figure 7.41. As stated in Section 7.7, if the Manhattan or independent-joint models are used, then the configurations remain on a grid of points. This enables discrete value iterations to be performed. A discrete feedback plan and navigation function, as considered in Section 8.2.3, can even be computed. If the Euclidean motion model is used, which is more natural, then the transitions allow a continuum of possible configurations. This case can finally be handled by using interpolation over the configuration space, as described in this section.

Approximating the cost functional

A discrete cost functional must be derived from the continuous cost functional, (8.39). The final term is just assigned as $l_F(x_F) = l_F(x(t_f))$. The cost at each stage is

$$l_d(x_k, u_k) = \int_0^{\Delta t} l(x(t), u(t))dt, \tag{8.65}$$

and $l_d(x_k, u_k)$ is used in the place of $l(x_k, u_k)$ in (8.56). For many problems, the integral does not need to be computed repeatedly. To obtain Euclidean shortest paths, $l_d(x_k, u_k) = \|u_k\|$ can be safely assigned for all $x_k \in X$ and $u_k \in U(x_k)$. A reasonable approximation to (8.65) if Δt is small is $l(x(t), u(t))\Delta t$.

Handling obstacles

A simple way to handle obstacles is to determine for each $x \in S$ whether $x \in \mathcal{C}_{obs}$. This can be computed and stored in an array before the value iterations are performed. For rigid robots, this can be efficiently computed using *fast Fourier transforms* [516]. For each $x \in \mathcal{C}_{obs}$, $G^*(x) = \infty$. No value iterations are performed on these states; their values must remain at infinity. During the evaluation of (8.59) (or a higher dimensional version), different actions are attempted. For each action, it is required that all of the interpolation neighbors of x_{k+1} lie in $\mathcal{C}_{free}$. If one of them lies in $\mathcal{C}_{obs}$, then that action produces infinite cost. This has the effect of automatically reducing the interpolation region, $R(S)$, to all cubes who vertices all lie in $\mathcal{C}_{free}$, as shown in Figure 8.21b. All samples in $\mathcal{C}_{obs}$ are assumed to be deleted from S in the remainder of this section; however, the full grid is still used for interpolation so that infinite values represent the obstacle region.

Note that as expressed so far, it is possible that points in $\mathcal{C}_{obs}$ may lie in $R(S)$ because collision detection is performed only on the samples. In practice, either the grid resolution must be made fine enough to minimize the chance of this error occurring or distance information from a collision detection algorithm must be used to infer that a sufficiently large ball around each sample is collision free. If an interpolation region cannot be assured to lie in $\mathcal{C}_{free}$, then the resolution may have to be increased, at least locally.

Handling the goal region

Recall that backward value iterations start with the final cost-to-go function and iterate backward. Initially, the final cost-to-go is assigned as infinity at all states except those in the goal. To properly initialize the final cost-to-go function, there must exist some subset of X over which the zero value can be obtained by interpolation. Let $G = S \cap X_G$. The requirement is that the interpolation region $R(G)$ must be nonempty. If this is not satisfied, then the grid resolution needs to be increased or the goal set needs to be enlarged. If X_g is a single point, then it needs to be enlarged, regardless of the resolution (unless an alternative way to interpolate near a goal point is developed). In the interpolation region shown in Figure 8.21c, all states in the vicinity of x_G yield an interpolated cost-to-go value of zero. If such a region did not exist, then all costs would remain at infinity during the evaluation of (8.59) from any state. Note that Δt must be chosen large enough to ensure that new samples can reach G.

Using G^* as a navigation function

After the cost-to-go values stabilize, the resulting cost-to-go function, G^* can be used as a navigation function. Even though G^* is defined only over $S \subset X$, the value of the navigation function can be obtained using interpolation over any point in $R(S)$. The optimal action is selected as the one that satisfies the min in (8.6). This means that the state trajectory does not have to visit the grid points as in the Manhattan model. A trajectory can visit any point in $R(S)$, which enables trajectories to converge to the true optimal solution as Δt and the grid spacing tend to zero.

Topological considerations

So far there has been no explicit consideration of the topology of $\mathcal{C}$. Assuming that $\mathcal{C}$ is a manifold, the concepts discussed so far can be applied to any open set on which coordinates are defined. In practice, it is often convenient to use the manifold representations of Section 4.1.2. The manifold can be expressed as a cube, $[0, 1]^n$, with some faces identified to obtain $[0, 1]^n / \sim$. Over the interior of the cube, all of the concepts explained in this section work without modification. At the boundary, the samples used for interpolation must take the identification into account. Furthermore, actions, u_k, and next states, x_{k+1}, must function correctly on the boundary. One must be careful, however, in declaring that some solution is optimal, because Euclidean shortest paths depend on the manifold parameterization. This ambiguity is usually resolved by formulating the cost in terms of some physical quantity, such as time or energy. This often requires modeling dynamics, which will be covered in Part IV.

Value iteration with interpolation is extremely general. It is a generic algorithm for approximating the solution to optimal control problems. It can be applied to solve many of the problems in Part IV by restricting $U(x)$ to take into account complicated differential constraints. The method can also be extended to problems that involve explicit uncertainty in predictability. This version of value iteration is covered in Section 10.6.

8.5.2.3 Obtaining Dijkstra-like algorithms

For motion planning problems, it is expected that $x(t + \Delta t)$, as computed from (8.62), is always close to $x(t)$ relative to the size of X. This suggests the use of a Dijkstra-like algorithm to compute optimal feedback plans more efficiently. As discussed for the finite case in Section 2.3.3, many values remain unchanged during the value iterations, as indicated in Example 2.5. Dijkstra's algorithm maintains a data structure that focuses the computation on the part of the state space where values are changing. The same can be done for the continuous case by carefully considering the sample points [610].

During the value iterations, there are three kinds of sample points, just as in the discrete case (recall from Section 2.3.3):

1. **Dead:** The cost-to-go has stabilized to its optimal value.
2. **Alive:** The current cost-to-go is finite, but it is not yet known whether the value is optimal.
3. **Unvisited:** The cost-to-go value remains at infinity because the sample has not been reached.

The sets are somewhat harder to maintain for the case of continuous state spaces because of the interaction between the sample set S and the interpolated region $R(S)$.

Imagine the first value iteration. Initially, all points in G are set to zero values. Among the collection of samples S, how many can reach $R(G)$ in a single stage? We expect that samples very far from G will not be able to reach $R(G)$; this keeps their values are infinity. The samples that are close to G should reach it. It would be convenient to prune away from consideration all samples that are too far from G to lower their value. In every iteration, we eliminate iterating over samples that are too far away from those already reached. It is also unnecessary to iterate over the dead samples because their values no longer change.

To keep track of reachable samples, it will be convenient to introduce the notion of a *backprojection*, which will be studied further in Section 10.1. For a single state, $x \in X$, its *backprojection* is defined as

$$B(x) = \{x' \in X \mid \exists u' \in U(x') \text{ such that } x = f(x', u')\}. \qquad (8.66)$$

The backprojection of a set, $X' \subseteq X$, of points is just the union of backprojections for each point:

$$B(X') = \bigcup_{x \in X'} B(x). \qquad (8.67)$$

Now consider a version of value iteration that uses backprojections to eliminate some states from consideration because it is known that their values cannot change. Let i refer to the number of stages considered by the current value iteration. During the first iteration, $i = 1$, which means that all one-stage trajectories are considered. Let S be the set of samples (assuming already that none lie in C_{obs}). Let D_i and A_i refer to the *dead* and *alive* samples, respectively. Initially, $D_1 = G$, the set of samples in the goal set. The first set, A_1, of alive samples is assigned by using the concept of a frontier. The *frontier* of a set $S' \subseteq S$ of sample points is

$$\text{Front}(S') = (B(R(S')) \setminus S') \cap S. \qquad (8.68)$$

This is the set of sample points that can reach $R(S')$ in one stage, excluding those already in S'. Figure 8.22 illustrates the frontier. Using (8.68), A_1 is defined as $A_1 = \text{Front}(D_1)$.

Now the approach is described for iteration i. The cost-to-go update (8.56) is computed at all points in A_i. If $G_{k+1}^*(s) = G_k^*(s)$ for some $s \in A_i$, then s is declared dead and moved to D_{i+1}. Samples are never removed from the dead set; therefore, all points in D_i are also added to D_{i+1}. The next active set, A_{i+1}, includes all samples in A_i, excluding those that were moved to the dead set. Furthermore, all samples in $\text{Front}(A_i)$ are added to A_{i+1} because these will produce a finite cost-to-go value in the next iteration. The iterations continue as usual until some stage, m, is reached for which A_m is empty, and D_m includes

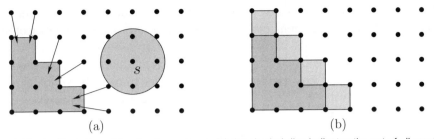

Figure 8.22: An illustration of the frontier concept: (a) the shaded disc indicates the set of all reachable points in one stage, from the sample on the left. The sample cannot reach in one stage the shaded region on the right, which represents $R(S')$. (b) The frontier is the set of samples that can reach $R(S')$. The inclusion of the frontier increases the interpolation region beyond $R(S')$.

all samples from which the goal can be reached (under the approximation assumptions made in this section).

For efficiency purposes, an approximation to Front may be used, provided that the true frontier is a proper subset of the approximate frontier. For example, the frontier might add all new samples within a specified radius of points in S'. In this case, the updated cost-to-go value for some $s \in A_i$ may remain infinite. If this occurs, it is of course not added to D_{i+1}. Furthermore, it is deleted from A_i in the computation of the next frontier (the frontier should only be computed for samples that have finite cost-to-go values).

The approach considered so far can be expected to reduce the amount of computations in each value iteration by eliminating the evaluation of (8.56) on unnecessary samples. The same cost-to-go values are obtained in each iteration because only samples for which the value cannot change are eliminated in each iteration. The resulting algorithm still does not, however, resemble Dijkstra's algorithm because value iterations are performed over all of A_i in each stage.

To make a version that behaves like Dijkstra's algorithm, a queue Q will be introduced. The algorithm removes the smallest element of Q in each iteration. The interpolation version first assigns $G^*(s) = 0$ for each $s \in G$. It also maintains a set D of dead samples, which is initialized to $D = G$. For each $s \in \text{Front}(G)$, the cost-to-go update (8.56) is computed. The priority Q is initialized to $\text{Front}(G)$, and elements are sorted by their current cost-to-go values (which may not be optimal). The algorithm iteratively removes the smallest element from Q (because its optimal cost-to-go is known to be the current value) and terminates when Q is empty. Each time the smallest element, $s_s \in Q$, is removed, it is inserted into D. Two procedures are then performed: 1) Some elements in the queue need to have their cost-to-go values recomputed using (8.56) because the value $G^*(s_s)$ is known to be optimal, and their values may depend on it. These are the samples in Q that lie in $\text{Front}(D)$ (in which D just got extended to include s_s). 2) Any samples in $B(R(D))$ that are not in Q are inserted into Q after computing their cost-to-go values using (8.56). This enables the active set of samples to grow as the set of dead samples grows. Dijkstra's algorithm with interpolation does not compute values that are identical to those produced by value iterations because G^*_{k+1} is not explicitly stored when G^*_k is computed. Each computed value is *some* cost-to-go, but it is only known to be the optimal when the sample is placed into D. It can be shown, however, that the method converges because computed values are no higher than what would have been computed in a value iteration. This is also the basis of dynamic programming using Gauss-Seidel iterations [98].

A specialized, wavefront-propagation version of the algorithm can be made for the special case of finding solutions that reach the goal in the smallest number of stages. The algorithm is similar to the one shown in Figure 8.4. It starts with an initial wavefront $W_0 = G$ in which $G^*(s) = 0$ for each $s \in G$. In each iteration, the optimal cost-to-go value i is increased by one, and the wavefront, W_{i+1}, is computed from W_i as $W_{i+1} = \text{Front}(W_i)$. The algorithm terminates at the first iteration in which the wavefront is empty.

Further reading

There is much less related literature for this chapter in comparison to previous chapters. As explained in Section 8.1, there are historical reasons why feedback is usually separated from motion planning. Navigation functions [544, 832] were one of the most influential ideas in bringing feedback into motion planning; therefore, navigation functions were a common theme throughout the chapter. For other works that use or develop navigation functions, see [208, 276, 753]. The ideas of *progress measures* [319], Lyapunov functions (covered in Section 15.1.1), and cost-to-go functions are all closely related. For Lyapunov-based design of feedback control laws, see [280]. In the context of motion planning, the Error Detection and Recovery (EDR) framework also contains feedback ideas [286].

In [327], the *topological complexity* of C-spaces is studied by characterizing the minimum number of regions needed to cover $C \times C$ by defining a continuous path function over each region. This indicates limits on navigation functions that can be constructed, assuming that both q_I and q_G are variables (throughout this chapter, q_G was instead fixed). Further work in this direction includes [328, 329].

To gain better intuitions about properties of vector fields, [44] is a helpful reference, filled with numerous insightful illustrations. A good introduction to smooth manifolds that is particularly suited for control-theory concepts is [135]. Basic intuitions for 2D and 3D curves and surfaces can be obtained from [756]. Other sources for smooth manifolds and differential geometry include [4, 109, 236, 281, 874, 907, 960]. For discussions of piecewise-smooth vector fields, see [27, 637, 848, 998].

Sections 8.4.2 and 8.4.3 were inspired by [237, 646] and [711], respectively. Many difficulties were avoided because discontinuous vector fields were allowed in these approaches. By requiring continuity or smoothness, the subject of Section 8.4.4 was obtained. The material is based mainly on [832, 833]. Other work on navigation functions includes [251, 654, 655].

Section 8.5.1 was inspired mainly by [164, 682], and the approach based on neighborhood graphs is drawn from [983].

Value iteration with interpolation, the subject of Section 8.5.2, is sometimes forgotten in motion planning because computers were not powerful enough at the time it was developed [86, 87, 585, 586]. Presently, however, solutions can be computed for challenging problems with several dimensions (e.g., 3 or 4). Convergence of discretized value iteration to solving the optimal continuous problem was first established in [94], based on Lipschitz conditions on the state transition equation and cost functional. Analyses that take interpolation into account, and general discretization issues, appear in [170, 294, 402, 568, 570]. A multi-resolution variant of value iteration was proposed in [725]. The discussion of Dijkstra-like versions of value iteration was based on [610, 946]. The level-set method is also closely related [535, 537, 536, 864].

Exercises

1. Suppose that a very fast path planning algorithm runs on board of a mobile robot (for example, it may find an answer in a few milliseconds, which is reasonable using trapezoidal decomposition in $\mathbb{R}^2$). Explain how this method can be used to simulate having a feedback plan on the robot. Explain the issues and trade-offs between having a fast on-line algorithm that computes open-loop plans vs. a better off-line algorithm that computes a feedback plan.

2. Use Dijkstra's algorithm to construct navigation functions on a 2D grid with obstacles. Experiment with adding a penalty to the cost functional for getting too close to obstacles.

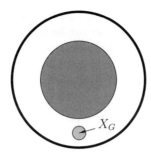

Figure 8.23: Consider designing a continuous vector field that flows into X_G.

3. If there are alternative routes, the NF2 algorithm does not necessarily send the state along the route that has the largest minimum clearance. Fix the NF2 algorithm so that it addresses this problem.

4. Tangent space problems:

   (a) For the manifold of unit quaternions, find basis vectors for the tangent space in $\mathbb{R}^4$ at any point.

   (b) Find basis vectors for the tangent space in $\mathbb{R}^9$, assuming that matrices in $SO(3)$ are parameterized with quaternions, as shown in (4.20).

5. Extend the algorithm described in Section 8.4.3 to make it work for polygons that have holes. See Example 8.16 for a similar problem.

6. Give a complete algorithm that uses the vertical cell decomposition for a polygonal obstacle region in $\mathbb{R}^2$ to construct a vector field that serves as a feedback plan. The vector field may be discontinuous.

7. Figure 8.23 depicts a 2D example for which X_{free} is an open annulus. Consider designing a vector field for which all integral curves flow into X_G and the vector field is continuous outside of X_G. Either give a vector field that achieves this or explain why it is not possible.

8. Use the maximum-clearance roadmap idea from Section 6.2.3 to define a cell decomposition and feedback motion plan (vector field) that maximizes clearance. The vector field may be discontinuous.

9. Develop an algorithm that computes an exact cover for a polygonal configuration space and ensures that if two neighborhoods intersect, then their intersection always contains an open set (i.e., the overlap region is two-dimensional). The neighborhoods in the cover should be polygonal.

10. Using a distance measurement and Euler angles, determine the expression for a collision-free ball that can be inferred (make the ball as large as possible). This should generalize (8.54).

11. Using a distance measurement and quaternions, determine the expression for a collision-free ball (once again, make it as large as possible).

12. Generalize the multi-linear interpolation scheme in (8.59) from 2 to n dimensions.

13. Explain the convergence problems for value iteration that can result if $\|u\| = 1$ is used to constraint the set of allowable actions, instead of $\|u\| \leq 1$.

Implementations

14. Experiment with numerical methods for solving the function (8.49) in two dimensions under various boundary conditions. Report on the efficiency and accuracy of the methods. How well can they be applied in higher dimensions?

15. Implement value iteration with interpolation (it is not necessary to use the method in Figure 8.20) for a polygonal robot that translates and rotates among polygonal obstacles in $\mathcal{W} = \mathbb{R}^2$. Define the cost functional so that the distance traveled is obtained with respect to a weighted Euclidean metric (the weights that compare rotation to translation can be set arbitrarily).

16. Evaluate the efficiency of the interpolation method shown in Figure 8.20 applied to multi-linear interpolation given by generalizing (8.59) as in Exercise 12. You do not need to implement the full value iteration approach (alternatively, this could be done, which provides a better comparison of the overall performance).

17. Implement the method of Section 8.4.2 of computing vector fields on a triangulation. For given input polygons, have your program draw a needle diagram of the computed vector field. Determine how fast the vector field can be recomputed as the goal changes.

18. Optimal navigation function problems:

    (a) Implement the algorithm illustrated in Figure 8.13. Show the level sets of the optimal cost-to-go function.

    (b) Extend the algorithm and implementation to the case in which there are polygonal holes in X_{free}.

19. Adapt value iteration with interpolation so that a point robot moving in the plane can keep track of a predictable moving point called a *target*. The cost functional should cause a small penalty to be added if the target is not visible. Optimizing this should minimize the amount of time that the target is not visible. Assume that the initial configuration of the robot is given. Compute optimal feedback plans for the robot.

20. Try to experimentally construct navigation functions by adding potential functions that repel the state away from obstacles and attract the state toward x_G. For simplicity, you may assume that $X = \mathbb{R}^2$ and the obstacles are discs. Start with a single disc and then gradually construct more complicated obstacle regions. How difficult is it to ensure that the resulting potential function has no local minima outside of x_G?

PART III

Decision-Theoretic Planning

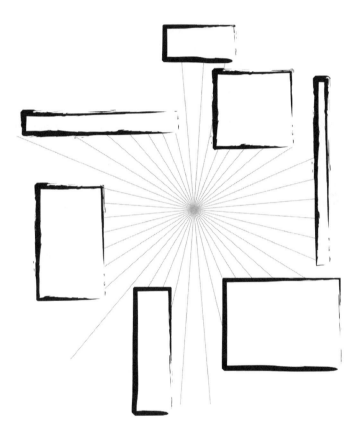

Overview of Part III: Decision-Theoretic Planning

Planning Under Uncertainty

As in Part II, it also seems appropriate to give two names to Part III. It is officially called *decision-theoretic planning*, but it can also be considered as *planning under uncertainty*. All of the concepts in Parts I and II avoided models of uncertainties. Chapter 8 considered plans that can overcome some uncertainties, but there was no explicit modeling of uncertainty.

In this part, uncertainties generally interfere with two aspects of planning:

1. **Predictability:** Due to uncertainties, it is not known what will happen in the future when certain actions are applied. This means that future states are not necessarily predictable.

2. **Sensing:** Due to uncertainties, the current state is not necessarily known. Information regarding the state is obtained from initial conditions, sensors, and the memory of previously applied actions.

These two kinds of uncertainty are independent in many ways. Each has a different effect on the planning problem.

Making a single decision

Chapter 9 provides an introduction to Part III by presenting ways to represent uncertainty in the process of making a single decision. The view taken in this chapter is that uncertainty can be modeled as interference from another decision maker. A special decision maker called *nature* will be introduced. The task is to make good decisions, in spite of actions applied by nature. Either *worst-case* or *probabilistic* models can be used to characterize nature's decision-making process. Some planning problems might involve multiple rational decision makers. This leads to game theory, which arises from the uncertainty about how other players will behave when they have conflicting goals. All of the concepts in Chapter 9 involve making a single decision; therefore, a state space is generally not necessary because there would only be one application of the state transition equation. One purpose of the chapter is to introduce and carefully evaluate the assumptions that are typically made in different forms of decision theory. This forms the basis of more complicated problems that follow, especially sequential decision making and control theory.

Uncertainty in predictability

Chapter 10 takes the concepts from Chapter 9 and iterates them over multiple stages. This brings in the notions of states and state transitions, and can be considered as a blending of discrete planning concepts from Chapter 2 with the uncertainty concepts of Chapter 9. Some coverage of continuous state spaces and continuous time is also given, which extends ideas from Part II. The state transition equation is generally extended to allow future states to depend on unknown actions taken by nature. In a game-theoretic setting, the state transitions may even depend on the actions of more than two decision makers.

For all of the models in Chapter 10, only uncertainty in predictability exists; the current state is always known. A plan is defined as a function that indicates the appropriate action to take from any current state. Plans are not formulated as a sequence of actions because future states are unpredictable, and responses to the future states may be required at the time they are achieved. Thus, for a fixed plan, the execution may be different each time: Different actions are applied and different states are reached. Plans are generally evaluated using worst-case, expected-case, or game-equilibrium analysis.

Uncertainty in sensing: The information space

Chapter 11 introduces perhaps the most important concept of this book: the *information space*. If there is uncertainty in sensing the current state, then the planning problem naturally lives in an information space. An analogy can be made to the configuration space and motion planning. Before efforts to unify motion planning by using configuration space concepts [591, 660, 854], most algorithms were developed on a case-by-case basis. For example, robot manipulators and mobile robots have very different characteristics when defined in the world. However, once viewed in the configuration space, it is easier to consider general algorithms, such as those from Chapters 5 and 6.

A similar kind of unification should be possible for planning problems that involve sensing uncertainties (i.e., are unable to determine the current state). Presently, the methods in the literature are developed mainly around individual models and problems, as basic motion planning once was. Therefore, it is difficult to provide a perspective as unified as the techniques in Part II. Nevertheless, the concepts from Chapter 11 are used to provide a unified introduction to many planning problems that involve sensing uncertainties in Chapter 12. As in the case of the configuration space, some effort is required to learn the information space concepts; however, it will pay great dividends if the investment is made.

Chapter 12 presents several different problems and solutions for planning under sensing uncertainty. The problems include exploring new environments with robots, playing a pursuit-evasion game with cameras, and manipulating objects with little or no sensing. The chapter provides many interesting applications of information space concepts, but it should also leave you with the feeling that much more remains to be done. Planning in information spaces remains a challenging research problem throughout much of robotics, control theory, and artificial intelligence.

9

Basic Decision Theory

This chapter serves as a building block for modeling and solving planning problems that involve more than one decision maker. The focus is on making a single decision in the presence of other decision makers that may interfere with the outcome. The planning problems in Chapters 10 to 12 will be viewed as a sequence of decision-making problems. The ideas presented in this chapter can be viewed as making a one-stage plan. With respect to Chapter 2, the present chapter reduces the number of stages down to one and then introduces more sophisticated ways to model a single stage. Upon returning to multiple stages in Chapter 10, it will quickly be seen that many algorithms from Chapter 2 extend nicely to incorporate the decision-theoretic concepts of this chapter.

Since there is no information to carry across stages, there will be no need for a state space. Instead of designing a *plan* for a *robot*, in this chapter we will refer to designing a *strategy* for a *decision maker* (DM). The *planning problem* reduces down to a *decision-making problem*. In later chapters, which describe sequential decision making, planning terminology will once again be used. It does not seem appropriate yet in this chapter because making a single decision appears too degenerate to be referred to as planning.

A consistent theme throughout Part III will be the interaction of multiple DMs. In addition to the primary DM, which has been referred to as the robot, there will be one or more other DMs that cannot be predicted or controlled by the robot. A special DM called *nature* will be used as a universal way to model uncertainties. Nature will usually be fictitious in the sense that it is not a true entity that makes intelligent, rational decisions for its own benefit. The introduction of nature merely serves as a convenient modeling tool to express many different forms of uncertainty. In some settings, however, the DMs may actually be intelligent opponents who make decisions out of their own self-interest. This leads to *game theory*, in which all decision makers (including the robot) can be called *players*.

Section 9.1 provides some basic review and perspective that will help in understanding and relating later concepts in the chapter. Section 9.2 covers making a single decision under uncertainty, which is typically referred to as *decision theory*. Sections 9.3 and 9.4 address *game theory*, in which two or more DMs make their decisions simultaneously and have conflicting interests. In *zero-sum game theory*, which is covered in Section 9.3, there are two DMs that have diametrically opposed interests. In *nonzero-sum game theory*, covered in Section 9.4, any number of DMs come together to form a *noncooperative game*, in which any degree of conflict or competition is allowable among them. Section 9.5 concludes the chapter by covering justifications and criticisms of the general models formulated in this chapter. It useful when trying to apply decision-theoretic models to planning problems in general.

This chapter was written without any strong dependencies on Part II. In fact, even the concepts from Chapter 2 are not needed because there are no stages or state spaces.

Occasional references to Part II will be given, but these are not vital to the understanding. Most of the focus in this chapter is on discrete spaces.

9.1 Preliminary concepts

9.1.1 Optimization

9.1.1.1 Optimizing a single objective

Before progressing to complicated decision-making models, first consider the simple case of a single decision maker that must make the best decision. This leads to a familiar *optimization* problem, which is formulated as follows.

Formulation 9.1 (Optimization)

1. A nonempty set U called the *action space*. Each $u \in U$ is referred to as an *action*.
2. A function $L : U \to \mathbb{R} \cup \{\infty\}$ called the *cost function*.

Compare Formulation 9.1 to Formulation 2.2. State space, X, and state transition concepts are no longer needed because there is only one decision. Since there is no state space, there is also no notion of initial and goal states. A *strategy* simply consists of selecting the best action.

What does it mean to be the "best" action? If U is finite, then the best action, $u^* \in U$ is

$$u^* = \operatorname*{argmin}_{u \in U} \left\{ L(u) \right\}. \tag{9.1}$$

If U is infinite, then there are different cases. Suppose that $U = (-1, 1)$ and $L(u) = u$. Which action produces the lowest cost? We would like to declare that -1 is the lowest cost, but $-1 \notin U$. If we had instead defined $U = [-1, 1]$, then this would work. However, if $U = (-1, 1)$ and $L(u) = u$, then there is no action that produces minimum cost. For any action $u \in U$, a second one, $u' \in U$, can always be chosen for which $L(u') < L(u)$. However, if $U = (-1, 1)$ and $L(u) = |u|$, then (9.1) correctly reports that $u = 0$ is the best action. There is no problem in this case because the minimum occurs in the interior, as opposed to on the boundary of U. In general it is important to be aware that an optimal value may not exist.

There are two ways to fix this frustrating behavior. One is to require that U is a closed set and is bounded (both were defined in Section 4.1). Since closed sets include their boundary, this problem will be avoided. The bounded condition prevents a problem such as optimizing $U = \mathbb{R}$, and $L(u) = u$. What is the best $u \in U$? Smaller and smaller values can be chosen for u to produce a lower cost, even though $\mathbb{R}$ is a closed set.

The alternative way to fix this problem is to define and use the notion of an *infimum*, denoted by inf. This is defined as the largest lower bound that can be placed on the cost. In the case of $U = (-1, 1)$ and $L(u) = u$, this is

$$\inf_{u \in (0,1)} \left\{ L(u) \right\} = -1. \tag{9.2}$$

The only difficulty is that there is no action $u \in U$ that produces this cost. The infimum essentially uses the closure of U to evaluate (9.2). If U happened to be closed already, then u would be included in U. Unbounded problems can also be handled. The infimum for the case of $U = \mathbb{R}$ and $L(u) = u$ is $-\infty$.

As a general rule, if you are not sure which to use, it is safer to write inf in the place were you would use min. The infimum happens to yield the minimum whenever a minimum exists. In addition, it gives a reasonable answer when no minimum exists. It may look embarrassing, however, to use inf in cases where it is obviously not needed (i.e., in the case of a finite U).

It is always possible to make an "upside-down" version of an optimization problem by multiplying L by -1. There is no fundamental change in the result, but sometimes it is more natural to formulate a problem as one of maximization instead of minimization. This will be done, for example, in the discussion of utility theory in Section 9.5.1. In such cases, a *reward function*, R, is defined instead of a cost function. The task is to select an action $u \in U$ that *maximizes* the reward. It will be understood that a maximization problem can easily be converted into a minimization problem by setting $L(u) = -R(u)$ for all $u \in U$. For maximization problems, the infimum can be replaced by the *supremum*, sup, which is the least upper bound on $R(u)$ over all $u \in U$.

For most problems in this book, the selection of an optimal $u \in U$ in a single decision stage is straightforward; planning problems are instead complicated by many other aspects. It is important to realize, however, that optimization itself is an extremely challenging if U and L are complicated. For example, U may be finite but extremely large, or U may be a high-dimensional (e.g., 1000) subset of $\mathbb{R}^n$. Also, the cost function may be extremely difficult or even impossible to express in a simple closed form. If the function is simple enough, then standard calculus tools based on first and second derivatives may apply. It most real-world applications, however, more sophisticated techniques are needed. Many involve a form of gradient descent and therefore only ensure that a local minimum is found. In many cases, sampling-based techniques are needed. In fact, many of the sampling ideas of Section 5.2, such as dispersion, were developed in the context of optimization. For some classes of problems, combinatorial solutions may exist. For example, *linear programming* involves finding the min or max of a collection of linear functions, and many combinatorial approaches exist [261, 266, 667, 734]. This optimization problem will appear in Section 9.4.

Given the importance of sampling-based and combinatorial methods in optimization, there are interesting parallels to motion planning. Chapters 5 and 6 each followed these two philosophies, respectively. Optimal motion planning actually corresponds to an optimization problem on the space of paths, which is extremely difficult to characterize. In some special cases, as in Section 6.2.4, it is possible to find optimal solutions, but in general, such problems are extremely challenging. *Calculus of variations* is a general approach for addressing optimization problems over a space of paths that must satisfy differential constraints [844]; this will be covered in Section 13.4.1.

9.1.1.2 Multiobjective optimization

Suppose that there is a collection of cost functions, each of which evaluates an action. This leads to a generalization of Formulation 9.1 to multiobjective optimization.

Formulation 9.2 (Multiobjective Optimization)

1. A nonempty set U called the *action space*. Each $u \in U$ is referred to as an *action*.

2. A vector-valued *cost function* of the form $L : U \to \mathbb{R}^d$ for some integer d. If desired, ∞ may also be allowed for any of the cost components.

A version of this problem was considered in Section 7.7.2, which involved the optimal coordination of multiple robots. Two actions, u and u', are called *equivalent* if $L(u) = L(u')$. An action u is said to *dominate* an action u' if they are not equivalent and $L_i(u) \leq L_i(u')$ for all i such that $1 \leq i \leq d$. This defines a partial ordering, $\leq$, on the set of actions. Note that many actions may be *incomparable*. An action is called *Pareto optimal* if it is not dominated by any others. This means that it is minimal with respect to the partial ordering.

Example 9.1 (Simple Example of Pareto Optimality) Suppose that $U = \{1, 2, 3, 4, 5\}$ and $d = 2$. The costs are assigned as $L(1) = (4, 0)$, $L(2) = (3, 3)$, $L(3) = (2, 2)$, $L(4) = (5, 7)$, and $L(5) = (9, 0)$. The actions 2, 4, and 5 can be eliminated because they are dominated by other actions. For example, $(3, 3)$ is dominated by $(2, 2)$; hence, action $u = 3$ is preferable to $u = 2$. The remaining two actions, $u = 1$ and $u = 3$, are Pareto optimal. ∎

Based on this simple example, the notion of Pareto optimality seems mostly aimed at discarding dominated actions. Although there may be multiple Pareto-optimal solutions, it at least narrows down U to a collection of the best alternatives.

Example 9.2 (Pennsylvania Turnpike) Imagine driving across the state of Pennsylvania and being confronted with the Pennsylvania Turnpike, which is a toll highway that once posted threatening signs about speed limits and the according fines for speeding. Let $U = \{50, 51, \ldots, 100\}$ represent possible integer speeds, expressed in miles per hour (mph). A posted sign indicates that the speeding fines are 1) \$50 for being caught driving between 56 and 65 mph, 2) \$100 for being caught between 66 and 75, 3) \$200 between 76 and 85, and 4) \$500 between 86 and 100. Beyond 100 mph, it is assumed that the penalty includes jail time, which is so severe that it will not be considered.

The two criteria for a driver are 1) the time to cross the state, and 2) the amount of money spent on tickets. It is assumed that you will be caught violating the speed limit. The goal is to minimize both. What are the resulting Pareto-optimal driving speeds? Compare driving 56 mph to driving 57 mph. Both cost the same amount of money, but driving 57 mph takes less time. Therefore, 57 mph dominates 56 mph. In fact, 65 mph dominates all speeds down to 56 mph because the cost is the same, and it reduces the time the most. Based on this argument, the Pareto-optimal driving speeds are 55, 65, 75, 85, and 100. It is up to the individual drivers to decide on the particular best action for them; however, it is clear that no speeds outside of the Pareto-optimal set are sensible. ∎

The following example illustrates the main frustration with Pareto optimality. Removing nondominated solutions may not be useful enough. In come cases, there may even be a continuum of Pareto-optimal solutions. Therefore, the Pareto-optimal concept is not always useful. Its value depends on the particular application.

Example 9.3 (A Continuum of Pareto-Optimal Solutions) Let $U = [0, 1]$ and $d = 2$. Let $L(u) = (u, 1 - u)$. In this case, every element of U is Pareto optimal. This can be seen by noting that a slight reduction in one criterion causes an increase in the other. Thus, any two actions are incomparable. ∎

9.1.2 Probability theory review

This section reviews some basic probability concepts and introduces notation that will be used throughout Part III.

Probability space

A *probability space* is a three-tuple, $(S, \mathcal{F}, P)$, in which the three components are

1. **Sample space:** A nonempty set S called the *sample space*, which represents all possible outcomes.

2. **Event space:** A collection $\mathcal{F}$ of subsets of S, called the *event space*. If S is discrete, then usually $\mathcal{F} = \text{pow}(S)$. If S is continuous, then $\mathcal{F}$ is usually a sigma-algebra on S, as defined in Section 5.1.3.

3. **Probability function:** A function, $P : \mathcal{F} \to \mathbb{R}$, that assigns probabilities to the events in $\mathcal{F}$. This will sometimes be referred to as a *probability distribution* over S.

The probability function, P, must satisfy several basic axioms:

1. $P(E) \geq 0$ for all $E \in \mathcal{F}$.
2. $P(S) = 1$.
3. $P(E \cup F) = P(E) + P(F)$ if $E \cap F = \emptyset$, for all $E, F \in \mathcal{F}$.

If S is discrete, then the definition of P over all of $\mathcal{F}$ can be inferred from its definition on single elements of S by using the axioms. It is common in this case to write $P(s)$ for some $s \in S$, which is slightly abusive because s is not an event. It technically should be $P(\{s\})$ for some $\{s\} \in \mathcal{F}$.

Example 9.4 (Tossing a Die)   Consider tossing a six-sided cube or die that has numbers 1 to 6 painted on its sides. When the die comes to rest, it will always show one number. In this case, $S = \{1, 2, 3, 4, 5, 6\}$ is the sample space. The event space is $\text{pow}(S)$, which is all 2^6 subsets of S. Suppose that the probability function is assigned to indicate that all numbers are equally likely. For any individual $s \in S$, $P(\{s\}) = 1/6$. The events include all subsets so that any probability statement can be formulated. For example, what is the probability that an even number is obtained? The event $E = \{2, 4, 6\}$ has probability $P(E) = 1/2$ of occurring.   ∎

The third probability axiom looks similar to the last axiom in the definition of a measure space in Section 5.1.3. In fact, P is technically a special kind of measure space as mentioned in Example 5.12. If S is continuous, however, this measure cannot be captured by defining probabilities over the singleton sets. The probabilities of singleton sets are usually zero. Instead, a *probability density function*, $p : S \to \mathbb{R}$, is used to define the probability measure. The probability function, P, for any event $E \in \mathcal{F}$ can then be determined via integration:

$$P(E) = \int_E p(x)\,dx, \tag{9.3}$$

in which $x \in E$ is the variable of integration. Intuitively, P indicates the total probability mass that accumulates over E.

Conditional probability

A *conditional probability* is expressed as $P(E|F)$ for any two events $E, F \in \mathcal{F}$ and is called the "probability of E, given F." Its definition is

$$P(E|F) = \frac{P(E \cap F)}{P(F)}. \tag{9.4}$$

Two events, E and F, are called *independent* if and only if $P(E \cap F) = P(E)P(F)$; otherwise, they are called *dependent*. An important and sometimes misleading concept is *conditional independence*. Consider some third event, $G \in \mathcal{F}$. It might be the case that E and F are dependent, but when G is given, they become independent. Thus, $P(E \cap F) \neq P(E)P(F)$; however, $P(E \cap F | G) = P(E|G)P(F|G)$. Such examples occur frequently in practice. For example, E might indicate someone's height, and F is their reading level. These will generally be dependent events because children are generally shorter and have a lower reading level. If we are given the person's age as an event G, then height is no longer important. It seems intuitive that there should be no correlation between height and reading level once the age is given.

The definition of conditional probability, (9.4), imposes the constraint that

$$P(E \cap F) = P(F)P(E|F) = P(E)P(F|E), \tag{9.5}$$

which nicely relates $P(E|F)$ to $P(F|E)$. This results in *Bayes' rule*, which is a convenient way to swap E and F:

$$P(F|E) = \frac{P(E|F)P(F)}{P(E)}. \tag{9.6}$$

The probability distribution, $P(F)$, is referred to as the *prior*, and $P(F|E)$ is the *posterior*. These terms indicate that the probabilities come before and after E is considered, respectively.

If all probabilities are conditioned on some event, $G \in \mathcal{F}$, then *conditional Bayes' rule* arises, which only differs from (9.6) by placing the condition G on all probabilities:

$$P(F|E, G) = \frac{P(E|F, G)P(F|G)}{P(E|G)}. \tag{9.7}$$

Marginalization

Let the events $F_1, F_2, \ldots, F_n$ be any partition of S. The probability of an event E can be obtained through *marginalization* as

$$P(E) = \sum_{i=1}^{n} P(E|F_i)P(F_i). \tag{9.8}$$

One of the most useful applications of marginalization is in the denominator of Bayes' rule. A substitution of (9.8) into the denominator of (9.6) yields

$$P(F|E) = \frac{P(E|F)P(F)}{\sum\limits_{i=1}^{n} P(E|F_i)P(F_i)}. \tag{9.9}$$

This form is sometimes easier to work with because $P(E)$ appears to be eliminated.

Random variables

Assume that a probability space $(S, \mathcal{F}, P)$ is given. A *random variable*[1] X is a function that maps S into $\mathbb{R}$. Thus, X assigns a real value to every element of the sample space. This enables statistics to be conveniently computed over a probability space. If S is already a subset of $\mathbb{R}$, X may by default represent the identity function.

---

[1] This is a terrible name, which often causes confusion. A random variable is not "random," nor is it a "variable." It is simply a function, $X : S \rightarrow \mathbb{R}$. To make matters worse, a capital letter is usually used to denote it, whereas lowercase letters are usually used to denote functions.

Expectation

The *expectation* or *expected value* of a random variable X is denoted by $E[X]$. It can be considered as a kind of weighted average for X, in which the weights are obtained from the probability distribution. If S is discrete, then

$$E[X] = \sum_{s \in S} X(s) P(s). \qquad (9.10)$$

If S is continuous, then[2]

$$E[X] = \int_S X(s) p(s) ds. \qquad (9.11)$$

One can then define *conditional expectation*, which applies a given condition to the probability distribution. For example, if S is discrete and an event F is given, then

$$E[X|F] = \sum_{s \in S} X(s) P(s|F). \qquad (9.12)$$

Example 9.5 (Tossing Dice) Returning to Example 9.4, the elements of S are already real numbers. Hence, a random variable X can be defined by simply letting $X(s) = s$. Using (9.11), the expected value, $E[X]$, is 3.5. Note that the expected value is not necessarily a value that is "expected" in practice. It is impossible to actually obtain 3.5, even though it is not contained in S. Suppose that the expected value of X is desired only over trials that result in numbers greater then 3. This can be described by the event $F = \{4, 5, 6\}$. Using conditional expectation, (9.12), the expected value is $E[X|F] = 5$.

Now consider tossing two dice in succession. Each element $s \in S$ is expressed as $s = (i, j)$ in which $i, j \in \{1, 2, 3, 4, 5, 6\}$. Since $S \not\subset \mathbb{R}$, the random variable needs to be slightly more interesting. One common approach is to count the sum of the dice, which yields $X(s) = i + j$ for any $s \in S$. In this case, $E[X] = 7$. ∎

9.1.3 Randomized strategies

Up until now, any actions taken in a plan have been *deterministic*. The plans in Chapter 2 specified actions with complete certainty. Formulation 9.1 was solved by specifying the best action. It can be viewed as a *strategy* that trivially makes the same decision every time.

In some applications, the decision maker may not want to be predictable. To achieve this, randomization can be incorporated into the strategy. If U is discrete, a *randomized strategy*, w, is specified by a probability distribution, $P(u)$, over U. Let W denote the set of all possible randomized strategies. When the strategy is applied, an action $u \in U$ is chosen by sampling according to the probability distribution, $P(u)$. We now have to make a clear distinction between *defining the strategy* and *applying the strategy*. So far, the two have been equivalent; however, a randomized strategy must be *executed* to determine the resulting action. If the strategy is executed repeatedly, it is assumed that each trial is independent of the actions obtained in previous trials. In other words, $P(u_k|u_i) = P(u_k)$, in which $P(u_k|u_i)$ represents the probability that the strategy chooses action u_k in trial k,

---

[2] Using the language of measure theory, both definitions are just special cases of the Lebesgue integral. Measure theory nicely unifies discrete and continuous probability theory, thereby avoiding the specification of separate cases. See [348, 549, 839].

given that u_i was chosen in trial i for some $i < k$. If U is continuous, then a randomized strategy may be specified by a probability density function, $p(u)$. In decision-theory and game-theory literature, deterministic and randomized strategies are often referred to as *pure* and *mixed*, respectively.

Example 9.6 (Basing Decisions on a Coin Toss) Let $U = \{a, b\}$. A randomized strategy w can be defined as

1. Flip a fair coin, which has two possible outcomes: heads (H) or tails (T).
2. If the outcome is H, choose a; otherwise, choose b.

Since the coin is fair, w is defined by assigning $P(a) = P(b) = 1/2$. Each time the strategy is applied, it not known what action will be chosen. Over many trials, however, it converges to choosing a half of the time. ∎

A deterministic strategy can always be viewed as a special case of a randomized strategy, if you are not bothered by events that have probability zero. A deterministic strategy, $u_i \in U$, can be simulated by a random strategy by assigning $P(u) = 1$ if $u = u_i$, and $P(u) = 0$ otherwise. Only with probability zero can different actions be chosen (possible, but not probable!).

Imagine using a randomized strategy to solve a problem expressed using Formulation 9.1. The first difficulty appears to be that the cost cannot be predicted. If the strategy is applied numerous times, then we can define the average cost. As the number of times tends to infinity, this average would converge to the expected cost, denoted by $\bar{L}(w)$, if L is treated as a random variable (in addition to the cost function). If U is discrete, the expected cost of a randomized strategy w is

$$\bar{L}(w) = \sum_{u \in U} L(u)P(u) = \sum_{u \in U} L(u)w. \tag{9.13}$$

An interesting question is whether there exists some $w \in W$ such that $\bar{L}(w) < L(u)$, for all $u \in U$. In other words, do there exist randomized strategies that are better than all deterministic strategies, using Formulation 9.1? The answer is *no* because the best strategy is always to assign probability one to the action, u^*, that minimizes L. This is equivalent to using a deterministic strategy. If there are two or more actions that obtain the optimal cost, then a randomized strategy could arbitrarily distribute all of the probability mass between these. However, there would be no further reduction in cost. Therefore, randomization seems pointless in this context, unless there are other considerations.

One important example in which a randomized strategy is of critical importance is when making decisions in competition with an intelligent adversary. If the problem is repeated many times, an opponent could easily learn any deterministic strategy. Randomization can be used to weaken the prediction capabilities of an opponent. This idea will be used in Section 9.3 to obtain better ways to play zero-sum games.

Following is an example that illustrates the advantage of randomization when repeatedly playing against an intelligent opponent.

Example 9.7 (Matching Pennies) Consider a game in which two players repeatedly play a simple game of placing pennies on the table. In each trial, the players must place their coins simultaneously with either heads (H) facing up or tails (T) facing up. Let a two-letter string denote the outcome. If the outcome is HH or TT (the players choose the same), then Player 1 pays Player 2 one Peso; if the outcome is HT or TH, then Player 2 pays Player 1 one Peso. What happens if Player 1 uses a deterministic strategy? If Player 2 can determine the strategy, then he can choose his strategy so that he always wins the game. However, if Player 1 chooses the best randomized strategy, then he can expect at best to break even on average. What randomized strategy achieves this?

A generalization of this to three actions is the famous game of Rock-Paper-Scissors [958]. If you want to design a computer program that repeatedly plays this game against smart opponents, it seems best to incorporate randomization. ∎

9.2 A game against nature

9.2.1 Modeling nature

For the first time in this book, uncertainty will be directly modeled. There are two DMs:

Robot: This is the name given to the primary DM throughout the book. So far, there has been only one DM. Now that there are two, the name is more important because it will be used to distinguish the DMs from each other.

Nature: This DM is a mysterious force that is unpredictable to the robot. It has its own set of actions, and it can choose them in a way that interferes with the achievements of the robot. Nature can be considered as a synthetic DM that is constructed for the purposes of modeling uncertainty in the decision-making or planning process.

Imagine that the robot and nature each make a decision. Each has a set of actions to choose from. Suppose that the cost depends on which actions are chosen by each. The cost still represents the effect of the outcome on the robot; however, the robot must now take into account the influence of nature on the cost. Since nature is unpredictable, the robot must formulate a model of its behavior. Assume that the robot has a set, U, of actions, as before. It is now assumed that nature also has a set of actions. This is referred to as the *nature action space* and is denoted by Θ. A *nature action* is denoted as $\theta \in \Theta$. It now seems appropriate to call U the *robot action space*; however, for convenience, it will often be referred to as the *action space*, in which the *robot* is implied.

This leads to the following formulation, which extends Formulation 9.1.

Formulation 9.3 (A Game Against Nature)

1. A nonempty set U called the *(robot) action space*. Each $u \in U$ is referred to as an *action*.

2. A nonempty set Θ called the *nature action space*. Each $\theta \in \Theta$ is referred to as a *nature action*.

3. A function $L : U \times \Theta \to \mathbb{R} \cup \{\infty\}$, called the *cost function*.

The cost function, L, now depends on $u \in U$ and $\theta \in \Theta$. If U and Θ are finite, then it is convenient to specify L as a $|U| \times |\Theta|$ matrix called the *cost matrix*.

Example 9.8 (A Simple Game Against Nature) Suppose that U and Θ each contain three actions. This results in nine possible outcomes, which can be specified by the following cost matrix:

Θ

U

1	−1	0
−1	2	−2
2	−1	1

The robot action, $u \in U$, selects a row, and the nature action, $\theta \in \Theta$, selects a column. The resulting cost, $L(u, \theta)$, is given by the corresponding matrix entry. ∎

In Formulation 9.3, it appears that both DMs act at the same time; nature does not know the robot action before deciding. In many contexts, nature may know the robot action. In this case, a different nature action space can be defined for every $u \in U$. This generalizes Formulation 9.3 to obtain:

Formulation 9.4 (Nature Knows the Robot Action)

1. A nonempty set U called the *action space*. Each $u \in U$ is referred to as an *action*.
2. For each $u \in U$, a nonempty set $\Theta(u)$ called the *nature action space*.
3. A function $L : U \times \Theta \to \mathbb{R} \cup \{\infty\}$, called the *cost function*.

If the robot chooses an action $u \in U$, then nature chooses from $\Theta(u)$.

9.2.2 Nondeterministic vs. probabilistic models

What is the best decision for the robot, given that it is engaged in a game against nature? This depends on what information the robot has regarding how nature chooses its actions. It will always be assumed that the robot does not know the precise nature action to be chosen; otherwise, it is pointless to define nature. Two alternative models that the robot can use for nature will be considered. From the robot's perspective, the possible models are

Nondeterministic: I have no idea what nature will do.

Probabilistic: I have been observing nature and gathering statistics.

Under both models, it is assumed that the robot knows Θ in Formulation 9.3 or $\Theta(u)$ for all $u \in U$ in Formulation 9.4. The nondeterministic and probabilistic terminology are borrowed from Erdmann [315]. In some literature, the term *possibilistic* is used instead of *nondeterministic*. This is an excellent term, but it is unfortunately too similar to *probabilistic* in English.

Assume first that Formulation 9.3 is used and that U and Θ are finite. Under the nondeterministic model, there is no additional information. One reasonable approach in this case is to make a decision by assuming the worst. It can even be imagined that nature knows what action the robot will take, and it will spitefully choose a nature action that drives the cost as high as possible. This pessimistic view is sometimes humorously referred to as Murphy's Law ("If anything can go wrong, it will.") [113] or Sod's Law. In this case, the best action, $u^* \in U$, is selected as

$$u^* = \operatorname*{argmin}_{u \in U} \left\{ \max_{\theta \in \Theta} \left\{ L(u, \theta) \right\} \right\}. \tag{9.14}$$

The action u^* is the lowest cost choice using *worst-case analysis*. This is sometimes referred to as a *minimax* solution because of the min and max in (9.14). If U or Θ is infinite, then the min or max may not exist and should be replaced by inf or sup, respectively.

Worst-case analysis may seem too pessimistic in some applications. Perhaps the assumption that all actions in Θ are equally likely may be preferable. This can be handled as a special case of the probabilistic model, which is described next.

Under the probabilistic model, it is assumed that the robot has gathered enough data to reliably estimate $P(\theta)$ (or $p(\theta)$ if Θ is continuous). In this case, it is imagined that nature applies a randomized strategy, as defined in Section 9.1.3. It assumed that the applied nature actions have been observed over many trials, and in the future they will continue to be chosen in the same manner, as predicted by the distribution $P(\theta)$. Instead of worst-case analysis, *expected-case analysis* is used. This optimizes the average cost to be received over numerous independent trials. In this case, the best action, $u^* \in U$, is

$$u^* = \operatorname*{argmin}_{u \in U} \left\{ E_\theta \left[L(u, \theta) \right] \right\}, \tag{9.15}$$

in which E_θ indicates that the expectation is taken according to the probability distribution (or density) over θ. Since Θ and $P(\theta)$ together form a probability space, $L(u, \theta)$ can be considered as a random variable for each value of u (it assigns a real value to each element of the sample space).[3] Using $P(\theta)$, the expectation in (9.15) can be expressed as

$$E_\theta[L(u, \theta)] = \sum_{\theta \in \Theta} L(u, \theta) P(\theta). \tag{9.16}$$

Example 9.9 (Nondeterministic vs. Probabilistic)   Return to Example 9.8. Let $U = \{u_1, u_2, u_3\}$ represent the robot actions, and let $\Theta = \{\theta_1, \theta_2, \theta_3\}$ represent the nature actions.

Under the nondeterministic model of nature, $u^* = u_1$, which results in $L(u^*, \theta) = 1$ in the worst case using (9.14). Under the probabilistic model, let $P(\theta_1) = 1/5$, $P(\theta_2) = 1/5$, and $P(\theta_3) = 3/5$. To find the optimal action, (9.15) can be used. This involves computing the expected cost for each action:

$$\begin{aligned}
E_\theta[L(u_1, \theta)] &= (1)1/5 + (-1)1/5 + (0)3/5 = 0 \\
E_\theta[L(u_2, \theta)] &= (-1)1/5 + (2)1/5 + (-2)3/5 = -1 \\
E_\theta[L(u_3, \theta)] &= (2)1/5 + (-1)1/5 + (1)3/5 = 4/5.
\end{aligned} \tag{9.17}$$

The best action is $u^* = u_2$, which produces the lowest expected cost, -1.

If the probability distribution had instead been $P = [1/10 \ 4/5 \ 1/10]$, then $u^* = u_1$ would have been obtained. Hence the best decision depends on $P(\theta)$; if this information is statistically valid, then it enables more informed decisions to be made. If such information is not available, then the nondeterministic model may be more suitable.

It is possible, however, to assign $P(\theta)$ as a uniform distribution in the absence of data. This means that all nature actions are equally likely; however, conclusions based on this are dangerous; see Section 9.5.   ∎

In Formulation 9.4, the nature action space $\Theta(u)$ depends on $u \in U$, the robot action. Under the nondeterministic model, (9.14) simply becomes

$$u^* = \operatorname*{argmin}_{u \in U} \left\{ \max_{\theta \in \Theta(u)} L(u, \theta) \right\}. \tag{9.18}$$

Unfortunately, these problems do not have a nice matrix representation because the size of $\Theta(u)$ can vary for different $u \in U$. In the probabilistic case, $P(\theta)$ is replaced by a conditional probability distribution $P(\theta|u)$. Estimating this distribution requires observing numerous independent trials for each possible $u \in U$. The behavior of nature can now

---

[3] Alternatively, a random variable may be defined over $U \times \Theta$, and conditional expectation would be taken, in which u is given.

depend on the robot action; however, nature is still characterized by a randomized strategy. It does not adapt its strategy across multiple trials. The expectation in (9.16) now becomes

$$E_\theta\Big[L(u, \theta)\Big] = \sum_{\theta \in \Theta(u)} L(u, \theta) P(\theta|u), \tag{9.19}$$

which replaces $P(\theta)$ by $P(\theta|u)$.

Regret

It is important to note that the models presented here are not the only accepted ways to make good decisions. In game theory, the key idea is to minimize "regret." This is the feeling you get after making a bad decision and wishing that you could change it after the game is finished. Suppose that after you choose some $u \in U$, you are told which $\theta \in \Theta$ was applied by nature. The regret is the amount of cost that you could have saved by picking a different action, given the nature action that was applied.

For each combination of $u \in U$ and $\theta \in \Theta$, the *regret*, T, is defined as

$$T(u, \theta) = \max_{u' \in U} \Big\{ L(u, \theta) - L(u', \theta) \Big\}. \tag{9.20}$$

For Formulation 9.3, if U and Θ are finite, then a $|\Theta| \times |U|$ *regret matrix* can be defined.

Suppose that minimizing regret is the primary concern, as opposed to the actual cost received. Under the nondeterministic model, the action that minimizes the worst-case regret is

$$u^* = \underset{u \in U}{\operatorname{argmin}} \Big\{ \max_{\theta \in \Theta} \Big\{ T(u, \theta) \Big\} \Big\}. \tag{9.21}$$

In the probabilistic model, the action that minimizes the expected regret is

$$u^* = \underset{u \in U}{\operatorname{argmin}} \Big\{ E_\theta\Big[T(u, \theta) \Big] \Big\}. \tag{9.22}$$

The only difference with respect to (9.14) and (9.15) is that L has been replaced by T. In Section 9.3.2, regret will be discussed in more detail because it forms the basis of optimality concepts in game theory.

Example 9.10 (Regret Matrix)   The regret matrix for Example 9.8 is

$$\Theta$$

2	0	2
0	3	0
3	0	3

U

Using the nondeterministic model, $u^* = u_1$, which results in a worst-case regret of 2 using (9.21). Under the probabilistic model, let $P(\theta_1) = P(\theta_2) = P(\theta_3) = 1/3$. In this case, $u^* = u_1$ or $u^* = u_2$, because in both cases the expected regret is 1 using (9.22).

9.2.3 Making use of observations

Formulations 9.3 and 9.4 do not allow the robot to receive any information (other than L) prior to making its decision. Now suppose that the robot has a sensor that it can check just prior to choosing the best action. This sensor provides an *observation* or measurement that contains information about which nature action might be chosen. In some contexts, the nature action can be imagined as a kind of *state* that has already been selected. The observation then provides information about this. For example, nature might select the current temperature in Bangkok. An observation could correspond to a thermometer in Bangkok that takes a reading.

Formulating the problem

Let Y denote the *observation space*, which is the set of all possible observations, $y \in Y$. For convenience, suppose that Y, U, and Θ are all discrete. It will be assumed as part of the model that some constraints on θ are known once y is given. Under the nondeterministic model a set $Y(\theta) \subseteq Y$ is specified for every $\theta \in \Theta$. The set $Y(\theta)$ indicates the possible observations, given that the nature action is θ. Under the probabilistic model a conditional probability distribution, $P(y|\theta)$, is specified. Examples of sensing models will be given in Section 9.2.4. Many others appear in Sections 11.1.1 and 11.5.1, although they are expressed with respect to a state space X that reduces to Θ in this section. As before, the probabilistic case also requires a prior distribution, $P(\Theta)$, to be given. This results in the following formulation.

Formulation 9.5 (A Game Against Nature with an Observation)

1. A finite, nonempty set U called the *action space*. Each $u \in U$ is referred to as an *action*.

2. A finite, nonempty set Θ called the *nature action space*.

3. A finite, nonempty set Y called the *observation space*.

4. A set $Y(\theta) \subset Y$ or probability distribution $P(y|\theta)$ specified for every $\theta \in \Theta$. This indicates which observations are possible or probable, respectively, if θ is the nature action. In the probabilistic case a prior, $P(\theta)$, must also be specified.

5. A function $L : U \times \Theta \to \mathbb{R} \cup \{\infty\}$, called the *cost function*.

Consider solving Formulation 9.5. A strategy is now more complicated than simply specifying an action because we want to completely characterize the behavior of the robot before the observation has been received. This is accomplished by defining a *strategy* as a function, $\pi : Y \to U$. For each possible observation, $y \in Y$, the strategy provides an action. We now want to search the space of possible strategies to find the one that makes the best decisions over all possible observations. In this section, Y is actually a special case of an information space, which is the main topic of Chapters 11 and 12. Eventually, a strategy (or plan) will be conditioned on an information state, which generalizes an observation.

Optimal strategies

Now consider finding the optimal strategy, denoted by π^*, under the nondeterministic model. The sets $Y(\theta)$ for each $\theta \in \Theta$ must be used to determine which nature actions are possible for each observation, $y \in Y$. Let $\Theta(y)$ denote this, which is obtained as

$$\Theta(y) = \{\theta \in \Theta \mid y \in Y(\theta)\}. \tag{9.23}$$

The optimal strategy, π^*, is defined by setting

$$\pi^*(y) = \operatorname*{argmin}_{u \in U} \left\{ \max_{\theta \in \Theta(y)} \left\{ L(u, \theta) \right\} \right\}, \tag{9.24}$$

for each $y \in Y$. Compare this to (9.14), in which the maximum was taken over all Θ. The advantage of having the observation, y, is that the set is restricted to $\Theta(y) \subseteq \Theta$.

Under the probabilistic model, an operation analogous to (9.23) must be performed. This involves computing $P(\theta|y)$ from $P(y|\theta)$ to determine the information that y contains regarding θ. Using Bayes' rule, (9.9), with marginalization on the denominator, the result is

$$P(\theta|y) = \frac{P(y|\theta)P(\theta)}{\displaystyle\sum_{\theta \in \Theta} P(y|\theta)P(\theta)}. \tag{9.25}$$

To see the connection between the nondeterministic and probabilistic cases, define a probability distribution, $P(y|\theta)$, that is nonzero only if $y \in Y(\theta)$ and use a uniform distribution for $P(\theta)$. In this case, (9.25) assigns nonzero probability to precisely the elements of $\Theta(y)$ as given in (9.23). Thus, (9.25) is just the probabilistic version of (9.23). The optimal strategy, π^*, is specified for each $y \in Y$ as

$$\pi^*(y) = \operatorname*{argmin}_{u \in U} \left\{ E_\theta \left[L(u, \theta) \,\middle|\, y \right] \right\} = \operatorname*{argmin}_{u \in U} \left\{ \sum_{\theta \in \Theta} L(u, \theta) P(\theta|y) \right\}. \tag{9.26}$$

This differs from (9.15) and (9.16) by replacing $P(\theta)$ with $P(\theta|y)$. For each u, the expectation in (9.26) is called the *conditional Bayes' risk*. The optimal strategy, π^*, always selects the strategy that minimizes this risk. Note that $P(\theta|y)$ in (9.26) can be expressed using (9.25), for which the denominator (9.26) represents $P(y)$ and does not depend on u; therefore, it does not affect the optimization. Due to this, $P(y|\theta)P(\theta)$ can be used in the place of $P(\theta|y)$ in (9.26), and the same π^* will be obtained. If the spaces are continuous, then probability densities are used in the place of all probability distributions, and the method otherwise remains the same.

Nature acts twice

A convenient, alternative formulation can be given by allowing nature to act twice:

1. First, a nature action, $\theta \in \Theta$, is chosen but is unknown to the robot.

2. Following this, a *nature observation action* is chosen to interfere with the robot's ability to sense θ.

Let ψ denote a *nature observation action*, which is chosen from a *nature observation action space*, $\Psi(\theta)$. A *sensor mapping*, h, can now be defined that yields $y = h(\theta, \psi)$ for each $\theta \in \Theta$ and $\psi \in \Psi(\theta)$. Thus, for each of the two kinds of nature actions, $\theta \in \Theta$ and $\psi \in \Psi$, an observation, $y = h(\theta, \psi)$, is given. This yields an alternative way to express Formulation 9.5:

Formulation 9.6 (Nature Interferes with the Observation)

1. A nonempty, finite set U called the *action space*.

2. A nonempty, finite set Θ called the *nature action space*.

3. A nonempty, finite set Y called the *observation space*.

4. For each $\theta \in \Theta$, a nonempty set $\Psi(\theta)$ called the *nature observation action space*.

5. A sensor mapping $h : \Theta \times \Psi \rightarrow Y$.

6. A function $L : U \times \Theta \rightarrow \mathbb{R} \cup \{\infty\}$ called the *cost function*.

This nicely unifies the nondeterministic and probabilistic models with a single function h. To express a nondeterministic model, it is assumed that any $\psi \in \Psi(\theta)$ is possible.

Using h,

$$\Theta(y) = \{\theta \in \Theta \mid \exists \psi \in \Psi(\theta) \text{ such that } y = h(\theta, \psi)\}. \tag{9.27}$$

For a probabilistic model, a distribution $P(\psi|\theta)$ is specified (often, this may reduce to $P(\psi)$). Suppose that when the domain of h is restricted to some $\theta \in \Theta$, then it forms an injective mapping from Ψ to Y. In other words, every nature observation action leads to a unique observation, assuming θ is fixed. Using $P(\psi)$ and h, $P(y|\theta)$ is derived as

$$P(y|\theta) = \begin{cases} P(\psi|\theta) & \text{for the unique } \psi \text{ such that } y = h(\theta, \psi). \\ 0 & \text{if no such } \psi \text{ exists.} \end{cases} \tag{9.28}$$

If the injective assumption is lifted, then $P(\psi|\theta)$ is replaced by a sum over all ψ for which $y = h(\theta, \psi)$. In Formulation 9.6, the only difference between the nondeterministic and probabilistic models is the characterization of ψ, which represents a kind of measurement interference. A strategy still takes the form $\pi : \Theta \to U$. A hybrid model is even possible in which one nature action is modeled nondeterministically and the other probabilistically.

Receiving multiple observations

Another extension of Formulation 9.5 is to allow multiple observations, $y_1, y_2, \ldots, y_n$, before making a decision. Each y_i is assumed to belong to an observation space, Y_i. A strategy, π, now depends on all observations:

$$\pi : Y_1 \times Y_2 \times \cdots \times Y_n \to U. \tag{9.29}$$

Under the nondeterministic model, $Y_i(\theta)$ is specified for each i and $\theta \in \Theta$. The set $\Theta(y)$ is replaced by

$$\Theta(y_1) \cap \Theta(y_2) \cap \cdots \cap \Theta(y_n) \tag{9.30}$$

in (9.24) to obtain the optimal action, $\pi^*(y_1, \ldots, y_n)$.

Under the probabilistic model, $P(y_i|\theta)$ is specified instead. It is often assumed that the observations are conditionally independent given θ. This means for any y_i, θ, and y_j such that $i \neq j$, $P(y_i|\theta, y_j) = P(y_i|\theta)$. The condition $P(\theta|y)$ in (9.26) is replaced by $P(\theta|y_1, \ldots, y_n)$. Applying Bayes' rule, and using the conditional independence of the y_i's given θ, yields

$$P(\theta|y_1, \ldots, y_n) = \frac{P(y_1|\theta)P(y_2|\theta) \cdots P(y_n|\theta)P(\theta)}{P(y_1, \ldots, y_n)}. \tag{9.31}$$

The denominator can be treated as a constant factor that does not affect the optimization. Therefore, it does not need to be explicitly computed unless the optimal expected cost is needed in addition to the optimal action.

Conditional independence allows a dramatic simplification that avoids the full specification of $P(y|\theta)$. Sometimes the conditional independence assumption is used when it is incorrect, just to exploit this simplification. Therefore, a method that uses conditional independence of observations is often called *naive Bayes*.

9.2.4 Examples of optimal decision making

The framework presented so far characterizes *statistical decision theory*, which covers a broad range of applications and research issues. Virtually any context in which a decision must be made automatically, by a machine or a person following specified rules, is a candidate for using these concepts. In Chapters 10 through 12, this decision problem will be repeatedly embedded into complicated planning problems. Planning will be viewed as a sequential decision-making process that iteratively modifies states in a state space. Most often, each decision step will be simpler than what usually arises in common applications of decision theory. This is because planning problems are complicated by many other factors. If the decision step in a particular application is already too hard to solve, then an extension to planning appears hopeless.

It is nevertheless important to recognize the challenges in general that arise when modeling and solving decision problems under the framework of this section. Some examples are presented here to help illustrate its enormous power and scope.

9.2.4.1 Pattern classification

An active field over the past several decades in computer vision and machine learning has been *pattern classification* [273, 297, 714]. The general problem involves using a set of data to perform classifications. For example, in computer vision, the data correspond to information extracted from an image. These indicate observed features of an object that are used by a vision system to try to classify the object (e.g., "I am looking at a bowl of Vietnamese noodle soup").

The presentation here represents a highly idealized version of pattern classification. We will assume that all of the appropriate model details, including the required probability distributions, are available. In some contexts, these can be obtained by gathering statistics over large data sets. In many applications, however, obtaining such data is expensive or inaccessible, and classification techniques must be developed in lieu of good information. Some problems are even *unsupervised*, which means that the set of possible classes must also be discovered automatically. Due to issues such as these, pattern classification remains a challenging research field.

The general model is that nature first determines the class, then observations are obtained regarding the class, and finally the robot action attempts to guess the correct class based on the observations. The problem fits under Formulation 9.5. Let Θ denote a finite set of *classes*. Since the robot must guess the class, $U = \Theta$. A simple cost function is defined to measure the mismatch between u and θ:

$$L(u, \theta) = \begin{cases} 0 & \text{if } u = \theta \text{ (correct classification} \\ 1 & \text{if } u \neq \theta \text{ (incorrect classification) .} \end{cases} \tag{9.32}$$

The nondeterministic model yields a cost of 1 if it is *possible* that a classification error can be made using action u. Under the probabilistic model, the expectation of (9.32) gives the probability that a classification error will be made given an action u.

The next part of the formulation considers information that is used to make the classification decision. Let Y denote a *feature space*, in which each $y \in Y$ is called a *feature* or *feature vector* (often $y \in \mathbb{R}^n$). The feature in this context is just an observation, as given in Formulation 9.5. The best *classifier* or *classification rule* is a strategy $\pi : Y \to U$ that provides the smallest classification error in the worst case or expected case, depending on the model.

A Bayesian classifier

The probabilistic approach is most common in pattern classification. This results in a *Bayesian classifier*. Here it is assumed that $P(y|\theta)$ and $P(\theta)$ are given. The distribution of

Shape	0	A E F H
	1	B C D G
Ends	0	B D
	1	
	2	A C G
	3	F E
	4	H
Holes	0	C E F G H
	1	A D
	2	B

Figure 9.1: A mapping from letters to feature values.

features for a given class is indicated by $P(y|\theta)$. The overall frequency of class occurrences is given by $P(\theta)$. If large, preclassified data sets are available, then these distributions can be reliably learned. The feature space is often continuous, which results in a density $p(y|\theta)$, even though $P(\theta)$ remains a discrete probability distribution. An optimal classifier, π^*, is designed according to (9.26). It performs classification by receiving a feature vector, y, and then declaring that the class is $u = \pi^*(y)$. The expected cost using (9.32) is the probability of error.

Example 9.11 (Optical Character Recognition) An example of classification is given by a simplified *optical character recognition* (OCR) problem. Suppose that a camera creates a digital image of a page of text. Segmentation is first performed to determine the location of each letter. Following this, the individual letters must be classified correctly. Let $\Theta = \{A, B, C, D, E, F, G, H\}$, which would ordinarily include all of the letters of the alphabet.

Suppose that there are three different image processing algorithms:

Shape extractor: This returns $s = 0$ if the letter is composed of straight edges only, and $s = 1$ if it contains at least one curve.

End counter: This returns e, the number of segment ends. For example, O has none and X has four.

Hole counter: This returns h, the number of holes enclosed by the character. For example, X has none and O has one.

The feature vector is $y = (s, e, h)$. The values that should be reported under ideal conditions are shown in Figure 9.1. These indicate $\Theta(s)$, $\Theta(e)$, and $\Theta(h)$. The intersection of these yields $\Theta(y)$ for any combination of s, e, and h.

Imagine doing classification under the nondeterministic model, with the assumption that the features always provide correct information. For $y = (0, 2, 1)$, the only possible letter is A. For $y = (1, 0, 2)$, the only letter is B. If each (s, e, h) is consistent with only one or no letters, then a perfect classifier can be constructed. Unfortunately, $(0, 3, 0)$ is consistent with both E and F. In the worst case, the cost of using (9.32) is 1.

One way to fix this is to introduce a new feature. Suppose that an image processing algorithm is used to detect corners. These are places at which two segments meet at a right (90 degrees) angle. Let c denote the number of corners, and let the new feature vector be $y = (s, e, h, c)$. The new algorithm nicely distinguishes E from F, for which $c = 2$ and $c = 1$, respectively. Now all letters can be correctly classified without errors.

Of course, in practice, the image processing algorithms occasionally make mistakes. A Bayesian classifier can be designed to maximize the probability of success. Assume conditional independence of the observations, which means that the classifier can be considered *naive*. Suppose that the four image processing algorithms are run over a training data set and the results are recorded. In each case, the correct classification is determined by hand to obtain probabilities $P(s|\theta)$, $P(e|\theta)$, $P(h|\theta)$, and $P(c|\theta)$. For example, suppose that the hole counter receives the letter A as input. After running the algorithm over many occurrences of A in text, it may be determined that $P(h = 1| \theta = A) = 0.9$, which is the correct answer. With smaller probabilities, perhaps $P(h = 0| \theta = A) = 0.09$ and $P(h = 2| \theta = A) = 0.01$. Assuming that the output of each image processing algorithm is independent given the input letter, a joint probability can be assigned as

$$P(y|\theta) = P(s, e, h, c|\theta) = P(s|\theta)P(e|\theta)P(h|\theta)P(c|\theta). \tag{9.33}$$

The value of the prior $P(\theta)$ can be obtained by running the classifier over large amounts of hand-classified text and recording the relative numbers of occurrences of each letter. It is interesting to note that some context-specific information can be incorporated. If the text is known to be written in Spanish, then $P(\theta)$ should be different than from text written in English. Tailoring $P(\theta)$ to the type of text that will appear improves the performance of the resulting classifier.

The classifier makes its decisions by choosing the action that minimizes the probability of error. This error is proportional to

$$\sum_{\theta \in \Theta} P(s|\theta)P(e|\theta)P(h|\theta)P(c|\theta)P(\theta), \tag{9.34}$$

by neglecting the constant $P(y)$ in the denominator of Bayes' rule in (9.26). ∎

9.2.4.2 Parameter estimation

Another important application of the decision-making framework of this section is *parameter estimation* [91, 270]. In this case, nature selects a *parameter*, $\theta \in \Theta$, and Θ represents a *parameter space*. Through one or more independent trials, some observations are obtained. Each observation should ideally be a direct measurement of Θ, but imperfections in the measurement process distort the observation. Usually, $\Theta \subseteq Y$, and in many cases, $Y = \Theta$. The robot action is to guess the parameter that was chosen by nature. Hence, $U = \Theta$. In most applications, all of the spaces are continuous subsets of $\mathbb{R}^n$. The cost function is designed to increase as the error, $\|u - \theta\|$, becomes larger.

Example 9.12 (Parameter Estimation)   Suppose that $U = Y = \Theta = \mathbb{R}$. Nature therefore chooses a real-valued parameter, which is estimated. The cost of making a mistake is

$$L(u, \theta) = (u - \theta)^2. \tag{9.35}$$

Suppose that a Bayesian approach is taken. The prior probability density $p(\theta)$ is given as uniform over an interval $[a, b] \subset \mathbb{R}$. An observation is received, but it is noisy. The noise can be modeled as a second action of nature, as described in Section 9.2.3. This leads to a density $p(y|\theta)$. Suppose that the noise is modeled with a Gaussian, which results in

$$p(y|\theta) = \frac{1}{\sqrt{2\pi\sigma^2}} e^{-(y-\theta)^2/2\sigma^2}, \tag{9.36}$$

in which the mean is θ and the standard deviation is σ.

The optimal parameter estimate based on y is obtained by selecting $u \in \mathbb{R}$ to minimize

$$\int_{-\infty}^{\infty} L(u, \theta) p(\theta|y) d\theta, \tag{9.37}$$

in which

$$p(\theta|y) = \frac{p(y|\theta) p(\theta)}{p(y)}, \tag{9.38}$$

by Bayes' rule. The term $p(y)$ does not depend on θ, and it can therefore be ignored in the optimization. Using the prior density, $p(\theta) = 0$ outside of $[a, b]$; hence, the domain of integration can be restricted to $[a, b]$. The value of $p(\theta) = 1/(b - a)$ is also a constant that can be ignored in the optimization. Using (9.36), this means that u is selected to optimize

$$\int_{a}^{b} L(u, \theta) p(y|\theta) d\theta, \tag{9.39}$$

which can be expressed in terms of the standard error function, $\text{erf}(x)$ (the integral from 0 to a constant, of a Gaussian density over an interval).

If a sequence, $y_1, \ldots, y_k$, of independent observations is obtained, then (9.39) is replaced by

$$\int_{a}^{b} L(u, \theta) p(y_1|\theta) \cdots p(y_k|\theta) d\theta. \tag{9.40}$$

■

9.3 Two-player zero-sum games

Section 9.2 involved one real decision maker (DM), the robot, playing against a fictitious DM called nature. Now suppose that the second DM is a clever opponent that makes decisions in the same way that the robot would. This leads to a symmetric situation in which two decision makers simultaneously make a decision, without knowing how the other will act. It is assumed in this section that the DMs have diametrically opposing interests. They are two players engaged in a game in which a loss for one player is a gain for the other, and vice versa. This results in the most basic form of *game theory*, which is referred to as a *zero-sum game*.

9.3.1 Game formulation

Suppose there are two *players*, P_1 and P_2, that each have to make a decision. Each has a finite set of actions, U and V, respectively. The set V can be viewed as the "replacement" of Θ from Formulation 9.3 by a set of actions chosen by a true opponent. Each player has a cost function, which is denoted as $L_i : U \times V \to \mathbb{R}$ for $i = 1, 2$. An important constraint for zero-sum games is

$$L_1(u, v) = -L_2(u, v), \tag{9.41}$$

which means that a cost for one player is a reward for the other. This is the basis of the term *zero sum*, which means that the two costs can be added to obtain zero. In zero-sum games the interests of the players are completely opposed. In Section 9.4 this constraint will be lifted to obtain more general games.

In light of (9.41) it is pointless to represent two cost functions. Instead, the superscript will be dropped, and L will refer to the cost, L_1, of P_1. The goal of P_1 is to minimize L. Due to (9.41), the goal of P_2 is to maximize L. Thus, L can be considered as a *reward* for P_2, but a *cost* for P_1.

A formulation can now be given:

Formulation 9.7 (A Zero-Sum Game)

1. Two players, P_1 and P_2.

2. A nonempty, finite set U called the *action space for* P_1. For convenience in describing examples, assume that U is a set of consecutive integers from 1 to $|U|$. Each $u \in U$ is referred to as an *action of* P_1.

3. A nonempty, finite set V called the *action space for* P_2. Assume that V is a set of consecutive integers from 1 to $|V|$. Each $v \in V$ is referred to as an *action of* P_2.

4. A function $L : U \times V \to \mathbb{R} \cup \{-\infty, \infty\}$ called the *cost function* for P_1. This also serves as a *reward function* for P_2 because of (9.41).

Before discussing what it means to solve a zero-sum game, some additional assumptions are needed. Assume that the players know each other's cost functions. This implies that the motivation of the opponent is completely understood. The other assumption is that the players are *rational*, which means that they will try to obtain the best cost whenever possible. P_1 will not choose an action that leads to higher cost when a lower cost action is available. Likewise, P_2 will not choose an action that leads to lower cost. Finally, it is assumed that both players make their decisions simultaneously. There is no information regarding the decision of P_1 that can be exploited by P_2, and vice versa.

Formulation 9.7 is often referred to as a *matrix game* because L can be expressed with a cost matrix, as was done in Section 9.2. Here the matrix indicates costs for P_1 and P_2, instead of the robot and nature. All of the required information from Formulation 9.7 is specified by a single matrix; therefore, it is a convenient form for expressing zero-sum games.

Example 9.13 (Matrix Representation of a Zero-Sum Game)   Suppose that U, the action set for P_1, contains three actions and V contains four actions. There should be $3 \times 4 = 12$ values in the specification of the cost function, L. This can be expressed as a cost matrix,

$$
\begin{array}{c}
\\
U
\end{array}
\begin{array}{c}
V \\
\begin{array}{|c|c|c|c|}
\hline
1 & 3 & 3 & 2 \\
\hline
0 & -1 & 2 & 1 \\
\hline
-2 & 2 & 0 & 1 \\
\hline
\end{array}
\end{array}
\quad , \tag{9.42}
$$

in which each row corresponds to some $u \in U$, and each column corresponds to some $v \in V$. Each entry yields $L(u, v)$, which is the cost for P_1. This representation is similar to that shown in Example 9.8, except that the nature action space, Θ, is replaced by V. The cost for P_2 is $-L(u, v)$.   ∎

9.3.2 Deterministic strategies

What constitutes a good solution to Formulation 9.7? Consider the game from the perspective of P_1. It seems reasonable to apply worst-case analysis when trying to account for the action that will be taken by P_2. This results in a choice that is equivalent to assuming that P_2 is nature acting under the nondeterministic model, as considered in Section 9.2.2. For a matrix game, this is computed by first determining the maximum cost over each row. Selecting the action that produces the minimum among these represents the lowest cost that P_1 can guarantee for itself. Let this selection be referred to as a *security strategy* for P_1.

For the matrix game in (9.42), the security strategy is illustrated as

$$
\begin{array}{c}
 & V \\
U & \begin{array}{|cccc|c}
1 & 3 & 3 & 2 & \rightarrow 3 \\
0 & -1 & 2 & 1 & \rightarrow \mathbf{2} \\
-2 & 2 & 0 & 1 & \rightarrow \mathbf{2}
\end{array}
\end{array}, \tag{9.43}
$$

in which $u = 2$ and $u = 3$ are the best actions. Each yields a cost no worse than 2, regardless of the action chosen by P_2.

This can be formalized using the existing notation. A security strategy, u^*, for P_1 is defined in general as

$$
u^* = \operatorname*{argmin}_{u \in U} \left\{ \max_{v \in V} \left\{ L(u, v) \right\} \right\}. \tag{9.44}
$$

There may be multiple security strategies that satisfy the argmin; however, this does not cause trouble, as will be explained shortly. Let the resulting worst-case cost be denoted by $\overline{L}^*$, and let it be called the *upper value* of the game. This is defined as

$$
\overline{L}^* = \max_{v \in V} \left\{ L(u^*, v) \right\}. \tag{9.45}
$$

Now swap roles, and consider the game from the perspective of P_2, which would like to maximize L. It can also use worst-case analysis, which means that it would like to select an action that guarantees a high cost, in spite of the action of P_1 to potentially reduce it. A security strategy, v^*, for P_2 is defined as

$$
v^* = \operatorname*{argmax}_{v \in V} \left\{ \min_{u \in U} \left\{ L(u, v) \right\} \right\}. \tag{9.46}
$$

Note the symmetry with respect to (9.44). There may be multiple security strategies for P_2. A security strategy v^* is just an "upside-down" version of the worst-case analysis applied in Section 9.2.2. The *lower value*, $\underline{L}^*$, is defined as

$$
\underline{L}^* = \min_{u \in U} \left\{ L(u, v^*) \right\}. \tag{9.47}
$$

Returning to the matrix game in (9.42), the last column is selected by applying (9.46):

$$
\begin{array}{c}
 & V \\
U & \begin{array}{|c|c|c|c|}
\hline
1 & 3 & 3 & 2 \\
\hline
0 & -1 & 2 & 1 \\
\hline
-2 & 2 & 0 & 1 \\
\hline
\downarrow & \downarrow & \downarrow & \downarrow \\
-2 & -1 & 0 & \mathbf{1} \\
\hline
\end{array}
\end{array}. \tag{9.48}
$$

An interesting relationship between the upper and lower values is that $\underline{L}^* \leq \overline{L}^*$ for any game using Formulation 9.7. This is shown by observing that

$$
\underline{L}^* = \min_{u \in U} \left\{ L(u, v^*) \right\} \leq L(u^*, v^*) \leq \max_{v \in V} \left\{ L(u^*, v) \right\} = \overline{L}^*, \tag{9.49}
$$

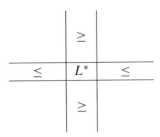

Figure 9.2: A saddle point can be detected in a matrix by finding a value L^* that is lowest among all elements in its column and greatest among all elements in its row.

in which $L(u^*, v^*)$ is the cost received when the players apply their respective security strategies. If the game is played by rational DMs, then the resulting cost always lies between $\underline{L}^*$ and $\overline{L}^*$.

Regret

Suppose that the players apply security strategies, $u^* = 2$ and $v^* = 4$. This results in a cost of $L(2, 4) = 1$. How do the players feel after the outcome? P_1 may feel satisfied because given that P_2 selected $v^* = 4$, it received the lowest cost possible. On the other hand, P_2 may regret its decision in light of the action chosen by P_1. If it had known that $u = 2$ would be chosen, then it could have picked $v = 2$ to receive cost $L(2, 2) = 2$, which is better than $L(2, 4) = 1$. If the game were to be repeated, then P_2 would want to change its strategy in hopes of tricking P_1 to obtain a higher reward.

Is there a way to keep both players satisfied? Any time there is a gap between $\underline{L}^*$ and $\overline{L}^*$, there is regret for one or both players. If r_1 and r_2 denote the amount of regret experienced by P_1 and P_2, respectively, then the total regret is

$$r_1 + r_2 = \overline{L}^* - \underline{L}^*. \tag{9.50}$$

Thus, the only way to satisfy both players is to obtain upper and lower values such that $\underline{L}^* = \overline{L}^*$. These are properties of the game, however, and they are not up to the players to decide. For some games, the values are equal, but for many $\underline{L}^* < \overline{L}^*$. Fortunately, by using randomized strategies, the upper and lower values always coincide; this is covered in Section 9.3.3.

Saddle points

If $\underline{L}^* = \overline{L}^*$, the security strategies are called a *saddle point*, and $L^* = \underline{L}^* = \overline{L}^*$ is called the *value* of the game. If this occurs, the order of the max and min can be swapped without changing the value:

$$L^* = \min_{u \in U} \left\{ \max_{v \in V} \left\{ L(u, v) \right\} \right\} = \max_{v \in V} \left\{ \min_{u \in U} \left\{ L(u, v) \right\} \right\}. \tag{9.51}$$

A saddle point is sometimes referred to as an *equilibrium* because the players have no incentive to change their choices (because there is no regret). A saddle point is defined as any $u^* \in U$ and $v^* \in V$ such that

$$L(u^*, v) \leq L(u^*, v^*) \leq L(u, v^*) \tag{9.52}$$

for all $u \in U$ and $v \in V$. Note that $L^* = L(u^*, v^*)$. When looking at a matrix game, a saddle point is found by finding the simple pattern shown in Figure 9.2.

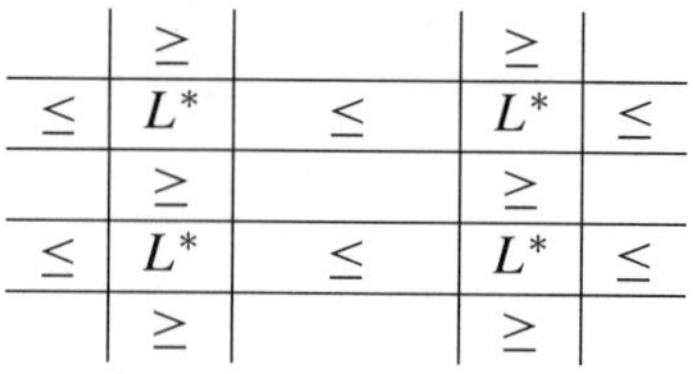

		$\geq$				$\geq$		
$\leq$		L^*		$\leq$		L^*		$\leq$
		$\geq$				$\geq$		
$\leq$		L^*		$\leq$		L^*		$\leq$
		$\geq$				$\geq$		

Figure 9.3: A matrix could have more than one saddle point, which may seem to lead to a coordination problem between the players. Fortunately, there is no problem, because the same value will be received regardless of which saddle point is selected by each player.

Example 9.14 (A Deterministic Saddle Point) Here is a matrix game that has a saddle point:

$$
U \quad
\begin{array}{|c|c|c|}
\hline
3 & 3 & 5 \\
\hline
1 & -1 & 7 \\
\hline
0 & -2 & 4 \\
\hline
\end{array}
\quad . \tag{9.53}
$$

with V labeling the columns.

By applying (9.52) (or using Figure 9.2), the saddle point is obtained when $u = 3$ and $v = 3$. The result is that $L^* = 4$. In this case, neither player has regret after the game is finished. P_1 is satisfied because 4 is the lowest cost it could have received, given that P_2 chose the third column. Likewise, 4 is the highest cost that P_2 could have received, given that P_1 chose the bottom row. ∎

What if there are multiple saddle points in the same game? This may appear to be a problem because the players have no way to coordinate their decisions. What if P_1 tries to achieve one saddle point while P_2 tries to achieve another? It turns out that if there is more than one saddle point, then there must at least be four, as shown in Figure 9.3. As soon as we try to make two "+" patterns like the one shown in Figure 9.2, they intersect, and four saddle points are created. Similar behavior occurs as more saddle points are added.

Example 9.15 (Multiple Saddle Points) This game has multiple saddle points and follows the pattern in Figure 9.3:

$$
U \quad
\begin{array}{|c|c|c|c|c|}
\hline
4 & 3 & 5 & 1 & 2 \\
\hline
-1 & 0 & -2 & 0 & -1 \\
\hline
-4 & 1 & 4 & 3 & 5 \\
\hline
-3 & 0 & -1 & 0 & -2 \\
\hline
3 & 2 & -7 & 3 & 8 \\
\hline
\end{array}
\quad . \tag{9.54}
$$

with V labeling the columns.

Let (i, j) denote the pair of choices for P_1 and P_2, respectively. Both $(2, 2)$ and $(4, 4)$ are saddle points with value $V = 0$. What if P_1 chooses $u = 2$ and P_2 chooses $v = 4$? This is not a problem because $(2, 4)$ is also a saddle point. Likewise, $(4, 2)$ is another saddle point. In general, no problems are caused by the existence of multiple saddle points because the resulting cost is independent of which saddle point is attempted by each player. ∎

9.3.3 Randomized strategies

The fact that some zero-sum games do not have a saddle point is disappointing because regret is unavoidable in these cases. Suppose we slightly change the rules. Assume that the same game is repeatedly played by P_1 and P_2 over numerous trials. If they use a deterministic strategy, they will choose the same actions every time, resulting in the same costs. They may instead switch between alternative security strategies, which causes fluctuations in the costs. What happens if they each implement a randomized strategy? Using the idea from Section 9.1.3, each strategy is specified as a probability distribution over the actions. In the limit, as the number of times the game is played tends to infinity, an expected cost is obtained. One of the most famous results in game theory is that on the space of randomized strategies, a saddle point always exists for any zero-sum matrix game; however, expected costs must be used. Thus, if randomization is used, there will be no regrets. In an individual trial, regret may be possible; however, as the costs are averaged over all trials, both players will be satisfied.

9.3.3.1 Extending the formulation

Since a game under Formulation 9.7 can be nicely expressed as a matrix, it is tempting to use linear algebra to conveniently express expected costs. Let $|U| = m$ and $|V| = n$. As in Section 9.1.3, a randomized strategy for P_1 can be represented as an m-dimensional vector,

$$w = [w_1 \; w_2 \; \ldots \; w_m]. \tag{9.55}$$

The probability axioms of Section 9.1.2 must be satisfied: 1) $w_i \geq 0$ for all $i \in \{1, \ldots, m\}$, and 2) $w_1 + \cdots + w_m = 1$. If w is considered as a point in $\mathbb{R}^m$, then the two constraints imply that it must lie on an $(m-1)$-dimensional simplex (recall Section 6.3.1). If $m = 3$, this means that w lies in a triangular subset of $\mathbb{R}^3$. Similarly, let z represent a randomized strategy for P_2 as an n-dimensional vector,

$$z = [z_1 \; z_2 \; \ldots \; z_n]^T, \tag{9.56}$$

that also satisfies the probability axioms. In (9.56), ^{T} denotes *transpose*, which yields a column vector that satisfies the dimensional constraints required for an upcoming matrix multiplication.

Let $\bar{L}(w, z)$ denote the expected cost that will be received if P_1 plays w and P_2 plays z. This can be computed as

$$\bar{L}(w, z) = \sum_{i=1}^{m} \sum_{j=1}^{n} L(i, j) w_i z_j. \tag{9.57}$$

Note that the cost, $L(i, j)$, makes use of the assumption in Formulation 9.7 that the actions are consecutive integers. The expected cost can be alternatively expressed using the cost matrix, A. In this case

$$\bar{L}(w, z) = wAz, \tag{9.58}$$

in which the product wAz yields a scalar value that is precisely (9.57). To see this, first consider the product Az. This yields an m-dimensional vector in which the ith element is the expected cost that P_1 would receive if it tries $u = i$. Thus, it appears that P_1 views P_2 as a nature player under the probabilistic model. Once w and Az are multiplied, a scalar value is obtained, which averages the costs in the vector Az according the probabilities of w.

Let W and Z denote the set of all randomized strategies for P_1 and P_2, respectively. These spaces include strategies that are equivalent to the deterministic strategies considered in Section 9.3.2 by assigning probability one to a single action. Thus, W and Z can be considered as expansions of the set of possible strategies in comparison to what was available in the deterministic setting. Using W and Z, *randomized security strategies* for P_1 and P_2 are defined as

$$w^* = \operatorname*{argmin}_{w \in W} \left\{ \max_{z \in Z} \left\{ \bar{L}(w, z) \right\} \right\} \tag{9.59}$$

and

$$z^* = \operatorname*{argmax}_{z \in Z} \left\{ \min_{w \in W} \left\{ \bar{L}(w, z) \right\} \right\}, \tag{9.60}$$

respectively. These should be compared to (9.44) and (9.46). The differences are that the space of strategies has been expanded, and expected cost is now used.

The *randomized upper value* is defined as

$$\overline{\mathcal{L}}^* = \max_{z \in Z} \left\{ \bar{L}(w^*, z) \right\}, \tag{9.61}$$

and the *randomized lower value* is

$$\underline{\mathcal{L}}^* = \min_{w \in W} \left\{ \bar{L}(w, z^*) \right\}. \tag{9.62}$$

Since W and Z include the deterministic security strategies, $\overline{\mathcal{L}}^* \leq \overline{L}^*$ and $\underline{\mathcal{L}}^* \geq \underline{L}^*$. These inequalities imply that the randomized security strategies may have some hope in closing the gap between the two values in general.

The most fundamental result in zero-sum game theory was shown by von Neumann [956, 957], and it states that $\underline{\mathcal{L}}^* = \overline{\mathcal{L}}^*$ for any game in Formulation 9.7. This yields the *randomized value* $\mathcal{L}^* = \underline{\mathcal{L}}^* = \overline{\mathcal{L}}^*$ for the game. This means that there will never be expected regret if the players stay with their security strategies. If the players apply their randomized security strategies, then a *randomized saddle point* is obtained. This saddle point cannot be seen as a simple pattern in the matrix A because it instead exists over W and Z.

The guaranteed existence of a randomized saddle point is an important result because it demonstrates the value of randomization when making decisions against an intelligent opponent. In Example 9.7, it was intuitively argued that randomization seems to help when playing against an intelligent adversary. When playing the game repeatedly with a deterministic strategy, the other player could learn the strategy and win every time. Once a randomized strategy is used, the players will not experience regret.

9.3.3.2 Computation of randomized saddle points

So far it has been established that a randomized saddle point always exists, but how can one be found? Two key observations enable a combinatorial solution to the problem:

1. The security strategy for each player can be found by considering only deterministic strategies for the opposing player.

2. If the strategy for the other player is fixed, then the expected cost is a linear function of the undetermined probabilities.

First consider the problem of determining the security strategy for P_1. The first observation means that (9.59) does not need to consider randomized strategies for P_2. Inside of the argmin, w is fixed. What randomized strategy, $z \in Z$, maximizes $\bar{L}(w, z) = wAz$? If w is fixed, then wA can be treated as a constant n-dimensional vector, s. This means $\bar{L}(w, z) = s \cdot z$, in which $\cdot$ is the inner (dot) product. Now the task is to select z to maximize $s \cdot z$.

This involves selecting the largest element of s; suppose this is s_i. The maximum cost over all $z \in Z$ is obtained by placing all of the probability mass at action i. Thus, the strategy $z_i = 1$ and $z_j = 0$ for $i \neq j$ gives the highest cost, and it is deterministic.

Using the first observation, for each $w \in W$, only n possible responses by P_2 need to be considered. These are the n deterministic strategies, each of which assigns $z_i = 1$ for a unique $i \in \{1, \ldots, n\}$.

Now consider the second observation. The expected cost, $\bar{L}(w, z) = wAz$, is a linear function of w, if z is fixed. Since z only needs to be fixed at n different values due to the first observation, w is selected at the point at which the smallest maximum value among the n linear functions occurs. This is the minimum value of the *upper envelope* of the collection of linear functions. Such envelopes were mentioned in Section 6.5.2. Example 9.16 will illustrate this. The domain for this optimization can conveniently be set as a triangle in $\mathbb{R}^{m-1}$. Even though $W \subset \mathbb{R}^m$, the last coordinate, w_m, is not needed because it is always $w_m = 1 - (w_1 + \cdots + w_{m-1})$. The resulting optimization falls under *linear programming*, for which many combinatorial algorithms exist [261, 266, 667, 734].

In the explanation above, there is nothing particular to P_1 when trying to find its security strategy. The same method can be applied to determine the security strategy for P_2; however, every minimization is replaced by a maximization, and vice versa. In summary, the min in (9.60) needs only to consider the deterministic strategies in W. If w becomes fixed, then $\bar{L}(w, z) = wAz$ is once again a linear function, but this time it is linear in z. The best randomized action is chosen by finding the point $z \in Z$ that gives the highest minimum value among m linear functions. This is the minimum value of the *lower envelope* of the collection of linear functions. The optimization occurs over $\mathbb{R}^{n-1}$ because the last coordinate, z_n, is obtained directly from $z_n = 1 - (z_1 + \cdots + z_{n-1})$.

This computation method is best understood through an example.

Example 9.16 (Computing a Randomized Saddle Point) The simplest case is when both players have only two actions. Let the cost matrix be defined as

$$
\begin{array}{c}
\quad V \\
U \quad \begin{array}{|c|c|} \hline 3 & 0 \\ \hline -1 & 1 \\ \hline \end{array}
\end{array} .
\tag{9.63}
$$

Consider computing the security strategy for P_1. Note that W and Z are only one-dimensional subsets of $\mathbb{R}^2$. A randomized strategy for P_1 is $w = [w_1 \; w_2]$, with $w_1 \geq 0$, $w_2 \geq 0$, and $w_1 + w_2 = 1$. Therefore, the domain over which the optimization is performed is $w_1 \in [0, 1]$ because w_2 can always be derived as $w_2 = 1 - w_1$. Using the first observation above, only the two deterministic strategies for P_2 need to be considered. When considered as linear functions of w, these are

$$
3w_1 + 0(1 - w_1)
\tag{9.64}
$$

for $z_1 = 1$ and

$$
w_1 + (-1)(1 - w_1)
\tag{9.65}
$$

for $z_2 = 1$. The lines are plotted in Figure 9.4a. The security strategy is determined by the minimum point along the upper envelope shown in the figure. This is indicated by the thickened line, and it is always a piecewise-linear function in general. The lowest point occurs at $w_1 = 2/5$, and the resulting value is $\mathcal{L}^* = 3/5$. Therefore, $w^* = [2/5 \; 3/5]$.

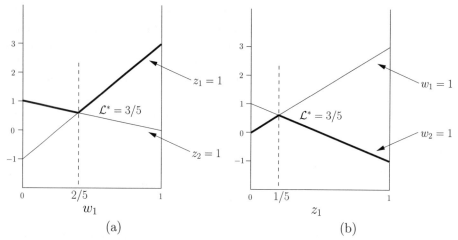

Figure 9.4: (a) Computing the randomized security strategy, w^*, for P_1. (b) Computing the randomized security strategy, z^*, for P_2.

A similar procedure can be used to obtain z^*. The lines that correspond to the deterministic strategies of P_1 are shown in Figure 9.4b. The security strategy is obtained by finding the maximum value along the lower envelope of the lines, which is shown as the thickened line in the figure. This results in $z^* = [1/5 \;\; 4/5]^T$, and once again, the value is observed as $\mathcal{L}^* = 3/5$ (this must coincide with the previous one because the randomized upper and lower values are the same!). ∎

This procedure appears quite simple if there are only two actions per player. If $n = m = 100$, then the upper and lower envelopes are piecewise-linear functions in $\mathbb{R}^{99}$. This may be computationally impractical because all existing linear programming algorithms have running time at least exponential in dimension [266].

9.4 Nonzero-sum games

This section parallels the development of Section 9.3, except that the more general case of nonzero-sum games is considered. This enables games with any desired degree of conflict to be modeled. Some decisions may even benefit all players. One of the main applications of the subject is in economics, where it helps to explain the behavior of businesses in competition.

The saddle-point solution will be replaced by the *Nash equilibrium*, which again is based on eliminating regret. Since the players do not necessarily oppose each other, it is possible to model a game that involves any number of players. For nonzero games, new difficulties arise, such as the nonuniqueness of Nash equilibria and the computation of randomized Nash equilibria does not generally fit into linear programming.

9.4.1 Two-player games

To help make the connection to Section 9.3 smoother, two-player games will be considered first. This case is also easier to understand because the notation is simpler. The ideas are then extended without difficulty from two players to many players. The game is formulated as follows.

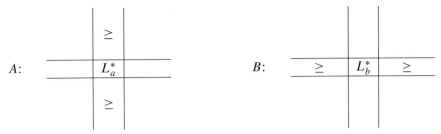

Figure 9.5: A Nash equilibrium can be detected in a pair of matrices by finding some (i, j) such that $L_a^* = L_1(i, j)$ is the lowest among all elements in column j of A, and $L_b^* = L_2(i, j)$ is the lowest among all elements in row i of B. Compare this with Figure 9.2.

Formulation 9.8 (A Two-Player Nonzero-Sum Game)

1. The same components as in Formulation 9.7, except the cost function.

2. A function, $L_1 : U \times V \to \mathbb{R} \cup \{\infty\}$, called the *cost function for* P_1.

3. A function, $L_2 : U \times V \to \mathbb{R} \cup \{\infty\}$, called the *cost function for* P_2.

The only difference with respect to Formulation 9.7 is that now there are two, independent cost functions, L_1 and L_2, one for each player. Each player would like to minimize its cost. There is no maximization in this problem; that appeared in zero-sum games because P_2 had opposing interests from P_1. A zero-sum game can be modeled under Formulation 9.7 by setting $L_1 = L$ and $L_2 = -L$.

Paralleling Section 9.3, first consider applying deterministic strategies to solve the game. As before, one possibility is that a player can apply its security strategy. To accomplish this, it does not even need to look at the cost function of the other player. It seems somewhat inappropriate, however, to neglect the consideration of both cost functions when making a decision. In most cases, the security strategy results in regret, which makes it inappropriate for nonzero-sum games.

A strategy that avoids regret will now be given. A pair (u^*, v^*) of actions is defined to be a *Nash equilibrium* if

$$L(u^*, v^*) = \min_{u \in U} \left\{ L(u, v^*) \right\} \tag{9.66}$$

and

$$L(u^*, v^*) = \min_{v \in V} \left\{ L(u^*, v) \right\}. \tag{9.67}$$

These expressions imply that neither P_1 nor P_2 has regret. Equation (9.66) indicates that P_1 is satisfied with its action, u^*, given the action, v^*, chosen by P_2. P_1 cannot reduce its cost any further by changing its action. Likewise, (9.67) indicates that P_2 is satisfied with its action v^*.

The game in Formulation 9.8 can be completely represented using two cost matrices. Let A and B denote the cost matrices for P_1 and P_2, respectively. Recall that Figure 9.2 showed a pattern for detecting a saddle point. A Nash equilibrium can be detected as shown in Figure 9.5. Think about the relationship between the two. If $A = -B$, then B can be negated and superimposed on top of A. This will yield the pattern in Figure 9.2 (each $\geq$ becomes $\leq$ because of negation). The values L_a^* and L_b^* coincide in this case. This observation implies that if $A = -B$, then the Nash equilibrium is actually the same concept as a saddle point. It applies, however, to much more general games.

Example 9.17 (A Deterministic Nash Equilibrium) Consider the game specified by the cost matrices A and B:

$$
A: \quad U
\begin{array}{c}
V \\
\begin{array}{|c|c|c|}
\hline
9 & 4 & 7 \\
\hline
6 & -1 & 5 \\
\hline
1 & 4 & 2 \\
\hline
\end{array}
\end{array}
\qquad
B: \quad U
\begin{array}{c}
V \\
\begin{array}{|c|c|c|}
\hline
2 & 1 & 6 \\
\hline
5 & 0 & 2 \\
\hline
2 & 2 & 5 \\
\hline
\end{array}
\end{array}
\qquad (9.68)
$$

By applying (9.66) and (9.67), or by using the patterns in Figure 9.5, it can be seen that $u = 3$ and $v = 1$ is a Nash equilibrium. The resulting costs are $L_1 = 1$ and $L_2 = 2$. Another Nash equilibrium appears at $u = 2$ and $v = 2$. This yields costs $L_1 = -1$ and $L_2 = 0$, which is better for both players.

For zero-sum games, the existence of multiple saddle points did not cause any problem; however, for nonzero-sum games, there are great troubles. In the example shown here, one Nash equilibrium is clearly better than the other for both players. Therefore, it may seem reasonable that a rational DM would choose the better one. The issue of multiple Nash equilibria will be discussed next.   ∎

9.4.1.1 Dealing with multiple Nash equilibria

Example 9.17 was somewhat disheartening due to the existence of multiple Nash equilibria. In general, there could be any number of equilibria. How can each player know which one to play? If they each choose a different one, they are not guaranteed to fall into another equilibrium as in the case of saddle points of zero-sum games. Many of the equilibria can be eliminated by using Pareto optimality, which was explained in Section 9.1.1 and also appeared in Section 7.7.2 as a way to optimally coordinate multiple robots. The idea is to formulate the selection as a multi-objective optimization problem, which fits into Formulation 9.2.

Consider two-dimensional vectors of the form (x_i, y_i), in which x and y represent the costs L_1 and L_2 obtained under the implementation of a Nash equilibrium denoted by π_i. For two different equilibria π_1 and π_2, the cost vectors (x_1, y_1) and (x_2, y_2) are obtained. In Example 9.17, these were $(1, 2)$ and $(-1, 0)$. In general, π_1 is said to be *better* than π_2 if $x_1 \leq x_2$, $y_1 \leq y_2$, and at least one of the inequalities is strict. In Example 9.17, the equilibrium that produces $(-1, 0)$ is clearly better than obtaining $(1, 2)$ because both players benefit.

The definition of "better" induces a partial ordering on the space of Nash equilibria. It is only partial because some vectors are incomparable. Consider, for example, $(-1, 1)$ and $(1, -1)$. The first one is preferable to P_1, and the second is preferred by P_2. In game theory, the Nash equilibria that are minimal with respect to this partial ordering are called *admissible*. They could alternatively be called *Pareto optimal*.

The best situation is when a game has one Nash equilibrium. If there are multiple Nash equilibria, then there is some hope that only one of them is admissible. In this case, it is hoped that the rational players are intelligent enough to figure out that any nonadmissible equilibria should be discarded. Unfortunately, there are many games that have multiple admissible Nash equilibria. In this case, analysis of the game indicates that the players must communicate or collaborate in some way to eliminate the possibility of regret. Otherwise, regret is unavoidable in the worst case. It is also possible that there are no Nash equilibria, but, fortunately, by allowing randomized strategies, a randomized

Nash equilibrium is always guaranteed to exist. This will be covered after the following two examples.

Example 9.18 (The Battle of the Sexes) Consider a game specified by the cost matrices A and B:

$$A : \quad U \begin{array}{c} \\ \overset{\displaystyle V}{\begin{array}{|c|c|} \hline -2 & 0 \\ \hline 0 & -1 \\ \hline \end{array}} \end{array} \qquad B : \quad U \begin{array}{c} \\ \overset{\displaystyle V}{\begin{array}{|c|c|} \hline -1 & 0 \\ \hline 0 & -2 \\ \hline \end{array}} \end{array} . \qquad (9.69)$$

This is a famous game called the "Battle of the Sexes." Suppose that a man and a woman have a relationship, and they each have different preferences on how to spend the evening. The man prefers to go shopping, and the woman prefers to watch a football match. The game involves selecting one of these two activities. The best case for either one is to do what they prefer while still remaining together. The worst case is to select different activities, which separates the couple. This game is somewhat unrealistic because in most situations some cooperation between them is expected.

Both $u = v = 1$ and $u = v = 2$ are Nash equilibria, which yield cost vectors $(-2, -1)$ and $(-1, -2)$, respectively. Neither solution is better than the other; therefore, they are both admissible. There is no way to avoid the possibility of regret unless the players cooperate (you probably already knew this). ∎

The following is one of the most famous nonzero-sum games.

Example 9.19 (The Prisoner's Dilemma) The following game is very simple to express, yet it illustrates many interesting issues. Imagine that a heinous crime has been committed by two people. The authorities know they are guilty, but they do not have enough evidence to convict them. Therefore, they develop a plan to try to trick the suspects. Each suspect (or player) is placed in an isolated prison cell and given two choices. Each player can cooperate with the authorities, $u = 1$ or $v = 1$, or refuse, $u = 2$ or $v = 2$. By cooperating, the player admits guilt and turns over evidence to the authorities. By refusing, the player claims innocence and refuses to help the authorities.

The cost L_i represents the number of years that the player will be sentenced to prison. The cost matrices are assigned as

$$A : \quad U \begin{array}{c} \\ \overset{\displaystyle V}{\begin{array}{|c|c|} \hline 8 & 0 \\ \hline 30 & 2 \\ \hline \end{array}} \end{array} \qquad B : \quad U \begin{array}{c} \\ \overset{\displaystyle V}{\begin{array}{|c|c|} \hline 8 & 30 \\ \hline 0 & 2 \\ \hline \end{array}} \end{array} . \qquad (9.70)$$

The motivation is that both players receive 8 years if they both cooperate, which is the sentence for being convicted of the crime and being rewarded for cooperating with the authorities. If they both refuse, then they receive 2 years because the authorities have insufficient evidence for a longer term. The interesting cases occur if one refuses and the other cooperates. The one who refuses is in big trouble because the evidence provided by the other will be used against him. The one who cooperates gets to go free (the cost is 0); however, the other is convicted on the evidence and spends 30 years in prison.

What should the players do? What would you do? If they could make a coordinated decision, then it seems that a good choice would be for both to refuse, which results in costs $(2, 2)$. In this case, however, there would be regret because each player would think that he had a chance to go free (receiving cost 0 by refusing). If they were to play the game a second time, they might be inclined to change their decisions.

The Nash equilibrium for this problem is for both of them to cooperate, which results in $(8, 8)$. Thus, they pay a price for not being able to communicate and coordinate their strategy. This solution is also a security strategy for the players, because it achieves the lowest cost using worst-case analysis.   ■

9.4.1.2 Randomized Nash equilibria

What happens if a game has no Nash equilibrium over the space of deterministic strategies? Once again the problem can be alleviated by expanding the strategy space to include randomized strategies. In Section 9.3.3 it was explained that every zero-sum game under Formulation 9.7 has a randomized saddle point on the space of randomized strategies. It was shown by Nash that every nonzero-sum game under Formulation 9.8 has a randomized Nash equilibrium [733]. This is a nice result; however, there are a couple of concerns. There may still exist other admissible equilibria, which means that there is no reliable way to avoid regret unless the players collaborate. The other concern is that randomized Nash equilibria unfortunately cannot be computed using the linear programming approach of Section 9.3.3. The required optimization is instead a form of nonlinear programming [96, 667, 734], which does not necessarily admit a nice, combinatorial solution.

Recall the definition of randomized strategies from Section 9.3.3. For a pair (w, z) of randomized strategies, the expected costs, $\bar{L}^1(w, z)$ and $\bar{L}^2(w, z)$, can be computed using (9.57). A pair (w^*, z^*) of strategies is said to be a *randomized Nash equilibrium* if

$$\bar{L}^1(w^*, z^*) = \min_{w \in W} \left\{ \bar{L}^1(w, z^*) \right\} \tag{9.71}$$

and

$$\bar{L}^2(w^*, z^*) = \min_{z \in Z} \left\{ \bar{L}^2(w^*, z) \right\}. \tag{9.72}$$

In game-theory literature, this is usually referred to as a *mixed Nash equilibrium*. Note that (9.71) and (9.72) are just generalizations of (9.66) and (9.67) from the space of deterministic strategies to the space of randomized strategies.

Using the cost matrices A and B, the Nash equilibrium conditions can be written as

$$w^* A z^* = \min_{w \in W} \left\{ w A z^* \right\} \tag{9.73}$$

and

$$w^* B z^* = \min_{z \in Z} \left\{ w^* B z \right\}. \tag{9.74}$$

Unfortunately, the computation of randomized Nash equilibria is considerably more challenging than computing saddle points. The main difficulty is that Nash equilibria are not necessarily security strategies. By using security strategies, it is possible to decouple the decisions of the players into separate linear programming problems, as was seen in Example 9.16. For the randomized Nash equilibrium, the optimization between the players remains coupled. The resulting optimization is often referred to as the *linear complementarity problem*. This can be formulated as a nonlinear programming problem [667, 734], which means that it is a nonlinear optimization that involves both equality and inequality constraints on the domain (in this particular case, a *bilinear programming* problem is obtained [60]).

Example 9.20 (Finding a Randomized Nash Equilibrium)   To get an idea of the kind of optimization that is required, recall Example 9.18. A randomized Nash equilibrium that is distinct from the two deterministic equilibria can be found. Using the cost matrices from Example 9.18, the expected cost for P_1 given randomized strategies w and z is

$$\bar{L}^1(w, z) = wAz$$

$$= \begin{pmatrix} w_1 & w_2 \end{pmatrix} \begin{pmatrix} -2 & 0 \\ 0 & -1 \end{pmatrix} \begin{pmatrix} z_1 \\ z_2 \end{pmatrix} \qquad (9.75)$$

$$= -2w_1z_1 - w_2z_2$$

$$= -3w_1z_1 + w_1 + z_1,$$

in which the final step uses the fact that $w_2 = 1 - w_1$ and $z_2 = 1 - z_1$. Similarly, the expected cost for P_2 is

$$\bar{L}^2(w, z) = wBz$$

$$= \begin{pmatrix} w_1 & w_2 \end{pmatrix} \begin{pmatrix} -1 & 0 \\ 0 & -2 \end{pmatrix} \begin{pmatrix} z_1 \\ z_2 \end{pmatrix} \qquad (9.76)$$

$$= -w_1z_1 - 2w_2z_2$$

$$= -3w_1z_1 + 2w_1 + 2z_1.$$

If z is fixed, then the final equation in (9.75) is linear in w; likewise, if w is fixed, then (9.76) is linear in z. In the case of computing saddle points for zero-sum games, we were allowed to make this assumption; however, it is not possible here. We must choose (w^*, z^*) to simultaneously optimize (9.75) while $z = z^*$ and (9.76) while $w = w^*$.

It turns out that this problem is simple enough to solve with calculus. Using the classical optimization method of taking derivatives, a candidate solution can be found by computing

$$\frac{\partial \bar{L}^1(w_1, z_1)}{\partial w_1} = 1 - 3z_1 \qquad (9.77)$$

and

$$\frac{\partial \bar{L}^2(w_1, z_1)}{\partial z_1} = 2 - 3w_1. \qquad (9.78)$$

Extrema occur when both of these simultaneously become 0. Solving $1 - 3z_1 = 0$ and $2 - 3w_1 = 0$ yields $(w^*, z^*) = (2/3, 1/3)$, which is a randomized Nash equilibrium. The deterministic Nash equilibria are not detected by this method because they occur on the boundary of W and Z, where the derivative is not defined. ∎

The computation method in Example 9.20 did not appear too difficult because there were only two actions per player, and half of the matrix costs were 0. In general, two complicated equations must be solved simultaneously. The expressions, however, are always second-degree polynomials. Furthermore, they each become linear with respect to the other variables if w or z is held fixed.

Summary of possible solutions

The solution possibilities to remember for a nonzero-sum game under Formulation 9.8 are as follows.

1. There may be multiple, admissible (deterministic) Nash equilibria.
2. There may be no (deterministic) Nash equilibria.
3. There is always at least one randomized Nash equilibrium.

9.4.2 More than two players

The ideas of Section 9.4.1 easily generalize to any number of players. The main difficulty is that complicated notation makes the concepts appear more difficult. Keep in mind, however, that there are no fundamental differences. A nonzero-sum game with n players is formulated as follows.

Formulation 9.9 (An n-Player Nonzero-Sum Game)

1. A set of n players, $P_1, P_2, \ldots, P_n$.

2. For each player P_i, a finite, nonempty set U^i called the *action space* for P_i. For convenience, assume that each U^i is a set of consecutive integers from 1 to $|U^i|$. Each $u^i \in U^i$ is referred to as an *action* of P_i.

3. For each player P_i, a function, $L_i : U^1 \times U^2 \times \cdots \times U^n \to \mathbb{R} \cup \{\infty\}$ called the *cost function for P_i*.

A matrix formulation of the costs is no longer possible because there are too many dimensions. For example, if $n = 3$ and $|U^i| = 2$ for each player, then $L_i(u^1, u^2, u^3)$ is specified by a $2 \times 2 \times 2$ cube of 8 entries. Three of these cubes are needed to specify the game. Thus, it may be helpful to just think of L_i as a multivariate function and avoid using matrices.[4]

The Nash equilibrium idea generalizes by requiring that each P_i experiences no regret, given the actions chosen by the other $n - 1$ players. Formally, a set $(u^{1*}, \ldots, u^{n*})$ of actions is said to be a (deterministic) *Nash equilibrium* if

$$L_i(u^{1*}, \ldots, u^{i*}, \ldots, u^{n*}) = \min_{u^i \in U^i} \left\{ L_i(u^{1*}, \ldots, u^{(i-1)*}, u^i, u^{(i+1)*}, \ldots, u^{n*}) \right\} \qquad (9.79)$$

for every $i \in \{1, \ldots, n\}$.

For $n > 2$, any of the situations summarized at the end of Section 9.4.1 can occur. There may be no deterministic Nash equilibria or multiple Nash equilibria. The definition of an admissible Nash equilibrium is extended by defining the notion of *better* over n-dimensional cost vectors. Once again, the minimal vectors with respect to the resulting partial ordering are considered *admissible* (or *Pareto optimal*). Unfortunately, multiple admissible Nash equilibria may still exist.

It turns out that for any game under Formulation 9.9, there exists a randomized Nash equilibrium. Let z^i denote a randomized strategy for P_i. The expected cost for each P_i can be expressed as

$$\bar{L}^i(z^1, z^2, \ldots, z^n) = \sum_{i_1=1}^{m_1} \sum_{i_2=1}^{m_2} \cdots \sum_{i_n=1}^{m_n} L_i(i_1, i_2, \ldots, i_n) z^1_{i_1} z^2_{i_2} \cdots z^n_{i_n}. \qquad (9.80)$$

Let Z^i denote the space of randomized strategies for P_i. An assignment, $(z^{1*}, \ldots, z^{n*})$, of randomized strategies to all of the players is called a *randomized Nash equilibrium* if

$$\bar{L}^i(z^{1*}, \ldots, z^{i*}, \ldots, z^{n*}) = \min_{z^i \in Z^i} \left\{ \bar{L}^i(z^{1*}, \ldots, z^{(i-1)*}, z^i, z^{(i+1)*}, \ldots, z^{n*}) \right\} \qquad (9.81)$$

for all $i \in \{1, \ldots, n\}$.

As might be expected, computing a randomized Nash equilibrium for $n > 2$ is even more challenging than for $n = 2$. The method of Example 9.20 can be generalized to

---

[4] If you enjoy working with tensors, these could be used to capture n-player cost functions [109].

n-player games; however, the expressions become even more complicated. There are n equations, each of which appears linear if the randomized strategies are fixed for the other $n - 1$ players. The result is a collection of n-degree polynomials over which n optimization problems must be solved simultaneously.

Example 9.21 (A Three-Player Nonzero-Sum Game)   Suppose there are three players, P_1, P_2, and P_3, each of which has two actions, 1 and 2. A deterministic strategy is specified by a vector such as $(1, 2, 1)$, which indicates $u^1 = 1$, $u^2 = 2$, and $u^3 = 1$.

Now some costs will be defined. For convenience, let

$$L(i, j, k) = \Big(L_1(i, j, k), \; L_2(i, j, k), \; L_3(i, j, k) \Big) \tag{9.82}$$

for each $i, j, k \in \{1, 2\}$. Let the costs be

$$
\begin{aligned}
&L(1, 1, 1) = (1, 1, -2) && L(1, 1, 2) = (-4, 3, 1) \\
&L(1, 2, 1) = (2, -4, 2) && L(1, 2, 2) = (-5, -5, 10) \qquad (9.83) \\
&L(2, 1, 1) = (3, -2, -1) && L(2, 1, 2) = (-6, -6, 12) \\
&L(2, 2, 1) = (2, 2, -4) && L(2, 2, 2) = (-2, 3, -1).
\end{aligned}
$$

There are two deterministic Nash equilibria, which yield the costs $(2, -4, 2)$ and $(3, -2, -1)$. These can be verified using (9.79). Each player is satisfied with the outcome given the actions chosen by the other players. Unfortunately, both Nash equilibria are both admissible. Therefore, some collaboration would be needed between the players to ensure that no regret will occur.   ∎

9.5 Decision theory under scrutiny

Numerous models for decision making were introduced in this chapter. These provide a foundation for planning under uncertainty, which is the main focus of Part III. Before constructing planning models with this foundation, it is important to critically assess how appropriate it may be in applications. You may have had many questions while reading Sections 9.1 to 9.4. How are the costs determined? Why should we believe that optimizing the *expected* cost is the right thing to do? What happens if prior probability distributions are not available? Is worst-case analysis too conservative? Can we be sure that players in a game will follow the assumed rational behavior? Is it realistic that players know each other's cost functions? The purpose of this section is to help shed some light on these questions. A building is only as good as its foundation. Any mistakes made by misunderstanding the limitations of decision theory will ultimately work their way into planning formulations that are constructed from them.

9.5.1 Utility theory and rationality

This section provides some justification for using cost functions and then minimizing their expected value under Formulations 9.3 and 9.4. The resulting framework is called *utility theory*, which is usually formulated using rewards instead of costs. As stated in Section 9.1.1, a cost can be converted into a reward by multiplying by -1 and then swapping each maximization with minimization. We will therefore talk about a reward R with the intuition that a higher reward is better.

9.5.1.1 Comparing rewards

Imagine assigning reward values to various outcomes of a decision-making process. In some applications numerical values may come naturally. For example, the reward might be the amount of money earned in a financial investment. In robotics applications, one could negate time to execute a task or the amount of energy consumed. For example, the reward could indicate the amount of remaining battery life after a mobile robot builds a map.

In some applications the source of rewards may be subjective. For example, what is the reward for washing dishes, in comparison to sweeping the floor? Each person would probably assign different rewards, which may even vary from day to day. It may be based on their enjoyment or misery in performing the task, the amount of time each task would take, the perceptions of others, and so on. If decision theory is used to automate the decision process for a human "client," then it is best to consult carefully with the client to make sure you know their preferences. In this situation, it may be possible to sort their preferences and then assign rewards that are consistent with the ordering.

Once the rewards are assigned, consider making a decision under Formulation 9.1, which does not involve nature. Each outcome corresponds directly to an action, $u \in U$. If the rewards are given by $R : U \to \mathbb{R}$, then the cost, L, can be defined as $L(u) = -R(u)$ for every $u \in U$. Satisfying the client is then a matter of choosing u to minimize L.

Now consider a game against nature. The decision now involves comparing probability distributions over the outcomes. The space of all probability distributions may be enormous, but this is simplified by using expectation to map each probability distribution (or density) to a real value. The concern should be whether this projection of distributions onto real numbers will fail to reflect the true preferences of the client. The following example illustrates the effect of this.

Example 9.22 (Do You Like to Gamble?)   Suppose you are given three choices:

1. You can have 1000 Euros.
2. We will toss an unbiased coin, and if the result is heads, then you will receive 2000 Euros. Otherwise, you receive nothing.
3. With probability 2/3, you can have 3000 Euros; however, with probability 1/3, you have to give me 3000 Euros.

The expected reward for each of these choices is 1000 Euros, but would you really consider these to be equivalent? Your love or disdain for gambling is not being taken into account by the expectation. How should such an issue be considered in games against nature? ∎

To begin to fix this problem, it is helpful to consider another scenario. Many people would probably agree that having more money is preferable (if having too much worries you, then you can always give away the surplus to your favorite charities). What is interesting, however, is that being wealthy decreases the perceived value of money. This is illustrated in the next example.

Example 9.23 (Reality Television)   Suppose you are lucky enough to appear on a popular reality television program. The point of the show is to test how far you will go in making a fool out of yourself, or perhaps even torturing yourself, to earn some money. You are asked to do some unpleasant task (such as eating cockroaches, or holding your head under water for a long time, and so on.). Let u_1 be the action to agree to do the task, and let u_2

mean that you decline the opportunity. The prizes are expressed in U.S. dollars. Imagine that you are a starving student on a tight budget.

Below are several possible scenarios that could be presented on the television program. Consider how you would react to each one.

1. Suppose that u_1 earns you \$1 and u_2 earns you nothing. Purely optimizing the reward would lead to choosing u_1, which means performing the unpleasant task. However, is this worth \$1? The problem so far is that we are not taking into account the amount of discomfort in completing a task. Perhaps it might make sense to make a reward function that shifts the dollar values by subtracting the amount for which you would be just barely willing to perform the task.

2. Suppose that u_1 earns you \$10,000 and u_2 earns you nothing. \$10,000 is assumed to be an enormous amount of money, clearly worth enduring any torture inflicted by the television program. Thus, u_1 is preferable.

3. Now imagine that the television host first gives you \$10 million just for appearing on the program. Are you still willing to perform the unpleasant task for an extra \$10,000? Probably not. What is happening here? Your sense of value assigned to money seems to decrease as you get more of it, right? It would not be too interesting to watch the program if the contestants were all wealthy oil executives.

4. Suppose that you have performed the task and are about to win the prize. Just to add to the drama, the host offers you a gambling opportunity. You can select action u_1 and receive \$10,000, or be a gambler by selecting u_2 and have probability $1/2$ of winning \$25,000 by the tossing of a fair coin. In terms of the expected reward, the clear choice is u_2. However, you just completed the unpleasant task and expect to earn money. The risk of losing it all may be intolerable. Different people will have different preferences in this situation.

5. Now suppose once again that you performed the task. This time your choices are u_1, to receive \$100, or u_2, to have probability $1/2$ of receiving \$250 by tossing a fair coin. The host is kind enough, though, to let you play 100 times. In this case, the expected totals for the two actions are \$10,000 and \$12,500, respectively. This time it seems clear that the best choice is to gamble. After 100 independent trials, we would expect that, with extremely high probability, over \$10,000 would be earned. Thus, reasoning by expected-case analysis seems valid if we are allowed numerous, independent trials. In this case, with high probability a value close to the expected reward should be received. ∎

Based on these examples, it seems that the client or evaluator of the decision-making system must indicate preferences between probability distributions over outcomes. There is a formal way to ensure that once these preferences are assigned, a cost function can be designed for which its expectation faithfully reflects the preferences over distributions. This results in *utility theory*, which involves the following steps:

1. Require that the client is *rational* when assigning preferences. This notion is defined through axioms.

2. If the preferences are assigned in a way that is consistent with the axioms, then a utility function is guaranteed to exist. When expected utility is optimized, the preferences match exactly those of the client.

3. The cost function can be derived from the utility function.

The client must specify preferences among probability distributions of outcomes. Suppose that Formulation 9.2 is used. For convenience, assume that U and Θ are finite.

Let X denote a *state space* based on outcomes.[5] Let $f : U \times \Theta \to X$ denote a mapping that assigns a state to every outcome. A simple example is to declare that $X = U \times \Theta$ and make f the identity map. This makes the outcome space and state space coincide. It may be convenient, though, to use f to collapse the space of outcomes down to a smaller set. If two outcomes map to the same state using f, then it means that the outcomes are indistinguishable as far as rewards or costs are concerned.

Let z denote a probability distribution over X, and let Z denote the set of all probability distributions over X. Every $z \in Z$ is represented as an n-dimensional vector of probabilities in which $n = |X|$; hence, it is considered as an element of $\mathbb{R}^n$. This makes it convenient to "blend" two probability distributions. For example, let $\alpha \in (0, 1)$ be a constant, and let z_1 and z_2 be any two probability distributions. Using scalar multiplication, a new probability distribution, $\alpha z_1 + (1 - \alpha) z_2$, is obtained, which is a *blend* of z_1 and z_2. Conveniently, there is no need to normalize the result. It is assumed that z_1 and z_2 initially have unit magnitude. The blend has magnitude $\alpha + (1 - \alpha) = 1$.

The modeler of the decision process must consult the client to represent preferences among elements of Z. Let $z_1 \prec z_2$ mean that z_2 is strictly preferred over z_1. Let $z_1 \approx z_2$ mean that z_1 and z_2 are equivalent in preference. Let $z_1 \preceq z_2$ mean that either $z_1 \prec z_2$ or $z_1 \approx z_2$. The following example illustrates the assignment of preferences.

Example 9.24 (Indicating Preferences) Suppose that $U = \Theta = \{1, 2\}$, which leads to four possible outcomes: $(1, 1)$, $(1, 2)$, $(2, 1)$, and $(2, 2)$. Imagine that nature represents a machine that generates 1 or 2 according to a probability distribution. The action is to guess the number that will be generated by the machine. If you pick the same number, then you win that number of gold pieces. If you do not pick the same number, then you win nothing, but also lose nothing.

Consider the construction of the state space X by using f. The outcomes $(2, 1)$ and $(1, 2)$ are identical concerning any conceivable reward. Therefore, these should map to the same state. The other two outcomes are distinct. The state space therefore needs only three elements and can be defined as $X = \{0, 1, 2\}$. Let $f(2, 1) = f(1, 2) = 0$, $f(1, 1) = 1$, and $f(2, 2) = 2$. Thus, the last two states indicate that some gold will be earned.

The set Z of probability distributions over X is now considered. Each $z \in Z$ is a three-dimensional vector. As an example, $z_1 = [1/2 \ 1/4 \ 1/4]$ indicates that the state will be 0 with probability $1/2$, 1 with probability $1/4$, and 2 with probability $1/4$. Suppose $z_2 = [1/3 \ 1/3 \ 1/3]$. Which distribution would you prefer? It seems in this case that z_2 is uniformly better than z_1 because there is a greater chance of winning gold. Thus, we declare $z_1 \prec z_2$. The distribution $z_3 = [1 \ 0 \ 0]$ seems to be the worst imaginable. Hence, we can safely declare $z_3 \prec z_1$ and $z_1 \prec z_2$.

The procedure of determining the preferences can become quite tedious for complicated problems. In the current example, Z is a 2D subset of $\mathbb{R}^3$. This subset can be partitioned into a finite set of regions over which the client may be able to clearly indicate preferences. One of the major criticisms of this framework is the impracticality of determining preferences over Z [834].

After the preferences are determined, is there a way to ensure that a real-value function on X exists for which the expected value exactly reflects the preferences? If the axioms of rationality are satisfied by the assignment of preferences, then the answer is *yes*. These axioms are covered next. ∎

---

[5] In most utility theory literature, this is referred to as a *reward space*, $\mathcal{R}$ [91].

9.5.1.2 Axioms of rationality

To meet the goal of designing a utility function, it turns out that the preferences must follow rules called the *axioms of rationality*. They are sensible statements of consistency among the preferences. As long as these are followed, then a utility function is guaranteed to exist (detailed arguments appear in [270, 834]). The decision maker is considered *rational* if the following axioms are followed when defining $\prec$ and $\approx$:[6]

1. If $z_1, z_2 \in Z$, then either $z_1 \preceq z_2$ or $z_2 \preceq z_1$.
   "You must be able to make up your mind."

2. If $z_1 \preceq z_2$ and $z_2 \preceq z_3$, then $z_1 \preceq z_3$.
   "Preferences must be transitive."

3. If $z_1 \prec z_2$, then

$$\alpha z_1 + (1 - \alpha)z_3 \prec \alpha z_2 + (1 - \alpha)z_3, \tag{9.84}$$

   for any $z_3 \in Z$ and $\alpha \in (0, 1)$.
   "Evenly blending in a new distribution does not alter preference."

4. If $z_1 \prec z_2 \prec z_3$, then there exists some $\alpha \in (0, 1)$ and $\beta \in (0, 1)$ such that

$$\alpha z_1 + (1 - \alpha)z_3 \prec z_2 \tag{9.85}$$

   and

$$z_2 \prec \beta z_1 + (1 - \beta)z_3. \tag{9.86}$$

   "There is no heaven or hell."

Each axiom has an intuitive interpretation that makes practical sense. The first one simply indicates that the preference direction can always be inferred for a pair of distributions. The second axiom indicates that preferences must be transitive.[7] The last two axioms are somewhat more complicated. In the third axiom, z_2 is strictly preferred to z_1. An attempt is made to cause confusion by blending in a third distribution, z_3. If the same "amount" of z_3 is blended into both z_1 and z_2, then the preference should not be affected. The final axiom involves z_1, z_2, and z_3, each of which is strictly better than its predecessor. The first equation, (9.85), indicates that if z_2 is strictly better than z_1, then a tiny amount of z_3 can be blended into z_1, with z_2 remaining preferable. If z_3 had been like "heaven" (i.e., infinite reward), then this would not be possible. Similarly, (9.86) indicates that a tiny amount of z_1 can be blended into z_3, and the result remains better than z_2. This means that z_1 cannot be "hell," which would have infinite negative reward.[8]

9.5.1.3 Constructing a utility function

If the preferences have been determined in a way consistent with the axioms, then it can be shown that a *utility function* always exists. This means that there exists a function

---

[6] Alternative axiom systems exist [270, 842].

[7] For some reasonable problems, however, transitivity is not desirable. See the Candorcet and Simpson paradoxes in [834].

[8] Some axiom systems allow infinite rewards, which lead to utility and cost functions with infinite values, but this is not considered here.

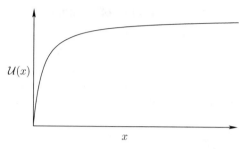

Figure 9.6: The utility of new amounts of money decreases as the total accumulation of wealth increases. The utility function may even bounded.

$\mathcal{U} : X \rightarrow \mathbb{R}$ such that, for all $z_1, z_2 \in Z$,

$$z_1 \prec z_2 \text{ if and only if } E_{z_1}[\mathcal{U}] < E_{z_2}[\mathcal{U}], \tag{9.87}$$

in which E_{z_i} denotes the expected value of $\mathcal{U}$, which is being treated as a random variable under the probability distribution z_i. The existence of $\mathcal{U}$ implies that it is safe to determine the best action by maximizing the expected utility.

A reward function can be defined using a utility function, $\mathcal{U}$, as $R(u, \theta) = \mathcal{U}(f(u, \theta))$. The utility function can be converted to a cost function as $L(u, \theta) = -R(u, \theta) = -\mathcal{U}(f(u, \theta))$. Minimizing the expected cost, as was recommended under Formulations 9.3 and 9.4 with probabilistic uncertainty, now seems justified under the assumption that $\mathcal{U}$ was constructed correctly to preserve preferences.

Unfortunately, establishing the existence of a utility function does not produce a systematic way to construct it. In most circumstances, one is forced to design $\mathcal{U}$ by a trial-and-error process that involves repeatedly checking the preferences. In the vast majority of applications, people create utility and cost functions without regard to the implications discussed in this section. Thus, undesirable conclusions may be reached in practice. Therefore, it is important not to be too confident about the quality of an optimal decision rule.

Note that if worst-case analysis had been used, then most of the problems discussed here could have been avoided. Worst-case analysis, however, has its weaknesses, which will be discussed in Section 9.5.3.

Example 9.25 (The Utility of Money)   We conclude the section by depicting a utility function that is often applied to money. Suppose that the state space $X = \mathbb{R}$, which corresponds to the amount of U.S. dollars earned. The utility of money applied by most people indicates that the value of new increments of money decreases as the total accumulated wealth increases. The utility function may even be bounded. Imagine there is some maximum dollar amount, such as $\$10^{100}$, after which additional money has no value. A typical utility curve is shown in Figure 9.6 [91]. ∎

9.5.2 Concerns regarding the probabilistic model

Section 9.5.1 addressed the source of cost functions and the validity of taking their expectations. This section raises concerns over the validity of the probability distributions used in Section 9.2. The two main topics are criticisms of Bayesian methods in general and problems with constructing probability distributions.

9.5.2.1 Bayesians vs. frequentists

For the past century and a half, there has been a fundamental debate among statisticians on the *meaning* of probabilities. Virtually everyone is satisfied with the axioms of probability, but beyond this, what is their meaning when making inferences? The two main camps are the *frequentists* and the *Bayesians*. A form of Bayes' rule was published in 1763 after the death of Bayes [82]. During most of the nineteenth century Bayesian analysis tended to dominate literature; however, during the twentieth century, the frequentist philosophy became more popular as a more rigorous interpretation of probabilities. In recent years, the credibility of Bayesian methods has been on the rise again.

As seen so far, a Bayesian interprets probabilities as the degree of belief in a hypothesis. Under this philosophy, it is perfectly valid to begin with a prior distribution, gather a few observations, and then make decisions based on the resulting posterior distribution from applying Bayes' rule.

From a frequentist perspective, Bayesian analysis makes far too liberal use of probabilities. The frequentist believes that probabilities are only defined as the quantities obtained in the limit after the number of independent trials tends to infinity. For example, if an unbiased coin is tossed over numerous trials, the probability $1/2$ represents the value to which the ratio between heads and the total number of trials will converge as the number of trials tends to infinity. On the other hand, a Bayesian might say that the probability that the *next* trial results in heads is $1/2$. To a frequentist, this interpretation of probability is too strong.

Frequentists have developed a version of decision theory based on their philosophy; comparisons between the two appear in [834]. As an example, a frequentist would advocate optimizing the following *frequentist risk* to obtain a decision rule:

$$R(\theta, \pi) = \int_y L(\pi(y), \theta) P(y|\theta) dy, \qquad (9.88)$$

in which π represents the strategy, $\pi : Y \rightarrow U$. The frequentist risk averages over all data, rather than making a decision based on a single observation, as advocated by Bayesians in (9.26). The probability $P(y|\theta)$ is assumed to be obtained in the limit as the number of independent data trials tends to infinity. The main drawback in using (9.88) is that the optimization depends on θ. The resulting best decision rule must depend on θ, which is unknown. In some limited cases, it may be possible to select some π that optimizes (9.88) for all θ, but this rarely occurs. Thus, the frequentist risk can be viewed as a constraint on the desirability of strategies, but it usually is not powerful enough to select a single one. This problem is reminiscent of Pareto optimality, which was discussed in Section 9.1.1. The frequentist approach attempts to be more conservative and rigorous, with the result being that weaker statements are made regarding decisions.

9.5.2.2 The source of prior distributions

Suppose that the Bayesian method has been adopted. The most widespread concern in all Bayesian analyses is the source of the prior distribution. In Section 9.2, this is represented as $P(\theta)$ (or $p(\theta)$), which represents a distribution (or density) over the nature action space. The best way to obtain $P(\theta)$ is by estimating the distribution over numerous independent trials. This brings its definition into alignment with frequentist views. This was possible with Example 9.11, in which $P(\theta)$ could be reliably estimated from the frequency of occurrence of letters across numerous pages of text. The distribution could even be adapted to a particular language or theme.

In most applications that use decision theory, however, it is impossible or too costly to perform such experiments. What should be done in this case? If a prior distribution is simply "made up," then the resulting posterior probabilities may be suspect. In fact, it may be invalid to call them probabilities at all. Sometimes the term *subjective probabilities* is used in this case. Nevertheless, this is commonly done because there are few other options. One of these options is to resort to frequentist decision theory, but, as mentioned, it does not work with single observations.

Fortunately, as the number of observations increases, the influence of the prior on the Bayesian posterior distributions diminishes. If there is only one observation, or even none as in Formulation 9.3, then the prior becomes very influential. If there is little or no information regarding $P(\theta)$, the distribution should be designed as carefully as possible. It should also be understood that whatever conclusions are made with this assumption, they are biased by the prior. Suppose this model is used as the basis of a planning approach. You might feel satisfied computing the "optimal" plan, but this notion of optimality could still depend on some arbitrary initial bias due to the assignment of prior values.

If there is no information available, then it seems reasonable that $P(\theta)$ should be as uniform as possible over Θ. This was referred to by Laplace as the "principle of insufficient reason" [584]. If there is no reason to believe that one element is more likely than another, then they should be assigned equal values. This can also be justified by using Shannon's entropy measure from information theory [50, 250, 866]. In the discrete case, this is

$$-\sum_{\theta \in \Theta} P(\theta) \lg P(\theta), \tag{9.89}$$

and in the continuous case it is

$$-\int_{\Theta} p(\theta) \lg p(\theta) d\theta. \tag{9.90}$$

This entropy measure was developed in the context of communication systems to estimate the minimum number of bits needed to encode messages delivered through a noisy medium. It generally indicates the amount of uncertainty associated with the distribution. A larger value of entropy implies a greater amount of uncertainty.

It turns out that the entropy function is maximized when $P(\theta)$ is a uniform distribution, which seems to justify the principle of insufficient reason. This can be considered as a *noninformative prior*. The idea is even applied quite frequently when $\Theta = \mathbb{R}$, which leads to an *improper prior*. The density function cannot maintain a constant, nonzero value over all of $\mathbb{R}$ because its integral would be infinite. Since the decisions made in Section 9.2 do not depend on any normalizing factors, a constant value can be assigned for $p(\theta)$ and the decisions are not affected by the fact that the prior is improper.

The main difficulty with applying the entropy argument in the selection of a prior is that Θ itself may be chosen in a number of arbitrary ways. Uniform assignments to different choices of Θ ultimately yield different information regarding the priors. Consider the following example.

Example 9.26 (A Problem with Noninformative Priors)   Consider a decision about what activities to do based on the weather. Imagine that there is absolutely no information about what kind of weather is possible. One possible assignment is $\Theta = \{p, c\}$, in which p means "precipitation" and c means "clear." Maximizing (9.89) suggests assigning $P(p) = P(c) = 1/2$.

After thinking more carefully, perhaps we would like to distinguish between different kinds of precipitation. A better set of nature actions would be $\Theta = \{r, s, c\}$, in which c still means "clear," but precipitation p has been divided into r for "rain" and s for "snow." Now maximizing (9.89) assigns probability $1/3$ to each nature action. This is clearly different from the original assignment. Now that we distinguish between different kinds of precipitation, it seems that precipitation is much more likely to occur. Does our preference to distinguish between different forms of precipitation really affect the weather? ∎

Example 9.27 (Noninformitive Priors for Continuous Spaces) Similar troubles can result in continuous spaces. Recall the parameter estimation problem described in Example 9.12. Suppose instead that the task is to estimate a line based on some data points that were supposed to fall on the line but missed due to noise in the measurement process.

What initial probability density should be assigned to Θ, the set of all lines? Suppose that the line lives in $Z = \mathbb{R}^2$. The line equation can be expressed as

$$\theta_1 z_1 + \theta_2 z_2 + \theta_3 = 0. \tag{9.91}$$

The problem is that if the parameter vector, $\theta = [\theta_1 \ \theta_2 \ \theta_3]$, is multiplied by a scalar constant, then the same line is obtained. Thus, even though $\theta \in \mathbb{R}^3$, a constraint must be added. Suppose we require that

$$\theta_1^2 + \theta_2^2 + \theta_3^1 = 1 \tag{9.92}$$

and $\theta_1 \geq 0$. This mostly fixes the problem and ensures that each parameter value corresponds to a unique line (except for some duplicate cases at $\theta_1 = 0$, but these can be safely neglected here). Thus, the parameter space is the upper half of a sphere, $\mathbb{S}^2$. The maximum-entropy prior suggests assigning a uniform probability density to Θ. This may feel like the right thing to do, but this notion of uniformity is biased by the particular constraint applied to the parameter space to ensure uniqueness. There are many other choices. For example, we could replace (9.92) by constraints that force the points to lie on the upper half of the surface of cube, instead of a sphere. A uniform probability density assigned in this new parameter space certainly differs from one over the sphere.

In some settings, there is a natural representation of the parameter space that is invariant to certain transformations. Section 5.1.4 introduced the notion of Haar measure. If the Haar measure is used as a noninformative prior, then a meaningful notion of uniformity may be obtained. For example, suppose that the parameter space is $SO(3)$. Uniform probability mass over the space of unit quaternions, as suggested in Example 5.14, is an excellent choice for a noninformative prior because it is consistent with the Haar measure, which is invariant to group operations applied to the events. Unfortunately, a Haar measure does not exist for most spaces that arise in practice.[9] ∎

9.5.2.3 Incorrect assumptions on conditional distributions

One final concern is that many times even the distribution $P(y|\theta)$ is incorrectly estimated because it is assumed arbitrarily to belong to a family of distributions. For example, it is often very easy to work with Gaussian densities. Therefore, it is tempting to assume that $p(y|\theta)$ is Gaussian. Experiments can be performed to estimate the mean and variance

[9] A locally compact topological group is required [348, 839].

parameters. Even though some best fit will be found, it does not necessarily imply that a Gaussian is a good representation. Conclusions based on this model may be incorrect, especially if the true distribution has a different shape, such as having a larger tail or being multimodal. In many cases, *nonparametric* methods may be needed to avoid such biases. Such methods do not assume a particular family of distributions. For example, imagine estimating a probability distribution by making a histogram that records the frequency of y occurrences for a fixed value of θ. The histogram can then be normalized to contain a representation of the probability distribution without assuming an initial form.

9.5.3 Concerns regarding the nondeterministic model

Given all of the problems with probabilistic modeling, it is tempting to abandon the whole framework and work strictly with the nondeterministic model. This only requires specifying Θ, without indicating anything about the relative likelihoods of various actions. Therefore, most of the complicated issues presented in Sections 9.5.1 and 9.5.2 vanish. Unfortunately, this advantage comes at a substantial price. Making decisions with worst-case analysis under the nondeterministic model has its own shortcomings. After considering the trade-offs, you can decide which is most appropriate for a particular application of interest.

The first difficulty is to ensure that Θ is sufficiently large to cover all possibilities. Consider Formulation 9.6, in which nature acts twice. Through a nature observation action space, $\Psi(\theta)$, interference is caused in the measurement process. Suppose that $\Theta = \mathbb{R}$ and $h(\theta, \psi) = \theta + \psi$. In this case, $\Psi(\theta)$ can be interpreted as the measurement error. What is the maximum amount of error that can occur? Perhaps a sonar is measuring the distance from the robot to a wall. Based on the sensor specifications, it may be possible to construct a nice bound on the error. Occasionally, however, the error may be larger than this bound. Sonars sometimes fail to hear the required echo to compute the distance. In this case the reported distance is ∞. Due to reflections, extremely large errors can sometimes occur. Although such errors may be infrequent, if we want *guaranteed* performance, then large or even infinite errors should be included in $\Psi(\theta)$. The problem is that worst-case reasoning could always conclude that the sensor is useless by reporting ∞. Any statistically valid information that could be gained from the sensor would be ignored. Under the probabilistic model, it is easy to make $\Psi(\theta)$ quite large and then assign very small probabilities to larger errors. The problem with nondeterministic uncertainty is that $\Psi(\theta)$ needs to be smaller to make appropriate decisions; however, theoretically "guaranteed" performance may not truly be guaranteed in practice.

Once a nondeterministic model is formulated, the optimal decision rule may produce results that seem absurd for the intended application. The problem is that the DM cannot tolerate any risk. An action is applied only if the result can be guaranteed. The hope of doing better than the worst case is not taken into account. Consider the following example:

Example 9.28 (A Problem with Conservative Decision Making) Suppose that a friend offers you the choice of either a check for 1000 Euros or 1 Euro in cash. With the check, you must take it to the bank, and there is a small chance that your friend will have insufficient funds in the account. In this case, you will receive nothing. If you select the 1 Euro in cash, then you are guaranteed to earn something.

The following cost matrix reflects the outcomes (ignoring utility theory):

$$
\Theta \quad
\begin{array}{c}
U \\
\begin{array}{|c|c|}
\hline
1 & 1000 \\
\hline
1 & 0 \\
\hline
\end{array}
\end{array}
\quad . \qquad (9.93)
$$

Using probabilistic analysis, we might conclude that it is best to take the check. Perhaps the friend is even known to be very wealthy and responsible with banking accounts. This information, however, cannot be taken into account in the decision-making process. Using worst-case analysis, the optimal action is to take the 1 Euro in cash. You may not feel too good about it, though. Imagine the regret if you later learn that the account had sufficient funds to cash the check for 1000 Euros. ∎

Thus, it is important to remember the price that one must pay for wanting results that are absolutely guaranteed. The probabilistic model offers the flexibility of incorporating statistical information. Sometimes the probabilistic model can be viewed as a generalization of the nondeterministic model. If it is assumed that nature acts after the robot, then the nature action can take this into account, as incorporated into Formulation 9.4. In the nondeterministic case, $\Theta(u)$ is specified, and in the probabilistic case, $P(\theta|u)$ is specified. The distribution $P(\theta|u)$ can be designed so that nature selects with very high probability the $\theta \in \Theta$ that maximizes $L(u, \theta)$. In Example 9.28, this would mean that the probability that the check would bounce (resulting in no earnings) would by very high, such as 0.999999. In this case, even the optimal action under the probabilistic model is to select the 1 Euro in cash. For virtually any decision problem that is modeled using worst-case analysis, it is possible to work backward and derive possible priors for which the same decision would be made using probabilistic analysis. In Example 9.4, it seemed as if the decision was based on assuming that with very high probability, the check would bounce, even though there were no probabilistic models.

This means that worst-case analysis under the nondeterministic model can be considered as a special case of a probabilistic model in which the prior distribution assigns high probabilities to the worst-case outcomes. The justification for this could be criticized in the same way that other prior assignments are criticized in Bayesian analysis. What is the basis of this particular assignment?

9.5.4 Concerns regarding game theory

One of the most basic limitations of game theory is that each player must know the cost functions of the other players. As established in Section 9.5.1, it is even quite difficult to determine an appropriate cost function for a single decision maker. It is even more difficult to determine costs and motivations of other players. In most practical settings this information is not available. One possibility is to model uncertainty associated with knowledge of the cost function of another player. Bayesian analysis could be used to reason about the cost based on observations of actions chosen by the player. Issues of assigning priors once again arise. One of the greatest difficulties in allowing uncertainties in the cost functions is that a kind of "infinite reflection" occurs [394]. For example, if I am playing a game, does the other player know my cost function? I may be uncertain about this. Furthermore, does the other player know that I do not completely know its cost function? This kind of second-guessing can occur indefinitely, leading to a nightmare of nested reasoning and assignments of prior distributions.[10]

The existence of saddle points or Nash equilibria was assured by using randomized strategies. Mathematically, this appears to be a clean solution to a frustrating problem; however, it also represents a substantial change to the model. Many games are played just once. For the expected-case results to converge, the game must be played an infinite number of times. If a game is played once, or only a few times, then the players are very likely to experience regret, even though the theory based on expected-case analysis indicates that regret is eliminated.

Another issue is that intelligent human players may fundamentally alter their strategies after playing a game several times. It is very difficult for humans to simulate a randomized strategy (assuming they even want to, which is unlikely). There are even international tournaments in which the players repeatedly engage in classic games such as Rock-Paper-Scissors or the Prisoner's Dilemma. For an interesting discussion of a tournament in which people designed programs that repeatedly compete on the Prisoner's Dilemma, see [918]. It was observed that even some cooperation often occurs after many iterations, which secures greater rewards for both players, even though they cannot communicate. A famous strategy arose in this context called Tit-for-Tat (written by Anatol Rapoport), which in each stage repeated the action chosen by the other player in the last stage. The approach is simple yet surprisingly successful.

In the case of nonzero-sum games, it is particularly disheartening that multiple Nash equilibria may exist. Suppose there is only one admissible equilibrium among several Nash equilibria. Does it really seem plausible that an adversary would think very carefully about the various Nash equilibria and pick the admissible one? Perhaps some players are conservative and even play security strategies, which completely destroys the assumptions of minimizing regret. If there are multiple admissible Nash equilibria, it appears that regret is unavoidable unless there is some collaboration between players. This result is unfortunate if such collaboration is impossible.

Further reading

Section 9.1 covered very basic concepts, which can be found in numerous books and on the Internet. For more on Pareto optimality, see [849, 910, 953, 1005]. Section 9.2 is inspired mainly by decision theory books. An excellent introduction is [91]. Other sources include [270, 273, 676, 834]. The "game against nature" view is based mainly on [111]. Pattern classification, which is an important form of decision theory, is covered in [19, 273, 297, 714]. Bayesian networks [781] are a popular representation in artificial intelligence research and often provide compact encodings of information for complicated decision-making problems.

Further reading on the game theory concepts of Sections 9.3 and 9.4 can be found in many books (e.g., [60, 762]). A fun book that has many examples and intuitions is [918]. For games that have infinite action sets, see [60]. The computation of randomized Nash equilibria remains a topic of active research. A survey of methods appears in [694]; see also [548, 702]. The coupled polynomial equations that appear in computing randomized Nash equilibria may seem to suggest applying algorithms from computational algebraic geometry, as were needed in Section 6.4 to solve this kind of problem in combinatorial motion planning. An approach that uses such tools is given in [263]. Contrary to the noncooperative games

---

[10] Readers familiar with the movie *The Princess Bride* may remember the humorous dialog between Vizzini and the Dread Pirate Roberts about which goblet contains the deadly Iocane powder.

defined in Section 9.4, *cooperative game theory* investigates ways in which various players can form coalitions to improve their rewards [782].

Parts of Section 9.5 were inspired by [91]. Utility theory appears in most decision theory books (e.g., [91]) and in some artificial intelligence books (e.g., [842]). An in-depth discussion of Bayesian vs. frequentist issues appears in [834]. For a thorough introduction to constructing cost models for decision making, see [542].

Exercises

1. Suppose that a single-stage two-objective decision-making problem is defined in which there are two objectives and a continuous set of actions, $U = [-10, 10]$. The cost vector is $L = [u^2 \ u - 1]$. Determine the set of Pareto-optimal actions.

2. Let

$$\Theta$$

$$U \quad \begin{array}{|c|c|c|c|} \hline -1 & 3 & 2 & -1 \\ \hline -1 & 0 & 7 & -1 \\ \hline 1 & 5 & 5 & -2 \\ \hline \end{array}$$

define the cost for each combination of choices by the decision maker and nature. Let nature's randomized strategy be $[1/5 \ \ 2/5 \ \ 1/10 \ \ 3/10]$.

   (a) Use nondeterministic reasoning to find the minimax decision and worst-case cost.

   (b) Use probabilistic reasoning to find the best expected-case decision and expected cost.

3. Many reasonable decision rules are possible, other than those considered in this chapter.

   (a) Exercise 2(a) reflects extreme pessimism. Suppose instead that extreme optimism is used. Select the choice that optimizes the best-case cost for the matrix in Exercise 2.

   (b) One approach is to develop a coefficient of optimism, $\alpha \in [0, 1]$, which allows one to interpolate between the two extreme scenarios. Thus, a decision, $u \in U$, is chosen by minimizing

$$\alpha \max_{\theta \in \Theta} \left\{ L(u, \theta) \right\} + (1 - \alpha) \min_{\theta \in \Theta} \left\{ L(u, \theta) \right\}. \tag{9.94}$$

   Determine the optimal decision for this scenario under all possible choices for $\alpha \in [0, 1]$. Give your answer as a list of choices, each with a specified range of α.

4. Suppose that after making a decision, you observe the choice made by nature. How does the cost that you received compare with the best cost that could have been obtained if you chose something else, given this choice by nature? This difference in costs can be considered as *regret* or minimum "Doh!"[11] Psychologists have argued that some people make choices based on minimizing regret. It reflects how badly you wish you had done something else after making the decision.

   (a) Develop an expression for the worst-case regret, and use it to make a minimax regret decision using the matrix from Exercise 2.

   (b) Develop an expression for the expected regret, and use it to make a minimum expected regret decision.

5. Using the matrix from Exercise 2, consider the set of all probability distributions for nature. Characterize the set of all distributions for which the minimax decision and the best expected decision results in the same choice. This indicates how to provide reverse justification for priors.

---

[11] In 2001, the Homer Simpson term "Doh!" was added to the Oxford English Dictionary as an expression of regret.

6. Consider a Bayesian decision-theory scenario with cost function L. Show that the decision rule never changes if $L(u, \theta)$ is replaced by $aL(u, \theta) + b$, for any $a > 0$ and $b \in \mathbb{R}$.

7. Suppose that there are two classes, $\Omega = \{\omega_1, \omega_2\}$, with $P(\omega_1) = P(\omega_2) = \frac{1}{2}$. The observation space, Y, is $\mathbb{R}$. Recall from probability theory that the normal (or Gaussian) probability density function is

$$p(y) = \frac{1}{\sigma\sqrt{2\pi}} e^{-(y-\mu)^2/2\sigma^2}, \tag{9.95}$$

in which μ denotes the mean and σ^2 denotes the variance. Suppose that $p(y|\omega_1)$ is a normal density in which $\mu = 0$ and $\sigma^2 = 1$. Suppose that $p(y|\omega_2)$ is a normal density in which $\mu = 6$ and $\sigma^2 = 4$. Find the optimal classification rule, $\gamma : Y \rightarrow \Omega$. You are welcome to solve the problem numerically (by computer) or graphically (by careful function plotting). Carefully explain how you arrived at the answer in any case.

8. Let

$$\Theta$$

	2	−2	−2	1
U	−1	−2	−2	6
	4	0	−3	4

give the cost for each combination of choices by the decision maker and nature. Let nature's randomized strategy be $[1/4 \ \ 1/2 \ \ 1/8 \ \ 1/8]$.

(a) Use nondeterministic reasoning to find the minimax decision and worst-case cost.

(b) Use probabilistic reasoning to find the best expected-case decision and expected cost.

(c) Characterize the set of all probability distributions for which the minimax decision and the best expected decision results in the same choice.

9. In a *constant-sum game*, the costs for any $u \in U$ and $v \in V$ add to yield

$$L_1(u, v) + L_2(u, v) = c \tag{9.96}$$

for some constant c that is independent of u and v. Show that any constant-sum game can be transformed into a zero-sum game, and that saddle point solutions can be found using techniques for the zero-sum formulation.

10. Formalize Example 9.7 as a zero-sum game, and compute security strategies for the players. What is the expected value of the game?

11. Suppose that for two zero-sum games, there exists some nonzero $c \in \mathbb{R}$ for which the cost matrix of one game is obtained by multiplying all entries by c in the cost matrix of the other. Prove that these two games must have the same deterministic and randomized saddle points.

12. In the same spirit as Exercise 11, prove that two zero-sum games have the same deterministic and randomized saddle points if c is added to all matrix entries.

13. Prove that multiple Nash equilibria of a nonzero-sum game specified by matrices A and B are interchangeable if (A, B) as a game yields the same Nash equilibria as the game $(A, -A)$.

14. Analyze the game of Rock-Paper-Scissors. For each player, assign a cost of 1 for losing, 0 for a tie, and -1 for winning. Specify the cost functions. Is it possible to avoid regret? Does it have a deterministic Nash equilibrium? Can you find a randomized Nash equilibrium?

15. Compute the randomized equilibrium point for the following zero-sum game:

$$V$$

$$U \quad \begin{array}{|c|c|} \hline 0 & -1 \\ \hline -1 & 2 \\ \hline \end{array} \quad . \tag{9.97}$$

Indicate the randomized strategies for the players and the resulting expected value of the game.

Implementations

16. Consider estimating the value of an unknown parameter, $\theta \in \mathbb{R}$. The prior probability density is a normal,

$$p(\theta) = \frac{1}{\sigma\sqrt{2\pi}} e^{-(\theta-\mu)^2/2\sigma^2}, \tag{9.98}$$

with $\mu = 0$ and $\sigma = 4$. Suppose that a sequence, $y_1, y_2, \ldots, y_k$, of k observations is made and that each $p(y_i|\theta)$ is a normal density with $\mu = \theta$ and $\sigma = 9$. Suppose that u represents your guess of the parameter value. The task is select u to minimize the expectation of the cost, $L(u, \theta) = (u - \theta)^2$. Suppose that the "true" value of θ is 4. Determine the u^*, the minimal action with respect to the expected cost after observing: $y_i = 4$ for every $i \in \{1, \ldots, k\}$.

(a) Determine u^* for $k = 1$.

(b) Determine u^* for $k = 10$.

(c) Determine u^* for $k = 1000$.

This experiment is not very realistic because the observations should be generated by sampling from the normal density, $p(y_i|\theta)$. Repeat the exercise using values drawn with the normal density, instead of $y_k = 4$, for each k.

17. Implement an algorithm that computes a randomized saddle point for zero-sum games. Assume that one player has no more than two actions and the other may have any finite number of actions.

18. Suppose that a K-stage decision-making problem is defined using multiple objectives. There is a finite state space X and a finite action set $U(x)$ for each $x \in X$. A state transition equation, $x_{k+1} = f(x_k, u_k)$, gives the next state from a current state and input. There are N cost functionals of the form

$$L_i(u_1, \ldots, u_K) = \sum_{k=1}^{K} l(x_k, u_k) + l_F(x_F), \tag{9.99}$$

in which $F = K + 1$. Assume that $l_F(x_F) = \infty$ if $x_F \in X_{goal}$ (for some goal region $X_{goal} \subset X$) and $l_F(x_F) = 0$ otherwise. Assume that there is no termination action (which simplifies the problem). Develop a value-iteration approach that finds the complete set of Pareto-optimal plans efficiently as possible. If two or more plans produce the same cost vector, then only one representative needs to be returned.

10

Sequential Decision Theory

Chapter 9 essentially took a break from planning by indicating how to make a single decision in the presence of uncertainty. In this chapter, we return to planning by formulating a sequence of decision problems. This is achieved by extending the discrete planning concepts from Chapter 2 to incorporate the effects of multiple decision makers. The most important new decision maker is nature, which causes unpredictable outcomes when actions are applied during the execution of a plan. State spaces and state transition equations reappear in this chapter; however, in contrast to Chapter 2, additional decision makers interfere with the state transitions. As a result of this effect, a plan needs to incorporate state feedback, which enables it to choose an action based on the current state. When the plan is determined, it is not known what future states will arise. Therefore, feedback is required, as opposed to specifying a plan as a sequence of actions, which sufficed in Chapter 2. This was only possible because actions were predictable.

Keep in mind throughout this chapter that the current state is always known. The only uncertainty that exists is with respect to predicting future states. Chapters 11 and 12 will address the important and challenging case in which the current state is not known. This requires defining sensing models that attempt to measure the state. The main result is that planning occurs in an *information space*, as opposed to the state space. Most of the ideas of this chapter extend into information spaces when uncertainties in prediction and in the current state exist together.

The problems considered in this chapter have a wide range of applicability. Most of the ideas were developed in the context of stochastic control theory [95, 567, 570]. The concepts can be useful for modeling problems in mobile robotics because future states are usually unpredictable and can sometimes be modeled probabilistically [1004] or using worst-case analysis [593]. Many other applications exist throughout engineering, operations research, and economics. Examples include process scheduling, gambling strategies, and investment planning.

As usual, the focus here is mainly on arriving in a goal state. Both nondeterministic and probabilistic forms of uncertainty will be considered. In the nondeterministic case, the task is to find plans that are guaranteed to work in spite of nature. In some cases, a plan can be computed that has optimal worst-case performance while achieving the goal. In the probabilistic case, the task is to find a plan that yields optimal expected-case performance. Even though the outcome is not predictable in a single-plan execution, the idea is to reduce the average cost, if the plan is executed numerous times on the same problem.

10.1 Introducing sequential games against nature

This section extends many ideas from Chapter 2 to the case in which nature interferes with the outcome of actions. Section 10.1.1 defines the planning problem in this context, which is a direct extension of Section 2.1. Due to unpredictability, *forward projections* and *backprojections* are introduced in Section 10.1.2 to characterize possible future and past states, respectively. Forward projections characterize the future states that will be obtained under the application of a plan or a sequence of actions. In Chapter 2 this concept was not needed because the sequence of future states could always be derived from a plan and initial state. Section 10.1.3 defines the notion of a plan and uses forward projections to indicate how its execution may differ every time the plan is applied.

10.1.1 Model definition

The formulation presented in this section is an extension of Formulation 2.3 that incorporates the effects of nature at every stage. Let X denote a discrete state space, and let $U(x)$ denote the set of actions available to the decision maker (or robot) from state $x \in X$. At each stage k it is assumed that a *nature action* θ_k is chosen from a set $\Theta(x_k, u_k)$. This can be considered as a multi-stage generalization of Formulation 9.4, which introduced $\Theta(u)$. Now Θ may depend on the state in addition to the action because both x_k and u_k are available in the current setting. This implies that nature acts with the knowledge of the action selected by the decision maker. It is always assumed that during stage k, the decision maker does not know the particular nature action that will be chosen. It does, however, know the set $\Theta(x_k, u_k)$ for all $x_k \in X$ and $u_k \in U(x_k)$.

As in Section 9.2, there are two alternative nature models: nondeterministic or probabilistic. If the nondeterministic model is used, then it is only known that nature will make a choice from $\Theta(x_k, u_k)$. In this case, making decisions using worst-case analysis is appropriate.

If the probabilistic model is used, then a probability distribution over $\Theta(x_k, u_k)$ is specified as part of the model. The most important assumption to keep in mind for this case is that nature is *Markovian*. In general, this means that the probability depends only on local information. In most applications, this locality is with respect to time. In our formulation, it means that the distribution over $\Theta(x_k, u_k)$ depends only on information obtained at the current stage. In other settings, Markovian could mean a dependency on a small number of stages, or even a local dependency in terms of spatial relationships, as in a *Markov random field* [233, 379].

To make the Markov assumption more precise, the state and action histories as defined in Section 8.2.1 will be used again here. Let

$$\tilde{x}_k = (x_1, x_2, \ldots, x_k) \tag{10.1}$$

and

$$\tilde{u}_k = (u_1, u_2, \ldots, u_k). \tag{10.2}$$

These represent all information that is available up to stage k. Without the Markov assumption, it could be possible that the probability distribution for nature is conditioned on all of $\tilde{x}_k$ and $\tilde{u}_k$, to obtain $P(\theta_k | \tilde{x}_k, \tilde{u}_k)$. The Markov assumption declares that for all $\theta \in \Theta(x_k, u_k)$,

$$P(\theta_{k+1} | \tilde{x}_k, \tilde{u}_k) = P(\theta_{k+1} | x_k, u_k), \tag{10.3}$$

which drops all history except the current state and action. Once these two are known, there is no extra information regarding the nature action that could be gained from any portion of the histories.

The effect of nature is defined in the state transition equation, which produces a new state, x_{k+1}, once x_k, u_k, and θ_k are given:

$$x_{k+1} = f(x_k, u_k, \theta_k). \tag{10.4}$$

From the perspective of the decision maker, θ_k is not given. Therefore, it can only infer that a particular set of states will result from applying u_k and x_k:

$$X_{k+1}(x_k, u_k) = \{x_{k+1} \in X \mid \exists\theta_1 \in \Theta(x_k, u_k) \text{ such that } x_{k+1} = f(x_k, u_k, \theta_k)\}. \tag{10.5}$$

In (10.5), the notation $X_{k+1}(x_k, u_k)$ indicates a set of possible values for x_{k+1}, given x_k and u_k. The notation $X_k(\cdot)$ will generally be used to indicate the possible values for x_k that can be derived using the information that appears in the argument.

In the probabilistic case, a probability distribution over X can be derived for stage $k + 1$, under the application of u_k from x_k. As part of the problem, $P(\theta_k | x_k, u_k)$ is given. Using the state transition equation, $x_{k+1} = f(x_k, u_k, \theta_k)$,

$$P(x_{k+1} | x_k, u_k) = \sum_{\theta_k \in \Theta'} P(\theta_k | x_k, u_k) \tag{10.6}$$

can be derived, in which

$$\Theta' = \{\theta_k \in \Theta(x_k, u_k) \mid x_{k+1} = f(x_k, u_k, \theta_k)\}. \tag{10.7}$$

The calculation of $P(x_{k+1} | x_k, u_k)$ simply involves accumulating all of the probability mass that could lead to x_{k+1} from the application of various nature actions.

Putting these parts of the model together and adding some of the components from Formulation 2.3, leads to the following formulation:

Formulation 10.1 (Discrete Planning with Nature)

1. A nonempty *state space* X which is a finite or countably infinite set of *states*.
2. For each state, $x \in X$, a finite, nonempty *action space* $U(x)$. It is assumed that U contains a special *termination action*, which has the same effect as the one defined in Formulation 2.3.
3. A finite, nonempty *nature action space* $\Theta(x, u)$ for each $x \in X$ and $u \in U(x)$.
4. A *state transition function* f that produces a state, $f(x, u, \theta)$, for every $x \in X$, $u \in U$, and $\theta \in \Theta(x, u)$.
5. A set of *stages*, each denoted by k, that begins at $k = 1$ and continues indefinitely. Alternatively, there may be a fixed, maximum stage $k = K + 1 = F$.
6. An *initial state* $x_I \in X$. For some problems, this may not be specified, in which case a solution plan must be found from all initial states.
7. A *goal set* $X_G \subset X$.
8. A stage-additive cost functional L. Let $\tilde{\theta}_K$ denote the history of nature actions up to stage K. The cost functional may be applied to any combination of state, action, and nature histories to yield

$$L(\tilde{x}_F, \tilde{u}_K, \tilde{\theta}_K) = \sum_{k=1}^{K} l(x_k, u_k, \theta_k) + l_F(x_F), \tag{10.8}$$

in which $F = K + 1$. If the termination action u_T is applied at some stage k, then for all $i \geq k$, $u_i = u_T$, $x_i = x_k$, and $l(x_i, u_T, \theta_i) = 0$.

Using Formulation 10.1, either a feasible or optimal planning problem can be defined. To obtain a feasible planning problem, let $l(x_k, u_k, \theta_k) = 0$ for all $x_k \in X$, $u_k \in U$, and $\theta_k \in \Theta_k(u_k)$. Furthermore, let

$$l_F(x_F) = \begin{cases} 0 & \text{if } x_F \in X_G \\ \infty & \text{otherwise.} \end{cases} \tag{10.9}$$

To obtain an optimal planning problem, in general $l(x_k, u_k, \theta_k)$ may assume any nonnegative, finite value if $x_k \notin X_G$. For problems that involve probabilistic uncertainty, it is sometimes appropriate to assign a high, finite value for $l_F(x_F)$ of $x_F \notin X_G$, as opposed to assigning an infinite cost for failing to achieve the goal.

Note that in each stage, the cost term is generally allowed to depend on the nature action θ_k. If probabilistic uncertainty is used, then Formulation 10.1 is often referred to as a *controlled Markov process* or *Markov decision process* (MDP). If the actions are removed from the formulation, then it is simply referred to as a *Markov process*. In most statistical literature, the name *Markov chain* is used instead of *Markov process* when there are discrete stages (as opposed to continuous-time Markov processes). Thus, the terms *controlled Markov chain* and *Markov decision chain* may be preferable.

In some applications, it may be convenient to avoid the explicit characterization of nature. Suppose that $l(x_k, u_k, \theta_k) = l(x_k, u_k)$. If nondeterministic uncertainty is used, then $X_{k+1}(x_k, u_k)$ can be specified for all $x_k \in X$ and $u_k \in U(x_k)$ as a substitute for the state transition equation; this avoids having to refer to nature. The application of an action u_k from a state x_k directly leads to a specified subset of X. If probabilistic uncertainty is used, then $P(x_{k+1}|x_k, u_k)$ can be directly defined as the alternative to the state transition equation. This yields a probability distribution over X, if u_k is applied from some x_k, once again avoiding explicit reference to nature. Most of the time we will use a state transition equation that refers to nature; however, it is important to keep these alternatives in mind. They arise in many related books and research articles.

As used throughout Chapter 2, a directed state transition graph is sometimes convenient for expressing the planning problem. The same idea can be applied in the current setting. As in Section 2.1, X is the vertex set; however, the edge definition must change to reflect nature. A directed edge exists from state x to x' if there exists some $u \in U(x)$ and $\theta \in \Theta(x, u)$ such that $x' = f(x, u, \theta)$. A weighted graph can be made by associating the cost term $l(x_k, u_k, \theta_k)$ with each edge. In the case of a probabilistic model, the probability of the transition occurring may also be associated with each edge.

Note that both the decision maker and nature are needed to determine which vertex will be reached. As the decision maker contemplates applying an action u from the state x, it sees that there may be several outgoing edges due to nature. If a different action is contemplated, then this set of possible outgoing edges changes. Once nature applies its action, then the particular edge is traversed to arrive at the new state; however, this is not completely controlled by the decision maker.

Example 10.1 (Traversing the Number Line) Let $X = \mathbb{Z}$, $U = \{-2, 2, u_T\}$, and $\Theta = \{-1, 0, 1\}$. The action sets of the decision maker and nature are the same for all states. For the state transition equation, $x_{k+1} = f(x_k, u_k, \theta_k) = x_k + u_k + \theta_k$. For each stage, unit cost is received. Hence $l(x, u, \theta) = 1$ for all x, θ, and $u \neq u_T$. The initial state is $x_I = 100$, and the goal set is $X_G = \{-1, 0, 1\}$.

Consider executing a sequence of actions, $(-2, -2, \ldots, -2)$, under the nondeterministic uncertainty model. This means that we attempt to move left two units in each stage.

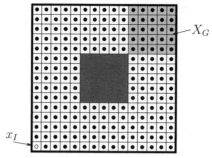

Figure 10.1: A grid-based shortest path problem with interference from nature.

After the first -2 is applied, the set of possible next states is $\{97, 98, 99\}$. Nature may slow down the progress to be only one unit per stage, or it may speed up the progress so that X_G is three units closer per stage. Note that after 100 stages, the goal is guaranteed to be achieved, in spite of any possible actions of nature. Once X_G is reached, u_T should be applied. If the problem is changed so that $X_G = \{0\}$, it becomes impossible to guarantee that the goal will be reached because nature may cause the goal to be overshot.

Now let $U = \{-1, 1, u_T\}$ and $\Theta = \{-2, -1, 0, 1, 2\}$. Under nondeterministic uncertainty, the problem can no longer be solved because nature is now powerful enough to move the state completely in the wrong direction in the worst case. A reasonable probabilistic version of the problem can, however, be defined and solved. Suppose that $P(\theta) = 1/5$ for each $\theta \in \Theta$. The transition probabilities can be defined from $P(\theta)$. For example, if $x_k = 100$ and $u_k = -1$, then $P(x_{k+1}|x_k, u_k) = 1/5$ if $97 \le x_k \le 101$, and $P(x_{k+1}|x_k, u_k) = 0$ otherwise. With the probabilistic formulation, there is a nonzero probability that the goal, $X_G = \{-1, 0, 1\}$, will be reached, even though in the worst-case reaching the goal is not guaranteed.

Example 10.2 (Moving on a Grid) A grid-based robot planning model can be made. A simple example is shown in Figure 10.1. The state space is a subset of a 15×15 integer grid in the plane. A state is represented as (i, j), in which $1 \le i, j \le 15$; however, the points in the center region (shown in Figure 10.1) are not included in X.

Let $A = \{0, 1, 2, 3, 4\}$ be a set of actions, which denote "stay," "right," "up," "left," and "down," respectively. Let $U = A \cup u_T$. For each $x \in X$, let $U(x)$ contain u_T and whichever actions are applicable from x (some are not applicable along the boundaries).

Let $\Theta(x, u)$ represent the set of all actions in A that are applicable after performing the move implied by u. For example, if $x = (2, 2)$ and $u = 3$, then the robot is attempting to move to $(1, 2)$. From this state, there are three neighboring states, each of which corresponds to an action of nature. Thus, $\Theta(x, u)$ in this case is $\{0, 1, 2, 4\}$. The action $\theta = 3$ does not appear because there is no state to the left of $(1, 2)$. Suppose that the probabilistic model is used, and that every nature action is equally likely.

The state transition function f is formed by adding the effect of both u_k and θ_k. For example, if $x_k = (i, j)$, $u_k = 1$, and $\theta_k = 2$, then $x_{k+1} = (i + 1, j + 1)$. If θ_k had been 3, then the two actions would cancel and $x_{k+1} = (i, j)$. Without nature, it would have been assumed that $\theta_k = 0$. As always, the state never changes once u_T is applied, regardless of nature's actions.

For the cost functional, let $l(x_k, u_k) = 1$ (unless $u_k = u_T$; in this case, $l(x_k, u_T) = 0$). For the final stage, let $l_F(x_F) = 0$ if $x_F \in X_G$; otherwise, let $l_F(x_F) = \infty$. A reasonable task is to get the robot to terminate in X_G in the minimum expected number of stages. A feedback plan is needed, which will be introduced in Section 10.1.3, and the optimal plan for this problem can be efficiently computed using the methods of Section 10.2.1.

This example can be easily generalized to moving through a complicated labyrinth in two or more dimensions. If the grid resolution is high, then an approximation to motion planning is obtained. Rather than forcing motions in only four directions, it may be preferable to allow any direction. This case is covered in Section 10.6, which addresses planning in continuous state spaces. ∎

10.1.2 Forward projections and backprojections

A *forward projection* is a useful concept for characterizing the behavior of plans during execution. Before uncertainties were considered, a plan was executed exactly as expected. When a sequence of actions was applied to an initial state, the resulting sequence of states could be computed using the state transition equation. Now that the state transitions are unpredictable, we would like to imagine what states are possible several stages into the future. In the case of nondeterministic uncertainty, this involves computing a set of possible future states, given a current state and plan. In the probabilistic case, a probability distribution over states is computed instead.

Nondeterministic forward projections

To facilitate the notation, suppose in this section that $U(x) = U$ for all $x \in X$. In Section 10.1.3 this will be lifted.

Suppose that the initial state, $x_1 = x_I$, is known. If the action $u_1 \in U$ is applied, then the set of possible next states is

$$X_2(x_1, u_1) = \{x_2 \in X \mid \exists \theta_1 \in \Theta(x_1, u_1) \text{ such that } x_2 = f(x_1, u_1, \theta_1)\}, \tag{10.10}$$

which is just a special version of (10.5). Now suppose that an action $u_2 \in U$ will be applied. The forward projection must determine which states could be reached from x_1 by applying u_1 followed by u_2. This can be expressed as

$$X_3(x_1, u_1, u_2) = \{x_3 \in X \mid \exists \theta_1 \in \Theta(x_1, u_1) \text{ and } \exists \theta_2 \in \Theta(x_2, u_2)$$
$$\text{such that } x_2 = f(x_1, u_1, \theta_1) \text{ and } x_3 = f(x_2, u_2, \theta_2)\}. \tag{10.11}$$

This idea can be repeated for any number of iterations but becomes quite cumbersome in the current notation. It is helpful to formulate the forward projection recursively. Suppose that an action history $\tilde{u}_k$ is fixed. Let $X_{k+1}(X_k, u_k)$ denote the forward projection at stage $k + 1$, given that X_k is the forward projection at stage k. This can be computed as

$$X_{k+1}(X_k, u_k) = \{x_{k+1} \in X \mid \exists x_k \in X_k \text{ and } \exists \theta_k \in \Theta(x_k, u_k)$$
$$\text{such that } x_{k+1} = f(x_k, u_k, \theta_k)\}. \tag{10.12}$$

This may be applied any number of times to compute X_{k+1} from an initial condition $X_1 = \{x_1\}$.

Example 10.3 (Nondeterministic Forward Projections)   Recall the first model given in Example 10.1, in which $U = \{-2, 2, u_T\}$ and $\Theta = \{-1, 0, 1\}$. Suppose that $x_1 = 0$, and $u = 2$ is applied. The one-stage forward projection is $X_2(0, 2) = \{1, 2, 3\}$. If $u = 2$ is applied again, the two-stage forward projection is $X_3(0, 2, 2) = \{2, 3, 4, 5, 6\}$. Repeating this process, the k-stage forward projection is $\{k, \ldots, 3k\}$. ∎

Probabilistic forward projections

The probabilistic forward projection can be considered as a Markov process because the "decision" part is removed once the actions are given. Suppose that x_k is given and u_k is applied. What is the probability distribution over x_{k+1}? This was already specified in (10.6) and is the one-stage forward projection. Now consider the two-stage probabilistic forward projection, $P(x_{k+2}|x_k, u_k, u_{k+1})$. This can be computed by marginalization as

$$P(x_{k+2}|x_k, u_k, u_{k+1}) = \sum_{x_{k+1} \in X} P(x_{k+2}|x_{k+1}, u_{k+1}) P(x_{k+1}|x_k, u_k). \qquad (10.13)$$

Computing further forward projections requires nested summations, which marginalize all of the intermediate states. For example, the three-stage forward projection is

$$P(x_{k+3}|x_k, u_k, u_{k+1}, u_{k+2}) =$$
$$\sum_{x_{k+1} \in X} \sum_{x_{k+2} \in X} P(x_{k+3}|x_{k+2}, u_{k+2}) P(x_{k+2}|x_{k+1}, u_{k+1}) P(x_{k+1}|x_k, u_k). \qquad (10.14)$$

A convenient expression of the probabilistic forward projections can be obtained by borrowing nice algebraic properties from linear algebra. For each action $u \in U$, let its *state transition matrix* M_u be an $n \times n$ matrix, for $n = |X|$, of probabilities. The matrix is defined as

$$M_u = \begin{pmatrix} m_{1,1} & m_{1,2} & \cdots & m_{1,n} \\ m_{2,1} & m_{2,2} & \cdots & m_{2,n} \\ \vdots & \vdots & & \vdots \\ m_{n,1} & m_{n,2} & \cdots & m_{n,n} \end{pmatrix}, \qquad (10.15)$$

in which

$$m_{i,j} = P(x_{k+1} = i \mid x_k = j, u). \qquad (10.16)$$

For each j, the jth column of M_u must sum to one and can be interpreted as the probability distribution over X that is obtained if u_k is applied from state $x_k = j$.

Let v denote an n-dimensional column vector that represents any probability distribution over X. The product $M_u v$ yields a column vector that represents the probability distribution over X that is obtained after starting with v and applying u. The matrix multiplication performs n inner products, each of which is a marginalization as shown in (10.13). The forward projection at any stage, k, can now be expressed using a product of $k - 1$ state transition matrices. Suppose that $\tilde{u}_{k-1}$ is fixed. Let $v = [0 \ 0 \ \cdots 0 \ 1 \ 0 \ \cdots \ 0]$, which indicates that x_1 is known (with probability one). The forward projection can be computed as

$$v' = M_{u_{k-1}} M_{u_{k-2}} \cdots M_{u_2} M_{u_1} v. \qquad (10.17)$$

The ith element of v' is $P(x_k = i \mid x_1, \tilde{u}_{k-1})$.

Example 10.4 (Probabilistic Forward Projections) Once again, use the first model from Example 10.1; however, now assign probability $1/3$ to each nature action. Assume that, initially, $x_1 = 0$, and $u = 2$ is applied in every stage. The one-stage forward projection yields probabilities

$$[1/3 \ \ 1/3 \ \ 1/3] \qquad (10.18)$$

over the sequence of states $(1, 2, 3)$. The two-stage forward projection yields

$$[1/9 \quad 2/9 \quad 3/9 \quad 2/9 \quad 1/9] \tag{10.19}$$

over $(2, 3, 4, 5, 6)$. ∎

Backprojections

Sometimes it is helpful to define the set of possible previous states from which one or more current states could be obtained. For example, they will become useful in defining graph-based planning algorithms in Section 10.2.3. This involves maintaining a *backprojection*, which is a counterpart to the forward projection that runs in the opposite direction. Backprojections were considered in Section 8.5.2 to keep track of the active states in a Dijkstra-like algorithm over continuous state spaces. In the current setting, backprojections need to address uncertainty.

Consider the case of nondeterministic uncertainty. Let a state $x \in X$ be given. Under a fixed action u, what previous states, $x' \in X$, could possibly lead to x? This depends only on the possible choices of nature and is expressed as

$$\text{WB}(x, u) = \{x' \in X \mid \exists \theta \in \Theta(x', u) \text{ such that } x = f(x', u, \theta)\}. \tag{10.20}$$

The notation $\text{WB}(x, u)$ refers to the *weak backprojection of x under u*, and gives the set of all states from which x may possibly be reached in one stage.

The backprojection is called "weak" because it does not guarantee that x is reached, which is a stronger condition. By guaranteeing that x is reached, a *strong backprojection of x under u* is defined as

$$\text{SB}(x, u) = \{x' \in X \mid \forall \theta \in \Theta(x', u), \ x = f(x', u, \theta)\}. \tag{10.21}$$

The difference between (10.20) and (10.21) is either *there exists* an action of nature that enables x to be reached, or x is reached *for all* actions of nature. Note that $\text{SB}(x, u) \subseteq \text{WB}(x, u)$. In many cases, $\text{SB}(x, u) = \emptyset$, and $\text{WB}(x, u)$ is rarely empty. The backprojection that was introduced in (8.66) of Section 8.5.2 did not involve uncertainty; hence, the distinction between weak and strong backprojections did not arise.

Two useful generalizations will now be made: 1) A backprojection can be defined from a set of states; 2) the action does not need to be fixed. Instead of a fixed state, x, consider a set $S \subseteq X$ of states. What are the states from which an element of S could possibly be reached in one stage under the application of u? This is the *weak backprojection of S under u*:

$$\text{WB}(S, u) = \{x' \in X \mid \exists \theta \in \Theta(x', u) \text{ such that } f(x', u, \theta) \in S\}, \tag{10.22}$$

which can also be expressed as

$$\text{WB}(S, u) = \bigcup_{x \in S} \text{WB}(x, u). \tag{10.23}$$

Similarly, the *strong backprojection of S under u* is defined as

$$\text{SB}(S, u) = \{x' \in X \mid \forall \theta \in \Theta(x', u), \ f(x', u, \theta) \in S\}. \tag{10.24}$$

Note that $\text{SB}(S, u)$ cannot be formed by the union of $SB(x, u)$ over all $x \in S$. Another observation is that for each $x_k \in \text{SB}(S, u_k)$, we have $X_{k+1}(x_k, u_k) \subseteq S$.

Now the dependency on u will be removed. This yields a backprojection of a set S. These are states from which there exists an action that possibly reaches S. The *weak backprojection of S* is

$$\mathrm{WB}(S) = \{x' \in X \mid \exists u \in U(x) \text{ such that } x \in \mathrm{WB}(S, u)\}, \qquad (10.25)$$

and the *strong backprojection of S* is

$$\mathrm{SB}(S) = \{x' \in X \mid \exists u \in U(x) \text{ such that } x \in \mathrm{SB}(S, u)\}. \qquad (10.26)$$

Note that $\mathrm{SB}(S) \subseteq \mathrm{WB}(S)$.

Example 10.5 (Backprojections) Once again, consider the model from the first part of Example 10.1. The backprojection $\mathrm{WB}(0, 2)$ represents the set of all states from which $u = 2$ can be applied and $x = 0$ is possibly reached; the result is $\mathrm{WB}(0, 2) = \{-3, -2, -1\}$. The state 0 cannot be reached with certainty from any state in $\mathrm{WB}(0, 2)$. Therefore, $\mathrm{SB}(0, 2) = \emptyset$.

Now consider backprojections from the goal, $X_G = \{-1, 0, 1\}$, under the action $u = 2$. The weak backprojection is

$$\mathrm{WB}(X_G, 2) = \mathrm{WB}(-1, 2) \cup \mathrm{WB}(0, 2) \cup \mathrm{WB}(1, 2) = \{-4, -3, -2, -1, 0\}. \qquad (10.27)$$

The strong backprojection is $\mathrm{SB}(X_G, 2) = \{-2\}$. From any of the other states in $\mathrm{WB}(X_G, 2)$, nature could cause the goal to be missed. Note that $\mathrm{SB}(X_G, 2)$ cannot be constructed by taking the union of $\mathrm{SB}(x, 2)$ over every $x \in X_G$.

Finally, consider backprojections that do not depend on an action. These are $\mathrm{WB}(X_G) = \{-4, -3, \ldots, 4\}$ and $\mathrm{SB}(X_G) = X_G$. In the latter case, all states in X_G lie in $\mathrm{SB}(X_G)$ because u_T can be applied. Without allowing u_T, we would obtain $\mathrm{SB}(X_G) = \{-2, 2\}$. ■

Other kinds of backprojections are possible, but we will not define them. One possibility is to make backprojections over multiple stages, as was done for forward projections. Another possibility is to define them for the probabilistic case. This is considerably more complicated. An example of a probabilistic backprojection is to find the set of all states from which a state in S will be reached with at least probability p.

10.1.3 A plan and its execution

In Chapter 2, a plan was specified by a sequence of actions. This was possible because the effect of actions was completely predictable. Throughout most of Part II, a plan was specified as a path, which is a continuous-stage version of the action sequence. Section 8.2.1 introduced plans that are expressed as a function on the state space. This was optional because uncertainty was not explicitly modeled (except perhaps in the initial state).

As a result of unpredictability caused by nature, it is now important to separate the definition of a plan from its execution. The same plan may be executed many times from the same initial state; however, because of nature, different future states will be obtained. This requires the use of feedback in the form of a plan that maps states to actions.

Defining a plan

Let a *(feedback) plan* for Formulation 10.1 be defined as a function $\pi : X \to U$ that produces an action $\pi(x) \in U(x)$, for each $x \in X$. Although the future state may not be known due to nature, if π is given, then it will at least be known what action will be taken from any future state. In other works, π has been called a *feedback policy, feedback control law, reactive plan* [342], and *conditional plan*.

For some problems, particularly when K is fixed at some finite value, a *stage-dependent plan* may be necessary. This enables a different action to be chosen for every stage, even from the same state. Let $\mathcal{K}$ denote the set $\{1, \ldots, K\}$ of stages. A stage-dependent plan is defined as $\pi : X \times \mathcal{K} \to U$. Thus, an action is given by $u = \pi(x, k)$. Note that the definition of a K-step plan, which was given Section 2.3, is a special case of the current definition. In that setting, the action depended only on the stage because future states were always predictable. Here they are no longer predictable and must be included in the domain of π. Unless otherwise mentioned, it will be assumed by default that π is *not* stage-dependent.

Note that once π is formulated, the state transitions appear to be a function of only the current state and nature. The next state is given by $f(x, \pi(x), \theta)$. The same is true for the cost term, $l(x, \pi(x), \theta)$.

Forward projections under a fixed plan

Forward projections can now be defined under the constraint that a particular plan is executed. The specific expression of actions is replaced by π. Each time an action is needed from a state $x \in X$, it is obtained as $\pi(x)$. In this formulation, a different $U(x)$ may be used for each $x \in X$, assuming that π is correctly defined to use whatever actions are actually available in $U(x)$ for each $x \in X$.

First we will consider the nondeterministic case. Suppose that the initial state x_1 and a plan π are known. This means that $u_1 = \pi(x_1)$, which can be substituted into (10.10) to compute the one-stage forward projection. To compute the two-stage forward projection, u_2 is determined from $\pi(x_2)$ for use in (10.11). A recursive formulation of the nondeterministic forward projection under a fixed plan is

$$X_{k+1}(x_1, \pi) = \{x_{k+1} \in X \mid \exists \theta_k \in \Theta(x_k, \pi(x_k)) \text{ such that} \tag{10.28}$$
$$x_k \in X_k(x_1, \pi) \text{ and } x_{k+1} = f(x_k, \pi(x_k), \theta_k)\}.$$

The probabilistic forward projection in (10.10) can be adapted to use π, which results in

$$P(x_{k+2} | x_k, \pi) = \sum_{x_{k+1} \in X} P(x_{k+2} | x_{k+1}, \pi(x_{k+1})) P(x_{k+1} | x_k, \pi(x_k)). \tag{10.29}$$

The basic idea can be applied $k - 1$ times to compute $P(x_k | x_1, \pi)$.

A state transition matrix can be used once again to express the probabilistic forward projection. In (10.15), all columns correspond to the application of the action u. Let M_π, be the forward projection due to a fixed plan π. Each column of M_π may represent a different action because each column represents a different state x_k. Each entry of M_π is

$$m_{i,j} = P(x_{k+1} = i \mid x_k = j, \ \pi(x_k)). \tag{10.30}$$

The resulting M_π defines a Markov process that is induced under the application of the plan π.

Graph representations of a plan

The game against nature involves two decision makers: nature and the robot. Once the plan is formulated, the decisions of the robot become fixed, which leaves nature as the only remaining decision maker. Using this interpretation, a directed graph can be defined in the same way as in Section 2.1, except nature actions are used instead of the robot's actions. It can even be imagined that nature itself faces a discrete feasible planning problem as in Formulation 2.1, in which $\Theta(x, \pi(x))$ replaces $U(x)$, and there is no goal set. Let $\mathcal{G}_\pi$ denote a *plan-based state transition graph*, which arises under the constraint that π is executed. The vertex set of $\mathcal{G}_\pi$ is X. A directed edge in $\mathcal{G}_\pi$ exists from x to x' if there exists some $\theta \in \Theta(x, \pi(x))$ such that $x' = f(x, \pi(x), \theta)$. Thus, from each vertex in $\mathcal{G}_\pi$, the set of outgoing edges represents all possible transitions to next states that are possible, given that the action is applied according to π. In the case of probabilistic uncertainty, $\mathcal{G}_\pi$ becomes a weighted graph in which each edge is assigned the probability $P(x'|x, \pi(x), \theta)$. In this case, $\mathcal{G}_\pi$ corresponds to the graph representation commonly used to depict a Markov chain.

A nondeterministic forward projection can easily be derived from $\mathcal{G}_\pi$ by following the edges outward from the current state. The outward edges lead to the states of the one-stage forward projection. The outward edges of these states lead to the two-stage forward projection, and so on. The probabilistic forward projection can also be derived from $\mathcal{G}_\pi$.

The cost of a feedback plan

Consider the cost-to-go of executing a plan π from a state $x_1 \in X$. The resulting cost depends on the sequences of states that are visited, actions that are applied by the plan, and the applied nature actions. In Chapter 2 this was obtained by adding the cost terms, but now there is a dependency on nature. Both worst-case and expected-case analyses are possible, which generalize the treatment of Section 9.2 to state spaces and multiple stages.

Let $\mathcal{H}(\pi, x_1)$ denote the set of state-action-nature histories that could arise from π when applied using x_1 as the initial state. The cost-to-go, $G_\pi(x_1)$, under a given plan π from x_1 can be measured using *worst-case analysis* as

$$G_\pi(x_1) = \max_{(\tilde{x}, \tilde{u}, \tilde{\theta}) \in \mathcal{H}(\pi, x_1)} \left\{ L(\tilde{x}, \tilde{u}, \tilde{\theta}) \right\}, \tag{10.31}$$

which is the maximum cost over all possible trajectories from x_1 under the plan π. If any of these fail to terminate in the goal, then the cost becomes infinity. In (10.31), $\tilde{x}$, $\tilde{u}$, and $\tilde{\theta}$ are infinite histories, although their influence on the cost is expected to terminate early due to the application of u_T.

An optimal plan using worst-case analysis is any plan for which $G_\pi(x_1)$ is minimized over all possible plans (all ways to assign actions to the states). In the case of feasible planning, there are usually numerous equivalent alternatives. Sometimes the task may be only to find a feasible plan, which means that all trajectories must reach the goal, but the cost does not need to be optimized.

Using probabilistic uncertainty, the cost of a plan can be measured using *expected-case analysis* as

$$G_\pi(x_1) = E_{\mathcal{H}(\pi, x_1)} \left[L(\tilde{x}, \tilde{u}, \tilde{\theta}) \right], \tag{10.32}$$

in which E denotes the mathematical expectation taken over $\mathcal{H}(\pi, x_1)$ (i.e., the plan is evaluated in terms of a weighted sum, in which each term has a weight for the probability of a state-action-nature history and its associated cost, $L(\tilde{x}, \tilde{u}, \tilde{\theta})$). This can also be interpreted as the expected cost over trajectories from x_1. If any of these have nonzero probability and fail to terminate in the goal, then $G_\pi(x_1) = \infty$. In the probabilistic setting, the task is usually to find a plan that minimizes $G_\pi(x_1)$.

An interesting question now emerges: Can the same plan, π, be optimal from every initial state $x_1 \in X$, or do we need to potentially find a different optimal plan for each initial state? Fortunately, a single plan will suffice to be optimal over all initial states. Why? This behavior was also observed in Section 8.2.1. If π is optimal from some x_1, then it must also be optimal from every other state that is potentially visited by executing π from x_1. Let x denote some visited state. If π was not optimal from x, then a better plan would exist, and the goal could be reached from x with lower cost. This contradicts the optimality of π because solutions must travel through x. Let π^* denote a plan that is optimal from every initial state.

10.2 Algorithms for computing feedback plans

10.2.1 Value iteration

Fortunately, the value iteration method of Section 2.3.1.1 extends nicely to handle uncertainty in prediction. This was the main reason why value iteration was introduced in Chapter 2. Value iteration was easier to describe in Section 2.3.1.1 because the complications of nature were avoided. In the current setting, value iteration retains most of its efficiency and can easily solve problems that involve thousands or even millions of states.

The state space, X, is assumed to be finite throughout Section 10.2.1. An extension to the case of a countably infinite state space can be developed if cost-to-go values over the entire space do not need to be computed incrementally.

Only backward value iteration is considered here. Forward versions can be defined alternatively.

Nondeterministic case

Suppose that the nondeterministic model of nature is used. A dynamic programming recurrence, (10.39), will be derived. This directly yields an iterative approach that computes a plan that minimizes the worst-case cost. The following presentation shadows that of Section 2.3.1.1; therefore, it may be helpful to refer back to this periodically.

An optimal plan π^* will be found by computing optimal cost-to-go functions. For $1 \leq k \leq F$, let G_k^* denote the worst-case cost that could accumulate from stage k to F under the execution of the optimal plan (compare to (2.5))

$$G_k^*(x_k) = \min_{u_k} \max_{\theta_k} \min_{u_{k+1}} \max_{\theta_{k+1}} \cdots \min_{u_K} \max_{\theta_K} \left\{ \sum_{i=k}^{K} l(x_i, u_i, \theta_i) + l_F(x_F) \right\}. \tag{10.33}$$

Inside of the min's and max's of (10.33) are the last $F - k$ terms of the cost functional, (10.8). For simplicity, the ranges of each u_i and θ_i in the min's and max's of (10.33) have not been indicated. The optimal cost-to-go for $k = F$ is

$$G_F^*(x_F) = l_F(x_F), \tag{10.34}$$

which is the same as (2.6) for the predictable case.

Now consider making K passes over X, each time computing G_k^* from G_{k+1}^*, as k ranges from F down to 1. In the first iteration, G_F^* is copied from l_F. In the second iteration, G_K^* is computed for each $x_K \in X$ as (compare to (2.7))

$$G_K^*(x_K) = \min_{u_K} \max_{\theta_K} \left\{ l(x_K, u_K, \theta_K) + l_F(x_F) \right\}, \tag{10.35}$$

in which $u_K \in U(x_K)$ and $\theta_K \in \Theta(x_K, u_K)$. Since $l_F = G_F^*$ and $x_F = f(x_K, u_K, \theta_K)$, substitutions are made into (10.35) to obtain (compare to (2.8))

$$G_K^*(x_K) = \min_{u_K} \max_{\theta_K} \left\{ l(x_K, u_K, \theta_K) + G_F^*(f(x_K, u_K, \theta_K)) \right\}, \qquad (10.36)$$

which computes the costs of all optimal one-step plans from stage K to stage $F = K + 1$.

More generally, G_k^* can be computed once G_{k+1}^* is given. Carefully study (10.33), and note that it can be written as (compare to (2.9))

$$G_k^*(x_k) = \min_{u_k} \max_{\theta_k} \left\{ \min_{u_{k+1}} \max_{\theta_{k+1}} \cdots \min_{u_K} \max_{\theta_K} \left\{ l(x_k, u_k, \theta_k) + \right.\right.$$
$$\left.\left. \sum_{i=k+1}^{K} l(x_i, u_i, \theta_i) + l_F(x_F) \right\} \right\} \qquad (10.37)$$

by pulling the first cost term out of the sum and by separating the minimization over u_k from the rest, which range from u_{k+1} to u_K. The second min and max do not affect the $l(x_k, u_k, \theta_k)$ term; thus, $l(x_k, u_k, \theta_k)$ can be pulled outside to obtain (compare to (2.10))

$$G_k^*(x_k) = \min_{u_k} \max_{\theta_k} \left\{ l(x_k, u_k, \theta_k) + \right.$$
$$\left. \min_{u_{k+1}} \max_{\theta_{k+1}} \cdots \min_{u_K} \max_{\theta_K} \left\{ \sum_{i=k+1}^{K} l(x_i, u_i, \theta_i) + l(x_F) \right\} \right\}. \qquad (10.38)$$

The inner min's and max's represent G_{k+1}^*, which yields the recurrence (compare to (2.11))

$$G_k^*(x_k) = \min_{u_k \in U(x_k)} \left\{ \max_{\theta_k} \left\{ l(x_k, u_k, \theta_k) + G_{k+1}^*(x_{k+1}) \right\} \right\}. \qquad (10.39)$$

Probabilistic case

Now consider the probabilistic case. A value iteration method can be obtained by once again shadowing the presentation in Section 2.3.1.1. For k from 1 to F, let G_k^* denote the expected cost from stage k to F under the execution of the optimal plan (compare to (2.5)):

$$G_k^*(x_k) = \min_{u_k, \ldots, u_K} \left\{ E_{\theta_k, \ldots, \theta_K} \left[\sum_{i=k}^{K} l(x_i, u_i, \theta_i) + l_F(x_F) \right] \right\}. \qquad (10.40)$$

The optimal cost-to-go for the boundary condition of $k = F$ again reduces to (10.34).

Once again, the algorithm makes K passes over X, each time computing G_k^* from G_{k+1}^*, as k ranges from F down to 1. As before, G_F^* is copied from l_F. In the second iteration, G_K^* is computed for each $x_K \in X$ as (compare to (2.7))

$$G_K^*(x_K) = \min_{u_K} \left\{ E_{\theta_K} \left[l(x_K, u_K, \theta_K) + l_F(x_F) \right] \right\}, \qquad (10.41)$$

in which $u_K \in U(x_K)$ and the expectation occurs over θ_K. Substitutions are made into (10.41) to obtain (compare to (2.8))

$$G_K^*(x_K) = \min_{u_K} \left\{ E_{\theta_K} \left[l(x_K, u_K, \theta_K) + G_F^*(f(x_K, u_K, \theta_K)) \right] \right\}. \qquad (10.42)$$

The general iteration is

$$G_k^*(x_k) = \min_{u_k} \left\{ E_{\theta_k} \left[\min_{u_{k+1},\dots,u_K} \left\{ E_{\theta_{k+1},\dots,\theta_K} \left[l(x_k, u_k, \theta_k) + \sum_{i=k+1}^{K} l(x_i, u_i, \theta_i) + l_F(x_F) \right] \right\} \right] \right\},$$
(10.43)

which is obtained once again by pulling the first cost term out of the sum and by separating the minimization over u_k from the rest. The second min and expectation do not affect the $l(x_k, u_k, \theta_k)$ term, which is pulled outside to obtain (compare to (2.10))

$$G_k^*(x_k) = \min_{u_k} \left\{ E_{\theta_k} \left[l(x_k, u_k, \theta_k) + \min_{u_{k+1},\dots,u_K} \left\{ E_{\theta_{k+1},\dots,\theta_K} \left[\sum_{i=k+1}^{K} l(x_i, u_i, \theta_i) + l(x_F) \right] \right\} \right] \right\}.$$
(10.44)

The inner min and expectation define G_{k+1}^*, yielding the recurrence (compare to (2.11) and (10.39))

$$\begin{aligned} G_k^*(x_k) &= \min_{u_k \in U(x_k)} \left\{ E_{\theta_k} \left[l(x_k, u_k, \theta_k) + G_{k+1}^*(x_{k+1}) \right] \right\} \\ &= \min_{u_k \in U(x_k)} \left\{ \sum_{\theta \in \Theta(x_k, u_k)} \left(l(x_k, u_k, \theta_k) + G_{k+1}^*(f(x_k, u_k, \theta_k)) \right) P(\theta_k | x_k, u_k) \right\}. \end{aligned}$$
(10.45)

If the cost term does not depend on θ_k, it can be written as $l(x_k, u_k)$, and (10.45) simplifies to

$$G_k^*(x_k) = \min_{u_k \in U(x_k)} \left\{ l(x_k, u_k) + \sum_{x_{k+1} \in X} G_{k+1}^*(x_{k+1}) P(x_{k+1} | x_k, u_k) \right\}.$$
(10.46)

The dependency of state transitions on θ_k is implicit through the expression of $P(x_{k+1} | x_k, u_k)$, for which the definition uses $P(\theta_k | x_k, u_k)$ and the state transition equation f. The form given in (10.46) may be more convenient than (10.45) in implementations.

Convergence issues

If the maximum number of stages is fixed in the problem definition, then convergence is assured. Suppose, however, that there is no limit on the number of stages. Recall from Section 2.3.2 that each value iteration increases the total path length by one. The actual stage indices were not important in backward dynamic programming because arbitrary shifting of indices does not affect the values. Eventually, the algorithm terminated because optimal cost-to-go values had been computed for all reachable states from the goal. This resulted in a *stationary cost-to-go function* because the values no longer changed. States that are reachable from the goal converged to finite values, and the rest remained at infinity. The only problem that prevents the existence of a stationary cost-to-go function, as mentioned in Section 2.3.2, is negative cycles in the graph. In this case, the best plan would be to loop around the cycle forever, which would reduce the cost to $-\infty$.

In the current setting, a stationary cost-to-go function once again arises, but cycles once again cause difficulty in convergence. The situation is, however, more complicated due to the influence of nature. It is helpful to consider a plan-based state transition graph, $\mathcal{G}_\pi$. First consider the nondeterministic case. If there exists a plan π from some state x_1 for which all possible actions of nature cause the traversal of cycles that accumulate

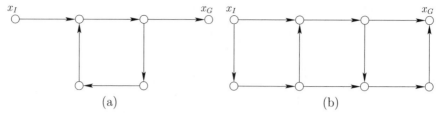

Figure 10.2: Plan-based state transition graphs. (a) The goal is possibly reachable, but not guaranteed reachable because an infinite cycle could occur. (b) The goal is guaranteed reachable because all flows lead to the goal.

negative cost, then the optimal cost-to-go at x_1 converges to $-\infty$, which prevents the value iterations from terminating. These cases can be detected in advance, and each such initial state can be avoided (some may even be in a different connected component of the state space).

It is also possible that there are unavoidable positive cycles. In Section 2.3.2, the cost-to-go function behaved differently depending on whether the goal set was reachable. Due to nature, the goal set may be possibly reachable or guaranteed reachable, as illustrated in Figure 10.2. To be *possibly reachable* from some initial state, there must exist a plan, π, for which there exists a sequence of nature actions that will lead the state into the goal set. To be *guaranteed reachable*, the goal must be reached in spite of *all* possible sequences of nature actions. If the goal is possibly reachable, but not guaranteed reachable, from some state x_1 and all edges have positive cost, then the cost-to-go value of x_1 tends to infinity as the value iterations are repeated. For example, every plan-based state transition graph may contain a cycle of positive cost, and in the worst case, nature may cause the state to cycle indefinitely. If convergence of the value iterations is only evaluated at states from which the goal set is guaranteed to be reachable, and if there are no negative cycles, then the algorithm should terminate when all cost-to-go values remain unchanged.

For the probabilistic case, there are three situations:

1. The value iterations arrive at a stationary cost-to-go function after a finite number of iterations.

2. The value iterations do not converge in any sense.

3. The value iterations converge only asymptotically to a stationary cost-to-go function. The number of iterations tends to infinity as the values converge.

The first two situations have already occurred. The first one occurs if there exists a plan, π, for which $\mathcal{G}_\pi$ has no cycles. The second situation occurs if there are negative or positive cycles for which all edges in the cycle have probability one. This situation is essentially equivalent to that for the nondeterministic case. Worst-case analysis assumes that the worst possible nature actions will be applied. For the probabilistic case, the nature actions are forced by setting their probabilities to one.

The third situation is unique to the probabilistic setting. This is caused by positive or negative cycles in $\mathcal{G}_\pi$ for which the edges have probabilities in $(0, 1)$. The optimal plan may even have such cycles. As the value iterations consider longer and longer paths, a cycle may be traversed more times. However, each time the cycle is traversed, the probability diminishes. The probabilities diminish exponentially in terms of the number of stages, whereas the costs only accumulate linearly. The changes in the cost-to-go function gradually decrease and converge only to stationary values as the number of iterations tends

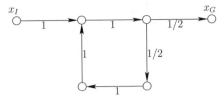

Figure 10.3: A plan-based state transition graph that causes asymptotic convergence. The probabilities of the transitions are shown on the edges. Longer and longer paths exist by traversing the cycle, but the probabilities become smaller.

to infinity. If some approximation error is acceptable, then the iterations can be terminated once the maximum change over all of X is within some ϵ threshold. The required number of value iterations to obtain a solution of the desired quality depends on the probabilities of following the cycles and on their costs. If the probabilities are lower, then the algorithm converges sooner.

Example 10.6 (A Cycle in the Transition Graph) Suppose that a plan, π, is chosen that yields the plan-based state transition graph shown in Figure 10.3. A probabilistic model is used, and the probabilities are shown on each edge. For simplicity, assume that each transition results in unit cost, $l(x, u, \theta) = 1$, over all x, u, and θ.

The expected cost from x_I is straightforward to compute. With probability $1/2$, the cost to reach x_G is 3. With probability $1/4$, the cost is 7. With probability $1/8$, the cost is 11. Each time another cycle is taken, the cost increases by 4, but the probability is cut in half. This leads to the infinite series

$$G_\pi(x_I) = 3 + 4 \sum_{i=1}^{\infty} \frac{1}{2^{i+1}} = 5. \qquad (10.47)$$

The infinite sum is part of the standard geometric series and converges to $1/2$; hence (10.47) converges to 5.

Even though the cost converges to a finite value, this only occurs in the limit. An infinite number of value iterations would theoretically be required to obtain this result. For most applications, an approximate solution suffices, and very high precision can be obtained with a small number of iterations (e.g., after 20 iterations, the change is on the order of one-billionth). Thus, in general, it is sensible to terminate the value iterations after the maximum cost-to-go change is less than a threshold based directly on precision.

Note that if nondeterministic uncertainty is used, then the value iterations do not converge because, in the worst case, nature will cause the state to cycle forever. Even though the goal is not guaranteed reachable, the probabilistic uncertainty model allows reasonable solutions. ∎

Using the plan

Assume that there is no limit on the number of stages. After the value iterations terminate, cost-to-go functions are determined over X. This is not exactly a plan, because an *action* is required for each $x \in X$. The actions can be obtained by recording the $u \in U(x)$ that produced the minimum cost value in (10.45) or (10.39).

Assume that the value iterations have converged to a stationary cost-to-go function. Before uncertainty was introduced, the optimal actions were determined by (2.19). The nondeterministic and probabilistic versions of (2.19) are

$$\pi^*(x) = \operatorname*{argmin}_{u \in U(x)} \left\{ \max_{\theta \in \Theta(x,u)} \left\{ l(x, u, \theta) + G^*(f(x, u, \theta)) \right\} \right\} \qquad (10.48)$$

and

$$\pi^*(x) = \operatorname*{argmin}_{u \in U(x)} \left\{ E_\theta \left[l(x, u, \theta) + G^*(f(x, u, \theta)) \right] \right\}, \qquad (10.49)$$

respectively. For each $x \in X$ at which the optimal cost-to-go value is known, one evaluation of (10.45) yields the best action.

Conveniently, the optimal action can be recovered directly during execution of the plan, rather than storing actions. Each time a state x_k is obtained during execution, the appropriate action $u_k = \pi^*(x_k)$ is selected by evaluating (10.48) or (10.49) at x_k. This means that the cost-to-go function itself can be interpreted as a representation of the optimal plan, once it is understood that a local operator is required to recover the action. It may seem strange that such a local computation yields the global optimum; however, this works because the cost-to-go function already encodes the global costs. This behavior was also observed for continuous state spaces in Section 8.4.1, in which a navigation function served to define a feedback motion plan. In that context, a gradient operator was needed to recover the direction of motion. In the current setting, (10.48) and (10.49) serve the same purpose.

10.2.2 Policy iteration

The value iterations of Section 10.2.1 work by iteratively updating cost-to-go values on the state space. The optimal plan can alternatively be obtained by iteratively searching in the space of plans. This leads to a method called *policy iteration* [86]; the term *policy* is synonymous with *plan*. The method will be explained for the case of probabilistic uncertainty, and it is assumed that X is finite. With minor adaptations, a version for nondeterministic uncertainty can also be developed.

Policy iteration repeatedly requires computing the cost-to-go for a given plan, π. Recall the definition of G_π from (10.32). First suppose that there are no uncertainties, and that the state transition equation is $x' = f(x, u)$. The dynamic programming equation (2.18) from Section 2.3.2 can be used to derive the cost-to-go for each state $x \in X$ under the application of π. Make a copy of (2.18) for each $x \in X$, and instead of the min, use the given action $u = \pi(x)$, to yield

$$G_\pi(x) = l(x, \pi(x)) + G_\pi(f(x, \pi(x))). \qquad (10.50)$$

In (10.50), the G^* has been replaced by G_π because there are no variables to optimize (it is simply the cost of applying π). Equation (10.50) can be thought of as a trivial form of dynamic programming in which the choice of possible plans has been restricted to a single plan, π. If the dynamic programming recurrence (2.18) holds over the space of all plans, it must certainly hold over a space that consists of a single plan; this is reflected in (10.50).

If there are n states, (10.50) yields n equations, each of which gives an expression of $G_\pi(x)$ for a different state. For the states in which $x \in X_G$, it is known that $G_\pi(x) = 0$. Now that this is known, the cost-to-go for all states from which X_G can be reached in one stage can be computed using (10.50) with $G_\pi(f(x, \pi(x))) = 0$. Once these cost-to-go values are computed, another wave of values can be computed from states that can reach

POLICY ITERATION ALGORITHM

1. Pick an initial plan π, in which u_T is applied at each $x \in X_G$ and all other actions are chosen arbitrarily.
2. Use (10.53) to compute G_π for each $x \in X$ under the plan π.
3. Substituting the computed G_π values for G^*, use (10.51) to compute a better plan, π':

$$\pi'(x) = \operatorname*{argmin}_{u \in U(x)} \left\{ l(x, u) + \sum_{x' \in X} G_\pi(x') P(x'|x, u) \right\}. \tag{10.54}$$

4. If π' produces at least one lower cost-to-go value than π, then let $\pi = \pi'$ and repeat Steps 2 and 3. Otherwise, declare π to be the optimal plan, π^*.

Figure 10.4: The policy iteration algorithm iteratively searches the space of plans by evaluating and improving plans.

these in one stage. This process continues until the cost-to-go values are computed for all states. This is similar to the behavior of Dijkstra's algorithm.

This process of determining the cost-to-go should not seem too mysterious. Equation (10.50) indicates how the costs differ between neighboring states in the state transition graph. Since all of the differences are specified and an initial condition is given for X_G, all others can be derived by adding up the differences expressed in (10.50). Similar ideas appear in the Hamilton-Jacobi-Bellman equation and Pontryagin's minimum principle, which are covered in Section 15.2.

Now we turn to the case in which there are probabilistic uncertainties. The probabilistic analog of (2.18) is (10.49). For simplicity, consider the special case in which $l(x, u, \theta)$ does not depend on θ, which results in

$$\pi^*(x) = \operatorname*{argmin}_{u \in U(x)} \left\{ l(x, u) + \sum_{x' \in X} G^*(x') P(x'|x, u) \right\}, \tag{10.51}$$

in which $x' = f(x, u)$. The cost-to-go function, G^*, satisfies the dynamic programming recurrence

$$G^*(x) = \min_{u \in U(x)} \left\{ l(x, u) + \sum_{x' \in X} G^*(x') P(x'|x, u) \right\}. \tag{10.52}$$

The probabilistic analog to (10.50) can be made from (10.52) by restricting the set of actions to a single plan, π, to obtain

$$G_\pi(x) = l(x, \pi(x)) + \sum_{x' \in X} G_\pi(x') P(x'|x, \pi(x)), \tag{10.53}$$

in which $x' = f(x, \pi(x))$.

The cost-to-go for each $x \in X$ under the application of π can be determined by writing (10.53) for each state. Note that all quantities except G_π are known. This means that if there are n states, then there are n linear equations and n unknowns ($G_\pi(x)$ for each $x \in X$). The same was true when (10.50) was used, except the equations were much simpler. In the probabilistic setting, a system of n linear equations must be solved to determine G_π. This may be performed using classical linear algebra techniques, such as *singular value decomposition (SVD)* [401, 961].

Now that we have a method for evaluating the cost of a plan, the policy iteration method is straightforward, as specified in Figure 10.4. Note that in Step 3, the cost-to-go

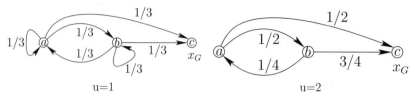

Figure 10.5: The probabilistic state transition graphs for $u = 1$ and $u = 2$. Transitions out of c are not shown because it is assumed that a termination action is always applied from x_g.

G_π, which was developed for one plan, π, is used to evaluate other plans. The result is the cost that will be obtained if a new action is tried in the first stage and then π is used for all remaining stages. If a new action cannot reduce the cost, then π must have already been optimal because it means that (10.54) has become equivalent to the stationary dynamic programming equation, (10.49). If it is possible to improve π, then a new plan is obtained. The new plan must be strictly better than the previous plan, and there is only a finite number of possible plans in total. Therefore, the policy iteration method converges after a finite number of iterations.

Example 10.7 (An Illustration of Policy Iteration) A simple example will now be used to illustrate policy iteration. Let $X = \{a, b, c\}$ and $U = \{1, 2, u_T\}$. Let $X_G = \{c\}$. Let $l(x, u) = 1$ for all $x \in X$ and $u \in U \setminus \{u_T\}$ (if u_T is applied, there is no cost). The probabilistic state transition graphs for each action are shown in Figure 10.5. The first step is to pick an initial plan. Let $\pi(a) = 1$ and $\pi(b) = 1$; let $\pi(c) = u_T$ because $c \in X_G$.

Now use (10.53) to compute G_π. This yields three equations:

$$G_\pi(a) = 1 + G_\pi(a)P(a \mid a, 1) + G_\pi(b)P(b \mid a, 1) + G_\pi(c)P(c \mid a, 1) \tag{10.55}$$

$$G_\pi(b) = 1 + G_\pi(a)P(a \mid b, 1) + G_\pi(b)P(b \mid b, 1) + G_\pi(c)P(c \mid b, 1) \tag{10.56}$$

$$G_\pi(c) = 0 + G_\pi(a)P(a \mid c, u_T) + G_\pi(b)P(b \mid c, u_T) + G_\pi(c)P(c \mid c, u_T). \tag{10.57}$$

Each equation represents a different state and uses the appropriate action from π. The final equation reduces to $G_\pi(c) = 0$ because of the basic rules of applying a termination condition. After substituting values for $P(x'|x, u)$ and using $G_\pi(c) = 0$, the other two equations become

$$G_\pi(a) = 1 + \tfrac{1}{3}G_\pi(a) + \tfrac{1}{3}G_\pi(b) \tag{10.58}$$

and

$$G_\pi(b) = 1 + \tfrac{1}{3}G_\pi(a) + \tfrac{1}{3}G_\pi(b). \tag{10.59}$$

The solutions are $G_\pi(a) = G_\pi(b) = 3$.

Now use (10.54) for each state with $G_\pi(a) = G_\pi(b) = 3$ and $G_\pi(c) = 0$ to find a better plan, π'. At state a, it is found by solving

$$\pi'(a) = \operatorname*{argmin}_{u \in U} \left\{ l(x, a) + \sum_{x' \in X} G_\pi(x')P(x'|x, a) \right\}. \tag{10.60}$$

The best action is $u = 2$, which produces cost $5/2$ and is computed as

$$l(x, 2) + \sum_{x' \in X} G_\pi(x')P(x'|x, 2) = 1 + 0 + (3)\tfrac{1}{2} + (0)\tfrac{1}{4} = \tfrac{5}{2}. \tag{10.61}$$

Thus, $\pi'(a) = 2$. Similarly, $\pi'(b) = 2$ can be computed, which produces cost $7/4$. Once again, $\pi'(c) = u_T$, which completes the determination of an improved plan.

BACKPROJECTION ALGORITHM

1.   Initialize $S = X_G$, and let $\pi(x) = u_T$ for each $x \in X_G$.

2.   For each $x \in X \setminus S$, if there exists some $u \in U(x)$ such that $x \in \text{SB}(S, u)$ then: 1) let $\pi(x) = u$, and 2) insert x into S.

3.   If Step 2 failed to extend S, then exit. This implies that $\text{SB}(S) = S$, which means no more progress can be made. Otherwise, go to Step 2.

Figure 10.6: A general algorithm for computing a feasible plan under nondeterministic uncertainty.

Since an improved plan has been found, replace π with π' and return to Step 2. The new plan yields the equations

$$G_\pi(a) = 1 + \tfrac{1}{2}G_\pi(b) \tag{10.62}$$

and

$$G_\pi(b) = 1 + \tfrac{1}{4}G_\pi(a). \tag{10.63}$$

Solving these yields $G_\pi(a) = 12/7$ and $G_\pi(b) = 10/7$. The next step attempts to find a better plan using (10.54), but it is determined that the current plan cannot be improved. The policy iteration method terminates by correctly reporting that $\pi^* = \pi$.   ∎

Policy iteration may appear preferable to value iteration, especially because it usually converges in fewer iterations than value iteration. The equation solving that determines the cost of a plan effectively considers multiple stages at once. However, for most planning problems, X is large and the large linear system of equations that must be solved at every iteration can become unwieldy. In some applications, either the state space may be small enough or sparse matrix techniques may allow efficient solutions over larger state spaces. In general, value-based methods seem preferable for most planning problems.

10.2.3 Graph search methods

Value iteration is quite general; however, in many instances, most of the time is wasted on states that do not update their values because either the optimal cost-to-go is already known or the goal is not yet reached. Policy iteration seems to alleviate this problem, but it is limited to small state spaces. These shortcomings motivate the consideration of alternatives, such as extending the graph search methods of Section 2.2. In some cases, Dijkstra's algorithm can even be extended to quickly obtain optimal solutions, but a strong assumption is required on the structure of solutions. In the nondeterministic setting, search methods can be developed that produce only feasible solutions, without regard for optimality. For the methods in this section, X need not be finite, as long as the search method is systematic, in the sense defined in Section 2.2.

Backward search with backprojections

A backward search can be conducted by incrementally growing a plan outward from X_G by using backprojections. A complete algorithm for computing feasible plans under nondeterministic uncertainty is outlined in Figure 10.6. Let S denote the set of states for which the plan has been computed. Initially, $S = X_G$ and, if possible, S may grow until $S = X$. The plan definition starts with $\pi(x) = u_T$ for each $x \in X_G$ and is incrementally extended to new states during execution.

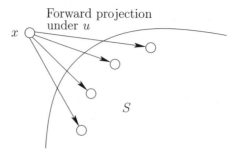

Figure 10.7: A state x can be added to S if there exists an action $u \in U(x)$ such that the one-stage forward projection is contained in S.

Step 2 takes every state x that is not already in S and checks whether it should be added. This requires determining whether some action, u, can be applied from x, with the next state guaranteed to lie in S, as shown in Figure 10.7. If so, then $\pi(x) = u$ is assigned and S is extended to include x. If no such progress can be made, then the algorithm must terminate. Otherwise, every state is checked again by returning to Step 2. This is necessary because S has grown, and in the next iteration new states may lie in its strong backprojection.

For efficiency reasons, the $X \setminus S$ set in Step 2 may be safely replaced with the smaller set, $\text{WB}(S) \setminus S$, because it is impossible for other states in X to be affected. Depending on the problem, this condition may provide a quick way to prune many hopeless states from consideration. As an example, consider a grid-like environment in which a maximum of two steps in any direction is possible at a given time. A simple distance test can be implemented to eliminate many states from possible inclusion into S in Step 2.

As long as the consideration of states to include in S is systematic, as considered in Section 2.2, numerous variations of the algorithm in Figure 10.6 are possible. One possibility is to keep track of the cost-to-go and grow S based on incrementally inserting minimal-cost states. This leads to a nondeterministic version of Dijkstra's algorithm, which is covered next.

Nondeterministic Dijkstra

Figure 10.8 shows an extension of Dijkstra's algorithm for solving the problem of Formulation 10.1 under nondeterministic uncertainty. It can also be considered as a variant of the algorithm in Figure 10.6 because it grows S by using backprojections. The algorithm in Figure 10.8 represents a backward-search version of Dijkstra's algorithm; therefore, it maintains the worst-case cost-to-go, G, which sometimes becomes the optimal, worst-case cost-to-go, G^*. Initially, $G = 0$ for states in the goal, and $G = \infty$ for all others.

Step 1 performs the initialization. Step 2 selects the state in A that has the smallest value. As in Dijkstra's algorithm for deterministic problems, it is known that the cost-to-go for this state is the smallest possible. It is therefore declared in Step 3 that $G^*(x_s) = G(x_s)$, and π^* is extended to include x_s.

Step 4 updates the costs for some states and expands the active set, A. Which costs could be immediately affected by the insertion of x_s into S? These are states $x_k \in X \setminus S$ for which there exists some $u_k \in U(x_k)$ that produces a one-stage forward projection, $X_{k+1}(x_k, u_k)$, such that: 1) $x_s \in X_{k+1}(x_k, u_k)$ and 2) $X_{k+1}(x_k, u_k) \subseteq S$. This is depicted in Figure 10.9. Let the set of states that satisfy these constraints be called the *frontier set*,

NONDETERMINISTIC DIJKSTRA

1. Initialize $S = \emptyset$ and $A = X_G$. Associate u_T with every $x \in A$. Assign $G(x) = 0$ for all $x \in A$ and $G(x) = \infty$ for all other states.

2. Unless A is empty, remove the $x_s \in A$ and its corresponding u, for which G is smallest. If A was empty, then exit (no further progress is possible).

3. Designate $\pi^*(x_s) = u$ as part of the optimal plan and insert x_s into S. Declare $G^*(x_s) = G(x_s)$.

4. Compute $G(x_s)$ using (10.64) for any x in the frontier set, Front(x_s, S), and insert Front(x_s, A) into A and with associated actions for each inserted state. For states already in A, retain whichever G value is lower, either its original value or the new computed value. Go to Step 2.

Figure 10.8: A Dijkstra-based algorithm for computing an optimal feasible plan under nondeterministic uncertainty.

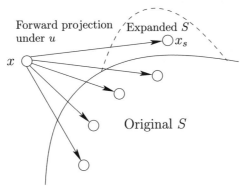

Figure 10.9: The worst-case cost-to-go is computed for any state x such that there exists a $u \in U(x)$ for which the one-stage forward projection is contained in the updated S and one state in the forward projection is x_s.

denoted by Front(x_s, S). For each $x \in$ Front(x_s, S), let $U_f(x) \subseteq U(x)$ denote the set of all actions for which the forward projection satisfies the two previous conditions.

The frontier set can be interpreted in terms of backprojections. The weak backprojection WB(x_s) yields all states that can possibly reach x_s in one step. However, the cost-to-go is only finite for states in SB(S) (here S already includes x_s). The states in S should certainly be excluded because their optimal costs are already known. These considerations reduce the set of candidate frontier states to $(\text{WB}(x_s) \cap \text{SB}(S)) \setminus S$. This set is still too large because the same action, u, must produce a one-stage forward projection that includes x_s and is a subset of S.

The worst-case cost-to-go is computed for all $x \in$ Front(x_s, S) as

$$G(x) = \min_{u \in U_f(x)} \left\{ \max_{\theta \in \Theta(x, u)} \left\{ l(x, u, \theta) + G(f(x, u, \theta)) \right\} \right\}, \tag{10.64}$$

in which the restricted action set, $U_f(x)$, is used. If x was already in A and a previous $G(x)$ was computed, then the minimum of its previous value and (10.64) is kept.

Probabilistic Dijkstra

A probabilistic version of Dijkstra's algorithm does not exist in general; however, for some problems, it can be made to work. The algorithm in Figure 10.8 is adapted to the probabilistic case by using

$$G(x) = \min_{u \in U_f(x)} \left\{ E_\theta \left[l(x, u, \theta) + G(f(x, u, \theta)) \right] \right\} \tag{10.65}$$

in the place of (10.64). The definition of Front remains the same, and the nondeterministic forward projections are still applied to the probabilistic problem. Only edges in the transition graph that have nonzero probability are actually considered as possible future states. Edges with zero probability are precluded from the forward projection because they cannot affect the computed cost values.

The probabilistic version of Dijkstra's algorithm can be successfully applied if there exists a plan, π, for which from any $x_k \in X$ there is probability one that $G_\pi(x_{k+1}) < G_\pi(x_k)$. What does this condition mean? From any x_k, all possible next states that have nonzero probability of occurring must have a lower cost value. If all edge costs are positive, this means that all paths in the multi-stage forward projection will make monotonic progress toward the goal. In the deterministic case, this always occurs if $l(x, u)$ is always positive. If nonmonotonic paths are possible, then Dijkstra's algorithm breaks down because the region in which cost-to-go values change is no longer contained within a propagating band, which arises in Dijkstra's algorithm for deterministic problems.

10.3 Infinite-horizon problems

In stochastic control theory and artificial intelligence research, most problems considered to date do not specify a goal set. Therefore, there are no associated termination actions. The task is to develop a plan that minimizes the expected cost (or maximize expected reward) over some number of stages. If the number of stages is finite, then it is straightforward to apply the value iteration method of Section 10.2.1. The adapted version of backward value iteration simply terminates when the first stage is reached. The problem becomes more challenging if the number of stages is infinite. This is called an *infinite-horizon problem*.

The number of stages for the planning problems considered in Section 10.1 is also infinite; however, it was expected that if the goal could be reached, termination would occur in a finite number of iterations. If there is no termination condition, then the costs tend to infinity. There are two alternative cost models that force the costs to become finite. The *discounted cost model* shrinks the per-stage costs as the stages extend into the future; this yields a geometric series for the total cost that converges to a finite value. The *average cost-per-stage model* divides the total cost by the number of stages. This essentially normalizes the accumulating cost, once again preventing its divergence to infinity. Some of the computation methods of Section 10.2 can be adapted to these models. This section formulates these two infinite-horizon cost models and presents computational solutions.

10.3.1 Problem formulation

Both of the cost models presented in this section were designed to force the cumulative cost to become finite, even though there is an infinite number of stages. Each can be considered as a minor adaptation of cost functional used in Formulation 10.1.

The following formulation will be used throughout Section 10.3.

Formulation 10.2 (Infinite-Horizon Problems)

1. A nonempty, finite *state space* X.

2. For each state $x \in X$, a finite *action space* $U(x)$ (there is no termination action, contrary to Formulation 10.1).

3. A finite *nature action space* $\Theta(x, u)$ for each $x \in X$ and $u \in U(x)$.

4. A *state transition function* f that produces a state, $f(x, u, \theta)$, for every $x \in X$, $u \in U(x)$, and $\theta \in \Theta(x, u)$.

5. A set of *stages*, each denoted by k, that begins at $k = 1$ and continues indefinitely.

6. A stage-additive cost functional, $L(\tilde{x}, \tilde{u}, \tilde{\theta})$, in which $\tilde{x}$, $\tilde{u}$, and $\tilde{\theta}$ are infinite state, action, and nature histories, respectively. Two alternative forms of L will be given shortly.

In comparison to Formulation 10.1, note that here there is no initial or goal state. Therefore, there are no termination actions. Without the specification of a goal set, this may appear to be a strange form of planning. A feedback plan, π, still takes the same form; $\pi(x)$ produces an action $u \in U(x)$ for each $x \in X$.

As a possible application, imagine a robot that delivers materials in a factory from several possible source locations to several destinations. The robot operates over a long work shift and has a probabilistic model of when requests to deliver materials will arrive. Formulation 10.2 can be used to define a problem in which the goal is to minimize the average amount of time that materials wait to be delivered. This strategy should not depend on the length of the shift; therefore, an infinite number of stages is reasonable. If the shift is too short, the robot may focus only on one delivery, or it may not even have enough time to accomplish that.

Discounted cost

In Formulation 10.2, the cost functional in Item 6 must be defined carefully to ensure that finite values are always obtained, even though the number of stages tends to infinity. The *discounted cost model* provides one simple way to achieve this by rapidly decreasing costs in future stages. Its definition is based on the standard geometric series. For any real parameter $\alpha \in (0, 1)$,

$$\lim_{K \to \infty} \left(\sum_{k=0}^{K} \alpha^k \right) = \frac{1}{1 - \alpha}. \tag{10.66}$$

The simplest case, $\alpha = 1/2$, yields $1 + 1/2 + 1/4 + 1/8 + \cdots$, which clearly converges to 2.

Now let $\alpha \in (0, 1)$ denote a *discount factor*, which is applied in the definition of a cost functional:

$$L(\tilde{x}, \tilde{u}, \tilde{\theta}) = \lim_{K \to \infty} \left(\sum_{k=0}^{K} \alpha^k l(x_k, u_k, \theta_k) \right). \tag{10.67}$$

Let l_k denote the cost, $l(x_k, u_k, \theta_k)$, received at stage k. For convenience in this setting, the first stage is $k = 0$, as opposed to $k = 1$, which has been used previously. As the maximum stage, K, increases, the diminished importance of costs far in the future can easily be observed, as indicated in Figure 10.10.

Stage	L_K^*
$K = 0$	l_0
$K = 1$	$l_0 + \alpha l_1$
$K = 2$	$l_0 + \alpha l_1 + \alpha^2 l_2$
$K = 3$	$l_0 + \alpha l_1 + \alpha^2 l_2 + \alpha^3 l_3$
$K = 4$	$l_0 + \alpha l_1 + \alpha^2 l_2 + \alpha^3 l_3 + \alpha^4 l_4$

$\vdots$

Figure 10.10: The cost magnitudes decease exponentially over the stages.

The rate of cost decrease depends strongly on α. For example, if $\alpha = 1/2$, the costs decrease very rapidly. If $\alpha = 0.999$, the convergence to zero is much slower. The trade-off is that with a large value of α, more stages are taken into account, and the designed plan is usually of higher quality. If a small value of α is used, methods such as value iteration converge much more quickly; however, the solution quality may be poor because of "short sightedness."

The term $l(x_k, u_k, \theta_k)$ in (10.67) assumes different values depending on x_k, u_k, and θ_k. Since there are only a finite number of possibilities, they must be bounded by some positive constant c.[1] Hence,

$$\lim_{K \to \infty} \left(\sum_{k=0}^{K} \alpha^k l(x_k, u_k, \theta_k) \right) \leq \lim_{K \to \infty} \left(\sum_{k=0}^{K} \alpha^k c \right) \leq \frac{c}{1 - \alpha}, \tag{10.68}$$

which means that $L(\tilde{x}, \tilde{u}, \tilde{\theta})$ is bounded from above, as desired. A similar lower bound can be constructed, which ensures that the resulting total cost is always finite.

Average cost-per-stage

An alternative to discounted cost is to use the *average cost-per-stage model*, which keeps the cumulative cost finite by dividing out the total number of stages:

$$L(\tilde{x}, \tilde{u}, \tilde{\theta}) = \lim_{K \to \infty} \left(\frac{1}{K} \sum_{k=0}^{K-1} l(x_k, u_k, \theta_k) \right). \tag{10.69}$$

Using the maximum per-stage cost bound c, it is clear that (10.69) grows no larger than c, even as $K \to \infty$. This model is sometimes preferable because the cost does not depend on an arbitrary parameter, α.

10.3.2 Solution techniques

Straightforward adaptations of the value and policy iteration methods of Section 10.2 exist for infinite-horizon problems. These will be presented here; however, it is important to note that many other important issues exist regarding their convergence and numerical stability [98]. There are several other variants of these algorithms that are too involved to cover here but nevertheless are important because they address many of these additional issues. The main point in this section is to understand the simple relationship to the problems considered so far in Sections 10.1 and 10.2.

---

[1] The state space X may even be infinite, but this requires that the set of possible costs is bounded.

Value iteration for discounted cost

A backward value iteration solution will be presented that follows naturally from the method given in Section 10.2.1. For notational convenience, let the first stage be designated as $k = 0$ so that α^{k-1} may be replaced by α^k. In the probabilistic case, the expected optimal cost-to-go is

$$G^*(x) = \lim_{K \to \infty} \left(\min_{\tilde{u}} \left\{ E_{\tilde{\theta}} \left[\sum_{k=1}^{K} \alpha^k l(x_k, u_k, \theta_k) \right] \right\} \right). \tag{10.70}$$

The expectation is taken over all nature histories, each of which is an infinite sequence of nature actions. The corresponding expression for the nondeterministic case is

$$G^*(x) = \lim_{K \to \infty} \left(\min_{\tilde{u}} \left\{ \max_{\tilde{\theta}} \left\{ \sum_{k=1}^{K} \alpha^k l(x_k, u_k, \theta_k) \right\} \right\} \right). \tag{10.71}$$

Since the probabilistic case is more common, it will be covered here. The nondeterministic version is handled in a similar way (see Exercise 17). As before, backward value iterations will be performed because they are simpler to express. The discount factor causes a minor complication that must be fixed to make the dynamic programming recurrence work properly.

One difficulty is that the stage index now appears in the cost function, in the form of α^k. This means that the shift-invariant property from Section 2.3.1.1 is no longer preserved. We must therefore be careful about assigning stage indices. This is a problem because for backward value iteration the final stage index has been unknown and unimportant.

Consider a sequence of discounted decision-making problems, by increasing the maximum stage index: $K = 0$, $K = 1$, $K = 2, \ldots$. Look at the neighboring cost expressions in Figure 10.10. What is the difference between finding the optimal cost-to-go for the $K + 1$-stage problem and the K-stage problem? In Figure 10.10 the last three terms of the cost for $K = 4$ can be obtained by multiplying all terms for $K = 3$ by α and adding a new term, l_0. The only difference is that the stage indices need to be shifted by one on each l_i that was borrowed from the $K = 3$ case. In general, the optimal costs of a K-stage optimization problem can serve as the optimal costs of the $K + 1$-stage problem if they are first multiplied by α. The $K + 1$-stage optimization problem can be solved by optimizing over the sum of the first-stage cost plus the optimal cost for the K-stage problem, discounted by α.

This can be derived using straightforward dynamic programming arguments as follows. Suppose that K is fixed. The cost-to-go can be expressed recursively for k from 0 to K as

$$G_k^*(x_k) = \min_{u_k \in U(x_k)} \left\{ E_{\theta_k} \left[\alpha^k l(x_k, u_k, \theta_k) + G_{k-1}^*(x_{k+1}) \right] \right\}, \tag{10.72}$$

in which $x_{k+1} = f(x_k, u_k, \theta_k)$. The problem, however, is that the recursion depends on k through α^k, which makes it appear nonstationary.

The idea of using neighboring cost values as shown in Figure 10.10 can be applied by making a notational change. Let $J_{K-k}^*(x_k) = \alpha^{-k} G_k^*(x_k)$. This reverses the direction of the stage indices to avoid specifying the final stage and also scales by α^{-k} to correctly compensate for the index change. Substitution into (10.72) yields

$$\alpha^k J_{K-k}^*(x_k) = \min_{u_k \in U(x_k)} \left\{ E_{\theta_k} \left[\alpha^k l(x_k, u_k, \theta_k) + \alpha^{k+1} J_{K-k-1}^*(x_{k+1}) \right] \right\}. \tag{10.73}$$

Dividing by α^k and then letting $i = K - k$ yields

$$J_i^*(x_k) = \min_{u_k \in U(x_k)} \left\{ E_{\theta_k} \left[l(x_k, u_k, \theta_k) + \alpha J_{i-1}^*(x_{k+1}) \right] \right\},$$ (10.74)

in which J_i^* represents the expected cost for a finite-horizon discounted problem in which $K = i$. Note that (10.74) expresses J_i^* in terms of J_{i-1}^*, but x_k is given, and the right-hand side uses x_{k+1}. The indices appear to run in opposite directions because this is simply backward value iteration with a notational change that reverses some of the indices. The particular stage indices of x_k and x_{k+1} are not important in (10.74), as long as $x_{k+1} = f(x_k, u_k, \theta_k)$ (for example, the substitutions $x = x_k$, $x' = x_{k+1}$, $u = u_k$, and $\theta = \theta_k$ can be safely made).

Value iteration proceeds by first letting $J_0^*(x_0) = 0$ for all $x \in X$. Successive cost-to-go functions are computed by iterating (10.74) over the state space. Under the cycle-avoiding assumptions of Section 10.2.1, the convergence is usually asymptotic due to the infinite horizon. The discounting gradually causes the cost differences to diminish until they are within the desired tolerance. The stationary form of the dynamic programming recurrence, which is obtained in the limit as i tends to infinity, is

$$J^*(x) = \min_{u \in U(x)} \left\{ E_{\theta_k} \left[l(x, u, \theta) + \alpha J^*(f(x, u, \theta)) \right] \right\}.$$ (10.75)

If the cost terms do not depend on nature, then the simplified form is

$$J^*(x) = \min_{u \in U(x)} \left\{ l(x, u) + \alpha \sum_{x' \in X} J^*(x') P(x'|x, u) \right\}.$$ (10.76)

As explained in Section 10.2.1, the optimal action, $\pi^*(x)$, is assigned as the $u \in U(x)$ that satisfies (10.75) or (10.76) at x.

Policy iteration for discounted cost

The policy iteration method may alternatively be applied to the probabilistic discounted-cost problem. Recall the method given in Figure 10.4. The general approach remains the same: A search is conducted over the space of plans by solving a linear system of equations in each iteration. In Step 2, (10.53) is replaced by

$$J_\pi(x) = l(x, u) + \alpha \sum_{x' \in X} J_\pi(x') P(x'|x, u),$$ (10.77)

which is a special form of (10.76) for evaluating a fixed plan. In Step 3, (10.54) is replaced by

$$\pi'(x) = \operatorname*{argmin}_{u \in U(x)} \left\{ l(x, u) + \alpha \sum_{x' \in X} J_\pi(x') P(x'|x, u) \right\}.$$ (10.78)

Using these alterations, the policy iteration algorithm proceeds in the same way as in Section 10.2.2.

Solutions for the average cost-per-stage model

A value iteration algorithm for the average cost model can be obtained by simply neglecting to divide by K. Selecting actions that optimize the total cost also optimizes the average cost as the number of stages approaches infinity. This may cause costs to increase toward $\pm\infty$; however, only a finite number of iterations can be executed in practice.

The backward value iterations of Section 10.2.1 can be followed with very little modification. Initially, let $G^*(x_F) = 0$ for all $x_F \in X$. The value iterations are computed using the standard form

$$G_k^*(x_k) = \min_{u_k \in U(x_k)} \left\{ \sum_{\theta \in \Theta(x_k, u_k)} \Big(l(x_k, u_k, \theta_k) + G_{k+1}^*(f(x_k, u_k, \theta_k)) \Big) P(\theta_k | x_k, u_k) \right\}. \quad (10.79)$$

The iterations continue until convergence occurs. To determine whether a solution of sufficient quality has been obtained, a reasonable criterion for is

$$\max_{x \in X} \left\{ \big| G_k^*(x)/N - G_{k+1}^*(x)/(N-1) \big| \right\} < \epsilon, \quad (10.80)$$

in which ϵ is the error tolerance and N is the number of value iterations that have been completed (it is required in (10.80) that $N > 1$). Once (10.80) has been satisfied, the iterations can be terminated.

A numerical problem may exist with the growing values obtained for $G^*(x)$. This can be alleviated by periodically reducing all values by some constant factor to ensure that the numbers fit within the allowable floating point range. In [98], a method called *relative value iteration* is presented, which selects one state, $s \in X$, arbitrarily and expresses the cost-to-go values by subtracting off the cost at s. This trims down all values simultaneously to keep them bounded while still maintaining the convergence properties of the algorithm.

Policy iteration can alternatively be performed by using the method given in Figure 10.4 with only minor modification.

10.4 Reinforcement learning

10.4.1 The general philosophy

This section briefly introduces the basic ideas of a framework that has been highly popular in the artificial intelligence community in recent years. It was developed and used primarily by machine learning researchers [19, 75], and therefore this section is called *reinforcement learning*. The problem generally involves computing optimal plans for probabilistic infinite-horizon problems. The basic idea is to combine the problems of learning the probability distribution, $P(\theta|x, u)$, and computing the optimal plan into the same algorithm.

Terminology

Before detailing the method further, some explanation of existing names seems required. Consider the term *reinforcement learning*. In machine learning, most decision-theoretic models are expressed in terms of *reward* instead of *cost*. Thus, the task is to make decisions or find plans that *maximize* a *reward functional*. Choosing good actions under this model appears to provide positive reinforcement in the form of a reward. Therefore, the term *reinforcement* is used. Using cost and minimization instead, some alternative names may be *decision-theoretic learning* or *cost-based learning*.

The term *learning* is associated with the problem because estimating the probability distribution $P(\theta|x, u)$ or $P(x'|x, u)$ is clearly a learning problem. However, it is important to remember that there is also the planning problem of computing cost-to-go functions (or reward-to-go functions) and determining a plan that optimizes the costs (or rewards). Therefore, the term *reinforcement planning* may be just as reasonable.

The general framework is referred to as *neuro-dynamic programming* in [99] because the formulation and resulting algorithms are based on dynamic programming. Most often,

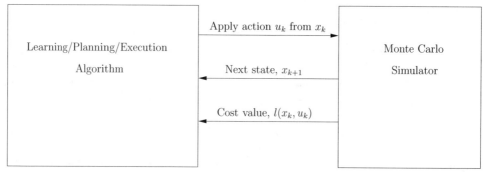

Figure 10.11: The general framework for reinforcement learning (or simulation-based dynamic programming).

a variant of value iteration is obtained. The *neuro* part refers to a family of functions that can be used to approximate plans and cost-to-go values. This term is fairly specific, however, because other function families may be used. Furthermore, for some problems (e.g., over small, finite state spaces), the cost values and plans are represented without approximation.

The name *simulation-based methods* is used in [97], which is perhaps one of the most accurate names (when used in the context of dynamic programming). Thus, *simulation-based dynamic programming* or *simulation-based planning* nicely reflects the framework explained here. The term *simulation* comes from the fact that a Monte Carlo simulator is used to generate samples for which the required distributions are learned during planning. You are, of course, welcome to use your favorite name, but keep in mind that under all of the names, the idea remains the same. This will be helpful to remember if you intend to study related literature.

The general framework

The framework is usually applied to infinite-horizon problems under probabilistic uncertainty. The discounted-cost model is most popular; however, we will mostly work with Formulation 10.1 because it is closer to the main theme of this book. It has been assumed so far that when planning under Formulation 10.1, all model components are known, including $P(x_{k+1}|x_k, u_k)$. This can be considered as a *traditional* framework, in which there are three general phases:

Learning phase: The transition probabilities are estimated by visiting states in X, trying actions, and gathering statistics. When this phase concludes, the model of the environment is completely known.

Planning phase: An algorithm computes a feedback plan using a method such as value iteration or policy iteration.

Execution phase: The plan is executed on a machine that is connected to the same environment on which the learning phase was applied.

The simulation-based framework combines all three of these phases into one. Learning, planning, and execution are all conducted by a machine that initially knows nothing about the state transitions or even the cost terms. Ideally, the machine should be connected to a physical environment for which the Markov model holds. However, in nearly all implementations, the machine is instead connected to a Monte Carlo simulator as shown in Figure 10.11. Based on the current state, the algorithm sends an action, u_k, to the simulator, and the simulator computes its effect by sampling according to its internal probability distributions. Obviously, the designer of the simulator knows the transition probabilities, but these are not given directly to the planning algorithm. The simulator then sends the next state, x_{k+1}, and cost, $l(x_k, u_k)$, back to the algorithm.

For simplicity, $l(x_k, u_k)$ is used instead of allowing the cost to depend on the particular nature action, which would yield $l(x_k, u_k, \theta_k)$. The explicit characterization of nature is usually not needed in this framework. The probabilities $P(x_{k+1}|x_k, u_k)$ are directly learned without specifying nature actions. It is common to generalize the cost term from $l(x_k, u_k)$ to $l(x_k, u_k, x_{k+1})$, but this is avoided here for notational convenience. The basic ideas remain the same, and only slight variations of the coming equations are needed to handle this generalization.

The simulator is intended to simulate "reality," in which the machine interacts with the physical world. It replaces the environment in Figure 1.16b from Section 1.4. Using the interpretation of that section, the algorithms presented in this context can be considered as a plan as shown in Figure 1.18b. If the learning component is terminated, then the resulting feedback plan can be programmed into another machine, as shown in Figure 1.18a. This step is usually not performed, however, because often it is assumed that the machine continues to learn over its lifetime.

One of the main issues is *exploration vs. exploitation* [75]. Some repetitive exploration of the state space is needed to gather enough data that reliably estimate the model. For true theoretical convergence, each state-action pair must be tried infinitely often. On the other hand, information regarding the model should be exploited to efficiently accomplish tasks. These two goals are often in conflict. Focusing too much on exploration will not optimize costs. Focusing too much on exploitation may prevent useful solutions from being developed because better alternatives have not yet been discovered.

10.4.2 Evaluating a plan via simulation

The simulation method is based on averaging the information gained incrementally from samples. Suppose that you receive a sequence of costs, $c_1, c_2, \ldots$, and would like to incrementally compute their average. You are not told the total number of samples in advance, and at any point you are required to report the current average. Let m_i denote the average of the first i samples,

$$m_i = \frac{1}{i} \sum_{j=1}^{i} c_j. \tag{10.81}$$

To efficiently compute m_i from m_{i-1}, multiply m_{i-1} by $i-1$ to recover the total, add c_i, and then divide by i:

$$m_i = \frac{(i-1)m_{i-1} + c_i}{i}. \tag{10.82}$$

This can be manipulated into

$$m_i = m_{i-1} + \frac{1}{i}(c_i - m_{i-1}). \tag{10.83}$$

Now consider the problem of estimating the expected cost-to-go, $G_\pi(x)$, at every $x \in X$ for some fixed plan, π. If $P(x'|x, u)$ and the costs $l(x, u)$ were known, then it could be computed by solving

$$G_\pi(x) = l(x, u) + \sum_{x'} P(x'|x, u) G_\pi(x'). \tag{10.84}$$

However, without this information, we must rely on the simulator.

From each $x \in X$, suppose that 1000 trials are conducted, and the resulting costs to get to the goal are recorded and averaged. Each trial is an iterative process in which π selects the action, and the simulator indicates the next state and its incremental cost. Once the goal state is reached, the costs are totaled to yield the measured cost-to-go for that trial (this assumes that $\pi(x) = u_T$ for all $x \in X_G$). If c_i denotes this total cost at trial i, then the average, m_i, over i trials provides an estimate of $G_\pi(x)$. As i tends to infinity, we expect m_i to converge to $G_\pi(x)$. The update formula (10.83) can be conveniently used to maintain the improving sequence of cost-to-go estimates. Let $\hat{G}_\pi(x)$ denote the current estimate of $G_\pi(x)$. The update formula based on (10.83) can be expressed as

$$\hat{G}_\pi(x) := \hat{G}_\pi(x) + \frac{1}{i}(l(x_1, u_1) + l(x_2, u_2) + \cdots + l(x_K, u_K) - \hat{G}_\pi(x)), \tag{10.85}$$

in which := means assignment, in the sense used in some programming languages.

It turns out that a single trial can actually yield update values for multiple states [75, 98]. Suppose that a trial is performed from x that results in the sequence $x_1 = x$, $x_2, \ldots, x_k, \ldots, x_K, x_F$ of visited states. For every state, x_k, in the sequence, a cost-to-go value can be measured by recording the cost that was accumulated from x_k to x_K:

$$c_k(x_k) = \sum_{j=k}^{K} l(x_j, u_j). \tag{10.86}$$

It is much more efficient to make use of (10.85) on every state that is visited along the path.

Temporal differences

Rather than waiting until the end of each trial to compute $c_i(x_i)$, it is possible to update each state, x_i, immediately after it is visited and $l(x_i, u_i)$ is received from the simulator. This leads to a well-known method of estimating the cost-to-go called *temporal differences* [930]. It is very similar to the method already given but somewhat more complicated. It will be introduced here because the method frequently appears in reinforcement learning literature, and an extension of it leads to a nice simulation-based method for updating the estimated cost-to-go.

Once again, consider the sequence $x_1, \ldots, x_K, x_F$ generated by a trial. Let d_k denote a *temporal difference*, which is defined as

$$d_k = l(x_k, u_k) + \hat{G}_\pi(x_{k+1}) - \hat{G}_\pi(x_k). \tag{10.87}$$

Note that both $l(x_k, u_k) + \hat{G}_\pi(x_{k+1})$ and $\hat{G}_\pi(x_k)$ could each serve as an estimate of $G_\pi(x_k)$. The difference is that the right part of (10.87) utilizes the latest cost obtained from the simulator for the first step and then uses $\hat{G}_\pi(x_{k+1})$ for an estimate of the remaining cost. In this and subsequent expressions, every action, u_k, is chosen using the plan: $u_k = \pi(x_k)$.

Let v_k denote the number of times that x_k has been visited so far, for each $1 \le k \le K$, including previous trials and the current visit. The following update algorithm can be used during the trial. When x_2 is reached, the value at x_1 is updated as

$$\hat{G}_\pi(x_1) := \hat{G}_\pi(x_1) + \frac{1}{v_1}d_1. \tag{10.88}$$

When x_3 is reached, the values at x_1 and x_2 are updated as

$$\hat{G}_\pi(x_1) := \hat{G}_\pi(x_1) + \frac{1}{v_1}d_2,$$
$$\hat{G}_\pi(x_2) := \hat{G}_\pi(x_2) + \frac{1}{v_2}d_2. \tag{10.89}$$

Now consider what has been done so far at x_1. The temporal differences partly collapse:

$$\hat{G}_\pi(x_1) := \hat{G}_\pi(x_1) + \frac{1}{v_1}d_1 + \frac{1}{v_1}d_2$$
$$= \hat{G}_\pi(x_1) + \frac{1}{v_1}(l(x_1, u_1) + \hat{G}_\pi(x_2) - \hat{G}_\pi(x_1) + l(x_2, u_2) + \hat{G}_\pi(x_3) - \hat{G}_\pi(x_2))$$
$$= \hat{G}_\pi(x_1) + \frac{1}{v_1}(l(x_1, u_1) + l(x_2, u_2) - \hat{G}_\pi(x_1) + \hat{G}_\pi(x_3)). \tag{10.90}$$

When x_4 is reached, similar updates are performed. At x_k, the updates are

$$\hat{G}_\pi(x_1) := \hat{G}_\pi(x_1) + \frac{1}{v_1}d_k,$$
$$\hat{G}_\pi(x_2) := \hat{G}_\pi(x_2) + \frac{1}{v_2}d_k,$$
$$\vdots \tag{10.91}$$
$$\hat{G}_\pi(x_k) := \hat{G}_\pi(x_k) + \frac{1}{v_k}d_k.$$

The updates are performed in this way until $x_F \in X_G$ is reached. Now consider what was actually computed for each x_k. The temporal differences form a telescoping sum that collapses, as shown in (10.90) after two iterations. After all iterations have been completed, the value at x_k has been updated as

$$\hat{G}_\pi(x_k) := \hat{G}_\pi(x_k) + \frac{1}{v_k}d_k + \frac{1}{v_{k+1}}d_{k+1} + \cdots + \frac{1}{v_K}d_K + \frac{1}{v_F}d_F$$
$$= \hat{G}_\pi(x_k) + \frac{1}{v_k}(l(x_1, u_1) + l(x_2, u_2) + \cdots + l(x_K, u_K) - \hat{G}_\pi(x_k) + \hat{G}_\pi(x_F))$$
$$= \hat{G}_\pi(x_k) + \frac{1}{v_k}(l(x_1, u_1) + l(x_2, u_2) + \cdots + l(x_K, u_K) - \hat{G}_\pi(x_k)). \tag{10.92}$$

The final $\hat{G}_\pi(x_F)$ was deleted because its value is zero, assuming that the termination action is applied by π. The resulting final expression is equivalent to (10.85) if each visited state in the sequence was distinct. This is often not true, which makes the method discussed above differ slightly from the method of (10.85) because the count, v_k, may change during the trial in the temporal difference scheme. This difference, however, is negligible, and the temporal difference method computes estimates that converge to $\hat{G}_\pi$ [98, 99].

The temporal difference method presented so far can be generalized in a way that often leads to faster convergence in practice. Let $\lambda \in [0, 1]$ be a specified parameter. The $TD(\lambda)$ temporal difference method replaces the equations in (10.91) with

$$\hat{G}_\pi(x_1) := \hat{G}_\pi(x_1) + \lambda^{k-1}\left(\frac{1}{v_1}d_k\right),$$

$$\hat{G}_\pi(x_2) := \hat{G}_\pi(x_2) + \lambda^{k-2}\left(\frac{1}{v_2}d_k\right),$$

$$\vdots \qquad\qquad (10.93)$$

$$\hat{G}_\pi(x_{k-1}) := \hat{G}_\pi(x_{k-1}) + \lambda\left(\frac{1}{v_{k-1}}d_k\right),$$

$$\hat{G}_\pi(x_k) := \hat{G}_\pi(x_k) + \frac{1}{v_k}d_k.$$

This has the effect of discounting costs that are received far away from x_k. The method in (10.91) was the special case of $\lambda = 1$, yielding $TD(1)$.

Another interesting special case is $TD(0)$, which becomes

$$\hat{G}_\pi(x_k) = \hat{G}_\pi(x_k) + \frac{1}{v_k}\left(l(x_k, u_k) + \hat{G}_\pi(x_{k+1}) - \hat{G}_\pi(x_{k+1})\right). \qquad (10.94)$$

This form appears most often in reinforcement learning literature (although it is applied to the discounted-cost model instead). Experimental evidence indicates that lower values of λ help to improve the convergence rate. Convergence for all values of λ is proved in [99].

One source of intuition about why (10.94) works is that it is a special case of a *stochastic iterative algorithm* or the *Robbins-Monro algorithm* [90, 99, 569]. This is a general statistical estimation technique that is used for solving systems of the form $h(y) = y$ by using a sequence of samples. Each sample represents a measurement of $h(y)$ using Monte Carlo simulation. The general form of this iterative approach is to update y as

$$y := (1 - \rho)y + \rho h(y), \qquad (10.95)$$

in which $\rho \in [0, 1]$ is a parameter whose choice affects the convergence rate. Intuitively, (10.95) updates y by interpolating between its original value and the most recent sample of $h(y)$. Convergence proofs for this algorithm are not given here; see [99] for details. The typical behavior is that a smaller value of ρ leads to more reliable estimates when there is substantial noise in the simulation process, but this comes at the cost of slowing the convergence rate. The convergence is asymptotic, which requires that all edges (that have nonzero probability) in the plan-based state transition graph should be visited infinitely often.

A general approach to obtaining $\hat{G}_\pi$ can be derived within the stochastic iterative framework by generalizing $TD(0)$:

$$\hat{G}_\pi(x) := (1 - \rho)\hat{G}_\pi(x) + \rho\left(l(x, u) + \hat{G}_\pi(x')\right). \qquad (10.96)$$

The formulation of $TD(0)$ in (10.94) essentially selects the ρ parameter by the way it was derived, but in (10.96) any $\rho \in (0, 1)$ may be used.

It may appear incorrect that the update equation does not take into account the transition probabilities. It turns out that they are taken into account in the simulation process because transitions that are more likely to occur have a stronger effect on (10.96). The same thing occurs when the mean of a nonuniform probability density function is estimated by using samples from the distribution. The values that occur with higher frequency make stronger contributions to the average, which automatically gives them the appropriate weight.

10.4.3 Q-learning: Computing an optimal plan

This section moves from evaluating a plan to computing an optimal plan in the simulation-based framework. The most important idea is the computation of *Q-factors*, $Q^*(x, u)$. This is an extension of the optimal cost-to-go, G^*, that records optimal costs for each possible combination of a state, $x \in X$, and action $u \in U(x)$. The interpretation of $Q^*(x, u)$ is the expected cost received by starting from state x, applying u, and then following the optimal plan from the resulting next state, $x' = f(x, u, \theta)$. If u happens to be the same action as would be selected by the optimal plan, $\pi^*(x)$, then $Q^*(x, u) = G^*(x)$. Thus, the Q-value can be thought of as the cost of making an arbitrary choice in the first stage and then exhibiting optimal decision making afterward.

Value iteration

A simulation-based version of value iteration can be constructed from Q-factors. The reason for their use instead of G^* is that a minimization over $U(x)$ will be avoided in the dynamic programming. Avoiding this minimization enables a sample-by-sample approach to estimating the optimal values and ultimately obtaining the optimal plan. The optimal cost-to-go can be obtained from the Q-factors as

$$G^*(x) = \min_{u \in U(x)} \left\{ Q^*(x, u) \right\}. \tag{10.97}$$

This enables the dynamic programming recurrence in (10.46) to be expressed as

$$Q^*(x, u) = l(x, u) + \sum_{x' \in X} P(x'|x, u) \min_{u' \in U(x')} \left\{ Q^*(x', u') \right\}. \tag{10.98}$$

By applying (10.97) to the right side of (10.98), it can also be expressed using G^* as

$$Q^*(x, u) = l(x, u) + \sum_{x' \in X} P(x'|x, u) G^*(x'). \tag{10.99}$$

If $P(x'|x, u)$ and $l(x, u)$ were known, then (10.98) would lead to an alternative, storage-intensive way to perform value iteration. After convergence occurs, (10.97) can be used to obtain the G^* values. The optimal plan is constructed as

$$\pi^*(x) = \operatorname*{argmin}_{u \in U(x)} \left\{ Q^*(x, u) \right\}. \tag{10.100}$$

Since the costs and transition probabilities are unknown, a simulation-based approach is needed. The stochastic iterative algorithm idea can be applied once again. Recall that (10.96) estimated the cost of a plan by using individual samples and required a convergence-rate parameter, ρ. Using the same idea here, a simulation-based version of value iteration can be derived as

$$\hat{Q}^*(x, u) := (1 - \rho)\hat{Q}^*(x, u) + \rho \left(l(x, u) + \min_{u' \in U(x')} \left\{ \hat{Q}^*(x', u') \right\} \right), \tag{10.101}$$

in which x' is the next state and $l(x, u)$ is the cost obtained from the simulator when u is applied at x. Initially, all Q-factors are set to zero. Sample trajectories that arrive at the goal can be generated using simulation, and (10.101) is applied to the resulting states and costs in each stage. Once again, the update equation may appear to be incorrect because the transition probabilities are not explicitly mentioned, but this is taken into account automatically through the simulation.

In most literature, Q-learning is applied to the discounted cost model. This yields a minor variant of (10.101):

$$\hat{Q}^*(x, u) := (1 - \rho)\hat{Q}^*(x, u) + \rho \left(l(x, u) + \alpha \min_{u' \in U(x')} \left\{ \hat{Q}^*(x', u') \right\} \right), \qquad (10.102)$$

in which the discount factor α appears because the update equation is derived from (10.76).

Policy iteration

A simulation-based policy iteration algorithm can be derived using Q-factors. Recall from Section 10.2.2 that methods are needed to: 1) evaluate a given plan, π, and 2) improve the plan by selecting better actions. The plan evaluation previously involved linear equation solving. Now any plan, π, can be evaluated without even knowing $P(x'|x, u)$ by using the methods of Section 10.4.2. Once $\hat{G}_\pi$ is computed reliably from every $x \in X$, further simulation can be used to compute $Q_\pi(x, u)$ for each $x \in X$ and $u \in U$. This can be achieved by defining a version of (10.99) that is constrained to π:

$$Q_\pi(x, u) = l(x, u) + \sum_{x' \in X} P(x'|x, u)G_\pi(x'). \qquad (10.103)$$

The transition probabilities do not need to be known. The Q-factors are computed by simulation and averaging. The plan can be improved by setting

$$\pi'(x) = \operatorname*{argmin}_{u \in U(x)} \left\{ Q^*(x, u) \right\}, \qquad (10.104)$$

which is based on (10.97).

10.5 Sequential game theory

So far in the chapter, the sequential decision-making process has only involved a game against nature. In this section, other decision makers are introduced to the game. The single-stage games and their equilibrium concepts from Sections 9.3 and 9.4 will be extended into a sequence of games. Section 10.5.1 introduces sequential zero-sum games that are represented using game trees, which help visualize the concepts. Section 10.5.2 covers sequential zero-sum games using the state-space representation. Section 10.5.3 briefly covers extensions to other games, including nonzero-sum games and games that involve nature. The formulations in this section will be called *sequential game theory*. Another common name for them is *dynamic game theory* [60]. If there is a continuum of stages, which is briefly considered in Section 13.5, then *differential game theory* is obtained [60, 480, 786, 985].

10.5.1 Game trees

In most literature, sequential games are formulated in terms of *game trees*. A state-space representation, which is more in alignment with the representations used in this chapter, will be presented in Section 10.5.2. The tree representation is commonly referred to as the *extensive form* of a game (as opposed to the *normal form*, which is the cost matrix

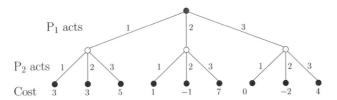

Figure 10.12: A 3 × 3 matrix game expressed using a game tree.

representation used in Chapter 9). The representation is helpful for visualizing many issues in game theory. It is perhaps most helpful for visualizing information states; this aspect of game trees will be deferred until Section 11.7, after information spaces have been formally introduced. Here, game trees are presented for cases that are simple to describe without going deeply into information spaces.

Before a sequential game is introduced, consider representing a single-stage game in a tree form. Recall Example 9.14, which is a zero-sum, 3 × 3 matrix game. It can be represented as a *game tree* as shown in Figure 10.12. At the root, P_1 has three choices. At the next level, P_2 has three choices. Based on the choices by both, one of nine possible leaves will be reached. At this point, a cost is obtained, which is written under the leaf. The entries of the cost matrix, (9.53), appear across the leaves of the tree. Every nonleaf vertex is called a *decision vertex*: One player must select an action.

There are two possible interpretations of the game depicted in Figure 10.12:

1. Before it makes its decision, P_2 knows which action was applied by P_1. This does not correspond to the zero-sum game formulation introduced in Section 9.3 because P_2 seems as powerful as nature. In this case, it is not equivalent to the game in Example 9.14.

2. P_2 does not know the action applied by P_1. This is equivalent to assuming that both P_1 and P_2 make their decisions at the same time, which is consistent with Formulation 9.7. The tree could have alternatively been represented with P_2 acting first.

Now imagine that P_1 and P_2 play a *sequence* of games. A sequential version of the zero-sum game from Section 9.3 will be defined by extending the game tree idea given so far to more levels. This will model the following *sequential game*:

Formulation 10.3 (Zero-Sum Sequential Game in Tree Form)

1. Two players, P_1 and P_2, take turns playing a game. A stage as considered previously is now stretched into two *substages*, in which each player acts individually. It is usually assumed that P_1 always starts, followed by P_2, then P_1 again, and so on. Player alternations continue until the game ends. The model reflects the rules of many popular games such as chess or poker. Let $\mathcal{K} = \{1, \ldots, K\}$ denote the set of stages at which P_1 and P_2 both take a turn.

2. As each player takes a turn, it chooses from a nonempty, finite set of actions. The available set could depend on the decision vertex.

3. At the end of the game, a cost for P_1 is incurred based on the sequence of actions chosen by each player. The cost is interpreted as a reward for P_2.

4. The amount of information that each player has when making its decision must be specified. This is usually expressed by indicating what portions of the action histories are known. For example, if P_1 just acted, does P_2 know its choice? Does it know what action P_1 chose in some previous stage?

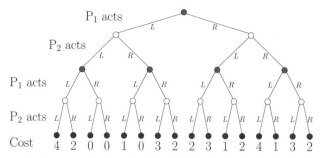

P₁ acts

P₂ acts

P₁ acts

P₂ acts

Cost

Figure 10.13: A two-player, two-stage game expressed using a game tree.

The *game tree* can now be described in detail. Figure 10.13 shows a particular example for two stages (hence, $K = 2$ and $\mathcal{K} = \{1, 2\}$). Every vertex corresponds to a point at which a decision needs to be made by one player. Each edge emanating from a vertex represents an action. The root of the tree indicates the beginning of the game, which usually means that P_1 chooses an action. The leaves of the tree represent the end of the game, which are the points at which a cost is received. The cost is usually shown below each leaf. One final concern is to specify the information available to each player, just prior to its decision. Which actions among those previously applied by itself or other players are known?

For the game tree in Figure 10.13, there are two players and two stages. Therefore, there are four levels of decision vertices. The action sets for the players are $U = V = \{L, R\}$, for "left" and "right." Since there are always two actions, a binary tree is obtained. There are 16 possible outcomes, which correspond to all pairwise combinations of four possible two-stage plans for each player.

For a single-stage game, both deterministic and randomized strategies were defined to obtain saddle points. Recall from Section 9.3.3 that randomized strategies were needed to guarantee the existence of a saddle point. For a sequential game, these are extended to *deterministic* and *randomized plans*, respectively. In Section 10.1.3, a (deterministic) plan was defined as a mapping from the state space to an action space. This definition can be applied here for each player; however, we must determine what is a "state" for the game tree. This depends on the information that each player has available when it plays.

A general framework for representing information in game trees is covered in Section 11.7. Three simple kinds of information will be discussed here. In every case, each player knows its own actions that were applied in previous stages. The differences correspond to knowledge of actions applied by the other player. These define the "state" that is used to make the decisions in a plan.

The three information models considered here are as follows.

Alternating play: The players take turns playing, and all players know all actions that have been previously applied. This is the situation obtained, for example, in a game of chess. To define a plan, let N_1 and N_2 denote the set of all vertices from which P_1 and P_2 must make a decision, respectively. In Figure 10.13, N_1 is the set of dark vertices and N_2 is the set of white vertices. Let $U(n_1)$ and $V(n_2)$ be the action spaces for P_1 and P_2, respectively, which depend on the vertex. A *(deterministic) plan for* P_1 is defined as a function, π_1, on N_1 that yields an action $u \in U(n_1)$ for each $n_1 \in N_1$. Similarly, a *(deterministic) plan for* P_2 is defined as a function, π_2, on N_2 that yields an action $v \in V(n_2)$ for each $n_2 \in N_2$. For the randomized case, let $W(n_1)$ and $Z(n_2)$ denote the sets of all probability distributions over $U(n_1)$ and $V(n_2)$, respectively. A *randomized plan* *for* P_1 is defined as a function that yields some $w \in W(n_1)$ for each $n_1 \in N_1$. Likewise, a *randomized plan for* P_2 is defined as a function that maps from N_2 into $Z(n_2)$.

Stage-by-stage: Each player knows the actions applied by the other in all previous stages; however, there is no information about actions chosen by others in the current stage. This effectively means that both players act simultaneously in each stage. In this case, a deterministic or randomized plan for P_1 is defined as in the alternating play case; however, plans for P_2 are defined as functions on N_1, instead of N_2. This is because at the time it makes its decision, P_2 has available precisely the same information as P_1. The action spaces for P_2 must conform to be dependent on elements of N_1, instead of N_2; otherwise, P_2 would not know what actions are available. Therefore, they are defined as $V(n_1)$ for each $n_1 \in N_1$.

Open loop: Each player has no knowledge of the previous actions of the other. They only know how many actions have been applied so far, which indicates the stage of the game. Plans are defined as functions on $\mathcal{K}$, the set of stages, because the particular vertex is not known. Note that an open-loop plan is just a sequence of actions in the deterministic case (as in Section 2.3) and a sequence of probability distributions in the randomized case. Again, the action spaces must conform to the information. Thus, they are $U(k)$ and $V(k)$ for each $k \in \mathcal{K}$.

For a single-stage game, as in Figure 10.12, the stage-by-stage and open-loop models are equivalent.

10.5.1.1 Determining a security plan

The notion of a security strategy from Section 9.3.2 extends in a natural way to sequential games. This yields a *security plan* in which each player performs worst-case analysis by treating the other player as nature under nondeterministic uncertainty. A security plan and its resulting cost can be computed by propagating costs from the leaves up to the root. The computation of the security plan for P_1 for the game in Figure 10.13 is shown in Figure 10.14. The actions that would be chosen by P_2 are determined at all vertices in the second-to-last level of the tree. Since P_2 tries to maximize costs, the recorded costs at each of these vertices is the maximum over the costs of its children. At the next higher level, the actions that would be chosen by P_1 are determined. At each vertex, the minimum cost among its children is recorded. In the next level, P_2 is considered, and so on, until the root is reached. At this point, the lowest cost that P_1 could secure is known. This yields the *upper value,* $\overline{L}^*$, for the sequential game. The security plan is defined by providing the action that selects the lowest cost child vertex, for each $n_1 \in N_1$. If P_2 responds rationally to the security plan of P_1, then the path shown in bold in Figure 10.14d will be followed. The execution of P_1's security plan yields the action sequence (L, L) for P_1 and (R, L) for P_2. The upper value is $\overline{L}^* = 1$.

A security plan for P_2 can be computed similarly; however, the order of the decisions must be swapped. This is not easy to visualize, unless the order of the players is swapped in the tree. If P_2 acts first, then the resulting tree is as shown in Figure 10.15. The costs on the leaves appear in different order; however, for the same action sequences chosen by P_1 and P_2, the costs obtained at the end of the game are the same as those in Figure 10.14. The resulting *lower value* for the game is found to be $\underline{L}^* = 1$. The resulting security plan is defined by assigning the action to each $n_2 \in N_2$ that maximizes the cost value of its children. If P_1 responds rationally to the security plan of P_2, then the actions executed will be (L, L) for P_1 and (R, L) for P_2. Note that these are the same as those obtained from executing the security plan of P_1, even though they appear different in the trees because

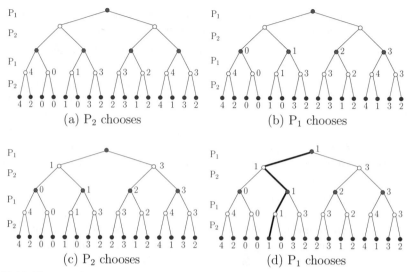

Figure 10.14: The security plan for P_1 is determined by propagating costs upward from the leaves. The choices involved in the security plan are shown in the last picture. An upper value of 1 is obtained for the game.

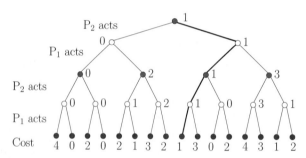

Figure 10.15: The security plan can be found for P_2 by swapping the order of P_1 and P_2 (the order of the costs on the leaves also become reshuffled).

the player order was swapped. In many cases, however, different action sequences will be obtained.

As in the case of a single-stage game, $\underline{L}^* = \overline{L}^*$ implies that the game has a deterministic saddle point and the *value* of the sequential game is $L^* = \underline{L}^* = \overline{L}^*$. This particular game has a unique, deterministic saddle point. This yields predictable, identical choices for the players, even though they perform separate, worst-case analyses.

A substantial reduction in the cost of computing the security strategies can be obtained by recognizing when certain parts of the tree do not need to be explored because they cannot yield improved costs. This idea is referred to as *alpha-beta pruning* in AI literature (see [842], pp. 186–187 for references and a brief history). Suppose that the tree is searched in depth-first order to determine the security strategy for P_1. At some decision vertex for P_1, suppose it has been determined that a cost c would be secured if a particular action, u, is applied; however, there are still other actions for which it is not known what costs could be secured. Consider determining the cost that could be secured for one of these remaining actions, denoted by u'. This requires computing how P_2 will maximize cost to respond to u'. As soon as P_2 has at least one option for which the cost, c', is greater than c, the other children of P_2 do not need to be explored. Why? This is because P_1 would never

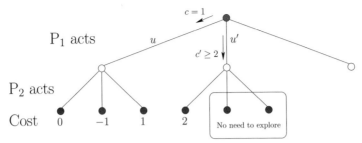

Figure 10.16: If the tree is explored in depth-first order, there are situations in which some children (and hence whole subtrees) do not need to be explored. This is an example that eliminates children of P_2. Another case exists, which eliminates children of P_1.

choose u' if P_2 could respond in a way that leads to a higher cost than what P_1 can already secure by choosing u. Figure 10.16 shows a simple example. This situation can occur at any level in the tree, and when an action does not need to be considered, an entire subtree is eliminated. In other situations, children of P_1 can be eliminated because P_2 would not make a choice that allows P_1 to improve the cost below a value that P_2 can already secure for itself.

10.5.1.2 Computing a saddle point

The security plan for P_1 constitutes a valid solution to the game under the alternating play model. P_2 has only to choose an optimal response to the plan of P_1 at each stage. Under the stage-by-stage model, the "solution" concept is a saddle point, which occurs when the upper and lower values coincide. The procedure just described could be used to determine the value and corresponding plans; however, what happens when the values do not coincide? In this case, *randomized security plans* should be developed for the players. As in the case of a single-stage game, a *randomized upper value* $\overline{\mathcal{L}}^*$ and a *randomized lower value* $\underline{\mathcal{L}}^*$ are obtained. In the space of randomized plans, it turns out that a saddle point always exists. This implies that the game always has a *randomized value*, $\mathcal{L}^* = \underline{\mathcal{L}}^* = \overline{\mathcal{L}}^*$. This saddle point can be computed from the bottom up, in a manner similar to the method just used to compute security plans.

Return to the example in Figure 10.13. This game actually has a deterministic saddle point, as indicated previously. It still, however, serves as a useful illustration of the method because any deterministic plan can once again be interpreted as a special case of a randomized plan (all of the probability mass is placed on a single action). Consider the bottom four subtrees of Figure 10.13, which are obtained by using only the last two levels of decision vertices. In each case, P_1 and P_2 must act in parallel to end the sequential game. Each subtree can be considered as a matrix game because the costs are immediately obtained after the two players act.

This leads to an alternative way to depict the game in Figure 10.13, which is shown in Figure 10.17. The bottom two layers of decision vertices are replaced by matrix games. Now compute the randomized value for each game and place it at the corresponding leaf vertex, as shown in Figure 10.18. In the example, there are only two layers of decision vertices remaining. This can be represented as the game

$$
U \quad \begin{array}{c} V \\ \begin{array}{|c|c|} \hline 0 & 1 \\ \hline 2 & 3 \\ \hline \end{array} \end{array} \quad , \tag{10.105}
$$

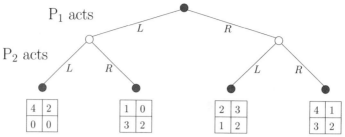

Figure 10.17: Under the stage-by-stage model, the game in Figure 10.13 can instead be represented as a tree in which each player acts once, and then they play a matrix game to determine the cost.

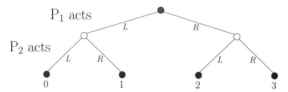

Figure 10.18: Each matrix in Figure 10.17 can be replaced by its randomized value. This clips one level from the original tree. For this particular example, the randomized value is also a deterministic value. Note that these are exactly the costs that appeared in Figure 10.14c. This occurred because each of the matrix games has a deterministic value; if they do not, then the costs will not coincide.

which has a value of 1 and occurs if P_1 applies L and P_2 applies R. Thus, the solution to the original sequential game has been determined by solving matrix games as an alternative to the method applied to obtain the security plans. The benefit of the new method is that if any matrix does not have a deterministic saddle point, its randomized value can instead be computed. A randomized strategy must be played by the players if the corresponding decision vertex is reached during execution.

10.5.1.3 Converting the tree to a single-stage game

Up to this point, solutions have been determined for the alternating-play and the stage-by-stage models. The open-loop model remains. In this case, there is no exchange of information between the players until the game is finished and they receive their costs. Therefore, imagine that players engaged in such a sequential game are equivalently engaged in a large, single-stage game. Recall that a plan under the open-loop model is a function over $\mathcal{K}$. Let Π_1 and Π_2 represent the sets of possible plans for P_1 and P_2, respectively. For the game in Figure 10.13, Π_i is a set of four possible plans for each player, which will be specified in the following order: (L, L), (L, R), (R, L), and (R, R). These can be arranged into a 4×4 matrix game:

$$
\Pi_1 \qquad
\begin{array}{|c|c|c|c|}
\hline
4 & 2 & 1 & 0 \\
\hline
0 & 0 & 3 & 2 \\
\hline
2 & 3 & 4 & 1 \\
\hline
1 & 2 & 3 & 2 \\
\hline
\end{array}
\qquad . \tag{10.106}
$$

with Π_2 labeling the columns above.

This matrix game does not have a deterministic saddle point. Unfortunately, a four-dimensional linear programming problem must be solved to find the randomized value and equilibrium. This is substantially different than the solution obtained for the other two information models.

The matrix-game form can also be derived for sequential games defined under the stage-by-stage model. In this case, however, the space of plans is even larger. For the example in Figure 10.13, there are 32 possible plans for each player (there are 5 decision vertices for each player, at which two different actions can be applied; hence, $|\Pi_i| = 2^5$ for $i = 1$ and $i = 2$). This results in a 32×32 matrix game! This game should admit the same saddle point solution that we already determined. The advantage of using the tree representation is that this enormous game was decomposed into many tiny matrix games. By treating the problem stage-by-stage, substantial savings in computation results. This power arises because the dynamic programming principle was implicitly used in the tree-based computation method of decomposing the sequential game into small matrix games. The connection to previous dynamic programming methods will be made clearer in the next section, which considers sequential games that are defined over a state space.

10.5.2 Sequential games on state spaces

An apparent problem in the previous section is that the number of vertices grows exponentially in the number of stages. In some games, however, there may be multiple action sequences that lead to the same state. This is true of many popular games, such as chess, checkers, and tic-tac-toe. In this case, it is convenient to define a state space that captures the complete set of unique game configurations. The player actions then transform the state. If there are different action sequences that lead to the same state, then separate vertices are not needed. This converts the game tree into a *game graph* by declaring vertices that represent the same state to be equivalent. The game graph is similar in many ways to the transition graphs discussed in Section 10.1, in the sequential game against nature. The same idea can be applied when there are opposing players.

We will arrive at a sequential game that is played over a state space by collapsing the game tree into a game graph. We will also allow the more general case of costs occurring on any transition edges, as opposed to only the leaves of the original game tree. Only the stage-by-stage model from the game tree is generalized here. Generalizations that use other information models are considered in Section 11.7. In the formulation that follows, P_2 can be can viewed as the replacement for nature in Formulation 10.1. The new formulation is still a generalization of Formulation 9.7, which was a single-stage, zero-sum game. To keep the concepts simpler, all spaces are assumed to be finite. The formulation is as follows.

Formulation 10.4 (Sequential Zero-Sum Game on a State Space)

1. Two players, P_1 and P_2.

2. A finite, nonempty *state space* X.

3. For each state $x \in X$, a finite, nonempty *action space* $U(x)$ for P_1.

4. For each state $x \in X$, a finite, nonempty *action space* $V(x)$ for P_2. To allow an extension of the alternating play model from Section 10.5.1, $V(x, u)$ could alternatively be defined, to enable the set of actions available to P_2 to depend on the action $u \in U$ of P_1.

5. A *state transition function* f that produces a state, $f(x, u, v)$, for every $x \in X, u \in U(x)$, and $v \in V(x)$.

6. A set $\mathcal{K}$ of K *stages*, each denoted by k, which begins at $k = 1$ and ends at $k = K$. Let $F = K + 1$, which is the final stage, after the last action is applied.

7. An *initial state* $x_I \in X$. For some problems, this may not be specified, in which case a solution must be found from all initial states.

8. A stage-additive cost functional L. Let $\tilde{v}_K$ denote the history of P_2's actions up to stage K. The cost functional may be applied to any combination of state and action histories to yield

$$L(\tilde{x}_F, \tilde{u}_K, \tilde{v}_K) = \sum_{k=1}^{K} l(x_k, u_k, v_k) + l_F(x_F). \qquad (10.107)$$

It will be assumed that both players always know the current state. Note that there are no termination actions in the formulation. The game terminates after each player has acted K times. There is also no direct formulation of a goal set. Both termination actions and goal sets can be added to the formulation without difficulty, but this is not considered here. The action sets can easily be extended to allow a dependency on the stage, to yield $U(x, k)$ and $V(x, k)$. The methods presented in this section can be adapted without trouble. This is avoided, however, to make the notation simpler.

Defining a plan for each player

Each player must now have its own plan. As in Section 10.1, it seems best to define a plan as a mapping from states to actions, because it may not be clear what actions will be taken by the other decision maker. In Section 10.1, the other decision maker was nature, and here it is a rational opponent. Let π_1 and π_2 denote plans for P_1 and P_2, respectively. Since the number of stages in Formulation 10.4 is fixed, stage-dependent plans of the form $\pi_1 : X \times \mathcal{K} \to U$ and $\pi_2 : X \times \mathcal{K} \to V$ are appropriate (recall that stage-dependent plans were defined in Section 10.1.3). Each produces an action $\pi_1(x, k) \in U(x)$ and $\pi_2(x, k) \in V(x)$, respectively.

Now consider different solution concepts for Formulation 10.4. For P_1, a *deterministic plan* is a function $\pi_1 : X \times \mathcal{K} \to U$, that produces an action $u = \pi(x) \in U(x)$, for each state $x \in X$ and stage $k \in \mathcal{K}$. For P_2 it is instead $\pi_2 : X \times \mathcal{K} \to V$, which produces an action $v = \pi(x) \in V(x)$, for each $x \in X$ and $k \in \mathcal{K}$. Now consider defining a randomized plan. Let $W(x)$ and $Z(x)$ denote the sets of all probability distributions over $U(x)$ and $V(x)$, respectively. A *randomized plan for* P_1 yields some $w \in W(x)$ for each $x \in X$ and $k \in \mathcal{K}$. Likewise, a *randomized plan for* P_2 yields some $w \in Z(x)$ for each $x \in X$ and $k \in \mathcal{K}$.

Saddle points in a sequential game

A saddle point will be obtained once again by defining security strategies for each player. Each player treats the other as nature, and if the same worst-case value is obtained, then the result is a saddle point for the game. If the values are different, then a randomized plan is needed to close the gap between the upper and lower values.

Upper and lower values now depend on the initial state, $x_1 \in X$. There was no equivalent for this in Section 10.5.1 because the root of the game tree is the only possible starting point.

If sequences, $\tilde{u}_K$ and $\tilde{v}_K$, of actions are applied from x_1, then the state history, $\tilde{x}_F$, can be derived by repeatedly using the state transition function, f. The *upper value* from x_1 is defined as

$$\overline{L}^*(x_1) = \min_{u_1} \max_{v_1} \min_{u_2} \max_{v_2} \cdots \min_{u_K} \max_{v_K} \left\{ L(\tilde{x}_F, \tilde{u}_K, \tilde{v}_K) \right\}, \qquad (10.108)$$

which is identical to (10.33) if P_2 is replaced by nature. Also, (10.108) generalizes (9.44) to multiple stages. The *lower value* from x_1, which generalizes (9.46), is

$$\underline{L}^*(x_1) = \max_{v_1} \min_{u_1} \max_{v_2} \min_{u_2} \cdots \max_{v_K} \min_{u_K} \left\{ L(\tilde{x}_F, \tilde{u}_K, \tilde{v}_K) \right\}. \tag{10.109}$$

If $\overline{L}^*(x_1) = \underline{L}^*(x_2)$, then a deterministic saddle point exists from x_1. This implies that the order of max and min can be swapped inside of every stage.

Value iteration

A value-iteration method can be derived by adapting the derivation that was applied to (10.33) to instead apply to (10.108). This leads to the dynamic programming recurrence

$$\overline{L}^*_k(x_k) = \min_{u_k \in U(x_k)} \left\{ \max_{v_k \in V(x_k)} \left\{ l(x_k, u_k, v_k) + \overline{L}^*_{k+1}(x_{k+1}) \right\} \right\}, \tag{10.110}$$

which is analogous to (10.39). This can be used to iteratively compute a *security plan for* P_1. The *security plan for* P_2 can be computed using

$$\underline{L}^*_k(x_k) = \max_{v_k \in V(x_k)} \left\{ \min_{u_k \in U(x_k)} \left\{ l(x_k, u_k, v_k) + \underline{L}^*_{k+1}(x_{k+1}) \right\} \right\}, \tag{10.111}$$

which is the dynamic programming equation derived from (10.109).

Starting from the final stage, F, the upper and lower values are determined directly from the cost function:

$$\overline{L}^*_F(x_F) = \underline{L}^*_F(x_F) = l_F(x_F). \tag{10.112}$$

Now compute $\overline{L}^*_K$ and $\underline{L}^*_K$. From every state, x_K, (10.110) and (10.111) are evaluated to determine whether $\overline{L}^*_K(x_K) = \underline{L}^*_K(x_K)$. If this occurs, then $L^*_L(x_K) = \overline{L}^*_K(x_K) = \underline{L}^*_K(x_K)$ is the *value* of the game from x_K at stage K. If it is determined that from any particular state, $x_K \in X$, the upper and lower values are not equal, then there is no deterministic saddle point from x_K. Furthermore, this will prevent the existence of deterministic saddle points from other states at earlier stages; these are encountered in later value iterations. Such problems are avoided by allowing randomized plans, but the optimization is more complicated because linear programming is repeatedly involved.

Suppose for now that $\overline{L}^*_K(x_K) = \underline{L}^*_K(x_K)$ for all $x_K \in X$. The value iterations proceed in the usual way from $k = K$ down to $k = 1$. Again, suppose that at every stage, $\overline{L}^*_k(x_k) = \underline{L}^*_k(x_k)$ for all $x_k \in X$. Note that L^*_{k+1} can be written in the place of $\overline{L}^*_{k+1}$ and $\underline{L}^*_{k+1}$ in (10.110) and (10.111) because it is assumed that the upper and lower values coincide. If they do not, then the method fails because randomized plans are needed to obtain a randomized saddle point.

Once the resulting values are computed from each $x_1 \in X_1$, a security plan π^*_1 for P_1 is defined for each $k \in \mathcal{K}$ and $x_k \in X$ as any action u that satisfies the min in (10.110). A security plan π^*_2 is similarly defined for P_2 by applying any action v that satisfies the max in (10.111).

Now suppose that there exists no deterministic saddle point from one or more initial states. To avoid regret, randomized security plans must be developed. These follow by direct extension of the randomized security strategies from Section 9.3.3. The vectors w and z will be used here to denote probability distributions over $U(x)$ and $V(x)$, respectively. The probability vectors are selected from $W(x)$ and $Z(x)$, which correspond to the set of all probability distributions over $U(x)$ and $V(x)$, respectively. For notational convenience, assume $U(x) = \{1, \ldots, m(x)\}$ and $V(x) = \{1, \ldots, n(x)\}$, in which $m(x)$ and $n(x)$ are positive integers.

Recall (9.61) and (9.62), which defined the randomized upper and lower values of a single-stage game. This idea is generalized here to randomized upper and lower value of a *sequential* game. Their definitions are similar to (10.108) and (10.109), except that: 1) the alternating min's and max's are taken over probability distributions on the space of actions, and 2) the expected cost is used.

The dynamic programming principle can be applied to the *randomized upper value* to derive

$$\overline{\mathcal{L}}_k^*(x_k) = \min_{w \in W(x_k)} \left\{ \max_{z \in Z(x_k)} \left\{ \sum_{i=1}^{m(x_k)} \sum_{j=1}^{n(x_k)} \Big(l(x_k, i, j) + \overline{\mathcal{L}}_{k+1}^*(x_{k+1}) \Big) w_i z_j \right\} \right\}, \qquad (10.113)$$

in which $x_{k+1} = f(x_k, i, j)$. The *randomized lower value* is similarly obtained as

$$\underline{\mathcal{L}}_k^*(x_k) = \max_{z \in Z(x_k)} \left\{ \min_{w \in W(x_k)} \left\{ \sum_{i=1}^{m(x_k)} \sum_{j=1}^{n(x_k)} \Big(l(x_k, i, j) + \underline{\mathcal{L}}_{k+1}^*(x_{k+1}) \Big) w_i z_j \right\} \right\}. \qquad (10.114)$$

In many games, the cost term may depend only on the state: $l(x, u, v) = l(x)$ for all $x \in X$, $u \in U(x)$ and $v \in V(x)$. In this case, (10.113) and (10.114) simplify to

$$\overline{\mathcal{L}}_k^*(x_k) = \min_{w \in W(x_k)} \left\{ \max_{z \in Z(x_k)} \left\{ l(x_k) + \sum_{i=1}^{m(x_k)} \sum_{j=1}^{n(x_k)} \overline{\mathcal{L}}_{k+1}^*(x_{k+1}) w_i z_j \right\} \right\} \qquad (10.115)$$

and

$$\underline{\mathcal{L}}_k^*(x_k) = \max_{z \in Z(x_k)} \left\{ \min_{w \in W(x_k)} \left\{ l(x_k) + \sum_{i=1}^{m(x_k)} \sum_{j=1}^{n(x_k)} \underline{\mathcal{L}}_{k+1}^*(x_{k+1}) w_i z_j \right\} \right\}, \qquad (10.116)$$

which is similar to the simplification obtained in (10.46), in which θ_k was assumed not to appear in the cost term. The summations are essentially generalizations of (9.57) to the multiple-stage case. If desired, these could even be written as matrix multiplications, as was done in Section 9.3.3.

Value iteration can be performed over the equations above to obtain the randomized values of the sequential game. Since the upper and lower values are always the same, there is no need to check for discrepancies between the two. In practice, it is best in every evaluation of (10.113) and (10.114) (or their simpler forms) to first check whether a deterministic saddle exists from x_k. Whenever one does not exist, the linear programming problem formulated in Section 9.3.3 must be solved to determine the value and the best randomized plan for each player. This can be avoided if a deterministic saddle exists from the current state and stage.

10.5.3 Other sequential games

Most of the ideas presented so far in Section 10.5 extend naturally to other sequential game problems. This subsection briefly mentions some of these possible extensions.

Nash equilibria in sequential games

Formulations 10.3 and 10.4 can be extended to sequential nonzero-sum games. In the case of game trees, a *cost vector*, with one element for each player, is written at each of the

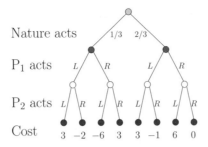

Figure 10.19: This is a single-stage, zero-sum game that involves nature. It is assumed that all players act at the same time.

leaves. Under the stage-by-stage model, deterministic and randomized Nash equilibria can be computed using the bottom-up technique that was presented in Section 10.5.1. This will result in the computation of a single Nash equilibrium. To represent all Nash equilibria is considerably more challenging. As usual, the game tree is decomposed into many matrix games; however, in each case, all Nash equilibria must be found and recorded along with their corresponding costs. Instead of propagating a single cost up the tree, a set of cost vectors, along with the actions associated with each cost vector, must be propagated up the tree to the root. As in the case of a single-stage game, nonadmissible Nash equilibria can be removed from consideration. Thus, from every matrix game encountered in the computation, only the admissible Nash equilibria and their costs should be propagated upward.

Formulation 10.4 can be extended by introducing the cost functions L_1 and L_2 for P_1 and P_2, respectively. The value-iteration approach can be extended in a way similar to the extension of the game tree method. Multiple value vectors and their corresponding actions must be maintained for each combination of state and stage. These correspond to the admissible Nash equilibria.

The nonuniqueness of Nash equilibria causes the greatest difficulty in the sequential game setting. There are typically many more equilibria in a sequential game than in a single-stage game. Therefore, the concept is not very useful in the design of a planning approach. It may be more useful, for example, in modeling the possible outcomes of a complicated economic system. A thorough treatment of the subject appears in [60].

Introducing nature

A nature player can easily be introduced into a game. Suppose, for example, that nature is introduced into a zero-sum game. In this case, there are three players: P_1, P_2, and nature. Figure 10.19 shows a game tree for a single-stage, zero-sum game that involves nature. It is assumed that all three players act at the same time, which fits the stage-by-stage model. Many other information models are possible. Suppose that probabilistic uncertainty is used to model nature, and it is known that nature chooses the left branch with probability $1/3$ and the right branch with probability $2/3$. Depending on the branch chosen by nature, it appears that P_1 and P_2 will play a specific 2×2 matrix game. With probability $1/3$, the cost matrix will be

$$
U \quad
\begin{array}{c}
V \\
\begin{array}{|c|c|}
\hline
3 & -2 \\
\hline
-6 & 3 \\
\hline
\end{array}
\end{array}
\quad , \tag{10.117}
$$

and with probability 2/3 it will be

$$
U \quad
\begin{array}{c}
V \\
\begin{array}{|c|c|}
\hline
3 & -1 \\
\hline
6 & 0 \\
\hline
\end{array}
\end{array} \quad .
\tag{10.118}
$$

Unfortunately, P_1 and P_2 do not know which matrix game they are actually playing. The regret can be eliminated in the expected sense, if the game is played over many independent trials. Let A_1 and A_2 denote (10.117) and (10.118), respectively. Define a new cost matrix as $A = (1/3)A_1 + (2/3)A_2$ (a scalar multiplied by a matrix scales every value of the matrix). The resulting matrix is

$$
U \quad
\begin{array}{c}
V \\
\begin{array}{|c|c|}
\hline
3 & 0 \\
\hline
2 & 1 \\
\hline
\end{array}
\end{array} \quad .
\tag{10.119}
$$

This matrix game has a deterministic saddle point in which P_1 chooses L (row 2) and P_2 chooses R (column 1), which yields a cost of 2. This means that they can play a deterministic strategy to obtain an expected cost of 2, if the game play is averaged over many independent trials. If this matrix did not admit a deterministic saddle point, then a randomized strategy would be needed. It is interesting to note that randomization is not needed for this example, even though P_1 and P_2 each play against both nature and an intelligent adversary.

Several other variations are possible. If nature is modeled nondeterministically, then a matrix of worst-case regrets can be formed to determine whether it is possible to eliminate regret. A sequential version of games such as the one in Figure 10.19 can be considered. In each stage, there are three substages in which nature, P_1, and P_2 all act. The bottom-up approach from Section 10.5.1 can be applied to decompose the tree into many single-stage games. Their costs can be propagated upward to the root in the same way to obtain an equilibrium solution.

Formulation 10.4 can be easily extended to include nature in games over state spaces. For each x, a nature action set is defined as $\Theta(x)$. The state transition equation is defined as

$$
x_{k+1} = f(x_k, u_k, v_k, \theta_k),
\tag{10.120}
$$

which means that the next state depends on all three player actions, in addition to the current state. The value-iteration method can be extended to solve problems of this type by properly considering the effect of nature in the dynamic programming equations. In the probabilistic case, for example, an expectation over nature is needed in every iteration. The resulting sequential game is often referred to as a *Markov game* [777].

Introducing more players

Involving more players poses no great difficulty, other than complicating the notation. For example, suppose that a set of n players, $P_1, P_2, \ldots, P_n$, takes turns playing a game. Consider using a game tree representation. A stage is now stretched into n *substages*, in which each player acts individually. Suppose that P_1 always starts, followed by P_2, and so on, until P_n. After P_n acts, then the next stage is started, and P_1 acts. The circular sequence of player alternations continues until the game ends. Again, many different information models are possible. For example, in the stage-by-stage model, each player does not know the action chosen by the other $n-1$ players in the current stage. The bottom-up computation method can be used to compute Nash equilibria; however, the problems with nonuniqueness must once again be confronted.

A state-space formulation that generalizes Formulation 10.4 can be made by introducing action sets $U^i(x)$ for each player P_i and state $x \in X$. Let u_k^i denote the action chosen by P_i at stage k. The state transition becomes

$$x_{k+1} = f(x_k, u_k^1, u_k^2, \ldots, u_k^n). \tag{10.121}$$

There is also a cost function, L_i, for each P_i. Value iteration, adapted to maintain multiple equilibria and cost vectors can be used to compute Nash equilibria.

10.6 Continuous state spaces

Virtually all of the concepts covered in this chapter extend to continuous state spaces. This enables them to at least theoretically be applied to configuration spaces. Thus, a motion planning problem that involves uncertainty or noncooperating robots can be modeled using the concepts of this chapter. Such problems also inherit the feedback concepts from Chapter 8. This section covers feedback motion planning problems that incorporate uncertainty due to nature. In particular contexts, it may be possible extend some of the methods of Sections 8.4 and 8.5. Solution feedback plans must ensure that the goal is reached in spite of nature's efforts. Among the methods in Chapter 8, the easiest to generalize is value iteration with interpolation, which was covered in Section 8.5.2. Therefore, it is the main focus of the current section. For games in continuous state spaces, see Section 13.5.

10.6.0.1 Extending the value-iteration method

The presentation follows in the same way as in Section 8.5.2, by beginning with the discrete problem and making various components continuous. Begin with Formulation 10.1 and let X be a bounded, open subset of $\mathbb{R}^n$. Assume that $U(x)$ and $\Theta(x, u)$ are finite. The value-iteration methods of Section 10.2.1 can be directly applied by using the interpolation concepts from Section 8.5.2 to compute the cost-to-go values over X. In the nondeterministic case, the recurrence is (10.39), in which G_{k+1}^* is represented on a finite sample set $S \subset X$ and is evaluated on all other points in $R(S)$ by interpolation (recall from Section 8.5.2 that $R(S)$ is the interpolation region of S). In the probabilistic case, (10.45) or (10.46) may once again be used, but G_{k+1}^* is evaluated by interpolation.

If $U(x)$ is continuous, then it can be sampled to evaluate the min in each recurrence, as suggested in Section 8.5.2. Now suppose $\Theta(x, u)$ is continuous. In the nondeterministic case, $\Theta(x, u)$ can be sampled to evaluate the max in (10.39) or it may be possible to employ a general optimization technique directly over $\Theta(x, u)$. In the probabilistic case, the expectation must be taken over a continuous probability space. A probability density function, $p(\theta|x, u)$, characterizes nature's action. A probabilistic state transition density function can be derived from this as $p(x_{k+1}|x_k, u_k)$. Using these densities, the continuous versions of (10.45) and (10.46) become

$$G_k^*(x_k) = \min_{u_k \in U(x_k)} \left\{ \int_{\Theta(x_k, u_k)} \left(l(x_k, u_k, \theta_k) + G_{k+1}^*(f(x_k, u_k, \theta_k)) \right) p(\theta_k|x_k, u_k) d\theta_k \right\}$$

$$\tag{10.122}$$

and

$$G_k^*(x_k) = \min_{u_k \in U(x_k)} \left\{ l(x_k, u_k) + \int_X G_{k+1}^*(x_{k+1}) p(x_{k+1}|x_k, u_k) dx_{k+1} \right\}, \qquad (10.123)$$

respectively. Sampling can be used to evaluate the integrals. One straightforward method is to approximate $p(\theta|x, u)$ by a discrete distribution. For example, in one dimension, this can be achieved by partitioning $\Theta(x, u)$ into intervals, in which each interval is declared to be a discrete nature action. The probability associated with the discrete nature action is just the integral of $p(\theta|x, u)$ over the associated interval.

Section 8.5.2 concluded by describing Dijkstra-like algorithms for continuous spaces. These were derived mainly by using backprojections, (8.66), to conclude that some samples cannot change their values because they are too far from the active set. The same principle can be applied in the current setting; however, the weak backprojection, (10.20), must be used instead. Using the weak backprojection, the usual value iterations can be applied while removing all samples that are not in the active set. For many problems, however, the size of the active set may quickly become unmanageable because the weak backprojection often causes much faster propagation than the original backprojection. Continuous-state generalizations of the Dijkstra-like algorithms in Section 10.2.3 can be made; however, this requires the additional condition that in every iteration, it must be possible to extend D by forcing the next state to lie in $R(D)$, in spite of nature.

10.6.0.2 Motion planning with nature

Recall from Section 8.5.2 that value iteration with interpolation can be applied to motion planning problems that are approximated in discrete time. Nature can even be introduced into the discrete-time approximation. For example, (8.62) can be replaced by

$$x(t + \Delta t) = x(t) + \Delta t \, (u + \theta), \qquad (10.124)$$

in which θ is chosen from a bounded set, $\Theta(x, u)$. Using (10.124), value iterations can be performed as described so far. An example of a 2D motion planning problem under this model using probabilistic uncertainty is shown in Figure 10.20. It is interesting that when the plan is executed from a fixed initial state, a different trajectory is obtained each time. The average cost over multiple executions, however, is close to the expected optimum.

Interesting hybrid system examples can be made in which nature is only allowed to interfere with the mode. Recall Formulation 7.3 from Section 7.3. Nature can be added to yield the following formulation.

Formulation 10.5 (Hybrid System Motion Planning with Nature)

1. Assume all of the definitions from Formulation 7.3, except for the transition functions, f_m and f. The state is represented as $x = (q, m)$.

2. A finite *nature action space* $\Theta(x, u)$ for each $x \in X$ and $u \in U(x)$.

3. A *mode transition function* f_m that produces a state $f_m(x, u, \theta)$ for every $x \in X, u \in U(x)$, and $\theta \in \Theta(x, u)$.

4. A *state transition function* f that is derived from f_m by changing the mode and holding the configuration fixed. Thus, $f((q, m), u) = (q, f_m(q, m, \theta))$ (the only difference with respect to Formulation 7.3 is that θ has been included).

5. An unbounded *time interval* $T = [0, \infty)$.

(a) Motion planning game against nature   (a) Optimal navigation function

(c) Vector field   (d) Simulated executions

Figure 10.20: (a) A 2D planning problem is shown in which nature is probabilistic (uniform density over an interval of angles) and can interfere with the direction of motion. Contact with obstacles is actually allowed in this problem. (b) Level sets of the computed, optimal cost-to-go (navigation) function. (c) The vector field derived from the navigation function. (d) Several dozen execution trials are superimposed [608].

6.   A continuous-time cost-functional,

$$L(\tilde{x}_{t_F}, \tilde{u}_{t_F}) = \int_0^{t_F} l(x(t), u(t))dt + l_F(x(t_F)). \tag{10.125}$$

Value iteration proceeds in the same way for such hybrid problems. Interpolation only needs to be performed over the configuration space. Along the mode "axis" no interpolation is needed because the mode set is already finite. The resulting computation time grows linearly in the number of modes. A 2D motion planning example for a point robot, taken from [616], is shown in Figures 10.21 and 10.22. In this case, the environment contains a door that is modeled as a stationary Markov process. The configuration space is sampled using a 40×40 grid. There are two modes: door open or door closed. Thus, the configuration space has two layers, one for each mode. The robot wishes to minimize the expected time to reach the goal. The navigation function for each layer cannot be computed independently because each takes into account the transition probabilities for the mode. For example, if the door is almost always open, then its plan would be different from one in which the door is almost always closed. If the door is almost always open,

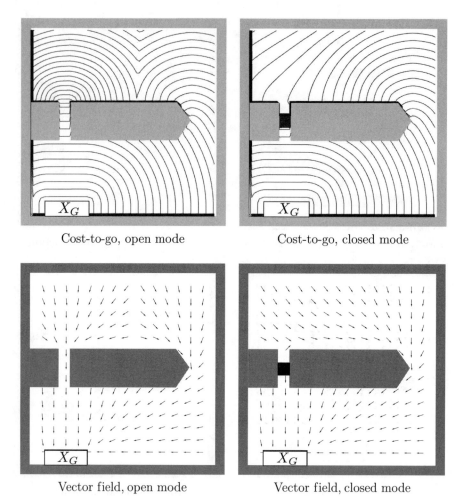

Cost-to-go, open mode   Cost-to-go, closed mode

Vector field, open mode   Vector field, closed mode

Figure 10.21: Level sets of the optimal navigation function and resulting vector field are shown for a stochastic, hybrid motion planning problem. There are two modes, which correspond to whether a door is closed. The goal is to reach the rectangle at the bottom left [616]

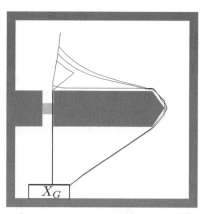

Figure 10.22: Several executions from the same initial state are shown. A different trajectory results each time because of the different times when the door is open or closed.

then the robot should go toward the door, even if it is currently closed, because it is highly likely that it will open soon. Numerous variations can be made on this example. More modes could be added, and other interpretations are possible, such as hazardous regions and shelters (the mode might be imagined as rain occurring and the robot must run for shelter) or requests to deliver objects [616, 872, 873].

Further reading

Since this chapter considers sequential versions of single-stage decision problems, the suggested reading at the end of Chapter 9 is also relevant here. The probabilistic formulation in Section 10.1 is a basic problem of stochastic control theory [97, 567]. The framework is also popular in artificial intelligence [81, 269, 474, 842]. For an early, influential work on stochastic control, see [111], in which the notion of sequential games against nature is developed. The forward projection and backprojection topics are not as common in control theory and are instead inspired from [283, 315, 662]. The nondeterministic formulation is obtained by eliminating probabilities from the formulation; worst-case analysis also appears extensively in control theory [58, 59, 303]. A case for using randomized strategies in robotics is made in [316].

Section 10.2 is based on classical dynamic programming work, but with emphasis on the *stochastic shortest-path problem*. For more reading on value and policy iteration in this context, see [97]. Section 10.2.3 is based on extending Dijkstra's algorithm. For convergence issues due to approximations of continuous problems, see [94, 570, 723]. For complexity results for games against nature, see [767, 770].

Section 10.3 was inspired by coverage in [97]. For further reading on reinforcement learning, the subject of Section 10.4, see [19, 76, 99, 896].

Section 10.5 was based on material in [60], but with an emphasis on unifying concepts from previous sections. Also contained in [60] are sequential game formulations on continuous spaces and even in continuous time. In continuous time, these are called *differential games*, and they are introduced in Section 13.5. Dynamic programming principles extend nicely into game theory. Furthermore, they extend to Pareto optimality [244].

The main purpose of Section 10.6 is to return to motion planning by considering continuous state spaces. Few works exist on combining stochastic optimal control with motion planning. The presented material is based mainly on [602, 608, 616, 869, 870].

Exercises

1. Show that $SB(S, u)$ cannot be expressed as the union of all $SB(x, u)$ for $x \in S$.

2. Show that for any $S \subset X$ and any state transition equation, $x' = f(x, u, \theta)$, it follows that $SB(S) \subseteq WB(S)$.

3. Generalize the strong and weak backprojections of Section 10.1.2 to work for multiple stages.

4. Assume that nondeterministic uncertainty is used, and there is no limit on the number of stages. Determine an expression for the forward projection at any stage $k > 1$, given that π is applied.

5. Give an algorithm for computing nondeterministic forward projections that uses matrices with binary entries. What is the asymptotic running time and space for your algorithm?

6. Develop a variant of the algorithm in Figure 10.6 that is based on *possibly* achieving the goal, as opposed to *guaranteeing* that it is achieved.

7. Develop a forward version of value iteration for nondeterministic uncertainty, by paralleling the derivation in Section 10.2.1.

8. Do the same as in Exercise 7, but for probabilistic uncertainty.

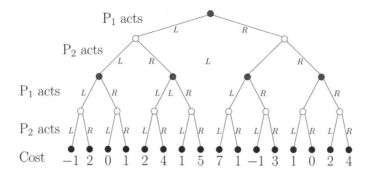

Figure 10.23: A two-player, two-stage game expressed using a game tree.

9. Give an algorithm that computes probabilistic forward projections directly from the plan-based state transition graph, $\mathcal{G}_\pi$.

10. Augment the nondeterministic value-iteration method of Section 10.2.1 to detect and handle states from which the goal is *possibly* reachable but not *guaranteed* reachable.

11. Derive a generalization of (10.39) for the case of stage-dependent state-transition equations, $x_{k+1} = f(x_k, u_k, \theta_k, k)$, and cost terms, $l(x_k, u_k, \theta_k, k)$, under nondeterministic uncertainty.

12. Do the same as in Exercise 11, but for probabilistic uncertainty.

13. Extend the policy-iteration method of Figure 10.4 to work for the more general case of nature-dependent cost terms, $l(x_k, u_k, \theta_k)$.

14. Derive a policy-iteration method that is the nondeterministic analog to the method in Figure 10.4. Assume that the cost terms do not depend on nature.

15. Can policy iteration be applied to solve problems under Formulation 2.3, which involve no uncertainties? Explain what happens in this case.

16. Show that the probabilistic infinite-horizon problem under the discounted-cost model is equivalent in terms of cost-to-go to a particular stochastic shortest-path problem (under Formulation 10.1). [Hint: See page 378 of [97].]

17. Derive a value-iteration method for the infinite-horizon problem with the discounted-cost model and nondeterministic uncertainty. This method should compute the cost-to-go given in (10.71).

18. Figure 10.23 shows a two-stage, zero-sum game expressed as a game tree. Compute the randomized value of this sequential game and give the corresponding randomized security plans for each player.

19. Generalize alpha-beta pruning beyond game trees so that it works for sequential games defined on a state space, starting from a fixed initial state.

20. Derive (10.110) and (10.111).

21. Extend Formulation 2.4 to allow nondeterministic uncertainty. This can be accomplished by specifying sets of possible effects of operators.

22. Extend Formulation 2.4 to allow probabilistic uncertainty. For this case, assign probabilities to the possible operator effects.

Implementations

23. Implement probabilistic backward value iteration and study the convergence issue depicted in Figure 10.3. How does this affect performance in problems for which there are many

cycles in the state transition graph? How does performance depend on particular costs and transition probabilities?

24. Implement the nondeterministic version of Dijkstra's algorithm and test it on a few examples.

25. Implement and test the probabilistic version of Dijkstra's algorithm. Make sure that the condition $G_\pi(x_{k+1}) < G_\pi(x_k)$ from 10.2.3 is satisfied. Study the performance of the algorithm on problems for which the condition is almost violated.

26. Experiment with the simulation-based version of value iteration, which is given by (10.101). For some simple examples, characterize how the performance depends on the choice of ρ.

27. Implement a recursive algorithm that uses dynamic programming to determine the upper and lower values for a sequential game expressed using a game tree under the stage-by-stage model.

11

Sensors and Information Spaces

Up until now it has been assumed everywhere that the current state is known. What if the state is not known? In this case, information regarding the state is obtained from sensors during the execution of a plan. This situation arises in most applications that involve interaction with the physical world. For example, in robotics it is virtually impossible for a robot to precisely know its state, except in some limited cases. What should be done if there is limited information regarding the state? A classical approach is to take all of the information available and try to estimate the state. In robotics, the state may include both the map of its environment and the robot configuration. If the estimates are sufficiently reliable, then we may safely pretend that there is no uncertainty in state information. This enables many of the planning methods introduced so far to be applied with little or no adaptation.

The more interesting case occurs when state estimation is altogether avoided. It may be surprising, but many important tasks can be defined and solved without ever requiring that specific states are sensed, even though a state space is defined for the planning problem. To achieve this, the planning problem will be expressed in terms of an *information space*. Information spaces serve the same purpose for sensing problems as the configuration spaces of Chapter 4 did for problems that involve geometric transformations. Each information space represents the place where a problem that involves sensing uncertainty naturally lives. Successfully formulating and solving such problems depends on our ability to manipulate, simplify, and control the information space. In some cases elegant solutions exist, and in others there appears to be no hope at present of efficiently solving them. There are many exciting open research problems associated with information spaces and sensing uncertainty in general.

Recall the situation depicted in Figure 11.1, which was also shown in Section 1.4. It is assumed that the state of the environment is not known. There are three general sources of information regarding the state:

1. The *initial conditions* can provide powerful information before any actions are applied. It might even be the case that the initial state is given. At the other extreme, the initial conditions might contain no information.

2. The *sensor observations* provide measurements related to the state during execution. These measurements are usually incomplete or involve disturbances that distort their values.

3. The *actions* already executed in the plan provide valuable information regarding the state. For example, if a robot is commanded to move east (with no other uncertainties except an unknown state), then it is expected that the state is further east than it was previously. Thus, the applied actions provide important clues for deducing possible states.

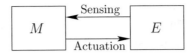

Figure 11.1: The state of the environment is not known. The only information available to make inferences is the history of sensor observations, actions that have been applied, and the initial conditions. This history becomes the *information state*.

Keep in mind that there are generally two ways to use the information space:

1. *Take all of the information available, and try to estimate the state.* This is the classical approach. Pretend that there is no longer any uncertainty in state, but prove (or hope) that the resulting plan works under reasonable estimation error. A plan is generally expressed as $\pi : X \to U$.

2. *Solve the task entirely in terms of an information space.* Many tasks may be achieved without ever knowing the exact state. The goals and analysis are formulated in the information space, without the need to achieve particular states. For many problems this results in dramatic simplifications. A plan is generally expressed as $\pi : \mathcal{I} \to U$ for an information space, $\mathcal{I}$.

The first approach may be considered somewhat traditional and can be handled by the concepts of Chapter 8 once a good estimation technique is defined. Most of the focus of the chapter is on the second approach, which represents a powerful way to express and solve planning problems.

For brevity, "information" will be replaced by "I" in many terms. Hence, information spaces and information states become I-spaces and I-states, respectively. This is similar to the shortening of configuration spaces to C-spaces.

Sections 11.1 to 11.3 first cover information spaces for discrete state spaces. This case is much easier to formulate than information spaces for continuous spaces. In Sections 11.4 to 11.6, the ideas are extended from discrete state spaces to continuous state spaces. It is helpful to have a good understanding of the discrete case before proceeding to the continuous case. Section 11.7 extends the formulation of information spaces to game theory, in which multiple players interact over the same state space. In this case, each player in the game has its own information space over which it makes decisions.

11.1 Discrete state spaces

11.1.1 Sensors

As the name suggests, *sensors* are designed to sense the state. Throughout all of this section it is assumed that the state space, X, is finite or countably infinite, as in Formulations 2.1 and 2.3. A *sensor* is defined in terms of two components: 1) an *observation space*, which is the set of possible readings for the sensor, and 2) a *sensor mapping*, which characterizes the readings that can be expected if the current state or other information is given. Be aware that in the planning model, the state is not really given; it is only assumed to be given when modeling a sensor. The sensing model given here generalizes the one given in Section 9.2.3. In that case, the sensor provided information regarding θ instead of x because state spaces were not needed in Chapter 9.

Let Y denote an *observation space*, which is a finite or countably infinite set. Let h denote the *sensor mapping*. Three different kinds of sensor mappings will be considered, each of which is more complicated and general than the previous one:

1. **State sensor mapping:** In this case, $h : X \to Y$, which means that given the state, the observation is completely determined.

2. **State-nature sensor mapping:** In this case, a finite set, $\Psi(x)$, of *nature sensing actions* is defined for each $x \in X$. Each nature sensing action, $\psi \in \Psi(x)$, interferes with the sensor observation. Therefore, the state-nature mapping, h, produces an observation, $y = h(x, \psi) \in Y$, for every $x \in X$ and $\psi \in \Psi(x)$. The particular ψ chosen by nature is assumed to be unknown during planning and execution. However, it is specified as part of the sensing model.

3. **History-based sensor mapping:** In this case, the observation could be based on the current state or any previous states. Furthermore, a nature sensing action could be applied. Suppose that the current stage is k. The set of nature sensing actions is denoted by $\Psi_k(x)$, and the particular nature sensing action is $\psi_k \in \Psi_k(x)$. This yields a very general sensor mapping,

$$y_k = h_k(x_1, \ldots, x_k, \psi_k), \tag{11.1}$$

in which y_k is the observation obtained in stage k. Note that the mapping is denoted as h_k because the domain is different for each k. In general, any of the sensor mappings may be stage-dependent, if desired.

Many examples of sensors will now be given. These are provided to illustrate the definitions and to provide building blocks that will be used in later examples of I-spaces. Examples 11.1 to 11.6 all involve state sensor mappings.

Example 11.1 (Odd/Even Sensor) Let $X = \mathbb{Z}$, the set of integers, and let $Y = \{0, 1\}$. The sensor mapping is

$$y = h(x) = \begin{cases} 0 & \text{if } x \text{ is even} \\ 1 & \text{if } x \text{ is odd.} \end{cases} \tag{11.2}$$

The limitation of this sensor is that it only tells whether $x \in X$ is odd or even. When combined with other information, this might be enough to infer the state, but in general it provides incomplete information. ∎

Example 11.2 (Mod Sensor) Example 11.1 can be easily generalized to yield the remainder when x is divided by k for some fixed integer k. Let $X = \mathbb{Z}$, and let $Y = \{0, 1, \ldots, k - 1\}$. The sensor mapping is

$$y = h(x) = x \bmod k. \tag{11.3}$$

∎

Example 11.3 (Sign Sensor) Let $X = \mathbb{Z}$, and let $Y = \{-1, 0, 1\}$. The sensor mapping is

$$y = h(x) = \operatorname{sgn} x. \tag{11.4}$$

This sensor provides very limited information because it only indicates on which side of the boundary $x = 0$ the state may lie. It can, however, precisely determine whether $x = 0$. ∎

Example 11.4 (Selective Sensor) Let $X = \mathbb{Z} \times \mathbb{Z}$, and let $(i, j) \in X$ denote a state in which $i, j \in \mathbb{Z}$. Suppose that only the first component of (i, j) can be observed. This yields the sensor mapping

$$y = h(i, j) = i. \tag{11.5}$$

An obvious generalization can be made for any state space that is formed from Cartesian products. The sensor may reveal the values of one or more components, and the rest remain hidden. ∎

Example 11.5 (Bijective Sensor) Let X be any state space, and let $Y = X$. Let the sensor mapping be any bijective function $h : X \to Y$. This sensor provides information that is equivalent to knowing the state. Since h is bijective, it can be inverted to obtain $h^{-1} : Y \to X$. For any $y \in Y$, the state can be determined as $x = h^{-1}(y)$.

A special case of the *bijective sensor* is the *identity sensor*, for which h is the identity function. This was essentially assumed to exist for all planning problems covered before this chapter because it immediately yields the state. However, any bijective sensor could serve the same purpose. ∎

Example 11.6 (Null Sensor) Let X be any state space, and let $Y = \{0\}$. The *null sensor* is obtained by defining the sensor mapping as $h(x) = 0$. The sensor reading remains fixed and hence provides no information regarding the state. ∎

From the examples so far, it is tempting to think about partitioning X based on sensor observations. Suppose that in general a state mapping, h, is not bijective, and let $H(y)$ denote the following subset of X:

$$H(y) = \{x \in X \mid y = h(x)\}, \tag{11.6}$$

which is the *preimage* of y. The set of preimages, one for each $y \in Y$, form a partition of X. In some sense, this indicates the "resolution" of the sensor. A bijective sensor partitions X into singleton sets because it contains perfect information. At the other extreme, the null sensor partitions X into a single set, X itself. The sign sensor appears slightly more useful because it partitions X into three sets: $H(1) = \{1, 2, \ldots\}$, $H(-1) = \{\ldots, -2, -1\}$, and $H(0) = \{0\}$. The preimages of the selective sensor are particularly interesting. For each $i \in \mathbb{Z}$, $H(i) = \mathbb{Z}$. The partitions induced by the preimages may remind those with an algebra background of the construction of quotient groups via homomorphisms [772].

Next consider some examples that involve a state-action sensor mapping. There are two different possibilities regarding the model for the nature sensing action:

1. **Nondeterministic:** In this case, there is no additional information regarding which $\psi \in \Psi(x)$ will be chosen.

2. **Probabilistic:** A probability distribution is known. In this case, the probability, $P(\psi|x)$, that ψ will be chosen is known for each $\psi \in \Psi(x)$.

These two possibilities also appeared in Section 10.1.1, for nature actions that interfere with the state transition equation.

It is sometimes useful to consider the state-action sensor model as a probability distribution over Y for a given state. Recall the conversion from $P(\psi|\theta)$ to $P(y|\theta)$ in (9.28). By replacing Θ by X, the same idea can be applied here. Assume that if the domain of h is restricted to some $x \in X$, it forms an injective (one-to-one) mapping from Ψ to Y. In this case,

$$P(y|x) = \begin{cases} P(\psi|x) & \text{for the unique } \psi \text{ such that } y = h(x, \psi). \\ 0 & \text{if no such } \psi \text{ exists.} \end{cases} \tag{11.7}$$

If the injective assumption is lifted, then $P(\psi|x)$ is replaced by a sum over all ψ for which $y = h(x, \psi)$.

Example 11.7 (Sensor Disturbance) Let $X = \mathbb{Z}$, $Y = \mathbb{Z}$, and $\Psi = \{-1, 0, 1\}$. The idea is to construct a sensor that would be the identity sensor if it were not for the interference of nature. The sensor mapping is

$$y = h(x, \psi) = x + \psi. \tag{11.8}$$

It is always known that $|x - y| \leq 1$. Therefore, if y is received as a sensor reading, one of the following must be true: $x = y - 1$, $x = y$, or $x = y + 1$. ∎

Example 11.8 (Disturbed Sign Sensor) Let $X = \mathbb{Z}$, $Y = \{-1, 0, 1\}$, and $\Psi = \{-1, 0, 1\}$. Let the sensor mapping be

$$y = h(x, \psi) = \operatorname{sgn}(x + \psi). \tag{11.9}$$

In this case, if $y = 0$, it is no longer known for certain whether $x = 0$. It is possible that $x = -1$ or $x = 1$. If $x = 0$, then it is possible for the sensor to read $-1, 0$, or 1. ∎

Example 11.9 (Disturbed Odd/Even Sensor) It is not hard to construct examples for which some mild interference from nature destroys all of the information. Let $X = \mathbb{Z}$, $Y = \{0, 1\}$, and $\Psi = \{0, 1\}$. Let the sensor mapping be

$$y = h(x, \psi) = \begin{cases} 0 & \text{if } x + \psi \text{ is even.} \\ 1 & \text{if } x + \psi \text{ is odd.} \end{cases} \tag{11.10}$$

Under the nondeterministic model for the nature sensing action, the sensor provides no useful information regarding the state. Regardless of the observation, it is never known whether x is even or odd. Under a probabilistic model, however, this sensor may provide some useful information. ∎

It is once again informative to consider preimages. For a state-action sensor mapping, the preimage is

$$H(y) = \{x \in X \mid \exists \psi \in \Psi(x) \text{ for which } y = h(x, \psi)\}. \tag{11.11}$$

In comparison to state sensor mappings, the preimage sets are larger for state-action sensor mappings. Also, they do not generally form a partition of X. For example, the preimages of Example 11.8 are $H(1) = \{0, 1, \ldots\}$, $H(0) = \{-1, 0, 1\}$, and $H(-1) = \{\ldots, -2, -1, 0\}$. This is not a partition because every preimage contains 0. If desired, $H(y)$ can be directly defined for each $y \in Y$, instead of explicitly defining nature sensing actions.

Finally, one example of a history-based sensor mapping is given.

Example 11.10 (Delayed-Observation Sensor) Let $X = Y = \mathbb{Z}$. A *delayed-observation sensor* can be defined for some fixed positive integer i as $y_k = x_{k-i}$. It indicates what the state was i stages ago. In this case, it gives a perfect measurement of the old state value. Many other variants are possible. For example, it might only give the sign of the state from i stages ago. ∎

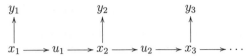

Figure 11.2: In each stage, k, an observation, $y_k \in Y$, is received and an action $u_k \in U$ is applied. The state, x_k, however, is hidden from the decision maker.

11.1.2 Defining the history information space

This section defines the most basic and natural I-space. Many others will be derived from it, which is the topic of Section 11.2. Suppose that X, U, and f have been defined as in Formulation 10.1, and the notion of stages has been defined as in Formulation 2.2. This yields a state sequence $x_1, x_2, \ldots$, and an action sequence $u_1, u_2, \ldots$, during the execution of a plan. However, in the current setting, the state sequence is not known. Instead, at every stage, an observation, y_k, is obtained. The process depicted in Figure 11.2.

In previous formulations, the action space, $U(x)$, was generally allowed to depend on x. Since x is unknown in the current setting, it would seem strange to allow the actions to depend on x. This would mean that inferences could be made regarding the state by simply noticing which actions are available.[1] Instead, it will be assumed by default that U is fixed for all $x \in X$. In some special contexts, however, $U(x)$ may be allowed to vary.

Initial conditions

As stated at the beginning of the chapter, the initial conditions provide one of the three general sources of information regarding the state. Therefore, three alternative types of initial conditions will be allowed:

1. **Known State:** The initial state, $x_1 \in X$, is given. This initializes the problem with perfect state information. Assuming nature actions interfere with the state transition function, f, uncertainty in the current state will generally develop.

2. **Nondeterministic:** A set of states, $X_1 \subset X$, is given. In this case, the initial state is only known to lie within a particular subset of X. This can be considered as a generalization of the first type, which only allowed singleton subsets.

3. **Probabilistic:** A probability distribution, $P(x_1)$, over X is given.

In general, let η_0 denote the initial condition, which may be any one of the three alternative types.

History

Suppose that the kth stage has passed. What information is available? It is assumed that at every stage, a sensor observation is made. This results in a *sensing history*,

$$\tilde{y}_k = (y_1, y_2, \ldots, y_k). \tag{11.12}$$

At every stage an action can also be applied, which yields an *action history*,

$$\tilde{u}_{k-1} = (u_1, u_2, \ldots, u_{k-1}). \tag{11.13}$$

Note that the action history only runs to u_{k-1}; if u_k is applied, the state x_{k+1} and stage $k+1$ are obtained, which lie beyond the current stage, k. By combining the sensing and action histories, the *history* at stage k is $(\tilde{u}_{k-1}, \tilde{y}_k)$.

---

[1] Such a problem could be quite interesting to study, but it will not be considered here.

History information states

The history, $(\tilde{u}_{k-1}, \tilde{y}_k)$, in combination with the initial condition, η_0, yields the *history I-state*, which is denoted by η_k. This corresponds to all information that is known up to stage k. In spite of the fact that the states, $x_1, \ldots, x_k$, might not be known, the history I-states are always known because they are defined directly in terms of available information. Thus, the history I-state is

$$\eta_k = (\eta_0, \tilde{u}_{k-1}, \tilde{y}_k). \tag{11.14}$$

When representing I-spaces, we will generally ignore the problem of nesting parentheses. For example, (11.14) is treated a single sequence, instead of a sequence that contains two sequences. This distinction is insignificant for the purposes of decision making.

The history I-state, η_k, can also be expressed as

$$\eta_k = (\eta_{k-1}, u_{k-1}, y_k), \tag{11.15}$$

by noticing that the history I-state at stage k contains all of the information from the history I-state at stage $k-1$. The only new information is the most recently applied action, u_{k-1}, and the current sensor observation, y_k.

The history information space

The history I-space is simply the set of all possible history I-states. Although the history I-states appear to be quite complicated, it is helpful to think of them abstractly as points in a new space. To define the set of all possible history I-states, the sets of all initial conditions, actions, and observations must be precisely defined.

The set of all observation histories is denoted as $\tilde{Y}_k$ and is obtained by a Cartesian product of k copies of the observation space:

$$\tilde{Y}_k = \underbrace{Y \times Y \ldots \times Y}_{k}. \tag{11.16}$$

Similarly, the set of all action histories is $\tilde{U}_{k-1}$, the Cartesian product of $k-1$ copies of the action space U.

It is slightly more complicated to define the set of all possible initial conditions because three different types of initial conditions are possible. Let $\mathcal{I}_0$ denote the *initial condition space*. Depending on which of the three types of initial conditions are used, one of the following three definitions of $\mathcal{I}_0$ is used:

1. **Known State:** If the initial state, x_1, is given, then $\mathcal{I}_0 \subseteq X$. Typically, $\mathcal{I}_0 = X$; however, it might be known in some instances that certain initial states are impossible. Therefore, it is generally written that $\mathcal{I}_0 \subseteq X$.

2. **Nondeterministic:** If X_1 is given, then $\mathcal{I}_0 \subseteq \text{pow}(X)$ (the power set of X). Again, a typical situation is $\mathcal{I}_0 = \text{pow}(x)$; however, it might be known that certain subsets of X are impossible as initial conditions.

3. **Probabilistic:** Finally, if $P(x)$ is given, then $\mathcal{I}_0 \subseteq \mathcal{P}(X)$, in which $\mathcal{P}(x)$ is the set of all probability distributions over X.

The *history I-space at stage k* is expressed as

$$\mathcal{I}_k = \mathcal{I}_0 \times \tilde{U}_{k-1} \times \tilde{Y}_k. \tag{11.17}$$

Each $\eta_k \in \mathcal{I}_k$ yields an initial condition, an action history, and an observation history. It will be convenient to consider I-spaces that do not depend on k. This will be defined by taking a union (be careful not to mistakenly think of this construction as a Cartesian product). If there are K stages, then the *history I-space* is

$$\mathcal{I}_{hist} = \mathcal{I}_0 \cup \mathcal{I}_1 \cup \mathcal{I}_2 \cup \cdots \cup \mathcal{I}_K. \tag{11.18}$$

Most often, the number of stages is not fixed. In this case, $\mathcal{I}_{hist}$ is defined to be the union of $\mathcal{I}_k$ over all $k \in \{0\} \cup \mathbb{N}$:

$$\mathcal{I}_{hist} = \mathcal{I}_0 \cup \mathcal{I}_1 \cup \mathcal{I}_2 \cup \cdots . \tag{11.19}$$

This construction is related to the state space obtained for time-varying motion planning in Section 7.1. The history I-space is stage-dependent because information accumulates over time. In the discrete model, the reference to time is only implicit through the use of stages. Therefore, stage-dependent I-spaces are defined. Taking the union of all of these is similar to the state space that was formed in Section 7.1 by making time be one axis of the state space. For the history I-space, $\mathcal{I}_{hist}$, the stage index k can be imagined as an "axis."

One immediate concern regarding the history I-space $\mathcal{I}_{hist}$ is that its I-states may be arbitrarily long because the history grows linearly with the number of stages. For now, it is helpful to imagine $\mathcal{I}_{hist}$ abstractly as another kind of state space, without paying close attention to how complicated each $\eta \in \mathcal{I}_{hist}$ may be to represent. In many contexts, there are ways to simplify the I-space. This is the topic of Section 11.2.

11.1.3 Defining a planning problem

Planning problems will be defined directly on the history I-space, which makes it appear as an ordinary state space in many ways. Keep in mind, however, that it was derived from another state space for which perfect state observations could not be obtained. In Section 10.1, a feedback plan was defined as a function of the state. Here, a feedback plan is instead a function of the I-state. Decisions cannot be based on the state because it will be generally unknown during the execution of the plan. However, the I-state is always known; thus, it is logical to base decisions on it.

Let π_K denote a *K-step information-feedback plan*, which is a sequence $(\pi_1, \pi_2, \ldots, \pi_K)$ of K functions, $\pi_k : \mathcal{I}_k \to U$. Thus, at every stage k, the I-state $\eta_k \in \mathcal{I}_k$ is used as a basis for choosing the action $u_k = \pi_k(\eta_k)$. Due to interference of nature through both the state transition equation and the sensor mapping, the action sequence $(u_1, \ldots, u_K)$ produced by a plan, π_K, will not be known until the plan terminates.

As in Formulation 2.3, it will be convenient to assume that U contains a *termination action*, u_T. If u_T is applied at stage k, then it is repeatedly applied forever. It is assumed once again that the state x_k remains fixed after the termination condition is applied. Remember, however, x_k is still unknown in general; it becomes fixed but unknown. Technically, based on the definition of the history I-space, the I-state must change after u_T is applied because the history grows. These changes can be ignored, however, because no new decisions are made after u_T is applied. A plan that uses a termination condition can be specified as $\pi = (\pi_1, \pi_2, \ldots)$ because the number of stages may vary each time the plan is executed. Using the history I-space definition in (11.19), an *information-feedback plan* is expressed as

$$\pi : \mathcal{I} \to U. \tag{11.20}$$

We are almost ready to define the planning problem. This will require the specification of a cost functional. The cost depends on the histories of states $\tilde{x}$ and actions $\tilde{u}$ as in Section 10.1. The planning formulation involves the following components, summarizing most of the concepts introduced so far in Section 11.1 (see Formulation 10.1 for similarities):

Formulation 11.1 (Discrete Information Space Planning)

1. A nonempty *state space* X that is either finite or countably infinite.

2. A nonempty, finite *action space* U. It is assumed that U contains a special *termination action*, which has the same effect as defined in Formulation 2.3.

3. A finite *nature action space* $\Theta(x, u)$ for each $x \in X$ and $u \in U$.

4. A *state transition function* f that produces a state, $f(x, u, \theta)$, for every $x \in X$, $u \in U$, and $\theta \in \Theta(x, u)$.

5. A finite or countably infinite *observation space* Y.

6. A finite *nature sensing action space* $\Psi(x)$ for each $x \in X$.

7. A *sensor mapping* h which produces an observation, $y = h(x, \psi)$, for each $x \in X$ and $\psi \in \Psi(x)$. This definition assumes a state-nature sensor mappings. A state sensor mapping or history-based sensor mapping, as defined in Section 11.1.1, could alternatively be used.

8. A set of *stages*, each denoted by k, which begins at $k = 1$ and continues indefinitely.

9. An *initial condition* η_0, which is an element of an *initial condition space*, $\mathcal{I}_0$.

10. A *history I-space* $\mathcal{I}_{hist}$ which is the union of $\mathcal{I}_0$ and $\mathcal{I}_k = \mathcal{I}_0 \times \tilde{U}_{k-1} \times \tilde{Y}_k$ for every stage $k \in \mathbb{N}$.

11. Let L denote a stage-additive cost functional, which may be applied to any pair $(\tilde{x}_{K+1}, \tilde{u}_K)$ of state and action histories to yield

$$L(\tilde{x}_{K+1}, \tilde{u}_K) = \sum_{k=1}^{K} l(x_k, u_k) + l_F(x_{K+1}). \qquad (11.21)$$

If the termination action u_T is applied at some stage k, then for all $i \geq k$, $u_i = u_T$, $x_i = x_k$, and $l(x_i, u_T) = 0$. Either a feasible or optimal planning problem can be defined, as in Formulation 10.1; however, the plan here is specified as $\pi : \mathcal{I} \to U$.

A *goal set* may be defined as $X_G \subset X$. Alternatively, the goal could be expressed as a desirable set of history I-states. After Section 11.2, it will be seen that the goal can be expressed in terms of I-states that are derived from histories.

Some immediate extensions of Formulation 11.1 are possible, but we avoid them here simplify notation in the coming concepts. One extension is to allow different action sets, $U(x)$, for each $x \in X$. Be careful, however, because information regarding the current state can be inferred if the action set $U(x)$ is given, and it varies depending on x. Another extension is to allow the costs to depend on nature, to obtain $l(x_k, u_k, \theta_k)$, instead of $l(x_k, u_k)$ in (11.21).

The cost of a plan

The next task is to extend the definition of the cost-to-go under a fixed plan, which was given in Section 10.1.3, to the case of imperfect state information. Consider evaluating the quality of a plan, so that the "best" one might be selected. Suppose that the nondeterministic uncertainty is used to model nature and that a nondeterministic initial condition is given. If a plan π is fixed, some state and action trajectories are possible, and others are not. It is impossible to know in general what histories will occur; however, the plan constrains the choices substantially. Let $\mathcal{H}(\pi, \eta_0)$ denote the set of state-action histories that could arise from π applied to the initial condition η_0.

The cost of a plan π from an initial condition η_0 is measured using *worst-case analysis* as

$$G_\pi(\eta_0) = \max_{(\tilde{x}, \tilde{u}) \in \mathcal{H}(\pi, \eta_0)} \left\{ L(\tilde{x}, \tilde{u}) \right\}. \tag{11.22}$$

Note that $\tilde{x}$ includes x_1, which is usually not known. It may be known only to lie in X_1, as specified by η_0. Let Π denote the set of all possible plans. An optimal plan using worst-case analysis is any plan for which (11.22) is minimized over all $\pi \in \Pi$ and $\eta_0 \in \mathcal{I}_0$. In the case of feasible planning, there are usually numerous equivalent alternatives.

Under probabilistic uncertainty, the cost of a plan can be measured using *expected-case analysis* as

$$G_\pi(\eta_0) = E_{\mathcal{H}(\pi, \eta_0)} \left[L(\tilde{x}, \tilde{u}) \right], \tag{11.23}$$

in which E denotes the mathematical expectation of the cost, with the probability distribution taken over $\mathcal{H}(\pi, \eta_0)$. The task is to find a plan $\pi \in \Pi$ that minimizes (11.23).

The information space is just another state space

It will become important throughout this chapter and Chapter 12 to view the I-space as an ordinary state space. It only seems special because it is derived from another state space, but once this is forgotten, it exhibits many properties of an ordinary state space in planning. One nice feature is that the state in this special space is always known. Thus, by converting from an original state space to its I-space, we also convert from having imperfect state information to always knowing the state, albeit in a larger state space.

One important consequence of this interpretation is that the state transition equation can be lifted into the I-space to obtain an *information transition function*, $f_\mathcal{I}$. Suppose that there are no sensors, and therefore no observations. In this case, future I-states are predictable, which leads to

$$\eta_{k+1} = f_\mathcal{I}(\eta_k, u_k). \tag{11.24}$$

The function $f_\mathcal{I}$ generates η_{k+1} by concatenating u_k onto η_k.

Now suppose that there are observations, which are generally unpredictable. In Section 10.1, the nature action $\theta_k \in \Theta(x, u)$ was used to model the unpredictability. In terms of the information transition equation, y_{k+1} serves the same purpose. When the decision is made to apply u_k, the observation y_{k+1} is not yet known (just as θ_k is unknown in Section 10.1). In a sequential game against nature with perfect state information, x_{k+1} is directly observed at the next stage. For the information transition equation, y_{k+1} is instead observed, and η_{k+1} can be determined. Using the history I-state representation, (11.14), simply concatenate u_k and y_{k+1} onto the histories in η_k to obtain η_{k+1}. The information transition equation is expressed as

$$\eta_{k+1} = f_\mathcal{I}(\eta_k, u_k, y_{k+1}), \tag{11.25}$$

with the understanding that y_{k+1} plays the same role as θ_k in the case of perfect state information and unpredictable future states. Even though nature causes future I-states to be unpredictable, the current I-state is always known. A plan, $\pi : \mathcal{I} \to U$, now seems like a state-feedback plan, if the I-space is viewed as a state space. The transitions are all specified by $f_\mathcal{I}$.

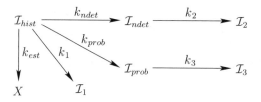

Figure 11.3: Many alternative information mappings may be proposed. Each leads to a derived information space.

The costs in this new state space can be derived from the original cost functional, but a maximization or expectation is needed over all possible states given the current information. This will be covered in Section 12.1.

11.2 Derived information spaces

The history I-space appears to be quite complicated. Every I-state corresponds to a history of actions and observations. Unfortunately, the length of the I-state sequence grows linearly with the number of stages. To overcome this difficulty, it is common to map history I-states to some simpler space. In many applications, the ability to perform this simplification is critical to finding a practical solution. In some cases, the simplification fully preserves the history I-space, meaning that completeness, and optimality if applicable, is not lost. In other cases, we are willing to tolerate a simplification that destroys much of the structure of the history I-space. This may be necessary to obtain a dramatic reduction in the size of the I-space.

11.2.1 Information mappings

Consider a function that maps the history I-space into a space that is simpler to manage. Formally, let $\kappa : \mathcal{I}_{hist} \to \mathcal{I}_{der}$ denote a function from a history I-space, $\mathcal{I}_{hist}$, to a *derived I-space*, $\mathcal{I}_{der}$. The function, κ, is called an *information mapping*, or *I-map*. The derived I-space may be any set; hence, there is great flexibility in defining an I-map.[2] Figure 11.3 illustrates the idea. The starting place is $\mathcal{I}_{hist}$, and mappings are made to various derived I-spaces. Some generic mappings, κ_1, κ_2, and κ_3, are shown, along with some very important kinds, $\mathcal{I}_{est}$, $\mathcal{I}_{ndet}$ and $\mathcal{I}_{prob}$. The last two are the subjects of Sections 11.2.2 and 11.2.3, respectively. The other important I-map is κ_{est}, which uses the history to estimate the state; hence, the derived I-space is X (see Example 11.11). In general, an I-map can even map any derived I-space to another, yielding $\kappa : \mathcal{I}_{der} \to \mathcal{I}'_{der}$, for any I-spaces $\mathcal{I}_{der}$ and $\mathcal{I}'_{der}$. Note that any composition of I-maps yields an I-map. The derived I-spaces $\mathcal{I}_2$ and $\mathcal{I}_3$ from Figure 11.3 are obtained via compositions.

Making smaller information-feedback plans

The primary use of an I-map is to simplify the description of a plan. In Section 11.1.3, a plan was defined as a function on the history I-space, $\mathcal{I}_{hist}$. Suppose that an I-map, κ, is introduced that maps from $\mathcal{I}_{hist}$ to $\mathcal{I}_{der}$. A feedback plan on $\mathcal{I}_{der}$ is defined as $\pi : \mathcal{I}_{der} \to U$. To execute a plan defined on $\mathcal{I}_{der}$, the derived I-state is computed at each stage k by applying κ to η_k to obtain $\kappa(\eta_k) \in \mathcal{I}_{der}$. The action selected by π is $\pi(\kappa(\eta_k)) \in U$.

---

[2] Ideally, the mapping should be *onto* $\mathcal{I}_{der}$; however, to facilitate some definitions, this will not be required.

To understand the effect of using $\mathcal{I}_{der}$ instead of $\mathcal{I}_{hist}$ as the domain of π, consider the set of possible plans that can be represented over $\mathcal{I}_{der}$. Let Π_{hist} and Π_{der} be the sets of all plans over $\mathcal{I}_{hist}$ and $\mathcal{I}_{der}$, respectively. Any $\pi \in \Pi_{der}$ can be converted into an equivalent plan, $\pi' \in \Pi_{hist}$, as follows: For each $\eta \in \mathcal{I}_{hist}$, define $\pi'(\eta) = \pi(\kappa(\eta))$.

It is not always possible, however, to construct a plan, $\pi \in \Pi_{der}$, from some $\pi' \in \mathcal{I}_{hist}$. The problem is that there may exist some $\eta_1, \eta_2 \in \mathcal{I}_{hist}$ for which $\pi'(\eta_1) \neq \pi'(\eta_2)$ and $\kappa(\eta_1) = \kappa(\eta_2)$. In words, this means that the plan in Π_{hist} requires that two histories cause different actions, but in the derived I-space the histories cannot be distinguished. For a plan in Π_{der}, both histories must yield the same action.

An I-map κ has the potential to collapse $\mathcal{I}_{hist}$ down to a smaller I-space by inducing a partition of $\mathcal{I}_{hist}$. For each $\eta_{der} \in \mathcal{I}_{der}$, let the preimage $\kappa^{-1}(\eta_{der})$ be defined as

$$\kappa^{-1}(\eta_{der}) = \{\eta \in \mathcal{I}_{hist} \mid \eta_{der} = \kappa(\eta)\}. \tag{11.26}$$

This yields the set of history I-states that map to η_{der}. The induced partition can intuitively be considered as the "resolution" at which the history I-space is characterized. If the sets in (11.26) are large, then the I-space is substantially reduced. The goal is to select κ to make the sets in the partition as large as possible; however, one must be careful to avoid collapsing the I-space so much that the problem can no longer be solved.

Example 11.11 (State Estimation)   In this example, the I-map is the classical approach that is conveniently taken in numerous applications. Suppose that a technique has been developed that uses the history I-state $\eta \in \mathcal{I}_{hist}$ to compute an estimate of the current state. In this case, the I-map is $\kappa_{est} : \mathcal{I}_{hist} \to X$. The derived I-space happens to be X in this case! This means that a plan is specified as $\pi : X \to U$, which is just a state-feedback plan.

Consider the partition of $\mathcal{I}_{hist}$ that is induced by κ_{est}. For each $x \in X$, the set $\kappa_{est}^{-1}(x)$, as defined in (11.26), is the set of all histories that lead to the same state estimate. A plan on X can no longer distinguish between various histories that led to the same state estimate. One implication is that the ability to encode the amount of uncertainty in the state estimate has been lost. For example, it might be wise to make the action depend on the covariance in the estimate of x; however, this is not possible because decisions are based only on the estimate itself. ∎

Example 11.12 (Stage Indices)   Consider an I-map, κ_{stage}, that returns only the current stage index. Thus, $\kappa_{stage}(\eta_k) = k$. The derived I-space is the set of stages, which is $\mathbb{N}$. A feedback plan on the derived I-space is specified as $\pi : \mathbb{N} \to U$. This is equivalent to specifying a plan as an action sequence, $(u_1, u_2, \dots,)$, as in Section 2.3.2. Since the feedback is trivial, this is precisely the original case of planning without feedback, which is also refereed to as an open-loop plan. ∎

Constructing a derived information transition equation

As presented so far, the full history I-state is needed to determine a derived I-state. It may be preferable, however, to discard histories and work entirely in the derived I-space. Without storing the histories on the machine or robot, a derived information transition equation needs to be developed. The important requirement in this case is as follows:

If η_k is replaced by $\kappa(\eta_k)$, then $\kappa(\eta_{k+1})$ must be correctly determined using only $\kappa(\eta_k)$, u_k, and y_{k+1}.

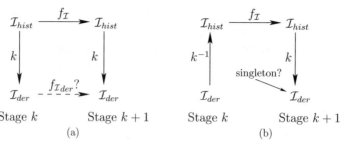

Stage k Stage $k+1$ Stage k Stage $k+1$

(a)   (b)

Figure 11.4: (a) For an I-map to be sufficient, the same result must be reached in the lower right, regardless of the path taken from the upper left. (b) The problem is that κ images may contain many histories, which eventually map to multiple derived I-states.

Whether this requirement can be met depends on the particular I-map. Another way to express the requirement is that if $\kappa(\eta_k)$ is given, then the full history η does not contain any information that could further constrain $\kappa(\eta_{k+1})$. The information provided by κ is *sufficient* for determining the next derived I-states. This is similar to the concept of a *sufficient statistic*, which arises in decision theory [91]. If the requirement is met, then κ is called a *sufficient I-map*. One peculiarity is that the sufficiency is relative to $\mathcal{I}_{der}$, as opposed to being absolute in some sense. For example, any I-map that maps onto $\mathcal{I}_{der} = \{0\}$ is sufficient because $\kappa(\eta_{k+1})$ is always known (it remains fixed at 0). Thus, the requirement for sufficiency depends strongly on the particular derived I-space.

For a sufficient I-map, a *derived information transition equation* is determined as

$$\kappa(\eta_{k+1}) = f_{\mathcal{I}_{der}}(\kappa(\eta_k), u_k, y_{k+1}). \tag{11.27}$$

The implication is that $\mathcal{I}_{der}$ is the new I-space in which the problem "lives." There is no reason for the decision maker to consider histories. This idea is crucial to the success of many planning algorithms. Sections 11.2.2 and 11.2.3 introduce nondeterministic I-spaces and probabilistic I-spaces, which are two of the most important derived I-spaces and are obtained from sufficient I-maps. The I-map κ_{stage} from Example 11.12 is also sufficient. The estimation I-map from Example 11.11 is usually not sufficient because some history is needed to provide a better estimate.

The diagram in Figure 11.4a indicates the problem of obtaining a sufficient I-map. The top of the diagram shows the history I-state transitions before the I-map was introduced. The bottom of the diagram shows the attempted derived information transition equation, $f_{\mathcal{I}_{der}}$. The requirement is that the derived I-state obtained in the lower right must be the same regardless of which path is followed from the upper left. Either $f_{\mathcal{I}}$ can be applied to η, followed by κ, or κ can be applied to η, followed by some $f_{\mathcal{I}_{der}}$. The problem with the existence of $f_{\mathcal{I}_{der}}$ is that κ is usually not invertible. The preimage $\kappa^{-1}(\eta_{der})$ of some derived I-state $\eta_{der} \in \mathcal{I}_{der}$ yields a set of histories in $\mathcal{I}_{hist}$. Applying $f_{\mathcal{I}}$ to all of these yields a set of possible next-stage history I-states. Applying κ to these may yield a set of derived I-states because of the ambiguity introduced by κ^{-1}. This chain of mappings is shown in Figure 11.4b. If a singleton is obtained under all circumstances, then this yields the required values of $f_{\mathcal{I}_{der}}$. Otherwise, new uncertainty arises about the current derived I-state. This could be handled by defining an information space over the information space, but this nastiness will be avoided here.

Since I-maps can be defined from any derived I-space to another, the concepts presented in this section do not necessarily require $\mathcal{I}_{hist}$ as the starting point. For example, an I-map,

$\kappa : \mathcal{I}_{der} \to \mathcal{I}'_{der}$, may be called *sufficient with respect to* $\mathcal{I}_{der}$ rather than with respect to $\mathcal{I}_{hist}$.

11.2.2 Nondeterministic information spaces

This section defines the I-map κ_{ndet} from Figure 11.3, which converts each history I-state into a subset of X that corresponds to all possible current states. Nature is modeled nondeterministically, which means that there is no information about what actions nature will choose, other than that they will be chosen from Θ and Ψ. Assume that the state-action sensor mapping from Section 11.1.1 is used. Consider what inferences may be drawn from a history I-state, $\eta_k = (\eta_0, \tilde{u}_{k-1}, \tilde{y}_k)$. Since the model does not involve probabilities, let η_0 represent a set $X_1 \subseteq X$. Let $\kappa_{ndet}(\eta_k)$ be the minimal subset of X in which x_k is known to lie given η_k. This subset is referred to as a *nondeterministic I-state*. To remind you that $\kappa_{ndet}(\eta_k)$ is a subset of X, it will now be denoted as $X_k(\eta_k)$. It is important that $X_k(\eta_k)$ be as small as possible while consistent with η_k.

Recall from (11.6) that for every observation y_k, a set $H(y_k) \subseteq X$ of possible values for x_k can be inferred. This could serve as a crude estimate of the nondeterministic I-state. It is certainly known that $X_k(\eta_k) \subseteq H(y_k)$; otherwise, x_k, would not be consistent with the current sensor observation. If we carefully progress from the initial conditions while applying constraints due to the state transition equation, the appropriate subset of $H(y_k)$ will be obtained.

From the state transition function f, define a set-valued function F that yields a subset of X for every $x \in X$ and $u \in U$ as

$$F(x, u) = \{x' \in X \mid \exists \theta \in \Theta(x, u) \text{ for which } x' = f(x, u, \theta)\}. \qquad (11.28)$$

Note that both F and H are set-valued functions that eliminate the direct appearance of nature actions. The effect of nature is taken into account in the set that is obtained when these functions are applied. This will be very convenient for computing the nondeterministic I-state.

An inductive process will now be described that results in computing the nondeterministic I-state, $X_k(\eta_k)$, for any stage k. The base case, $k = 1$, of the induction proceeds as

$$X_1(\eta_1) = X_1(\eta_0, y_1) = X_1 \cap H(y_1). \qquad (11.29)$$

The first part of the equation replaces η_1 with (η_0, y_1), which is a longer way to write the history I-state. There are not yet any actions in the history. The second part applies set intersection to make consistent the two pieces of information: 1) The initial state lies in X_1, which is the initial condition, and 2) the states in $H(y_1)$ are possible given the observation y_1.

Now assume inductively that $X_k(\eta_k) \subseteq X$ has been computed and the task is to compute $X_{k+1}(\eta_{k+1})$. From (11.15), $\eta_{k+1} = (\eta_k, u_k, y_{k+1})$. Thus, the only new pieces of information are that u_k was applied and y_{k+1} was observed. These will be considered one at a time.

Consider computing $X_{k+1}(\eta_k, u_k)$. If x_k was known, then after applying u_k, the state could lie anywhere within $F(x_k, u_k)$, using (11.28). Although x_k is actually not known, it is at least known that $x_k \in X_k(\eta_k)$. Therefore,

$$X_{k+1}(\eta_k, u_k) = \bigcup_{x_k \in X_k(\eta_k)} F(x_k, u_k). \qquad (11.30)$$

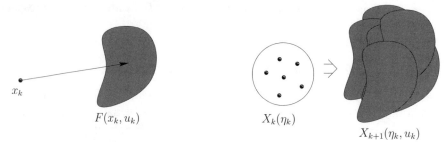

Figure 11.5: The first step in computing the nondeterministic I-state is to take the union of $F(x_k, u_k)$ over all possible $x_k \in X_k(\eta_k)$.

This can be considered as the set of all states that can be reached by starting from some state in $X_k(\eta_k)$ and applying any actions $u_k \in U$ and $\theta_k \in \Theta(x_k, u_k)$. See Figure 11.5.

The next step is to take into account the observation y_{k+1}. This information alone indicates that x_{k+1} lies in $H(y_{k+1})$. Therefore, an intersection is performed to obtain the nondeterministic I-state,

$$X_{k+1}(\eta_{k+1}) = X_{k+1}(\eta_k, u_k, y_{k+1}) = X_{k+1}(\eta_k, u_k) \cap H(y_{k+1}). \qquad (11.31)$$

Thus, it has been shown how to compute $X_{k+1}(\eta_{k+1})$ from $X_k(\eta_k)$. After starting with (11.29), the nondeterministic I-states at any stage can be computed by iterating (11.30) and (11.31) as many times as necessary.

Since the nondeterministic I-state is always a subset of X, the *nondeterministic I-space*, $\mathcal{I}_{ndet} = \text{pow}(X)$, is obtained (shown in Figure 11.3). If X is finite, then $\mathcal{I}_{ndet}$ is also finite, which was not the case with $\mathcal{I}_{hist}$ because the histories continued to grow with the number of stages. Thus, if the number of stages is unbounded or large in comparison to the size of X, then nondeterministic I-states seem preferable. It is also convenient that κ_{ndet} is a sufficient I-map, as defined in Section 11.2.1. This implies that a planning problem can be completely expressed in terms of $\mathcal{I}_{ndet}$ without maintaining the histories. The goal region, X_G, can be expressed directly as a nondeterministic I-state. In this way, the planning task is to terminate in a nondeterministic I-state, $X_k(\eta_k)$, for which $X_k(\eta_k) \subseteq X_G$.

The sufficiency of κ_{ndet} is obtained because (11.30) and (11.31) show that $X_{k+1}(\eta_{k+1})$ can be computed from $X_k(\eta_k)$, u_k, and y_{k+1}. This implies that a derived information transition equation can be formed. The nondeterministic I-space can also be treated as "just another state space." Although many history I-states may map to the same nondeterministic I-state, it has been assumed for decision-making purposes that particular history is irrelevant, once $X_k(\eta_k)$ is given.

The following example is not very interesting in itself, but it is simple enough to illustrate the concepts.

Example 11.13 (Three-State Example) Let $X = \{0, 1, 2\}$, $U = \{-1, 0, 1\}$, and $\Theta(x, u) = \{0, 1\}$ for all $x \in X$ and $u \in U$. The state transitions are given by $f(x, u, \theta) = (x + u + \theta) \mod 3$. Regarding sensing, $Y = \{0, 1, 2, 3, 4\}$ and $\Psi(x) = \{0, 1, 2\}$ for all $x \in X$. The sensor mapping is $y = h(x, \psi) = x + \psi$.

The history I-space appears very cumbersome for this example, which only involves three states. The nondeterministic I-space for this example is

$$\mathcal{I}_{ndet} = \{\emptyset, \{0\}, \{1\}, \{2\}, \{0, 1\}, \{1, 2\}, \{0, 2\}, \{0, 1, 2\}\}, \qquad (11.32)$$

which is the power set of $X = \{0, 1, 2\}$. Note, however, that the empty set, $\emptyset$, can usually be deleted from $\mathcal{I}_{ndet}$.[3] Suppose that the initial condition is $X_1 = \{0, 2\}$ and that the initial state is $x_1 = 0$. The initial state is unknown to the decision maker, but it is needed to ensure that valid observations are made in the example.

Now consider the execution over a number of stages. Suppose that the first observation is $y_1 = 2$. Based on the sensor mapping, $H(y_1) = H(2) = \{0, 1, 2\}$, which is not very helpful because $H(2) = X$. Applying (11.29) yields $X_1(\eta_1) = \{0, 2\}$. Now suppose that the decision maker applies the action $u_1 = 1$ and nature applies $\theta_1 = 1$. Using f, this yields $x_2 = 2$. The decision maker does not know θ_1 and must therefore take into account any nature action that could have been applied. It uses (11.30) to infer that

$$X_2(\eta_1, u_1) = F(2, 1) \cup F(0, 1) = \{0, 1\} \cup \{1, 2\} = \{0, 1, 2\}. \qquad (11.33)$$

Now suppose that $y_2 = 3$. From the sensor mapping, $H(3) = \{1, 2\}$. Applying (11.31) yields

$$X_2(\eta_2) = X_2(\eta_1, u_1) \cap H(y_2) = \{0, 1, 2\} \cap \{1, 2\} = \{1, 2\}. \qquad (11.34)$$

This process may be repeated for as many stages as desired. A path is generated through $\mathcal{I}_{ndet}$ by visiting a sequence of nondeterministic I-states. If the observation $y_k = 4$ is ever received, the state, x_k, becomes immediately known because $H(4) = \{2\}$. ∎

11.2.3 Probabilistic information spaces

This section defines the I-map κ_{prob} from Figure 11.3, which converts each history I-state into a probability distribution over X. A Markov, probabilistic model is assumed in the sense that the actions of nature only depend on the current state and action, as opposed to state or action histories. The set union and intersection of (11.30) and (11.31) are replaced in this section by marginalization and Bayes' rule, respectively. In a sense, these are the probabilistic equivalents of union and intersection. It will be very helpful to compare the expressions from this section to those of Section 11.2.2.

Rather than write $\kappa_{prob}(\eta)$, standard probability notation will be applied to obtain $P(x|\eta)$. Most expressions in this section of the form $P(x_k|\cdot)$ have an analogous expression in Section 11.2.2 of the form $X_k(\cdot)$. It is helpful to recognize the similarities.

The first step is to construct probabilistic versions of H and F. These are $P(x_k|y_k)$ and $P(x_{k+1}|x_k, u_k)$, respectively. The latter term was given in Section 10.1.1. To obtain $P(x_k|y_k)$, recall from Section 11.1.1 that $P(y_k|x_k)$ is easily derived from $P(\psi_k|x_k)$. To obtain $P(x_k|y_k)$, Bayes' rule is applied:

$$P(x_k|y_k) = \frac{P(y_k|x_k)P(x_k)}{P(y_k)} = \frac{P(y_k|x_k)P(x_k)}{\displaystyle\sum_{x_k \in X} P(y_k|x_k)P(x_k)}. \qquad (11.35)$$

In the last step, $P(y_k)$ was rewritten using marginalization, (9.8). In this case x_k appears as the sum index; therefore, the denominator is only a function of y_k, as required. Bayes' rule requires knowing the prior, $P(x_k)$. In the coming expressions, this will be replaced by a probabilistic I-state.

---

[3] One notable exception is in the theory of nondeterministic finite automata, in which it is possible that all copies of the machine die and there is no possible current state [892].

Now consider defining probabilistic I-states. Each is a probability distribution over X and is written as $P(x_k|\eta_k)$. The initial condition produces $P(x_1)$. As for the nondeterministic case, probabilistic I-states can be computed inductively. For the base case, the only new piece of information is y_1. Thus, the probabilistic I-state, $P(x_1|\eta_1)$, is $P(x_1|y_1)$. This is computed by letting $k = 1$ in (11.35) to yield

$$P(x_1|\eta_1) = P(x_1|y_1) = \frac{P(y_1|x_1)P(x_1)}{\sum_{x_1 \in X} P(y_1|x_1)P(x_1)}. \tag{11.36}$$

Now consider the inductive step by assuming that $P(x_k|\eta_k)$ is given. The task is to determine $P(x_{k+1}|\eta_{k+1})$, which is equivalent to $P(x_{k+1}|\eta_k, u_k, y_{k+1})$. As in Section 11.2.2, this will proceed in two parts by first considering the effect of u_k, followed by y_{k+1}. The first step is to determine $P(x_{k+1}|\eta_k, u_k)$ from $P(x_k|\eta_k)$. First, note that

$$P(x_{k+1}|\eta_k, x_k, u_k) = P(x_{k+1}|x_k, u_k) \tag{11.37}$$

because η_k contains no additional information regarding the prediction of x_{k+1} once x_k is given. Marginalization, (9.8), can be used to eliminate x_k from $P(x_{k+1}|x_k, u_k)$. This must be eliminated because it is not given. Putting these steps together yields

$$\begin{aligned}
P(x_{k+1}|\eta_k, u_k) &= \sum_{x_k \in X} P(x_{k+1}|x_k, u_k, \eta_k)P(x_k|\eta_k) \\
&= \sum_{x_k \in X} P(x_{k+1}|x_k, u_k)P(x_k|\eta_k),
\end{aligned} \tag{11.38}$$

which expresses $P(x_{k+1}|\eta_k, u_k)$ in terms of given quantities. Equation (11.38) can be considered as the probabilistic counterpart of (11.30).

The next step is to take into account the observation y_{k+1}. This is accomplished by making a version of (11.35) that is conditioned on the information accumulated so far: η_k and u_k. Also, k is replaced with $k + 1$. The result is

$$P(x_{k+1}|y_{k+1}, \eta_k, u_k) = \frac{P(y_{k+1}|x_{k+1}, \eta_k, u_k)P(x_{k+1}|\eta_k, u_k)}{\sum_{x_{k+1} \in X} P(y_{k+1}|x_{k+1}, \eta_k, u_k)P(x_{k+1}|\eta_k, u_k)}. \tag{11.39}$$

This can be considered as the probabilistic counterpart of (11.31). The left side of (11.39) is equivalent to $P(x_{k+1}|\eta_{k+1})$, which is the probabilistic I-state for stage $k + 1$, as desired. There are two different kinds of terms on the right. The expression for $P(x_{k+1}|\eta_k, u_k)$ is given in (11.38). Therefore, the only remaining term to calculate is $P(y_{k+1}|x_{k+1}, \eta_k, u_k)$. Note that

$$P(y_{k+1}|x_{k+1}, \eta_k, u_k) = P(y_{k+1}|x_{k+1}) \tag{11.40}$$

because the sensor mapping depends only on the state (and the probability model for the nature sensing action, which also depends only on the state). Since $P(y_{k+1}|x_{k+1})$ is specified as part of the sensor model, we have now determined how to obtain $P(x_{k+1}|\eta_{k+1})$ from $P(x_k|\eta_k)$, u_k, and y_{k+1}. Thus, $\mathcal{I}_{prob}$ is another I-space that can be treated as just another state space.

The probabilistic I-space $\mathcal{I}_{prob}$ (shown in Figure 11.3) is the set of all probability distributions over X. The update expressions, (11.38) and (11.39), establish that the I-map κ_{prob} is sufficient, which means that the planning problem can be expressed entirely in terms of $\mathcal{I}_{prob}$, instead of maintaining histories. A goal region can be specified as

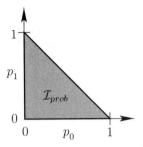

Figure 11.6: The probabilistic I-space for the three-state example is a 2-simplex embedded in $\mathbb{R}^3$. This simplex can be projected into $\mathbb{R}^2$ to yield the depicted triangular region in $\mathbb{R}^2$.

constraints on the probabilities. For example, from some particular $x \in X$, the goal might be to reach any probabilistic I-state for which $P(x_k|\eta_k) > 1/2$.

Example 11.14 (Three-State Example Revisited) Now return to Example 11.13, but this time use probabilistic models. For a probabilistic I-state, let p_i denote the probability that the current state is $i \in X$. Any probabilistic I-state can be expressed as $(p_0, p_1, p_2) \in \mathbb{R}^3$. This implies that the I-space can be nicely embedded in $\mathbb{R}^3$. By the axioms of probability (given in Section 9.1.2), $p_0 + p_1 + p_2 = 1$, which can be interpreted as a plane equation in $\mathbb{R}^3$ that restricts $\mathcal{I}_{prob}$ to a 2D set. Also following the axioms of probability, for each $i \in \{0, 1, 2\}$, $0 \leq p_i \leq 1$. This means that $\mathcal{I}_{prob}$ is restricted to a triangular region in $\mathbb{R}^3$. The vertices of this triangular region are $(0, 0, 1)$, $(0, 1, 0)$, and $(1, 0, 0)$; these correspond to the three different ways to have perfect state information. In a sense, the distance away from these points corresponds to the amount of uncertainty in the state. The uniform probability distribution $(1/3, 1/3, 1/3)$ is equidistant from the three vertices. A projection of the triangular region into $\mathbb{R}^2$ is shown in Figure 11.6. The interpretation in this case is that p_1 and p_2 specify a point in $\mathbb{R}^2$, and p_3 is automatically determined from $p_3 = 1 - p_1 - p_2$.

The triangular region in $\mathbb{R}^3$ is an uncountably infinite set, even though the history I-space is countably infinite for a fixed initial condition. This may seem strange, but there is no mistake because for a fixed initial condition, it is generally impossible to reach all of the points in $\mathcal{I}_{prob}$. If the initial condition can be any point in $\mathcal{I}_{prob}$, then all of the probabilistic I-space is covered because $\mathcal{I}_0 = \mathcal{I}_{prob}$, in which $\mathcal{I}_0$ is the initial condition space. ∎

11.2.4 Limited-memory information spaces

Limiting the amount of memory provides one way to reduce the sizes of history I-states. Except in special cases, this usually does not preserve the feasibility or optimality of the original problem. Nevertheless, such I-maps are very useful in practice when there appears to be no other way to reduce the size of the I-space. Furthermore, they occasionally do preserve the desired properties of feasibility, and sometimes even optimality.

Previous i stages

Under this model, the history I-state is truncated. Any actions or observations received earlier than i stages ago are dropped from memory. An I-map, κ_i, is defined as

$$\kappa_i(\eta_k) = (u_{k-i}, \ldots, u_{k-1}, y_{k-i+1}, \ldots, y_k), \tag{11.41}$$

for any integer $i > 0$ and $k > i$. If $i \leq k$, then the derived I-state is the full history I-state, (11.14). The advantage of this approach, if it leads to a solution, is that the length of the I-state no longer grows with the number of stages. If X and U are finite, then the derived I-space is also finite. Note that κ_i is sufficient in the sense defined in Section 11.2.1 because enough history is passed from stage to stage to determine the derived I-states.

Sensor feedback

An interesting I-map is obtained by removing all but the last sensor observation from the history I-state. This yields an I-map, $\kappa_{sf} : \mathcal{I}_{hist} \rightarrow Y$, which is defined as $\kappa(\eta_k) = y_k$. The model is referred to as *sensor feedback*. In this case, all decisions are made directly in terms of the current sensor observation. The derived I-space is Y, and a plan on the derived I-space is $\pi : Y \rightarrow U$, which is called a *sensor-feedback plan*. In some literature, this may be referred to as a purely *reactive plan*. Many problems for which solutions exist in the history I-space cannot be solved using sensor feedback. Neglecting history prevents the complicated deductions that are often needed regarding the state. In some sense, sensor feedback causes short-sightedness that could unavoidably lead to repeating the same mistakes indefinitely. However, it may be worth determining whether such a sensor-feedback solution plan exists for some particular problem. Such plans tend to be simpler to implement in practice because the actions can be connected directly to the sensor output. Certainly, if a sensor-feedback solution plan exists for a problem, and feasibility is the only concern, then it is pointless to design and implement a plan in terms of the history I-space or some larger derived I-space. Note that this I-map is sufficient, even though it ignores the entire history.

11.3 Examples for discrete state spaces

11.3.1 Basic nondeterministic examples

First, we consider a simple example that uses the sign sensor of Example 11.3.

Example 11.15 (Using the Sign Sensor) This example is similar to Example 10.1, except that it involves sensing uncertainty instead of prediction uncertainty. Let $X = \mathbb{Z}$, $U = \{-1, 1, u_T\}$, $Y = \{-1, 0, 1\}$, and $y = h(x) = \text{sgn} x$. For the state transition equation, $x_{k+1} = f(x_k, u_k) = x_k + u_k$. No nature actions interfere with the state transition equation or the sensor mapping. Therefore, future history I-states are predictable. The information transition equation is $\eta_{k+1} = f_{\mathcal{I}}(\eta_k, u_k)$. Suppose that initially, $\eta_0 = X$, which means that any initial state is possible. The goal is to terminate at $0 \in X$.

The general expression for a history I-state at stage k is

$$\eta_k = (X, u_1, \ldots, u_{k-1}, y_1, \ldots, y_k). \tag{11.42}$$

A possible I-state is $\eta_5 = (X, -1, 1, 1, -1, 1, 1, 1, 1, 0)$. Using the nondeterministic I-space from Section 11.2.2, $\mathcal{I}_{ndet} = \text{pow}(X)$, which is uncountably infinite. By looking carefully at the problem, however, it can be seen that most of the nondeterministic I-states are not reachable. If $y_k = 0$, it is known that $x_k = 0$; hence, $X_k(\eta_k) = \{0\}$. If $y_k = 1$, it will always be the case that $X_k(\eta_k) = \{1, 2, \ldots\}$. If $y_k = -1$, then $X_k(\eta_k) = \{\ldots, -2, -1\}$. From this a plan, π, can be specified over the three nondeterministic I-states mentioned above. For the first one, $\pi(X_k(\eta_k)) = u_T$. For the other two, $\pi(X_k(\eta_k)) = -1$ and $\pi(X_k(\eta_k)) = 1$, respectively. Based on the sign, the plan tries to move toward 0. If different initial conditions are allowed, then more nondeterministic I-states can be reached, but this was not required as the problem was defined. Note that optimal-length solutions are produced by the plan.

The solution can even be implemented with sensor feedback because the action depends only on the current sensor value. Let $\pi : Y \to U$ be defined as

$$\pi(y) = \begin{cases} -1 & \text{if } y = 1 \\ 1 & \text{if } y = -1 \\ u_T & \text{if } y = 0. \end{cases} \tag{11.43}$$

This provides dramatic memory savings over defining a plan on $\mathcal{I}_{hist}$.   ■

The next example provides a simple illustration of solving a problem without ever knowing the current state. This leads to the *goal recognizability* problem [662] (see Section 12.5.1).

Example 11.16 (Goal Recognizability)   Let $X = \mathbb{Z}$, $U = \{-1, 1, u_T\}$, and $Y = \mathbb{Z}$. For the state transition equation, $x_{k+1} = f(x_k, u_k) = x_k + u_k$. Now suppose that a variant of Example 11.7 is used to model sensing: $y = h(x, \psi) = x + \psi$ and $\Psi = \{-5, -4, \dots, 5\}$. Suppose that once again, $\eta_0 = X$. In this case, it is impossible to guarantee that a goal, $X_G = \{0\}$, is reached because of the goal recognizability problem. The disturbance in the sensor mapping does not allow precise enough state measurements to deduce the precise achievement of the state. If the goal region, X_G, is enlarged to $\{-5, -4, \dots, 5\}$, then the problem can be solved. Due to the disturbance, the nondeterministic I-state is always a subset of a consecutive sequence of 11 states. It is simple to derive a plan that moves this interval until the nondeterministic I-state becomes a subset of X_G. When this occurs, then the plan applies u_T. In solving this problem, the exact state never had to be known.   ■

The problem shown in Figure 11.7 serves two purposes. First, it is an example of *sensorless planning* [323, 396], which means that there are no observations (see Sections 11.5.4 and 12.5.2). This is an interesting class of problems because it appears that no information can be gained regarding the state. Contrary to intuition, it turns out for this example and many others that plans can be designed that estimate the state. The second purpose is to illustrate how the I-space can be dramatically collapsed using the I-map concepts of Section 11.2.1. The standard nondeterministic I-space for this example contains 2^{19} I-states, but it can be mapped to a much smaller derived I-space that contains only a few elements.

Example 11.17 (Moving in an L-Shaped Corridor)   The state space X for the example shown in Figure 11.7 has 19 states, each of which corresponds to a location on one of the white tiles. For convenience, let each state be denoted by (i, j). There are 10 *bottom states*, denoted by $(1, 1), (2, 1), \dots, (10, 1)$, and 10 *left states*, denoted by $(1, 1), (1, 2), \dots, (1, 10)$. Since $(1, 1)$ is both a bottom state and a left state, it is called the *corner state*.

There are no sensor observations for this problem. However, nature interferes with the state transitions, which leads to a form of nondeterministic uncertainty. If an action is applied that tries to take one step, nature may cause two or three steps to be taken. This can be modeled as follows. Let

$$U = \{(1, 0), (-1, 0), (0, 1), (0, -1)\} \tag{11.44}$$

and let $\Theta = \{1, 2, 3\}$. The state transition equation is defined as $f(x, u, \theta) = x + \theta u$ whenever such motion is not blocked (by hitting a dead end). For example, if $x = (5, 1)$,

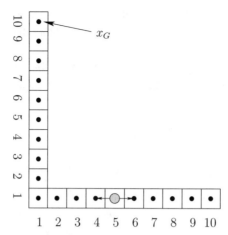

Figure 11.7: An example that involves 19 states. There are no sensor observations; however, actions can be chosen that enable the state to be estimated. The example provides an illustration of reducing the I-space via I-maps.

$u = (-1, 0)$, and $\theta = 2$, then the resulting next state is $(5, 1) + 2(-1, 0) = (3, 1)$. If blocking is possible, the state changes as much as possible until it becomes blocked. Due to blocking, it is even possible that $f(x, u, \theta) = x$.

Since there are no sensor observations, the history I-state at stage k is

$$\eta_k = (\eta_0, u_1, \ldots, u_{k-1}). \tag{11.45}$$

Now use the nondeterministic I-space, $\mathcal{I}_{ndet} = \text{pow}(X)$. The initial state, $x_1 = (10, 1)$, is given, which means that the initial I-state, η_0, is $\{(10, 1)\}$. The goal is to arrive at the I-state, $\{(1, 10)\}$, which means that the task is to design a plan that moves from the lower right to the upper left.

With perfect information, this would be trivial; however, without sensors the uncertainty may grow very quickly. For example, after applying the action $u_1 = (-1, 0)$ from the initial state, the nondeterministic I-state becomes $\{(7, 1), (8, 1), (9, 1)\}$. After $u_2 = (-1, 0)$ it becomes $\{(4, 1), \ldots, (8, 1)\}$. A nice feature of this problem, however, is that uncertainty can be reduced without sensing. Suppose that for 100 stages, we repeatedly apply $u_k = (-1, 0)$. What is the resulting I-state? As the corner state is approached, the uncertainty is reduced because the state cannot be further changed by nature. It is known that each action, $u_k = (-1, 0)$, decreases the X coordinate by at least one each time. Therefore, after nine or more stages, it is known that $\eta_k = \{(1, 1)\}$. Once this is known, then the action $(0, 1)$ can be applied. This will again increase uncertainty as the state moves through the set of left states. If $(0, 1)$ is applied nine or more times, then it is known for certain that $x_k = (1, 10)$, which is the required goal state.

A successful plan has now been obtained: 1) Apply $(-1, 0)$ for nine stages, 2) then apply $(0, 1)$ for nine stages. This plan could be defined over $\mathcal{I}_{ndet}$; however, it is simpler to use the I-map κ_{stage} from Example 11.12 to define a plan as $\pi : \mathbb{N} \to U$. For k such that $1 \le k \le 9$, $\pi(k) = (-1, 0)$. For k such that $10 \le k \le 18$, $\pi(k) = (0, 1)$. For $k > 18$, $\pi(k) = u_T$. Note that the plan works even if the initial condition is any subset of X. From this point onward, assume that any subset may be given as the initial condition.

Some alternative plans will now be considered by making other derived I-spaces from $\mathcal{I}_{ndet}$. Let κ_3 be an I-map from $\mathcal{I}_{ndet}$ to a set $\mathcal{I}_3$ of three derived I-states. Let $\mathcal{I}_3 = \{g, l, a\}$,

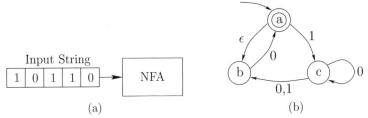

Figure 11.8: (a) An nondeterministic finite automaton (NFA) is a state machine that reads an input string and decides whether to accept it. (b) A graphical depiction of an NFA.

in which g denotes "goal," l denotes "left," and a denotes "any." The I-map, κ_3, is

$$X(\eta) = \begin{cases} g & \text{if } X(\eta) = \{(1, 10)\} \\ l & \text{if } X(\eta) \text{ is a subset of the set of left states} \\ a & \text{otherwise.} \end{cases} \quad (11.46)$$

Based on the successful plan described so far, a solution on $\mathcal{I}_3$ is defined as $\pi(g) = u_T$, $\pi(l) = (0, 1)$, and $\pi(a) = (-1, 0)$. This plan is simpler to represent than the one on $\mathbb{N}$; however, there is one drawback. The I-map κ_3 is not sufficient. This implies that more of the nondeterministic I-state needs to be maintained during execution. Otherwise, there is no way to know when certain transitions occur. For example, if $(-1, 0)$ is applied from a, how can the robot determine whether l or a is reached in the next stage? This can be easily determined from the nondeterministic I-state.

To address this problem, consider a new I-map, $\kappa_{19} : \mathcal{I}_{ndet} \to \mathcal{I}_{19}$, which is sufficient. There are 19 derived I-states, which include g as defined previously, l_j for $1 \leq j \leq 9$, and a_i for $2 \leq i \leq 10$. The I-map is defined as $\kappa_{19}(X(\eta)) = g$ if $X(\eta) = \{(1, 10)\}$. Otherwise, $\kappa_{19}(X(\eta)) = l_i$ for the smallest value of i such that $X(\eta)$ is a subset of $\{(1, i), \dots, (1, 10)\}$. If there is no such value for i, then $\kappa_{19}(X(\eta)) = a_i$, for the smallest value of i such that $X(\eta)$ is a subset of $\{(1, 1), \dots, (1, 10), (2, 1), \dots, (i, 1)\}$. Now the plan is defined as $\pi(g) = u_T$, $\pi(l_i) = (0, 1)$, and $\pi(a_i) = (-1, 0)$. Although the plan is larger, the robot does not need to represent the full nondeterministic I-state during execution. The correct transitions occur. For example, if $u_k = (-1, 0)$ is applied at a_5, then a_4 is obtained. If $u = (-1, 0)$ is applied at a_2, then l_1 is obtained. From there, $u = (0, 1)$ is applied to yield l_2. These actions can be repeated until eventually l_9 and g are reached. The resulting plan, however, is not an improvement over the original open-loop one. ∎

11.3.2 Nondeterministic finite automata

An interesting connection lies between the ideas of this chapter and the theory of finite automata, which is part of the theory of computation (see [465, 892]). In Section 2.1, it was mentioned that determining whether there exists some string that is accepted by a DFA is equivalent to a discrete feasible planning problem. If unpredictability is introduced into the model, then a *nondeterministic finite automaton* (NFA) is obtained, as depicted in Figure 11.8. This represents one of the simplest examples of nondeterminism in theoretical computer science. Such nondeterministic models serve as a powerful tool for defining models of computation and their associated complexity classes. It turns out that these models give rise to interesting examples of information spaces.

An NFA is typically described using a directed graph as shown in Figure 11.8b, and is considered as a special kind of finite state machine. Each vertex of the graph represents a state, and edges represent possible transitions. An *input string* of finite length is read by the machine. Typically, the input string is a binary sequence of 0's and 1's. The initial state is designated by an inward arrow that has no source vertex, as shown pointing into state a in Figure 11.8b. The machine starts in this state and reads the first symbol of the input string. Based on its value, it makes appropriate transitions. For a DFA, the next state must be specified for each of the two inputs 0 and 1 from each state. From a state in an NFA, there may be any number of outgoing edges (including zero) that represent the response to a single symbol. For example, there are two outgoing edges if 0 is read from state c (the arrow from c to b actually corresponds to two directed edges, one for 0 and the other for 1). There are also edges designated with a special ϵ symbol. If a state has an outgoing ϵ, the state may immediately transition along the edge without reading another symbol. This may be iterated any number of times, for any outgoing ϵ edges that may be encountered, without reading the next input symbol. The nondeterminism arises from the fact that there are multiple choices for possible next states due to multiple edges for the same input and ϵ transitions. There is no sensor that indicates which state is actually chosen.

The interpretation often given in the theory of computation is that when there are multiple choices, the machine clones itself and one copy runs each choice. It is like having multiple universes in which each different possible action of nature is occurring simultaneously. If there are no outgoing edges for a certain combination of state and input, then the clone dies. Any states that are depicted with a double boundary, such as state a in Figure 11.8, are called *accept states*. When the input string ends, the NFA is said to *accept* the input string if there exists at least one alternate universe in which the final machine state is an accept state.

The formulation usually given for NFAs seems very close to Formulation 2.1 for discrete feasible planning. Here is a typical NFA formulation [892], which formalizes the ideas depicted in Figure 11.8:

Formulation 11.2 (Nondeterministic Finite Automaton)

1. A finite state space X.
2. A finite *alphabet* Σ which represents the possible input symbols. Let $\Sigma_\epsilon = \Sigma \cup \{\epsilon\}$.
3. A *transition function*, $\delta : X \times \Sigma_\epsilon \to \text{pow}(X)$. For each state and symbol, a set of outgoing edges is specified by indicating the states that are reached.
4. A *start state* $x_0 \in X$.
5. A set $A \subseteq X$ of *accept states*.

Example 11.18 (Three-State NFA) The example in Figure 11.8 can be expressed using Formulation 11.2. The components are $X = \{a, b, c\}$, $\Sigma = \{0, 1\}$, $\Sigma_\epsilon = \{0, 1, \epsilon\}$, $x_0 = a$, and $A = \{a\}$. The state transition equation requires the specification of a state for every $x \in X$ and symbol in Σ_ϵ:

$$
\begin{array}{c|ccc}
 & 0 & 1 & \epsilon \\
\hline
a & \emptyset & \{c\} & \{b\} \\
b & \{a\} & \emptyset & \emptyset \\
c & \{b, c\} & \{b\} & \emptyset .
\end{array}
\tag{11.47}
$$

Now consider reformulating the NFA and its acceptance of strings as a kind of planning problem. An input string can be considered as a plan that uses no form of feedback; it is a fixed sequence of actions. The feasible planning problem is to determine whether any string exists that is accepted by the NFA. Since there is no feedback, there is no sensing model. The initial state is known, but subsequent states cannot be measured. The history I-state η_k at stage k reduces to $\eta_k = \tilde{u}_{k-1} = (u_1, \ldots, u_{k-1})$, the action history. The nondeterminism can be accounted for by defining nature actions that interfere with the state transitions. This results in the following formulation, which is described in terms of Formulation 11.2.

Formulation 11.3 (An NFA Planning Problem)

1. A finite state space X.
2. An action space $U = \Sigma \cup \{u_T\}$.
3. A *state transition function*, $F : X \times U \to \mathrm{pow}(X)$. For each state and symbol, a set of outgoing edges is specified by indicating the states that are reached.
4. An *initial state* $x_0 = x_1$.
5. A set $X_G = A$ of *goal states*.

The history I-space $\mathcal{I}_{hist}$ is defined using

$$\mathcal{I}_k = \tilde{U}_{k-1} \tag{11.48}$$

for each $k \in \mathbb{N}$ and taking the union as defined in (11.19). Assume that the initial state of the NFA is always fixed; therefore, it does not appear in the definition of $\mathcal{I}_{hist}$.

For expressing the planning task, it is best to use the nondeterministic I-space $\mathcal{I}_{ndet} = \mathrm{pow}(X)$ from Section 11.2.2. Thus, each nondeterministic I-state, $X(\eta) \in \mathcal{I}_{ndet}$, is the subset of X that corresponds to the possible current states of the machine. The initial condition could be any subset of X because ϵ transitions can occur from x_1. Subsequent nondeterministic I-states follow directly from F. The task is to compute a plan of the form

$$\pi = (u_1, u_2, \ldots, u_K, u_T), \tag{11.49}$$

which results in $X_{K+1}(\eta_{K+1}) \in \mathcal{I}_{ndet}$ with $X_{K+1}(\eta_{K+1}) \cap X_G \neq \emptyset$. This means that at least one possible state of the NFA must lie in X_G after the termination action is applied. This condition is much weaker than a typical planning requirement. Using worst-case analysis, a typical requirement would instead be that *every* possible NFA state lies in X_G.

The problem given in Formulation 11.3 is not precisely a specialization of Formulation 11.1 because of the state transition function. For convenience, F was directly defined, instead of explicitly requiring that f be defined in terms of nature actions, $\Theta(x, u)$, which in this context depend on both x and u for an NFA. There is one other small issue regarding this formulation. In the planning problems considered in this book, it is always assumed that there is a current state. For an NFA, it was already mentioned that if there are no outgoing edges for a certain input, then the clone of the machine dies. This means that potential current states cease to exist. It is even possible that every clone dies, which leaves no current state for the machine. This can be easily enabled by directly defining F; however, planning problems must always have a current state. To resolve this issue, we could augment X in Formulation 11.3 to include an extra *dead* state, which signifies the death of a clone when there are no outgoing edges. A dead state can never lie in X_G, and once a transition to a dead state occurs, the state remains dead for all time. In this section, the state space will not be augmented in this way; however, it is important to note that the NFA formulation can easily be made consistent with Formulation 11.3.

The planning model can now be compared to the standard use of NFAs in the theory of computation. A *language* of an NFA is defined to be the set of all input strings that it accepts. The planning problem formulated here determines whether there exists a string (which is a plan that ends with termination actions) that is accepted by the NFA. Equivalently, a planning algorithm determines whether the language of an NFA is empty. Constructing the set of all successful plans is equivalent to determining the language of the NFA.

Example 11.19 (Planning for the Three-State NFA)   The example in Figure 11.8 can be expressed using Formulation 11.2. The components are $X = \{a, b, c\}$, $\Sigma = \{0, 1\}$, $\Sigma_\epsilon = \{0, 1, \epsilon\}$, $x_0 = a$, and $F = \{a\}$. The function $F(x, u)$ is defined as

$$
\begin{array}{c|cc}
 & 0 & 1 \\
\hline
a & \emptyset & \{c\} \\
b & \{a, b\} & \emptyset \\
c & \{b, c\} & \{b\}.
\end{array}
\tag{11.50}
$$

The nondeterministic I-space is

$$X(\eta) = \{\emptyset, \{a\}, \{b\}, \{c\}, \{a, b\}, \{a, c\}, \{b, c\}, \{a, b, c\}\}, \tag{11.51}$$

in which the initial condition is $\eta_0 = \{a, b\}$ because an ϵ transition occurs immediately from a. An example plan that solves the problem is $(1, 0, 0, u_T, \dots)$. This corresponds to sending an input string "100" through the NFA depicted in Figure 11.8. The sequence of nondeterministic I-states obtained during the execution of the plan is

$$\{a, b\} \xrightarrow{1} \{c\} \xrightarrow{0} \{b, c\} \xrightarrow{0} \{a, b, c\} \xrightarrow{u_T} \{a, b, c\}. \tag{11.52}$$

■

A basic theorem from the theory of finite automata states that for the set of strings accepted by an NFA, there exists a DFA (deterministic) that accepts the same set [892]. This is proved by constructing a DFA directly from the nondeterministic I-space. Each nondeterministic I-state can be considered as a state of a DFA. Thus, the DFA has 2^n states, if the original NFA has n states. The state transitions of the DFA are derived directly from the transitions between nondeterministic I-states. When an input (or action) is given, then a transition occurs from one subset of X to another. A transition is made between the two corresponding states in the DFA. This construction is an interesting example of how the I-space is a new state space that arises when the states of the original state space are unknown. Even though the I-space is usually larger than the original state space, its states are always known. Therefore, the behavior appears the same as in the case of perfect state information. This idea is very general and may be applied to many problems beyond DFAs and NFAs; see Section 12.1.2

11.3.3 The probabilistic case: POMDPs

Example 11.14 generalizes nicely to the case of n states. In operations research and artificial intelligence literature, these are generally referred to as *partially observable*

Markov decision processes or *POMDPs* (pronounced "pom dee peez"). For the case of three states, the probabilistic I-space, $\mathcal{I}_{prob}$, is a 2-simplex embedded in $\mathbb{R}^3$. In general, if $|X| = n$, then $\mathcal{I}_{prob}$ is an $(n-1)$-simplex embedded in $\mathbb{R}^n$. The coordinates of a point are expressed as $(p_0, p_1, \ldots, p_{n-1}) \in \mathbb{R}^n$. By the axioms of probability, $p_0 + \cdots + p_{n-1} = 1$, which implies that $\mathcal{I}_{prob}$ is an $(n-1)$-dimensional subspace of $\mathbb{R}^n$. The vertices of the simplex correspond to the n cases in which the state is known; hence, their coordinates are $(0, 0, \ldots, 0, 1)$, $(0, 0, \ldots, 0, 1, 0)$, $\ldots$, $(1, 0, \ldots, 0)$. For convenience, the simplex can be projected into $\mathbb{R}^{n-1}$ by specifying a point in $\mathbb{R}^{n-1}$ for which $p_1 + \cdots + p_{n-2} \leq 1$ and then choosing the final coordinate as $p_{n-1} = 1 - p_1 + \cdots + p_{n-2}$. Section 12.1.3 presents algorithms for planning for POMDPs.

11.4 Continuous state spaces

This section takes many of the concepts that have been developed in Sections 11.1 and 11.2 and generalizes them to continuous state spaces. This represents an important generalization because the configuration space concepts, on which motion planning was defined in Part II, are all based on continuous state spaces. In this section, the state space might be a configuration space, $X = \mathcal{C}$, as defined in Chapter 4 or any other continuous state space. Since it may be a configuration space, many interesting problems can be drawn from robotics.

During the presentation of the concepts of this section, it will be helpful to recall analogous concepts that were already developed for discrete state spaces. In many cases, the formulations appear identical. In others, the continuous case is more complicated, but it usually maintains some of the properties from the discrete case. It will be seen after introducing continuous sensing models in Section 11.5.1 that some problems formulated in continuous spaces are even more elegant and easy to understand than their discrete counterparts.

11.4.1 Discrete-stage information spaces

Assume here that there are discrete stages. Let $X \subseteq \mathbb{R}^m$ be an n-dimensional manifold for $n \leq m$ called the *state space*.[4] Let $Y \subseteq \mathbb{R}^m$ be an n_y-dimensional manifold for $n_y \leq m$ called the *observation space*. For each $x \in X$, let $\Psi(x) \subseteq \mathbb{R}^m$ be an n_n-dimensional manifold for $n_n \leq m$ called the set of *nature sensing actions*. The three kinds of sensors mappings, h, defined in Section 11.1.1 are possible, to yield either a *state mapping*, $y = h(x)$, a *state-nature mapping* $y = h(x, \psi)$, or a *history-based*, $y = h_k(x_1, \ldots, x_k, y)$. For the case of a state mapping, the preimages, $H(y)$, once again induce a partition of X. Preimages can also be defined for state-action mappings, but they do not necessarily induce a partition of X.

Many interesting sensing models can be formulated in continuous state spaces. Section 11.5.1 provides a kind of sensor catalog. There is once again the choice of nondeterministic or probabilistic uncertainty if nature sensing actions are used. If nondeterministic uncertainty is used, the expressions are the same as the discrete case. Probabilistic models

---

[4] If you did not read Chapter 4 and are not familiar with manifold concepts, then assume $X = \mathbb{R}^n$; it will not make much difference. Make similar assumptions for Y, $\Psi(x)$, U, and $\Theta(x, u)$.

are defined in terms of a probability density function, $p : \Psi \rightarrow [0, \infty)$,[5] in which $p(\psi)$ denotes the continuous-time replacement for $P(\psi)$. The model can also be expressed as $p(y|x)$, in that same manner that $P(y|x)$ was obtained for discrete state spaces.

The usual three choices exist for the initial conditions: 1) Either $x_1 \in X$ is given; 2) a subset $X_1 \in X$ is given; or 3) a probability density function, $p(x)$, is given. The initial condition spaces in the last two cases can be enormous. For example, if $X = [0, 1]$ and any subset is possible as an initial condition, then $\mathcal{I}_0 = \text{pow}(\mathbb{R})$, which has higher cardinality than $\mathbb{R}$. If any probability density function is possible, then $\mathcal{I}_0$ is a space of functions.[6]

The I-space definitions from Section 11.1.2 remain the same, with the understanding that all of the variables are continuous. Thus, (11.17) and (11.19) serve as the definitions of $\mathcal{I}_k$ and $\mathcal{I}$. Let $U \subseteq \mathbb{R}^m$ be an n_u-dimensional manifold for $n_u \leq m$. For each $x \in X$ and $u \in U$, let $\Theta(x, u)$ be an n_θ-dimensional manifold for $n_\theta \leq m$. A discrete-stage I-space planning problem over continuous state spaces can be easily formulated by replacing each discrete variable in Formulation 11.1 by its continuous counterpart that uses the same notation. Therefore, the full formulation is not given.

11.4.2 Continuous-time information spaces

Now assume that there is a continuum of stages. Most of the components of Section 11.4.1 remain the same. The spaces X, Y, $\Psi(x)$, U, and $\Theta(x, u)$ remain the same. The sensor mapping also remains the same. The main difference occurs in the state transition equation because the effect of nature must be expressed in terms of velocities. This was already introduced in Section 10.6. In that context, there was only uncertainty in predictability. In the current context there may be uncertainties in both predictability and in sensing the current state.

For the discrete-stage case, the history I-states were based on action and observation sequences. For the continuous-time case, the history instead becomes a function of time. As defined in Section 7.1.1, let T denote a *time interval*, which may be bounded or unbounded. Let $\tilde{y}_t : [0, t] \rightarrow Y$ be called the *observation history* up to time $t \in T$. Similarly, let $\tilde{u}_t : [0, t) \rightarrow U$ and $\tilde{x}_t : [0, t] \rightarrow X$ be called the *action history* and *state history*, respectively, up to time $t \in T$.

Thus, the three kinds of sensor mappings in the continuous-time case are as follows:

1. A *state-sensor mapping* is expressed as $y(t) = h(x(t))$, in which $x(t)$ and $y(t)$ are the state and observation, respectively, at time $t \in T$.

2. A *state-nature mapping* is expressed as $y(t) = h(x(t), \psi(t))$, which implies that nature chooses some $\psi(t) \in \Psi(x(t))$ for each $t \in T$.

3. A *history-based sensor mapping*, which could depend on all of the states obtained so far. Thus, it depends on the entire function $\tilde{x}_t$. This could be denoted as $y(t) = h(\tilde{x}_t, \psi(t))$ if nature can also interfere with the observation.

---

[5] Assume that all continuous spaces are measure spaces and all probability density functions are measurable functions over these spaces.

[6] To appreciate of the size of this space, it can generally be viewed as an infinite-dimensional vector space (recall Example 8.5). Consider, for example, representing each function with a series expansion. To represent any analytic function exactly over [0, 1], an infinite sequence of real-valued coefficients may be needed. Each sequence can be considered as an infinitely long vector, and the set of all such sequences forms an infinite-dimensional vector space. See [348, 839] for more background on function spaces and functional analysis.

If $\tilde{u}_t$ and $\tilde{y}_t$ are combined with the initial condition η_0, the *history I-state at time t* is obtained as

$$\eta_t = (\eta_0, \tilde{u}_t, \tilde{y}_t). \tag{11.53}$$

The *history I-space at time t* is the set of all possible η_t and is denoted as $\mathcal{I}_t$. Note that $\mathcal{I}_t$ is a space of functions because each $\eta_t \in \mathcal{I}_t$ is a function of time. Recall that in the discrete-stage case, every $\mathcal{I}_k$ was combined into a single history I-space, $\mathcal{I}_{hist}$, using (11.18) or (11.19). The continuous-time analog is obtained as

$$\mathcal{I}_{hist} = \bigcup_{t \in T} \mathcal{I}_t, \tag{11.54}$$

which is an irregular collection of functions because they have different domains; this irregularity also occurred in the discrete-stage case, in which $\mathcal{I}_{hist}$ was composed of sequences of varying lengths.

A continuous-time version of the cost functional in Formulation 11.1 can be given to evaluate the execution of a plan. Let L denote a cost functional that may be applied to any state-action history $(\tilde{x}_t, \tilde{u}_t)$ to yield

$$L(\tilde{x}_t, \tilde{u}_t) = \int_0^t l(x(t'), u(t'))dt' + l_F(x(t)), \tag{11.55}$$

in which $l(x(t'), u(t'))$ is the instantaneous cost and $l_F(x(t))$ is a final cost.

11.4.3 Derived information spaces

For continuous state spaces, the motivation to construct derived I-spaces is even stronger than in the discrete case because the I-space quickly becomes unwieldy.

11.4.3.1 Nondeterministic and probabilistic I-spaces for discrete stages

The concepts of I-maps and derived I-spaces from Section 11.2 extend directly to continuous spaces. In the nondeterministic case, κ_{ndet} once again transforms the initial condition and history into a subset of X. In the probabilistic case, κ_{prob} yields a probability density function over X. First, consider the discrete-stage case.

The nondeterministic I-states are obtained exactly as defined in Section 11.2.2, except that the discrete sets are replaced by their continuous counterparts. For example, $F(x, u)$ as defined in (11.28) is now a continuous set, as are X and $\Theta(x, u)$. Since probabilistic I-states are probability density functions, the derivation in Section 11.2.3 needs to be modified slightly. There are, however, no important conceptual differences. Follow the derivation of Section 11.2.3 and consider which parts need to be replaced.

The replacement for (11.35) is

$$p(x_k|y_k) = \frac{p(y_k|x_k)p(x_k)}{\displaystyle\int_X p(y_k|x_k)p(x_k)dx_k}, \tag{11.56}$$

which is based in part on deriving $p(y_k|x_k)$ from $p(\psi_k|x_k)$. The base of the induction, which replaces (11.36), is obtained by letting $k = 1$ in (11.56). By following the explanation given from (11.37) to (11.40), but using instead probability density functions, the following update equations are obtained:

$$
\begin{aligned}
p(x_{k+1}|\eta_k, u_k) &= \int_X p(x_{k+1}|x_k, u_k, \eta_k)p(x_k|\eta_k)dx_k \\
&= \int_X p(x_{k+1}|x_k, u_k)p(x_k|\eta_k)dx_k,
\end{aligned}
\tag{11.57}
$$

and

$$
p(x_{k+1}|y_{k+1}, \eta_k, u_k) = \frac{p(y_{k+1}|x_{k+1})p(x_{k+1}|\eta_k, u_k)}{\displaystyle\int_X p(y_{k+1}|x_{k+1})p(x_{k+1}|\eta_k, u_k)dx_{k+1}}.
\tag{11.58}
$$

11.4.3.2 Approximating nondeterministic and probabilistic I-spaces

Many other derived I-spaces extend directly to continuous spaces, such as the limited-memory models of Section 11.2.4 and Examples 11.11 and 11.12. In the present context, it is extremely useful to try to collapse the I-space as much as possible because it tends to be unmanageable in most practical applications. Recall that an I-map, $\kappa : \mathcal{I}_{hist} \to \mathcal{I}_{der}$, partitions $\mathcal{I}_{hist}$ into sets over which a constant action must be applied. The main concern is that restricting plans to $\mathcal{I}_{der}$ does not inhibit solutions.

Consider making derived I-spaces that approximate nondeterministic or probabilistic I-states. Approximations make sense because X is usually a metric space in the continuous setting. The aim is to dramatically simplify the I-space while trying to avoid the loss of critical information. A trade-off occurs in which the quality of the approximation is traded against the size of the resulting derived I-space. For the case of nondeterministic I-states, *conservative approximations* are formulated, which are sets that are guaranteed to contain the nondeterministic I-state. For the probabilistic case, *moment-based approximations* are presented, which are based on general techniques from probability and statistics to approximate probability densities. To avoid unnecessary complications, the presentation will be confined to the discrete-stage model.

Conservative approximations

Suppose that nondeterministic uncertainty is used and an approximation is made to the nondeterministic I-states. An I-map, $\kappa_{app} : \mathcal{I}_{ndet} \to \mathcal{I}_{app}$, will be defined in which $\mathcal{I}_{app}$ is a particular family of subsets of X. For example, $\mathcal{I}_{app}$ could represent the set of all ball subsets of X. If $X = \mathbb{R}^2$, then the balls become discs, and only three parameters (x, y, r) are needed to parameterize $\mathcal{I}_{app}$ (x, y for the center and r for the radius). This implies that $\mathcal{I}_{app} \subset \mathbb{R}^3$; this appears to be much simpler than $\mathcal{I}_{ndet}$, which could be a complicated collection of regions in $\mathbb{R}^2$. To make $\mathcal{I}_{app}$ even smaller, it could be required that x, y, and r are integers (or are sampled with some specified dispersion, as defined in Section 5.2.3). If $\mathcal{I}_{app}$ is bounded, then the number of derived I-states would become finite. Of course, this comes an at expense because $\mathcal{I}_{ndet}$ may be poorly approximated.

For a fixed sequence of actions $(u_1, u_2, \dots)$ consider the sequence of nondeterministic I-states:

$$
X_1(\eta_1) \xrightarrow{u_1, y_2} X_2(\eta_2) \xrightarrow{u_2, y_3} X_3(\eta_3) \xrightarrow{u_3, y_4} \cdots,
\tag{11.59}
$$

which is also depicted in Figure 11.9. The I-map $\mathcal{I}_{app}$ must select a bounding region for every nondeterministic I-state. Starting with a history I-state, η, the nondeterministic I-state $X_k(\eta_k)$ can first be computed, followed by applying $\mathcal{I}_{app}$ to yield a bounding region.

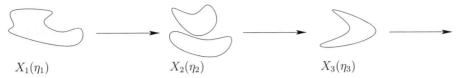

$X_1(\eta_1)$ $\qquad\qquad$ $X_2(\eta_2)$ $\qquad\qquad$ $X_3(\eta_3)$

Figure 11.9: The nondeterministic I-states may be complicated regions that are difficult or impossible to compute.

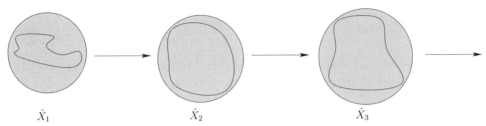

$\hat{X}_1$ $\qquad\qquad$ $\hat{X}_2$ $\qquad\qquad$ $\hat{X}_3$

Figure 11.10: The nondeterministic I-states can be approximated by bounding spheres.

If there is a way to efficiently compute $X_k(\eta_k)$ for any η_k, then a plan on $\mathcal{I}_{app}$ could be much simpler than those on $\mathcal{I}_{ndet}$ or $\mathcal{I}_{hist}$.

If it is difficult to compute $X_k(\eta_k)$, one possibility is to try to define a derived information transition equation, as discussed in Section 11.2.1. The trouble, however, is that $\mathcal{I}_{app}$ is usually not a sufficient I-map. Imagine wanting to compute $\kappa_{app}(X_{k+1}(\eta_{k+1}))$, which is a bounding approximation to $X_{k+1}(\eta_{k+1})$. This can be accomplished by starting with $X_k(\eta_k)$, applying the update rules (11.30) and (11.31), and then applying κ_{app} to $X_{k+1}(\eta_{k+1})$. In general, this does not produce the same result as starting with the bounding volume $\mathcal{I}_{app}(X_k(\eta_k))$, applying (11.30) and (11.31), and then applying κ_{app}.

Thus, it is not possible to express the transitions entirely in $\mathcal{I}_{app}$ without some further loss of information. However, if this loss of information is tolerable, then an information-destroying approximation may nevertheless be useful. The general idea is to make a bounding region for the nondeterministic I-state in each iteration. Let $\hat{X}_k$ denote this bounding region at stage k. Be careful in using such approximations. As depicted in Figures 11.9 and 11.10, the sequences of derived I-states diverge. The sequence in Figure 11.10 is *not* obtained by simply bounding each calculated I-state by an element of $\mathcal{I}_{app}$; the entire sequence is different.

Initially, $\hat{X}_1$ is chosen so that $X_1(\eta_1) \subseteq \hat{X}_1$. In each inductive step, $\hat{X}_k$ is treated as if it were the true nondeterministic I-state (not an approximation). Using (11.30) and (11.31), the update for considering u_k and y_{k+1} is

$$\hat{X}'_{k+1} = \left(\bigcup_{x_k \in \hat{X}_k} F(x_k, u_k) \right) \cap H(y_{k+1}). \tag{11.60}$$

In general, $\hat{X}'_{k+1}(\eta_{k+1})$ might not lie in $\mathcal{I}_{app}$. Therefore, a bounding region, $\hat{X}_{k+1} \in \mathcal{I}_{app}$, must be selected to approximate $\hat{X}'$ under the constraint that $\hat{X}'_{k+1} \subseteq \hat{X}_{k+1}$. This completes the inductive step, which together with the base case yields a sequence

$$\hat{X}_1 \xrightarrow{u_1, y_2} \hat{X}_2 \xrightarrow{u_2, y_3} \hat{X}_3 \xrightarrow{u_3, y_4} \cdots , \tag{11.61}$$

which is depicted in Figure 11.10.

Both a plan, $\pi : \mathcal{I}_{app} \to U$, and information transitions can now be defined over $\mathcal{I}_{app}$. To ensure that a plan is sound, the approximation must be conservative. If in some iteration, $\hat{X}_{k+1}(\eta_{k+1}) \subset \hat{X}'_{k+1}(\eta_{k+1})$, then the true state may not necessarily be included in the approximate derived I-state. This could, for example, mean that a robot is in a collision state, even though the derived I-state indicates that this is impossible. This bad behavior is generally avoided by keeping conservative approximations. At one extreme, the approximations can be made very conservative by always assigning $\hat{X}_{k+1}(\eta_{k+1}) = X$. This, however, is useless because the only possible plans must apply a single, fixed action for every stage. Even if the approximations are better, it might still be impossible to cause transitions in the approximated I-state. To ensure that solutions exist to the planning problem, it is therefore important to make the bounding volumes as close as possible to the derived I-states.

This trade-off between the simplicity of bounding volumes and the computational expense of working with them was also observed in Section 5.3.2 for collision detection. Dramatic improvement in performance can be obtained by working with simpler shapes; however, in the present context this could come at the expense of failing to solve the problem. Using balls as described so far might not seem to provide very tight bounds. Imagine instead using solid ellipsoids. This would provide tighter approximations, but the dimension of $\mathcal{I}_{app}$ grows quadratically with the dimension of X. A sphere equation generally requires $n + 1$ parameters, whereas the ellipsoid equation requires $\binom{n}{2} + 2n$ parameters. Thus, if the dimension of X is high, it may be difficult or even impossible to use ellipsoid approximations. Nonconvex bounding shapes could provide even better approximations, but the required number of parameters could easily become unmanageable, even if $X = \mathbb{R}^2$. For very particular problems, however, it may be possible to design a family of shapes that is both manageable and tightly approximates the nondeterministic I-states. This leads to many interesting research issues.

Moment-based approximations

Since the probabilistic I-states are functions, it seems natural to use function approximation methods to approximate $\mathcal{I}_{prob}$. One possibility might be to use the first m coefficients of a Taylor series expansion. The derived I-space then becomes the space of possible Taylor coefficients. The quality of the approximation is improved as m is increased, but also the dimension of the derived I-space rises.

Since we are working with probability density functions, it is generally preferable to use moments as approximations instead of Taylor series coefficients or other generic function approximation methods. The first and second moments are the familiar *mean* and *covariance*, respectively. These are preferable over other approximations because the mean and covariance exactly represent the Gaussian density, which is the most basic and fundamental density in probability theory. Thus, approximating the probabilistic I-space with first and second moments is equivalent to assuming that the resulting probability densities are always Gaussian. Such approximations are frequently made in practice because of the convenience of working with Gaussians. In general, higher order moments can be used to obtain higher quality approximations at the expense of more coefficients. Let $\kappa_{mom} : \mathcal{I}_{prob} \rightarrow \mathcal{I}_{mom}$ denote a moment-based I-map.

The same issues arise for κ_{mom} as for κ_{app}. In most cases, κ_{mom} is not a sufficient I-map. The moments are computed in the same way as the conservative approximations. The update equations (11.57) and (11.58) are applied for probabilistic I-states; however, after each step, κ_{mom} is applied to the resulting probability density function. This traps the derived I-states in $\mathcal{I}_{mom}$. The moments could be computed after each of (11.57) and

(11.58) or after both of them have been applied (different results may be obtained). The later case may be more difficult to compute, depending on the application.

First consider using the mean (first moment) to represent some probabilistic I-state, $p(x|\eta)$. Let x_i denote the ith coordinate of x. The mean, $\bar{x}_i$, with respect to x_i is generally defined as

$$\bar{x}_i = \int_X x_i \, p(x|\eta) dx. \tag{11.62}$$

This leads to the vector mean $\bar{x} = (\bar{x}_1, \ldots, \bar{x}_n)$. Suppose that we would like to construct $\mathcal{I}_{mom}$ using only the mean. Since there is no information about the covariance of the density, working with $\bar{x}$ is very similar to estimating the state. The mean value serves as the estimate, and $\mathcal{I}_{mom} = X$. This certainly helps to simplify the I-space, but there is no way to infer the amount of uncertainty associated with the I-state. Was the probability mass concentrated greatly around $\bar{x}$, or was the density function very diffuse over X?

Using second moments helps to alleviate this problem. The covariance with respect to two variables, x_i and x_i, is

$$\sigma_{i,j} = \int_X x_i x_j \, p(x|\eta) dx. \tag{11.63}$$

Since $\sigma_{ij} = \sigma_{ji}$, the second moments can be organized into a symmetric *covariance matrix*,

$$\Sigma = \begin{pmatrix} \sigma_{1,1} & \sigma_{1,2} & \cdots & \sigma_{1,n} \\ \sigma_{2,1} & \sigma_{2,2} & \cdots & \sigma_{2,n} \\ \vdots & \vdots & & \vdots \\ \sigma_{n,1} & \sigma_{n,2} & \cdots & \sigma_{n,n} \end{pmatrix} \tag{11.64}$$

for which there are $\binom{n}{2} + n$ unique elements, corresponding to every $x_{i,i}$ and every way to pair x_i with x_j for each distinct i and j such that $1 \le i, j \le n$. This implies that if first and second moments are used, then the dimension of $\mathcal{I}_{mom}$ is $\binom{n}{2} + 2n$. For some problems, it may turn out that all probabilistic I-states are indeed Gaussians. In this case, the mean and covariance exactly capture the probabilistic I-space. The I-map in this case is sufficient. This leads to a powerful tool called the Kalman filter, which is the subject of Section 11.6.1.

Higher quality approximations can be made by taking higher order moments. The *rth moment* is defined as

$$\int_X x_{i_1} x_{i_2} \cdots x_{i_r} \, p(x|\eta) dx, \tag{11.65}$$

in which $i_1, i_2, \ldots, i_r$ are r integers chosen with replacement from $\{1, \ldots, n\}$.

The moment-based approximation is very similar to the conservative approximations for nondeterministic uncertainty. The use of mean and covariance appears very similar to using ellipsoids for the nondeterministic case. The level sets of a Gaussian density are ellipsoids. These level sets generalize the notion of confidence intervals to confidence ellipsoids, which provides a close connection between the nondeterministic and probabilistic cases. The domain of a Gaussian density is $\mathbb{R}^n$, which is not bounded, contrary to the nondeterministic case. However, for a given confidence level, it can be approximated as a bounded set. For example, an elliptical region can be computed in which 99.9% of the probability mass falls. In general, it may be possible to combine the idea of moments and bounding volumes to construct a derived I-space for the probabilistic case. This could yield the guaranteed correctness of plans while also taking probabilities into account. Unfortunately, this would once again increase the dimension of the derived I-space.

11.4.3.3 Derived I-spaces for continuous time

The continuous-time case is substantially more difficult, both to express and to compute in general forms. In many special cases, however, there are elegant ways to compute it. Some of these will be covered in Section 11.5 and Chapter 12. To help complete the I-space framework, some general expressions are given here. In general, I-maps and derived I-spaces can be constructed following the ideas of Section 11.2.1.

Since there are no discrete transition rules, the derived I-states cannot be expressed in terms of simple update rules. However, they can at least be expressed as a function that indicates the state $x(t)$ that will be obtained after $\tilde{u}_t$ and $\tilde{\theta}_t$ are applied from an initial state $x(0)$. Often, this is obtained via some form of integration (see Section 14.1), although this may not be explicitly given. In general, let $X_t(\eta_t) \subset X$ denote a nondeterministic I-state at time t; this is the replacement for X_k from the discrete-stage case. The initial condition is denoted as X_0, as opposed to X_1, which was used in the discrete-stage case.

More definitions are needed to precisely characterize $X_t(\eta_t)$. Let $\tilde{\theta}_t : [0, t) \to \Theta$ denote the history of nature actions up to time t. Similarly, let $\tilde{\psi}_t : [0, t] \to \Psi$ denote the history of nature sensing actions. Suppose that the initial condition is $X_0 \subset X$. The nondeterministic I-state is defined as

$$X_t(\eta_t) = \{x \in X \mid \exists x' \in X_0, \ \exists \tilde{\theta}_t, \text{ and } \exists \tilde{\psi}_t \text{ such that}$$
$$x = \Phi(x', \tilde{u}_t, \tilde{\theta}_t) \text{ and } \forall t' \in [0, t], \ y(t') = h(x(t'), \psi(t'))\}. \tag{11.66}$$

In words, this means that a state $x(t)$ lies in $X_t(\eta_t)$ if and only if there exists an initial state $x' \in X_0$, a nature history $\tilde{\theta}_t$, and a nature sensing action history, $\tilde{\psi}_t$ such that the transition equation causes arrival at $x(t)$ and the observation history $\tilde{y}_t$ agrees with the sensor mapping over all time from 0 to t.

It is also possible to derive a probabilistic I-state, but this requires technical details from continuous-time stochastic processes and stochastic differential equations. In some cases, the resulting expressions work out very nicely; however, it is difficult to formulate a general expression for the derived I-state because it depends on many technical assumptions regarding the behavior of the stochastic processes. For details on such systems, see [570].

11.5 Examples for continuous state spaces

11.5.1 Sensor models

A remarkable variety of sensing models arises in applications that involve continuous state spaces. This section presents a catalog of different kinds of sensor models that is inspired mainly by robotics problems. The models are gathered together in one place to provide convenient reference. Some of them will be used in upcoming sections, and others are included to help in the understanding of I-spaces. For each sensor, there are usually two different versions, based on whether nature sensing actions are included.

Linear sensing models

Developed mainly in control theory literature, *linear sensing models* are some of the most common and important. For all of the sensors in this family, assume that $X = Y = \mathbb{R}^n$ (nonsingular linear transformations allow the sensor space to effectively have lower

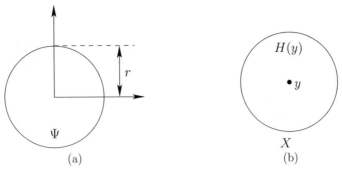

Figure 11.11: A simple sensing model in which the observation error is no more than r: (a) the nature sensing action space; (b) the preimage in X based on observation y.

dimension, if desired). The simplest case in this family is the *identity sensor*, in which $y = h(x)$. In this case, the state is immediately known. If this sensor is available at every stage, then the I-space collapses to X by the I-map $\kappa_{sf} : \mathcal{I}_{hist} \to X$.

Now nature sensing actions can be used to corrupt this perfect state observation to obtain $y = h(x, \psi) = x + \psi$. Suppose that y is an estimate of x, the current state, with error bounded by a constant $r \in (0, \infty)$. This can be modeled by assigning for every $x \in X$, $\Psi(x)$ as a closed ball of radius r, centered at the origin:

$$\Psi = \{\psi \in \mathbb{R}^n \mid \|\psi\| \leq r\}. \tag{11.67}$$

Figure 11.11 illustrates the resulting nondeterministic sensing model. If the observation y is received, then it is known that the true state lies within a ball in X of radius r, centered at y. This ball is the preimage, $H(y)$, as defined in (11.11). To make the model probabilistic, a probability density function can be defined over Ψ. For example, it could be assumed that $p(\psi)$ is a uniform density (although this model is not very realistic in many applications because there is a boundary at which the probability mass discontinuously jumps to zero).

A more typical probabilistic sensing model can be made by letting $\Psi(x) = \mathbb{R}^n$ and defining a probability density function over all of $\mathbb{R}^n$. (Note that the nondeterministic version of this sensor is completely useless.) One of the easiest choices to work with is the multivariate Gaussian probability density function,

$$p(\psi) = \frac{1}{\sqrt{(2\pi)^n |\Sigma|}} e^{-\frac{1}{2}\psi^T \Sigma \psi}, \tag{11.68}$$

in which Σ is the covariance matrix (11.64), $|\Sigma|$ is its determinant, and $\psi^T \Sigma \psi$ is a quadratic form, which multiplies out to yield

$$\psi^T \Sigma \psi = \sum_{i=1}^{n} \sum_{j=1}^{n} \sigma_{i,j} \psi_i \psi_j. \tag{11.69}$$

If $p(x)$ is a Gaussian and y is received, then $p(y|x)$ must also be Gaussian under this model. This will become very important in Section 11.6.1.

The sensing models presented so far can be generalized by applying linear transformations. For example, let C denote a nonsingular $n \times n$ matrix with real-valued entries. If the sensor mapping is $y = h(x) = Cx$, then the state can still be determined immediately because the mapping $y = Cx$ is bijective; each $H(y)$ contains a unique point of X. A linear transformation can also be formed on the nature sensing action. Let W denote an

$n \times n$ matrix. The sensor mapping is

$$y = h(x) = Cx + W\psi. \tag{11.70}$$

In general, C and W may even be singular, and a linear sensing model is still obtained. Suppose that $W = 0$. If C is singular, however, it is impossible to infer the state directly from a single sensor observation. This generally corresponds to a projection from an n-dimensional state space to a subset of Y whose dimension is the rank of C. For example, if

$$C = \begin{pmatrix} 0 & 1 \\ 0 & 0 \end{pmatrix}, \tag{11.71}$$

then $y = Cx$ yields $y_1 = x_2$ and $y_2 = 0$. Only x_2 of each $(x_1, x_2) \in X$ can be observed because C has rank 1. Thus, for some special cases, singular matrices can measure some state variables while leaving others invisible. For a general singular matrix C, the interpretation is that X is projected into some k-dimensional subspace by the sensor, in which k is the rank of C. If W is singular, this means that the effect of nature is limited. The degrees of freedom with which nature can distort the sensor observations is the rank of W. These concepts motivate the next set of sensor models.

Simple projection sensors

Several common sensor models can be defined by observing particular coordinates of X while leaving others invisible. This is the continuous version of the selective sensor from Example 11.4. Imagine, for example, a mobile robot that rolls in a 2D world, $\mathcal{W} = \mathbb{R}^2$, and is capable of rotation. The state space (or configuration space) is $X = \mathbb{R}^2 \times \mathbb{S}^1$. For visualization purposes, it may be helpful to imagine that the robot is very tiny, so that it can be interpreted as a point, to avoid the complicated configuration space constructions of Section 4.3.[7] Let $p = (p_1, p_2)$ denote the coordinates of the point, and let $s \in \mathbb{S}^1$ denote its orientation. Thus, a state in $\mathbb{R}^2 \times \mathbb{S}^1$ is specified as (p_1, p_2, s) (rather than (x, y, θ), which may cause confusion with important spaces such as X, Y, and Θ).

Suppose that the robot can estimate its position but does not know its orientation. This leads to a *position sensor* defined as $Y = \mathbb{R}^2$, with $y_1 = p_1$ and $y_2 = p_2$ (also denoted as $y = h(x) = p$). The third state variable, s, of the state remains unknown. Of course, any of the previously considered nature sensing action models can be added. For example, nature might cause errors that are modeled with Gaussian probability densities.

A *compass* or *orientation sensor* can likewise be made by observing only the final state variable, s. In this case, $Y = \mathbb{S}^1$ and $y = s$. Nature sensing actions can be included. For example, the sensed orientation may be y, but it is only known that $|s - y| \le \epsilon$ for some constant ϵ, which is the maximum sensor error. A Gaussian model cannot exactly be applied because its domain is unbounded and $\mathbb{S}^1$ is bounded. This can be fixed by truncating the Gaussian or by using a more appropriate distribution.

The position and orientation sensors generalize nicely to a 3D world, $\mathcal{W} = \mathbb{R}^3$. Recall from Section 4.2 that in this case the state space is $X = SE(3)$, which can be represented as $\mathbb{R}^3 \times \mathbb{RP}^3$. A position sensor measures the first three coordinates, whereas an orientation sensor measures the last three coordinates. A physical sensor that measures orientation in $\mathbb{R}^3$ is often called a *gyroscope*. These are usually based on the principle of precession, which means that they contain a spinning disc that is reluctant to change its orientation

---

[7] This can also be handled, but it just adds unnecessary complication to the current discussion.

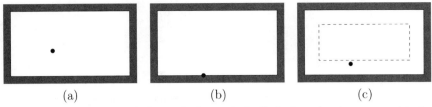

Figure 11.12: Boundary sensors indicate whether contact with the boundary has occurred. In the latter case, a proximity sensor may indicate whether the boundary is within a specified distance.

due to angular momentum. For the case of a linkage of bodies that are connected by revolute joints, a point in the state space gives the angles between each pair of attached links. A *joint encoder* is a sensor that yields one of these angles.

Dynamics of mechanical systems will not be considered until Part IV; however, it is worth pointing out several sensors. In these problems, the state space will be expanded to include velocity parameters and possibly even acceleration parameters. In this case, a *speedometer* can sense a velocity vector or a scalar speed. Sensors even exist to measure *angular velocity*, which indicates the speed with which rotation occurs. Finally, an *accelerometer* can be used to sense acceleration parameters. With any of these models, nature sensing actions can be used to account for measurement errors.

Boundary sensors

If the state space has an interesting boundary, as in the case of $\mathcal{C}_{free}$ for motion planning problems, then many important *boundary sensors* can be formulated based on the detection of the boundary. Figure 11.12 shows several interesting cases on which sensors are based.

Suppose that the state space is a closed set with some well-defined boundary. To provide a connection to motion planning, assume that $X = \mathrm{cl}(\mathcal{C}_{free})$, the closure of $\mathcal{C}_{free}$. A *contact sensor* determines whether the boundary is being contacted. In this case, $Y = \{0, 1\}$ and h is defined as $h(x) = 1$ if $x \in \partial X$, and $h(x) = 0$ otherwise. These two cases are shown in Figures 11.12a and 11.12b, respectively. Using this sensor, there is no information regarding where along the boundary the contact may be occurring. In mobile robotics, it may be disastrous if the robot is in contact with obstacles. Instead, a *proximity sensor* is often used, which yields $h(x) = 1$ if the state or position is within some specified constant, r, of ∂X, and $h(x) = 0$ otherwise. This is shown in Figure 11.12.

In robot manipulation, haptic interfaces, and other applications in which physical interaction occurs between machines and the environment, a *force sensor* may be used. In addition to simply indicating contact, a force sensor can indicate the magnitude and direction of the force. The robot model must be formulated so that it is possible to derive the anticipated force value from a given state.

Landmark sensors

Many important sensing models can be defined in terms of *landmarks*. A landmark is a special point or region in the state space that can be detected in some way by the sensor. The measurements of the landmark can be used to make inferences about the current state. An ancient example is using stars to navigate on the ocean. Based on the location of the stars relative to a ship, its orientation can be inferred. You may have found landmarks useful for trying to find your way through an unfamiliar city. For example, mountains around the perimeter of Mexico City or the Eiffel Tower in Paris might be used to infer your heading. Even though the streets of Paris are very complicated, it might be possible

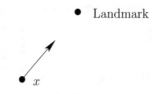

Figure 11.13: The most basic landmark sensor indicates only its direction.

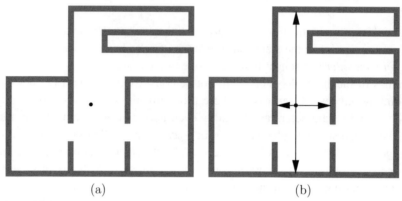

<table>
<tr><td>(a)</td><td>(b)</td></tr>
</table>

Figure 11.14: (a) A mobile robot is dropped into an unknown environment. (b) Four sonars are used to measure distances to the walls.

to walk to the Eiffel Tower by walking toward it whenever it is visible. Such models are common in the *competitive ratio* framework for analyzing on-line algorithms [677].

In general, a set of states may serve as landmarks. A common model is to make x_G a single landmark. In robotics applications, these landmarks may be instead considered as points in the world, $\mathcal{W}$. Generalizations from points to landmark regions are also possible. The ideas, here, however, will be kept simple to illustrate the concept. Following this presentation, you can imagine a wide variety of generalizations. Assume for all examples of landmarks that $X = \mathbb{R}^2$, and let a state be denoted by $x = (x_1, x_2)$.

For the first examples, suppose there is only one landmark, $l \in X$, with coordinates (l_1, l_2). A *homing sensor* is depicted in Figure 11.13 and yields values in $Y = \mathbb{S}^1$. The sensor mapping is $h(x) = \text{atan2}(l_1 - x_1, l_2 - x_2)$, in which atan2 gives the angle in the proper quadrant.

Another possibility is a *Geiger counter sensor* (radiation level), in which $Y = [0, \infty)$ and $h(x) = \|x - l\|$. In this case, only the distance to the landmark is reported, but there is no directional information.

A contact sensor could also be combined with the landmark idea to yield a sensor called a *pebble*. This sensor reports 1 if the pebble is "touched"; otherwise, it reports 0. This idea can be generalized nicely to regions. Imagine that there is a *landmark region*, $X_l \subset X$. If $x \in X_l$, then the *landmark region detector* reports 1; otherwise, it reports 0.

Many useful and interesting sensing models can be formulated by using the ideas explained so far with multiple landmarks. For example, using three homing sensors that are not collinear, it is possible to reconstruct the exact state. Many interesting problems can be made by populating the state space with landmark regions and their associated detectors. In mobile robotics applications, this can be implemented by placing stationary cameras or other sensors in an environment. The sensors can indicate which cameras can currently view the robot. They might also provide the distance from each camera.

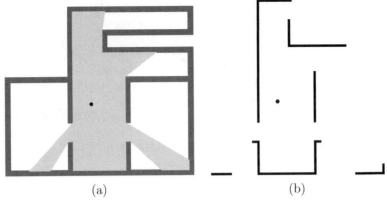

(a) $\qquad\qquad\qquad$ (b)

Figure 11.15: A range scanner or visibility sensor is like having a continuum of sonars, even with much higher accuracy. A distance value is provided for each $s \in \mathbb{S}^1$.

Depth-mapping sensors

In many robotics applications, the robot may not have a map of the obstacles in the world. In this case, sensing is used to both learn the environment and to determine its position and orientation within the environment. Suppose that a robot is dropped into an environment as shown in Figure 11.14a. For problems such as this, the state represents both the position of the robot and the obstacles themselves. This situation is explained in further detail in Section 12.3. Here, some sensor models for problems of this type are given. These are related to the boundary and proximity sensors of Figure 11.12, but they yield more information when the robot is not at the boundary.

One of the oldest sensors used in mobile robotics is an acoustic *sonar*, which emits a high-frequency sound wave in a specific direction and measures the time that it takes for the wave to reflect off a wall and return to the sonar (often the sonar serves as both a speaker and a microphone). Based on the speed of sound and the time of flight, the distance to the wall can be estimated. Sometimes, the wave never returns; this can be modeled with nature. Also, errors in the distance estimate can be modeled with nature. In general, the observation space Y for a single sonar is $[0, \infty]$, in which ∞ indicates that the wave did not return. The interpretation of Y could be the time of flight, or it could already be transformed into estimated distance. If there are k sonars, each pointing in a different direction, then $Y = [0, \infty]^k$, which indicates that one reading can be obtained for each sonar. For example, Figure 11.14b shows four sonars and the distances that they can measure. Each observation therefore yields a point in $\mathbb{R}^4$.

Modern laser scanning technology enables very accurate distance measurements with very high angular density. For example, the SICK LMS-200 can obtain a distance measurement for at least every 1/2 degree and sweep the full 360 degrees at least 30 times a second. The measurement accuracy in an indoor environment is often on the order of a few millimeters. Imagine the limiting case, which is like having a continuum of sonars, one for every angle in $\mathbb{S}^1$. This results in a sensor called a *range scanner* or *visibility sensor*, which provides a distance measurement for each $s \in \mathbb{S}^1$, as shown in Figure 11.15.

A weaker sensor can be made by only indicating points in $\mathbb{S}^1$ at which discontinuities (or gaps) occur in the depth scan. Refer to this as a *gap sensor*; an example is shown in Figure 11.16. It might even be the case that only the circular ordering of these gaps is given around $\mathbb{S}^1$, without knowing the relative angles between them, or the distance to each gap. A planner based on this sensing model is presented in Section 12.3.4.

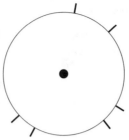

Figure 11.16: A gap sensor indicates only the directions at which discontinuities in depth occur, instead of providing distance information.

Odometry sensors

A final category will be given, which provides interesting examples of history-based sensor mappings, as defined for discrete state spaces in Section 11.1.1. Mobile robots often have *odometry sensors*, which indicate how far the robot has traveled, based on the amount that the wheels have turned. Such measurements are often inaccurate because of wheel slippage, surface imperfections, and small modeling errors. For a given state history, $\tilde{x}_t$, a sensor can estimate the total distance traveled. For this model, $Y = [0, \infty)$ and $y = h(\tilde{x}_t)$, in which the argument, $\tilde{x}_t$, to h is the entire state history up to time t. Another way to model odometry is to have a sensor indicate the estimated distance traveled since the last stage. This avoids the dependency on the entire history, but it may be harder to model the resulting errors in distance estimation.

In some literature (e.g., [352]) the action history, $\tilde{u}_k$, is referred to as odometry. This interpretation is appropriate in some applications. For example, each action might correspond to turning the pedals one full revolution on a bicycle. The number of times the pedals have been turned could serve as an odometry reading. Since this information already appears in η_k, it is not modeled in this book as part of the sensing process. For the bicycle example, there might be an odometry sensor that bases its measurements on factors other than the pedal motions. It would be appropriate to model this as a history-based sensor.

Another kind of history-based sensor is to observe a *wall clock* that indicates how much time has passed since the initial stage. This, in combination with other information, such as the speed of the robot, could enable strong inferences to be made about the state.

11.5.2 Simple projection examples

This section gives examples of I-spaces for which the sensor mapping is $y = h(x)$ and h is a projection that reveals some of the state variables, while concealing others. The examples all involve continuous time, and the focus is mainly on the nondeterministic I-space $\mathcal{I}_{ndet}$. It is assumed that there are no actions, which means that $U = \emptyset$. Nature actions, $\Theta(x)$, however, will be allowed. Since there are no robot actions and no nature sensing actions, all of the uncertainty arises from the fact that h is a projection and the nature actions that affect the state transition equation are not known. This is a very important and interesting class of problems in itself. The examples can be further complicated by allowing some control from the action set, U; however, the purpose here is to illustrate I-space concepts. Therefore, it will not be necessary.

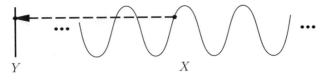

Figure 11.17: The state space is the set of points traced out by a sine curve in $\mathbb{R}^2$.

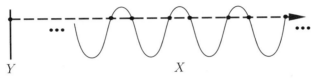

Figure 11.18: The preimage, $H(y)$, of an observation y is a countably infinite set of points along X.

Example 11.20 (Moving on a Sine Curve) Suppose that the state space is the set of points that lie on the sine curve in the plane:

$$X = \{(x_1, x_2) \in \mathbb{R}^2 \mid x_2 = \sin x_1\}. \tag{11.72}$$

Let $U = \emptyset$, which results in no action history. The observation space is $Y = [-1, 1]$ and the sensor mapping yields $y = h(x) = x_2$, the height of the point on the sine curve, as shown in Figure 11.17.

The nature action space is $\Theta = \{-1, 1\}$, in which -1 means to move at unit speed in the $-x_1$ direction along the sine curve, and 1 means to move at unit speed in the x_1 direction along the curve. Thus, for some nature action history $\tilde{\theta}_t$, a state trajectory $\tilde{x}_t$ that moves the point along the curve can be determined by integration.

A history I-state takes the form $\eta_t = (X_0, \tilde{y}_t)$, which includes the initial condition $X_0 \subseteq X$ and the observation history $\tilde{y}_t$ up to time t. The nondeterministic I-states are very interesting for this problem. For each observation y, the preimage $H(y)$ is a countably infinite set of points that corresponds to the intersection of X with a horizontal line at height y, as shown in Figure 11.18.

The uncertainty for this problem is always characterized by the number of intersection points that might contain the true state. Suppose that $X_0 = X$. In this case, there is no state trajectory that can reduce the amount of uncertainty. As the point moves along X, the height is always known because of the sensor, but the x_1 coordinate can only be narrowed down to being any of the intersection points.

Suppose instead that $X_0 = \{x_0\}$, in which x_0 is some particular point along X. If y remains within $(0, 1)$ over some any period of time starting at $t = 0$, then $x(t)$ is known because the exact segment of the sine curve that contains the state is known. However, if the point reaches an extremum, which results in $y = 0$ or $y = 1$, then it is not known which way the point will travel. From this point, the sensor cannot disambiguate moving in the $-x_1$ direction from the x_1 direction. Therefore, the uncertainty grows, as shown in Figure 11.19. After the observation $y = 1$ is obtained, there are two possibilities for the current state, depending on which action was taken by nature when $y = 1$; hence, the nondeterministic I-state contains two states. If the motion continues until $y = -1$, then there will be four states in the nondeterministic I-state. Unfortunately, the uncertainty can only grow in this example. There is no way to use the sensor to reduce the size of the nondeterministic I-states. ∎

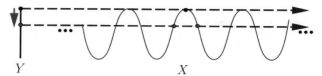

Figure 11.19: A bifurcation occurs when $y = 1$ or $y = -1$ is received. This irreversibly increases the amount of uncertainty in the state.

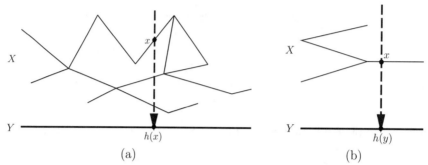

(a)   (b)

Figure 11.20: (a) Imagine trying to infer the location of a point on a planar graph while observing only a single coordinate. (b) This simple example involves a point moving along a graph that has four edges. When the point is on the rightmost edge, there is no uncertainty; however, uncertainty exists when the point travels along the other edges.

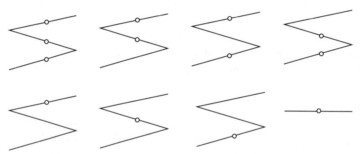

Figure 11.21: Pieces of the nondeterministic I-space $\mathcal{I}_{ndet}$ are obtained by the different possible sets of edges on which the point may lie.

The previous example can be generalized to observing a single coordinate of a point that moves around in a planar topological graph, as shown in Figure 11.20a. Most of the model remains the same as for Example 11.20, except that the state space is now a graph. The set of nature actions, $\Theta(x)$, needs to be extended so that if x is a vertex of the graph, then there is one input for each incident edge. These are the possible directions along which the point could move.

Example 11.21 (Observing a Point on a Graph)   Consider the graph shown in Figure 11.20b, in which there are four edges.[8] When the point moves on the interior of the leftmost edge of the graph, then the state can be inferred from the sensor. The set $H(y)$ contains a single point on the leftmost edge. If the point moves in the interior of one of the other edges, then $H(y)$ contains three points, one for each edge above y. This leads to seven possible cases for the nondeterministic I-state, as shown in Figure 11.21. Any subset of these edges may be possible for the nondeterministic I-state, except for the empty set.

---

[8] This example was significantly refined after a helpful discussion with Rob Ghrist.

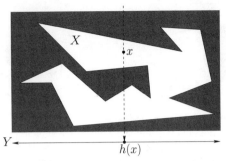

Figure 11.22: The graph can be generalized to a planar region, and layers in the nondeterministic I-space will once again be obtained.

The eight pieces of $\mathcal{I}_{ndet}$ depicted in Figure 11.21 are connected together in an interesting way. Suppose that the point is on the rightmost edge and moves left. After crossing the vertex, the I-state must be the case shown in the upper right of Figure 11.21, which indicates that the point could be on one of two edges. If the point travels right from one of the I-states of the left edges, then the I-state shown in the bottom right of Figure 11.20 is always reached; however, it is not necessarily possible to return to the same I-state on the left. Thus, in general, there are directional constraints on $\mathcal{I}_{ndet}$. Also, note that from the I-state on the lower left of Figure 11.20, it is impossible to reach the I-state on the lower right by moving straight right. This is because it is known from the structure of the graph that this is impossible. ∎

The graph example can be generalized substantially to reflect a wide variety of problems that occur in robotics and other areas. For example, Figure 11.22 shows a polygon in which a point can move. Only one coordinate is observed, and the resulting nondeterministic I-space has layers similar to those obtained for Example 11.21. These ideas can be generalized to any dimension. Interesting models can be constructed using the simple projection sensors, such as a position sensor or compass, from Section 11.5.1. In Section 12.4, such layers will appear in a pursuit-evasion game that uses visibility sensors to find moving targets.

11.5.3 Examples with nature sensing actions

This section illustrates the effect of nature sensing actions, but only for the nondeterministic case. General methods for computing probabilistic I-states are covered in Section 11.6.

Example 11.22 (Above or Below Disc?) This example involves continuous time. Suppose that the task is to gather information and determine whether the state trajectory travels above or below some designated region of the state space, as shown in Figure 11.23.

Let $X = \mathbb{R}^2$. Motions are generated by integrating the velocity $(\dot{x}, \dot{y})$, which is expressed as $\dot{x} = \cos(u(t) + \theta(t))$ and $\dot{y} = \sin(u(t) + \theta(t))$. For simplicity, assume $u(t) = 0$ is applied for all time, which is a command to move right. The nature action $\theta(t) \in \Theta = [-\pi/4, \pi/4]$ interferes with the outcome. The robot tries to make progress by moving in the positive x_1 direction; however, the interference of nature makes it difficult to predict the x_2 direction. Without nature, there should be no change in the x_2 coordinate; however, with nature, the error in the x_2 direction could be as much as t, after t seconds have passed. Figure 11.24 illustrates the possible resulting motions.

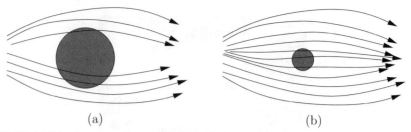

Figure 11.23: (a) It is always possible to determine whether the state trajectory went above or below the designated region. (b) Now the ability to determine whether the trajectory went above or below the hole depends on the particular observations. In some cases, it may not be possible.

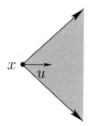

Figure 11.24: Nature interferes with the commanded direction, so that the true state could be anywhere within a circular section.

Sensor observations will be made that alleviate the growing cone of uncertainty; use the sensing model from Figure 11.11, and suppose that the measurement error r is 1. Suppose there is a disc in $\mathbb{R}^2$ of radius larger than 1, as shown in Figure 11.23a. Since the true state is never further than 1 from the measured state, it is always possible to determine whether the state passed above or below the disc. Multiple possible observation histories are shown in Figure 11.23a. The observation history need not even be continuous, but it is drawn that way for convenience. For a disc with radius less than 1, there may exist some observation histories for which it is impossible to determine whether the true state traveled above or below the disc; see Figure 11.23b. For other observation histories, it may still be possible to make the determination; for example, from the uppermost trajectory shown in Figure 11.23b it is known for certain that the true state traveled above the disc. ∎

Example 11.23 (A Simple Mobile Robot Model) In this example, suppose that a robot is modeled as a point that moves in $X = \mathbb{R}^2$. The sensing model is the same as in Example 11.22, except that discrete stages are used instead of continuous time. It can be imagined that each stage represents a constant interval of time (e.g., 1 second).

To control the robot, a motion command is given in the form of an action $u_k \in U = \mathbb{S}^1$. Nature interferes with the motions in two ways: 1) The robot tries to travel some distance d, but there is some error $\epsilon_d > 0$, for which the true distance traveled, d', is known satisfy $|d' - d| < \epsilon_d$; and 2) the robot tries to move in a direction u, but there is some error, $\epsilon_u > 0$, for which the true direction u' is known to satisfy $|u - u'| < \epsilon_u$. These two independent errors can be modeled by defining a 2D nature action set, $\Theta(x)$. The transition equation is then defined so that the forward projection $F(x, u)$ is as shown in Figure 11.25.

Some nondeterministic I-states will now be constructed. Suppose that the initial state x_1 is known, and history I-states take the form

$$\eta_k = (x_1, u_1, \dots, u_{k-1}, y_1, \dots, y_k). \tag{11.73}$$

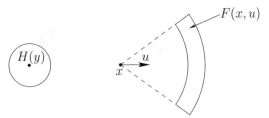

Figure 11.25: A simple mobile robot motion model in which the sensing model is as given in Figure 11.11 and then nature interferes with commanded motions to yield an uncertainty region that is a circular ring.

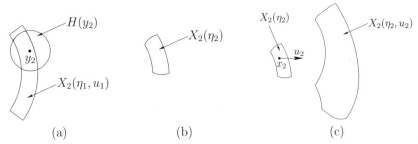

Figure 11.26: (a) Combining information from $X_2(\eta_1, u_1)$ and the observation y_2; (b) the intersection must be taken between $X_2(\eta_1, u_1)$ and $H(y_2)$. (c) The action u_2 leads to a complicated nondeterministic I-state that is the union of $F(x_2, u_2)$ over all $x_2 \in X_2(\eta_2)$.

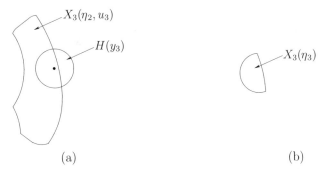

Figure 11.27: After the sensor observation, y_3, the intersection must be taken between $X_3(\eta_2, u_2)$ and $H(y_3 x)$.

The first sensor observation, y_1, is useless because the initial state is known. Equation (11.29) is applied to yield $H(y_1) \cap \{x_1\} = \{x_1\}$. Suppose that the action $u_1 = 0$ is applied, indicating that the robot should move horizontally to the right. Equation (11.30) is applied to yield $X_2(\eta_1, u_1)$, which looks identical to the $F(x, u)$ shown in Figure 11.25. Suppose that an observation y_2 is received as shown in Figure 11.26a. Using this, $X_2(\eta_2)$ is computed by taking the intersection of $H(y_2)$ and $X_2(\eta_1, u_1)$, as shown in Figure 11.26b.

The next step is considerably more complicated. Suppose that $u_2 = 0$ and that (11.30) is applied to compute $X_3(\eta_2, u_2)$ from $X_2(\eta_2)$. The shape shown in Figure 11.26c is obtained by taking the union of $F(x_2, u_2)$ for all possible $x_2 \in X_2(\eta_2)$. The resulting shape is composed of circular arcs and straight line segments (see Exercise 13). Once y_3 is obtained, an intersection is taken once again to yield $X_3(\eta_3) = X_3(\eta_2, u_2) \cap H(y_3)$, as shown in Figure 11.27. The process repeats in the same way for the desired number of stages. The complexity of the region in Figure 11.26c provides motivation for the

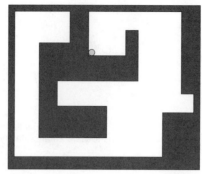

Figure 11.28: A top view of a tray that must be tilted to roll the ball into the desired corner.

approximation methods of Section 11.4.3. For example, the nondeterministic I-states could be nicely approximated by ellipsoidal regions. ∎

11.5.4 Gaining information without sensors

For some problems, it is remarkable that uncertainty may be reduced without even using sensors. Recall Example 11.17. This is counterintuitive because it seems that information regarding the state can only be gained from sensing. It is possible, however, to also gain information from the knowledge that some actions have been executed and the effect that should have in terms of the state transitions. The example presented in this section is inspired by work on *sensorless manipulation planning* [323, 398], which is covered in more detail in Section 12.5.2. This topic underscores the advantages of reasoning in terms of an I-space, as opposed to requiring that accurate state estimates can be made.

Example 11.24 (Tray Tilting) The state space, $X \subset \mathbb{R}^2$, indicates the position of a ball that rolls on a flat surface, as shown Figure 11.28. The ball is confined to roll within the polygonal region shown in the figure. It can be imagined that the ball rolls in a tray on which several barriers have been glued to confine its motion (try this experiment at home!). If the tray is tilted, it is assumed that the ball rolls in a direction induced by gravity (in the same way that a ball rolls to the bottom of a pinball machine).

The tilt of the tray is considered as an action that can be chosen by the robot. It is assumed that the initial position of the ball (initial state) is unknown and there are no sensors that can be used to estimate the state. The task is to find some tilting motions that are guaranteed to place the ball in the position shown in Figure 11.28, regardless of its initial position.

The problem could be modeled with continuous time, but this complicates the design. If the tray is tilted in a particular orientation, it is assumed that the ball rolls in a direction, possibly following the boundary, until it comes to rest. This can be considered as a discrete-stage transition: The ball is in some rest state, a tilt action is applied, and a then it enters another rest state. Thus, a discrete-stage state transition equation, $x_{k+1} = f(x_k, u_k)$, is used.

To describe the tilting actions, we can formally pick directions for the upward normal vector to the tray from the upper half of $\mathbb{S}^2$; however, this can be reduced to a one-dimensional set because the steepness of the tilt is not important, as long as the ball rolls to its new equilibrium state. Therefore, the set of actions can be considered as $U = \mathbb{S}^1$, in which a direction $u \in \mathbb{S}^1$ indicates the direction that the ball rolls due to gravity. Before

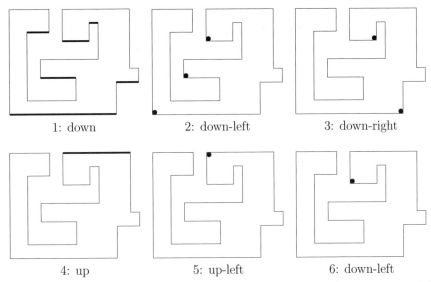

Figure 11.29: A plan is shown that places the ball in the desired location using a sequence of six tilts, regardless of its initial position and in spite of the fact that there are no sensors. The thickened black lines and black dots indicate the possible locations for the ball: the nondeterministic I-states. Under each picture, the direction that the ball rolls due to the action is written.

any action is applied, it is assumed that the tray is initially level (its normal is parallel to the direction of gravity). In practice, one should be more careful and model the motion of the tray between a pair of actions; this is neglected here because the example is only for illustrative purposes. This extra level of detail could be achieved by introducing new state variables that indicate the orientation of the tray or by using continuous-time actions. In the latter case, the action is essentially providing the needed state information, which means that the action function would have to be continuous. Here it is simply assumed that a sequence of actions from $\mathbb{S}^1$ is applied.

The initial condition is $X_1 = X$ and the history I-state is

$$\eta_k = (X_1, u_1, u_2, \ldots, u_{k-1}). \tag{11.74}$$

Since there are no observations, the path through the I-space is predictable. Therefore, a plan, π, is simply an action sequence, $\pi = (u_1, u_2, \ldots, u_K)$, for any desired K.

It is surprisingly simple to solve this task by reasoning in terms of nondeterministic I-states, each of which corresponds to a set of possible locations for the ball. A sequence of six actions, as shown in Figure 11.29, is sufficient to guarantee that the ball will come to rest at the goal position, regardless of its initial position. ■

11.6 Computing probabilistic information states

The probabilistic I-states can be quite complicated in practice because each element of $\mathcal{I}_{prob}$ is a probability distribution or density function. Therefore, substantial effort has been invested in developing efficient techniques for computing probabilistic I-states efficiently. This section can be considered as a continuation of the presentations in Sections 11.2.3 (and part of Section 11.4, for the case of continuous state spaces). Section 11.6.1 covers Kalman filtering, which provides elegant computations of probabilistic I-states. It is designed for problems in which the state transitions and sensor mapping are linear, and all acts of nature are modeled by multivariate Gaussian densities. Section 11.6.2 covers a general sampling-based planning approach, which is approximate but applies to a broader class of problems. One of these methods, called *particle filtering*, has become very popular in recent years for mobile robot localization.

11.6.1 Kalman filtering

This section covers the most successful and widely used example of a derived I-space that dramatically collapses the history I-space. In the special case in which both f and h are linear functions, and $p(\theta)$, $p(\psi)$, and $p(x_1)$ are Gaussian, all probabilistic I-states become Gaussian. This means that the probabilistic I-space, $\mathcal{I}_{prob}$, does not need to represent every conceivable probability density function. The probabilistic I-state is always trapped in the subspace of $\mathcal{I}_{prob}$ that corresponds only to Gaussians. The subspace is denoted as $\mathcal{I}_{gauss}$. This implies that an I-map, $\kappa_{mom} : \mathcal{I}_{prob} \to \mathcal{I}_{gauss}$, can be applied without any loss of information.

The model is called *linear-Gaussian* (or *LG*). Each Gaussian density on $\mathbb{R}^n$ is fully specified by its n-dimensional mean vector μ and an $n \times n$ symmetric covariance matrix, Σ. Therefore, $\mathcal{I}_{gauss}$ can be considered as a subset of $\mathbb{R}^m$ in which $m = 2n + \binom{n}{2}$. For example, if $X = \mathbb{R}^n$, then $\mathcal{I}_{gauss} \subset \mathbb{R}^5$, because two independent parameters specify the mean and three independent parameters specify the covariance matrix (not four, because of symmetry). It was mentioned in Section 11.4.3 that moment-based approximations can be used in general; however, for an LG model it is important to remember that $\mathcal{I}_{gauss}$ is an *exact* representation of $\mathcal{I}_{prob}$.

In addition to the fact that the $\mathcal{I}_{prob}$ collapses nicely, κ_{mom} is a sufficient I-map, and convenient expressions exist for incrementally updating the derived I-states entirely in terms of the computed means and covariance. This implies that we can work directly with $\mathcal{I}_{gauss}$, without any regard for the original histories or even the general formulas for the probabilistic I-states from Section 11.4.1. The update expressions are given here without the full explanation, which is lengthy but not difficult and can be found in virtually any textbook on stochastic control (e.g., [97, 567]).

For Kalman filtering, all of the required spaces are Euclidean, but they may have different dimensions. Therefore, let $X = \mathbb{R}^n$, $U = \Theta = \mathbb{R}^m$, and $Y = \Psi = \mathbb{R}^r$. Since Kalman filtering relies on linear models, everything can be expressed in terms of matrix transformations. Let A_k, B_k, C_k, G_k, and H_k each denote a matrix with constant real-valued entries and which may or may not be singular. The dimensions of the matrices will be inferred from the equations in which they will appear (the dimensions have to be defined correctly to make the multiplications work out right). The k subscript is used to indicate that a different matrix may be used in each stage. In many applications, the matrices will be the same in each stage, in which case they can be denoted by A, B, C, G, and H. Since Kalman filtering can handle the more general case, the subscripts are included (even though they slightly complicate the expressions).

In general, the state transition equation, $x_{k+1} = f_k(x_k, u_k, \theta_k)$, is defined as

$$x_{k+1} = A_k x_k + B_k u_k + G_k \theta_k, \tag{11.75}$$

in which the matrices A_k, B_k, and G_k are of appropriate dimensions. The notation f_k is used instead of f, because the Kalman filter works even if f is different in every stage.

Example 11.25 (Linear-Gaussian Example) For a simple example of (11.75), suppose $X = \mathbb{R}^3$ and $U = \Theta = \mathbb{R}^2$. A particular instance is

$$x_{k+1} = \begin{pmatrix} 0 & \sqrt{2} & 1 \\ 1 & -1 & 4 \\ 2 & 0 & 1 \end{pmatrix} x_k + \begin{pmatrix} 1 & 0 \\ 0 & 1 \\ 1 & 1 \end{pmatrix} u_k + \begin{pmatrix} 1 & 1 \\ 0 & -1 \\ 0 & 1 \end{pmatrix} \theta_k. \tag{11.76}$$

∎

The general form of the sensor mapping $y_k = h_k(x_k, \psi_k)$ is

$$y_k = C_k x_k + H_k \psi_k, \tag{11.77}$$

in which the matrices C_k and H_k are of appropriate dimension. Once again, h_k is used instead of h because a different sensor mapping can be used in every stage.

So far the linear part of the model has been given. The next step is to specify the Gaussian part. In each stage, both nature actions θ_k and ψ_k are modeled with zero-mean Gaussians. Thus, each has an associated covariance matrix, denoted by Σ_θ and Σ_ψ, respectively. Using the model given so far and starting with an initial Gaussian density over X, all resulting probabilistic I-states will be Gaussian [567].

Every derived I-state in $\mathcal{I}_{gauss}$ can be represented by a mean and covariance. Let μ_k and Σ_k denote the mean and covariance of $P(x_k|\eta_k)$. The expressions given in the remainder of this section define a derived information transition equation that computes μ_{k+1} and Σ_{k+1}, given μ_k, Σ_k, u_k, and y_{k+1}. The process starts by computing μ_1 and Σ_1 from the initial conditions.

Assume that an initial condition is given that represents a Gaussian density over $\mathbb{R}^n$. Let this be denoted by μ_0, and Σ_0. The first I-state, which incorporates the first observation y_1, is computed as $\mu_1 = L_1 y_1$ and

$$\Sigma_1 = (I - L_1 C_1) \Sigma_0, \tag{11.78}$$

in which I is the identity matrix and

$$L_1 = \Sigma_0 C_1^T \left(C_1 \Sigma_0 C_1^T + H_1 \Sigma_\psi H_1 \right)^{-1}. \tag{11.79}$$

Although the expression for L_1 is complicated, note that all matrices have been specified as part of the model. The only unfortunate part is that a matrix inversion is required, which sometimes leads to numerical instability in practice; see [567] or other sources for an alternative formulation that alleviates this problem.

Now that μ_1 and Σ_1 have been expressed, the base case is completed. The next part is to give the iterative updates from stage k to stage $k + 1$. Using μ_k, the mean at the next stage is computed as

$$\mu_{k+1} = A_k \mu_k + L_{k+1}(y_{k+1} - C_{k+1} A_k \mu_k), \tag{11.80}$$

in which L_{k+1} will be defined shortly. The covariance is computed in two steps; one is based on applying u_k, and the other arises from considering y_{k+1}. Thus, after u_k is applied, the covariance becomes

$$\Sigma'_{k+1} = A_k \Sigma_k A_k^T + G_k \Sigma_\theta G_k^T. \tag{11.81}$$

After y_{k+1} is received, the covariance Σ_{k+1} is computed from Σ'_{k+1} as

$$\Sigma_{k+1} = (I - L_{k+1} C_{k+1}) \Sigma'_{k+1}. \tag{11.82}$$

The expression for L_k is

$$L_k = \Sigma'_k C_k^T \left(C_k \Sigma'_k C_k^T + H_k \Sigma_\psi H_k \right)^{-1}. \tag{11.83}$$

To obtain L_{k+1}, substitute $k + 1$ for k in (11.83). Note that to compute μ_{k+1} using (11.80), Σ'_{k+1} must first be computed because (11.80) depends on L_{k+1}, which in turn depends on Σ'_{k+1}.

The most common use of the Kalman filter is to provide reliable estimates of the state x_k by using μ_k. It turns out that the optimal expected-cost feedback plan for a cost functional that is a quadratic form can be obtained for LG systems in a closed-from expression; see Section 15.2.2. This model is often called LQG, to reflect the fact that it is linear, quadratic-cost, and Gaussian. The optimal feedback plan can even be expressed directly in terms of μ_k, without requiring Σ_k. This indicates that the I-space may be collapsed down to X; however, the corresponding I-map is not sufficient. The covariances are still needed to compute the means, as is evident from (11.80) and (11.83). Thus, an optimal plan can be specified as $\pi : X \to U$, but the derived I-states in $\mathcal{I}_{gauss}$ need to be represented for the I-map to be sufficient.

The Kalman filter provides a beautiful solution to the class of linear Gaussian models. It is even successfully applied quite often in practice for problems that do not even satisfy these conditions. This is called the *extended Kalman filter*. The success may be explained by recalling that the probabilistic I-space may be approximated by mean and covariance in a second-order moment-based approximation. In general, such an approximation may be inappropriate, but it is nevertheless widely used in practice.

11.6.2 Sampling-based approaches

Since probabilistic I-space computations over continuous spaces involve the evaluation of complicated, possibly high-dimensional integrals, there is strong motivation for using sampling-based approaches. If a problem is nonlinear and/or non-Gaussian, such approaches may provide the only practical way to compute probabilistic I-states. Two approaches are considered here: grid-based sampling and particle filtering. One of the most common applications of the techniques described here is mobile robot localization, which is covered in Section 12.2.

A grid-based approach

Perhaps the most straightforward way to numerically compute probabilistic I-states is to approximate probability density functions over a grid and use numerical integration to evaluate the integrals in (11.57) and (11.58).

A grid can be used to compute a discrete probability distribution that approximates the continuous probability density function. Consider, for example, using the Sukharev grid shown in Figure 5.5a, or a similar grid adapted to the state space. Consider approximating some probability density function $p(x)$ using a finite set, $S \subset X$. The Voronoi region surrounding each point can be considered as a "bucket" that holds probability mass. A probability is associated with each sample and is defined as the integral of $p(x)$ over the Voronoi region associated with the point. In this way, the samples S and their discrete probability distribution, $P(s)$ for all $s \in S$ approximate $p(x)$ over X. Let $P(s_k)$ denote the probability distribution over S_k, the set of grid samples at stage k.

In the initial step, $P(s)$ is computed from $p(x)$ by numerically evaluating the integrals of $p(x_1)$ over the Voronoi region of each sample. This can alternatively be estimated by drawing random samples from the density $p(x_1)$ and then recording the number of samples that fall into each bucket (Voronoi region). Normalizing the counts for the buckets yields a probability distribution, $P(s_1)$. Buckets that have little or no points can be eliminated from future computations, depending on the desired accuracy. Let S_1 denote the samples for which nonzero probabilities are associated.

Now suppose that $P(s_k|\eta_k)$ has been computed over S_k and the task is to compute $P(s_{k+1}|\eta_{k+1})$ given u_k and y_{k+1}. A discrete approximation, $P(s_{k+1}|s_k, u_k)$, to $p(x_{k+1}|x_k, u_k)$ can be computed using a grid and buckets in the manner described above. At this point the densities needed for (11.57) have been approximated by discrete distributions. In this case, (11.38) can be applied over S_k to obtain a grid-based distribution over S_{k+1} (again, any buckets that do not contain enough probability mass can be discarded). The resulting distribution is $P(s_{k+1}|\eta_k, u_k)$, and the next step is to consider y_{k+1}. Once again, a discrete distribution can be computed; in this case, $p(x_{k+1}|y_{k+1})$ is approximated by $P(s_{k+1}|y_{k+1})$ by using the grid samples. This enables (11.58) to be replaced by the discrete counterpart (11.39), which is applied to the samples. The resulting distribution, $P(s_{k+1}|\eta_{k+1})$, represents the approximate probabilistic I-state.

Particle filtering

As mentioned so far, the discrete distributions can be estimated by using samples. In fact, it turns out that the Voronoi regions over the samples do not even need to be carefully considered. One can work directly with a collection of samples drawn randomly from the initial probability density, $p(x_1)$. The general method is referred to as *particle filtering* and has yielded good performance in applications to experimental mobile robotics. Recall Figure 1.7 and see Section 12.2.3.

Let $S \subset X$ denote a finite collection of samples. A probability distribution is defined over S. The collection of samples, together with its probability distribution, is considered as an approximation of a probability density over X. Since S is used to represent probabilistic I-states, let P_k denote the probability distribution over S_k, which is computed at stage k using the history I-state η_k. Thus, at every stage, there is a new sample set, S_k, and probability distribution, P_k.

The general method to compute the probabilistic I-state update proceeds as follows. For some large number, m, of iterations, perform the following:

1. Select a state $x_k \in S_k$ according to the distribution P_k.
2. Generate a new sample, x_{k+1}, for S_{k+1} by generating a single sample according to the density $p(x_{k+1}|x_k, u_k)$.
3. Assign the weight, $w(x_{k+1}) = p(y_{k+1}|x_{k+1})$.

After the m iterations have completed, the weights over S_{k+1} are normalized to obtain a valid probability distribution, P_{k+1}. It turns out that this method provides an approximation that converges to the true probabilistic I-states as m tends to infinity. Other methods exist, which provide faster convergence [539]. One of the main difficulties with using particle filtering is that for some problems it is difficult to ensure that a sufficient concentration of samples exists in the places where they are needed the most. This is a general issue that plagues many sampling-based algorithms, including the motion planning algorithms of Chapter 5.

11.7 Information spaces in game theory

This section unifies the sequential game theory concepts from Section 10.5 with the I-space concepts from this chapter. Considerable attention is devoted to the modeling of information in game theory. The problem is complicated by the fact that each player has its own frame of reference, and hence its own I-space. Game solution concepts, such as saddle points or Nash equilibria, depend critically on the information available to each player as it makes it decisions. Paralleling Section 10.5, the current section first covers I-states in game trees, followed by I-states for games on state spaces. The presentation in this section will be confined to the case in which the state space and stages are finite. The formulation of I-spaces extends naturally to countably infinite or continuous state spaces, action spaces, and stages [60].

11.7.1 Information States in Game Trees

Recall from Section 10.5.1 that an important part of formulating a sequential game in a game tree is specifying the information model. This was described in Step 4 of Formulation 10.3. Three information models were considered in Section 10.5.1: alternating play, stage-by-stage, and open loop. These and many other information models can be described using I-spaces.

From Section 11.1, it should be clear that an I-space is always defined with respect to a state space. Even though Section 10.5.1 did not formally introduce a state space, it is not difficult to define one. Let the state space X be N, the set of all vertices in the game tree. Assume that two players are engaged in a sequential zero-sum game. Using notation from Section 10.5.1, N_1 and N_2 are the decision vertices of P_1 and P_2, respectively. Consider the nondeterministic I-space $\mathcal{I}_{ndet}$ over N. Let η denote a nondeterministic I-state; thus, each $\eta \in \mathcal{I}_{ndet}$ is a subset of N.

There are now many possible ways in which the players can be confused while making their decisions. For example, if some η contains vertices from both N_1 and N_2, the player does not know whether it is even its turn to make a decision. If η additionally contains some leaf vertices, the game may be finished without a player even being aware of it. Most game tree formulations avoid these strange situations. It is usually assumed that the players at least know when it is their turn to make a decision. It is also usually assumed that they know the stage of the game. This eliminates many sets from $\mathcal{I}_{ndet}$.

While playing the game, each player has its own nondeterministic I-state because the players may hide their decisions from each other. Let η_1 and η_2 denote the nondeterministic I-states for P_1 and P_2, respectively. For each player, many sets in $\mathcal{I}_{ndet}$ are eliminated. Some are removed to avoid the confusions mentioned above. We also impose the constraint that $\eta_i \subseteq N_i$ for $i = 1$ and $i = 2$. We only care about the I-state of a player when it is that player's turn to make a decision. Thus, the nondeterministic I-state should tell us which decision vertices in N_i are possible as P_i faces a decision. Let $\mathcal{I}_1$ and $\mathcal{I}_2$ represent the nondeterministic I-spaces for P_1 and P_2, respectively, with all impossible I-states eliminated.

The I-spaces $\mathcal{I}_1$ and $\mathcal{I}_2$ are usually defined directly on the game tree by circling vertices that belong to the same I-state. They form a partition of the vertices in each level of the

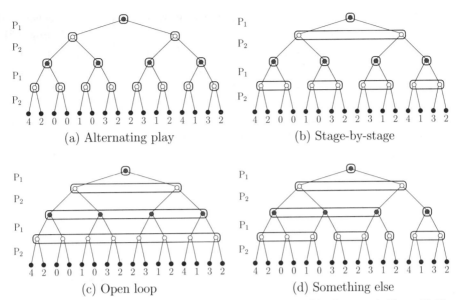

Figure 11.30: Several different information models are illustrated for the game in Figure 10.13.

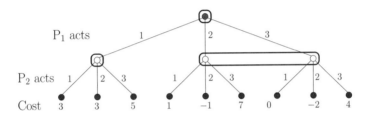

Figure 11.31: A single-stage game that has an information model unlike those in Section 10.5.1.

tree (except the leaves). In fact, $\mathcal{I}_i$ even forms a partition of N_i for each player. Figure 11.30 shows four information models specified in this way for the example in Figure 10.13. The first three correspond directly to the models allowed in Section 10.5.1. In the alternating-play model, each player always knows the decision vertex. This corresponds to a case of perfect state information. In the stage-by-stage model, P_1 always knows the decision vertex; P_2 knows the decision vertex from which P_1 made its last decision, but it does not know which branch was chosen. The open-loop model represents the case that has the poorest information. Only P_1 knows its decision vertex at the beginning of the game. After that, there is no information about the actions chosen. In fact, the players cannot even remember their own previous actions. Figure 11.30d shows an information model that does not fit into any of the three previous ones. In this model, very strange behavior results. If P_1 and P_2 initially choose right branches, then the resulting decision vertex is known; however, if P_2 instead chooses the left branch, then P_1 will forget which action it applied (as if the action of P_2 caused P_1 to have amnesia!). Here is a single-stage example:

Example 11.26 (An Unusual Information Model) Figure 11.31 shows a game that does not fit any of the information models in Section 10.5.1. It is actually a variant of the game considered before in Figure 10.12. The game is a kind of hybrid that partly looks like the alternating-play model and partly like the stage-by-stage model. This particular problem can be solved in the usual way, from the bottom up. A value is computed for each of the nondeterministic I-states, for the level in which P_2 makes a decision. The left I-state has value 5, which corresponds to P_1 choosing 1 and P_2 responding with 3. The right I-state has value 4, which results from the deterministic saddle point in a 2×3 matrix game played between P_1 and P_2. The overall game has a deterministic saddle point in which P_1 chooses 3 and P_2 chooses 3. This results in a value of 4 for the game.   ■

Plans are now defined directly as functions on the I-spaces. A *(deterministic) plan for* P_1 is defined as a function π_1 on $\mathcal{I}_1$ that yields an action $u \in U(\eta_1)$ for each $\eta_1 \in \mathcal{I}_1$, and $U(\eta_1)$ is the set of actions that can be inferred from the I-state η_1; assume that this set is the same for all decision vertices in η_1. Similarly, a *(deterministic) plan for* P_2 is defined as a function π_2 on $\mathcal{I}_2$ that yields an action $v \in V(\eta_2)$ for each $\eta_2 \in \mathcal{I}_2$.

There are generally two alternative ways to define a randomized plan in terms of I-spaces. The first choice is to define a *globally randomized plan*, which is a probability distribution over the set of all deterministic plans. During execution, this means that an entire deterministic plan will be sampled in advance according to the probability distribution. An alternative is to sample actions as they are needed at each I-state. This is defined as follows. For the randomized case, let $W(\eta_1)$ and $Z(\eta_2)$ denote the sets of all probability distributions over $U(\eta_1)$ and $V(\eta_2)$, respectively. A *locally randomized plan for* P_1 is defined as a function that yields some $w \in W(\eta_1)$ for each $\eta_1 \in \mathcal{I}_1$. Likewise, a *locally randomized plan for* P_2 is a function that maps from $\mathcal{I}_2$ into $Z(\eta_2)$. Locally randomized plans expressed as functions of I-states are often called *behavioral strategies* in game theory literature.

A randomized saddle point on the space of locally randomized plans does not exist for all sequential games [60]. This is unfortunate because this form of randomization seems most natural for the way decisions are made during execution. At least for the stage-by-stage model, a randomized saddle point always exists on the space of locally randomized plans. For the open-loop model, randomized saddle points are only guaranteed to exist using a globally randomized plan (this was actually done in Section 10.5.1). To help understand the problem, suppose that the game tree is a balanced, binary tree with k stages (hence, $2k$ levels). For each player, there are 2^k possible deterministic plans. This means that $2^k - 1$ probability values may be assigned independently (the last one is constrained to force them to sum to 1) to define a globally randomized plan over the space of deterministic plans. Defining a locally randomized plan, there are k I-states for each player, one for each search stage. At each stage, a probability distribution is defined over the action set, which contains only two elements. Thus, each of these distributions has only one independent parameter. A randomized plan is specified in this way using $k - 1$ independent parameters. Since $k - 1$ is much less than $2^k - 1$, there are many globally randomized plans that cannot be expressed as a locally randomized plan. Unfortunately, in some games the locally randomized representation removes the randomized saddle point.

This strange result arises mainly because players can forget information over time. A player with *perfect recall* remembers its own actions and also never forgets any information that it previously knew. It was shown by Kuhn that the space of all globally randomized plans is equivalent to the space of all locally randomized plans if and only if the players have perfect memory [565]. Thus, by sticking to games in which all players have perfect recall, a randomized saddle point always exists in the space locally randomized plans. The result of Kuhn even holds for the more general case of the existence of randomized Nash equilibria on the space of locally randomized plans.

The nondeterministic I-states can be used in game trees that involve more players. Accordingly, deterministic, globally randomized, and locally randomized plans can be defined. The result of Kuhn applies to any number of players, which ensures the existence of a randomized Nash equilibrium on the space of locally randomized strategies if (and only if) the players have perfect recall. It is generally preferable to exploit this fact and decompose the game tree into smaller matrix games, as described in Section 10.5.1. It turns out that the precise condition that allows this is that it must be *ladder-nested* [60]. This means that there are decision vertices, other than the root, at which 1) the player that must make a decision knows it is at that vertex (the nondeterministic I-state is a singleton set), and 2) the nondeterministic I-state will not leave the subtree rooted at that vertex (vertices outside of the subtree cannot be circled when drawing the game tree). In this case, the game tree can be decomposed at these special decision vertices and replaced with the game value(s). Unfortunately, there is still the nuisance of multiple Nash equilibria.

It may seem odd that nondeterministic I-states were defined without being derived from a history I-space. Without much difficulty, it is possible to define a sensing model that leads to the nondeterministic I-states used in this section. In many cases, the I-state can be expressed using only a subset of the action histories. Let $\tilde{u}_k$ and $\tilde{v}_k$ denote the action histories of P_1 and P_2, respectively. The history I-state for the alternating-play model at stage k is $(\tilde{u}_{k-1}, \tilde{v}_{k-1})$ for P_1 and $(\tilde{u}_k, \tilde{v}_{k-1})$ for P_2. The history I-state for the stage-by-stage model is $(\tilde{u}_{k-1}, \tilde{v}_{k-1})$ for both players. The nondeterministic I-states used in this section can be derived from these histories. For other models, such as the one in Figure 11.31, a sensing model is additionally needed because only partial information regarding some actions appears. This leads into the formulation covered in the next section, which involves both sensing models and a state space.

11.7.2 Information spaces for games on state spaces

I-space concepts can also be incorporated into sequential games that are played over state spaces. The resulting formulation naturally extends Formulation 11.1 of Section 11.1 to multiple players. Rather than starting with two players and generalizing later, the full generality of having n players is assumed up front. The focus in this section is primarily on *characterizing* I-spaces for such games, rather than solving them. Solution approaches depend heavily on the particular information models; therefore, they will not be covered here.

As in Section 11.7.1, each player has its own frame of reference and therefore its own I-space. The I-state for each player indicates its information regarding a common game state. This is the same state as introduced in Section 10.5; however, each player may have different observations and may not know the actions of others. Therefore, the I-state is different for each decision maker. In the case of perfect state sensing, these I-spaces all collapse to X.

Suppose that there are n players. As presented in Section 10.5, each player has its own action space, U^i; however, here it is not allowed to depend on x, because the state may generally be unknown. It can depend, however, on the I-state. If nature actions may interfere with the state transition equation, then (10.120) is used (if there are two players); otherwise, (10.121) is used, which leads to predictable future states if the actions of all of the players are given. A single nature action, $\theta \in \Theta(x, u^1, u^2, \ldots, u^n)$, is used to model the effect of nature across all players when uncertainty in prediction exists.

Any of the sensor models from Section 11.1.1 may be defined in the case of multiple players. Each has its own observation space Y^i and sensor mapping h^i. For each player, nature may interfere with observations through nature sensing actions, $\Psi^i(x)$. A state-action sensor mapping appears as $y^i = h^i(x, \psi^i)$; state sensor mappings and history-based sensor mappings may also be defined.

Consider how the game appears to a single player at stage k. What information might be available for making a decision? Each player produces the following in the most general case: 1) an initial condition, η_0^i; 2) an action history, $\tilde{u}_{k-1}^i$; and 3) and an observation history, $\tilde{y}_k^i$. It must be specified whether one player knows the previous actions that have been applied by other players. It might even be possible for one player to receive the observations of other players. If P_i receives all of this information, its history I-state at stage k is

$$\eta_k^i = (\eta_0^i, \tilde{u}_{k-1}^1, \tilde{u}_{k-1}^2, \ldots, \tilde{u}_{k-1}^n, \tilde{y}_k^1, \tilde{y}_k^2, \ldots, \tilde{y}_k^n). \qquad (11.84)$$

In most situations, however, η_k^i only includes a subset of the histories from (11.84). A typical situation is

$$\eta_k^i = (\eta_0^i, \tilde{u}_{k-1}^i, \tilde{y}_k^i), \qquad (11.85)$$

which means that P_i knows only its own actions and observations. Another possibility is that all players know all actions that have been applied, but they do not receive the observations of other players. This results in

$$\eta_k^i = (\eta_0^i, \tilde{u}_{k-1}^1, \tilde{u}_{k-1}^2, \ldots, \tilde{u}_{k-1}^n, \tilde{y}_k^i). \qquad (11.86)$$

Of course, many special cases may be defined by generalizing many of the examples in this chapter. For example, an intriguing sensorless game may be defined in which the history I-state consists only of actions. This could yield

$$\eta_k^i = (\eta_0^i, \tilde{u}_{k-1}^1, \tilde{u}_{k-1}^2, \ldots, \tilde{u}_{k-1}^n), \qquad (11.87)$$

or even a more secretive game in which the actions of other players are not known:

$$\eta_k^i = (\eta_0^i, \tilde{u}_{k-1}^i). \qquad (11.88)$$

Once the I-state has been decided upon, a history I-space $\mathcal{I}_{hist}^i$ for each player is defined as the set of all history I-states. In general, I-maps and derived I-spaces can be defined to yield alternative simplifications of each history I-space.

Assuming all spaces are finite, the concepts given so far can be organized into a sequential game formulation that is the imperfect state information counterpart of Formulation 10.4:

Formulation 11.4 (Sequential Game with I-Spaces)

1. A set of n players, $P_1, P_2, \ldots, P_n$.

2. A nonempty, finite *state space* X.

3. For each P_i, a finite *action space* U^i. We also allow a more general definition, in which the set of available choices depends on the history I-state; this can be written as $U^i(\eta^i)$.

4. A finite *nature action space* $\Theta(x, u^1, \ldots, u^n)$ for each $x \in X$, and $u^i \in U^i$ for each i such that $1 \le i \le m$.

5. A *state transition function* f that produces a state, $f(x, u^1, \ldots, u^n, \theta)$, for every $x \in X$, $\theta \in \Theta(x, u)$, and $u^i \in U^i$ for each i such that $1 \le i \le n$.

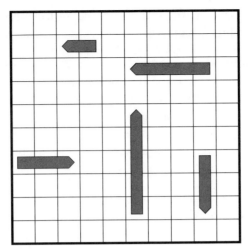

Figure 11.32: In the Battleship game, each player places several ships on a grid. The other player must guess the locations of ships by asking whether a particular tile is occupied.

6. For each P_i, a finite *observation space* Y^i.

7. For each P_i, a finite *nature sensing action space* $\Psi^i(x)$ for each $x \in X$.

8. For each P_i, a *sensor mapping* h^i which produces an observation, $y = h^i(x, \psi^i)$, for each $x \in X$ and $\psi^i \in \Psi^i(x)$. This definition assumes a state-nature sensor mapping. A state sensor mapping or history-based sensor mapping, as defined in Section 11.1.1, may alternatively be used.

9. A set of K *stages*, each denoted by k, which begins at $k = 1$ and ends at $k = K$. Let $F = K + 1$.

10. For each P_i, an *initial condition* η_0^i, which is an element of an *initial condition space* $\mathcal{I}_0^i$.

11. For each P_i, a *history I-space* $\mathcal{I}_{hist}^i$ which is the set of all history I-states, formed from action and observation histories, and may include the histories of other players.

12. For each P_i, let L^i denote a stage-additive cost functional,

$$L^i(\tilde{x}_F, \tilde{u}_K^1, \ldots, \tilde{u}_K^2) = \sum_{k=1}^{K} l(x_k, u_k^1, \ldots, u_k^n) + l_F(x_F). \qquad (11.89)$$

Extensions exist for cases in which one or more of the spaces are continuous; see [60]. It is also not difficult to add goal sets and termination conditions and allow the stages to run indefinitely.

An interesting specialization of Formulation 11.4 is when all players have identical cost functions. This is not equivalent to having a single player because the players have different I-states. For example, a task may be for several robots to search for a treasure, but they have limited communication between them. This results in different I-states. They would all like to cooperate, but they are unable to do so without knowing the state. Such problems fall under the subject of *team theory* [227, 453, 533].

As for the games considered in Formulation 10.4, each player has its own plan. Since the players do not necessarily know the state, the decisions are based on the I-state. The definitions of a deterministic plan, a globally randomized plan, and a locally randomized plan are essentially the same as in Section 11.7.1. The only difference is that more general I-spaces are defined in the current setting. Various kinds of solution concepts, such as saddle points and Nash equilibria, can be defined for the general game in Formulation 11.4.

The existence of locally randomized saddle points and Nash equilibria depends on general on the particular information model [60].

Example 11.27 (Battleship Game)   Many interesting I-spaces arise from classical board games. A brief illustration is provided here from Battleship, which is a sequential game under the alternating-turn model. Two players, P_1 and P_2, each having a collection of battleships that it arranges secretly on a 10×10 grid; see Figure 11.32.

A state is the specification of the exact location of all ships on each player's grid. The state space yields the set of all possible ship locations for both players. Each player always knows the location of its own ships. Once they are placed on the grid, they are never allowed to move.

The players take turns guessing a single grid tile, expressed as a row and column, that it suspects contains a ship. The possible observations are "hit" and "miss," depending on whether a ship was at that location. In each turn, a single guess is made, and the players continue taking turns until one player has observed a hit for every tile that was occupied by a ship.

This is an interesting game because once a "hit" is discovered, it is clear that a player should search for other hits in the vicinity because there are going to be several contiguous tiles covered by the same ship. The only problem is that the precise ship position and orientation are unknown. A good player essentially uses the nondeterministic I-state to improve the chances that a hit will occur next.   ∎

Example 11.28 (The Princess and the Monster)   This is a classic example from game theory that involves no sensing. A princess and a monster move about in a 2D environment. A simple motion model is assumed; for example, they take single steps on a grid. The princess is trying not to be discovered by the monster, and the game is played in complete darkness. The game ends when the monster and the princess are on the same grid point. There is no form of feedback that can be used during the game; however, it is possible to construct nondeterministic I-states for the players. For most environments, it is impossible for the monster to be guaranteed to win; however, for some environments it is guaranteed to succeed. This example can be considered as a special kind of *pursuit-evasion game*. A continuous-time pursuit-evasion game that involves I-spaces is covered in Section 12.4.   ∎

Further reading

The basic concept of an information space can be traced back to work of Kuhn [565] in the context of game trees. There, the nondeterministic I-state is referred to as an *information set*. After spreading throughout game theory, the concept was also borrowed into stochastic control theory (see [97, 567]). The term *information space* is used extensively in [60] in the context of sequential and differential game theory. For further reading on I-spaces in game theory, see [60, 762]. In artificial intelligence literature, I-states are referred to as *belief states* and are particularly important in the study of POMDPs; see the literature suggested at the end of Chapter 12. The *observability problem* in control theory also results in I-spaces [194, 310, 481, 913], in which *observers* are used to reconstruct the current state from the history I-state. In robotics literature, they have been called *hyperstates* [398] and *knowledge states* [317]. Concepts closely related to I-spaces also appear as *perceptual equivalence classes* in [289] and also appear in the *information invariants* framework of Donald [288]. I-spaces were proposed as a general way to represent planning under sensing uncertainty in [69, 607, 608]. For further reading on sensors in general, see [354].

The Kalman filter is covered in great detail in numerous other texts; see for example, [228, 567, 913]. The original reference is [503]. For more on particle filters, see [45, 295, 352, 539].

Exercises

1. Forward projections in $\mathcal{I}_{ndet}$:

    (a) Starting from a nondeterministic I-state, $X_k(\eta_k)$, and applying an action u_k, derive an expression for the nondeterministic one-stage forward projection by extending the presentation in Section 10.1.2.

    (b) Determine an expression for the two-stage forward projection starting from $X_k(\eta_k)$ and applying u_k and u_{k+1}.

2. Forward projections in $\mathcal{I}_{prob}$:

    (a) Starting from a probabilistic I-state, $P(x_k|\eta_k)$, and applying an action u_k, derive an expression for the probabilistic one-stage forward projection.

    (b) Determine an expression for the two-stage forward projection starting from $P(x_k|\eta_k)$ and applying u_k and u_{k+1}.

3. Determine the strong and weak backprojections on $\mathcal{I}_{hist}$ for a given history I-state, η_k. These should give sets of possible $\eta_{k-1} \in \mathcal{I}_{hist}$.

4. At the end of Section 11.3.2, it was mentioned that an equivalent DFA can be constructed from an NFA.

    (a) Give an explicit DFA that accepts the same set of strings as the NFA in Figure 11.8b.

    (b) Express the problem of determining whether the NFA in Figure 11.8b accepts any strings as a planning problem using Formulation 2.1.

5. This problem involves computing probabilistic I-states for Example 11.14. Let the initial I-state be

$$P(x_1) = [1/3 \ \ 1/3 \ \ 1/3], \tag{11.90}$$

in which the ith entry in the vector indicates $P(x_1 = i + 1)$. Let $U = \{0, 1\}$. For each action, a state transition matrix can be specified, which gives the probabilities $P(x_{k+1}|x_k, u_k)$. For $u = 0$, let $P(x_{k+1}|x_k, u_k = 0)$ be

$$\begin{pmatrix} 4/5 & 1/5 & 0 \\ 1/10 & 4/5 & 1/10 \\ 0 & 1/5 & 4/5 \end{pmatrix}. \tag{11.91}$$

The jth entry of the ith row yields $P(x_{k+1} = i \mid x_k = j, u_k = 0)$. For $u = 1$, let $P(x_{k+1} \mid x_k, u_k = 1)$ be

$$\begin{pmatrix} 1/10 & 5/5 & 1/10 \\ 0 & 1/5 & 4/5 \\ 0 & 0 & 1 \end{pmatrix}. \tag{11.92}$$

The sensing model is specified by three vectors:

$$P(y_k|x_k = 0) = [4/5 \ \ 1/5], \tag{11.93}$$

$$P(y_k|x_k = 1) = [1/2 \ \ 1/2], \tag{11.94}$$

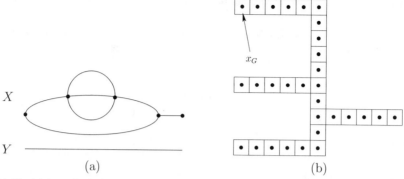

Figure 11.33: (a) A topological graph in which a point moves (note that two vertices are vertically aligned). (b) An exercise that is a variant of Example 11.17.

and

$$P(y_k|x_k = 2) = [1/5 \ \ 4/5], \tag{11.95}$$

in which the ith component yields $P(y_k = i \mid x_k)$. Suppose that $k = 3$ and the history I-state obtained so far is

$$(\eta_0, u_1, u_2, y_1, y_2, y_3) = (\eta_0, 1, 0, 1, 0, 0). \tag{11.96}$$

The task is to compute the probabilistic I-state. Starting from $P(x_1)$, compute the following distributions: $P(x_1|\eta_1)$, $P(x_2|\eta_1, u_1)$, $P(x_2|\eta_2)$, $P(x_3|\eta_2, u_2)$, $P(x_3|\eta_3)$.

6. Explain why it is not possible to reach every nondeterministic I-state from every other one for Example 11.7. Give an example of a nondeterministic I-state that cannot be reached from the initial I-state. Completely characterize the reachability of nondeterministic I-states from all possible initial conditions.

7. In the same spirit as Example 11.21, consider a point moving on the topological graph shown in Figure 11.33. Fully characterize the connectivity of $\mathcal{I}_{ndet}$ (you may exploit symmetries to simplify the answer).

8. Design an I-map for Example 11.17 that is not necessarily sufficient but leads to a solution plan defined over only three derived I-states.

9. Consider the discrete problem in Figure 11.33b, using the same sensing and motion model as in Example 11.17.

   (a) Develop a sufficient I-map and a solution plan that uses as few derived I-states as possible.

   (b) Develop an I-map that is not necessarily sufficient, and a solution plan that uses as few derived I-states as possible.

10. Suppose that there are two I-maps, $\kappa_1 : \mathcal{I}_1 \to \mathcal{I}_2$ and $\kappa_2 : \mathcal{I}_2 \to \mathcal{I}_3$, and it is given that κ_1 is sufficient with respect to $\mathcal{I}_1$, and κ_2 is sufficient with respect to $\mathcal{I}_2$. Determine whether the I-map $\kappa_2 \circ \kappa_1$ is sufficient with respect to $\mathcal{I}_1$, and prove your claim.

11. Propose a solution to Example 11.16 that uses fewer nondeterministic I-states.

12. Suppose that a point robot moves in $\mathbb{R}^2$ and receives observations from three homing beacons that are not collinear and originate from known locations. Assume that the robot can calibrate the three observations on $\mathbb{S}^1$.

   (a) Prove that the robot can always recover its position in $\mathbb{R}^2$.

   (b) What can the robot infer if there are only two beacons?

13. Nondeterministic I-state problems:

    (a) Prove that the nondeterministic I-states for Example 11.23 are always a single connected region whose boundary is composed only of circular arcs and line segments.

    (b) Design an algorithm for efficiently computing the nondeterministic I-states from stage to stage.

14. Design an algorithm that takes as input a simply connected rectilinear region (i.e., described by a polygon that has all right angles) and a goal state, and designs a sequence of tray tilts that guarantees the ball will come to rest at the goal. Example 11.24 provides an illustration.

15. Extend the game-theoretic formulation from Section 11.7.2 of history I-spaces to continuous time.

16. Consider the "where did I come from?" problem.

    (a) Derive an expression for $X_1(\eta_k)$.

    (b) Derive an expression for $P(x_1|\eta_k)$.

17. In the game of Example 11.27, could there exist a point in the game at which one player has not yet observed every possible "hit" yet it knows the state of the game (i.e., the exact location of all ships)? Explain.

18. When playing blackjack in casinos, many *card-counting* strategies involve remembering simple statistics of the cards, rather than the entire history of cards seen so far. Define a game of blackjack and card counting as an example of history I-states and an I-map that dramatically reduces the size of the I-space, and an information-feedback plan.

Implementations

19. Implement the Kalman filter for the case of a robot moving in the plane. Show the confidence ellipsoids obtained during execution. Be careful of numerical issues (see [567]).

20. Implement probabilistic I-state computations for a point robot moving in a 2D polygonal environment. Compare the efficiency and accuracy of grid-based approximations to particle filtering.

21. Design and implement an algorithm that uses nondeterministic I-states to play a good game of Battleship, as explained in Example 11.27.

12

Planning Under Sensing Uncertainty

The main purpose of Chapter 11 was to introduce information space (I-space) concepts and to provide illustrative examples that aid in understanding. This chapter addresses planning under sensing uncertainty, which amounts to planning in an I-space. Section 12.1 covers general-purpose algorithms, for which it will quickly be discovered that only problems with very few states can be solved because of the explosive growth of the I-space. In Chapter 6, it was seen that general-purpose motion planning algorithms apply only to simple problems. Ways to avoid this were either to develop sampling-based techniques or to focus on a narrower class of problems. It is intriguing to apply sampling-based planning ideas to I-spaces, but as of yet this idea remains largely unexplored. Therefore, the majority of this chapter focuses on planning algorithms designed for narrower classes of problems. In each case, interesting algorithms have been developed that can solve problems that are much more complicated than what could be solved by the general-purpose algorithms. This is because they exploit some structure that is specific to the problem.

An important philosophy when dealing with an I-space is to develop an I-map that reduces its size and complexity as much as possible by obtaining a simpler derived I-space. Following this, it may be possible to design a special-purpose algorithm that efficiently solves the new problem by relying on the fact that the I-space does have the full generality. This idea will appear repeatedly throughout the chapter. The most common derived I-space is $\mathcal{I}_{ndet}$ from Section 11.2.2; $\mathcal{I}_{prob}$, from Section 11.2.3, will also arise.

After Section 12.1, the problems considered in the remainder of the chapter are inspired mainly by robotics applications. Section 12.2 addresses the localization problem, which means that a robot must use sensing information to determine its location. This is essentially a matter of maintaining derived I-states and computing plans that lead to the desired derived I-space. Section 12.3 generalizes localization to problems in which the robot does not even know its environment. In this case, the state space and I-space take into account both the possible environments in which the robot might be and the possible locations of the robot within each environment. This section is fundamental to robotics because it is costly and difficult to build precise maps of a robot's environment. By careful consideration of the I-space, a complete representation may be safely avoided in many applications.

Section 12.4 covers a kind of pursuit-evasion game that can be considered as a formal version of the children's game of "hide and seek." The pursuer carries a lantern and must illuminate an unpredictable evader that moves with unbounded speed. The nondeterministic I-states for this problem characterize the set of possible evader locations. The problem is solved by performing a cell decomposition of $\mathcal{I}_{ndet}$ to obtain a finite, graph-search problem. The method is based on finding critical curves in the I-space, much like the critical-curve method in Section 6.3.4 for moving a line-segment robot.

Section 12.5 concludes the chapter with manipulation planning under imperfect state information. This differs from the manipulation planning considered in Section 7.3.2

because it was assumed there that the state is always known. Section 12.5.1 presents the preimage planning framework, which was introduced two decades ago to address manipulation planning problems that have bounded uncertainty models for the state transitions and the sensors. Many important I-space ideas and complexity results were obtained from this framework and the body of literature on which it was based; therefore, it will be covered here. Section 12.5.2 addresses problems in which the robots have very limited sensing information and rely on the information gained from the physical interaction of objects. In some cases, these methods surprisingly do not even require sensing.

12.1 General methods

This section presents planning methods for the problems introduced in Section 11.1. They are based mainly on general-purpose dynamic programming, without exploiting any particular structure to the problem. Therefore, their application is limited to small state spaces; nevertheless, they are worth covering because of their extreme generality. The basic idea is to use either the nondeterministic or probabilistic I-map to express the problem entirely in terms of the derived I-space, $\mathcal{I}_{ndet}$ or $\mathcal{I}_{prob}$, respectively. Once the derived information transition equation (recall Section 11.2.1) is defined, it can be imagined that $\mathcal{I}_{ndet}$ or $\mathcal{I}_{prob}$ is a state space in which perfect state measurements are obtained during execution (because the I-state is always known).

12.1.1 The information space as a big state space

Recall that any problem specified using Formulation 11.1 can be converted using derived I-states into a problem under Formulation 10.1. By building on the discussion from the end of Section 11.1.3, this can be achieved by treating the I-space as a big state space in which each state is an I-state in the original problem formulation. Some of the components were given previously, but here a complete formulation is given.

Suppose that a problem has been specified using Formulation 11.1, resulting in the usual components: X, U, Θ, f, Y, h, x_I, X_G, and L. The following concepts will work for any sufficient I-map; however, the presentation will be limited to two important cases: κ_{ndet} and κ_{prob}, which yield derived I-spaces $\mathcal{I}_{ndet}$ and $\mathcal{I}_{prob}$, respectively (recall Sections 11.2.2 and 11.2.3).

The components of Formulation 10.1 will now be specified using components of the original problem. To avoid confusion between the two formulations, an arrow will be placed above all components of the new formulation. Figure 12.1 summarizes the coming definitions. The new state space, $\vec{X}$, is defined as $\vec{X} = \mathcal{I}_{der}$, and a state, $\vec{x} \in \vec{X}$, is a derived I-state, $\vec{x} = \eta_{der}$. Under nondeterministic uncertainty, $\vec{x}_k$ means $X_k(\eta_k)$, in which η_k is the history I-state. Under probabilistic uncertainty, $\vec{x}_k$ means $P(x_k|\eta_k)$. The action space remains the same: $\vec{U} = U$.

The strangest part of the formulation is the new nature action space, $\vec{\Theta}(\vec{x}, \vec{u})$. The observations in Formulation 11.1 behave very much like nature actions because they are not selected by the robot, and, as will be seen shortly, they are the only unpredictable part of the new state transition equation. Therefore, $\vec{\Theta}(\vec{x}, \vec{u}) \subseteq Y$, the original observation space. A new nature action, $\vec{\theta} \in \vec{\Theta}$, is just an observation, $\vec{\theta}(\vec{x}, \vec{u}) = y$. The set $\vec{\Theta}(\vec{x}, \vec{u})$ generally depends on $\vec{x}$ and $\vec{u}$ because some observations may be impossible to receive from some states. For example, if a sensor that measures a mobile robot position is never

Item	Notation	Explanation
State	$\vec{x} = \eta_{der}$	Derived I-state
State space	$\vec{X} = \mathcal{I}_{der}$	Derived I-space
Action space	$\vec{U} = U$	Original action space
Nature action space	$\vec{\Theta} \subseteq Y$	Original observation space
State transition equation	$\vec{f}(\vec{x}, \vec{u}, \vec{\theta})$	Nature action is just y
Initial state	$\vec{x}_I = \eta_0$	Initial I-state, $\eta_0 \in \mathcal{I}_{der}$
Goal set	$\vec{X}_G$	Subsets of original X_G
Cost functional	$\vec{L}$	Derived from original L

Figure 12.1: The derived I-space can be treated as an ordinary state space on which planning with perfect state information can be performed.

wrong by more than 1 meter, then observations that are further than 1 meter from the true robot position are impossible.

A derived state transition equation is defined with $\vec{f}(\vec{x}_k, \vec{u}_k, \vec{\theta}_k)$ and yields a new state, $\vec{x}_{k+1}$. Using the original notation, this is just a function that uses $\kappa(\eta_k)$, u_k, and y_k to compute the next derived I-state, $\kappa(\eta_{k+1})$, which is allowed because we are working with sufficient I-maps, as described in Section 11.2.1.

Initial states and goal sets are optional and can be easily formulated in the new representation. The initial I-state, η_0, becomes the new initial state, $\vec{x}_I = \eta_0$. It is assumed that η_0 is either a subset of X or a probability distribution, depending on whether planning occurs in $\mathcal{I}_{ndet}$ or $\mathcal{I}_{prob}$. In the nondeterministic case, the new goal set $\vec{X}_G$ can be derived as

$$\vec{X}_G = \{X(\eta) \in \mathcal{I}_{ndet} \mid X(\eta) \subseteq X_G\}, \tag{12.1}$$

which is the set of derived I-states for which it is *guaranteed* that the true state lies in X_G. A probabilistic version can be made by requiring that all states assigned nonzero probability by $P(x|\eta)$ lie in X_G. Instead of being nonzero, a threshold could be used. For example, the goal may require being only 98% certain that the goal is reached.

The only remaining portion of Formulation 10.1 is the cost functional. We will develop a cost model that uses only the state and action histories. A dependency on nature would imply that the costs depend directly on the observation, $y = \vec{\theta}$, which was not assumed in Formulation 11.1. The general K-stage cost functional from Formulation 10.1 appears in this context as

$$\vec{L}(\vec{x}_k, \vec{u}_k) = \sum_{k=1}^{K} \vec{l}(\vec{x}_k, \vec{u}_k) + \vec{l}_F(\vec{x}_F), \tag{12.2}$$

with the usual cost assumptions regarding the termination action.

The cost functional $\vec{L}$ must be derived from the cost functional L of the original problem. This is expressed in terms of states, which are unknown. First consider the case of $\mathcal{I}_{prob}$. The state x_k at stage k follows the probability distribution $P(x_k|\eta_k)$, as derived in Section 11.2.3. Using $\vec{x}_k$, an expected cost is assigned as

$$\vec{l}(\vec{x}_k, \vec{u}_k) = \vec{l}(\eta_k, u_k) = \sum_{x_k \in X} P(x_k|\eta_k)l(x_k, u_k) \tag{12.3}$$

and

$$\vec{l}_F(\vec{x}_F) = \vec{l}_F(\eta_F) = \sum_{x_F \in X} P(x_F|\eta_K)l_F(x_F). \tag{12.4}$$

Ideally, we would like to make analogous expressions for the case of $\mathcal{I}_{ndet}$; however, there is one problem. Formulating the worst-case cost for each stage is too pessimistic. For example, it may be possible to obtain high costs in two consecutive stages, but each of these may correspond to following different paths in X. There is nothing to constrain the worst-case analysis to the *same* path. In the probabilistic case there is no problem because probabilities can be assigned to paths. For the nondeterministic case, a cost functional can be defined, but the stage-additive property needed for dynamic programming is destroyed in general. Under some restrictions on allowable costs, the stage-additive property is preserved.

The state x_k at stage k is known to lie in $X_k(\eta_k)$, as derived in Section 11.2.2. For every history I-state, $\eta_k = \vec{x}_k$, and $u_k \in U$, assume that $l(x_k, u_k)$ is invariant over all $x_k \in X_k(\eta_k)$. In this case,

$$\vec{l}(\vec{x}_k, \vec{u}_k) = \vec{l}(\eta_k, u_k) = l(x_k, u_k), \tag{12.5}$$

in which $x_k \in X_k(\eta_k)$, and

$$\vec{l}_F(\vec{x}_F) = \vec{l}_F(\eta_F) = l_F(x_F), \tag{12.6}$$

in which $x_F \in X_F(\eta_F)$.

A plan on the derived I-space, $\mathcal{I}_{ndet}$ or $\mathcal{I}_{prob}$, can now also be considered as a plan on the new state space $\vec{X}$. Thus, state feedback is now possible, but in a larger state space $\vec{X}$ instead of X. The outcomes of actions are still generally unpredictable due to the observations. An interesting special case occurs when there are no observations. In this case, the I-state is predictable because it is derived only from actions that are chosen by the robot. In this case, the new formulation does not need nature actions, which reduces it down to Formulation 2.3. Due to this, feedback is no longer needed if the initial I-state is given. A plan can be expressed once again as a sequence of actions. Even though the *original* states are not predictable, the future *information* states are! This means that the state trajectory in the new state space is completely predictable as well.

12.1.2 Algorithms for nondeterministic I-spaces

Now that the problem of planning in $\mathcal{I}_{ndet}$ has been expressed using Formulation 10.1, the methods of Section 10.2 directly apply. The main limitation of their use is that the new state space $\vec{X}$ is exponentially larger than X. If X contains n states, then $\vec{X}$ contains $2^n - 1$ states. Thus, even though some methods in Section 10.2 can solve problems in practice that involve a million states, this would only be about 20 states in the original state space. Handling substantially larger problems requires developing application-specific methods that exploit some special structure of the I-space, possibly by defining an I-map that leads to a smaller derived I-space.

Value iteration

The value-iteration method from Section 10.2.1 can be applied without modification. In the first step, initialize G_F^* using (12.6). Using the notation for the new problem, the dynamic programming recurrence, (10.39), becomes

$$G_k^*(\vec{x}_k) = \min_{\vec{u}_k \in U} \left\{ \max_{\vec{\theta}_k} \left[\vec{l}(\vec{x}_k, \vec{u}_k) + G_{k+1}^*(\vec{x}_{k+1}) \right] \right\}, \tag{12.7}$$

in which $\vec{x}_{k+1} = \vec{f}(\vec{x}_k, \vec{u}_k, \vec{\theta}_k)$.

The main difficulty in evaluating (12.7) is to determine the set $\vec{\Theta}(\vec{x}_k, \vec{u}_k)$, over which the maximization occurs. Suppose that a state-nature sensor mapping is used, as defined in Section 11.1.1. From the I-state $\vec{x}_k = X_k(\eta_k)$, the action $\vec{u}_k = u_k$ is applied. This yields a forward projection $X_{k+1}(\eta_k, u_k)$. The set of all possible observations is

$$\vec{\Theta}(\vec{x}_k, \vec{u}_k) = \{y_{k+1} \in Y \mid \exists x_{k+1} \in X_{k+1}(\eta_k, u_k) \text{ and } \exists \psi_{k+1} \in \Psi$$
$$\text{such that } y_{k+1} = h(x_{k+1}, \psi_{k+1})\}. \tag{12.8}$$

Without using forward projections, a longer, equivalent expression is obtained:

$$\vec{\Theta}(\vec{x}_k, \vec{u}_k) = \{y_{k+1} \in Y \mid \exists x_k \in X_k(\eta_k), \exists \theta_k \in \Theta, \text{ and } \exists \psi_{k+1} \in \Psi$$
$$\text{such that } y_{k+1} = h(f(x_k, u_k, \theta_k), \psi_{k+1})\}. \tag{12.9}$$

Other variants can be formulated for different sensing models.

Policy iteration

The policy iteration method of Section 10.2.2 can be applied in principle, but it is unlikely to solve challenging problems. For example, if $|X| = 10$, then each iteration will require solving matrices that have 1 million entries! At least they are likely to be sparse in many applications.

Graph-search methods

The methods from Section 10.2.3, which are based on backprojections, can also be applied to this formulation. These methods must initially set $S = \vec{X}_G$. If S is initially nonempty, then backprojections can be attempted using the general algorithm in Figure 10.6. Dijkstra's algorithm, as given in Figure 10.8, can be applied to yield a plan that is worst-case optimal.

The sensorless case

If there are no sensors, then better methods can be applied because the formulation reduces from Formulation 10.1 to Formulation 2.3. The simpler value iterations of Section 2.3 or Dijkstra's algorithm can be applied to find a solution. If optimality is not required, then any of the search methods of Section 2.2 can even be applied. For example, one can even imagine performing a bidirectional search on $\vec{X}$ to attempt to connect $\vec{x}_I$ to some $\vec{x}_G$.

12.1.3 Algorithms for probabilistic I-spaces (POMDPs)

For the probabilistic case, the methods of Section 10.2 cannot be applied because $\mathcal{I}_{prob}$ is a continuous space. Dynamic programming methods for continuous state spaces, as covered in Section 10.6, are needed. The main difficulty is that the dimension of $\vec{X}$ grows linearly with the number of states in X. If there are n states in X, the dimension of $\vec{X}$ is $n - 1$. Since the methods of Section 10.6 suffer from the curse of dimensionality, the general dynamic programming techniques are limited to problems in which X has only a few states.

Approximate value iteration

The continuous-space methods from Section 10.6 can be directly applied to produce an approximate solution by interpolating over $\vec{X}$ to determine cost-to-go values. The initial cost-to-go value G_F^* over the collection of samples is obtained by (12.6). Following (10.46), the dynamic programming recurrence is

$$G_k^*(\vec{x}_k) = \min_{\vec{u}_k \in \vec{U}} \left\{ \vec{l}(\vec{x}_k, \vec{u}_k) + \sum_{\vec{x}_{k+1} \in \vec{X}} G_{k+1}^*(\vec{x}_{k+1}) P(\vec{x}_{k+1} | \vec{x}_k, \vec{u}_k) \right\}. \qquad (12.10)$$

If $\vec{\Theta}(\vec{x}, \vec{u})$ is finite, the probability mass is distributed over a finite set of points, $y = \vec{\theta} \in \vec{\Theta}(\vec{x}, \vec{u})$. This in turn implies that $P(\vec{x}_{k+1} | \vec{x}_k, \vec{u}_k)$ is also distributed over a finite subset of $\vec{X}$. This is somewhat unusual because $\vec{X}$ is a continuous space, which ordinarily requires the specification of a probability density function. Since the set of future states is finite, this enables a sum to be used in (12.10) as opposed to an integral over a probability density function. This technically yields a probability *density* over $\vec{X}$, but this density must be expressed using Dirac functions.[1] An approximation is still needed, however, because the x_{k+1} points may not be exactly the sample points on which the cost-to-go function G_{k+1}^* is represented.

Exact methods

If the total number of stages is small, it is possible in practice to compute exact representations. Some methods are based on an observation that the cost-to-come is piecewise linear and convex [497]. A linear-programming problem results, which can be solved using the techniques that were described for finding randomized saddle points of zero-sum games in Section 9.3. Due to the numerous constraints, methods have been proposed that dramatically reduce the number that need to be considered in some circumstances (see the suggested reading on POMDPs at the end of the chapter).

An exact, discrete representation can be computed as follows. Suppose that the initial condition space $\mathcal{I}_0$ consists of one initial condition, η_0 (or a finite number of initial conditions), and that there are no more than K stages at which decisions are made. Since $\Theta(x, u)$ and $\Psi(x)$ are assumed to be finite, there is a finite number of possible final I-states, $\eta_F = (\eta_0, \tilde{u}_K, \tilde{y}_F)$. For each of these, the distribution $P(x_F | \eta_F)$ can be computed, which is alternatively represented as $\vec{x}_F$. Following this, (12.4) is used to compute $G^*(\vec{x}_F)$ for each possible $\vec{x}_F$. The number of these states is unfortunately exponential in the total number of stages, but at least there are finitely many. The dynamic programming recurrence (12.10) can be applied for $k = K$ to roll back one stage. It is known that each possible $\vec{x}_{k+1}$ will be a point in $\vec{X}$ at which a value was computed because values were computed for possible all I-states. Therefore, interpolation is not necessary. Equation 12.10 can be applied repeatedly until the first stage is reached. In each iteration, no interpolation is needed because the cost-to-go G_{k+1}^* was computed for each possible next I-state. Given the enormous size of $\mathcal{I}$, this method is practical only for very small problems.

The sensorless case

In the case of having no observations, the path through $\mathcal{I}_{prob}$ becomes predictable. Suppose that a feasible planning problem is formulated. For example, there are complicated

---

[1] These are single points that are assigned a nonzero probability mass, which is not allowed, for example, in the construction of a continuous probability density function.

constraints on the probability distributions over X that are permitted during the execution of the plan. Since $\breve{X} = \mathcal{I}_{prob}$ is a continuous space, it is tempting to apply motion planning techniques from Chapter 5 to find a successful path. The adaptation of such techniques may be possible, but they must be formulated to use actions and state transition functions, which was not done in Chapter 5. Such adaptations of these methods, however, will be covered in Chapter 14. They could be applied to this problem to search the I-space and produce a sequence of actions that traverses it while satisfying hard constraints on the probabilities.

12.2 Localization

Localization is a fundamental problem in robotics. Using its sensors, a mobile robot must determine its location within some map of the environment. There are both passive and active versions of the localization problem:

Passive localization: The robot applies actions, and its position is inferred by computing the nondeterministic or probabilistic I-state. For example, if the Kalman filter is used, then probabilistic I-states are captured by mean and covariance. The mean serves as an estimate of the robot position, and the covariance indicates the amount of uncertainty.

Active localization: A plan must be designed that attempts to reduce the localization uncertainty as much as possible. How should the robot move so that it can figure out its location?

Both versions of localization will be considered in this section.

In many applications, localization is an incremental problem. The initial configuration may be known, and the task is to maintain good estimates as motions occur. A more extreme version is the *kidnapped-robot problem*, in which a robot initially has no knowledge of its initial configuration. Either case can be modeled by the appropriate initial conditions. The kidnapped-robot problem is more difficult and is assumed by default in this section.

12.2.1 Discrete localization

Many interesting lessons about realistic localization problems can be learned by first studying a discrete version of localization. Problems that may or may not be solvable can be embedded in more complicated problems, which may even involve continuous state spaces. The discrete case is often easier to understand, which motivates its presentation here. To simplify the presentation, only the nondeterministic I-space $\mathcal{I}_{ndet}$ will be considered; see Section 12.2.3 for the probabilistic case.

Suppose that a robot moves on a 2D grid, which was introduced in Example 2.1. It has a map of the grid but does not know its initial location or orientation within the grid. An example is shown in Figure 12.2a.

To formulate the problem, it is helpful to include in the state both the position of the robot and its orientation. Suppose that the robot may be oriented in one of four directions, which are labeled N, E, W, and S, for "north," "east," "west," and "south," respectively. Although the robot is treated as a point, its orientation is important because it does not have a compass. If it chooses to move in a particular direction, such as straight ahead, it does not necessarily know which direction it will be heading with respect to the four directions.

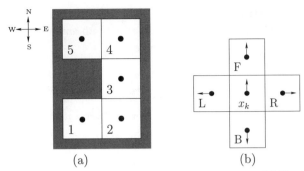

Figure 12.2: (a) This map is given to the robot for localization purposes. (b) The four possible actions each take one step, if possible, and reorient the robot as shown.

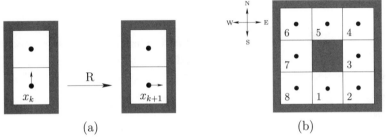

Figure 12.3: (a) If a direction is blocked because of an obstacle, then the orientation changes, but the position remains fixed. In this example, the R action is applied. (b) Another map is given to the robot for localization purposes. In this case, the robot cannot localize itself exactly.

Thus, a state, $x \in X$, is written as $x = (p, d)$, in which p is a position and d is one of the four directions. A set of states at the same position will be denoted with special superscripts that point in the possible directions. For example, $3^{\llcorner}$ indicates the set of states for which $p = 3$ and the direction may be north (N) or east (E), because the superscript points in the north and east directions.

The robot is given four actions,

$$U = \{F, B, R, L\}, \tag{12.11}$$

which represent "forward," "backward," "right motion," and "left motion," respectively. These motions occur with respect to the current orientation of the robot, which may be unknown. See Figure 12.2b. For the F action, the robot moves forward one grid element and maintains its orientation. For the B action, the robot changes its orientation by 180 degrees and then moves forward one grid element. For the R action, the robot turns right by 90 degrees and then moves forward one grid element. The L action behaves similarly. If it is not possible to move because of an obstacle, it is assumed that the robot changes its orientation (in the case of B, R, or L) but does not change its position. This is depicted in Figure 12.3a.

The robot has one simple sensor that can only detect whether it was able to move in the direction that was attempted. The sensor space is $Y = \{0, 1\}$, and the sensor mapping is $h : X \times X \to Y$. This yields $y = h(x_{k-1}, x_k) = 1$ if x_{k-1} and x_k place the robot at different positions, and $h(x_{k-1}, x_k) = 0$ otherwise. Thus, the sensor indicates whether the robot has moved after the application of an action.

Nondeterministic uncertainty will be used, and the initial I-state η_0 is always assumed to be X (this can easily be extended to allow starting with any nonempty subset of X). A history I-state at stake k in its general form appears as

$$\eta_0 = (X, \tilde{u}_{k-1}, y_2, \ldots, y_k). \tag{12.12}$$

One special adjustment was made in comparison to (11.14). There is no observation y_1 because the sensor mapping requires a previous state to report a value. Thus, the observation history starts with y_2. An example history I-state for stage $k = 5$ is

$$\eta_5 = (X, R, R, F, L, 1, 0, 1, 1), \tag{12.13}$$

in which $\eta_0 = X$, $\tilde{u}_4 = (R, R, F, L)$, and $(y_2, y_3, y_4, y_5) = (1, 0, 1, 1)$.

The *passive localization* problem starts with a given map, such as the one shown in Figure 12.2a, and a history I-state, η_k, and computes the nondeterministic I-state $X_k(\eta_k) \subseteq X$. The *active localization problem* is to compute some k and sequence of actions, $(u_1, \ldots, u_{k-1})$, such that the nondeterministic I-state is as small as possible. In the best case, $X_k(\eta_k)$ might become a singleton set, which means that the robot knows its position and orientation on the map. However, due to *symmetries*, which will be presented shortly in an example, it might not be possible.

Solving the passive localization problem

The passive problem requires only that the nondeterministic I-states are computed correctly as the robot moves. A couple of examples of this are given.

Example 12.1 (An Easy Localization Problem)   Consider the example given in Figure 12.2a. Suppose that the robot is initially placed in position 1 facing east. The initial condition is $\eta_0 = X$, which can be represented as

$$\eta_0 = 1^{\uparrow} \cup 2^{\uparrow} \cup 3^{\uparrow} \cup 4^{\uparrow} \cup 5^{\uparrow}, \tag{12.14}$$

the collection of all 20 states in X. Suppose that the action sequence (F, L, F, L) is applied. In each case, a motion occurs, which results in the observation history $(y_2, y_3, y_4, y_5) = (1, 1, 1, 1)$.

After the first action, $u_1 = F$, the history I-state is $\eta_2 = (X, F, 1)$. The nondeterministic I-state is

$$X_2(\eta_2) = 1^{\rightarrow} \cup 2^{\ulcorner} \cup 3^{\uparrow} \cup 4^{\llcorner} \cup 5^{\rightarrow}, \tag{12.15}$$

which means that any position is still possible, but the successful forward motion removed some orientations from consideration. For example, $1^{\uparrow}$ is not possible because the previous state would have to be directly south of 1, which is an obstacle.

After the second action, $u_2 = L$,

$$X_3(\eta_3) = 3^{\uparrow} \cup 5^{\rightarrow}, \tag{12.16}$$

which yields only two possible current states. This can be easily seen in Figure 12.2a by observing that there are only two states from which a forward motion can be followed by a left motion. The initial state must have been either $1^{\rightarrow}$ or $3^{\uparrow}$.

After $u_3 = F$ is applied, the only possibility remaining is that x_3 must have been $3^{\uparrow}$. This yields

$$X_4(\eta_4) = 4^{\uparrow}, \tag{12.17}$$

which exactly localizes the robot: It is at position 4 facing north. After the final action $u_4 = L$ is applied it is clear that

$$X_5(\eta_5) = 5^{\rightarrow} , \tag{12.18}$$

which means that in the final state, x_5, the robot is at position 1 facing west. Once the exact robot state is known, no new uncertainty will accumulate because the effects of all actions are predictable. Although it was not shown, it is also possible to prune the possible states by the execution of actions that do not produce motions.   ∎

Example 12.2 (A Problem that Involves Symmetries) Now extend the map from Figure 12.2a so that it forms a loop as shown in Figure 12.2b. In this case, it is impossible to determine the precise location of the robot. For simplicity, consider only actions that produce motion (convince yourself that allowing the other actions cannot fix the problem).

Suppose that the robot is initially in position 1 facing east. If the action sequence $(F, L, F, L, \ldots)$ is executed, the robot will travel around in cycles. The problem is that it is also possible to apply the same action sequence from position 3 facing north. Every action successfully moves the robot, which means that, to the robot, the information appears identical. The other two cases in which this sequence can be applied to travel in cycles are 1) from 5 heading west, and 2) from 7 heading south. A similar situation occurs from 2 facing east, if the sequence $(L, F, L, F, \ldots)$ is applied. Can you find the other three starting states from which this sequence moves the robot at every stage? Similar symmetries exist when traveling in clockwise circles and making right turns instead of left turns.

The state space for this problem contains 32 states, obtained from four directions at each position. After executing some motions, the nondeterministic I-state can be reduced down to a *symmetry class* of no more than four possible states. How can this be proved? One way is to use the algorithm that is described next.   ∎

Solving the active localization problem

From the previous two examples, it should be clear how to compute nondeterministic I-states and therefore solve the passive localization problem on a grid. Now consider constructing a plan that solves the active localization problem. Imagine using a computer to help in this task. There are two general approaches:

> **Precomputed Plan:** In this approach, a planning algorithm running on a computer accepts a map of the environment and computes an information-feedback plan that immediately indicates which action to take based on all possible I-states that could result (a derived I-space could be used). During execution, the actions are immediately determined from the stored, precomputed plan.

> **Lazy Plan:** In this case the map is still given, but the appropriate action is computed just as it is needed during each stage of execution. The computer runs on-board of the robot and must compute which action to take based on the current I-state.

The issues are similar to those of the sampling-based roadmap in Section 5.6. If faster execution is desired, then the precomputed plan may be preferable. If it would consume too much time or space, then a lazy plan may be preferable.

Using either approach, it will be helpful to recall the formulation of Section 12.1.1, which considers $\mathcal{I}_{ndet}$ as a new state space, $\vec{X}$, in which state feedback can be used. Even though there are no nature sensing actions, the observations are not predictable because the state is generally unknown. This means that $\vec{\theta}$ is unknown, and future new states, $\vec{x}_{k+1}$, are unpredictable once $\vec{x}_k$ and $\vec{u}_k$ are given. A plan must therefore use feedback, which means that it needs information learned during execution to solve the problem. The state transition function $\vec{f}$ on the new state space was illustrated for the localization problem in Examples 12.1 and 12.2. The initial state $\vec{x}_I$ is the set of all original states. If there are no symmetries, the goal set $\vec{X}_G$ is the set of all singleton subsets of X; otherwise, it is the set of all smallest possible I-states that are reachable (this does not need to be constructed in advance). If desired, cost terms can be defined to produce an optimal planning problem. For example, $\vec{l}(\vec{x}, \vec{u}) = 2$ if a motion occurs, or $\vec{l}(\vec{x}, \vec{u}) = 1$ otherwise.

Consider the approach of precomputing a plan. The methods of Section 12.1.2 can generally be applied to compute a plan, $\pi : \vec{X} \to U$, that solves the localization problem from any initial nondeterministic I-state. The approach may be space-intensive because an action must be stored for every state in $\vec{X}$. If there are n grid tiles, then $|\vec{X}| = 2^n - 1$. If the initial I-state is always X, then it may be possible to restrict π to a much smaller portion of $\vec{X}$. From any $\vec{x} \in \vec{X}_G$, a search based on backprojections can be conducted. If the initial I-state is added to S, then the partial plan will reliably localize the robot. Parts of $\vec{X}$ for which π is not specified will never be reached and can therefore be ignored.

Now consider the lazy approach. An algorithm running on the robot can perform a kind of search by executing actions and seeing which I-states result. This leads to a directed graph over $\vec{X}$ that is incrementally revealed through the robot's motions. The graph is directed because the information regarding the state generally improves. For example, once the robot knows its state (or symmetry class of states), it cannot return to an I-state that represents greater uncertainty. In many cases, the robot may get lucky during execution and localize itself using much less memory than would be required for a precomputed plan.

The robot needs to recognize that the same positions have been reached in different ways, to ensure a systematic search. Even though the robot does not necessarily know its position on the map, it can usually deduce whether it has been to some location previously. One way to achieve this is to assign (i, j) coordinates to the positions already visited. It starts with $(0, 0)$ assigned to the initial position. If F is applied, then suppose that position $(1, 0)$ is reached, assuming the robot moves to a new grid cell. If R is applied, then $(0, 1)$ is reached if the robot is not blocked. The point $(2, 1)$ may be reachable by (F, F, R) or (R, F, F). One way to interpret this is that a local coordinate frame in $\mathbb{R}^2$ is attached to the robot's initial position. Let this be referred to as the *odometric coordinates*. The orientation between this coordinate frame and the map is not known in the beginning, but a transformation between the two can be computed if the robot is able to localize itself exactly.

A variety of search algorithms can now be defined by starting in the initial state $\vec{x}_I$ and trying actions until a goal condition is satisfied (e.g., no smaller nondeterministic I-states are reachable). There is, however, a key difference between this search and the search conducted by the algorithms in Section 2.2.1. Previously, the search could continue from any state that has been explored previously without any additional cost. In the current setting, there are two issues:

> **Reroute paths:** Most search algorithms enable new states to be expanded from any previously considered states at any time. For the lazy approach, the robot must move to a state and apply an action to determine whether a new state can be reached. The robot is capable of returning to any previously considered state by using its odometric coordinates.

This induces a cost that does not exist in the previous search problem. Rather than being able to jump from place to place in a search tree, the search is instead a long, continuous path that is traversed by the robot. Let the jump be referred to as a *reroute path*. This will become important in Section 12.3.2.

Information improvement: The robot may not even be able to return to a previous nondeterministic I-state. For example, if the robot follows (F, F, R) and then tries to return to the same state using (B, L, F), it will indeed know that it returned to the same state, but the state remains unknown. It might be the case, however, that after executing (F, F, R), it was able to narrow down the possibilities for its current state. Upon returning using (B, L, F), the nondeterministic I-state will be different.

The implication of these issues is that the search algorithm should take into account the cost of moving the robot and that the search graph is directed. The second issue is really not a problem because even though the I-state may be different when returning to the same position, it will always be at least as good as the previous one. This means that if η_1 and η_2 are the original and later history I-states from the same position, it will always be true that $X(\eta_2) \subseteq X(\eta_1)$. Information always improves in this version of the localization problem. Thus, while trying to return to a previous I-state, the robot will find an improved I-state.

Other information models

The model given so far in this section is only one of many interesting alternatives. Suppose, for example, that the robot carries a compass that always indicates its direction. In this case, there is no need to keep track of the direction as part of the state. The robot can use the compass to specify actions directly with respect to global directions. Suppose that $U = \{N, E, W, S\}$, which denote the directions, "north," "east," "west," and "south," respectively. Examples 12.1 and 12.2 now become trivial. The first one is solved by applying the action sequence (E, N). The symmetry problems vanish for Example 12.2, which can also be solved by the sequence (E, N) because (1, 2, 3) is the only sequence of positions that is consistent with the actions and compass readings.

Other interesting models can be made by giving the robot less information. In the models so far, the robot can easily infer its current position relative to its starting position. Even though it is not necessarily known where this starting position lies on the map, it can always be expressed in relative coordinates. This is because the robot relies on different forms of odometry. For example, if the direction is E and the robot executes the sequence (L, L, L), it is known that the direction is S because three lefts make a right. Suppose that instead of a grid, the robot must explore a graph. It moves discretely from vertex to vertex by applying an action that traverses an edge. Let this be a planar graph that is embedded in $\mathbb{R}^2$ and is drawn with straight line segments. The number of available actions can vary at each vertex. We can generally define $U = \mathbb{S}^1$, with the behavior that the robot only rotates without translating whenever a particular direction is blocked (this is a generalization of the grid case). A sensor can be defined that indicates which actions will lead to translations from the current vertex. In this case, the model nicely generalizes the original model for the grid. If the robot knows the angles between the edges that arrive at a vertex, then it can use angular odometry to make a local coordinate system in $\mathbb{R}^2$ that keeps track of its relative positions.

The situation can be made very confusing for the robot. Suppose that instead of $U = \mathbb{S}^1$, the action set at each vertex indicates which edges can be traversed. The robot can traverse an edge by applying an action, but it does not know anything about the direction relative to other edges. In this case, angular odometry can no longer be used. It could not, for example, tell the difference between traversing a rhombus, trapezoid, or a rectangle. If angular odometry is possible, then some symmetries can be avoided by noting the angles between the edges at each vertex. However, the new model does not allow this. All vertices that have the same degree would appear identical.

12.2.2 Combinatorial methods for continuous localization

Now consider localization for the case in which X is a continuous region in $\mathbb{R}^2$. Assume that X is bounded by a simple polygon (a closed polygonal chain; there are no interior holes). A map of X in $\mathbb{R}^2$ is given to the robot. The robot velocity $\dot{x}$ is directly commanded by the action u, yielding a motion model $\dot{x} = u$, for which U is a unit ball centered at the origin. This enables a plan to be specified as a continuous path in X, as was done throughout Part II. Therefore, instead of specifying velocities using u, a path is directly specified, which is simpler. For models of the form $\dot{x} = u$ and the more general form $\dot{x} = f(x, u)$, see Section 8.4 and Chapter 13, respectively.

The robot uses two different sensors:

1. **Compass:** A perfect compass solves all orientation problems that arose in Section 12.2.1.
2. **Visibility:** The visibility sensor, which was shown in Figure 11.15, provides perfect distance measurements in all directions.

There are no nature sensing actions for either sensor.

As in Section 12.2.1, localization involves computing nondeterministic I-states. In the current setting there is no need to represent the orientation as part of the state space because of the perfect compass and known orientation of the polygon in $\mathbb{R}^2$. Therefore, the nondeterministic I-states are just subsets of X. Imagine computing the nondeterministic I-state for the example shown in Figure 11.15, but without any history. This is $H(y) \subseteq X$, which was defined in (11.6). Only the current sensor reading is given. This requires computing states from which the distance measurements shown in Figure 11.15b could be obtained. This means that a translation must be found that perfectly overlays the edges shown in Figure 11.15b on top of the polygon edges that are shown in Figure 11.15a. Let ∂X denote the boundary of X. The distance measurements from the visibility sensor must correspond exactly to a subset of ∂X. For the example, these could only be obtained from one state, which is shown in Figure 11.15a. Therefore, the robot does not even have to move to localize itself for this example.

As in Section 8.4.3, let the *visibility polygon* $V(x)$ refer to the set of all points visible from x, which is shown in Figure 11.15a. To perform the required computations efficiently, the polygon must be processed to determine the different ways in which the visibility polygon could appear from various points in X. This involves carefully determining which edges of ∂X could appear on $\partial V(x)$. The state space X can be decomposed into a finite number of cells, and over each region the invariant is that same set of edges is used to describe $V(x)$ [138, 418]. An example is shown in Figure 12.4. Two different kinds of rays must be extended to make the decomposition. Figure 12.5 shows the case in which a pair of vertices is mutually visible and an outward ray extension is possible. The other case is shown in Figure 12.6, in which rays are extended outward at every reflex vertex (a vertex whose interior angle is more than π, as considered in Section 6.2.4).

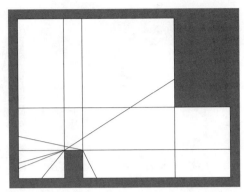

Figure 12.4: An example of the visibility cell decomposition. Inside of each cell, the visibility polygon is composed of the same edges of ∂X.

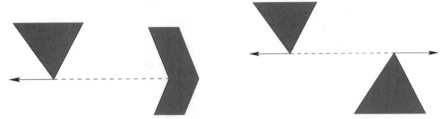

Figure 12.5: Rays are extended outward, whenever possible, from each pair of mutually visible vertices. The case on the right is a bitangent, as shown in Figure 6.10; however, here the edges extend outward instead of inward as required for the visibility graph.

Figure 12.6: A reflex vertex: If the interior angle at a vertex is greater than π, then two outward rays are extended from the incident edges.

The resulting decomposition generates $O(n^2 r)$ cells in the worse case, in which n is the number of edges that form ∂X and r is the number of reflex vertices (note that $r < n$). Once the measurements are obtained from the sensor, the cell or cells in which the edges or distance measurements match perfectly need to be computed to determine $H(y)$ (the set of points in X from which the current distance measurements could be obtained). An algorithm based on the idea of a *visibility skeleton* is given in [418], which performs these computations in time $O(m + \lg n + s)$ and uses $O(n^5)$ space, in which n is the number of vertices in ∂X, m is the number of vertices in $V(x)$, and $s = |H(y)|$, the size of the nondeterministic I-state. This method assumes that the environment is preprocessed to perform rapid queries during execution; without preprocessing, $H(y)$ can be computed in time $O(mn)$.

What happens if there are multiple states that match the distance data from the visibility sensor? Since the method in [418] only computes $H(y) \subseteq X$, some robot motions must be planned to further reduce the uncertainty. This provides yet another interesting illustration

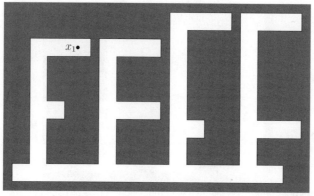

Figure 12.7: Consider this example, in which the initial state is not known [300].

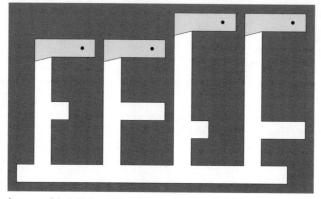

Figure 12.8: The four possible initial positions for the robot in Figure 12.7 based on the visibility sensor.

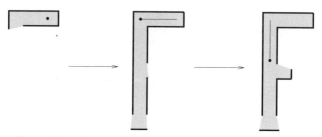

Figure 12.9: These motions completely disambiguate the state.

of the power of I-spaces. Even though the state space is continuous, an I-state in this case is used to disambiguate the state from a finite collection of possibilities.

The following example is taken from [300].

Example 12.3 (Visibility-Based Localization) Consider the environment shown in Figure 12.7, with the initial state as shown. Based on the visibility sensor observation, the initial state could be any one of the four possibilities shown in Figure 12.8. Thus, $H(y_1)$ contains four states, in which y_1 is the initial sensor observation. Suppose that the motion sequence shown in Figure 12.9 is executed. After the first step, the position of the robot is narrowed down to two possibilities, as shown in Figure 12.10. This occurs because the corridor is longer for the remaining two possibilities. After the second motion, the state is completely determined because the short side corridor is detected. ∎

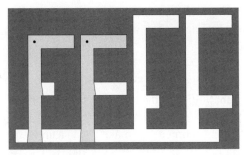

Figure 12.10: There are now only two possible states.

The localization problem can be solved in general by using the visibility cell decomposition, as shown in Figure 12.4. Initially, $X_1(\eta_1) = H(y_1)$ is computed from the initial visibility polygon, which can be efficiently performed using the visibility skeleton [418]. Suppose that $X_1(\eta_1)$ contains k states. In this case, k translated copies of the map are overlaid so that all of the possible states in $X_1(\eta_1)$ coincide. A motion is then executed that reduces the amount of uncertainty. This could be performed, by example, by crossing a cell boundary in the overlay that corresponds to one or more, but not all, of the k copies. This enables some possible states to be eliminated from the next I-state, $X_2(\eta_2)$. The overlay is used once again to obtain another disambiguating motion, which results in $X_3(\eta_3)$. This process continues until the state is known. In [300], a motion plan is given that enables the robot to localize itself by traveling no more than k times as far as the optimal distance that would need to be traveled to verify the given state. This particular localization problem might not seem too difficult after seeing Example 12.3, but it turns out that the problem of localizing using optimal motions is NP-hard if any simple polygon is allowed. This was proved in [300] by showing that every abstract decision tree can be realized as a localization problem, and the abstract decision tree problem is already known to be NP-hard.

Many interesting variations of the localization problem in continuous spaces can be constructed by changing the sensing model. For example, suppose that the robot can only measure distances up to a limit; all points beyond the limit cannot be seen. This corresponds to many realistic sensing systems, such as infrared sensors, sonars, and range scanners on mobile robots. This may substantially enlarge $H(y)$. Suppose that the robot can take distance measurements only in a limited number of directions, as shown in Figure 11.14b. Another interesting variant can be made by removing the compass. This introduces the orientation confusion effects observed in Section 12.2.1. One can even consider interesting localization problems that have little or no sensing [754, 755], which yields I-spaces that are similar to that for the tray tilting example in Figure 11.28.

12.2.3 Probabilistic methods for localization

The localization problems considered so far have involved only nondeterministic uncertainty. Furthermore, it was assumed that nature does not interfere with the state transition equation or the sensor mapping. If nature is involved in the sensor mapping, then future I-states are not predictable. For the active localization problem, this implies that a localization plan must use information feedback. In other words, the actions must be conditioned on I-states so that the appropriate decisions are taken after new observations are made. The passive localization problem involves computing probabilistic I-states from the sensing and action histories. The formulation and solution of localization problems that involve nature and nondeterministic uncertainty will be left to the reader. Only the probabilistic case will be covered here.

Discrete problems

First consider adding probabilities to the discrete grid problem of Section 12.2.1. A state is once again expressed as $x = (p, d)$. The initial condition is a probability distribution, $P(x_1)$, over X. One reasonable choice is to make $P(x_1)$ a uniform probability distribution, which makes each direction and position equally likely. The robot is once again given four actions, but now assume that nature interferes with state transitions. For example, if $u_k = F$, then perhaps with high probability the robot moves forward, but with low probability it may move right, left, or possibly not move at all, even if it is not blocked.

The sensor mapping from Section 12.2.1 indicated whether the robot moved. In the current setting, nature can interfere with this measurement. With low probability, it may incorrectly indicate that the robot moved, when in fact it remained stationary. Conversely, it may also indicate that the robot remained still, when in fact it moved. Since the sensor depends on the previous two states, the mapping is expressed as

$$y_k = h(x_k, x_{k-1}, \psi_k). \tag{12.19}$$

With a given probability model, $P(\psi_k)$, this can be expressed as $P(y_k|x_k, x_{k-1})$.

To solve the passive localization problem, the expressions from Section 11.2.3 for computing the derived I-states are applied. If the sensor mapping used only the current state, then (11.36), (11.38), and (11.39) would apply without modification. However, since h depends on both x_k and x_{k-1}, some modifications are needed. Recall that the observations start with y_2 for this sensor. Therefore, $P(x_1|\eta_1) = P(x_1|y_1) = P(x_1)$, instead of applying (11.36).

After each stage, $P(x_{k+1}|\eta_{k+1})$ is computed from $P(x_k|\eta_k)$ by first applying (11.38) to take into account the action u_k. Equation (11.39) takes into account the sensor observation, y_{k+1}, but $P(y_{k+1}|x_{k+1}, \eta_k, u_k)$ is not given because the sensor mapping also depends on x_{k-1}. It reduces using marginalization as

$$P(y_k|\eta_{k-1}, u_{k-1}, x_k) = \sum_{x_{k-1} \in X} P(y_k|\eta_{k-1}, u_{k-1}, x_{k-1}, x_k)P(x_{k-1}|\eta_{k-1}, u_{k-1}, x_k). \tag{12.20}$$

The first factor in the sum can be reduced to the sensor model,

$$P(y_k|\eta_{k-1}, u_{k-1}, x_{k-1}, x_k) = P(y_k|x_{k-1}, x_k), \tag{12.21}$$

because the observations depend only on x_{k-1}, x_k, and the nature sensing action, ψ_k. The second term in (12.20) can be computed using Bayes' rule as

$$P(x_{k-1}|\eta_{k-1}, u_{k-1}, x_k) = \frac{P(x_k|\eta_{k-1}, u_{k-1}, x_{k-1})P(x_{k-1}|\eta_{k-1}, u_{k-1})}{\displaystyle\sum_{x_{k-1} \in X} P(x_k|\eta_{k-1}, u_{k-1}, x_{k-1})P(x_{k-1}|\eta_{k-1}, u_{k-1})}, \tag{12.22}$$

in which $P(x_k|\eta_{k-1}, u_{k-1}, x_{k-1})$ simplifies to $P(x_k|u_{k-1}, x_{k-1})$. This is directly obtained from the state transition probability, which is expressed as $P(x_{k+1}|x_k, u_k)$ by shifting the stage index forward. The term $P(x_{k-1}|\eta_{k-1}, u_{k-1})$ is given by (11.38). The completes the computation of the probabilistic I-states, which solves the passive localization problem.

Solving the active localization problem is substantially harder because a search occurs on $\mathcal{I}_{prob}$. The same choices exist as for the discrete localization problem. Computing an

Figure 12.11: Four frames from an animation that performs probabilistic localization of an indoor mobile robot using sonars [352].

information-feedback plan over the whole I-space $\mathcal{I}_{prob}$ is theoretically possible but impractical for most environments. The search-based idea that was applied to incrementally grow a directed graph in Section 12.2.1 could also be applied here. The success of the method depends on clever search heuristics developed for this particular problem.

Continuous problems

Localization in a continuous space using probabilistic models has received substantial attention in recent years [260, 450, 625, 828, 888, 962]. It is often difficult to localize mobile robots because of noisy sensor data, modeling errors, and high demands for robust operation over long time periods. Probabilistic modeling and the computation of probabilistic I-states have been quite successful in many experimental systems, both for indoor and outdoor mobile robots. Figure 12.11 shows localization successfully being solved using sonars only. The vast majority of work in this context involves passive localization because the robot is often completing some other task, such as reaching a particular part of the environment. Therefore, the focus is mainly on *computing* the probabilistic I-states, rather than performing a difficult search on $\mathcal{I}_{prob}$.

Probabilistic localization in continuous spaces most often involves the definition of the probability densities $p(x_{k+1}|x_k, u_k)$ and $p(y_k|x_k)$ (in the case of a state sensor mapping). If the stages represent equally spaced times, then these densities usually remain fixed for every stage. The state space is usually $X = SE(2)$ to account for translation and rotation, but it may be $X = \mathbb{R}^2$ for translation only. The density $p(x_{k+1}|x_k, u_k)$ accounts for the unpredictability that arises when controlling a mobile robot over some fixed time interval. A method for estimating this distribution for nonholonomic robots by solving stochastic differential equations appears in [1004].

The density $p(y_k|x_k)$ indicates the relative likelihood of various measurements when given the state. Most often this models distance measurements that are obtained from a laser range scanner, an array of sonars, or even infrared sensors. Suppose that a robot moves around in a 2D environment and takes depth measurements at various orientations. In the robot body frame, there are n angles at which a depth measurement is taken. Ideally, the measurements should look like those in Figure 11.15b; however, in practice, the data contain substantial noise. The observation $y \in Y$ is an n-dimensional vector of noisy depth measurements.

One common way to define $p(y|x)$ is to assume that the error in each distance measurement follows a Gaussian density. The mean value of the measurement can easily be calculated as the true distance value once x is given, and the variance should be determined from experimental evaluation of the sensor. If it is assumed that the vector of measurements is modeled as a set of independent, identically distributed random variables, a simple product of Guassian densities is obtained for $p(y|x)$.

Once the models have been formulated, the computation of probabilistic I-states directly follows from Sections 11.2.3 and 11.4.1. The initial condition is a probability density function, $p(x_1)$, over X. The marginalization and Bayesian update rules are then applied to construct a sequence of density functions of the form $p(x_k|\eta_k)$ for every stage, k.

In some limited applications, the models used to express $p(x_{k+1}|x_k, u_k)$ and $p(y_k|x_k)$ may be linear and Gaussian. In this case, the Kalman filter of Section 11.6.1 can be easily applied. In most cases, however, the densities will not have this form. Moment-based approximations, as discussed in Section 11.4.3, can be used to approximate the densities. If second-order moments are used, then the so-called *extended Kalman filter* is obtained, in which the Kalman filter update rules can be applied to a *linear-Gaussian* approximation to the original problem. In recent years, one of the most widely accepted approaches in experimental mobile robotics is to use sampling-based techniques to directly compute and estimate the probabilistic I-states. The particle-filtering approach, described in general in Section 11.6.2, appears to provide good experimental performance when applied to localization. The application of particle filtering in this context is often referred to as *Monte Carlo localization*; see the references at the end of this chapter.

12.3 Environment uncertainty and mapping

After reading Section 12.2, you may have already wondered what happens if the map is not given. This leads to a fascinating set of problems that are fundamental to robotics. If the state represents configuration, then the I-space allows tasks to be solved without knowing the exact configuration. If, however, the state also represents the environment, then the I-space allows tasks to be solved without even having a complete representation of the environment! This is obviously very powerful because building a representation of a robot's environment is very costly and subject to errors. Furthermore, it is likely to become quickly outdated.

12.3.1 Grid problems

To gain a clear understanding of the issues, it will once again be helpful to consider discrete problems. The discussion here is a continuation of Section 12.2.1. In that section, the state represented a position, p, and a direction, d. Now suppose that the state is represented as (p, d, e), in which e represents the particular environment that contains the robot. This will require defining a space of environments, which is rarely represented explicitly. It is often expressed as a constraint on the types of environments that can exist. For example, the set of environments could be defined as all connected 2D grid-planning problems. The set of simply connected grid-planning problems is even further constrained.

One question immediately arises: When are two maps of an environment equivalent? Recall the maps shown in Figures 12.2a and 12.3b. The map in Figure 12.3b appears the same for every 90-degree rotation; however, the map in Figure 12.2a appears to be different. Even if it appears different, it should still be the same environment, right? Imagine mapping a remote island without having a compass that indicates the direction to the north pole. An orientation (which way is up?) for the map can be chosen arbitrarily without any harm. If a map of the environment is made by "drawing" on $\mathbb{R}^2$, it should seem that two maps are equivalent if a transformation in $SE(2)$ (i.e., translation and rotation) can be applied to overlay one perfectly on top of the other.

When defining an environment space, it is important to clearly define what it means for two environments to be equivalent. For example, if we are required to build a map by exploration, is it required to also provide the exact translation and orientation? This may or may not be required, but it is important to specify this in the problem description. Thus, we will allow any possibility: If the maps only differ by a transformation in $SE(2)$, they may or may not be defined as equivalent, depending on the application.

To consider some examples, it will be convenient to define some finite or infinite sets of environments. Suppose that planning on a 2D grid is once again considered. In this section, assume that each grid point p has integer coordinates $(i, j) \in \mathbb{Z} \times \mathbb{Z}$, as defined in Section 2.1. Let E denote a set of environments. Once again, there are four possible directions for the robot to face; let D denote this set. The state space is

$$X = \mathbb{Z} \times \mathbb{Z} \times D \times E. \qquad (12.23)$$

Assume in general that an environment, $e \in E$, is specified by indicating a subset of $\mathbb{Z} \times \mathbb{Z}$ that corresponds to the positions of all of the *white* tiles on which the robot can be placed. All other tiles are *black*, which means that they are obstacles. If any subset of $\mathbb{Z} \times \mathbb{Z}$ is allowed, then $E = \text{pow}(\mathbb{Z} \times \mathbb{Z})$. This includes many useless maps, such as a checkerboard that spans the entire plane; this motivates some restrictions on E. For example, E can be restricted to be the subset of $\text{pow}(\mathbb{Z} \times \mathbb{Z})$ that corresponds to all maps that include a white tile at the origin, $(0, 0)$, and for which all other white tiles are reachable from it and lie within a bounded region.

Examples will be given shortly, but first think about the kinds of problems that can be formulated:

1. **Map building:** The task is to visit every reachable tile and construct a map. Depending on how E is defined, this may identify a particular environment in E or a set of environments that are consistent with the exploration. This may also be referred to as *simultaneous localization and mapping*, or *SLAM*, because constructing a complete map usually implies that the robot position and orientation are eventually known [486, 970]. Thus, the complete state, $x \in X$, as given in (12.23) is determined by the map-building process. For the grid problem considered here, this point is trivial, but the problem becomes more difficult for the case of probabilistic uncertainty in a continuous environment. See Section 12.3.5 for this case.

2. **Determining the environment:** Imagine that a robot is placed into a building at random and then is switched on. The robot is told that it is in one of a fixed (i.e., 10) number of buildings. It must move to determine which one. As the number of possible environments

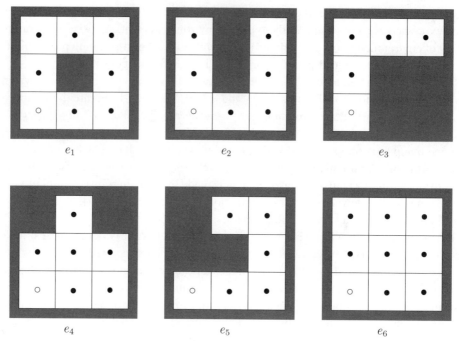

Figure 12.12: A set of possible 2D grid environments. In each case, the "up" direction represents north and the white circle represents the origin, $p = (0, 0)$.

is increased, the problem appears to be more like map building. In fact, map building can be considered as a special case in which little or no constraints are initially imposed on the set of possible environments.

3. **Navigation:** In this case, a goal position is to be reached, even though the robot has no map. The location of the goal relative to the robot can be specified through a sensor. The robot is allowed to solve this problem without fully exploring the environment. Thus, the final nondeterministic I-state after solving the task could contain numerous possible environments. Only a part of the environment is needed to solve the problem.

4. **Searching:** In this case, a goal state can only be identified when it is reached (or detected by a short-range sensor). There are no additional sensors to help in the search. The environment must be systematically explored, but the search may terminate early if the goal is found. A map does not necessarily have to be constructed. Searching can be extended to *pursuit-evasion*, which is covered in Section 12.4.

Simple examples of determining the environment and navigation will now be given.

Example 12.4 (Determining the Environment) Suppose that the robot is told that it was placed into one of the environments shown in Figure 12.12. Let the initial position of the robot be $(0, 0)$, which is shown as a white circle. Let the initial direction be east and the environment be e_3. These facts are unknown to the robot. Use the same actions and state transition model as in Section 12.2.1. The current state space includes the environment, but the environment never changes. Only information regarding which environment the robot is in will change. The sensing model again only indicates whether the robot has changed its position from the application of the last action.

The initial condition is X, because any position, orientation, and environment are possible. Some nondeterministic I-states will now be determined. Let $(u_1, u_2, u_3) = (F, R, R)$. From this sequence of actions, the sensor observations (y_2, y_3, y_4) report that the robot has

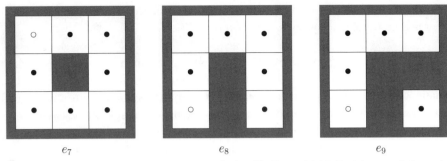

Figure 12.13: Add these environments to the set depicted in Figure 12.12. Each is essentially equivalent to an environment already given and generally does not affect the planning problem.

not yet changed its position. The orientation was changed to west, but this is not known to the robot (it does, however, know that it is now pointing in the opposite direction with respect to its initial orientation). What can now be inferred? The robot has discovered that it is on a tile that is bounded on three sides by obstacles. This means that e_1 and e_6 are ruled out as possible environments. In the remaining four environments, the robot deduces that it must be on one of the end tiles: 1) the upper left of e_2, 2) the upper right of e_2, 3) the bottom of e_3, 4) the rightmost of e_3, 5) the top of e_4, 6) the lower left of e_5, or 7) the upper left of e_5. It can also make strong inferences regarding its orientation. It even knows that the action $u_4 = R$ would cause it to move because all four directions cannot be blocked.

Apply $(u_4, u_5) = (R, F)$. The robot should move two times, to arrive in the upper left of e_3 facing north. In this case, any of e_2, e_3, e_4, or e_5 are still possible; however, it now knows that its position at stage 4 could not have been in the upper left of e_5. If the robot is in e_3, it knows that it must be in the upper left, but it still does not know its orientation (it could be north or west). The robot could also be in the lower left or lower right of e_2.

Now let $(u_6, u_7) = (R, F)$, which moves the robot twice. At this point, e_4 and e_5 are ruled out, and the set of possible environments is $\{e_2, e_3\}$ (one orientation from e_2 is also ruled out). If $u_8 = R$ is applied, then the sensor observation y_9 reports that the robot does not move. This rules out e_2. Finally, the robot can deduce that it is in the upper right of e_3 facing south. It can also deduce that in its initial state it was in the lower left of e_3 facing east. Thus, all of the uncertainty has been eliminated through the construction of the nondeterministic I-states.

Now consider adding the environments shown in Figure 12.13 to the set and starting the problem over again. Environment e_7 is identical to e_1, except that the origin is moved, and e_8 is identical to e_2, except that it is rotated by 180 degrees. In these two cases, there exist no inputs that enable the robot to distinguish between e_1 and e_7 or between e_2 and e_8. It is reasonable to declare these environments to be pairwise equivalent. The only distinction between them is the way that the map is drawn.

If the robot executes the same action sequence as given previously, then it will also not be able to distinguish e_3 from e_9. It is impossible for the robot to deduce whether there is a white tile somewhere that is not reachable. A general environment space may include such variations, and this will prevent the robot from knowing the precise environment. However, this usually presents no additional difficulty in solving a planning problem. Therefore, it might make sense to declare e_3 and e_9 to be equivalent. The fact that tasks can be achieved without knowing the precise environment is very important. In a sense, the environment is observed at some "resolution" that is sufficient for solving a problem;

further details beyond that are unimportant. Since the robot can ignore unnecessary details, cheaper and more reliable systems can often be built.   ∎

Example 12.5 (Reaching a Goal State)   Suppose once again that the set of environments shown in Figure 12.12 is given. This time, also assume that the position $p = (0, 0)$ and orientation east are known. The environment is e_4, but it is unknown to the robot. The task is to reach the position $(2, 0)$, which means that the robot must move two tiles to the east. The plan $(u_1, u_2) = (F, F)$ achieves the goal without providing much information about the environment. After $u_1 = F$ is applied, it is known that the environment is not e_3; however, after this, no additional information is gathered regarding the environment because it is not relevant to solving the problem. If the goal had been to reach $(2, 2)$, then more information would be obtained regarding the environment. For example, if the plan is (F, L, R, L), then it is known that the environment is e_6.   ∎

Algorithms for determining the environment

To determine the environment (which includes the map-building problem), it is sufficient to reach and remember all of the tiles. If the robot must determine its environment from a small set of possibilities, an optimal worst-case plan can be precomputed. This can be computed on $\vec{X} = \mathcal{I}_{ndet}$ by using value iteration or the nondeterministic version of Dijkstra's algorithm from Section 10.2.3. When the robot is dropped into the environment, it applies the optimal plan to deduce its position, orientation, and environment. If the set of possible environments is too large (possibly infinite), then a lazy approach is most suitable. This includes the map-building problem, for which there may be little or no assumptions about the environment. A lazy approach to the map-building problem simply has to ensure that every tile is visited. One additional concern may be to minimize the amount of reroute paths, which were mentioned in Section 12.2.1. A simple algorithm that solves the problem while avoiding excessive rerouting is depth-first search, from Section 2.2.2.

Algorithms for navigation

The navigation task is to reach a prescribed goal, even though no environment map is given. It is assumed that the goal is expressed in coordinates relative to the robot's initial position and orientation (these are odometric coordinates). If the goal can only be identified when the robot is on the goal tile, then searching is required, which is covered next. As seen in Example 12.5, the robot is not required to learn the whole environment to solve a navigation problem. The search algorithms of Section 2.2 may be applied. For example, the A^* method will find the optimal route to the goal, and a reasonable heuristic underestimate of the cost-to-go can be defined by assuming that all tiles are empty. Although such a method will work, the reroute costs are not being taken into account. Thus, the optimal path eventually computed by A^* may be meaningless unless other robots will later use this information to reach the same goal in the same environment. For the unfortunate robot that went first, a substantial amount of exploration steps might have been wasted because A^* is not designed for exploration during execution. Even though the search algorithms in Section 2.2 assumed that the search graph was gradually revealed during execution, as opposed to being given in advance, they allow the current state in the search to jump around arbitrarily. In the current setting, this would require teleporting the robot to different parts of the environment. Section 12.3.2 covers a navigation algorithm that extends Dijkstra's algorithm to work correctly when the costs are discovered during execution. It can be nicely applied to the grid-based navigation problem presented in this section, even when the environment is initially unknown.

Algorithms for maze searching

A fascinating example of using an I-map to dramatically reduce the I-space was given a long time ago by Blum and Kozen [121]. Map building requires space that is linear in the number of tiles; however, it is possible to ensure that the environment has been systematically searched using much less space. For 2D grid environments, the searching problem can be solved without maintaining a complete map. It must systematically visit every tile; however, this does not imply that it must remember all of the places that it has visited. It is important only to ensure that the robot does not become trapped in an infinite loop before covering all tiles. It was shown in [121] that any maze can be searched using space that is only logarithmic in the number of tiles. This implies that many different environments have the same representation in the machine. Essentially, an I-map was developed that severely collapses $\mathcal{I}_{ndet}$ down to a smaller derived I-space.

Assume that the robot motion model is the same as has been given so far in this section; however, no map of the environment is initially given. Whatever direction the robot is facing initially can be declared to be north without any harm. It is assumed that any planar 2D grid is possible; therefore, there are identical maps for each of the four orientations. The north direction of one of these maps might be mislabeled by arbitrarily declaring the initial direction to be north, but this is not critical for the coming approach. It is assumed that the robot is a finite automaton that carries a binary counter. The counter will be needed because it can store values that are arbitrarily large, which is not possible for the automaton alone.

To keep the robot from wandering around in circles forever, two important pieces of information need to be maintained:

1. The *latitude*, which is the number of tiles in the north direction from the robot's initial position.

2. When a loop path is executed, it needs to know its *orientation*, which means whether the loop travels clockwise or counterclockwise.

Both of these can be computed from the history I-state, which takes the same form as in (12.12), except in the current setting, X is given by (12.23) and E is the set of all bounded environments (bounded means that the white tiles can be contained in a large rectangle). From the history I-state, let $\tilde{u}'_k$ denote the subsequence of the action history that corresponds to actions that produce motions. The latitude, $l(\tilde{u}'_k)$, can be computed by counting the number of actions that produce motions in the north direction and subtracting those that produce motions in the south direction. The loop orientation can be determined by angular odometry (which is equivalent to having a compass in this problem [288]). Let the value $r(\tilde{u}'_k)$ give the number of right turns in $\tilde{u}'_k$ minus the number of left turns in $\tilde{u}'_k$. Note that making four rights yields a clockwise loop and $r(\tilde{u}'_k) = 4$. Making four lefts yields a counterclockwise loop and $r(\tilde{u}'_k) = -4$. In general, it can be shown that for any loop path that does not intersect itself, either $r(\tilde{u}'_k) = 4$, which means that it travels clockwise, or $r(\tilde{u}'_k) = -4$, which means that it travels counterclockwise.

It was stated that a finite automaton and a binary counter are needed. The counter is used to keep track of $l(\tilde{u}'_k)$ as the robot moves. It turns out that an additional counter is not needed to measure the angular odometry because the robot can instead perform mod-3 arithmetic when counting right and left turns. If the result is $r(\tilde{u}'_k) = 1 \mod 3$

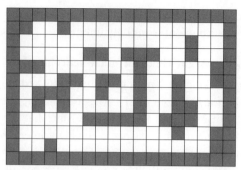

Figure 12.14: An example that has six obstacles.

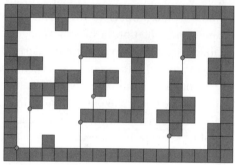

Figure 12.15: The obstacles are connected together by extending a thin obstacle downward from their unique points.

after forming a loop, then the robot traveled counterclockwise. If the result is $r(\tilde{u}'_k) = 2$ mod 3, then the robot traveled clockwise. This observation avoids using an unlimited number of bits, contrary to the case of maintaining latitude. The construction so far can be viewed as part of an I-map that maps the history I-states into a much smaller derived I-space.

The plan will be described in terms of the example shown in Figure 12.14. For any environment, there are obstacles in the interior (this example has six), and there is an outer boundary. Using the latitude and orientation information, a unique point can be determined on the boundary of each obstacle and on the outer boundary. The *unique point* is defined as the westernmost vertex among the southernmost vertices of the obstacle. These are shown by small discs in Figure 12.15. By using the latitude and orientation information, the unique point can always be found (see Exercise 4).

To solve the problem, the robot moves to a boundary and traverses it by performing *wall following*. The robot can use its sensing information to move in a way that keeps the wall to its left. Assuming that the robot can always detect a unique point along the boundary, it can imagine that the obstacles are connected as shown in Figure 12.15. There is a fictitious thin obstacle that extends southward from each unique point. This connects the obstacles together in a way that appears to be an extension of the outer boundary. In other words, imagine that the obstacles are protruding from the walls, as opposed to "floating" in the interior. By refusing to cross these fictitious obstacles, the robot moves around the boundary of all obstacles in a single closed-loop path. The strategy so far does not ensure that every cell will be visited. Therefore, the modification shown in Figure 12.16 is needed to ensure that every tile is visited by zig-zag motions. It is interesting to compare the solution to the spanning-tree coverage planning approach in Section 7.6,

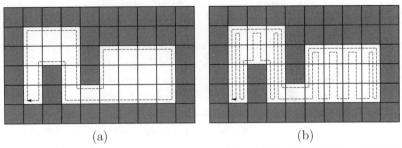

(a)   (b)

Figure 12.16: (a) A clockwise loop produced by wall following. (b) An alternative loop that visits all of the tiles in the interior.

Figure 12.17: The Automated Cross-Country Unmanned Vehicle (XUV) is equipped with laser radar and other sensors, and uses Stentz's algorithm to navigate (courtesy of General Dynamics Robotic Systems).

which assumed a complete map was given and the goal was to optimize the distance traveled.

If there is some special object in the environment that can be detected when reached by the robot, then the given strategy is always guaranteed to find it, even though at the end, it does not even have a map!

The resulting approach can be considered as an information-feedback plan on the I-space. In this sense, Blum and Kozen were the "planner" that found a plan that solves any problem. Alternative plans do not need to be computed from the problem data because the plan can handle all possible environments without modification. This is the power of working directly with an I-space over the set of environments, as opposed to requiring state estimation.

12.3.2 Stentz's algorithm (D*)

Imagine exploring an unknown planet using a robotic vehicle. The robot moves along the rugged terrain while using a range scanner to make precise measurements of the ground in its vicinity. As the robot moves, it may discover that some parts were easier to traverse than it originally thought. In other cases, it might realize that some direction it was intending to go is impassable due to a large bolder or a ravine. If the goal is to arrive at some specified coordinates, this problem can be viewed as a navigation problem in an unknown environment. The resulting solution is a lazy approach, as discussed in Section 12.2.1.

This section presents *Stentz's algorithm* [914], which has been used in many outdoor vehicle navigation applications, such as the vehicle shown in Figure 12.17. The algorithm can be considered as a dynamic version of the backward variant of Dijkstra's algorithm. Thus, it maintains cost-to-go values, and the search grows outward from the goal, as opposed to cost-to-come values from x_I in the version of Dijkstra's algorithm in Section 2.3.3. The method applies to any optimal planning problem. In terms of the state transition graph, it is assumed that the costs of edge transitions are unknown (equivalently, each cost $l(x, u)$ is unknown). In the navigation problem, a positive cost indicates the difficulty of traveling from state x to state $x' = f(x, u)$.

To work with a concrete problem, imagine that a planet surface is partitioned into a high-resolution grid. The state space is simply a bounded set of grid tiles; hence, $X \subseteq \mathbb{Z} \times \mathbb{Z}$. Each grid tile is assigned a positive, real value, $c(x)$, that indicates the difficulty of its traversal. The actions $U(x)$ at each grid point can be chosen using standard grid neighbors (e.g., four-neighbors or eight-neighbors). This now defines a state transition graph over X. From any $x' \in X$ and $u' \in U(x')$ such that $x = f(x', u')$, the cost term is assigned using c as $l(x', u') = c(x)$. This model is a generalization of the grid in Section 12.3.1, in which the tiles were either empty or occupied; here any positive real value is allowed. In the coming explanation, the costs may be more general than what is permitted by starting from $c(x)$, and the state transition graph does not need to be derived from a grid. Some initial values are assigned arbitrarily for all $l(x, u)$. For example, in the planetary exploration application, the cost of traversing a level, unobstructed surface may be uniformly assumed.

The task is to navigate to some goal state, x_G. The method works by initially constructing a feedback plan, π, on a subset of X that includes both x_I and x_G. The plan, π, is computed by iteratively applying the procedure in Figure 12.18 until the optimal cost-to-go is known at x_I. A priority queue, Q, is maintained as in Dijkstra's algorithm; however, Stentz's algorithm allows the costs of elements in Q to be modified due to information sensed during execution. Let $G_{best}(x)$ denote the lowest cost-to-go associated with x during the time it spends in Q. Assume that Q is sorted according to G_{best}. Let $G_{cur}(x)$ denote its current cost-to-go value, which may actually be more than $G_{best}(x)$ if some cost updates caused it to increase. Suppose that some $u \in U(x)$ can be applied to reach a state $x' = f(x, u)$. Let $G_{via}(x, x')$ denote the cost-to-go from x by traveling via x',

$$G_{via}(x, x') = G_{cur}(x') + l(x, u). \tag{12.24}$$

If $G_{via}(x, x') < G_{cur}(x)$, then it indicates that $G_{cur}(x)$ could be reduced. If $G_{cur}(x') \leq G_{best}(x)$, then it is furthermore known that $G_{cur}(x')$ is optimal. If both of these conditions are met, then $G_{cur}(x)$ is updated to $G_{via}(x, x')$.

After the iterations of Figure 12.18 finish, the robot executes π, which generates a sequence of visited states. Let x_k denote the current state during execution. If it is discovered that if $\pi(x_k) = u_k$ would be applied, the received cost would not match the cost $l(x_k, u_k)$ in the current model, then the costs need to be updated. More generally, the robot may have to be able to update costs within a region around x_k that corresponds to the sensor field of view. For the description below, assume that an update, $l(x_k, u_k)$, is obtained for x_k only (the more general case is handled similarly). First, $l(x_k, u_k)$ is updated to the newly measured value. If x_k happened to be dead (visited, but no longer in Q), then it is inserted again into Q, with cost $G_{cur}(x_k)$. The steps in Figure 12.18 are performed until $G_{cur}(x_k) \leq G_{best}(x)$ for all $x \in Q$. Following this, the plan execution continues until either the goal is reached or another cost mismatch is discovered. At any time during execution, the robot motions are optimal given the current information about the costs [914].

STENTZ'S ALGORITHM

1. Remove x from Q, which is the state with the lowest $G_{best}(x)$ value.

2. If $G_{best}(x) < G_{cur}(x)$, then x has increased its value while on Q. If x can improve its cost by traveling via a neighboring state for which the optimal cost-to-go is known, it should do so. Thus, for every $u \in U(x)$, test for $x' = f(x, u)$ whether $G_{via}(x, x') < G_{cur}(x)$ and $G_{cur}(x') \le G_{best}(x)$. If so, then update $G_{cur}(x) := G_{via}(x, x')$ and $\pi(x) := u$.

3. This and the remaining steps are repeated for each x' such that there exists $u' \in U(x')$ for which $x = f(x', u')$. If x' is unvisited, then assign $\pi(x') := u'$, and place x' onto Q with cost $G_{via}(x', x)$.

4. If the cost-to-go from x' appears incorrect because $\pi(x') = u'$ but $G_{via}(x', x) \ne G_{cur}(x')$, then an update is needed. Place x' onto Q with cost $G_{via}(x', x)$.

5. If $\pi(x') \ne u'$ but $G_{via}(x', x) < G_{cur}(x')$, then from x' it is better to travel via x than to use $\pi(x')$. If $G_{cur}(x) = G_{best}(x)$, then $\pi(x') := u'$ and x' is inserted into Q because the optimal cost-to-go for x is known. Otherwise, x (instead of x') is inserted into Q with its current value, $G_{cur}(x)$.

6. One final condition is needed to avoid generating cycles in π. If x' is dead (visited, but no longer in Q), it may need to be inserted back into Q with cost $G_{cur}(x')$. This must be done if $\pi(x') \ne u'$, $G_{via}(x, x') < G_{cur}(x)$, and $G_{cur}(x) > G_{best}(x)$

Figure 12.18: Stentz's algorithm, often called D^* (pronounced "dee star"), is a variant of Dijkstra's algorithm that dynamically updates cost values as the cost terms are learned during execution. The steps here are only one iteration of updating the costs after a removal of a state from Q.

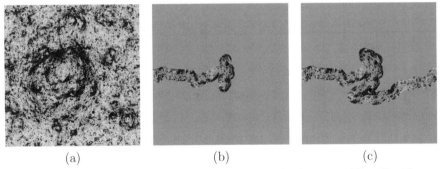

| (a) | (b) | (c) |

Figure 12.19: An example of executing Stentz's algorithm (courtesy of Tony Stentz).

Figure 12.19 illustrates the execution of the algorithm. Figure 12.19a shows a synthetic terrain that was generated by a stochastic fractal. Darker gray values indicate higher cost. In the center, very costly terrain acts as a barrier, for which an escape route exists in the downward direction. The initial state is the middle of the left edge of the environment, and the goal state is the right edge. The robot initially plans a straight-line path and then incrementally updates the path in each step as it moves. In Figure 12.19b, the robot has encountered the costly center and begins to search for a way around. Finally, the goal is reached, as shown in Figure 12.19c. The executed path is actually the result of executing a series of optimal paths, each of which is based on the known information at the time a single action is applied.

Interpretation in terms of I-spaces

An alternative formulation will now be given to help understand the connection to I-spaces of a set of environments. The state space, as defined previously, could instead be defined as a *configuration space*, $C = \mathbb{Z} \times \mathbb{Z}$. Let $q \in C$ denote a configuration. Suppose that each possible environment corresponds to one way to assign costs to all of the edges in a configuration transition graph. The set E of all possible environments for this problem seems to be all possible ways to assign costs, $l(q, u)$. The state space can now be defined as $C \times E$, and for each state, $x = (q, e) \in X$, the configuration and complete set of costs are specified. Initially, it is guessed that the robot is in some particular $e \in E$. If a cost mismatch is discovered, this means that a different environment model is now assumed because a transition cost is different from what was expected. The costs should actually be written as $l(x, u) = l(q, e, u)$, which indicates the dependency of the costs on the particular environment is assumed.

A nondeterministic I-state corresponds to a set of possible cost assignments, along with their corresponding configurations. Since the method requires assigning costs that have not yet been observed, it takes a guess and assumes that one particular environment in the nondeterministic I-state is the correct one. As cost mismatches are discovered, it is realized that the previous guess lies outside of the updated nondeterministic I-state. Therefore, the guess is changed to incorporate the new cost information. As this process evolves, the nondeterministic I-state continues to shrink. Note, however, that in the end, the robot may solve the problem while being incorrect about the precise $e \in E$. Some tiles are never visited, and their true costs are therefore unknown. A default assumption about their costs was made to solve the problem; however, the true $e \in E$ can only be known if all tiles are visited. It is only true that the final assumed default values lie within the final nondeterministic I-state.

12.3.3 Planning in unknown continuous environments

We now move from discrete to continuous environments but continue to use nondeterministic uncertainty. First, several *bug algorithms* [507, 670, 508] are presented, which represent a family of motion plans that solve planning problems using ideas that are related in many ways to the maze exploration ideas of Section 12.3.1. In addition to bug algorithms, the concept of competitive ratios is also briefly covered.

The following model will be used for bug algorithms. Suppose that a point robot is placed into an unknown 2D environment that may contain any finite number of bounded obstacles. It is assumed that the boundary of each obstacle and the outer boundary (if it exists) are piecewise-analytic (here, *analytic* implies that each piece is smooth and switches its curvature sign only a finite number of times). Thus, the obstacles could be polygons, smooth curves, or some combination of curved and linear parts. The set E of possible environments is overwhelming, but it will be managed by avoiding its explicit construction. The robot configuration is characterized by its position and orientation.

There are two main sensors:[2]

1. A *goal sensor* indicates the current Euclidean distance to the goal and the direction to the goal, expressed with respect to an absolute "north."

2. A *local visibility sensor* provides the exact shape of the boundary within a small distance from the robot. The robot must be in contact or almost in contact to observe part of the boundary; otherwise, the sensor provides no useful information.

---

[2] This is just one possible sensing model. Alternative combinations of sensors may be used, provided that they enable the required motions and decisions to be executed in the coming motion strategies.

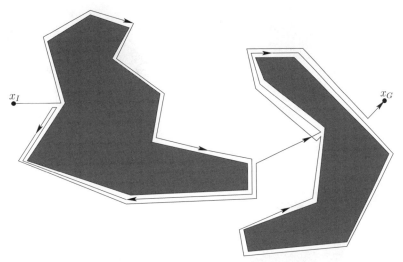

Figure 12.20: An illustration of the Bug1 strategy.

The goal sensor essentially encodes the robot's position in polar coordinates (the goal is the origin). Therefore, unique (x, y) coordinates can be assigned to any position visited by the robot. This enables it to incrementally trace out obstacle boundaries that it has already traversed. The local visibility sensor provides just enough information to allow wall-following motions; the range of the sensor is very short so that the robot cannot learn anything more about the structure of the environment.

Some strategies will now be considered for the robot. Each of these can be considered as an information-feedback plan on a nondeterministic I-space.

The Bug1 strategy

A strategy called *Bug1* was developed in [670] and is illustrated in Figure 12.20. The execution is as follows:

1. Move toward the goal until an obstacle or the goal is encountered. If the goal is reached, then stop.

2. Turn left and follow the entire perimeter of the contacted obstacle. Once the full perimeter has been visited, then return to the point at which the goal was closest, and go to Step 1.

Determining that the entire perimeter has been traversed may seem to require a pebble or marker; however, this can be inferred by finding the point at which the goal sensor reading repeats.

The worst case is conceptually simple to understand. The total distance traveled by the robot is no greater than

$$d + \frac{3}{2} \sum_{i=1}^{M} p_i, \qquad (12.25)$$

in which d is the Euclidean distance from the initial position to the goal position, p_i is the perimeter of the ith obstacle, and M is the number of obstacles. This means that the boundary of each obstacle is followed no more than $3/2$ times. Figure 12.21 shows an example in which each obstacle is traversed $3/2$ times. This bound relies on the fact that the robot can always recall the shortest path along the boundary to the point from which it needs to leave. This seems reasonable because the robot can infer its distance traveled

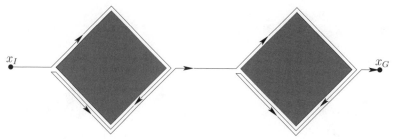

Figure 12.21: A bad example for Bug1. The perimeter of each obstacle is spanned one and a half times.

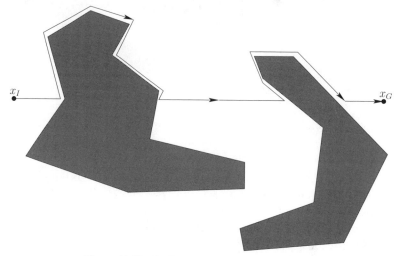

Figure 12.22: An illustration of the Bug2 strategy.

along the boundary from the goal sensor. If this was not possible, then the 3/2 would have to be replaced by 2 because the robot could nearly traverse the full boundary twice in the worst case.

The Bug2 strategy

An alternative to Bug1 is the *Bug2 strategy*, which is illustrated in Figure 12.22. The robot always attempts to move along a line that connects the initial and goal positions. When the robot is on this line, the goal direction will be either the same as from the initial state or it will differ by π radians (if the robot is on the other side of the goal). The first step is the same as for Bug1. In the second step, the robot follows the perimeter only until the line is reached and it is able to move in the direction toward the goal. From there, it goes to Step 1. As expressed so far, it is possible that infinite cycles occur. Therefore, a small modification is needed. If the robot detects that it is about to leave from a point on the boundary from which it has already visited, it instead continues further along the boundary until arriving at a point on the line that it has not yet visited. From there, it leaves the line and goes to Step 1.

For the Bug2 strategy, the total distance traveled is no more than

$$d + \frac{1}{2} \sum_{i=1}^{M} n_i \, p_i, \tag{12.26}$$

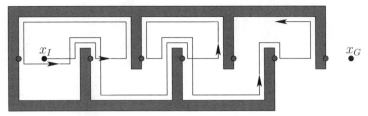

Figure 12.23: A bad case for Bug2. Only part of the resulting path is shown. Points from which the robot can leave the boundary are indicated.

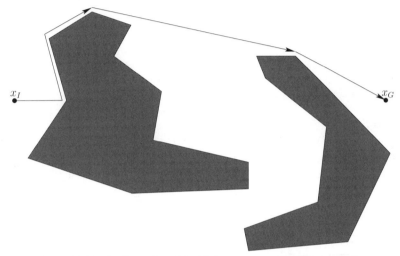

Figure 12.24: An illustration of the VisBug strategy with unlimited radius.

in which n_i is the number of times the ith obstacle crosses the line segment between the initial position and the goal position. An example that illustrates the trouble caused by the crossings is shown in Figure 12.23.

Using range data

The *VisBug* [669] and *TangentBug* [508, 595] strategies incorporate distance measurements made by a range or visibility sensor to improve the efficiency. The TangentBug strategy will be described here and is illustrated in Figure 12.24. Suppose that in addition to the sensors described previously, it is also equipped with a sensor that produces measurements as shown in Figure 12.25. The strategy is as follows:

1. Move toward the goal, either through the interior of the space or by wall following, until it is realized that the robot is trapped in a local minimum or the goal is reached. This is similar to the gradient-descent motion of the potential-field planner of Section 5.4.3. If the goal is reached, then stop; otherwise, go to the next step.

2. Execute motions along the boundary. First, pick a direction by comparing the previous heading to the goal direction. While moving along the boundary, keep track of two distances: d_f and d_r. The distance d_f is the minimal distance from the goal, observed while traveling along the boundary. The distance d_r is the length of the shortest path from the current position to the goal, assuming that the only obstacles are those visible by the range sensor. The robot stops following the boundary if $d_r < d_f$. In this case, go to Step 1. If the robot loops around the entire obstacle without this condition occurring, then the algorithm reports that the goal is not reachable.

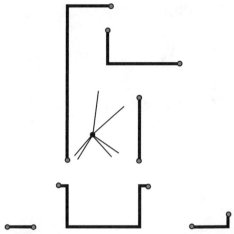

Figure 12.25: The candidate motions with respect to the range sensor are the directions in which there is a discontinuity in the depth map. The distances from the robot to the small circles are used to select the desired motion.

A one-parameter family of TangentBug algorithms can be made by setting a depth limit for the range sensor. As the maximum depth is decreased, the robot becomes more short-sighted and performance degrades. It is shown in [508] that the distance traveled is no greater than

$$d + \sum_{i=1}^{M} p_i + \sum_{i=1}^{M} p_i m_i, \tag{12.27}$$

in which m_i is the number of local minima for the ith obstacle and d is the initial distance to the goal. The bound is taken over M obstacles, which are assumed to intersect a disc of radius d, centered at the goal (all others can be ignored). A variant of the TangentBug, called WedgeBug, was developed in [595] for planetary rovers that have a limited field of view.

Competitive ratios

A popular way to evaluate algorithms that utilize different information has emerged from the algorithms community. The idea is to compute a *competitive ratio*, which places an *on-line algorithm* in competition with an algorithm that receives more information [677, 893]. The idea can generally be applied to plans. First a cost is formulated, such as the total distance that the robot travels to solve a navigation task. A competitive ratio can then be defined as

$$\max_{e \in E} \frac{\text{Cost of executing the plan that does not know } e \text{ in advance.}}{\text{Cost of executing the plan that knows } e \text{ in advance}}. \tag{12.28}$$

The maximum is taken over all $e \in E$, which is usually an infinite set, as in the case of the bug algorithms. A competitive ratio for a navigation problem can be made by comparing the optimal distance to the total distance traveled by the robot during the execution of the on-line algorithm. Since E is infinite, many plans fail to produce a finite competitive ratio. The bug algorithms, while elegant, represent such an example. Imagine a goal that is very close, but a large obstacle boundary needs to be explored. An obstacle boundary can be made arbitrarily large while making the optimal distance to the goal very small. When evaluated in (12.28), the result over all environments is unbounded. In some contexts, the

Figure 12.26: (a) A lost cow must find its way to the gate, but it does not know in which direction the gate lies. (b) If there is no bound on the distance to the gate, then a doubling spiral strategy works well, producing a competitive ratio of 9.

ratio may still be useful if expressed as a function of the representation. For example, if E is a polygon with n edges, then an $O(\sqrt{n})$ competitive ratio means that (12.28) is bounded over all n by $c\sqrt{n}$ for some $c \in \mathbb{R}$. For competitive ratio analysis in the context of bug algorithms, see [377].

A nice illustration of competitive ratio analysis and issues is provided by the *lost-cow problem* [61]. As shown in Figure 12.26a, a short-sighted cow is following along an infinite fence and wants to find the gate. This makes a convenient one-dimensional planning problem. If the location of the gate is given, then the cow can reach it directly by traveling directly. If the cow is told that the gate is no more than distance 1 away, then it can move one unit in one direction and return to try the other direction if the gate has not been found. The competitive ratio in this case (the set of environments corresponds to all gate placements) is 3. What if the cow is not even told how far away the gate may be? In this case, the best strategy is a *spiral search*, which is to zig-zag back and forth while iteratively doubling the distance traveled in each direction, as shown in Figure 12.26b. In other words: left one unit, right one unit, left two units, right two units, left four units, and so on. The competitive ratio for this strategy turns out to be 9, which is optimal. This approach resembles iterative deepening, which was covered in Section 2.2.2.

12.3.4 Optimal navigation without a geometric model

This section presents *gap navigation trees* (GNTs) [943, 945], which are a data structure and associated planning algorithm for performing optimal navigation in the continuous environments that were considered in Section 12.3.3. It is assumed in this section that the robot is equipped with a gap sensor, as depicted in Figure 11.16 of Section 11.5.1. At every instant in time, the robot has available one action for each gap that is visible in the gap sensor. If an action is applied, then the robot moves toward the corresponding gap. This can be applied over continuous time, which enables the robot to "chase" a particular gap. The robot has no other sensing information: It has no compass and no ability to measure distances. Therefore, it is impossible to construct a map of the environment that contains metric information.

Assume that the robot is placed into an unknown but simply connected planar environment, X. The GNT can be extended to the case of multiply connected environments; however, in this case there are subtle issues with distinguishability, and it is only possible to guarantee optimality within a homotopy class of paths [944]. By analyzing the way that critical events occur in the gap sensor, a tree representation can be built that indicates how to move optimally in the environment, even though precise measurements cannot be taken. Since a gap sensor cannot even measure distances, it may seem unusual that the robot can move along shortest paths without receiving any distance (or metric) information. This will once again illustrate the power of I-spaces.

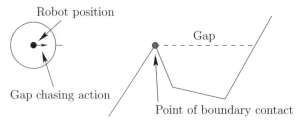

Figure 12.27: A gap-chasing action is applied, which moves the robot straight in the direction of the gap until the boundary is contacted. Once this occurs, a new part of the environment becomes visible.

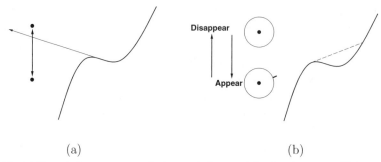

(a)   (b)

Figure 12.28: (a) The robot crosses a ray that extends from an inflectional tangent. (b) A gap appears or disappears from the gap sensor, depending on the direction.

The appearance of the environment *relative to the position of the robot* is encoded as a tree that indicates how the gaps change as the robot moves. It provides the robot with sufficient information to move to any part of the environment while traveling along the shortest path. It is important to understand that the tree does not correspond to some static map of the environment. It expresses how the environment appears relative to the robot and may therefore change as the robot moves in the environment.

The root of the tree represents the gap sensor. For each gap that currently appears in the sensor, an edge is connected to the root. Let these edges be called *root edges*. Each root edge corresponds to an action that can be applied by the robot. By selecting a root edge, the action moves the robot along a straight line toward that gap. Thus, there is a simple control model that enables the robot to move precisely toward a particular point along the boundary, ∂X, as shown in Figure 12.27.

Let $V(x)$ be the *visibility region*, which is the set of all points in X that are visible from x. Let $X \setminus V(x)$ be called the *shadow region*, which is the set of all points *not* visible from x. Let each connected component of the shadow region be called a *shadow component*. Every gap in the gap sensor corresponds to a line segment in X that touches ∂X in two places (for example, see Figure 11.15a). Each of these segments forms a boundary between the visibility region and a shadow component. If the robot would like to travel to this shadow component, the shortest way is to move directly to the gap. When moving toward a gap, the robot eventually reaches ∂X, at which point a new action must be selected.

Critical gap events

As the robot moves, several important events can occur in the gap sensor:

1. **Disappear:** A gap disappears because the robot crosses an *inflection ray* as shown in Figure 12.28. This means that some previous shadow component is now visible.

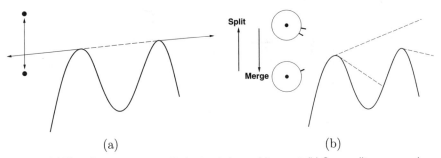

Figure 12.29: (a) The robot crosses a ray that extends from a bitangent. (b) Gaps split or merge, depending on the direction.

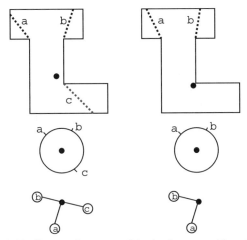

Figure 12.30: If a gap disappears, it is simply removed from the GNT.

2. **Appear:** A gap appears because the robot crosses an inflection ray in the opposite direction. This means that a new shadow component exists, which represents a freshly hidden portion of the environment.

3. **Split:** A gap splits into two gaps because the robot crosses a *bitangent ray*, as shown in Figure 12.29 (this was also shown in Figure 12.5). This means that one shadow component splits into two shadow components.

4. **Merge:** Two gaps merge into one because the robot crosses a bitangent ray in the oppose direction. In this case, two shadow components merge into one.

This is a complete list of possible events, under a *general position* assumption that precludes environments that cause degeneracies, such as three gaps that merge into one or the appearance of a gap precisely where two other gaps split.

As each of these gap events occurs, it needs to be reflected in the tree. If a gap disappears, as shown in Figure 12.30, then the corresponding edge and vertex are simply removed. If a merge event occurs, then an intermediate vertex is inserted as shown in Figure 12.31. This indicates that if that gap is chased, it will split into the two original gaps. If a split occurs, as shown in Figure 12.32, then the intermediate vertex is removed. The appearance of a gap is an important case, which generates a *primitive vertex* in the tree, as shown in

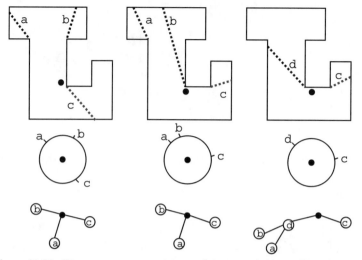

Figure 12.31: If two gaps merge, an intermediate vertex is inserted into the tree.

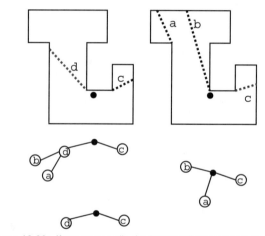

Figure 12.32: If two gaps split, the intermediate vertex is removed.

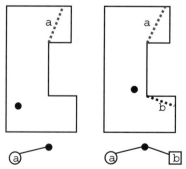

Figure 12.33: The appearance of a gap results in a primitive vertex, which is denoted by a square.

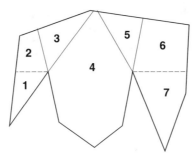

Figure 12.34: A simple environment for illustrating the gap navigation tree.

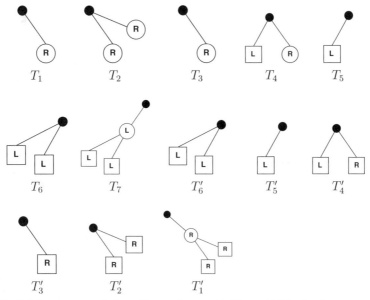

Figure 12.35: Building a representation of the environment in Figure 12.34 using the gap navigation tree. The sequence is followed from left to right. For convenience, the "R" or "L" inside of each vertex indicates whether the shadow component is to the right or left of the gap, respectively. This information is not needed by the algorithm, but it helps in understanding the representation.

Figure 12.33. Note that a primitive vertex can never split because chasing it will result in its disappearance.

A simple example will now be considered.

Example 12.6 (Gap Navigation Tree) Suppose that the robot does not know the environment in Figure 12.34. It moves from cells 1 to 7 in order and then returns to cell 1. The following sequence of trees occurs: $T_1, \ldots, T_7, T_6', \ldots, T_1'$, as shown in Figure 12.35. The root vertex is shown as a solid black disc. Vertices that are not known to be primitive are shown as circles; primitive vertices are squares. Note that if any leaf vertex is a circle, then it means that the shadow region of R that is hidden by that gap has not been completely explored. Note that once the robot reaches cell 5, it has seen the whole environment. This occurs precisely when all leaf vertices are primitive. When the robot returns to the first region, the tree is larger because it knows that the region on the right is composed of two smaller regions to the right. If all leaves are squares, this means that the environment has been completely explored. ∎

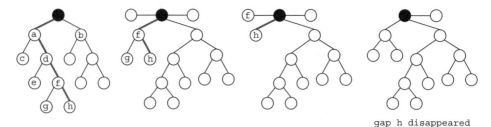

gap h disappeared

Figure 12.36: Optimal navigation to a specified part of the environment is achieved by "chasing" the desired vertex in the GNT until it disappears. This will make a portion of the environment visible. In the example, the gap labeled "h" is chased.

In the example, all of the interesting parts of the environment were explored. From this point onward, all leaf vertices will be primitive vertices because all possible splits have been discovered. In a sense, the environment has been completely learned, at the level of resolution possible with the gap sensor. A simple strategy for exploring the environment is to chase any gaps that themselves are nonprimitive leaf vertices or that have children that are nonprimitive leaf vertices. A leaf vertex in the tree can be *chased* by repeatedly applying actions that chase its corresponding gap in the gap sensor. This may cause the tree to incrementally change; however, there is no problem if the action is selected to chase whichever gap hides the desired leaf vertex, as shown in Figure 12.36. Every nonprimitive leaf vertex will either split or disappear. After all nonprimitive leaf vertices have been chased, all possible splits have been performed and only primitive leaves remain. In this case, the environment has been completely learned.

Using the GNTs for optimal navigation

Since there is no precise map of the environment, it is impossible to express a goal state using coordinates in $\mathbb{R}^2$. However, a goal can be expressed in terms of the vertex that must be chased to make the state visible. For example, imagine showing the robot an object while it explores. At first, the object is visible, but a gap may appear that hides the object. After several merges, a vertex deep in the tree may correspond to the location from which the object is visible. The robot can navigate back to the object optimally by chasing the vertex that first hid the object by its appearance. Once this vertex and its corresponding gap disappear, the object becomes visible. At this time the robot can move straight toward the object (assuming an additional sensor that indicates the direction of the object). It was argued in [945] that when the robot chases a vertex in the GNT, it precisely follows the paths of the shortest-path roadmap, which was introduced in Section 6.2.4. Each pair of successive gap events corresponds to the traversal of a bitangent edge.

I-space interpretation

In terms of an I-space over the set of environments, the GNT considers large sets of environments to be equivalent. This means that an I-map was constructed on which the derived I-space is the set of possible GNTs. Under this I-map, many environments correspond to the same GNT. Due to this, the robot can accomplish interesting tasks without requesting further information. For example, if two environments differ only by rotation or scale, the GNT representations are identical. Surprisingly, the robot does not even need to be concerned about whether the environment boundary is polygonal or curved. The only important concern is how the gaps events occur. For example, the environments in Figure 12.37

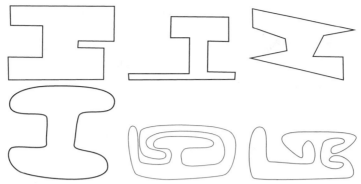

Figure 12.37: These environments yield the same GNTs and are therefore equivalent at the resolution of the derived I-space. The robot cannot measure distances and does not even care whether walls are straight or curved; it is not relevant to the navigation task. Nevertheless, it executes optimal motions in terms of the Euclidean distance traveled.

all produce the same GNTs and are therefore indistinguishable to the robot. In the same way that the maze exploring algorithm of Section 12.3.1 did not need a complete map to locate an object, the GNT does not need one to perform optimal navigation.

12.3.5 Probabilistic localization and mapping

The problems considered so far in Section 12.3 have avoided probabilistic modeling. Suppose here that probabilistic models exist for the state transitions and the observations. Many problems can be formulated by replacing the nondeterministic models in Section 12.3.1 by probabilistic models. This would lead to probabilistic I-states that represent distributions over a set of possible grids and a configuration within each grid. If the problem is left in its full generality, the I-space is enormous to the point that is seems hopeless to approach problems in the manner used to far. If optimality is not required, then in some special cases progress may be possible.

The current problem is to construct a map of the environment while simultaneously localizing the robot with the respect to the map. Recall Figure 1.7 from Section 1.2. The section covers a general framework that has been popular in mobile robotics in recent years (see the literature suggested at the end of the chapter). The discussion presented here can be considered as a generalization of the discussion from Section 12.2.3, which was only concerned with the localization portion of the current problem. Now the environment is not even known. The current problem can be interpreted as localization in a state space defined as

$$X = C \times E, \tag{12.29}$$

in which C is a configuration space and E is the environment space. A state, x_k, is represented as $x_k = (q_k, e)$; there is no k subscript for e because the environment is assumed to be static). The history I-state provides the data to use in the process of determining the state. As for localization in Section 12.2, there are both passive and active versions of the problem. An incremental version of the active problem is sometimes called the *next-best-view problem* [67, 240, 796]. The difficulty is that the robot has opposing goals of: 1) trying to turn on the sensor at places that will gain as much new data as possible, and 2) this minimization of redundancy can make it difficult to fuse all of the measurements into a global map. The passive problem will be described here; the methods can be used to provide information for solving the active problem.

Suppose that the robot is a point that translates and rotates in $\mathbb{R}^2$. According to Section 4.2, this yields $\mathcal{C} = \mathbb{R}^2 \times \mathbb{S}^1$, which represents $SE(2)$. Let $q \in \mathcal{C}$ denote a configuration, which yields the position and orientation of the robot. Assume that configuration transitions are modeled probabilistically, which requires specifying a probability density, $p(q_{k+1}|q_k, u_k)$. This can be lifted to the state space to obtain $p(x_{k+1}|x_k, u_k)$ by assuming that the configuration transitions are independent of the environment (assuming no collisions ever occur). This replaces q_k and q_{k+1} by x_k and x_{k+1}, respectively, in which $x_k = (q_k, e)$ and $x_{k+1} = (q_{k+1}, e)$ for any $e \in E$.

Suppose that observations are obtained from a depth sensor, which ideally would produce measurements like those shown in Figure 11.15b; however, the data are assumed to be noisy. The probabilistic model discussed in Section 12.2.3 can be used to define $p(y|x)$. Now imagine that the robot moves to several parts of the environment, such as those shown in Figure 11.15a, and performs a sensor sweep in each place. If the configuration q_k is not known from which each sweep y_k was performed, how can the data sets be sewn together to build a correct, global map of the environment? This is trivial after considering the knowledge of the configurations, but without it the problem is like putting together pieces of a jigsaw puzzle. Thus, the important data in each stage form a vector, (y_k, q_k). If the sensor observations, y_k, are not tagged with a configuration, q_k, from which they are taken, then the jigsaw problem arises. If information is used to tightly constrain the possibilities for q_k, then it becomes easier to put the pieces together. This intuition leads to the following approach.

The EM algorithm

The problem is often solved in practice by applying the *expectation-maximization* (EM) algorithm [108]. In the general framework, there are three different spaces:

1. A set of parameters, which are to be determined through some measurement and estimation process. In our problem, this represents E, because the main goal is to determine the environment.

2. A set of data, which provide information that can be used to estimate the parameter. In the localization and mapping problem, this corresponds to the history I-space $\mathcal{I}_K$. Each history I-state $\eta_K \in \mathcal{I}_K$ is $\eta_K = (p(x), \tilde{u}_{K-1}, \tilde{y}_K)$, in which $p(x)$ is a prior probability density over X.

3. A set of hidden variables, which are unknown but need to be estimated to complete the process of determining the parameters. In the localization and mapping problem, this is the configuration space $\mathcal{C}$.

Since both the parameters and the hidden variables are unknown, the choice between the two may seem arbitrary. It will turn out that expressions can be derived to nicely express the probability density for the hidden variables, but the parameters are much more complicated.

The EM algorithm involves an expectation step followed by a maximization step. The two steps are repeated as necessary until a solution with the desired accuracy is obtained. The method is guaranteed to converge under general conditions [271, 977, 978]. In practice, it appears to work well even under cases that are not theoretically guaranteed to converge [940].

From this point onward, let $E, \mathcal{I}_K$, and C denote the three spaces for the EM algorithm because they pertain directly to the problem. Suppose that a robot has moved in the environment for $K - 1$ stages, resulting in a final stage, K. At each stage, $k \in \{1, \ldots, K\}$, an observation, y_k, is made using its sensor. This could, for example, represent a set of distance measurements made by sonars or a range scanner. Furthermore, an action, u_k, is applied for $k = 1$ to $k = K$. A prior probability density function, $p(x)$, is initially assumed over X. This leads to the history I-state, η_k, as defined in (11.14).

Now imagine that K stages have been executed, and the task is to estimate e. From each q_k, a measurement, y_k, of part of the environment is taken. The EM algorithm generates a sequence of improved estimates of e. In each execution of the two EM steps, a new estimate of $e \in E$ is produced. Let $\hat{e}_i$ denote this estimate after the ith iteration. Let $\tilde{q}_K$ denote the configuration history from stage 1 to stage K. The expectation step computes the expected likelihood of η_K given $\hat{e}_i$. This can be expressed as[3]

$$
\begin{aligned}
Q(e, \hat{e}_{i-1}) &= E\left[p(\eta_K, \tilde{q}_K \mid e) \mid \eta_K, \hat{e}_{i-1} \right] \\
&= \int_C p(\eta_K, \tilde{q}_K \mid e) p(\tilde{q}_K \mid \eta_K, \hat{e}_{i-1}) d\tilde{q}_K,
\end{aligned}
\tag{12.30}
$$

in which the expectation is taken over the configuration histories. Since η_K is given and the expectation removes $\tilde{q}_k$, (12.30) is a function only of e and $\hat{e}_{i-1}$. The term $p(\eta_K, \tilde{q}_K \mid e)$ can be expressed as

$$
p(\eta_K, \tilde{q}_K \mid e) = p(\tilde{q}_K \mid \eta_K, e) p(\eta_K \mid e),
\tag{12.31}
$$

in which $p(\eta_K)$ is a prior density over the I-space, given nothing but the environment e. The factor $p(\tilde{q}_K \mid \eta_K, e)$ differs from the second factor of the integrand in (12.30) only by using e or $\hat{e}_{i-1}$. The main difficulty in evaluating (12.30) is to evaluate $p(\tilde{q}_k \mid \eta_K, \hat{e}_{i-1})$ (or the version that uses e). This is essentially a localization problem with a given map, as considered in Section 12.2.3. The information up to stage k can be applied to yield the probabilistic I-state $p(q_k \mid \eta_k, \hat{e}_{i-1})$ for each q_k; however, this neglects the information from the remaining stages. This new information can be used to make inferences about old configurations. For example, based on current measurements and memory of the actions that were applied, we have better information regarding the configuration several stages ago. In [941] a method of computing $p(q_k \mid \eta_k, \hat{e}_{i-1})$ is given that computes two terms: One is $p(q_k \mid \eta_k)$, and the other is a backward probabilistic I-state that starts at stage K and runs down to $k + 1$.

Note that once determined, (12.30) is a function only of e and $\hat{e}_{i-1}$. The maximization step involves selecting an $\hat{e}_i$ that minimizes (12.30):

$$
\hat{e}_i = \operatorname*{argmax}_{e \in E} Q(e, \hat{e}_{i-1}).
\tag{12.32}
$$

This optimization is often too difficult, and convergence conditions exist if $\hat{e}_i$ is chosen such that $Q(\hat{e}_i, \hat{e}_{i-1}) > Q(\hat{e}_{i-1}, \hat{e}_{i-1})$. Repeated iterations of the EM algorithm result in a kind of gradient descent that arrives at a local minimum in E.

One important factor in the success of the method is in the representation of E. In the EM computations, one common approach is to use a set of landmarks, which were mentioned in Section 11.5.1. These are special places in the environment that can be identified by

---

[3] In practice, a logarithm is applied to $p(\eta_K, q_k \mid e)$ because densities that contain exponentials usually arise. Taking the logarithm makes the expressions simpler without affecting the result of the optimization. The log is not applied here because this level of detail is not covered.

sensors, and if correctly classified, they dramatically improve localization. In [941], the landmarks are indicated by a user as the robot travels. Classification and positioning errors can both be modeled probabilistically and incorporated into the EM approach. Another idea that dramatically simplifies the representation of E is to approximate environments with a fine-resolution grid. Probabilities are associated with grid cells, which leads to a data structure called an *occupancy grid* [309, 688, 852]. In any case, E must be carefully defined to ensure that reasonable prior distributions can be made for $p(e)$ to initialize the EM algorithm as the robot first moves.

12.4 Visibility-based pursuit-evasion

This section considers *visibility-based pursuit-evasion* [615, 932], which was described in Section 1.2 as a game of hide-and-seek. The topic provides an excellent illustration of the power of I-space concepts.

12.4.1 Problem formulation

The problem considered in this section is formulated as follows.

Formulation 12.1 (Visibility-Based Pursuit-Evasion)

1. A given, continuous environment region $R \subset \mathbb{R}^2$, which is an open set that is bounded by a simple closed curve. The boundary ∂R is often a polygon, but it may be any piecewise-analytic closed curve.

2. An *unbounded time interval* $T = [0, \infty)$.

3. An *evader*, which is a moving point in R. The evader position $e(t)$ at time $t \in T$ is determined by a continuous *position function*, $\tilde{e} : [0, 1] \to R$.[4]

4. A *pursuer*, which is a moving point in R. The evader position function $\tilde{e}$ is unknown to the pursuer.

5. A *visibility sensor*, which defines a set $V(r) \subseteq R$ for each $r \in R$.

The task is to find a path, $\tilde{p} : [0, 1] \to R$, for the pursuer for which the evader is guaranteed to be detected, regardless of its position function. This means that $\exists t \in T$ such that $e(t) \in V(p(t))$. The speed of the pursuer is not important; therefore, the time domain may be lengthened as desired, if the pursuer is slow.

It will be convenient to solve the problem by verifying that there is no evader. In other words, find a path for the pursuer that upon completion guarantees that there are no remaining places where the evader could be hiding. This ensures that during execution of the plan, the pursuer will encounter any evader. In fact, there can be any number of evaders, and the pursuer will find all of them. The approach systematically eliminates any possible places where evaders could hide.

The state yields the positions of the pursuer and the evader, $x = (p, e)$, which results in the state space $X = R \times R \subset \mathbb{R}^4$. Since the evader position is unknown, the current state is unknown, and I-spaces arise. The observation space Y is a collection of subsets of R. For each $p \in R$, the sensor yields a visibility polygon, $V(p) \subseteq R$ (this is denoted by $y = h(p, e)$ using notation of Section 11.1.1). Consider the history I-state at time t. The

---

[4] Following from standard function notation, it is better to use $\tilde{e}(t)$ instead of $e(t)$ to denote the position at time t; however, this will not be followed.

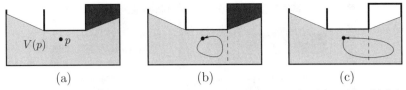

Figure 12.38: (a) Suppose the pursuer comes near the end of a contaminated corridor. (b) If the pursuer moves in a loop path, the nondeterministic I-state gradually changes, but returns to its original value. (c) However, if a critical boundary is crossed, then the nondeterministic I-state fundamentally changes.

initial pursuer position $p(0)$ is given (any position can be chosen arbitrarily, if it is not given), and the evader may lie anywhere in R. The input history $\tilde{u}_t$ can be expressed as the pursuer history $\tilde{p}_t$.[5] Thus, the history I-state is

$$\eta_t = ((p(0), R), \tilde{p}_t, \tilde{y}_t), \qquad (12.33)$$

in which $(p(0), R) \subset X$ reflects the initial condition in which $p(0)$ is known, and the evader position $e(0)$ may lie anywhere in R.

Consider the nondeterministic I-space, $\mathcal{I}_{ndet}$. Since the pursuer position is always known, the interesting part of R is the subset in which the evader may lie. Thus, the nondeterministic I-state can be expressed as $X_t(\eta_t) = (p(t), E(\eta_t))$, in which $E(\eta_t)$ is the set of possible evader positions given η_t. As usual for nondeterministic I-states, $E(\eta_t)$ is the smallest set that is consistent with all of the information in η_t.

Consider how $E(\eta_t)$ varies over time. After the first instant of time, $V(p(0))$ is observed, and it is known that the evader lies in $R \setminus V(p(0))$, which is the shadow region (defined in Section 12.3.4) from $p(0)$. As the pursuer moves, $E(\eta_t)$ varies. Suppose you are told that the pursuer is now at position $p(t)$, but you are not yet told η_t. What options seem possible for $E(\eta_t)$? These depend on the history, but the only interesting possibilities are that each shadow component may or may not contain the evader. For some of these components, we may be certain that it does not. For example, consider Figure 12.38. Suppose that the pursuer initially believes that the end of the corridor may contain the evader. If it moves along the smaller closed-loop path, the nondeterministic I-state gradually varies but returns to the same value when the loop is completed. However, if the pursuer traverses the larger loop, it becomes certain upon completing the loop that the corridor does not contain the evader. The dashed line that was crossed in this example may inspire you to think about cell decompositions based on critical boundaries, as in the algorithm in Section 6.3.4. This idea will be pursued shortly to develop a complete algorithm for solving this problem. Before presenting a complete algorithm, however, first consider some interesting examples.

Example 12.7 (When Is a Problem Solvable?) Figure 12.39 shows four similar problems. The evader position is never shown because the problem is solved by ensuring that no evader could be left hiding. Note that the speed of the pursuer is not relevant to the nondeterministic I-states. Therefore, a solution can be defined by simply showing the pursuer path. The first three examples are straightforward to solve. However, the fourth example does not have a solution because there are at least three distinct hiding places (can

---

[5] To follow the notation of Section 11.4 more closely, the motion model $\dot{p} = u$ can be used, in which u represents the velocity of the pursuer. Nature actions can be used to model the velocity of the evader to obtain $\dot{e}$. By integrating $\dot{p}$ over time, $p(t)$ can be obtained for any t. This means that $\tilde{p}_t$ can be used as a simpler representation of the input history, instead of directly referring to velocities.

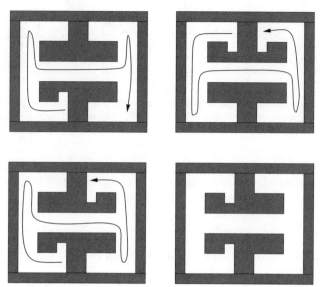

Figure 12.39: Three problems that can be easily solved with one pursuer, and a minor variant for which no solution exists.

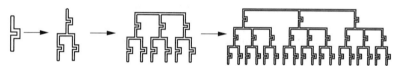

Figure 12.40: Each collection of corridors requires one more pursuer than the one before it because a new pursuer must guard the junction.

you find them?). Let $V(V(p))$ denote the set of all points visible from at least one point in $V(p)$. The condition that prevents the problem from being solved is that there exist three positions, p_1, p_2, p_3, such that $V(V(p_i)) \cap V(V(p_j)) = \emptyset$ for each $i, j \in \{1, 2, 3\}$ with $i \neq j$. As one hiding place is reached, the evader can sneak between the other two. In the worst case, this could result in an endless chase with the evader always eluding discovery. We would like an algorithm that systematically searches $\mathcal{I}_{ndet}$ and determines whether a solution exists. ■

Since one pursuer is incapable of solving some problems, it is tempting to wonder whether two pursuers can solve any problem. The next example gives an interesting sequence of environments that implies that for any positive integer k, there is an environment that requires exactly k pursuers to solve.

Example 12.8 (A Sequence of Hard Problems) Each environment in the sequence shown in Figure 12.40 requires one more pursuer than the previous one [417]. The construction is based on recursively ensuring there are three isolated hiding places, as in the last problem of Figure 12.39. Each time this occurs, another pursuer is needed. The sequence recursively appends three environments that require k pursuers, to obtain a problem that requires $k + 1$. An extra pursuer is always needed to guard the junction where the three environments are attached together. The construction is based on the notion of 3-separability, from pursuit-evasion on a graph, which was developed in [776]. ■

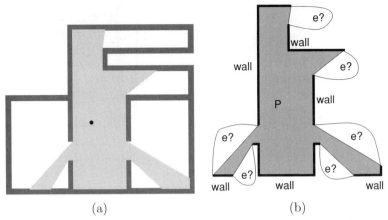

Figure 12.41: Recall Figure 11.15. Beyond each gap is a portion of the environment that may or may not contain the evader.

The problem can be made more challenging by considering multiply connected environments (environments with holes). A single pursuer cannot solve any of the these problems. Determining the minimum number of pursuers required to solve such a problem is NP-hard [417].

12.4.2 A complete algorithm

Now consider designing a complete algorithm that solves the problem in the case of a single pursuer. To be *complete*, it must find a solution if one exists; otherwise, it correctly reports that no solution is possible. Recall from Figure 12.38 that the nondeterministic I-state changed in an interesting way only after a critical boundary was crossed. The pursuit-evasion problem can be solved by carefully analyzing all of the cases in which these critical changes can occur. It turns out that these are exactly the same cases as considered in Section 12.3.4: crossing inflection rays and bitangent rays. Figure 12.38 is an example of crossing an inflection ray. Figure 12.41 indicates the connection between the gaps of Section 12.3.4 and the parts of the environment that may contain the evader.

Recall that the shadow region is the set of all points not visible from some $p(t)$; this is expressed as $R \setminus V(p(t))$. Every critical event changes the number of shadow components. If an inflection ray is crossed, then a shadow component either appears or disappears, depending on the direction. If a bitangent ray is crossed, then either two components merge into one or one component splits into two. To keep track of the nondeterministic I-state, it must be determined whether each component of the shadow region is *cleared*, which means it certainly does not contain the evader, or *contaminated*, which means that it might contain the evader. Initially, all components are labeled as contaminated, and as the pursuer moves, cleared components can emerge. Solving the pursuit-evasion problem amounts to moving the pursuer until all shadow components are cleared. At this point, it is known that there are no places left where the evader could be hiding.

If the pursuer crosses an inflection ray and a new shadow component appears, it must always be labeled as cleared because this is a portion of the environment that was just visible. If the pursuer crosses a bitangent ray and a split occurs, then the labels are distributed across the two components: A contaminated shadow component splits into two contaminated components, and a cleared component splits into two cleared components.

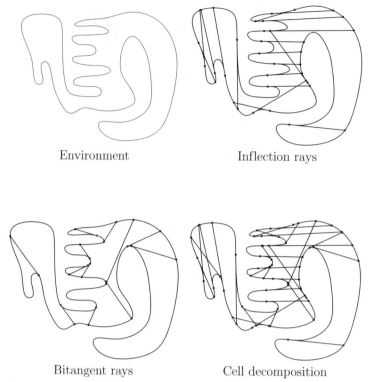

Figure 12.42: The environment is decomposed into cells based on inflections and bitangents, which are the only critical visibility events.

If the bitangent ray is crossed in the other direction, resulting in a merge of components, then the situation is more complicated. If one component is cleared and the other is contaminated, then the merged component is contaminated. The merged component may only be labeled as cleared if both of the original components are already cleared. Note that among the four critical cases, only the merge has the potential to undo the work of the pursuer. In other words, it may lead to *recontamination*.

Consider decomposing R into cells based on inflection rays and bitangent rays, as shown in Figure 12.42. These cells have the following *information-conservative property*: If the pursuer travels along any loop path that stays within a 2D cell, then the I-state remains the same upon returning to the start. This implies that the particular path taken by the pursuer through a cell is not important. A solution to the pursuit-evasion problem can be described as a sequence of adjacent 2D cells that must be visited. Due to the information-conservative property, the particular path through a sequence of cells can be chosen arbitrarily.

Searching the cells for a solution is more complicated than searching for paths in Chapter 6 because the search must be conducted in the I-space. The pursuer may visit the same cell in R on different occasions but with different knowledge about which components are cleared and contaminated. A directed graph, $\mathcal{G}_I$, can be constructed as follows. For each 2D cell in R and each possible labeling of shadow components, a vertex is defined in $\mathcal{G}_I$. For example, if the shadow region of a cell has three components, then there are $2^3 = 8$ corresponding vertices in $\mathcal{G}_I$. An edge exists in $\mathcal{G}_I$ between two vertices if: 1) their corresponding cells are adjacent, and 2) the labels of the components are consistent with the changes induced by crossing the boundary between the two cells. The second condition means that the labeling rules for an appear, disappear, split, or merge must be followed. For example, if crossing the boundary causes a split of a contaminated shadow component, then the new components must be labeled contaminated and all other components must retain the same label. Note that $\mathcal{G}_I$ is directed because many motions in the $\mathcal{I}_{ndet}$ are not reversible. For example, if a contaminated region disappears, it cannot reappear as contaminated by reversing the path. Note that the information in this directed graph does not improve monotonically as in the case of lazy discrete localization from Section 12.2.1. In the current setting, information is potentially worse when shadow components merge because contamination can spread.

To search $\mathcal{G}_I$, start with any vertex for which all shadow region components are labeled as contaminated. The particular starting cell is not important. Any of the search algorithms from Section 2.2 may be applied to find a goal vertex, which is any vertex of $\mathcal{G}_I$ for which all shadow components are labeled as cleared. If no such vertices are reachable from the initial state, then the algorithm can correctly declare that no solution exists. If a goal vertex is found, then the path in $\mathcal{G}_I$ gives the sequence of cells that must be visited to solve the problem. The actual path through R is then constructed from the sequence of cells. Some of the cells may not be convex; however, their shape is simple enough that a sophisticated motion planning algorithm is not needed to construct a path that traverses the cell sequence.

The algorithm presented here is conceptually straightforward and performs well in practice; however, its worst-case running time is exponential in the number of inflection rays. Consider a polygonal environment that is expressed with n edges. There can be as many as $O(n)$ inflections and $O(n^2)$ bitangents. The number of cells is bounded by $O(n^3)$ [415]. Unfortunately, $\mathcal{G}_I$ has an exponential number of vertices because there can be as many as $O(n)$ shadow components, and there are 2^n possible labelings if there are n components. Note that $\mathcal{G}_I$ does not need to be computed prior to the search. It can be revealed incrementally during the planning process. The most efficient complete algorithm, which is more complicated, solves the pursuit-evasion problem in time $O(n^2)$ and was derived by first proving that any problem that can be solved by a pursuer using the visibility polygon can be solved by a pursuer that uses only two beams of light [773]. This simplifies $V(p(t))$ from a 2D region in R to two rotatable rays that emanate from $p(t)$ and dramatically reduces the complexity of the I-space.

12.4.3 Other variations

Numerous variations of the pursuit-evasion problem presented in this section can be considered. The problem becomes much more difficult if there are multiple pursuers. A cell decomposition can be made based on changing shadow components; however, some of the cell boundaries are algebraic surfaces due to complicated interactions between the visibility polygons of different pursuers. Thus, it is difficult to implement a complete algorithm. On the other hand, straightforward heuristics can be used to guide multiple pursuers. A single pursuer can use the complete algorithm described in this section. When this pursuer fails, it can move to some part of the environment and then wait while a second pursuer applies the complete single-pursuer algorithm on each shadow component. This idea can be applied recursively for any number of robots.

The problem can be made more complicated by placing a velocity bound on the evader. Even though this makes the pursuer more powerful, it is more difficult to design

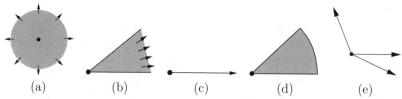

Figure 12.43: Several evader detection models: (a) omnidirectional sensing with unlimited distance; (b) visibility with a limited field of view; (c) a single visibility ray that is capable of rotating; (d) limited distance and a rotating viewing cone, which corresponds closely to a camera model; and (e) three visibility rays that are capable of rotating.

a complete algorithm that correctly exploits this additional information. No complete algorithms currently exist for this case.

Figure 12.43 shows several alternative detection models that yield different definitions of $V(p(t))$. Each requires different pursuit-evasion algorithms because the structure of the I-space varies dramatically across different sensing models. For example, using the model in Figure 12.43c, a single pursuer is required to move along the ∂X. Once it moves into the interior, the shadow region always becomes a single connected component. This model is sometimes referred to as a *flashlight*. If there are two flashlights, then one flashlight may move into the interior while the other protects previous work. The case of limited depth, as shown in Figure 12.43, is very realistic in practice, but unfortunately it is the most challenging. The number of required pursuers generally depends on metric properties of the environment, such as its minimum "thickness." The method presented in this section was extended to the case of a limited field of view in [383]; critical curves are obtained that are similar to those in Section 6.3.4. See the literature overview at the end of the chapter for more related material.

12.5 Manipulation planning with sensing uncertainty

One of the richest sources of interesting I-spaces is manipulation planning. As robots interact with obstacles or objects in the world, the burden of estimating the state becomes greater. The classical way to address this problem is to highly restrict the way in which the robot can interact with obstacles. Within the manipulation planning framework of Section 7.3.2, this means that a robot must grasp and carry objects to their desired destinations. Any object must be lying in a stable configuration upon grasping, and it must be returned to a stable configuration after grasping.

As the assumptions on the classical manipulation planning framework are lifted, it becomes more difficult to predict how the robot and other bodies will behave. This immediately leads to the challenges of uncertainty in predictability, which was the basis of Chapter 10. The next problem is to design sensors that enable plans to be achieved in spite of this uncertainty. For each sensing model, an I-space arises.

Section 12.5.1 covers the preimage planning framework [313, 662], under which many interesting issues covered in Chapters 10 and 11 are addressed for a specific manipulation planning problem. I-states, forward projections, backprojections, and termination actions were characterized in this context. Furthermore, several algorithmic complexity results regarding planning under uncertainty have been proved within this framework.

Section 12.5.2 covers methods that clearly illustrate the power of reasoning directly in terms of the I-space. The philosophy is to allow nonprehensile forms of manipulation (e.g., pushing, squeezing, throwing) and to design simple sensors, or even to avoid sensing altogether. This dramatically reduces the I-space while still allowing feasible plans to exist. This contradicts the intuition that more information is better. Using less information leads to greater uncertainty in the state, but this is not important in some problems. It is only important is that the I-space becomes simpler.

12.5.1 Preimage planning

The *preimage planning* framework (or *LMT framework*, named after its developers, Lozano-Pérez, Mason, and Taylor) was developed as a general way to perform manipulation planning under uncertainty [313, 662]. Although the concepts apply to general configuration spaces, they will be covered here for the case in which $C = \mathbb{R}^2$ and C_{obs} is polygonal. This is a common assumption throughout most of the work done within this framework. This could correspond to a simplified model of a robot hand that translates in $\mathcal{W} = \mathbb{R}^2$, while possibly carrying a part. A popular illustrative task is the *peg-in-hole problem*, in which the part is a peg that must be inserted into a hole that is slightly larger. This operation is frequently performed as manufacturing robots assemble products. Using the configuration space representation of Section 4.3.2, the robot becomes a point moving in $\mathbb{R}^2$ among polygonal obstacles.

The distinctive features of the models used in preimage planning are as follows:

1. The robot can execute *compliant motions*, which means that it can slide along the boundary of C_{obs}. This differs from the usual requirement in Part II that the robot must avoid obstacles.

2. There is nondeterministic uncertainty in prediction. An action determines a motion direction, but nature determines how much error will occur during execution. A bounded error model is assumed.

3. There is nondeterministic uncertainty in sensing, and the true state cannot be reliably estimated.

4. The goal region is usually an edge of C_{obs}, but it may more generally be any subset of $cl(C_{free})$, the closure of C_{free}.

5. A hierarchical planning model is used, in which the robot is issued a sequence of *motion commands*, each of which is terminated by applying u_T based on the I-state.

Each of these will now be explained in more detail.

Compliant motions

It will be seen shortly that the possibility of executing *compliant motions* is crucial for reducing uncertainty in the robot position. Let C_{con} denote the obstacle boundary, ∂C_{obs} (also, $C_{con} = \partial C_{free}$). A model of robot motion while $q \in C_{con}$ needs to be formulated. In general, this is complicated by friction. A simple *Coulomb friction* model is assumed here; see [684] for more details on modeling friction in the context of manipulation planning. Suppose that the net force F is applied by a robot at some $q \in C_{con}$. The force could be maintained by using the *generalized damper model* of robot control [966].

The resulting motion is characterized using a *friction cone*, as shown in Figure 12.44a. A basic principle of Newtonian mechanics is that the obstacle applies a reaction force (it may be helpful to look ahead to Section 13.3, which introduces mechanics). If F points into the surface and is normal to it, then the reaction force provided by the obstacle will cancel F, and there will be no motion. If F is not perpendicular to the surface, then sliding may

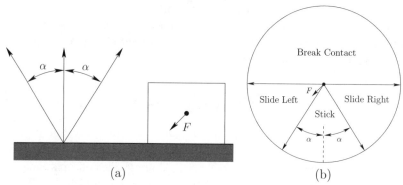

Figure 12.44: The compliant motion model. If a force F is applied by the robot at $q \in \mathcal{C}_{con}$, then it moves along the boundary only if $-F$ points outside of the friction cone.

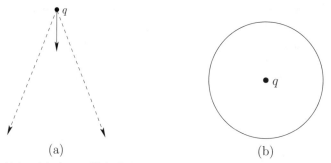

Figure 12.45: Nature interferes with both the configuration transitions and the sensor observations.

occur. At one extreme, F may be parallel to the surface. In this case, it must slide along the boundary. In general, F can be decomposed into parallel and perpendicular components. If the parallel component is too small relative to the perpendicular component, then the robot becomes stuck. The friction cone shown in Figure 12.44a indicates precisely the conditions under which motion occurs. The parameter α captures the amount of friction (more friction leads to larger α). Figure 12.44b indicates the behaviors that occur for various directions of F. The diagram is obtained by inverting the friction cone. If F points into the bottom region, then *sticking* occurs, which means that the robot cannot move. If F points away from the obstacle boundary, then contact is broken (this is reasonable, unless the boundary is sticky). For the remaining two cases, the robot slides along the boundary.

Sources of uncertainty

Nature interferes with both the configuration transitions and with the sensor. Let $U = [0, 2\pi)$, which indicates the direction in $\mathbb{R}^2$ that the robot is commanded to head. Nature interferes with this command, and the actual direction lies within an interval of $\mathbb{S}^1$. As shown in Figure 12.45a, the forward projection (recall from Section 10.1.2) for a fixed action $u \in U$ yields a cone of possible future configurations. (A precise specification of the motion model is given using differential equations in Example 13.15.) The sensing model, shown in Figure 12.45b, was already given in Section 11.5.1. The nature sensing actions form a disc given by (11.67), and $y = q + \psi$, in which q is the true configuration, ψ is the nature sensing action, and y is the observation. The result appears in Figure 11.11.

Goal region

Since contact with the obstacle is allowed, the goal region can be defined to include edges of $\mathcal{C}_{obs}$ in addition to points in $\mathcal{C}_{free}$. Most often, a single edge of $\mathcal{C}_{obs}$ is chosen as the goal region.

Motion commands

The planning problem can now be described. It may be tempting to express the model using continuous time, as opposed to discrete stages. This is a viable approach, but leads to planning under differential constraints, which is the topic of Part IV and is considerably more complicated. In the preimage-planning framework, a hierarchical approach is taken. A restricted kind of plan called a *motion command*, μ, will be defined, and the goal is achieved by constructing a sequence of motion commands. This has the effect of converting the continuous-time decision-making problem into a planning problem that involves discrete stages. Each time a motion command is applied, the robot must apply a termination action to end it. At that point another motion command can be issued. Thus, imagine that a high-level module issues motion commands, and a low-level module executes each until a termination condition is met.

For some action $u \in U$, let $M_u = \{u, u_T\}$, in which u_T is the termination action. A *motion command* is a feedback plan, $\mu : \mathcal{I}_{hist} \to M_u$, in which $\mathcal{I}_{hist}$ is the standard history I-space, based on initial conditions, the action history, and the sensing history. The motion command is executed over continuous time. At $t = 0$, $\mu(\eta_0) = u$. Using a history I-state η gathered during execution, the motion command will eventually yield $\mu(\eta) = u_T$, which terminates it. If the goal was not achieved, then the high-level module can apply another motion command.

Preimages

Now consider how to construct motion commands. Using the hierarchical approach, the main task of terminating in the goal region can be decomposed into achieving intermediate subgoals. The *preimage* $P(\mu, G)$ of a motion command μ and subgoal $G \subset \text{cl}(\mathcal{C}_{free})$ is the set of all history I-states from which μ is guaranteed to be achieved in spite of all interference from nature. Each motion command must recognize that the subgoal has been achieved so that it can apply its termination action. Once a subgoal is achieved, the resulting history I-state must lie within the required set of history I-states for the next motion command in the plan. Let $\mathcal{M}$ denote the set of all allowable motion commands that can be defined. This can actually be considered as an action space for the high-level module.

Planning with motion commands

A high-level open-loop plan,[6]

$$\pi = (\mu_1, \mu_2, \ldots, \mu_k), \tag{12.34}$$

can be constructed, which is a sequence of k motion commands. Although the precise path executed by the robot is unpredictable, the sequence of motion commands is assumed to be predictable. Each motion command μ_i for $1 < i < k$ must terminate with an I-state

---

[6] Note that this open-loop plan is composed of closed-loop motion commands. This is perfectly acceptable using hierarchical modeling.

$\eta \in P(\mu_{i+1}, G_{i+1})$. The preimage of μ_1 must include η_0, the initial I-state. The goal is achieved by the last motion command, μ_k.

More generally, the particular motion command chosen need not be predictable, and may depend on the I-state during execution. In this case, the high-level feedback plan $\pi : \mathcal{I}_{hist} \to \mathcal{M}$ can be developed, in which a motion command $\mu = \pi(\eta)$ is chosen based on the history I-state η that results after the previous motion command terminates. Such variations are covered in [283, 313, 591].

The high-level planning problem can be solved using discrete planning algorithms from Chapters 2 and 10. The most popular method within the preimage planning framework is to perform a backward search from the goal. Although this sounds simple enough, the set of possible motion commands is infinite, and it is difficult to sample μ in a way that leads to completeness. Another complication is that termination is based on the history I-state. Planning is therefore quite challenging. It was even shown in [313], by a reduction from the Turing machine halting problem [892], that the preimage in general is uncomputable by any algorithm. It was shown in [735] that the 3D version of preimage planning, in which the obstacles are polyhedral, is PSPACE-hard. It was then shown in [174] that it is even NEXPTIME-hard.[7]

Backprojections

Erdmann proposed a practical way to compute effective motion commands by separating the reachability and recognizability issues [313, 314]. Reachability refers to characterizing the set of points that are guaranteed to be reachable. Recognizability refers to knowing that the subgoal has been reached based on the history I-state. Another way to interpret the separation is that the effects of nature on the configuration transitions is separated from the effects of nature on sensing.

For reachability analysis, the sensing uncertainty is neglected. The notions of forward projections and backprojections from Section 10.1.2 can then be used. The only difference here is that they are applied to continuous spaces and motion commands (instead of u). Let S denote a subset of $cl(\mathcal{C}_{free})$. Both weak backprojections, $WB(S, \mu)$, and strong backprojections, $SB(S, \mu)$, can be defined. Furthermore, *nondirectional backprojections* [285], $WB(S)$ and $SB(S)$, can be defined, which are analogous to (10.25) and (10.26), respectively.

Figure 12.46 shows a simple problem in which the task is to reach a goal edge with a motion command that points downward. This is inspired by the peg-in-hole problem. Figure 12.47 illustrates several backprojections from the goal region for the problem in Figure 12.46. The action is $u = 3\pi/2$; however, the actual motion lies within the shown cone due to nature. First suppose that contact with the obstacle is not allowed, except at the goal region. The strong backprojection is given in Figure 12.47a. Starting from any point in the triangular region, the goal is guaranteed to be reached in spite of nature. The weak backprojection is the unbounded region shown in Figure 12.47b. This indicates configurations from which it is *possible* to reach the goal. The weak backprojection will not be considered further because it is important here to *guarantee* that the goal is reached. This is accomplished by the strong backprojection. From here onward, it will be assumed that *backprojection* by default means a strong backprojection. Using weak

---

[7] NEXPTIME is the complexity class of all problems that can be solved in nondeterministic exponential time. This is beyond the complexity classes shown in Figure 6.40.

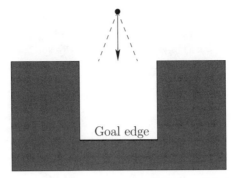

Figure 12.46: A simple example that resembles the peg-in-hole problem.

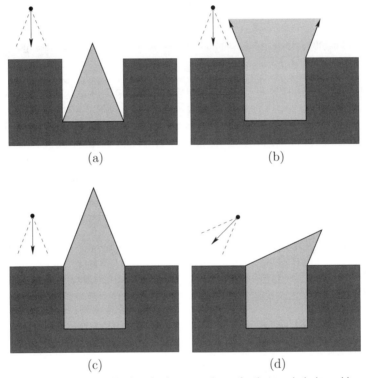

Figure 12.47: Several backprojections are shown for the peg-in-hole problem.

backprojections, it is possible to develop an alternative framework of *error detection and recovery* (EDR), which was introduced by Donald in [283].

Now assume that compliant motions are possible along the obstacle boundary. This has the effect of enlarging the backprojections. Suppose for simplicity that there is no friction ($\alpha = 0$ in Figure 12.44a). The backprojection is shown in Figure 12.47c. As the robot comes into contact with the side walls, it slides down until the goal is reached. It is not important to keep track of the exact configuration while this occurs. This illustrates the power of compliant motions in reducing uncertainty. This point will be pursued further in Section 12.5.2. Figure 12.47d shows the backprojection for a different motion command.

Now consider computing backprojections in a more general setting. The backprojection can be defined from any subset of cl($\mathcal{C}_{free}$) and may allow a friction cone with parameter α. To be included in a backprojection, points from which sticking is possible must be avoided.

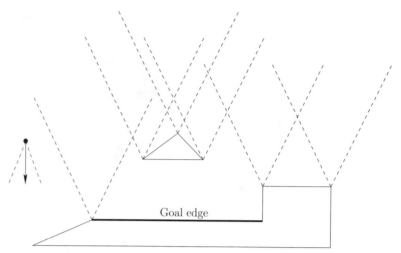

Figure 12.48: Erdmann's backprojection algorithm traces out the boundary after constructing cones based on friction.

Note that sticking is possible even if $\alpha = 0$. For example, in Figure 12.46, nature may allow the motion to be exactly perpendicular to the obstacle boundary. In this case, sticking occurs on horizontal edges because there is no tangential motion. In general, it must be determined whether sticking is *possible* at each edge and vertex of $\mathcal{C}_{obs}$. Possible sticking from an edge depends on u, α, and the maximum directional error contributed by nature. The robot can become stuck at a vertex if it is possible to become stuck at either incident edge.

Computing backprojections

Many algorithms have been developed to compute backprojections. The first algorithm was given in [313, 314]. Assume that the goal region is one or more segments contained in edges of $\mathcal{C}_{con}$. The algorithm proceeds for a fixed motion command, μ, which is based on a direction $u \in U$ as follows:

1. Mark every obstacle vertex at which sticking is possible. Also mark any point on the boundary of the goal region if it is possible to slide away from the goal.

2. For every marked vertex, extend two rays with directions based on the maximum possible deviations allowed by nature when executing u. This inverts the cone shown in Figure 12.45a. The extended rays are shown in Figure 12.48 for the frictionless case ($\alpha = 0$).

3. Starting at every goal edge, trace out the boundary of the backprojection region. Every edge encountered defines a half-plane of configurations from which the robot is guaranteed to move into. In Figure 12.48, this corresponds to being below a ray. When tracing out the backprojection boundary, the direction at each intersection vertex is determined based on including the points in the half-plane.

The resulting backprojection is shown in Figure 12.49. A more general algorithm that applies to goal regions that include polygonal regions in $\mathcal{C}_{free}$ was given in [285] (some details are also covered in [591]). It uses the plane-sweep principle (presented in Section 6.2.2) to yield an algorithm that computes the backprojection in time $O(n \lg n)$, in which n is the number of edges used to define $\mathcal{C}_{obs}$. The backprojection itself has no more than $O(n)$ edges. Algorithms for computing nondirectional backprojections are given in [142, 285]. One difficulty in this case is that the backprojection boundary may be quite

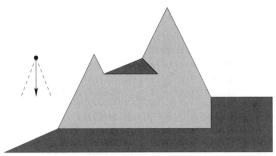

Figure 12.49: The computed backprojection. Sliding is guaranteed from the steeper edge of the triangle; hence, it is included in the backprojection. From the other top edge, sticking is possible.

complicated. An incremental algorithm for computing a nondirectional backprojection of size $O(n^2)$ in time $O(n^2 \lg n)$ is given in [142].

Once an algorithm that computes backprojections has been obtained, it needs to be adapted to compute preimages. Using the sensing model shown in Figure 12.45b, a preimage can be obtained by shrinking the subgoal region G. Let ϵ denote the radius of the ball in Figure 12.45b. Let $G' \subset G$ denote a subset of the subgoal in which a strip of thickness ϵ has been removed. If the sensor returns $y \in G'$, then it is guaranteed that $q \in G$. This yields a method of obtaining preimages by shrinking the subgoals. If ϵ is too large, however, this may fail to yield a successful plan, even though one exists.

The high-level plan can be found by performing a backward search that computes backprojections from the goal region (reduced by ϵ). There is still the difficulty of $\mathcal{M}$ being too large, which controls the branching factor in the search. One possibility is to compute nondirectional backprojections. Another possibility is to discretize $\mathcal{M}$. For example, in [591, 593], $\mathcal{M}$ is reduced to four principle directions, and plans are computed for complicated environments by using sticking edges as subgoals. Using discretization, however, it becomes more difficult to ensure the completeness of the planning algorithm.

The preimage planning framework may seem to apply only to a very specific model, but it can be extended and adapted to a much more general setting. It was extended to semi-algebraic obstacle models in [176], which gives a planning method that runs in time doubly exponential in the C-space dimension (based on cylindrical algebraic decomposition, which was covered in Section 6.4.2). In [149], probabilistic backprojections were introduced by assigning a uniform probability density function to the nature action spaces considered in this section. This was in turn generalized further to define backprojections and preimages as the level sets of optimal cost-to-go functions in [600, 608]. Dynamic programming methods can then be applied to compute plans.

12.5.2 Nonprehensile manipulation

Manipulation by grasping is very restrictive. People manipulate objects in many interesting ways that do not involve grasping. Objects may be pushed, flipped, thrown, squeezed, twirled, smacked, blown, and so on. A classic example from the kitchen is flipping a pancake over by a flick of the wrist while holding the skillet. These are all examples of *nonprehensile manipulation*, which means manipulation without grasping.

The temptation to make robots grasp objects arises from the obsession with estimating and controlling the state. This task is more daunting for nonprehensile manipulation because there are times at which the object appears to be out of direct control. This leads to greater uncertainty in predictability and a larger sensing burden. By planning in the I-space, however, it may be possible to avoid all of these problems. Several works have emerged which show that manipulation goals can be achieved with little or no sensing at all. This leads to a form of *minimalism* [177, 323, 684], in which the sensors are designed in a way that simplifies the I-space, as opposed to worrying about accurate estimation. The search for minimalist robotic systems is completely aligned with trying to find derived I-spaces that are as small as possible, as mentioned in Section 11.2.1. Sensing systems should be simple, yet still able to achieve the task. Preferably, completeness should not be lost. Most work in this area is concerned primarily with finding feasible solutions, as opposed to optimal solutions. This enables further simplifications of the I-space.

This section gives an example that represents an extreme version of this minimalism. A *sensorless manipulation* system is developed. At first this may seem absurd. From the forward projections in Section 10.1.2, it may seem that uncertainty can only grow if nature causes uncertainty in the configuration transitions and there are no sensors. To counter the intuition, compliant motions have the ability to reduce uncertainty. This is consistent with the discussion in Section 11.5.4. Simply knowing that some motion commands have been successfully applied may reduce the amount of uncertainty. In an early demonstration of sensorless manipulation, it was shown that an Allen wrench (L-shaped wrench) resting in a tray can be placed into a known orientation by simply tilting the tray in a few directions [323]. The same orientation is achieved in the end, regardless of the initial wrench configuration. Also, no sensors are needed. This can be considered as a more complicated extension of the ball rolling in a tray that was shown in Figure 11.29. This is also an example of compliant motions, as shown in Figure 12.44; however, in the present setting F is caused by gravity.

Squeezing parts

Another example of sensorless manipulation will now be described, which was developed by Goldberg and Mason in [396, 397, 398]; see also [684]. A Java implementation of the algorithm appears in [133]. Suppose that convex, polygonal parts arrive individually along a conveyor belt in a factory. They are to be used in an assembly operation and need to be placed into a given orientation. Figure 12.50 shows a top view of a *parallel-jaw gripper*. The robot can perform a squeeze operation by bringing the jaws together. Figure 12.50a shows the part before squeezing, and Figure 12.50b shows it afterward. A simple model is assumed for the mechanics. The jaws move at constant velocity toward each other, and it is assumed that they move slowly enough so that dynamics can be neglected. To help slide the part into place, one of the jaws may be considered as a frictionless contact (this is a real device; see [177]). The robot can perform a squeeze operation at any orientation in $[0, 2\pi)$ (actually, only $[0, \pi)$ is needed due to symmetry). Let $U = [0, 2\pi)$ denote the set of all squeezing actions. Each squeezing action terminates on its own after the part can be squeezed no further (without crushing the part).

The planning problem can be modeled as a game against nature. The initial orientation, $x \in [0, 2\pi)$, of the part is chosen by nature and is unknown. The state space is $\mathbb{S}^1$. For a given part, the task is to design a sequence,

$$\pi = (u_1, u_2, \ldots, u_n), \tag{12.35}$$

of squeeze operations that leads to a known orientation for the part, regardless of its initial state. Note that there is no specific requirement on the final state. After i motion

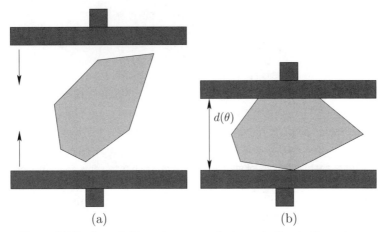

Figure 12.50: A parallel-jaw gripper can orient a part without using sensors.

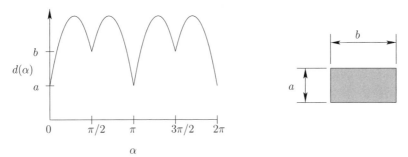

Figure 12.51: The diameter function for a rectangle.

commands have terminated, the history I-state is the sequence

$$\eta = (u_1, u_2, \ldots, u_i) \tag{12.36}$$

of squeezes applied so far. The nondeterministic I-space $\mathcal{I}_{ndet}$ will now be used. The requirement can be stated as obtaining a singleton, nondeterministic I-state (includes only one possible orientation). If the part has symmetries, then the task is instead to determine a single symmetry class (which includes only a finite number of orientations)

Consider how a part in an unknown orientation behaves. Due to rotational symmetry, it will be convenient to describe the effect of a squeeze operation based on the relative angle between the part and the robot. Therefore, let $\alpha = u - x$, assuming arithmetic modulo 2π. Initially, α may assume any value in $[0, 2\pi)$. It turns out that after one squeeze, α is always forced into one of a finite number of values. This can be explained by representing the *diameter function* $d(\alpha)$, which indicates the maximum thickness that can be obtained by taking a slice of the part at orientation α. Figure 12.51 shows the slice for a rectangle. The local minima of the distance function indicate orientations at which the part will stabilize as shown in Figure 12.50b. As the part changes its orientation during the squeeze operation, the α value changes in a way that gradually decreases $d(\alpha)$. Thus, $[0, 2\pi)$ can be divided into regions of attraction, as shown in Figure 12.52. These behave much like the funnels in Section 8.5.1.

The critical observation to solve the problem without sensors is that with each squeeze the uncertainty can grow no worse, and is usually reduced. Assume u is fixed. For the state transition equation $x' = f(x, u)$, the same x' will be produced for an interval of values

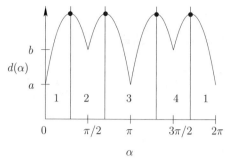

Figure 12.52: There are four regions of attraction, each of which represents an interval of orientations.

for x. Due to rotational symmetry, it is best to express this in terms of α. Let $s(\alpha)$ denote relative orientation obtained after a squeeze. Since α is a function of x and u, this can be expressed as a *squeeze function*, $s : \mathbb{S}^1 \to \mathbb{S}^1$, defined as

$$s(\alpha) = f(x, u) - u. \tag{12.37}$$

The forward projection with respect to an interval, A, of α values can also be defined:

$$S(A) = \bigcup_{\alpha \in A} s(\alpha). \tag{12.38}$$

Any interval $A \subset [0, 2\pi)$ can be interpreted as a nondeterministic I-state, based on the history of squeezes that have been performed. It is defined, however, with respect to relative orientations, instead of the original states. The algorithms discussed in Section 12.1.2 can be applied to $\mathcal{I}_{ndet}$. A backward search algorithm is given in [397] that starts with a singleton, nondeterministic I-state. The planning proceeds by performing a backward search on $\mathcal{I}_{ndet}$. In each iteration, the interval, A, of possible relative orientations increases until eventually all of $\mathbb{S}^1$ is reached (or the period of symmetry, if symmetries exist).

The algorithm is greedy in the sense that it attempts to force A to be as large as possible in every step. Note from Figure 12.52 that the regions of attraction are maximal at the minima of the diameter function. Therefore, only the minima values are worth considering as choices for α. Let B denote the preimage of the function s. In the first step, the algorithm finds the α for which $B(\alpha)$ is largest (in terms of length in $\mathbb{S}^1$). Let α_0 denote this relative orientation, and let $A_0 = B(\alpha_0)$. For each subsequent iteration, let A_i denote the largest interval in $[0, 2\pi)$ that satisfies

$$|S(A_{i-1})| < |A_i|, \tag{12.39}$$

in which $|\cdot|$ denotes interval length. This implies that there exists a squeeze operation for which any relative orientation in $S(A_{i-1})$ can be forced into A_i by a single squeeze. This iteration is repeated, generating A_{-1}, A_{-2}, and so on, until the condition in (12.39) can no longer be satisfied. It was shown in [397] that for any polygonal part, the A_i intervals increase until all of $\mathbb{S}^1$ (or the period of symmetry) is obtained.

Suppose that the sequence $(A_{-k}, \ldots, A_0)$ has been computed. This must be transformed into a plan that is expressed in terms of a fixed coordinate frame for the robot. The k-step action sequence $(u_1, \ldots, u_k)$ is recovered from

$$u_i = s(\beta_{i-1}) - a_i - \tfrac{1}{2}(|A_{i-k}| - |S(A_{i-k-1})|) + u_{i-1} \tag{12.40}$$

and $u_{-k} = 0$ [397]. Each a_i in (12.40) is the left endpoint of A_i. There is some freedom of choice in the alignment, and the third term in (12.40) selects actions in the middle to

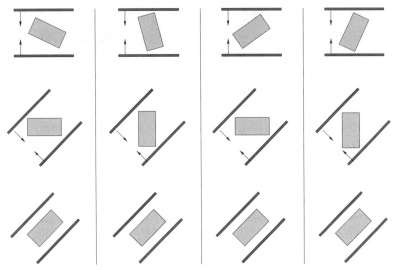

Figure 12.53: A two-step squeeze plan [397].

improve robustness with respect to orientation errors. By exploiting a proof in [197] that no more than $O(n)$ squeeze operations are needed for a part with n edges, the complete algorithm runs in time $O(n^2)$.

Example 12.9 (Squeezing a Rectangle) Figure 12.53 shows a simple example of a plan that requires two squeezes to orient the rectangular part when placed in any initial orientation. Four different executions of the plan are shown, one in each column. After the first squeeze, the part orientation is a multiple of $\pi/2$. After the second squeeze, the orientation is known. Even though the execution looks different every time, no feedback is necessary because the I-state contains no sensor information. ∎

Further reading

The material from this chapter could easily be expanded into an entire book on planning under sensing uncertainty. Several key topics were covered, but numerous others remain. An incomplete set of suggestions for further reading is given here.

Since Section 12.1 involved converting the I-space into an ordinary state space, many methods and references in Chapter 10 are applicable. For POMDPs, a substantial body of work has been developed in operations research and stochastic control theory [567, 658, 717, 900] and more recently in artificial intelligence [497, 650, 651, 740, 775, 794, 806, 808, 838, 1002, 1003]. Many of these algorithms compress or approximate $\mathcal{I}_{prob}$, possibly yielding nonoptimal solutions, but handling problems that involve dozens of states.

Localization, the subject of Section 12.2, is one of the most fundamental problems in robotics; therefore, there are hundreds of related references. Localization in a graph has been considered [299, 344]. The combinatorial localization presentation was based on [300, 418]. Ambiguities due to symmetry also appeared in [80]. Combinatorial localization with very little sensing is presented in [755]. For further reading on probabilistic localization, see [43, 260, 424, 450, 488, 496, 552, 624, 625, 757, 828, 888, 889, 962]. In [935, 936], localization uncertainty is expressed in terms of a sensor-uncertainty field, which is a derived I-space.

Section 12.3 was synthesized from many sources. For more on the maze searching method from Section 12.3.1 and its extension to exploring a graph, see [121]. The issue of distinguishability and

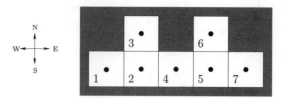

Figure 12.54: An environment for grid-based localization.

pebbles arises again in [89, 288, 289, 671, 843, 944]. For more on competitive ratios and combinatorial approaches to on-line navigation, see [118, 262, 272, 334, 377, 510, 540, 677, 771, 814].

For more on Stentz's algorithm and related work, see [546, 914]. A multi-resolution approach to terrain exploration appears in [764]. For material on bug algorithms, see [508, 571, 595, 669, 670, 812, 884]. Related sensor-based planning work based on generalized Voronoi diagrams appears in [220, 221]; also related is [831]. Gap navigation trees were introduced in [943, 944, 945]. For other work on minimal mapping, see [487, 827, 875]. Landmark-based navigation is considered in [371, 593, 885].

There is a vast body of literature on probabilistic methods for mapping and localization, much of which is referred to as SLAM [942]; see also [184, 223, 277, 720, 774, 982]. One of the earliest works is [898]. An early application of dynamic programming in this context appears in [587]. A well-known demonstration of SLAM techniques is described in [161]. For an introduction to the EM algorithm, see [108]; its convergence is addressed in [271, 977, 978]. For more on mobile robotics in general, see [136, 298].

The presentation of Section 12.4 was based mainly on [417, 615]. Pursuit-evasion problems in general were first studied in differential game theory [60, 425, 480]. Pursuit-evasion in a graph was introduced in [776], and related theoretical analysis appears in [107, 583, 718]. Visibility-based pursuit-evasion was introduced in [932], and the first complete algorithm appeared in [615]. An algorithm that runs in $O(n^2)$ for a single pursuer in a simple polygon was given in [773]. Variations that consider curved environments, beams of light, and other considerations appear in [210, 256, 306, 606, 621, 748, 890, 891, 931, 933, 981]. Pursuit-evasion in three dimensions is discussed in [617]. For versions that involve minimal sensing and no prior given map, see [419, 506, 812, 843, 988]. The problem of visually tracking a moving target both with [83, 403, 404, 605, 726, 731] and without [325, 473, 871] obstacles is closely related to pursuit-evasion. For a survey of combinatorial algorithms for computing visibility information, see [759]. Art gallery and sensor placement problems are also related [143, 758, 876]. The bitangent events also arise in the visibility complex [799] and in aspect graphs [785], which are related visibility-based data structures.

Section 12.5 was inspired mostly by the works in [285, 313, 323, 398, 662, 967]. Many works are surveyed in [684]. A probabilistic version of preimage planning was considered in [150, 151, 608]. Visual preimages are considered in [351]. Careful analysis of manipulation uncertainty appears in [147, 148]. For more on preimage planning, see [591, 593]. The error detection and recovery (EDR) framework uses many preimage planning ideas but allows more problems to be solved by permitting fixable errors to occur during execution [283, 286, 287]. Compliant motions are also considered in [142, 285, 489, 681, 683, 779]. The effects of friction in the C-space are studied in [318]. For more work on orienting parts, see [177, 324, 396, 397, 813, 969]. For more forms of nonprehensile manipulation, see [12, 14, 112, 320, 673, 674, 922]. A humorous paper, which introduces the concept of the "principle of virtual dirt," is [682]; the idea later appears in [842] and in the Roomba autonomous vacuum cleaner from the iRobot Corporation.

Exercises

1. For the environment in Figure 12.1a, give the nondeterministic I-states for the action sequence (L, L, F, B, F, R, F, F), if the initial state is the robot in position 3 facing north and the initial I-state is $\eta_0 = X$.

2. Describe how to apply the algorithm from Figure 10.6 to design an information-feedback plan that takes a map of a grid and performs localization.

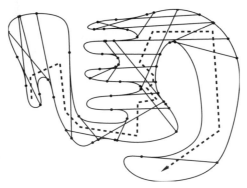

Figure 12.55: A path followed by the robot in an initially unknown environment. The robot finishes in the lower right.

3. Suppose that a robot operates in the environment shown in Figure 12.54 using the same motion and sensing model as in Example 12.1. Design an information-feedback plan that is as simple as possible and successfully localizes the robot, regardless of its initial state. Assume the initial condition $\eta_0 = X$.

4. Prove that the robot can use the latitude and orientation information to detect the unique point of each obstacle boundary in the maze searching algorithm of Section 12.3.1.

5. Suppose once again that a robot is placed into one of the six environments shown in Figure 12.12. It is initially in the upper right cell facing north; however, the initial condition is $\eta_0 = X$. Determine the sequence of sensor observations and nondeterministic I-states as the robot executes the action sequence (F, R, B, F, L, L, F).

6. Prove that the counter in the maze searching algorithm of Section 12.3.1 can be replaced by two pebbles, and the robot can still solve the problem by simulating the counter. The robot can place either pebble on a tile, detect them when the robot is on the same tile, and can pick them up to move them to other tiles.

7. Continue the trajectory shown in Figure 12.23 until the goal is reached using the Bug2 strategy.

8. Show that the competitive ratio for the doubling spiral motion applied to the lost-cow problem of Figure 12.26 is 9.

9. Generalize the lost-cow problem so that there are n fences that emanate from the current cow location ($n = 2$ for the original problem).

   (a) If the cow is told that the gate is along only one unknown fence and is no more than one unit away, what is the competitive ratio of the best plan that you can think of?

   (b) Suppose the cow does not know the maximum distance to the gate. Propose a plan that solves the problem and establish its competitive ratio.

10. Suppose a point robot is dropped into the environment shown in Figure 12.42. Indicate the gap navigation trees that are obtained as the robot moves along the path shown in Figure 12.55.

11. Construct an example for which the worst case bound, (12.25), for Bug1 is obtained.

12. Some environments are so complicated that in the pursuit-evasion problem they require the same region to be visited multiple times. Find a solution for a single pursuer with omnidirectional visibility to the problem in Figure 12.56a.

13. Find a pursuit-evasion solution for a single pursuer with omnidirectional visibility to the problem in Figure 12.56b, in which any number of pairs of "feet" may appear on the bottom of the polygon.

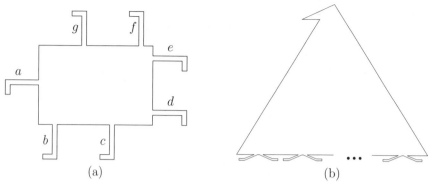

Figure 12.56: Two pursuit-evasion problems that involve recontamination.

14. Prove that for a polygonal environment, if there are three points, p_1, p_2, and p_3, for which $V(V(p_1))$, $V(V(p_2))$, and $V(V(p_3))$ are pairwise-disjoint, then the problem requires more than one pursuer.

15. Prove that the diameter function for the squeezing algorithm in Section 12.5.2 has no more than $O(n^2)$ vertices. Give a sequence of polygons that achieves this bound. What happens for a regular polygon?

16. Develop versions of (12.8) and (12.9) for state-nature sensor mappings.

17. Develop versions of (12.8) and (12.9) for history-based sensor mappings.

18. Describe in detail the I-map used for maze searching in Section 12.3.1. Indicate how this is an example of dramatically reducing the size of the I-space, as described in Section 11.2. Is a sufficient I-map obtained?

19. Describe in detail the I-map used in the Bug1 algorithm. Is a sufficient I-map obtained?

20. Suppose that several teams of point robots move around in a simple polygon. Each robot has an omnidirectional visibility sensor and would like to keep track of information for each shadow region. For each team and shadow region, it would like to record one of three possibilities: 1) There are definitely no team members in the region; 2) there may possibly be one or more; 3) there is definitely at least one.

    (a) Define a nondeterministic I-space based on labeling gaps that captures the appropriate information. The I-space should be defined with respect to one robot (each will have its own).

    (b) Design an algorithm that keeps track of the nondeterministic I-state as the robot moves through the environments and observes others.

21. Recall the sequence of connected corridors shown in Figure 12.40. Try to adapt the polygons so that the same number of pursuers is needed, but there are fewer polygon edges. Try to use as few edges as possible.

Implementations

22. Solve the probabilistic passive localization problem of Section 12.2.3 for 2D grids. Implement your solution and demonstrate it on several interesting examples.

23. Implement the exact value-iteration method described in Section 12.1.3 to compute optimal cost-to-go functions. Test the implementation on several small examples. How large can you make K, Θ, and Ψ?

24. Develop and implement a graph search algorithm that searches on $\mathcal{I}_{ndet}$ to perform robot localization on a 2D grid. Test the algorithm on several interesting examples. Try developing search heuristics that improve the performance.

25. Implement the Bug1, Bug2, and VisBug (with unlimited radius) algorithms. Design a good set of examples for illustrating their relative strengths and weaknesses.

26. Implement software that computes probabilistic I-states for localization as the robot moves in a grid.

27. Implement the method of Section 12.3.4 for simply connected environments and demonstrate it in simulation for polygonal environments.

28. Implement the pursuit-evasion algorithm for a single pursuer in a simple polygon.

29. Implement the part-squeezing algorithm presented in Section 12.5.2.

PART IV

Planning Under Differential Constraints

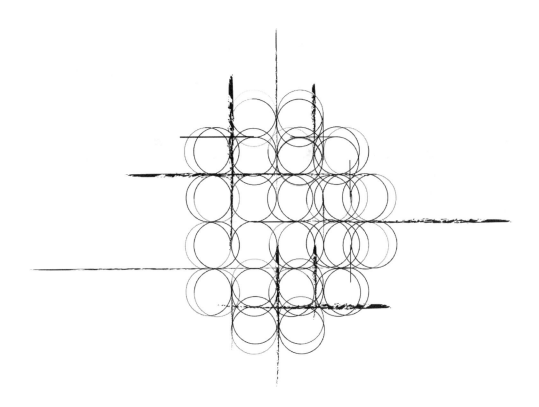

Overview of Part IV: Planning Under Differential Constraints

Part IV is a continuation of Part II. It is generally not necessary to read Part III before starting Part IV. In the models and methods studied in Part II, it was assumed that a path can be easily determined between any two configurations in the absence of obstacles. For example, the sampling-based roadmap approach assumed that two nearby configurations could be connected by a "straight line" in the configuration space. The constraints on the path are *global* in the sense that the restrictions are on the set of allowable configurations.

The next few chapters introduce *differential constraints*, which restrict the allowable velocities at each point. These can be considered as *local* constraints, in contrast to the global constraints that arise due to obstacles. Some weak differential constraints, such as smoothness requirements, arose in Chapter 8. Part IV goes much further by covering differential consraints in full detail and generality.

Differential constraints arise everywhere. In robotics, most problems involve differential constraints that arise from the kinematics and dynamics of a robot. One approach is to ignore them in the planning process and hope that the differential constraints can be appropriately handled in making refinements. This corresponds to applying the techniques of Part II in robotics applications and then using control techniques to ensure that a computed path is executed as closely as possible. If it is practical, a better approach is to consider differential constraints in the planning process. This yields plans that directly comply with the natural motions of a mechanical system.

Chapter 13 is similar in spirit to Chapter 3. It explains how to construct and represent models that have differential constraints, whereas Chapter 3 did the same for geometric models. It also provides background and motivation for Part IV by giving a catalog of numerous models that can be used in planning algorithms. Differential models are generally expressed as $\dot{x} = f(x, u)$, which is the continuous-time counterpart of the state transition equation, $x_{k+1} = f(x_k, u_k)$. Thus, the focus of Chapter 13 it to define transition functions.

Chapter 14 covers sampling-based planning algorithms for problems that involve differential constraints. There is no chapter on combinatorial algorithms in this context because they exist only in extremely limited cases. Differential constraints seem to destroy most of the nice properties that are needed by combinatorial approaches. Rather than develop complete algorithms, the focus is on resolution-complete planning algorithms. This is complicated by the discretization of three spaces (state space, action space, and time), whereas in Chapter 5 resolution completeness only involved discretization of the C-space. The main topics are extending the incremental sampling and searching framework of Section 5.4, extending feedback motion planning of Chapter 8, and developing decoupled methods for trajectory planning.

Chapter 15 overviews powerful ideas and tools that come mainly from control theory. The planning methods of Chapter 14 can be greatly enhanced by utilizing the material from Chapter 15. The two chapters are complementary in that Chapter 14 is mainly algorithmic and Chapter 15 is mainly about mathematical techniques. The main topics of Chapter 15 are system stability, optimality concepts (Hamilton-Jacobi-Bellman equation and Pontryagin's minimum principle), shortest paths for wheeled vehicles, nonholonomic system theory, and nonholonomic steering methods. The term *nonholonomic* comes from mechanics and refers to differential constraints that cannot be fully integrated to remove time derivatives of the state variables.

13

Differential Models

This chapter provides a continuous-time counterpart to the state transition equation, $x_{k+1} = f(x_k, u_k)$, which was crucial in Chapter 2. On a continuous state space, X (assumed to be a smooth manifold), it will be defined as $\dot{x} = f(x, u)$, which intentionally looks similar to the discrete version. It will still be referred to as a state transition equation. It will also be called a *system* (short for *control system*), which is a term used in control theory. There are no obstacle regions in this chapter. Obstacles will appear again when planning algorithms are covered in Chapter 14. In continuous time, the state transition function $f(x, u)$ yields a velocity as opposed to the next state. Since the transitions are no longer discrete, it does not make sense to talk about a "next" state. Future states that satisfy the differential constraints are obtained by integration of the velocity. Therefore, it is natural to specify only velocities. This relies on the notions of tangent spaces and vector fields, as covered in Section 8.3.

This chapter presents many example models that can be used in the planning algorithms of Chapter 14. Section 13.1 develops differential constraints for the case in which X is the C-space of one or more bodies. These constraints commonly occur for wheeled vehicles (e.g., a car cannot move sideways). To represent dynamics, constraints on acceleration are needed. Section 13.2 therefore introduces the *phase space*, which enables any problem with dynamics to be expressed as velocity constraints on an enlarged state space. This collapses the higher order derivatives down to being only first-order, but it comes at the cost of increasing the dimension of the state space. Section 13.3 introduces the basics of Newton-Euler mechanics and concludes with expressing the dynamics of a free-floating rigid body. Section 13.4 introduces some concepts from advanced mechanics, including the Lagrangian and Hamiltonian. It also provides a model of the dynamics of a kinematic chain of bodies, which applies to typical robot manipulators. Section 13.5 introduces differential models that have more than one decision maker.

13.1 Velocity constraints on the configuration space

In this section, it will be assumed that $X = \mathcal{C}$, which is a C-space of one or more rigid bodies, as defined in Section 4.2. Differential models in this section are all expressed as constraints on the set of allowable velocities at each point in $\mathcal{C}$. This results in first-order differential equations because only velocities are constrained, as opposed to accelerations or higher order derivatives.

To carefully discuss velocities, it will be assumed that $\mathcal{C}$ is a smooth manifold, as defined in Section 8.3.2, in addition to a topological manifold, as defined in Section 4.1.2. It may be helpful to keep the cases $\mathcal{C} = \mathbb{R}^2$ and $\mathcal{C} = \mathbb{R}^3$ in mind. The velocities are straightforward to define without resorting to manifold technicalities, and the dimension is low enough that the concepts can be visualized.

13.1.1 Implicit vs. parametric representations

There are two general ways to represent differential constraints: parametric and implicit. Many parallels can be drawn to the parametric and implicit ways of specifying functions in general. Parametric representations are generally easier to understand and are simpler to use in applications. Implicit representations are more general but are often more difficult to utilize. The intuitive difference is that implicit representations express velocities that are *prohibited*, whereas parametric representations directly express the velocities that are *allowed*. In this chapter, a parametric representation is obtained wherever possible; nevertheless, it is important to understand both.

13.1.1.1 Implicit representation

The planar case

For purposes of illustration, suppose that $\mathcal{C} = \mathbb{R}^2$. A configuration is expressed as $q = (x, y) \in \mathbb{R}^2$, and a velocity is expressed as $(\dot{x}, \dot{y})$. Each $(\dot{x}, \dot{y})$ is an element of the tangent space $T_q(\mathbb{R}^2)$, which is a two-dimensional vector space at every (x, y). Think about the kinds of constraints that could be imposed. At each $q \in \mathbb{R}^2$, restricting the set of velocities yields some set $U(q) \subset T_q(\mathbb{R}^2)$. The parametric and implicit representations will be alternative ways to express $U(q)$ for all $q \in \mathbb{R}^2$.

Here are some interesting, simple constraints. Each yields a definition of $U(q)$ as the subset of $T_q(\mathbb{R}^2)$ that satisfies the constraints.

1. $\dot{x} > 0$: In this case, imagine that you are paddling a boat on a swift river that flows in the positive x direction. You can obtain any velocity you like in the y direction, but you can never flow against the current. This means that all integral curves increase monotonically in x over time.

2. $\dot{x} \geq 0$: This constraint allows you to stop moving in the x direction. A velocity perpendicular to the current can be obtained (for example, $(0, 1)$ causes motion with unit speed in the positive y direction).

3. $\dot{x} > 0$, $\dot{y} > 0$: Under this constraint, integral curves must monotonically increase in both x and y.

4. $\dot{x} = 0$: In the previous three examples, the set of allowable velocities remained two-dimensional. Under the constraint $\dot{x} = 0$, the set of allowable velocities is only one-dimensional. All vectors of the form $(0, \dot{y})$ for any $\dot{y} \in \mathbb{R}$ are allowed. This means that no motion in the x direction is allowed. Starting at any (x_0, y_0), the integral curves will be of the form $(x_0, y(t))$ for all $t \in [0, \infty)$, which confines each one to a vertical line.

5. $a\dot{x} + b\dot{y} = 0$: This constraint is qualitatively the same as the previous one. The difference is that now the motions can be restricted along any collection of parallel lines by choosing a and b. For example, if $a = b = 1$, then only diagonal motions are allowed.

6. $a\dot{x} + b\dot{y} + c = 0$: This constraint is similar to the previous one. The integral curves are once again confined to lines, but the addition of the constant $c \neq 0$ implies that the $(0, 0)$ velocity vector is not allowed. Traveling along a line is allowed, but there is no way to stop.

7. $\dot{x}^2 + \dot{y}^2 \leq 1$: This constraint was used in Chapter 8. It has no effect on the existence of solutions to the feasible motion planning problem because motion in any direction is still allowed. The constraint only enforces a maximum speed.

8. $\dot{x}^2 + \dot{y}^2 \geq 1$: This constraint allows motions in any direction and at any speed greater than 1. It is impossible to stop or slow down below unit speed.

Many other constraints can be imagined, including some that define very complicated regions in $\mathbb{R}^2$ for each $U(q)$. Ignoring the fact that $\dot{x}$ and $\dot{y}$ represent derivatives, the geometric modeling concepts from Section 3.1 can even be used to define complicated constraints at each q. In fact, the constraints expressed above in terms of $\dot{x}$ and $\dot{y}$ are simple examples of the semi-algebraic model, which was introduced in Section 3.1.2. Just replace x and y from that section by $\dot{x}$ and $\dot{y}$ here.

If at every q there exists some open set O such that $(0, 0) \in O$ and $O \subseteq U(q)$, then there is no effect on the existence of solutions to the feasible motion planning problem. Velocities in all directions are still allowed. This holds true for velocity constraints on any smooth manifold [925].

So far, the velocities have been constrained in the same way at every $q \in \mathbb{R}^2$, which means that $U(q)$ is the same for all $q \in \mathbb{R}^2$. Constraints of this kind are of the form $g(\dot{x}, \dot{y}) \bowtie 0$, in which $\bowtie$ could be $=$, $<$, $>$, $\leq$, or $\geq$, and g_i is a function from $\mathbb{R}^2$ to $\mathbb{R}$. Typically, the $=$ relation drops the dimension of $U(x)$ by one, and the others usually leave it unchanged.

Now consider the constraint $\dot{x} = x$. This results in a different one-dimensional set, $U(q)$, of allowable velocities at each $q \in \mathbb{R}^2$. At each $q = (x, y)$, the set of allowable velocities must be of the form $(x, \dot{y})$ for any $\dot{y} \in \mathbb{R}$. This means that as x increases, the velocity in the x direction must increase proportionally. Starting at any positive x value, there is no way to travel to the y-axis. However, starting on the y-axis, the integral curves will always remain on it! Constraints of this kind can generally be expressed as $g(x, y, \dot{x}, \dot{y}) \bowtie 0$, which allows the dependency on x or y.

General configuration spaces

Velocity constraints can be considered in the same way on a general C-space. Assume that $\mathcal{C}$ is a smooth manifold (a manifold was not required to be smooth in Chapter 4 because derivatives were not needed there). All constraints are expressed using a coordinate neighborhood, as defined in Section 8.3.2. For expressing differential models, this actually makes an n-dimensional manifold look very much like $\mathbb{R}^n$. It is implicitly understood that a change of coordinates may occasionally be needed; however, this does not complicate the expression of constraints. This makes it possible to ignore many of the manifold technicalities and think about the constraints as if they are applied to $\mathbb{R}^n$.

Now consider placing velocity constraints on $\mathcal{C}$. Imagine how complicated velocity constraints could become if any semi-algebraic model is allowed. Velocity constraints on $\mathcal{C}$ could be as complicated as any $\mathcal{C}_{obs}$. It is not even necessary to use algebraic primitives. In general, the constraints can be expressed as

$$g(q, \dot{q}) \bowtie 0, \tag{13.1}$$

in which $\bowtie$ could once again be $=$, $<$, $>$, $\leq$, or $\geq$. The same expressive power can be maintained even after eliminating some of these relations. For example, any constraint of the form (13.1) can be expressed as a combination of constraints of the form $g(q, \dot{q}) = 0$ and $g(q, \dot{q}) < 0$. All of the relations are allowed here, however, to make the formulations simpler.

Constraints expressed in the form shown in (13.1) are called *implicit*. As explained in Chapters 3 and 4, it can be very complicated to obtain a parametric representation of the solutions of implicit equations. This was seen, for example, in Section 4.4, in which it was difficult to characterize the set of configurations that satisfy closure constraints. Nevertheless, we will be in a much better position in terms of developing planning algorithms if a parametric representation of the constraints can be obtained. Fortunately, most constraints that are derived from robots, vehicles, and other mechanical systems can be expressed in parametric form.

13.1.1.2 Parametric constraints

The parametric way of expressing velocity constraints gives a different interpretation to $U(q)$. Rather than directly corresponding to a velocity, each $u \in U(q)$ is interpreted as an abstract action vector. The set of allowable velocities is then obtained through a function that maps an action vector into $T_q(\mathcal{C})$. This yields the *configuration transition equation* (or *system*)

$$\dot{q} = f(q, u), \tag{13.2}$$

in which f is a continuous-time version of the state transition function that was developed in Section 2.1. Note that (13.2) actually represents n scalar equations, in which n is the dimension of $\mathcal{C}$. The system will nevertheless be referred to as a single equation in the vector sense. Usually, $U(q)$ is fixed for all $q \in \mathcal{C}$. This will be assumed unless otherwise stated. In this case, the fixed action set is denoted as U.

There are two interesting ways to interpret (13.2):

1. **Subspace of the tangent space:** If q is fixed, then f maps from U into $T_q(\mathcal{C})$. This parameterizes the set of allowable velocities at q because a velocity vector, $f(q, u)$, is obtained for every $u \in U(q)$.

2. **Vector field:** If u is fixed, then f can be considered as a function that maps each $q \in \mathcal{C}$ into $T_q(\mathcal{C})$. This means that f defines a vector field over $\mathcal{C}$ for every fixed $u \in U$.

Example 13.1 (Two Interpetations of $\dot{q} = f(q, u)$) Suppose that $\mathcal{C} = \mathbb{R}^2$, which yields a two-dimensional velocity vector space at every $q = (x, y) \in \mathbb{R}^2$. Let $U = \mathbb{R}$, and $\dot{q} = f(q, u)$ be defined as $\dot{x} = u$ and $\dot{y} = x$.

To obtain the first interpretation of $\dot{q} = f(q, u)$, hold $q = (x, y)$ fixed; for each $u \in U$, a velocity vector $(\dot{x}, \dot{y}) = (u, x)$ is obtained. The set of all allowable velocity vectors at $q = (x, y)$ is

$$\{(\dot{x}, \dot{y}) \in \mathbb{R}^2 \mid \dot{y} = x\}. \tag{13.3}$$

Suppose that $q = (1, 2)$. In this case, any vector of the form $(u, 1)$ for any $u \in \mathbb{R}$ is allowable.

To obtain the second interpretation, hold u fixed. For example, let $u = 1$. The vector field $(\dot{x}, \dot{y}) = (1, x)$ over $\mathbb{R}^2$ is obtained. ∎

It is important to specify U when defining the configuration transition equation. We previously allowed, but discouraged, the action set to depend on q. Any differential constraints expressed as $\dot{q} = f(q, u)$ for any U can be alternatively expressed as $\dot{q} = u$ by defining

$$U(q) = \{\dot{q} \in \mathbb{R}^n \mid \exists u \in U \text{ such that } \dot{q} = f(q, u)\} \tag{13.4}$$

for each $q \in \mathcal{C}$. In this definition, $U(q)$ is not necessarily a subset of U. It is usually more convenient, however, to use the form $\dot{q} = f(q, u)$ and keep the same U for all q. The common interpretation of U is that it is a set of fixed actions that can be applied from any point in the C-space.

In the context of ordinary motion planning, a configuration transition equation did not need to be specifically mentioned. This issue was discussed in Section 8.4. Provided that U contains an open subset that contains the origin, motion in any direction is allowed. The configuration transition equation for basic motion planning was simply $\dot{q} = u$. Since this does not impose constraints on the direction, it was not explicitly mentioned. For the coming models in this chapter, constraints will be imposed on the velocities that restrict the possible directions. This requires planning algorithms that handle differential models and is the subject of Chapter 14.

13.1.1.3 Conversion from implicit to parametric form

There are trade-offs between the implicit and parametric ways to express differential constraints. The implicit representation is more general; however, the parametric form is more useful because it explicitly gives the possible actions. For this reason, it is often desirable to derive a parametric representation from an implicit one. Under very general conditions, it is theoretically possible. As will be explained shortly, this is a result of the implicit function theorem. Unfortunately, the theoretical existence of such a conversion does not help in actually performing the transformations. In many cases, it may not be practical to determine a parametric representation.

To model a mechanical system, it is simplest to express constraints in the implicit form and then derive the parametric representation $\dot{q} = f(q, u)$. So far there has been no appearance of u in the implicit representation. Since u is interpreted as an action, it needs to be specified while deriving the parametric representation. To understand the issues, it is helpful to first assume that all constraints in implicit form are linear equations in $\dot{q}$ of the form

$$g_1(q)\dot{q}_1 + g_2(q)\dot{q}_2 + \cdots + g_n(q)\dot{q}_n = 0, \tag{13.5}$$

which are called *Pfaffian constraints*. These constraints are linear only under the assumption that q is known. It is helpful in the current discussion to imagine that q is fixed at some known value, which means that each of the $g_i(q)$ coefficients in (13.5) is a constant.

Suppose that k Pfaffian constraints are given for $k \le n$ and that they are linearly independent.[1] Recall the standard techniques for solving linear equations. If $k = n$, then a unique solution exists. If $k < n$, then a continuum of solutions exists, which forms an $(n - k)$-dimensional hyperplane. It is impossible to have $k > n$ because there can be no more than n linearly independent equations.

If $k = n$, only one velocity vector satisfies the constraints for each $q \in C$. A vector field can therefore be derived from the constraints, and the problem is not interesting from a planning perspective because there is no choice of velocities. If $k < n$, then $n - k$ components of $\dot{q}$ can be chosen independently, and then the remaining k are computed to satisfy the Pfaffian constraints (this can be accomplished using linear algebra techniques such as singular value decomposition [401, 961]). The components of $\dot{q}$ that can be chosen independently can be considered as $n - k$ scalar actions. Together these form an $(n - k)$-dimensional action vector, $u = (u_1, \ldots, u_{n-k})$. Suppose without loss of generality that the first $n - k$ components of $\dot{q}$ are specified by u. The configuration transition equation

---

[1] If the coefficients are placed into an $k \times n$ matrix, its rank is k.

can then be written as

$$\dot{q}_1 = u_1 \qquad\qquad \dot{q}_{n-k+1} = f_{n-k+1}(q, u)$$
$$\dot{q}_2 = u_2 \qquad\qquad \dot{q}_{n-k+2} = f_{n-k+2}(q, u)$$
$$\vdots \qquad\qquad\qquad \vdots \qquad\qquad\qquad\qquad (13.6)$$
$$\dot{q}_{n-k} = u_{n-k} \qquad\qquad \dot{q}_n = f_n(q, u),$$

in which each f_i is a linear function of u and is derived from the Pfaffian constraints after substituting u_i for $\dot{q}_i$ for each i from 1 to $n - k$ and then solving for the remaining components of $\dot{q}$. For some values of q, the constraints may become linearly dependent. This only weakens the constraints, which means the dimension of u can be increased at any q for which independence is lost. Such points are usually isolated and will not be considered further.

Example 13.2 (Pfaffian Constraints) Suppose that $\mathcal{C} = \mathbb{R}^3$, and there is one constraint of the form (13.5)

$$2\dot{q}_1 - \dot{q}_2 - \dot{q}_3 = 0. \qquad\qquad (13.7)$$

For this problem, $n = 3$ and $k = 1$. There are two action variables because $n - k = 2$. The configuration transition equation is

$$\dot{q}_1 = u_1$$
$$\dot{q}_2 = u_2 \qquad\qquad\qquad (13.8)$$
$$\dot{q}_3 = -2u_1 + u_2,$$

in which the last component was obtained by substituting u_1 and u_2, respectively, for $\dot{q}_1$ and $\dot{q}_2$ in (13.7) and then solving for $\dot{q}_3$.

The constraint given in (13.7) does not even depend on q. The same ideas apply for more general Pfaffian constraints, such as

$$(\cos q_3)\dot{q}_1 - (\sin q_3)\dot{q}_2 - \dot{q}_3 = 0. \qquad\qquad (13.9)$$

Following the same procedure, the configuration transition equation becomes

$$\dot{q}_1 = u_1$$
$$\dot{q}_2 = u_2 \qquad\qquad\qquad (13.10)$$
$$\dot{q}_3 = -(\cos q_3)u_1 + (\sin q_3)u_2.$$

∎

The ideas presented so far naturally extend to equality constraints that are not linear in $\dot{x}$. At each q, an $(n - k)$-dimensional set of actions, $U(q)$, is guaranteed to exist if the Jacobian $\partial(g_1, \ldots, g_k)/\partial(\dot{q}_1, \ldots, \dot{q}_n)$ (recall (6.28) or see [511]) of the constraint functions has rank k at q. This follows from the *implicit function theorem* [511].

Suppose that there are inequality constraints of the form $g(q, \dot{q}) \le 0$, in addition to equality constraints. Using the previous concepts, the actions may once again be assigned directly as $\dot{q}_i = u_i$ for all i such that $1 \le i \le n - k$. Without inequality constraints, there are no constraints on u, which means that $U = \mathbb{R}^n$. Since u is interpreted as an input to some physical system, U will often be constrained. In a physical system, for example, the amount of energy consumed may be proportional to u. After performing the $\dot{q}_i = u_i$ substitutions, the inequality constraints indicate limits on u. These limits are expressed in

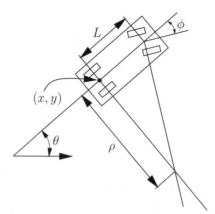

Figure 13.1: The simple car has three degrees of freedom, but the velocity space at any configuration is only two-dimensional.

terms of q and the remaining components of $\dot{q}$, which are the variables $\dot{q}_{n-k+1}, \ldots, \dot{q}_n$. For many problems, the inequality constraints are simple enough that constraints directly on U can be derived. For example, if u_1 represents scalar acceleration applied to a car, then it may have a simple bound such as $|u_1| \leq 1$.

One final complication that sometimes occurs is that the action variables may already be specified in the equality constraints: $g(q, \dot{q}, u) = 0$. In this case, imagine once again that q is fixed. If there are k independent constraints, then by the implicit function theorem, $\dot{q}$ can be solved to yield $\dot{q} = f(q, u)$ (although theoretically possible, it may be difficult in practice). If the Jacobian $\partial(f_1, \ldots, f_n)/\partial(u_1, \ldots, u_k)$ has rank k at q, then actions can be applied to yield any velocity on a k-dimensional hyperplane in $T_q(\mathcal{C})$. If $k = n$, then there are enough independent action variables to overcome the constraints. Any velocity in $T_q(\mathcal{C})$ can be achieved through a choice of u. This is true only if there are no inequality constraints on U.

13.1.2 Kinematics for wheeled systems

The most common family of examples in robotics arises from wheels that are required to roll in the direction they are pointing. Most wheels are not designed to slide sideways. This imposes velocity constraints on rolling vehicles. As a result, there are usually less action variables than degrees of freedom. Such systems are therefore called *underactuated*. It is interesting that, in many cases, vehicles can execute motions that overcome the constraint. For example, a car can parallel park itself anywhere that it could reach if all four wheels could turn to any orientation. This leads to formal concepts such as *nonholonomic constraints* and *small-time local controllability*, which are covered in Section 15.4.

13.1.2.1 A simple car

One of the easiest examples to understand is the *simple car*, which is shown in Figure 13.1. We all know that a car cannot drive sideways because the back wheels would have to slide instead of roll. This is why parallel parking is challenging. If all four wheels could be turned simultaneously toward the curb, it would be trivial to park a car. The complicated maneuvers for parking a simple car arise because of rolling constraints.

The car can be imagined as a rigid body that moves in the plane. Therefore, its C-space is $\mathcal{C} = \mathbb{R}^2 \times \mathbb{S}^1$. Figure 13.1 indicates several parameters associated with the car.

A configuration is denoted by $q = (x, y, \theta)$. The body frame of the car places the origin at the center of rear axle, and the x-axis points along the main axis of the car. Let s denote the (signed) speed[2] of the car. Let ϕ denote the steering angle (it is negative for the wheel orientation shown in Figure 13.1). The distance between the front and rear axles is represented as L. If the steering angle is fixed at ϕ, the car travels in a circular motion, in which the radius of the circle is ρ. Note that ρ can be determined from the intersection of the two axes shown in Figure 13.1 (the angle between these axes is ϕ).

Using the current notation, the task is to represent the motion of the car as a set of equations of the form

$$\dot{x} = f_1(x, y, \theta, s, \phi)$$
$$\dot{y} = f_2(x, y, \theta, s, \phi) \tag{13.11}$$
$$\dot{\theta} = f_3(x, y, \theta, s, \phi).$$

In a small time interval, Δt, the car must move approximately in the direction that the rear wheels are pointing. In the limit as Δt tends to zero, this implies that $dy/dx = \tan\theta$. Since $dy/dx = \dot{y}/\dot{x}$ and $\tan\theta = \sin\theta/\cos\theta$, this condition can be written as a Pfaffian constraint (recall (13.5)):

$$-\dot{x}\sin\theta + \dot{y}\cos\theta = 0. \tag{13.12}$$

The constraint is satisfied if $\dot{x} = \cos\theta$ and $\dot{y} = \sin\theta$. Furthermore, any scalar multiple of this solution is also a solution; the scaling factor corresponds directly to the speed s of the car. Thus, the first two scalar components of the configuration transition equation are $\dot{x} = s\cos\theta$ and $\dot{y} = s\sin\theta$.

The next task is to derive the equation for $\dot{\theta}$. Let w denote the distance traveled by the car (the integral of speed). As shown in Figure 13.1, ρ represents the radius of a circle that is traversed by the center of the rear axle, if the steering angle is fixed. Note that $dw = \rho d\theta$. From trigonometry, $\rho = L/\tan\phi$, which implies

$$d\theta = \frac{\tan\phi}{L} dw. \tag{13.13}$$

Dividing both sides by dt and using the fact that $\dot{w} = s$ yields

$$\dot{\theta} = \frac{s}{L}\tan\phi. \tag{13.14}$$

So far, the motion of the car has been modeled, but no action variables have been specified. Suppose that the speed s and steering angle ϕ are directly specified by the action variables u_s and u_ϕ, respectively. The convention of using a u variable with the old variable name appearing as a subscript will be followed. This makes it easy to identify the actions in a configuration transition equation. A two-dimensional action vector, $u = (u_s, u_\phi)$, is obtained. The configuration transition equation for the simple car is

$$\dot{x} = u_s\cos\theta$$
$$\dot{y} = u_s\sin\theta \tag{13.15}$$
$$\dot{\theta} = \frac{u_s}{L}\tan u_\phi.$$

---

[2] Having a signed speed is somewhat unorthodox. If the car moves in reverse, then s is negative. A more correct name for s would be velocity in the x direction of the body frame, but this is too cumbersome.

As expressed in (13.15), the transition equation is not yet complete without specifying U, the set of actions of the form $u = (u_s, u_\phi)$. First suppose that any $u_s \in \mathbb{R}$ is possible. What steering angles are possible? The interval $[-\pi/2, \pi/2]$ is sufficiently large for the steering angle u_ϕ because any other value is equivalent to one between $-\pi/2$ and $\pi/2$. Steering angles of $\pi/2$ and $-\pi/2$ are problematic. To derive the expressions for $\dot{x}$ and $\dot{y}$, it was assumed that the car moves in the direction that the rear wheels are pointing. Imagine you are sitting on a tricycle and turn the front wheel perpendicular to the rear wheels (assigning $u_\phi = \pi/2$). If you are able to pedal, then the tricycle should rotate in place. This means that $\dot{x} = \dot{y} = 0$ because the center of the rear axle does not translate.

This strange behavior is not allowed for a standard automobile. A car with rear-wheel drive would probably skid the front wheels across the pavement. If a car with front-wheel drive attempted this, it should behave as a tricycle; however, this is usually not possible because the front wheels would collide with the front axle when turned to $\phi = \pi/2$. Therefore, the simple car should have a maximum steering angle, $\phi_{max} < \pi/2$, and we require that $|\phi| \leq \phi_{max}$. Observe from Figure 13.1 that a maximum steering angle implies a *minimum turning radius*, ρ_{min}. For the case of a tricycle, $\rho_{min} = 0$. You may have encountered the problem of a minimum turning radius while trying to make an illegal U-turn. It is sometimes difficult to turn a car around without driving it off of the road.

Now return to the speed u_s. On level pavement, a real vehicle has a top speed, and its behavior should change dramatically depending on the speed. For example, if you want to drive along the minimum turning radius, you should not drive at 140km/hr. It seems that the maximum steering angle should reduce at higher speeds. This enters the realm of dynamics, which will be allowed after phase spaces are introduced in Section 13.2. Following this, some models of cars with dynamics will be covered in Sections 13.2.4 and 13.3.3.

It has been assumed implicitly that the simple car is moving slowly to safely neglect dynamics. A bound such as $|u_s| \leq 1$ can be placed on the speed without affecting the configurations that it can reach. The speed can even be constrained as $u_s \in \{-1, 0, 1\}$ without destroying reachability. Be careful, however, about a bound such as $0 \leq u_s \leq 1$. In this case, the car cannot drive in reverse! This clearly affects the set of reachable configurations. Imagine a car that is facing a wall and is unable to move in reverse. It may be forced to hit the wall as it moves.

Based on these considerations regarding the speed and steering angle, several interesting variations are possible:

Tricycle: $U = [-1, 1] \times [-\pi/2, \pi/2]$. Assuming front-wheel drive, the "car" can rotate in place if $u_\phi = \pi/2$ or $u_\phi = \pi/2$. This is unrealistic for a simple car. The resulting model is similar to that of the simple unicycle, which appears later in (13.18).

Simple Car [599]: $U = [-1, 1] \times (-\phi_{max}, \phi_{max})$. By requiring that $|u_\phi| \leq \phi_{max} < \pi/2$, a car with minimum turning radius $\rho_{min} = L/\tan \phi_{max}$ is obtained.

Reeds-Shepp Car [817, 924]: Further restrict the speed of the simple car so that $u_s \in \{-1, 0, 1\}$.[3] This model intuitively makes u_s correspond to three discrete "gears": reverse, park, or forward. An interesting question under this model is: What is the shortest possible path (traversed in $\mathbb{R}^2$ by the center of the rear axle) between two configurations in the absence of obstacles? This is answered in Section 15.3.

---

[3] In many works, the speed $u_s = 0$ is not included. It appears here so that a proper termination condition can be defined.

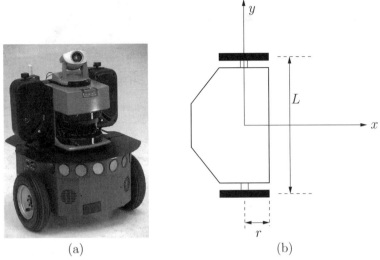

(a)   (b)

Figure 13.2: (a) The Pioneer 3-DX8 (courtesy of ActivMedia Robotics: MobileRobots.com), and many other mobile robots use a differential drive. In addition to the two drive wheels, a caster wheel (as on the bottom of an office chair) is placed in the rear center to prevent the robot from toppling over. (b) The parameters of a generic differential-drive robot.

Dubins Car [296]: Remove the reverse speed $u_s = -1$ from the Reeds-Shepp car to obtain $u_s \in \{0, 1\}$ as the only possible speeds. The shortest paths in $\mathbb{R}^2$ for this car are quite different than for the Reeds-Shepp car; see Section 15.3.

The car that was shown in Figure 1.12a of Section 1.2 is even more restricted than the Dubins car because it is additionally forced to turn left.

Basic controllability issues have been studied thoroughly for the simple car. These will be covered in Section 15.4, but it is helpful to develop intuitive notions here to assist in understanding the planning algorithms of Chapter 14. The simple car is considered *non-holonomic* because there are differential constraints that cannot be completely integrated. This means that the car configurations are not restricted to a lower dimensional subspace of $\mathcal{C}$. The Reeds-Shepp car can be maneuvered into an arbitrarily small parking space, provided that a small amount of clearance exists. This property is called *small-time local controllability* and is presented in Section 15.1.3. The Dubins car is nonholonomic, but it does not possess this property. Imagine the difficulty of parallel parking without using the reverse gear. In an infinitely large parking lot without obstacles, however, the Dubins car can reach any configuration.

13.1.2.2 A differential drive

Most indoor mobile robots do not move like a car. For example, consider the mobile robotics platform shown in Figure 13.2a. This is an example of the most popular way to drive indoor mobile robots. There are two main wheels, each of which is attached to its own motor. A third wheel (not visible in Figure 13.2a) is placed in the rear to passively roll along while preventing the robot from falling over.

To construct a simple model of the constraints that arise from the differential drive, only the distance L between the two wheels, and the wheel radius, r, are necessary. See Figure 13.2b. The action vector $u = (u_r, u_l)$ directly specifies the two angular wheel

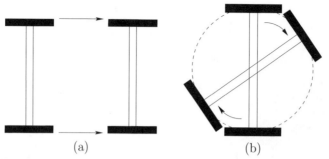

Figure 13.3: (a) Pure translation occurs when both wheels move at the same angular velocity; (b) pure rotation occurs when the wheels move at opposite velocities.

velocities (e.g., in radians per second). Consider how the robot moves as different actions are applied. See Figure 13.3. If $u_l = u_r > 0$, then the robot moves forward in the direction that the wheels are pointing. The speed is proportional to r. In general, if $u_l = u_r$, then the distance traveled over a duration t of time is rtu_l (because tu_l is the total angular displacement of the wheels). If $u_l = -u_r \neq 0$, then the robot rotates clockwise because the wheels are turning in opposite directions. This motivates the placement of the body-frame origin at the center of the axle between the wheels. By this assignment, no translation occurs if the wheels rotate at the same rate but in opposite directions.

Based on these observations, the configuration transition equation is

$$\dot{x} = \frac{r}{2}(u_l + u_r)\cos\theta$$
$$\dot{y} = \frac{r}{2}(u_l + u_r)\sin\theta \qquad (13.16)$$
$$\dot{\theta} = \frac{r}{L}(u_r - u_l).$$

The translational part contains $\cos\theta$ and $\sin\theta$ parts, just like the simple car because the differential drive moves in the direction that its drive wheels are pointing. The translation speed depends on the average of the angular wheel velocities. To see this, consider the case in which one wheel is fixed and the other rotates. This initially causes the robot to translate at $1/2$ of the speed in comparison to both wheels rotating. The rotational speed $\dot{\theta}$ is proportional to the change in angular wheel speeds. The robot's rotation rate grows linearly with the wheel radius but reduces linearly with respect to the distance between the wheels.

It is sometimes preferable to transform the action space. Let $u_\omega = (u_r + u_l)/2$ and $u_\psi = u_r - u_l$. In this case, u_ω can be interpreted as an action variable that means "translate," and u_ψ means "rotate." Using these actions, the configuration transition equation becomes

$$\dot{x} = ru_\omega\cos\theta$$
$$\dot{y} = ru_\omega\sin\theta \qquad (13.17)$$
$$\dot{\theta} = \frac{r}{L}u_\psi.$$

In this form, the configuration transition equation resembles (13.15) for the simple car (try setting $u_\psi = \tan u_\phi$ and $u_s = ru_\omega$). A differential drive can easily simulate the motions of the simple car. For the differential drive, the rotation rate can be set independently of

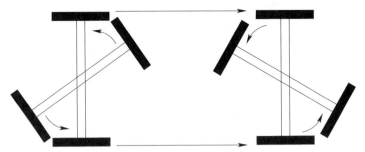

Figure 13.4: The shortest path traversed by the center of the axle is simply the line segment that connects the initial and goal positions in the plane. Rotations appear to be cost-free.

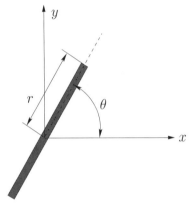

Figure 13.5: Viewed from above, the unicycle model has an action u_ω that changes the wheel orientation θ.

the translational velocity. The simple car, however, has the speed u_s appearing in the $\dot{\theta}$ expression. Therefore, the rotation rate depends on the translational velocity.

Recall the question asked about shortest paths for the Reeds-Shepp and Dubins cars. The same question for the differential drive turns out to be uninteresting because the differential drive can cause the center of its axle to follow any continuous path in $\mathbb{R}^2$. As depicted in Figure 13.4, it can move between any two configurations by: 1) first rotating itself to point the wheels to the goal position, which causes no translation; 2) translating itself to the goal position; and 3) rotating itself to the desired orientation, which again causes no translation. The total distance traveled by the center of the axle is always the Euclidean distance in $\mathbb{R}^2$ between the two desired positions.

This may seem like a strange effect due to the placement of the coordinate origin. Rotations seem to have no cost. This can be fixed by optimizing the total amount of wheel rotation or time required, if the speed is held fixed [65]. Suppose that $u_r, u_l \in \{-1, 0, 1\}$. Determining the minimum time required to travel between two configurations is quite interesting and is covered in Section 15.3. This properly takes into account the cost of rotating the robot, even if it does not cause a translation.

13.1.2.3 A simple unicycle

Consider the simple model of a unicycle, which is shown in Figure 13.5. Ignoring balancing concerns, there are two action variables. The rider of the unicycle can set the pedaling speed and the orientation of the wheel with respect to the z-axis. Let σ denote the pedaling angular velocity, and let r be the wheel radius. The speed of the unicycle is $s = r\sigma$. In this

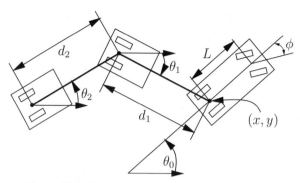

Figure 13.6: The parameters for a car pulling trailers.

model, the speed is set directly by an action variable u_s (alternatively, the pedaling rate could be an action variable u_σ, and the speed is derived as $s = ru_\sigma$). Let ω be the angular velocity of the unicycle orientation in the xy plane (hence, $\omega = \dot{\theta}$). Let ω be directly set by an action variable u_ω. The configuration transition equation is

$$
\begin{aligned}
\dot{x} &= u_s \cos \theta \\
\dot{y} &= u_s \sin \theta \\
\dot{\theta} &= u_\omega.
\end{aligned}
\tag{13.18}
$$

This is just the differential drive equation (13.17) with $L = 1$ and the substitution $u_s = ru_\sigma$. Thus, a differential drive can simulate a unicycle. This may seem strange; however, it is possible because these models do not consider dynamics. Note that the unicycle can also simulate the simple-car model. Therefore, the tricycle and unicycle models are similar.

13.1.2.4 A car pulling trailers

An interesting extension of the simple car can be made by attaching one or more trailers. You may have seen a train of luggage carts on the tarmac at airports. There are many subtle issues for modeling the constraints for these models. The form of equations is very sensitive to the precise point at which the trailer is attached and also on the choice of body frames. One possibility for expressing the kinematics is to use the expressions in Section 3.3; however, these may lead to complications when analyzing the constraints. It is somewhat of an art to find a simple expression of the constraints. The model given here is adapted from [730].[4]

Consider a simple car that pulls k trailers as shown in Figure 13.6. Each trailer is attached to the center of the rear axle of the body in front of it. The important new parameter is the *hitch length* d_i which is the distance from the center of the rear axle of trailer i to the point at which the trailer is hitched to the next body. Using concepts from Section 3.3.1, the car itself contributes $\mathbb{R}^2 \times \mathbb{S}^1$ to $\mathcal{C}$, and each trailer contributes an $\mathbb{S}^1$ component to $\mathcal{C}$. The dimension of $\mathcal{C}$ is therefore $k + 3$. Let θ_i denote the orientation of the ith trailer, expressed with respect to the world frame.

---

[4] The original model required a continuous steering angle.

The configuration transition equation is

$$\dot{x} = s \cos \theta_0$$

$$\dot{y} = s \sin \theta_0$$

$$\dot{\theta}_0 = \frac{s}{L} \tan \phi$$

$$\dot{\theta}_1 = \frac{s}{d_1} \sin(\theta_1 - \theta_0)$$

$$\vdots$$

$$\dot{\theta}_i = \frac{s}{d_i} \left(\prod_{j=1}^{i-1} \cos(\theta_{j-1} - \theta_j) \right) \sin(\theta_{i-1} - \theta_i)$$

$$\vdots$$

$$\dot{\theta}_k = \frac{s}{d_k} \left(\prod_{j=1}^{k-1} \cos(\theta_{j-1} - \theta_j) \right) \sin(\theta_{k-1} - \theta_k).$$

(13.19)

An interesting variation of this model is to allow the trailer wheels to be steered. For a single trailer, this leads to a model that resembles a *firetruck* [165].

13.1.3 Other examples of velocity constraints

The differential models seen so far were obtained from wheels that roll along a planar surface. Many generalizations are possible by considering other ways in which bodies can contact each other. In robotics, many interesting differential models arise in the context of manipulation. This section briefly covers some other examples of velocity constraints on the C-space. Once again, dynamics is neglected for now. Such models are sometimes classified as *quasi-static* because even though motions occur, some aspects of the model treat the bodies as if they were static. Such models are often realistic when moving at slow enough speeds.

13.1.3.1 Pushing a box

Imagine using a differential drive robot to push a box around on the floor, as shown in Figure 13.7a. It is assumed that the box is a convex polygon, one edge of which contacts the front of the robot. There are frictional contacts between the box and floor and also between the box and robot. Suppose that the robot is moving slowly enough so that dynamics are insignificant. It is assumed that the box cannot move unless the robot is moving. This prohibits manipulations such as "kicking" the box across the room. The term *stable pushing* [12, 674, 684] refers to the case in which the robot moves the box as if the box were rigidly attached to the robot.

As the robot pushes the box, the box may slide or rotate, as shown in Figures 13.7b and 13.7c, respectively. These cases are considered illegal because they do not constitute stable pushing. What motions of the robot are possible? Begin with the configuration transition equation of the differential drive robot, and then determine which constraints need to be placed on U to maintain stable pushing. Suppose that (13.17) is used. It is clear that only forward motion is possible because the robot immediately breaks contact with the box if the robot moves in the opposite direction. Thus, s must be positive (also,

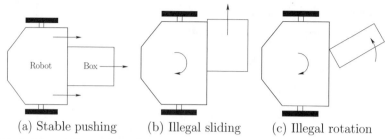

(a) Stable pushing   (b) Illegal sliding   (c) Illegal rotation

Figure 13.7: Lynch and Mason showed that pushing a box is very much like driving the simple car: (a) With careful motions, the box will act as if it is attached to the robot. b) If it turns too sharply, however, the box will slide away; this induces limits on the steering angle. c) The box may alternatively rotate from sharp turns [674].

to fit the quasi-static model, s should be small enough so that dynamical effects become insignificant). How should the rotation rate ψ be constrained? Constraints on ψ depend on the friction model (e.g., Coulomb), the shape of the box, and the particular edge that is being pushed. Details on these constraints are given in [674, 684]. This leads to an interval $[a, b] \subseteq [-\pi/2, \pi/2]$, in which $a < 0$ and $b > 0$, and it is required that $\psi \in [a, b]$. This combination of constraints produces a motion model that is similar to the Dubins car. The main difference is that the maximum steering angle in the left and right directions may be different.

To apply this model for planning, it seems that the C-space should be $\mathbb{R}^2 \times \mathbb{S}^1 \times \mathbb{R}^2 \times \mathbb{S}^1$ because there are two rigid bodies. The manipulation planning framework of Section 7.3.2 can be applied to obtain a hybrid system and manipulation graph that expresses the various ways in which the robot can contact the box or fail to contact the box. For example, the robot may be able to push the box along one of several possible edges. If the robot becomes stuck, it can change the pushing edge to move the box in a new direction.

13.1.3.2 Flying an airplane

The Dubins car model from Section 13.1.2 can be extended to 3D worlds to provide a simple aircraft flight model that may be reasonable for air traffic analysis. First suppose that the aircraft maintains a fixed altitude and is capable only of yaw rotations. In this case, (13.15) could be used directly by imposing the constraint that $s = 1$ (or some suitable positive speed). This is equivalent to the Dubins car, except that $s = 0$ is prohibited because it would imply that the aircraft can instantaneously stop in the air. This model assumes that the aircraft is small relative to the C-space. A more precise model should take into account pitch and roll rotations, disturbances, and dynamic effects. These would become important, for example, in studying the flight stability of an aircraft design. Such concerns are neglected here.

Now consider an aircraft that can change its altitude, in addition to executing motions like the Dubins car. In this case let $\mathcal{C} = \mathbb{R}^3 \times \mathbb{S}^1$, in which the extra $\mathbb{R}$ represents the altitude with respect to flying over a flat surface. A configuration is represented as $q = (x, y, z, \theta)$. Let u_z denote an action that directly causes a change in the altitude: $\dot{z} = u_z$. The steering action u_ϕ is the same as in the Dubins car model. The configuration transition equation is

$$
\begin{aligned}
\dot{x} &= \cos\theta & \dot{z} &= u_z \\
\dot{y} &= \sin\theta & \dot{\theta} &= u_\omega.
\end{aligned}
\tag{13.20}
$$

For a fixed value of $u = (u_z, u_\omega)$ such that $u_z \neq 0$ and $u_\omega \neq 0$, a helical path results. The central axis of the helix is parallel to the z-axis, and projection of the path down to the xy plane is a circle or circular arc. Maximum absolute values should be set for u_z and u_ω based on the maximum possible altitude and yaw rate changes of the aircraft.

13.1.3.3 Rolling a ball

Instead of a wheel, consider rolling a ball in the plane. Place a ball on a table and try rolling it with your palm placed flat on top of it. It should feel like there are two degrees of freedom: rolling forward and rolling side to side. The ball should not be able to spin in place. The directions can be considered as two action variables. The total degrees of freedom of the ball is five, however, because it can achieve any orientation in $SO(3)$ and any (x, y) position in the plane; thus, $\mathcal{C} = \mathbb{R}^2 \times SO(3)$. Given that there are only two action variables, is it possible to roll the ball into any configuration? It is shown in [635, 494] that this is possible, even for the more general problem of one sphere rolling on another (the plane is a special case of a sphere with infinite radius). This problem can actually arise in robotic manipulation when a spherical object come into contact (e.g., a robot hand may have fingers with spherical tips); see [105, 679, 728, 732].

The resulting transition equation was shown in [719] (also see [728]) to be

$$
\begin{aligned}
\dot{\theta} &= -u_2 \\
\dot{\phi} &= \frac{u_1}{\cos\theta} \\
\dot{x} &= -u_1\rho\sin\psi - u_2\rho\cos\psi \\
\dot{y} &= -u_1\rho\cos\psi + u_2\rho\sin\psi \\
\dot{\psi} &= -u_1\tan\theta.
\end{aligned}
\tag{13.21}
$$

In these equations, x and y are the position on the contact point in the plane, and θ and ϕ are the position of the contact point in the ball frame and are expressed using spherical coordinates. The radius of the ball is ρ. Finally, ψ expresses the orientation of the ball with respect to the contact point.

13.1.3.4 Trapped on a surface

It is possible that the constraints cause the configuration to be trapped on a lower dimensional surface. Let $\mathcal{C} = \mathbb{R}^2$, and consider the system

$$
\dot{x} = yu \qquad\qquad \dot{y} = -xu, \tag{13.22}
$$

for $(x, y) \in \mathbb{R}^2$ and $u \in U = \mathbb{R}$. What are the integral curves for a constant action $u \neq 0$? From any point $(x, y) \in \mathbb{R}^2$, the trajectory follows a circle of radius $\sqrt{x^2 + y^2}$ centered at the origin. The speed along the circle is determined by $|u|$, and the direction is determined by the sign of u. Therefore, (13.22) indicates that the configuration is confined to a circle. Other than that, there are no further constraints.

Suppose that the initial configuration is given as (x_0, y_0). Since the configuration is confined to a circle, the C-space could alternatively be defined as $\mathcal{C} = \mathbb{S}^1$. Each point on $\mathbb{S}^1$ can be mapped to the circle that has radius $r = \sqrt{x_0^2 + y_0^2}$ and center at $(0, 0)$. In this case, there are no differential constraints on the velocities, provided that motions are trapped on the circle. Any velocity in the one-dimensional tangent space at points on the circle is allowed. This model is equivalent to (13.22).

Now consider the possible trajectories that are constrained to traverse a circle,

$$h(x, y) = x^2 + y^2 - r^2 = 0. \tag{13.23}$$

This means that for all time t,

$$h(x(t), y(t)) = x(t)^2 + y(t)^2 - r^2 = 0. \tag{13.24}$$

To derive a constraint on velocities, take the derivative with respect to time, which yields

$$\frac{dh(x, y)}{dt} = 2x\dot{x} + 2y\dot{y} = 0. \tag{13.25}$$

This is an example of a Pfaffian constraint, as given in (13.5). The parametric form of this differential constraint happens to be (13.22). Any velocity vector that is a multiple of $(y, -x)$ satisfies (13.25). When expressed as a differential constraint, the radius r does not matter. This is because it is determined from the initial configuration.

What just occurred here is a special case of a *completely integrable* differential model. In general, if the model $\dot{q} = f(q, u)$ can be expressed as the time derivative of constraints of the form $h(q) = 0$, then the configuration transition equation is said to be *completely integrable*. Obtaining an implicit differential model from constraints of the form $h_i(q) = 0$ is not difficult. Each constraint is differentiated to obtain

$$\frac{dh_i(q)}{dt} = 0. \tag{13.26}$$

For example, such constraints arise from closed kinematic chains, as in Section 4.4, and the implicit differential model just expresses the condition that velocities must lie in the tangent space to the constraints. It may be difficult, however, to obtain a parametric form of the differential model. Possible velocity vectors can be computed at any particular q, however, by using the linear algebra techniques described in Section 7.4.1.

It is even quite difficult to determine whether a differential model is completely integrable, which means that the configurations are trapped on a lower dimensional surface. For some systems, to be described by (13.41), this will be solved by the Frobenius Theorem in 15.4.2. If such systems are not completely integrable, they are called *nonholonomic*; otherwise, they are called *holonomic*. In general, even if a model is theoretically integrable, actually performing the integration is another issue. In most cases, it is difficult or impossible to integrate the model.

Therefore, it is sometimes important to work directly with constraints in differential form, even if they are integrable. Furthermore, methods for planning under differential constraints can be applied to problems that have constraints of the form $h(q) = 0$. This, for example, implies that motion planning for closed kinematic chains can be performed by planning algorithms designed to handle differential constraints.

13.2 Phase space representation of dynamical systems

The differential constraints defined in Section 13.1 are often called *kinematic* because they can be expressed in terms of velocities on the C-space. This formulation is useful for many problems, such as modeling the possible directions of motions for a wheeled mobile robot. It does not, however, enable dynamics to be expressed. For example, suppose that the simple car is traveling quickly. Taking dynamics into account, it should not be able to instantaneously start and stop. For example, if it is heading straight for a wall at full speed, any reasonable model should not allow it to apply its brakes from only one millimeter away and expect it to avoid collision. Due to momentum, the required stopping distance depends on the speed. You may have learned this from a drivers education course.

To account for momentum and other aspects of dynamics, higher order differential equations are needed. There are usually constraints on acceleration $\ddot{q}$, which is defined as $d\dot{q}/dt$. For example, the car may only be able to decelerate at some maximum rate without skidding the wheels (or tumbling the vehicle). Most often, the actions are even expressed in terms of higher order derivatives. For example, the floor pedal of a car may directly set the acceleration. It may be reasonable to consider the amount that the pedal is pressed as an action variable. In this case, the configuration must be obtained by two integrations. The first yields the velocity, and the second yields the configuration.

The models for dynamics therefore involve acceleration $\ddot{q}$ in addition to velocity $\dot{q}$ and configuration q. Once again, both implicit and parametric models exist. For an implicit model, the constraints are expressed as

$$g_i(\ddot{q}, \dot{q}, q) = 0. \tag{13.27}$$

For a parametric model, they are expressed as

$$\ddot{q} = f(\dot{q}, q, u). \tag{13.28}$$

13.2.1 Reducing degree by increasing dimension

Taking into account constraints on higher order derivatives seems substantially more complicated. This section explains a convenient trick that converts constraints that have higher order derivatives into a new set of constraints that has only first-order derivatives. This involves the introduction of a *phase space*, which has more dimensions than the original C-space. Thus, there is a trade-off because the dimension is increased; however, it is widely accepted that increasing the dimension of the space is often easier than dealing with higher order derivatives. In general, the term *state space* will refer to either C-spaces or phase spaces derived from them.

13.2.1.1 The scalar case

To make the discussion concrete, consider the following differential equation:

$$\ddot{y} - 3\dot{y} + y = 0, \tag{13.29}$$

in which y is a scalar variable, $y \in \mathbb{R}$. This is a second-order differential equation because of $\ddot{y}$. A *phase space* can be defined as follows. Let $x = (x_1, x_2)$ denote a two-dimensional *phase vector*, which is defined by assigning $x_1 = y$ and $x_2 = \dot{y}$. The terms state space and state vector will be used interchangeably with phase space and phase vector, respectively, in contexts in which the phase space is defined. Substituting the equations into (13.29) yields

$$\ddot{y} - 3x_2 + x_1 = 0. \tag{13.30}$$

So far, this does not seem to have helped. However, $\ddot{y}$ can be expressed as either $\dot{x}_2$ or $\ddot{x}_1$. The first choice is better because it is a lower order derivative. Using $\dot{x}_2 = \ddot{y}$, the differential equation becomes

$$\dot{x}_2 - 3x_2 + x_1 = 0. \tag{13.31}$$

Is this expression equivalent to (13.29)? By itself it is not. There is one more constraint, $x_2 = \dot{x}_1$. In implicit form, $\dot{x}_1 - x_2 = 0$. The key to making the phase space approach work correctly is to relate some of the phase variables by derivatives.

Using the phase space, we just converted the second-order differential equation (13.29) into two first-order differential equations,

$$
\begin{aligned}
\dot{x}_1 &= x_2 \\
\dot{x}_2 &= 3x_2 - x_1,
\end{aligned}
\tag{13.32}
$$

which are obtained by solving for $\dot{x}_1$ and $\dot{x}_2$. Note that (13.32) can be expressed as $\dot{x} = f(x)$, in which f is a function that maps from $\mathbb{R}^2$ into $\mathbb{R}^2$.

The same approach can be used for any differential equation in implicit form, $g(\ddot{y}, \dot{y}, y) = 0$. Let $x_1 = y$, $x_2 = \dot{y}$, and $\dot{x}_2 = \ddot{y}$. This results in the implicit equations $g(\dot{x}_2, x_2, x_1) = 0$ and $\dot{x}_1 = x_2$. Now suppose that there is a scalar action $u \in U = \mathbb{R}$ represented in the differential equations. Once again, the same approach applies. In implicit form, $g(\ddot{y}, \dot{y}, y, u) = 0$ can be expressed as $g(\dot{x}_2, x_2, x_1, u) = 0$.

Suppose that a given acceleration constraint is expressed in parametric form as $\ddot{y} = h(\dot{y}, y, u)$. This often occurs in the dynamics models of Section 13.3. This can be converted into a *phase transition equation* or *state transition equation* of the form $\dot{x} = f(x, u)$, in which $f : \mathbb{R}^2 \times \mathbb{R} \to \mathbb{R}^2$. The expression is

$$
\begin{aligned}
\dot{x}_1 &= x_2 \\
\dot{x}_2 &= h(x_2, x_1, u).
\end{aligned}
\tag{13.33}
$$

For a second-order differential equation, two initial conditions are usually given. The values of $y(0)$ and $\dot{y}(0)$ are needed to determine the exact position $y(t)$ for any $t \geq 0$. Using the phase space representation, no higher order initial conditions are needed because any point in phase space indicates both y and $\dot{y}$. Thus, given an initial point in the phase and $u(t)$ for all $t \geq 0$, $y(t)$ can be determined.

Example 13.3 (Double Integrator) The *double integrator* is a simple yet important example that nicely illustrates the phase space. Suppose that a second-order differential equation is given as $\ddot{q} = u$, in which q and u are chosen from $\mathbb{R}$. In words, this means that the action directly specifies acceleration. Integrating[5] once yields the velocity $\dot{q}$ and performing a double integration yields the position q. If $q(0)$ and $\dot{q}(0)$ are given, and $u(t')$ is specified for all $t' \in [0, t)$, then $\dot{q}(t)$ and $q(t)$ can be determined for any $t > 0$.

A two-dimensional phase space $X = \mathbb{R}^2$ is defined in which

$$
x = (x_1, x_2) = (q, \dot{q}).
\tag{13.34}
$$

The state (or phase) transition equation $\dot{x} = f(x, u)$ is

$$
\begin{aligned}
\dot{x}_1 &= x_2 \\
\dot{x}_2 &= u.
\end{aligned}
\tag{13.35}
$$

To determine the state trajectory, initial values $x_1(0) = q_0$ (position) and $x_2(0) = \dot{q}_0$ (velocity) must be given in addition to the action history. If u is constant, then the state trajectory is quadratic because it is obtained by two integrations of a constant function. ∎

---

[5] Wherever integrals are performed, it will be assumed that the integrands are integrable.

13.2.1.2 The vector case

The transformation to the phase space can be extended to differential equations in which there are time derivatives in more than one variable. Suppose that q represents a configuration, expressed using a coordinate neighborhood on a smooth n-dimensional manifold $\mathcal{C}$. Second-order constraints of the form $g(\ddot{q}, \dot{q}, q) = 0$ or $g(\ddot{q}, \dot{q}, q, u) = 0$ can be expressed as first-order constraints in a $2n$-dimensional state space. Let x denote the $2n$-dimensional phase vector. By extending the method that was applied to the scalar case, x is defined as $x = (q, \dot{q})$. For each integer i such that $1 \leq i \leq n$, $x_i = q_i$. For each i such that $n + 1 \leq i \leq 2n$, $x_i = \dot{q}_i$. These substitutions can be made directly into an implicit constraint to reduce the order to one.

Suppose that a set of n differential equations is expressed in parametric form as $\ddot{q} = h(q, \dot{q}, u)$. In the phase space, there are $2n$ differential equations. The first n correspond to the phase space definition $\dot{x}_i = x_{n+i}$, for each i such that $1 \leq i \leq n$. These hold because $x_{n+i} = \dot{q}$ and $\dot{x}_i$ is the time derivative of $\dot{q}_i$ for $i \leq n$. The remaining n components of $\dot{x} = f(x, u)$ follow directly from h by substituting the first n components of x in the place of q and the remaining n in the place of $\dot{q}$ in the expression $h(q, \dot{q}, u)$. The result can be denoted as $h(x, u)$ (obtained directly from $h(q, \dot{q}, u)$). This yields the final n equations as $\dot{x}_i = h_i(x, u)$, for each i such that $n + 1 \leq i \leq 2n$. These $2n$ equations define a *phase (or state) transition equation* of the form $\dot{x} = f(x, u)$. Now it is clear that constraints on acceleration can be manipulated into velocity constraints on the phase space. This enables the tangent space concepts from Section 8.3 to express constraints that involve acceleration. Furthermore, the state space X is the tangent bundle (defined in (8.9) for $\mathbb{R}^n$ and later in (15.67) for any smooth manifold) of $\mathcal{C}$ because q and $\dot{q}$ together indicate a tangent space $T_q(\mathcal{C})$ and a particular tangent vector $\dot{q} \in T_q(\mathcal{C})$.

13.2.1.3 Higher order differential constraints

The phase space idea can even be applied to differential equations with order higher than two. For example, a constraint may involve the time derivative of acceleration $q^{(3)}$, which is often called *jerk*. If the differential equations involve jerk variables, then a $3n$-dimensional phase space can be defined to obtain first-order constraints. In this case, each q_i, $\dot{q}_i$, and $\ddot{q}_i$ in a constraint such as $g(q^{(3)}, \ddot{q}, \dot{q}, q, u) = 0$ is defined as a phase variable. Similarly, kth-order differential constraints can be reduced to first-order constraints by introducing a kn-dimensional phase space.

Example 13.4 (Chain of Integrators) A simple example of higher order differential constraints is the *chain of integrators*.[6] This is a higher order generalization of Example 13.3. Suppose that a kth-order differential equation is given as $q^{(k)} = u$, in which q and u are scalars, and $q^{(k)}$ denotes the kth derivative of q with respect to time.

A k-dimensional phase space X is defined in which

$$x = (q, \dot{q}, \ddot{q}, q^{(3)}, \ldots, q^{(k-1)}). \tag{13.36}$$

The state (or phase) transition equation $\dot{x} = f(x, u)$ is $\dot{x}_i = x_{i+1}$ for each i such that $1 \leq i \leq n - 1$, and $\dot{x}_n = u$. Together, these n individual equations are equivalent to $q^{(k)} = u$.

The initial state specifies the initial position and all time derivatives up to order $k - 1$. Using these and the action u, the state trajectory can be obtained by a chain of integrations. ∎

---

[6] It is called this because in block diagram representations of systems it is depicted as a chain of integrator blocks.

You might be wondering whether derivatives can be eliminated completely by introducing a phase space that has high enough dimension. This does actually work. For example, if there are second-order constraints, then a $3n$-dimensional phase space can be introduced in which $x = (q, \dot{q}, \ddot{q})$. This enables constraints such as $g(q, \dot{q}, \ddot{q}) = 0$ to appear as $g(x) = 0$. The trouble with using such formulations is that the state must follow the constraint surface in a way that is similar to traversing the solution set of a closed kinematic chain, as considered in Section 4.4. This is why tangent spaces arose in that context. In either case, the set of allowable velocities becomes constrained at every point in the space.

Problems defined using phase spaces typically have an interesting property known as *drift*. This means that for some $x \in X$, there does *not* exist any $u \in U$ such that $f(x, u) = 0$. For the examples in Section 13.1.2, such an action always existed. These were examples of *driftless systems*. This was possible because the constraints did not involve dynamics. In a dynamical system, it is impossible to instantaneously stop due to momentum, which is a form of drift. For example, a car will "drift" into a brick wall if it is 3 meters way and traveling 100 km/hr in the direction of the wall. There exists no action (e.g., stepping firmly on the brakes) that could instantaneously stop the car. In general, there is no way to instantaneously stop in the phase space.

13.2.2 Linear systems

Now that the phase space has been defined as a special kind of state space that can handle dynamics, it is convenient to classify the kinds of differential models that can be defined based on their mathematical form. The class of *linear systems* has been most widely studied, particularly in the context of control theory. The reason is that many powerful techniques from linear algebra can be applied to yield good control laws [194]. The ideas can also be generalized to linear systems that involve optimality criteria [28, 573], nature [97, 567], or multiple players [60].

Let $X = \mathbb{R}^n$ be a phase space, and let $U = \mathbb{R}^m$ be an action space for $m \leq n$. A *linear system* is a differential model for which the state transition equation can be expressed as

$$\dot{x} = f(x, u) = Ax + Bu, \tag{13.37}$$

in which A and B are constant, real-valued matrices of dimensions $n \times n$ and $n \times m$, respectively.

Example 13.5 (Linear System Example)   For a simple example of (13.37), suppose $X = \mathbb{R}^3$, $U = \mathbb{R}^2$, and let

$$\begin{pmatrix} \dot{x}_1 \\ \dot{x}_2 \\ \dot{x}_3 \end{pmatrix} = \begin{pmatrix} 0 & \sqrt{2} & 1 \\ 1 & -1 & 4 \\ 2 & 0 & 1 \end{pmatrix} \begin{pmatrix} x_1 \\ x_2 \\ x_3 \end{pmatrix} + \begin{pmatrix} 1 & 0 \\ 0 & 1 \\ 1 & 1 \end{pmatrix} \begin{pmatrix} u_1 \\ u_2 \end{pmatrix}. \tag{13.38}$$

Performing the matrix multiplications reveals that all three equations are linear in the state and action variables. Compare this to the discrete-time linear Gaussian system shown in Example 11.25.   ■

Recall from Section 13.1.1 that k linear constraints *restrict* the velocity to an $(n - k)$-dimensional hyperplane. The linear model in (13.37) is in parametric form, which means that each action variable may *allow* an independent degree of freedom. In this case,

$m = n - k$. In the extreme case of $m = 0$, there are no actions, which results in $\dot{x} = Ax$. The phase velocity $\dot{x}$ is fixed for every point $x \in X$. If $m = 1$, then at every $x \in X$ a one-dimensional set of velocities may be chosen using u. This implies that the direction is fixed, but the magnitude is chosen using u. In general, the set of allowable velocities at a point $x \in \mathbb{R}^n$ is an m-dimensional linear subspace of the tangent space $T_x(\mathbb{R}^n)$ (if B is nonsingular).

In spite of (13.37), it may still be possible to reach all of the state space from any initial state. It may be costly, however, to reach a nearby point because of the restriction on the tangent space; it is impossible to command a velocity in some directions. For the case of nonlinear systems, it is sometimes possible to quickly reach any point in a small neighborhood of a state, while remaining in a small region around the state. Such issues fall under the general topic of controllability, which will be covered in Sections 15.1.3 and 15.4.3.

Although not covered here, the *observability* of the system is an important topic in control [194, 481]. In terms of the I-space concepts of Chapter 11, this means that a sensor of the form $y = h(x)$ is defined, and the task is to determine the current state, given the history I-state. If the system is observable, this means that the nondeterministic I-state is a single point. Otherwise, the system may only be partially observable. In the case of linear systems, if the sensing model is also linear,

$$y = h(x) = Cy, \tag{13.39}$$

then simple matrix conditions can be used to determine whether the system is observable [194]. Nonlinear observability theory also exists [481].

As in the case of discrete planning problems, it is possible to define differential models that depend on time. In the discrete case, this involves a dependency on stages. For the continuous-stage case, a *time-varying linear system* is defined as

$$\dot{x} = f(x(t), u(t), t) = A(t)x(t) + B(t)u(t). \tag{13.40}$$

In this case, the matrix entries are allowed to be functions of time. Many powerful control techniques can be easily adapted to this case, but it will not be considered here because most planning problems are *time-invariant* (or stationary).

13.2.3 Nonlinear systems

Although many powerful control laws can be developed for linear systems, the vast majority of systems that occur in the physical world fail to be linear. Any differential models that do not fit (13.37) or (13.40) are called *nonlinear systems*. All of the models given in Section 13.1.2 are nonlinear systems for the special case in which $X = C$.

One important family of nonlinear systems actually appears to be linear in some sense. Let X be a smooth n-dimensional manifold, and let $U \subseteq \mathbb{R}^m$. Let $U = \mathbb{R}^m$ for some $m \leq n$. Using a coordinate neighborhood, a nonlinear system of the form

$$\dot{x} = f(x) + \sum_{i=1}^{m} g_i(x)u_i \tag{13.41}$$

for smooth functions f and g_i is called a *control-affine system* or *affine-in-control system*.[7] These have been studied extensively in nonlinear control theory [481, 848]. They are linear in the actions but nonlinear with respect to the state. See Section 15.4.1 for further reading on control-affine systems.

For a control-affine system it is not necessarily possible to obtain zero velocity because f causes drift. The important special case of a *driftless* control-affine system occurs if $f \equiv 0$. This is written as

$$\dot{x} = \sum_{i=1}^{m} g_i(x)u_i. \tag{13.42}$$

By setting $u_i = 0$ for each i from 1 to m, zero velocity, $\dot{x} = 0$, is obtained.

Example 13.6 (Nonholonomic Integrator)   One of the simplest examples of a driftless control-affine system is the *nonholonomic integrator* introduced in control literature by Brockett in [144]. It some times referred to as *Brockett's system*, or the *Heisenberg system* because it arises in quantum mechanics [114]. Let $X = \mathbb{R}^3$, and let the set of actions $U = \mathbb{R}^2$. The state transition equation for the nonholonomic integrator is

$$\begin{aligned} \dot{x}_1 &= u_1 \\ \dot{x}_2 &= u_2 \\ \dot{x}_3 &= x_1 u_2 - x_2 u_1. \end{aligned} \tag{13.43}$$

∎

Many nonlinear systems can be expressed implicitly using Pfaffian constraints, which appeared in Section 13.1.1, and can be generalized from C-spaces to phase spaces. In terms of X, a Pfaffian constraint is expressed as

$$g_1(x)\dot{x}_1 + g_2(x)\dot{x}_2 + \cdots + g_n(x)\dot{x}_n = 0. \tag{13.44}$$

Even though the equation is linear in $\dot{x}$, a nonlinear dependency on x is allowed.

Both holonomic and nonholonomic models may exist for phase spaces, just as in the case of C-spaces in Section 13.1.3. The Frobenius Theorem, which is covered in Section 15.4.2, can be used to determine whether control-affine systems are completely integrable.

13.2.4 Extending models by adding integrators

The differential models from Section 13.1 may seem realistic in many applications because actions are required to undergo instantaneous changes. For example, in the simple car, the steering angle and speed may be instantaneously changed to any value. This implies that the car is capable of instantaneous acceleration changes. This may be a reasonable approximation if the car is moving slowly (for example, to analyze parallel-parking maneuvers). The model is ridiculous, however, at high speeds.

---

[7] Be careful not to confuse control-affine systems with *affine control systems*, which are of the form $\dot{x} = Ax + Bu + w$, for some constant matrices A, B and a constant vector w.

Suppose a state transition equation of the form $\dot{x} = f(x, u)$ is given in which the dimension of X is n. The model can be enhanced as follows:

1. Select an action variable u_i.
2. Rename the action variable as a new state variable, $x_{n+1} = u_i$.
3. Define a new action variable u_i' that takes the place of u_i.
4. Extend the state transition equation by one dimension by introducing $\dot{x}_{n+1} = u_i'$.

This enhancement will be referred to as *placing an integrator in front of u_i*. This procedure can be applied incrementally as many times as desired, to create a chain of integrators from any action variable. It can also be applied to different action variables.

13.2.4.1 Better unicycle models

Improvements to the models in Section 13.1 can be made by placing integrators in front of action variables. For example, consider the unicycle model (13.18). Instead of directly setting the speed using u_s, suppose that the speed is obtained by integration of an action u_a that represents acceleration. The equation $\dot{s} = u_a$ is used instead of $s = u_s$, which means that the action sets the *change* in speed. If u_a is chosen from some bounded interval, then the speed is a continuous function of time.

How should the transition equation be represented in this case? The set of possible values for u_a imposes a second-order constraint on x and y because double integration is needed to determine their values. By applying the phase space idea, s can be considered as a phase variable. This results in a four-dimensional phase space, in which each state is (x, y, θ, s). The state (or phase) transition equation is

$$\dot{x} = s \cos\theta \qquad\qquad \dot{\theta} = u_\omega$$
$$\dot{y} = s \sin\theta \qquad\qquad \dot{s} = u_a, \qquad\qquad (13.45)$$

which should be compared to (13.18). The action u_s was replaced by s because now speed is a phase variable, and an extra equation was added to reflect the connection between speed and acceleration.

The integrator idea can be applied again to make the unicycle orientations a continuous function of time. Let u_α denote an angular acceleration action. Let ω denote the angular velocity, which is introduced as a new state variable. This results in a five-dimensional phase space and a model called the *second-order unicycle*:

$$\dot{x} = s \cos\theta \qquad\qquad \dot{s} = u_a$$
$$\dot{y} = s \sin\theta \qquad\qquad \dot{\omega} = u_\alpha \qquad\qquad (13.46)$$
$$\dot{\theta} = \omega,$$

in which $u = (u_a, u_\alpha)$ is a two-dimensional action vector. In some contexts, s may be fixed at a constant value, which implies that u_a is fixed to $u_a = 0$.

13.2.4.2 A continuous-steering car

As another example, consider the simple car. As formulated in (13.15), the steering angle is allowed to change discontinuously. For simplicity, suppose that the speed is fixed at $s = 1$. To make the steering angle vary continuously over time, let u_ω be an action that represents the velocity of the steering angle: $\dot{\phi} = u_\omega$. The result is a four-dimensional state space, in which each state is represented as (x, y, θ, ϕ). This yields a *continuous-steering car,*

$$\dot{x} = \cos\theta \qquad\qquad \dot{\theta} = \frac{\tan\phi}{L}$$
$$\dot{y} = \sin\theta \qquad\qquad \dot{\phi} = u_\omega, \qquad\qquad (13.47)$$

in which there are two action variables, u_s and u_ω. This model was used for planning in [851].

A second integrator can be applied to make the steering angle a C^1 smooth function of time. Let ω be a state variable, and let u_α denote the angular acceleration of the steering angle. In this case, the state vector is $(x, y, \theta, \phi, \omega)$, and the state transition equation is

$$\dot{x} = \cos\theta \qquad\qquad \dot{\phi} = \omega$$
$$\dot{y} = \sin\theta \qquad\qquad \dot{\omega} = u_\alpha \qquad\qquad (13.48)$$
$$\dot{\theta} = \frac{\tan\phi}{L}.$$

Integrators can be applied any number of times to make any variables as smooth as desired. Furthermore, the rate of change in each case can be bounded due to limits on the phase variables and on the action set.

13.2.4.3 Smooth differential drive

A *second-order differential drive* model can be made by defining actions u_l and u_r that accelerate the motors, instead of directly setting their velocities. Let ω_l and ω_r denote the left and right motor angular velocities, respectively. The resulting state transition equation is

$$\dot{x} = \frac{r}{2}(\omega_l + \omega_r)\cos\theta \qquad\qquad \dot{\omega}_l = u_l$$
$$\dot{y} = \frac{r}{2}(\omega_l + \omega_r)\sin\theta \qquad\qquad \dot{\omega}_r = u_r \qquad\qquad (13.49)$$
$$\dot{\theta} = \frac{r}{L}(\omega_r - \omega_l).$$

In summary, an important technique for making existing models somewhat more realistic is to insert one or more integrators in front of any action variables. The dimension of the phase space increases with the introduction of each integrator. A single integrator forces an original action to become continuous over time. If the new action is bounded, then the rate of change of the original action is bounded in places where it is differentiable (it is Lipschitz in general, as expressed in (8.16)). Using a double integrator, the original action is forced to be C^1 smooth. Chaining more integrators on an action variable further constrains its values. In general, k integrators can be chained in front of an original action to force it to be C^{k-1} smooth and respect Lipschitz bounds.

One important limitation, however, is that to make realistic models, other variables may depend on the new phase variables. For example, if the simple car is traveling fast, then we should not be able to turn as sharply as in the case of a slow-moving car (think about how sharply you can turn the wheel while parallel parking in comparison to driving on the highway). The development of better differential models ultimately requires careful consideration of mechanics. This provides motivation for Sections 13.3 and 13.4.

13.3 Basic Newton-Euler mechanics

Mechanics is a vast and difficult subject. It is virtually impossible to provide a thorough introduction in a couple of sections. Here, the purpose instead is to overview some of the main concepts and to provide some models that may be used with the planning algorithms in Chapter 14. The presentation in this section and in Section 13.4 should hopefully stimulate some further studies in mechanics (see the suggested literature at the end of the chapter). On the other hand, if you are only interested in *using* the differential models, then you can safely skip their derivations. Just keep in mind that all differential models produced in this section end with the form $\dot{x} = f(x, u)$, which is ready to use in planning algorithms.

There are two important points to keep in mind while studying mechanics:

1. The models are based on maintaining consistency with experimental observations about how bodies behave in the physical world. These observations depend on the kind of experiment. In a particular application, many effects may be insignificant or might not even be detectable by an experiment. For example, it is difficult to detect relativistic effects using a radar gun that measures automobile speed. It is therefore important to specify any simplifying assumptions regarding the world and the kind of experiments that will be performed in it.

2. The approach is usually to express some laws that translate into constraints on the allowable velocities in the phase space. This means that implicit representations are usually obtained in mechanics, and they must be converted into parametric form. Furthermore, most treatments of mechanics do not explicitly mention action variables; these arise from the intention of *controlling* the physical world. From the perspective of mechanics, the actions can be assumed to be already determined. Thus, constraints appear as $g(\dot{x}, x) = 0$, instead of $g(\dot{x}, x, u) = 0$.

Several formulations of mechanics arrive at the same differential constraints, but from different mathematical reasoning. The remainder of this chapter overviews three schools of thought, each of which is more elegant and modern than the one before. The easiest to understand is Newton-Euler mechanics, which follows from Newton's famous laws of physics and is covered in this section. Lagrangian mechanics is covered in Section 13.4.1 and arrives at the differential constraints using very general principles of optimization on a space of functions (i.e., calculus of variations). Hamiltonian mechanics, covered in Section 13.4.4, defines a higher dimensional state space on which the differential constraints can once again be obtained by optimization.

13.3.1 The Newtonian model

The most basic formulation of mechanics goes back to Newton and Euler, and parts of it are commonly studied in basic physics courses. Consider a *world* $\mathcal{W}$ defined as in Section 3.1, except here a 1D world $\mathcal{W} = \mathbb{R}$ is allowed, in addition to 2D and 3D worlds. A notion of time is also needed. The space of motions that can be obtained in the space-time continuum can be formalized as a Galilean group [39]; however, the presentation here will utilize standard intuitive notions of time and Euclidean space. It is also assumed that any relativistic effects due to curvature of the time-space continuum are nonexistent (Newton and Euler did not know about this, and it is insignificant for most small-scale mechanical systems on or near the earth).

Inertial coordinate frames

Central to Newton-Euler mechanics is the idea that points in $\mathcal{W}$ are expressed using an *inertial coordinate frame*. Imagine locating the origin and axes of $\mathcal{W}$ somewhere in our universe. They need to be fixed in a way that does not interfere with our observations of the basic laws of motion. Imagine that we are playing racquetball in an indoor court and want to model the motion of the ball as it bounces from wall to wall. If the coordinate frame is rigidly attached to the ball, it will appear that the ball never moves; however, the walls, earth, and the rest of the universe will appear to spin wildly around the ball (imagine we have camera that points along some axis of the ball frame – you could quickly become ill trying to follow the movie). If the coordinate frame is fixed with respect to the court, then sensible measurements of the ball positions would result (the movie would also be easier to watch). For all practical purposes, we can consider this fixed coordinate frame to be inertial. Note, however, that the ball will dance around wildly if the coordinate frame is instead fixed with respect to the sun. The rotation and revolution of the earth would cause the ball to move at incredible speeds. In reality, inertial frames do not exist; nevertheless, it is a reasonable assumption for earth-based mechanical systems that an inertial frame may be fixed to the earth.

The properties that inertial frames should technically possess are 1) the laws of motions appear the same in any inertial frame, and 2) any frame that moves at constant speed without rotation with respect to an inertial frame is itself inertial. As an example of the second condition, suppose that the racquetball experiment is performed inside of a big truck that is driving along a highway. Ignoring vibrations, if the truck moves at constant speed on a straight stretch of road, then an inertial coordinate frame can be fixed to the truck itself, and the ball will appear to bounce as if the court was not moving. If, however, the road curves or the truck changes its speed, the ball will not bounce the right way. If we still believe that the frame attached to the truck is inertial, then the laws of motion will appear strange. The inertial frame must be attached to the earth in this case to correctly model the behavior of the truck and ball together.

Closed system

Another important aspect of the Newton-Euler model is that the system of bodies for which motions are modeled is *closed*, which means that no bodies other than those that are explicitly modeled can have any affect on the motions (imagine, for example, the effect if we forget to account for a black hole that is a few hundred meters away from the racquetball court).

Newton's laws

The motions of bodies are based on three laws that were experimentally verified by Newton and should hold in any inertial frame:

1. An object at rest tends to stay at rest, and an object in motion tends to stay in motion with fixed speed, unless a nonzero resultant[8] force acts upon it.

2. The relationship between a body mass m, its acceleration a, and an applied force f is $f = ma$.

3. The interaction forces between two bodies are of equal magnitude and in opposite directions.

---

[8] This is the sum of all forces acting on the point.

Based on these laws, the differential constraints on a system of moving bodies can be modeled.

13.3.2 Motions of particles

The Newton-Euler model is described in terms of particles. Each *particle* is considered as a point that has an associated mass m. Forces may act on any particle. The motion of a rigid body, covered in Section 13.3.3, is actually determined by modeling the body as a collection of particles that are stuck together. Therefore, it is helpful to first understand how particles behave.

13.3.2.1 Motion of a single particle

Consider the case of a single particle of mass m that moves in $\mathcal{W} = \mathbb{R}$. The force becomes a scalar, $f \in \mathbb{R}$. Let $q(t)$ denote the position of the particle in $\mathcal{W}$ at time t. Using this notation, acceleration is $\ddot{q}$, and Newton's second law becomes $f = m\ddot{q}$. This can be solved for $\ddot{q}$ to yield

$$\ddot{q} = f/m. \tag{13.50}$$

If f is interpreted as an action variable u, and if $m = 1$, then (13.50) is precisely the double integrator $\ddot{q} = u$ from Example 13.3. Phase variables $x_1 = q$ and $x_2 = \dot{q}$ can be introduced to obtain a state vector $x = (q, \dot{q})$. This means that for a fixed u, the motion of the particle from any initial state can be captured by a vector field on $\mathbb{R}^2$. The state transition equation is

$$\begin{aligned} \dot{x}_1 &= x_2 \\ \dot{x}_2 &= \frac{u}{m}, \end{aligned} \tag{13.51}$$

in which $x_1 = q$, $x_2 = \dot{q}$, and $u = f$. Let $U = [-f_{max}, f_{max}]$, in which f_{max} represents the maximum magnitude of force that can be applied to the particle. Forces of arbitrarily high magnitude are not allowed because this would be physically unrealistic.

Now generalize the particle motion to $\mathcal{W} = \mathbb{R}^2$ and $\mathcal{W} = \mathbb{R}^3$. Let n denote the dimension of $\mathcal{W}$, which may be $n = 2$ or $n = 3$. Let q denote the position of the particle in $\mathcal{W}$. Once again, Newton's second law yields $f = m\ddot{q}$, but in this case there are n independent equations of the form $f_i = m\ddot{q}_i$. Each of these may be considered as an independent example of the double integrator, scaled by m. Each component f_i of the force can be considered as an action variable u_i. A $2n$-dimensional state space can be defined as $x = (q, \dot{q})$. The state transition equation for $n = 2$ becomes

$$\begin{aligned} \dot{x}_1 &= x_3 & \dot{x}_3 &= u_1/m \\ \dot{x}_2 &= x_4 & \dot{x}_4 &= u_2/m, \end{aligned} \tag{13.52}$$

and for $n = 3$ it becomes

$$\begin{aligned} \dot{x}_1 &= x_4 & \dot{x}_4 &= u_1/m \\ \dot{x}_2 &= x_5 & \dot{x}_5 &= u_2/m \\ \dot{x}_3 &= x_6 & \dot{x}_6 &= u_3/m. \end{aligned} \tag{13.53}$$

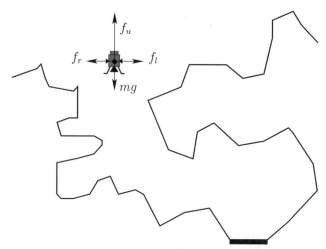

Figure 13.8: There are three thrusters on the lunar lander, and it is under the influence of lunar gravity. It is treated as a particle; therefore, no rotations are possible. Four orthogonal forces may act on the lander: Three arise from thrusters that can be switched on or off, and the remaining arises from the acceleration of gravity.

For a fixed action, these equations define vector fields on $\mathbb{R}^4$ and $\mathbb{R}^6$, respectively. The action set should also be bounded, as in the one-dimensional case. Suppose that

$$U = \{u \in \mathbb{R}^n \mid \|u\| \leq f_{max}\}. \tag{13.54}$$

Now suppose that multiple forces act on the same particle. In this case, the vector sum

$$F = \sum f \tag{13.55}$$

yields the *resultant force* over all f taken from a collection of forces. The resultant force F represents a single force that is equivalent, in terms of its effect on the particle, to the combined forces in the collection. This enables Newton's second law to be formulated as $F = m\ddot{q}$. The next two examples illustrate state transition equations that arise from a collection of forces, some of which correspond to actions.

Example 13.7 (Lunar Lander) Using the Newton-Euler model of a particle, an example will be constructed for which $X = \mathbb{R}^4$. A lunar lander is modeled as a particle with mass m in a 2D world shown in Figure 13.8. It is not allowed to rotate, implying that $C = \mathbb{R}^2$. There are three thrusters on the lander, which are on the left, right, and bottom of the lander. The forces acting on the lander are shown in Figure 13.8. The activation of each thruster is considered as a binary switch. Each has its own associated binary action variable, in which the value 1 means that the thruster is firing and 0 means the thruster is dormant. The left and right lateral thrusters provide forces of magnitude f_l and f_r, respectively, when activated (note that the left thruster provides a force to the right, and vice versa). The upward thruster, mounted to the bottom of the lander, provides a force of magnitude f_u when activated. Let g denote the scalar acceleration constant for gravity (this is approximately 1.622 m/s^2 for the moon).

From (13.55) and Newton's second law, $F = m\ddot{q}$. In the horizontal direction, this becomes

$$m\ddot{q}_1 = u_l f_l - u_r f_r, \tag{13.56}$$

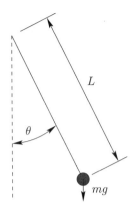

Figure 13.9: The pendulum is a simple and important example of a nonlinear system.

and in the vertical direction,

$$m\ddot{q}_2 = u_u f_u - mg. \tag{13.57}$$

Opposing forces are subtracted because only the magnitudes are given by f_l, f_r, f_u, and g. If they were instead expressed as vectors in $\mathbb{R}^2$, then they would be added.

The lunar lander model can be transformed into a four-dimensional phase space in which $x = (q_1, q_2, \dot{q}_1, \dot{q}_2)$. By replacing $\ddot{q}_1$ and $\ddot{q}_2$ with $\dot{x}_3$ and $\dot{x}_4$, respectively, (13.56) and (13.57) can be written as

$$\dot{x}_3 = \frac{1}{m}(u_l f_l - u_r f_r) \tag{13.58}$$

and

$$\dot{x}_4 = \frac{u_2 f_u}{m} - g. \tag{13.59}$$

Using $\dot{x}_1 = x_3$ and $\dot{x}_2 = x_4$, the state transition equation becomes

$$\begin{aligned} \dot{x}_1 &= x_3 & \dot{x}_3 &= \frac{f_s}{m}(u_l f_l - u_r f_r) \\ \dot{x}_2 &= x_4 & \dot{x}_4 &= \frac{u_u f_u}{m} - g, \end{aligned} \tag{13.60}$$

which is in the desired form, $\dot{x} = f(x, u)$. The action space U consists of eight elements, which indicate whether each of the three thrusters is turned on or off. Each action vector is of the form (u_l, u_r, u_u), in which each component is 0 or 1. $\blacksquare$

The next example illustrates the importance of Newton's third law.

Example 13.8 (Pendulum) A simple and very important model is the pendulum shown in Figure 13.9. Let m denote the mass of the attached particle (the string is assumed to have no mass). Let g denote the acceleration constant due to gravity. Let L denote the length of the pendulum string. Let θ denote the angular displacement of the pendulum, which characterizes the pendulum configuration. Using Newton's second law and assuming the pendulum moves in a vacuum (no wind resistance), the constraint

$$mL\ddot{\theta} = -mg\sin\theta \tag{13.61}$$

is obtained. A 2D state space can be formulated in which $x_1 = \theta$ and $x_2 = \dot{\theta}$. This leads to

$$\dot{x}_1 = x_2$$
$$\dot{x}_2 = -\frac{g}{L}\sin x_1, \tag{13.62}$$

which has no actions (the form of (13.62) is $\dot{x} = f(x)$).

A linear drag term $kL\dot{\theta}$ can be added to the model to account for wind resistance. This yields

$$mL\ddot{\theta} = -mg\sin\theta - kL\dot{\theta}, \tag{13.63}$$

which becomes

$$\dot{x}_1 = x_2$$
$$\dot{x}_2 = -\frac{g}{L}\sin x_1 - \frac{k}{m}x_2 \tag{13.64}$$

in the state space form.

Now consider applying a force u_f on the particle, in a direction perpendicular to the string. This action can be imagined as having a thruster attached to the side of the particle. This adds the term u_f to (13.63). Its sign depends on the choice of the perpendicular vector (thrust to the left or to the right). The state transition equation $\dot{x} = f(x, u)$ then becomes

$$\dot{x}_1 = x_2$$
$$\dot{x}_2 = -\frac{g}{L}\sin x_1 - \frac{k}{m}x_2 + \frac{1}{mL}u_f. \tag{13.65}$$

∎

Although sufficient information has been given to specify differential models for a particle, several other concepts are useful to introduce, especially in the extension to multiple particles and rigid bodies. The main idea is that conservation laws can be derived from Newton's laws. The *linear momentum* (or just *momentum*) d of the particle is defined as

$$d = m\dot{q}. \tag{13.66}$$

This is obtained by integrating $f = m\ddot{q}$ with respect to time.

It will be convenient when rigid-body rotations are covered to work with the *moment of momentum* (or *angular momentum*). A version of momentum that is based on moments can be obtained by first defining the *moment of force* (or *torque*) for a force f acting at a point $q \in W$ as

$$n = q \times f, \tag{13.67}$$

in which $\times$ denotes the vector cross product in $\mathbb{R}^3$. For a particle that has linear momentum d, the *moment of momentum* e is defined as

$$e = q \times d. \tag{13.68}$$

It can be shown that

$$\frac{de}{dt} = n, \tag{13.69}$$

which is equivalent to Newton's second law but is expressed in terms of momentum. For the motion of a particle in a closed system, the linear momentum and moment of momentum are *conserved* if there are no external forces acting on it. This is essentially a restatement of Newton's first law.

This idea can alternatively be expressed in terms of energy, which depends on the same variables as linear momentum. The *kinetic energy* of a particle is

$$T = \frac{1}{2} m \dot{q} \cdot \dot{q}, \tag{13.70}$$

in which $\cdot$ is the familiar inner product (or dot product). The total kinetic energy of a system of particles is obtained by summing the kinetic energies of the individual particles.

13.3.2.2 Motion of a set of particles

The concepts expressed so far naturally extend to a set of particles that move in a closed system. This provides a smooth transition to rigid bodies, which are modeled as a collection of infinitesimal particles that are "stuck together," causing forces between neighboring particles to cancel. In the present model, the particles are independently moving. If a pair of particles collides, then, by Newton's third law, they receive forces of equal magnitude and opposite directions at the instant of impact.

It can be shown that all momentum expressions extend to sums over the particles [684]. For a set of particles, the linear momentum of each can be summed to yield the linear momentum of the system as

$$D = \sum d. \tag{13.71}$$

The total external force can be determined as

$$F = \sum f_i, \tag{13.72}$$

which is a kind of resultant force for the whole system. The relationship $dD/dt = F$ holds, which extends the case of a single particle. The total mass can be summed to yield

$$M = \sum m, \tag{13.73}$$

and the *center of mass* of the system is

$$p = \frac{1}{M} \sum m q, \tag{13.74}$$

in which m and q are the mass and position of each particle, respectively. The expressions $D = M \dot{p}$ and $F = M \ddot{p}$ hold, which are the analogs of $d = m \dot{q}$ and $f = m \ddot{q}$ for a single particle.

So far the translational part of the motion has been captured; however, rotation of the system is also important. This was the motivation for introducing the moment concepts. Let the total moment of force (or total torque) be

$$N = \sum q \times f, \tag{13.75}$$

and let the moment of momentum of the system be

$$E = \sum q \times d. \tag{13.76}$$

It can be shown that $dE/dt = N$, which behaves in the same way as in the single-particle case.

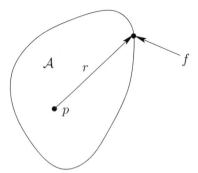

Figure 13.10: A force f acting on $\mathcal{A}$ at r produces a moment about p of $r \times f$.

The ideas given so far make a system of particles appear very much as a single particle. It is important, however, when conducting a simulation of their behavior to consider the collisions between the particles. Detecting these collisions and calculating the resulting impact forces ensures that correct motions are obtained.

As the number of particles tends to infinity, consider the limiting case of a rigid body. In this case, the particles are "sewn" together, which cancels their internal forces. It will be sufficient only to handle the forces that act on the boundary of the rigid body. The expressions for the motion of a rigid body are given in Section 13.3.3. The expressions can alternatively be obtained using other concepts, such as those in Section 13.4.

13.3.3 Motion of a rigid body

For a free-floating 3D rigid body, recall from Section 4.2.2 that its C-space $\mathcal{C}$ has six dimensions. Suppose that actions are applied to the body as external forces. These directly cause accelerations that result in second-order differential equations. By defining a state to be $(q, \dot{q})$, first-order differential equations can be obtained in a twelve-dimensional phase space X.

Let $\mathcal{A} \subseteq \mathbb{R}^3$ denote a free-floating rigid body. Let $\sigma(r)$ denote the *body density* at $r \in \mathcal{A}$. Let m denote the total mass of $\mathcal{A}$, which is defined using the density as

$$m = \int_{\mathcal{A}} \sigma(r) dr, \tag{13.77}$$

in which $dr = dr_1 dr_2 dr_3$ represents a volume element in $\mathbb{R}^3$. Let $p \in \mathbb{R}^3$ denote the *center of mass* of $\mathcal{A}$, which is defined for $p = (p_1, p_2, p_3)$ as

$$p_i = \frac{1}{m} \int_{\mathcal{A}} r_i \sigma(r) dr. \tag{13.78}$$

Suppose that a collection of external forces acts on $\mathcal{A}$ (it is assumed that all internal forces in $\mathcal{A}$ cancel each other out). Each force f acts at a point on the boundary, as shown in Figure 13.10 (note that any point along the line of force may alternatively be used). The set of forces can be combined into a single force and moment that both act about the center of mass p. Let F denote the total external force acting on $\mathcal{A}$. Let N denote the total external moment about the center of mass of $\mathcal{A}$. These are given by

$$F = \sum f \tag{13.79}$$

and

$$N = \sum r \times f \qquad (13.80)$$

for the collection of external forces. The terms F and N are often called the *resultant force* and *resultant moment* of a collection of forces. It was shown by Poinsot that every system of forces is equivalent to a single force and a moment parallel to the line of action of the force. The result is called a *wrench*, which is the force-based analog of a screw; see [684] for a nice discussion.

Actions of the form $u \in U$ can be expressed as external forces and/or moments that act on the rigid body. For example, a thruster may exert a force on the body when activated. For a given u, the total force and moment can be resolved to obtain $F(u)$ and $N(u)$.

Important frames

Three different coordinate frames will become important during the presentation:

1. **Inertial frame:** The global coordinate frame that is fixed with respect to all motions of interest.
2. **Translating frame:** A moving frame that has its origin at the center of mass of $\mathcal{A}$ and its axes aligned with the inertial frame.
3. **Body frame:** A frame that again has its origin at the center of mass of $\mathcal{A}$, but its axes are rigidly attached to $\mathcal{A}$. This is the same frame that was used to define bodies in Chapter 3.

The translational part

The state transition equation involves 12 scalar equations. Six of these are straightforward to obtain by characterizing the linear velocity. For this case, it can be imagined that the body does not rotate with respect to the inertial frame. The linear momentum is $D = m\dot{p}$, and Newton's second law implies that

$$F(u) = \frac{dD}{dt} = m\ddot{p}. \qquad (13.81)$$

This immediately yields half of the state transition equation by solving for $\ddot{p}$. This yields a 3D version of the double integrator in Example 13.3, scaled by m. Let (p_1, p_2, p_3) denote the coordinates of p. Let (v_1, v_2, v_3) denote the linear velocity the center of mass. Three scalar equations of the state transition equation are $\dot{p}_i = v_i$ for $i = 1, 2, 3$. Three more are obtained as $\dot{v}_i = F_i(u)/m$ for $i = 1, 2, 3$. If there are no moments and the body is not rotating with respect to the inertial frame, then these six equations are sufficient to describe its motion. This may occur for a spacecraft that is initially at rest, and its thrusters apply a total force only through the center of mass.

The rotational part

The six equations derived so far are valid even if $\mathcal{A}$ rotates with respect to the inertial frame. They are just the translational part of the motion. The rotational part can be decoupled from the translational part by using the translating frame. All translational aspects of the motion have already been considered. Imagine that $\mathcal{A}$ is only rotating while its center of mass remains fixed. Once the rotational part of the motion has been determined, it can be combined with the translational part by simply viewing things from the inertial frame. Therefore, the motion of $\mathcal{A}$ is now considered with respect to the translating frame, which makes it appear to be pure rotation.

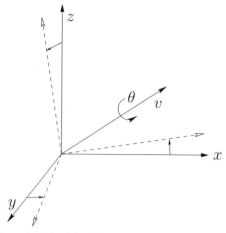

Figure 13.11: The angular velocity is defined as a rotation rate of the coordinate frame about an axis.

Unfortunately, characterizing the rotational part of the motion is substantially more complicated than the translation case and the 2D rotation case. This should not be surprising in light of the difficulties associated with 3D rotations in Chapters 3 and 4.

Following from Newton's second law, the change in the moment of momentum is

$$N(u) = \frac{dE}{dt}. \tag{13.82}$$

The remaining challenge is to express the right-hand side of (13.82) in a form that can be inserted into the state transition equation.

Differential rotations

To express the change in the moment of momentum in detail, the concept of a differential rotation is needed. In the plane, it is straightforward to define $\omega = \dot{\theta}$; however, for $SO(3)$, it is more complicated. One choice is to define derivatives with respect to yaw-pitch-roll variables, but this leads to distortions and singularities, which are problematic for the Newton-Euler formulation. Instead, a differential rotation is defined as shown in Figure 13.11. Let v denote a unit vector in $\mathbb{R}^3$, and let θ denote a rotation that is analogous to the 2D case. Let ω denote the angular velocity vector,

$$\omega = v\frac{d\theta}{dt}. \tag{13.83}$$

This provides a natural expression for angular velocity.[9] The change in a rotation matrix R with respect to time is

$$\dot{R} = \omega \times R. \tag{13.84}$$

This relationship can be used to derive expressions that relate ω to yaw-pitch-roll angles or quaternions. For example, using the yaw-pitch-roll matrix (3.42) the conversion from

---

[9] One important issue to be aware of is that the integral of ω is not path-invariant (see Example 2.15 of [994]).

ω to the change yaw, pitch, and roll angles is

$$
\begin{pmatrix} \dot{\gamma} \\ \dot{\beta} \\ \dot{\alpha} \end{pmatrix} = \frac{1}{\cos \beta} \begin{pmatrix} \cos \alpha & \sin \alpha & 0 \\ -\sin \alpha \cos \beta & \cos \alpha \cos \beta & 0 \\ \cos \alpha \sin \beta & \sin \alpha \sin \beta & -\cos \beta \end{pmatrix} \begin{pmatrix} \omega_1 \\ \omega_2 \\ \omega_3 \end{pmatrix}. \tag{13.85}
$$

Inertia matrix

An *inertia matrix* (also called an *inertia tensor* or *inertia operator*) will be derived by considering $\mathcal{A}$ as a collection of particles that are rigidly attached together (all contact forces between them cancel due to Newton's third law). The expression $\sigma(r)dr$ in (13.77) represents the mass of an infinitesimal particle of $\mathcal{A}$. The *moment of momentum* of the infinitesimal particle is $r \times \dot{r}\sigma(r)dr$. This means that the total moment of momentum of $\mathcal{A}$ is

$$
E = \int_{\mathcal{A}(q)} (r \times \dot{r})\, \sigma(r) dr. \tag{13.86}
$$

By using the fact that $\dot{r} = \omega \times r$, the expression becomes

$$
E = \int_{\mathcal{A}(q)} r \times (\omega \times r)\, \sigma(r) dr. \tag{13.87}
$$

Observe that r now appears twice in the integrand. By doing some algebraic manipulations, ω can be removed from the integrand, and a function that is quadratic in the r variables is obtained (since r is a vector, the function is technically a quadratic form). The first step is to apply the identity $a \times (b \times c) = (a \cdot c)b - (a \cdot b)c$ to obtain

$$
E = \int_{\mathcal{A}(q)} \big((r \cdot r)\omega - (r \cdot \omega)r\big)\sigma(r)dr. \tag{13.88}
$$

The angular velocity can be moved to the right to obtain

$$
E = \left(\int_{\mathcal{A}(q)} \big((r \cdot r)I_3 - rr^T\big)\sigma(r)dr \right) \omega, \tag{13.89}
$$

in which the integral now occurs over a 3×3 matrix and I_3 is the 3×3 identity matrix.

Let I be called the *inertia matrix* and be defined as

$$
I(q) = \left(\int_{\mathcal{A}(q)} \big((r \cdot r)I_3 - rr^T\big)\sigma(r)dr \right). \tag{13.90}
$$

Using the definition,

$$
E = I\omega. \tag{13.91}
$$

This simplification enables a concise expression of (13.82) as

$$
N(u) = \frac{dE}{dt} = \frac{d(I\omega)}{dt} = I\frac{d\omega}{dt} + \frac{dI}{dt}\omega, \tag{13.92}
$$

which makes use of the chain rule.

Simplifying the inertia matrix

Now the inertia matrix will be considered more carefully. It is a symmetric 3×3 matrix, which can be expressed as

$$I(q) = \begin{pmatrix} I_{11}(q) & I_{12}(q) & I_{13}(q) \\ I_{12}(q) & I_{22}(q) & I_{23}(q) \\ I_{13}(q) & I_{23}(q) & I_{33}(q) \end{pmatrix}. \qquad (13.93)$$

For each $i \in \{1, 2, 3\}$, the entry $I_{ii}(q)$ is called a *moment of inertia*. The three cases are

$$I_{11}(q) = \int_{A(q)} (r_2^2 + r_3^2)\sigma(r)dr, \qquad (13.94)$$

$$I_{22}(q) = \int_{A(q)} (r_1^2 + r_3^2)\sigma(r)dr, \qquad (13.95)$$

and

$$I_{33}(q) = \int_{A(q)} (r_1^2 + r_2^2)\sigma(r)dr. \qquad (13.96)$$

The remaining entries are defined as follows. For each $i, j \in \{1, 2, 3\}$ such that $i \neq j$, the *product of inertia* is

$$H_{ij}(q) = \int_{A(q)} r_i r_j \sigma(r)dr, \qquad (13.97)$$

and $I_{ij}(q) = -H_{ij}(q)$.

One problem with the formulation so far is that the inertia matrix changes as the body rotates because all entries depend on the orientation q. Recall that it was derived by considering A as a collection of infinitesimal particles in the translating frame. It is possible, however, to express the inertia matrix in the body frame of A. In this case, the inertia matrix can be denoted as I because it does not depend on the orientation of A with respect to the translational frame. The original inertia matrix is then recovered by applying a rotation that relates the body frame to the translational frame: $I(q) = RI$, in which R is a rotation matrix. It can be shown (see Equation (2.91) and Section 3.2 of [994]) that after performing this substitution, (13.92) simplifies to

$$N(u) = I\frac{d\omega}{dt} + \omega \times (I\omega). \qquad (13.98)$$

The body frame of A must have its origin at the center of mass p; however, its orientation has not been constrained. For different orientations, different inertia matrices will be obtained. Since I captures the physical characteristics of A, any two inertia matrices differ only by a rotation. This means for a given A, all inertia matrices that can be defined by different body frame orientations have the same eigenvalues and eigenvectors. Consider the positive definite quadratic form $x^T I x = 1$, which represents the equation of an ellipsoid. A standard technique in linear algebra is to compute the principle axes of an ellipsoid, which turn out to be the eigenvectors of I. The lengths of the ellipsoid axes are given by the eigenvalues. An axis-aligned expression of the ellipsoid can be obtained by defining $x' = Rx$, in which R is the matrix formed by columns of eigenvectors. Therefore, there exists an orientation of the body frame in which the inertia matrix simplifies to

$$I = \begin{pmatrix} I_{11} & 0 & 0 \\ 0 & I_{22} & 0 \\ 0 & 0 & I_{33} \end{pmatrix} \tag{13.99}$$

and the diagonal elements are the eigenvalues. If the body happens to be an ellipsoid, the principle axes correspond to the ellipsoid axes. Moment of inertia tables are given in many texts [693]; in these cases, the principle axes are usually chosen as the axis of the body frame because they result in the simplest expression of I.

Completing the state transition equation

Assume that the body frame of $\mathcal{A}$ aligns with the principle axes. The remaining six equations of motion can finally be given in a nice form. Using (13.99), the expression (13.98) reduces to [684]

$$\begin{pmatrix} N_1(u) \\ N_2(u) \\ N_3(u) \end{pmatrix} = \begin{pmatrix} I_{11} & 0 & 0 \\ 0 & I_{22} & 0 \\ 0 & 0 & I_{33} \end{pmatrix} \begin{pmatrix} \dot{\omega}_1 \\ \dot{\omega}_2 \\ \dot{\omega}_3 \end{pmatrix} + $$
$$\begin{pmatrix} 0 & -\omega_3 & \omega_2 \\ \omega_3 & 0 & -\omega_1 \\ -\omega_2 & \omega_1 & 0 \end{pmatrix} \begin{pmatrix} I_{11} & 0 & 0 \\ 0 & I_{22} & 0 \\ 0 & 0 & I_{33} \end{pmatrix} \begin{pmatrix} \omega_1 \\ \omega_2 \\ \omega_3 \end{pmatrix}. \tag{13.100}$$

Multiplying out (13.100) yields

$$N_1(u) = I_{11}\dot{\omega}_1 + (I_{33} - I_{22})\omega_2\omega_3$$
$$N_2(u) = I_{22}\dot{\omega}_2 + (I_{11} - I_{33})\omega_3\omega_1 \tag{13.101}$$
$$N_3(u) = I_{33}\dot{\omega}_3 + (I_{22} - I_{11})\omega_1\omega_2.$$

To prepare for the state transition equation form, solving for $\dot{\omega}$ yields

$$\dot{\omega}_1 = \big(N_1(u) + (I_{22} - I_{33})\omega_2\omega_3\big)/I_{11}$$
$$\dot{\omega}_2 = \big(N_2(u) + (I_{33} - I_{11})\omega_3\omega_1\big)/I_{22} \tag{13.102}$$
$$\dot{\omega}_3 = \big(N_3(u) + (I_{11} - I_{22})\omega_1\omega_2\big)/I_{33}.$$

One final complication is that ω needs to be related to angles that are used to express an element of $SO(3)$. The mapping between these depends on the particular parameterization of $SO(3)$. Suppose that quaternions of the form (a, b, c, d) are used to express rotation. Recall that a can be recovered once b, c, and d are given using $a^2 + b^2 + c^2 + d^2 = 1$. The relationship between ω and the time derivatives of the quaternion components is obtained by using (13.84) (see [693], p. 433):

$$\dot{b} = \omega_3 c - \omega_2 d$$
$$\dot{c} = \omega_1 d - \omega_3 b \tag{13.103}$$
$$\dot{d} = \omega_2 b - \omega_1 c.$$

This finally completes the specification of $\dot{x} = f(x, u)$, in which

$$x = (p_1, p_2, p_3, v_1, v_2, v_3, b, c, d, \omega_1, \omega_2, \omega_3) \tag{13.104}$$

is a twelve-dimensional phase vector. For convenience, the full specification of the state transition equation is

$$
\begin{aligned}
\dot{p}_1 &= v_1 & \dot{b} &= \omega_3 c - \omega_2 d \\
\dot{p}_2 &= v_2 & \dot{c} &= \omega_1 d - \omega_3 b \\
\dot{p}_3 &= v_3 & \dot{d} &= \omega_2 b - \omega_1 c \qquad (13.105) \\
\dot{v}_1 &= F_1(u)/m & \dot{\omega}_1 &= \big(N_1(u) + (I_{22} - I_{33})\omega_2\omega_3\big)/I_{11} \\
\dot{v}_2 &= F_2(u)/m & \dot{\omega}_2 &= \big(N_2(u) + (I_{33} - I_{11})\omega_3\omega_1\big)/I_{22} \\
\dot{v}_3 &= F_3(u)/m & \dot{\omega}_3 &= \big(N_3(u) + (I_{11} - I_{22})\omega_1\omega_2\big)/I_{33}.
\end{aligned}
$$

The relationship between inertia matrices and ellipsoids is actually much deeper than presented here. The kinetic energy due to rotation only is elegantly expressed as

$$
T = \tfrac{1}{2}\omega^T I \omega. \qquad (13.106)
$$

A fascinating interpretation of rotational motion in the absence of external forces was given by Poinsot [39, 684]. As the body rotates, its motion is equivalent to that of the inertia ellipsoid, given by (13.106), rolling (without sliding) down a plane with normal vector $I\omega$ in $\mathbb{R}^3$.

The 2D case

The dynamics of a 2D rigid body that moves in the plane can be handled as a special case of a 3D body. Let $\mathcal{A} \subset \mathbb{R}^2$ be a 2D body, expressed in its body frame. The total external forces acting on $\mathcal{A}$ can be expressed in terms of a two-dimensional total force through the center of mass and a moment through the center of mass. The phase space for this model has six dimensions. Three come from the degrees of freedom of $SE(2)$, two come from linear velocity, and one comes from angular velocity.

The translational part is once again expressed as

$$
F(u) = \frac{dD}{dt} = m\ddot{p}. \qquad (13.107)
$$

This provides four components of the state transition equation.

All rotations must occur with respect to the z-axis in the 2D formulation. This means that the angular velocity ω is a scalar value. Let θ denote the orientation of $\mathcal{A}$. The relationship between ω and θ is given by $\dot{\theta} = \omega$, which yields one more component of the state transition equation.

At this point, only one component remains. Recall (13.92). By inspecting (13.101) it can be seen that the inertia-based terms vanish. In that formulation, ω_3 is equivalent to the scalar ω for the 2D case. The final terms of all three equations vanish because $\omega_1 = \omega_2 = 0$. The first terms of the first two equations also vanish because $\dot{\omega}_1 = \dot{\omega}_2 = 0$. This leaves $N_3(u) = I_{33}\dot{\omega}_3$. In the 2D case, this can be notationally simplified to

$$
N(u) = \frac{dE}{dt} = \frac{d(I\omega)}{dt} = I\frac{d\omega}{dt} = I\dot{\omega}, \qquad (13.108)
$$

in which I is now a scalar. Note that for the 3D case, the angular velocity can change, even when $N(u) = 0$. In the 2D case, however, this is not possible. In both cases, the moment of momentum is conserved; in the 2D case, this happens to imply that ω is fixed. The sixth component of the state transition equation is obtained by solving (13.108) for $\dot{\omega}$.

The state transition equation for a 2D rigid body in the plane is therefore

$$\dot{p}_1 = v_1 \qquad\qquad \dot{v}_1 = F_1(u)/m$$
$$\dot{p}_2 = v_2 \qquad\qquad \dot{v}_2 = F_2(u)/m \qquad (13.109)$$
$$\dot{\theta} = \omega \qquad\qquad \dot{\omega} = N(u)/I.$$

A car with tire skidding

This section concludes by introducing a car model that considers it as a skidding rigid body in the plane. This model was suggested by Jim Bernard. The C-space is $\mathcal{C} = \mathbb{R}^2 \times \mathbb{S}^1$, in which $q = (x, y, \theta)$. Suppose that as the car moves at high speeds, the tires are able to skid laterally in a direction perpendicular to the main axis of the car (i.e., parallel to the rear axle). Let ω denote the angular velocity of the car. Let v denote the lateral skidding velocity, which is another state variable. This results in a five-dimensional state space in which each state is a vector of the form $(x, y, \theta, \omega, v)$.

The position of the rear axle center can be expressed as

$$\dot{x} = s\cos\theta - v\sin\theta$$
$$\dot{y} = s\sin\theta + v\cos\theta, \qquad (13.110)$$

which yields two components of the state transition equation. Let $\omega = \dot{\theta}$ denote the angular velocity, which yields one more component of the state transition equation. This leaves only two equations, which are derived from 2D rigid body mechanics (which will be covered in Section 13.3.3). The state transition is

$$\dot{x} = s\cos\theta - v\sin\theta$$
$$\dot{y} = s\sin\theta + v\cos\theta$$
$$\dot{\theta} = \omega \qquad (13.111)$$
$$\dot{\omega} = (af_f - bf_r)/I$$
$$\dot{v} = -s\omega + (f_f + f_r)/m,$$

in which f_f and f_r are the front and rear tire forces, m is the mass, I is the moment of inertia, and a and b are the distances from the center of mass to the front and rear axles, respectively. The first force is

$$f_f = c_f\big((v + a\omega)/s + \phi\big), \qquad (13.112)$$

in which c_f is the front cornering stiffness, and ϕ is the steering angle. The second force is

$$f_r = c_r(v - b\omega)/s, \qquad (13.113)$$

in which c_r is the rear cornering stiffness. The steering angle can be designated as an action variable: $u_\phi = \phi$. An integrator can be placed in front of the speed to allow accelerations. This increases the state space dimension by one.

Reasonable values for the parameters for an automotive application are: $m = 1460$ kg, $c_f = 17000$, $c_r = 20000$, $a = 1.2$ m, $b = 1.5$ m, $I = 2170$ kg/m^2, and $s = 27$ m/sec. This state transition equation involves a linear tire skidding model, which is a poor approximation in many applications. Nonlinear tire models provide better approximations to the actual behavior of cars [93]. For a thorough introduction to the dynamics of cars, see [825].

13.4 Advanced mechanics concepts

Newton-Euler mechanics has the advantage that it starts with very basic principles, but it has frustrating restrictions that make modeling more difficult for complicated mechanical systems. One of the main limitations is that all laws must be expressed in terms of an inertial frame with orthogonal axes. This section introduces the basic ideas of Lagrangian and Hamiltonian mechanics, which remove these restrictions by reducing mechanics to finding an optimal path using any coordinate neighborhood of the C-space. The optimality criterion is expressed in terms of energy. The resulting techniques can be applied on any coordinate neighborhood of a smooth manifold. The Lagrangian formulation is usually best for determining the motions of one or more bodies. Section 13.4.1 introduces the basic Lagrangian concepts based on the calculus of variations. Section 13.4.2 presents a general form of the Euler-Lagrange equations, which is useful for determining the motions of numerous dynamical systems, including chains of bodies. The Lagrangian is also convenient for systems that involve additional differential constraints, such as friction or rolling wheels. These cases are briefly covered in Section 13.4.3. The Hamiltonian formulation in Section 13.4.4 is based on a special phase space and provides an alternative to the Lagrangian formulation. The technique generalizes to Pontryagin's minimum principle, a powerful optimal control technique that is covered in Section 15.2.3.

13.4.1 Lagrangian mechanics

13.4.1.1 Calculus of variations

Lagrangian mechanics is based on the *calculus of variations*, which is the subject of optimization over a space of paths. One of the most famous variational problems involves constraining a particle to travel along a curve (imagine that the particle slides along a frictionless track). The problem is to find the curve for which the ball travels from one point to the other, starting at rest, and being accelerated only by gravity. The solution is a cycloid function called the *Brachistochrone curve* [844]. Before this problem is described further, recall the classical optimization problem from calculus in which the task is to find extremal values (minima and maxima) of a function. Let $\tilde{x}$ denote a smooth function from $\mathbb{R}$ to $\mathbb{R}$, and let $x(t)$ denote its value for any $t \in \mathbb{R}$. From standard calculus, the extremal values of $\tilde{x}$ are all $t \in \mathbb{R}$ for which $\dot{x} = 0$. Suppose that at some $t' \in \mathbb{R}$, $\tilde{x}$ achieves a local minimum. To serve as a local minimum, tiny perturbations of t' should result in larger function values. Thus, there exists some $d > 0$ such that $x(t' + \epsilon) > x(t')$ for any $\epsilon \in [-d, d]$. Each ϵ represents a possible perturbation of t'.

The calculus of variations addresses a harder problem in which optimization occurs over a space of functions. For each function, a value is assigned by a criterion called a *functional*.[10] A procedure analogous to taking the derivative of the function and setting it to zero will be performed. This will be arrived at by considering tiny perturbations of an entire function, as opposed to the ϵ perturbations mentioned above. Each perturbation is itself a function, which is called a *variation*. For a function to minimize a functional, any small enough perturbation of it must yield a larger functional value. In the case of optimizing a function of one variable, there are only two directions for the perturbation: $\pm \epsilon$. See Figure 13.12. In the calculus of variations, there are many different "directions" because of the uncountably infinite number of ways to construct a small variation function that

---

[10] This is the reason why a cost *functional* has been used throughout the book. It is a function on a space of functions.

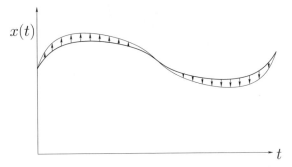

Figure 13.12: The variation is a "small" function that is added to $\tilde{x}$ to perturb it.

perturbs the original function (the set of all variations is an infinite-dimensional function space; recall Example 8.5).

Let $\tilde{x}$ denote a smooth function from $T = [t_0, t_1]$ into $\mathbb{R}$. The functional is defined by integrating a function over the domain of $\tilde{x}$. Let L be a smooth, real-valued function of three variables, a, b, and c.[11] The arguments of L may be any $a, b \in \mathbb{R}$ and $c \in T$ to yield $L(a, b, c)$, but each has a special interpretation. For some smooth function $\tilde{x}$, L is used to evaluate it at a particular $t \in T$ to obtain $L(x, \dot{x}, t)$. A *functional* Φ is constructed using L to evaluate the whole function $\tilde{x}$ as

$$\Phi(\tilde{x}) = \int_T L(x(t), \dot{x}(t), t) dt. \tag{13.114}$$

The problem is to select an $\tilde{x}$ that optimizes Φ. The approach is to take the derivative of Φ and set it equal to zero, just as in standard calculus; however, differentiating Φ with respect to $\tilde{x}$ is not standard calculus. This usually requires special conditions on the class of possible functions (e.g., smoothness) and on the vector space of variations, which are implicitly assumed to hold for the problems considered in this section.

Example 13.9 (Shortest-Path Functional) As an example of a functional, consider

$$L(x, \dot{x}, t) = \sqrt{1 + \dot{x}^2}. \tag{13.115}$$

When evaluated on a function $\tilde{x}$, this yields the arc length of the path. ■

Another example of a functional has already been seen in the context of motion planning. The cost functional (8.39) assigns a cost to a path taken through the state space. This provided a natural way to formulate optimal path planning. A discrete, approximate version was given by (7.26).

Let h be a smooth function over T, and let $\epsilon \in \mathbb{R}$ be a small constant. Consider the function defined as $x(t) + \epsilon h(t)$ for all $t \in [0, 1]$. If $\epsilon = 0$, then (13.114) remains the same. As ϵ is increased or decreased, then $\Phi(\tilde{x} + \epsilon h)$ may change. The function h is like the "direction" in a directional derivative. If for any smooth function h, their exists some $\epsilon > 0$ such that the value $\Phi(\tilde{x} + \epsilon h)$ increases, then $\tilde{x}$ is called an *extremal* of Φ. Any small perturbation to $\tilde{x}$ causes the value of Φ to increase. Therefore, $\tilde{x}$ behaves like a local minimum in a standard optimization problem.

---

[11] Unfortunately, L is used here to represent a cost function, on which a functional Φ will be based. This conflicts with using l as a cost function and L as the functional in motion planning formulations. This notational collision remains because L is standard notation for the Lagrangian. Be careful to avoid confusion.

Let $g = \epsilon h$ for some $\epsilon > 0$ and function h. The differential of a functional can be approximated as [39]

$$\Phi(\tilde{x} + g) - \Phi(\tilde{x}) = \int_T \Big(L(x(t) + g(t), \dot{x}(t) + \dot{g}(t), t) - L(x(t), \dot{x}(t), t) \Big) dt + \cdots$$

$$= \int_T \left(\frac{\partial L}{\partial x} g + \frac{\partial L}{\partial \dot{x}} \dot{g} \right) dt + \cdots \qquad (13.116)$$

$$= \int_T \left(\frac{\partial L}{\partial x} g - \frac{d}{dt} \frac{\partial L}{\partial \dot{x}} g \right) dt + \left(\frac{\partial L}{\partial \dot{x}} g \right) \Big|_{t_0}^{t_1} + \cdots,$$

in which $\cdots$ represents higher order terms that will vanish in the limit. The last step follows from integration by parts:

$$\left(\frac{\partial L}{\partial \dot{x}} g \right) \Big|_{t_0}^{t_1} = \int_T \frac{\partial L}{\partial \dot{x}} \dot{g} dt + \int_T \frac{d}{dt} \frac{\partial L}{\partial \dot{x}} h dt, \qquad (13.117)$$

which is just $uv = \int v \, du + \int u \, dv$. Consider the value of (13.116) as ϵ becomes small, and assume that $h(t_0) = h(t_1) = 0$. For $\tilde{x}$ to be an extremal function, the change expressed in (13.116) should tend to zero as the variations approach zero. Based on further technical assumptions, including the *Fundamental Lemma of the Calculus of Variations* (see Section 12 of [39]), the *Euler-Lagrange equation*,

$$\frac{d}{dt} \frac{\partial L}{\partial \dot{x}} - \frac{\partial L}{\partial x} = 0, \qquad (13.118)$$

is obtained as a necessary condition for $\tilde{x}$ to be an extremum. Intuition can be gained by studying the last line of (13.116). The integral attains a zero value precisely when (13.118) is satisfied. The other terms vanish because $h(t_0) = h(t_1) = 0$, and higher order terms disappear in the limit process.

The partial derivatives of L with respect to $\dot{x}$ and x are defined using standard calculus. The derivative $\partial L / \partial \dot{x}$ is evaluated by treating $\dot{x}$ as an ordinary variable (i.e., as $\partial L / \partial b$ when the variables are named as in $L(a, b, c)$). Following this, the derivative of $\partial L / \partial \dot{x}$ with respect to t is taken. To illustrate this process, consider the following example.

Example 13.10 (A Simple Variational Problem)   Let L be a functional defined as

$$L(x, \dot{x}, t) = x^3 + \dot{x}^2. \qquad (13.119)$$

The partial derivatives with respect to x and $\dot{x}$ are

$$\frac{\partial L}{\partial x} = 3x^2 \qquad (13.120)$$

and

$$\frac{\partial L}{\partial \dot{x}} = 2\dot{x}. \qquad (13.121)$$

Taking the time derivative of (13.121) yields

$$\frac{d}{dt} \frac{\partial L}{\partial \dot{x}} = 2\ddot{x} \qquad (13.122)$$

Substituting these into the Euler-Lagrange equation (13.118) yields

$$\frac{d}{dt} \frac{\partial L}{\partial \dot{x}} - \frac{\partial L}{\partial x} = 2\ddot{x} - 3x^2 = 0. \qquad (13.123)$$

This represents a second-order differential constraint that constrains the acceleration as $\ddot{x} = 3x^2/2$. By constructing a 2D phase space, the constraint could be expressed using first-order differential equations. ∎

13.4.1.2 Hamilton's principle of least action

Now sufficient background has been given to return to the dynamics of mechanical systems. The path through the C-space of a system of bodies can be expressed as the solution to a calculus of variations problem that optimizes the difference between kinetic and potential energy. The calculus of variations principles generalize to any coordinate neighborhood of $\mathcal{C}$. In this case, the Euler-Lagrange equation is

$$\frac{d}{dt}\frac{\partial L}{\partial \dot{q}} - \frac{\partial L}{\partial q} = 0, \tag{13.124}$$

in which q is a vector of n coordinates. It is actually n scalar equations of the form

$$\frac{d}{dt}\frac{\partial L}{\partial \dot{q}_i} - \frac{\partial L}{\partial q_i} = 0. \tag{13.125}$$

The coming presentation will use (13.124) to obtain a phase transition equation. This will be derived by optimizing a functional defined as the change in kinetic and potential energy. Kinetic energy for particles and rigid bodies was defined in Section 13.3.1. In general, the kinetic energy function must be a quadratic function of $\dot{q}$. Its definition can be interpreted as an inner product on $\mathcal{C}$, which causes $\mathcal{C}$ to become a *Riemannian manifold* [158]. This gives the manifold a notion of the "angle" between velocity vectors and leads to well-defined notions of curvature and shortest paths called *geodesics*. Let $K(q, \dot{q})$ denote the kinetic energy, expressed using the manifold coordinates, which always takes the form

$$K(q, \dot{q}) = \tfrac{1}{2}\dot{q}^T M(q)\dot{q}, \tag{13.126}$$

in which $M(q)$ is an $n \times n$ matrix called the *mass matrix* or *inertia matrix*.

The next step is to define potential energy. A system is called *conservative* if the forces acting on a point depend only on the point's location, and the work done by the force along a path depends only on the endpoints of the path. The total energy is conserved under the motion of a conservative system. In this case, there exists a *potential function* $\phi : W \to \mathbb{R}$ such that $F = \partial\phi/\partial p$, for any $p \in W$. Let $V(q)$ denote the total *potential energy* of a collection of bodies, placed at configuration q.

It will be assumed that the dynamics are time-invariant. *Hamilton's principle of least action* states that the trajectory, $\tilde{q} : T \to \mathcal{C}$, of a mechanical system coincides with extremals of the functional,

$$\Phi(\tilde{q}) = \int_T \Big(K(q(t), \dot{q}(t)) - V(q(t)) \Big) dt, \tag{13.127}$$

using *any* coordinate neighborhood of $\mathcal{C}$. The principle can be seen for the case of $\mathcal{C} = \mathbb{R}^3$ by expressing Newton's second law in a way that looks like (13.124) [39]:

$$\frac{d}{dt}(m\dot{q}) - \frac{\partial V}{\partial q} = 0, \tag{13.128}$$

in which the force is replaced by the derivative of potential energy. This suggests applying the Euler-Lagrange equation to the functional

$$L(q, \dot{q}) = K(q, \dot{q}) - V(q), \tag{13.129}$$

in which it has been assumed that the dynamics are time-invariant; hence, $L(q, \dot{q}, t) = L(q, \dot{q})$. Applying the Euler-Lagrange equation to (13.127) yields the extremals.

The advantage of the Lagrangian formulation is that the C-space does not have to be $\mathcal{C} = \mathbb{R}^3$, described in an inertial frame. The Euler-Lagrange equation gives a necessary condition for the motions in any C-space of a mechanical system. The conditions can be expressed in terms of any coordinate neighborhood, as opposed to orthogonal coordinate systems, which are required by the Newton-Euler formulation. In mechanics literature, the q variables are often referred to as *generalized coordinates*. This simply means the coordinates given by any coordinate neighborhood of a smooth manifold.

Thus, the special form of (13.124) that uses (13.129) yields the appropriate constraints on the motion:

$$\frac{d}{dt}\frac{\partial L}{\partial \dot{q}} - \frac{\partial L}{\partial q} = \frac{d}{dt}\frac{\partial K(q, \dot{q})}{\partial \dot{q}} - \frac{\partial K(q, \dot{q})}{\partial q} + \frac{\partial V(q)}{\partial q} = 0. \tag{13.130}$$

Recall that this represents n equations, one for each coordinate q_i. Since $K(q, \dot{q})$ does not depend on time, the d/dt operator simply replaces $\dot{q}$ by $\ddot{q}$ in the calculated expression for $\partial K(q, \dot{q})/\partial \dot{q}$. The appearance of $\ddot{q}$ seems appropriate because the resulting differential equations are second-order, which is consistent with Newton-Euler mechanics.

Example 13.11 (A Falling Particle) Suppose that a particle with mass m is falling in $\mathbb{R}^3$. Let (q_1, q_2, q_3) denote the position of the particle. Let g denote the acceleration constant of gravity in the $-q_3$ direction. The potential energy is $V(q) = mgq_3$. The kinetic energy is

$$K(q, \dot{q}) = \tfrac{1}{2}m\dot{q} \cdot \dot{q} = \tfrac{1}{2}m(\dot{q}_1^2 + \dot{q}_2^2 + \dot{q}_3^2). \tag{13.131}$$

The Lagrangian is

$$L(q, \dot{q}) = K(q, \dot{q}) - V(q) = \tfrac{1}{2}m(\dot{q}_1^2 + \dot{q}_2^2 + \dot{q}_3^2) - mgq_3 = 0. \tag{13.132}$$

To obtain the differential constraints on the motion of the particle, use (13.130). For each i from 1 to 3,

$$\frac{d}{dt}\frac{\partial L}{\partial \dot{q}} = \frac{d}{dt}(m\dot{q}_i) = m\ddot{q}_i \tag{13.133}$$

Since $K(q, \dot{q})$ does not depend on q, the derivative $\partial K/\partial q_i = 0$ for each i. The derivatives with respect to potential energy are

$$\frac{\partial V}{\partial q_1} = 0 \qquad \frac{\partial V}{\partial q_2} = 0 \qquad \frac{\partial V}{\partial q_3} = mg. \tag{13.134}$$

Substitution into (13.130) yields three equations:

$$m\ddot{q}_1 = 0 \qquad m\ddot{q}_2 = 0 \qquad m\ddot{q}_3 + mg = 0. \tag{13.135}$$

These indicate that acceleration only occurs in the $-q_3$ direction, and this is due to gravity. The equations are consistent with Newton's laws. As usual, a six-dimensional phase space can be defined to obtain first-order differential constraints. ∎

The "least" part of Hamilton's principle is actually a misnomer. It is technically only a principle of "extremal" action because (13.130) can also yield motions that maximize the functional.

13.4.1.3 Applying actions

Up to this point, it has been assumed that no actions are applied to the mechanical system. This is the way the Euler-Lagrange equation usually appears in physics because the goal is to predict motion, rather than control it. Let $u \in \mathbb{R}^n$ denote an action vector. Actions can be applied to the Lagrangian formulation as *generalized forces* that "act" on the right side of the Euler-Lagrange equation. This results in

$$\frac{d}{dt}\frac{\partial L}{\partial \dot{q}} - \frac{\partial L}{\partial q} = u. \tag{13.136}$$

The actions force the mechanical system to deviate from its usual behavior. In some instances, the true actions may be expressed in terms of other variables, and then u is obtained by a transformation (recall transforming action variables for the differential drive vehicle of Section 13.1.2). In this case, u may be replaced in (13.136) by $\phi(u)$ for some transformation ϕ. In this case, the dimension of u need not be n.

13.4.1.4 Procedure for deriving the state transition equation

The following general procedure can be followed to derive the differential model using Lagrangian mechanics on a coordinate neighborhood of a smooth n-dimensional manifold:

1. Determine the degrees of freedom of the system and define the appropriate n-dimensional smooth manifold $\mathcal{C}$.

2. Express the kinetic energy as a quadratic form in the configuration velocity components:

$$K(q, \dot{q}) = \frac{1}{2}\dot{q}^T M(q)\dot{q} = \frac{1}{2}\sum_{i=1}^{n}\sum_{j=1}^{n} m_{ij}(q)\dot{q}_i\dot{q}_j. \tag{13.137}$$

3. Express the potential energy $V(q)$.

4. Let $L(q, \dot{q}) = K(q, \dot{q}) - V(q)$ be the Lagrangian function, and use the Euler-Lagrange equation (13.130) to determine the differential constraints.

5. Convert to phase space form by letting $x = (q, \dot{q})$. If possible, solve for $\dot{x}$ to obtain $\dot{x} = f(x, u)$.

Example 13.12 (2D Rigid Body Revisited) The equations in (13.109) can be alternatively derived using the Euler-Lagrange equation. Let $\mathcal{C} = \mathbb{R}^2 \times \mathbb{S}^1$, and let $(q_1, q_2, q_3) = (x, y, \theta)$ to conform to the notation used to express the Lagrangian.

The kinetic energy is the sum of kinetic energies due to linear and angular velocities, respectively. This yields

$$K(q, \dot{q}) = \tfrac{1}{2}m\dot{q} \cdot \dot{q} + \tfrac{1}{2}I\dot{q}_3^2, \tag{13.138}$$

in which m and I are the mass and moment of inertia, respectively. Assume there is no gravity; hence, $V(q) = 0$ and $L(q, \dot{q}) = K(q, \dot{q})$.

Suppose that generalized forces u_1, u_2, and u_3 can be applied to the configuration variables. Applying the Euler-Lagrange equation to $L(q, \dot{q})$ yields

$$\frac{d}{dt}\frac{\partial L}{\partial \dot{q}_1} - \frac{\partial L}{\partial q_1} = \frac{d}{dt}(m\dot{q}_1) = m\ddot{q}_1 = u_1$$

$$\frac{d}{dt}\frac{\partial L}{\partial \dot{q}_2} - \frac{\partial L}{\partial q_2} = \frac{d}{dt}(m\dot{q}_2) = m\ddot{q}_2 = u_2 \qquad (13.139)$$

$$\frac{d}{dt}\frac{\partial L}{\partial \dot{q}_3} - \frac{\partial L}{\partial q_3} = \frac{d}{dt}(I\dot{q}_3) = I\ddot{q}_3 = u_3.$$

These expressions are equivalent to those given in (13.109). One difference is that conversion to the phase space is needed. The second difference is that the action variables in (13.139) do not refer directly to forces and moments. They are instead interpreted as generalized forces that act on the configuration variables. A conversion should be performed if the original actions in (13.109) are required. ∎

13.4.2 General lagrangian expressions

As more complicated mechanics problems are considered, it is convenient to express the differential constraints in a general form. For example, evaluating (13.130) for a kinematic chain of bodies leads to very complicated expressions. The terms of these expressions, however, can be organized into standard forms that appear simpler and give some intuitive meanings to the components.

Suppose that the kinetic energy is expressed using (13.126), and let $m_{ij}(q)$ denote an entry of $M(q)$. Suppose that the potential energy is $V(q)$. By performing the derivatives expressed in (13.136), the Euler-Lagrange equation can be expressed as n scalar equations of the form [858]

$$\sum_{j=1}^{n} m_{ij}(q)\ddot{q}_j + \sum_{j=1}^{n}\sum_{k=1}^{n} h_{ijk}(q)\dot{q}_j\dot{q}_k + g_i(q) = u_i \qquad (13.140)$$

in which

$$h_{ijk} = \frac{\partial m_{ij}}{\partial q_k} - \frac{1}{2}\frac{\partial m_{jk}}{\partial q_i}. \qquad (13.141)$$

There is one equation for each i from 1 to n. The components of (13.140) have physical interpretations. The m_{ii} coefficients represent the inertia with respect to q_i. The m_{ij} represent the affect on q_j of accelerating q_i. The $h_{ijj}\dot{q}_j^2$ terms represent the centrifugal effect induced on q_i by the velocity of q_j. The $h_{ijk}\dot{q}_j\dot{q}_k$ terms represent the Coriolis effect induced on q_i by the velocities of q_j and q_k. The g_i term usually arises from gravity.

An alternative to (13.140) is often given in terms of matrices. It can be shown that the Euler-Lagrange equation reduces to

$$M(q)\ddot{q} + C(q, \dot{q})\dot{q} + g(q) = u, \qquad (13.142)$$

which represents n scalar equations. This introduces $C(q, \dot{q})$, which is an $n \times n$ *Coriolis matrix*. It turns out that many possible Coriolis matrices may produce equivalent different constraints. With respect to (13.140), the Coriolis matrix must be chosen so that

$$\sum_{j=1}^{n} c_{ij}\dot{q}_j = \sum_{j=1}^{n}\sum_{k=1}^{n} h_{ijk}\dot{q}_j\dot{q}_k. \qquad (13.143)$$

Using (13.141),

$$\sum_{j=1}^{n} c_{ij}\dot{q}_j = \sum_{j=1}^{n}\sum_{k=1}^{n} \left(\frac{\partial m_{ij}}{\partial q_k} - \frac{1}{2}\frac{\partial m_{jk}}{\partial q_i} \right) \dot{q}_j\dot{q}_k. \tag{13.144}$$

A standard way to determine $C(q, \dot{q})$ is by computing *Christoffel symbols*. By subtracting $\frac{1}{2}\frac{\partial m_{jk}}{\partial q_i}$ from the inside of the nested sums in (13.144), the equation can be rewritten as

$$\sum_{j=1}^{n} c_{ij}\dot{q}_j = \frac{1}{2}\sum_{j=1}^{n}\sum_{k=1}^{n} \frac{\partial m_{ij}}{\partial q_k}\dot{q}_j\dot{q}_k + \frac{1}{2}\sum_{j=1}^{n}\sum_{k=1}^{n} \left(\frac{\partial m_{ij}}{\partial q_k} - \frac{\partial m_{jk}}{\partial q_i} \right) \dot{q}_j\dot{q}_k. \tag{13.145}$$

This enables an element of $C(q, \dot{q})$ to be written as

$$c_{ij} = \sum_{k=1}^{n} c_{ijk}\dot{q}_k, \tag{13.146}$$

in which

$$c_{ijk} = \frac{1}{2} \left(\frac{\partial m_{ij}}{\partial q_k} + \frac{\partial m_{ik}}{\partial q_j} - \frac{\partial m_{jk}}{\partial q_i} \right). \tag{13.147}$$

This is called a *Christoffel symbol*, and it is obtained from (13.145). Note that $c_{ijk} = c_{ikj}$. Christoffel symbols arise in the study of affine connections in differential geometry and are usually denoted as Γ^i_{jk}. Affine connections provide a way to express acceleration without coordinates, in the same way that the tangent space was expressed without coordinates in Section 8.3.2. For affine connections in differential geometry, see [135]; for their application to mechanics, see [158].

13.4.2.1 Conversion to a phase transition equation

The final step is to convert the equations into phase space form. A $2n$-dimensional phase vector is introduced as $x = (q, \dot{q})$. The task is to obtain $\dot{x} = f(x, u)$, which represents $2n$ scalar equations. The first n equations are $\dot{x}_i = x_{n+i}$ for i from 1 to n. The final n equations are obtained by solving for $\ddot{q}$.

Suppose that the general form in (13.142) is used. Solving for $\ddot{q}$ yields

$$\ddot{q} = M(q)^{-1}(u - C(q, \dot{q})\dot{q} - g(q)). \tag{13.148}$$

The phase variables are then substituted in a straightforward manner. Each $\ddot{q}_i$ for i from 1 to n becomes $\dot{x}_{n+i}$, and $M(q)$, $C(q, \dot{q})$, and $g(q)$ are expressed in terms of x. This completes the specification of the phase transition equation.

Example 13.13 (Two-Link Manipulator) Figure 13.13 shows a two-link manipulator for which there are two revolute joints and two links, $\mathcal{A}_1$ and $\mathcal{A}_2$. Hence, $\mathcal{C} = \mathbb{S}^1 \times \mathbb{S}^1$. Let $q = (\theta_1, \theta_2)$ denote a configuration. Each of the two joints is controlled by a motor that applies a torque u_i. Let u_1 apply to the base, and let u_2 apply to the joint between $\mathcal{A}_1$ and $\mathcal{A}_2$. Let d_1 be the link length of $\mathcal{A}_1$. Let ℓ_i be the distance from the $\mathcal{A}_i$ origin to its center of mass. For each $\mathcal{A}_i$, let m_i and I_i be its mass and moment of inertia, respectively.

The kinetic energy of $\mathcal{A}_1$ is

$$K_1(\dot{q}) = \tfrac{1}{2}m_1\ell_1\dot{\theta}_1^2 + \tfrac{1}{2}I_1\dot{\theta}_1^2, \tag{13.149}$$

and the potential energy of $\mathcal{A}_1$ is

$$V_1(q) = m_1 g\ell_1 \sin\theta_1. \tag{13.150}$$

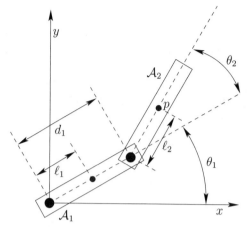

Figure 13.13: Parameter values for a two-link robot with two revolute joints.

The kinetic energy of $\mathcal{A}_2$ is

$$K_2(\dot{q}) = \tfrac{1}{2}p \cdot p + \tfrac{1}{2}I_2(\dot{\theta}_1 + \dot{\theta}_2)^2, \qquad (13.151)$$

in which p denotes the position of the center of mass of $\mathcal{A}_1$ and is given from (3.53) as

$$\begin{aligned} p_1 &= d_1 \cos\theta_1 + \ell_2 \cos\theta_2 \\ p_2 &= d_1 \sin\theta_1 + \ell_2 \sin\theta_2. \end{aligned} \qquad (13.152)$$

The potential energy of $\mathcal{A}_2$ is

$$V_2(q) = m_2 g(d_1 \sin\theta_1 + \ell_2 \sin\theta_2). \qquad (13.153)$$

At this point, the Lagrangian function can be formed as

$$L(q, \dot{q}) = K_1(\dot{\theta}_1) + K_2(\dot{\theta}_1, \dot{\theta}_2) - V_1(\theta_1) - V_2(\theta_1, \theta_2) \qquad (13.154)$$

and inserted into (13.118) to obtain the differential constraints in implicit form, expressed in terms of $\ddot{q}$, $\dot{q}$, and q. Conversion to the phase space is performed by solving the implicit constraints for $\ddot{q}$ and assigning $x = (q, \dot{q})$, in which x is a four-dimensional phase vector.

Rather than performing the computations directly using (13.118), the constraints can be directly determined using (13.140). The terms are

$$M(q) = \begin{pmatrix} m_{11} & m_{12} \\ m_{21} & m_{22} \end{pmatrix}, \qquad (13.155)$$

in which

$$\begin{aligned} m_{11} &= I_1 + m_1\ell_1^2 + I_2 + m_2(d_1^2 + \ell_2^2 + 2d_1\ell_2 \cos\theta_2) \\ m_{12} &= m_{21} = I_2 + m_2(l_2^2 + d_1\ell_2 \cos\theta_2) \\ m_{22} &= I_2 + m_2\ell_2^2, \end{aligned} \qquad (13.156)$$

and

$$c_{111} = \frac{1}{2} \frac{\partial m_{11}}{\partial \theta_1} = 0$$

$$c_{112} = c_{121} = \frac{1}{2} \frac{\partial m_{11}}{\partial \theta_2} = -m_2 l_1 \ell_2 p_2$$

$$c_{122} = \frac{\partial m_{12}}{\partial \theta_2} - \frac{1}{2} \frac{\partial m_{22}}{\partial \theta_1} = -m_2 l_1 \ell_2 p_2$$

$$c_{211} = \frac{\partial m_{21}}{\partial \theta_1} - \frac{1}{2} \frac{\partial m_{11}}{\partial \theta_2} = m_2 l_1 \ell_2 p_2 \qquad (13.157)$$

$$c_{212} = c_{221} = \frac{1}{2} \frac{\partial m_{22}}{\partial \theta_1} = 0$$

$$c_{222} = \frac{1}{2} \frac{\partial m_{22}}{\partial \theta_2} = 0.$$

The final term is defined as

$$g_1 = (m_1 \ell_1 + m_2 d_1) g p_1 + m_1 l_2 p_2 \qquad (13.158)$$
$$g_2 = m_2 \ell_2 g p_2.$$

The dynamics can alternatively be expressed using $M(q)$, $C(q, \dot{q})$, and $g(q)$ in (13.142). The Coriolis matrix is defined using (13.143) to obtain

$$C(q, \dot{q}) = -m_2 l_1 \ell_2 p_2 \begin{pmatrix} \dot{\theta}_2 & \dot{\theta}_1 + \dot{\theta}_2 \\ \dot{\theta}_1 & 0 \end{pmatrix}, \qquad (13.159)$$

in which p_2 is defined in (13.152) and is a function of q. For convenience, let

$$r = m_2 l_1 \ell_2 p_2. \qquad (13.160)$$

The resulting expression, which is now a special form of (13.142), is

$$m_{11} \ddot{\theta}_1 + m_{12} \ddot{\theta}_2 - 2r \dot{\theta}_1 \dot{\theta}_2 - r \dot{\theta}_2^2 + g_1(q) = u_1 \qquad (13.161)$$
$$m_{22} \ddot{\theta}_1 + m_{21} \ddot{\theta}_2 + r \dot{\theta}_1^2 + g_2(q) = u_2.$$

The phase transition equation is obtained by letting $x = (\theta_1, \theta_2, \dot{\theta}_1, \dot{\theta}_2)$ and substituting the state variables into (13.161). The variables $\ddot{\theta}_1$ and $\ddot{\theta}_2$ become $\dot{x}_3$ and $\dot{x}_4$, respectively. The equations must be solved for $\dot{x}_3$ and $\dot{x}_4$. An extension of this model to motors that have gear ratios and nonnegligible mass appears in [858]. ∎

The example provided here barely scratches the surface on the possible systems that can be elegantly modeled. Many robotics texts cover cases in which there are more links, different kinds of joints, and frictional forces [368, 728, 858, 908, 994].

The phase transition equation for chains of bodies could alternatively be derived using the Newton-Euler formulation of mechanics. Even though the Lagrangian form is more elegant, the Newton-Euler equations, when expressed recursively, are far more efficient for simulations of multibody dynamical systems [368, 865, 994].

13.4.3 Extensions of the Euler-Lagrange equations

Several extensions of the Euler-Lagrange equation can be constructed to handle complications that arise in addition to kinetic energy and potential energy in a conservative field. Each extension usually involves adding more terms to (13.129) to account for the new complication. Problems that can be handled in this way are closed kinematic chains, nonholonomic constraints, and nonconservative forces (such as friction).

13.4.3.1 Incorporating velocity constraints

The Lagrangian formulation of Section 13.4.1 can be extended to allow additional constraints placed on q and $\dot{q}$. This is very powerful for developing state transition equations for robots that have closed kinematic chains or wheeled bodies. If there are closed chains, then the configurations may be restricted to lie in a subset of $\mathcal{C}$. If a parameterization of the solution set is possible, then $\mathcal{C}$ can be redefined over the reduced C-space. This is usually not possible, however, because such a parametrization is difficult to obtain, as mentioned in Section 4.4. If there are wheels or other contact-based constraints, such as those in Section 13.1.3, then extra constraints on q and $\dot{q}$ exist. Dynamics can be incorporated into the models of Section 13.1 by extending the Euler-Lagrange equation.

The coming method will be based on Lagrange multipliers. Recall from standard calculus that to optimize a function h defined over $\mathbb{R}^n$, subject to an implicit constraint $g(x) = 0$, it is sufficient to consider only the extrema of

$$h(x) + \lambda g(x), \tag{13.162}$$

in which $\lambda \in \mathbb{R}$ represents a *Lagrange multiplier* [511]. The extrema are found by solving

$$\nabla h(x) + \lambda \nabla g(x) = 0, \tag{13.163}$$

which expresses n equations of the form

$$\frac{\partial h}{\partial x_i} + \lambda \frac{\partial g}{\partial x_i} = 0. \tag{13.164}$$

The same principle applies for handling velocity constraints on $\mathcal{C}$.

Suppose that there are velocity constraints on $\mathcal{C}$ as considered in Section 13.1. Consider implicit constraints, in which there are k equations of the form $g_i(q, \dot{q}) = 0$ for i from 1 to k. Parametric constraints can be handled as a special case of implicit constraints by writing

$$g_i(q, \dot{q}) = \dot{q}_i - f_i(q, u) = 0. \tag{13.165}$$

For any constraints that contain actions u, no extra difficulties arise. Each u_i is treated as a constant in the following analysis. Therefore, action variables will not be explicitly named in the expressions.

As before, assume time-invariant dynamics (see [792] for the time-varying case). Starting with $L(q, \dot{q})$ defined using (13.130), let the new criterion be

$$L_c(q, \dot{q}, \lambda) = L(q, \dot{q}) + \sum_{i=1}^{k} \lambda_i g_i(q, \dot{q}). \tag{13.166}$$

A functional Φ_c is defined by substituting L_c for L in (13.114).

The extremals of Φ_c are given by n equations,

$$\frac{d}{dt} \frac{\partial L_c}{\partial \dot{q}_i} - \frac{\partial L_c}{\partial q_i} = 0, \tag{13.167}$$

and k equations,

$$\frac{d}{dt} \frac{\partial L_c}{\partial \dot{\lambda}_i} - \frac{\partial L_c}{\partial \lambda_i} = 0. \tag{13.168}$$

The justification for this is the same as for (13.124), except now λ is included. The equations of (13.168) are equivalent to the constraints $g_i(q, \dot{q}) = 0$. The first term of each is zero because $\dot{\lambda}$ does not appear in the constraints, which reduces them to

$$\frac{\partial L_c}{\partial \lambda_i} = 0. \tag{13.169}$$

This already follows from the constraints on extremals of L and the constraints $g_i(q, \dot{q}) = 0$. In (13.167), there are n equations in $n + k$ unknowns. The k Lagrange multipliers can be eliminated by using the k constraints $g_i(q, \dot{q}) = 0$. This corresponds to Lagrange multiplier elimination in standard constrained optimization [511].

The expressions in (13.167) and the constraints $g_i(q, \dot{q})$ may be quite complicated, which makes the determination of a state transition equation challenging. General forms are given in Section 3.8 of [792]. An important special case will be considered here. Suppose that the constraints are Pfaffian,

$$g_i(q, \dot{q}) = \sum_{j=1}^{n} g_{ij}(q)\dot{q}_j = 0, \tag{13.170}$$

as introduced in Section 13.1. This includes the nonholonomic velocity constraints due to wheeled vehicles, which were presented in Section 13.1.2. Furthermore, this includes the special case of constraints of the form $g_i(q) = 0$, which models closed kinematic chains. Such constraints can be differentiated with respect to time to obtain

$$\frac{d}{dt} g_i(q) = \sum_{j=1}^{n} \frac{\partial g_i}{\partial q_j} \dot{q}_j = \sum_{j=1}^{n} g_{ij}(q)\dot{q}_j = 0, \tag{13.171}$$

which is in the Pfaffian form. This enables the dynamics of closed chains, considered in Section 4.4, to be expressed without even having a parametrization of the subset of $\mathcal{C}$ that satisfies the closure constraints. Starting in implicit form, differentiation is required to convert them into the Pfaffian form.

For the important case of Pfaffian constraints, (13.167) simplifies to

$$\frac{d}{dt} \frac{\partial L}{\partial \dot{q}_i} - \frac{\partial L}{\partial q_i} + \sum_{j=1}^{k} \lambda_j g_{ji}(q) = 0, \tag{13.172}$$

The Pfaffian constraints can be used to eliminate the Lagrange multipliers, if desired. Note that g_{ji} represents the ith term of the jth Pfaffian constraint. An action variable u_i can be placed on the right side of each constraint, if desired.

Equation (13.172) often appears instead as

$$\frac{d}{dt} \frac{\partial L}{\partial \dot{q}_i} - \frac{\partial L}{\partial q_i} = \sum_{l=1}^{k} \lambda_j g_{ji}(q, \dot{q}), \tag{13.173}$$

which is an alternative but equivalent expression of constraints because the Lagrange multipliers can be negated without affecting the existence of extremals. In this case, a nice interpretation due to D'Alembert can be given. Expressions that appear on the right of (13.173) can be considered as actions, as mentioned in Section 13.4.1. As stated previously, such actions are called generalized forces in mechanics. The *principle of virtual work* is obtained by integrating the reaction forces needed to maintain the constraints. These reaction forces are precisely given on the right side of (13.173). Due to the cancellation of forces, no true work is done by the constraints (if there is no friction).

Example 13.14 (A Particle on a Sphere)   Suppose that a particle travels on a unit sphere without friction or gravity. Let $(q_1, q_2, q_3) \in \mathbb{R}^3$ denote the position of the point. The Lagrangian function is the kinetic energy,

$$L(q, \dot{q}) = \tfrac{1}{2}m(\dot{q}_1^2 + \dot{q}_2^2 + \dot{q}_3^2), \tag{13.174}$$

in which m is the particle mass. For simplicity, assume that $m = 2$.

The constraint that the particle must travel on a sphere yields

$$g_1(q) = q_1^2 + q_2^2 + q_3^2 - 1 = 0. \tag{13.175}$$

This can be put into Pfaffian form by time differentiation to obtain

$$2q_1\dot{q}_1 + 2q_2\dot{q}_2 + 2q_3\dot{q}_3 = 0. \tag{13.176}$$

Since $k = 1$, there is a single Lagrange multiplier λ_1. Applying (13.172) yields three equations,

$$\ddot{q}_i - 2q_i\lambda_1 = 0, \tag{13.177}$$

for i from 1 to 3. The generic form of the solution is

$$c_1q_1 + c_2q_2 + c_3q_3 = 0, \tag{13.178}$$

in which the c_i are real-valued constants that can be determined from the initial position of the particle. This represents the equation of a plane through the origin. The intersection of the plane with the sphere is a great circle. This implies that the particle moves between two points by traveling along the great circle. These are the shortest paths (geodesics) on the sphere. ∎

The general forms in Section 13.4.2 can be extended to the constrained case. For example, (13.142) generalizes to

$$M(q)\ddot{q} + C(q, \dot{q})\dot{q} + g(q) + G(q)^T \lambda = u, \tag{13.179}$$

in which G is a $n \times k$ matrix that represents all of the g_{ji} Pfaffian coefficients. In this case, the Lagrange multipliers can be computed as [728]

$$\lambda = \left(G(q)M(q)^{-1}G(q)^T\right)^{-1} G(q)M(q)^{-1}\left(u - C(q, \dot{q})\dot{q}\right), \tag{13.180}$$

assuming G is time-invariant.

The phase transition equation can be determined in the usual way by performing the required differentiations, defining the $2n$ phase variables, and solving for $\dot{x}$. The result generalizes (13.148).

13.4.3.2 Nonconservative forces

The Lagrangian formulation has been extended so far to handle constraints on C that lower the dimension of the tangent space. The formation can also be extended to allow nonconservative forces. The most common and important example in mechanical systems is friction. The details of friction models will not be covered here; see [684]. As examples, friction can arise when bodies come into contact, as in the joints of a robot manipulator, and as bodies move through a fluid, such as air or water. The nonconservative forces can be expressed as additional generalized forces, expressed in an $n \times 1$ vector of the form

$B(q, \dot{q})$. Suppose that an action vector is also permitted. The modified Euler-Lagrange equation then becomes

$$\frac{d}{dt} \frac{\partial L}{\partial \dot{q}} - \frac{\partial L}{\partial q} = u - B(\dot{q}, q). \tag{13.181}$$

A common extension to (13.142) is

$$M(q)\ddot{q} + C(q, \dot{q})\dot{q} + N(q, \dot{q}) = u, \tag{13.182}$$

in which $N(q, \dot{q})$ generalizes $g(q)$ to include nonconservative forces. This can be generalized even further to include Pfaffian constraints and Lagrange multipliers,

$$M(q)\ddot{q} + C(q, \dot{q})\dot{q} + N(q, \dot{q}) + G(q)^T \lambda = u. \tag{13.183}$$

The Lagrange multipliers become [728]

$$\lambda = \left(G(q)M(q)^{-1}G(q)^T\right)^{-1} G(q)M(q)^{-1}\left(u - C(q, \dot{q})\dot{q} - N(q, \dot{q})\right). \tag{13.184}$$

Once again, the phase transition equation can be derived in terms of $2n$ phase variables and generalizes (13.148).

13.4.4 Hamiltonian mechanics

The Lagrangian formulation of mechanics is the most convenient for determining a state transition equation for a collection of bodies. Once the kinetic and potential energies are determined, the remaining efforts are straightforward computation of derivatives and algebraic manipulation. Hamiltonian mechanics provides an alternative formulation that is closely related to the Lagrangian. Instead of expressing second-order differential constraints on an n-dimensional C-space, it expresses first-order constraints on a $2n$-dimensional phase space. This idea should be familiar from Section 13.2. The new phase space considered here is an example of a *symplectic manifold*, which has many important properties, such as being orientable and having an even number of dimensions [39]. The standard phase vector is defined as $x = (q, \dot{q})$; however, instead of $\dot{q}$, n variables will be introduced and denoted as p. Thus, a transformation exists between $(q, \dot{q})$ and (p, q). The p variables are related to the configuration variables through a special function over the phase space called the *Hamiltonian*. Although the Hamiltonian formulation usually does not help in the determination of $\dot{x} = f(x, u)$, it is covered here because its generalization to optimal control problems is quite powerful. This generalization is called Pontryagin's minimum principle and is covered in Section 15.2.3. In the context of mechanics, it provides a general expression of energy conservation laws, which aids in proving many theoretical results [39, 399].

The relationship between $(q, \dot{q})$ and (p, q) can be obtained by using the *Legendre transformation* [39, 399]. Consider a real-valued function f of two variables, $x, y \in \mathbb{R}$. Its *total differential* [511] is

$$df = u \, dx + v \, dy, \tag{13.185}$$

in which

$$u = \frac{\partial f}{\partial x} \quad \text{and} \quad v = \frac{\partial f}{\partial y}. \tag{13.186}$$

Consider constructing a total differential that depends on du and dy, instead of dx and dy. Let g be a function of u and y defined as

$$g(u, y) = ux - f. \tag{13.187}$$

The total differential of g is

$$dg = x \, du + u \, dx - df. \tag{13.188}$$

Using (13.185) to express df, this simplifies to

$$dg = x \, du - v \, dy. \tag{13.189}$$

The x and v variables are now interpreted as

$$x = \frac{\partial g}{\partial u} \qquad\qquad v = -\frac{\partial g}{\partial y}, \tag{13.190}$$

which appear to be a kind of inversion of (13.186). This idea will be extended to vector form to arrive the Hamiltonian formulation.

Assume that the dynamics do not depend on the particular time (the extension to time-varying dynamics is not difficult; see [39, 399]). Let $L(q, \dot{q})$ be the Lagrangian function defined (13.129). Let $p \in \mathbb{R}^n$ represent a *generalized momentum* vector (or *adjoint variables*), which serves the same purpose as u in (13.185). Each p_i is defined as

$$p_i = \frac{\partial L}{\partial \dot{q}_i}. \tag{13.191}$$

In some literature, p is instead denoted as λ because it can also be interpreted as a vector of Lagrange multipliers. The *Hamiltonian function* is defined as

$$H(p, q) = p \cdot \dot{q} - L(q, \dot{q}) = \sum_{i=1}^{n} p_i \dot{q}_i - L(q, \dot{q}) \tag{13.192}$$

and can be interpreted as the total energy of a conservative system [399]. This is a vector-based extension of (13.187) in which L and H replace f and g, respectively. Also, p and q are the vector versions of u and x, respectively.

Considered as a function of p and q only, the total differential of H is

$$dH = \sum_{i=1}^{n} \frac{\partial H}{\partial p_i} dp_i + \sum_{i=1}^{n} \frac{\partial H}{\partial q_i} dq_i. \tag{13.193}$$

Using (13.192), dH can be expressed as

$$dH = \sum_{i=1}^{n} \dot{q}_i \, dp_i + \sum_{i=1}^{n} p_i \, d\dot{q}_i - \sum_{i=1}^{n} \frac{\partial L}{\partial \dot{q}_i} d\dot{q}_i - \sum_{i=1}^{n} \frac{\partial L}{\partial q_i} dq_i. \tag{13.194}$$

The $d\dot{q}_i$ terms all cancel by using (13.191), to obtain

$$dH = \sum_{i=1}^{n} \dot{q}_i \, dp_i - \sum_{i=1}^{n} \frac{\partial L}{\partial q_i} dq_i. \tag{13.195}$$

Using (13.118),

$$\dot{p} = \frac{\partial L}{\partial q_i}. \tag{13.196}$$

This implies that

$$dH = \sum_{i=1}^{n} \dot{q}_i \, dp_i - \sum_{i=1}^{n} \dot{p}_i \, dq_i. \tag{13.197}$$

Equating (13.197) and (13.193) yields $2n$ equations called *Hamilton's equations*:

$$\dot{q}_i = \frac{\partial H}{\partial p_i} \qquad\qquad \dot{p}_i = \frac{\partial H}{\partial q_i}, \tag{13.198}$$

for each i from 1 to n. These equations are analogous to (13.190).

Hamilton's equations are equivalent to the Euler-Lagrange equation. Extremals in both cases yield equivalent differential constraints. The difference is that the Lagrangian formulation uses $(q, \dot{q})$ and the Hamiltonian uses (p, q). The Hamiltonian results in first-order partial differential equations. It was assumed here that the dynamics are time-invariant and the motions occur in a conservative field. In this case, $dH = 0$, which corresponds to conservation of total energy. In the time-varying case, the additional equation $\partial H/\partial t = -\partial L/\partial t$ appears along with Hamilton's equations. As stated previously, Hamilton's equations are primarily of interest in establishing basic results in theoretical mechanics, as opposed to determining the motions of particular systems. For example, the Hamiltonian is used to establish Louisville's theorem, which states that phase flows preserve volume, implying that a Hamiltonian system cannot be asymptotically stable [39]. Asymptotic stability is covered in Section 15.1.1. Pontryagin's minimum principle, an extension of Hamilton's equations to optimal control theory, is covered in 15.2.3.

13.5 Multiple decision makers

Differential models can be extended to model the interaction of multiple decision makers. This leads to continuous-time extensions of sequential decision making, from Formulation 10.1, and sequential games, from Formulation 10.4. A differential version of the state transition equation can be made for these extensions.

13.5.1 Differential decision making

To make a *differential game against nature* that extends Formulation 10.1 to continuous time, suppose that nature actions $\theta(t)$ are chosen from Θ. A differential model can be defined as

$$\dot{x} = f(x, u, \theta). \tag{13.199}$$

The state space X and action space U are used in the same way as throughout this chapter. The difference only comes in the state transition equation. State-dependent nature action spaces may also be used.

As observed repeatedly throughout Part III, nature can be modeled nondeterministically or probabilistically. In the nondeterministic case, (13.199) is equivalent to a *differential inclusion* [54]:

$$\dot{x} \in \{\dot{x}' \mid \exists \theta \in \Theta \text{ such that } \dot{x}' = f(x, u, \theta)\}. \tag{13.200}$$

Possible future values for $\dot{x}$ can be computed using forward projections. Reachable sets, which will be introduced in Section 14.2.1, can be defined that characterize the evolution of future possible states over time. Plans constructed under this model usually use worst-case analysis.

Example 13.15 (Nondeterministic Forward Projection)   As a simple example of using (13.199), consider expressing the uncertainty model used in the preimage planning framework of Section 12.5.1.

At each time $t \geq 0$, nature chooses some $\theta \in \Theta(t)$. The state transition equation is

$$\dot{x} = x + u + \theta. \tag{13.201}$$

The cone shown in Figure 12.45 is just the nondeterministic forward projection under the application of a constant $u \in U$.   ∎

In the probabilistic case, restrictions must be carefully placed on the nature action trajectory (e.g., a Weiner process [911]). Under such conditions, (13.199) becomes a *stochastic differential equation*. Planning in this case becomes continuous-time stochastic control [570], and the task is to optimize the expected cost.

Example 13.16 (A Simple Car and Nature)   Uncertainty can be introduced into any of the models of this chapter. For example, recall the simple car, (13.15). Suppose that nature interferes with the steering action so that it is not precisely known in which direction the car will drive. Let $\Theta = [-\theta_{max}, \theta_{max}]$, in which $\theta_{max} \in (0, \pi/2)$ represents the maximum amount of steering angle error that can be caused by nature. The simple-car model can be modified to account for this error as

$$\begin{aligned}
\dot{x} &= u_s \cos\theta \\
\dot{y} &= u_s \sin\theta \\
\dot{\theta} &= \frac{u_s}{L} \tan(u_\phi + \gamma),
\end{aligned} \tag{13.202}$$

in which the domain of tan must be extended to $\mathbb{R}$ or other suitable restrictions must be imposed. At each time t, a nature action[12] $\gamma \in \Theta$ causes the true heading of the car to be perturbed from the commanded direction u_ϕ. Under nondeterministic uncertainty, the maximum amount that the car deviates from the commanded direction must be determined by the planning algorithm. A probability density function $p(\gamma)$ can be assigned to obtain a probabilistic model. When integrated over time, (13.202) yields probability density functions over future car configurations [1004].   ∎

In a similar way, parameters that account for nature can be introduced virtually anywhere in the models of this chapter. Some errors may be systematic, which reflect mistakes or simplifications made in the modeling process. These correspond to a constant nature action applied at the outset. In this case, nature is not allowed to vary its action over time. Other errors could correspond to noise, which is expected to yield different nature actions over time.

13.5.2 Differential game theory

The extension of sequential game theory to the continuous-time case is called *differential game theory* (or *dynamic game theory* [60]), a subject introduced by Isaacs [480]. All of the variants considered in Sections 9.3, 9.4, 10.5 are possible:

---

[12] The notation γ is used instead of θ to avoid conflicting with the car orientation variable θ in this particular example.

1. There may be any number of players.

2. The game may be zero-sum or nonzero-sum.

3. The state may or may not be known. If the state is unknown, then interesting I-spaces arise, similar to those of Section 11.7.

4. Nature can interfere with the game.

5. Different equilibrium concepts, such as saddle points and Nash equilibria, can be defined.

See [60] for a thorough overview of differential games. Two players, P_1 and P_2, can be engaged in a *differential game* in which each has a continuous set of actions. Let U and V denote the action spaces of P_1 and P_2, respectively. A state transition equation can be defined as

$$\dot{x} = f(x, u, v), \tag{13.203}$$

in which x is the state, $u \in U$, and $v \in V$.

Linear differential games are an important family of games because many techniques from optimal control theory can be extended to solve them [60].

Example 13.17 (Linear Differential Games)   The linear system model (13.37) can be extended to incorporate two players. Let $X = \mathbb{R}^n$ be a phase space. Let $U = \mathbb{R}^{m_1}$ and $V = \mathbb{R}^{m_2}$ be an action spaces for $m_1, m_2 \leq n$. A *linear differential game* is expressed as

$$\dot{x} = Ax + Bu + Cv, \tag{13.204}$$

in which A, B, and C are constant, real-valued matrices of dimensions $n \times n$, $n \times m_1$, and $n \times m_2$, respectively. The particular solution to such games depends on the cost functional and desired equilibrium concept. For the case of a quadratic cost, closed-form solutions exist. These extend techniques that are developed for linear systems with one decision maker; see Section 15.2.2 and [60].

The original work of Isaacs [480] contains many interesting examples of *pursuit-evasion differential games*. One of the most famous is described next.

Example 13.18 (Homicidal Chauffeur)   In the *homicidal chauffeur* game, the pursuer is a Dubins car and the evader is a point robot that can translate in any direction. Both exist in the same world, $\mathcal{W} = \mathbb{R}^2$. The speeds of the car and robot are s_1 and s_2, respectively. It is assumed that $|s_1| > |s_2|$, which means that the pursuer moves faster than the evader. The transition equation is given by extending (13.15) to include two state variables that account for the robot position:

$$\begin{aligned}
\dot{x}_1 &= s_1 \cos \theta_1 & \dot{x}_2 &= s_2 \cos v \\
\dot{y}_1 &= s_1 \sin \theta_1 & \dot{y}_2 &= s_2 \sin v \\
\dot{\theta}_1 &= \frac{s_1}{L} \tan u_\phi.
\end{aligned} \tag{13.205}$$

The state space is X is $\mathbb{R}^4 \times \mathbb{S}^1$, and the action spaces are $U = [-\phi_{max}, \phi_{max}]$ and $V = [0, 2\pi)$.

The task is to determine whether the pursuer can come within some prescribed distance ϵ of the evader:

$$(x_1 - x_2)^2 + (y_1 - y_2)^2 < \epsilon^2. \tag{13.206}$$

If this occurs, then the pursuer wins; otherwise, the evader wins. The solution depends on the L, s_1, s_2, ϵ, and the initial state. Even though the pursuer moves faster, the evader may escape because it does not have a limited turning radius. For given values of L, s_1, s_2, and ϵ, the state space X can be partitioned into two regions that correspond to whether the pursuer or evader wins [60, 480]. To gain some intuition about how this partition may appear, imagine the motions that a bullfighter must make to avoid a fast, charging bull (yes, bulls behave very much like a fast Dubins car when provoked). ∎

Another interesting pursuit-evasion game arises in the case of one car attempting to intercept another [697].

Example 13.19 (A Game of Two Cars)   Imagine that there are two simple cars that move in the same world, $\mathcal{W} = \mathbb{R}^2$. Each has a transition equation given by (13.15). The state transition equation for the game is

$$
\begin{aligned}
\dot{x}_1 &= u_s \cos \theta_1 &\qquad \dot{x}_2 &= v_s \cos \theta_2 \\
\dot{y}_1 &= u_s \sin \theta_1 &\qquad \dot{y}_2 &= v_s \sin \theta_2 &\qquad (13.207)\\
\dot{\theta}_1 &= \frac{u_s}{L_1} \tan u_\phi &\qquad \dot{\theta}_2 &= s\frac{v_s}{L_2} \tan v_\phi.
\end{aligned}
$$

The pursuit-evasion game becomes very interesting if both players are restricted to be Dubins cars. ∎

Further reading

This chapter was synthesized from numerous sources. Many important, related subjects were omitted. For some mechanics of bodies in contact and manipulation in general, see [684]. Three-dimensional vehicle models were avoided because they are complicated by $SO(3)$; see [436]. For computational issues associated with simulating dynamical systems, see [249, 865].

For further reading on velocity constraints on the C-space, see [599, 728] and Sections 15.3 to 15.5. For more problems involving rolling spheres, see [530] and references therein. The rolling-ball problem is sometimes referred to as the Chaplygin ball. A nonholonomic manipulator constructed from rolling-ball joints was developed and analyzed in [732]. The kinematics of curved bodies in contact was studied in [635, 719]. For motion planning in this context, see [103, 105, 225, 679]. Other interesting nonholonomic systems include the snakeboard [476, 632], roller racer [559], rollerblader [216], Trikke [215], and examples in [114] (e.g., the Chaplygin sled).

Phase space representations are a basic part of differential equations, physics, and control theory; see [44, 194].

Further reading in mechanics is somewhat complicated by two different levels of treatment. Classical mechanics texts do not base the subject on differential geometry, which results in cumbersome formulations and unusual terminology (e.g., generalized coordinates). Modern mechanics texts overcome this problem by cleanly formulating everything in terms of geodesics on Riemannian manifolds; however, this many be more difficult to absorb for readers without background in differential geometry. An excellent source for modern mechanics is [39]. One of the most famous texts for classical mechanics is [399]. For an on-line book that covers the calculus of variations, including constrained Lagrangians, see [793]. The constrained Lagrangian presentation is based on Chapter 3 of [792], Section 2.4 of [399], and parts of [407]. Integral constraints on the Lagrangian are covered in [793], in addition to algebraic and differential constraints. Lagrangian mechanics under inequality constraints is considered in [792]. The presentation of the Hamiltonian in Section 13.4.4 is based on Chapter 7 of [399] and Section 15 of [39]. For advanced, modern treatments of mechanics in the language of affine connections and Christoffel

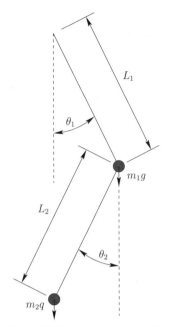

Figure 13.14: A double pendulum.

symbols, see [3, 158, 680]. Another source, which is also heavily illustrated, is [361]. For further reading on robot dynamics, see [30, 206, 728, 858, 908, 994]. For dynamics of automobiles, see [391].

For further reading on differential game theory, primary sources are [60, 426, 480]; see also [34, 58, 786, 985, 991, 992, 993, 997]. Lower bounds for the algorithmic complexity of pursuit-evasion differential games are presented in [824].

Exercises

1. Let $\mathcal{C} = \mathbb{R}^4$. There are two Pfaffian constraints, $\dot{q}_1 + \dot{q}_2 + \dot{q}_3 + \dot{q}_4 = 0$ and $\dot{q}_2 - \dot{q}_4 = 0$. Determine the appropriate number of action variables and express the differential constraints in the form $\dot{q} = f(q, u)$.

2. Introduce a phase space and convert $2\ddot{y} - 10\dot{y}^2 + 5y = 0$ into the form $\dot{x} = f(x)$.

3. Introduce a phase space and convert $y^{(4)} + y = 0$ into the form $\dot{x} = f(x)$.

4. Derive the configuration transition equation (13.19) for a car pulling trailers.

5. Use the main idea of Section 13.2.4 to develop a smooth-steering extension of the car pulling trailers, (13.19).

6. Suppose that two identical differential-drive robots are connected together at their centers with a rigid bar of length d. The robots are attached at each end of the rod, and each attachment forms a revolute joint. There are four wheels to control; however, some combinations of wheel rotations cause skidding. Assuming that skidding is not allowed, develop a motion model of the form $\dot{q} = f(q, u)$, in which $\mathcal{C}$ and U are chosen to reflect the true degrees of freedom.

7. Extend the lunar lander model to a general rigid body with a thruster that does not apply forces through the center of mass.

8. Develop a model for a 3D rotating rigid body fired out of a canon at a specified angle above level ground under gravity. Suppose that thrusters are placed on the body, enabling it to be controlled before it impacts the ground. Develop general phase transition equations.

9. Add gravity with respect to q_2 in Example 13.12 and derive the new state transition equation using the Euler-Lagrange equation.

10. Use the constrained Lagrangian to derive the equations of motion of the pendulum in Example 13.8.

11. Define a phase space, and determine an equation of the form $\dot{x} = f(x)$ for the double pendulum shown in Figure 13.14.

12. Extend Example 13.13 to obtain the dynamics of a three-link manipulator. The third link, $\mathcal{A}_3$, is attached to the other two by a revolute joint. The new parameters are θ_3, d_2, ℓ_3, m_3, and I_3.

13. Solve Example 13.14 by parameterizing the sphere with standard spherical coordinates and using the unconstrained Lagrangian. Verify that the same answer is obtained.

14. Convert the equations in (13.161) into phase space form, to obtain the phase transition equation in the form $\dot{x} = f(x, u)$. Express the right side of the equation in terms of the basic parameters, such as mass, moment of inertia, and lengths.

15. Define the Hamiltonian for a free-floating 2D rigid body under gravity and develop Hamilton's equations.

Implementations

16. Make a 3D spacecraft (rigid-body) simulator that allows any number of binary thrusters to be placed in any position and orientation.

17. Make a simulator for the two-link manipulator in Example 13.13.

14

Sampling-Based Planning
Under Differential Constraints

After Chapter 13, it seems that differential constraints arise nearly everywhere. For example, they may arise when wheels roll, aircraft fly, and when the dynamics of virtually any mechanical system is considered. This makes the basic model used for motion planning in Part II invalid for many applications because differential constraints were neglected. Formulation 4.1, for example, was concerned only with obstacles in the C-space.

This chapter incorporates the differential models of Chapter 13 into sampling-based motion planning. The detailed modeling (e.g., Lagrangian mechanics) of Chapter 13 is not important here. This chapter works directly with a given system, expressed as $\dot{x} = f(x, u)$. The focus is limited to *sampling-based* approaches because very little can be done with combinatorial methods if differential constraints exist. However, if there are no obstacles, then powerful analytical techniques may apply. This subject is complementary to motion planning with obstacles and is the focus of Chapter 15.

Section 14.1 provides basic definitions and concepts for motion planning under differential constraints. It is particularly important to explain the distinctions made in literature between nonholonomic planning, kinodynamic planning, and trajectory planning, all of which are cases of planning under differential constraints. Another important point is that obstacles may be somewhat more complicated in phase spaces, which were introduced in Section 13.2. Section 14.2 introduces sampling over the space of action trajectories, which is an essential part of later planning algorithms.

Section 14.3 revisits the incremental sampling and searching framework of Section 5.4 and extends it to handle differential constraints. This leads to several sampling-based planning approaches, which are covered in Section 14.4. Familiar choices such as dynamic programming or the RDTs of Section 5.5 appear once again. The resulting planning methods can be used for a wide variety of problems that involve differential constraints on C-spaces or phase spaces.

Section 14.5 briefly covers feedback motion planning under differential constraints. Approximate, optimal plans can be obtained by a simple adaptation of value iteration from Section 8.5.2. Section 14.6 describes decoupled methods, which start with a collision-free path that ignores differential constraints, and then perform refinements to obtain the desired trajectory. Such approaches often lose completeness and optimality, but they offer substantial computational savings in many settings. Section 14.7 briefly surveys numerical techniques for optimizing a trajectory subjected to differential constraints; the techniques can be used to improve solutions computed by planning algorithms.

14.1 Introduction

14.1.1 Problem formulation

Motion planning under differential constraints can be considered as a variant of classical *two-point boundary value problems* (BVPs) [443]. In that setting, initial and goal states are given, and the task is to compute a path through a state space that connects initial and goal states while satisfying differential constraints. Motion planning involves the additional complication of avoiding obstacles in the state space. Techniques for solving BVPs are unfortunately not well-suited for motion planning because they are not designed for handling obstacle regions. For some methods, adaptation may be possible; however, the obstacle constraints usually cause these classical methods to become inefficient or incomplete. Throughout this chapter, the BVP will refer to motion planning with differential constraints and no obstacles. BVPs that involve more than two points also exist; however, they are not considered in this book.

It is assumed that the differential constraints are expressed in a state transition equation, $\dot{x} = f(x, u)$, on a smooth manifold X, called the *state space*, which may be a C-space $\mathcal{C}$ or a phase space of a C-space. A solution path will not be directly expressed as in Part II but is instead derived from an action trajectory via integration of the state transition equation.

Let the action space U be a bounded subset of $\mathbb{R}^m$. A planning algorithm computes an *action trajectory* $\tilde{u}$, which is a function of the form $\tilde{u} : [0, \infty) \to U$. The action at a particular time t is expressed as $u(t)$. To be consistent with standard notation for functions, it seems that this should instead be denoted as $\tilde{u}(t)$. This abuse of notation was intentional, to make the connection to the discrete-stage case clearer and to distinguish an action, $u \in U$, from an action trajectory $\tilde{u}$. If the action space is state-dependent, then $u(t)$ must additionally satisfy $u(t) \in U(x(t)) \subseteq U$. For state-dependent models, this will be assumed by default. It will also be assumed that a termination action u_T is used, which makes it possible to specify all action trajectories over $[0, \infty)$ with the understanding that at some time t_F, the termination action is applied.

The connection between the action and state trajectories needs to be formulated. Starting from some initial state $x(0)$ at time $t = 0$, a *state trajectory* is derived from an action trajectory $\tilde{u}$ as

$$x(t) = x(0) + \int_0^t f(x(t'), u(t'))dt', \tag{14.1}$$

which integrates the state transition equation $\dot{x} = f(x, u)$ from the initial condition $x(0)$. Let $\tilde{x}(x(0), \tilde{u})$ denote the state trajectory over all time, obtained by integrating (14.1). Differentiation of (14.1) leads back to the state transition equation. Recall from Section 13.1.1 that if u is fixed, then the state transition equation defines a vector field. The state transition equation is an alternative expression of (8.14) from Section 8.3, which is the expression for an integral curve of a vector field. The state trajectory is the integral curve in the present context.

The problem of motion planning under differential constraints can be formulated as an extension of the Piano Mover's Problem in Formulation 4.1. The main differences in this extension are 1) the introduction of time, 2) the state or phase space, and 3) the state transition equation. The resulting formulation follows.

Formulation 14.1 (Motion Planning Under Differential Constraints)

1. A *world* $\mathcal{W}$, a *robot* $\mathcal{A}$ (or $\mathcal{A}_1, \ldots, \mathcal{A}_m$ for a linkage), an *obstacle region* $\mathcal{O}$, and a *configuration space* $\mathcal{C}$, which are defined the same as in Formulation 4.1.

2. An unbounded *time interval* $T = [0, \infty)$.

3. A smooth manifold X, called the *state space*, which may be $X = \mathcal{C}$ or it may be a phase space derived from $\mathcal{C}$ if dynamics is considered; see Section 13.2. Let $\kappa : X \to \mathcal{C}$ denote a function that returns the configuration $q \in \mathcal{C}$ associated with $x \in X$. Hence, $q = \kappa(x)$.

4. An obstacle region X_{obs} is defined for the state space. If $X = \mathcal{C}$, then $X_{obs} = \mathcal{C}_{obs}$. For general phase spaces, X_{obs} is described in detail in Section 14.1.3. The notation $X_{free} = X \setminus X_{obs}$ indicates the states that avoid collision and satisfy any additional global constraints.

5. For each state $x \in X$, a bounded *action space* $U(x) \subseteq \mathbb{R}^m \cup \{u_T\}$, which includes a termination action u_T and m is some fixed integer called the *number of action variables*. If the termination action is applied, it is assumed that $f(x, u_T) = 0$ (and no cost accumulates, if a cost functional is used). Let U denote the union of $U(x)$ over all $x \in X$.

6. A system is specified using a state transition equation $\dot{x} = f(x, u)$, defined for every $x \in X$ and $u \in U(x)$. This could arise from any of the differential models of Chapter 13.

7. A state $x_I \in X_{free}$ is designated as the *initial state*.

8. A set $X_G \subset X_{free}$ is designated as the *goal region*.

9. A complete algorithm must compute an *action trajectory* $\tilde{u} : T \to U$, for which the state trajectory $\tilde{x}$, resulting from (14.1), satisfies: 1) $x(0) = x_I$, and 2) there exists some $t > 0$ for which $u(t) = u_T$ and $x(t) \in X_G$.

Additional constraints may be placed on $\tilde{u}$, such as continuity or smoothness over time. At the very least, $\tilde{u}$ must be chosen so that the integrand of (14.1) is integrable over time. Let $\mathcal{U}$ denote the set of all *permissible action trajectories* over $T = [0, \infty)$. By default, $\mathcal{U}$ is assumed to include any integrable action trajectory. If desired, continuity and smoothness conditions can be enforced by introducing new phase variables. The method of placing integrators in front of action variables, which was covered in Section 13.2.4, can usually achieve the desired constraints. If optimizing a criterion is additionally important, then the cost functional given by (8.39) can be used. The existence of optimal solutions requires that U is a closed set, in addition to being bounded.

A final time does not need to be stated because of the termination action u_T. As usual, once u_T is applied, cost does not accumulate any further and the state remains fixed. This might seem strange for problems that involve dynamics because momentum should keep the state in motion. Keep in mind that the termination action is a trick to make the formulation work correctly. In many cases, the goal corresponds to a subset of X in which the velocity components are zero. In this case, there is no momentum and hence no problem. If the goal region includes states that have nonzero velocity, then it is true that a physical system may keep moving after u_T has been applied; however, the cost functional will not measure any additional cost. The task is considered to be completed after u_T is applied, and the simulation is essentially halted. If the mechanical system eventually collides due to momentum, then this is the problem of the user who specified a goal state that involves momentum.

The overwhelming majority of solution techniques are sampling-based. This is motivated primarily by the extreme difficultly of planning under differential constraints. The standard Piano Mover's Problem from Formulation 4.1 is a special case of Formulation 14.1 and is already PSPACE-hard [820]. Optimal planning is also NP-hard, even for a point in a 3D polyhedral environment without differential constraints [174]. The only known methods for exact planning under differential constraints in the presence of obstacles are for the double integrator system $\ddot{q} = u$, for $C = \mathbb{R}$ [750] and $C = \mathbb{R}^2$ [173].

Section 14.1.2 provides some perspective on motion planning problems under differential constraints that fall under Formulation 14.1, which assumes that the initial state is given and future states are predictable. Section 14.5 briefly addresses the broader problem of feedback motion planning under differential constraints.

14.1.2 Different kinds of planning problems

There are many ways to classify motion planning problems under differential constraints. Some planning approaches rely on particular properties of the system; therefore, it is helpful to characterize these general differences. The different kinds of problems described here are specializations of Formulation 14.1. In spite of differences based on the kinds of models described below, all of them can be unified under the topic of planning under differential constraints.

One factor that affects the differential model is the way in which the task is decomposed. For example, the task of moving a robot usually requires the consideration of mechanics. Under the classical robotics approach that was shown in Figure 1.19, the motion planning problem is abstracted away from the mechanics of the robot. This enables the motion planning ideas of Part II to be applied. This decomposition is arbitrary. The mechanics of the robot can be considered directly in the planning process. Another possibility is that only part of the constraints may be considered. For example, perhaps only the rolling constraints of a vehicle are considered in the planning process, but dynamics are handled by another planning module. Thus, it is important to remember that the kinds of differential constraints that appear in the planning problem depend not only on the particular mechanical system, but also on how the task is decomposed.

14.1.2.1 Terms from planning literature

Nonholonomic planning

The term *nonholonomic planning* was introduced by Laumond [596] to describe the problem of motion planning for wheeled mobile robots (see [598, 636] for overviews). It was informally explained in Section 13.1 that *nonholonomic* refers to differential constraints that cannot be completely integrated. This means they cannot be converted into constraints that involve no derivatives. A more formal definition of *nonholonomic* will be given in Section 15.4. Most planning research has focused on velocity constraints on C, as opposed to a phase space X. This includes most of the models given in Section 13.1, which are specified as nonintegrable velocity constraints on the C-space C. These are often called *kinematic constraints*, to distinguish them from constraints that arise due to dynamics.

In mechanics and control, the term nonholonomic also applies to nonintegrable velocity constraints on a phase space [114, 115]. Therefore, it is perfectly reasonable for the term nonholonomic planning to refer to problems that also involve dynamics. However, in most applications to date, the term nonholonomic planning is applied to problems that have kinematic constraints only. This is motivated primarily by the early consideration of planning for wheeled mobile robots. In this book, it will be assumed that nonholonomic planning refers to planning under nonintegrable velocity constraints on $\mathcal{C}$ or any phase space X.

For the purposes of sampling-based planning, complete integrability is actually not important. In many cases, even if it can be theoretically established that constraints are integrable, it does not mean that performing the integration is practical. Furthermore, even if integration can be performed, each constraint may be implicit and therefore not easily parameterizable. Suppose, for example, that constraints arise from closed kinematic chains. Usually, a parameterization is not available. By differentiating the closure constraint, a velocity constraint is obtained on $\mathcal{C}$. This can be treated in a sampling-based planner as if it were a nonholonomic constraint, even though it can easily be integrated.

Kinodynamic planning

The term *kinodynamic planning* was introduced by Canny, Donald, Reif, and Xavier [292] to refer to motion planning problems for which velocity and acceleration bounds must be satisfied. This means that there are second-order constraints on $\mathcal{C}$. The original work used the double integrator model $\ddot{q} = u$ for $\mathcal{C} = \mathbb{R}^2$ and $\mathcal{C} = \mathbb{R}^3$. A scalar version of this model appeared Example 13.3. More recently, the term has been applied by some authors to virtually any motion planning problem that involves dynamics. Thus, any problem that involves second-order (or higher) differential constraints can be considered as a form of kinodynamic planning. Thus, if x includes velocity variables, then kinodynamic planning includes any system, $\dot{x} = f(x, u)$.

Note that kinodynamic planning is not necessarily a form of nonholonomic planning; in most cases considered so far, it is not. A problem may even involve both nonholonomic and kinodynamic planning. This requires the differential constraints to be both nonintegrable and at least second-order. This situation often results from constrained Lagrangian analysis, covered in Section 13.4.3. The car with dynamics which was given Section 13.3.3 is both kinodynamic and nonholonomic.

Trajectory planning

The term *trajectory planning* has been used for decades in robotics to refer mainly to the problem of determining both a path and velocity function for a robot arm (e.g., PUMA 560). This corresponds to finding a path in the phase space X in which $x \in X$ is defined as $x = (q, \dot{q})$. Most often the problem is solved using the refinement approach mentioned in Section 1.4 by first computing a path through $\mathcal{C}_{free}$. For each configuration q along the path, a velocity $\dot{q}$ must be computed that satisfies the differential constraints. An inverse control problem may also exist, which involves computing for each t, the action $u(t)$ that results in the desired $\dot{q}(t)$. The refinement approach is often referred to as *time scaling* of a path through $\mathcal{C}$ [459]. In recent times, trajectory planning seems synonymous with kinodynamic planning, assuming that the constraints are second-order (x includes only configuration and velocity variables). One distinction is that trajectory planning still perhaps bears the historical connotations of an approach that first plans a path through $\mathcal{C}_{free}$.

14.1.2.2 Terms from control theory

A significant amount of terminology that is appropriate for planning has been developed in the control theory community. In some cases, there are even conflicts with planning terminology. For example, the term *motion planning* has been used to refer to nonholonomic planning in the absence of obstacles [158, 730]. This can be considered as a kind of BVP. In some cases, this form of planning is referred to as the *steering problem* (see [599, 728]) and will be covered in Section 15.5. The term *motion planning* is reserved in this book for problems that involve obstacle avoidance and possibly other constraints.

Open-loop control laws

Differential models, such as any of those from Chapter 13, are usually referred to as *control systems* or just *systems*, a term that we have used already. These are divided into *linear* and *nonlinear* systems, as described in Sections 13.2.2 and 13.2.3, respectively. Formulation 14.1 can be considered in control terminology as the design of an *open-loop control law* for the system (subjected to nonconvex constraints on the state space). The *open-loop* part indicates that no feedback is used. Only the action trajectory needs to be specified over time (the feedback case is called *closed-loop*; recall Section 8.1). Once the initial state is given, the state trajectory can be inferred from the action trajectory. It may also be qualified as a *feasible* open-loop control law, to indicate that it satisfies all constraints but is not necessarily optimal. It is then interesting to consider designing an *optimal* open-loop control law. This is extremely challenging, even for problems that appear to be very simple. Elegant solutions exist for some restricted cases, including linear systems and some wheeled vehicle models, but in the absence of obstacles. These are covered in Chapter 15.

Drift

The term *drift* arose in Section 13.2.1 and implies that from some states it is impossible to instantaneously stop. This difficulty arises in mechanical systems due to momentum. Infinite deceleration, and therefore infinite energy, would be required to remove all kinetic energy from a mechanical system in an instant of time. Kinodynamic and trajectory planning generally involve drift. Nonholonomic planning problems may be *driftless* if only velocity constraints exist on the C-space; the models of Section 13.1.2 are driftless. From a planning perspective, systems with drift are usually more challenging than driftless systems.

Underactuation

Action variables, the components of u, are often referred to as *actuators*, and a system is called *underactuated* if the number of actuators is strictly less than the dimension of C. In other words, there are less independent action variables than the degrees of freedom of the mechanical system. Underactuated nonlinear systems are typically nonholonomic. Therefore, a substantial amount of nonholonomic system theory and planning for non-holonomic systems involves applications to underactuated systems. As an example of an underactuated system, consider a free-floating spacecraft in $\mathbb{R}^3$ that has three thrusters. The amount of force applied by each thruster can be declared as an action variable; however, the system is underactuated because there are only three actuators, and the dimension of C is six. Other examples appeared Section 13.1.2. If the system is not underactuated, it is called *fully actuated*, which means that the number of actuators is equal to the dimension of C. Kinodynamic planning has mostly addressed fully actuated systems.

Symmetric systems

Finally, one property of systems that is important in some planning algorithms is *symmetry*.[1] A system $\dot{x} = f(x, u)$ is symmetric if the following condition holds. If there exists

---

[1] Sometimes in control theory, the term symmetry applies to Lie groups. This is a different concept and means that the system is invariant with respect to transformations in a group such as $SE(3)$. For example, the dynamics of a car should not depend on the direction in which the car is pointing.

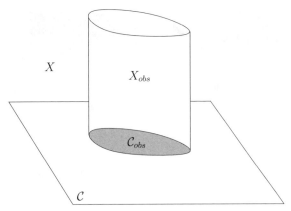

Figure 14.1: An obstacle region $\mathcal{C}_{obs} \subset \mathcal{C}$ generates a cylindrical obstacle region $X_{obs} \subset X$ with respect to the phase variables.

an action trajectory that brings the system from some x_I to some x_G, then there exists another action trajectory that brings the system from x_G to x_I by visiting the same points in X, but in reverse time. At each point along the path, this means that the velocity can be negated by a different choice of action. Thus, it is possible for a symmetric system to reverse any motions. This is usually not possible for systems with drift. An example of a symmetric system is the differential drive of Section 13.1.2. For the simple car, the Reeds-Shepp version is symmetric, but the Dubins version is not because the car cannot travel in reverse.

14.1.3 Obstacles in the phase space

In Formulation 14.1, the specification of the obstacle region in Item 4 was intentionally left ambiguous. Now it will be specified in more detail. If $X = \mathcal{C}$, then $X_{obs} = \mathcal{C}_{obs}$, which was defined in (4.34) for a rigid robot and in (4.36) for a robot with multiple links. The more interesting case occurs if X is a phase space that includes velocity variables in addition to configuration information.

Any state for which its associated configuration lies in $\mathcal{C}_{obs}$ must also be a member of X_{obs}. The velocity is irrelevant if a collision occurs in the world $\mathcal{W}$. In most cases that involve a phase space, the obstacle region X_{obs} is therefore defined as

$$X_{obs} = \{x \in X \mid \kappa(x) \in \mathcal{C}_{obs}\}, \tag{14.2}$$

in which $\kappa(x)$ is the configuration associated with the state $x \in X$. If the first n variables of X are configuration parameters, then X_{obs} has the cylindrical structure shown in Figure 14.1 with respect to the other variables. If κ is a complicated mapping, as opposed to simply selecting the configuration coordinates, then the structure might not appear cylindrical. In these cases, (14.2) still indicates the correct obstacle region in X.

14.1.3.1 Additional constraints on phase variables

In many applications, additional constraints may exist on the phase variables. These are called *phase constraints* and are generally of the form $h_i(x) \leq 0$. For example, a car or hovercraft may have a maximum speed for safety reasons. Therefore, simple bounds on the velocity variables will exist. For example, it might be specified that $\|\dot{q}\| \leq \dot{q}_{max}$ for some constant $\dot{q}_{max} \in (0, \infty)$. Such simple bounds are often incorporated directly into the definition of X by placing limits on the velocity variables.

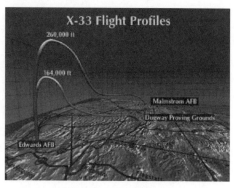

NASA/Lockheed Martin X-33   Re-entry trajectory

Figure 14.2: In the NASA/Lockheed Martin X-33 re-entry problem, there are complicated constraints on the phase variables, which avoid states that cause the craft to overheat or vibrate uncontrollably. (Courtesy of NASA)

In other cases, however, constraints on velocity may be quite complicated. For example, the problem of computing the re-entry trajectory of the NASA/Lockheed Martin X-33 reusable spacecraft[2] (see Figure 14.2) requires remaining within a complicated, narrow region in the phase space. Even though there are no hard obstacles in the traditional sense, many bad things can happen by entering the wrong part of the phase space. For example, the craft may overheat or vibrate uncontrollably [162, 203, 665]. For a simpler example, imagine constraints on X to ensure that an SUV or a double-decker tour bus (as often seen in London, for example) will not tumble sideways while turning.

The additional constraints can be expressed implicitly as $h_i(x) \leq 0$. As part of determining whether some state x lies in X_{free} or X_{obs}, it must be substituted into each constraint to determine whether it is satisfied. If a state lies in X_{free}, it will generally be called *violation-free*, which implies that it is both collision-free and does not violate any additional phase constraints.

14.1.3.2 The region of inevitable collision

One of the most challenging aspects of planning can be visualized in terms of the *region of inevitable collision*, denoted by X_{ric}. This is the set of states from which entry into X_{obs} will eventually occur, regardless of any actions that are applied. As a simple example, imagine that a robotic vehicle is traveling 100 km/hr toward a large wall and is only 2 meters away. Clearly the robot is doomed. Due to momentum, collision will occur regardless of any efforts to stop or turn the vehicle. At low enough speeds, X_{ric} and X_{obs} are approximately the same; however, X_{ric} grows dramatically as the speed increases.

Let $\mathcal{U}_\infty$ denote the set of all trajectories $\tilde{u} : [0, \infty) \to U$ for which the termination action u_T is *never* applied (we do not want inevitable collision to be avoided by simply applying u_T). The *region of inevitable collision* is defined as

$$X_{ric} = \{x(0) \in X \mid \text{ for any } \tilde{u} \in \mathcal{U}_\infty , \ \exists t > 0 \text{ such that } x(t) \in X_{obs}\}, \qquad (14.3)$$

in which $x(t)$ is the state at time t obtained by applying (14.1) from $x(0)$. This does not include cases in which motions are eventually blocked, but it is possible to bring the system to a state with zero velocity. Suppose that the Dubins car from Section 13.1.2 is

---

[2] This project was canceled in 2001, but similar crafts have been under development.

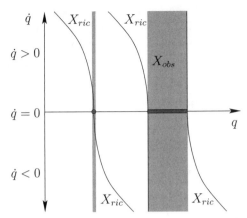

Figure 14.3: The region of inevitable collision grows quadratically with the speed.

used and the car is unable to back its way out of a dead-end alley. In this case, it can avoid collision by stopping and remaining motionless. If it continues to move, it will eventually have no choice but to collide. This case appears more like being trapped and technically does not fit under the definition of X_{ric}. For driftless systems, $X_{ric} = X_{obs}$.

Example 14.1 (Region of Inevitable Collision) Figure 14.3 shows a simple illustration of X_{ric}. Suppose that $\mathcal{W} = \mathbb{R}$, and the robot is a particle (or point mass) that moves according to the double integrator model $\ddot{q} = u$ (for mass, assume $m = 1$). For simplicity, suppose that u represents a force that must be chosen from $U = [-1, 1]$. The C-space is $\mathcal{C} = \mathbb{R}$, the phase space is $X = \mathbb{R}^2$, and a phase (or state) is expressed as $x = (q, \dot{q})$. Suppose that there are two obstacles in $\mathcal{C}$: a point and an interval. These are shown in Figure 14.3 along the q-axis. In the cylinder above them, X_{obs} appears. In the slice at $\dot{q} = 0$, $X_{ric} = X_{obs} = \mathcal{C}_{obs}$. As $\dot{q}$ increases, X_{ric} becomes larger, even though X_{obs} remains fixed. Note that X_{ric} only grows toward the left because $\dot{q} > 0$ indicates a positive velocity, which causes momentum in the positive q direction. As this momentum increases, the distance required to stop increases quadratically. From a speed of $\dot{q} = v$, the minimum distance required to stop is $v^2/2$, which can be calculated by applying the action $u = -1$ and integrating $\ddot{q} = u$ twice. If $\dot{q} > 0$ and q is to the right of an obstacle, then it will safely avoid the obstacle, regardless of its speed. If $\dot{q} < 0$, then X_{ric} extends to the right instead of the left. Again, this is due to the required stopping distance. ∎

In higher dimensions and for more general systems, the problem becomes substantially more complicated. For example, in $\mathbb{R}^2$ the robot can swerve to avoid small obstacles. In general, the particular direction of motion becomes important. Also, the topology of X_{ric} may be quite different from that of X_{obs}. Imagine that a small airplane flies into a cave that consists of a complicated network of corridors. Once the plane enters the cave, there may be no possible actions that can avoid collision. The entire part of the state space that corresponds to the plane in the cave would be included in X_{ric}. Furthermore, even parts of the state space from which the plane cannot avoid entering the cave must be included.

In sampling-based planning under differential constraints, X_{ric} is not computed because it is too complicated.[3] It is not even known how to make a "collision detector" for X_{ric}. By

---

[3] It may, however, be possible to compute crude approximations of X_{ric} and use them in planning.

working instead with X_{obs}, challenges arise due to momentum. There may be large parts of the state space that are never worth exploring because they lie in X_{ric}. Unfortunately, there is no practical way at present to accurately determine whether states lie in X_{ric}. As the momentum and amount of clutter increase, this becomes increasingly problematic.

14.2 Reachability and completeness

This section provides preliminary concepts for sampling-based planning algorithms. In Chapter 5, sampling over C was of fundamental importance. The most important consideration was that a sequence of samples should be *dense* so that samples get arbitrarily close to any point in C_{free}. Planning under differential constraints is complicated by the specification of solutions by an action trajectory instead of a path through X_{free}. For sampling-based algorithms to be resolution complete, sampling and searching performed on the space of action trajectories must somehow lead to a dense set in X_{free}.

14.2.1 Reachable sets

For the algorithms in Chapter 5, resolution completeness and probabilistic completeness rely on having a sampling sequence that is dense on C. In the present setting, this would require dense sampling on X. Differential constraints, however, substantially complicate the sampling process. It is generally not reasonable to prescribe precise samples in X that must be reached because reaching them may be impossible or require solving a BVP. Since paths in X are obtained indirectly via action trajectories, completeness analysis begins with considering which points can be reached by integrating action trajectories.

14.2.1.1 Reachable set

Assume temporarily that there are no obstacles: $X_{free} = X$. Let $\mathcal{U}$ be the set of all permissible action trajectories on the time interval $[0, \infty)$. From each $\tilde{u} \in \mathcal{U}$, a state trajectory $\tilde{x}(x_0, \tilde{u})$ is defined using (14.1). Which states in X are visited by these trajectories? It may be possible that all of X is visited, but in general some states may not be reachable due to differential constraints.

Let $R(x_0, \mathcal{U}) \subseteq X$ denote the *reachable set* from x_0, which is the set of all states that are visited by any trajectories that start at x_0 and are obtained from some $\tilde{u} \in \mathcal{U}$ by integration. This can be expressed formally as

$$R(x_0, \mathcal{U}) = \{x_1 \in X \mid \exists \tilde{u} \in \mathcal{U} \text{ and } \exists t \in [0, \infty) \text{ such that } x(t) = x_1\}, \qquad (14.4)$$

in which $x(t)$ is given by (14.1) and requires that $x(0) = x_0$.

The following example illustrates some simple cases.

Example 14.2 (Reachable Sets for Simple Inequality Constraints)   Suppose that $X = C = \mathbb{R}^2$, and recall some of the simple constraints from Section 13.1.1. Let a point in $\mathbb{R}^2$ be denoted as $q = (x, y)$. Let the state transition equation be $\dot{x} = u_1$ and $\dot{y} = u_2$, in which $(u_1, u_2) \in U = \mathbb{R}^2$.

Several constraints will now be imposed on U, to define different possible action spaces. Suppose it is required that $u_1 > 0$ (this was $\dot{x} > 0$ in Section 13.1.1). The reachable set $R(q_0, \mathcal{U})$ from any $q_0 = (x_0, y_0) \in \mathbb{R}^2$ is an open half-plane that is defined by the set of all points to the right of the vertical line $x = x_0$. In the case of $u_1 \leq 0$, then $R(q_0, \mathcal{U})$ is a closed half-plane to the left of the same vertical line. If U is defined as the set of all

$(u_1, u_2) \in \mathbb{R}^2$ such that $u_1 > 0$ and $u_2 > 0$, then the reachable set from any point is a quadrant.

For the constraint $au_1 + bu_2 = 0$, the reachable set from any point is a line in $\mathbb{R}^2$ with normal vector (a, b). The location of the line depends on the particular q_0. Thus, a family of parallel lines is obtained by considering reachable states from different initial states. This is an example of a *foliation* in differential geometry, and the lines are called *leaves* [874].

In the case of $u_1^2 + u_2^2 \leq 1$, the reachable set from any (x_0, y_0) is $\mathbb{R}^2$. Thus, any state can reach any other state. ∎

So far the obstacle region has not been considered. Let $\mathcal{U}_{free} \subseteq \mathcal{U}$ denote the set of all action trajectories that produce state trajectories that map into X_{free}. In other words, $\mathcal{U}_{free}$ is obtained by removing from $\mathcal{U}$ all action trajectories that cause entry into X_{obs} for some $t > 0$. The reachable set that takes the obstacle region into account is denoted $R(x_0, \mathcal{U}_{free})$, which replaces $\mathcal{U}$ by $\mathcal{U}_{free}$ in (14.4). This assumes that for the trajectories in $\mathcal{U}_{free}$, the termination action can be applied to avoid inevitable collisions due to momentum. A smaller reachable set could have been defined that eliminates trajectories for which collision inevitably occurs without applying u_T.

The completeness of an algorithm can be expressed in terms of reachable sets. For any given pair $x_I, x_G \in X_{free}$, a complete algorithm must report a solution action trajectory if $x_G \in R(x_I, \mathcal{U}_{free})$, or report failure otherwise. Completeness is too difficult to achieve, except for very limited cases [173, 750]; therefore, sampling-based notions of completeness are more valuable.

14.2.1.2 Time-limited reachable set

Consider the set of all states that can be reached up to some fixed time limit. Let the *time-limited reachable set* $R(x_0, \mathcal{U}, t)$ be the subset of $R(x_0, \mathcal{U})$ that is reached up to and including time t. Formally, this is

$$R(x_0, \mathcal{U}, t) = \{x_1 \in X \mid \exists \tilde{u} \in \mathcal{U} \text{ and } \exists t' \in [0, t] \text{ such that } x(t') = x_1\}. \tag{14.5}$$

For the last case in Example 14.2, the time-limited reachable sets are closed discs of radius t centered at (x_0, y_0). A version of (14.5) that takes the obstacle region into account can be defined as $R(x_0, \mathcal{U}_{free}, t)$.

Imagine an animation of $R(x_0, \mathcal{U}, t)$ that starts at $t = 0$ and gradually increases t. The boundary of $R(x_0, \mathcal{U}, t)$ can be imagined as a propagating wavefront that begins at x_0. It eventually reaches the boundary of $R(x_0, \mathcal{U})$ (assuming it has a boundary; it does not if $R(x_0, \mathcal{U}) = X$). The boundary of $R(x_0, \mathcal{U}, t)$ can actually be interpreted as a level set of the optimal cost-to-come from x_0 for a cost functional that measures the elapsed time. The boundary is also a kind of forward projection, as considered for discrete spaces in Section 10.1.2. In that context, possible future states due to nature were specified in the forward projection. In the current setting, possible future states are determined by the unspecified actions of the robot. Rather than looking k stages ahead, the time-limited reachable set looks for duration t into the future. In the present context there is essentially a continuum of stages.

Example 14.3 (Reachable Sets for Simple Cars) Nice illustrations of reachable sets can be obtained from the simple car models from Section 13.1.2. Suppose that $X = C = \mathbb{R}^2 \times \mathbb{S}^1$ and $X_{obs} = \emptyset$.

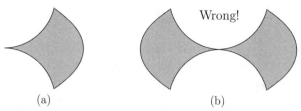

(a)   (b)

Figure 14.4: (a) The time-limited reachable set for the Dubins car facing to the right; (b) this is *not* the time-limited reachable set for the Reeds-Shepp car!

Recall that the Dubins car can only drive forward. From an arbitrary configuration, the time-limited reachable set appears as shown in Figure 14.4a. The time limit t is small enough so that the car cannot rotate by more than $\pi/2$. Note that Figure 14.4a shows a 2D projection of the reachable set that gives translation only. The true reachable set is a 3D region in $\mathcal{C}$. If $t > 2\pi$, then the car will be able to drive in a circle. For any q, consider the limiting case as t approaches infinity, which results in $R(q, \mathcal{U})$. Imagine a car driving without reverse on an infinitely large, flat surface. It is possible to reach any desired configuration by driving along a circle, driving straight for a while, and then driving along a circle again. Therefore, $R(q, \mathcal{U}) = \mathcal{C}$ for any $q \in \mathcal{C}$. The lack of a reverse gear means that some extra maneuvering space may be needed to reach some configurations.

Now consider the Reeds-Shepp car, which is allowed to travel in reverse. Any time-limited reachable set for this car must include all points from the corresponding reachable set for the Dubins car because new actions have been added to U but none have been removed. It is tempting to assert that the time-limited reachable set appears as in Figure 14.4b; however, this is wrong. In an arbitrarily small amount of time (or space) a car with reverse can be wiggled sideways. This is achieved in practice by familiar parallel-parking maneuvers. It turns out in this case that $R(q, \mathcal{U}, t)$ always contains an open set around q, which means that it grows in all directions (see Section 15.3.2). The property is formally referred to as small-time controllability and is covered in Section 15.4. ∎

14.2.1.3 Backward reachable sets

The reachability definitions have a nice symmetry with respect to time. Rather than describing all points reachable from some $x \in X$, it is just as easy to describe all points from which some $x \in X$ can be reached. This is similar to the alternative between forward and backward projections in Section 10.1.2.

Let the *backward reachable set* be defined as

$$B(x_f, \mathcal{U}) = \{x_0 \in X \mid \exists \tilde{u} \in \mathcal{U} \text{ and } \exists t \in [0, \infty) \text{ such that } x(t) = x_f\}, \qquad (14.6)$$

in which $x(t)$ is given by (14.1) and requires that $x(0) = x_0$. Note the intentional similarity to (14.4). The *time-limited backward reachable set* is defined as

$$B(x_f, \mathcal{U}, t) = \{x_0 \in X \mid \exists \tilde{u} \in \mathcal{U} \text{ and } \exists t' \in [0, t] \text{ such that } x(t') = x_f\}, \qquad (14.7)$$

which once again requires that $x(0) = x_0$ in (14.1). Completeness can even be defined in terms of backward reachable sets by defining a backward-time counterpart to $\mathcal{U}$.

At this point, there appear to be close parallels between forward, backward, and bidirectional searches from Chapter 2. The same possibilities exist in sampling-based planning under differential constraints. The forward and backward reachable sets indicate

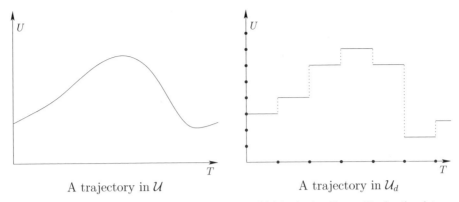

A trajectory in $\mathcal{U}$ A trajectory in $\mathcal{U}_d$

Figure 14.5: The discrete-time model results in $\mathcal{U}_d \subset \mathcal{U}$, which is obtained by partitioning time into regular intervals and applying a constant action over each interval. The action is chosen from a finite subset U_d of U.

the possible states that can be reached under such schemes. The algorithms explore subsets of these reachable sets.

14.2.2 The discrete-time model

This section introduces a simple and effective way to sample the space of action trajectories. Section 14.2.3 covers the more general case. Under differential constraints, sampling-based motion planning algorithms all work by sampling the space of action trajectories. This results in a reduced set of possible action trajectories. To ensure some form of completeness, a motion planning algorithm should carefully construct and refine the sample set. As in Chapter 5, the qualities of a sample set can be expressed in terms of dispersion and denseness. The main difference in the current setting is that the algorithms here work with a sample sequence over $\mathcal{U}$, as opposed to over $\mathcal{C}$ as in Chapter 5. This is required because solution paths can no longer be expressed directly on $\mathcal{C}$ (or X).

The *discrete-time model* is depicted in Figure 14.5 and is characterized by three aspects:

1. Time T is partitioned into intervals of length Δt. This enables stages to be assigned, in which stage k indicates that $(k-1)\Delta t$ units of time have elapsed.

2. A finite subset U_d of the action space U is chosen. If U is already finite, then this selection may be $U_d = U$.

3. The action $u(t) \in U_d$ must remain constant over each time interval.

The first two discretize time and the action spaces. The third condition is needed to relate the time discretization to the space of action trajectories. Let $\mathcal{U}_d$ denote the set of all action trajectories allowed under a given time discretization. Note that $\mathcal{U}_d$ completely specifies the discrete-time model.

For some problems, U may already be finite. Imagine, for example, a model of firing one of several thrusters (turn them *on* or *off*) on a free-floating spacecraft. In this case no discretization of U is necessary. In the more general case, U may be a continuous set. The sampling methods of Section 5.2 can be applied to determine a finite subset $U_d \subseteq U$.

Any action trajectory in $\mathcal{U}_d$ can be conveniently expressed as an *action sequence* $(u_1, u_2, \ldots, u_k)$, in which each $u_i \in U_d$ gives the action to apply from time $(i-1)\Delta t$ to time $i\Delta t$. After stage k, it is assumed that the termination action is applied.

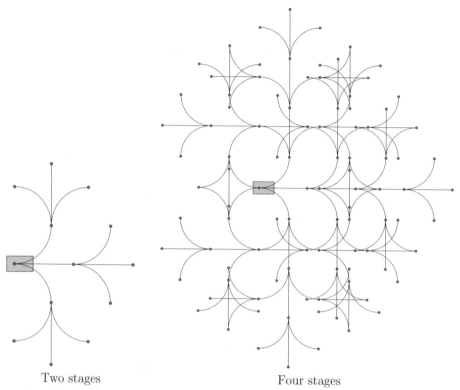

Two stages   Four stages

Figure 14.6: A reachability tree for the Dubins car with three actions. The *k*th stage produces 3^k new vertices.

14.2.2.1 Reachability graph

After time discretization has been performed, the reachable set can be adapted to $\mathcal{U}_d$ to obtain $R(x_0, \mathcal{U}_d)$. An interesting question is: What is the effect of sampling on the reachable set? In other words, how do $R(x_0, \mathcal{U})$ and $R(x_0, \mathcal{U}_d)$ differ? This can be addressed by defining a reachability graph, which will be revealed incrementally by a planning algorithm.

Let $T_r(x_0, \mathcal{U}_d)$ denote a *reachability tree*, which encodes the set of all trajectories from x_0 that can be obtained by applying trajectories in $\mathcal{U}_d$. Each vertex of $T_r(x_0, \mathcal{U}_d)$ is a reachable state, $x \in R(x_0, \mathcal{U}_d)$. Each edge of $T_r(x_0, \mathcal{U}_d)$ is directed; its source represents a starting state, and its destination represents the state obtained by applying a constant action $u \in U_d$ over time Δt. Each edge e represents an action trajectory segment, $e : [0, \Delta t] \to U$. This can be transformed into a state trajectory, $\tilde{x}_e$, via integration using (14.1), from 0 to Δt of $f(x, u)$ from the source state of e.

Thus, in terms of $\tilde{x}_e$, T_r can be considered as a topological graph in X (T_r will be used as an abbreviation of $T_r(x_0, \mathcal{U}_d)$). The *swath* $S(T_r)$ of T_r is

$$S(T_r) = \bigcup_{e \in E} \bigcup_{t \in [0, \Delta t]} x_e(t), \tag{14.8}$$

in which $x_e(t)$ denotes the state obtained at time t from edge e. (Recall topological graphs from Example 4.6 and the swath from Section 5.5.1.)

Example 14.4 (Reachability Tree for the Dubins Car) Several stages of the reachability tree for the Dubins car are shown in Figure 14.6. Suppose that there are three actions (straight, right-turn, left-turn), and Δt is chosen so that if the right-turn or left-turn action is applied, the car travels enough to rotate by $\pi/2$. After the second stage, there are nine leaves in the tree, as shown in Figure 14.6a. Each stage produces 3^k new leaves. In Figure 14.6b, 81 new leaves are added in stage $k = 4$, which yields a total of $81 + 27 + 9 + 3 + 1$ vertices. In many cases, the same state is reachable by different action sequences. The swath after the first four stages is the set of all points visited so far. This is a subset of $\mathcal{C}$ that is the union of all vertices and all points traced out by $\tilde{x}_e$ for each $e \in E$. ∎

From Example 14.4 it can be seen that it is sometimes possible to arrive at the same state using two or more alternative action trajectories. Since each action trajectory can be expressed as an action sequence, the familiar issue arises from classical AI search of detecting whether the same state has been reached from different action sequences. For some systems, the reachability problem can be dramatically simplified by exploiting this information. If the same state is reached from multiple action sequences, then only one vertex needs to be represented.

This yields a directed *reachability graph* $\mathcal{G}_r(x_0, \mathcal{U}_d)$, which is obtained from $T_r(x_0, \mathcal{U}_d)$ by merging its duplicate states. If every action sequence arrives at a unique state, then the reachability graph reduces to the reachability tree. However, if multiple action sequences arrive at the same state, this is represented as a single vertex $\mathcal{G}_r$. From this point onward, the reachability graph will be primarily used. As for a reachability tree, a reachability graph can be interpreted as a topological graph in X, and its swath $S(\mathcal{G}_r)$ is defined by adapting (14.8).

The simplest case of arriving at the same state was observed in Example 2.1. The discrete grid in the plane can be modeled using the terminology of Chapter 13 as a system of the form $\dot{x} = u_1$ and $\dot{y} = u_2$ for a state space $X = \mathbb{R}^2$. The discretized set U_d of actions is $\{(1, 0), (0, 1), (-1, 0), (0, -1)\}$. Let $\Delta t = 1$. In this case, the reachability graph becomes the familiar 2D grid. If $(0, 0)$ is the initial state, then the grid vertices consist of all states in which both coordinates are integers.

Through careless discretization of an arbitrary system, such a nice grid usually does not arise. However, in many cases a discretization can be carefully chosen so that the states become trapped on a grid or lattice. This has some advantages in sampling-based planning. Section 14.4.1 covers a method that exploits such structure for the system $\ddot{q} = u$. It can even be extended to more general systems, provided that the system can be expressed as $\ddot{q} = g(q, \dot{q}, u)$ and it is not underactuated. It was shown recently that by a clever choice of discretization, a very large class of nonholonomic systems[4] can also be forced onto a lattice [765]. This is usually difficult to achieve, and under most discretizations the vertices of the reachability graph are dense in the reachable set.

It is also possible to define backward versions of the reachability tree and reachability graph, in the same way that backward reachable sets were obtained. These indicate initial states and action sequences that will reach a given goal state and are no more difficult to define or compute than their forward counterparts. They might appear more difficult, but keep in mind that the initial states are not fixed; thus, no BVP appears. The initial states can be obtained by reverse-time integration of the state transition equation; see Section 14.3.2.

14.2.2.2 Resolution completeness for $\dot{x} = u$

Sampling-based notions of completeness can be expressed in terms of reachable sets and the reachability graph. The requirement is to sample $\mathcal{U}$ in a way that causes the vertices

---

[4] The class is all driftless, nilpotent systems. The term nilpotent will be defined in Section 15.5.

of the reachability graph to eventually become dense in the reachable set, while also making sure that the reachability graph is systematically searched. All of the completeness concepts can be expressed in terms of forward or backward reachability graphs. Only the forward case will be described because the backward case is very similar.

To help bridge the gap with respect to motion planning as covered in Part II, first suppose: 1) $X = C = \mathbb{R}^2$, 2) a state is denoted as $q = (x, y)$, 3) $U = [-1, 1]^2$, and 4) the state transition equation is $\dot{x} = u_1$ and $\dot{y} = u_2$. Suppose that the discrete-time model is applied to $\mathcal{U}$. Let $\Delta t = 1$ and

$$U_d = \{(-1, 0), (0, -1), (1, 0), (0, 1)\}, \tag{14.9}$$

which yields the Manhattan motion model from Example 7.4. Staircase paths are produced as was shown in Figure 7.40. In the present setting, these paths are obtained by integrating the action trajectory. From some state x_I, the reachability graph represents the set of all possible staircase paths with unit step size that can be obtained via (14.1).

Suppose that under this model, X_{free} is a bounded, open subset of $\mathbb{R}^2$. The connection to resolution completeness from Chapter 5 can be expressed clearly in this case. For any fixed Δt, a grid of a certain resolution is implicitly defined via the reachability graph. The task is to find an action sequence that leads to the goal (or a vertex close to it in the reachability graph) while remaining in X_{free}. Such a sequence can be found by a systematic search, as considered in Section 2.2. If the search is systematic, then it will correctly determine whether the reachability graph encodes a solution. If no solution exists, then the planning algorithm can decrease Δt by a constant factor (e.g., 2), and perform the systematic search again. This process repeats indefinitely until a solution is found. The algorithm runs forever if no solution exists (in practice, of course, one terminates early and gives up). The approach just described is resolution complete in the sense used in Chapter 5, even though all paths are expressed using action sequences.

The connection to ordinary motion planning is clear for this simple model because the action trajectories integrate to produce motions that follow a grid. As the time discretization is improved, the staircase paths can come arbitrarily close to some solution path. Looking at Figure 14.5, it can be seen that as the sampling resolution is improved with respect to U and T, the trajectories obtained via discrete-time approximations converge to any trajectory that can be obtained by integrating some $\tilde{u}$. In general, convergence occurs as Δt and the dispersion of the sampling in U are driven to zero. This also holds in the same way for the more general case in which $\dot{x} = u$ and X is any smooth manifold. Imagine placing a grid down on X and refining it arbitrarily by reducing Δt.

14.2.2.3 Resolution completeness for $\dot{x} = f(x, u)$

Beyond the trivial case of $\dot{x} = u$, the reachability graph is usually not a simple grid. Even if X is bounded, the reachability graph may have an infinite number of vertices, even though Δt is fixed and U_d is finite. For a simple example, consider the Dubins car under the discretization $\Delta t = 1$. Fix $u_\phi = -\phi_{max}$ (turn left) for all $t \in T$. This branch alone generates a countably infinite number of vertices in the reachability graph. The circumference of the circle is $2\pi\rho_{min}$, in which ρ_{min} is the minimum turning radius. Let $\rho_{min} = 1$. Since the circumference is an irrational number, it is impossible to revisit the initial point by traveling k seconds for some integer k. It is even impossible to revisit any point on the circle. The set of vertices in the reachability graph is actually dense in the circle. This did not happen in Figure 14.6 because Δt and the circumference were rationally related (i.e., one can be obtained from the other via multiplication by a rational number). Consider what happens in the current example when $\rho_{min} = 1/\pi$ and $\Delta t = 1$.

Suppose that $\dot{x} = f(x, u)$ and the discrete-time model is used. To ensure convergence of the discrete-time approximation, f must be well-behaved. This can be established by requiring that all of the derivatives of f with respect to u and x are bounded above and below by a constant. More generally, f is assumed to be Lipschitz, which is an equivalent condition for cases in which the derivatives exist, but it also applies at points that are not differentiable. If U is finite, then the Lipschitz condition is that there exists some $c \in (0, \infty)$ such that

$$\| f(x, u) - f(x', u) \| \leq c \| x - x' \| \tag{14.10}$$

for all $x, x' \in X$, for all $u \in U$, and $\| \cdot \|$ denotes a norm on X. If U is infinite, then the condition is that there must exist some $c \in (0, \infty)$ such that

$$\| f(x, u) - f(x', u') \| \leq c(\| x - x' \| + \| u - u' \|), \tag{14.11}$$

for all $x, x' \in X$, and for all $u, u' \in U$. Intuitively, the Lipschitz condition indicates that if x and u are approximated by x' and u', then the error when substituted into f will be manageable. If convergence to optimal trajectories with respect to a cost functional is important, then Lipschitz conditions are also needed for $l(x, u)$. Under such mild assumptions, if Δt and the dispersion of samples of U_d is driven down to zero, then the trajectories obtained from integrating discrete action sequences come arbitrarily close to solution trajectories. In other words, action sequences provide arbitrarily close approximations to any $\tilde{u} \in U$. If f is Lipschitz, then the integration of (14.14) yields approximately the same result for $\tilde{u}$ as the approximating action sequence.

In the limit as Δt and the dispersion of U_d approach zero, the reachability graph becomes dense in the reachable set $R(x_I, \mathcal{U})$. Ensuring a systematic search for the case of a grid was not difficult because there is only a finite number of vertices at each resolution. Unfortunately, the reachability graph may generally have a countably infinite number of vertices for some fixed discrete-time model, even if X is bounded.

To see that resolution-complete algorithms nevertheless exist if the reachability graph is countably infinite, consider *triangular enumeration*, which proves that $\mathbb{N} \times \mathbb{N}$ is countable, in which $\mathbb{N}$ is the set of natural numbers. The proof proceeds by giving a sequence that starts at $(0, 0)$ and proceeds by sweeping diagonally back and forth across the first quadrant. In the limit, all points are covered. The same idea can be applied to obtain resolution-complete algorithms. A sequence of discrete-time models can be made for which the time step Δt and the dispersion of the sampling of U approach zero. Each discretization produces a reachability graph that has a countable number of vertices.

A resolution-complete algorithm can be made by performing the same kind of zig-zagging that was used to show that $\mathbb{N} \times \mathbb{N}$ is countable. See Figure 14.7; suppose that U is finite and $U_d = U$. Along the horizontal axis is a sequence of improving discrete-time models. Each model generates its own reachability graph, for which a systematic search eventually explores all of its vertices. Imagine this exploration occurs one step at a time, in which one new vertex is reached in each step. The vertical axis in Figure 14.7 indicates the number of vertices reached so far by the search algorithm. A countably infinite set of computers could explore all of reachability graphs in parallel. With a single computer, it can still be assured that everything is eventually explored by zig-zagging as shown. Thus a resolution-complete algorithm always exists if U is finite. If U is not finite, then U_d must also be refined as the time step is decreased. Of course, there are numerous other

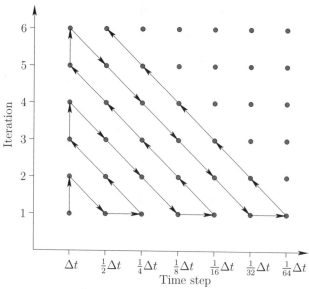

Figure 14.7: By systematically alternating between exploring different reachability graphs, resolution completeness can be achieved, even if each reachability graph has a countably infinite number of vertices.

ways to systematically explore all of the reachability graphs. The challenging task is to find a way that leads to good performance in practice.

The discussion so far has assumed that a sampling-based algorithm can uncover a subgraph of the reachability graph. This neglects numerical issues such as arithmetic precision and numerical integration error. Such issues can additionally be incorporated into a resolution completeness analysis [198].

14.2.3 Motion primitives

The discrete-time model of Section 14.2.2 is just one of many possible ways to discretize the space of action trajectories. It will now be considered as a special case of specifying *motion primitives*. The restriction to constant actions over fixed time intervals may be too restrictive in many applications. Suppose we want to automate the motions of a digital actor for use in a video game or film. Imagine having a database of interesting motion primitives. Such primitives could be extracted, for example, from motion capture data [35, 556]. For example, if the actor is designed for kung-fu fighting, then each motion sequence may correspond to a basic move, such a kick or punch. It is unlikely that such motion primitives correspond to constant actions over a fixed time interval. The durations of the motion primitives will usually vary.

Such models can generally be handled by defining a more general kind of discretization. The discrete-time model can be used to formulate a discrete-time state transition equation of the form

$$x_{k+1} = f_d(x_k, u_k), \tag{14.12}$$

in which $x_k = x((k-1)\Delta t)$, $x_{k+1} = x(k\Delta t)$, and u_k is the action in U_d that is applied from time $(k-1)\Delta t$ to time $k\Delta t$. Thus, f_d is a function $f_d : X \times U_d \to X$ that represents an approximation to f, the original state transition function. Every constant action $u \in U_d$ applied over Δt can be considered as a motion primitive.

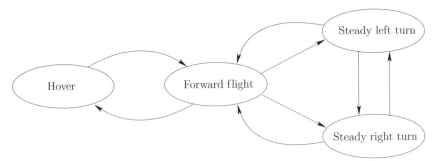

Figure 14.8: A maneuver automaton, proposed by Frazzoli [362], captures the constraints on allowable sequences of motion primitives.

Now generalize the preceding construction to allow more general motion primitives. Let $\tilde{u}^p$ denote a motion primitive, which is a function from an interval of time into U. Let the interval of time start at 0 and stop at $t_F(\tilde{u}^p)$, which is a final time that depends on the particular primitive. From any state $x \in X_{free}$, suppose that a set $\mathcal{U}^p(x)$ of motion primitives is available. The set may even be infinite, in which case some additional sampling must eventually be performed over the space of motion primitives by a local planning method. A state transition equation that operates over discrete stages can be defined as

$$x_{k+1} = f_p(x_k, \tilde{u}_k^p), \tag{14.13}$$

in which $\tilde{u}_k^p$ is a motion primitive that must be chosen from $\mathcal{U}^p(x_k)$. The time discretization model and (14.12) can be considered as a special case in which the motion primitives are all constant over a fixed time interval $[0, \Delta t)$. Note that in (14.13) the stage index k does not necessarily correspond to time $(k-1)\Delta t$. The index k merely represents the fact that $k-1$ motion primitives have been applied so far, and it is time to decide on the kth motion primitive. The current time is determined by summing the durations of all $k-1$ primitives applied so far. If a set $\mathcal{U}^p(x)$ of primitives is given for all $x \in X$, then a reachability graph and its swath can be defined by simple extensions of the discrete-time case. The discrete-time model $\mathcal{U}_d$ can now be interpreted as a special set of motion primitives.

For some motion primitives, it may not be possible to immediately sequence them without applying transitional motions. For example, in [364], two different kinds of motion primitives, called *trim trajectories* and *maneuvers*, are defined for autonomous helicopter flight. The trim trajectories correspond to steady motions, and maneuvers correspond to unsteady motions that are needed to make transitions between steady motions. Transitions from one trim trajectory to another are only permitted through the execution of a maneuver. The problem can be nicely modeled as a hybrid system in which each motion primitive represents a mode [362] (recall hybrid system concepts from Sections 7.3, 8.3.1, and 10.6). The augmented state space is $X \times M$, in which M is a set of modes. The transition equation (14.13) can be extended over the augmented state space so that motion primitives can change modes in addition to changing the original state. The possible trajectories for the helicopter follow paths in a graph called the *maneuver automaton*. An example from [362] is shown in Figure 14.8. Every edge and every vertex corresponds to a mode in the maneuver automaton. Each edge or vertex actually corresponds to a parameterized family of primitives, from which a particular one is chosen based on the state. A similar state machine is proposed in [455] for animating humans, and the motion primitives are called *behaviors*.

Discretizations based on general motion primitives offer great flexibility, and in many cases dramatic performance improvements can be obtained in a sampling-based planning algorithm. The main drawback is that the burden of establishing resolution completeness is increased.

14.3 Sampling-based motion planning revisited

Now that the preliminary concepts have been defined for motion planning under differential constraints, the focus shifts to extending the sampling-based planning methods of Chapter 5. This primarily involves extending the incremental sampling and searching framework from Section 5.4 to incorporate differential constraints. Following the general framework, several popular methods are covered in Section 14.4 as special cases of the framework. If an efficient BVP solver is available, then it may also be possible to extend sampling-based roadmaps of Section 5.6 to handle differential constraints.

14.3.1 Basic components

This section describes how Sections 5.1 to 5.3 are adapted to handle phase spaces and differential constraints.

14.3.1.1 Distance and volume in X

Recall from Chapter 5 that many sampling-based planning algorithms rely on measuring distances or volumes in $\mathcal{C}$. If $X = \mathcal{C}$, as in the wheeled systems from Section 13.1.2, then the concepts of Section 5.1 apply directly. The equivalent is needed for a general state space X, which may include phase variables in addition to the configuration variables. In most cases, the topology of the phase variables is trivial. For example, if $x = (q, \dot{q})$, then each $\dot{q}_i$ component is constrained to an interval of $\mathbb{R}$. In this case the velocity components are just an axis-aligned rectangular region in $\mathbb{R}^{n/2}$, if n is the dimension of X. It is straightforward in this case to extend a measure and metric defined on $\mathcal{C}$ up to X by forming the Cartesian product.

A metric can be defined using the Cartesian product method given by (5.4). The usual difficulty arises of arbitrarily weighting different components and combining them into a single scalar function. In the case of $\mathcal{C}$, this has involved combining translations and rotation. For X, this additionally includes velocity components, which makes it more difficult to choose meaningful weights.

Riemannian metrics

A rigorous way to define a metric on a smooth manifold is to define a *metric tensor* (or *Riemannian tensor*), which is a quadratic function of two tangent vectors. This can be considered as an inner product on X, which can be used to measure angles. This leads to the definition of the *Riemannian metric*, which is based on the shortest paths (called *geodesics*) in X [135]. An example of this appeared in the context of Lagrangian mechanics in Section 13.4.1. The kinetic energy, (13.70), serves as the required metric tensor, and the geodesics are the motions taken by the dynamical system to conserve energy. The metric can be defined as the length of the geodesic that connects a pair of points. If the chosen Riemannian metric has some physical significance, as in the case of Lagrangian mechanics, then the resulting metric provides meaningful information. Unfortunately, it may be difficult or expensive to compute its value.

The ideal distance function

The ideal way to define distance on X is to use a cost functional and then define the distance from $x \in X_{free}$ to $x' \in X_{free}$ as the optimal cost-to-go from x to x' while remaining in X_{free}. In some cases, it has been also referred to as the *nonholonomic metric*, *Carnot-Caratheodory metric*, or *sub-Riemannian metric* [599]. Note that this not a true metric, as mentioned in Section 5.1.2, because the cost may not be symmetric. For example, traveling a small distance forward with Dubins car is much shorter than traveling a small distance backward. If there are obstacles, it may not even be possible to reach configurations behind the car.

This concept of distance should be somewhat disturbing because it requires optimally solving the motion planning problem of Formulation 14.1. Thus, it cannot be practical for efficient use in a motion planning algorithm. Nevertheless, understanding this ideal notion of distance can be very helpful in designing practical distance functions on X. For example, rather than using a weighted Euclidean metric (often called *Mahalanobis metric*) for the Dubins car, a distance function can be defined based on the length of the shortest path between two configurations. These lengths are straightforward to compute, and are based on the optimal curve families that will be covered in Section 15.3. This distance function neglects obstacles, but it should still provide better distance information than the weighted Euclidean metric. It may also be useful for car models that involve dynamics.

The general idea is to get as close as possible to the optimal cost-to-go without having to perform expensive computations. It is often possible to compute a useful underestimate of the optimal cost-to-go by neglecting some of the constraints, such as obstacles or dynamics. This may help in applying A^* search heuristics.

Defining measure

As mentioned already, it is straightforward to extend a measure on $\mathcal{C}$ to X if the topology associated with the phase variables is trivial. It may not be possible, however, to obtain an invariant measure. In most cases, $\mathcal{C}$ is a transformation group, in which the Haar measure exists, thereby yielding the "true" volume in a sense that is not sensitive to parameterizations of $\mathcal{C}$. This was observed for $SO(3)$ in Section 5.1.4. For a general state space X, a Haar measure may not exist. If a Riemannian metric is defined, then intrinsic notions of surface integration and volume exist [135]; however, these may be difficult to exploit in a sampling-based planning algorithm.

14.3.1.2 Sampling theory

Section 14.2.2 already covered some of the sampling issues. There are at least two continuous spaces: X, and the time interval T. In most cases, the action space U is also continuous. Each continuous space must be sampled in some way. In the limit, it is important that any sample sequence is dense in the space on which sampling occurs. This was required for the resolution completeness concepts of Section 14.2.2.

Sampling of T and U can be performed by directly using the random or deterministic methods of Section 5.2. Time is just an interval of $\mathbb{R}$, and U is typically expressed as a convex m-dimensional subset of $\mathbb{R}^m$. For example, U is often an axis-aligned rectangular subset of $\mathbb{R}^m$.

Some planning methods may require sampling on X. The definitions of discrepancy and dispersion from Section 5.2 can be easily adapted to any measure space and metric space, respectively. Even though it may be straightforward to define a good criterion, generating samples that optimize the criterion may be difficult or impossible.

A convenient way to avoid this problem is to work in a coordinate neighborhood of X. This makes the manifold appear as an n-dimensional region in $\mathbb{R}^n$, which in many cases is rectangular. This enables the sampling concepts of Section 5.2 to be applied in a straightforward manner. While this is the most straightforward approach, the sampling quality depends on the particular parameterization used to define the coordinate neighborhood. Note that when working with a coordinate neighborhood (for example, by imagining that X is a cube), appropriate identifications must be taken into account.

14.3.1.3 Collision detection

As in Chapter 5, efficient collision detection algorithms are a key enabler of sampling-based planning. If $X = C$, then the methods of Section 5.3 directly apply. If X includes phase constraints, then additional tests must be performed. These constraints are usually given and are therefore straightforward to evaluate. Recall from Section 4.3 that this is not efficient for the obstacle constraints on C due to the complicated mapping between obstacles in $\mathcal{W}$ and obstacles in C.

If only pointwise tests are performed, the trajectory segment between the points is not guaranteed to stay in X_{free}. This problem was addressed in Section 5.3.4 by using distance information from collision checking algorithms. The same problem exists for the phase constraints of the form $h_i(x) \leq 0$. In this general form there is no additional information that can be used to ensure that some neighborhood of x is contained in X_{free}. Fortunately, the phase constraints are not complicated in most applications, and it is possible to ensure that x is at least some distance away from the constraint boundary. In general, careful analysis of each phase constraint is required to ensure that the state trajectory segments are violation-free.

In summary, determining whether $x \in X_{free}$ involves

1. Using a collision detection algorithm as in Section 5.3 to ensure that $\kappa(x) \in C_{free}$.
2. Checking x to ensure that other constraints of the form $h_i(x) \leq 0$ have been satisfied.

Entire trajectory segments should theoretically be checked. Often times, in practice, only individual points are checked, which is more efficient but technically incorrect.

14.3.2 System simulator

A new component is needed for sampling-based planning under differential constraints because of (14.1). Motions are now expressed in terms of an action trajectory, but collision detection and constraint satisfaction tests must be performed in X. Therefore, the system, $\dot{x} = f(x, u)$ needs to be integrated frequently during the planning process. Similar to the modeling of collision detection as a "black box," the integration process is modeled as a module called the *system simulator*. See Figure 14.9. Since the systems considered in this chapter are time-invariant, the starting time for any required integration can always be shifted to start at $t = 0$. Integration can be considered as a module that implements (14.1) by computing the state trajectory resulting from a given initial state $x(0)$, an action trajectory $\tilde{u}_t$, and time t. The incremental simulator encapsulates the details of integrating

Figure 14.9: Using a system simulator, the system $\dot{x} = f(x, u)$ is integrated from $x(0)$ using $\tilde{u}_t : [0, t] \to U$ to produce a state trajectory $\tilde{x}_t : [0, t] \to X$. Sometimes $\tilde{x}$ is specified as a parameterized path, but most often it is approximated as a sequence of samples in X.

the state transition equation so that they do not need to be addressed in the design of planners. However, that information from the particular state transition equation may still be important in the design of the planning algorithm.

Closed-form solutions

According to (14.1), the action trajectory must be integrated to produce a state trajectory. In some cases, this integration leads to a closed-form expression. For example, if the system is a chain of integrators, then a polynomial expression can easily be obtained for $x(t)$. For example, suppose q is a scalar and $\ddot{q} = u$. If $q(0) = \dot{q}(0) = 0$ and a constant action $u = 1$ is applied, then $x(t) = t^2/2$. If $\dot{x} = f(x, u)$ is a linear system (which includes chains of integrators; recall the definition from Section 13.2.2), then a closed-form expression for the state trajectory can always be obtained. This is based on matrix exponentials and is given in many control theory texts (e.g., [194]).

Euler method

For most systems, the integration must be performed numerically. A system simulator based on numerical integration can be constructed by breaking t into smaller intervals and iterating classical methods for computing numerical solutions to differential equations. The Euler method is the simplest of these methods. Let Δt denote a small time interval over which the approximation will be made. This can be considered as an internal parameter of the system simulator. In practice, this Δt is usually much smaller than the Δt used in the discrete-time model of Section 14.2.2. Suppose that $x(0)$ and $u(0)$ are given and the task is to estimate $x(\Delta t)$.

By performing integration over time, the state transition equation can be used to determine the state after some fixed amount of time Δt has passed. For example, if $x(0)$ is given and $u(t')$ is known over the interval $t' \in [0, \Delta t]$, then the state at time Δt can be determined as

$$x(\Delta t) = x(0) + \int_0^{\Delta t} f(x(t), u(t))dt. \tag{14.14}$$

The integral cannot be evaluated directly because $x(t)$ appears in the integrand and is unknown for time $t > 0$.

Using the fact that

$$f(x, u) = \dot{x} = \frac{dx}{dt} \approx \frac{x(\Delta t) - x(0)}{\Delta t}, \tag{14.15}$$

solving for $x(\Delta t)$ yields the classic *Euler integration method*

$$x(\Delta t) \approx x(0) + \Delta t \ f(x(0), u(0)). \tag{14.16}$$

The approximation error depends on how quickly $x(t)$ changes over time and on the length of the interval Δt. If the planning algorithm applies a motion primitive $\tilde{u}^p$, it gives $t_F(\tilde{u}^p)$

as the time input, and the system simulator may subdivide the time interval to maintain higher accuracy. This allows the developer of the planning algorithm to ignore numerical accuracy issues.

Runge-Kutta methods

Although Euler integration is efficient and easy to understand, it generally yields poor approximations. Taking a Taylor series expansion of $\tilde{x}$ at $t = 0$ yields

$$x(\Delta t) = x(0) + \Delta t \; \dot{x}(0) + \frac{(\Delta t)^2}{2!}\ddot{x}(0) + \frac{(\Delta t)^3}{3!}x^{(3)}(0) + \cdots . \qquad (14.17)$$

Comparing to (14.16), it can be seen that the Euler method just uses the first term of the Taylor series, which is an exact representation (if $\tilde{x}$ is analytic). Thus, the neglected terms reflect the approximation error. If $x(t)$ is roughly linear, then the error may be small; however, if $\dot{x}(t)$ or higher order derivatives change quickly, then poor approximations are obtained.

Runge-Kutta methods are based on using higher order terms of the Taylor series expansion. One of the most widely used and efficient numerical integration methods is the fourth-order Runge-Kutta method. It is simple to implement and yields good numerical behavior in most applications. Also, it is generally recommended over Euler integration. The technique can be derived by performing a Taylor series expansion at $x(\frac{1}{2}\Delta t)$. This state itself is estimated in the approximation process.

The fourth-order *Runge-Kutta integration method* is

$$x(\Delta t) \approx x(0) + \frac{\Delta t}{6}(w_1 + 2w_2 + 2w_3 + w_4), \qquad (14.18)$$

in which

$$
\begin{aligned}
w_1 &= f(x(0), u(0)) \\
w_2 &= f(x(0) + \tfrac{1}{2}\Delta t \; w_1, \; u(\tfrac{1}{2}\Delta t)) \\
w_3 &= f(x(0) + \tfrac{1}{2}\Delta t \; w_2, \; u(\tfrac{1}{2}\Delta t)) \\
w_4 &= f(x(0) + \Delta t \; w_3, \; u(\Delta t)).
\end{aligned}
\qquad (14.19)
$$

Although this is more expensive than Euler integration, the improved accuracy is usually worthwhile in practice. Note that the action is needed at three different times: 0, $\frac{1}{2}\Delta t$, and Δt. If the action is constant over $[0, \Delta t)$, then the same value is used at all three times.

The approximation error depends on how quickly higher order derivatives of $\tilde{x}$ vary over time. This can be expressed using the remaining terms of the Taylor series. In practice, it may be advantageous to adapt Δt over successive iterations of Runge-Kutta integration. In [249], for example, it is suggested that Δt is scaled by $(\Delta t / \Delta x)^{1/5}$, in which $\Delta x = \|x(\Delta t) - x(0)\|$, the Euclidean distance in $\mathbb{R}^n$.

Multistep methods

Runge-Kutta methods represent a popular trade-off between simplicity and efficiency. However, by focusing on the integration problem more carefully, it is often possible to improve efficiency further. The Euler and Runge-Kutta methods are often referred to as *single-step methods*. There exist *multi-step methods*, which rely on the fact that a sequence of integrations will be performed, in a manner analogous to incremental collision detection in Section 5.3.3. The key issues are ensuring that the methods properly initialize, ensuring numerical stability over time, and estimating error to adaptively adjust the step size. Many books on numerical analysis cover multi-step methods [52, 443, 865]. One of the most popular families is the *Adams methods*.

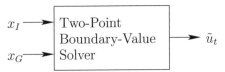

Figure 14.10: Some methods in Chapter 15 can solve two-point boundary value problems in the absence of X_{obs}. This is difficult to obtain for most systems, but it is more powerful than the system simulator. It is very valuable, for example, in making a sampling-based roadmap that satisfies differential constraints.

Multistep methods require more investment to understand and implement. For a particular application, the decision to pursue this route should be based on the relative costs of planning, collision detection, and numerical integration. If integration tends to dominate and efficiency is critical, then multi-step methods could improve running times dramatically over Runge-Kutta methods.

Black-box simulators

For some problems, a state transition equation might not be available; however, it is still possible to compute future states given a current state and an action trajectory. This might occur, for example, in a complex software system that simulates the dynamics of a automobile or a collection of parts that bounce around on a table. In computer graphics applications, simulations may arise from motion capture data. Some simulators may even work internally with implicit differential constraints of the form $g_i(x, \dot{x}, u) = 0$, instead of $\dot{x} = f(x, u)$. In such situations, many sampling-based planners can be applied because they rely only on the existence of the system simulator. The planning algorithm is thus shielded from the particular details of how the system is represented and integrated.

Reverse-time system simulation

Some planning algorithms require integration in the reverse-time direction. For some given $x(0)$ and action trajectory that runs from $-\Delta t$ to 0, the *backward system simulator* computes a state trajectory, $\tilde{x} : [-t, 0] \rightarrow X$, which when integrated from $-\Delta t$ to 0 under the application of $\tilde{u}_t$ yields $x(0)$. This may seem like an *inverse control problem* [858] or a BVP as shown in Figure 14.10; however, it is much simpler. Determining the action trajectory for given initial and goal states is more complicated; however, in reverse-time integration, the action trajectory and final state are given, and the initial state does not need to be fixed.

The reverse-time version of (14.14) is

$$x(-\Delta t) = x(0) + \int_0^{-\Delta t} f(x(t), u(t))dt = x(0) + \int_0^{\Delta t} -f(x(t), u(t))dt, \qquad (14.20)$$

which relies on the fact that $\dot{x} = f(x, u)$ is time-invariant. Thus, reverse-time integration is obtained by simply negating the state transition equation. The Euler and Runge-Kutta methods can then be applied in the usual way to $-f(x(t), u(t))$.

14.3.3 Local planning

The methods of Chapter 5 were based on the existence of a local planning method (LPM) that is simple and efficient. This represented an important part of both the incremental sampling and searching framework of Section 5.4 and the sampling-based roadmap framework of Section 5.6. In the absence of obstacles and differential constraints, it is trivial to define an LPM that connects two configurations. They can, for example, be connected using the shortest path (geodesic) in $\mathcal{C}$. The sampling-based roadmap approach from Section 5.6 relies on this simple LPM.

In the presence of differential constraints, the problem of constructing an LPM that connects two configurations or states is considerably more challenging. Recall from Section 14.1 that this is the classical BVP, which is difficult to solve for most systems. There are two main alternatives to handle this difficulty in a sampling-based planning algorithm:

1. Design the sampling scheme, which may include careful selection of motion primitives, so that the BVP can be trivially solved.

2. Design the planning algorithm so that as few as possible BVPs need to be solved. The LPM in this case does not specify precise goal states that must be reached.

Under the first alternative, the BVP solver can be considered as a black box, as shown in Figure 14.10, that efficiently connects x_I to x_G in the absence of obstacles. In the case of the Piano Mover's Problem, this was obtained by moving along the shortest path in $\mathcal{C}$. For many of the wheeled vehicle systems from Section 13.1.2, *steering methods* exist that could serve as an efficient BVP solver; see Section 15.5. Efficient techniques also exist for linear systems and are covered in Section 15.2.2.

If the BVP is efficiently solved, then virtually any sampling-based planning algorithm from Chapter 5 can be adapted to the case of differential constraints. This is achieved by using the module in Figure 14.10 as the LPM. For example, a sampling-based roadmap can use the computed solution in the place of the shortest path through $\mathcal{C}$. If the BVP solver is not efficient enough, then this approach becomes impractical because it must typically be used thousands of times to build a roadmap. The existence of an efficient module as shown in Figure 14.10 magically eliminates most of the complications associated with planning under differential constraints. The only remaining concern is that the solutions provided by the BVP solver could be quite long in comparison to the shortest path in the absence of differential constraints (for example, how far must the Dubins car travel to move slightly backward?).

Under the second alternative, it is assumed that solving the BVP is very costly. The planning method in this case should avoid solving BVPs whenever possible. Some planning algorithms may only require an LPM that *approximately* reaches intermediate goal states, which is simpler for some systems. Other planning algorithms may not require the LPM to make any kind of connection. The LPM may return a motion primitive that appears to make some progress in the search but is not designed to connect to a prescribed state. This usually involves incremental planning methods, which are covered in Section 14.4 and extends the methods of Sections 5.4 and 5.5 to handle differential constraints.

14.3.4 General framework under differential constraints

The framework presented here is a direct extension of the sampling and searching framework from Section 5.4.1 and includes the extension of Section 5.5 to allow the selection of any point in the swath of the search graph. This replaces the vertex selection method (VSM) by a swath-point selection method (SSM). The framework also naturally extends the discrete search framework of Section 2.2.4. The components are are follows:

1. **Initialization:** Let $\mathcal{G}(V, E)$ represent an undirected *search graph*, for which the vertex set V contains a vertex for x_I and possibly other states in X_{free}, and the edge set E is empty. The graph can be interpreted as a topological graph with a swath $S(\mathcal{G})$.

2. **Swath-point Selection Method (SSM):** Choose a vertex $x_{cur} \in S(\mathcal{G})$ for expansion.

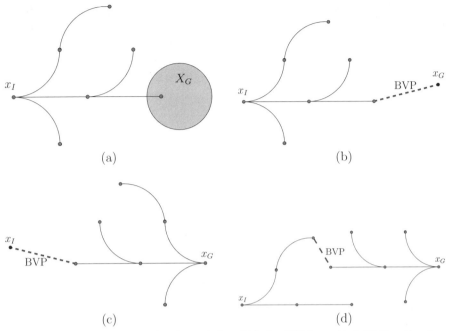

Figure 14.11: (a) Forward, unidirectional search for which the BVP is avoided. (b) Reaching the goal precisely causes a BVP. (c) Backward, unidirectional search also causes a BVP. (d) For bidirectional search, the BVP arises when connecting the trees.

3. **Local Planning Method (LPM):** Generate a motion primitive $\tilde{u}^p : [0, t_F] \rightarrow X_{free}$ such that $u(0) = x_{cur}$ and $u(t_F) = x_r$ for some $x_r \in X_{free}$, which may or may not be a vertex in $\mathcal{G}$. Using the system simulator, a collision detection algorithm, and by testing the phase constraints, $\tilde{u}^p$ must be verified to be violation-free. If this step fails, then go to Step 2.

4. **Insert an Edge in the Graph:** Insert $\tilde{u}^p$ into E. Upon integration, $\tilde{u}^p$ yields a state trajectory from x_{cur} to x_r. If x_r is not already in V, it is added. If x_{cur} lies in the interior of an edge trajectory for some $e \in E$, then e is split by the introduction of a new vertex at x_{cur}.

5. **Check for a Solution:** Determine whether $\mathcal{G}$ encodes a solution path. In some applications, a small gap in the state trajectory may be tolerated.

6. **Return to Step 2:** Iterate unless a solution has been found or some termination condition is satisfied. In the latter case, the algorithm reports failure.

The general framework may be applied in the same ways as in Section 5.4.1 to obtain unidirectional, bidirectional, and multidirectional searches. The issues from the Piano Mover's Problem extend to motion planning under differential constraints. For example, bug traps cause the same difficulties, and as the number of trees increases, it becomes difficult to coordinate the search.

The main new complication is due to BVPs. See Figure 14.11. Recall from Section 14.1.1 that for most systems it is important to reduce the number of BVPs that must be solved during planning as much as possible. Assume that connecting precisely to a prescribed state is difficult. Figure 14.11a shows the best situation, in which forward, unidirectional search is used to enter a large goal region. In this case, no BVPs need to be solved. As the goal region is reduced, the problem becomes more challenging. Figure 14.11b shows the limiting case in which X_G is a point $\{x_G\}$. This requires the planning algorithm to solve at least one BVP.

Figure 14.11c shows the case of backward, unidirectional search. This has the effect of moving the BVP to x_I. Since x_I is precisely given (there is no "initial region"), the BVP cannot be avoided as in the forward case. If an algorithm produces a solution $\tilde{u}$ for which $x(0)$ is very close to x_I, and if X_G is large, then it may be possible to salvage the solution. The system simulator can be applied to $\tilde{u}$ from x_I instead of $x(0)$. It is known that $\tilde{x}(x(0), \tilde{u})$ is violation-free, and $\tilde{x}(x_I, \tilde{u})$ may travel close to $\tilde{x}(x(0), \tilde{u})$ at all times. This requires f to vary only a small amount with respect to changes in x (this would be implied by a small Lipschitz constant) and also for $\|x_I - x(0)\|$ to be small. One problem is that the difference between points on the two trajectories usually increases as time increases. If it is verified by the system simulator that $\tilde{x}(x_I, \tilde{u})$ is violation-free and the final state still lies in X_G, then a solution can be declared.

For bidirectional search, a BVP must be solved somewhere in the middle of a trajectory, as shown in Figure 14.11d. This complicates the problem of determining whether the two trees can be connected. Once again, if the goal region is large, it may be possible remove the gap in the middle of the trajectory by moving the starting state of the trajectory produced by the backward tree. Let $\tilde{u}_1$ and $\tilde{u}_2$ denote the action trajectories produced by the forward and backward trees, respectively. Suppose that their termination times are t_1 and t_2, respectively. The action trajectories can be concatenated to yield a function $\tilde{u} : [0, t_1 + t_2] \rightarrow U$ by shifting the domain of $\tilde{u}_2$ from $[0, t_2]$ to $[t_1, t_1 + t_2]$. If $t \leq t_1$, then $u(t) = u_1(t)$; otherwise, $u(t) = u_2(t - t_1)$. If there is a gap, the new state trajectory $\tilde{x}(x_I, \tilde{u})$ must be checked using the system simulator to determine whether it is violation-free and terminates in X_G. Multi-directional search becomes even more difficult because more BVPs are created. It is possible in principle to extend the ideas above to concatenate a sequence of action trajectories, which tries to remove all of the gaps.

Consider the relationship between the search graph and reachability graphs. In the case of unidirectional search, the search graph is always a subset of a reachability graph (assuming perfect precision and no numerical integration error). In the forward case, the reachability graph starts at x_I, and in the backward case it starts at x_G. In the case of bidirectional search, there are two reachability graphs. It might be the case that vertices from the two coincide, which is another way that the BVP can be avoided. Such cases are unfortunately rare, unless x_I and x_G are intentionally chosen to cause this. For example, the precise location of x_G may be chosen because it is known to be a vertex of the reachability graph from x_I. For most systems, it is difficult to force this behavior. Thus, in general, BVPs arise because the reachability graphs do not have common vertices. In the case of multi-directional search, numerous reachability graphs are being explored, none of which may have vertices that coincide with vertices of others.

14.4 Incremental sampling and searching methods

The general framework of Section 14.3.4 will now be specialized to obtain three important methods for planning under differential constraints.

14.4.1 Searching on a lattice

This section follows in the same spirit as Section 5.4.2, which adapted grid search techniques to motion planning. The difficulty in the current setting is to choose a discretization that leads to a lattice that can be searched using any of the search techniques of Section 2.2. The section is inspired mainly by kinodynamic planning work [290, 292, 444].

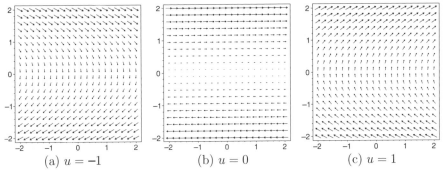

(a) $u = -1$ (b) $u = 0$ (c) $u = 1$

Figure 14.12: The reachability graph will be obtained by switching between these vector fields at every Δt. The middle one produces horizontal phase trajectories, and the others produce parabolic curves.

14.4.1.1 A double-integrator lattice

First consider the double integrator from Example 13.3. Let $\mathcal{C} = \mathcal{C}_{free} = \mathbb{R}$ and $\ddot{q} = u$. This models the motion of a free-floating particle in $\mathbb{R}$, as described in Section 13.3.2. The phase space is $X = \mathbb{R}^2$, and $x = (q, \dot{q})$. Let $U = [-1, 1]$. The coming ideas can be easily generalized to allow any acceleration bound $a_{max} > 0$ by letting $U = [-a_{max}, a_{max}]$; however, $a_{max} = 1$ will be chosen to simplify the presentation.

The differential equation $\ddot{q} = u$ can be integrated once to yield

$$\dot{q}(t) = \dot{q}(0) + ut, \tag{14.21}$$

in which $\dot{q}(0)$ is an initial speed. Upon integration of (14.21), the position is obtained as

$$q(t) = q(0) + \dot{q}(0)t + \tfrac{1}{2}ut^2, \tag{14.22}$$

which uses two initial conditions, $q(0)$ and $\dot{q}(0)$.

A discrete-time model exists for which the reachability graph is trapped on a lattice. This is obtained by letting $U_d = \{-1, 0, 1\}$ and Δt be any positive real number. The vector fields over X that correspond to the cases of $u = -1$, $u = 0$, and $u = 1$ are shown in Figure 14.12. Switching between these fields at every Δt and integrating yields the reachability graph shown in Figure 14.13.

This leads to a discrete-time transition equation of the form $x_{k+1} = f_d(x_k, u_k)$, in which $u_k \in U_d$, and k represents time $t = (k - 1)\Delta t$. Any action trajectory can be specified as an action sequence; for example a six-stage action sequence may be given by $(-1, 1, 0, 0, -1, 1)$. Start from $x_1 = x(0) = (q_1, \dot{q}_1)$. At any stage k and for any action sequence, the resulting state $x_k = (q_k, \dot{q}_k)$ can be expressed as

$$
\begin{aligned}
q_k &= q_1 + i\tfrac{1}{2}(\Delta t)^2 \\
\dot{q}_k &= \dot{q}_1 + j\Delta t,
\end{aligned}
\tag{14.23}
$$

in which i, j are integers that can be computed from the action sequence. Thus, any action sequence leads to a state that can be expressed using integer coordinates (i, j) in the plane. Starting at $x_1 = (0, 0)$, this forms the lattice of points shown in Figure 14.13. The lattice is slanted (with slope 1) because changing speed requires some motion. If infinite acceleration were allowed, then $\dot{q}$ could be changed instantaneously, which corresponds to moving vertically in X. As seen in (14.21), $\dot{q}$ changes linearly over time. If $\dot{q} \neq 0$, then the configuration changes quadratically. If $u = 0$, then it changes linearly, except when $\dot{q} = 0$; in this case, no motion occurs.

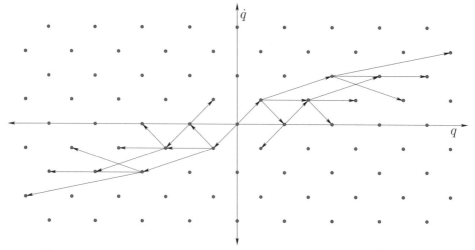

Figure 14.13: The reachability graph from the origin is shown after three stages (the true state trajectories are actually parabolic arcs when acceleration or deceleration occurs). Note that a lattice is obtained, but the distance traveled in one stage increases as $|\dot{q}|$ increases.

The neighborhood structure is not the same as those in Section 5.4.2 because of drift. For $u = 0$, imagine having a stack of horizontal conveyor belts that carry points to the right if they are above the q-axis, and to the left if they are below it (see Figure 14.12b). The speed of the conveyor belt is given by $\dot{q}$. If $u = 0$, the distance traveled along q is $\dot{q}\Delta t$. This causes horizontal motion to the right in the phase plane if $\dot{q} > 0$ and horizontal motion to the left if $\dot{q} < 0$. Observe in Figure 14.13 that larger motions result as $|\dot{q}|$ increases. If $\dot{q} = 0$, then no horizontal motion can occur. If $q \neq 0$, then the $\dot{q}$ coordinate changes by $\pm \frac{1}{2}u(\Delta t)^2$. This slowing down or speeding up also affects the position along q.

For most realistic problems, there is an upper bound on speed. Let $v_{max} > 0$ be a positive constant and assume that $|\dot{q}| \leq v_{max}$. Furthermore, assume that $\mathcal{C}$ is bounded (all values of $q \in \mathcal{C}$ are contained in an interval of $\mathbb{R}$). Since the reachability graph is a lattice and the states are now confined to a bounded subset of $\mathbb{R}^2$, the number of vertices in the reachability graph is finite. For any fixed Δt, the lattice can be searched using any of the algorithms of Section 2.2. The search starts on a reachability graph for which the initial vertex is x_I. Trajectories that are approximately time-optimal can be obtained by using breadth-first search (Dijkstra's algorithm could alternatively be used, but it is more expensive). Resolution completeness can be obtained by reducing Δt by a constant factor each time the search fails to find a solution. As mentioned in Section 5.4.2, it is not required to construct an entire grid resolution at once. Samples can be gradually added, and the connectivity can be updated efficiently using the union-find algorithm [245, 826]. A rigorous approximation algorithm framework will be presented shortly, which indicates how close the solution is to optimal, expressed in terms of input parameters to the algorithm.

Recall the problem of connecting to grid points, which was illustrated in Figure 5.14b. If the goal region X_G contains lattice points, then exact arrival at the goal occurs. If it does not contain lattice points, as in the common case of X_G being a single point, then some additional work is needed to connect a goal state to a nearby lattice point. This actually corresponds to a BVP, but it is easy to solve for the double integrator. The set of states that can be reached from some state x_G within time Δt lie within a cone, as shown

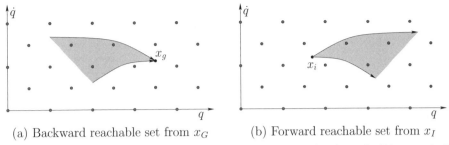

(a) Backward reachable set from x_G (b) Forward reachable set from x_I

Figure 14.14: The initial and goal states can be connected to lattice points that call within cones in X that represent time-limited reachable sets.

in Figure 14.14a. Lattice points that fall into the cone can be easily connected to x_G by applying a constant action in U. Likewise, x_I does not even have to coincide with a lattice point. Thus, it is straightforward to connect x_I to a lattice point, obtain a trajectory that arrives at a lattice point near x_G, and then connect it exactly to x_G.

14.4.1.2 Extensions and other considerations

Alternative lattices for the double integrator

Many alternative lattices can be constructed over X. Different discretizations of U and time can be used. Great flexibility is allowed if feasibility is the only concern, as opposed to optimality. Since $\mathcal{C} = \mathbb{R}$, it is difficult to define an obstacle avoidance problem; however, the concepts will be soon generalized to higher dimensions. In this case, finding a feasible trajectory that connects from some initial state to a goal state may be the main concern. Note, however, that if x_I and x_G are states with zero velocity, then the state could hover around close to the q-axis, and the speeds will be so slow that momentum is insignificant. This provides some incentive for at least reducing the travel time as much as possible, even if the final result is not optimal. Alternatively, the initial and goal states may not have zero velocity, in which case, any feasible solution may be desired. For example, suppose the goal is to topple a sports utility vehicle (SUV) as part of safety analysis.

To get a feeling for how to construct lattices, recall again the analogy to conveyor belts. A lattice can be designed by placing horizontal rows of sample points at various values of $\dot{q}$. These could, for example, be evenly spaced in the $\dot{q}$ direction as in Figure 14.13. Imagine the state lies on a conveyor belt. If desired, a move can be made to any other conveyor belt, say at $\dot{q}'$, by applying a nonzero action for some specific amount of time. If $\dot{q}' > \dot{q}$, then $u > 0$; otherwise, $u < 0$. If the action is constant, then after time $|\dot{q} - \dot{q}'|/u$ has passed, the state will arrive at $\dot{q}'$. Upon arrival, the position q on the conveyor belt might not coincide with a sample point. This is no problem because the action $u = 0$ can be applied until the state drifts to the next sample point. An alternative is to choose an action from U that drives directly to a lattice point within its forward, time-limited reachable set. Recall Figure 14.14; the cone can be placed on a lattice point to locate other lattice points that can be reached by application of a constant action in U over some time interval.

Recall from Figure 14.13 that longer distances are traveled over time Δt as $|\dot{q}|$ increases. This may be undesirable behavior in practice because the resolution is essentially much poorer at higher speeds. This can be compensated for by placing the conveyor belts closer together as $|\dot{q}|$ increases. As the speed increases, a shorter time interval is needed to change belts, and the distance traveled can be held roughly the same for all levels. This corresponds to the intuition that faster response times are needed at higher speeds.

A multi-resolution version can also be made [819]. The simple problem considered so far can actually be solved combinatorially, without any approximation error [750]; however, the lattice-based approach was covered because it can be extended to much harder problems, as will be explained next.

Multiple, independent double integrators

Now consider generalizing to a vector of n double integrators. In this case, $\mathcal{C} = \mathbb{R}^n$ and each $q \in \mathcal{C}$ is an n-dimensional vector. There are n action variables and n double integrators of the form $\ddot{q}_i = u_i$. The action space for each variable is $U_i = [-1, 1]$ (once again, any acceleration bound can be used). The phase space X is $\mathbb{R}^{2n}$, and each point is $x = (q_1, \ldots, q_n, \dot{q}_1, \ldots, \dot{q}_n)$. The ith double integrator produces two scalar equations of the phase transition equation: $\dot{x}_i = x_{n+i}$ and $\dot{x}_{n+i} = u_i$.

Even though there are n double integrators, they are decoupled in the state transition equation. The phase of one integrator does not depend on the phase of another. Therefore, the ideas expressed so far can be extended in a straightforward way to obtain a lattice over $\mathbb{R}^{2n}$. Each action is an n-dimensional vector u. Each U_i is discretized to yield values -1, 0, and 1. There are 3^n edges emanating from any lattice point for which $\dot{q}_i \neq 0$ for all i. For any double integrator for which $\dot{q}_i = 0$, there are only two choices because $u_i = 0$ produces no motion. The projection of the reachability graph down to (x_i, x_{n+i}) for any i from 1 to n looks exactly like Figure 14.13 and characterizes the behavior of the ith integrator.

The standard search algorithms can be applied to the lattice over $\mathbb{R}^{2n}$. Breadth-first search once again yields solutions that are approximately time-optimal. Resolution completeness can be obtained again by bounding X and allowing Δt to converge to zero. Now that there are more dimensions, a complicated obstacle region X_{obs} can be removed from X. The traversal of each edge then requires collision detection along each edge of the graph. Note that the state trajectories are linear or parabolic arcs. Numerical integration is not needed because (14.22) already gives the closed-form expression for the state trajectory.

Unconstrained mechanical systems

A lattice can even be obtained for the general case of a fully actuated mechanical system, which for example includes most robot arms. Recall from (13.4) that any system in the form $\dot{q} = f(q, u)$ can alternatively be expressed as $\dot{q} = u$, if $U(q)$ is defined as the image of f for a fixed q. The main purpose of using f is to make it easy to specify a fixed action space U that maps differently into the tangent space for each $q \in \mathcal{C}$.

A similar observation can be made regarding equations of the form $\ddot{q} = h(q, \dot{q}, u)$, in which $u \in U$ and U is an open subset of $\mathbb{R}^n$. Recall that this form was obtained for general unconstrained mechanical systems in Sections 13.3 and 13.4. For example, (13.148) expresses the dynamics of open-chain robot arms. Such equations can be expressed as $\ddot{q} = u'$ by directly specifying the set of allowable accelerations. Each u will map to a new action u' in an action space given by

$$U'(q, \dot{q}) = \{\ddot{q} \in \mathbb{R}^n \mid \exists u \in U \text{ such that } \ddot{q} = h(q, \dot{q}, u)\} \qquad (14.24)$$

for each $q \in \mathcal{C}$ and $\dot{q} \in \mathbb{R}^n$.

Each $u' \in U'(q, \dot{q})$ directly expresses an acceleration vector in $\mathbb{R}^n$. Therefore, using $u' \in U(q, \dot{q})$, the original equation expressed using h can be now written as $\ddot{q} = u'$. In its

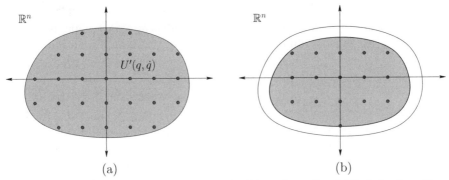

(a)   (b)

Figure 14.15: (a) The set, $U'(q, \dot{q})$, of new actions and grid-based sampling. (b) Reducing the set by some safety margin to account for its variation over time.

new form, this appears just like the multiple, independent double integrators. The main differences are

1. The set $U'(q, \dot{q})$ may describe a complicated region in $\mathbb{R}^n$, whereas U in the case of the true double integrators was a cube centered at the origin.

2. The set $U'(q, \dot{q})$ varies with respect to q and $\dot{q}$. Special concern must be given for this variation over the time sampling interval Δt. In the case of the true double integrators, U was fixed.

The first difference is handled by performing grid sampling over $\mathbb{R}^n$ and making an edge in the reachability graph for every grid point that falls into $U'(q, \dot{q})$; see Figure 14.15a. The grid resolution can be improved along with Δt to obtain resolution completeness. To address the second problem, think of $U'(q(t), \dot{q}(t))$ as a shape in $\mathbb{R}^n$ that moves over time. Choosing u' close to the boundary of $U'(q(t), \dot{q}(t))$ is dangerous because as t increases, u' may fall outside of the new action set. It is often possible to obtain bounds on how quickly the boundary of $U'(q, \dot{q})$ can vary over time (this can be determined, for example, by differentiating h with respect to q and $\dot{q}$). Based on the bound, a thin layer near the boundary of $U'(q, \dot{q})$ can be removed from consideration to ensure that all attempted actions remain in $U'(q(t), \dot{q}(t))$ during the whole interval Δt. See Figure 14.15b.

These ideas were applied to extend the approximation algorithm framework to the case of open-chain robot arms, for which h is given by (13.148). Suppose that U is an axis-aligned rectangle, which is often the case for manipulators because the bounds for each u_i correspond to torque limits for each motor. If q and $\dot{q}$ are fixed, then (13.140) applies a linear transformation to obtain $\ddot{q}$ from u. The rectangle is generally sheared into a parallelepiped (a n-dimensional extension of a parallelogram). Recall such transformations from Section 3.5 or linear algebra.

Approximation algorithm framework

The lattices developed in this section were introduced in [292] for analyzing the kinodynamic planning problem in the rigorous *approximation algorithm* framework for NP-hard problems [768]. Suppose that there are two or three independent double integrators. The analysis shows that the computed solutions are approximately optimal in the following sense. Let c_0 and c_1 be two positive constants that define a function

$$\delta(c_0, c_1)(\dot{q}) = c_0 + c_1 \|\dot{q}\|. \tag{14.25}$$

Let t_F denote the time at which the termination action is applied. A state trajectory is called $\delta(c_0, c_1)$-*safe* if for all $t \in [0, t_F]$, the ball of radius $\delta(c_0, c_1)(\dot{q})$ that is centered at $q(t)$ does not cause collisions with obstacles in $\mathcal{W}$. Note that the ball radius grows linearly as the speed increases. The robot can be imagined as a disk with a radius determined by speed. Let x_I, x_G, c_0, and c_1 be given (only a point goal region is allowed). Suppose that for a given problem, there exists a $\delta(c_0, c_1)$-safe state trajectory (resulting from integrating any $\tilde{u} \in \mathcal{U}$) that terminates in x_G after time t_{opt}. It was shown that by choosing the appropriate Δt (given by a formula in [292]), applying breadth-first search to the reachability lattice will find a $(1 - \epsilon)\delta(c_0, c_1)$-safe trajectory that takes time at most $(1 + \epsilon)t_{opt}$, and approximately connects x_I to x_G (which means that the closeness in X depends on ϵ). Furthermore, the running time of the algorithm is polynomial in $1/\epsilon$ and the number of primitives used to define polygonal obstacles.[5] One of the key steps in the analysis is to show that any state trajectory can be closely tracked using only actions from U_d and keeping them constant over Δt. One important aspect is that it does not necessarily imply that the computed solution is close to the true optimum, as it travels through X (only the execution times are close). Thus, the algorithm may give a solution from a different homotopy class from the one that contains the true optimal trajectory. The analysis was extended to the general case of open-chain robot arms in [290, 444].

Backward and bidirectional versions

There is a perfect symmetry to the concepts presented so far in this section. A reachability lattice similar to the one in Figure 14.13 can be obtained by integrating backward in time. This indicates action sequences and associated initial states from which a fixed state can be reached. Note that applying the ideas in the reverse direction does not require the system to be symmetric. Given that the graphs exist in both directions, bidirectional search can be performed. By using the forward and backward time-limited reachability cones, the initial and goal states can be connected to a common lattice, which is started, for example, at the origin.

Underactuated and nonholonomic systems

Many interesting systems cannot be expressed in the form $\ddot{q} = h(q, \dot{q}, u)$ with n independent action variables because of underactuation or other constraints. For example, the models in Section 13.1.2 are underactuated and nonholonomic. In this case, it is not straightforward to convert the equations into a vector of double integrators because the dimension of $U(q, \dot{q})$ is less than n, the dimension of $\mathcal{C}$. This makes it impossible to use grid-based sampling of $U(q, \dot{q})$. Nevertheless, it is still possible in many cases to discretize the system in a clever way to obtain a lattice. If this can be obtained, then a straightforward resolution-complete approach based on classical search algorithms can be developed. If X is bounded (or a bounded region is obtained after applying the phase constraints), then the search is performed on a finite graph. If failure occurs, then the resolution can be improved in the usual way to eventually obtain resolution completeness. As stated in Section 14.2.2, obtaining such a lattice is possible for a large family of nonholonomic systems [765]. Next, a method is presented for handling reachability graphs that are not lattices.

---

[5] One technical point: It is actually only pseudopolynomial [768] in a_{max}, v_{max}, c_0, c_1, and the width of the bounding cube in $\mathcal{W}$. This means that the running time is polynomial if the representations of these parameters are treated as having constant size; however, it is not polynomial in the actual number of bits needed to truly represent them.

14.4.2 Incorporating state space discretization

If the reachability graph is not a lattice, which is typically the case with underactuated and nonholonomic systems, then state space discretization can be used to force it to behave like a lattice. If there are no differential constraints, then paths can be easily forced to travel along a lattice, as in the methods of Section 7.7.1. Under differential constraints, the state cannot be forced, for example, to follow a staircase path. Instead of sampling X and forcing trajectories to visit specific points, X can be partitioned into small cells, within which no more than one vertex is allowed in the search graph. This prevents a systematic search algorithm from running forever if the search graph has an infinite number of vertices in some bounded region. For example, with the Dubins car, if u is fixed to an integer, an infinite number of vertices on a circle is obtained, as mentioned in Section 14.2.2. The ideas in this section are inspired mainly by the Barraquand-Latombe dynamic programming method [74], which has been mainly applied to the models in Section 13.1.2. In the current presentation, however, the approach is substantially generalized. Here, optimality is not even necessarily required (but can be imposed, if desired).

Decomposing X into cells

At the outset, X is decomposed into a collection of cells without considering collision detection. Suppose that X is an n-dimensional rectangular subset of $\mathbb{R}^n$. If X is more generally a smooth manifold, then the rectangular subset can be defined in a coordinate neighborhood. If desired, identifications can be used to respect the topology of X; however, coordinate changes are technically needed at the boundaries to properly express velocities (recall Section 8.3).

The most common cell decomposition is obtained by splitting X into n-dimensional cubes of equal size by quantizing each coordinate. This will be called a *cubical partition*. Assume in general that X is partitioned into a collection $\mathcal{D}$ of n-dimensional cells. Let $D \in \mathcal{D}$ denote a *cell*, which is a subset of X. It is assumed here that all cells have dimension n. In the case of cubes, this means that points on common boundaries between cubes are declared to belong to only one neighboring cube (thus, the cells may be open, closed, or neither).

Note that X is partitioned into cells, and not X_{free}, as might be expected from the methods in Chapter 6. This means that collision detection and other constraints on X are ignored when defining $\mathcal{D}$. The cells are defined in advance, just as grids were declared in Section 5.4.2. In the case of a cubical partition, the cells are immediately known upon quantization of each coordinate axis.

Searching

The algorithm fits directly into the framework of Section 14.3.4. A search graph is constructed incrementally from x_I by applying any systematic search algorithm. It is assumed that the system has been discretized in some way. Most often, the discrete-time model of Section 14.2.2 is used, which results in a fixed Δt and a finite set U_d of actions.

In the basic search algorithms of Section 2.2.1, it is important to keep track of which vertices have been explored. Instead of applying this idea to vertices, it is applied here to cells. A cell D is called *visited* if the search graph that has been constructed so far contains a vertex in D; otherwise, D is called *unvisited*. Initially, only the cell that contains x_I is marked as *visited*. All others are initialized to *unvisited*. These labels are used to prune the reachability graph during the search, as shown in Figure 14.16.

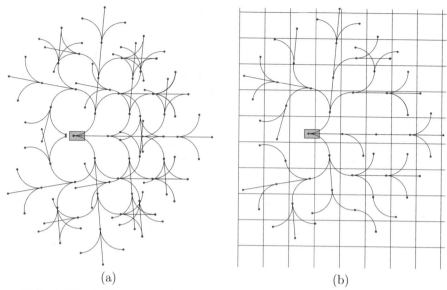

(a)   (b)

Figure 14.16: (a) The first four stages of a dense reachability graph for the Dubins car. (b) One possible search graph, obtained by allowing at most one vertex per cell. Many branches are pruned away. In this simple example, there are no cell divisions along the θ-axis.

CELL-BASED_SEARCH(x_I, x_G)

1   Q.insert(x_I);
2    $\mathcal{G}$.init(x_I);
3   **while** $Q \neq \emptyset$ **and** x_G is *unvisited*
4        $x_{cur} \rightarrow Q$.pop();
5   **for each** $(\tilde{u}_t, x) \in$ REACHED(x_{cur})
6   **if** x is *unvisited*
7   Q.insert(x);
8                $\mathcal{G}$.add_vertex(x);
9                $\mathcal{G}$.add_edge($\tilde{u}_t$);
10   Mark cell that contains x as *visited*;
11   Return $\mathcal{G}$;

Figure 14.17: Searching by using a cell decomposition of X.

The basic algorithm outline is shown in Figure 14.17. Let Q represent a priority queue in which the elements are vertices of the search graph. If optimization of a cost functional is required, then Q may be sorted by the cost accumulated along the path constructed so far from x_I to x. This cost can be assigned in many different ways. It could simply represent the time (number of Δt steps), or it could count the number of times the action has changed. As the algorithm explores, new candidate vertices are encountered. They are only saved in the search graph and placed into Q if they lie in a cell marked *unvisited* and are violation-free. Upon encountering such a cell, it becomes marked as *visited*. The REACHED function generates a set of violation-free trajectory segments. Under the discrete-time model, this means applying each $u \in U_d$ over time Δt and reporting only those states reached without violating the constraints (including collision avoidance).

As usual, the BVP issue may arise if X_G is small relative to the cell size. If X_G is large enough to include entire cells, then this issue is avoided. If x_G is a single point, then it may only be possible to approximately reach x_G. Therefore, the algorithm must accept reaching x_G to within a specified tolerance. This can be modeled by defining X_G to be larger; therefore, tolerance is not explicitly mentioned.

Maintaining the cells

There are several alternatives for maintaining the cells. The main operation that needs to be performed efficiently is *point location* [266]: determine which cell contains a given state. The original method in [74] preallocates an n-dimensional array. The collision-checking is even performed in advance. Any cell that contains at least one point in X_{obs} can be labeled as *occupied*. This allows cells that contain collision configurations to be avoided without having to call the collision detection module. For a fixed dimension, this scheme finds the correct cell and updates the labels in constant time. Unfortunately, the space requirement is exponential in dimension.

An alternative is to use a hash table to maintain the collection of cells that are labeled as *visited*. This may be particularly valuable if optimality is not important and if it is expected that solutions will be found before most of the cells are reached. The point location problem can be solved efficiently without explicitly storing a multi-dimensional array.

Suppose that the cubical decomposition is not necessarily used. One general approach is to define $\mathcal{D}$ as the Voronoi regions of a collection P of m samples $\{p_1, \ldots, p_m\}$ in X. The "name" of each cell corresponds uniquely to a sample in P. The cell that contains some $x \in X$ is defined as the nearest sample in P, using some predetermined metric on X. As a special case, the cubical decomposition defines the cells based on a Sukharev grid (recall Figure 5.5a). If the dimension of X is not too high, then efficient nearest-neighbor schemes can be used to determine the appropriate cell in near-logarithmic time in the number of points in P (in practice, Kd-trees, mentioned in Section 5.5.2, should perform well). For maintaining a cubical decomposition, this approach would be cumbersome; however, it works for *any* sample set P. If no solution is found for a given P, then the partition could be improved by adding more samples. This allows any dense sequence to be used to guide the exploration of X while ensuring resolution completeness, which is discussed next.

Resolution issues

One of the main complications in using state discretization is that there are three spaces over which sampling occurs: time, the action space, and the state space. Assume the discrete-time model is used. If obtaining optimal solutions is important, then very small cells should be used (e.g., 50 to 100 per axis). This limits its application to state spaces of a few dimensions. The time interval Δt should also be made small, but if it is too small relative to the cell size, then it may be impossible to leave a cell. If only feasibility is the only requirement, then larger cells may be used, and Δt must be appropriately increased. A course quantization of U may cause solutions to be missed, particularly if Δt is large. As Δt decreases, the number of samples in U_d becomes less important.

To obtain resolution completeness, the sampling should be improved each time the search fails. Each time that the search is started, the sampling dispersion for at least one of the three spaces should be decreased. The possibilities are 1) the time interval Δt may be reduced, 2) more actions may be added to U_d, or 3) more points may be added to P to reduce the cell size. If the dispersion approaches zero for all three spaces, and if X_G contains an open subset of X_{free}, then resolution completeness is obtained. If X_G is only a point, then solutions that come within some $\epsilon > 0$ must be tolerated.

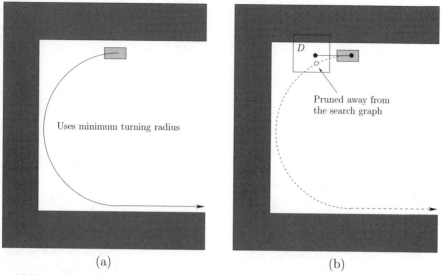

(a)   (b)

Figure 14.18: (a) The Dubins car is able to turn around if it turns left as sharply as possible. (b) Unfortunately, the required vertex is pruned because one cell along the required trajectory already contains a vertex. This illustrates how missing a possible action can cause serious problems many stages later.

Recall that resolution completeness assumes that f has bounded derivatives or at least satisfies a Lipschitz condition (14.11). The actual rate of convergence is mainly affected by three factors: 1) the rate at which f varies with respect to changes in u and x (characterized by Lipschitz constants), 2) the required traversal of narrow regions in X_{free}, and 3) the controllability of the system. The last condition will be studied further for nonholonomic systems in Section 15.4. For a concrete example, consider making a U-turn with a Dubins car that has a very large turning radius, as shown in Figure 14.18. A precise turn may be required to turn around, and this may depend on an action that was chosen many stages earlier. The Dubins car model does not allow zig-zagging (e.g., parallel parking) maneuvers to make local corrections to the configuration.

Backward and bidirectional versions

As usual, both backward and bidirectional versions of this approach can be made. If the X_G is large (or the goal tolerance is large) and the BVP is costly to solve, then the backward version seems less desirable if the BVP is hard. The forward direction is preferred because the BVP can be avoided altogether.

For a bidirectional algorithm, the same collection $\mathcal{D}$ of cells can be used for both trees. The problem could be considered solved if the same cell is reached by both trees; however, one must be careful to still ensure that the remaining BVP can be solved. It must be possible to find an action trajectory segment that connects a vertex from the initial-based tree to a vertex of the goal-based tree. Alternatively, connections made to within a tolerance may be acceptable.

14.4.3 RDT-based methods

The rapidly exploring dense tree (RDT) family of methods, which includes the RRT, avoids maintaining a lattice altogether. RDTs were originally developed for handling

---

SIMPLE_RDT_WITH_DIFFERENTIAL_CONSTRAINTS(x_0)

1    $\mathcal{G}$.init(x_0);
2   **for** $i = 1$ **to** k **do**
3        $x_n \leftarrow$ NEAREST($S(\mathcal{G}), \alpha(i)$);
4        $(\tilde{u}^p, x_r) \leftarrow$ LOCAL_PLANNER($x_n, \alpha(i)$);
5        $\mathcal{G}$.add_vertex(x_r);
6        $\mathcal{G}$.add_edge($\tilde{u}^p$);

Figure 14.19: Extending the basic RDT algorithm to handle differential constraints. In comparison to Figure 5.16, an LPM computes x_r, which becomes the new vertex, instead of $\alpha(i)$. In some applications, line 4 may fail, in which case lines 5 and 6 are skipped.

differential constraints, even though most of their practical application has been to the Piano Mover's Problem. This section extends the ideas of Section 5.5 from $\mathcal{C}$ to X and incorporates differential constraints. The methods covered so far in Section 14.4 produce approximately optimal solutions if the graph is searched using dynamic programming and the resolution is high enough. By contrast, RDTs are aimed at returning only feasible trajectories, even as the resolution improves. They are often successful at producing a solution trajectory with relatively less sampling. This performance gain is enabled in part by the lack of concern for optimality.

Let α denote an infinite, dense sequence of samples in X. Let $\rho : X \times X \rightarrow [0, \infty]$ denote a distance function on X, which may or may not be a proper metric. The distance function may not be symmetric, in which case $\rho(x_1, x_2)$ represents the directed distance from x_1 to x_2.

The RDT is a search graph as considered so far in this section and can hence be interpreted as a subgraph of the reachability graph under some discretization model. For simplicity, first assume that the discrete-time model of Section 14.2.2 is used, which leads to a finite action set U_d and a fixed time interval Δt. The set $\mathcal{U}^p$ of motion primitives is all action trajectories for which some $u \in U_d$ is held constant from time 0 to Δt. The more general case will be handled at the end of this section.

Paralleling Section 5.5.1, the RDT will first be defined in the absence of obstacles. Hence, let $X_{free} = X$. The construction algorithm is defined in Figure 14.19; it may be helpful to compare it to Figure 5.16, which was introduced on $\mathcal{C}$ for the Piano Mover's Problem. The RDT, denoted by $\mathcal{G}$, is initialized with a single vertex at some $x_0 \in X$. In each iteration, a new edge and vertex are added to $\mathcal{G}$. Line 3 uses ρ to choose x_n, which is the nearest point to $\alpha(i)$ in the swath of $\mathcal{G}$. In the RDT algorithm of Section 5.5, each sample of α becomes a vertex. Due to the BVP and the particular motion primitives in $\mathcal{U}^p$, it may be difficult or impossible to precisely reach $\alpha(i)$. Therefore, line 4 calls an LPM to determine a primitive $\tilde{u}^p \in \mathcal{U}^p$ that produces a new state x_r upon integration from x_n. The result is depicted in Figure 14.20. For the default case in which $\mathcal{U}^p$ represents the discrete-time model, the action is chosen by applying all $u \in U$ over time Δt and selecting the one that minimizes $\rho(x_r, \alpha(i))$. One additional constraint is that if x_n has been chosen in a previous iteration, then $\tilde{u}^p$ must be a motion primitive that has not been previously tried from x_n; otherwise, duplicate edges would result in $\mathcal{G}$ or time would be wasted performing collision checking for reachability graph edges that are already known to be in collision. The remaining steps add the new vertex and edge from x_n. If x_n is contained in the trajectory produced by an edge e, then e is split as described in Section 5.5.1.

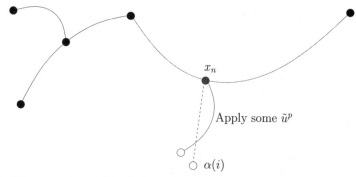

Figure 14.20: If the nearest point S lies in the state trajectory segment associated to an edge, then the edge is split into two, and a new vertex is inserted into $\mathcal{G}$.

Efficiently finding nearest points

The issues of Section 5.5.2 arise again for RDTs under differential constraints. In fact, the problem is further complicated because the edges in $\mathcal{G}$ are generally curved. This prevents the use of simple point-segment distance tests. Furthermore, an exact representation of the state trajectory is usually not known. Instead, it is approximated numerically by the system simulator. For these reasons, it is best to use the approximate method of determining the nearest point in the swath, which is a straightforward extension of the discussion in Section 5.5.2; recall Figure 5.22. Intermediate vertices may be inserted if the applied motion primitive yields a state trajectory that travels far in X_{free}. If the dimension is low enough (e.g., less than 20), then efficient nearest-neighbor algorithms (Section 5.5.2) can be used to offset the cost of maintaining intermediate vertices.

Handling obstacles

Now suppose that $X_{obs} \neq \emptyset$. In Section 5.5.1, the RDT was extended until a stopping configuration q_s was reached, just in front of an obstacle. There are two new complications under differential constraints. The first is that motion primitives are used. If Δt is small, then in many cases the time will expire before the boundary is reached. This can be alleviated by using a large Δt and then taking only the violation-free portion of the trajectory. In this case, the trajectory may even be clipped early to avoid overshooting $\alpha(i)$. The second complication is due to X_{ric}. If momentum is substantial, then pulling the tree as close as possible to obstacles will increase the likelihood that the RDT becomes trapped. Vertices close to obstacles will be selected often because they have large Voronoi regions, but expansion is not possible. In the case of the Piano Mover's Problem, this was much less significant because the tree could easily follow along the boundary. In most experimental work, it therefore seems best to travel only part of the way (perhaps half) to the boundary.

Tree-based planners

Planning algorithms can be constructed from RDTs in the same way as in Section 5.5. Forward, backward, and bidirectional versions can be made. The main new complication is the familiar BVP that the other sampling-based methods of this section have also suffered from. If it is expensive or even impossible to connect nearby states, then the usual complications arise. If X_G contains a sizable open set, then a forward, single-tree planner with a gentle bias toward the goal could perform well while avoiding the BVP. However, if X_G is a point, then a tolerance must be set on how close the RDT must get to the goal before it can declare that it has a solution. For systems with drift, the search time often increases dramatically as this tolerance decreases.

Bidirectional search offers great performance advantages in many cases, but the BVP exists when attempting connections between the two trees. One possibility is to set the tolerance very small and then concatenate the two action trajectories, as described in Section 14.3.4. If it succeeds, then the planning algorithm successfully terminates. Unfortunately, the performance once again depends greatly on the tolerance, particularly if the drift is substantial. Recent studies have shown that using a bidirectional RDT with a large connection tolerance and then closing the gap by using efficient variational techniques provides dramatic improvement in performance [200, 579]. Unfortunately, variational techniques are not efficient for all systems because they must essentially solve the BVP by performing a gradient descent in the trajectory space; see Section 14.7.

Distance function issues

The RDT construction algorithm is heavily influenced by the distance function ρ. This was also true for RDTs applied to the Piano Mover's Problem; however, it becomes more critical and challenging to design a good metric in the presence of differential constraints. For example, the metric given by Example 5.3 is inappropriate for measuring the distance between configurations for the Dubins car. A more appropriate metric is to use length of the shortest path from q to q' (this length is easy to compute; see Section 15.5). Such a metric would be more appropriate than the one in Example 5.3 for comparing the configurations, even for car models that involve dynamics and obstacles.

Although many challenging problems can be solved using weighted Euclidean metrics [614], dramatic improvements can be obtained by exploiting particular properties of the system. This problem might seem similar to the choice of a potential function for the randomized potential field planer of Section 5.4.3; however, since RDTs approach many different samples in $\alpha(i)$, instead of focusing only on the goal, the performance degradation is generally not as severe as the local minimum problem for a potential field planner. There are many more opportunities to escape in an RDT. Metrics that would fail miserably as a potential function often yield good performance in an RDT-based planner.

The ideal distance function, as mentioned in Section 14.3, is to use the optimal cost-to-go, denoted here as ρ^*. Of course, computing ρ^* is at least as hard as solving the motion planning problem. Therefore, this idea does not seem practical. However, it is generally useful to consider ρ^* because the performance of RDT-based planners generally degrades as ρ, the actual metric used in the RDT, and ρ^* diverge. An effort to make a crude approximation to ρ^*, even if obstacles are neglected, often leads to great improvements in performance. An excellent example of this appears in [365], in which value iteration was used to compute the optimal cost-to-go in the absence of obstacles for an autonomous helicopter using the maneuver automaton model of Figure 14.8.

Ensuring resolution completeness

Suppose that the discrete-time model is used. If α is dense in X, then each RDT vertex is visited a countably infinite number of times after it is constructed. By ensuring that the same motion primitive is never applied twice from the same vertex, all available motion primitives will eventually be tried. This ensures that the full reachability graph is explored for a fixed Δt. Since the reachability graph is not necessarily finite, obtaining resolution completeness is more challenging. The scheme described in Figure 14.7 can be applied by periodically varying Δt during execution, and using smaller and smaller of values of

Δt in later iterations. If U is finite, refinements can also be made to U_d. This leads to a resolution-complete RDT.

Designing good motion primitives

Up to this point, only the discrete-time model has been considered. Although it is the most straightforward and general, there are often many better motion primitives that can be used. For a particular system, it may be possible to design a nice family of trajectories off-line in the absence of obstacles and then use them as motion primitives in the RDT construction. If possible, it is important to carefully analyze the system under consideration to try to exploit any special structure it may have or techniques that might have been developed for it. For motion planning of a vehicle, symmetries can be exploited to apply the primitives from different states. For example, in flying a helicopter, the yaw angle and the particular position (unless it is close to the ground) may not be important. A family of trajectories designed for one yaw angle and position should work well for others.

Using more complicated motion primitives may increase the burden on the LPM. In some cases, a simple control law (e.g., PID [51]) may perform well. Ideally, the LPM should behave like a good steering method, which could be obtained using methods in Chapter 15. It is important to note, though, that the RDT's ability to solve problems does not hinge on this. It will greatly improve performance if there are excellent motion primitives and a good steering method in the LPM. The main reason for this is that the difficulties of the differential constraints have essentially been overcome once this happens (except for the adverse effects of drift). Although having good motion primitives can often improve performance in practice, it can also increase the difficulty of ensuring resolution completeness.

14.4.4 Other methods

Extensions of virtually any other method in Chapter 5 can be made to handle differential constraints. Several possibilities are briefly mentioned in this section.

Randomized potential fields

The randomized potential field method of Section 5.4.3 can be easily adapted to handle differential constraints. Instead of moving in any direction to reduce the potential value, motion primitives are applied and integrated to attempt to reduce the value. For example, under the discrete-time model, each $u \in U_d$ can be applied over Δt, and the one for which the next state has the lowest potential value should be selected as part of the descent. Random walks can be tried whenever no such action exists, but once again, motion in any direction is not possible. Random actions can be chosen instead. The main problems with the method under differential constraints are 1) it is extremely challenging to design a good potential function, and 2) random actions do not necessarily provide motions that are similar to those of a random walk. Section 15.1.2 discusses Lyapunov functions, which serve as good potential functions in the presence of differential constraints (but usually neglect obstacles). In the place of random walks, other planning methods, such as an RDT, could be used to try to escape local minima.

Other tree-based planners

Many other tree-based planners can be extended to handle differential constraints. For example, an extension of the expansive space planner from Section 5.4.4 to kinodynamic planning for spacecrafts appears in [469]. Recently, a new tree-based method, called the *path-directed subdivision tree*, has been proposed for planning under differential constraints [575]. The method works by choosing points at random in the swath, applying random actions, and also using a space-partition data structure to control the exploration.

Sampling-based roadmap planners

As stated already, it is generally difficult to construct sampling-based roadmaps unless the BVP can be efficiently solved. The steering methods of Section 15.5 can serve this purpose [934, 861]. In principle, any of the single-query methods of Section 14.4 could be used; however, it may be too costly to use them numerous times, which is required in the roadmap construction algorithm.

14.5 Feedback planning under differential constraints

14.5.1 Problem definition

Formulation 14.1 assumed that feedback is not necessary. If the initial state is given, then the solution takes the form of an action trajectory, which upon integration yields a time-parametrized path through X_{free}. This extended the Piano Mover's Problem of Section 4.3.1 to include phase spaces and differential constraints. Now suppose that feedback is required. The reasons may be that the initial state is not given or the plan execution might not be predictable due to disturbances or errors in the system model. Recall the motivation from Section 8.1.

With little effort, the feedback motion planning framework from Chapter 8 can be extended to handle differential constraints. Compare Formulations 8.2 and 14.1. Feedback motion planning under differential constraints is obtained by making the following adjustments to Formulation 8.2:

1. In Formulation 8.2, $X = C_{free}$, which automatically removed C_{obs} from C by definition. Now let X be any C-space or phase space, and let X_{obs} be defined as in Formulation 8.2. This leads to X_{free}, as defined in Formulation 14.1.

2. In Formulation 8.2, the state transition equation was $\dot{x} = u$, which directly specified velocities in the tangent space $T_x(X)$. Now let any system, $\dot{x} = f(x, u)$, be used instead. In this case, $U(x)$ is no longer a subset of $T_x(X)$. It still includes the special termination action u_T.

3. Formulation 14.1 includes x_I, which is now removed for the feedback case to be consistent with Formulation 8.2.

4. A feedback plan is now defined as a function $\pi : X_{free} \to U$. For a given state $x \in X_{free}$, an action $\pi(x)$ is produced. Composing π with f yields a velocity in $T_x(X)$ given by $\dot{x} = f(x, \pi(x))$. Therefore, π defines a vector field on X_{free}.

Let t_F denote the time at which u_T is applied. Both feasible and optimal planning can be defined using a cost functional,

$$L(\tilde{x}_{t_F}, \tilde{u}_{t_F}) = \int_0^{t_F} l(x(t), u(t))dt + l_F(x(t_F)), \qquad (14.26)$$

which is identical to that given in Section 8.4.1. This now specifies the problem of feedback motion planning under differential constraints.

The most important difference with respect to Chapter 8 is that $\dot{x} = u$ is replaced with $\dot{x} = f(x, u)$, which allows complicated differential models of Chapter 13 to be used. The vector field that results from π must satisfy the differential constraints imposed by $\dot{x} = f(x, u)$. In Section 8.4.4, simple constraints on the allowable vector fields were imposed, such as velocity bounds or smoothness; however, these constraints were not as severe as the models in Chapter 13. For example, the Dubins car does not allow motions in the reverse direction, whereas the constraints in Section 8.4.4 permit motions in any direction.

14.5.2 Dynamic programming with interpolation

As observed in Section 14.4, motion planning under differential constraints is extremely challenging. Additionally requiring feedback complicates the problem even further. If $X_{obs} = \emptyset$, then a feedback plan can be designed using numerous techniques from control theory. See Section 15.2.2 and [194, 526, 848]. In many cases, designing feedback plans is no more difficult than computing an open-loop trajectory. However, if $X_{obs} \neq \emptyset$, feedback usually makes the problem much harder.

Fortunately, dynamic programming once again comes to the rescue. In Section 2.3, value iteration yielded feedback plans for discrete state spaces and state transition equations. It is remarkable that this idea can be generalized to the case in which U and X are continuous and there is a continuum of stages (called time). Most of the tools required to apply dynamic programming in the current setting were already introduced in Section 8.5.2. The main ideas in that section were to represent the optimal cost-to-go G^* by interpolation and to use a discrete-time approximation to the motion planning problem.

The discrete-time model of Section 14.2.2 can be used in the current setting to obtain a discrete-stage state transition equation of the form $x_{k+1} = f_d(x_k, u_k)$. The cost functional is approximated as in Section 8.5.2 by using (8.65). This integral can be evaluated numerically by using the result of the system simulator and yields the cost-per-stage as $l_d(x_k, u_k)$. Using backward value iteration, the dynamic programming recurrence is

$$G_k^*(x_k) = \min_{u_k \in U_d} \left\{ l_d(x_k, u_k) + G_{k+1}^*(x_{k+1}) \right\}, \tag{14.27}$$

which is similar to (2.11) and (8.56). The finite set U_d of action samples is used if U is not already finite. The system simulator is applied to determine whether some points along the trajectory lie in X_{obs}. In this case, $l_d(x_k, u_k) = \infty$, which prevents actions from being chosen that violate constraints.

As in Section 8.5.2, a set $P \subset X$ of samples is used to approximate G^* over X. The required values at points in $X \setminus P$ are obtained by interpolation. For example, the barycentric subdivision scheme of Figure 8.20 may be applied here to interpolate over simplexes in $O(n \lg n)$ time, in which n is the dimension of X.

As usual, backward value iteration starts at some final stage F and proceeds backward through the stage indices. Termination occurs when all of the cost-to-go values stabilize. The initialization at stage F yields $G_F^*(x) = 0$ for $x \in X_G \cap P$; otherwise, $G_F^*(x) = \infty$. Each subsequent iteration is performed by evaluating (14.27) on each $x \in P$ and using interpolation to obtain $G_{k+1}^*(x_{k+1})$.

The resulting stationary cost-to-go function G^* can serve as a navigation function over X_{free}, as described in Section 8.5.2. Recall from Chapter 8 that a navigation function is converted into a feedback plan by applying a local operator. The local operator in the present setting is

$$\pi(x) = \min_{u \in U_d} \left\{ l_d(x, u) + G^*(x) \right\}, \tag{14.28}$$

which yields an action for any state in X_{free} that falls into an interpolation neighborhood of some samples in P.

Unfortunately, the method presented here is only useful in spaces of a few dimensions. If $X = \mathcal{C}$, then it may be applied, for example, to the systems in Section 13.1.2. If dynamics are considered, then in many circumstances the dimension is too high because the dimension of X is usually twice that of $\mathcal{C}$. For example, if $\mathcal{A}$ is a rigid body in the plane, then the dimension of X is six, which is already at the usual limit of practical use.

It is interesting to compare the use of dynamic programming here with that of Sections 14.4.1 and 14.4.2, in which a search graph was constructed. If Dijkstra's algorithm is used (or even breadth-first search in the case of time optimality), then by the dynamic programming principle, the resulting solutions are approximately optimal. To ensure convergence, resolution completeness arguments were given based on Lipschitz conditions on f. It was important to allow the resolution to improve as the search failed to find a solution. Instead of computing a search graph, value iteration is based on computing cost-to-go functions. In that same way that both forward and backward versions of the tree-based approaches were possible, both forward and backward value iteration can be used here. Providing resolution completeness is more difficult, however, because x_I is not fixed. It is therefore not known whether some resolution is good enough for the intended application. If x_I is known, then G^* can be used to generate a trajectory from x_I using the system simulator. If the trajectory fails to reach X_G, then the resolution can be improved by adding more samples to P and U_d or by reducing Δt. Under Lipschitz conditions on f, the approach converges to the true optimal cost-to-go [94, 170, 568]. Therefore, value iteration can be considered resolution complete with respect to a given x_I. The convergence even extends to computing optimal feedback plans with additional actions that are taken by nature, which is modeled nondeterministically or probabilistically. This extends the value iteration method of Section 10.6.

The relationship between the methods based on a search graph and on value iteration can be brought even closer by constructing Dijkstra-like versions of value iteration, as described at the end of Section 8.5.2. These extend Dijkstra's algorithm, which was viewed for the finite case in Section 2.3.3 as an improvement to value iteration. The improvement to value iteration is made by recognizing that in most evaluations of (14.27), the cost-to-go value does not change. This is caused by two factors: 1) From some states, no trajectory has yet been found that leads to X_G; therefore, the cost-to-go remains at infinity. 2) The optimal cost-to-go from some state might already be computed; no future iterations would improve the cost.

A forward or backward version of a Dijkstra-like algorithm can be made. Consider the backward case. The notion of a backprojection was used in Section 8.5.2 to characterize the set of states that can reach another set of states in one stage. This was used in (8.68) to define the *frontier* during the execution of the Dijkstra-like algorithm. There is essentially no difference in the current setting to handle the system $\dot{x} = f(x, u)$. Once the discrete-time approximation has been made, the definition of the backprojection is essentially the same as in (8.66) of Section 8.5.2. Using the discrete-time model of Section 14.2.2, the backprojection of a state $x \in X_{free}$ is

$$B(x) = \{x' \in X_{free} \mid \exists u \in U_d \text{ such that } x = f_d(x', u)\}. \tag{14.29}$$

The backprojection is closely related to the backward time-limited reachable set from Section 14.2.1. The backprojection can be considered as a discrete, one-stage version, which indicates the states that can reach x through the application of a constant action $u \in U_d$ over time Δt. As mentioned in Section 8.5.2, computing an overapproximation to the frontier set may be preferable in practice. This can be obtained by approximating the backprojections, which are generally more complicated under differential constraints than for the case considered in Section 8.5.2. One useful simplification is to ignore collisions with obstacles in defining $B(x)$. Also, a simple bounding volume of the true backprojection may be used. The trade-offs are similar to those in collision detection, as mentioned in Section 5.3.2. Sometimes the structure of the particular system greatly helps in determining the backprojections. A nice wavefront propagation algorithm can be obtained, for example, for a double integrator; this is exploited in Section 14.6.3. For more on value iteration and Dijkstra-like versions, see [610].

14.6 Decoupled planning approaches

14.6.1 Different ways to decouple the big problem

As sampling-based algorithms continue to improve along with computation power, it becomes increasingly feasible in practice to directly solve challenging planning problems under differential constraints. There are many situations, however, in which computing such solutions is still too costly due to expensive numerical integration, collision detection, and complicated obstacles in a high-dimensional state space. Decoupled approaches become appealing because they divide the big problem into modules that are each easier to solve. For versions of the Piano Mover's Problem, such methods were already seen in Chapter 7. Section 7.1.3 introduced the velocity-tuning method to handle time-varying obstacles, and Section 7.2.2 presented decoupled approaches to coordinating multiple robots.

Ideally, we would like to obtain feedback plans on any state space in the presence of obstacles and differential constraints. This assumes that the state can be reliably measured during execution. Section 14.5 provided the best generic techniques for solving the problem, but they are unfortunately limited to a few dimensions. If there is substantial sensing uncertainty, then the feedback plan must be defined on the I-space, which was covered in Chapter 11. Back in Section 1.4, Figure 1.19 showed a popular model of decoupling the big planning problem into a sequence of refinements. A typical decoupled approach involves four modules:

1. Use a motion planning algorithm to find a collision-free path $\tau : [0, 1] \to \mathcal{C}_{free}$.

2. Transform τ into a new path τ' so that velocity constraints on $\mathcal{C}$ (if there are any) are satisfied. This might, for example, ensure that the Dubins car can actually follow the path. At the very least, some path-smoothing is needed in most circumstances.

3. Compute a timing function $\sigma : [0, t_F] \to [0, 1]$ for τ' so that $\tau' \circ \sigma$ is a time-parameterized path through $\mathcal{C}_{free}$ with the following requirement. The state trajectory $\tilde{x}$ must satisfy $\dot{x} = f(x(t), u(t))$ and $u(t) \in U(x(t))$ for all time, until u_T is applied at time t_F.

4. Design a feedback plan (or feedback control law) $\pi : X \to U$ that tracks $\tilde{x}$. The plan should attempt to minimize the error between the desired state and the measured state during execution.

PLAN-AND-TRANSFORM APPROACH

1. Compute a path $\tau : [0, 1] \to \mathcal{C}_{free}$ using a motion planning algorithm, such as one from Part II.

2. Choose some $s_1, s_2 \in [0, 1]$ such that $s_1 < s_2$ and use an LPM to attempt to replace the portion of τ from $\tau(s_1)$ to $\tau(s_2)$ with a path γ that satisfies the differential constraints.

3. If τ now satisfies the differential constraints over all $[0, 1]$, then the algorithm terminates. Otherwise, go to Step 2.

Figure 14.21: A general outline of the plan-and-transform approach.

Given recent techniques and computation power, the significance of this approach may diminish somewhat; however, it remains an important way to decompose and solve problems. Be aware, however, that this decomposition is arbitrary. If every module can be solved, then it is sufficient for producing a solution; however, such a decomposition is not necessary. At any step along the way, completeness may be lost because of poor choices in earlier modules. It is often difficult for modules to take into account problems that may arise later.

Various ways to merge the modules have been considered. The methods of Section 14.4 solve either: 1) the first two modules simultaneously, if paths that satisfy $\dot{q} = f(q, u)$ are computed through $\mathcal{C}_{free}$, or 2) the first three modules simultaneously, if paths that satisfy $\dot{x} = f(x, u)$ are computed through X_{free}. Section 14.5 solved all four modules simultaneously but was limited to low-dimensional state spaces.

Now consider keeping the modules separate. Planning methods from Part II can be applied to solve the first module. Section 14.6.2 will cover methods that implement the second module. Section 14.6.3 will cover methods that solve the third module, possibly while also solving the second module. The fourth module is a well-studied control problem that is covered in numerous texts [526, 848, 858].

14.6.2 Plan and transform

For the decoupled approach in this section, assume that $X = \mathcal{C}$, which means there are only velocity constraints, as covered in Section 13.1. The system may be specified as $\dot{q} = f(q, u)$ or implicitly as a set of constraints of the form $g_i(q, \dot{q}) = 0$. The ideas in this section can easily be extended to phase spaces. The method given here was developed primarily by Laumond (see [599]) and was also applied to the simple car of Section 13.1.2 in [590]; other applications of the method are covered in [599].

An outline of the *plan-and-transform* approach is shown in Figure 14.21. In the first step, a collision-free path $\tau : [0, 1] \to \mathcal{C}_{free}$ is computed by ignoring differential constraints. The path is then iteratively modified until it satisfies the constraints. In each iteration, a subinterval $[s_1, s_2] \subseteq [0, 1]$ is selected by specifying some $s_1, s_2 \in [0, 1]$ so that $s_1 < s_2$. These points may be chosen using random sequences or may be chosen deterministically. The approach may use binary subdivision to refine intervals and gradually improve the resolution on $[0, 1]$ over the iterations.

For each chosen interval $[s_1, s_2]$, an LPM is used to compute a path segment $\gamma : [0, 1] \to \mathcal{C}_{free}$ that satisfies the conditions $\gamma(0) = \tau(s_1)$ and $\gamma(1) = \tau(s_2)$. It might be the case that the LPM fails because it cannot connect the two configurations or a collision may occur. In this case, another subinterval is chosen, and the process repeats. Each time

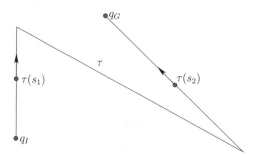

Figure 14.22: An initial path that ignores differential constraints.

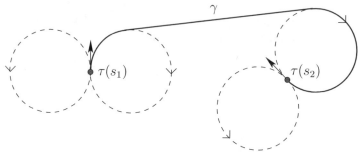

Figure 14.23: A path for the Dubins car can always be found by connecting a bitangent to two circles generated by the minimum turning radius. The path is not necessarily optimal; see Section 15.3.1 for optimal paths.

the LPM succeeds, τ is updated to τ' as

$$\tau'(s) = \begin{cases} \tau(s) & \text{if } s < s_1 \\ \gamma((s - s_1)/(s_2 - s_1)) & \text{if } s \in [s_1, s_2] \\ \tau(s) & \text{if } s > s_2. \end{cases} \qquad (14.30)$$

The argument to γ reparameterizes it to run from s_1 to s_2, instead of 0 to 1.

Example 14.5 (Plan-and-Transform for the Dubins Car) For a concrete example, suppose that the task is to plan a path for the Dubins car. Figure 14.22 shows a path τ that might be computed by a motion planning algorithm that ignores differential constraints. Two sharp corners cannot be traversed by the car. Suppose that s_1 and s_2 are chosen at random, and appear at the locations shown in Figure 14.22. The portion of τ between $\tau(s_1)$ and $\tau(s_2)$ needs to be replaced by a path that can be executed by the Dubins car. Note that matching the orientations at $\tau(s_1)$ and $\tau(s_2)$ is important because they are part of the configuration.

A replacement path γ is shown in Figure 14.23. This is obtained by implementing the following LPM. For the Dubins car, a path between any configurations can be found by drawing circles at the starting and stopping configurations as shown in the figure. Each circle corresponds to the sharpest possible left turn or right turn. It is straightforward to find a line that is tangent to one circle from each configuration and also matches the direction of flow for the car (the circles are like one-way streets). Using γ, the path τ is updated to obtain τ', which is shown in Figure 14.24, and satisfies the differential constraints for the Dubins car. This problem was very simple, and in practice dozens of iterations may be necessary to replace path segments. Also, if randomization is used, then intervals of the form $[0, s]$ and $[s, 1]$ must not be neglected. ∎

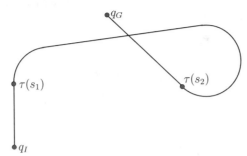

Figure 14.24: Upon replacement, the resulting path τ' can be followed by the Dubins car.

Example 14.5 seemed easy because of the existence of a simple local planner. Also, there were no obstacles. Imagine that τ instead traveled through a narrow, zig-zagging corridor. In this case, a solution might not even exist because of sharp corners that cannot be turned by the Dubins car. If there had been an single obstacle that happened to intersect the loop in Figure 14.24, then the replacement would have failed. In general, there is no guarantee that the replacement segment is collision-free. It is important for the LPM to construct path segments that are as close as possible to the original path. For the Dubins car, this is not possible in many cases. For example, moving the Dubins car a small distance backward requires moving along the circles shown in Figure 14.23. Even as the distance between two configurations is reduced, the distance that the car needs to travel does not approach zero. This is true even if the shortest possible paths are used for the Dubins car.

What property should an LPM have to ensure resolution completeness of the plan-and-transform approach? A sufficient condition is given in [599]. Let ρ denote a metric on X. An LPM is said to satisfy the *topological property* if and only if the following statement holds: For any $\epsilon > 0$, there exists some $\delta > 0$ such that for any pair $q, q' \in \mathcal{C}_{free}$ having $\rho(q, q') < \delta$ implies that $\rho(\tau(s), q) < \epsilon$ for all $s \in [0, 1]$. If an LPM satisfies the topological property, then any collision-free path through $\mathcal{C}_{free}$ can be transformed into one that satisfies the differential constraints. Suppose that a path τ has some clearance of at least ϵ in $\mathcal{C}_{free}$. By dividing the domain of τ into intervals so that the change in q is no more than δ over each interval, then the LPM will produce collision-free path segments for replacement.

It turns out that for the Reeds-Shepp car (which has reverse) such an LPM can be designed because it is *small-time locally controllable*, a property that will be covered in Sections 15.1.3 and 15.4. In general, many techniques from Chapter 15 may be useful for analyzing and designing effective LPMs.

An interesting adaptation of the plan-and-transform approach has been developed for problems that involve k implicit constraints of the form $g_i(q, \dot{q}) = 0$. An outline of the *multi-level* approach, which was introduced in [861], is shown in Figure 14.25 (a similar approach was also introduced in [335]). The idea is to sort the k constraints into a sequence and introduce them one at a time. Initially, a path is planned that ignores the constraints. This path is first transformed to satisfy $g_1(q, \dot{q}) = 0$ and avoid collisions by using the plan-and-transform method of Figure 14.21. If successful, then the resulting path is transformed into one that is collision-free and satisfies both $g_1(q, \dot{q}) = 0$ and $g_2(q, \dot{q}) = 0$. This process repeats by adding one constraint each time, until either the method fails or all k constraints have been taken into account.

MULTI-LEVEL APPROACH

1. Compute a path $\tau : [0, 1] \to \mathcal{C}_{free}$ using a standard motion planning algorithm (as in Part II), and let $i = 1$.

2. Transform τ into a collision free path that satisfies $g_j(q, \dot{q}) = 0$ for all j from 1 to i.

3. If the transformation failed in Step 2, then terminate and report failure.

4. If $i < k$, the number of implicit velocity constraints, then increment i and go to Step 2. Otherwise, terminate and successfully report τ as a path that satisfies all constraints.

Figure 14.25: The multi-level approach considers implicit constraints one at a time.

14.6.3 Path-constrained trajectory planning

This section assumes that a path $\tau : [0, 1] \to \mathcal{C}_{free}$ has been given. It may be computed by a motion planning algorithm from Part II or given by hand. The remaining task is to determine the speed along the path in a way that satisfies differential constraints on the phase space X. Assume that each state $x \in X$ represents both a configuration and its time derivative, to obtain $x = (q, \dot{q})$. Let n denote the dimension of $\mathcal{C}$; hence, the dimension of X is $2n$. Once a path is given, there are only two remaining degrees of freedom in X: 1) the position $s \in [0, 1]$ along the domain of τ, and 2) the speed $\dot{s} = ds/dt$ at each s. The full state, x, can be recovered from these two parameters. As the state changes, it must satisfy a given system, $\dot{x} = f(x, u)$. It will be seen that a 2D planning problem arises, which can be solved efficiently using many alternative techniques. Similar concepts appeared for decoupled versions of time-varying motion planning in Section 7.1. The presentation in the current section is inspired by work in time-scaling paths for robot manipulators [459, 878, 881], which was developed a couple of decades ago. At that time, computers were much slower, which motivated the development of strongly decoupled approaches.

14.6.3.1 Expressing systems in terms of s, $\dot{s}$, and $\ddot{s}$

Suppose that a system is given in the form

$$\ddot{q} = h(q, \dot{q}, u), \tag{14.31}$$

in which there are n action variables $u = (u_1, \ldots, u_n)$. It may be helpful to glance ahead to Example 14.6, which will illustrate the coming concepts for the simple case of double integrators $\ddot{q} = u$. The acceleration in $\mathcal{C}$ is determined from the state $x = (q, \dot{q})$ and action u. Assume $u \in U$, in which U is an n-dimensional subset of $\mathbb{R}^n$. If h is nonsingular at x, then an n-dimensional set of possible accelerations arises from choices of $u \in U$. This means it is fully actuated. If there were fewer than n action variables, then there would generally not be enough freedom to follow a specified path. Therefore, U must be n-dimensional. Which choices of u, however, constrain the motion to follow the given path τ? To determine this, the q, $\dot{q}$, and $\ddot{q}$ variables need to be related to the path domain s and its first and second time derivatives $\dot{s}$ and $\ddot{s}$, respectively. This leads to a subset of U that corresponds to actions that follow the path.

Suppose that s, $\dot{s}$, $\ddot{s}$, and a path τ are given. The configuration $q \in \mathcal{C}_{free}$ is

$$q = \tau(s). \tag{14.32}$$

Assume that all first and second derivatives of τ exist. The velocity $\dot{q}$ can be determined by the chain rule as

$$\dot{q} = \frac{d\tau}{ds}\frac{ds}{dt} = \frac{d\tau}{ds}\dot{s}, \tag{14.33}$$

in which the derivative $d\tau/ds$ is evaluated at s. The acceleration is obtained by taking another derivative, which yields

$$\ddot{q} = \frac{d}{dt}\left(\frac{d\tau}{ds}\dot{s}\right)$$
$$= \frac{d^2\tau}{ds^2}\frac{ds}{dt}\dot{s} + \frac{d\tau}{ds}\ddot{s} \tag{14.34}$$
$$= \frac{d^2\tau}{ds^2}\dot{s}^2 + \frac{d\tau}{ds}\ddot{s},$$

by application of the product rule. The full state $x = (q, \dot{q})$ can be recovered from $(s, \dot{s})$ using (14.32) and (14.33).

The next step is to obtain an equation that looks similar to (14.31), but is expressed in terms of s, $\dot{s}$, and $\ddot{s}$. A function $h'(s, \dot{s}, u)$ can be obtained from $h(q, \dot{q}, u)$ by substituting $\tau(s)$ for q and the right side of (14.33) for $\dot{q}$:

$$h'(s, \dot{s}, u) = h(\tau(s), \frac{d\tau}{ds}\dot{s}, u). \tag{14.35}$$

This yields

$$\ddot{q} = h'(s, \dot{s}, u). \tag{14.36}$$

For a given state x (which can be obtained from s and $\dot{s}$), the set of accelerations that can be obtained by a choice of u in (14.36) is the same as that for the original system in (14.31). The only difference is that x is now constrained to a 2D subset of X, which are the states that can be reached by selecting values for s and $\dot{s}$.

Applying (14.34) to the left side of (14.36) constrains the accelerations to cause motions that follow τ. This yields

$$\frac{d^2\tau}{ds^2}\dot{s}^2 + \frac{d\tau}{ds}\ddot{s} = h'(s, \dot{s}, u), \tag{14.37}$$

which can also be expressed as

$$\frac{d\tau}{ds}\ddot{s} = h'(s, \dot{s}, u) - \frac{d^2\tau}{ds^2}\dot{s}^2, \tag{14.38}$$

by moving the first term of (14.34) to the right. Note that n equations are actually represented in (14.38). For each i in which $d\tau_i/ds \neq 0$, a constraint of the form

$$\ddot{s} = \frac{1}{d\tau_i/ds}h_i'(s, \dot{s}, u_i) - \frac{d^2\tau_i}{ds^2}\dot{s}^2 \tag{14.39}$$

is obtained by solving for $\ddot{s}$.

14.6.3.2 Determining the allowable accelerations

The actions in U that cause τ to be followed can now be characterized. An action $u \in U$ follows τ if and only if every equation of the form (14.39) is satisfied. If $d\tau_i/ds \neq 0$ for all i from 1 to n, then n such equations exist. Suppose that u_1 is chosen, and the first equation is solved for $\ddot{s}$. The required values of the remaining action variables $u_2, \ldots, u_n$ can be

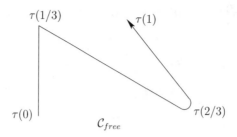

Figure 14.26: A bad path for path-constrained trajectory planning.

obtained by substituting the determined $\ddot{s}$ value into the remaining $n - 1$ equations. This means that the actions that follow τ are at most a one-dimensional subset of U.

If $d\tau_i/ds = 0$ for some i, then following the path requires that $\dot{q}_i = 0$. Instead of (14.39), the constraint is that $h_i(q, \dot{q}, u) = 0$. Example 14.6 will provide a simple illustration of this. If $d\tau_i/ds = 0$ for all i, then the configuration is not allowed to change. This occurs in the degenerate (and useless) case in which τ is a constant function.

In many cases, a value of u does not exist that satisfies all of the constraint equations. This means that the path cannot be followed at that particular state. Such states should be removed, if possible, by defining phase constraints on X. By a poor choice of path τ violating such a phase constraint may be unavoidable. There may exist some s for which no $u \in U$ can follow τ, regardless of $\dot{s}$.

Even if a state trajectory may be optimal in some sense, its quality ultimately depends on the given path $\tau : [0, 1] \to \mathcal{C}_{free}$. Consider the path shown in Figure 14.26. At $\tau(1/3)$, a "corner" is reached. This violates the differentiability assumption and would require infinite acceleration to traverse while remaining on τ. For some models, it may be possible to stop at $\tau(1/3)$ and then start again. For example, imagine a floating particle in the plane. It can be decelerated to rest exactly at $\tau(1/3)$ and then started in a new direction to exactly follow the curve. This assumes that the particle is fully actuated. If there are nonholonomic constraints on $\mathcal{C}$, as in the case of the Dubins car, then the given path must at least satisfy them before accelerations can be considered. The solution in this case depends on the existence of *decoupling vector fields* [159, 226].

It is generally preferable to round off any corners that might have been produced by a motion planning algorithm in constructing τ. This helps, but it still does not completely resolve the issue. The portion of the path around $\tau(2/3)$ is not desirable because of high curvature. At a fixed speed, larger accelerations are generally needed to follow sharp turns. The speed may have to be decreased simply because τ carelessly requires sharp turns in $\mathcal{C}$. Imagine developing an autonomous double-decker tour bus. It is clear that following the curve around $\tau(2/3)$ may cause the bus to topple at high speeds. The bus will have to slow down because it is a slave to the particular choice of τ.

14.6.3.3 The path-constrained phase space

Recall the approach in Section 14.4.1 that enabled systems of the form $\ddot{q} = h(q, \dot{q}, u)$ to be expressed as $\ddot{q} = u'$ for some suitable $U'(q, \dot{q}) \subseteq U$ (this was illustrated in Figure 14.15). This enabled many systems to be imagined as multiple, independent double integrators with phase-dependent constraints on the action space. The same idea can be applied here to obtain a single integrator.

Let S denote a 2D *path-constrained phase space*, in which each element is of the form $(s, \dot{s})$ and represents the position and velocity along τ. This parameterizes a 2D subset of the original phase space X. Each original state vector is $x = (q, \dot{q}) = (\tau(s), d\tau/ds\,\dot{s})$. Which accelerations are possible at points in S? At each $(s, \dot{s})$, a subset of U can be determined that satisfies the equations of the form (14.39). Each valid action yields an acceleration $\ddot{s}$. Let $U'(s, \dot{s}) \subseteq \mathbb{R}$ denote the set of all values of $\ddot{s}$ that can be obtained from an action $u \in U$ that satisfies (14.39) for each i (except the ones for which $d\tau_i/ds = 0$). Now the system can be expressed as $\ddot{s} = u'$, in which $u' \in U'(s, \dot{s})$. After all of this work, we have arrived at the double integrator. The main complication is that $U'(s, \dot{s})$ can be challenging to determine for some systems. It could consist of a single interval, disjoint intervals, or may even be empty. Assuming that $U'(s, \dot{s})$ has been characterized, it is straightforward to solve the remaining planning problem using techniques already presented in this chapter. One double integrator is not very challenging; hence, efficient sampling-based algorithms exist.

An obstacle region $S_{obs} \subset S$ will now be considered. This includes any states that belong to X_{free}. Given s and $\dot{s}$, the state x can be computed to determine whether any constraints on X are violated. Usually, τ is constructed to avoid obstacle collision; however, some phase constraints may also exist. The obstacle region S_{obs} also includes any points $(s, \dot{s})$ for which $U'(s, \dot{s})$ is empty. Let S_{free} denote $S \setminus S_{obs}$.

Before considering computation methods, we give some examples.

Example 14.6 (Path-Constrained Double Integrators) Consider the case of two double integrators. This could correspond physically to a particle moving in $\mathbb{R}^2$. Hence, $\mathcal{C} = \mathcal{W} = \mathbb{R}^2$. Let $U = [-1, 1]^2$ and $\ddot{q} = u$ for $u \in U$. The path τ will be chosen to force the particle to move along a line. For linear paths, $d\tau/ds$ is constant and $d^2\tau/ds^2 = 0$. Using these observations and the fact that $h'(s, \dot{s}, u) = u$, (14.39) simplifies to

$$\ddot{s} = \frac{u_i}{d\tau_i/ds}, \tag{14.40}$$

for $i = 1, 2$.

Suppose that $\tau(s) = (s, s)$, which means that the particle must move along a diagonal line through the origin of $\mathcal{C}$. This further simplifies (14.40) to $\ddot{s} = u_1$ and $\ddot{s} = u_2$. Hence any $u_1 \in [-1, 1]$ may be chosen, but u_2 must then be chosen as $u_2 = u_1$. The constrained system can be written as one double integrator $\ddot{s} = u'$, in which $u' \in [-1, 1]$. Both u_1 and u_2 are derived from u' as $u_1 = u_2 = u'$. Note that U' does not vary over S; this occurs because a linear path is degenerate.

Now consider constraining the motion to a general line:

$$\tau(s) = (a_1 s + b_1, \ a_2 s + b_2), \tag{14.41}$$

in which a_1 and a_2 are nonzero. In this case, (14.40) yields $\ddot{s} = u_1/a_1$ and $\ddot{s} = u_2/a_2$. Since each $u_i \in [-1, 1]$, each equation indicates that $\ddot{s} \in [-1/a_i, 1/a_i]$. The acceleration must lie in the intersection of these two intervals. If $|a_1| \geq |a_2|$, then $\ddot{s} \in [-1/a_1, 1/a_1]$. We can designate $u' = u_1$ and let $u_2 = u'a_2/a_1$. If $|a_1| > |a_2|$, then $\ddot{s} \in [-1/a_2, 1/a_2]$, $u' = u_2$, and $u_1 = u'a_1/a_2$.

Suppose that $a_1 = 0$ and $a_2 \neq 0$. The path is

$$\tau(s) = (q_1, \ a_2 s + b_2), \tag{14.42}$$

in which q_1 is fixed and the particle is constrained to move along a vertical line in $\mathcal{C} = \mathbb{R}^2$. In this case, only one constraint, $\ddot{s} = u_2$, is obtained from (14.40). However, u_1 is independently constrained to $u_1 = 0$ because horizontal motions are prohibited.

If n independent, double integrators are constrained to a line, a similar result is obtained. There are n equations of the form (14.40). The $i \in \{1, \ldots, n\}$ for which $|a_i|$ is largest determines the acceleration range as $\ddot{s} \in [-1/a_i, 1/a_i]$. The action u' is defined as $u' = u_i$, and the u_j for $j \neq i$ are obtained from the remaining $n - 1$ equations.

Now assume τ is nonlinear, in which case (14.39) becomes

$$\ddot{s} = \frac{u_i}{d\tau_i/ds} - \frac{d^2\tau_i}{ds^2}\dot{s}^2, \tag{14.43}$$

for each i for which $d\tau_i/ds \neq 0$. Now the set $U'(s, \dot{s})$ varies over S. As the speed $\dot{s}$ increases, it becomes less likely that $U'(s, \dot{s})$ is nonempty. In other words, it is less likely that a solution exists to all equations of the form (14.43). In a physical system, that means that staying on the path requires turning too sharply. At a high speed, this may require an acceleration $\ddot{q}$ that lies outside of $[-1, 1]^n$. ∎

The same ideas can be applied to systems that are much more complicated. This should not be surprising because in Section 14.4.1 systems of the form $\ddot{q} = h(q, \dot{q})$ were interpreted as multiple, independent double integrators of the form $\ddot{q} = u'$, in which $u' \in U'(q, \dot{q})$ provided the possible accelerations. Under this interpretation, and in light of Example 14.6, constraining the motions of a general system to a path τ just further restricts $U'(q, \dot{q})$. The resulting set of allowable accelerations may be at most one-dimensional.

The following example indicates the specialization of (14.39) for a robot arm.

Example 14.7 (Path-Constrained Manipulators)   Suppose that the system is described as (13.142) from Section 13.4.2. This is a common form that has been used for controlling robot arms for decades. Constraints of the form (14.39) can be derived by expressing q, $\dot{q}$, and $\ddot{q}$ in terms of s, $\dot{s}$, and $\ddot{s}$. This requires using (14.32), (14.33), and (14.34). Direct substitution into (13.142) yields

$$M(\tau(s))\left(\frac{d^2\tau}{ds^2}\dot{s}^2 + \frac{d\tau}{ds}\ddot{s}\right) + C\left(\tau(s), \frac{d\tau}{ds}\dot{s}\right)\frac{d\tau}{ds}\dot{s} + g(\tau(s)) = u. \tag{14.44}$$

This can be simplified to n equations of the form

$$\alpha_i(s)\ddot{s} + \beta_i(s)\dot{s}^2 + \gamma_i(s)\dot{s} = u_i. \tag{14.45}$$

Solving each one for $\ddot{s}$ yields a special case of (14.39). As in Example 14.6, each equation determines a bounding interval for $\ddot{s}$. The intersection of the intervals for all n equations yields the allowed interval for $\ddot{s}$. The action u' once again indicates the acceleration in the interval, and the original action variables u_i can be obtained from (14.45). If $d\tau_i/ds = 0$, then $\alpha_i(s) = 0$, which corresponds to the case in which the constraint does not apply. Instead, the constraint is that the vector u must be chosen so that $\dot{q}_i = 0$. ∎

14.6.3.4 Computing optimal solutions via dynamic programming

Dynamic programming with interpolation, as covered in Section 14.5, can be applied to solve the problem once it is formulated in terms of the path-constrained phase space $S \subset \mathbb{R}^2$. The domain of τ provides the constraint $0 \leq s \leq 1$. Assume that only forward progress along the path is needed; moving in the reverse direction should not be necessary. This implies that $\dot{s} > 0$. To make S bounded, an upper bound, $\dot{s}_{max}$, is usually assumed, beyond which it is known that the speed is too high to follow the path.

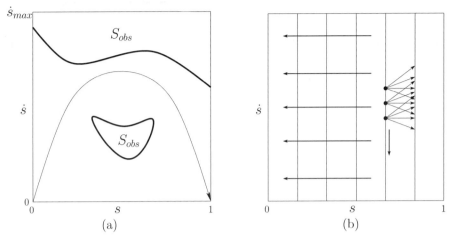

Figure 14.27: (a) Planning occurs in the path-constrained phase space. (b) Due to the forward-progress assumption, value iteration can be reduced to a quick wavefront propagation across regularly spaced vertical lines in S.

This results in the planning problem shown in Figure 14.27a. The system is expressed as $\ddot{s} = u'$, in which $u' \in U'(s, \dot{s})$. The initial phase in S is $(0, \dot{s}_i)$ and the goal phase is $(1, \dot{s}_g)$. Typically, $\dot{s}_i = \dot{s}_g = 0$. The region shown in Figure 14.27 is contained in the first quadrant of the phase space because only positive values of s and $\dot{s}$ are allowed (in Figure 14.13, q and $\dot{q}$ could be positive or negative). This implies that all motions are to the right. The actions determine whether accelerations or decelerations will occur.

Backward value iteration with interpolation can be easily applied by discretizing S and $U'(s, \dot{s})$. Due to the constraint $\dot{s} > 0$, making a Dijkstra-like version of the algorithm is straightforward. A simple wavefront propagation can even be performed, starting at $s = 1$ and progressing backward in vertical waves until $s = 0$ is reached. See Figure 14.27b. The backprojection (14.29) can be greatly simplified. Suppose that the s-axis is discretized into $m + 1$ regularly spaced values $s_0, \ldots, s_m$ at every Δs, for some fixed $\Delta s > 0$. Thus, $s_k = (k \Delta s)/m$. The index k can be interpreted as the stage. Starting at $k = m$, the final cost-to-go $G_m^*(s_m, \dot{s}_m)$ is defined as 0 if the corresponding phase represents the goal, and ∞ otherwise. At each s_k, the $\dot{s}$ values are sampled, and the cost-to-go function is represented using one-dimensional linear interpolation along the vertical axis. At each stage, the dynamic programming computation

$$G_k^*(s_k, \dot{s}_k) = \min_{u' \in U'(s_k, \dot{s}_k)} \left\{ l_d'(s_k, \dot{s}_k, u') + G_{k+1}^*(s_{k+1}, \dot{s}_{k+1}) \right\} \quad (14.46)$$

is performed at each $\dot{s}$ sample. This represents a special form of (14.27). Linear interpolation over discretized $\dot{s}$ values is used to evaluate $G_{k+1}^*(s_{k+1}, \dot{s}_{k+1})$. The cost term l_d' is obtained from l_d by computing the original state $x \in X$ from s and $\dot{s}$; however, if the trajectory segment enters S_{obs}, it receives infinite cost. The computations proceed until stage $k = 1$, at which time the optimal cost-to-go $G_1^*(s_1, \dot{s}_1)$ is computed. The optimal trajectory is obtained by using the cost-to-go function at each stage as a navigation function.

The dynamic programming approach is so general that it can even be extended to path-constrained trajectory planning in the presence of higher order constraints [882]. For example, if a system is specified as $q^{(3)} = h(q, \dot{q}, \ddot{q}, u)$, then a 3D path-constrained phase

---

BANG-BANG APPROACH

1. From the final state $(1, 0)$, apply reverse-time integration to $\ddot{s} = u'_{min}(s, \dot{s})$. Continue constructing the curve numerically until either the interior of S_{obs} is entered or $\dot{s} = 0$. In the latter case, the algorithm terminates with failure.

2. Let $(s_{cur}, \dot{s}_{cur}) = (0, 0)$.

3. Apply forward integration $\ddot{s} = u'_{max}(s, \dot{s})$ from $(s_{cur}, \dot{s}_{cur})$ until either the interior of S_{obs} is entered or the curve generated in Step 1 is crossed. In the latter case, the problem is solved.

4. Starting at the point where the trajectory from Step 3 crossed the limit curve, find next tangent point $(s_{tan}, \dot{s}_{tan})$ to the right along the limit curve. From $(s_{tan}, \dot{s}_{tan})$, perform reverse integration on $\ddot{s} = u'_{min}(s, \dot{s})$ until the curve from Step 3 is hit. Let $(s_{cur}, \dot{s}_{cur}) = (s_{tan}, \dot{s}_{tan})$ and go to Step 3.

Figure 14.28: The bang-bang approach finds a time-optimal, path-constrained trajectory with less searching than the dynamic programming approach.

---

space results, in which each element is expressed as $(s, \dot{s}, \ddot{s})$. The actions in this space are jerks, yielding $s^{(3)} = u'$ for $u' \in U'(s, \dot{s}, \ddot{s})$.

14.6.3.5 A bang-bang approach for time optimality

The dynamic programming approach is already very efficient because the search is confined to two dimensions. Nevertheless, trajectories that are time optimal can be computed even more efficiently if S_{obs} has some special structure. The idea is to find an alternating sequence between two motion primitives: one of maximum acceleration and one of maximum deceleration. This kind of switching between extreme opposites is often called *bang-bang control* and arises often in the development of time-optimal control laws (look ahead to Example 15.4). The method explained here was introduced in [123, 881]. One drawback of obtaining time-optimal trajectories is that they cannot be tracked (the fourth module from Section 14.6.1) if errors occur because the solutions travel on the boundary of the reachable set.

The approach was developed for robot arms, as considered in Example 14.7. Suppose that S_{obs} is a single connected component that is bounded above by $\dot{s}_{max}$, and on the sides it is bounded by $s = 0$ and $s = 1$. It is assumed that S arises only due to the vanishing of the interval of allowable values for $\ddot{s}$ (in this case, $U'(s, \dot{s})$ becomes empty). It is also assumed that the lower boundary of S_{obs} can be expressed as a differentiable function $\phi : [0, 1] \to S$, called the *limit curve*, which yields the maximum speed $\dot{s} = \phi(s)$ for every $s \in [0, 1]$. The method is extended to handle multiple obstacles in [881], but this case is not considered here. Assume also that $d\tau_i/ds \neq 0$ for every i; the case of $d\tau_i/ds = 0$ can also be handled in the method [880].

Let $u'_{min}(s, \dot{s})$ and $u'_{max}(s, \dot{s})$ denote the smallest and largest possible accelerations, respectively, from $(s, \dot{s}) \in S$. If $(s, \dot{s}) \notin S_{obs}$, then $u'_{min}(s, \dot{s}) < u'_{max}(s, \dot{s})$. At the limit curve, $u'_{min}(s, \phi(s)) = u'_{max}(s, \phi(s))$. Applying the only feasible action in this case generates a velocity that is tangent to the limit curve. This is called a *tangent point*, $(s_{tan}, \dot{s}_{tan})$, to ϕ. Inside of S_{obs}, no accelerations are possible.

The *bang-bang approach* is described in Figure 14.28, and a graphical illustration appears in Figure 14.29. Assume that the initial and goal phases are $(0, 0)$ and $(1, 0)$, respectively. Step 1 essentially enlarges the goal by constructing a maximum-deceleration curve that terminates at $(1, 0)$. A trajectory that contacts this curve can optimally reach

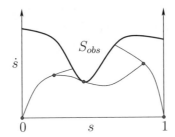

Figure 14.29: An illustration of the bang-bang approach to computing a time-optimal trajectory. The solution trajectory is obtained by connecting the dots.

$(1, 0)$ by switching to maximum deceleration. Steps 3 and 4 construct a maximum-acceleration curve followed by a maximum-deceleration curve. The acceleration curve runs until it pierces the limit curve. This constraint violation must be avoided. Therefore, a deceleration must be determined that departs earlier from the acceleration curve and just barely misses entering the interior of S_{obs}. This curve must become tangent to the limit curve; therefore, a search is made along the limit curve for the next possible tangent point. From there, reverse-time integration is used in Step 4 to generate a deceleration curve that contacts the acceleration curve. A portion of the solution has now been obtained in which an acceleration is followed by a deceleration that arrives at a tangent point of ϕ. It is possible that Step 4 is not reached because the curve that connects to the goal is contacted. Starting from the tangent point, Steps 3 and 4 are repeated until the goal curve is contacted.

14.7 Gradient-based trajectory optimization

This section provides a brief overview of a complementary problem to motion planning. Suppose that an algorithm in this chapter returns a feasible action trajectory. How can the solution be improved? *Trajectory optimization* refers to the problem of perturbing the trajectory while satisfying all constraints so that its quality can be improved. For example, it may be desirable to shorten a trajectory computed by an RRT, to remove some of the arbitrary changes in actions due to randomization. Trajectory optimization is considered complementary to motion planning because it usually requires an initial guess, which could be provided by a planning algorithm. Trajectory optimization can be considered as a kind of BVP, but one that improves an initial guess, as opposed to determining trajectories from scratch.

The optimization issue also exists for paths computed by sampling-based algorithms for the Piano Mover's Problem; however, without differential constraints, it is much simpler to shorten paths. The plan and transform method of Section 14.6.2 can be applied, and the LPM just connects pairs of configurations along the shortest path in $\mathcal{C}$. In the presence of differential constraints, the BVP must be faced.

In the most general setting, it is very difficult to improve trajectories. There are numerous methods from optimization literature; see [100, 153, 667] for overviews. The purpose of this section is to encourage further study by briefly mentioning the various kinds of methods that have been developed, instead of explaining them in detail. The methods fall under the area of *nonlinear programming* (NLP) (or *nonlinear optimization*), as opposed to *linear programming*, which was used to find randomized security strategies in Section 9.3. The optimization actually occurs in a space of possible trajectories, each of which is a function of time. Therefore, the calculus of variations, which was used in Section 13.4.1, becomes relevant to characterize extrema. The functional Φ from that setting becomes the cost functional L in the current setting. The system $\dot{x} = f(x, u)$ forms an additional set of constraints that must be satisfied, but u can be selected in the optimization.

To enable numerical computation methods, a family of trajectories is specified in terms of a parameter space. The optimization can then be viewed as an incremental search in the parameter space while satisfying all constraints. The direction of motion in each step is determined by computing the gradient of a cost functional with respect to the parameters while constrained to move in a direction tangent to the constraints. Hence, much of nonlinear programming can be considered as an application of Newton's method or gradient descent. As in standard optimization, second-order derivatives of the cost functional can be used to indicate when the search should terminate. The numerical issues associated with these methods are quite involved; several NLP software packages, such as the NAG Fortran Library or packages within Matlab, are available.

Nonlinear optimal control theory can be considered as a variant of NLP. The dynamic programming recurrence becomes a differential equation in the continuous-time setting, and Hamilton's equations (13.198) generalize to Pontryagin's minimum principle. These are covered in Section 15.2. The extra variables that arise in the minimum principle can be considered as Lagrange multipliers of a constrained optimization, in which $\dot{x} = f(x, u)$ is the constraint. The differential equations arising from dynamic programming or the minimum principle are difficult to solve analytically; therefore, in most cases, numerical techniques are used. The case of numerical dynamic programming was covered in Section 14.5.

Shooting methods constitute the simplest family of trajectory optimization methods. As a simple example, suppose that an action trajectory $\tilde{u} : [0, t_F] \rightarrow \mathbb{R}$ has been computed of the form

$$u(t) = w_1 + w_2 t, \tag{14.47}$$

in which w_1 and w_2 are some fixed parameters. Consider perturbing w_1 and w_2 by some small amount and applying the integration in (14.1). If f satisfies Lipschitz conditions, then a small perturbation should produce a small change in $\tilde{x}$. The resulting new trajectory can be evaluated by a cost functional to determine whether it is an improvement. It might, for example, have lower maximum curvature. Rather than picking a perturbation at random, the gradient of the cost functional with respect to the parameters can be computed. A small step in the parameter space along the negative gradient direction should reduce the cost. It is very likely, however, that perturbing w_1 and w_2 will move the final state $x(t_F)$. Usually, a termination condition, such as $x(t_F) = x_G$, must be enforced as a constraint in the optimization. This removes degrees of freedom from the optimization; therefore, more trajectory parameters are often needed.

Suppose more generally that a motion planning algorithm computes an action sequence based on the discrete-time model. Each action in the sequence remains constant for duration Δt. The time duration of each action can instead be defined as a parameter to be perturbed. Each action variable u_i over each interval could also be perturbed using by (14.47) with the initial condition that $w_1 = u_i$ and $w_2 = 0$. The dimension of the search has increased, but there are more degrees of freedom. In some formulations, the parameters may appear as implicit constraints; in this case, a BVP must be solved in each iteration. The minimum principle is often applied in this case [100]. More details on formulating and solving the trajectory optimization problem via shooting appear in [153].

Several difficulties are encountered when applying the shooting technique to trajectory optimization among obstacles. Each perturbation requires integration and collision-checking. For problems involving vehicles, the integrations can sometimes be avoided by exploiting symmetries [199]. For example, a path for the Dubins car can be perturbed by changing a steering angle over a short amount of time, and the rest of the trajectory can simply be transformed using a matrix of $SE(2)$. A critical problem is that following the negative gradient may suggest shortening the path in a way that causes collision. The problem can be alleviated by breaking the trajectory into segments, as in the plan-and-transform approach; however, this yields more optimizations. Another possible solution is to invent a penalty function for the obstacles; however, this is difficult due to local minima problems and the lack of representing the precise boundary of X_{obs}.

Another difficulty with shooting is that a small change in the action near the starting time may lead to great changes in the states at later times. One way to alleviate this problem is by *multiple shooting* (as opposed to *single shooting*, which has been described so far). In this case, the trajectory is initially broken into segments. These could correspond to the time boundaries imposed by a sequence of motion primitives. In this case, imagine perturbing each motion primitive separately. Extra constraints are needed in this case to indicate that all of the trajectory pieces must remain connected. The multiple shooting method can be generalized to a family of methods called *transcription* or *collocation* (see [100] for references). These methods again split the trajectory into segments, but each connection constraint relates more points along the trajectory than just the segment endpoints. One version of transcription uses implicit constraints, which require using another BVP solver, and another version uses parametric constraints, which dramatically increases the dimension of the search. The latter case is still useful in practice by employing fast, sparse-matrix computation methods.

One of the main difficulties with trajectory optimization methods is that they can become stuck in a local minimum in the space of trajectories. This means that their behavior depends strongly on the initial guess. It is generally impossible for them to find a trajectory that is not homotopic to the initial trajectory. They cannot recover from an initial guess in a bad homotopy class. If X_{obs} is complicated, then this issue becomes increasingly important. In many cases, variational techniques might not even find an optimal solution within a single homotopy class. Multiple local minima may exist if the closure of X_{free} contains positive curvature. If it does not, the space is called *nonpositively curved* (NPC) or CAT(0), which is a property that can be derived directly from the metric on X [141]. For these spaces, the locally optimal trajectory with respect to the metric is always the best within its homotopy class.

Further reading

The characterization and computation of reachable sets has been growing in interest [102, 104, 709, 710, 917, 955]. One motivation for studying reachability is *verification*, which ensures that a control system behaves as desired under all possible disturbances. This can actually be modeled as a game against nature, in which nature attempts to bring the system into an undesirable state (e.g., crashing an airplane). For recent progress on characterizing X_{ric}, see [357]. The triangularization argument for completeness appears in a similar context in [294]. The precise rate of convergence, expressed in terms of dispersion and Lipschitz conditions, for resolution-complete sampling-based motion planning methods under differential constraints is covered in [198]. For the computational complexity of control problems, see [116, 769]. For further reading on motion primitives in the context of planning, see [362, 364,

365, 395, 790, 797, 850]. For further reading on dynamical simulation and numerical integration, see [333, 443, 865].

Section 14.4.1 was based on [290, 292, 444]. For more works on kinodynamic planning, see [205, 239, 291, 358, 362, 614, 783, 999]. Section 14.4.2 was inspired by [74]. Section 14.4.3 was drawn from [614]. For more work on RRTs under differential constraints, see [140, 201, 226, 326, 362, 395, 512, 949]. For other works on nonholonomic planning, see the survey [599] and [68, 279, 336, 337, 356, 359, 485, 582, 636, 675]. Combinatorial approaches to nonholonomic planning have appeared in [13, 131, 349].

Section 14.5 was developed by adapting value iteration to motion planning problems. For general convergence theorems for value iteration with interpolation, see [170, 294, 402, 568, 570]. In [170], global constraints on the phase space are actually considered. The use of these techniques and the development of Dijkstra-like variants are covered in [610]. Related work exists in artificial intelligence [725] and control theory [946].

Decoupled approaches to planning, as covered in Section 14.6, are very common in robotics literature. For material related to the plan-and-transform method, see [335, 599, 861]. For more on decoupled trajectory planning and time scaling, see [355, 459, 460, 846, 878, 879, 882, 883], and see [106, 122, 123, 788, 881, 895, 880] for particular emphasis on time-optimal trajectories.

For more on gradient-based techniques in general, see [100] and references therein. Classical texts on the subject are [153, 667]. Gradient-based approaches to path deformation in the context of nonholonomic planning appear in [199, 345, 578].

The techniques presented in this chapter are useful in other fields beyond robotics. For aerospace applications of motion planning, see [88, 204, 439, 440, 789]. Motion planning problems and techniques have been gaining interest in computer graphics, particularly for generating animations of virtual humans (or digital actors); works in this area include [35, 88, 395, 502, 547, 557, 560, 594, 620, 652, 715, 805, 980]. In many of these works, *motion capture* is a popular way to generate a database of recorded motions that serves as a set of motion primitives in the planning approach.

Exercises

1. Characterize X_{ric} for the case of a point mass in $\mathcal{W} = \mathbb{R}^2$, with each coordinate modeled as a double integrator. Assume that $u_1 = 1$ and u_2 may take any value in $[-1, 1]$. Determine X_{ric} for:

   (a) A point obstacle at $(0, 0)$ in $\mathcal{W}$.

   (b) A segment from $(0, -1)$ to $(0, 1)$ in $\mathcal{W}$.

   Characterize the solutions in terms of the phase variables $q_1(0)$, $q_2(0)$, $\dot{q}_1(0)$, and $\dot{q}_2(0)$.

2. Extending the double integrator:

   (a) Develop a lattice for the triple integrator $q^{(3)} = u$ that extends naturally from the double-integrator lattice.

   (b) Describe how to develop a lattice for higher order integrators $q^{(n)}$ for $n > 3$.

3. Make a figure similar to Figure 14.6b, but for three stages of the Reeds-Shepp car.

4. Determine expressions for the upper and lower boundaries of the time-limited reachable sets shown in Figure 14.14. Express them as parabolas, with $\dot{q}$ as a function of q.

5. A reachability graph can be made by "rolling" a polyhedron in the plane. For example, suppose a solid, regular tetrahedron is placed on a planar surface. Assuming high friction, the tetrahedron can be flipped in one of four directions by pushing on the top. Construct the three-stage reachability graph for this problem.

6. Construct a four-stage reachability graph similar to the one shown in Figure 14.6b, but for the case of a differential drive robot modeled by (13.17). Use the three actions $(1, 0)$, $(0, 1)$, and $(1, 1)$. Draw the graph in the plane and indicate the configuration coordinates of each vertex.

7. Section 14.2.2 explained how resolution-complete algorithms exist for planning under differential constraints. Suppose that in addition to continuous state variables, there are discrete modes, as introduced in Section 7.3, to form a hybrid system. Explain how resolution-complete planning algorithms can be developed for this case. Extend the argument shown in Figure 14.7.

Implementations

8. Compare the performance and accuracy of Euler integration to fourth-order Runge-Kutta on trajectories generated for a single, double, and triple integrator. For accuracy, compare the results to solutions obtained analytically. Provide recommendations of which one to use under various conditions.

9. Improve Figure 14.13 by making a plot of the actual trajectories, which are parabolic in most cases.

10. In Figure 14.13, the state trajectory segments are longer as $|\dot{x}|$ increases. Develop a lattice that tries to keep all segments as close to the same length as possible by reducing Δt as $|\dot{x}|$ increases. Implement and experiment with different schemes and report on the results.

11. Develop an implementation for computing approximately time-optimal state trajectories for a point mass in a 2D polygonal world. The robot dynamics can be modeled as two independent double integrators. Search the double-integrator lattice in $X = \mathbb{R}^4$ to solve the problem. Animate the computed solutions.

12. Experiment with RDT methods applied to a spacecraft that is modeled as a 3D rigid body with thrusters. Develop software that computes collision-free trajectories for the robot. Carefully study the issues associated with choosing the metric on X.

13. Solve the problem of optimally bringing the Dubins car to a goal region in a polygonal world by using value iteration with interpolation.

14. Select and implement a planning algorithm that computes pushing trajectories for a differential drive robot that pushes a box in a polygonal environment. This was given as an example of a nonholonomic system in Section 13.1.3. To use the appropriate constraints on U, see [674].

15. Select and implement a planning algorithm that computes trajectories for parking a car while pulling a single trailer, using (13.19). Make an obstacle region in $\mathcal{W}$ that corresponds to a tight parking space and vary the amount of clearance. Also, experiment with driving the vehicle through an obstacle course.

16. Generate a 3D rendering of reachability graphs for the airplane model in (13.20). Assume that in each stage there are nine possible actions, based on combinations of flying to the right, left, or straight and decreasing, increasing, or maintaining altitude.

17. Implement the dynamic programming algorithm shown in Figure 14.27 for the two-link manipulator model given in Example 13.13.

18. Implement the bang-bang algorithm shown in Figure 14.28 for the two-link manipulator model given in Example 13.13.

19. For the Dubins car (or another system), experiment with generating a search graph based on Figure 14.7 by alternating between various step sizes. Plot in the plane, the vertices and state trajectories associated with the edges of the graph. Experiment with different schemes for generating a resolution-complete search graph in a rectangular region and compare the results.

20. Use value iteration with interpolation to compute the optimal cost-to-go for the Reeds-Shepp car. Plot level sets of the cost-to-go, which indicate the time-limited reachable sets. Compare the result to Figure 14.4.

15

System Theory and Analytical Techniques

This chapter is complementary to Chapter 14 in that it provides tools and concepts that can be used to develop better local planning methods (LPMs). Most of the material was developed in the field of control theory, which focuses mainly on characterizing the behavior of particular classes of systems, and controlling them in the absence of obstacles. The two-point boundary value problem (BVP), which was a frequent nuisance in Chapter 14, can be better understood and solved for many systems by using the ideas of this chapter. Keep in mind that throughout this chapter there are no obstacles. Although planning for this case was trivial in Part II, the presence of differential constraints brings many challenges.

The style in this chapter is to provide a brief survey of concepts and techniques, with the hope of inspiring further study in other textbooks and research literature. Modern control theory is a vast and fascinating subject, of which only the surface can be scratched in one chapter. Section 15.1 introduces stability and controllability concepts, both of which characterize possible arrivals in a goal state. Stability characterizes how the integral curves of a vector field behave around a goal point, and controllability indicates whether an action trajectory exists that arrives at a specified goal.

Section 15.2 revisits dynamic programming one last time. Here it becomes a partial differential equation expressed in terms of the optimal cost-to-go function. In some cases, it actually has a closed-form *solution*, as opposed to its main use in computer science, which is to obtain algorithm constraints. The powerful *Pontryagin's minimum principle*, which can be derived from dynamic programming, is also covered.

The remainder of the chapter is devoted to nonholonomic systems, which often arise from underactuated mechanical systems. Section 15.3 expresses the shortest paths between any pair of points for the Dubins car, the Reeds-Shepp car, and a differential drive, all of which were introduced in Section 13.1.2. The paths are a beautiful solution to the BVP and are particularly valuable as an LPM; for example, some have been used in the plan-and-transform method of Section 14.6.2. Section 15.4 addresses some basic properties of nonholonomic systems. The most important issues are determining whether nonholonomic constraints are actually integrable (which removes all $\dot{x}_i$ variables) and characterizing reachable sets that arise due to nonholonomic constraints. Section 15.5 attempts to do the same as Section 15.3, but for more challenging nonholonomic systems. In these cases, the BVP problem may not be solved optimally, and some methods may not even reach the goal point precisely. Nevertheless, when applicable, they can be used to build powerful LPMs in a sampling-based motion planning algorithm.

15.1 Basic system properties

This section provides a brief overview of two fundamental concepts in control theory: stability and controllability. Either can be considered as characterizing how a goal state

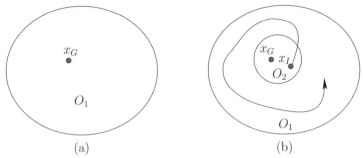

Figure 15.1: Lyapunov stability: (a) Choose any open set O_1 that contains x_G, and (b) there exists some open set O_2 from which trajectories will not be able to escape O_1. Note that convergence to x_G is not required.

is reached. Stability usually involves feedback and may only converge to the goal as time approaches infinity. Controllability assesses whether an action trajectory exists that leads exactly to a specified goal state. In both cases, there is no obstacle region in X.

15.1.1 Stability

The subject of stability addresses properties of a vector field with respect to a given point. Let X denote a smooth manifold on which the vector field is defined; X may be a C-space or a phase space. The given point is denoted as x_G and can be interpreted in motion planning applications as the goal state. Stability characterizes how x_G is approached from other states in X by integrating the vector field.

The given vector field f is considered as a velocity field, which is represented as

$$\dot{x} = f(x). \tag{15.1}$$

This looks like a state transition equation that is missing actions. If a system of the form $\dot{x} = f(x, u)$ is given, then u can be fixed by designing a feedback plan $\pi : X \to U$. This yields $\dot{x} = f(x, \pi(x))$, which is a vector field on X without any further dependency on actions. The dynamic programming approach in Section 14.5 computed such a solution. The process of designing a stable feedback plan is referred to in control literature as *feedback stabilization*.

Equilibrium points and Lyapunov stability

At the very least, it seems that the state should remain fixed at x_G, if it is reached. A point $x_G \in X$ is called an *equilibrium point* (or *fixed point*) of the vector field f if and only if $f(x_G) = 0$. This does not, however, characterize how trajectories behave in the vicinity of x_G. Let $x_I \in X$ denote some initial state, and let $x(t)$ refer to the state obtained at time t after integrating the vector field f from $x_I = x(0)$.

See Figure 15.1. An equilibrium point $x_G \in X$ is called *Lyapunov stable* if for any open neighborhood[1] O_1 of x_G there exists another open neighborhood O_2 of x_G such that $x_I \in O_2$ implies that $x(t) \in O_1$ for all $t > 0$. If $X = \mathbb{R}^n$, then some intuition can be obtained by using an equivalent definition that is expressed in terms of the Euclidean metric. An equilibrium point $x_G \in \mathbb{R}^n$ is called *Lyapunov stable* if, for any $t > 0$, there exists some $\delta > 0$ such that $\|x_I - x_G\| < \delta$ implies that $\|x(t) - x_G\| < \epsilon$. This means

---

[1] An *open neighborhood* of a point x means an open set that contains x.

that we can choose a ball around x_G with a radius as small as desired, and all future states will be trapped within this ball, as long as they start within a potentially smaller ball of radius δ. If a single δ can be chosen independently of every ϵ and x, then the equilibrium point is called *uniform* Lyapunov stable.

Asymptotic stability

Lyapunov stability is weak in that it does not even imply that $x(t)$ converges to x_G as t approaches infinity. The states are only required to hover around x_G. Convergence requires a stronger notion called *asymptotic stability*. A point x_G is an *asymptotically stable* equilibrium point of f if:

1.   It is a Lyapunov stable equilibrium point of f.
2.   There exists some open neighborhood O of x_G such that, for any $x_I \in O$, $x(t)$ converges[2] to x_G as t approaches infinity.

For $X = \mathbb{R}^n$, the second condition can be expressed as follows: There exists some $\delta > 0$ such that, for any $x_I \in X$ with $\|x_I - x_G\| < \delta$, the state $x(t)$ converges to x_G as t approaches infinity. It may seem strange that two requirements are needed for asymptotic stability. The first one bounds the amount of wiggling room for the integral curve, which is not captured by the second condition.

Asymptotic stability appears to be a reasonable requirement, but it does not imply anything about how long it takes to converge. If x_G is asymptotically stable and there exist some $m > 0$ and $\alpha > 0$ such that

$$\|x(t) - x_G\| \leq me^{-\alpha t}\|x_I - x_G\|, \tag{15.2}$$

then x_G is also called *exponentially stable*. This provides a convenient way to express the rate of convergence.

For use in motion planning applications, even exponential convergence may not seem strong enough. This issue was discussed in Section 8.4.1. For example, in practice, one usually prefers to reach x_G in finite time, as opposed to only being "reached" in the limit. There are two common fixes. One is to allow asymptotic stability and declare the goal to be reached if the state arrives in some small, predetermined ball around x_G. In this case, the enlarged goal will always be reached in finite time if x_G is asymptotically stable. The other fix is to require a stronger form of stability in which x_G must be exactly reached in finite time. To enable this, however, discontinuous vector fields such as the inward flow of Figure 8.5b must be used. Most control theorists are appalled by this because infinite energy is usually required to execute such trajectories. On the other hand, discontinuous vector fields may be a suitable representation in some applications, as mentioned in Chapter 8. Note that without feedback this issue does not seem as important. The state trajectories designed in much of Chapter 14 were expected to reach the goal in finite time. Without feedback there was no surrounding vector field that was expected to maintain continuity or smoothness properties. Section 15.1.3 introduces controllability, which is based on actually arriving at the goal in finite time, but it is also based on the existence of one trajectory for a given system $\dot{x} = f(x, u)$, as opposed to a family of trajectories for a given vector field $x = f(x)$.

---

[2] This convergence can be evaluated using the metric ρ on X.

Time-varying vector fields

The stability notions expressed here are usually introduced in the time-varying setting $\dot{x} = f(x, t)$. Since the vast majority of planning problems in this book are time-invariant, the presentation was confined to time-invariant vector fields. There is, however, one fascinating peculiarity in the topic of finding a feedback plan that stabilizes a system. *Brockett's condition* implies that for some time-invariant systems for which continuous, time-varying feedback plans exist, there does not exist a continuous time-invariant feedback plan [145, 158, 996]. This includes the class of driftless control systems, such as the simple car and the unicycle. This implies that to maintain continuity of the vector field, a time dependency must be introduced to allow the vector field to vary as x_G is approached! If continuity of the vector field is not important, then this concern vanishes.

Domains of attraction

The stability definitions given so far are often called *local* because they are expressed in terms of a neighborhood of x_G. *Global* versions can also be defined by extending the neighborhood to all of X. An equilibrium point is *globally asymptotically stable* if it is Lyapunov stable, and the integral curve from any $x_0 \in X$ converges to x_G as time approaches infinity. It may be the case that only points in some proper subset of X converge to x_G. The set of all points in X that converge to x_G is often called the *domain of attraction* of x_G. The funnels of Section 8.5.1 are based on domains of attraction. Also related is the backward reachable set from Section 14.2.1. In that setting, action trajectories were considered that lead to x_G in finite time. For the domain of attraction only asymptotic convergence to x_G is assumed, and the vector field is given (there are no actions to choose).

Limit cycles

For some vector fields, states may be attracted into a *limit cycle*. Rather than stabilizing to a point, the state trajectories converge to a loop path in X. For example, they may converge to following a circle. This occurs in a wide variety of mechanical systems in which oscillations are possible. Some of the basic issues, along with several interesting examples for $X = \mathbb{R}^2$, are covered in [44].

15.1.2 Lyapunov functions

Suppose a velocity field $\dot{x} = f(x)$ is given along with an equilibrium point, x_G. Can the various forms of stability be easily determined? One of the most powerful methods to prove stability is to construct a Lyapunov function. This will be introduced shortly, but first some alternatives are briefly mentioned.

If $f(x)$ is linear, which means that $f(x) = Ax$ for some constant $n \times n$ matrix A and $X = \mathbb{R}^n$, then stability questions with respect to the origin, $x_G = 0$, are answered by finding the eigenvalues of A [194]. The state $x = 0$ is asymptotically stable if and only if all eigenvalues of A have negative real parts. Consider the scalar case, $\dot{x} = ax$, for which $X = \mathbb{R}$ and a is a constant. The solution to this differential equation is $x(t) = x(0) \, e^{at}$, which converges to 0 only if $a < 0$. This can be easily extended to the case in which $X = \mathbb{R}^n$ and A is an $n \times n$ diagonal matrix for which each diagonal entry (or eigenvalue) is negative. For a general matrix, real or complex eigenvalues determine the stability (complex eigenvalues cause oscillations). Conditions also exist for Lyapunov stability. Every equilibrium state of $\dot{x} = Ax$ is Lyapunov stable if the eigenvalues of A all have nonpositive real parts, and the eigenvalues with zero real parts are distinct roots of the characteristic polynomial of A.

If $f(x)$ is nonlinear, then stability can sometimes be inferred by linearizing $f(x)$ about x_G and performing linear stability analysis. In many cases, however, this procedure is inconclusive (see Chapter 6 of [158]). Proving the stability of a vector field is a challenging task for most nonlinear systems. One approach is based on LaSalle's invariance principle [39, 158, 588] and is particularly useful for showing convergence to any of multiple goal states (see Section 5.4 of [848]). The other major approach is to construct a *Lyapunov function*, which is used as an intermediate tool to indirectly establish stability. If this method fails, then it still may be possible to show stability using other means. Therefore, it is a sufficient condition for stability, but not a necessary one.

Determining stability

Suppose a velocity field $\dot{x} = f(x)$ is given along with an equilibrium point x_G. Let ϕ denote a *candidate Lyapunov function*, which will be used as an auxiliary device for establishing the stability of f. An appropriate ϕ must be determined for the particular vector field f. This may be quite challenging in itself, and the details are not covered here. In a sense, the procedure can be characterized as "guess and verify," which is the way that many solution techniques for differential equations are described. If ϕ succeeds in establishing stability, then it is promoted to being called a *Lyapunov function* for f.

It will be important to characterize how ϕ varies in the direction of flow induced by f. This is measured by the *Lie derivative*,

$$\dot{\phi}(x) = \sum_{i=1}^{n} \frac{\partial \phi}{\partial x_i} f_i(x). \tag{15.3}$$

This results in a new function $\dot{\phi}(x)$, which indicates for each x the change in ϕ along the direction of $\dot{x} = f(x)$.

Several concepts are needed to determine stability. Let a function $h : [0, \infty) \to [0, \infty)$ be called a *hill* if it is continuous, strictly increasing, and $h(0) = 0$. This can be considered as a one-dimensional navigation function, which has a single local minimum at the goal, 0. A function $\phi : X \to [0, \infty)$ is called *locally positive definite* if there exists some open set $O \subseteq X$ and a hill function h such that $\phi(x_G) = 0$ and $\phi(x) \geq h(\|x\|)$ for all $x \in O$. If O can be chosen as $O = X$, and if X is bounded, then ϕ is called *globally positive definite* or just *positive definite*. In some spaces this may not be possible due to the topology of X; such issues arose when constructing navigation functions in Section 8.4.4. If X is unbounded, then h must additionally approach infinity as $\|x\|$ approaches infinity to yield a positive definite ϕ [848]. For $X = \mathbb{R}^n$, a quadratic form $x^T M x$, for which M is a positive definite matrix, is a globally positive definite function. This motivates the use of quadratic forms in Lyapunov stability analysis.

The Lyapunov theorems can now be stated [158, 848]. Suppose that ϕ is locally positive definite at x_G. If there exists an open set O for which $x_G \in O$, and $\dot{\phi}(x) \leq 0$ on all $x \in O$, then f is Lyapunov stable. If $-\dot{\phi}(x)$ is also locally positive definite on O, then f is asymptotically stable. If ϕ and $-\dot{\phi}$ are both globally positive definite, then f is globally asymptotically stable.

Example 15.1 (Establishing Stability via Lyapunov Functions) Let $X = \mathbb{R}$. Let $\dot{x} = f(x) = -x^5$, and we will attempt to show that $x = 0$ is stable. Let the candidate Lyapunov function be $\phi(x) = \frac{1}{2}x^2$. The Lie derivative (15.3) produces $\dot{\phi}(x) = -x^6$. It is clear that

ϕ and $-\dot{\phi}$ are both globally positive definite; hence, 0 is a global, asymptotically stable equilibrium point of f. ∎

Lyapunov functions in planning

Lyapunov functions are closely related to navigation functions and optimal cost-to-go functions in planning. In the optimal discrete planning problem of Sections 2.3 and 8.2, the cost-to-go values can be considered as a discrete Lyapunov function. By applying the computed actions, a kind of discrete vector field can be imagined over the search graph. Each applied optimal action yields a reduction in the optimal cost-to-go value, until 0 is reached at the goal. Both the optimal cost-to-go and Lyapunov functions ensure that the trajectories do not become trapped in a local minimum. Lyapunov functions are more general than cost-to-go functions because they do not require optimality. They are more like navigation functions, as considered in Chapter 8. The requirements for a discrete navigation function, as given in Section 8.2.2, are very similar to the positive definite condition given in this section. Imagine that the navigation function shown in Figure 8.3 is a discrete approximation to a Lyapunov function over $\mathbb{R}^2$. In general, a Lyapunov function indicates some form of distance to x_G, although it may not be optimal. Nevertheless, it is based on making monotonic progress toward x_G. Therefore, it may serve as a distance function in many sampling-based planning algorithms of Chapter 14. Since it respects the differential constraints imposed by the system, it may provide a better indication of how to make progress during planning in comparison to a Euclidean metric that ignores these considerations. Lyapunov functions should be particularly valuable in the RDT method of Section 14.4.3, which relies heavily on the distance function over X.

15.1.3 Controllability

Now suppose that a system $\dot{x} = f(x, u)$ is given on a smooth manifold X as defined throughout Chapter 13 and used extensively in Chapter 14. The system can be considered as a parameterized family of vector fields in which u is the parameter. For stability, it was assumed that this parameter was fixed by a feedback plan to obtain some $\dot{x} = f(x)$. This section addresses *controllability*, which indicates whether one state is reachable from another via the existence of an action trajectory $\tilde{u}$. It may be helpful to review the reachable set definitions from Section 14.2.1.

Classical controllability

Let $\mathcal{U}$ denote the set of permissible action trajectories for the system, as considered in Section 14.1.1. By default, this is taken as any $\tilde{u}$ for which (14.1) can be integrated. A system $\dot{x} = f(x, u)$ is called *controllable* if for all $x_I, x_G \in X$, there exists a time $t > 0$ and action trajectory $\tilde{u} \in \mathcal{U}$ such that upon integration from $x(0) = x_I$, the result is $x(t) = x_G$. Controllability can alternatively be expressed in terms of the reachable sets of Section 14.2.1. The system is controllable if $x_G \in R(x_I, \mathcal{U})$ for all $x_I, x_G \in X$.

A system is therefore controllable if a solution exists to any motion planning problem in the absence of obstacles. In other words, a solution always exists to the two-point boundary value problem (BVP).

Example 15.2 (Classical Controllability)   All of the vehicle models in Section 13.1.2 are controllable. For example, in an infinitely large plane, the Dubins car can be driven between any two configurations. Note, however, that if the plane is restricted by obstacles, then this is not necessarily possible with the Dubins car. As an example of a system that is not controllable, let $X = \mathbb{R}$, $\dot{x} = u$, and $U = [0, 1]$. In this case, the state cannot decrease. For example, there exists no action trajectory that brings the state from $x_I = 1$ to $x_G = 0$. ∎

Many methods for determining controllability of a system are covered in standard textbooks on control theory. If the system is linear, as given by (13.37) with dimensions m and n, then it is controllable if and only if the $n \times nm$ *controllability matrix*

$$M = \begin{bmatrix} B \vdots AB \vdots A^2 B \vdots \cdots \vdots A^{n-1} B \end{bmatrix} \tag{15.4}$$

has full rank [194]. This is called the *Kalman rank condition* [504]. If the system is nonlinear, then the controllability matrix can be evaluated on a linearized version of the system. Having full rank is sufficient to establish controllability from a single point (see Proposition 11.2 in [848]). If the rank is not full, however, the system may still be controllable. A fascinating property of some nonlinear systems is that they may be able to produce motions in directions that do not seem to be allowed at first. For example, the simple car given in Section 13.1.2 cannot slide sideways; however, it is possible to wiggle the car sideways by performing parallel-parking maneuvers. A method for determining the controllability of such systems is covered in Section 15.4.

For fully actuated systems of the form $\ddot{q} = h(q, \dot{q}, u)$, controllability can be determined by converting the system into double-integrator form, as considered in Section 14.4.1. Let the system be expressed as $\ddot{q} = u'$, in which $u' \in U'(q, \dot{q})$. If $U'(q, \dot{q})$ contains an open neighborhood of the origin of $\mathbb{R}^n$, and the same neighborhood can be used for any $x \in X$, then the system is controllable. If a nonlinear system is underactuated, as in the simple car, then controllability issues become considerably more complicated. The next concept is suitable for such systems.

STLC: Controllability that handles obstacles

The controllability concept discussed so far has no concern for how far the trajectory travels in X before x_G is reached. This issue becomes particularly important for underactuated systems and planning among obstacles. These concerns motivate a natural question: Is there a form of controllability that is naturally suited for obstacles? It should declare that if a state is reachable from another in the absence of differential constraints, then it is also reachable with the given system $\dot{x} = f(x, u)$. This can be expressed using time-limited reachable sets. Let $R(x, \mathcal{U}, t)$ denote the set of all states reachable in time less than or equal to t, starting from x. A system $\dot{x} = f(x, u)$ is called *small-time locally controllable* (STLC) from x_I if there exists some $t > 0$ such that $x_I \in \text{int}(R(x_I, \mathcal{U}, t'))$ for all $t' \in (0, t]$ (here, int denotes the interior of a set, as defined in Section 4.1.1). If the system $\dot{x} = f(x, u)$ is STLC from every $x_I \in X$, then the whole system is said to be STLC.

Consider using this definition to answer the question above. Since $\text{int}(R(x_I, \mathcal{U}, t'))$ is an open set, there must exist some small $\epsilon > 0$ for which the open ball $B(x_I, \epsilon)$ is a strict subset of $\text{int}(R(x_I, \mathcal{U}, t'))$. See Figure 15.2. Any point on the boundary of $B(x_I, \epsilon)$ can be reached, which means that a step of size ϵ can be taken in any direction, even though differential constraints exist. With obstacles, however, we have to be careful that the trajectory from x_I to the surface of $B(x_I, \epsilon)$ does not wander too far away.

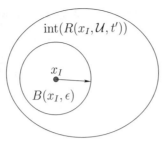

Figure 15.2: If the system is STLC, then motions can be made in any direction, in an arbitrarily small amount of time.

Suppose that there is an obstacle region X_{obs}, and a violation-free state trajectory $\tilde{x}$ is given that terminates in x_G at time t_F and does not necessarily satisfy a given system. If the system is STLC, then it is always possible to find another trajectory, based on $\tilde{x}$, that satisfies the differential constraints. Apply the plan-and-transform method of Section 14.6.2. Suppose that intervals for potential replacement are chosen using binary recursive subdivision. Also suppose that an LPM exists that computes that shortest trajectory between any pair of states; this trajectory ignores obstacles but respects the differential constraints. Initially, $[0, t_F]$ is replaced by a trajectory from the LPM, and if it is not violation-free, then $[0, t_F]$ is subdivided into $[0, t_F/2]$ and $[t_F/2, t_F]$, and replacement is attempted on the smaller intervals. This idea can be applied recursively until eventually the segments are small enough that they must be violation-free.

This final claim is implied by the STLC property. No matter how small the intervals become, there must exist a replacement trajectory. If an interval is large, then there may be sufficient time to wander far from the original trajectory. However, as the time interval decreases, there is not enough time to deviate far from the original trajectory. (This discussion assumes mild conditions on f, such as being Lipschitz.) Suppose that the trajectory is protected by a collision-free tube of radius ϵ. Thus, all points along the trajectory are at least ϵ from the boundary of X_{free}. The time intervals can be chosen small enough to ensure that the trajectory deviations are less than ϵ from the original trajectory. Therefore, STLC is a very important property for a system to possess for planning in the presence of obstacles. Section 15.4 covers some mathematical tools for determining whether a nonlinear system is STLC.

A concept closely related to controllability is *accessibility*, which is only concerned with the dimension of the reachable set. Let n be the dimension of X. If there exists some $t > 0$ for which the dimension of $R(x_I, \mathcal{U}, t)$ is n, then the system is called *accessible* from x_I. Alternatively, this may be expressed as requiring that $\text{int}(R(x_I, \mathcal{U}, t)) \neq \emptyset$.

Example 15.3 (Accessibility) Recall the system from Section 13.1.3 in which the state is trapped on a circle. In this case $X = \mathbb{R}^2$, and the state transition equation was specified by $\dot{x} = yu$ and $\dot{y} = -xu$. This system is not accessible because the reachable sets have dimension one. ∎

A small-time version of accessibility can also be defined by requiring that there exists some t such that $\text{int}(R(x_I, \mathcal{U}, t')) \neq \emptyset$ for all $t' \in (0, t]$. Accessibility is particularly important for systems with drift.

15.2 Continuous-time dynamic programming

Dynamic programming has been a recurring theme throughout most of this book. So far, it has always taken the form of computing optimal cost-to-go (or cost-to-come) functions over some sequence of stages. Both value iteration and Dijkstra-like algorithms have emerged. In computer science, dynamic programming is a fundamental insight in the development of algorithms that compute optimal solutions to problems. In its original form, however, dynamic programming was developed to solve the optimal control problem [86]. In this setting, a discrete set of stages is replaced by a continuum of stages, known as *time*. The dynamic programming recurrence is instead a partial differential equation, called the Hamilton-Jacobi-Bellman (HJB) equation. The HJB equation can be solved using numerical algorithms; however, in some cases, it can be *solved analytically*.[3] Section 15.2.2 briefly describes an analytical solution in the case of linear systems. Section 15.2.3 covers Pontryagin's minimum principle, which can be derived from the dynamic programming principle, and generalizes the optimization performed in Hamiltonian mechanics (recall Section 13.4.4).

15.2.1 Hamilton-Jacobi-Bellman equation

The HJB equation is a central result in optimal control theory. Many other principles and design techniques follow from the HJB equation, which itself is just a statement of the dynamic programming principle in continuous time. A proper derivation of all forms of the HJB equation would be beyond the scope of this book. Instead, a time-invariant formulation that is most relevant to planning will be given here. Also, an informal derivation will follow, based in part on [97].

15.2.1.1 The discrete case

Before entering the continuous realm, the concepts will first be described for discrete planning, which is often easier to understand. Recall from Section 2.3 that if X, U, and the stages are discrete, then optimal planning can be performed by using value iteration or Dijkstra's algorithm on the search graph. The stationary, optimal cost-to-go function G^* can be used as a navigation function that encodes the optimal feedback plan. This was suggested in Section 8.2.2, and an example was shown in Figure 8.3.

Suppose that G^* has been computed under Formulation 8.1 (or Formulation 2.3). Let the state transition equation be denoted as

$$x' = f_d(x, u). \qquad (15.5)$$

The dynamic programming recurrence for G^* is

$$G^*(x) = \min_{u \in U(x)} \left\{ l(x, u) + G^*(x') \right\}, \qquad (15.6)$$

which may already be considered as a discrete form of the Hamilton-Jacobi-Bellman equation. To gain some insights into the coming concepts, however, some further manipulations will be performed.

Let u^* denote the optimal action that is applied in the min of (15.6). Imagine that u^* is hypothesized as the optimal action but needs to be tested in (15.6) to make sure. If it is

---

[3] It is often surprising to computer scientists that dynamic programming in this case does not yield an algorithm. It instead yields a closed-form solution to the problem.

truly optimal, then

$$G^*(x) = l(x, u^*) + G^*(f_d(x, u^*)).$$ (15.7)

This can already be considered as a discrete form of the Pontryagin minimum principle, which will appear in Section 15.2.3. By rearranging terms, a nice interpretation is obtained:

$$G^*(f_d(x, u^*)) - G^*(x) = -l(x, u^*).$$ (15.8)

In a single stage, the optimal cost-to-go drops by $l(x, u^*)$ when G^* is used as a navigation function (multiply (15.8) by -1). The optimal single-stage cost is revealed precisely when taking one step toward the goal along the optimal path. This incremental change in the cost-to-go function while moving in the best direction forms the basis of both the HJB equation and the minimum principle.

15.2.1.2 The continuous case

Now consider adapting to the continuous case. Suppose X and U are both continuous, but discrete stages remain, and verify that (15.5) to (15.8) still hold true. Their present form can be used for any system that is approximated by discrete stages. Suppose that the discrete-time model of Section 14.2.2 is used to approximate a system $\dot{x} = f(x, u)$ on a state space X that is a smooth manifold. In that model, U was discretized to U_d, but here it will be left in its original form. Let Δt represent the time discretization.

The HJB equation will be obtained by approximating (15.6) with the discrete-time model and letting Δt approach zero. The arguments here are very informal; see [97, 573, 913] for more details. Using discrete-time approximation, the dynamic programming recurrence is

$$G^*(x) = \min_{u \in U(x)} \left\{ l_d(x, u) + G^*(x') \right\},$$ (15.9)

in which l_d is a discrete-time approximation to the cost that accumulates over stage k and is given as

$$l_d(x, u) \approx l(x, u)\Delta t.$$ (15.10)

It is assumed that as Δt approaches zero, the total discretized cost converges to the integrated cost of the continuous-time formulation.

Using the linear part of a Taylor series expansion about x, the term $G^*(x')$ can be approximated as

$$G^*(x') \approx G^*(x) + \sum_{i=1}^{n} \frac{\partial G^*}{\partial x_i} f_i(x, u)\Delta t.$$ (15.11)

This approximates $G^*(x')$ by its tangent plane at x. Substitution of (15.11) and (15.10) into (15.9) yields

$$G^*(x) \approx \min_{u \in U(x)} \left\{ l(x, u)\,\Delta t + G^*(x) + \sum_{i=1}^{n} \frac{\partial G^*}{\partial x_i} f_i(x, u)\,\Delta t \right\}.$$ (15.12)

Subtracting $G^*(x)$ from both sides of (15.12) yields

$$\min_{u \in U(x)} \left\{ l(x, u)\,\Delta t + \sum_{i=1}^{n} \frac{\partial G^*}{\partial x_i} f_i(x, u)\,\Delta t \right\} \approx 0.$$ (15.13)

Taking the limit as Δt approaches zero and then dividing by Δt yields the *HJB equation*:

$$\min_{u \in U(x)} \left\{ l(x, u) + \sum_{i=1}^{n} \frac{\partial G^*}{\partial x_i} f_i(x, u) \right\} = 0. \tag{15.14}$$

Compare the HJB equation to (15.6) for the discrete-time case. Both indicate how the cost changes when moving in the best direction. Substitution of u^* for the optimal action into (15.14) yields

$$\sum_{i=1}^{n} \frac{\partial G^*}{\partial x_i} f_i(x, u^*) = -l(x, u^*). \tag{15.15}$$

This is just the continuous-time version of (15.8). In the current setting, the left side indicates the derivative of the cost-to-go function along the direction obtained by applying the optimal action from x.

The HJB equation, together with a boundary condition that specifies the final-stage cost, sufficiently characterizes the optimal solution to the planning problem. Since it is expressed over the whole state space, solutions to the HJB equation yield optimal feedback plans. Unfortunately, the HJB equation cannot be solved analytically in most settings. Therefore, numerical techniques, such as the value iteration method of Section 14.5, must be employed. There is, however, an important class of problems that can be directly solved using the HJB equation; see Section 15.2.2.

15.2.1.3 Variants of the HJB equation

Several versions of the HJB equation exist. The one presented in (15.14) is suitable for planning problems such as those expressed in Chapter 14. If the cost-to-go functions are time-dependent, then the HJB equation is

$$\min_{u \in U(x)} \left\{ l(x, u, t) + \frac{\partial G^*}{\partial t} + \sum_{i=1}^{n} \frac{\partial G^*}{\partial x_i} f_i(x, u, t) \right\} = 0, \tag{15.16}$$

and G^* is a function of both x and t. This can be derived again using a Taylor expansion, but with x and t treated as the variables. Most textbooks on optimal control theory present the HJB equation in this form or in a slightly different form by pulling $\partial G^*/\partial t$ outside of the min and moving it to the right of the equation:

$$\min_{u \in U(x)} \left\{ l(x, u, t) + \sum_{i=1}^{n} \frac{\partial G^*}{\partial x_i} f_i(x, u, t) \right\} = -\frac{\partial G^*}{\partial t}. \tag{15.17}$$

In differential game theory, the HJB equation generalizes to the *Hamilton-Jacobi-Isaacs* (HJI) equations [60, 480]. Suppose that the system is given as (13.203) and a zero-sum game is defined using a cost term of the form $l(x, u, v, t)$. The HJI equations characterize saddle equilibria and are given as

$$\min_{u \in U(x)} \max_{v \in V(x)} \left\{ l(x, u, v, t) + \frac{\partial G^*}{\partial t} + \sum_{i=1}^{n} \frac{\partial G^*}{\partial x_i} f_i(x, u, v, t) \right\} = 0 \tag{15.18}$$

and

$$\max_{v \in V(x)} \min_{u \in U(x)} \left\{ l(x, u, v, t) + \frac{\partial G^*}{\partial t} + \sum_{i=1}^{n} \frac{\partial G^*}{\partial x_i} f_i(x, u, v, t) \right\} = 0. \tag{15.19}$$

There are clear similarities between these equations and (15.16). Also, the swapping of the min and max operators resembles the definition of saddle points in Section 9.3.

15.2.2 Linear-quadratic problems

This section briefly describes a problem for which the HJB equation can be directly solved to yield a closed-form expression, as opposed to an algorithm that computes numerical approximations. Suppose that a linear system is given by (13.37), which requires specifying the matrices A and B. The task is to design a feedback plan that asymptotically stabilizes the system from any initial state. This is an infinite-horizon problem, and no termination action is applied.

An optimal solution is requested with respect to a cost functional based on matrix quadratic forms. Let Q be a nonnegative definite[4] $n \times n$ matrix, and let R be a positive definite $n \times n$ matrix. The *quadratic cost functional* is defined as

$$L(\tilde{x}, \tilde{u}) = \frac{1}{2} \int_0^\infty \left(x(t)^T Q x(t) + u(t)^T R u(t) \right) dt. \tag{15.20}$$

To guarantee that a solution exists that yields finite cost, several assumptions must be made on the matrices. The pair (A, B) must be *stabilizable*, and (A, Q) must be *detectable*; see [28] for specific conditions and a full derivation of the solution presented here.

Although it is not done here, the HJB equation can be used to derive the *algebraic Riccati equation*,

$$SA + A^T S - S B R^{-1} B^T S + Q = 0, \tag{15.21}$$

in which all matrices except S were already given. Methods exist that solve for S, which is a unique solution in the space of nonnegative definite $n \times n$ matrices.

The linear vector field

$$\dot{x} = \left(A - B R^{-1} B^T S \right) x \tag{15.22}$$

is asymptotically stable (the real parts of all eigenvalues of the matrix are negative). This vector field is obtained if u is selected using a feedback plan π defined as

$$\pi(x) = -R^{-1} B^T S x. \tag{15.23}$$

The feedback plan π is in fact optimal, and the optimal cost-to-go is simply

$$G^*(x) = \tfrac{1}{2} x^T S x. \tag{15.24}$$

Thus, for linear systems with quadratic cost, an elegant solution exists without resorting to numerical approximations. Unfortunately, the solution techniques do not generalize to nonlinear systems or linear systems among obstacles. Hence, the planning methods of Chapter 14 are justified.

However, many variations and extensions of the solutions given here do exist, but only for other problems that are expressed as linear systems with quadratic cost. In every case, some variant of Riccati equations is obtained by application of the HJB equation. Solutions to time-varying systems are derived in [28]. If there is Gaussian uncertainty in predictability, then the linear-quadratic Gaussian (LQG) problem is obtained [567].

---

[4] Nonnegative definite means $x^T Q x \geq 0$ for all $x \in \mathbb{R}$, and positive definite means $x^T R x > 0$ for all $x \in \mathbb{R}^n$.

Linear-quadratic problems and solutions even exist for differential games of the form (13.204) [60].

15.2.3 Pontryagin's minimum principle

Pontryagin's minimum principle[5] is closely related to the HJB equation and provides conditions that an optimal trajectory must satisfy. Keep in mind, however, that the minimum principle provides *necessary* conditions, but not *sufficient conditions*, for optimality. In contrast, the HJB equation offered sufficient conditions. Using the minimum principle alone, one is often not able to conclude that a trajectory is optimal. In some cases, however, it is quite useful for finding candidate optimal trajectories. Any trajectory that fails to satisfy the minimum principle cannot be optimal.

To understand the minimum principle, we first return to the case of discrete planning. As mentioned previously, the minimum principle is essentially given by (15.7). This can be considered as a specialization of the HJB equation to the special case of applying the optimal action u^*. This causes the min to disappear, but along with it the global properties of the HJB equation also vanish. The minimum principle expresses conditions along the optimal trajectory, as opposed to the cost-to-go function over the whole state space. Therefore, it can at best assure local optimality in the space of possible trajectories.

The minimum principle for the continuous case is essentially given by (15.15), which is the continuous-time counterpart to (15.7). However, it is usually expressed in terms of adjoint variables and a Hamiltonian function, in the spirit of Hamiltonian mechanics from Section 13.4.4.

Let λ denote an n-dimensional vector of *adjoint variables*, which are defined as

$$\lambda_i = \frac{\partial G^*}{\partial x_i}. \tag{15.25}$$

The *Hamiltonian function* is defined as

$$H(x, u, \lambda) = l(x, u) + \sum_{i=1}^{n} \lambda_i f_i(x, u), \tag{15.26}$$

which is exactly the expression inside of the min of the HJB equation (15.14) after using the adjoint variable definition from (15.25). This can be compared to the Hamiltonian given by (13.192) in Section 13.4.4 (p from that context becomes λ here). The two are not exactly the same, but they both are motivated by the same basic principles.

Under the execution of the optimal action trajectory $\tilde{u}^*$, the HJB equation implies that

$$H(x(t), u(t)^*, \lambda(t)) = 0 \tag{15.27}$$

for all $t \geq 0$. This is just an alternative way to express (15.15). The fact that H remains constant appears very much like a conservation law, which was the basis of Hamiltonian mechanics in Section 13.4.4. The use of the Hamiltonian in the minimum principle is more general.

---

[5] This is often called Pontryagin's maximum principle, because Pontryagin originally defined it as a maximization [804]. The Hamiltonian used in most control literature is negated with respect to Pontryagin's Hamiltonian; therefore, it becomes minimized. Both names are in common use.

Using the HJB equation (15.14), the optimal action is given by

$$u^*(t) = \operatorname*{argmin}_{u \in U(x)} \{H(x(t), u(t), \lambda(t))\}. \tag{15.28}$$

In other words, the Hamiltonian is minimized precisely at $u(t) = u^*(t)$.

The missing piece of information so far is how λ evolves over time. It turns out that a system of the form

$$\dot\lambda = g(x, \lambda, u^*) \tag{15.29}$$

can be derived by differentiating the Hamiltonian (or, equivalently, the HJB equation) with respect to x. This yields two coupled systems, $\dot x = f(x, u^*)$ and (15.29). These can in fact be interpreted as a single system in a $2n$-dimensional phase space, in which each phase vector is (x, λ). This is analogous to the phase interpretation in Section 13.4.4 for Hamiltonian mechanics, which results in (13.198).

Remember that λ is defined in (15.25) just to keep track of the change in G^*. It would be helpful to have an explicit form for (15.29). Suppose that u^* is selected by a feedback plan to yield $u^* = \pi^*(x)$. In this case, the Hamiltonian can be interpreted as a function of only x and λ. Under this assumption, differentiating the Hamiltonian (15.26) with respect to x_i yields

$$\frac{\partial l(x, \pi^*(x))}{\partial x_i} + \sum_{j=1}^{n} \frac{\partial \lambda_j}{\partial x_i} f_j(x, \pi^*(x)) + \sum_{j=1}^{n} \lambda_j \frac{\partial f_i(x, \pi^*(x))}{\partial x_j}. \tag{15.30}$$

This validity of this differentiation requires a technical lemma that asserts that the derivatives of $\pi(x)$ can be disregarded (see Lemma 3.3.1 of [97]). Also, it will be assumed that U is convex in the arguments that follow, even though there exist proofs of the minimum principle that do not require this.

The second term in (15.30) is actually $\dot\lambda_i$, although it is hard to see at first. The total differential of λ_i with respect to the state is

$$d\lambda_i = \sum_{j=1}^{n} \frac{\partial \lambda_i}{\partial x_j} dx_i. \tag{15.31}$$

Dividing both sides by dt yields

$$\frac{d\lambda_i}{dt} = \sum_{j=1}^{n} \frac{\partial \lambda_i}{\partial x_j} \frac{dx_i}{dt} = \sum_{j=1}^{n} \frac{\partial \lambda_i}{\partial x_j} \dot x_i. \tag{15.32}$$

Each $\dot x_i$ is given by the state transition equation: $\dot x_i = f_i(x, \pi^*(x))$. Therefore,

$$\dot\lambda = \frac{d\lambda_i}{dt} = \frac{d}{dt} \frac{\partial G^*}{\partial x_i} = \sum_{j=1}^{n} \frac{\partial \lambda_i}{\partial x_j} f_j(x, \pi^*(x)). \tag{15.33}$$

Substituting (15.33) into (15.30) and setting the equation to zero (because the Hamiltonian is zero along the optimal trajectory) yields

$$\frac{\partial l(x, \pi^*(x))}{\partial x_i} + \dot\lambda_i + \sum_{j=1}^{n} \lambda_j \frac{\partial f_i(x, \pi^*(x))}{\partial x_j} = 0. \tag{15.34}$$

Solving for $\dot{\lambda}_i$ yields

$$\dot{\lambda}_i = -\frac{\partial l(x, \pi^*(x))}{\partial x_i} - \sum_{j=1}^{n} \lambda_j \frac{\partial f_i(x, \pi^*(x))}{\partial x_j}. \tag{15.35}$$

Conveniently, this is the same as

$$\dot{\lambda}_i = -\frac{\partial H}{\partial x_i}, \tag{15.36}$$

which yields the *adjoint transition equation*, as desired.

The transition equations given by $\dot{x} = f(x, u)$ and (15.36) specify the evolution of the system given by the minimum principle. These are analogous to Hamilton's equations (13.198), which were given in Section 13.4.4. The generalized momentum in that context becomes the adjoint variables here.

When applying the minimum principle, it is usually required to use the fact that the optimal action at all times must satisfy (15.28). Often, this is equivalently expressed as

$$H(x(t), u^*(t), \lambda(t)) \le H(x(t), u(t), \lambda(t)), \tag{15.37}$$

which indicates that the Hamiltonian increases or remains the same whenever deviation from the optimal action occurs (the Hamiltonian cannot decrease).

Example 15.4 (Optimal Planning for the Double Integrator)   Recall the double integrator system from Example 13.3. Let $\ddot{q} = u$, $\mathcal{C} = \mathbb{R}$, and $U = [-1, 1] \cup \{u_T\}$. Imagine a particle that moves in $\mathbb{R}$. The action is a force in either direction and has at most unit magnitude. The state transition equation is $\dot{x}_1 = x_2$ and $\dot{x}_2 = u$, and $X = \mathbb{R}^2$. The task is to perform optimal motion planning between any two states $x_I, x_G \in X$. From a given initial state x_I, a goal state x_G must be reached in minimum time. The cost functional is defined in this case as $l(x, u) = 1$ for all $x \in X$ and and $u \in U$ such that $u \ne u_T$.

Using (15.26), the Hamiltonian is defined as

$$H(x, u, \lambda) = 1 + \lambda_1 x_2 + \lambda_2 u. \tag{15.38}$$

The optimal action trajectory is obtained from (15.28) as

$$u^*(t) = \operatorname*{argmin}_{u \in [-1, 1]} \{1 + \lambda_1(t)x_2(t) + \lambda_2(t)u(t)\}. \tag{15.39}$$

If $\lambda_2(t) < 0$, then $u^*(t) = 1$, and if $\lambda_2(t) > 0$, then $u^*(t) = -1$. Thus, the action may be assigned as $u^*(t) = -\operatorname{sgn}(\lambda_2(t))$, if $\lambda_2(t) \ne 0$. Note that these two cases are the "bangs" of the bang-bang control from Section 14.6.3, and they are also the extremal actions used for the planning algorithm in Section 14.4.1. At the boundary case in which $\lambda_2(t) = 0$, any action in $[-1, 1]$ may be chosen.

The only remaining task is to determine the values of the adjoint variables over time. The adjoint transition equation is obtained from (15.36) as $\dot{\lambda}_1 = 0$ and $\dot{\lambda}_2 = -\lambda_1$. The solutions are $\lambda_1(t) = c_1$ and $\lambda_2(t) = c_2 - c_1 t$, in which c_1 and c_2 are constants that can be determined at $t = 0$ from (15.38) and (15.39). The optimal action depends only on the sign of $\lambda_2(t)$. Since its solution is the equation of a line, it can change signs at most once. Therefore, there are four possible kinds of solutions, depending on the particular x_I and x_G:

1.   Pure acceleration, $u^*(t) = 1$, is applied for all time.

2.   Pure deceleration, $u^*(t) = -1$, is applied for all time.

3. Pure acceleration is applied up to some time t' and is followed immediately by pure deceleration until the final time.

4. Pure deceleration is applied up to some time t' followed immediately by pure acceleration until the final time.

For the last two cases, t' is often called the *switching time*, at which point a discontinuity in $\tilde{u}^*$ occurs. These two are bang-bang solutions, which were described in Section 14.6.3. ∎

This was one of the simplest possible examples, and the optimal solution was easily found because the adjoint variables are linear functions of time. Section 15.3 covers optimal solutions for the Dubins car, the Reeds-Shepp car, and the differential drive, all of which can be established using the minimum principle combined with some geometric arguments. As systems become more complicated, such analysis is unfortunately too difficult. In these cases, sampling-based methods, such as those of Chapter 14, must be used to determine optimal trajectories.

One common complication is the existence of *singular arcs* along the solution trajectory. These correspond to a degeneracy in H with respect to u over some duration of time. This could be caused, for example, by having H independent of u. In Example 15.4, H became independent of u when $\lambda_2(t) = 0$; however, there was no singular arc because this could only occur for an instant of time. If the duration had been longer, then there would be an interval of time over which the optimal action could not be determined. In general, if the Hessian (recall definition from (8.48)) of H with respect to u is a positive definite matrix, then there are no singular arcs (this is often called the Legendre-Clebsch condition). The minimum principle in this case provides a sufficient condition for local optimality in the space of possible state trajectories. If the Hessian is not positive definite for some interval $[t_1, t_2]$ with $t_1 < t_2$, then additional information is needed to determine the optimal trajectory over the singular arc from $x^*(t_1)$ to $x^*(t_2)$.

Note that all of this analysis ignores the existence of obstacles. There is nothing to prevent the solutions from attempting to enter an obstacle region. The action set $U(x)$ and cost $l(x, u)$ can be adjusted to account for obstacles; however, determining an optimal solution from the minimum principle becomes virtually impossible, except in some special cases.

There are other ways to derive the minimum principle. Recall from Section 13.4.4 that Hamilton's equations can be derived from the Euler-Lagrange equation. It should not be surprising that the minimum principle can also be derived using variational principles [97, 792]. The minimum principle can also be interpreted as a form of constrained optimization. This yields the interpretation of λ as Lagrange multipliers. A very illuminating reference for further study of the minimum principle is Pontryagin's original works [804].

Time optimality

Interesting interpretations of the minimum principle exist for the case of optimizing the time to reach the goal [427, 904]. In this case, $l(x, u) = 1$ in (15.26), and the cost term can be ignored. For the remaining portion, let λ be defined as

$$\lambda_i = -\frac{\partial G^*}{\partial x_i}, \qquad (15.40)$$

instead of using (15.25). In this case, the Hamiltonian can be expressed as

$$H(x, u, \lambda) = \sum_{i=1}^{n} \lambda_i f_i(x, u) = \left\langle -\frac{\partial G^*}{\partial x}, f(x, u) \right\rangle, \qquad (15.41)$$

which is an inner product between $f(x, u)$ and the negative gradient of G^*. Using (15.40), the Hamiltonian should be maximized instead of minimized (this is equivalent to Pontryagin's original formulation [804]). An inner product of two vectors increases as their directions become closer to parallel. Optimizing (15.41) amounts to selecting u so that $\dot{x}$ is as close as possible to the direction of steepest descent of G^*. This is nicely interpreted by considering how the boundary of the reachable set $R(x_0, \mathcal{U}, t)$ propagates through X. By definition, the points on $\partial R(x_0, \mathcal{U}, t)$ must correspond to time-optimal trajectories. Furthermore, $\partial R(x_0, \mathcal{U}, t)$ can be interpreted as a propagating wavefront that is perpendicular to $-\partial G^*/\partial x$. The minimum principle simply indicates that u should be chosen so that $\dot{x}$ points into the propagating boundary, as close to being orthogonal as possible [427].

15.3 Optimal paths for some wheeled vehicles

For some of the wheeled vehicle models of Section 13.1.2, the shortest path between any pair of configurations was completely characterized. In this section, $X = \mathcal{C} = \mathbb{R}^2 \times \mathbb{S}^1$, which corresponds to the C-space for a rigid body in the plane. For each model, the path length in $\mathcal{C}$ must be carefully defined to retain some physical significance in the world $\mathcal{W} = \mathbb{R}^2$ in which the vehicle travels. For example, in the case of the simple car, the distance in $\mathcal{W}$ traveled by the center of the rear axle will be optimized. If the coordinate frame is assigned appropriately, this corresponds to optimizing the path length in the $\mathbb{R}^2$ subspace of $\mathcal{C}$ while ignoring orientation. Keep in mind that the solutions given in this section depend heavily on the particular cost functional that is optimized.

Sections 15.3.1–15.3.3 cover the shortest paths for the Dubins car, the Reeds-Shepp car, and a differential-drive model, respectively. In each case, the paths can be elegantly described as combinations of a few motion primitives. Due to symmetries, it is sufficient to describe the optimal paths from a fixed initial configuration $q_I = (0, 0, 0)$ to any goal configuration $q_G \in \mathcal{C}$. If the optimal path is desired from a different $q_I \in \mathcal{C}$, then it can be recovered from rigid-body transformations applied to q_I and q_G (the whole path can easily be translated and rotated without effecting its optimality, provided that q_G does not move relative to q_I). Alternatively, it may be convenient to fix q_G and consider optimal paths from all possible q_I.

Once q_I (or q_G) is fixed, $\mathcal{C}$ can be partitioned into cells that correspond to sets of placements for q_G (or q_I). Inside of each cell, the optimal curve is described by a fixed sequence of parameterized motion primitives. For example, one cell for the Dubins car indicates "turn left," "go straight," and then "turn right." The curves are ideally suited for use as an LPM in a sampling-based planning algorithm.

This section mainly focuses on presenting the solutions. Establishing their correctness is quite involved and is based in part on Pontryagin's minimum principle from Section 15.2.3. Other important components are Filipov's existence theorem (see [904]) and Boltyanskii's sufficient condition for optimality (which also justifies dynamic programming) [132]. Substantially more details and justifications of the curves presented in Sections 15.3.1 and

Symbol	Steering: u
S	0
L	1
R	-1

Figure 15.3: The three motion primitives from which all optimal curves for the Dubins car can be constructed.

15.3.2 appear in [904, 905, 924]. The corresponding details for the curves of Section 15.3.3 appear in [65].

15.3.1 Dubins curves

Recall the Dubins version of the simple car given in Section 13.1.2. The system was specified in (13.15). It is assumed here that the car moves at constant forward speed, $u_s = 1$. The other important constraint is the maximum steering angle ϕ_{max}, which results in a minimum turning radius ρ_{min}. As the car travels, consider the length of the curve in $\mathcal{W} = \mathbb{R}^2$ traced out by a pencil attached to the center of the rear axle. This is the location of the body-frame origin in Figure 13.1. The task is to minimize the length of this curve as the car travels between any q_I and q_G. Due to ρ_{min}, this can be considered as a bounded-curvature shortest-path problem. If $\rho_{min} = 0$, then there is no curvature bound, and the shortest path follows a straight line in $\mathbb{R}^2$. In terms of a cost functional of the form (8.39), the criterion to optimize is

$$L(\tilde{q}, \tilde{u}) = \int_0^{t_F} \sqrt{\dot{x}(t)^2 + \dot{y}(t)^2} dt, \tag{15.42}$$

in which t_F is the time at which q_G is reached, and a configuration is denoted as $q = (x, y, \theta)$. If q_G is not reached, then it is assumed that $L(\tilde{q}, \tilde{u}) = \infty$.

Since the speed is constant, the system can be simplified to

$$\dot{x} = \cos\theta$$
$$\dot{y} = \sin\theta \tag{15.43}$$
$$\dot{\theta} = u,$$

in which u is chosen from the interval $U = [-\tan\phi_{max}, \tan\phi_{max}]$. This implies that (15.42) reduces to optimizing the time t_F to reach q_G because the integrand reduces to 1. For simplicity, assume that $\tan\phi = 1$. The following results also hold for any $\phi_{max} \in (0, \pi/2)$.

It was shown in [296] that between any two configurations, the shortest path for the Dubins car can always be expressed as a combination of no more than three motion primitives. Each motion primitive applies a constant action over an interval of time. Furthermore, the only actions that are needed to traverse the shortest paths are $u \in \{-1, 0, 1\}$. The primitives and their associated symbols are shown in Figure 15.3. The S primitive drives the car straight ahead. The L and R primitives turn as sharply as possible to the left and right, respectively. Using these symbols, each possible kind of shortest path can be designated as a sequence of three symbols that corresponds to the order in which the primitives are applied. Let such a sequence be called a *word*. There is no need to have two consecutive primitives of the same kind because they can be merged into one. Under this observation, ten possible words of length three are possible. Dubins showed that only

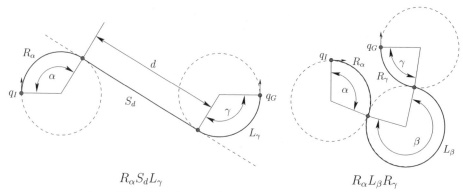

Figure 15.4: The trajectories for two words are shown in $\mathcal{W} = \mathbb{R}^2$.

these six words are possibly optimal:

$$\{LRL, \ RLR, \ LSL, \ LSR, \ RSL, \ RSR\}. \tag{15.44}$$

The shortest path between any two configurations can always be characterized by one of these words. These are called the *Dubins curves*.

To be more precise, the duration of each primitive should also be specified. For L or R, let a subscript denote the total amount of rotation that accumulates during the application of the primitive. For S, let a subscript denote the total distance traveled. Using such subscripts, the Dubins curves can be more precisely characterized as

$$\{L_\alpha \, R_\beta \, L_\gamma, \ R_\alpha \, L_\beta \, R_\gamma, \ L_\alpha \, S_d \, L_\gamma, \ L_\alpha \, S_d \, R_\gamma, \ R_\alpha \, S_d \, L_\gamma, \ R_\alpha \, S_d \, R_\gamma\}, \tag{15.45}$$

in which $\alpha, \gamma \in [0, 2\pi)$, $\beta \in (\pi, 2\pi)$, and $d \geq 0$. Figure 15.4 illustrates two cases. Note that β must be greater than π (if it is less, then some other word becomes optimal).

It will be convenient to invent a compressed form of the words to group together paths that are qualitatively similar. This will be particularly valuable when Reeds-Shepp curves are introduced in Section 15.3.2 because there are 46 of them, as opposed to 6 Dubins curves. Let C denote a symbol that means "curve," and represents either R or L. Using C, the six words in (15.44) can be compressed to only two *base words*:

$$\{CCC, \ CSC\}. \tag{15.46}$$

In this compressed form, remember that two consecutive Cs must be filled in by distinct turns (RR and LL are not allowed as subsequences). In compressed form, the base words can be specified more precisely as

$$\{C_\alpha \, C_\beta \, C_\gamma, \ C_\alpha \, S_d \, C_\gamma\}, \tag{15.47}$$

in which $\alpha, \gamma \in [0, 2\pi)$, $\beta \in (\pi, 2\pi)$, and $d \geq 0$.

Powerful information has been provided so far for characterizing the shortest paths; however, for a given q_I and q_G, two problems remain:

1. Which of the six words in (15.45) yields the shortest path between q_I and q_G?

2. What are the values of the subscripts, α, β, γ, and d for the particular word?

To use the Dubins curves as an LPM, these questions should be answered efficiently. One simple approach is to try all six words and choose the shortest one. The parameters

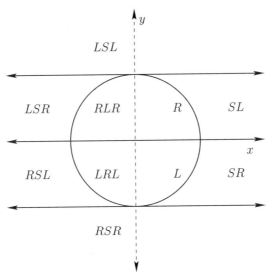

Figure 15.5: A slice at $\theta = \pi$ of the partition into word-invariant cells for the Dubins car. The circle is centered on the origin.

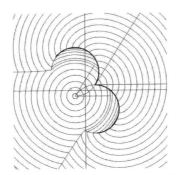

Figure 15.6: Level sets of the Dubins metric are shown in the plane. Along two circular arcs, the metric is discontinuous (courtesy of Philippe Souères).

for each word can be determined by tracing out minimum-radius circles from q_I and q_G, as shown in Figure 14.23. Another way is to use the precise characterization of the regions over which a particular word is optimal. Suppose that q_G is fixed at $(0, 0, 0)$. Based on the possible placements of q_I, the C-space can be partitioned into cells for which the same word is optimal. The cells and their boundaries are given precisely in [904]. As an example, a slice of the cell decomposition for $\theta = \pi$ is shown in Figure 15.5.

In addition to use as an LPM, the resulting cost of the shortest path may be a useful distance function in many sampling-based planning algorithms. This is sometimes called the *Dubins metric* (it is not, however, a true metric because it violates the symmetry axiom). This can be considered as the optimal cost-to-go G^*. It could have been computed approximately using the dynamic programming approach in Section 14.5; however, thanks to careful analysis, the exact values are known. One interesting property of the Dubins metric is that it is discontinuous; see Figure 15.6. Compare the cost of traveling $\pi/2$ using the R primitive to the cost of traveling to a nearby point that would require a smaller turning radius than that achieved by the R primitive. The required action does not exist in U, and the point will have to be reached by a longer sequence of primitives. The discontinuity in G^* is enabled by the fact that the Dubins car fails to possess the STLC property from Section 15.1.3. For STLC systems, G^* is continuous.

15.3.2 Reeds-Shepp curves

Now consider the shortest paths of the Reeds-Shepp car. The only difference in comparison to the Dubins car is that travel in the reverse direction is now allowed. The same criterion (15.42) is optimized, which is the distance traveled by the center of the rear axle. The shortest path is equivalent to the path that takes minimum time, as for the Dubins car. The simplified system in (15.43) can be enhanced to obtain

$$\dot{x} = u_1 \cos \theta$$
$$\dot{y} = u_1 \sin \theta \qquad\qquad (15.48)$$
$$\dot{\theta} = u_1 u_2,$$

in which $u_1 \in \{-1, 1\}$ and $u_2 \in [-\tan \phi_{max}, \tan \phi_{max}]$. The first action variable, u_1, selects the gear, which is forward ($u_1 = 1$) or reverse ($u_1 = -1$). Once again, assume for simplicity that $u_2 \in [-1, 1]$. The results stated here apply to any $\phi_{max} \in (0, \pi/2)$.

It was shown in [817] that there are no more than 48 different words that describe the shortest paths for the Reeds-Shepp car. The base word notation from Section 15.3.1 can be extended to nicely express the shortest paths. A new symbol, " | ", is used in the words to indicate that the "gear" is shifted from forward to reverse or reverse to forward. Reeds and Shepp showed that the shortest path for their car can always be expressed with one of the following base words:

$$\{C|C|C, \quad CC|C, \quad C|CC, \quad CSC, \quad CC_\beta|C_\beta C, \quad C|C_\beta C_\beta|C,$$
$$C|C_{\pi/2}SC, \quad CSC_{\pi/2}|C, \quad C|C_{\pi/2}SC_{\pi/2}|C\}. \qquad (15.49)$$

As many as five primitives could be needed to execute the shortest path. A subscript of $\pi/2$ is given in some cases because the curve must be followed for precisely $\pi/2$ radians. For some others, β is given as a subscript to indicate that it must match the parameter of another primitive. The form given in (15.49) is analogous to (15.46) for the Dubins car. The parameter ranges can also be specified, to yield a form analogous to (15.47). The result is shown in Figure 15.7. Example curves for two cases are shown in Figure 15.9.

Now the base words will be made more precise by specifying the particular motion primitive. Imagine constructing a list of words analogous to (15.44) for the Dubins car. There are six primitives as shown in Figure 15.8. The symbols S, L, and R are used again. To indicate the forward or reverse gear, $+$ and $-$ superscripts will be used as shown in Figure 15.8.[6]

Figure 15.10 shows 48 different words, which result from uncompressing the base words expressed using C, S, and " | " in (15.49). Each shortest path is a word with length at most five. There are substantially more words than for the Dubins car. Each base word in (15.49) expands into four or eight words using the motion primitives. To uncompress

---

[6] This differs conceptually from the notation used in [904]. There, r^- corresponds to L^- here. The L here means that the steering wheel is positioned for a left turn, but the car is in reverse. This aids in implementing the rule that R and L cannot be consecutive in a word.

Base	α	β	γ	d
$C_\alpha|C_\beta|C_\gamma$	$[0, \pi]$	$[0, \pi]$	$[0, \pi]$	$-$
$C_\alpha|C_\beta C_\gamma$	$[0, \beta]$	$[0, \pi/2]$	$[0, \beta]$	$-$
$C_\alpha C_\beta|C_\gamma$	$[0, \beta]$	$[0, \pi/2]$	$[0, \beta]$	$-$
$C_\alpha S_d C_\gamma$	$[0, \pi/2]$	$-$	$[0, \pi/2]$	$(0, \infty)$
$C_\alpha C_\beta|C_\beta C_\gamma$	$[0, \beta]$	$[0, \pi/2]$	$[0, \beta]$	$-$
$C_\alpha|C_\beta C_\beta|C_\gamma$	$[0, \beta]$	$[0, \pi/2]$	$[0, \beta]$	$-$
$C_\alpha|C_{\pi/2} S_d C_{\pi/2}|C_\gamma$	$[0, \pi/2]$	$-$	$[0, \pi/2]$	$(0, \infty)$
$C_\alpha|C_{\pi/2} S_d C_\gamma$	$[0, \pi/2]$	$-$	$[0, \pi/2]$	$(0, \infty)$
$C_\alpha S_d C_{\pi/2}|C_\gamma$	$[0, \pi/2]$	$-$	$[0, \pi/2]$	$(0, \infty)$

Figure 15.7: The interval ranges are shown for each motion primitive parameter for the Reeds-Shepp optimal curves.

Symbol	Gear: u_1	Steering: u_2
S^+	1	0
S^-	-1	0
L^+	1	1
L^-	-1	1
R^+	1	-1
R^-	-1	-1

Figure 15.8: The six motion primitives from which all optimal curves for the Reeds-Shepp car can be constructed.

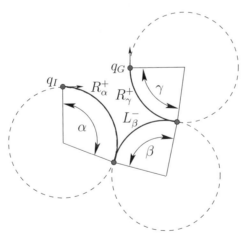

Figure 15.9: An example of the $R_\alpha^+ L_\beta^- R_\gamma^+$ curve. This uses reverse to generate a curve that is shorter than the one in Figure 15.4b for the Dubins car.

each base word, the rule that R and L cannot be applied consecutively is maintained. This yields four possibilities for the first six compressed words. The remaining three involve an intermediate S primitive, which allows eight possible sequences of Rs and Ls for each one. Two of the 48 words were eliminated in [924]. Each of the remaining 46 words can actually occur for a shortest path and are called the *Reeds-Shepp curves*.

For use as an LPM, the problem appears once again of determining the particular word and parameters for a given q_I and q_G. This was not difficult for Dubins curves, but now

Base word	Sequences of motion primitives
$C\|C\|C$	$(L^+R^-L^+)(L^-R^+L^-)(R^+L^-R^+)(R^-L^+R^-)$
$CC\|C$	$(L^+R^+L^-)(L^-R^-L^+)(R^+L^+R^-)(R^-L^-R^+)$
$C\|CC$	$(L^+R^-L^-)(L^-R^+L^+)(R^+L^-R^-)(R^-L^+R^+)$
CSC	$(L^+S^+L^+)(L^-S^-L^-)(R^+S^+R^+)(R^-S^-R^-)$
	$(L^+S^+R^+)(L^-S^-R^-)(R^+S^+L^+)(R^-S^-L^-)$
$CC_\beta\|C_\beta C$	$(L^+R_\beta^+L_\beta^-R^-)(L^-R_\beta^-L_\beta^+R^+)(R^+L_\beta^+R_\beta^-L^-)(R^-L_\beta^-R_\beta^+L^+)$
$C\|C_\beta C_\beta\|C$	$(L^+R_\beta^-L_\beta^-R^+)(L^-R_\beta^+L_\beta^+R^-)(R^+L_\beta^-R_\beta^-L^+)(R^-L_\beta^+R_\beta^+L^-)$
$C\|C_{\pi/2}SC$	$(L^+R_{\pi/2}^-S^-R^-)(L^-R_{\pi/2}^+S^+R^+)(R^+L_{\pi/2}^-S^-L^-)(R^-L_{\pi/2}^+S^+L^+)$
	$(L^+R_{\pi/2}^-S^-L^-)(L^-R_{\pi/2}^+S^+L^+)(R^+L_{\pi/2}^-S^-R^-)(R^-L_{\pi/2}^+S^+R^+)$
$CSC_{\pi/2}\|C$	$(L^+S^+L_{\pi/2}^+R^-)(L^-S^-L_{\pi/2}^-R^+)(R^+S^+R_{\pi/2}^+L^-)(R^-S^-R_{\pi/2}^-L^+)$
	$(R^+S^+L_{\pi/2}^+R^-)(R^-S^-L_{\pi/2}^-R^+)(L^+S^+R_{\pi/2}^+L^-)(L^-S^-R_{\pi/2}^-L^+)$
$C\|C_{\pi/2}SC_{\pi/2}\|C$	$(L^+R_{\pi/2}^-S^-L_{\pi/2}^-R^+)(L^-R_{\pi/2}^+S^+L_{\pi/2}^+R^-)$
	$(R^+L_{\pi/2}^-S^-R_{\pi/2}^-L^+)(R^-L_{\pi/2}^+S^+R_{\pi/2}^+L^-)$

Figure 15.10: The 48 curves of Reeds and Shepp. Sussmann and Tang [924] showed that $(L^-R^+L^-)$ and $(R^-L^+R^-)$, which appear in the first row, can be eliminated. Hence, only 46 words are needed to describe the shortest paths.

there are 46 possibilities. The naive approach of testing every word and choosing the shortest one may be too costly. The precise cell boundaries in $\mathcal{C}$ over which each word applies are given in [904]. The cell boundaries are unfortunately quite complicated, which makes the point location algorithm difficult to implement. A simple way to prune away many words from consideration is to use intervals of validity for θ. For some values of θ, certain compressed words are impossible as shortest paths. A convenient table of words that become active over ranges of θ is given in [904]. Once again, the length of the shortest path can serve as a distance function in sampling-based planning algorithms. The resulting *Reeds-Shepp metric* is continuous because the Reeds-Shepp car is STLC, which will be established in Section 15.4.

15.3.3 Balkcom-Mason curves

In recent years, two more families of optimal curves have been determined [65, 213]. Recall the differential-drive system from Section 13.1.2, which appears in many mobile robot systems. In many ways, it appears that the differential drive is a special case of the simple car. The expression of the system given in (13.17) can be made to appear identical to the Reeds-Shepp car system in (15.48). For example, letting $r = 1$ and $L = 1$ makes them equivalent by assigning $u_\omega = u_1$ and $u_\psi = u_2$. Consider the distance traveled by a point attached to the center of the differential-drive axle using (15.42). Minimizing this distance for any q_I and q_G is trivial, as shown in Figure 13.4 of Section 13.1.2. The center point can be made to travel in a straight line in $\mathcal{W} = \mathbb{R}^2$. This would be possible for the Reeds-Shepp car if $\rho_{min} = 0$, which implies that $\phi_{max} = \pi/2$. It therefore appeared for many years that no interesting curves exist for the differential drive.

The problem, however, with measuring the distance traveled by the axle center is that pure rotations are cost-free. This occurs when the wheels rotate at the same speed but with opposite angular velocities. The center does not move; however, the time duration, energy expenditure, and wheel rotations that occur are neglected. By incorporating one or more of these into the cost functional, a challenging optimization arises. Balkcom and Mason

Symbol	Left wheel: u_l	Right wheel: u_r
⟰	1	1
⟱	-1	-1
⤺	-1	1
⤻	1	-1

Figure 15.11: The four motion primitives from which all optimal curves for the differential-drive robot can be constructed.

bounded the speed of the differential drive and minimized the total time that it takes to travel from q_I to q_G. Using (13.16), the action set is defined as $U = [-1, 1] \times [-1, 1]$, in which the maximum rotation rate of each wheel is one (an alternative bound can be used without loss of generality). The criterion to optimize is

$$L(\tilde{q}, \tilde{u}) = \int_0^{t_F} \sqrt{\dot{x}(t)^2 + \dot{y}(t)^2} + |\dot{\theta}(t)|dt, \qquad (15.50)$$

which takes θ into account, whereas it was neglected in (15.42). This criterion is once again equivalent to minimizing the time to reach q_G. The resulting model will be referred to as the *Balkcom-Mason drive*. An alternative criterion is the total amount of wheel rotation; this leads to an alternative family of optimal curves [213].

It was shown in [65] that only the four motion primitives shown in Figure 15.11 are needed to express time-optimal paths for the differential-drive robot. Each primitive corresponds to holding one action variable fixed at its limit for an interval of time. Using the symbols in Figure 15.11 (which were used in [65]), words can be formed that describe the optimal path. It has been shown that the word length is no more than five. Thus, any shortest paths may be expressed as a piecewise-constant action trajectory in which there are no more than five pieces. Every piece corresponds to one of the primitives in Figure 15.11.

It is convenient in the case of the Balkcom-Mason drive to use the same symbols for both base words and for precise specification of primitives. Symmetry transformations will be applied to each base word to yield a family of eight words that precisely specify the sequences of motion primitives. Nine base words describe the shortest paths:

$$\{⤺, \ ⟱, \ ⟱⤺, \ ⤺⟱⤺, \ ⟰⤺_\pi⟱, \ ⤺⟱⤺, \ ⟱⤺⤺, \ ⤺⟱⤺⟰, \ ⟰⤺⟱⤺⟰\}. \qquad (15.51)$$

This is analogous to the compressed forms given in (15.46) and (15.49). The motions are depicted in Figure 15.12.

Figure 15.13 shows 40 distinct *Balkcom-Mason curves* that result from applying symmetry transformations to the base words of (15.51). There are 72 entries in Figure 15.13, but many are identical. The transformation T_1 indicates that the directions of ⟰ and ⟱ are flipped from the base word. The transformation T_2 reverses the order of the motion primitives. The transformation T_3 flips the directions of ⤺ and ⤻. The transformations commute, and there are seven possible ways to combine them, which contributes to a row of Figure 15.13.

To construct an LPM or distance function, the same issues arise as for the Reeds-Shepp and Dubins cars. Rather than testing all 40 words to find the shortest path, simple tests can be defined over which a particular word becomes active [65]. A slice of the precise cell decomposition and the resulting optimal cost-to-go (which can be called the *Balkcom-Mason metric*) are shown in Figure 15.14.

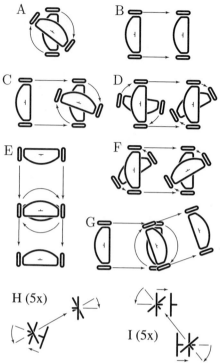

Figure 15.12: Each of the nine base words is depicted [65]. The last two are only valid for small motions; they are magnified five times and the robot outline is not drawn.

	Base	T_1	T_2	T_3	$T_2 \circ T_1$	$T_3 \circ T_1$	$T_3 \circ T_2$	$T_3 \circ T_2 \circ T_1$
A.	↷	↷	↷	↶	↷	↶	↷	↷
B.	⇓	⇑	⇓	⇓	⇑	⇑	⇓	⇑
C.	⇓↷	⇑↷	↷⇓	⇓↶	↷⇑	⇑↷	↶⇓	↶⇑
D.	↷⇓↷	↷⇑↷	↷⇓↷	↶⇓↶	↷⇑↷	↷⇑↷	↶⇓↷	↷⇑↶
E.	⇑↷$_\pi$⇓	⇓↷$_\pi$⇑	⇓↷$_\pi$⇑	⇑↷$_\pi$⇓	⇑↷$_\pi$⇓	⇓↷$_\pi$⇑	⇓↷$_\pi$⇑	⇑↷$_\pi$⇓
F.	↶⇓↷	↷⇑↷	↶⇓↷	↶⇓↷	↷⇑↷	↷⇑↶	↶⇓↷	↷⇑↶
G.	⇓↷⇑	⇑↷⇓	⇑↷⇓	⇓↶⇑	⇓↶⇑	⇑↷⇓	⇑↶⇓	⇓↶⇑
H.	↷⇓↷⇑	↷↷↷⇓	⇑↷⇓↷	↶↷↓↷⇑	⇓↷↑↷	↷↷⇑↓	⇑↷⇓↷	⇓↷↑↷
I.	⇑↷⇓↷⇑	⇓↷↑↷⇓	⇑↷⇓↷⇑	↷↷⇓↷⇑	⇓↷↑↷⇓	⇓↷↑↷⇓	↷↷⇓↷⇑	⇓↷↑↷⇓

Figure 15.13: The 40 optimal curve types for the differential-drive robot, sorted by symmetry class [65].

15.4 Nonholonomic system theory

This section gives some precision to the term *nonholonomic*, which was used loosely in Chapters 13 and 14. Furthermore, small-time controllability (STLC), which was defined in Section 15.1.3, is addressed. The presentation given here barely scratches the surface of this subject, which involves deep mathematical principles from differential geometry, algebra, control theory, and mechanics. The intention is to entice the reader to pursue further study of these topics; see the suggested literature at the end of the chapter.

15.4.1 Control-affine systems

Nonholonomic system theory is restricted to a special class of nonlinear systems. The techniques of Section 15.4 utilize ideas from linear algebra. The main concepts will be formulated in terms of linear combinations of vector fields on a smooth manifold X. Therefore, the formulation is restricted to *control-affine systems*, which were briefly

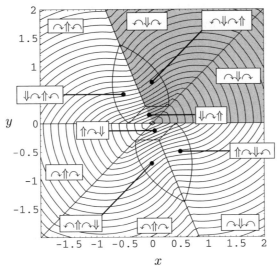

Figure 15.14: A slice of the optimal curves is shown for $q_I = (x, y, \frac{\pi}{4})$ and $q_G = (0, 0, 0)$ [65]. Level sets of the optimal cost-to-go G^* are displayed. The coordinates correspond to a differential drive with $r = L = 1$ in (13.16).

introduced in Section 13.2.3. For these systems, $\dot{x} = f(x, u)$ is of the form

$$\dot{x} = h_0(x) + \sum_{i=1}^{m} h_i(x)u_i, \tag{15.52}$$

in which each h_i is a vector field on X.

The vector fields are expressed using a coordinate neighborhood of X. Usually, $m < n$, in which n is the dimension of X. Unless otherwise stated, assume that $U = \mathbb{R}^m$. In some cases, U may be restricted.

Each action variable $u_i \in \mathbb{R}$ can be imagined as a coefficient that determines how much of $h_i(x)$ is blended into the result $\dot{x}$. The *drift term* $h_0(x)$ always remains and is often such a nuisance that the *driftless* case will be the main focus. This means that $h_0(x) = 0$ for all $x \in X$, which yields

$$\dot{x} = \sum_{i=1}^{m} h_i(x)u_i. \tag{15.53}$$

The driftless case will be used throughout most of this section. The set $h_1, \ldots, h_m$, is referred to as the *system vector fields*. It is essential that U contains at least an open set that contains the origin of $\mathbb{R}^m$. If the origin is not contained in U, then the system is no longer driftless.[7]

Control-affine systems arise in many mechanical systems. Velocity constraints on the C-space frequently are of the Pfaffian form (13.5). In Section 13.1.1, it was explained that under such constraints, a configuration transition equation (13.6) can be derived that is linear if q is fixed. This is precisely the driftless form (15.53) using $X = \mathcal{C}$. Most of the models in Section 13.1.2 can be expressed in this form. The Pfaffian constraints on configuration are often called *kinematic constraints* because they arise due to the

---

[7] Actually, if the convex hull of U contains an open set that contains the origin, then a driftless system can be simulated by rapid switching.

kinematics of bodies in contact, such as a wheel rolling. The more general case of (15.52) for a phase space X arises from *dynamic constraints* that are obtained from Euler-Lagrange equation (13.118) or Hamilton's equations (13.198) in the formulation of the mechanics. These constraints capture conservation laws, and the drift term usually appears due to momentum.

Example 15.5 (A Simplified Model for Differential Drives and Cars)   Both the simple-car and the differential-drive models of Section 13.1.2 can be expressed in the form (15.53) after making simplifications. The simplified model, (15.48), can be used to conveniently express versions of both of them by using different restrictions to define U. The third equation of (15.48) can be reduced to $\dot{\theta} = u_2$ without affecting the set of velocities that can be achieved. To conform to (15.53), the equations of (15.48) can be written in a linear-algebra form as

$$\begin{pmatrix} \dot{x} \\ \dot{y} \\ \dot{\theta} \end{pmatrix} = \begin{pmatrix} \cos\theta \\ \sin\theta \\ 0 \end{pmatrix} u_1 + \begin{pmatrix} 0 \\ 0 \\ 1 \end{pmatrix} u_2. \tag{15.54}$$

This makes it clear that there are two system vector fields, which can be combined by selecting the scalar values u_1 and u_2. One vector field allows pure translation, and the other allows pure rotation. Without restrictions on U, this system behaves like a differential drive because the simple car cannot execute pure rotation. Simulating the simple car with (15.54) requires restrictions on U (such as requiring that u_1 be 1 or -1, as in Section 15.3.2). This is equivalent to the unicycle from Figure 13.5 and (13.18).

Note that (15.54) can equivalently be expressed as

$$\begin{pmatrix} \dot{x} \\ \dot{y} \\ \dot{\theta} \end{pmatrix} = \begin{pmatrix} \cos\theta & 0 \\ \sin\theta & 0 \\ 0 & 1 \end{pmatrix} \begin{pmatrix} u_1 \\ u_2 \end{pmatrix} \tag{15.55}$$

by organizing the vector fields into a matrix.   ■

In (15.54), the vector fields were written as column vectors that combine linearly using action variables. This suggested that control-affine systems can be alternatively expressed using matrix multiplication in (15.55). In general, the vector fields can be organized into an $n \times m$ matrix as

$$H(x) = \begin{bmatrix} h_1(x) & h_2(x) & \cdots & h_m(x) \end{bmatrix}. \tag{15.56}$$

In the driftless case, this yields

$$\dot{x} = H(x)u \tag{15.57}$$

as an equivalent way to express (15.53)

It is sometimes convenient to work with Pfaffian constraints,

$$g_1(x)\dot{x}_1 + g_2(x)\dot{x}_2 + \cdots + g_n(x)\dot{x}_n = 0, \tag{15.58}$$

instead of a state transition equation. As indicated in Section 13.1.1, a set of k independent Pfaffian constraints can be converted into a state transition equation with $m = (n - k)$ action variables. The resulting state transition equation is a driftless control-affine system. Thus, Pfaffian constraints provide a dual way of specifying driftless control-affine systems. The k Pfaffian constraints can be expressed in matrix form as

$$G(x)\dot{x} = 0, \tag{15.59}$$

which is the dual of (15.57), and $G(x)$ is a $k \times n$ matrix formed from the g_i coefficients of each Pfaffian constraint. Systems with drift can be expressed in a Pfaffian-like form by constraints

$$g_0(x) + g_1(x)\dot{x}_1 + g_2(x)\dot{x}_2 + \cdots + g_n(x)\dot{x}_n = 0. \tag{15.60}$$

15.4.2 Determining whether a system is nonholonomic

The use of linear algebra in Section 15.4.1 suggests further development of algebraic concepts. This section briefly introduces concepts that resemble ordinary linear algebra but apply to linear combinations of vector fields. This provides the concepts and tools needed to characterize important system properties in the remainder of this section. This will enable the assessment of whether a system is nonholonomic and also whether it is STLC. Many of the constructions are named after Sophus Lie (pronounced "lee"), a mathematician who in the nineteenth century contributed many ideas to algebra and geometry that happen to be relevant in the study of nonholonomic systems (although that application came much later).

15.4.2.1 Completely integrable or nonholonomic?

Every control-affine system must be one or the other (not both) of the following:

1. **Completely integrable:** This means that the Pfaffian form (15.59) can be obtained by differentiating k equations of the form $f_i(x) = 0$ with respect to time. This case was interpreted as being trapped on a surface in Section 13.1.3. An example of being trapped on a circle in $\mathbb{R}^2$ was given in (13.22).

2. **Nonholonomic:** This means that the system is not completely integrable. In this case, it might even be possible to reach all of X, even if the number of action variables m is much smaller than n, the dimension of X.

In this context, the term *holonomic* is synonymous with completely integrable, and *nonintegrable* is synonymous with nonholonomic. The term nonholonomic is sometimes applied to non-Pfaffian constraints [591]; however, this will be avoided here, in accordance with mechanics literature [114].

The notion of integrability used here is quite different from that required for (14.1). In that case, the state transition equation needed to be integrable to obtain integral curves from any initial state. This was required for all systems considered in this book. By contrast, *complete integrability* implies that the system can be expressed without even using derivatives. This means that all integral curves can eventually be characterized by constraints that do not involve derivatives.

To help understand complete integrability, the notion of an integral curve will be generalized from one to m dimensions. A manifold $M \subseteq X$ is called an *integral manifold* of a set of Pfaffian constraints if at every $x \in M$, all vectors in the tangent space $T_x(M)$ satisfy the constraints. For a set of completely integrable Pfaffian constraints, a partition of X into integral manifolds can be obtained by defining maximal integral manifolds from every $x \in X$. The resulting partition is called a *foliation*, and the maximal integral manifolds are called *leaves* [874].

Example 15.6 (A Foliation with Spherical Leaves)   As an example, suppose $X = \mathbb{R}^n$ and consider the Pfaffian constraint

$$x_1 \dot{x}_1 + x_2 \dot{x}_2 + \cdots x_n \dot{x}_n = 0. \tag{15.61}$$

This is completely integrable because it can be obtained by differentiating the equation of a sphere,

$$x_1^2 + x_2^2 + \cdots x_n^2 - r^2 = 0, \tag{15.62}$$

with respect to time (r is a constant). The particular sphere that is obtained via integration depends on an initial state. The foliation is the collection of all concentric spheres that are centered at the origin. For example, if $X = \mathbb{R}^3$, then a maximal integral manifold arises for each point of the form $(0, 0, r)$. In each case, it is a sphere of radius r. The foliation is generated by selecting every $r \in [0, \infty)$. ∎

The task in this section is to determine whether a system is completely integrable. Imagine someone is playing a game with you. You are given an control-affine system and asked to determine whether it is completely integrable. The person playing the game with you can start with equations of the form $h_i(x) = 0$ and differentiate them to obtain Pfaffian constraints. These can then be converted into the parametric form to obtain the state transition equation (15.53). It is easy to construct challenging problems; however, it is very hard to solve them. The concepts in this section can be used to determine only whether it is possible to win such a game. The main tool will be the Frobenius theorem, which concludes whether a system is completely integrable. Unfortunately, the conclusion is obtained without producing the integrated constraints $h_i(x) = 0$. Therefore, it is important to keep in mind that "integrability" does not mean that *you* can integrate it to obtain a nice form. This is a challenging problem of reverse engineering. On the other hand, it is easy to go in the other direction by differentiating the constraints to make a challenging game for someone else to play.

15.4.2.2 Distributions

A distribution[8] expresses a set of vector fields on a smooth manifold. Suppose that a driftless control-affine system (15.53) is given. Recall the vector space definition from Section 8.3.1 or from linear algebra. Also recall that a state transition equation can be interpreted as a vector field if the actions are fixed and as a vector space if the state is instead fixed. For $U = \mathbb{R}^m$ and a fixed $x \in X$, the state transition equation defines a vector space in which each h_i evaluated at x is a basis vector and each u_i is a coefficient. For example, in (15.54), the vector fields h_1 and h_2 evaluated at $q = (0, 0, 0)$ become $[1 \ \ 0 \ \ 0]^T$ and $[0 \ \ 0 \ \ 1]^T$, respectively. These serve as the basis vectors. By selecting values of $u \in \mathbb{R}^2$, a 2D vector space results. Any vector of the form $[a \ \ 0 \ \ b]^T$ can be represented by setting $u_1 = a$ and $u_2 = b$. More generally, let $\triangle(x)$ denote the vector space obtained in this way for any $x \in X$.

The dimension of a vector space is the number of independent basis vectors. Therefore, the dimension of $\triangle(x)$ is the rank of $H(x)$ from (15.56) when evaluated at the particular $x \in X$. Now consider defining $\triangle(x)$ for every $x \in X$. This yields a parameterized family of vector spaces, one for each $x \in X$. The result could just as well be interpreted as a parameterized family of vector fields. For example, consider actions for i from 1 to m of

---

[8] This distribution has nothing to do with probability theory. It is just an unfortunate coincidence of terminology.

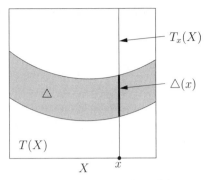

Figure 15.15: The distribution $\triangle$ can be imagined as a slice of the tangent bundle $T(X)$. It restricts the tangent space at every $x \in X$.

the form $u_i = 1$ and $u_j = 0$ for all $i \neq j$. If the action is held constant over all $x \in X$, then it selects a single vector field h_i from the collection of m vector fields:

$$\dot{x} = h_i(x). \tag{15.63}$$

Using constant actions, an m-dimensional vector space can be defined in which each vector field h_i is a basis vector (assuming the h_i are linearly independent), and the $u_i \in \mathbb{R}$ are the coefficients:

$$u_1 h_1(x) + u_2 h_2(x) + \cdots + u_m h_m(x). \tag{15.64}$$

This idea can be generalized to allow the u_i to vary over X. Thus, rather than having u constant, it can be interpreted as a feedback plan $\pi : X \to U$, in which the action at x is given by $u = \pi(x)$. The set of all vector fields that can be obtained as

$$\pi_1(x)h_1(x) + \pi_2(x)h_2(x) + \cdots + \pi_m(x)h_m(x) \tag{15.65}$$

is called the *distribution* of the set $\{h_1, \ldots, h_m\}$ of vector fields and is denoted as $\triangle$. If $\triangle$ is obtained from an control-affine system, then $\triangle$ is called the *system distribution*. The resulting set of vector fields is not quite a vector space because the nonzero coefficients π_i do not necessarily have a multiplicative inverse. This is required for the coefficients of a vector field and was satisfied by using $\mathbb{R}$ in the case of constant actions. A distribution is instead considered algebraically as a *module* [472]. In most circumstances, it is helpful to imagine it as a vector space (just do not try to invert the coefficients!). Since a distribution is almost a vector space, the span notation from linear algebra is often used to define it:

$$\triangle = \text{span}\{h_1, h_2, \ldots, h_m\}. \tag{15.66}$$

Furthermore, it *is* actually a vector space with respect to constant actions $u \in \mathbb{R}^m$. Note that for each fixed $x \in X$, the vector space $\triangle(x)$ is obtained, as defined earlier. A vector field f is said to *belong* to a distribution $\triangle$ if it can be expressed using (15.65). If for all $x \in X$, the dimension of $\triangle(x)$ is m, then $\triangle$ is called a *nonsingular distribution* (or *regular distribution*). Otherwise, $\triangle$ is called a *singular distribution*, and the points $x \in X$ for which the dimension of $\triangle(x)$ is less than m are called *singular points*. If the dimension of $\triangle(x)$ is a constant c over all $x \in X$, then c is called the *dimension* of the distribution and is denoted by $\dim(\triangle)$. If the vector fields are smooth, and if π is restricted to be smooth, then a *smooth distribution* is obtained, which is a subset of the original distribution.

As depicted in Figure 15.15, a nice interpretation of the distribution can be given in terms of the tangent bundle of a smooth manifold. The tangent bundle was defined for

$X = \mathbb{R}^n$ in (8.9) and generalizes to any smooth manifold X to obtain

$$T(X) = \bigcup_{x \in X} T_x(X). \tag{15.67}$$

The tangent bundle is a $2n$-dimensional manifold in which n is the dimension of X. A phase space for which $x = (q, \dot{q})$ is actually $T(\mathcal{C})$. In the current setting, each element of $T(X)$ yields a state and a velocity, $(x, \dot{x})$. Which pairs are possible for a driftless control-affine system? Each $\triangle(x)$ indicates the set of possible $\dot{x}$ values for a fixed x. The point x is sometimes called the *base* and $\triangle(x)$ is called the *fiber* over x in $T(X)$. The distribution $\triangle$ simply specifies a subset of $T_x(X)$ for every $x \in X$. For a vector field f to belong to $\triangle$, it must satisfy $f(x) \in \triangle(x)$ for all $x \in X$. This is just a restriction to a subset of $T(X)$. If $m = n$ and the system vector fields are independent, then any vector field is allowed. In this case, $\triangle$ includes any vector field that can be constructed from the vectors in $T(X)$.

Example 15.7 (The Distribution for the Differential Drive)   The system in (15.54) yields a two-dimensional distribution:

$$\triangle = \operatorname{span}\{[\cos\theta \quad \sin\theta \quad 0]^T, \ [0 \ \ 0 \ \ 1]^T\}. \tag{15.68}$$

The distribution is nonsingular because for any (x, y, θ) in the coordinate neighborhood, the resulting vector space $\triangle(x, y, \theta)$ is two-dimensional.   ∎

Example 15.8 (A Singular Distribution)   Consider the following system, which is given in [481]:

$$\begin{pmatrix} \dot{x}_1 \\ \dot{x}_2 \\ \dot{x}_3 \end{pmatrix} = h_1(x)u_1 + h_2(x)u_2 + h_3(x)u_3$$

$$= \begin{pmatrix} x_1 \\ 1 + x_3 \\ 1 \end{pmatrix} u_1 + \begin{pmatrix} x_1 x_2 \\ (1 + x_3)x_2 \\ x_2 \end{pmatrix} u_2 + \begin{pmatrix} x_1 \\ x_1 \\ 0 \end{pmatrix} u_3. \tag{15.69}$$

The distribution is

$$\triangle = \operatorname{span}\{h_1, h_2, h_3\}. \tag{15.70}$$

The first issue is that for any $x \in \mathbb{R}^3$, $h_2(x) = h_1(x)x_2$, which implies that the vector fields are linearly dependent over all of $\mathbb{R}^3$. Hence, this distribution is singular because $m = 3$ and the dimension of $\triangle(x)$ is 2 if $x_1 \neq 0$. If $x_1 = 0$, then the dimension of $\triangle(x)$ drops to 1. The dimension of $\triangle$ is not defined because the dimension of $\triangle(x)$ depends on x.   ∎

A distribution can alternatively be defined directly from Pfaffian constraints. Each $g_i(x) = 0$ is called an *annihilator* because enforcing the constraint eliminates many vector fields from consideration. At each $x \in X$, $\triangle(x)$ is defined as the set of all velocity vectors that satisfy all k Pfaffian constraints. The constraints themselves can be used to form a *codistribution*, which is a kind of dual to the distribution. The codistribution can be interpreted as a vector space in which each constraint is a basis vector. Constraints can be added together or multiplied by any $c \in \mathbb{R}$, and there is no effect on the resulting distribution of allowable vector fields.

15.4.2.3 Lie brackets

The key to establishing whether a system is nonholonomic is to construct motions that combine the effects of two action variables, which may produce motions in a direction that

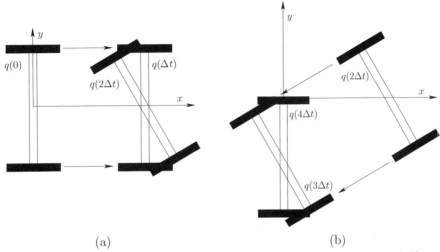

Figure 15.16: (a) The effect of the first two primitives. (b) The effect of the last two primitives.

seems impossible from the system distribution. To motivate the coming ideas, consider the differential-drive model from (15.54). Apply the following piecewise-constant action trajectory over the interval $[0, 4\Delta t]$:

$$
u(t) = \begin{cases} (1, 0) & \text{for } t \in [0, \Delta t) \\ (0, 1) & \text{for } t \in [\Delta t, 2\Delta t) \\ (-1, 0) & \text{for } t \in [2\Delta t, 3\Delta t) \\ (0, -1) & \text{for } t \in [3\Delta t, 4\Delta t] \,. \end{cases} \tag{15.71}
$$

The action trajectory is a sequence of four motion primitives: 1) translate forward, 2) rotate forward, 3) translate backward, and 4) rotate backward.

The result of all four motion primitives in succession from $q_I = (0, 0, 0)$ is shown in Figure 15.16. It is fun to try this at home with an axle and two wheels (Tinkertoys work well, for example). The result is that the differential drive moves sideways![9] From the transition equation (15.54) such motions appear impossible. This is a beautiful property of nonlinear systems. The state may wiggle its way in directions that do not seem possible. A more familiar example is parallel parking a car. It is known that a car cannot directly move sideways; however, some wiggling motions can be performed to move it sideways into a tight parking space. The actions we perform while parking resemble the primitives in (15.71).

Algebraically, the motions of (15.71) appear to be checking for commutativity. Recall from Section 4.2.1 that a group G is called *commutative* (or *Abelian*) if $ab = ba$ for any $a, b \in G$. A *commutator* is a group element of the form $aba^{-1}b^{-1}$. If the group is commutative, then $aba^{-1}b^{-1} = e$ (the identity element) for any $a, b \in G$. If a nonidentity element of G is produced by the commutator, then the group is not commutative. Similarly, if the trajectory arising from (15.71) does not form a loop (by returning to the starting point), then the motion primitives do not commute. Therefore, a sequence of motion primitives in (15.71) will be referred to as the *commutator motion*. It will turn out that if the commutator motion cannot produce any velocities not allowed by the system

---

[9] It also moves slightly forward; however, this can be eliminated by either lengthening the time of the third primitive or by considering the limit as Δ approaches zero.

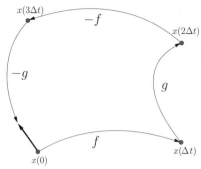

Figure 15.17: The velocity obtained by the Lie bracket can be approximated by a sequence of four motion primitives.

distribution, then the system is completely integrable. This means that if we are trapped on a surface, then it is impossible to leave the surface by using commutator motions.

Now generalize the differential drive to any driftless control-affine system that has two action variables:

$$\dot{x} = f(x)u_1 + g(x)u_2. \tag{15.72}$$

Using the notation of (15.53), the vector fields would be h_1 and h_2; however, f and g are chosen here to allow subscripts to denote the components of the vector field in the coming explanation.

Suppose that the commutator motion (15.71) is applied to (15.72) as shown in Figure 15.17. Determining the resulting motion requires some general computations, as opposed to the simple geometric arguments that could be made for the differential drive. If would be convenient to have an expression for the velocity obtained in the limit as Δt approaches zero. This can be obtained by using Taylor series arguments. These are simplified by the fact that the action history is piecewise constant.

The coming derivation will require an expression for $\ddot{x}$ under the application of a constant action. For each action, a vector field of the form $\dot{x} = h(x)$ is obtained. Upon differentiation, this yields

$$\ddot{x} = \frac{dh}{dt} = \frac{\partial h}{\partial x}\frac{dx}{dt} = \frac{\partial h}{\partial x}\dot{x} = \frac{\partial h}{\partial x}h(x). \tag{15.73}$$

This follows from the chain rule because h is a function of x, which itself is a function of t. The derivative $\partial h/\partial x$ is actually an $n \times n$ Jacobian matrix, which is multiplied by the vector $\dot{x}$. To further clarify (15.73), each component can be expressed as

$$\ddot{x}_i = \frac{d}{dt}h_i(x(t)) = \sum_{j=1}^{n}\frac{\partial h_i}{\partial x_j}h_j. \tag{15.74}$$

Now the state trajectory under the application of (15.71) will be determined using the Taylor series, which was given in (14.17). The state trajectory that results from the first motion primitive $u = (1, 0)$ can be expressed as

$$\begin{aligned} x(\Delta t) &= x(0) + \Delta t \, \dot{x}(0) + \tfrac{1}{2}(\Delta t)^2 \, \ddot{x}(0) + \cdots \\ &= x(0) + \Delta t \, f(x(0)) + \frac{1}{2}(\Delta t)^2 \left.\frac{\partial f}{\partial x}\right|_{x(0)} f(x(0)) + \cdots, \end{aligned} \tag{15.75}$$

which makes use of (15.73) in the second line. The Taylor series expansion for the second primitive is

$$x(2\Delta t) = x(\Delta t) + \Delta t \; g(x(\Delta t)) + \frac{1}{2}(\Delta t)^2 \left. \frac{\partial g}{\partial x}\right|_{x(\Delta t)} g(x(\Delta t)) + \cdots . \tag{15.76}$$

An expression for $g(x(\Delta t))$ can be obtained by using the Taylor series expansion in (15.75) to express $x(\Delta t)$. The first terms after substitution and simplification are

$$x(2\Delta t) = x(0) + \Delta t \; g + (\Delta t)^2 \left(\frac{1}{2}\frac{\partial f}{\partial x}f + \frac{\partial g}{\partial x}f + \frac{1}{2}\frac{\partial g}{\partial x}g \right) + \cdots . \tag{15.77}$$

To simplify the expression, the evaluation at $x(0)$ has been dropped from every occurrence of f and g and their derivatives.

The idea of substituting previous Taylor series expansions as they are needed can be repeated for the remaining two motion primitives. The Taylor series expansion for the result after the third primitive is

$$x(3\Delta t) = x(0) + \Delta t \; g + (\Delta t)^2 \left(\frac{\partial g}{\partial x}f - \frac{\partial f}{\partial x}g + \frac{1}{2}\frac{\partial g}{\partial x}g \right) + \cdots . \tag{15.78}$$

Finally, the Taylor series expansion after all four primitives have been applied is

$$x(4\Delta t) = x(0) + (\Delta t)^2 \left(\frac{\partial g}{\partial x}f - \frac{\partial f}{\partial x}g \right) + \cdots . \tag{15.79}$$

Taking the limit yields

$$\lim_{\Delta t \to 0} \frac{x(4\Delta t) - x(0)}{(\Delta t)^2} = \frac{\partial g}{\partial x}f - \frac{\partial f}{\partial x}g, \tag{15.80}$$

which is called the *Lie bracket* of f and g and is denoted by $[f, g]$. Similar to (15.74), the ith component can be expressed as

$$[f, g]_i = \sum_{j=1}^n \left(f_j \frac{\partial g_i}{\partial x_j} - g_j \frac{\partial f_i}{\partial x_j} \right). \tag{15.81}$$

The Lie bracket is an important operation in many subjects, and is related to the Poisson and Jacobi brackets that arise in physics and mathematics.

Example 15.9 (Lie Bracket for the Differential Drive) The Lie bracket should indicate that sideways motions are possible for the differential drive. Consider taking the Lie bracket of the two vector fields used in (15.54). Let $f = [\cos\theta \;\; \sin\theta \;\; 0]^T$ and $g = [0 \;\; 0 \;\; 1]^T$. Rename h_1 and h_2 to f and g to allow subscripts to denote the components of a vector field.

By applying (15.81), the Lie bracket $[f, g]$ is

$$[f, g]_1 = f_1 \frac{\partial g_1}{\partial x} - g_1 \frac{\partial f_1}{\partial x} + f_2 \frac{\partial g_1}{\partial y} - g_2 \frac{\partial f_1}{\partial y} + f_3 \frac{\partial g_1}{\partial \theta} - g_3 \frac{\partial f_1}{\partial \theta} = \sin\theta$$

$$[f, g]_2 = f_1 \frac{\partial g_2}{\partial x} - g_1 \frac{\partial f_2}{\partial x} + f_2 \frac{\partial g_2}{\partial y} - g_2 \frac{\partial f_2}{\partial y} + f_3 \frac{\partial g_2}{\partial \theta} - g_3 \frac{\partial f_2}{\partial \theta} = -\cos\theta \qquad (15.82)$$

$$[f, g]_3 = f_1 \frac{\partial g_3}{\partial x} - g_1 \frac{\partial f_3}{\partial x} + f_2 \frac{\partial g_3}{\partial y} - g_2 \frac{\partial f_3}{\partial y} + f_3 \frac{\partial g_3}{\partial \theta} - g_3 \frac{\partial f_3}{\partial \theta} = 0.$$

The resulting vector field is $[f, g] = [\sin\theta \;\; -\cos\theta \;\; 0]^T$, which indicates the sideways motion, as desired. When evaluated at $q = (0, 0, 0)$, the vector $[0 \;\; -1 \;\; 0]^T$ is obtained.

This means that performing short commutator motions wiggles the differential drive sideways in the $-y$ direction, which we already knew from Figure 15.16. ∎

Example 15.10 (Lie Bracket of Linear Vector Fields)   Suppose that each vector field is a linear function of x. The $n \times n$ Jacobians $\partial f/\partial x$ and $\partial g/\partial x$ are constant.

As a simple example, recall the nonholonomic integrator (13.43). In the linear-algebra form, the system is

$$\begin{pmatrix} \dot{x}_1 \\ \dot{x}_2 \\ \dot{x}_3 \end{pmatrix} = \begin{pmatrix} 1 \\ 0 \\ -x_2 \end{pmatrix} u_1 + \begin{pmatrix} 0 \\ 1 \\ x_1 \end{pmatrix} u_2. \tag{15.83}$$

Let $f = h_1$ and $g = h_2$. The Jacobian matrices are

$$\frac{\partial f}{\partial x} = \begin{pmatrix} 0 & 0 & 0 \\ 0 & 0 & 0 \\ 0 & -1 & 0 \end{pmatrix} \quad \text{and} \quad \frac{\partial g}{\partial x} = \begin{pmatrix} 0 & 0 & 0 \\ 0 & 0 & 0 \\ 1 & 0 & 0 \end{pmatrix}. \tag{15.84}$$

Using (15.80),

$$\frac{\partial g}{\partial x} f - \frac{\partial f}{\partial x} g = \begin{pmatrix} 0 & 0 & 0 \\ 0 & 0 & 0 \\ 1 & 0 & 0 \end{pmatrix} \begin{pmatrix} 1 \\ 0 \\ -x_2 \end{pmatrix} - \begin{pmatrix} 0 & 0 & 0 \\ 0 & 0 & 0 \\ 0 & -1 & 0 \end{pmatrix} \begin{pmatrix} 0 \\ 1 \\ -x_1 \end{pmatrix} = \begin{pmatrix} 0 \\ 0 \\ 2 \end{pmatrix}. \tag{15.85}$$

This result can be verified using (15.81). ∎

15.4.2.4 The Frobenius theorem

The Lie bracket is the only tool needed to determine whether a system is completely integrable (holonomic) or nonholonomic (not integrable). Suppose that a system of the form (15.53) is given. Using the m system vector fields $h_1, \dots, h_m$ there are $\binom{m}{2}$ Lie brackets of the form $[h_i, h_j]$ for $i < j$ that can be formed. A distribution $\triangle$ is called *involutive* [135] if for each of these brackets there exist m coefficients $c_k \in \mathbb{R}$ such that

$$[h_i, h_j] = \sum_{k=1}^{m} c_k h_k. \tag{15.86}$$

In other words, every Lie bracket can be expressed as a linear combination of the system vector fields, and therefore it already belongs to $\triangle$. The Lie brackets are unable to escape $\triangle$ and generate new directions of motion. We did not need to consider all n^2 possible Lie brackets of the system vector fields because it turns out that $[h_i, h_j] = -[h_j, h_i]$ and consequently $[h_i, h_i] = 0$. Therefore, the definition of involutive is not altered by looking only at the $\binom{m}{2}$ pairs.

If the system is smooth and the distribution is nonsingular, then the Frobenius theorem immediately characterizes integrability:

A system is completely integrable if and only if it is involutive.

Proofs of the Frobenius theorem appear in numerous differential geometry and control theory books [135, 158, 481, 848]. There also exist versions that do not require the distribution to be nonsingular.

Determining integrability involves performing Lie brackets and determining whether (15.86) is satisfied. The search for the coefficients can luckily be avoided by using linear algebra tests for linear independence. The $n \times m$ matrix $H(x)$, which was defined in (15.56), can be augmented into an $n \times (m + 1)$ matrix $H'(x)$ by adding $[h_i, h_j]$ as a new column. If the rank of $H'(x)$ is $m + 1$ for any pair h_i and h_j, then it is immediately known that the system is nonholonomic. If the rank of $H'(x)$ is m for all Lie brackets, then the system is completely integrable. Driftless linear systems, which are expressed as $\dot{x} = Bu$ for a fixed matrix B, are completely integrable because all Lie brackets are zero.

Example 15.11 (The Differential Drive Is Nonholonomic)   For the differential drive model in (15.54), the Lie bracket $[f, g]$ was determined in Example 15.9 to be $[\sin \theta - \cos \theta \ 0]^T$. The matrix $H'(q)$, in which $q = (x, y, \theta)$, is

$$H'(q) = \begin{pmatrix} \cos \theta & 0 & \sin \theta \\ \sin \theta & 0 & -\cos \theta \\ 0 & 1 & 0 \end{pmatrix}. \tag{15.87}$$

The rank of $H'(q)$ is 3 for all $q \in C$ (the determinant of $H'(q)$ is 1). Therefore, by the Frobenius theorem, the system is nonholonomic. ∎

Example 15.12 (The Nonholonomic Integrator Is Nonholonomic)   We would hope that the nonholonomic integrator is nonholonomic. In Example 15.10, the Lie bracket was determined to be $[0 \ 0 \ 2]^T$. The matrix $H'(q)$ is

$$H'(q) = \begin{pmatrix} 1 & 0 & 0 \\ 0 & 1 & 0 \\ -x_2 & x_1 & 2 \end{pmatrix}, \tag{15.88}$$

which clearly has full rank for all $q \in C$. ∎

Example 15.13 (Trapped on a Sphere)   Suppose that the following system is given:

$$\begin{pmatrix} \dot{x}_1 \\ \dot{x}_2 \\ \dot{x}_3 \end{pmatrix} = \begin{pmatrix} x_2 \\ -x_1 \\ 0 \end{pmatrix} u_1 + \begin{pmatrix} x_3 \\ 0 \\ -x_1 \end{pmatrix} u_2, \tag{15.89}$$

for which $X = \mathbb{R}^3$ and $U = \mathbb{R}^2$. Since the vector fields are linear, the Jacobians are constant (as in Example 15.10):

$$\frac{\partial f}{\partial x} = \begin{pmatrix} 0 & 1 & 0 \\ -1 & 0 & 0 \\ 0 & 0 & 0 \end{pmatrix} \quad \text{and} \quad \frac{\partial g}{\partial x} = \begin{pmatrix} 0 & 0 & 1 \\ 0 & 0 & 0 \\ -1 & 0 & 0 \end{pmatrix}. \tag{15.90}$$

Using (15.80),

$$\frac{\partial g}{\partial x} f - \frac{\partial f}{\partial x} g = \begin{pmatrix} 0 & 0 & 1 \\ 0 & 0 & 0 \\ -1 & 0 & 0 \end{pmatrix} \begin{pmatrix} x_2 \\ -x_1 \\ 0 \end{pmatrix} - \begin{pmatrix} 0 & 1 & 0 \\ -1 & 0 & 0 \\ 0 & 0 & 0 \end{pmatrix} \begin{pmatrix} x_3 \\ 0 \\ -x_1 \end{pmatrix} = \begin{pmatrix} 0 \\ x_3 \\ -x_2 \end{pmatrix}. \tag{15.91}$$

This yields the matrix

$$H'(x) = \begin{pmatrix} x_2 & -x_1 & 0 \\ x_3 & 0 & -x_1 \\ 0 & x_3 & -x_2 \end{pmatrix}. \tag{15.92}$$

The determinant is zero for all $x \in \mathbb{R}^3$, which means that $[f, g]$ is never linearly indepen-dent of f and g. Therefore, the system is completely integrable.[10]

The system can actually be constructed by differentiating the equation of a sphere. Let

$$f(x) = x_1^2 + x_2^2 + x_3^2 - r^2 = 0, \qquad (15.93)$$

and differentiate with respect to time to obtain

$$x_1 \dot{x}_1 + x_2 \dot{x}_2 + x_3 \dot{x}_3 = 0, \qquad (15.94)$$

which is a Pfaffian constraint. A parametric representation of the set of vectors that satisfy (15.94) is given by (15.89). For each $(u_1, u_2) \in \mathbb{R}^2$, (15.89) yields a vector that satisfies (15.94). Thus, this was an example of being trapped on a sphere, which we would expect to be completely integrable. It was difficult, however, to suspect this using only (15.89). ∎

15.4.3 Determining controllability

Determining complete integrability is the first step toward determining whether a driftless control-affine system is STLC. The Lie bracket attempts to produce motions in directions that do not seem to be allowed by the system distribution. At each q, a velocity not in $\triangle(q)$ may be produced by the Lie bracket. By working further with Lie brackets, it is possible to completely characterize *all* of the directions that are possible from each q. So far, the Lie brackets have only been applied to the system vector fields $h_1, \ldots, h_m$. It is possible to proceed further by applying Lie bracket operations on Lie brackets. For example, $[h_1, [h_1, h_2]]$ can be computed. This might generate a vector field that is linearly independent of all of the vector fields considered in Section 15.4.2 for the Frobenius theorem. The main idea in this section is to apply the Lie bracket recursively until no more independent vector fields can be found. The result is called the Lie algebra. If the number of independent vector fields obtained in this way is the dimension of X, then it turns out that the system is STLC.

15.4.3.1 The Lie algebra

The notion of a Lie algebra is first established in general. Let V be any vector space with coefficients in $\mathbb{R}$. In V, the vectors can be added or multiplied by elements of $\mathbb{R}$; however, there is no way to "multiply" two vectors to obtain a third. The Lie algebra introduces a product operation to V. The product is called a *bracket* or *Lie bracket* (considered here as a generalization of the previous Lie bracket) and is denoted by $[\cdot, \cdot] : V \times V \to V$.

To be a *Lie algebra* obtained from V, the bracket must satisfy the following three axioms:

1. **Bilinearity:** For any $a, b \in \mathbb{R}$ and $u, v, w \in V$,

$$\begin{aligned} [au + bv, w] &= a[u, w] + b[v, w] \\ [u, av + bw] &= a[u, w] + b[u, w]. \end{aligned} \qquad (15.95)$$

2. **Skew symmetry:** For any $u, v \in V$,

$$[u, v] = -[v, u]. \qquad (15.96)$$

   This means that the bracket is anti-commutative.

---

[10] This system is singular at the origin. A variant of the Frobenius theorem given here is technically needed.

3. **Jacobi identity:** For any $u, v, w \in V$,

$$[[u, v], w] + [[v, w], u] + [[w, u], v] = 0. \tag{15.97}$$

Note that the bracket is not even associative.

Let $\mathcal{L}(V)$ denote the *Lie algebra* of V. This is a vector space that includes all elements of V and any new elements that can be obtained via Lie bracket operations. The Lie algebra $\mathcal{L}(V)$ includes every vector that can be obtained from any finite number of nested Lie bracket operations. Thus, describing a Lie algebra requires characterizing all vectors that are obtained under the algebraic closure of the bracket operation. Since $\mathcal{L}(V)$ is a vector space, this is accomplished by finding a basis of independent vectors of which all elements of $\mathcal{L}(V)$ can be expressed as a linear combination.

Example 15.14 (The Vector Cross Product) Let V be the vector space over $\mathbb{R}^3$ that is used in vector calculus. The basis elements are often denoted as $\hat{\imath}, \hat{\jmath}$, and $\hat{k}$. A bracket for this vector space is simply the cross product

$$[u, v] = u \times v. \tag{15.98}$$

It can be verified that the required axioms of a Lie bracket are satisfied.

One interesting property of the cross product that is exploited often in analytic geometry is that it produces a vector outside of the span of u and v. For example, let W be the two-dimensional subspace of vectors

$$W = \text{span}\{\hat{\imath}, \hat{\jmath}\}. \tag{15.99}$$

The cross product always yields a vector that is a multiple of $\hat{k}$, which lies outside of V if the product is nonzero. This behavior is very similar to constructing vector fields that lie outside of $\triangle$ using the Lie bracket in Section 15.4.2. ∎

Example 15.15 (Lie Algebra on Lie Groups) Lie groups are the most important application of the Lie algebra concepts. Recall from Section 4.2.1 the notion of a matrix group. Important examples throughout this book have been $SO(n)$ and $SE(n)$. If interpreted as a smooth manifold, these matrix groups are examples of *Lie groups* [64]. In general, a *Lie group* G is both a differentiable manifold and a group with respect to some operation $\circ$ if and only if:

1. The product $a \circ b$, interpreted as a function from $G \times G \to G$, is smooth.
2. The inverse a^{-1}, interpreted as a function from G to G, is smooth.

The two conditions are needed to prevent the group from destroying the nice properties that come with the smooth manifold. An important result in the study of Lie groups is that all compact finite-dimensional Lie groups can be represented as matrix groups.

For any Lie group, a Lie algebra can be defined on a special set of vector fields. These are defined using the *left translation* mapping $L_g : x \mapsto gx$. The vector field formed from the differential of L_g is called a *left-invariant vector field*. A Lie algebra can be defined on the set of these fields. The Lie bracket definition depends on the particular group. For the case of $GL(n)$, the Lie bracket is

$$[A, B] = AB - BA. \tag{15.100}$$

In this case, the Lie bracket clearly appears to be a test for commutativity. If the matrices commute with respect to multiplication, then the Lie bracket is zero. The Lie brackets for

$SO(n)$ and $SE(n)$ are given in many texts on mechanics and control [158, 848]. The Lie algebra of left-invariant vector fields is an important structure in the study of nonlinear systems and mechanics. ∎

15.4.3.2 Lie algebra of the system distribution

Now suppose that a set $h_1, \ldots, h_m$ of vector fields is given as a driftless control-affine system, as in (15.53). Its associated distribution $\triangle$ is interpreted as a vector space with coefficients in $\mathbb{R}$, and the Lie bracket operation was given by (15.81). It can be verified that the Lie bracket operation in (15.81) satisfies the required axioms for a Lie algebra.

As observed in Examples 15.9 and 15.10, the Lie bracket may produce vector fields outside of $\triangle$. By defining the Lie algebra of $\triangle$ to be all vector fields that can be obtained by applying Lie bracket operations, a potentially larger distribution $\mathcal{L}(\triangle)$ is obtained. The Lie algebra can be expressed using the span notation by including $h_1, \ldots, h_m$ and all independent vector fields generated by Lie brackets. Note that no more than n independent vector fields can possibly be produced.

Example 15.16 (The Lie Algebra of the Differential Drive) The Lie algebra of the differential drive (15.54) is

$$\mathcal{L}(\triangle) = \text{span}\{[\cos\theta \ \ \sin\theta \ \ 0]^T, \ [0 \ \ 0 \ \ 1]^T, \ [\sin\theta \ \ -\cos\theta \ \ 0]^T\}. \qquad (15.101)$$

This uses the Lie bracket that was computed in (15.82) to obtain a three-dimensional Lie algebra. No further Lie brackets are needed because the maximum number of independent vector fields has been already obtained. ∎

Example 15.17 (A Lie Algebra That Involves Nested Brackets) The previous example was not very interesting because the Lie algebra was generated after computing only one bracket. Suppose that $X = \mathbb{R}^5$ and $U = \mathbb{R}^2$. In this case, there is room to obtain up to three additional, linearly independent vector fields. The dimension of the Lie algebra may be any integer from 2 to 5.

Let the system be

$$\begin{pmatrix} \dot{x}_1 \\ \dot{x}_2 \\ \dot{x}_3 \\ \dot{x}_4 \\ \dot{x}_5 \end{pmatrix} = \begin{pmatrix} 1 \\ 0 \\ x_2 \\ x_3 \\ x_4 \end{pmatrix} u_1 + \begin{pmatrix} 0 \\ 1 \\ 0 \\ 0 \\ 0 \end{pmatrix} u_2. \qquad (15.102)$$

This is a *chained-form system*, which is a concept that becomes important in Section 15.5.2.

The first Lie bracket produces

$$[h_1, h_2] = [0 \ \ 0 \ \ -1 \ \ 0 \ \ 0]^T. \qquad (15.103)$$

Other vector fields that can be obtained by Lie brackets are

$$[h_1, [h_1, h_2]] = [0 \ \ 0 \ \ 0 \ \ 1 \ \ 0]^T \qquad (15.104)$$

and

$$[h_1, [h_1, [h_1, h_2]]] = [0 \ \ 0 \ \ 0 \ \ 0 \ \ 1]^T. \qquad (15.105)$$

The resulting five vector fields are independent over all $x \in \mathbb{R}^5$. This includes h_1, h_2, and the three obtained from Lie bracket operations. Independence can be established by placing them into a 5×5 matrix,

$$\begin{pmatrix} 1 & 0 & 0 & 0 & 0 \\ 0 & 1 & 0 & 0 & 0 \\ x_2 & 0 & -1 & 0 & 0 \\ x_3 & 0 & 0 & 1 & 0 \\ x_4 & 0 & 0 & 0 & 1 \end{pmatrix}, \tag{15.106}$$

which has full rank for all $x \in \mathbb{R}^5$. No additional vector fields can possibly be independent. Therefore, the five-dimensional Lie algebra is

$$\mathcal{L}(\triangle) = \text{span}\{h_1, \; h_2, \; [h_1, h_2], \; [h_1, [h_1, h_2]], \; [h_1, [h_1, [h_1, h_2]]]\}. \tag{15.107}$$

∎

15.4.3.3 Philip Hall basis of a Lie algebra

Determining the basis of a Lie algebra may be a long and tedious process. The combinations of Lie brackets in Example 15.17 were given; however, it is not known in advance which ones will produce independent vector fields. Numerous Lie brackets may be needed, including some that are nested, such as $[[h_1, h_2], h_3]$. The maximum depth of nested Lie bracket operations is not known a priori. Therefore, a systematic search must be performed (this can in fact be modeled as a discrete planning problem) by starting with $h_1, \ldots, h_m$ and iteratively generating new, independent vector fields using Lie brackets.

One popular approach is to generate the *Philip Hall basis* (or *P. Hall basis*) of the Lie algebra $\mathcal{L}(\triangle)$. The construction of the basis essentially follows breadth-first search, in which the search depth is defined to be the number of nested levels of bracket operations. The *order* (or *depth*) d of a Lie product is defined recursively as follows. For the base case, let $d(h_i) = 1$ for any of the system vector fields. For any Lie product $[\phi_1, \phi_2]$, let

$$d([\phi_1, \phi_2]) = d(\phi_1) + d(\phi_2). \tag{15.108}$$

Thus, the order is just the nesting depth (plus one) of the Lie bracket operations. For example, $d([h_1, h_2]) = 2$ and $d([h_1, [h_2, h_3]]) = 3$.

In addition to standard breadth-first search, pruning should be automatically performed to ensure that the skew symmetry and Jacobi identities are always utilized to eliminate redundancy. A *P. Hall basis* is a sequence, $\mathcal{PH} = (\phi_1, \phi_2, \ldots)$, of Lie products for which:

1. The system vector fields h_i are the first m elements of $\mathcal{PH}$.

2. If $d(\phi_i) < d(\phi_j)$, then $i < j$.

3. Each $[\phi_i, \phi_j] \in \mathcal{PH}$ if and only if: a) $\phi_i, \phi_j \in \mathcal{PH}$ and $i < j$, and b) either $\phi_j = h_i$ for some i or $\phi_j = [\phi_l, \phi_r]$ for some $\phi_l, \phi_r \in \mathcal{PH}$ such that $l \leq i$.

It is shown in many algebra books (e.g., [863]) that this procedure results in a basis for the Lie algebra $\mathcal{L}(\triangle)$. Various algorithms for computing the basis are evaluated in [301].

Example 15.18 (P. Hall Basis Up to Depth Three) The P. Hall basis sorts the Lie products into the following sequence, which is obtained up to depth $d = 3$:

$$
\begin{array}{llll}
h_1, & h_2, & h_3, & \\
[h_1, h_2], & [h_2, h_3], & [h_3, h_1], & \\
[h_1, [h_1, h_2]], & [h_1, [h_1, h_3]], & [h_2, [h_1, h_2]], & [h_2, [h_1, h_3]], \\
[h_2, [h_2, h_3]], & [h_3, [h_1, h_2]], & [h_3, [h_1, h_3]], & [h_3, [h_2, h_3]].
\end{array}
$$

So far, the only Lie product eliminated by the Jacobi identity is $[h_1, [h_2, h_3]]$ because

$$[h_1, [h_2, h_3]] = [h_2, [h_1, h_3]] - [h_3, [h_1, h_2]]. \tag{15.109}$$

Note that all of the Lie products given here may not be linearly independent vector fields. For a particular system, linear independence tests should be performed to delete any linearly dependent vector fields from the basis. ∎

When does the sequence $\mathcal{PH}$ terminate? Recall that $\dim(\mathcal{L}(\triangle))$ can be no greater than n, because $\mathcal{L}_x(\triangle) \subseteq T_x(X)$. In other words, at every state $x \in X$, the number of possible independent velocity vectors is no more than the dimension of the tangent space at x. Therefore, $\mathcal{PH}$ can be terminated once n independent vector fields are obtained because there is no possibility of finding more. For some systems, there may be a depth k after which all Lie brackets are zero. Such systems are called *nilpotent* of order k. This occurs, for example, if all components of all vector fields are polynomials. If the system is not nilpotent, then achieving termination may be difficult. It may be the case that $\dim(\mathcal{L}(\triangle))$ is strictly less than n, but this is usually not known in advance. It is difficult to determine whether more Lie brackets are needed to increase the dimension or the limit has already been reached.

15.4.3.4 Controllability of driftless systems

The controllability of a driftless control-affine system (15.53) can be characterized using the *Lie algebra rank condition* (or *LARC*). Recall the definition of STLC from Section 15.1.3. Assume that either $U = \mathbb{R}^m$ or U at least contains an open set that contains the origin of $\mathbb{R}^m$. The *Chow-Rashevskii theorem* [114, 158, 848] states:

A driftless control-affine system, (15.53), is small-time locally controllable (STLC) at a point $x \in X$ if and only if $\dim(\mathcal{L}_x(\triangle)) = n$, the dimension of X.

If the condition holds for every $x \in X$, then the whole system is STLC. Integrability can also be expressed in terms of $\dim(\mathcal{L}(\triangle))$. Assume as usual that $m < n$. The three cases are:

$$\begin{array}{lll} 1. \ \dim(\mathcal{L}(\triangle)) = m & \text{the system is completely integrable;} \\ 2. \ m < \dim(\mathcal{L}(\triangle)) < n & \text{the system is nonholonomic, but not STLC;} & (15.110) \\ 3. \ \dim(\mathcal{L}(\triangle)) = n & \text{the system is nonholonomic and STLC.} \end{array}$$

Example 15.19 (Controllability Examples) The differential drive, nonholonomic integrator, and the system from Example 15.17 are all STLC by the Chow-Rashevskii theorem because $\dim(\mathcal{L}(\triangle)) = n$. This implies that the state can be changed in any direction, even though there are differential constraints. The state can be made to follow arbitrarily close to any smooth curve in X. A method that achieves this based on the Lie algebra is given in Section 15.5.1. The fact that these systems are STLC assures the existence of an LPM that satisfies the topological property of Section 14.6.2. ∎

15.4.3.5 Handling control-affine systems with drift

Determining whether a system with drift (15.52), is STLC is substantially more difficult. Imagine a mechanical system, such as a hovercraft, that is moving at a high speed. Due to momentum, it is impossible from most states to move in certain directions during an arbitrarily small interval of time. One can, however, ask whether a system is STLC from a state $x \in X$ for which $h_0(x) = 0$. For a mechanical system, this usually means that it starts at rest. If a system with drift is STLC, this intuitively means that it can move in any direction by hovering around states that are close to zero velocity for the mechanical system.

The Lie algebra techniques can be extended to determine controllability for systems with drift; however, the tools needed are far more complicated. See Chapter 7 of [158] for more complete coverage. Even if $\dim(\mathcal{L}(\triangle)) = n$, it does not necessarily imply that the system is STLC. It does at least imply that the system is accessible, which motivates the definition given in Section 15.1.3. Thus, the set of achievable velocities still has dimension n; however, motions in all directions may not be possible due to drift. To obtain STLC, a sufficient condition is that the set of possible values for $\dot{x}$ contains an open set that contains the origin.

The following example clearly illustrates the main difficultly with establishing whether a system with drift is STLC.

Example 15.20 (Accessible, Not STLC) The following simple system clearly illustrates the difficulty caused by drift and was considered in [744]. Let $X = \mathbb{R}^2$, $U = \mathbb{R}$, and the state transition equation be

$$
\begin{aligned}
\dot{x}_1 &= u \\
\dot{x}_2 &= x_1^2.
\end{aligned}
\tag{15.111}
$$

This system is clearly not controllable in any sense because x_2 cannot be decreased. The vector fields are $h_0(x) = [0 \; x_1^2]^T$ and $h_1(x) = [1 \; 0]^T$. The first independent Lie bracket is

$$
[h_1, [h_0, h_1]] = [0 \; -2].
\tag{15.112}
$$

The two-dimensional Lie algebra is

$$
\mathcal{L}(\triangle) = \text{span}\{h_1, [h_1, [h_0, h_1]]\},
\tag{15.113}
$$

which implies that the system is accessible. It is not STLC, however, because the bracket $[h_1, [h_0, h_1]]$ was constructed using h_0 and was combined in an unfortunate way. This bracket is indicating that changing x_2 is possible; however, we already know that it is not possible to decrease x_2. Thus, some of the vector fields obtained from Lie brackets that involve h_0 may have directional constraints. ∎

In Example 15.20, $[h_1, [h_0, h_1]]$ was an example of a *bad bracket* [926] because it obstructed controllability. A method of classifying brackets as *good* or *bad* has been developed, and there exist theorems that imply whether a system with drift is STLC by satisfying certain conditions on the good and bad brackets. Intuitively, there must be enough good brackets to neutralize the obstructions imposed by the bad brackets [158, 926].

15.5 Steering methods for nonholonomic systems

This section briefly surveys some methods that solve the BVP for nonholonomic systems. This can be considered as a motion planning problem under differential constraints but in the absence of obstacles. For linear systems, optimal control techniques can be used, as covered in Section 15.2.2. For mechanical systems that are fully actuated, standard control techniques such as the acceleration-based control model in (8.47) can be applied.

If a mechanical system is underactuated, then it is likely to be nonholonomic. As observed in Section 15.4, it is possible to generate motions that appear at first to be prohibited. Suppose that by the Chow-Rashevskii theorem, it is shown that a driftless system is STLC. This indicates that it should be possible to design an LPM that successfully connects any pair of initial and goal states. The next challenge is to find an action trajectory $\tilde{u}$ that actually causes x_I to reach x_G upon integration in (14.1). Many methods in Chapter 14 could actually be used, but it is assumed that these would be too slow. The methods in this section exploit the structure of the system (e.g, its Lie algebra) and the fact that there are no obstacles to more efficiently solve the planning problem.

15.5.1 Using the P. Hall basis

The steering method presented in this section is due to Lafferriere and Sussmann [577]. It is assumed here that a driftless control-affine system is given, in which X is a Lie group, as introduced in Example 15.15. Furthermore, the system is assumed to be STLC. The steering method sketched in this section follows from the Lie algebra $\mathcal{L}(\triangle)$. The idea is to apply piecewise-constant motion primitives to move in directions given by the P. Hall basis. If the system is nilpotent, then this method reaches the goal state exactly. Otherwise, it leads to an approximate method that can be iterated to get arbitrarily close to the goal. Furthermore, some systems are *nilpotentizable* by using feedback [445].

The main idea is to start with (15.53) and construct an *extended system*

$$\dot{x} = \sum_{i=1}^{s} b_i(x)v_i, \tag{15.114}$$

in which each v_i is an action variable, and b_i is a vector field in $\mathcal{PH}$, the P. Hall basis. For every $i \leq m$, each term of (15.114) is $b_i(x)v_i = h_i(x)u_i$, which comes from the original system. For $i > m$, each b_i represents a Lie product in $\mathcal{PH}$, and v_i is a *fictitious action variable*. It is called fictitious because the velocity given by b_i for $i > m$ cannot necessarily be achieved by using a single action variable of the system. In general, s may be larger than n because at each $x \in X$ a different subset of $\mathcal{PH}$ may be needed to obtain n independent vectors. Also, including more basis elements simplifies some of the coming computations.

Example 15.21 (Extended System for the Nonholonomic Integrator) The extended system for the nonholonomic integrator (15.83) is

$$\begin{pmatrix} \dot{x}_1 \\ \dot{x}_2 \\ \dot{x}_3 \end{pmatrix} = \begin{pmatrix} 1 \\ 0 \\ -x_2 \end{pmatrix} v_1 + \begin{pmatrix} 0 \\ 1 \\ x_1 \end{pmatrix} v_2 + \begin{pmatrix} 0 \\ 0 \\ 2 \end{pmatrix} v_3. \tag{15.115}$$

The first two terms correspond to the original system. The last term arises from the Lie bracket $[h_1, h_2]$. Only one fictitious action variable is needed because the three P. Hall vector fields are independent at every $x \in X$.

It is straightforward to move this system along a grid-based path in $\mathbb{R}^3$. Motions in the x_1 and x_2 directions are obtained by applying $v_1 = u_1$ and $v_2 = u_2$, respectively. To move the system in the x_3 direction, the commutator motion in (15.71) should be performed. This corresponds to applying v_3. The steering method described in this section yields a generalization of this approach. Higher degree Lie products can be used, and motion in any direction can be achieved. ∎

Suppose some x_I and x_G are given. There are two phases to the steering method:

1. Determine an action trajectory $\tilde{v}$ for the extended system, for which $x(0) = x_I$ and $x(t_F) = x_G$ for some $t_F > 0$.

2. Convert $\tilde{v}$ into an action trajectory $\tilde{u}$ that eliminates the fictitious variables and uses the actual m action variables $u_1, \ldots, u_m$.

The first phase is straightforward. For the extended system, any velocity in the tangent space, $T_x(X)$, can be generated. Start with any smooth path $\tau : [0, 1] \to X$ such that $\tau(0) = x_I$ and $\tau(1) = x_G$. The velocity $\dot{\tau}(t)$ along the path τ is a velocity vector in $T_{\tau(t)}(X)$ that can be expressed as a linear combination of the $b_i(\tau(t))$ vectors using linear algebra. The coefficients of this combination are the v_i values. The second phase is much more complicated and will be described shortly. If the system is nilpotent, then $\tilde{u}$ should bring the system precisely from x_I to x_G. By the way it is constructed, it will also be clear how to refine $\tilde{u}$ to come as close as desired to the trajectory produced by $\tilde{v}$.

Formal calculations

The second phase is solved using formal algebraic computations. This means that the particular vector fields, differentiation, manifolds, and so on, can be ignored. The concepts involve pure algebraic manipulation. To avoid confusion with previous definitions, the term *formal* will be added to many coming definitions. Recall from Section 4.4.1 the formal definitions of the algebra of polynomials (e.g., $\mathbb{F}[x_1, \ldots, x_n]$). Let $A(y_1, \ldots, y_m)$ denote the *formal noncommutative algebra*[11] of polynomials in the variables $y_1, \ldots, y_m$. The y_i here are treated as symbols and have no other assumed properties (e.g, they are not necessarily vector fields). When polynomials are multiplied in this algebra, no simplifications can be made based on commutativity. The algebra can be converted into a Lie algebra by defining a Lie bracket. For any two polynomials $p, q \in A(y_1, \ldots, y_m)$, define the *formal Lie bracket* to be $[p, q] = pq - qp$. The formal Lie bracket yields an equivalence relation on the algebra; this results in a *formal Lie algebra* $L(y_1, \ldots, y_m)$ (there are many equivalent expressions for the same elements of the algebra when the formal Lie bracket is applied). Nilpotent versions of the formal algebra and formal Lie algebra can be made by forcing all monomials of degree $k + 1$ to be zero. Let these be denoted by $A_k(y_1, \ldots, y_m)$ and $L_k(y_1, \ldots, y_m)$, respectively. The P. Hall basis can be applied to obtain a basis of the formal Lie algebra. Example 15.18 actually corresponds to the basis of $L_3(h_1, h_2, h_3)$ using formal calculations.

The exponential map

The steering problem will be solved by performing calculations on $L_k(y_1, \ldots, y_m)$. The *formal power series* of $A(y_1, \ldots, y_m)$ is the set of all linear combinations of monomials, including those that have an infinite number of terms. Similarly, the *formal Lie series* of $L(y_1, \ldots, y_m)$ can be defined.

The *formal exponential map* is defined for any $p \in A(y_1, \ldots, y_m)$ as

$$e^p = 1 + p + \frac{1}{2!}p^2 + \frac{1}{3!}p^3 + \cdots . \tag{15.116}$$

---

[11] Intuitively, being an algebra means that polynomials can be added and multiplied; for all of the required axioms, see [472].

In the nilpotent case, the *formal exponential map* is defined for any $p \in A_k(y_1, \ldots, y_m)$ as

$$e^p = \sum_{i=0}^{k} \frac{p^i}{i!}. \tag{15.117}$$

The formal series is truncated because all terms with exponents larger than k vanish.

A *formal Lie group* is constructed as

$$G_k(y_1, \ldots, y_m) = \{e^p \mid p \in L_k(y_1, \ldots, y_m)\}. \tag{15.118}$$

If the formal Lie algebra is not nilpotent, then a formal Lie group $G(y_1, \ldots, y_m)$ can be defined as the set of all e^p, in which p is represented using a formal Lie series.

The following example is taken from [577]:

Example 15.22 (Formal Lie Groups) Suppose that the generators x and y are given. Some elements of the formal Lie group $G(x, y)$ are

$$e^x = I + x + \tfrac{1}{2}x^2 + \tfrac{1}{6}x^3 + \cdots, \tag{15.119}$$

$$e^{[x,y]} = I + [x, y] + \tfrac{1}{2}[x, y]^2 + \cdots, \tag{15.120}$$

and

$$e^{x-y+3[x,y]} = I + x - y + 3[x, y] + \cdots, \tag{15.121}$$

in which I is the formal Lie group identity. Some elements of the formal Lie group $G_2(x, y)$ are

$$e^x = I + x + \tfrac{1}{2}x^2, \tag{15.122}$$

$$e^{[x,y]} = I + [x, y], \tag{15.123}$$

and

$$e^{x-y+3[x,y]} = I + x - y + 3[x, y] + \tfrac{1}{2}(x - y)^2. \tag{15.124}$$

∎

To be a group, the axioms given in Section 4.2.1 must be satisfied. The identity is I, and associativity clearly follows from the series representations. Each e^p has an inverse, e^{-p}, because $e^p e^{-p} = I$. The only remaining axiom to satisfy is closure. This is given by the *Campbell-Baker-Hausdorff-Dynkin formula* (or *CBHD formula*), for which the first terms for any $p, q \in G(y_1, \ldots, y_m)$ are

$$\begin{aligned}
\exp(p)\exp(q) = \exp(p + q + \tfrac{1}{2}[p, q] + \tfrac{1}{12}[[p, q], q] - \tfrac{1}{12}[[p, q], p] \\
+ \tfrac{1}{24}[p, [q, [p, q]]] + \cdots),
\end{aligned} \tag{15.125}$$

in which $\exp(x)$ alternatively denotes e^x for any x. The formula also applies to $G_k(y_1, \ldots, y_m)$, but it becomes truncated into a finite series. This fact will be utilized later. Note that $e^p e^q \neq e^{p+q}$, which differs from the standard definition of exponentiation.

The CBHD formula is often expressed as

$$e^p e^q e^{-p} = \exp\left(\sum_{i=0}^{\infty} \frac{\mathrm{Ad}_p^i \, q}{i!}\right), \tag{15.126}$$

in which $\text{Ad}_p^0 q = q$, and $\text{Ad}_p^i q = [p, \text{Ad}_p^{i-1} q]$. The operator Ad provides a compact way to express some nested Lie bracket operations. Additional terms of (15.125) can be obtained using (15.126).

The Chen-Fliess series

The P. Hall basis from Section 15.4.3 applies in general to any Lie algebra. Let $B_1, \ldots, B_s$ denote a P. Hall basis for the nilpotent formal Lie algebra $L_k(y_1, \ldots, y_m)$. An important theorem in the study of formal Lie groups is that every $S \in G_k(y_1, \ldots, y_m)$ can be expressed in terms of the P. Hall basis of its formal Lie algebra as

$$S = e^{z_s B_s} e^{z_{s-1} B_{s-1}} \cdots e^{z_2 B_2} e^{z_1 B_1}, \tag{15.127}$$

which is called the *Chen-Fliess series*. The z_i are sometimes called the backward P. Hall coordinates of S (there is a forward version, for which the terms in (15.127) go from 1 to s, instead of s to 1).

Returning to the system vector fields

Now the formal algebra concepts can be applied to the steering problem. The variables become the system vector fields: $y_i = h_i$ for all i from 1 to m. For the P. Hall basis elements, each B_i becomes b_i. The Lie group becomes the state space X, and the Lie algebra is the familiar Lie algebra over the vector fields, which was introduced in Section 15.4.3. Consider how an element of the Lie group must evolve over time. This can be expressed using the differential equation

$$\dot{S}(t) = S(t)(v_1 b_1 + v_2 b_2 + \cdots + v_s b_s), \tag{15.128}$$

which is initialized with $S(0) = I$. Here, S can be interpreted as a matrix, which may, for example, belong to $SE(3)$.

The solution at every time $t > 0$ can be written using the Chen-Fliess series, (15.127):

$$S(t) = e^{z_s(t)b_s} e^{z_{s-1}(t)b_{s-1}} \cdots e^{z_2(t)b_2} e^{z_1(t)b_1}. \tag{15.129}$$

This indicates that $S(t)$ can be obtained by integrating b_1 for time $z_1(t)$, followed by b_2 for time $z_2(t)$, and so on until b_s is integrated for time $z_s(t)$. Note that the backward P. Hall coordinates now vary over time. If we determine how they evolve over time, then the differential equation in (15.128) is solved.

The next step is to figure out how the backward P. Hall coordinates evolve. Differentiating (15.129) with respect to time yields

$$\dot{S}(t) = \sum_{j=1}^{s} e^{z_s b_s} \cdots e^{z_{j+1} b_{j+1}} \dot{z}_j b_j e^{z_j b_j} \cdots e^{z_1 b_1}. \tag{15.130}$$

The Chen-Fliess-Sussmann equation

There are now two expressions for $\dot{S}$, which are given by (15.128) and (15.130). By equating them, s equations of the form

$$\sum_{j=1}^{s} p_{j,k} \dot{z}_j = v_k \tag{15.131}$$

are obtained, in which $p_{j,k}$ is a polynomial in z_i variables. This makes use of the series representation for each exponential; see Example 15.23.

The evolution of the backward P. Hall coordinates is therefore given by the *Chen-Fliess-Sussmann (CFS) equation*:

$$\dot{z} = Q(z)v, \tag{15.132}$$

in which $Q(z)$ is an $s \times s$ matrix, and $z(0) = 0$. The entries in $Q(z)$ are polynomials; hence, it is possible to integrate the system analytically to obtain expressions for the $z_i(t)$.

A simple example is given, which was worked out in [301]:

Example 15.23 (The CFS Equation for the Nonholonomic Integrator) The extended system for the nonholonomic integrator was given in (15.115). The differential equation (15.128) for the Lie group is

$$\dot{S}(t) = S(t)(v_1 b_1 + v_2 b_2 + v_3 b_3), \tag{15.133}$$

because $s = 3$.

There are two expressions for its solution. The Chen-Fliess series (15.129) becomes

$$S(t) = e^{z_3(t)b_3} e^{z_2(t)b_2} e^{z_1(t)b_1}. \tag{15.134}$$

The initial condition $S(0) = I$ is satisfied if $z_i(0) = 0$ for i from 1 to 3. The second expression for $\dot{S}(t)$ is (15.130), which in the case of the nonholonomic integrator becomes

$$\begin{aligned}
\dot{S}(t) = {} & \dot{z}_3(t)b_3 e^{z_3(t)b_3} e^{z_2(t)b_2} e^{z_1(t)b_1} \\
& + e^{z_3(t)b_3} \dot{z}_2(t)b_2 e^{z_2(t)b_2} e^{z_1(t)b_1} \\
& + e^{z_3(t)b_3} e^{z_2(t)b_2} \dot{z}_1(t)b_1 e^{z_1(t)b_1}.
\end{aligned} \tag{15.135}$$

Note that

$$S^{-1}(t) = e^{-z_1(t)b_1} e^{-z_2(t)b_2} e^{-z_3(t)b_3}. \tag{15.136}$$

Equating (15.133) and (15.135) yields

$$\begin{aligned}
S^{-1}\dot{S} = v_1 b_1 + v_2 b_2 + v_3 b_3 = {} & e^{-z_1 b_1} e^{-z_2 b_2} e^{-z_3 b_3} \dot{z}_3 b_3 e^{z_3 b_3} e^{z_2 b_2} e^{z_1 b_1} \\
& + e^{-z_1 b_1} e^{-z_2 b_2} \dot{z}_2 b_2 e^{z_2 b_2} e^{z_1 b_1} \\
& + e^{-z_1 b_1} \dot{z}_1 b_1 e^{z_1 b_1},
\end{aligned} \tag{15.137}$$

in which the time dependencies have been suppressed to shorten the expression. The formal Lie series expansions, appropriately for the exponentials, are now used. For $i = 1, 2$,

$$e^{z_i b_i} = (I + z_i b_i + \tfrac{1}{2} z_i^2 b_i^2) \tag{15.138}$$

and

$$e^{-z_i b_i} = (I - z_i b_i - \tfrac{1}{2} z_i^2 b_i^2). \tag{15.139}$$

Also,

$$e^{z_3 b_3} = (I + z_3 b_3) \tag{15.140}$$

and

$$e^{-z_3 b_3} = (I - z_3 b_3). \tag{15.141}$$

The truncation is clearly visible in (15.140) and (15.141). The b_3^2 terms are absent because b_3 is a polynomial of degree two, and its square would be of degree four.

Substitution into (15.137), performing noncommutative multiplication, and applying the Lie bracket definition yields

$$\dot{z}_1 b_1 + \dot{z}_2 (b_2 - z_1 b_3) + \dot{z}_3 b_3 = v_1 b_1 + v_2 b_2 + v_3 b_3. \tag{15.142}$$

Equating like terms yields the Chen-Fliess-Sussmann equation

$$\begin{aligned} \dot{z}_1 &= v_1 \\ \dot{z}_2 &= v_2 \\ \dot{z}_3 &= v_3 + z_1 v_2. \end{aligned} \tag{15.143}$$

Recall that $\tilde{v}$ is given. By integrating (15.143) from $z(0) = 0$, the backward P. Hall coordinate trajectory $\tilde{z}$ is obtained. ∎

Using the original action variables

Once the CFS equation has been determined, the problem is almost solved. The action trajectory $\tilde{v}$ was determined from the given state trajectory $\tilde{v}$ and the backward P. Hall coordinate trajectory $\tilde{z}$ is determined by (15.143). The only remaining problem is that the action variables from v_{m+1} to v_s are fictitious because their associated vector fields are not part of the system. They were instead obtained from Lie bracket operations. When these are applied, they interfere with each other because many of them may try to use the same u_i variables from the original system at the same time.

The CBHD formula is used to determine the solution in terms of the system action variables $u_1, \ldots, u_m$. The differential equation now becomes

$$\dot{S}(t) = S(t)(u_1 h_1 + u_2 h_2 + \cdots + u_m h_m), \tag{15.144}$$

which is initialized with $S(0) = I$ and uses the original system instead of the extended system.

When applying vector fields over time, the CBHD formula becomes

$$\exp(tf)\exp(tg) =$$
$$\exp(tf + tg + \frac{t^2}{2}[f, g] + \frac{t^3}{12}[[f, g], g] - \frac{t^3}{12}[[f, g], f] + \frac{t^4}{24}[f, [g, [f, g]]] + \cdots). \tag{15.145}$$

If the system is nilpotent, then this series is truncated, and the exact effect of sequentially combining constant motion primitives can be determined. This leads to a procedure for determining a finite sequence of constant motion primitives that generate a motion in the same direction as prescribed by the extended system and the action trajectory $\tilde{v}$.

15.5.2 Using sinusoidal action trajectories

The steering method presented in this section is based on initial work by Brockett [144] and a substantial generalization of it by Murray and Sastry [730]. The approach applies to several classes of systems for which the growth of independent vector fields occurs as quickly as possible. This means that when the P. Hall basis is constructed, no elements need to be removed due to linear dependency on previous Lie products or system vector fields. For these systems, the approach applies sinusoids of integrally related frequencies to some action variables. This changes some state variables while others are automatically fixed. For more details beyond the presentation here, see [599, 728, 730, 848].

15.5.2.1 Steering the nonholonomic integrator

The main idea of the method can be clearly illustrated for the nonholonomic integrator,

$$\dot{x}_1 = u_1$$
$$\dot{x}_2 = u_2 \quad\quad\quad (15.146)$$
$$\dot{x}_3 = x_1 u_2 - x_2 u_1,$$

which was considered throughout Section 15.5.1. This case will be explained in detail, and the methods obtained by generalizing the principles will subsequently be stated. The presentation given here is based on [730, 848].

As was previously indicated, growing independent vector fields as quickly as possible is important. For the nonholonomic integrator, $[h_1, h_2]$, is linearly independent of h_1 and h_2, as observed in Example 15.12; thus, it satisfies this property. Consider steering the system from some $x_I = x(0)$ to some $x_G = x(1)$ while optimizing the cost functional

$$\int_0^1 \left(u_1(t)^2 + u_2(t)^2\right)dt. \quad\quad\quad (15.147)$$

The problem can be solved by using the constrained Lagrangian formulation, which was given in Section 13.4.3. The first step is to eliminate the u variables. From (15.146), the cost can be expressed in terms of $\dot{x}_1$ and $\dot{x}_2$ by using $\dot{x}_1 = u_1$ and $\dot{x}_2 = u_2$. The third equation in (15.146) can be written as

$$\dot{x}_3 = x_1 \dot{x}_2 - x_2 \dot{x}_1 \quad\quad\quad (15.148)$$

and will be interpreted as a constraint on the Lagrangian, which is combined using a (scalar) Lagrange multiplier as explained in Section 13.4.3. Define the Lagrangian as

$$L(x, \dot{x}) = (\dot{x}_1^2 + \dot{x}_2^2) + \lambda\left(\dot{x}_3 - x_1 \dot{x}_2 + x_2 \dot{x}_1\right), \quad\quad\quad (15.149)$$

in which the first term comes from the integrand of (15.147), and the second term comes from (15.148).

The Euler-Lagrange equation (13.118) yields

$$\ddot{x}_1 + \lambda \dot{x}_2 = 0$$
$$\ddot{x}_2 - \lambda \dot{x}_1 = 0 \quad\quad\quad (15.150)$$
$$\dot{\lambda} = 0.$$

Note that $\dot{\lambda} = 0$ implies that $\lambda(t)$ is constant for all time. To obtain a differential equation that characterizes the optimal action trajectory, use the fact that for $i = 1, 2$, $\dot{x}_i = u_i$ and $\ddot{x}_i = \dot{u}_i$. This yields the equations $\dot{u}_1 = -\lambda \dot{u}_2$ and $\dot{u}_2 = \lambda \dot{u}_1$. These can be represented as second-order linear differential equations. Based on its roots, the solution is

$$u_1(t) = u_1(0)\cos\lambda t - u_2(0)\sin\lambda t$$
$$u_2(t) = u_1(0)\sin\lambda t + u_2(0)\cos\lambda t. \quad\quad\quad (15.151)$$

Given initial and goal states, the optimal action trajectory is found by determining $u_1(0)$, $u_2(0)$, and λ. Suppose that $x_I = x(0) = (0, 0, 0)$ and $x_G = x(1) = (0, 0, a)$ for some $a \in \mathbb{R}$. Other cases can be obtained by applying transformations in $SE(3)$ to the solution.

The state trajectories for x_1 and x_2 can be obtained by integration of (15.151) because $u_i = \dot{x}_i$ for $i = 1$ and $i = 2$. Starting from $x_1(0) = x_2(0) = 0$, this yields

$$x_1(t) = \frac{1}{\lambda}\big(u_1(0)\sin\lambda t + u_2(0)\cos\lambda t - u_2(0)\big)$$
$$x_2(t) = \frac{1}{\lambda}\big(-u_1(0)\cos\lambda t + u_2(0)\sin\lambda t + u_1(0)\big). \tag{15.152}$$

To maintain the constraint that $x_1(1) = x_2(1) = 0$, λ must be chosen as $\lambda = 2k\pi$ for some integer n. Integration of $\dot{x}_3$ yields

$$x_3(t) = \int_0^1 \big(x_1 u_2 - x_2 u_1\big)dt = \frac{1}{\lambda}\big(u_1^2(0) + u_2^2(0)\big) = a. \tag{15.153}$$

The cost is

$$\int_0^1 \big(u_1^2(t) + u_2^2(t)\big)dt = u_1^2(0) + u_2^2(0) = \lambda a. \tag{15.154}$$

The minimum cost is therefore achieved for $k = -1$, which yields $\lambda = 2\pi$ and $\|u\| = 2\pi a$. This fixes the magnitude of $u(0)$, but any direction may be chosen.

The steering problem can be solved in two phases:

1. Apply any action trajectory to steer x_1 and x_2 to their desired values while neglecting to consider x_3.

2. Apply the solution just developed to steer x_3 to the goal while x_1 and x_2 return to their values obtained in the first phase.

This idea can be generalized to other systems.

15.5.2.2 First-order controllable systems

The approach developed for the nonholonomic integrator generalizes to systems of the form

$$\begin{aligned} \dot{x}_i &= u_i && \text{for } i \text{ from 1 to } m \\ \dot{x}_{ij} &= x_i u_j - x_j u_i && \text{for all } i, j \text{ so that } i < j \text{ and } 1 \le j \le m \end{aligned} \tag{15.155}$$

and

$$\begin{aligned} \dot{x}_i &= u_i && \text{for } i \text{ from 1 to } m \\ \dot{x}_{ij} &= x_i u_j && \text{for all } i, j \text{ such that } i < j \text{ and } 1 \le j \le m. \end{aligned} \tag{15.156}$$

Brockett showed in [144] that for such *first-order controllable systems*, the optimal action trajectory is obtained by applying a sum of sinusoids with integrally related frequencies for each of the m action variables. If m is even, then the trajectory for each variable is a sum of $m/2$ sinusoids at frequencies $2\pi, 2 \cdot 2\pi, \ldots, (m/2) \cdot 2\pi$. If m is odd, there are instead $(m-1)/2$ sinusoids; the sequence of frequencies remains the same. Suppose m is even (the odd case is similar). Each action is selected as

$$u_i = \sum_{k=1}^{m/2} a_{ik}\sin 2\pi kt + b_{ik}\cos 2\pi kt. \tag{15.157}$$

The other state variables evolve as

$$x_{ij} = x_{ij}(0) + \frac{1}{2} \sum_{k=1}^{m/2} \frac{1}{k}(a_{jk}b_{ik} - a_{ik}b_{jk}),$$ (15.158)

which provides a constraint similar to (15.153). The periodic behavior of these action trajectories causes the x_i variables to return to their original values while steering the x_{ij} to their desired values. In a sense this is a vector-based generalization in which the scalar case was the nonholonomic integrator.

Once again, a two-phase steering approach is obtained:

1. Apply any action trajectory that brings every x_i to its goal value. The evolution of the x_{ij} states is ignored in this stage.

2. Apply sinusoids of integrally related frequencies to the action variables. Choose each $u_i(0)$ so that x_{ij} reaches its goal value. In this stage, the x_i variables are ignored because they will return to their values obtained in the first stage.

This method has been generalized even further to *second-order controllable systems*:

$$\begin{aligned} \dot{x}_i &= u_i && \text{for } i \text{ from 1 to } m \\ \dot{x}_{ij} &= x_i u_j && \text{for all } i, j \text{ such that } i < j \text{ and } 1 \leq j \leq m \\ \dot{x}_{ijk} &= x_{ij} u_k && \text{for all } (i, j, k) \in J, \end{aligned}$$ (15.159)

in which J is the set of all unique triples formed from distinct $i, j, k \in \{1, \ldots, m\}$ and removing unnecessary permutations due to the Jacobi identity for Lie brackets. For this problem, a three-phase steering method can be developed by using ideas similar to the first-order controllable case. The first phase determines x_i, the second handles x_{ij}, and the third resolves x_{ijk}. See [730, 848] for more details.

15.5.2.3 Chained-form systems

Example 15.17 considered a special case of a *chained-form system*. The system in (15.102) can be generalized to any n as

$$\begin{aligned} \dot{x}_1 &= u_1 && \dot{x}_4 = x_3 u_1 \\ \dot{x}_2 &= u_2 && \vdots \\ \dot{x}_3 &= x_2 u_1 && \dot{x}_n = x_{n-1} u_1. \end{aligned}$$ (15.160)

This can be considered as a system with *higher order controllability*. For these systems, a multi-phase approach is obtained:

1. Apply any action trajectory for u_1 and u_2 that brings x_1 and x_2 to their goal values. The evolution of the other states is ignored in this stage.

2. This phase is repeated for each k from 3 to n. Steer x_k to its desired value by applying

$$u_1 = a \sin 2\pi kt \quad \text{and} \quad u_2 = b \cos 2\pi kt,$$ (15.161)

in which a and b are chosen to satisfy the constraint

$$x_k(1) = x_k(0) + \left(\frac{a}{4\pi}\right)^{(k-2)} \frac{b}{(k-2)!}.$$ (15.162)

Each execution of this phase causes the previous $k - 1$ state variables to return to their previous values.

For a proof of the correctness of the second phase, and more information in general, see [730, 848]. It may appear that very few systems fit the forms given in this section; however, it is sometimes possible to transform systems to fit this form. Recall that the original simple car model in (13.15) was simplified to (15.54). Transformation methods for putting systems into chained form have been developed. For systems that still cannot be put in this form, Fourier techniques can be used to obtain approximate steering methods that are similar in spirit to the methods in this section. When the chained-form system is expressed using Pfaffian constraints, the result is often referred to as the *Goursat normal form*. The method can be extended even further to *multi-chained-form systems*.

15.5.3 Other steering methods

The steering methods presented so far are perhaps the most widely known; however, several other alternatives exist. Most of these follow in the spirit of the methods in Sections 15.5.1 and 15.5.2 by exploiting the properties of a specific class of systems. Some alternatives are briefly surveyed here. This is an active field of research; it is likely that new methods will be developed in the coming years.

Differentially flat systems

Differential flatness has become an important concept in the development of steering methods. It was introduced by Fliess, Lévine, Martin, and Rouchon in [346]; see also [729]. Intuitively, a system is said to be *differentially flat* if a set of variables called *flat outputs* can be found for which all states and actions can be determined from them without integration. This specifically means that for a system $\dot{x} = f(x, u)$ with $X = \mathbb{R}^n$ and $U = \mathbb{R}^m$, there exist *flat outputs* of the form

$$y = h(x, u, \dot{u}, \ldots, u^{(k)}) \tag{15.163}$$

such that there exist functions g and g' for which

$$x = g(y, \dot{y}, \ldots, y^{(j)}) \tag{15.164}$$

and

$$u = g'(y, \dot{y}, \ldots, y^{(j)}). \tag{15.165}$$

One example is the simple car pulling trailers, expressed in (13.19); the flat outputs are the position in $\mathcal{W} = \mathbb{R}^2$ of the last trailer. This property was used for motion planning in [581]. Recent works on the steering of differentially flat systems include [581, 816, 836].

Decoupling vector fields

For mechanical systems in which dynamics is considered, the steering problem becomes complicated by drift. One recent approach is based on establishing that a system is *kinematically controllable*, which means that the system is STLC on the C-space, if traversed using trajectories that start and stop at zero velocity states [159]. The method finds *decoupling vector fields* on the C-space. Any path that is the integral curve of a decoupling vector field in the C-space is executable by the full system with dynamics. If a mechanical system admits such vector fields, then it was proved in [159] that a steering method for $\mathcal{C}$ can be lifted into one for X, the phase space of the mechanical system. This idea was applied to generate an efficient LPM in an RRT planner in [226].

Averaging methods

By decomposing the state trajectory into a low-frequency part that accounts for the long-range evolution of states and a high-frequency part that accounts for small oscillations over short ranges, *averaging methods* enable perturbations to be systematically made to state trajectories. This yields other steering methods based on sinusoidal action trajectories [114, 423, 626, 627].

Variational techniques

As might be expected, the general-purpose gradient-based optimization techniques of Section 14.7 can be applied to the steering of nonholonomic systems. Such methods are based on Newton iterations on the space of possible state trajectories. This leads to a gradient descent that arrives at a local optimum while satisfying the differential constraints. For details on applying such techniques to steer nonholonomic systems, see [278, 336, 599, 902, 927].

Pontryagin's minimum principle

The minimum principle can be helpful in developing a steering method. Due to the close connection between the Euler-Lagrange equation and Hamilton's equations, as mentioned in Section 13.4.4, this should not be surprising. The Euler-Lagrange equation was used in Section 15.5.2 to determine an optimal steering method for the nonholonomic integrator. A steering methodology based on the minimum principle is described in [848]. The optimal curves of Section 15.3 actually represent steering methods obtained from the minimum principle. Unfortunately, for the vast majority of problems, numerical techniques are needed to solve the resulting differential equations. It is generally expected that techniques developed for specific classes, such as the nilpotent, chained-form, or differentially flat systems, perform much better than general-purpose numerical techniques applied to the Euler-Lagrange equation, Hamilton's equations or Pontryagin's minimum principle.

Dynamic programming

The numerical dynamic programming approach of Section 14.5 can be applied to provide optimal steering for virtual any system. To apply it here, the obstacle region X_{free} is empty. The main drawback, however, is that the computational cost is usually too high, particularly if the dimension of X is high. On the other hand, it applies in a very general setting, and Lie group symmetries can be used to apply precomputed trajectories from any initial state. This is certainly a viable approach with systems for which the state space is $SE(2)$ or $SO(3)$.

Further reading

The basic stability and controllability concepts from Section 15.1 appear in many control textbooks, especially ones that specialize in nonlinear control; see [526, 848] for an introduction to nonlinear control. More advanced concepts appear in [158]. For illustrations of many convergence properties in vector fields, see [44]. For linear system theory, see [194]. Brockett's condition and its generalization appeared in [145, 996]. For more on stabilization and feedback control of nonholonomic systems, see [158, 848, 964]. For Lyapunov-based design for feedback control, see [280].

For further reading on the Hamilton-Jacobi-Bellman equation, see [87, 97, 495, 792, 913]. For numerical approaches to its solution (aside from value iteration), see [2, 255, 710]. Linear-quadratic problems are covered in [28, 573]. Pontryagin's original works provide an unusually clear explanation of the minimum principle [804]. For other sources, see [97, 412, 792]. A generalization that incorporates state-space constraints appears in [928].

Works on which Section 15.3 is based are [65, 130, 213, 296, 817, 904, 905, 924]. Optimal curves have been partially characterized in other cases; see [229, 904]. One complication is that optimal curves often involve infinite switching [372, 1000]. There is also interest in nonoptimal curves that nevertheless have good properties, especially for use as a local planning method for car-like robots [31, 360, 523, 797, 850]. For feedback control of car-like robots, see [114, 666].

For further reading on nonholonomic system theory beyond Section 15.4, there are many excellent sources: [85, 114, 115, 158, 481, 728, 744, 848]. A generalization of the Chow-Rashevskii theorem to hybrid systems is presented in [727]. Controllability of a car pulling trailers is studied in [597]. Controllability of a planar hovercraft with thrusters is considered in [672]. The term holonomic is formed from two Greek words meaning "integrable" and "law" [137].

Section 15.5 is based mainly on the steering methods in [577] (Section 15.5.1) and [144, 730] (Section 15.5.2). The method of Section 15.5.1 is extended to time-varying systems in [301]. A multi-rate version is developed in [716]. In [483], it was improved by using a Lyndon basis, as opposed to the P. Hall basis. Another steering method that involves series appears in [156, 157]. For more on chained-form systems, see [860, 903]. For a variant that uses polynomials and the Goursat normal form, instead of sinusoids, see [848]. For other steering methods, see the references suggested in Section 15.5.3.

Exercises

1. Characterize the stability at $(0, 0)$ of the vector field on $X = \mathbb{R}^2$, given by $\dot{x}_1 = x_2$ and $\dot{x}_2 = -x_2^3 - x_1$. Use the Lyapunov function $\phi(x_1, x_2) = x_1^2 + x_2^2$.

2. Repeat Example 15.4, but instead use the cost term $l(x, u) = u^2$.

3. Repeat Example 15.4, but instead for a triple integrator $q^{(3)} = u$ and $U = [-1, 1]$.

4. Determine the precise conditions under which each of the four cases of Example 15.4 occurs. Define a feedback motion plan that causes time-optimal motions.

5. Note that some of the six optimal words for the Dubins car do not appear for the Reeds-Shepp car. For each of these, illustrate why it does not appear.

6. Retrace the steps of the Taylor series argument for deriving the Lie bracket in Section 15.4.2. Arrive at (15.81) by showing all steps in detail (smaller steps are skipped in Section 15.4.2).

7. Determine whether the following system is nonholonomic and STLC:

$$\dot{q}_1 = u_1 \qquad\qquad \dot{q}_4 = q_2^2 u_1$$
$$\dot{q}_2 = u_2 \qquad\qquad \dot{q}_5 = q_1^2 u_2 \qquad\qquad (15.166)$$
$$\dot{q}_3 = q_1 u_2 - q_2 u_1.$$

8. Prove that linear systems $\dot{x} = Ax + Bu$ for constant matrices A and B cannot be nonholonomic.

9. Determine whether the following system is nonholonomic and STLC:

$$\begin{pmatrix} \dot{x} \\ \dot{y} \\ \dot{\theta} \\ \dot{\psi} \end{pmatrix} = \begin{pmatrix} \cos\theta \\ \sin\theta \\ 0 \\ -\sin\psi \end{pmatrix} u_1 + \begin{pmatrix} 0 \\ 0 \\ 1 \\ 1 \end{pmatrix} u_2. \qquad\qquad (15.167)$$

10. Using the commutator motion and constant actions for the differential drive, develop a lattice over its configuration space.

11. Consider a smooth nonlinear system that has only one action variable and an n-dimensional state space for $n > 1$. Are such systems always completely integrable, always nonholonomic, or is either possible?

12. Generalize Example 15.17 to $\mathbb{R}^n$ with two action variables. Determine whether the system is STLC for any $n > 5$.

13. Show that the vector cross product on $\mathbb{R}^3$ indeed produces a Lie algebra when used as a bracket operation.

14. Derive the CFS equation for the following system:

$$\dot{q}_1 = u_1 \qquad\qquad \dot{q}_3 = q_1 u_2 - q_2 u_1$$
$$\dot{q}_2 = u_2 \qquad\qquad \dot{q}_4 = q_2^2 u_1. \qquad\qquad (15.168)$$

Implementations

15. Implement software that computes the P. Hall basis up to any desired order (this is only symbolic computation; the Lie brackets are not expanded).

16. Implement software that displays the appropriate optimal path for the Dubins car, between any given q_I and q_G.

17. Apply the planning algorithm in Section 14.4.2 to numerically determine the Dubins curves. Use Dijkstra's algorithm for the search, and use a high-resolution grid. Can your software obtain the same set of curves as Dubins?

18. Experiment with using Dubins curves as a local planning method (LPM) and metric in an RRT-based planning algorithm. Does using the curves improve execution time? Do they lead to better solutions?

Bibliography

[1] D. Aarno, D. Kragic, and H. I. Christensen. Artificial potential biased probabilistic roadmap method. In *Proceedings IEEE International Conference on Robotics & Automation*, 2004.

[2] R. Abgrall. Numerical discretization of the first-order Hamilton-Jacobi equation on triangular meshes. *Communications on Pure and Applied Mathematics*, 49(12):1339–1373, December 1996.

[3] R. Abraham and J. Marsden. *Foundations of Mechanics*. Addison-Wesley, Reading, MA, 2002.

[4] R. Abraham, J. Marsden, and T. Ratiu. *Manifolds, Tensor Analysis, and Applications, 2nd Ed.* Springer-Verlag, Berlin, 1988.

[5] A. Abrams and R. Ghrist. Finding topology in a factory: Configuration spaces. *The American Mathematics Monthly*, 109:140–150, February 2002.

[6] E. U. Acar and H. Choset. Complete sensor-based coverage with extended-range detectors: A hierarchical decomposition in terms of critical points and Voronoi diagrams. In *Proceedings IEEE/RSJ International Conference on Intelligent Robots and Systems*, 2001.

[7] E. U. Acar and H. Choset. Robust sensor-based coverage of unstructured environments. In *Proceedings IEEE/RSJ International Conference on Intelligent Robots and Systems*, 2001.

[8] C. C. Adams. *The Knot Book: An Elementary Introduction to the Mathematical Theory of Knots*. W. H. Freeman, New York, 1994.

[9] P. Agarwal, M. de Berg, D. Halperin, and M. Sharir. Efficient generation of k-directional assembly sequences. In *ACM Symposium on Discrete Algorithms*, pages 122–131, 1996.

[10] P. K. Agarwal, N. Amenta, B. Aronov, and M. Sharir. Largest placements and motion planning of a convex polygon. In J.-P. Laumond and M. Overmars, editors, *Robotics: The Algorithmic Perspective*. A.K. Peters, Wellesley, MA, 1996.

[11] P. K. Agarwal, B. Aronov, and M. Sharir. Motion planning for a convex polygon in a polygonal environment. *Discrete and Computational Geometry*, 22:201–221, 1999.

[12] P. K. Agarwal, J.-C. Latombe, R. Motwani, and P. Raghavan. Nonholonomic path planning for pushing a disk among obstacles. In *Proceedings IEEE International Conference on Robotics & Automation*, 1997.

[13] P. K. Agarwal, P. Raghavan, and H. Tamaki. Motion planning for a steering constrained robot through moderate obstacles. In *Proceedings ACM Symposium on Computational Geometry*, 1995.

[14] S. Akella, W. H. Huang, K. M. Lynch, and M. T. Mason. Parts feeding on a conveyor with a one joint robot. *Algorithmica*, 26(3/4):313–344, March/April 2000.

[15] S. Akella and S. Hutchinson. Coordinating the motions of multiple robots with specified trajectories. In *Proceedings IEEE International Conference on Robotics & Automation*, pages 624–631, 2002.

[16] R. Alami, J.-P. Laumond, and T. Siméon. Two manipulation planning algorithms. In J.-P. Laumond and M. Overmars, editors, *Algorithms for Robotic Motion and Manipulation*. A.K. Peters, Wellesley, MA, 1997.

[17] R. Alami, T. Siméon, and J.-P. Laumond. A geometrical approach to planning manipulation tasks. In *Proceedings*

International Symposium on Robotics Research, pages 113–119, 1989.

[18] G. Allgower and K. Georg. *Numerical Continuation Methods*. Springer-Verlag, Berlin, 1990.

[19] E. Alpaydin. *Machine Learning*. MIT Press, Cambridge, MA, 2004.

[20] H. Alt, R. Fleischer, M. Kaufmann, K. Mehlhorn, S. Näher, S. Schirra, and C. Uhrig. Approximate motion planning and the complexity of the boundary of the union of simple geometric figures. In *Proceedings ACM Symposium on Computational Geometry*, pages 281–289, 1990.

[21] N. M. Amato, O. B. Bayazit, L. K. Dale, C. Jones, and D. Vallejo. Choosing good distance metrics and local planners for probabilistic roadmap methods. In *Proceedings IEEE International Conference on Robotics & Automation*, pages 630–637, 1998.

[22] N. M. Amato, O. B. Bayazit, L. K. Dale, C. Jones, and D. Vallejo. OBPRM: An obstacle-based PRM for 3D workspaces. In *Proceedings Workshop on Algorithmic Foundations of Robotics*, pages 155–168, 1998.

[23] N. M. Amato, O. B. Bayazit, L. K. Dale, C. Jones, and D. Vallejo. Choosing good distance metrics and local planners for probabilistic roadmap methods. *IEEE Transactions on Robotics & Automation*, 16(4):442–447, Aug 2000.

[24] N. M. Amato, K. A. Dill, and G. Song. Using motion planning to map protein folding landscapes and analyze folding kinetics of known native structures. In *Proceedings 6th ACM International Conference on Computational Molecular Biology (RECOMB)*, pages 2–11, 2002.

[25] N. M. Amato and G. Song. Using motion planning to study protein folding pathways. *Journal of Computational Biology*, 9(2):149–168, 2002.

[26] N. M. Amato and Y. Wu. A randomized roadmap method for path and manipulation planning. In *Proceedings IEEE International Conference on Robotics & Automation*, pages 113–120, 1996.

[27] F. Ancona and A. Bressan. Patchy vector fields and asymptotic stabilization.

ESAIM-Control, Optimisation and Calculus of Variations, 4:445–471, 1999.

[28] B. D. Anderson and J. B. Moore. *Optimal Control: Linear-Quadratic Methods*. Prentice-Hall, Englewood Cliffs, NJ, 1990.

[29] J. Angeles. *Spatial Kinematic Chains. Analysis, Synthesis, and Optimisation*. Springer-Verlag, Berlin, 1982.

[30] J. Angeles. *Fundamentals of Robotic Mechanical Systems: Theory, Methods, and Algorithms*. Springer-Verlag, Berlin, 2003.

[31] D. A. Anisi, J. Hamberg, and X. Hu. Nearly time-optimal paths for a ground vehicle. *Journal of Control Theory and Applications*, November 2003.

[32] E. Anshelevich, S. Owens, F. Lamiraux, and L. E. Kavraki. Deformable volumes in path planning applications. In *Proceedings IEEE International Conference on Robotics & Automation*, pages 2290–2295, 2000.

[33] M. Apaydin, D. Brutlag, C. Guestrin, D. Hsu J.-C. Latombe, and C. Varm. Stochastic roadmap simulation: An efficient representation and algorithm for analyzing molecular motion. *Journal of Computational Biology*, 10:257–281, 2003.

[34] M. D. Ardema and J. M. Skowronski. Dynamic game applied to coordination control of two arm robotic system. In R. P. Hämäläinen and H. K. Ehtamo, editors, *Differential Games – Developments in Modelling and Computation*, pages 118–130. Springer-Verlag, Berlin, 1991.

[35] O. Arikan and D. Forsyth. Interactive motion generation from examples. In *Proceedings ACM SIGGRAPH*, 2002.

[36] E. M. Arkin and R. Hassin. Approximation algorithms for the geometric covering traveling salesman problem. *Discrete Applied Mathematics*, 55:194–218, 1994.

[37] B. Armstrong, O. Khatib, and J. Burdick. The explicit dynamic model and inertial parameters of the Puma 560 arm. In *Proceedings IEEE International Conference on Systems, Man, & Cyberetics*, pages 510–518, 1986.

[38] M. A. Armstrong. *Basic Topology*. Springer-Verlag, New York, 1983.

[39] V. I. Arnold. *Mathematical Methods of Classical Mechanics, 2nd Ed.* Springer-Verlag, Berlin, 1989.

[40] D. S. Arnon. Geometric reasoning with logic and algebra. *Artificial Intelligence Journal*, 37(1–3):37–60, 1988.

[41] B. Aronov, M. de Berg, A. F. van der Stappen, P. Svestka, and J. Vleugels. Motion planning for multiple robots. *Discrete and Computational Geometry*, 22:505–525, 1999.

[42] B. Aronov and M. Sharir. On translational motion planning of a convex polyhedron in 3-space. *SIAM Journal on Computing*, 26(6):1875–1803, December 1997.

[43] K. Arras, N. Tomatis, B. Jensen, and R. Siegwart. Multisensor on-the-fly localization: Precision and reliability for applications. *Robotics and Autonomous Systems*, 34(2–3):131–143, 2001.

[44] D. K. Arrowsmith and C. M. Place. *Dynamical Systems: Differential Equations, Maps, and Chaotic Behaviour.* Chapman & Hall/CRC, New York, 1992.

[45] S. Arulampalam, S. Maskell, N. Gordon, and T. Clapp. A tutorial on particle filters for on-line non-linear/non-Gaussian Bayesian tracking. *IEEE Transactions on Signal Processing*, 50(2):174–188, 2002.

[46] J. Arvo. Fast random rotation matrices. In D. Kirk, editor, *Graphics Gems III*, pages 117–120. Academic, New York, 1992.

[47] S. Arya and D. M. Mount. Algorithms for fast vector quantization. In *IEEE Data Compression Conference*, pages 381–390, March 1993.

[48] S. Arya and D. M. Mount. Approximate nearest neighbor queries in fixed dimensions. In *Proceedings ACM-SIAM Symposium on Discrete Algorithms*, pages 271–280, 1993.

[49] S. Arya, D. M. Mount, N. S. Netanyahu, R. Silverman, and A. Y. Wu. An optimal algorithm for approximate nearest neighbor searching. *Journal of the ACM*, 45:891–923, 1998.

[50] R. B. Ash. *Information Theory.* Dover, New York, 1990.

[51] K. J. Astrom and T. Hagglund. *PID Controllers: Theory, Design, and Tuning, 2nd Ed.* The Instrument, Systems, and Automation Society, Research Triangle Park, NC, 1995.

[52] K. E. Atkinson. *An Introduction to Numerical Analysis.* Wiley, New York, 1978.

[53] A. Atramentov and S. M. LaValle. Efficient nearest neighbor searching for motion planning. In *Proceedings IEEE International Conference on Robotics and Automation*, pages 632–637, 2002.

[54] J.-P. Aubin and A. Cellina. *Differential Inclusions.* Springer-Verlag, Berlin, 1984.

[55] F. Aurenhammer. Voronoi diagrams – A survey of a fundamental geometric structure. *ACM Computing Surveys*, 23:345–405, 1991.

[56] F. Avnaim, J.-D. Boissonnat, and B. Faverjon. A practical exact planning algorithm for polygonal objects amidst polygonal obstacles. In *Proceedings IEEE International Conference on Robotics & Automation*, pages 1656–1660, 1988.

[57] J. Bañon. Implementation and extension of the ladder algorithm. In *Proceedings IEEE International Conference on Robotics & Automation*, pages 1548–1553, 1990.

[58] T. Başar. Game theory and H^∞-optimal control: The continuous-time case. In R. P. Hämäläinen and H. K. Ehtamo, editors, *Differential Games – Developments in Modelling and Computation*, pages 171–186. Springer-Verlag, Berlin, 1991.

[59] T. Başar and P. R. Kumar. On worst case design strategies. *Computers and Mathematics with Applications*, 13(1–3):239–245, 1987.

[60] T. Başar and G. J. Olsder. *Dynamic Noncooperative Game Theory, 2nd Ed.* Academic, London, 1995.

[61] R. A. Baeza, J. C. Culberson, and G. J. E. Rawlins. Searching in the plane. *Information and Computation*, 106(2):234–252, 1993.

[62] B. Baginski. The Z^3 method for fast path planning in dynamic environments. In *Proceedings IASTED Conference on Applications of Control and Robotics*, pages 47–52, 1996.

[63] B. Baginski. *Motion Planning for Manipulators with Many Degrees of*

Freedom – The BB-Method. PhD thesis, Technical University of Munich, 1998.

[64] A. Baker. *Matrix Groups.* Springer-Verlag, Berlin, 2002.

[65] D. J. Balkcom and M. T. Mason. Time optimal trajectories for bounded velocity differential drive vehicles. *International Journal of Robotics Research,* 21(3):199–217, 2002.

[66] D. J. Balkcom and M. T. Mason. Introducing robotic origami folding. In *Proceedings IEEE International Conference on Robotics & Automation,* 2004.

[67] J. E. Banta, Y. Zhien, X. Z. Wang, G. Zhang, M. T. Smith, and M. A. Abidi. A "best-next-view" algorithm for three-dimensional scene reconstruction using range images. In *Proceedings SPIE, vol. 2588,* pages 418–29, 1995.

[68] J. Barraquand and P. Ferbach. A penalty function method for constrained motion planning. In *Proceedings IEEE International Conference on Robotics & Automation,* pages 1235–1242, 1994.

[69] J. Barraquand and P. Ferbach. Motion planning with uncertainty: The information space approach. In *Proceedings IEEE International Conference on Robotics & Automation,* pages 1341–1348, 1995.

[70] J. Barraquand, L. Kavraki, J.-C. Latombe, T.-Y. Li, R. Motwani, and P. Raghavan. A random sampling scheme for robot path planning. In G. Giralt and G. Hirzinger, editors, *Proceedings International Symposium on Robotics Research,* pages 249–264. Springer-Verlag, New York, 1996.

[71] J. Barraquand and J.-C. Latombe. A Monte-Carlo algorithm for path planning with many degrees of freedom. In *Proceedings IEEE International Conference on Robotics & Automation,* pages 1712–1717, 1990.

[72] J. Barraquand and J.-C. Latombe. Nonholonomic multibody mobile robots: Controllability and motion planning in the presence of obstacles. In *Proceedings IEEE International Conference on Robotics & Automation,* pages 2328–2335, 1991.

[73] J. Barraquand and J.-C. Latombe. Robot motion planning: A distributed representation approach. *International Journal of*

Robotics Research, 10(6):628–649, December 1991.

[74] J. Barraquand and J.-C. Latombe. Nonholonomic multibody mobile robots: Controllability and motion planning in the presence of obstacles. *Algorithmica,* 10:121–155, 1993.

[75] A. G. Barto and R. S. Sutton. *Reinforcement Learning: An Introduction.* MIT Press, Cambridge, MA, 1998.

[76] A. G. Barto, R. S. Sutton, and C. J. C. H. Watkins. Learning and sequential decision making. In M. Gabriel and J.W. Moore, editors, *Learning and Computational Neuroscience: Foundations of Adaptive Networks,* pages 539–602. MIT Press, Cambridge, MA, 1990.

[77] J. Basch, L. J. Guibas, D. Hsu, and A. T. Nguyen. Disconnection proofs for motion planning. In *Proceedings IEEE International Conference on Robotics & Automation,* pages 1765–1772, 2001.

[78] S. Basu, R. Pollack, and M. F. Roy. Computing roadmaps of semi-algebraic sets on a variety. *Journal of the American Society of Mathematics,* 3(1):55–82, 1999.

[79] S. Basu, R. Pollack, and M.-F. Roy. *Algorithms in Real Algebraic Geometry.* Springer-Verlag, Berlin, 2003.

[80] K. Basye and T. Dean. Map learning with indistinguishable locations. In M. Henrion, L. N. Kanal, and J. F. Lemmer, editors, *Uncertainty in Artificial Intelligence 5,* pages 331–340. Elsevier Science, New York, 1990.

[81] K. Basye, T. Dean, J. Kirman, and M. Lejter. A decision-theoretic approach to planning, perception, and control. *IEEE Expert,* 7(4):58–65, August 1992.

[82] T. Bayes. An essay towards solving a problem in the doctrine of chances. *Philosophical Transactions of the Royal Society of London,* 53, 1763.

[83] C. Becker, H. González-Baños, J.-C. Latombe, and C. Tomasi. An intelligent observer. In *Preprints of International Symposium on Experimental Robotics,* pages 94–99, 1995.

[84] K. E. Bekris, B. Y. Chen, A. Ladd, E. Plaku, and L. E. Kavraki. Multiple query probabilistic roadmap planning using single query primitives. In *Proceedings IEEE/RSJ International*

Conference on Intelligent Robots and Systems, 2003.

[85] A. Bellaiche, F. Jean, and J. J. Risler. Geometry of nonholonomic systems. In J.-P. Laumond, editor, *Robot Motion Planning and Control*, pages 55–92. Springer-Verlag, Berlin, 1998.

[86] R. E. Bellman. *Dynamic Programming*. Princeton University Press, Princeton, NJ, 1957.

[87] R. E. Bellman and S. E. Dreyfus. *Applied Dynamic Programming*. Princeton University Press, Princeton, NJ, 1962.

[88] I. Belousov, C. Esteves, J.-P. Laumond, and E. Ferre. Motion planning for large space manipulators with complicated dynamics. In *Proceedings IEEE/RSJ International Conference on Intelligent Robots and Systems*, 2005.

[89] M. A. Bender, A. Fernandez, D. Ron, A. Sahai, and S. Vadhan. The power of a pebble: Exploring and mapping directed graphs. In *Proceedings Annual Symposium on Foundations of Computer Science*, 1998.

[90] A. Benveniste, M. Metivier, and P. Prourier. *Adaptive Algorithms and Stochastic Approximations*. Springer-Verlag, Berlin, 1990.

[91] J. O. Berger. *Statistical Decision Theory*. Springer-Verlag, Berlin, 1980.

[92] M. Bern. Triangulations and mesh generation. In J. E. Goodman and J. O'Rourke, editors, *Handbook of Discrete and Computational Geometry, 2nd Ed.*, pages 563–582. Chapman and Hall/CRC Press, New York, 2004.

[93] J. Bernard, J. Shannan, and M. Vanderploeg. Vehicle rollover on smooth surfaces. In *Proceedings SAE Passenger Car Meeting and Exposition*, Dearborn, MI, 1989.

[94] D. P. Bertsekas. Convergence in discretization procedures in dynamic programming. *IEEE Transactions on Automatic Control*, 20(3):415–419, June 1975.

[95] D. P. Bertsekas. *Dynamic Programming: Deterministic and Stochastic Models*. Prentice-Hall, Englewood Cliffs, NJ, 1987.

[96] D. P. Bertsekas. *Nonlinear Programming*. Athena Scientific, Belmont, MA, 1999.

[97] D. P. Bertsekas. *Dynamic Programming and Optimal Control, Vol. I, 2nd Ed.* Athena Scientific, Belmont, MA, 2001.

[98] D. P. Bertsekas. *Dynamic Programming and Optimal Control, Vol. II, 2nd Ed.* Athena Scientific, Belmont, MA, 2001.

[99] D. P. Bertsekas and J. N. Tsitsiklis. *Neuro-Dynamic Programming*. Athena Scientific, Belmont, MA, 1996.

[100] J. T. Betts. Survey of numerical methods for trajectory optimization. *Journal of Guidance, Control, and Dynamics*, 21(2):193–207, March–April 1998.

[101] A. Beygelzimer, S. M. Kakade, and J. Langford. Cover trees for nearest neighbor. University of Pennsylvania, Available from http://www.cis.upenn.edu/~skakade/papers/ml/cover_tree.pdf, 2005.

[102] A. Bhatia and E. Frazzoli. Incremental search methods for reachability analysis of continuous and hybrid systems. In R. Alur and G. J. Pappas, editors, *Hybrid Systems: Computation and Control*, pages 67–78. Springer-Verlag, Berlin, 2004. Lecture Notes in Computer Science, 2993.

[103] S. Bhattacharya and S. K. Agrawal. Design, experiments and motion planning of a spherical rolling robot. In *Proceedings IEEE International Conference on Robotics & Automation*, pages 1207–1212, 2000.

[104] A. Bicchi, A. Marigo, and B. Piccoli. On the reachability of quantized control systems. *IEEE Transactions on Automatic Control*, 47(4):546–563, April 2002.

[105] A. Bicchi, D. Prattichizzo, and S. Sastry. Planning motions of rolling surfaces. In *Proceedings IEEE Conference Decision & Control*, 1995.

[106] Z. Bien and J. Lee. A minimum-time trajectory planning method for two robots. *IEEE Transactions on Robotics & Automation*, 8(3):414–418, June 1992.

[107] D. Bienstock and P. Seymour. Monotonicity in graph searching. *Journal of Algorithms*, 12:239–245, 1991.

[108] J. Bilmes. A gentle tutorial on the EM algorithm and its application to parameter estimation for Gaussian mixture and hidden Markov models. Technical Report ICSI-TR-97-021, International

Computer Science Institute (ICSI), Berkeley, CA, 1997.

[109] R. L. Bishop and S. I. Goldberg. *Tensor Analysis on Manifolds*. Dover, New York, 1980.

[110] H. S. Black. Stabilized feedback amplifiers. *Bell Systems Technical Journal*, 13:1–18, 1934.

[111] D. Blackwell and M. A. Girshik. *Theory of Games and Statistical Decisions*. Dover, New York, 1979.

[112] S. Blind, C. McCullough, S. Akella, and J. Ponce. Manipulating parts with an array of pins: A method and a machine. *International Journal of Robotics Research*, 20(10):808–818, December 2001.

[113] A. Bloch. *Murphy's Law and Other Reasons Why Things Go Wrong*. Price Stern Sloan Adult, New York, 1977.

[114] A. M. Bloch. *Nonholonomic Mechanics and Control*. Springer-Verlag, Berlin, 2003.

[115] A. M. Bloch and P. E. Crouch. Nonholonomic control systems on Riemannian manifolds. *SIAM Journal on Control and Optimization*, 33:126–148, 1995.

[116] V. D. Blondel and J. N. Tsitsiklis. A survey of computational complexity results in systems and control. *Automatica*, 36(9):1249–1274, September 2000.

[117] A. Blum, S. Chawla, D. Karger, T. Lane, A. Meyerson, and M. Minkoff. Approximation algorithms for orienteering and discounted-reward TSP. In *Proceedings IEEE Symposium on Foundations of Computer Science*, 2003.

[118] A. Blum, P. Raghavan, and B. Schieber. Navigating in unfamiliar geometric terrains. In *Proceedings ACM Symposium on Computational Geometry*, pages 494–504, 1991.

[119] A. L. Blum and M. L. Furst. Fast planing through planning graph analysis. In *Proceedings International Joint Conference on Artificial Intelligence*, pages 1636–1642, 1995.

[120] L. Blum, F. Cucker, and M. Schub abd S. Smale. *Complexity and Real Computation*. Springer-Verlag, Berlin, 1998.

[121] M. Blum and D. Kozen. On the power of the compass (or, why mazes are easier to search than graphs). In *Proceedings Annual Symposium on Foundations*

of Computer Science, pages 132–142, 1978.

[122] J. E. Bobrow. Optimal robot path planning using the minimum-time criterion. *IEEE Transactions on Robotics & Automation*, 4(4):443–450, August 1988.

[123] J. E. Bobrow, S. Dubowsky, and J. S. Gibson. Time-optimal control of robotic manipulators along specified paths. *International Journal of Robotics Research*, 4(3):3–17, 1985.

[124] H. Bode. Feedback: The history of an idea. In R. Bellman and R. Kalaba, editors, *Selected Papers on Mathematical Trends in Control Theory*, pages 106–123. Dover, New York, 1969.

[125] R. Bohlin. Path planning in practice; lazy evaluation on a multi-resolution grid. In *Proceedings IEEE/RSJ International Conference on Intelligent Robots and Systems*, 2001.

[126] R. Bohlin. *Robot Path Planning*. PhD thesis, Chalmers University, Gothenburg, Sweden, 2002.

[127] R. Bohlin and L. Kavraki. Path planning using Lazy PRM. In *Proceedings IEEE International Conference on Robotics & Automation*, 2000.

[128] K.-F. Böhringer, B. R. Donald, and N. C. MacDonald. Upper and lower bounds for programmable vector fields with applications to MEMS and vibratory plate parts feeders. In J.-P. Laumond and M. Overmars, editors, *Algorithms for Robotic Motion and Manipulation*. A. K. Peters, Wellesley, MA, 1997.

[129] J.-D. Boissonnat and M. Yvinec. *Algorithmic Geometry*. Cambridge University Press, Cambridge, U.K., 1998.

[130] J.-.D. Boissonnat, A. Cérézo, and J. Leblond. Shortest paths of bounded curvature in the plane. *Journal of Intelligent and Robotic Systems*, 11:5–20, 1994.

[131] J.-D. Boissonnat and S. Lazard. A polynomial-time algorithm for computing a shortest path of bounded curvature amidst moderate obstacles. In *Proceedings ACM Symposium on Computational Geometry*, pages 242–251, 1996.

[132] V. G. Boltyanskii. Sufficient conditions for optimality and the justification of the dynamic programming method. *SIAM Journal on Control*, 4:326–361, 1966.

[133] G. Boo and K. Goldberg. Orienting polygonal parts without sensors: An implementation in Java. Alpha Lab, UC Berkeley. Available from http://www.ieor.berkeley.edu/~goldberg/feeder-S05/, 2005.

[134] V. Boor, M. H. Overmars, and A. F. van der Stappen. The Gaussian sampling strategy for probabilistic roadmap planners. In *Proceedings IEEE International Conference on Robotics & Automation*, pages 1018–1023, 1999.

[135] W. M. Boothby. *An Introduction to Differentiable Manifolds and Riemannian Geometry. Revised 2nd Ed.* Academic, New York, 2003.

[136] J. Borenstein, B. Everett, and L. Feng. *Navigating Mobile Robots: Systems and Techniques.* A.K. Peters, Wellesley, MA, 1996.

[137] A. V. Borisov and I .S. Mamaev. On the history of the development of nonholonomic dynamics. *Regular and Chaotic Dynamics*, 7(1):43–47, 2002.

[138] P. Bose, A. Lubiv, and J. I. Munro. Efficient visibility queries in simple polygons. In *Proceedings Canadian Conference on Computational Geometry*, pages 23–28, 1992.

[139] M. S. Branicky, V. S. Borkar, and S. K. Mitter. A unified framework for hybrid control: Model and optimal control theory. *IEEE Transactions on Automatic Control*, 43(1):31–45, 1998.

[140] M. S. Branicky, M. M. Curtiss, J. Levine, and S. Morgan. RRTs for nonlinear, discrete, and hybrid planning and control. In *Proceedings IEEE Conference Decision & Control*, 2003.

[141] M. Bridson and A. Haefliger. *Metric Spaces of Non-Positive Curvature.* Springer-Verlag, Berlin, 1999.

[142] A. Briggs. An efficient algorithm for one-step compliant motion planning with uncertainty. In *Proceedings ACM Symposium on Computational Geometry*, 1989.

[143] A. J. Briggs and B. R. Donald. Robust geometric algorithms for sensor planning. In J.-P. Laumond and M. Overmars, editors, *Proceedings Workshop on Algorithmic Foundations of Robotics.* A.K. Peters, Wellesley, MA, 1996.

[144] R. W. Brockett. Control theory and singular Riemannian geometry. In P. A. Fuhrman, editor, *New Directions in Applied Mathematics*, pages 11–27. Springer-Verlag, Berlin, 1981.

[145] R. W. Brockett. Asymptotic stability and feedback stabilization. In R. W. Brockett, R. S. Millman, and H. J. Sussmann, editors, *Differential Geometric Control Theory*, pages 181–191. Birkhäuser, Boston, MA, 1983.

[146] R. A. Brooks and T. Lozano-Pérez. A subdivision algorithm in configuration space for findpath with rotation. *IEEE Transactions on Systems, Man, & Cybernetics*, SMC-15(2):224–233, 1985.

[147] R. C. Brost. Automatic grasp planning in the presence of uncertainty. *International Journal of Robotics Research*, 7(1):3–17, 1988.

[148] R. C. Brost. *Analysis and Planning of Planar Manipulation Tasks.* PhD thesis, Carnegie Mellon University, Pittsburgh, PA, 1991.

[149] R. C. Brost and A. D. Christiansen. Probabilistic analysis of manipulation tasks: A research agenda. In *Proceedings IEEE International Conference on Robotics & Automation*, volume 3, pages 549–556, 1993.

[150] R. C. Brost and A. D. Christiansen. Probabilistic analysis of manipulation tasks: A computational framework. Technical Report SAND92-2033, Sandia National Laboratories, Albuquerque, NM, January 1994.

[151] R. C. Brost and A. D. Christiansen. Probabilistic analysis of manipulation tasks: A computational framework. *International Journal of Robotics Research*, 15(1):1–23, February 1996.

[152] J. Bruce and M. Veloso. Real-time randomized path planning for robot navigation. In *Proceedings IEEE/RSJ International Conference on Intelligent Robots and Systems*, 2002.

[153] A. E. Bryson and Y.-C. Ho. *Applied Optimal Control.* Hemisphere Publishing Corp., New York, 1975.

[154] M. Buckland. *AI Techniques for Game Programming.* Premier Press, Portland, OR, 2002.

[155] S. J. Buckley. Fast motion planning for multiple moving robots. In *Proceedings*

IEEE International Conference on Robotics & Automation, pages 322–326, 1989.

[156] F. Bullo. Series expansions for the evolution of mechanical control systems. *SIAM Journal on Control and Optimization*, 40(1):166–190, 2001.

[157] F. Bullo. Series expansions for analytic systems linear in control. *Automatica*, 38(9):1425–1432, September 2002.

[158] F. Bullo and A. D. Lewis. *Geometric Control of Mechanical Systems*. Springer-Verlag, Berlin, 2004.

[159] F. Bullo and K. M. Lynch. Kinematic controllability for decoupled trajectory planning in underactuated mechanical systems. *IEEE Transactions on Robotics and Automation*, 17(4):402–412, 2001.

[160] J. W. Burdick. *Kinematic Analysis and Design of Redundant Manipulators*. PhD thesis, Stanford University, Stanford, CA, 1988.

[161] W. Burgard, A. B. Cremers, D. Fox, D. Hähnel, G. Lakemeyer, D. Schulz, W. Steiner, and S. Thrun. The interactive museum tour-guide robot. In *Proceedings AAAI National Conference on Artificial Intelligence*, pages 11–18, 1998.

[162] J. J. Burken, P. Lu, and Z. Wu. Reconfigurable flight control designs with application to the X-33 vehicle. Technical Report TM-1999-206582, NASA, Washington, DC, 1999.

[163] B. Burns and O. Brock. Sampling-based motion planning using predictive models. In *Proceedings IEEE International Conference on Robotics & Automation*, 2005.

[164] R. R. Burridge, A. A. Rizzi, and D. E. Koditschek. Sequential composition of dynamically dexterous robot behaviors. *International Journal of Robotics Research*, 18(6):534–555, 1999.

[165] L. G. Bushnell, D. M. Tilbury, and S. S. Sastry. Steering three-input nonholonomic systems: the fire truck example. *International Journal of Robotics Research*, 14(4):366–381, 1995.

[166] Z. J. Butler, A. A. Rizzi, and R. L. Hollis. Contact sensor-based coverage of rectilinear environments. In *IEEE Symposium on Intelligent Control*, 1999.

[167] Z. J. Butler and D. Rus. Distributed motion planning for modular robots

with unit-compressible modules. *International Journal of Robotics Research*, 22(9):699–716, 2003.

[168] S. Cambon, F. Gravot, and R. Alami. A robot task planner and merges symbolic and geometric reasoning. In *Proceedings European Conference on Artificial Intelligence*, 2004.

[169] S. Cameron. A comparison of two fast algorithms for computing the distance between convex polyhedra. *IEEE Transactions on Robotics & Automation*, 13(6):915–920, December 1997.

[170] F. Camilli and M. Falcone. Approximation of optimal control problems with state constraints: Estimates and applications. In B. S. Mordukhovich and H. J. Sussmann, editors, *Nonsmooth Analysis and Geometric Methods in Deterministic Optimal Control*, pages 23–57. Springer-Verlag, Berlin, 1996. Mathematics and its Applications, Vol. 78.

[171] J. Canny. Constructing roadmaps of semi-algebraic sets I. *Artificial Intelligence Journal*, 37:203–222, 1988.

[172] J. Canny. Computing roadmaps of general semi-algebraic sets. *The Computer Journal*, 36(5):504–514, 1993.

[173] J. Canny, A. Rege, and J. Reif. An exact algorithm for kinodynamic planning in the plane. *Discrete and Computational Geometry*, 6:461–484, 1991.

[174] J. Canny and J. Reif. New lower bound techniques for robot motion planning problems. In *Proceedings IEEE Symposium on Foundations of Computer Science*, pages 49–60, 1987.

[175] J. F. Canny. *The Complexity of Robot Motion Planning*. MIT Press, Cambridge, MA, 1988.

[176] J. F. Canny. On computability of fine motion plans. In *Proceedings IEEE International Conference on Robotics & Automation*, pages 177–182, 1989.

[177] J. F. Canny and K. Y. Goldberg. "RISC" industrial robots: Recent results and current trends. In *Proceedings IEEE International Conference on Robotics & Automation*, pages 1951–1958, 1994.

[178] J. F. Canny and M. Lin. An opportunistic global path planner. *Algorithmica*, 10:102–120, 1993.

[179] S. Carpin and E. Pagello. On parallel RRTs for multi-robot systems. In

Proceedings 8th Conference of the Italian Association for Artificial Intelligence, pages 834–841, 2002.

[180] S. Carpin and G. Pillonetto. Merging the adaptive random walks planner with the randomized potential field planner. In *Proceedings IEEE International Workshop on Robot Motion and Control*, pages 151–156, 2005.

[181] S. Carpin and G. Pillonetto. Robot motion planning using adaptive random walks. *IEEE Transactions on Robotics & Automation*, 21(1):129–136, 2005.

[182] A. Casal. *Reconfiguration Planning for Modular Self-Reconfigurable Robots*. PhD thesis, Stanford University, Stanford, CA, 2002.

[183] S. Caselli and M. Reggiani. ERPP: An experience-based randomized path planner. In *Proceedings IEEE International Conference on Robotics & Automation*, 2000.

[184] J. Castellanos, J. Montiel, J. Neira, and J. Tardós. The SPmap: A probabilistic framework for simultaneous localization and mapping. *IEEE Transactions on Robotics & Automation*, 15(5):948–953, 1999.

[185] D. Challou, D. Boley, M. Gini, and V. Kumar. A parallel formulation of informed randomized search for robot motion planning problems. In *Proceedings IEEE International Conference on Robotics & Automation*, pages 709–714, 1995.

[186] D. D. Champeaux. Bidirectional heuristic search again. *Journal of the ACM*, 30(1):22–32, January 1983.

[187] D. D. Champeaux and L. Sint. An improved bidirectional heuristic search algorithm. *Journal of the ACM*, 24(2):177–191, April 1977.

[188] H. Chang and T. Y. Li. Assembly maintainability study with motion planning. In *Proceedings IEEE International Conference on Robotics & Automation*, pages 1012–1019, 1995.

[189] S. Charentus. *Modeling and Control of a Robot Manipulator Composed of Several Stewart Platforms*. PhD thesis, Université Paul Sabatier, Toulouse, France, 1990. In French.

[190] S. Chawla. *Graph Algorithms for Planning and Partitioning*. PhD thesis, Carnegie Mellon University, Pittsburgh, PA, June 2005.

[191] B. Chazelle. Approximation and decomposition of shapes. In J. T. Schwartz and C. K. Yap, editors, *Algorithmic and Geometric Aspects of Robotics*, pages 145–185. Lawrence Erlbaum Associates, Hillsdale, NJ, 1987.

[192] B. Chazelle. Triangulating a simple polygon in linear time. *Discrete and Computational Geometry*, 6(5):485–524, 1991.

[193] B. Chazelle. *The Discrepancy Method*. Cambridge University Press, Cambridge, U.K., 2000.

[194] C.-T. Chen. *Linear System Theory and Design*. Holt, Rinehart, and Winston, New York, 1984.

[195] P. C. Chen and Y. K. Hwang. SANDROS: A motion planner with performance proportional to task difficulty. In *Proceedings IEEE International Conference on Robotics & Automation*, pages 2346–2353, 1992.

[196] P. C. Chen and Y. K. Hwang. SANDROS: A dynamic search graph algorithm for motion planning. *IEEE Transactions on Robotics & Automation*, 14(3):390–403, 1998.

[197] Y.-B. Chen and D. J. Ierardi. The complexity of oblivious plans for orienting and distinguishing polygonal parts. *Algorithmica*, 14:367–397, 1995.

[198] P. Cheng. *Sampling-Based Motion Planning with Differential Constraints*. PhD thesis, University of Illinois, Urbana, IL, August 2005.

[199] P. Cheng, E. Frazzoli, and S. M. LaValle. Exploiting group symmetries to improve precision in kinodynamic and nonholonomic planning. In *IEEE/RSJ International Conference on Intelligent Robots and Systems*, 2003.

[200] P. Cheng, E. Frazzoli, and S. M. LaValle. Improving the performance of sampling-based planners by using a symmetry-exploiting gap reduction algorithm. In *Proceedings IEEE International Conference on Robotics and Automation*, 2004.

[201] P. Cheng and S. M. LaValle. Reducing metric sensitivity in randomized trajectory design. In *Proceedings IEEE/RSJ*

International Conference on Intelligent Robots and Systems, pages 43–48, 2001.

[202] P. Cheng and S. M. LaValle. Resolution complete rapidly-exploring random trees. In *Proceedings IEEE International Conference on Robotics and Automation*, pages 267–272, 2002.

[203] P. Cheng, Z. Shen, and S. M. LaValle. Using randomization to find and optimize feasible trajectories for nonlinear systems. In *Proceedings Annual Allerton Conference on Communications, Control, Computing*, pages 926–935, 2000.

[204] P. Cheng, Z. Shen, and S. M. LaValle. RRT-based trajectory design for autonomous automobiles and spacecraft. *Archives of Control Sciences*, 11(3–4):167–194, 2001.

[205] M. Cherif. Kinodynamic motion planning for all-terrain wheeled vehicles. In *Proceedings IEEE International Conference on Robotics & Automation*, 1999.

[206] F. L. Chernousko, N. N. Bolotnik, and V. G. Gradetsky. *Manipulation Robots*. CRC Press, Boca Raton, FL, 1994.

[207] L. P. Chew and K. Kedem. A convex polygon among polygonal obstacles: Placement and high-clearance motion. *Computational Geometry: Theory and Applications*, 3:59–89, 1993.

[208] D. Chibisov, E. W. Mayr, and S. Pankratov. Spatial planning and geometric optimization: Combining configuration space and energy methods. In H. Hong and D. Wang, editors, *Automated Deduction in Geometry – ADG 2004*. Springer-Verlag, Berlin, 2006.

[209] S. Chien, R. Sherwood, D. Tran, B. Cichy, D. Mandl, S. Frye, B. Trout, S. Shulman, and D. Boyer. Using autonomy flight software to improve science return on Earth Observing One. *Journal of Aerospace Computing, Information, and Communication*, 2:196–216, April 2005.

[210] W.-P. Chin and S. Ntafos. Optimum watchman routes. *Information Processing Letters*, 28:39–44, 1988.

[211] G. Chirikjian, A. Pamecha, and I. Ebert-Uphoff. Evaluating efficiency of self-reconfiguration in a class of modular robots. *Journal of Robotic Systems*, 13(5):717–338, 1996.

[212] G. S. Chirikjian and A. B. Kyatkin. *Engineering Applications of Noncommutative Harmonic Analysis*. CRC Press, Boca Raton, FL, 2001.

[213] H. Chitsaz, S. M. LaValle, D. J. Balkcom, and M. T. Mason. Minimum wheel-rotation paths for differential-drive mobile robots. In *Proceedings IEEE International Conference on Robotics and Automation*, 2006.

[214] H. Chitsaz, J. M. O'Kane, and S. M. LaValle. Pareto-optimal coordination of two translating polygonal robots on an acyclic roadmap. In *Proceedings IEEE International Conference on Robotics and Automation*, 2004.

[215] S. Chitta, P. Cheng, E. Frazzoli, and V. Kumar. RoboTrikke: A novel undulatory locomotion system. In *Proceedings IEEE International Conference on Robotics & Automation*, 2005.

[216] S. Chitta and V. Kumar. Dynamics and generation of gaits for a planar rollerblader. In *Proceedings IEEE/RSJ International Conference on Intelligent Robots and Systems*, 2003.

[217] J. Choi, J. Sellen, and C. K. Yap. Precision-sensitive Euclidean shortest path in 3-space. In *Proceedings ACM Symposium on Computational Geometry*, pages 350–359, 1995.

[218] H. Choset. Coverage of known spaces: The boustrophedon cellular decomposition. *Autonomous Robots*, 9:247–253, 2000.

[219] H. Choset. Coverage for robotics – A survey of recent results. *Annals of Mathematics and Artificial Intelligence*, 31:113–126, 2001.

[220] H. Choset and J. Burdick. Sensor based motion planning: Incremental construction of the hierarchical generalized Voronoi graph. *International Journal of Robotics Research*, 19(2):126–148, 2000.

[221] H. Choset and J. Burdick. Sensor based motion planning: The hierarchical generalized Voronoi graph. *International Journal of Robotics Research*, 19(2):96–125, 2000.

[222] H. Choset, K. M. Lynch, S. Hutchinson, G. Kantor, W. Burgard, L. E. Kavraki, and S. Thrun. *Principles of Robot Motion: Theory, Algorithms, and*

Implementations. MIT Press, Cambridge, MA, 2005.

[223] H. Choset and K. Nagatani. Topological simultaneous localization and mapping (T-SLAM). *IEEE Transactions on Robotics & Automation*, 17(2):125–137, 2001.

[224] H. Choset and P. Pignon. Cover path planning: The boustrophedon decomposition. In *Proceedings International Conference on Field and Service Robotics*, Canberra, Australia, December 1997.

[225] P. Choudhury and K. Lynch. Rolling manipulation with a single control. In *Proceedings Conference on Control Applications*, September 2002.

[226] P. Choudhury and K. Lynch. Trajectory planning for second-order underactuated mechanical systems in presence of obstacles. In *Proceedings Workshop on Algorithmic Foundations of Robotics*, 2002.

[227] K.-C. Chu. Team decision theory and information structures in optimal control problems – Part II. *IEEE Transactions on Automatic Control*, 17(1):22–28, February 1972.

[228] C. K. Chui and G. Chen. *Kalman Filtering*. Springer-Verlag, Berlin, 1991.

[229] M. Chyba, H. Sussmann, H. Maurer, and G. Vossen. Underwater vehicles: The minimum time problem. In *Proceedings IEEE Conference Decision & Control*, The Bahamas, December 2004.

[230] C. M. Clark, S. M. Rock, and J.-C. Latombe. Motion planning for multiple mobile robots using dynamic networks. In *Proceedings IEEE International Conference on Robotics & Automation*, 2003.

[231] D. E. Clark, G. Jones, P. Willett P. W. Kenny, and R. C. Glen. Pharmacophoric pattern matching in files of three-dimensional chemical structures: Comparison of conformational searching algorithms for flexible searching. *Journal Chemical Information and Computational Sciences*, 34:197–206, 1994.

[232] K. L. Clarkson. Nearest neighbor searching in metric spaces: Experimental results for sb(s). Bell Labs. Available from http://cm.bell-labs.com/who/clarkson/Msb/readme.html, 2003.

[233] F. S. Cohen and D. B. Cooper. Simple parallel hierarchical and relaxation algorithms for segmenting noncausal Markovian random fields. *IEEE Transactions Pattern Analysis Machine Intelligence*, 9(2):195–219, March 1987.

[234] G. E. Collins. Quantifier elimination for real closed fields by cylindrical algebraic decomposition. In *Proceedings Second GI Conference on Automata Theory and Formal Languages*, pages 134–183, Berlin, 1975. Springer-Verlag. Lecture Notes in Computer Science, 33.

[235] G. E. Collins. Quantifier elimination by cylindrical algebraic decomposition – twenty years of progress. In B. F. Caviness and J. R. Johnson, editors, *Quantifier Elimination and Cylindrical Algebraic Decomposition*, pages 8–23. Springer-Verlag, Berlin, 1998.

[236] L. Conlon. *Differentiable Manifolds, 2nd Ed.* Birkhäuser, Boston, MA, 2001.

[237] D. C. Conner, A. A. Rizzi, and H. Choset. Composition of local potential functions for global robot control and navigation. In *Proceedings IEEE/RSJ International Conference on Intelligent Robots and Systems*, pages 3546–3551, 2003.

[238] C. Connolly and R. Grupen. The application of harmonic potential functions to robotics. *Journal of Robotic Systems*, 10(7):931–946, 1993.

[239] C. Connolly, R. Grupen, and K. Souccar. A Hamiltonian framework for kinodynamic planning. In *Proceedings IEEE International Conference on Robotics & Automation*, 1995.

[240] C. I. Connolly. The determination of next best views. In *Proceedings IEEE International Conference on Robotics & Automation*, pages 432–435, 1985.

[241] C. I. Connolly. Applications of harmonic functions to robotics. In *IEEE Symposium on Intelligent Control*, pages 498–502, 1992.

[242] C. I. Connolly, J. B. Burns, and R. Weiss. Path planning using Laplace's equation. In *Proceedings IEEE International Conference on Robotics & Automation*, pages 2102–2106, May 1990.

[243] J. H. Conway and N. J. A. Sloane. *Sphere Packings, Lattices, and Groups.* Springer-Verlag, Berlin, 1999.

[244] H. W. Corley. Some multiple objective dynamic programs. *IEEE Transactions on Automatic Control*, 30(12):1221–1222, December 1985.

[245] T. H. Cormen, C. E. Leiserson, R. L. Rivest, and C. Stein. *Introduction to Algorithms (2nd Ed.).* MIT Press, Cambridge, MA, 2001.

[246] J. Cortés. *Motion Planning Algorithms for General Closed-Chain Mechanisms.* PhD thesis, Institut National Polytechnique de Toulouse, Toulouse, France, 2003.

[247] J. Cortés, T. Siméon M. Remaud-Siméon, and V. Tran. Geometric algorithms for the conformational analysis of long protein loops. *Journal of Computational Chemistry*, 25:956–967, 2004.

[248] J. Cortés, T. Siméon, and J.-P. Laumond. A random loop generator for planning the motions of closed kinematic chains using PRM methods. In *Proceedings IEEE International Conference on Robotics & Automation*, 2002.

[249] M. G. Coutinho. *Dynamic Simulations of Multibody Systems.* Springer-Verlag, Berlin, 2001.

[250] T. M. Cover and J. A. Thomas. *Elements of Information Theory.* Wiley, New York, 1991.

[251] N. Cowan. Composing navigation functions on Cartesian products of manifolds with boundary. In *Proceedings Workshop on Algorithmic Foundations of Robotics*, Zeist, The Netherlands, July 2004.

[252] D. Cox, J. Little, and D. O'Shea. *Ideals, Varieties, and Algorithms.* Springer-Verlag, Berlin, 1992.

[253] H. S. M. Coxeter. *Regular Polytopes.* Dover, New York, 1973.

[254] J. J. Craig. *Introduction to Robotics.* Addison-Wesley, Reading, MA, 1989.

[255] M. G. Crandall and P.-L. Lions. Viscosity solutions of Hamilton-Jacobi equations. *Transactions of the American Mathematical Society*, 277(1):1–42, 1983.

[256] D. Crass, I. Suzuki, and M. Yamashita. Searching for a mobile intruder in a corridor – The open edge variant of the polygon search problem. *International Journal Computational Geometry & Applications*, 5(4):397–412, 1995.

[257] J. C. Culberson. Sokoban is PSPACE-complete. In *Proceedings International Conference on Fun with Algorithms (FUN98)*, pages 65–76, Waterloo, Ontario, Canada, June 1998. Carleton Scientific.

[258] M. R. Cutkosky. *Robotic Grasping and Fine Manipulation.* Kluwer, Boston, MA, 1985.

[259] L. K. Dale and N. M. Amato. Probabilistic roadmap methods are embarrassingly parallel. In *Proceedings IEEE International Conference on Robotics & Automation*, 1999.

[260] F. Dallaert, D. Fox, W. Burgard, and S. Thrun. Monte Carlo localization for mobile robots. In *Proceedings IEEE International Conference on Robotics & Automation*, 1999.

[261] G. B. Dantzig. *Linear Programming and Extensions.* Princeton University Press, Princeton, NJ, 1963.

[262] A. Datta, C. A. Hipke, and S. Schuierer. Competitive searching in polygons—beyond generalized streets. In J. Staples, P. Eades, N. Katoh, and A. Moffat, editors, *Algorithms and Computation, ISAAC '95*, pages 32–41. Springer-Verlag, Berlin, 1995.

[263] R. S. Datta. Using computer algebra to compute Nash equilibria. In *Proceedings International Symposium on Symbolic and Algebraic Computation*, 2003.

[264] J. Davenport and J. Heintz. Real quantifier elimination is doubly exponential. *Journal of Symbolic Computation*, 5:29–35, 1988.

[265] S. Davies. Multidimensional triangulation and interpolation for reinforcement learning. In *Proceedings Neural Information Processing Systems*, 1996.

[266] M. de Berg, M. van Kreveld, M. Overmars, and O. Schwarzkopf. *Computational Geometry: Algorithms and Applications, 2nd Ed.* Springer-Verlag, Berlin, 2000.

[267] M. J. de Smith. *Distance and Path: The Development, Interpretation and Application of Distance Measurement in Mapping and Modelling.* PhD thesis,

University College, University of London, London, 2003.

[268] T. Dean and S. Kambhampati. Planning and scheduling. In A. B. Tucker, editor, *The CRC Handbook of Computer Science and Engineering*, pages 614–636. CRC Press, Boca Raton, FL, 1997.

[269] T. L. Dean and M. P. Wellman. *Planning and Control*. Morgan Kaufman, San Francisco, CA, 1991.

[270] M. H. DeGroot. *Optimal Statistical Decisions*. McGraw-Hill, New York, 1970.

[271] A. P. Dempster, N. M. Laird, and D. B. Rubin. Maximum-likelihood from incomplete data via the EM algorithm. *Journal of the Royal Statistical Society, Ser. B.*, 39:1–38, 1977.

[272] X. Deng, T. Kameda, and C. Papadimitriou. How to learn an unknown environment I: The rectilinear case. Available from http://www.cs.berkeley.edu/~christos/, 1997.

[273] P. A. Devijver and J. Kittler. *Pattern Recognition: A Statistical Approach*. Prentice-Hall, Englewood Cliffs, NJ, 1982.

[274] R. Dial. Algorithm 360: Shortest path forest with topological ordering. *Communications of the ACM*, 12:632–633, 1969.

[275] E. W. Dijkstra. A note on two problems in connexion with graphs. *Numerische Mathematik*, 1:269–271, 1959.

[276] D. V. Dimarogonas, M. M. Zavlanos, S. G. Loizou, and K. J. Kyriakopoulos. Decentralized motion control of multiple holonomic agents under input constraints. In *Proceedings IEEE Conference Decision & Control*, 2003.

[277] G. Dissanayake, P. Newman, S. Clark, H. F. Durrant-Whyte, and M. Csorba. A solution to the simultaneous localisation and map building (SLAM) problem. *IEEE Transactions on Robotics & Automation*, 17(3):229–241, 2001.

[278] A. W. Divelbiss and J. T. Wen. Nonholonomic path planning with inequality constraints. In *Proceedings IEEE International Conference on Robotics & Automation*, pages 52–57, 1994.

[279] A. W. Divelbiss and J. T. Wen. A path-space approach to nonholonomic planning in the presence of obstacles. *IEEE Transactions on Robotics & Automation*, 13(3):443–451, 1997.

[280] W. E. Dixon, A. Behal, D. M. Dawson, and S. Nagarkatti. *Nonlinear Control of Engineering Systems: A Lyapunov-Based Approach*. Birkhäuser, Boston, MA, 2003.

[281] M. P. do Carmo. *Riemannian Geometry*. Birkhäuser, Boston, MA, 1992.

[282] B. R. Donald. Motion planning with six degrees of freedom. Technical Report AI-TR-791, Artificial Intelligence Lab., Massachusetts Institute of Technology, Cambridge, MA, 1984.

[283] B. R. Donald. *Error Detection and Recovery for Robot Motion Planning with Uncertainty*. PhD thesis, Massachusetts Institute of Technology, Cambridge, MA, 1987.

[284] B. R. Donald. A search algorithm for motion planning with six degrees of freedom. *Artificial Intelligence Journal*, 31:295–353, 1987.

[285] B. R. Donald. The complexity of planar compliant motion planning under uncertainty. In *Proceedings ACM Symposium on Computational Geometry*, pages 309–318, 1988.

[286] B. R. Donald. A geometric approach to error detection and recovery for robot motion planning with uncertainty. *Artificial Intelligence Journal*, 37:223–271, 1988.

[287] B. R. Donald. Planning multi-step error detection and recovery strategies. *International Journal of Robotics Research*, 9(1):3–60, 1990.

[288] B. R. Donald. On information invariants in robotics. *Artificial Intelligence Journal*, 72:217–304, 1995.

[289] B. R. Donald and J. Jennings. Sensor interpretation and task-directed planning using perceptual equivalence classes. In *Proceedings IEEE International Conference on Robotics & Automation*, pages 190–197, 1991.

[290] B. R. Donald and P. Xavier. Provably good approximation algorithms for optimal kinodynamic planning for Cartesian robots and open chain manipulators. *Algorithmica*, 14(6):480–530, 1995.

[291] B. R. Donald and P. Xavier. Provably good approximation algorithms for

optimal kinodynamic planning: Robots with decoupled dynamics bounds. *Algorithmica*, 14(6):443–479, 1995.

[292] B. R. Donald, P. G. Xavier, J. Canny, and J. Reif. Kinodynamic planning. *Journal of the ACM*, 40:1048–66, November 1993.

[293] S. K. Donaldson. Self-dual connections and the topology of smooth 4-manifold. *Bulletin of the American Mathematical Society*, 8:81–83, 1983.

[294] A. L. Dontchev. Discrete approximations in optimal control. In B. S. Mordukhovich and H. J. Sussmann, editors, *Nonsmooth Analysis and Geometric Methods in Deterministic Optimal Control*, pages 59–80. Springer-Verlag, Berlin, 1996. Mathematics and Its Applications, Vol. 78.

[295] A. Doucet, N. de Freitas, and N. Gordon. *Sequential Monte Carlo Methods in Practice*. Springer-Verlag, Berlin, 2001.

[296] L. E. Dubins. On curves of minimal length with a constraint on average curvature, and with prescribed initial and terminal positions and tangents. *American Journal of Mathematics*, 79:497–516, 1957.

[297] R. O. Duda, P. E. Hart, and D. G. Stork. *Pattern Classification, 2nd Ed.* Wiley, New York, 2000.

[298] G. Dudek and M. Jenkin. *Computational Principles of Mobile Robotics*. Cambridge University Press, Cambridge, U.K., 2000.

[299] G. Dudek, M. Jenkin, E. Milios, and D. Wilkes. Map validation and self-location in a graph-like world. In *Proceedings AAAI National Conference on Artificial Intelligence*, pages 1648–1653, 1993.

[300] G. Dudek, K. Romanik, and S. Whitesides. Global localization: Localizing a robot with minimal travel. *SIAM Journal on Computing*, 27(2):583–604, April 1998.

[301] I. Duleba. *Algorithms of Motion Planning for Nonholonomic Robots*. Technical University of Wroclaw, Wroclaw, Poland, 1998.

[302] G. E. Dullerud and R. D'Andrea. Distributed control of heterogeneous systems. *IEEE Transactions on Automatic Control*, 49(12):2113–2128, 2004.

[303] G. E. Dullerud and F. Paganini. *A Course in Robust Control Theory*. Springer-Verlag, Berlin, 2000.

[304] H. Edelsbrunner. *Algorithms in Combinatorial Geometry*. Springer-Verlag, Berlin, 1987.

[305] C. Edwards and S. K. Spurgeon. *Sliding Mode Control: Theory and Applications*. CRC Press, Ann Arbor, MI, 1998.

[306] A. Efrat, L. J. Guibas, D. C. Lin, J. S. B. Mitchell, and T. M. Murali. Sweeping simple polygons with a chain of guards. In *Proceedings ACM-SIAM Symposium on Discrete Algorithms*, 2000.

[307] M. Egerstedt and X. Hu. Formation constrained multi-agent control. *IEEE Transactions on Robotics & Automation*, 17(6):947–951, December 2001.

[308] S. Ehmann and M.C. Lin. Accurate and fast proximity queries between polyhedra using convex surface decomposition. In *Proceedings Eurographics* 2001.

[309] A. Elfes. Using occupancy grids for mobile robot perception and navigation. *IEEE Computer*, 22(6):46–57, June 1989.

[310] G. Ellis. *Observers in Control Systems*. Elsevier, New York, 2002.

[311] I. Z. Emiris and B. Mourrain. Computer algebra methods for studying and computing molecular conformations. Technical report, INRIA, Sophia-Antipolis, France, 1997.

[312] A. G. Erdman, G. N. Sandor, and S. Kota. *Mechanism Design: Analysis and Synthesis, 4th Ed., Vol. 1*. Prentice Hall, Englewood Cliffs, NJ, 2001.

[313] M. A. Erdmann. On motion planning with uncertainty. Master's thesis, Massachusetts Institute of Technology, Cambridge, MA, August 1984.

[314] M. A. Erdmann. Using backprojections for fine motion planning with uncertainty. *International Journal of Robotics Research*, 5(1):19–45, 1986.

[315] M. A. Erdmann. *On Probabilistic Strategies for Robot Tasks*. PhD thesis, Massachusetts Institute of Technology, Cambridge, MA, 1989.

[316] M. A. Erdmann. Randomization in robot tasks. *International Journal of Robotics Research*, 11(5):399–436, October 1992.

[317] M. A. Erdmann. Randomization for robot tasks: Using dynamic programming in the space of knowledge states. *Algorithmica*, 10:248–291, 1993.

[318] M. A. Erdmann. On a representation of friction in configuration space. *International Journal of Robotics Research*, 13(3):240–271, 1994.

[319] M. A. Erdmann. Understanding action and sensing by designing action-based sensors. *International Journal of Robotics Research*, 14(5):483–509, 1995.

[320] M. A. Erdmann. An exploration of nonprehensile two-palm manipulation using two zebra robots. In J.-P. Laumond and M. Overmars, editors, *Algorithms for Robotic Motion and Manipulation*, pages 239–254. A.K. Peters, Wellesley, MA, 1997.

[321] M. A. Erdmann and T. Lozano-Pérez. On multiple moving objects. In *Proceedings IEEE International Conference on Robotics & Automation*, pages 1419–1424, 1986.

[322] M. A. Erdmann and T. Lozano-Pérez. On multiple moving objects. *Algorithmica*, 2:477–521, 1987.

[323] M. A. Erdmann and M. T. Mason. An exploration of sensorless manipulation. *IEEE Transactions on Robotics & Automation*, 4(4):369–379, August 1988.

[324] M. A. Erdmann, M. T. Mason, and G. Vaněček. Mechanical parts orienting: The case of a polyhedron on a table. *Algorithmica*, 10:206–247, 1993.

[325] B. Espiau, F. Chaumette, and P. Rives. A new approach to visual servoing in robotics. *IEEE Transactions on Robotics & Automation*, 8(3):313–326, June 1992.

[326] J. Esposito, J. W. Kim, and V. Kumar. Adaptive RRTs for validating hybrid robotic control systems. In *Proceedings Workshop on Algorithmic Foundations of Robotics*, Zeist, The Netherlands, July 2004.

[327] M. Farber. Topological complexity of motion planning. *Discrete and Computational Geometry*, 29:211–221, 2003.

[328] M. Farber, S. Tabachnkov, and S. Yuzvinsky. Topological robotics: Motion planning in projective spaces. *International Mathematical Research Notices*, 34:1853–1870, 2003.

[329] M. Farber and S. Yuzvinsky. Topological robotics: Subspace arrangements and collision free motion planning. Technical Report math.AT/0210115, arXiv (online), 2004.

[330] B. Faverjon. Obstacle avoidance using an octree in the configuration space of a manipulator. In *Proceedings IEEE International Conference on Robotics & Automation*, pages 504–512, 1984.

[331] B. Faverjon. Hierarchical object models for efficient anti-collision algorithms. In *Proceedings IEEE International Conference on Robotics & Automation*, pages 333–340, 1989.

[332] B. Faverjon and P. Tournassoud. A local based method for path planning of manipulators with a high number of degrees of freedom. In *Proceedings IEEE International Conference on Robotics & Automation*, pages 1152–1159, 1987.

[333] R. Featherstone. *Robot Dynamics Algorithms*. Kluwer, Boston, MA, 1987.

[334] S. P. Fekete, R. Klein, and A. Nüchter. Online searching with an autonomous robot. In *Proceedings Workshop on Algorithmic Foundations of Robotics*, Zeist, The Netherlands, July 2004.

[335] P. Ferbach. A method of progressive constraints for nonholonomic motion planning. In *Proceedings IEEE International Conference on Robotics & Automation*, pages 2949–2955, 1996.

[336] C. Fernandes, L. Gurvits, and Z. X. Li. A variational approach to optimal nonholonomic motion planning. In *Proceedings IEEE International Conference on Robotics & Automation*, pages 680–685, 1991.

[337] C. Fernandes, L. Gurvits, and Z. X. Li. Near-optimal nonholonomic motion planning for a system of coupled rigid bodies. *IEEE Transactions on Automatic Control*, 30(3):450–463, March 1994.

[338] R. Fierro, A. Das, V. Kumar, and J. P. Ostrowski. Hybrid control of formations of robots. In *Proceedings IEEE International Conference on Robotics & Automation*, pages 157–162, 2001.

[339] R. E. Fikes and N. J. Nilsson. STRIPS: A new approach to the application of

theorem proving. *Artificial Intelligence Journal*, 2:189–208, 1971.

[340] A. F. Filipov. Differential equations with discontinuous right hand sides. *Translations of the American Mathematical Society*, 62, 1960.

[341] P. W. Finn, D. Halperin, L. E. Kavraki, J.-C. Latombe, R. Motwani, C. Shelton, and S. Venkatasubramanian. Geometric manipulation of flexible ligands. In M. C. Lin and D. Manocha, editors, *Applied Computational Geometry*, pages 67–78. Springer-Verlag, Berlin, 1996. Lecture Notes in Computer Science, 1148.

[342] R. J. Firby. An investigation into reactive planning in complex domains. In *Proceedings AAAI National Conference on Artificial Intelligence*, 1987.

[343] G. F. Fishman. *Monte Carlo: Concepts, Algorithms, and Applications*. Springer-Verlag, Berlin, 1996.

[344] R. Fleischer, K. Romanik, S. Schuierer, and G. Trippen. Optimal localization in trees. *Information and Computation*, 171(2):224–247, 2002.

[345] S. Fleury, P. Souères, J.-P. Laumond, and R. Chatila. Primitives for smoothing mobile robot trajectories. *IEEE Transactions on Robotics & Automation*, 11(3):441–448, 1995.

[346] M. Fliess, J. Lévine, P. Martin, and P. Rouchon. Flatness and defect of nonlinear systems: Introductory theory and examples. *International Journal of Control*, 61(6):1327–1361, 1995.

[347] H. Flordal, M. Fabian, and K. Akesson. Automatic implementation and verification of coordinating PLC-code for robotcells. In *Proceedings IFAC Symposium of Information Control Problems in Manufacturing*, 2004.

[348] G. B. Folland. *Real Analysis: Modern Techniques and Their Applications*. Wiley, New York, 1984.

[349] S. Fortune and G. Wilfong. Planning constrained motion. In *Proceedings ACM Symposium on Theory of Computing*, pages 445–459, 1988.

[350] M. Foskey, M. Garber, M. Lin, and D. Manocha. A Voronoi-based hybrid motion planner. In *Proceedings IEEE/RSJ International Conference on Intelligent Robots and Systems*, 2001.

[351] A. Fox and S. Hutchinson. Exploiting visual constraints in the synthesis of uncertainty-tolerant motion plans. *IEEE Transactions on Robotics & Automation*, 1(11):56–71, February 1995.

[352] D. Fox, S. Thrun, W. Burgard, and F. Dallaert. Particle filters for mobile robot localization. In A. Doucet, N. de Freitas, and N. Gordon, editors, *Sequential Monte Carlo Methods in Practice*, pages 401–428. Springer-Verlag, Berlin, 2001.

[353] D. Hähnel D. Fox, W. Burgard, and S. Thrun. A highly efficient FastSLAM algorithm for generating cyclic maps of large-scale environments from raw laser range measurements. In *Proceedings IEEE/RSJ International Conference on Intelligent Robots and Systems*, 2003.

[354] J. Fraden. *Handbook of Modern Sensors: Physics, Designs, and Applications*. Springer-Verlag, Berlin, 2003.

[355] T. Fraichard. Dynamic trajectory planning with dynamic constraints: A 'state-time space' approach. In *Proceedings IEEE/RSJ International Conference on Intelligent Robots and Systems*, pages 1393–1400, 1993.

[356] T. Fraichard and J.-M. Ahuactzin. Smooth path planning for cars. In *Proceedings IEEE International Conference on Robotics & Automation*, pages 3722–3727, 2001.

[357] T. Fraichard and H. Asama. Inevitable collision states – a step towards safer robots? *Advanced Robotics*, pages 1001–1024, 2004.

[358] T. Fraichard and C. Laugier. Kinodynamic planning in a structured and time-varying 2D workspace. In *Proceedings IEEE International Conference on Robotics & Automation*, pages 2: 1500–1505, 1992.

[359] T. Fraichard and A. Scheuer. Car-like robots and moving obstacles. In *Proceedings IEEE International Conference on Robotics & Automation*, pages 64–69, 1994.

[360] T. Fraichard and A. Scheuer. From Reeds and Shepp's to continuous-curvature paths. *IEEE Transactions on Robotics*, 20(6):1025–1035, December 2004.

[361] T. Frankel. *The Geometry of Physics.* Cambridge University Press, Cambridge, U.K., 2004.

[362] E. Frazzoli. *Robust Hybrid Control of Autonomous Vehicle Motion Planning.* PhD thesis, Massachusetts Institute of Technology, Cambridge, MA, June 2001.

[363] E. Frazzoli and F. Bullo. Decentralized algorithms for vehicle routing in a stochastic time-varying environment. In *Proceedings IEEE Conference Decision & Control*, pages 3357–3363, 2004.

[364] E. Frazzoli, M. A. Dahleh, and E. Feron. Real-time motion planning for agile autonomous vehicles. *AIAA Journal of Guidance and Control*, 25(1):116–129, 2002.

[365] E. Frazzoli, M. A. Dahleh, and E. Feron. Maneuver-based motion planning for nonlinear systems with symmetries. *IEEE Transactions on Robotics*, 21(6):1077–1091, December 2005.

[366] E. Freund and H. Hoyer. Path finding in multi robot systems including obstacle avoidance. *International Journal of Robotics Research*, 7(1):42–70, February 1988.

[367] J. H. Friedman, J. L. Bentley, and R. A. Finkel. An algorithm for finding best matches in logarithmic expected time. *ACM Transactions on Mathematical Software*, 3(3):209–226, September 1977.

[368] K. S. Fu, R. C. Gonzalez, and C. S. G. Lee. *Robotics: Control, Sensing, Vision, and Intelligence.* McGraw-Hill, New York, 1987.

[369] K. Fujimura and H. Samet. A hierarchical strategy for path planning among moving obstacles. Technical Report CAR-TR-237, Center for Automation Research, University of Maryland, November 1986.

[370] K. Fujimura and H. Samet. Planning a time-minimal motion among moving obstacles. *Algorithmica*, 10:41–63, 1993.

[371] T. Fukuda, S. Ito, N. Oota, F. Arai, Y. Abe, K. Tanake, and Y. Tanaka. Navigation system based on ceiling landmark recognition for autonomous mobile robot. In *Proceedings International Conference on Industrial Electronics, Control, and Instrumentation*, pages 1466–1471, 1993.

[372] A. T. Fuller. Relay control systems optimized for various performance criteria. In *Automatic and Remote Control (Proceedings First World Congress IFAC, Moscow, 1960)*, pages 510–519. Butterworths, London, 1961.

[373] J. Funge. *Artificial Intelligence for Computer Games.* A. K. Peters, Wellesley, MA, 2004.

[374] Y. Gabriely and E. Rimon. Spanning-tree based coverage of continuous areas by a mobile robot. Technical report, Dept. of Mechanical Engineering, Technion, Israel Institute of Technology, December 1999.

[375] Y. Gabriely and E. Rimon. Spanning-tree based coverage of continuous areas by a mobile robot. In *Proceedings IEEE International Conference on Robotics & Automation*, pages 1927–1933, 2001.

[376] Y. Gabriely and E. Rimon. Competitive on-line coverage of grid environments by a mobile robot. *Computational Geometry: Theory and Applications*, 24(3):197–224, April 2003.

[377] Y. Gabriely and E. Rimon. Competitive complexity of mobile robot on line motion planning problems. In *Proceedings Workshop on Algorithmic Foundations of Robotics*, pages 249–264, 2004.

[378] J. Gallier. *Curves and Surfaces in Geometric Modeling.* Morgan Kaufmann, San Francisco, CA, 2000.

[379] D. Geman and S. Geman. Stochastic relaxation, Gibbs distributions, and the Bayesian restoration of images. *IEEE Transactions Pattern Analysis Machine Intelligence*, 6(6):721–741, November 1984.

[380] M. R. Genesereth and N. Nilsson. *Logical Foundations of Artificial Intelligence.* Morgan Kaufmann, San Francisco, CA, 1987.

[381] R. Geraerts and M. Overmars. Sampling techniques for probabilistic roadmap planners. In *Proceedings International Conference on Intelligent Autonomous Systems*, 2004.

[382] R. Geraerts and M. H. Overmars. A comparative study of probabilistic roadmap

planners. In *Proceedings Workshop on Algorithmic Foundations of Robotics*, December 2002.

[383] B. Gerkey, S. Thrun, and G. Gordon. Clear the building: Pursuit-evasion with teams of robots. In *Proceedings AAAI National Conference on Artificial Intelligence*, 2004.

[384] M. Ghallab, D. Nau, and P. Traverso. *Automated Planning: Theory and Practice*. Morgan Kaufman, San Francisco, CA, 2004.

[385] A. K. Ghose, M. E. Logan, A. M. Treasurywala, H. Wang, R. C. Wahl, B. E. Tomczuk, M. R. Gowravaram, E. P. Jaeger, and J. J. Wendoloski. Determination of pharmacophoric geometry for collagenase inhibitors using a novel computational method and its verification using molecular dynamics, NMR, and X-ray crystallography. *Journal of the American Chemical Society*, 117:4671–4682, 1995.

[386] S. K. Ghosh and D. M. Mount. An output sensitive algorithm for computing visibility graphs. *SIAM Journal on Computing*, 20:888–910, 1991.

[387] R. Ghrist. Shape complexes for metamorphic robot systems. In *Proceedings Workshop on Algorithmic Foundations of Robotics*, December 2002.

[388] R. Ghrist, J. M. O'Kane, and S. M. LaValle. Computing Pareto Optimal Coordinations on Roadmaps. *The International Journal of Robotics Research*, 24(11):997–1010, 2005.

[389] E. G. Gilbert and D. W. Johnson. Distance functions and their application to robot path planning in the presence of obstacles. *IEEE Transactions on Robotics & Automation*, 1(1):21–30, March 1985.

[390] E. G. Gilbert, D. W. Johnson, and S. S. Keerth. A fast procedure for computing the distance between complex objects in three-dimensional space. *IEEE Journal of Robotics & Automation*, RA-4(2):193–203, Apr 1988.

[391] T. N. Gillespie. *Fundamentals of Vehicle Dynamics*. Society of Automotive Engineers, Warrendale, PA, 1992.

[392] B. Glavina. Solving findpath by combination of goal-directed and randomized search. In *Proceedings IEEE Inter-national Conference on Robotics & Automation*, pages 1718–1723, May 1990.

[393] B. Glavina. *Planning collision free motions for manipulators through a combination of goal oriented search and the creation of intermediate random subgoals*. PhD thesis, Technical University of Munich, 1991. In German.

[394] P. J. Gmytrasiewicz, E. H. Durfee, and D. K. Wehe. A decision-theoretic approach to coordinating multi-agent interactions. In *Proceedings International Joint Conference on Artificial Intelligence*, pages 62–68, 1991.

[395] J. Go, T. Vu, and J. J. Kuffner. Autonomous behaviors for interactive vehicle animations. In *Proceedings SIGGRAPH Symposium on Computer Animation*, 2004.

[396] K. Y. Goldberg. *Stochastic Plans for Robotic Manipulation*. PhD thesis, Carnegie Mellon University, Pittsburgh, PA, August 1990.

[397] K. Y. Goldberg. Orienting polygonal parts without sensors. *Algorithmica*, 10:201–225, 1993.

[398] K. Y. Goldberg and M. T. Mason. Bayesian grasping. In *Proceedings IEEE International Conference on Robotics & Automation*, 1990.

[399] H. Goldstein. *Classical Mechanics*. Addison-Wesley, Reading, MA, 1980.

[400] M. Goldwasser and R. Motwani. Intractability of assembly sequencing: Unit disks in the plane. In F. Dehne, A. Rau-Chaplin, J.-R. Sack, and R. Tamassia, editors, *WADS '97 Algorithms and Data Structures*, pages 307–320. Springer-Verlag, Berlin, 1997. Lecture Notes in Computer Science, 1272.

[401] G. H. Golub and C. F. Van Loan. *Matrix Computations (3rd ed)*. Johns Hopkins University Press, Baltimore, MD, 1996.

[402] R. Gonzalez and E. Rofman. On deterministic control problems: An approximation procedure for the optimal cost, parts I, II. *SIAM Journal on Control and Optimization*, 23:242–285, 1985.

[403] H. H. González-Baños, L. Guibas, J.-C. Latombe, S. M. LaValle, D. Lin, R. Motwani, and C. Tomasi. Motion planning with visibility constraints: Building autonomous observers. In Y. Shirai and S. Hirose, editors, *Proceedings Eighth*

International Symposium on Robotics Research, pages 95–101. Springer-Verlag, Berlin, 1998.

[404] H. H. Gonzalez-Banos, C.-Y. Lee, and J.-C. Latombe. Real-time combinatorial tracking of a target moving unpredictably among obstacles. In *Proceedings IEEE International Conference on Robotics & Automation*, 2002.

[405] J. E. Goodman and J. O'Rourke (eds). *Handbook of Discrete and Computational Geometry, 2nd Ed*. Chapman and Hall/CRC Press, New York, 2004.

[406] M. T. Goodrich and R. Tammasia. *Algorithm Design: Foundations, Analysis, and Internet Examples*. Wiley, New York, 2002.

[407] B. R. Gossick. *Hamilton's Principle and Physical Systems*. Academic, New York, 1967.

[408] S. Gottschalk, M. C. Lin, and D. Manocha. Obbtree: A hierarchical structure for rapid interference detection. In *Proceedings ACM SIGGRAPH*, 1996.

[409] V. E. Gough and S. G. Whitehall. Universal tyre test machine. In *Proceedings 9th International Technical Congress F.I.S.I.T.A.*, May 1962.

[410] E. J. Griffith and S. Akella. Coordinating multiple droplets in planar array digital microfluidic systems. *International Journal of Robotics Research*, 24(11):933–949, 2005.

[411] R. Grossman, A. Nerode, A. Ravn, and H. Rischel (eds). *Hybrid Systems*. Springer-Verlag, Berlin, 1993.

[412] L. Grüne. An adaptive grid scheme for the discrete Hamilton-Jacobi-Bellman equation. *Numerische Mathematik*, 75:319–337, 1997.

[413] G. Sánchez and J.-C. Latombe. On delaying collision checking in PRM planning: Application to multi-robot coordination. *International Journal of Robotics Research*, 21(1):5–26, 2002.

[414] L. Guibas and R. Seidel. Computing convolution by reciprocal search. In *Proceedings ACM Symposium on Computational Geometry*, pages 90–99, 1986.

[415] L. Guibas and J. Stolfi. Primitives for the manipulation of general subdivisions and the computation of Voronoi diagrams. *ACM Transactions on Graphics*, 4(2):74–123, 1985.

[416] L. J. Guibas, D. Hsu, and L. Zhang. H-Walk: Hierarchical distance computation for moving convex bodies. In *Proceedings ACM Symposium on Computational Geometry*, pages 265–273, 1999.

[417] L. J. Guibas, J.-C. Latombe, S. M. LaValle, D. Lin, and R. Motwani. Visibility-based pursuit-evasion in a polygonal environment. *International Journal of Computational Geometry and Applications*, 9(5):471–494, 1999.

[418] L. J. Guibas, R. Motwani, and P. Raghavan. The robot localization problem. In K. Goldberg, D. Halperin, J.-C. Latombe, and R. Wilson, editors, *Algorithmic Foundations of Robotics*, pages 269–282. A. K. Peters, Wellesley, MA, 1995.

[419] L. Guilamo, B. Tovar, and S. M. LaValle. Pursuit-evasion in an unknown environment using gap navigation trees. In *IEEE/RSJ International Conference on Intelligent Robots and Systems*, 2004.

[420] K. Gupta and Z. Guo. Motion planning with many degrees of freedom: Sequential search with backtracking. *IEEE Transactions on Robotics & Automation*, 6(11):897–906, 1995.

[421] K. Gupta and X. Zhu. Practical motion planning for many degrees of freedom: A novel approach within sequential framework. *Journal of Robotic Systems*, 2(12):105–118, 1995.

[422] S. K. Gupta, D. A. Bourne, K. Kim, and S. S. Krishnan. Automated process planning for robotic sheet metal bending operations. *Journal of Manufacturing Systems*, 17(5):338–360, 1998.

[423] L. Gurvits. Averaging approach to nonholonomic motion planning. In *Proceedings IEEE International Conference on Robotics & Automation*, pages 2541–2546, 1992.

[424] J.-S. Gutmann, T. Weigel, and B. Nebel. A fast, accurate, and robust method for self-localization in polygonal environments using laser-range-finders. *Advanced Robotics*, 14(8):651–668, 2001.

[425] O. Hájek. *Pursuit Games*. Academic, New York, 1975.

[426] K. Haji-Ghassemi. On differential games of fixed duration with phase coordinate restrictions on one player. *SIAM Journal on Control & Optimization*, 28(3):624–652, May 1990.

[427] H. Halkin. Mathematical foundation of system optimization. In G. Leitman, editor, *Topics in Optimization*. Academic, New York, 1967.

[428] P. R. Halmos. *Measure Theory*. Springer-Verlag, Berlin, 1974.

[429] D. Halperin. Arrangements. In J. E. Goodman and J. O'Rourke, editors, *Handbook of Discrete and Computational Geometry, 2nd Ed.*, pages 529–562. Chapman and Hall/CRC Press, New York, 2004.

[430] D. Halperin, J.-C. Latombe, and R. H. Wilson. A general framework for assembly planning: the motion space approach. In *Proceedings ACM Symposium on Computational Geometry*, pages 9–18, 1998.

[431] D. Halperin and M. Sharir. A near-quadratic algorithm for planning the motion of a polygon in a polygonal environment. *Discrete and Computational Geometry*, 16:121–134, 1996.

[432] D. Halperin and R. Wilson. Assembly partitioning along simple paths: the case of multiple translations. In *Proceedings IEEE International Conference on Robotics & Automation*, pages 1585–1592, 1995.

[433] J. H. Halton. On the efficiency of certain quasi-random sequences of points in evaluating multi-dimensional integrals. *Numerische Mathematik*, 2:84–90, 1960.

[434] J. M. Hammersley. Monte-Carlo methods for solving multivariable problems. *Annals of the New York Academy of Science*, 86:844–874, 1960.

[435] L. Han and N. M. Amato. A kinematics-based probabilistic roadmap method for closed chain systems. In B. R. Donald, K. M. Lynch, and D. Rus, editors, *Algorithmic and Computational Robotics: New Directions*, pages 233–246. A. K. Peters, Wellesley, MA, 2001.

[436] H. Harrison and T. Nettleton. *Advanced Engineering Dynamics*. Elsevier, New York, 1997.

[437] R. S. Hartenberg and J. Denavit. A kinematic notation for lower pair mechanisms based on matrices. *Journal of Applied Mechanics*, 77:215–221, 1955.

[438] R. S. Hartenberg and J. Denavit. *Kinematic Synthesis of Linkages*. McGraw-Hill, New York, 1964.

[439] J. W. Hartmann. *Counter-Intuitive Behavior in Locally Optimal Solar Sail Escape Trajectories*. PhD thesis, University of Illinois, Urbana, IL, May 2005.

[440] J. W. Hartmann, V. L. Coverstone, and J. E. Prussing. Optimal counter-intuitive solar sail escape trajectories. In *Proceedings AIAA/AAS Space Flight Mechanics Conference*, 2004. Paper AAS 04-279.

[441] R. Hartshorne. *Algebraic Geometry*. Springer-Verlag, Berlin, 1977.

[442] A. Hatcher. *Algebraic Topology*. Cambridge University Press, Cambridge, U.K., 2002. Available at http://www.math.cornell.edu/~hatcher/AT/ATpage.html.

[443] M. T. Heath. *Scientific Computing: An Introductory Survey, 2nd Ed.* McGraw-Hill, New York, 2002.

[444] G. Heinzinger, P. Jacobs, J. Canny, and B. Paden. Time-optimal trajectories for a robotic manipulator: A provably good approximation algorithm. In *Proceedings IEEE International Conference on Robotics & Automation*, pages 150–155, Cincinnati, OH, 1990.

[445] H. Hermes, A. Lundell, and D. Sullivan. Nilpotent bases for distributions and control systems. *Journal of Differential Equations*, 55(3):385–400, 1984.

[446] J. Hershberger and S. Suri. Efficient computation of Euclidean shortest paths in the plane. In *Proceedings IEEE Symposium on Foundations of Computer Science*, pages 508–517, 1995.

[447] S. Hert, S. Tiwari, and V. Lumelsky. A terrain-covering algorithm for an AUV. *Autonomous Robots*, 3:91–119, 1996.

[448] F. J. Hickernell. Lattice rules: How well do they measure up? In P. Bickel, editor, *Random and Quasi-Random Point Sets*, pages 109–166. Springer-Verlag, Berlin, 1998.

[449] F. J. Hickernell, H. S. Hong, P. L'Ecuyer, and C. Lemieux. Extensible lattice sequences for quasi-monte carlo quadrature. *SIAM Journal on Scientific Computing*, 22:1117–1138, 2000.

[450] R. Hinkel and T. Knieriemen. Environment perception with a laser radar in a fast moving robot. In *Proceedings Symposium on Robot Control*, pages 68.1–68.7, Karlsruhe, Germany, 1988.

[451] Y. Hirano, K. Kitahama, and S. Yoshizawa. Image-based object recognition and dextrous hand/arm motion planning using RRTs for grasping in cluttered scene. In *Proceedings IEEE/RSJ International Conference on Intelligent Robots and Systems*, 2005.

[452] M. W. Hirsch. *Differential Topology*. Springer-Verlag, Berlin, 1994.

[453] Y.-C. Ho and K.-C. Chu. Team decision theory and information structures in optimal control problems-Part I. In *IEEE Transactions on Automatic Control*, pages 15–22, 1972.

[454] J. G. Hocking and G. S. Young. *Topology*. Dover, New York, 1988.

[455] J. K. Hodgins and W. L. Wooten. Animating human athletes. In Y. Shirai and S. Hirose, editors, *Proceedings International Symposium on Robotics Research*, pages 356–367. Springer-Verlag, Berlin, 1998.

[456] R. L. Hoffman. Automated assembly in a CSG domain. In *Proceedings IEEE International Conference on Robotics & Automation*, pages 210–215, 1989.

[457] C. M. Hoffmann. *Geometric and Solid Modeling*. Morgan Kaufmann, San Francisco, CA, 1989.

[458] C. Holleman and L. E. Kavraki. A framework for using the workspace medial axis in PRM planners. In *Proceedings IEEE International Conference on Robotics & Automation*, pages 1408–1413, 2000.

[459] J. Hollerbach. Dynamic scaling of manipulator trajectories. Technical report, MIT A.I. Lab Memo 700, 1983.

[460] J. Hollerbach. Dynamic scaling of manipulator trajectories. In *Proceedings American Control Conference*, pages 752–756, 1983.

[461] L. S. Homem de Mello and A. C. Sanderson. Representations of mechanical assembly sequences. *IEEE Transactions on Robotics & Automation*, 7(2):211–227, 1991.

[462] H. H. Hoos and T. Stützle. *Stochastic Local Search: Foundations and Applications*. Morgan Kaufmann, San Francisco, 2004.

[463] J. Hopcroft, D. Joseph, and S. Whitesides. Movement problems for 2-dimensional linkages. In J. T. Schwartz, M. Sharir, and J. Hopcroft, editors, *Planning, Geometry, and Complexity of Robot Motion*, pages 282–329. Ablex, Norwood, NJ, 1987.

[464] J. E. Hopcroft, J. T. Schwartz, and M. Sharir. On the complexity of motion planning for multiple independent objects: PSPACE-hardness of the "warehouseman's problem". *International Journal of Robotics Research*, 3(4):76–88, 1984.

[465] J. E. Hopcroft, J. D. Ullman, and R. Motwani. *Introduction to Automata Theory, Languages, and Computation*. Addison-Wesley, Reading, MA, 2000.

[466] T. Horsch, F. Schwarz, and H. Tolle. Motion planning for many degrees of freedom: Random reflections at C-space obstacles. In *Proceedings IEEE International Conference on Robotics & Automation*, pages 3318–3323, San Diego, CA, April 1994.

[467] A. E. Howe and E. Dahlman. A critical assessment of benchmark comparison in planning. *Journal of Artificial Intelligence Research*, pages 1–33, 2002.

[468] D. Hsu, T. Jiang, J. Reif, and Z. Sun. The bridge test for sampling narrow passages with probabilistic roadmap planners. In *Proceedings IEEE International Conference on Robotics & Automation*, 2003.

[469] D. Hsu, R. Kindel, J.-C. Latombe, and S. Rock. Randomized kinodynamic motion planning with moving obstacles. In B. R. Donald, K. M. Lynch, and D. Rus, editors, *Algorithmic and Computational Robotics: New Directions*. A.K. Peters, Wellesley, MA, 2001.

[470] D. Hsu, J.-C. Latombe, and R. Motwani. Path planning in expansive configuration spaces. *International Journal Computational Geometry & Applications*, 4:495–512, 1999.

[471] W. Huang. Optimal line-sweep-based decompositions for coverage algorithms. In *Proceedings IEEE International Conference on Robotics & Automation*, pages 27–32, 2001.

[472] T. W. Hungerford. *Algebra*. Springer-Verlag, Berlin, 1984.

[473] S. A. Hutchinson, G. D. Hager, and P. I. Corke. A tutorial on visual servo control. *IEEE Transactions on Robotics & Automation*, 12(5):651–670, October 1996.

[474] M. Hutter. *Universal Artificial Intelligence*. Springer-Verlag, Berlin, 2005.

[475] Y. K. Hwang and N. Ahuja. Gross motion planning–A survey. *ACM Computing Surveys*, 24(3):219–291, September 1992.

[476] S. Iannitti and K. M. Lynch. Exact minimum control switch motion planning for the snakeboard. In *Proceedings IEEE/RSJ International Conference on Intelligent Robots and Systems*, 2003.

[477] C. Icking, G. Rote, E. Welzl, and C.-K. Yap. Shortest paths for line segments. *Algorithmica*, 10:182–200, 1992.

[478] P. Indyk. Nearest neighbors in high-dimensional spaces. In J. E. Goodman and J. O'Rourke, editors, *Handbook of Discrete and Computational Geometry, 2nd Ed.*, pages 877–892. Chapman and Hall/CRC Press, New York, 2004.

[479] P. Indyk and R. Motwani. Approximate nearest neighbors: Towards removing the curse of dimensionality. In *Proceedings ACM Symposium on Theory of Computing*, pages 604–613, 1998.

[480] R. Isaacs. *Differential Games*. Wiley, New York, 1965.

[481] A. Isidori. *Nonlinear Control Systems, 2nd Ed.* Springer-Verlag, Berlin, 1989.

[482] P. Isto. Constructing probabilistic roadmaps with powerful local planning and path optimization. In *Proceedings IEEE/RSJ International Conference on Intelligent Robots and Systems*, pages 2323–2328, 2002.

[483] G. Jacob. Lyndon discretization and exact motion planning. In *Proceedings European Control Conference*, 1991.

[484] H. Jacob, S. Feder, and J. Slotine. Real-time path planning using harmonic potential functions in dynamic environment. In *Proceedings IEEE International Conference on Robotics & Automation*, pages 874–881, 1997.

[485] P. Jacobs and J. Canny. Planning smooth paths for mobile robots. In *Proceedings*

[486] P. Jensfelt. *Approaches to Mobile Robot Localization*. PhD thesis, Royal Institute of Technology (KTH), Stockholm, Sweden, 2001.

[487] P. Jensfelt and H. I. Christensen. Pose tracking using laser scanning and minimalistic environmental models. *IEEE Transactions on Robotics & Automation*, 17(2):138–147, 2001.

[488] P. Jensfelt and S. Kristensen. Active global localisation for a mobile robot using multiple hypothesis tracking. *IEEE Transactions on Robotics & Automation*, 17(5):748–760, October 2001.

[489] X. Ji and J. Xiao. Planning motion compliant to complex contact states. *International Journal of Robotics Research*, 20(6):446–465, 2001.

[490] Y.-B. Jia. Computation on parametric curves with an application in grasping. *International Journal of Robotics Research*, 23(7-8):825–855, 2004.

[491] P. Jiménez, F. Thomas, and C. Torras. Collision detection algorithms for motion planning. In J.-P. Laumond, editor, *Robot Motion Planning and Control*, pages 1–53. Springer-Verlag, Berlin, 1998.

[492] D. Jordan and M. Steiner. Configuration spaces of mechanical linkages. *Discrete and Computational Geometry*, 22:297–315, 1999.

[493] D. A. Joseph and W. H. Plantiga. On the complexity of reachability and motion planning questions. In *Proceedings ACM Symposium on Computational Geometry*, pages 62–66, 1985.

[494] V. Jurdjevic. The geometry of the plate-ball problem. *Archives for Rational Mechanics and Analysis*, 124:305–328, 1993.

[495] V. Jurdjevic. *Geometric Control Theory*. Cambridge University Press, Cambridge, U.K., 1997.

[496] L. P. Kaelbling, A. Cassandra, and J. Kurien. Acting under uncertainty: Discrete Bayesian models for mobile robot navigation. In *Proceedings IEEE/RSJ International Conference on Intelligent Robots and Systems*, 1996.

[497] L. P. Kaelbling, M. L. Littman, and A. R. Cassandra. Planning and acting in

IEEE International Conference on Robotics & Automation, pages 2–7, 1989.

partially observable stochastic domains. *Artificial Intelligence Journal*, 101, 1998.

[498] S. Kagami, J. Kuffner, K. Nishiwaki, and K. Okada M. Inaba. Humanoid arm motion planning using stereo vision and RRT search. In *Proceedings IEEE/RSJ International Conference on Intelligent Robots and Systems*, 2003.

[499] D. W. Kahn. *Topology: An Introduction to the Point-Set and Algebraic Areas*. Dover, New York, 1995.

[500] H. Kaindl and G. Kainz. Bidirectional heuristic search reconsidered. *Journal of Artificial Intelligence Research*, pages 283–317, December 1997.

[501] M. Kallmann and M. Mataric. Motion planning using dynamic roadmaps. In *Proceedings IEEE International Conference on Robotics & Automation*, 2004.

[502] M. Kallmann, A. Aubel, T. Abaci, and D. Thalmann. Planning collision-free reaching motions for interactive object manipulation and grasping. *Eurographics*, 22(3), 2003.

[503] R. Kalman. A new approach to linear filtering and prediction problems. *Transactions of the ASME, Journal of Basic Engineering*, 82:35–45, 1960.

[504] R. E. Kalman, Y.-C. Ho, and K. S. Narendra. Controllability of dynamical systems. *Contributions to Differential Equations*, 1:189–213, 1963.

[505] M. H. Kalos and P. A. Whitlock. *Monte Carlo Methods*. Wiley, New York, 1986.

[506] T. Kameda, M. Yamashita, and I. Suzuki. On-line polygon search by a seven-state boundary 1-searcher. *IEEE Transactions on Robotics*, 2006. To appear.

[507] I. Kamon and E. Rivlin. Sensory-based motion planning with global proofs. *IEEE Transactions on Robotics & Automation*, 13(6):814–822, December 1997.

[508] I. Kamon, E. Rivlin, and E. Rimon. Range-sensor based navigation in three dimensions. In *Proceedings IEEE International Conference on Robotics & Automation*, 1999.

[509] K. Kant and S. W. Zucker. Toward efficient trajectory planning: The path-velocity decomposition. *International Journal of Robotics Research*, 5(3):72–89, 1986.

[510] M.-Y. Kao, J. H. Reif, and S. R. Tate. Searching in an unknown environment: An optimal randomized algorithm for the cow-path problem. In *SODA: ACM-SIAM Symposium on Discrete Algorithms*, pages 441–447, 1993.

[511] W. Kaplan. *Advanced Calculus*. Addison-Wesley, Reading, MA, 1984.

[512] T. Karatas and F. Bullo. Randomized searches and nonlinear programming in trajectory planning. In *IEEE Conference on Decision and Control*, 2001.

[513] R. M. Karp. On-line algorithms versus off-line algorithms: How much is it worth to know the future? In *Proceedings World Computer Congress*, 1992.

[514] L. Kauffman. *Knots and Applications*. World Scientific, River Edge, NJ, 1995.

[515] H. Kautz, D. McAllester, and B. Selman. Encoding plans in propositional logic. In *Proceedings International Conference on Knowledge Representation and Reasoning*, 1996.

[516] L. E. Kavraki. Computation of configuration-space obstacles using the Fast Fourier Transform. *IEEE Transactions on Robotics & Automation*, 11(3):408–413, 1995.

[517] L. E. Kavraki. Geometry and the discovery of new ligands. In J.-P. Laumond and M. Overmars, editors, *Algorithms for Robotic Motion and Manipulation*, pages 435–445. A.K. Peters, Wellesley, MA, 1997.

[518] L. E. Kavraki and M. Kolountzakis. Partitioning a planar assembly into two connected parts is NP-complete. *Information Processing Letters*, 55(3):159–165, 1995.

[519] L. E. Kavraki, P. Svestka, J.-C. Latombe, and M. H. Overmars. Probabilistic roadmaps for path planning in high-dimensional configuration spaces. *IEEE Transactions on Robotics & Automation*, 12(4):566–580, June 1996.

[520] Y. Ke and J. O'Rourke. Lower bounds on moving a ladder in two and three dimensions. *Discrete and Computational Geometry*, 3:197–217, 1988.

[521] K. Kedem, R. Livne, J. Pach, and M. Sharir. On the union of Jordan regions and collision-free translational motion amidst polygonal obstacles.

Discrete and Computational Geometry, 1:59–71, 1986.

[522] J. M. Keil. Polygon decomposition. In J. R. Sack and J. Urrutia, editors, *Handbook on Computational Geometry*. Elsevier, New York, 2000.

[523] A. Kelly and B. Nagy. Reactive nonholonomic trajectory generation via parametric optimal control. *International Journal of Robotics Research*, 22(7-8):583–601, 2003.

[524] J. F. Kenney and E. S. Keeping. *Mathematics of Statistics, Part 2, 2nd ed.* Van Nostrand, Princeton, NJ, 1951.

[525] L. Kettner. Designing a data structure for polyhedral surfaces. In *Proceedings ACM Symposium on Computational Geometry*, pages 146–154, 1998.

[526] H. K. Khalil. *Nonlinear Systems.* Macmillan, New York, 2002.

[527] W. Khalil and J. F. Kleinfinger. A new geometric notation for open and closed-loop robots. In *Proceedings IEEE International Conference on Robotics & Automation*, volume 3, pages 1174–1179, 1986.

[528] O. Khatib. *Commande dynamique dans l'espace opérational des robots manipulateurs en présence d'obstacles.* PhD thesis, Ecole Nationale de la Statistique et de l'Administration Economique, France, 1980.

[529] O. Khatib. Real-time obstacle avoidance for manipulators and mobile robots. *International Journal of Robotics Research*, 5(1):90–98, 1986.

[530] A. A. Kilin. The dynamics of Chaplygin ball: The qualitative and computer analysis. *Regular and Chaotic Dynamics*, 6(3):291–306, 2001.

[531] J. Kim and J. P. Ostrowski. Motion planning of aerial robot using rapidly-exploring random trees with dynamic constraints. In *Proceedings IEEE International Conference on Robotics & Automation*, 2003.

[532] J.-O. Kim and P. Khosla. Real-time obstacle avoidance using harmonic potential functions. Technical report, Carnegie Mellon University, Pittsburgh, PA, 1990.

[533] K. H. Kim and F. W. Roush. *Team Theory.* Ellis Horwood Limited, Chichester, U.K., 1987.

[534] J. T. Kimbrell. *Kinematic Analysis and Synthesis.* McGraw-Hill, New York, 1991.

[535] R. Kimmel, N. Kiryati, and A. M. Bruckstein. Multivalued distance maps for motion planning on surfaces with moving obstacles. *IEEE Transactions on Robotics & Automation*, 14(3):427–435, June 1998.

[536] R. Kimmel and J. Sethian. Computing geodesic paths on manifolds. *Proceedings of the National Academy of Sciences, USA*, 95(15):8431–8435, 1998.

[537] R. Kimmel and J. Sethian. Optimal algorithm for shape from shading and path planning. *Journal of Mathematical Imaging and Vision*, 14(3):234–244, 2001.

[538] C. L. Kinsey. *Topology of Surfaces.* Springer-Verlag, Berlin, 1993.

[539] G. Kitagawa. Monte Carlo filter and smoother for non-Gaussian nonlinear state space models. *Journal of Computational and Graphical Statistics*, 5(1), 1996.

[540] J. M. Kleinberg. On-line algorithms for robot navigation and server problems. Technical Report MIT/LCS/TR-641, MIT, Cambridge, MA, May 1994.

[541] J. M. Kleinberg. Two algorithms for nearest-neighbor search in high dimensions. In *Proceedings ACM Symposium on Theory of Computing*, pages 599–608, May 1997.

[542] S. A. Klugman, H. H. Panjer, and G. E. Willmot. *Loss Models: From Data to Decisions, 2nd Ed.* Wiley, New York, 2004.

[543] D. E. Knuth. *The Art of Computer Programming, Volume 2: Seminumerical Algorithms, 3rd Ed.* Addison-Wesley, Reading, MA, 1998.

[544] D. E. Koditschek. Exact robot navigation by means of potential functions: Some topological considerations. In *Proceedings IEEE International Conference on Robotics & Automation*, pages 1–6, 1987.

[545] D. E. Koditschek. An approach to autonomous robot assembly. *Robotica*, 12:137–155, 1994.

[546] S. Koenig and M. Likhachev. D^* lite. In *Proceedings AAAI National Conference*

on Artificial Intelligence, pages 476–483, 2002.

[547] Y. Koga, K. Kondo, J. Kuffner, and J.-C. Latombe. Planning motions with intentions. *Proceedings ACM SIGGRAPH*, pages 395–408, 1994.

[548] D. Koller, N. Megiddo, and B. von Stengel. Efficient computation of equilibria for extensive two-person games. *Games and Economic Behavior*, 14:247–259, 1996.

[549] A. N. Kolmogorov and S. V. Fomin. *Introductory Real Analysis*. Dover, New York, 1975.

[550] V. Koltun. Pianos are not flat: Rigid motion planning in three dimensions. In *Proceedings ACM-SIAM Symposium on Discrete Algorithms*, 2005.

[551] K. Kondo. Motion planning with six degrees of freedom by multistrategic bidirectional heuristic free-space enumeration. *IEEE Transactions on Robotics & Automation*, 7(3):267–277, 1991.

[552] K. Konolige. Markov localization using correlation. In *Proceedings International Joint Conference on Artificial Intelligence*, 1999.

[553] R. E. Korf. Search: A survey of recent results. In H. E. Shrobe, editor, *Exploring Artificial Intelligence: Survey Talks from the National Conference on Artificial Intelligence*. Moran Kaufmann, San Francisco, CA, 1988.

[554] R. E. Korf. Artificial intelligence search algorithms. In *Algorithms and Theory of Computation Handbook*. CRC Press, Boca Raton, FL, 1999.

[555] K. Kotay, D. Rus, M. Vora, and C. McGray. The self-reconfiguring robotic molecule: Design and control algorithms. In P. K. Agarwal, L. E. Kavraki, and M. T. Mason, editors, *Robotics: The Algorithmic Perspective*. A. K. Peters, Natick, MA, 1998.

[556] L. Kovar and M. Gleicher. Automated extraction and parameterization of motions in large data sets. In *Proceedings ACM SIGGRAPH*, 2004.

[557] L. Kovar, M. Gleicher, and F. Pighin. Motion graphs. In *Proceedings ACM SIGGRAPH*, 2002.

[558] K. Kozlowski, P. Dutkiewicz, and W. Wróblewski. *Modeling and Control of Robots*. Wydawnictwo Naukowe PWN, Warsaw, Poland, 2003. In Polish.

[559] P. S. Krishnaprasad and D. P. Tsakaris. Oscillations, SE(2)-snakes and motion control: A study of the roller racer. Technical report, Center for Dynamics and Control of Smart Structures, University of Maryland, 1998.

[560] J. J. Kuffner. *Autonomous Agents for Real-time Animation*. PhD thesis, Stanford University, Stanford, CA, 1999.

[561] J. J. Kuffner. *Some Computed Examples [using RRT-Connect]*. [Online], 2001. Available at http://www.kuffner.org/james/plan/examples.html.

[562] J. J. Kuffner. Effective sampling and distance metrics for 3D rigid body path planning. In *Proceedings IEEE International Conference on Robotics & Automation*, 2004.

[563] J. J. Kuffner and S. M. LaValle. An efficient approach to path planning using balanced bidirectional RRT search. Technical Report CMU-RI-TR-05-34, Robotics Institute, Carnegie Mellon University, Pittsburgh, PA, August 2005.

[564] J. J. Kuffner, K. Nishiwaki, M. Inaba, and H. Inoue. Motion planning for humanoid robots. In *Proceedings International Symposium on Robotics Research*, 2003.

[565] H. W. Kuhn. Extensive games and the problem of information. In H. W. Kuhn and A. W. Tucker, editors, *Contributions to the Theory of Games*, pages 196–216. Princeton University Press, Princeton, NJ, 1953.

[566] J. B. Kuipers. *Quaternions and Rotation Sequences: A Primer with Applications to Orbits, Aerospace, and Virtual Reality*. Princeton University Press, Princeton, NJ, 2002.

[567] P. R. Kumar and P. Varaiya. *Stochastic Systems*. Prentice-Hall, Englewood Cliffs, NJ, 1986.

[568] H. J. Kushner. Numerical methods for continuous control problems in continuous time. *SIAM Journal on Control and Optimization*, 28:999–1048, 1990.

[569] H. J. Kushner and D. S. Clark. *Stochastic Approximation Methods for Constrained and Unconstrained Systems*. Springer-Verlag, Berlin, 1978.

[570] H. J. Kushner and P. G. Dupuis. *Numerical Methods for Stochastic Control Problems in Continuous Time*. Springer-Verlag, Berlin, 1992.

[571] K. N. Kutulakos, C. R. Dyer, and V. J. Lumelsky. Provable strategies for vision-guided exploration in three dimensions. In *Proceedings IEEE International Conference on Robotics & Automation*, pages 1365–1371, 1994.

[572] J. B. H. Kwa. BS*: An admissible bidirectional staged heuristic search algorithm. *Artificial Intelligence Journal*, 38:95–109, 1989.

[573] H. Kwakernaak and R. Sivan. *Linear Optimal Control Systems*. Wiley, New York, 1972.

[574] A. Ladd and L. E. Kavraki. Motion planning for knot untangling. In *Proceedings Workshop on Algorithmic Foundations of Robotics*, Nice, France, December 2002.

[575] A. Ladd and L. E. Kavraki. Fast exploration for robots with dynamics. In *Proceedings Workshop on Algorithmic Foundations of Robotics*, Zeist, The Netherlands, July 2004.

[576] A. Ladd and L. E. Kavraki. Measure theoretic analysis of probabilistic path planning. *IEEE Transactions on Robotics & Automation*, 20(2):229–242, 2004.

[577] G. Laffierriere and H. J. Sussmann. Motion planning for controllable systems without drift. In *Proceedings IEEE International Conference on Robotics & Automation*, 1991.

[578] F. Lamiraux, D. Bonnafous, and O. Lefebvre. Reactive path deformation for non-holonomic mobile robots. *IEEE Transactions on Robotics*, 20(6):967–977, December 2004.

[579] F. Lamiraux, E. Ferre, and E. Vallee. Kinodynamic motion planning: Connecting exploration trees using trajectory optimization methods. In *Proceedings IEEE International Conference on Robotics & Automation*, pages 3987–3992, 2004.

[580] F. Lamiraux and L. Kavraki. Path planning for elastic plates under manipulation constraints. In *Proceedings IEEE International Conference on Robotics & Automation*, pages 151–156, 1999.

[581] F. Lamiraux and J.-P. Laumond. Flatness and small-time controllability of multibody mobile robots: Application to motion planning. *IEEE Transactions on Automatic Control*, 45(10):1878–1881, April 2000.

[582] F. Lamiraux, S. Sekhavat, and J.-P. Laumond. Motion planning and control for Hilare pulling a trailer. *IEEE Transactions on Robotics & Automation*, 15(4):640–652, August 1999.

[583] A. S. Lapaugh. Recontamination does not help to search a graph. *Journal of the ACM*, 40(2):224–245, April 1993.

[584] P.-S. Laplace. *Théorie Analityque des Probabilités*. Courceir, Paris, 1812.

[585] R. E. Larson. A survey of dynamic programming computational procedures. *IEEE Transactions on Automatic Control*, 12(6):767–774, December 1967.

[586] R. E. Larson and J. L. Casti. *Principles of Dynamic Programming, Part II*. Dekker, New York, 1982.

[587] R. E. Larson and W. G. Keckler. Optimum adaptive control in an unknown environment. *IEEE Transactions on Automatic Control*, 13(4):438–439, August 1968.

[588] J. P. LaSalle. Stability theory for ordinary differential equations. *Journal of Differential Equations*, 4:57–65, 1968.

[589] A. Lasota and M. C. Mackey. *Chaos, Fractals, and Noise: Stochastic Aspects of Dynamics, 2nd Ed*. Springer-Verlag, Berlin, 1995.

[590] J.-C. Latombe. A fast path planner for a car-like indoor mobile robot. In *Proceedings AAAI National Conference on Artificial Intelligence*, pages 659–665, 1991.

[591] J.-C. Latombe. *Robot Motion Planning*. Kluwer, Boston, MA, 1991.

[592] J.-C. Latombe. Motion planning: A journey of robots, molecules, digital actors, and other artifacts. *International Journal of Robotics Research*, 18(11):1119–1128, 1999.

[593] J.-C. Latombe, A. Lazanas, and S. Shekhar. Robot motion planning with uncertainty in control and sensing. *Artificial Intelligence Journal*, 52:1–47, 1991.

[594] M. Lau and J. J. Kuffner. Behavior planning for character animation. In *Proceedings Eurographics/SIGGRAPH Symposium on Computer Animation*, 2005.

[595] S. L. Laubach and J. W. Burdick. An autonomous sensor-based path-planning for planetary microrovers. In *Proceedings IEEE International Conference on Robotics & Automation*, 1999.

[596] J.-P. Laumond. Trajectories for mobile robots with kinematic and environment constraints. In *Proceedings International Conference on Intelligent Autonomous Systems*, pages 346–354, 1986.

[597] J.-P. Laumond. Controllability of a multibody mobile robot. *IEEE Transactions on Robotics & Automation*, 9(6):755–763, December 1993.

[598] J.-P. Laumond. *Robot Motion Planning and Control*. Springer-Verlag, Berlin, 1998. Available online at http://www.laas.fr/~jpl/book.html.

[599] J.-P. Laumond, S. Sekhavat, and F. Lamiraux. Guidelines in nonholonomic motion planning for mobile robots. In J.-P. Laumond, editor, *Robot Motion Planning and Control*, pages 1–53. Springer-Verlag, Berlin, 1998.

[600] S. M. LaValle. *A Game-Theoretic Framework for Robot Motion Planning*. PhD thesis, University of Illinois, Urbana, IL, July 1995.

[601] S. M. LaValle. Rapidly-exploring random trees: A new tool for path planning. Technical Report 98-11, Computer Science Dept., Iowa State University, Oct. 1998.

[602] S. M. LaValle. Robot motion planning: A game-theoretic foundation. *Algorithmica*, 26(3):430–465, 2000.

[603] S. M. LaValle, M. S. Branicky, and S. R. Lindemann. On the relationship between classical grid search and probabilistic roadmaps. *International Journal of Robotics Research*, 23(7/8):673–692, July/August 2004.

[604] S. M. LaValle, P. Finn, L. Kavraki, and J.-C. Latombe. A randomized kinematics-based approach to pharmacophore-constrained conformational search and database screening. *J.*

Computational Chemistry, 21(9):731–747, 2000.

[605] S. M. LaValle, H. H. González-Baños, C. Becker, and J.-C. Latombe. Motion strategies for maintaining visibility of a moving target. In *Proceedings IEEE International Conference on Robotics and Automation*, pages 731–736, 1997.

[606] S. M. LaValle and J. Hinrichsen. Visibility-based pursuit-evasion: The case of curved environments. *IEEE Transactions on Robotics and Automation*, 17(2):196–201, April 2001.

[607] S. M. LaValle and S. A. Hutchinson. An objective-based stochastic framework for manipulation planning. In *Proceedings IEEE/RSJ/GI International Conference on Intelligent Robots and Systems*, pages 1772–1779, September 1994.

[608] S. M. LaValle and S. A. Hutchinson. An objective-based framework for motion planning under sensing and control uncertainties. *International Journal of Robotics Research*, 17(1):19–42, January 1998.

[609] S. M. LaValle and S. A. Hutchinson. Optimal motion planning for multiple robots having independent goals. *IEEE Trans. on Robotics and Automation*, 14(6):912–925, December 1998.

[610] S. M. LaValle and P. Konkimalla. Algorithms for computing numerical optimal feedback motion strategies. *International Journal of Robotics Research*, 20(9):729–752, September 2001.

[611] S. M. LaValle and J. J. Kuffner. Randomized kinodynamic planning. In *Proceedings IEEE International Conference on Robotics and Automation*, pages 473–479, 1999.

[612] S. M. LaValle and J. J. Kuffner. Rapidly-exploring random trees: Progress and prospects. In *Proceedings Workshop on the Algorithmic Foundations of Robotics*, 2000.

[613] S. M. LaValle and J. J. Kuffner. Randomized kinodynamic planning. *International Journal of Robotics Research*, 20(5):378–400, May 2001.

[614] S. M. LaValle and J. J. Kuffner. Rapidly-exploring random trees: Progress and prospects. In B. R. Donald, K. M. Lynch, and D. Rus, editors, *Algorithmic*

and Computational Robotics: New Directions, pages 293–308. A K Peters, Wellesley, MA, 2001.

[615] S. M. LaValle, D. Lin, L. J. Guibas, J.-C. Latombe, and R. Motwani. Finding an unpredictable target in a workspace with obstacles. In *Proceedings IEEE International Conference on Robotics and Automation*, pages 737–742, 1997.

[616] S. M. LaValle and R. Sharma. On motion planning in changing, partially-predictable environments. *International Journal of Robotics Research*, 16(6):775–805, December 1997.

[617] S. Lazebnik. Visibility-based pursuit evasion in three-dimensional environments. Technical Report CVR TR 2001-01, Beckman Institute, University of Illinois, 2001.

[618] A. R. Leach and I. D. Kuntz. Conformational analysis of flexible ligands in macromolecular receptor sites. *Journal of Computational Chemistry*, 13(6):730–748, 1992.

[619] D. T. Lee and R. L. Drysdale. Generalization of Voronoi diagrams in the plane. *SIAM Journal on Computing*, 10:73–87, 1981.

[620] J. Lee, J. Chai, P. S. A. Reitsma, J. K. Hodgins, and N. S. Pollard. Interactive control of avatars with human motion data. In *Proceedings ACM SIGGRAPH*, 2002.

[621] J.-H. Lee, S. Y. Shin, and K.-Y. Chwa. Visibility-based pursuit-evasions in a polygonal room with a door. In *Proceedings ACM Symposium on Computational Geometry*, 1999.

[622] D. H. Lehmer. Mathematical methods in large-scale computing units. In *Proceedings 2nd Symposium on Large-Scale Digital Computing Machinery*, pages 141–146, Cambridge, MA, 1951. Harvard University Press.

[623] J. Lengyel, M. Reichert, B. R. Donald, and D. P. Greenberg. Real-time robot motion planning using rasterizing computer graphics hardware. *Computer Graphics*, 24(4):327–335, August 1990.

[624] S. Lenser and M. Veloso. Sensor resetting localization for poorly modelled mobile robots. In *Proceedings IEEE International Conference on Robotics & Automation*, 2000.

[625] J. Leonard, H. Durrant-Whyte, and I. Cox. Dynamic map building for an autonomous mobile robot. *International Journal of Robotics Research*, 11(4):89–96, 1992.

[626] N. E. Leonard and P. S. Krishnaprasad. Averaging for attitude control and motion planning. In *Proceedings IEEE Conference Decision & Control*, pages 3098–3104, December 1993.

[627] N. E. Leonard and P. S. Krishnaprasad. Motion control of drift-free left-invariant systems on lie groups. *IEEE Transactions on Automatic Control*, 40(9):1539–1554, 1995.

[628] D. Leven and M. Sharir. An efficient and simple motion planning algorithm for a ladder moving in a 2-dimensional space amidst polygonal barriers. *Journal of Algorithms*, 8:192–215, 1987.

[629] D. Leven and M. Sharir. Planning a purely translational motion for a convex object in two-dimensional space using generalized Voronoi diagrams. *Discrete and Computational Geometry*, 2:9–31, 1987.

[630] P. Leven and S. A. Hutchinson. Real-time path planning in changing environments. *IEEE Transactions on Robotics & Automation*, 21(12):999–1030, December 2002.

[631] P. Leven and S. A. Hutchinson. Using manipulability to bias sampling during the construction of probabilistic roadmaps. *IEEE Transactions on Robotics & Automation*, 19(6):1020–1026, December 2003.

[632] A. D. Lewis, J. P. Ostrowski, J. W. Burdick, and R. M. Murray. Nonholonomic mechanics and locomotion: The snakeboard example. In *Proceedings IEEE International Conference on Robotics & Automation*, pages 2391–2400, 1994.

[633] M. Li and P. Vitanyi. *An Introduction to Kolmogorov Complexity and Its Applications*. Springer-Verlag, Berlin, 1997.

[634] T.-Y. Li and Y.-C. Shie. An incremental learning approach to motion planning with roadmap management. In *Proceedings IEEE International Conference on Robotics & Automation*, 2002.

[635] Z. Li and J. F. Canny. Motion of two rigid bodies with rolling constraint. *IEEE*

Transactions on Robotics & Automation, 6(1):62–72, February 1990.

[636] Z. Li and J. F. Canny. *Nonholonomic Motion Planning*. Kluwer, Boston, MA, 1993.

[637] D. Liberzon. *Switching in Systems and Control*. Birkhäuser, Boston, MA, 2003.

[638] J.-M. Lien, S. L. Thomas, and N. M. Amato. A general framework for sampling on the medial axis of the free space. In *Proceedings IEEE International Conference on Robotics & Automation*, 2003.

[639] M. C. Lin and J. F. Canny. Efficient algorithms for incremental distance computation. In *Proceedings IEEE International Conference on Robotics & Automation*, 1991.

[640] M. C. Lin and D. Manocha. Collision and proximity queries. In J. E. Goodman and J. O'Rourke, editors, *Handbook of Discrete and Computational Geometry, 2nd Ed.*, pages 787–807. Chapman and Hall/CRC Press, New York, 2004.

[641] M. C. Lin, D. Manocha, J. Cohen, and S. Gottschalk. Collision detection: Algorithms and applications. In J.-P. Laumond and M. Overmars, editors, *Algorithms for Robotic Motion and Manipulation*, pages 129–142. A.K. Peters, Wellesley, MA, 1997.

[642] S. R. Lindemann and S. M. LaValle. Incremental low-discrepancy lattice methods for motion planning. In *Proceedings IEEE International Conference on Robotics and Automation*, pages 2920–2927, 2003.

[643] S. R. Lindemann and S. M. LaValle. Current issues in sampling-based motion planning. In P. Dario and R. Chatila, editors, *Proceedings International Symposium on Robotics Research*. Springer-Verlag, Berlin, 2004.

[644] S. R. Lindemann and S. M. LaValle. Incrementally reducing dispersion by increasing Voronoi bias in RRTs. In *Proceedings IEEE International Conference on Robotics and Automation*, 2004.

[645] S. R. Lindemann and S. M. LaValle. Steps toward derandomizing RRTs. In *IEEE Fourth International Workshop on Robot Motion and Control*, 2004.

[646] S. R. Lindemann and S. M. LaValle. Smoothly blending vector fields for global robot navigation. In *Proceedings IEEE Conference Decision & Control*, pages 3353–3559, 2005.

[647] S. R. Lindemann, A. Yershova, and S. M. LaValle. Incremental grid sampling strategies in robotics. In *Proceedings Workshop on Algorithmic Foundations of Robotics*, pages 297–312, 2004.

[648] A. Lingas. The power of non-rectilinear holes. In *Proceedings 9th International Colloquium on Automata, Languange, and Programming*, pages 369–383. Springer-Verlag, 1982. Lecture Notes in Computer Science, 140.

[649] F. Lingelbach. Path planning using probabilistic cell decomposition. In *Proceedings IEEE International Conference on Robotics & Automation*, 2004.

[650] M. Littman. The witness algorithm: Solving partially observable Markov decision processes. Technical Report CS-94-40, Brown University, Providence, RI, 1994.

[651] M. L. Littman, A. R. Cassandra, and L. P. Kaelbling. Learning policies for partially-observable environments: Scaling up. In *Proceedings International Conference on Machine Learning*, pages 362–370, 1995.

[652] C. K. Liu and Z. Popovic. Synthesis of complex dynamic character motion from simple animations. In *Proceedings ACM SIGGRAPH*, pages 408–416, 2002.

[653] Y. Liu and S. Arimoto. Path planning using a tangent graph for mobile robots among polygonal and curved obstacles. *International Journal of Robotics Research*, 11(4):376–382, 1992.

[654] S. G. Loizou and K.J. Kyriakopoulos. Closed loop navigation for multiple holonomic vehicles. In *Proceedings IEEE/RSJ International Conference on Intelligent Robots and Systems*, 2002.

[655] S. G. Loizou and K.J. Kyriakopoulos. Closed loop navigation for multiple non-holonomic vehicles. In *Proceedings IEEE International Conference on Robotics & Automation*, 2003.

[656] I. Lotan, F. Schwarzer, D. Halperin, and J.-C. Latombe. Efficient maintenance and self-collision testing for kinematic chains. In *Proceedings ACM Symposium on Computational Geometry*, pages 43–52, 2002.

[657] I. Lotan, H. van den Bedem, A. M. Deacon, and J.-C. Latombe. Computing protein structures from electron density maps: The missing loop problem. In *Proceedings Workshop on Algorithmic Foundations of Robotics*, 2004.

[658] W. S. Lovejoy. Computationally feasible bounds for partially observed Markov decision processes. *Operations Research*, 39(1):162–175, 1991.

[659] T. Lozano-Pérez. Automatic planning of manipulator transfer movements. *IEEE Transactions on Systems, Man, & Cybernetics*, 11(10):681–698, 1981.

[660] T. Lozano-Pérez. Spatial planning: A configuration space approach. *IEEE Transactions on Computing*, C-32(2):108–120, 1983.

[661] T. Lozano-Pérez. A simple motion-planning algorithm for general robot manipulators. *IEEE Journal of Robotics & Automation*, RA-3(3):224–238, Jun 1987.

[662] T. Lozano-Pérez, M. T. Mason, and R. H. Taylor. Automatic synthesis of fine-motion strategies for robots. *International Journal of Robotics Research*, 3(1):3–24, 1984.

[663] T. Lozano-Pérez and M. A. Wesley. An algorithm for planning collision-free paths among polyhedral obstacles. *Communications of the ACM*, 22(10):560–570, 1979.

[664] L. Lu and S. Akella. Folding cartons with fixtures: A motion planning approach. *IEEE Transactions on Robotics & Automation*, 16(4):346–356, Aug 2000.

[665] P. Lu and J. M. Hanson. Entry guidance for the X-33 vehicle. *Journal of Spacecraft and Rockets*, 35(3):342–349, 1998.

[666] A. De Luca, G. Oriolo, and C. Samson. Feedback control of a nonholonomic car-like robot. In J.-P. Laumond, editor, *Robot Motion Planning and Control*, pages 171–253. Springer-Verlag, Berlin, 1998.

[667] D. G. Luenberger. *Introduction to Linear and Nonlinear Programming*. Wiley, New York, 1973.

[668] V. J. Lumelsky and K. R. Harinarayan. Decentralized motion planning for multiple mobile robots: The cocktail party model. *Autonomous Robots*, 4(1):121–135, 1997.

[669] V. J. Lumelsky and T. Skewis. Incorporating range sensing in the robot navigation function. *IEEE Transactions on Systems, Man, & Cybernetics*, 20(5):1058–1069, 1990.

[670] V. J. Lumelsky and A. A. Stepanov. Path planning strategies for a point mobile automaton moving amidst unknown obstacles of arbitrary shape. *Algorithmica*, 2:403–430, 1987.

[671] V. J. Lumelsky and S. Tiwari. An algorithm for maze searching with azimuth input. In *Proceedings IEEE International Conference on Robotics & Automation*, pages 111–116, 1994.

[672] K. M. Lynch. Controllability of a planar body with unilateral thrusters. *IEEE Transactions on Automatic Control*, 44(6):1206–1211, 1999.

[673] K. M. Lynch and M. T. Mason. Pulling by pushing, slip with infinite friction, and perfectly rough surfaces. *International Journal of Robotics Research*, 14(2):174–183, 1995.

[674] K. M. Lynch and M. T. Mason. Stable pushing: Mechanics, controllability, and planning. *International Journal of Robotics Research*, 15(6):533–556, 1996.

[675] K. M. Lynch, N. Shiroma, H. Arai, and K. Tanie. Collision free trajectory planning for a 3-dof robot with a passive joint. *International Journal of Robotics Research*, 19(12):1171–1184, 2000.

[676] I. M. Makarov, T. M. Vinogradskaya, A. A. Rubchinsky, and V. B. Sokolov. *The Theory of Choice and Decision Making*. Mir Publishers, Moscow, 1987.

[677] M. S. Manasse, L. A. McGeoch, and D. D. Sleator. Competitive algorithms for on-line problems. In *Proceedings ACM Symposium on Theory of Computing*, pages 322–333, 1988.

[678] D. Manocha and J. Canny. Real time inverse kinematics of general 6R manipulators. In *Proceedings IEEE International Conference on Robotics & Automation*, pages 383–389, Nice, May 1992.

[679] A. Marigo and A. Bicchi. Rolling bodies with regular surface: Controllability theory and applications. *IEEE Transactions on Automatic Control*, 45(9):1586–1599, 2000.

[680] J. E. Marsden and T. S. Ratiu. *Introduction to Mechanics and Symmetry.* Springer-Verlag, Berlin, 1999.

[681] M. T. Mason. Compliance and force control for computer controlled manipulators. In M. Brady *et al.*, editor, *Robot Motion: Planning and Control*, pages 373–404. MIT Press, Cambridge, MA, 1982.

[682] M. T. Mason. The mechanics of manipulation. In *Proceedings IEEE International Conference on Robotics & Automation*, pages 544–548, 1985.

[683] M. T. Mason. Mechanics and planning of manipulator pushing operations. *International Journal of Robotics Research*, 5(3):53–71, 1986.

[684] M. T. Mason. *Mechanics of Robotic Manipulation.* MIT Press, Cambridge, MA, 2001.

[685] J. Matousek. *Geometric Discrepancy.* Springer-Verlag, Berlin, 1999.

[686] J. Matousek and J. Nesetril. *Invitation to Discrete Mathematics.* Oxford University Press, Oxford, U.K., 1998.

[687] M. Matsumoto and T. Nishimura. Mersenne twister: A 623-dimensionally equidistributed uniform pseudo-random number generator. *ACM Transactions on Modeling and Computer Simulation*, 8(1):3–30, January 1998.

[688] L. Matthies and A. Elfes. Integration of sonar and stereo range data using a grid-based representation. In *Proceedings IEEE International Conference on Robotics & Automation*, pages 727–733, 1988.

[689] O. Mayr. *The Origins of Feedback Control.* MIT Press, Cambridge, MA, 1970.

[690] E. Mazer, J. M. Ahuactzin, and P. Bessière. The Ariadne's clew algorithm. *Journal of Artificial Intelligence Research*, 9:295–316, November 1998.

[691] E. Mazer, G. Talbi, J. M. Ahuactzin, and P. Bessière. The Ariadne's clew algorithm. In *Proceedings International Conference of Society of Adaptive Behavior*, Honolulu, 1992.

[692] J. M. McCarthy. *Geometric Design of Linkages.* Springer-Verlag, Berlin, 2000.

[693] D. J. McGill and W. W. King. *An Introduction to Dynamics.* PWS, Boston, MA, 1995.

[694] R. McKelvey and A. McLennan. Computation of equilibria in finite games. In H. Amman, D. A. Kendrick, and J .Rust, editors, *The Handbook of Computational Economics*, pages 87–142. Elsevier, New York, 1996.

[695] N. Megiddo, S. L. Hakimi, M. R. Garey, D. S. Johnson, and C. H. Papadimitriou. The complexity of searching a graph. *Journal of the ACM*, 35(1):18–44, January 1988.

[696] J.-P. Merlet. *Parallel Robots.* Kluwer, Boston, MA, 2000.

[697] A. W. Merz. The game of two identical cars. *Journal of Optimization Theory and Applications*, 9(5):324–343, 1972.

[698] N. C. Metropolis and S. M. Ulam. The Monte-Carlo method. *Journal of the American Statistical Association*, 44:335–341, 1949.

[699] A. N. Michel and C. J. Herget. *Applied Algebra and Functional Analysis.* Dover, New York, 1993.

[700] R. J. Milgram and J. C. Trinkle. Complete path planning for closed kinematic chains with spherical joints. *International Journal of Robotics Research*, 21(9):773–789, 2002.

[701] R. J. Milgram and J. C. Trinkle. The geometry of configuration spaces for closed chains in two and three dimensions. *Homology, Homotopy, and Applications*, 6(1):237–267, 2004.

[702] D. A. Miller and S. W. Zucker. Copositive-plus Lemke algorithm solves polymatrix games. *Operations Research Letters*, 10:285–290, 1991.

[703] G. L. Miller, S.-H. Teng, W. Thurston, and S. A. Vavasis. Separators for sphere-packings and nearest neighbor graphs. *Journal of the ACM*, 44(1):1–29, January 1997.

[704] J. W. Milnor. *Morse Theory.* Princeton University Press, Princeton, NJ, 1963.

[705] B. Mirtich. V-Clip: Fast and robust polyhedral collision detection. Technical Report TR97-05, Mitsubishi Electronics Research Laboratory, 1997.

[706] B. Mirtich. Efficient algorithms for two-phase collision detection. In K. Gupta and A.P. del Pobil, editors, *Practical Motion Planning in Robotics: Current Approaches and Future Directions*, pages 203–223. Wiley, New York, 1998.

[707] B. Mishra. *Algorithmic Algebra.* Springer-Verlag, New York, 1993.

[708] B. Mishra. Computational real algebraic geometry. In J. E. Goodman and J. O'Rourke, editors, *Handbook of Discrete and Computational Geometry*, pages 537–556. CRC Press, New York, 1997.

[709] I. Mitchell, A. Bayen, and C. Tomlin. Computing reachable sets for continuous dynamic games using level set methods. *IEEE Transactions on Automatic Control*, 2003. Submitted.

[710] I. Mitchell and C. J. Tomlin. Overapproximating reachable sets by hamilton-jacobi projections. *Journal of Scientific Computation*, 19(1):323–346, 2003.

[711] J. S. B. Mitchell. Shortest paths among obstacles in the plane. *International Journal Computational Geometry & Applications*, 6(3):309–332, 1996.

[712] J. S. B. Mitchell. Shortest paths and networks. In J. E. Goodman and J. O'Rourke, editors, *Handbook of Discrete and Computational Geometry, 2nd Ed.*, pages 607–641. Chapman and Hall/CRC Press, New York, 2004.

[713] J. S. B. Mitchell and C. H. Papadimitriou. The weighted region problem. *Journal of the ACM*, 38:18–73, 1991.

[714] T. M. Mitchell. *Machine Learning.* McGraw-Hill, New York, 1997.

[715] L. Molina-Tanco and A. Hilton. Realistic synthesis of novel human movements from a database of motion capture examples. In *Proceedings IEEE Workshop on Human Motion*, 2000.

[716] S. Monaco and D. Normand-Cyrot. An introduction to motion planning under multirate digital control. In *Proceedings IEEE Conference Decision & Control*, pages 1780–1785, 1992.

[717] G. Monahan. A survey of partially observable Markov decision processes. *Management Science*, 101(1):1–16, 1982.

[718] B. Monien and I. H. Sudborough. Min cut is NP-complete for edge weighted graphs. *Theoretical Computer Science*, 58:209–229, 1988.

[719] D. J. Montana. The kinematics of contact and grasp. *International Journal of Robotics Research*, 7(3):17–32, 1988.

[720] M. Montemerlo, S. Thrun, D. Koller, and B. Wegbreit. FastSLAM: A factored solution to the simultaneous localization and mapping problem. In *Proceedings AAAI National Conference on Artificial Intelligence*, 1999.

[721] M. E. Mortenson. *Geometric Modeling, 2nd Ed.* Wiley, New York, 1997.

[722] R. Motwani and P. Raghavan. *Randomized Algorithms.* Cambridge University Press, Cambridge, U.K., 1995.

[723] R. Munos. Error bounds for approximate value iteration. In *Proceedings AAAI National Conference on Artificial Intelligence*, 2005.

[724] R. Munos and A. Moore. Barycentric interpolator for continuous space & time reinforcement learning. In *Proceedings Neural Information Processing Systems*, 1998.

[725] R. Munos and A. Moore. Variable resolution discretization in optimal control. *Machine Learning*, 49:291–323, 2001.

[726] T. Muppirala, R. Murrieta-Cid, and S. Hutchinson. Optimal motion strategies based on critical events to maintain visibility of a moving target. In *Proceedings IEEE International Conference on Robotics & Automation*, pages 3837–3842, 2005.

[727] T. Murphey. *Control of Multiple Model Systems.* PhD thesis, California Institute of Technology, May 2002.

[728] R. M. Murray, Z. Li, and S. Sastry. *A Mathematical Introduction to Robotic Manipulation.* CRC Press, Boca Raton, FL, 1994.

[729] R. M. Murray, M. Rathinam, and W. M. Sluis. Differential flatness of mechanical control systems. In *Proceedings ASME International Congress and Exposition*, 1995.

[730] R. M. Murray and S. Sastry. Nonholonomic motion planning: Steering using sinusoids. *IEEE Transactions on Automatic Control*, 38(5):700–716, 1993.

[731] R. Murrieta-Cid, A. Sarmiento, S. Bhattacharya, and S. Hutchinson. Maintaining visibility of a moving target at a fixed distance: The case of observer bounded speed. In *Proceedings IEEE International Conference on Robotics & Automation*, pages 479–484, 2004.

[732] Y. Nakamura, T. Suzuki, and M. Koinuma. Nonlinear behavior and control of a nonholonomic free-joint manipulator. *IEEE Transactions on Robotics & Automation*, 13(6):853–862, 1997.

[733] J. Nash. Noncooperative games. *Annals of Mathematics*, 54(2):286–295, 1951.

[734] S. G. Nash and A. Sofer. *Linear and Nonlinear Programming*. McGraw-Hill, New York, 1996.

[735] B. K. Natarajan. The complexity of fine motion planning. *International Journal of Robotics Research*, 7(2):36–42, 1988.

[736] B. K. Natarajan. On planning assemblies. In *Proceedings ACM Symposium on Computational Geometry*, pages 299–308, 1988.

[737] New York University. MathMol Library. Scientific Visualization Center. Available from http://www.nyu.edu/pages/mathmol/library/, 2005.

[738] A. Newell and H. Simon. GPS: A program that simulates human thought. In E. A. Feigenbaum and J. Feldman, editors, *Computers and Thought*. McGraw-Hill, New York, 1963.

[739] W. S. Newman and M. S. Branicky. Real-time configuration space transforms for obstacle avoidance. *International Journal of Robotics Research*, 10(6):650–667, 1991.

[740] A. Y. Ng and M. Jordan. PEGASUS: A policy search method for large MDPs and POMDPs. In *Proceedings Conference on Uncertainty in Artificial Intelligence*, 2000.

[741] H. Niederreiter. *Random Number Generation and Quasi-Monte-Carlo Methods*. Society for Industrial and Applied Mathematics, Philadelphia, 1992.

[742] H. Niederreiter and C. P. Xing. Nets, (t,s)-sequences, and algebraic geometry. In P. Hellekalek and G. Larcher, editors, *Random and Quasi-Random Point Sets*, pages 267–302. Springer-Verlag, Berlin, 1998. Lecture Notes in Statistics, 138.

[743] D. Nieuwenhuisen and M. H. Overmars. Useful cycles in probabilistic roadmap graphs. In *Proceedings IEEE International Conference on Robotics & Automation*, pages 446–452, 2004.

[744] H. Nijmeijer and A. J. van der Schaft. *Nonlinear Dynamical Control Systems*. Springer-Verlag, Berlin, 1990.

[745] N. J. Nilsson. A mobile automaton: An application of artificial intelligence techniques. In *1st International Conference on Artificial Intelligence*, pages 509–520, 1969.

[746] N. J. Nilsson. *Principles of Artificial Intelligence*. Tioga Publishing Company, Wellsboro, PA, 1980.

[747] N. J. Nilsson. *Artificial Intelligence: A New Synthesis*. Morgan Kaufmann, San Francisco, CA, 1998.

[748] S. Ntafos. Watchman routes under limited visibility. *Computational Geometry: Theory and Applications*, 1:149–170, 1992.

[749] P. A. O'Donnell and T. Lozano-Pérez. Deadlock-free and collision-free coordination of two robot manipulators. In *Proceedings IEEE International Conference on Robotics & Automation*, pages 484–489, 1989.

[750] C. O'Dunlaing. Motion planning with inertial constraints. *Algorithmica*, 2(4):431–475, 1987.

[751] C. O'Dunlaing, M. Sharir, and C. K. Yap. Retraction: A new approach to motion planning. In J .T .Schwartz, M. Sharir, and J. Hopcroft, editors, *Planning, Geometry, and Complexity of Robot Motion*, pages 193–213. Ablex, Norwood, NJ, 1987.

[752] C. O'Dunlaing and C. K. Yap. A retraction method for planning the motion of a disc. *Journal of Algorithms*, 6:104–111, 1982.

[753] P. Ögren. *Formations and Obstacle Avoidance in Mobile Robot Control*. PhD thesis, Royal Institute of Technology (KTH), Stockholm, Sweden, 2003.

[754] J. M. O'Kane. Global localization using odometry. In *Proceedings IEEE International Conference on Robotics and Automation*, 2005.

[755] J. M. O'Kane and S. M. LaValle. Almost-sensorless localization. In *Proceedings IEEE International Conference on Robotics and Automation*, 2005.

[756] B. O'Neill. *Elementary Differential Geometry*. Academic, New York, 1966.

[757] S. Oore, G. E. Hinton, and G. Dudek. A mobile robot that learns its place. *Neural Computation*, 9:683–699, 1997.

[758] J. O'Rourke. *Art Gallery Theorems and Algorithms*. Oxford University Press, New York, 1987.

[759] J. O'Rourke. Visibility. In J. E. Goodman and J. O'Rourke, editors, *Handbook of Discrete and Computational Geometry, 2nd Ed.*, pages 643–663. Chapman and Hall/CRC Press, New York, 2004.

[760] J. O'Rourke and S. Suri. Polygons. In J. E. Goodman and J. O'Rourke, editors, *Handbook of Discrete and Computational Geometry, 2nd Ed.*, pages 583–606. Chapman and Hall/CRC Press, New York, 2004.

[761] M. H. Overmars and J. van Leeuwen. Dynamic multidimensional data structures based on Quad- and K-D trees. *Acta Informatica*, 17:267–285, 1982.

[762] G. Owen. *Game Theory*. Academic, New York, 1982.

[763] B. Paden, A. Mees, and M. Fisher. Path planning using a Jacobian-based freespace generation algorithm. In *Proceedings IEEE International Conference on Robotics & Automation*, pages 1732–1737, 1989.

[764] D. K. Pai and L. M. Reissell. Multiresolution rough terrain motion planning. *IEEE Transactions on Robotics & Automation*, 14(5):709–717, 1998.

[765] S. Pancanti, L. Pallottino, D. Salvadorini, and A. Bicchi. Motion planning through symbols and lattices. In *Proceedings IEEE International Conference on Robotics & Automation*, pages 3914–3919, 2004.

[766] C. H. Papadimitriou. An algorithm for shortest-path planning in three dimensions. *Information Processing Letters*, 20(5):259–263, 1985.

[767] C. H. Papadimitriou. Games against nature. *Journal of Computer and System Sciences*, 31:288–301, 1985.

[768] C. H. Papadimitriou and K. J. Steiglitz. *Combinatorial Optimization: Algorithms and Complexity*. Prentice Hall, Englewood Cliffs, NJ, 1982.

[769] C. H. Papadimitriou and J. N. Tsitsiklis. Intractable problems in control theory. *SIAM Journal of Control and Optimization*, 24(4):639–654, July 1986.

[770] C. H. Papadimitriou and J. N. Tsitsiklis. The complexity of Markov decision processes. *Mathematics of Operations Research*, 12(3):441–450, August 1987.

[771] C. H. Papadimitriou and M. Yannakakis. Shortest paths without a map. *Theoretical Computer Science*, 84:127–150, 1991.

[772] A. Papantonopoulou. *Algebra: Pure and Applied*. Prentice Hall, Englewood Cliffs, NJ, 2002.

[773] S.-M. Park, J.-H. Lee, and K.-Y. Chwa. Visibility-based pursuit-evasion in a polygonal region by a searcher. Technical Report CS/TR-2001-161, Dept. of Computer Science, KAIST, Seoul, South Korea, January 2001.

[774] R. Parr and A. Eliazar. DP-SLAM: Fast, robust simultaneous localization and mapping without predetermined landmarks. In *Proceedings International Joint Conference on Artificial Intelligence*, 2003.

[775] R. Parr and S. Russell. Approximating optimal policies for partially observable stochastic domains. In *Proceedings International Joint Conference on Artificial Intelligence*, 1995.

[776] T. D. Parsons. Pursuit-evasion in a graph. In Y. Alavi and D. R. Lick, editors, *Theory and Application of Graphs*, pages 426–441. Springer-Verlag, Berlin, 1976.

[777] T. Parthasarathy and M. Stern. Markov games: A survey. In *Differential Games and Control Theory II*, pages 1–46. Marcel Dekker, New York, 1977.

[778] R. P. Paul. *Robot Manipulators: Mathematics, Programming, and Control*. MIT Press, Cambridge, MA, 1981.

[779] R. P. Paul and B. Shimano. Compliance and control. In *Proceedings of the Joint American Automatic Control Conference*, pages 1694–1699, 1976.

[780] J. Pearl. *Heuristics*. Addison-Wesley, Reading, MA, 1984.

[781] J. Pearl. *Probabilistic Reasoning in Intelligent Systems: Networks of Plausible Inference*. Morgan Kaufmann, San Francisco, CA, 1988.

[782] B. Peleg and P. Sudlölter. *Introduction to the Theory of Cooperative Games*. Springer-Verlag, Berlin, 2003.

[783] J. Peng and S. Akella. Coordinating multiple robots with kinodynamic constraints along specified paths. In J.-D. Boissonnat, J. Burdick, K. Goldberg, and S. Hutchinson, editors, *Algorithmic Foundations of Robotics V (WAFR*

2002), pages 221–237. Springer-Verlag, Berlin, 2002.

[784] J. Pertin-Troccaz. Grasping: A state of the art. In O. Khatib, J. J. Craig, and T. Lozano-Pérez, editors, *The Robotics Review 1*. MIT Press, Cambridge, MA, 1989.

[785] S. Petitjean, D. Kriegman, and J. Ponce. Computing exact aspect graphs of curved objects: algebraic surfaces. *International Journal of Computer Vision*, 9:231–255, Dec 1992.

[786] L. A. Petrosjan. *Differential Games of Pursuit*. World Scientific, Singapore, 1993.

[787] J. Pettré, J.-P. Laumond, and T. Siméon. A 2-stages locomotion planner for digital actors. In *Proceedings Eurographics/SIGGRAPH Symposium on Computer Animation*, pages 258–264, 2003.

[788] F. Pfeiffer and R. Johanni. A concept for manipulator trajectory planning. *IEEE Journal of Robotics & Automation*, RA-3(2):115–123, 1987.

[789] J. M. Phillips, N. Bedrosian, and L. E. Kavraki. Spacecraft rendezvous and docking with real-time randomized optimization. In *Proceedings AIAA Guidance, Navigation and Control Conference*, 2003.

[790] A. Piazzi, M. Romano, and C. G. Lo. Bianco. g^3 splines for the path planning of wheeled mobile robots. In *Proceedings European Control Conference*, 2003.

[791] L. Piegl. On NURBS: A survey. *IEEE Transactions on Computer Graphics & Applications*, 11(1):55–71, Jan 1991.

[792] D. A. Pierre. *Optimization Theory with Applications*. Dover, New York, 1986.

[793] R. W. Pike. *Optimization for Engineering Systems*. [Online], 2001. Available at http://www.mpri.lsu.edu/bookindex.html.

[794] J. Pineau, G. Gordon, and S. Thrun. Point-based value iteration. In *Proceedings International Joint Conference on Artificial Intelligence*, pages 1025–1032, 2003.

[795] C. Pisula, K. Hoff, M. Lin, and D. Manocha. Randomized path planning for a rigid body based on hardware accelerated Voronoi sampling. In *Proceedings Workshop on Algorithmic Foundations of Robotics*, 2000.

[796] R. Pito. A sensor based solution to the next best view problem. In *International Conference Pattern Recognition*, 1996.

[797] M. Pivtoraiko and A. Kelly. Generating near minimal spanning control sets for constrained motion planning in discrete state spaces. In *Proceedings IEEE/RSJ International Conference on Intelligent Robots and Systems*, 2005.

[798] E. Plaku and L. E. Kavraki. Distributed sampling-based roadmap of trees for large-scale motion planning. In *Proceedings IEEE International Conference on Robotics & Automation*, 2005.

[799] M. Pocchiola and G. Vegter. The visibility complex. *International Journal Computational Geometry & Applications*, 6(3):279–308, 1996.

[800] I. Pohl. Bi-directional and heuristic search in path problems. Technical report, Stanford Linear Accelerator Center, Stanford, CA, 1969.

[801] I. Pohl. Bi-directional search. In B. Meltzer and D. Michie, editors, *Machine Intelligence*, pages 127–140. Elsevier, New York, 1971.

[802] J. Ponce and B. Faverjon. On computing three-finger force-closure grasps of polygonal objects. *IEEE Transactions on Robotics & Automation*, 11(6):868–881, 1995.

[803] J. Ponce, S. Sullivan, A. Sudsang, J.-D. Boissonnat, and J.-P. Merlet. On computing four-finger equilibrium and force-closure grasps of polyhedral objects. *International Journal of Robotics Research*, 16(1):11–35, February 1997.

[804] L. S. Pontryagin, V. G. Boltyanskii, R. V. Gamkrelidze, and E. F. Mishchenko. *L. S. Pontryagin Selected Works, Volume 4: The Mathematical Theory of Optimal Processes*. Gordon and Breach, Montreux, Switzerland, 1986.

[805] J. Popovic, S. M. Seitz, M. A. Erdmann, and Z. Popovic A. P. Wiktin. Interactive manipulation of rigid body simulations. In *Proceedings ACM SIGGRAPH*, pages 209–217, 2002.

[806] J. M. Porta, M. T. J. Spaan, and N. Vlassis. Robot planning in partially observable continuous domains. In *Proceedings Robotics: Science and Systems*, 2005.

[807] H. Pottman and J. Wallner. *Computational Line Geometry*. Springer-Verlag, Berlin, 2001.

[808] P. Poupart and C. Boutilier. Value-directed compression of POMDPs. In *Proceedings Neural Information Processing Systems*, 2003.

[809] F. P. Preparata and M. I. Shamos. *Computational Geometry*. Springer-Verlag, Berlin, 1985.

[810] S. Quinlan. Efficient distance computation between nonconvex objects. In *Proceedings IEEE International Conference on Robotics & Automation*, pages 3324–3329, 1994.

[811] M. Rabin. Transaction protection by beacons. *Journal of Computation Systems Science*, 27(2):256–267, 1983.

[812] S. Rajko and S. M. LaValle. A pursuit-evasion bug algorithm. In *Proceedings IEEE International Conference on Robotics and Automation*, pages 1954–1960, 2001.

[813] A. Rao and K. Goldberg. Manipulating algebraic parts in the plane. *IEEE Transactions on Robotics & Automation*, 11(4):598–602, 1995.

[814] N. Rao, S. Kareti, W. Shi, and S. Iyenagar. Robot navigation in unknown terrains: Introductory survey of non-heuristic algorithms. Technical Report ORNL/TM-12410:1–58, Oak Ridge National Laboratory, July 1993.

[815] S. Ratering and M. Gini. Robot navigation in a known environment with unknown moving obstacles. In *Proceedings IEEE International Conference on Robotics & Automation*, pages 25–30, 1993.

[816] M. Rathinam and R. M. Murray. Configuration flatness of Lagrangian systems underactuated by one control. *SIAM Journal of Control and Optimization*, 36(1):164–179, 1998.

[817] J. A. Reeds and L. A. Shepp. Optimal paths for a car that goes both forwards and backwards. *Pacific Journal of Mathematics*, 145(2):367–393, 1990.

[818] J. Reif and Z. Sun. On frictional mechanical systems and their computational power. *SIAM Journal on Computing*, 32(6):1449–1474, 2003.

[819] J. Reif and H. Wang. Non-uniform discretization approximations for kinodynamic motion planning. In J.-P. Laumond and M. Overmars, editors, *Algorithms for Robotic Motion and Manipulation*, pages 97–112. A.K. Peters, Wellesley, MA, 1997.

[820] J. H. Reif. Complexity of the mover's problem and generalizations. In *Proceedings IEEE Symposium on Foundations of Computer Science*, pages 421–427, 1979.

[821] J. H. Reif and M. Sharir. Motion planning in the presence of moving obstacles. In *Proceedings IEEE Symposium on Foundations of Computer Science*, pages 144–154, 1985.

[822] J. H. Reif and M. Sharir. Motion planning in the presence of moving obstacles. *Journal of the ACM*, 41:764–790, 1994.

[823] J. H. Reif and Z. Sun. An efficient approximation algorithm for weighted region shortest path problem. In B. R. Donald, K. M. Lynch, and D. Rus, editors, *Algorithmic and Computational Robotics: New Directions*, pages 191–203. A.K. Peters, Wellesley, MA, 2001.

[824] J. H. Reif and S. R. Tate. Continuous alternation: The complexity of pursuit in continuous domains. *Algorithmica*, 10:157–181, 1993.

[825] J. Reimpell, H. Stoll, and J. W. Betzler. *The Automotive Chassis: Engineering Principles*. Society of Automotive Engineers, Troy, MI, 2001.

[826] E. M. Reingold, J. Nievergelt, and N. Deo. *Combinatorial Algorithms*. Prentice Hall, Englewood Cliffs, NJ, 1977.

[827] E. Remolina and B. Kuipers. Towards a general theory of topological maps. *Artificial Intelligence Journal*, 152(1):47–104, 2004.

[828] W. Rencken. Concurrent localisation and map building for mobile robots using ultrasonic sensors. In *Proceedings IEEE/RSJ International Conference on Intelligent Robots and Systems*, pages 2192–2197, 1993.

[829] E. Rimon and J. W. Burdick. Mobility of bodies in contact–I: A 2nd order mobility index for multiple-finger grasps. *IEEE Transactions on Robotics & Automation*, 14(5):696–708, 1998.

[830] E. Rimon and J. W. Burdick. Mobility of bodies in contact–II: How forces are generated by curvature effects. *IEEE Transactions on Robotics & Automation*, 14(5):709–717, 1998.

[831] E. Rimon and J. Canny. Construction of C-space roadmaps using local sensory data – What should the sensors look for? In *Proceedings IEEE International Conference on Robotics & Automation*, pages 117–124, 1994.

[832] E. Rimon and D. E. Koditschek. Exact robot navigation using artificial potential fields. *IEEE Transactions on Robotics & Automation*, 8(5):501–518, October 1992.

[833] A. A. Rizzi. Hybrid control as a method for robot motion programming. In *Proceedings IEEE International Conference on Robotics & Automation*, pages 832–837, 1998.

[834] C. P. Robert. *The Bayesian Choice, 2nd. Ed.* Springer-Verlag, Berlin, 2001.

[835] H. Rohnert. Shortest paths in the plane with convex polygonal obstacles. *Information Processing Letters*, 23:71–76, 1986.

[836] I. M. Ross and F. Fahroo. Pseudospectral methods for optimal motion planning of differentially flat systems. *IEEE Transactions on Automatic Control*, 49(8):1410–1413, 2004.

[837] J. J. Rotman. *Introduction to Algebraic Topology*. Springer-Verlag, Berlin, 1988.

[838] N. Roy and G. Gordon. Exponential family PCA for belief compression in POMDPs. In *Proceedings Neural Information Processing Systems*, 2003.

[839] H. L. Royden. *Real Analysis*. MacMillan, New York, 1988.

[840] W. Rudin. *Real Analysis*. McGraw-Hill, New York, 1987.

[841] W. Rudin. *Functional Analysis, 2nd Ed.* McGraw-Hill, New York, 1991.

[842] S. Russell and P. Norvig. *Artificial Intelligence: A Modern Approach, 2nd Edition*. Prentice-Hall, Englewood Cliffs, NJ, 2003.

[843] S. Sachs, S. Rajko, and S. M. LaValle. Visibility-based pursuit-evasion in an unknown planar environment. *International Journal of Robotics Research*, 23(1):3–26, January 2004.

[844] H. Sagan. *Introduction to the Calculus of Variations*. Dover, New York, 1992.

[845] H. Sagan. *Space-Filling Curves*. Springer-Verlag, Berlin, 1994.

[846] G. Sahar and J. M. Hollerbach. Planning minimum-time trajectories for robot arms. *International Journal of Robotics Research*, 5(3):97–140, 1986.

[847] G. Sánchez and J.-C. Latombe. A single-query bi-directional probabilistic roadmap planner with lazy collision checking. In *Proceedings International Symposium on Robotics Research*, 2001.

[848] S. Sastry. *Nonlinear Systems: Analysis, Stability, and Control*. Springer-Verlag, Berlin, 1999.

[849] Y. Sawaragi, H. Nakayama, and T. Tanino. *Theory of Multiobjective Optimization*. Academic, New York, 1985.

[850] A. Scheuer and T. Fraichard. Collision-free and continuous-curvature path planning for car-like robots. In *Proceedings IEEE International Conference on Robotics & Automation*, pages 867–873, 1997.

[851] A. Scheuer and C. Laugier. Planning sub-optimal and continuous-curvature paths for car-like robots. In *Proceedings IEEE/RSJ International Conference on Intelligent Robots and Systems*, pages 25–31, 1998.

[852] B. Schiele and J. Crowley. A comparison of position estimation techniques using occupancy grids. In *Proceedings IEEE International Conference on Robotics & Automation*, 1994.

[853] J. T. Schwartz and M. Sharir. On the Piano Movers' Problem: I. The case of a two-dimensional rigid polygonal body moving amidst polygonal barriers. *Communications on Pure and Applied Mathematics*, 36:345–398, 1983.

[854] J. T. Schwartz and M. Sharir. On the Piano Movers' Problem: II. General techniques for computing topological properties of algebraic manifolds. *Communications on Pure and Applied Mathematics*, 36:345–398, 1983.

[855] J. T. Schwartz and M. Sharir. On the Piano Movers' Problem: III. Coordinating the motion of several independent bodies. *International Journal of Robotics Research*, 2(3):97–140, 1983.

[856] J. T. Schwartz, M. Sharir, and J. Hopcroft. *Planning, Geometry, and Complexity of Robot Motion*. Ablex, Norwood, NJ, 1987.

[857] F. Schwarzer, M. Saha, and J.-C. Latombe. Exact collision checking of robot paths. In J.-D. Boissonnat, J. Burdick, K. Goldberg, and S. Hutchinson, editors, *Algorithmic Foundations of Robotics V (WAFR 2002)*. Springer-Verlag, Berlin, 2002.

[858] L. Sciavicco and B. Siciliano. *Modelling and Control of Robot Manipulators*. Springer-Verlag, Berlin, 1996.

[859] R. Sedgewick. *Algorithms in C++, 2nd Ed.* Addison-Wesley, Reading, MA, 2002.

[860] S. Sekhavat and J.-P. Laumond. Topological property for collision-free nonholonomic motion planning: The case of sinusoidal inputs for chained-form systems. *IEEE Transactions on Robotics & Automation*, 14(5):671–680, 1998.

[861] S. Sekhavat, P. Svestka, J.-P. Laumond, and M. H. Overmars. Multilevel path planning for nonholonomic robots using semiholonomic subsystems. *International Journal of Robotics Research*, 17:840–857, 1998.

[862] N. F. Sepetov, V. Krchnak, M. Stankova, S. Wade, K. S. Lam, and M. Lebl. Library of libraries: Approach to synthetic combinatorial library design and screening of "pharmacophore" motifs. *Proceedings of the National Academy of Sciences, USA*, 92:5426–5430, June 1995.

[863] J.-P. Serre. *Lie Algebras and Lie Groups*. Springer-Verlag, Berlin, 1992.

[864] J. A. Sethian. *Level set methods : Evolving interfaces in geometry, fluid mechanics, computer vision, and materials science*. Cambridge University Press, Cambridge, U.K., 1996.

[865] A. A. Shabana. *Computational Dynamics*. Wiley, New York, 2001.

[866] C. E. Shannon. A mathematical theory of communication. *The Bell Systems Technical Journal*, 27:379–423, 1948.

[867] M. Sharir. Algorithmic motion planning. In J. E. Goodman and J. O'Rourke, editors, *Handbook of Discrete and Computational Geometry, 2nd Ed.*, pages 1037–

1064. Chapman and Hall/CRC Press, New York, 2004.

[868] M. Sharir and P. K. Agarwal. *Davenport-Schinzel Sequences and Their Geometric Applications*. Cambridge University Press, Cambridge, U.K., 1995.

[869] R. Sharma. Locally efficient path planning in an uncertain, dynamic environment using a probabilistic model. *IEEE Transactions on Robotics & Automation*, 8(1):105–110, February 1992.

[870] R. Sharma. A probabilistic framework for dynamic motion planning in partially known environments. In *Proceedings IEEE International Conference on Robotics & Automation*, pages 2459–2464, Nice, France, May 1992.

[871] R. Sharma, J.-Y. Hervé, and P. Cucka. Dynamic robot manipulation using visual tracking. In *Proceedings IEEE International Conference on Robotics & Automation*, pages 1844–1849, 1992.

[872] R. Sharma, S. M. LaValle, and S. A. Hutchinson. Optimizing robot motion strategies for assembly with stochastic models of the assembly process. *IEEE Trans. on Robotics and Automation*, 12(2):160–174, April 1996.

[873] R. Sharma, D. M. Mount, and Y. Aloimonos. Probabilistic analysis of some navigation strategies in a dynamic environment. *IEEE Transactions on Systems, Man, & Cybernetics*, 23(5):1465–1474, September 1993.

[874] R. W. Sharpe. *Differential Geometry*. Springer-Verlag, Berlin, 1997.

[875] H. Shatkay and L. P. Kaelbling. Learning topological maps with weak local odometric information. In *Proceedings International Joint Conference on Artificial Intelligence*, 1997.

[876] T. Shermer. Recent results in art galleries. *Proceedings of the IEEE*, 80(9):1384–1399, September 1992.

[877] C. L. Shih, T.-T. Lee, and W. A. Gruver. A unified approach for robot motion planning with moving polyhedral obstacles. *IEEE Transactions on Systems, Man, & Cybernetics*, 20:903–915, 1990.

[878] Z. Shiller and S. Dubowsky. On the optimal control of robotic manipulators with actuator and end-effector constraints. In *Proceedings IEEE International*

Conference on Robotics & Automation, pages 614–620, 1985.

[879] Z. Shiller and S. Dubowsky. On computing time-optimal motions of robotic manipulators in the presence of obstacles. *IEEE Transactions on Robotics and Automation*, 7(6), Dec 1991.

[880] Z. Shiller and H.-H. Lu. Computation of path constrained time-optimal motions with dynamic singularities. *Transactions of the ASME, Journal of Dynamical Systems, Measurement, & Control*, 114:34–40, 1992.

[881] K. G. Shin and N. D. McKay. Minimum-time control of robot manipulators with geometric path constraints. *IEEE Transactions on Automatic Control*, 30(6):531–541, 1985.

[882] K. G. Shin and N. D. McKay. A dynamic programming approach to trajectory planning of robotic manipulators. *IEEE Transactions on Automatic Control*, 31(6):491–500, 1986.

[883] K. G. Shin and Q. Zheng. Minimum-time collision-free trajectory planning for dual-robot systems. *IEEE Transactions on Robotics & Automation*, 8(5):641–644, October 1992.

[884] A. M. Shkel and V. J. Lumelsky. Incorporating body dynamics into sensor-based motion planning: The maximum turn strategy. *IEEE Transactions on Robotics & Automation*, 13(6):873–880, December 1997.

[885] R. Sim and G. Dudek. Learning generative models of scene features. In *Proceedings IEEE Conference on Computer Vision and Pattern Recognition*, pages 920–929, 2001.

[886] T. Siméon, J.-P. Laumond and C. Nissoux. Visibility based probabilistic roadmaps for motion planning. *Advanced Robotics*, 14(6), 2000.

[887] T. Siméon, S. Leroy, and J.-P. Laumond. Path coordination for multiple mobile robots: A resolution complete algorithm. *IEEE Transactions on Robotics & Automation*, 18(1), February 2002.

[888] R. Simmons, R. Goodwin, K. Haigh, S. Koenig, and J. O'Sullivan. A layered architecture for office delivery robots. In *Proceedings First International Conference on Autonomous Agents*, Marina del Rey, CA, 1997.

[889] R. Simmons and S. Koenig. Probabilistic robot navigation in partially observable environments. In *Proceedings International Joint Conference on Artificial Intelligence*, pages 1080–1087, 1995.

[890] B. Simov, S. M. LaValle, and G. Slutzki. A complete pursuit-evasion algorithm for two pursuers using beam detection. In *Proceedings IEEE International Conference on Robotics and Automation*, pages 618–623, 2002.

[891] B. Simov, G. Slutzki, and S. M. LaValle. Pursuit-evasion using beam detection. In *Proceedings IEEE International Conference on Robotics and Automation*, 2000.

[892] M. Sipser. *Introduction to the Theory of Computation*. PWS, Boston, MA, 1997.

[893] D. Sleator and R. Tarjan. Amortized efficiency of list update and paging rules. *Communications of the ACM*, 28(2):202–208, 1985.

[894] I. H. Sloan and S. Joe. *Lattice Methods for Multiple Integration*. Oxford Science, Englewood Cliffs, NJ, 1994.

[895] J.-J. E. Slotine and H. S. Yang. Improving the efficiency of time-optimal path-following algorithms. *IEEE Transactions on Robotics & Automation*, 5(1):118–124, 1989.

[896] W. D. Smart and L. P. Kaelbling. Practical reinforcement learning in continuous spaces. In *Proceedings International Conference on Machine Learning*, 2000.

[897] D. Smith, J. Frank, and A. Jónsson. Bridging the gap between planning and scheduling. *Knowledge Engineering Review*, 15(1):47–83, 2000.

[898] R. C. Smith and P. Cheeseman. On the representation and estimation of spatial uncertainty. *International Journal of Robotics Research*, 5(4):56–68, 1986.

[899] S. J. J. Smith, D. S. Nau, and T. Throop. Computer bridge: A big win for AI planning. *AI Magazine*, 19(2):93–105, 1998.

[900] E. J. Sondik. The optimal control of partially observable Markov processes over the infinite horizon: Discounted costs. *Operations Research*, 9(2):149–168, 1978.

[901] G. Song and N. M. Amato. Using motion planning to study protein folding pathways. *Journal of Computational Biology*, 26(2):282–304, 2002.

[902] E. Sontag. Gradient technique for systems with no drift: A classical idea revisited. In *Proceedings IEEE Conference Decision & Control*, pages 2706–2711, December 1993.

[903] O. J. Sordalen. Conversion of a car with *n* trailers into a chained form. In *Proceedings IEEE International Conference on Robotics & Automation*, pages 1382–1387, 1993.

[904] P. Souères and J.-D. Boissonnat. Optimal trajectories for nonholonomic mobile robots. In J.-P. Laumond, editor, *Robot Motion Planning and Control*, pages 93–169. Springer-Verlag, Berlin, 1998.

[905] P. Souères and J.-P. Laumond. Shortest paths synthesis for a car-like robot. In *IEEE Transactions on Automatic Control*, pages 672–688, 1996.

[906] R. Spence and S. A. Hutchinson. Dealing with unexpected moving obstacles by integrating potential field planning with inverse dynamics control. In *Proceedings IEEE/RSJ International Conference on Intelligent Robots and Systems*, pages 1485–1490, 1992.

[907] M. Spivak. *Differential Geometry*. Publish or Perish, Houston, TX, 1979.

[908] M. W. Spong, S. Hutchinson, and M. Vidyasagar. *Robot Modeling and Control*. Wiley, New York, 2005.

[909] R. L Sproull. Refinements to nearest-neighbor searching in k-dimensional trees. *Algorithmica*, 6:579–589, 1991.

[910] W. Stadler. Fundamentals of multicriteria optimization. In W. Stadler, editor, *Multicriteria Optimization in Engineering and in the Sciences*, pages 1–25. Plenum Press, New York, 1988.

[911] H. Stark and J. W. Woods. *Probability, Random Processes, and Estimation Theory for Engineers*. Prentice-Hall, Englewood Cliffs, NJ, 1986.

[912] L. A. Steen and J. A. Seebach Jr. *Counterexamples in Topology*. Dover, New York, 1996.

[913] R. F. Stengel. *Optimal Control and Estimation*. Dover, New York, 1994.

[914] A. Stentz. Optimal and efficient path planning for partially-known environments. In *Proceedings IEEE International Conference on Robotics & Automation*, pages 3310–3317, 1994.

[915] D. Stewart. A platform with six degrees of freedom. In *Institution of Mechanical Engineers, Proceedings 1965–66, 180 Part 1*, pages 371–386, 1966.

[916] M. Stilman and J. J. Kuffner. Navigation among movable obstacles: Real-time reasoning in complex environments. In *Proceedings 2004 IEEE International Conference on Humanoid Robotics (Humanoids'04)*, 2004.

[917] D. Stipanovic, I. Hwang, and C. J. Tomlin. Computation of an overapproximation of the backward reachable set using subsystem level set functions, dynamics of continuous, discrete, and impulsive systems. *Series A: Mathematical Analysis*, 11:399–411, 2004.

[918] P. D. Straffin. *Game Theory and Strategy*. Mathematical Association of America, Washington, DC, 1993.

[919] M. Strandberg. Augmenting RRT-planners with local trees. In *Proceedings IEEE International Conference on Robotics & Automation*, pages 3258–3262, 2004.

[920] M. Strandberg. *Robot Path Planning: An Object-Oriented Approach*. PhD thesis, Royal Institute of Technology (KTH), Stockholm, Sweden, 2004.

[921] A. Sudsang, J. Ponce, and N. Srinivasa. Grasping and in-hand manipulation: Geometry and algorithms. *Algorithmica*, 26:466–493, 2000.

[922] A. Sudsang, F. Rothganger, and J. Ponce. Motion planning for disc-shaped robots pushing a polygonal object in the plane. *IEEE Transactions on Robotics & Automation*, 18(4):550–562, 2002.

[923] A. G. Sukharev. Optimal strategies of the search for an extremum. *U.S.S.R. Computational Mathematics and Mathematical Physics*, 11(4), 1971. Translated from Russian, *Zh. Vychisl. Mat. i Mat. Fiz.*, 11, 4, 910-924, 1971.

[924] H. Sussmann and G. Tang. Shortest paths for the Reeds-Shepp car: A worked out example of the use of geometric techniques in nonlinear optimal control. Technical Report SYNCON 91-10, Dept. of Mathematics, Rutgers University, Piscataway, NJ, 1991.

[925] H. J. Sussmann. A sufficient condition for local controllability. *SIAM Journal on Control and Optimization*, 16(5):790–802, 1978.

[926] H. J. Sussmann. A general theorem on local controllability. *SIAM Journal on Control and Optimization*, 25(1):158–194, 1987.

[927] H. J. Sussmann. A continuation method for nonholonomic path-finding problems. In *Proceedings IEEE Conference Decision & Control*, pages 2717–2723, December 1993.

[928] H. J. Sussmann. A very non-smooth maximum principle with state constraints. In *Proceedings IEEE Conference Decision & Control*, pages 917–922, December 2005.

[929] K. Sutner and W. Maass. Motion planning among time dependent obstacles. *Acta Informatica*, 26:93–122, 1988.

[930] R. S. Sutton. Learning to predict by the methods of temporal differences. *Machine Learning*, 3:9–44, 1988.

[931] I. Suzuki, Y. Tazoe, M. Yamashita, and T. Kameda. Searching a polygonal region from the boundary. *International Journal on Computational Geometry and Applications*, 11(5):529–553, 2001.

[932] I. Suzuki and M. Yamashita. Searching for a mobile intruder in a polygonal region. *SIAM Journal on Computing*, 21(5):863–888, October 1992.

[933] I. Suzuki, M. Yamashita, H. Umemoto, and T. Kameda. Bushiness and a tight worst-case upper bound on the search number of a simple polygon. *Information Processing Letters*, 66:49–52, 1998.

[934] P. Svestka and M. H. Overmars. Coordinated motion planning for multiple car-like robots using probabilistic roadmaps. In *Proceedings IEEE International Conference on Robotics & Automation*, pages 1631–1636, 1995.

[935] H. Takeda, C. Facchinetti, and J.-C. Latombe. Planning the motions of a mobile robot in a sensory uncertainty field. *IEEE Transactions Pattern Analysis Machine Intelligence*, 16(10):1002–1017, October 1994.

[936] H. Takeda and J.-C. Latombe. Sensory uncertainty field for mobile robot navigation. In *Proceedings IEEE International Conference on Robotics & Automation*, pages 2465–2472, Nice, France, May 1992.

[937] S. Tezuka. *Uniform Random Numbers: Theory and Practice*. Kluwer, Boston, MA, 1995.

[938] S. Tezuka. Quasi-Monte Carlo: The discrepancy between theory and practice. In K.-T. Fang, F. J. Hickernell, and H. Niederreiter, editors, *Monte Carlo and Quasi-Monte Carlo Methods 2000*, pages 124–140. Springer-Verlag, Berlin, 2002.

[939] M. Thorup. Undirected single source shortest paths in linear time. In *Proceedings IEEE Symposium on Foundations of Computer Science*, pages 12–21, 1997.

[940] S. Thrun. Probabilistic algorithms in robotics. *AI Magazine*, 21(4):93–109, 2000.

[941] S. Thrun, W. Burgard, and D. Fox. A probabilistic approach to concurrent mapping and localization for mobile robots. *Machine Learning*, 31(5):1–25, April 1998.

[942] S. Thrun, W. Burgard, and D. Fox. *Probabilistic Robotics*. MIT Press, Cambridge, MA, 2005.

[943] B. Tovar, L. Guilamo, and S. M. LaValle. Gap navigation trees: A minimal representation for visibility-based tasks. In *Proceedings Workshop on Algorithmic Foundations of Robotics*, pages 11–26, 2004.

[944] B. Tovar, S. M. LaValle, and R. Murrieta. Locally-optimal navigation in multiply-connected environments without geometric maps. In *IEEE/RSJ International Conference on Intelligent Robots and Systems*, 2003.

[945] B. Tovar, S. M. LaValle, and R. Murrieta. Optimal navigation and object finding without geometric maps or localization. In *Proceedings IEEE International Conference on Robotics and Automation*, pages 464–470, 2003.

[946] J. N. Tsitsiklis. Efficient algorithms for globally optimal trajectories. *IEEE Transactions on Automatic Control*, 40(9):1528–1538, September 1995.

[947] S. Udupa. *Collision Detection and Avoidance in Computer Controlled Manipulators*. PhD thesis, Dept. of

Electrical Engineering, California Institute of Technology, 1977.

[948] University of North Carolina. PQP: A proximity query package. GAMMA Research Group, Available from http://www.cs.unc.edu/~geom/SSV/, 2005.

[949] C. Urmson and R. Simmons. Approaches for heuristically biasing RRT growth. In *Proceedings IEEE/RSJ International Conference on Intelligent Robots and Systems*, 2003.

[950] J. van den Berg and M. Overmars. Roadmap-based motion planing in dynamic environments. In *Proceedings IEEE/RSJ International Conference on Intelligent Robots and Systems*, pages 1598–1605, 2004.

[951] J. van den Berg and M. Overmars. Prioritized motion planning for multiple robots. In *Proceedings IEEE/RSJ International Conference on Intelligent Robots and Systems*, pages 2217–2222, 2005.

[952] J. G. van der Corput. Verteilungsfunktionen I. *Akademie van Wetenschappen*, 38:813–821, 1935.

[953] D. Vanderpooten. Multiobjective programming: Basic concepts and approaches. In R. Slowinski and J. Teghem, editors, *Stochastic vs. Fuzzy Approaches to Multiobjective Mathematical Programming under Uncertainty*, pages 7–22. Kluwer, Boston, MA, 1990.

[954] G. Vegter. Computational topology. In J. E. Goodman and J. O'Rourke, editors, *Handbook of Discrete and Computational Geometry, 2nd Ed.*, pages 719–742. Chapman and Hall/CRC Press, New York, 2004.

[955] M. Vendittelli and J.-P. Laumond. Visible positions for a car-like robot amidst obstacles. In J.-P. Laumond and M. Overmars, editors, *Algorithms for Robotic Motion and Manipulation*, pages 213–228. A.K. Peters, Wellesley, MA, 1997.

[956] J. von Neumann. Zur Theorie der Gesellschaftsspiele. *Mathematische Annalen*, 100:295–320, 1928.

[957] J. von Neumann and O. Morgenstern. *Theory of Games and Economic Behavior*. Princeton University Press, Princeton, NJ, 1944.

[958] G. Walker and D. Walker. *The Official Rock Paper Scissors Strategy Guide*. Fireside, 2004.

[959] X. Wang and F. J. Hickernell. An historical overview of lattice point sets. In K.-T. Fang, F. J. Hickernell, and H. Niederreiter, editors, *Monte Carlo and Quasi-Monte Carlo Methods 2000*, pages 158–167. Springer-Verlag, Berlin, 2002.

[960] F. W. Warner. *Foundations of Differentiable Manifolds and Lie Groups*. Springer-Verlag, Berlin, 1983.

[961] D. S. Watkins. *Fundamentals of Matrix Computations, 2nd Ed.* Wiley, New York, 2002.

[962] G. Weiss, C. Wetzler, and E. von Puttkamer. Keeping track of position and orientation of moving indoor systems by correlation of range-finder scans. In *Proceedings IEEE/RSJ International Conference on Intelligent Robots and Systems*, pages 595–601, 1994.

[963] D. Weld. Recent advances in AI planning. *AI Magazine*, 20(2), 1999.

[964] J. T. Wen. Control of nonholonomic systems. In W. S. Levine, editor, *The Control Handbook*, pages 1359–1368. CRC Press, Boca Raton, FL, 1996.

[965] H. Weyl. Über die Gleichverteilung von Zahlen mod Eins. *Mathematische Annalen*, 77:313–352, 1916.

[966] D. Whitney. Force feedback control of manipulator fine motions. *Transactions of the ASME, Journal of Dynamical Systems, Measurement, & Control*, 99:91–97, 1977.

[967] D. E. Whitney. Real robots don't need jigs. In *Proceedings IEEE International Conference on Robotics & Automation*, 1986.

[968] H. Whitney. Local properties of analytic varieties. In S. Cairns, editor, *Differential and Combinatorial Topology*, pages 205–244. Princeton University Press, Princeton, NJ, 1965.

[969] J. Wiegley, K. Goldberg, M. Peshkin, and M. Brokowski. A complete algorithm for designing passive fences to orient parts. In *Proceedings IEEE International Conference on Robotics & Automation*, pages 1133–1139, 1996.

[970] O. Wijk. *Triangulation-Based Fusion of Sonar Data with Application in Mobile*

Robot Mapping and Localization. PhD thesis, Royal Institute of Technology (KTH), Stockholm, Sweden, 2001.

[971] S. A. Wilmarth, N. M. Amato, and P. F. Stiller. MAPRM: A probabilistic roadmap planner with sampling on the medial axis of the free space. In *Proceedings IEEE International Conference on Robotics & Automation*, pages 1024–1031, 1999.

[972] R. Wilson, L. Kavraki, J.-C. Latombe, and T. Lozano-Pérez. Two-handed assembly sequencing. *International Journal of Robotics Research*, 14(4):335–350, 1995.

[973] R. H. Wilson. *On Geometric Assembly Planning*. PhD thesis, Stanford University, Stanford, CA, March 1992.

[974] R. H. Wilson and J.-C. Latombe. Geometric reasoning about mechanical assembly. *Artificial Intelligence Journal*, 71(2):371–396, 1994.

[975] P. H. Winston. *Artificial Intelligence*. Addison-Wesley, Reading, MA, 1992.

[976] S. C. Wong, L. Middleton, and B. A. MacDonald. Performance metrics for robot coverage tasks. In *Proceedings Australasian Conference on Robotics and Automation*, 2002.

[977] C. F. J. Wu. On the convergence properties of the EM algorithm. *The Annals of Statistics*, 11(1):95–103, 1983.

[978] L. Xu and M. I. Jordan. On convergence properties of the EM algorithm for Gaussian mixtures. *Neural Computation*, 8:129–151, 1996.

[979] J. Yakey, S. M. LaValle, and L. E. Kavraki. Randomized path planning for linkages with closed kinematic chains. *IEEE Transactions on Robotics and Automation*, 17(6):951–958, December 2001.

[980] K. Yamane, J. J. Kuffner, and J. K. Hodgins. Synthesizing animations of human manipulation tasks. In *Proceedings ACM SIGGRAPH*, 2004.

[981] M. Yamashita, H. Umemoto, I. Suzuki, and T. Kameda. Searching for a mobile intruder in a polygonal region by a group of mobile searchers. *Algorithmica*, 31:208–236, 2001.

[982] B. Yamauchi, A. Schultz, and W. Adams. Mobile robot exploration and map-building with continuous localization. In *Proceedings IEEE International Conference on Robotics & Automation*, pages 3715–3720, 2002.

[983] L. Yang and S. M. LaValle. The sampling-based neighborhood graph: A framework for planning and executing feedback motion strategies. *IEEE Transactions on Robotics and Automation*, 20(3):419–432, June 2004.

[984] Q. Yang. *Intelligent Planning*. Springer-Verlag, Berlin, 1997.

[985] Y. Yavin and M. Pachter. *Pursuit-Evasion Differential Games*. Pergamon, Oxford, U.K., 1987.

[986] A. Yershova, L. Jaillet, T. Simeon, and S. M. LaValle. Dynamic-domain RRTs: Efficient exploration by controlling the sampling domain. In *Proceedings IEEE International Conference on Robotics and Automation*, 2005.

[987] A. Yershova and S. M. LaValle. Deterministic sampling methods for spheres and SO(3). In *Proceedings IEEE International Conference on Robotics and Automation*, 2004.

[988] A. Yershova, B. Tovar, R. Ghrist, and S. M. LaValle. Bitbots: Simple robots solving complex tasks. In *AAAI National Conference on Artificial Intelligence*, 2005.

[989] P. N. Yianilos. Data structures and algorithms for nearest neighbor search in general metric spaces. In *ACM-SIAM Symposium on Discrete Algorithms*, pages 311–321, 1993.

[990] M. Yim. *Locomotion with a Unit-Modular Reconfigurable Robot*. PhD thesis, Stanford University, Stanford, CA, December 1994. Stanford Technical Report STAN-CS-94-1536.

[991] J. Yong. On differential evasion games. *SIAM Journal on Control & Optimization*, 26(1):1–22, January 1988.

[992] J. Yong. On differential pursuit games. *SIAM Journal on Control & Optimization*, 26(2):478–495, March 1988.

[993] J. Yong. A zero-sum differential game in a finite duration with switching strategies. *SIAM Journal on Control & Optimization*, 28(5):1234–1250, September 1990.

[994] T. Yoshikawa. *Foundations of Robotics: Analysis and Control*. MIT Press, Cambridge, MA, 1990.

[995] Y. Yu and K. Gupta. On sensor-based roadmap: A framework for motion planning for a manipulator arm in unknown environments. In *Proceedings IEEE/RSJ International Conference on Intelligent Robots and Systems*, pages 1919–1924, 1998.

[996] J. Zabczyk. Some comments on stabilizability. *Applied Mathematics and Optimization*, 19(1):1–9, 1989.

[997] L. S. Zaremba. Differential games reducible to optimal control problems. In *Proceedings IEEE Conference Decision & Control*, pages 2449–2450, Tampa, FL, December 1989.

[998] M. Zefran and J. Burdick. Stabilization of systems with changing dynamics by means of switching. In *Proceedings IEEE International Conference on Robotics & Automation*, pages 1090–1095, 1998.

[999] M. Zefran, J. Desai, and V. Kumar. Continuous motion plans for robotic systems with changing dynamic behavior. In *Proceedings IEEE International Conference on Robotics & Automation*, 1996.

[1000] M. I. Zelikin and V. F. Borisov. *Theory of Chattering Control*. Birkhäuser, Boston, MA, 1994.

[1001] M. Zhang, R. A. White, L. Wang, R. N. Goldman, L. E. Kavraki, and B. Hassett. Improving conformational searches by geometric screening. *Bioinformatics*, 21(5):624–630, 2005.

[1002] N. L. Zhang and W. Zhang. Speeding up the convergence of value iteration in partially observable Markov decision processes. *Journal of Artificial Intelligence Research*, 14:29–51, 2001.

[1003] R. Zhou and E. A. Hansen. An improved grid-based approximation algorithm for POMDPs. In *Proceedings International Joint Conference on Artificial Intelligence*, 2001.

[1004] Y. Zhou and G. S. Chirikjian. Probabilistic models of dead-reckoning error in nonholonomic mobile robots. In *Proceedings IEEE International Conference on Robotics & Automation*, pages 1594–1599, 2003.

[1005] S. Zionts. Multiple criteria mathematical programming: An overview and several approaches. In P. Serafini, editor, *Mathematics of Multi-Objective Optimization*, pages 227–273. Springer-Verlag, Berlin, 1985.

Index

Ganesh Raghu • Roberto G. Carbone

Editors

Lung Transplantation

Evolving Knowledge and New Horizons

 Springer

Editors
Ganesh Raghu
Division of Pulmonary
Critical Care, and Sleep Medicine
Department of Medicine
University of Washington
Seattle, WA
USA

Roberto G. Carbone
Department of Internal Medicine
University of Genoa
Genoa
Italy

ISBN 978-3-319-91182-3   ISBN 978-3-319-91184-7   (eBook)
https://doi.org/10.1007/978-3-319-91184-7

Library of Congress Control Number: 2018950336

Printed on acid-free paper

This Springer imprint is published by the registered company Springer International Publishing AG part of Springer Nature
The registered company address is: Gewerbestrasse 11, 6330 Cham, Switzerland